A PEOPLE AND A NATION

Brief Edition

A PEOPLE AND A NATION

A History of the United States

Brief Seventh Edition

Mary Beth Norton
Cornell University

David M. Katzman
University of Kansas

David W. Blight
Yale University

Howard P. Chudacoff
Brown University

Fredrik Logevall
Cornell University

Beth Bailey
Temple University

Thomas G. Paterson
University of Connecticut

William M. Tuttle, Jr.
University of Kansas

Houghton Mifflin Company   Boston New York

Publisher: Charles Hartford
Sponsoring Editor: Sally Constable
Senior Development Editor: Jeffrey Greene
Editorial Assistant: Arianne Vanni
Senior Project Editor: Bob Greiner
Editorial Assistant: Katherine Leahey
Senior Art and Design Coordinator: Jill Haber Atkins
Senior Photo Editor: Jennifer Meyer Dare
Composition Buyer: Chuck Dutton
Manufacturing Buyer: Florence Cadran
Senior Marketing Manager: Sandra McGuire

Cover Image: Seymour Joseph Guy (1824–1910). Knowledge is Power. Oil on canvas on panel. Christie's Images / Superstock.

Printed in the U.S.A.

Library of Congress Catalog Number: 2005926283

Instructor's exam copy:
ISBN 13: 978-0-618-73025-4
ISBN 10: 0-618-73025-7

For orders, use student text ISBNs:
ISBN 13: 978-0-618-61150-8
ISBN 10: 0-618-61150-9

2 3 4 5 6 7 8 9-VH-09 08 07 06

BRIEF CONTENTS

MAPS *xv*

FIGURES *xv*

TABLES *xv*

PREFACE TO THE BRIEF SEVENTH EDITION *xvii*

PREFACE TO THE FULL-LENGTH SEVENTH EDITION *xix*

1 THREE OLD WORLDS CREATE A NEW, 1492–1600 *1*

2 EUROPEANS COLONIZE NORTH AMERICA, 1600–1640 *20*

3 NORTH AMERICA IN THE ATLANTIC WORLD, 1640–1720 *39*

4 AMERICAN SOCIETY TRANSFORMED, 1720–1770 *57*

5 SEVERING THE BONDS OF EMPIRE, 1754–1774 *74*

6 A REVOLUTION, INDEED, 1774–1783 *92*

7 FORGING A NATIONAL REPUBLIC, 1776–1789 *109*

8 THE EARLY REPUBLIC: CONFLICTS AT HOME AND ABROAD, 1789–1800 *127*

9 PARTISAN POLITICS AND WAR: THE DEMOCRATIC-REPUBLICANS IN POWER, 1801–1815 *142*

10 NATIONALISM, EXPANSION, AND THE MARKET ECONOMY, 1816–1845 *159*

11 REFORM AND POLITICS IN THE AGE OF JACKSON, 1824–1845 *181*

12 PEOPLE AND COMMUNITIES IN THE NORTH AND WEST, 1830–1860 *199*

13 PEOPLE AND COMMUNITIES IN A SLAVE SOCIETY: THE SOUTH, 1830–1860 *218*

14 SLAVERY AND AMERICA'S FUTURE: THE ROAD TO WAR, 1845–1861 *236*

15 TRANSFORMING FIRE: THE CIVIL WAR, 1861–1865 *256*

16 RECONSTRUCTION: AN UNFINISHED REVOLUTION, 1865–1877 *279*

17 THE DEVELOPMENT OF THE WEST, 1877–1900 *299*

18 THE MACHINE AGE, 1877–1920 *317*

19 THE VITALITY AND TURMOIL OF URBAN LIFE, 1877–1920 *337*

20 GILDED AGE POLITICS, 1877–1900 *358*

21 THE PROGRESSIVE ERA, 1895–1920 *376*

22 THE QUEST FOR EMPIRE, 1865–1914 *396*

23 AMERICANS IN THE GREAT WAR, 1914–1920 *415*

24 THE NEW ERA, 1920–1929 *434*

25 THE GREAT DEPRESSION AND THE NEW DEAL, 1929–1941 *453*

26 PEACESEEKERS AND WARMAKERS: AMERICANS IN THE WORLD, 1920–1941   *474*

27 THE SECOND WORLD WAR AT HOME AND ABROAD, 1941–1945   *492*

28 THE COLD WAR AND AMERICAN GLOBALISM, 1945–1961   *511*

29 AMERICA AT MIDCENTURY, 1945–1960   *532*

30 THE TUMULTUOUS SIXTIES, 1960–1968   *553*

31 CONTINUING DIVISIONS AND NEW LIMITS, 1969–1980   *574*

32 CONSERVATISM REVIVED, 1980–1992   *595*

33 GLOBAL BRIDGES IN THE NEW MILLENNIUM: AMERICA SINCE 1992   *615*

APPENDIX   *A-1*

INDEX   *I-1*

CONTENTS

MAPS *xv*

FIGURES *xv*

TABLES *xv*

PREFACE TO THE BRIEF SEVENTH EDITION *xvii*

PREFACE TO THE FULL-LENGTH SEVENTH EDITION *xix*

1 *T*hree Old Worlds Create a New, 1492–1600 *1*

American Societies *3*

North America in 1492 *5*

African Societies *7*

European Societies *9*

Early European Explorations *12*

The Voyages of Columbus, Cabot, and Their Successors *13*

Spanish Exploration and Conquest *14*

The Columbian Exchange *15*

LINKS TO THE WORLD: Maize *16*

Europeans in North America *17*

Summary *18*

LEGACY FOR A PEOPLE AND A NATION: Columbus Day *19*

2 *E*uropeans Colonize North America, 1600–1640 *20*

New Spain, New France, and New Netherland *22*

The Caribbean *25*

English Interest in Colonization *25*

LINKS TO THE WORLD: Wampum *26*

The Founding of Virginia *28*

Life in the Chesapeake *30*

The Founding of New England *32*

Life in New England *36*

Summary *37*

LEGACY FOR A PEOPLE AND A NATION: The Foxwoods Casino and the Mashantucket Pequot Museum *38*

3 *N*orth America in the Atlantic World, 1640–1720 *39*

The Growth of Anglo-American Settlements *41*

A Decade of Imperial Crisis: The 1670s *44*

African Slavery on the Mainland *46*

The Web of Empire and the Atlantic Slave Trade *47*

LINKS TO THE WORLD: International Piracy *48*

Enslavement of Africans and Indians *51*

Imperial Reorganization and the Witchcraft Crisis *53*

Summary *55*

LEGACY FOR A PEOPLE AND A NATION: Americans of African Descent *56*

4 *A*merican Society Transformed, 1720–1770 *57*

Population Growth and Ethnic Diversity *59*

Economic Growth and Development *62*

Colonial Cultures *64*

LINKS TO THE WORLD: Exotic Beverages *66*

Colonial Families *67*

Politics: Stability and Crisis in British America *69*

A Crisis in Religion *71*

Summary *72*

LEGACY FOR A PEOPLE AND A NATION: "Self-Made Men" *72*

5 Severing the Bonds of Empire, 1754–1774   74

Renewed Warfare Among Europeans and Indians   76

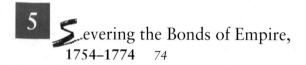 LINKS TO THE WORLD: The First Worldwide War   79

1763: A Turning Point   80
The Stamp Act Crisis   82
Resistance to the Townshend Acts   85
Confrontations in Boston   86
Tea and Turmoil   88
Summary   90

LEGACY FOR A PEOPLE AND A NATION: The Census and Reapportionment   90

6 A Revolution, Indeed, 1774–1783   92

Government by Congress and Committee   93
Contest in the Backcountry   95
Choosing Sides   96

LINKS TO THE WORLD: New Nations   98

War and Independence   99
The Struggle in the North   102
Life in the Army and on the Home Front   104
Victory in the South   105
Surrender at Yorktown   106
Summary   107

LEGACY FOR A PEOPLE AND A NATION: Revolutionary Origins   107

7 Forging a National Republic, 1776–1789   109

Creating a Virtuous Republic   111

LINKS TO THE WORLD: Novels   113

The First Emancipation and the Growth of Racism   114

Designing Republican Governments   116
Trials of the Confederation   119
Order and Disorder in the West   120
From Crisis to the Constitution   122
Opposition and Ratification   124
Summary   126

LEGACY FOR A PEOPLE AND A NATION: Women's Education   126

8 The Early Republic: Conflicts at Home and Abroad, 1789–1800   127

Building a Workable Government   128
Domestic Policy Under Washington and Hamilton   130
The French Revolution and the Development of Partisan Politics   132
Partisan Politics and Relations with Great Britain   134
John Adams and Political Dissent   135
Indians and African Americans at the End of the Century   137

LINKS TO THE WORLD: Haitian Refugees   138

Summary   140

LEGACY FOR A PEOPLE AND A NATION: Dissent During Wartime   140

9 Partisan Politics and War: The Democratic-Republicans in Power, 1801–1815   142

The Jefferson Presidency and Marshall Court   144
Louisiana and Lewis and Clark   146
A New Political Culture   148
Indian Resistance   150
American Shipping Imperiled   151
"Mr. Madison's War"   152

LINKS TO THE WORLD: Industrial Piracy   153

Peace and Consequences   *156*

Summary   *157*

LEGACY FOR A PEOPLE AND A NATION: States' Rights and Nullification   *157*

10 Nationalism, Expansion, and the Market Economy, 1816–1845   *159*

Postwar Nationalism   *161*

The Market Economy and Government's Role   *164*

Transportation Links   *167*

LINKS TO THE WORLD: The United States as a Developing Nation   *168*

Commercial Farming   *169*

The Rise of Manufacturing and Commerce   *170*

Workers and the Workplace   *172*

Americans on the Move   *174*

Native American Resistance and Removal   *175*

Summary   *179*

LEGACY FOR A PEOPLE AND A NATION: A Mixed Economy   *179*

11 Reform and Politics in the Age of Jackson, 1824–1845   *181*

From Revival to Reform   *183*

Abolitionism and the Women's Movement   *186*

LINKS TO THE WORLD: The International Antislavery Movement   *187*

Jacksonianism and Party Politics   *189*

Federalism at Issue: The Nullification and Bank Controversies   *191*

The Whig Challenge and the Second Party System   *193*

Manifest Destiny and Expansionism   *195*

Summary   *197*

LEGACY FOR A PEOPLE AND A NATION: The Bible Belt   *198*

12 People and Communities in the North and West, 1830–1860   *199*

Country Life   *201*

The West   *203*

LINKS TO THE WORLD: Gold in California   *204*

City Life   *205*

Extremes of Wealth   *209*

Family Life   *210*

Immigrant Lives in America   *211*

Free People of Color   *215*

Summary   *216*

LEGACY FOR A PEOPLE AND A NATION: White Fascination with and Appropriation of Black Culture   *217*

13 People and Communities in a Slave Society: The South, 1830–1860   *218*

The "Distinctive" South?   *219*

Free Southerners: Farmers, Free Blacks, and Planters   *221*

LINKS TO THE WORLD: "King Cotton" in the World Economy   *225*

Slave Life and Labor   *226*

Slave Culture   *229*

Slave Resistance and Rebellion   *231*

Harmony and Tension in a Slave Society   *232*

Summary   *234*

LEGACY FOR A PEOPLE AND A NATION: Reparations for Slavery   *234*

14 Slavery and America's Future: The Road to War, 1845–1861   *236*

The War with Mexico and Its Consequences   *238*

1850: Compromise or Armistice?   *241*

Slavery Expansion and Collapse of the Party System *244*

■ **LINKS TO THE WORLD: Annexation of Cuba** *245*

Slavery and the Nation's Future *249*

Disunion *250*

Summary *254*

LEGACY FOR A PEOPLE AND A NATION: Terrorist or Freedom Fighter? *254*

15 *T*ransforming Fire: The Civil War, 1861–1865 *256*

America Goes to War, 1861–1862 *258*

War Transforms the South *260*

Wartime Northern Economy and Society *263*

The Advent of Emancipation *265*

The Soldiers' War *267*

1863: The Tide of Battle Turns *268*

Disunity, South, North, and West *269*

1864–1865: The Final Test of Wills *272*

■ **LINKS TO THE WORLD: The Civil War in Britain** *273*

Summary *276*

LEGACY FOR A PEOPLE AND A NATION: The Confederate Battle Flag *277*

16 *R*econstruction: An Unfinished Revolution, 1865–1877 *279*

Wartime Reconstruction *281*

The Meanings of Freedom *282*

Johnson's Reconstruction Plan *284*

The Congressional Reconstruction Plan *286*

Reconstruction Politics in the South *289*

Reconstruction Reversed *292*

■ **LINKS TO THE WORLD: The Grants' Tour of the World** *294*

Summary *297*

LEGACY FOR A PEOPLE AND A NATION: The Fourteenth Amendment *297*

17 *T*he Development of the West, 1877–1900 *299*

The Economic Activities of Native Peoples *301*

The Transformation of Native Cultures *302*

The Extraction of Natural Resources *306*

Irrigation and Transportation *309*

Farming the Plains *310*

■ **LINKS TO THE WORLD: The Australian Frontier** *311*

The Ranching Frontier *314*

Summary *315*

LEGACY FOR A PEOPLE AND A NATION: The West and Rugged Individualism *316*

18 *T*he Machine Age, 1877–1920 *317*

Technology and the Triumph of Industrialism *319*

■ **LINKS TO THE WORLD: The Atlantic Cable** *321*

Mechanization and the Changing Status of Labor *324*

Labor Violence and the Union Movement *326*

Standards of Living *329*

The Corporate Consolidation Movement *333*

The Gospel of Wealth and Its Critics *334*

Summary *335*

LEGACY FOR A PEOPLE AND A NATION: Industrialism, Smoke, and Pollution Control *336*

19 *T*he Vitality and Turmoil of Urban Life, 1877–1920 *337*

Growth of the Modern City *338*

Urban Neighborhoods *343*

Living Conditions in the Inner City *345*

Managing the City *347*

Family Life   *350*
The New Leisure and Mass Culture   *352*
   LINKS TO THE WORLD: Japanese Baseball   *354*
Summary   *357*
LEGACY FOR A PEOPLE AND A NATION: Ethnic Food   *357*

20 Gilded Age Politics, 1877–1900   *358*

The Nature of Party Politics   *360*
Issues of Legislation   *360*
   LINKS TO THE WORLD: Missionaries   *361*
The Presidency Restrengthened   *364*
Discrimination, Disfranchisement, Response   *365*
Agrarian Unrest and Populism   *367*
The Depression and Protests of the 1890s   *370*
The Silver Crusade and the Election of 1896   *372*
Summary   *374*
LEGACY FOR A PEOPLE AND A NATION: Interpreting a Fairy Tale   *374*

21 The Progressive Era, 1895–1920   *376*

The Varied Progressive Impulse   *378*
Governmental and Legislative Reform   *381*
   LINKS TO THE WORLD: Russian Temperance   *382*
New Ideas in Social Institutions   *383*
Challenges to Racial and Sexual Discrimination   *385*
Theodore Roosevelt and the Revival of the Presidency   *388*
Woodrow Wilson and the Extension of Reform   *392*
Summary   *394*
LEGACY FOR A PEOPLE AND A NATION: Margaret Sanger, Planned Parenthood, and the Birth-Control Controversy   *394*

22 The Quest for Empire, 1865–1914   *396*

Imperial Dreams   *398*
Ambitions and Strategies   *402*
Crises in the 1890s: Hawai'i, Venezuela, and Cuba   *403*
The Spanish-American War and the Debate over Empire   *405*
Asian Encounters: War in the Philippines, Diplomacy in China   *407*
   LINKS TO THE WORLD: The U.S. System of Education in the Philippines   *408*
TR's World   *410*
Summary   *413*
LEGACY FOR A PEOPLE AND A NATION: The Status of Puerto Rico   *414*

23 Americans in the Great War, 1914–1920   *415*

Precarious Neutrality   *417*
The Decision for War   *418*
Winning the War   *420*
Mobilizing the Home Front   *423*
   LINKS TO THE WORLD: The Influenza Pandemic of 1918   *424*
Civil Liberties Under Challenge   *427*
Red Scare, Red Summer   *428*
The Defeat of Peace   *429*
Summary   *432*
LEGACY FOR A PEOPLE AND A NATION: Freedom of Speech and the ACLU   *432*

24 The New Era, 1920–1929   *434*

Big Business Triumphant   *435*
Politics and Government   *436*

Materialism Unbound   438
Cities, Migrants, and Suburbs   440
New Rhythms of Everyday Life   441
   LINKS TO THE WORLD: Pan American
   Airways   442
Lines of Defense   445
The Age of Play   448
Cultural Currents   449
The Election of 1928 and the End of the New
   Era   450
Summary   451
LEGACY FOR A PEOPLE AND A NATION: Intercollegiate
Athletics   452

25 The Great Depression and the
    New Deal, 1929–1941   453

Hoover and Hard Times: 1929–1933   455
Franklin D. Roosevelt and the Launching of the
   New Deal   459
Political Pressure and the Second New Deal   461
Labor   466
Federal Power and the Nationalization of
   Culture   467
   LINKS TO THE WORLD: The 1936 Olympic
   Games   469
The Limits of the New Deal   470
Summary   472
LEGACY FOR A PEOPLE AND A NATION: Social Security   473

26 Peaceseekers and Warmakers:
    Americans in the World,
    1920–1941   474

Searching for Peace and Order in the 1920s   476
The World Economy, Cultural Expansion, and Great
   Depression   477
U.S. Dominance in Latin America   480
The Course to War in Europe   481

Japan, China, and a New Order in Asia   483
U.S. Entry into World War II   484
   LINKS TO THE WORLD: Radio News   487
Summary   490
LEGACY FOR A PEOPLE AND A NATION: Presidential
Deception of the Public   490

27 The Second World War at Home
    and Abroad, 1941–1945   492

The United States at War   494
The Production Front and American Workers   496
Life on the Home Front   498
The Limits of American Ideals   500
   LINKS TO THE WORLD: War Brides   501
Life in the Military   504
Winning the War   505
Summary   509
LEGACY FOR A PEOPLE AND A NATION:
Atomic Waste   510

28 The Cold War and American
    Globalism, 1945–1961   511

From Allies to Adversaries   513
Containment in Action   517
The Cold War in Asia   519
The Korean War   520
Unrelenting Cold War   522
   LINKS TO THE WORLD: The People-to-People
   Campaign   524
The Struggle for the Third World   525
Summary   530
LEGACY FOR A PEOPLE AND A NATION: The National
Security State   531

29 America at Midcentury, 1945–1960 *532*

Shaping Postwar America   *534*
Domestic Politics in the Cold War Era   *536*
Cold War Fears and Anticommunism   *538*
The Struggle for Civil Rights   *540*
Creating a Middle-Class Nation   *543*
Men, Women, and Youth at Midcentury   *545*
   LINKS TO THE WORLD: Barbie   *548*
The Limits of the Middle-Class Nation   *549*
Summary   *551*
LEGACY FOR A PEOPLE AND A NATION: The Pledge of Allegiance   *551*

30 The Tumultuous Sixties, 1960–1968 *553*

Kennedy and the Cold War   *555*
Marching for Freedom   *557*
Liberalism and the Great Society   *560*
Johnson and Vietnam   *563*
A Nation Divided   *567*
1968   *570*
   LINKS TO THE WORLD: The British Invasion   *571*
Summary   *572*
LEGACY FOR A PEOPLE AND A NATION: The Immigration Act of 1965   *573*

31 Continuing Divisions and New Limits, 1969–1980 *574*

The New Politics of Identity   *576*
The Women's Movement and Gay Liberation   *578*
The End in Vietnam   *580*
Nixon, Kissinger, and the World   *582*
Presidential Politics and the Crisis of Leadership   *583*

   LINKS TO THE WORLD: OPEC and the 1973 Oil Embargo   *584*
Economic Crisis   *587*
An Era of Cultural Transformation   *590*
Renewed Cold War and Middle East Crisis   *591*
Summary   *593*
LEGACY FOR A PEOPLE AND A NATION: Human Rights   *594*

32 Conservatism Revived, 1980–1992 *595*

Reagan and the Conservative Resurgence   *597*
"Reaganomics"   *599*
Reagan and the World   *601*
   LINKS TO THE WORLD: CNN   *602*
A Polarized People: American Society in the 1980s   *606*
The End of the Cold War and Global Disorder   *610*
Summary   *613*
LEGACY FOR A PEOPLE AND A NATION: The Americans with Disabilities Act   *614*

33 Global Bridges in the New Millennium: America Since 1992 *615*

Social Strains and New Political Directions   *617*
"The New Economy" and Globalization   *619*
Paradoxes of Prosperity   *623*
September 11 and the War on Terrorism   *626*
Americans in the New Millennium   *630*
   LINKS TO THE WORLD: The Global AIDS Epidemic   *634*
Summary   *636*
LEGACY FOR A PEOPLE AND A NATION: The Internet   *636*

APPENDIX A-1

Documents   *A-1*

  Declaration of Independence in Congress, July 4, 1776   A-1

  Constitution of the United States of America and Amendments   A-2

Presidential Elections   *A-12*

Presidents and Vice Presidents   *A-17*

Justices of the Supreme Court   *A-19*

INDEX   *I-1*

SPECIAL FEATURES

Maps

1.1 Native Cultures of North America 6
1.2 Europe in 1490 9
2.1 European Settlements and Indians in Eastern North America, 1650 24
3.1 Atlantic Trade Routes 49
4.1 Major Origins and Destinations of Africans Enslaved in the Americas 60
5.1 European Settlements and Indians, 1754 78
6.1 The War in the North, 1775–1777 102
6.2 The War in the South 106
7.1 Western Land Claims and Cessions, 1782–1802 118
9.1 Louisiana Purchase 147
10.1 Missouri Compromise and the State of the Union, 1820 162
10.2 Removal of Native Americans from the South, 1820–1840 177
11.1 Westward Expansion, 1800–1860 196
12.1 Major American Cities in 1830 and 1860 206
14.1 The War with Mexico 239
14.2 The Kansas-Nebraska Act and Slavery Expansion, 1854 246
14.3 The Divided Nation: Slave and Free Areas, 1861 252
15.1 Battle of Gettysburg 269
15.2 Sherman's March to the Sea 275
16.1 The Reconstruction 288
16.2 Presidential Election of 1876 and the Compromise of 1877 296
17.1 The Development and Natural Resources of the West 306
18.1 Industrial Production, 1919 320
19.1 Urbanization, 1880 and 1920 340

21.1 Woman Suffrage Before 1920 389
22.1 Imperialism in Asia: Turn of the Century 409
22.2 U.S. Hegemony in the Caribbean and Latin America 411
23.1 American Troops at the Western Front, 1918 423
26.1 Japanese Expansion Before Pearl Harbor 485
26.2 The German Advance, 1939–1942 486
27.1 The Pacific War 485
27.2 The Allies on the Offensive in Europe, 1942–1945 506
28.1 Divided Europe 518
28.2 The Rise of the Third World: Newly Independent Nations Since 1943 526
30.1 Southeast Asia and the Vietnam War 565
31.1 The Continued Shift to the Sunbelt in the 1970s and 1980s 589
32.1 The United States in the Caribbean and Central America 605
33.1 The Middle East 629
33.2 Mapping America's Diversity 631

Figures

12.1 Major Sources of Immigration to the United States, 1831–1860 212
14.1 Voting Returns of Counties with Few Slaveholders, Eight Southern States, 1860 and 1861 253
15.1 Comparative Resources, Union and Confederate States, 1861 259
18.1 Distribution of Occupational Categories Among Employed Men and Women, 1880–1920 325

22.1   The Rise of U.S. Economic Power in the World   *400*

24.1   Changing Dimensions of Paid Female Labor, 1910–1930   *444*

24.2   Sources of Immigration, 1907 and 1927   *447*

25.1   The Economy Before and After the New Deal, 1929–1941   *463*

26.1   The United States in the World Economy   *478*

29.1   Birth Rate, 1945–1964   *535*

29.2   Marital Distribution of the Female Labor Force, 1944–1970   *546*

32.1   While the Rich Got Richer in the 1980s, the Poor Got Poorer   *603*

32.2   Poverty in America by Race, 1974–1990   *608*

33.1   The Changing American Family   *632*

Tables

2.1   The Founding of Permanent European Colonies in North America, 1565–1640   *23*

3.1   The Founding of English Colonies in North America, 1664–1681   *42*

5.1   The Colonial Wars, 1689–1763   *77*

18.1   American Living Standards, 1890–1910   *330*

24.1   Consumerism in the 1920s   *439*

25.1   New Deal Achievements   *462*

30.1   Great Society Achievement, 1964–1966   *562*

33.1   U.S. Military Personnel on Active Duty in Foreign Countires, 2001   *635*

PREFACE TO THE BRIEF SEVENTH EDITION

Creation of the Brief Edition

More than two decades have passed since the publication of the first brief edition of *A People and a Nation*. In that initial brief edition, as well as each subsequent one, the intent was to preserve the uniqueness and integrity of the complete work while condensing it. This Brief Seventh Edition once again reflects the scholarship, readability, and comprehensiveness of the full-length version. It also maintains the integration of social, cultural, political, economic, and foreign relations history that has been a hallmark of *A People and a Nation*.

The authors collectively mourn the death of William J. Brophy, who prepared the brief text for the previous six editions. His successors, though, have worked closely with us, ensuring that the changes in content and organization incorporated in the full-length Seventh Edition were retained in the condensation. The authors attained reductions by paring down details rather than deleting entire sections. The Brief Seventh Edition thus contains fewer statistics, fewer quotations, and fewer examples than the unabridged version. A sufficient number of quotations and examples were retained, however, to maintain the richness in style created by the authors.

The Brief Seventh Edition is available in both one- and two-volume formats. The two-volume format is divided as follows: Volume 1 contains Chapters 1 through 16, beginning with a discussion of three cultures—American, African, and European—that intersected during the exploration and colonization of the New World, and ending with a discussion of the Reconstruction era. Volume 2 contains Chapters 16 through 33, beginning its coverage at Reconstruction and extending the history of the American people to the present. The chapter on Reconstruction appears in both volumes to provide greater flexibility in matching a volume to the historical span covered by a specific course.

Changes in This Edition

While the preface to the full-length Seventh Edition elaborates on specific content changes, we note here that the authors paid increased attention to the following: ethnic and religious diversity in the United States; the environment and technology; the domestic, political, economic, and social impact of the nation's wars; and popular culture. The discussion of the relationship between America and the rest of the world from the colonial period to the present has been expanded throughout the book, as is exemplified in a feature now appearing in each chapter, "Links to the World." These emphases and the complete reorganization of the post-1960 chapters, as well as the updated scholarship on which they are based, are retained in the Brief Seventh Edition.

Although each author feels answerable for the whole of *A People and a Nation*, we take primary responsibility for particular chapters: Mary Beth Norton, Chapters 1–8; David M. Katzman, Chapters 9–12; David Blight, Chapters 13–16; Howard P. Chudacoff, Chapters 17–21 and 24; Fredrik Logevall, Chapters 22, 23, 26, 28, and shared responsibility for 30–33; Beth Bailey, Chapters 25, 27, 29, and shared responsibility for 30–33.

Teaching and Learning Aids

These supplements have been created with the diverse needs of today's students and instructors in mind.

For the Instructor

- The **Online Teaching Center** (http://college.hmco .com/pic/nortonbrief7e) includes PowerPoint slides of hundreds of maps, images, and other media related to each chapter in the book as well as web links and questions for use with Personal Response Systems. Instructors have access to 100 interactive maps and over 500 primary sources to use for assignments. In addition, there is an Instructor's Resource Manual that can aid in encouraging classroom discussions or constructively enhance a class presentation.

■ A **Class Prep CD-ROM** contains a computerized test bank prepared by George Warren of Central Piedmont Community College that includes search functions that allow instructors to design tests thematically by entering keywords. This CD contains the maps and images that are on the Online Teaching Center web site.

■ The **Blackboard/WebCT CD** provides instructors who want to offer all or part of their entire course online with much of the fundamental material for their course, including graded homework questions organized by topic. From this base, instructors can customize the course to meet their needs.

■ **Eduspace** provides the ability for instructors to create part or all of their courses online, using the widely recognized tools of Blackboard Learning System and content from Houghton Mifflin. Instructors can quickly and easily assign homework exercises, quizzes and tests, tutorials, and supplementary study materials and can modify or add content of their own. A powerful grade book in Eduspace allows instructors to monitor student progress and easily tabulate grades.

■ The **Houghton Mifflin U.S. History Transparency Set, Volumes I and II,** is a set of standard U.S. history transparencies, taken from illustrations and maps in the Houghton Mifflin survey texts. It includes 150 full-color maps.

■ **BiblioBase for U.S. History** is a database of hundreds of primary source documents—including speeches, essays, travel accounts, government documents, and memoirs—covering U.S. history from the fifteenth century to the present. This comprehensive database enables you to create a customized course pack of primary sources to complement any U.S. history text. You can search for documents by period, region, approach, theme, and type and then view the documents in their entirety before choosing your course pack selections.

■ The **Rand McNally Atlas of American History** is offered for packaging with the textbook. Please contact your sales representative for additional information.

For the Student

■ The **Online Study Center** (http://college.hmco .com/pic/nortonbrief7e) is a student web site that includes a wide array of interactive study content such as pre-class quizzes, ACE Practice Tests, vocabulary-building exercises, identification exercises, and interactive map activities, among other resources. This web site also contains the same primary sources and interactive maps that are on the Online Teaching Center.

■ **Icons** in the text direct students to interactive maps, primary sources, and ACE Practice Test questions.

Acknowledgments

For essential assistance in the preparation of this abridged edition, we are grateful to Jan Fitter and Debra Michals.

Author teams rely on review panels to help create and execute successful revision plans. For the revision of this Brief Seventh Edition, we were guided by the many historians whose thoughtful insights and recommendations helped us with the preparation of the full-length Seventh Edition. Their names appear in the preface to that edition that follows.

Finally, we want to thank the many people who have contributed their thoughts and labors to this work, especially the talented staff at Houghton Mifflin.

For the authors,
Mary Beth Norton,
Coordinating Author

PREFACE TO THE FULL-LENGTH SEVENTH EDITION

Some readers might think that a book entering its seventh edition would be little changed from the previous version. Nothing could be further from the truth. In this seventh edition, *A People and a Nation* has undergone major revisions, while still retaining the narrative strength and focus that characterized its earlier editions and made it so popular with students and teachers alike. In the years since the publication of the sixth edition, new documents have been uncovered, new interpretations advanced, and new themes (especially globalization) have come to the forefront of American historical scholarship. The authors—including two new members of our team—have worked diligently to incorporate those findings into this text.

Like other teachers and students, we are always re-creating our past, restructuring our memory, rediscovering the personalities and events that have influenced us, injured us, and bedeviled us. This book represents our continuing rediscovery of America's history—its diverse people and the nation they created and have nurtured. As this book demonstrates, there are many different Americans and many different memories. We have sought to present all of them, in both triumph and tragedy, in both division and unity.

About *A People and a Nation*

A People and a Nation, first published in 1982, was the first major textbook in the United States to fully integrate social and political history. Since the outset, the authors have been determined to tell the story of *all* the people of the United States. This book's hallmark has been its melding of social and political history, its movement beyond history's common focus on public figures and events to examine the daily life of America's people. All editions of the book have stressed the interaction of public policy and personal experience, the relationship between domestic concerns and foreign affairs, the various manifestations of popular culture, and the multiple origins of America and Americans. We have consistently built our narrative on a firm foundation in primary sources—on both well-known and obscure letters, diaries, public documents, oral histories, and artifacts of material culture. We have long challenged readers to think about the meaning of American history, not just to memorize facts. Both students and instructors have repeatedly told us how much they appreciate and enjoy our approach to the past.

As has been true since the first edition, each chapter opens with a dramatic vignette focusing on an individual or a group of people. These vignettes develop key questions, which then frame the chapters in succinct introductions and summaries. Numerous maps, tables, graphs, and charts provide readers with the necessary geographical and statistical context for observations in the text. Carefully selected illustrations—many of them unique to this book—offer readers visual insight into the topics under discussion, especially because the authors have written the captions. In this edition, as in all previous ones, we have sought to incorporate up-to-date scholarship, readability, a clear structure, critical thinking, and instructive illustrative material on every page.

What's New in This Edition

Planning for the seventh edition began at a two-day authors' meeting at the Houghton Mifflin headquarters in Boston. There we discussed the most recent scholarship in the field, the reviews of the sixth edition solicited from instructors, and the findings of our own continuing research. For this edition, we added two new colleagues, who experienced the intellectual exhilaration and rigor of such an authors' meeting for the first time. Beth Bailey, who has written acclaimed works on sexuality and popular culture in modern America, now writes the chapters and sections dealing with domestic matters after the 1920s. Fredrik Logevall, whose scholarship on the Vietnam War has won international recognition, now writes all the chapters and sections on foreign policy since the Civil War. These new authors have substantially reworked and reorganized the post-1945 chapters, in ways outlined below.

This seventh edition enhances the global perspective on American history that has characterized the book since its first edition. From the "Atlantic world" context of European colonies in North and South America to the discussion of international terrorism, the authors have incorporated the most recent globally oriented scholarship throughout the volume. We have worked to strengthen our treatment of the diversity of America's people by examining differences within the broad ethnic categories commonly employed and by paying greater attention to immigration, cultural and intellectual infusions from around the world, and America's growing religious diversity. At the same time, we have more fully integrated the discussion of such diversity into our narrative, so as not to artificially isolate any group from the mainstream. Treatments of environmental history and the history of technology have both been expanded. Finally, we have streamlined the useful chronologies that appear near the beginning of each chapter.

As always, the authors reexamined every sentence, interpretation, map, chart, illustration, and caption, refining the narrative, presenting new examples, and bringing to the text the latest findings of scholars in many areas of history, anthropology, sociology, and political science. More than a quarter of the chapter-opening vignettes are new, as is also true of the popular "Legacy" features introduced in the sixth edition.

To students who question the relevance of historical study, the legacies offer compelling and timely answers. Those brief essays, which follow the chapter summaries, explore the historical roots of contemporary topics. New subjects of legacies include the "self-made man" ideal, states' rights, reparations for slavery, Planned Parenthood, the Social Security system, the concern for human rights, and the Americans with Disabilities Act.

New "Links to the World"

keeping with the emphasis on globalization in this on, and building on the long-standing strength of

this text in the history of American foreign relations, we have introduced a new feature in each chapter: "Links to the World." Examining both inward and outward ties between America (and Americans) and the rest of the world, the "Links" appear at appropriate places in each chapter to explore specific topics at considerable length. Tightly constructed essays detail the often little-known connections between developments here and abroad. The topics range broadly over economic, political, social, technological, medical, and cultural history, vividly demonstrating that the geographical region that is now the United States has never lived in isolation from other peoples and countries. Examples include the impact of American maize (corn) on the rest of the world, the introduction of coffee and tea into the American colonies, the discovery of gold in California, proposals to annex Cuba, baseball in Japan, Pan American Airways, the influenza pandemic of 1918, the 1936 Olympics, Barbie dolls, CNN, and the AIDS epidemic. Each "Link" highlights global interconnections with unusual and lively examples that will both intrigue and inform students.

Themes in This Book

Several themes and questions stand out in our continuing effort to integrate political, social, and cultural history. We study the many ways Americans have defined themselves—gender, race, class, region, ethnicity, religion, sexual orientation—and the many subjects that have reflected their multidimensional experiences. We highlight the remarkably diverse everyday lives of the American people—in cities and on farms and ranches, in factories and in corporate headquarters, in neighborhoods and in legislatures, in love relationships and in hate groups, in recreation and in work, in the classroom and in military uniform, in secret national security conferences and in public foreign relations debates, in church and in voluntary associations, in polluted environments and in conservation areas. We pay particular attention to lifestyles, diet and dress, family life and structure, labor conditions, gender roles, migration and mobility, childbearing, and child rearing. We explore how Americans have entertained and informed themselves by discussing their music, sports, theater, print media, film, radio, television, graphic arts, and literature, in both "high" culture and popular culture. We study how technology has influenced Americans' lives, such as through the internal combustion engine and the computer.

Americans' personal lives have always interacted with the public realm of politics and government. To understand how Americans have sought to protect their different ways of life and to work out solutions to thorny problems, we emphasize their expectations of governments at the local, state, and federal levels; governments' role in providing answers; the lobbying of interest groups; the campaigns and outcomes of elections; and the hierarchy of power in any period. Because the United States has long been a major participant in world affairs, we explore America's participation in wars, interventions in other nations, empire-building, immigration patterns, images of foreign peoples, cross-national cultural ties, and international economic trends.

Section-by-Section Changes in This Edition

Mary Beth Norton, who had primary responsibility for Chapters 1 through 8 and served as coordinating author, expanded coverage of ancient North America (the Anasazi and Mississippians); Brazil, the Caribbean islands, and Nova Scotia; witchcraft, especially the 1692 Salem crisis; migration to the colonies from England, Ireland, and Germany; the trade in African and Indian slaves and the impact of that trade on African and Native American societies; the trans-Appalachian west in peace and war; and slavery and gradual emancipation after the Revolution. She also reorganized Chapter 3 to consolidate related materials on politics and the imperial context, and extensively revised and expanded Chapter 6 to reflect recent scholarship. There are new sections on the West during the revolutionary era and on the experiences of ordinary Americans in wartime, both in and out of the military.

David M. Katzman, with responsibility for Chapters 9 through 12, has continued (as in the sixth edition) to sharpen the chronological flow in these chapters. He has broadened the discussion of political culture and emerging partisanship in the young republic, reflecting the current rethinking of politics at that time. He has expanded coverage of religious life and the links between religion and social and po-

litical reform. The discussions of families, immigrant lives (especially the Irish), and African American identity, culture, and communities have all been completely revised. Throughout, there is greater attention paid to technology, global ties, and popular culture.

David W. Blight, who had primary responsibility for Chapters 13 through 16, enhanced the discussion of women and gender throughout these chapters. He also added material on the lives of freed people, before, during, and after the Civil War; the impact of the Fugitive Slave Law; the West in the Civil War and Reconstruction eras; and the home front during wartime. He revised the interpretation of the Denmark Vesey slave rebellion and increased coverage of the Underground Railroad, and of the role of the Mormons and westward expansion in the slavery crisis. In Chapter 15, he developed new sections on how the Civil War shaped the future of Indians in the far West, as well as the conflict's significance abroad, especially in England.

Howard P. Chudacoff, responsible for Chapters 17 through 21 and 24, has increased the coverage of technology throughout his chapters, adding discussions of farming technology, the machine tool industry, technological education in universities, birth-control devices, and the automobile. He has included new material on the environment as well, expanding his discussion of such topics as water supply and sewage disposal, the unanticipated effects of national parks, and the conservation movement. Topics related to ethnicity—including anti-Chinese violence and exclusion laws, Mexican immigration, and holiday celebrations by ethnic groups—also receive increased attention. He has reconfigured portions of Chapters 18, 19, and 21 to clarify the narrative.

Fredrik Logevall, with primary responsibility for Chapters 22, 23, 26, and 28, worked to internationalize the treatment of America's foreign relations by giving greater attention to the perspectives of nations with which we interacted, and by examining the foreign policy aims of such leaders as Joseph Stalin, especially in Chapters 23 and 26. He significantly expanded the coverage of U.S. relations with the Middle East, showing the increasing importance of America's dealings with that region during the past four decades. He has also brought a sense of contingency to the narrative of American foreign relations, suggesting that matters might have turned out quite differently at various key junctures had policy-makers reached different decisions. He made major changes in Chapter 28 (formerly Chapter 29), creating greater thematic unity and incorporating much new scholarship on the Cold War and relations with China and the Soviet Union. Throughout, Logevall builds on the excellent foundation laid by Thomas G. Paterson, who wrote these and the post-1960 foreign policy chapters in the previous six editions of this textbook, and who also served as the coordinating author for all six of those editions.

Beth Bailey, primarily responsible for Chapters 25, 27, and 29, integrated the experiences and actions of various groups into the main narrative while still focusing on the diversity of the American people in the modern era. In general, she enhanced coverage of the South and West (especially Latinos and Mexican immigrants in the Southwest) and added material on gender, sexuality, and popular culture. Throughout these chapters she placed Americans' fears about their nation's future in an international context. In Chapter 25, she strengthened the discussion of New Deal policies, showing how assumptions about race and gender structured these important social programs. Chapter 27 has a stronger chronological framework, as well as new treatments of culture and daily life during WWII, in combat and on the home front. Chapter 29 (formerly Chapter 28) has been extensively revised, assessing the myriad transformations of American society and culture in the 1950s, with particular attention to race, labor, masculinity, McCarthyism, and the impact of new federal policies. Bailey's work updates the domestic policy chapters written superbly in the previous six editions by William M. Tuttle, Jr.

Post-1960 Chapters

Bailey and Logevall shared responsibility for the new Chapters 30 through 33. In these completely revamped chapters, domestic and foreign topics are discussed in tandem rather than separately, demonstrating the extensive linkages between them. The two authors collaborated closely to create a fresh and lively, comprehensive, chronologically based narrative that places events in the United States in their appropriate international setting. The coverage of foreign relations includes increased attention to the Middle East and to the motivations of America's allies and opponents alike. The treatment of the Vietnam War now draws on Logevall's own scholarship, just as the discussion of recent popular culture and sexuality is based on Bailey's original research. Increased attention is given to the civil rights movement, the rise of second- and third-wave feminism, new patterns of immigration, and the growth of grassroots conservatism.

Teaching and Learning Aids

The supplements listed here accompany this Seventh Edition of *A People and a Nation*. They have been created with the diverse needs of today's students and instructors in mind, with extensive print and non-print resources available.

We are proud to announce the *History Companion*, your new primary source for history technology solutions. The *History Companion* has three components: the *Instructor Companion*, the *Student Study Companion*, and the *Student Research Companion*. Each of these components is described below: the *Instructor Companion* under instructor resources, and the *Student Research Companion* and *Student Study Companion* under student resources.

For the Instructor:

■ The *Instructor Companion* is an easily searchable CD-ROM that makes hundreds of historical images and maps instantly accessible in PowerPoint format. Each image is accompanied by notes that place it in its proper historical context and tips for ways it can be presented in the classroom. With this edition of *A People and a Nation*, this CD also includes a wealth of additional resources, including testing, lecture, and course planning tools. A computerized test bank is included complete with search functions, which allows instructors to design tests thematically by entering keywords to bring up particular questions. An Instructor's Resource Guide is also included that can aid in encouraging classroom discussions or constructively enhance a class presentation. This CD is free to instructors with the adoption of this Houghton Mifflin textbook.

- A print **Test Bank,** prepared by George Warren of Central Piedmont Community College, also accompanies the text and contains many multiple choice, identification, geography, and essay questions for use in creating exams.

- In addition, a series of **PowerPoint** slides, created by Barney Rickman of Valdosta State University, is included to assist in instruction and discussion of key topics and material.

- The **Blackboard/WebCT Basic CD** provides instructors who want to offer all or part of their entire course online with much of the fundamental material for their course. From this base, instructors can customize the course to meet their needs.

- The **Houghton Mifflin U.S. History Transparency Set, Volumes I and II,** is a set of standard U.S. history transparencies, taken from illustrations and maps in the Houghton Mifflin survey texts. It includes 150 full-color maps.

- **BiblioBase for U.S. History** is a database of hundreds of primary source documents—including speeches, essays, travel accounts, government documents, and memoirs—covering U.S. history from the fifteenth century to the present. This comprehensive database enables you to create a customized course pack of primary sources to complement any U.S. history text. You can search for documents by period, region, approach, theme, and type and then view the documents in their entirety before choosing your course pack selections.

- The **Rand McNally Atlas of American History** is offered for packaging with the textbook. Please contact your sales representative for additional information.

For the Student:

The **Houghton Mifflin History Companion** for *A People and a Nation,* Seventh Edition, has two student components.

- The *Student Study Companion* is a free online study guide that contains ACE self-tests, flash-cards, timelines, chronology exercises, graphic organizer exercises, map exercises, text feature exercises, web links, and Internet exercises. These study tools will help your students to be more successful.

- The *Student Research Companion* is a free Internet-based tool with 100 interactive maps and 500 primary sources. The primary sources include headnotes that provide pertinent background information, and both the maps and the primary sources include questions that students can answer and e-mail to their instructors.

- **Study Guide Volumes I and II,** by George Warren, offers students learning objectives, vocabulary exercises, identification suggestions, skill-building activities, multiple choice questions, essay questions, and map exercises in two volumes.

- **American Ethnic Identities: Online Activities** By using examples throughout American history, these informative and lively activities will broaden your understanding of the different ethnic groups that make up the United States.

Acknowledgments

The authors would like to thank the following persons for their assistance with the preparation of this edition: Shawn Alexander, David Anthony Tyeeme Clark, Mike Ezra, David Farber, Max Bailey/Farber, Steve Jacobson, Andrea Katzman, Eric Katzman, Julee Katzman, Theo Katzman, Ariela Katzman-Jacobson, Elieza Katzman-Jacobson, Iris Jane Katzman, Sharyn Brooks Katzman, Danyel Logevall, Chester Pach, Cheryl Ragar, Ann Schofield, Daniel Williams, and Norman Yetman.

At each stage of this revision, a sizable panel of historian reviewers read drafts of our chapters. Their suggestions, corrections, and pleas helped guide us through this momentous revision. We could not include all of their recommendations, but the book is better for our having heeded most of their advice. We heartily thank:

Marynita Anderson, *Nassau Community College*
Erica R. Armstrong, *University of Delaware*

Jim Barrett, *University of Illinois at Urbana-Champaign*

Virginia R. Boynton, *Western Illinois University*

Robert Cottrell, *California State University, Chico*

Bruce Dierenfield, *Canisius College*

Lisa Lindquist Dorr, *University of Alabama*

Latricia E. Gill-Brown, *Pensacola Junior College*

Melanie Gustafson, *University of Vermont*

Jorge Iber, *Texas Tech University*

Anthony E. Kaye, *Pennsylvania State University, University Park*

Carol A. Keller, *San Antonio College*

Kathleen Kennedy, *Western Washington University*

Anne Klejment, *University of St. Thomas*

Carolyn J. Lawes, *Old Dominion University*

Patrick K. Moore, *University of West Florida*

Jared Orsi, *Colorado State University*

Chester Pach, *Ohio University*

Marie Jenkins Schwartz, *University of Rhode Island*

Erik R. Seeman, *SUNY-Buffalo*

Sayuri G. Shimizu, *Michigan State University*

Manisha Sinha, *University of Massachusetts, Amherst*

Evelyn Sterne, *University of Rhode Island*

Benson Tong, *Wichita State University*

Michael M. Topp, *University of Texas, El Paso*

The authors once again thank the extraordinary Houghton Mifflin people who designed, edited, produced, and nourished this book. Their high standards and acute attention to both general structure and fine detail are cherished in the publishing industry. Many thanks, then, to Jean Woy, editor-in-chief; Sally Constable, sponsoring editor; Ann Hofstra Grogg, freelance development editor; Bob Greiner, senior project editor; Sandra McGuire, senior marketing manager; Henry Rachlin, senior designer; Carol Merrigan, senior production/design coordinator; Marie Barnes, senior manufacturing coordinator; Pembroke Herbert, photo researcher; Charlotte Miller, art editor; and Kisha Mitchell and Trinity Peacock-Broyles, editorial assistants.

THREE OLD WORLDS CREATE A NEW 1492–1600

*a*s they neared the village called Cofitachequi on May 1, 1540, the band of Spanish explorers led by Hernán de Soto beheld a surprising scene. Villagers came to meet the Europeans, carrying their female chief, or *cacica*. The Lady of Cofitachequi, a Spanish chronicler recorded, welcomed the weary Spaniards to her domain in today's western South Carolina, giving Soto a string of pearls from her neck. Later, she gave the hungry men huge quantities of corn and, seeing that they especially valued pearls, suggested they take the ones they would find in nearby burial chambers.

The Spanish explorers had landed at Tampa Bay, Florida, about a year earlier. They would wander through what is now the southeastern United States for three more years, encountering many different peoples, whom they often treated with great cruelty. Always they sought gold and silver. The people of Cofitachequi told the Spaniards they might find these treasures in another ruler's domain, about twelve days' travel away. When Soto left, he took the Lady with him as a captive, but she escaped and presumably returned home.

Why had the Lady greeted Soto's band so kindly? Perhaps she did not have enough men to resist the Europeans; her people had been devastated by an unknown "pestilence" two years earlier. Or possibly messengers had informed the Lady about Soto's vicious treatment of villages he had previously encountered. Whatever her reasoning, the strategy worked: Soto and his men moved on, and Cofitachequi survived to be recorded by Spanish, French, and finally English visitors over the next 130 years.

For thousands of years before 1492, human societies in the Americas had developed in isolation from the rest of the world. The era that began in the Christian fifteenth century brought that long-standing isolation to an end. As Europeans sought treasure and trade, peoples from different cultures came into regular contact for the first time. All were profoundly changed. The brief encounter between Soto and the Lady of Cofitachequi illustrates many of the

American Societies

North America in 1492

African Societies

European Societies

Early European Explorations

The Voyages of Columbus, Cabot, and Their Successors

Spanish Exploration and Conquest

The Columbian Exchange

LINKS TO THE WORLD
Maize

Europeans in North America

LEGACY FOR A PEOPLE AND A NATION
Columbus Day

Online Study Center
This icon will direct you to interactive map and primary source activities on the website http://college.hmco.com/pic/nortonbrief7e

CHRONOLOGY

12,000–10,000 B.C.E. • Paleo-Indians begin migrating from Asia to North America across the Beringia land bridge

7000 B.C.E. • Cultivation of food crops begins in America

c. 1000 B.C.E. • Olmec civilization appears

c. 300–600 C.E. • Height of influence of Teotihuacán

c. 600–900 C.E. • Classic Mayan civilization

1000 C.E. • Anasazi build settlements in modern states of Arizona and New Mexico

1001 • Norse establish settlement in "Vinland"

1050–1250 • Height of influence of Cahokia; prevalence of Mississippian culture in midwestern and southeastern United States

14th century • Aztec rise to power

1450s–80s • Portuguese explore and colonize islands in the Mediterranean Atlantic and São Tomé in Gulf of Guinea

1477 • Publication of Marco Polo's *Travels,* describing China

1492 • Columbus reaches Bahamas

1494 • Treaty of Tordesillas divides land claims between Spain and Portugal in Africa, India, and South America

1496 • Last Canary Island falls to Spain

1497 • Cabot reaches North America

1513 • León explores Florida

1518–30 • Smallpox epidemic devastates Indian population of West Indies and Central and South America

1519 • Cortés invades Mexico

1521 • Tenochtitlán surrenders to Cortés; Aztec Empire falls to Spaniards

1524 • Verrazzano sails along Atlantic coast of United States

1534–35 • Cartier explores St. Lawrence River

1539–42 • Soto explores southeastern United States

1540–42 • Coronado explores southwestern United States

1587–90 • Raleigh's Roanoke colony vanishes

1588 • Harriot publishes *A Briefe and True Report of the New Found Land of Virginia*

---

elements of contact: cruelty and kindness, greed and deception, trade and theft, surprise and sickness, captivity and enslavement. By the time Soto and his men landed in Florida in 1539, the age of European expansion and colonization was already well under way. The history of the tiny colonies that would become the United States must be seen in this broad context of European exploration and exploitation.

The continents that European sailors reached in the late fifteenth century had their own history. The residents of the Americas were the world's most skilled plant breeders; they had developed vegetable crops more nutritious and productive than those grown in Europe, Asia, or Africa. They had invented systems of writing and mathematics and had created calendars as accurate as those used on the other side of the Atlantic. In the Americas, as in Europe, states rose and fell as leaders succeeded or failed in expanding their political and economic power. But the arrival of Europeans immeasurably altered the Americans' struggles with one another.

After 1400, European nations tried to acquire valuable colonies and trading posts elsewhere in the world. Initially they were interested primarily in Asia and Africa, but many Europeans eventually focused their attention on the Americas. Their contests for trade and conquest changed the course of history on four continents. Even as Europeans slowly achieved dominance, their fates were shaped by the strategies of Americans and Africans. In the Americas of the fifteenth and sixteenth centuries, three old worlds came together to produce a new. ■

American Societies

*H*uman beings originated on the continent of Africa, where humanlike remains about 3 million years old have been found in what is now Ethiopia. Over many millennia, the growing population slowly dispersed to the other continents. Scholars have long believed that all the earliest inhabitants of the Americas crossed a land bridge known as Beringia (at the site of the Bering Strait) approximately 12,000 to 14,000 years ago. Yet striking new archaeological discoveries in both North and South America suggest that some parts of the Americas may have been settled much earlier, perhaps by seafarers crossing from northern Europe by island hopping from Iceland to Greenland to Baffin Island, much as the Vikings did many millennia later (see Map 1.1).

The first Americans are called Paleo-Indians. Nomadic hunters of game and gatherers of wild plants,

ANCIENT AMERICA

they spread throughout North and South America, probably moving as bands composed of extended families. By about 11,500 years ago the Paleo-Indians were making fine stone projectile points, which they attached to wooden spears and used to kill the large mammals then living in the Americas. But as the Ice Age ended and the human population increased, all the large American mammals except the bison (buffalo) disappeared. As their meat supply decreased, the Paleo-Indians found new ways to survive.

By approximately 9,000 years ago, the residents of what is now central Mexico began to cultivate food crops, especially maize (corn), squash, beans, and peppers. In the Andes Mountains of South America, people started to grow potatoes. As knowledge of agricultural techniques improved and spread throughout the Americas, vegetables and maize proved a more reliable source of food than hunting and gathering. Thus, most Americans started to adopt a more sedentary style of life so that they could tend fields regularly. Some established permanent settlements; others moved several times a year among fixed sites. All the American cultures emphasized producing sufficient food to support themselves. Trade existed, but no society ever became dependent on another group for items vital to its survival.

Wherever agriculture dominated the economy, complex civilizations flourished. Such societies, assured of steady supplies, were able to accumulate wealth, produce ornamental objects, trade with other groups, and create elaborate rituals and ceremonies. In North America, the successful cultivation of nutritious crops seems to have led to the growth and development of all the major civilizations: first the large city-states of Mesoamerica (modern Mexico and Guatemala), and then the urban clusters known collectively as the Mississippian culture and located in the present-day United States. Each of these societies reached its height of population and influence only after achieving success in agriculture. Each later collapsed after reaching the limits of its food supply.

Little is known about the first major Mesoamerican civilization, that of the Olmecs, who about 3,000

MESOAMERICAN CIVILIZATIONS

years ago lived near the Gulf of Mexico in cities dominated by temple pyramids. Two societies that developed approximately 1,000 years later, those of the Mayas and of Teotihuacán, are better recorded. Teotihuacán, founded in the Valley of Mexico about 300 B.C.E. (Before the Common Era), eventually became one of the largest urban areas in the world, housing perhaps 100,000 people in the fifth century C.E. (Common Era). Teotihuacán's commercial network extended hundreds of miles; many peoples prized its obsidian (a green glass), used to make fine knives and mirrors. Pilgrims must also have traveled long distances to visit Teotihuacán's impressive pyramids and the great temple of Quetzalcoatl—the feathered serpent, primary god of central Mexico.

On the Yucatán Peninsula, in today's eastern Mexico, the Mayas built urban centers containing tall pyramids and temples. They studied astronomy and created the first writing system in the Americas.

Their city-states, though, engaged in near-constant warfare with one another. Warfare and an inadequate food supply caused the collapse of the most powerful cities by 900 C.E., thus ending the classic era of Mayan civilization. By the time Spaniards arrived five hundred years later, only a few remnants of the once-mighty society remained.

Ancient native societies in what is now the United States learned to grow maize, squash, and

ANASAZI AND MISSISSIPPIANS

beans from Mesoamericans, but the exact relationship of the various cultures is unknown. (No Meso-american artifacts have been found north of the Rio Grande, but some items resembling Mississippian objects have been excavated in northern Mexico.) The Hohokam, Mogollon, and Anasazi peoples of the modern states of Arizona and New Mexico subsisted by combining hunting and gathering with agriculture in an arid region. Hohokam villagers constructed extensive irrigation systems, but even so, they occasionally had to relocate when water supplies failed. Between 900 and 1150 C.E., the Anasazi built fourteen "Great Houses" in Chaco Canyon, each a massive multistoried stone structure averaging two hundred rooms. The canyon served as a major regional trading and processing center for turquoise, used then as now to create beautiful ornamental objects. Scholars have not determined why the Anasazi disappeared or where they went, but a major drought could well have been responsible.

At almost the same time, the unrelated Mississippian culture flourished in what is now the midwestern and southeastern United States. Relying largely on maize, squash, nuts, pumpkins, and venison for food, the Mississippians lived in substantial settlements. The largest of their urban centers was the City of the Sun (now called Cahokia), near modern St. Louis. Located near the confluence of the Illinois, Missouri, and Mississippi Rivers, Cahokia, like Teotihuacán and Chaco Canyon, served as a focal point for both religion and trade. At its peak (in the eleventh and twelfth centuries C.E.), the City of the Sun covered more than 5 square miles and had a population of about twenty thousand—small by Mesoamerican standards but larger than London in the same era.

Although the Cahokians never seem to have invented a writing system, these sun worshipers

developed an accurate calendar, evidenced by a woodhenge—a large circle of timber posts aligned with the solstices and the equinox. The city's main pyramid (one of 120 of varying sizes), today called Monks Mound, was at the time of its construction the third largest structure in the Western Hemisphere; it remains the largest earthwork ever built in the Americas. It sat at the northern end of the Grand Plaza, surrounded by seventeen other mounds, some used for burials. Yet after 1250 C.E., the city was abandoned. Archaeologists believe that climate change and degradation of the environment, caused by overpopulation and the destruction of nearby forests, brought about the city's collapse.

The Aztecs' histories tell of the long migration of their people (who called themselves Mexica) into the

AZTECS

Valley of Mexico during the twelfth century. The uninhabited ruins of Teotihuacán, which by then had been deserted for at least two hundred years, awed and mystified the migrants. Their chronicles record that their primary deity, Huitzilopochtli—a war god represented by an eagle—directed them to establish their capital on an island where they saw an eagle eating a serpent, the symbol of Quetzalcoatl. That island city became Tenochtitlán, the center of a rigidly stratified society composed of hereditary classes of warriors, merchants, priests, common folk, and slaves.

The Aztecs conquered their neighbors, forcing them to pay tribute, including human beings who could be sacrificed to Huitzilopochtli. The war god's taste for blood was not easily quenched. At the 1502 coronation of Motecuhzoma II (Montezuma to the Spaniards), five thousand people are thought to have been sacrificed by having their still-beating hearts torn from their bodies.

The Aztecs believed that they lived in the age of the Fifth Sun. Four times previously, they wrote, the earth and all the people who lived on it had been destroyed. They predicted that their own world would end in earthquakes and hunger. In the Aztec year Thirteen Flint, volcanoes erupted, sickness and hunger spread, and an eclipse of the sun darkened the sky. Did some priest wonder whether the Fifth Sun was approaching its end? In time, the Aztecs learned that Thirteen Flint was called 1492 by the Europeans.

North America in 1492

*O*ver the centuries, the Americans who lived north of Mexico adapted their once-similar ways of life to very different climates and terrains, thus creating the diverse cultures that the Europeans encountered when they first arrived (see Map 1.1). Scholars often refer to such cultures by language group (such as Algonquian or Iroquoian), since neighboring Indian nations commonly spoke related languages. Bands that lived in environments not well suited to agriculture followed a nomadic lifestyle. Within the area of the present-day United States, these groups included the Paiutes and Shoshones, who inhabited the Great Basin (now Nevada and Utah). Because of the difficulty of finding sufficient food for more than a few people, such hunter-gatherer bands were small. The men hunted small animals, and the women gathered seeds and berries. Where large game was more plentiful and food supplies therefore more certain, as in present-day central and western Canada and the Great Plains, bands of hunters were somewhat larger.

In more favorable environments, larger groups combined agriculture with gathering, hunting, and fishing. Those who lived near the seacoasts, like the Chinooks of present-day Washington State and Oregon, consumed fish and shellfish in addition to growing crops and gathering seeds and berries. Residents of the interior (for example, the Arikaras of the Missouri River valley) hunted large animals while also cultivating maize, squash, and beans. The peoples of what is now eastern Canada and the northeastern United States also combined hunting and agriculture.

Societies that relied primarily on hunting large animals assigned that task to men and allotted food preparation and clothing production to women. Agricultural societies, by contrast, differed in their assignments of work to the sexes. The Pueblo peoples (descendants of the Anasazi) defined agricultural labor as men's work. In the east, large clusters of peoples speaking Algonquian, Iroquoian, and Muskogean languages allocated most agricultural chores to women. In all the farming societies, women gathered wild foods and prepared food for consumption or storage, while men were responsible for hunting.

SEXUAL DIVISION OF LABOR IN NORTH AMERICA

Everywhere in North America, women cared for young children, while older youths learned adult skills from the parent of the same sex. Young people usually chose their own marital partners, and in most societies couples could easily divorce. Populations in these societies remained at a level sustainable by existing food supplies, largely because of low birth rates. Mothers nursed infants and toddlers until the age of two or even longer, and taboos prevented couples from having sexual intercourse during that period.

The southwestern and eastern agricultural peoples had similar social organizations. The Pueblos lived in multistory buildings constructed on terraces along the sides of cliffs or other easily defended sites. Northern Iroquois villages (in modern New York State) were composed of large, rectangular, bark-covered structures, or longhouses. In the present-day southeastern United States, Muskogeans and southern Algonquians lived in large houses made of thatch. Defensive wood palisades and ditches surrounded most of the eastern villages.

SOCIAL ORGANIZATION

In all the agricultural societies, each dwelling housed an extended family defined matrilineally (through a female line of descent). Mothers, their married daughters, and their daughters' husbands and children all lived together. Matrilineal descent did not imply matriarchy, or the wielding of power by women, but rather served as a way to reckon kinship. Extended families were linked into clans defined by matrilineal ties. The nomadic bands of the Great Plains, by contrast, were most often related patrilineally (through the male line).

Long before Europeans arrived, residents of the continent fought one another for control of the best hunting and fishing territories, the most fertile agricultural lands, or the sources of essential items like salt (for preserving meat) and flint (for making knives and arrowheads). People captured in such wars were sometimes enslaved, but slavery was never an important source of labor in pre-Columbian America.

WAR AND POLITICS

American political structures varied considerably. Among Pueblo and Muskogean peoples, the village council was the highest political authority; no

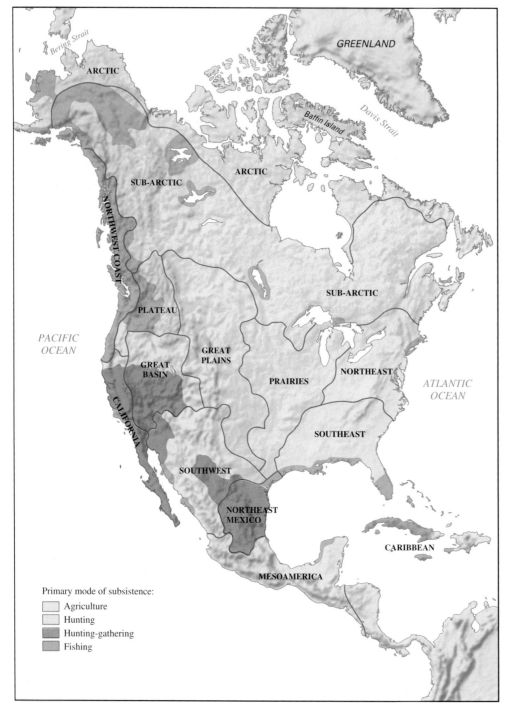

Primary mode of subsistence:
- Agriculture
- Hunting
- Hunting-gathering
- Fishing

Map 1.1   Native Cultures of North America

The natives of the North American continent effectively used the resources of the
regions in which they lived. As this map shows, coastal groups relied on fishing,
residents of fertile areas engaged in agriculture, and other peoples employed
hunting (often combined with gathering) as a primary mode of subsistence.

government structure connected the villages. Nomadic hunters also lacked formal links among separate bands. The Iroquois, by contrast, had an elaborate political hierarchy incorporating villages into nations and nations into a confederation; a council comprising representatives from each nation made crucial decisions concerning war and peace for the entire confederacy. In all the North American cultures, political power was divided between civil and war leaders, who wielded authority only so long as they retained the confidence of the people. Women assumed leadership roles more often among agricultural peoples than among nomadic hunters. Female sachems (rulers) led Algonquian villages in what is now Massachusetts, but women never became heads of Great Plains hunting bands. Iroquois women did not become chiefs, yet the clan matrons of each village chose its chief and could both start wars (by calling for the capture of prisoners to replace dead relatives) and stop them (by refusing to supply warriors with necessary foodstuffs).

Online Study Center
Improve Your Grade
   Primary Source: Dekanawida Myth & the
   Achievement of Iroquois Unity

Americans' religious beliefs varied even more than did their political systems, but all the peoples were

RELIGION

polytheistic, worshiping a multitude of gods. Each group's most important beliefs and rituals were closely tied to its means of subsistence. The major deities of agricultural peoples like the Pueblos and Muskogeans were associated with cultivation. The most important gods of hunters (such as those living on the Great Plains) were associated with animals. A band's economy and women's role in it helped to determine women's potential as religious leaders. Women held the most prominent positions in agricultural societies in which they were also the chief food producers, whereas in hunting societies, men took the lead in religious as well as political affairs.

A wide variety of cultures, comprising more than 5 million people, thus inhabited mainland North America when Europeans arrived. The diverse inhabitants of North America spoke well over one thousand different languages. For obvious reasons, they did not consider themselves one people, nor did they—for the most part—think of uniting to repel the European invaders.

African Societies

Fifteenth-century Africa also housed a variety of cultures adapted to different terrains and climates. In the north, along the Mediterranean Sea, lived the Berbers, who were Muslims, followers of the Islamic religion founded by the prophet Mohammed in the seventh century C.E.

On the east coast of Africa, Muslim city-states traded extensively with India, the Moluccas (part of modern Indonesia), and China. Waterborne commerce between the eastern Mediterranean and East Asia passed through the East African city-states; the rest followed the long land route across Central Asia known as the Silk Road.

South of the Mediterranean coast in the African interior lie the great Saharan and Libyan deserts. Below the deserts, much of the continent is divided between tropical rain forests (along the coasts) and grassy plains (in the interior). People speaking a variety of languages and pursuing different subsistence strategies lived in a wide belt south of the deserts. South of the Gulf of Guinea, the grassy landscape came to be dominated by Bantu-speaking peoples, who left their homeland in modern Nigeria about 2,000 years ago and slowly migrated south and east across the continent.

Online Study Center **Improve Your Grade**
   Interactive Map: Africa and Its Peoples, c. 1400

West Africa was a land of tropical forests and savanna grasslands where fishing, cattle herding, and

WEST AFRICA
(GUINEA)

agriculture supported the inhabitants. The northern region of West Africa, or Upper Guinea, was heavily influenced by the Islamic culture of the Mediterranean. Trade via camel caravans between Upper Guinea and the Muslim Mediterranean was sub-Saharan Africa's major connection to Europe and West Asia. In return for salt, dates, silk, and cotton cloth, Africans exchanged ivory, gold, and slaves with northern merchants.

The people of Upper Guinea's northernmost region, the so-called Rice Coast (present-day Gambia, Senegal, and Guinea), fished and cultivated rice. The Grain Coast, the next region to the south, was thinly populated and not readily accessible from the sea because it had only one good harbor (modern Freetown,

Sierra Leone). Its people concentrated on farming and raising livestock.

In the fifteenth century, most Africans in Lower Guinea were farmers who practiced traditional religions, not the precepts of Islam. As did the agricultural peoples of the Americas, they developed rituals intended to ensure good harvests. Throughout the region, individual villages composed of kin groups were linked into hierarchical kingdoms characterized by decentralized political and social authority.

The societies of West Africa, like those of the Americas, assigned different tasks to men and women.

COMPLEMENTARY GENDER ROLES

In general, the sexes shared agricultural duties. Men also hunted, managed livestock, and did most of the fishing. Women were responsible for child care, food preparation, and cloth manufacture. Everywhere in West Africa, women were the primary local traders.

Despite their different economies and the rivalries among states, the peoples of Lower Guinea had similar social systems organized on the basis of what anthropologists have called the dual-sex principle. In Lower Guinea, each sex handled its own affairs: just as male political and religious leaders governed men, so females ruled women. In the Dahomean kingdom, for example, every male official had his female counterpart; in the thirty little Akan States on the Gold Coast, chiefs inherited their status through the female line, and each male chief had a female assistant who supervised other women.

Throughout Upper Guinea, religious beliefs stressed complementary male and female roles. Both women and men served as heads of the cults and secret societies that directed the spiritual life of the villages. Young women were initiated into the Sandé cult, young men into Poro. Although West African women rarely held formal power over men, female religious leaders did govern other members of their sex within the Sandé cult.

West African law recognized both individual and communal landownership, but men seeking to

SLAVERY IN GUINEA

accumulate wealth needed access to labor, including slaves. West Africans held in slavery on their own continent therefore made up essential elements of the economy. Africans could be enslaved for life as punishment for crimes, but more often slaves were enemy captives or people who voluntarily enslaved themselves or their children to pay debts. An African who possessed bondspeople had a right to the products of their labor, although the degree to which slaves were exploited varied greatly. Some slaves were held as chattel; others could engage in trade, retaining a portion of their profits; and still others achieved prominent political or military positions. All, however, found it difficult to overcome the social stigma of enslavement, and they could be traded or sold at the will of their owners.

■ This decorative brass weight, created by the Asante peoples of Lower Guinea, was used for measuring gold dust. It depicts a family pounding fu-fu, a food made by mashing together plantains (a kind of banana), yams, and cassava. The paste was then shaped into balls to be eaten with soup. This weight, probably used in trading with Europeans, shows a scene combining foods of African origin (plantains and yams) with an import from the Americas (cassava), thus bringing the three continents together in ways both symbolic and real.   (© Trustees of the British Museum. Photo by Michael Holford)

European Societies

*I*n the fifteenth century, Europeans too were agricultural peoples. Split into numerous small, warring countries, Europe was divided linguistically, politically, and economically, yet in social terms Europeans' lives were more similar than different. European societies were hierarchical: a few families wielded autocratic power over the majority of the people. At the base of such hierarchies were people held in various forms of bondage. Although Europeans were not subjected to perpetual slavery, Christian doctrine permitted the enslavement of "heathens" (non-Christians), and serfdom restricted some Europeans' freedom, tying them to the land, if not to specific owners. In short, Europe's kingdoms resembled those of Africa and Mesoamerica but differed greatly from the more egalitarian societies found in America north of Mexico (see Map 1.2).

Most Europeans, like most Africans and Americans, lived in small villages. European farmers, who

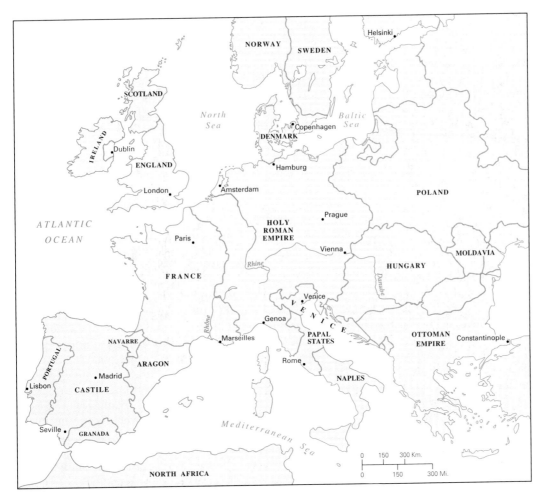

Map 1.2   Europe in 1490

The Europeans who ventured out into the Atlantic came from countries on the northwestern edge of the continent, which was divided into numerous competing nations.

SEXUAL DIVISION
OF LABOR IN
EUROPE

were called peasants, owned or leased separate landholdings, but they worked the fields communally. Because fields had to lie fallow (unplanted) every second or third year to regain fertility, a family could not ensure itself a regular food supply unless all villagers shared each year's work and crops. Men did most of the fieldwork; women helped out chiefly at planting and harvest. In some areas, men concentrated on herding livestock. Women's duties consisted primarily of child care and household tasks, including preserving food, milking cows, and caring for poultry. Since Europeans kept domesticated pigs, goats, sheep, and cattle for meat, hunting had little economic importance in their cultures.

In contrast to African and American societies, in which women often played prominent roles in politics and religion, men dominated all areas of life in Europe. A few women—notably Queen Elizabeth I of England—achieved status or power by right of birth, but the vast majority were excluded from positions of political authority. Husbands and fathers expected to control their families. European women generally held inferior social, economic, and political positions, yet within their own families they wielded power over children and servants.

Christianity was the dominant religion in Europe. In the West, authority rested in the Catholic

CHRISTIANITY

Church, based in Rome and led by the pope. The Catholic Church had an uneasy relationship with both secular rulers and the populace at large. Although European peoples were nominally Catholic, many adhered to local belief systems that the church deemed heretical and could not extinguish. Kings would ally themselves with the church when it suited their needs but often acted independently. Even so, the Christian nations of Europe from the twelfth century on publicly united in a goal of driving nonbelievers (especially Muslims) not only from European domains but also from the holy city of Jerusalem, which caused the series of wars known as the Crusades.

When the fifteenth century began, European nations were slowly recovering from the devastating epidemic of plague known as the

EFFECTS OF
PLAGUE AND
WARFARE

Black Death, which seems to have arrived in Europe from China, traveling with long-distance traders along the Silk Road to the eastern Mediterranean. From 1346 through the 1360s and 1370s, the plague killed an estimated one-third of Europe's people. A precipitous economic decline followed, as did severe social, political, and religious disruption because of the deaths of clergymen and other leading figures.

As plague ravaged the population, England and France waged the Hundred Years' War (1337–1453) over the English monarchy's claim to the French throne. The war interrupted overland trade routes through France that connected England and the Netherlands to the Italian city-states and thence to Central Asia. Merchants in the eastern Mediterranean found a new way to reach their northern markets by forging a regular maritime link with the Netherlands to replace the overland route. The use of a triangular, or lateen, sail (rather than the then-standard square rigging) improved the maneuverability of ships. Also of key importance was the perfection of navigational instruments like the astrolabe and the quadrant, which allowed oceangoing sailors to estimate their position (latitude) by measuring the relationship of the sun, moon, or certain stars to the horizon.

In the aftermath of the Hundred Years' War, European monarchs forcefully consolidated their previously diffuse political power

POLITICAL AND
TECHNOLOGICAL
CHANGE

and raised new revenues through increased taxation of an already hard-pressed peasantry. In England, Henry VII in 1485 founded the Tudor dynasty and began uniting a previously divided land. In France, the successors of Charles VII unified the kingdom. Most successful of all were Ferdinand of Aragón and Isabella of Castile, who married in 1469, founding a strongly Catholic Spain. In 1492 they defeated the Muslims, who had lived in Spain and Portugal for centuries, and thereafter expelled all Jews and Muslims from their domain.

The fifteenth century also brought technological change to Europe. Movable type and the printing press, invented in Germany in the 1450s, made information more accessible than ever before. Printing stimulated the Europeans' curiosity about fabled lands across the seas—lands they could now read about in books. The most important such work was Marco Polo's *Travels*, first published in 1477, which recounted a Venetian merchant's adventures in thirteenth-century China and, most intriguing, described that nation as bordered on the east by an ocean. Polo's account led

In the fifteenth and sixteenth centuries, caravels ventured into the open oceans, thereby changing the contours of the known world. This illustration from a manuscript account of William Barents's 1594 expedition into the Arctic Ocean shows the combination of square rigging and lateen sails that gave ships greater maneuverability and allowed them to navigate along unfamiliar coastlines far from their home ports.   (Bridgeman Art Library)

many Europeans to believe that they could trade directly with China in oceangoing vessels instead of relying on the Silk Road or the route through East Africa.

Technological advances and the growing strength of newly powerful national rulers made possible the European explorations of the fifteenth and sixteenth centuries. Each country craved easy access to African and Asian goods—spices like pepper, cloves, cinnamon, and nutmeg (to season the bland European diet), silk, dyes, perfumes, jewels, sugar, and gold. A desire to spread Christianity around the world supplemented the economic motive. This linking of materialist and spiritual goals might seem contradictory today, but fifteenth-century Europeans saw no necessary conflict between the two. Explorers and colonizers—especially Roman Catholics—honestly sought to convert "heathen" peoples, while at the same time hoping to increase their nation's wealth and standing among other countries.

MOTIVES FOR EXPLORATION

Early European Explorations

Before European mariners could discover new lands, they had to explore the oceans. To reach Asia, seafarers needed not just maneuverable vessels and navigational aids, but also knowledge of the sea, its currents, and especially its winds. How did the winds run? Where would Atlantic breezes take their ships?

Europeans answered these questions in the "Mediterranean Atlantic": the expanse of the Atlantic Ocean that is south and west of Iberia, the peninsula that includes Spain and Portugal, and bounded by the island groups of the Azores (on the west) and the Canaries (on the south), with the Madeiras in their midst. Europeans reached all three sets of islands during the fourteenth century. From their experience sailing in the Mediterranean Atlantic, mariners learned to exploit the prevailing winds—the Northeast Trades that would push them south along the coast of Africa and eventually toward the Caribbean; and the Westerlies, farther north, that returned them to Europe.

SAILING IN THE MEDITERRANEAN ATLANTIC

During the fifteenth century, armed with knowledge of the winds and currents of the Mediterranean Atlantic, Iberian seamen regularly visited the three island groups, all of which they could reach in two weeks or less. By the 1450s Portuguese colonists in the Madeiras were employing slaves (probably Jews and Muslims brought from Iberia) to grow large quantities of sugar for export to the mainland. By the 1470s Madeira had developed into a colonial plantation economy. For the first time in world history, a region had been settled explicitly to cultivate a valuable crop—sugar—to be sold elsewhere, and only a supply of enslaved laborers to do the backbreaking plantation work could ensure the system's continued success.

ISLANDS OF THE MEDITERRANEAN ATLANTIC

Meanwhile, the Guanche people of the Canary Islands fought the assaults of the French, Portuguese, and Spanish. However, the Guanches were weakened by European diseases, and one by one the islands fell to Europeans, who carried off the Guanches as slaves to the Madeiras or the Iberian Peninsula. Spain conquered the last island in 1496 and subsequently devoted the land to sugar cultivation. Collectively, the Canaries and Madeira became known as the Wine Islands because much of their sugar production was directed to making sweet wines.

For Portugal's Prince Henry the Navigator, the islands were steppingstones to Africa. He knew that vast wealth awaited the first European nation to tap the riches of Africa and Asia directly. Each year he dispatched ships southward along the African coast, attempting to discover an oceanic route to Asia. But not until after Prince Henry's death did Bartholomew Dias round the southern tip of Africa (1488) and Vasco da Gama finally reach India (1498).

PORTUGUESE TRADING POSTS IN AFRICA

Long before that, West African states had allowed the Portuguese to establish trading posts along their coasts. Charging the traders rent and levying duties on goods they imported, the African kingdoms set the terms of exchange and benefited considerably from their new, easier access to European manufactures. The Portuguese gained too, for they no longer had to rely on trans-Saharan camel caravans. Their vessels earned immense profits by swiftly transporting African gold, ivory, and slaves to Europe. By bargaining with African masters to purchase their slaves and then carrying those bondspeople to Iberia, the Portuguese introduced black slavery into Europe.

In the 1480s the Portuguese colonized an island off the African coast, previously uninhabited: São Tomé, located in the Gulf of Guinea. The soil of São Tomé proved ideal for raising sugar, and plantation agriculture there expanded rapidly. Planters imported large numbers of slaves from the mainland to work in the cane fields, thus creating the first economy based primarily on the bondage of black Africans.

By the 1490s, Europeans had learned three key lessons of colonization in the Mediterranean Atlantic. First, they had learned how to transplant their crops and livestock successfully to exotic locations. Second, they had discovered that the native peoples of those lands could be either conquered (the Guanches) or exploited (the Africans). Third, they had developed a viable model of plantation slavery and a system for supplying nearly unlimited quantities of such workers. The stage was set for a pivotal moment in world history.

LESSONS OF EARLY COLONIZATION

The Voyages of Columbus, Cabot, and Their Successors

C hristopher Columbus was well schooled in the lessons of the Mediterranean Atlantic. Born in 1451 in the Italian city-state of Genoa, Columbus was by the 1490s an experienced sailor and mapmaker. Like many mariners of the day, he was drawn to Portugal and its islands, especially Madeira, where he commanded a merchant vessel. At least once he voyaged to the Portuguese outpost on the Gold Coast. There he acquired an obsession with gold and came to understand the economic potential of the slave trade.

Like all accomplished seafarers and most educated people, Columbus knew the world was round. However, he differed from other cartographers in his estimate of the earth's size: he thought that China lay only 3,000 miles from the southern European coast. Thus, he argued, it would be easier to reach Asia by sailing west than by making the difficult voyage around the southern tip of Africa. Experts scoffed at this crackpot notion, accurately predicting that the two continents lay 12,000 miles apart. When Columbus in 1484 asked the Portuguese authorities to back his plan to sail west to Asia, they rejected the proposal.

Ferdinand and Isabella of Spain, jealous of Portugal's successes in Africa, were more receptive to

COLUMBUS'S VOYAGE

Columbus's ideas. Urged on by some Spanish noblemen and a group of Italian merchants residing in Castile, the monarchs agreed to finance the risky voyage. And so, on August 3, 1492, in command of the *Pinta*, the *Niña*, and the *Santa Maria*, Columbus set sail from the Spanish port of Palos.

On October 12, he and his men landed on an island in the Bahamas, which he renamed San Salvador. Later he went on to explore the islands now known as Cuba and Hispaniola. Because he thought he had reached the Indies, Columbus referred to the inhabitants of the region as Indians.

Three themes predominate in Columbus's log. First, he insistently asked the Taínos, the islands' residents,

COLUMBUS'S OBSERVATIONS

where he could find gold, pearls, and valuable spices. Each time, his informants replied (largely via signs) that such products could be obtained on other islands, on the mainland, or in cities in the interior. Second, he wrote repeatedly of the strange and beautiful plants and animals. Columbus's interest was more than aesthetic. "I believe that there are many plants and trees here that could be worth a lot in Spain for use as dyes, spices, and medicines," he observed, adding that he was carrying home to Europe "a sample of everything I can," so that experts could examine them.

Third, Columbus described the Taíno people, and he seized some to take back to Spain. The Taínos were, he said, very handsome, gentle, and friendly. He believed they would be likely converts to Catholicism. He also thought the islanders "ought to make good and skilled servants."

These records of the first encounter between Europeans and America and its residents revealed the

EUROPEANS AND "AMERICA"

themes that would be of enormous significance for centuries to come. Above all, Europeans wanted to extract profits from North and South America by exploiting their natural resources: plants, animals, and peoples alike. Christopher Columbus made three more voyages, exploring most of the major Caribbean islands and sailing along the coasts of Central and South America. Until the day he died in 1506 at the age of fifty-five, Columbus believed that he had reached Asia. Even before his death, others knew better. Because the Florentine Amerigo Vespucci, who explored the South American coast in 1499, was the first to publish the idea that a new continent had been discovered, Martin Waldseemüller in 1507 labeled the land "America." By then, Spain, Portugal, and Pope Alexander VI had signed the Treaty of Tordesillas (1494), confirming Portugal's dominance in Africa—and later Brazil—in exchange for Spanish preeminence in the rest of the Americas.

Five hundred years before Columbus, about the year 1001, the Norseman Leif Ericsson and other

NORSE AND OTHER NORTHERN VOYAGERS

Norse explorers sailed to North America across the Davis Strait, which separated their villages in Greenland from Baffin Island (see Map 1.1), settling at a site they named Vinland. Attacks by local residents forced them to depart after just a few years. In the 1960s, archaeologists determined that the Norse had established an outpost at what is now L'Anse aux Meadows, Newfoundland, but Vinland itself was probably located farther south.

Later Europeans did not know of the Norse explorers, but some historians argue that European sailors may have found the rich Newfoundland fishing grounds in the 1480s but kept their discoveries a secret so that they alone could fish there. Whether or not fishermen crossed the entire width of the Atlantic, they thoroughly explored its northern reaches, voyaging among the European continent, England, Ireland, and Iceland. Those who explored what would become the United States and Canada built on their knowledge. They learned that in the spring at the northernmost reaches of the Westerlies, sporadic shifts to easterly winds would push them west. Thus, those taking the northern route usually reached America along the coast of what is now Maine or the Canadian maritime provinces.

The European generally credited with "discovering" North America is John Cabot. More precisely,

JOHN CABOT'S EXPLORATIONS Cabot brought to Europe the first formal knowledge of the northern coastline of the continent and claimed the land for England. Like Columbus, Cabot was a master mariner from the Italian city-state of Genoa, and he was in Spain when Columbus returned from his first trip to America. Calculating that England—which traded with Asia only through a long series of middlemen stretching from Belgium to Venice to the Muslim world—would be eager to sponsor exploratory voyages, Cabot sought and won the support of King Henry VII. He set sail from Bristol in late May 1497, reaching his destination on June 24. Scholars disagree about the location of his landfall (some say it was Cape Breton Island, others Newfoundland), but all recognize the importance of his month-long exploration of the coast.

The voyages of Columbus, Cabot, and their successors finally brought the Eastern and Western Hemispheres together. The Portuguese explorer Pedro Álvares Cabral reached Brazil in 1500; John Cabot's son Sebastian followed his father to North America in 1507; France financed Giovanni da Verrazzano in 1524 and Jacques Cartier in 1534; and in 1609 and 1610 Henry Hudson explored the North American coast for the Dutch West India Company. These men were primarily searching for the legendary, nonexistent "Northwest Passage" through

the Americas, but their discoveries interested European nations in exploring North and South America.

Spanish Exploration and Conquest

*O*nly in the areas that Spain explored and claimed did colonization begin immediately. On his second voyage in 1493, Columbus brought to Hispaniola seventeen ships loaded with twelve hundred men, seeds, plants, livestock, chickens, and dogs—along with microbes, rats, and weeds. The settlement named Isabela (in the modern Dominican Republic) and its successors became the staging area for the Spanish invasion of America.

At first, Spanish explorers fanned out around the Caribbean basin. In 1513 Juan Ponce de León reached Florida, and Vasco Núñez de Balboa crossed the Isthmus of Panama to the Pacific Ocean. In the 1530s and 1540s, conquistadors traveled farther, exploring many regions claimed by the Spanish monarchs: Francisco Vásquez de Coronado journeyed through the southwestern portion of what is now the United States at approximately the same time as Hernán de Soto explored the southeast and encountered the Lady of Cofitachequi. Juan Rodriguez Cabrillo sailed along the California coast, and Francisco Pizarro acquired the richest silver mines in the world by conquering and enslaving the Incas in western South America. But the most important conquistador was Hernán Cortés.

Cortés, an adventurer who first arrived in the West Indies in 1504, embarked for the mainland in

CORTÉS AND MALINCHE 1519 in search of the wealthy cities rumored to exist there. As he moved his force inland from the Gulf of Mexico, local Mayas presented him with a gift of twenty young female slaves. One of them, Malinche, who had been sold into slavery by the Aztecs and raised by the Mayas, became Cortés's translator. Malinche bore Cortés a son, Martín—one of the first *mestizos*, or mixed-blood children—and eventually married one of his officers. When the Aztec capital Tenochtitlán fell to the Spaniards in 1521, Cortés and his men seized a fabulous treasure of gold and silver. Thus, not long after Columbus's first voyage, the Spanish monarchs controlled the richest, most extensive empire Europe had known since ancient Rome.

Spain established the model of colonization that other countries later attempted to imitate, a model with three major elements. First, the Crown maintained tight control over the colonies, imposing a hierarchical government that allowed little autonomy to New World jurisdictions. Second, most of the colonists sent from Spain were male. They took Indian—and later African—women as their sexual partners, thereby creating the racially mixed population that characterizes much of Latin America to the present day.

SPANISH COLONIZATION

Third, the colonies' wealth was based on the exploitation of both the native population and slaves imported from Africa. The *encomienda* system, which granted tribute from Indian villages to individual conquistadors as a reward for their services to the Crown, in effect legalized Indian slavery. Yet in 1542 a new code of laws reformed the system, forbidding Spaniards from enslaving Indians. In response, the conquerors, familiar with slavery in Spain, began to import Africans to increase the labor force under their direct control.

Spanish wealth derived from American suffering. The Spaniards deliberately leveled American cities, building cathedrals and monasteries on sites once occupied by Aztec, Incan, and Mayan temples. Some conquistadors sought to erase all vestiges of the great Indian cultures by burning the written records they found. With their traditional ways of life in disarray, devastated by disease, and compelled to labor for their conquerors, many demoralized residents of Mesoamerica accepted the Christian religion brought to New Spain by friars of the Franciscan and Dominican orders.

The friars devoted their energies to persuading Mesoamerican people to move into new towns and build Roman Catholic churches. In such towns, Indians were exposed to European customs and religious rituals designed to assimilate Catholic and pagan beliefs. Friars deliberately juxtaposed the cult of the Virgin Mary with that of the corn goddess, and the Indians adeptly melded aspects of their traditional worldview with Christianity, in a process called syncretism. Thousands of Indians residing in Spanish territory embraced Catholicism,

CHRISTIANITY IN NEW SPAIN

at least partly because it was the religion of their new rulers.

The Columbian Exchange

a broad mutual transfer of diseases, plants, and animals (called the Columbian Exchange by the historian Alfred Crosby) resulted directly from the European voyages of the fifteenth and sixteenth centuries and from Spanish colonization. The Eastern and Western Hemispheres had evolved separately for thousands of years, developing widely different forms of life. Many large mammals like cattle and horses were native to the connected continents of Europe, Asia, and Africa, but the Americas had no domesticated beasts larger than dogs and llamas. The vegetable crops of the Americas—particularly corn, beans, squash, cassava, and potatoes—were more nutritious and produced higher yields than those of Europe and Africa, such as wheat, millet, and rye. In time, native peoples learned to raise and consume European livestock, and Europeans and Africans became accustomed to planting and eating American crops. The diets of all three peoples were consequently vastly enriched.

Diseases carried from Europe and Africa, though, had a devastating impact on the Americas. Indians fell victim to microbes that had long infested the other continents and had repeatedly killed hundreds of thousands but had also left survivors with some measure of immunity. The statistics are staggering. When Columbus landed on Hispaniola in 1492, approximately half a million people resided there. Fifty years later, fewer than two thousand native inhabitants were still alive. Overall, historians estimate that the alien microorganisms could have reduced the American population by as much as 90 percent.

SMALLPOX AND OTHER DISEASES

The greatest killer was smallpox, spread primarily by direct human contact. One epidemic began on Hispaniola in December 1518 and was carried to the mainland by Spaniards in 1520. There it fatally weakened the defenders of Tenochtitlán. As an old Aztec man recalled, "It spread over the people as great destruction." Largely as a consequence, Tenochtitlán surrendered, and the Spaniards built Mexico City on its site.

Maize, to Mesoamericans, was a gift from Quetzalcoatl, the plumed serpent god. Cherokees told of an old woman whose blood produced the prized stalks after her grandson buried her body in a cleared, sunny field. For the Abenakis, the crop began when a beautiful maiden ordered a youth to drag her by the hair through a burned-over field. The long hair of the Cherokee grandmother and the Abenaki maiden turned into silk, the flower on the stalks that Europeans called Indian corn.

Sacred to all the Indian peoples who grew it, maize was a cereal crop, a main part of their diet. They dried the kernels; ground into meal, maize was cooked as a mush or shaped into flat cakes and baked, the forerunners of modern tortillas. Indians also heated the dried kernels until they popped open, just as is done today. Although the European invaders of North and South America initially disdained maize, they soon learned that it could be cultivated in a wide variety of conditions— from sea level to twelve thousand feet, from regions with abundant rainfall to dry lands with as little as twelve inches of rain a year. Corn was also highly productive, yielding almost twice as many calories per acre as wheat. So Europeans too came to rely on corn, growing it not only in their American settlements but also in their homelands.

Maize cultivation spread to Asia and Africa. Today, China is second only to the United States in total corn production, and corn is more widely grown in Africa than any other crop. Still, the United States produces 45 percent of the world's corn—almost half of it in the three states of Illinois, Iowa, and Nebraska—and corn is the nation's single largest crop. More than half of American corn is consumed by livestock. Much of the rest is processed into syrup, which sweetens carbonated beverages and candies, or into ethanol, a gasoline additive that reduces both pollution and dependence on fossil fuels. Corn is an ingredient in light beer and toothpaste. It is used in the manufacture of tires, wallpaper, cat litter, and aspirin. Remarkably, of the ten thousand products in a modern American grocery store, about one-fourth rely to some extent on corn.

Today this crop bequeathed to the world by ancient American plant breeders provides one-fifth of all the calories consumed by the earth's peoples. The gift of Quetzalcoatl has linked the globe.

The earliest known European drawing of maize, the American plant that was to have such an extraordinary impact on the entire world.   (Typ 565.42. 409 F[B], Department of Printing and Graphic Arts, Houghton Library, Harvard College Library)

Far to the north, where smaller American populations encountered only a few Europeans, disease also ravaged the countryside. A great epidemic, probably smallpox coupled with measles, swept through the villages along the coast north of Cape Cod from 1616 to 1618. Again the mortality rate may have been as high as 90 percent. Because of this dramatic depopulation of the area, English colonists were able to establish settlements virtually unopposed just a few years later.

The Americans, though, took a revenge of sorts. They gave the Europeans syphilis, a virulent venereal disease. The first recorded European case of the new ailment occurred in Barcelona, Spain, in 1493, shortly after Columbus's return from the Caribbean. Carried by soldiers, sailors, and prostitutes, it spread quickly through Europe and Asia, reaching as far as China by 1505.

SUGAR, HORSES, AND TOBACCO The exchange of three commodities had significant impacts on Europe and the Americas. Sugar, which was first domesticated in the East Indies, was being grown on the islands of the Mediterranean Atlantic by 1450. The insatiable European demand for sugar led Columbus to take Canary Island sugar canes to Hispaniola on his 1493 voyage. By the 1520s, plantations worked by African slaves in the Greater Antilles (the major Caribbean islands) regularly shipped cargoes of sugar to Spain. Half a century later, the Portuguese colony in Brazil (founded in 1532) was producing sugar on an even larger scale for the European market, and after 1640, sugar cultivation became the crucial component of English and French colonization in the Caribbean.

Horses, which like sugar were brought to America by Columbus in 1493, fell into the hands of North American Indians during the seventeenth century. Through trade and theft, horses spread among the peoples of the Great Plains, reaching most areas by 1750. Lakota, Comanches, and Crows, among others, came to use horses for transportation and hunting, calculated their wealth in the number of horses owned, and waged wars primarily from horseback. Women no longer had to carry the bands' belongings on their backs. And a mode of subsistence that had been based on hunting several different animals, in combination with gathering and agriculture, became one focused almost wholly on hunting buffalo.

In America, Europeans encountered tobacco, which at first they believed had beneficial medicinal effects. Smoking and chewing the "Indian weed" became a fad in Europe. Despite the efforts of such skeptics as King James I of England, who in 1604 pronounced smoking "harmfull to the brain, [and] dangerous to the Lungs," tobacco's popularity climbed.

The European and African invasion of the Americas therefore had a significant biological component, for the invaders carried plants and animals with them. Some creatures, such as livestock, they brought deliberately. Others, including rats, weeds, and diseases, arrived unexpectedly. And upon their return home, the Europeans deliberately took back such crops as corn, potatoes, and tobacco, along with that unanticipated stowaway, syphilis.

Europeans in North America

Northern Europeans, denied access to the wealth of Mesoamerica by the Spanish and beaten to South America by the Portuguese, were initially more interested in exploiting North America's abundant natural resources than in the difficult task of establishing colonies on the mainland. Following John Cabot's report of a plentiful supply of fish along the North American coast, Europeans rushed to reap the sea's bounty. By the 1570s, more than 350 ships, primarily from France and England, were capitalizing on the fisheries of the Newfoundland Banks each year.

European fishermen soon learned that they could augment their profits by exchanging cloth and metal goods like pots and knives for the *TRADE AMONG INDIANS AND EUROPEANS* native trappers' beaver pelts, which Europeans used to make fashionable hats. At first the Europeans conducted their trading from ships sailing along the coast, but later they established permanent outposts on the mainland to centralize and control the traffic in furs.

The Europeans' demand for furs, especially beaver, was matched by the Indians' desire for European goods that could make their lives easier and establish their superiority over their neighbors. Some bands began to concentrate so completely on trapping for the European market that they abandoned their traditional economies. The intensive trade in pelts also had serious ecological consequences. In some regions, beavers were completely wiped out. The disappearance of their dams led to soil erosion, especially when combined with the extensive clearing of forests by later European settlers.

Although their nation reaped handsome profits from fishing, English merchants and political leaders

CONTEST BETWEEN SPAIN AND ENGLAND

watched enviously as Spain's American possessions enriched that country immeasurably. In the mid-sixteenth century, English "sea dogs" like John Hawkins and Sir Francis Drake began to raid Spanish treasure fleets sailing home from the West Indies. Their actions helped to foment a war that in 1588 culminated in the defeat of a huge invasion force—the Spanish Armada—off the English coast. As part of the contest with Spain, English leaders started to think about planting colonies in the Western Hemisphere, thereby gaining better access to valuable trade goods and simultaneously preventing their enemy from dominating the Americas.

The first English colonial planners hoped to reproduce Spanish successes by dispatching to America men who would similarly exploit the native peoples for their own and their nation's benefit. In the mid-1570s, a group that included Sir Humphrey Gilbert and his younger half-brother, Sir Walter Raleigh, began to promote a scheme to establish outposts that could trade with the Indians and provide bases for attacks on New Spain. Approving the idea, Queen Elizabeth I authorized first Gilbert, and then Raleigh, to colonize North America.

Gilbert died trying, unsuccessfully, to plant a colony in Newfoundland, and Raleigh was only briefly

ROANOKE

more successful. After two preliminary expeditions, in 1587 he sent 117 colonists to the territory he named Virginia, after Elizabeth, the "Virgin Queen." They established a settlement on Roanoke Island, in what is now North Carolina, but in 1590 a resupply ship—delayed in leaving England because of the Spanish Armada—could not find them. The colonists had vanished, leaving only the name of a nearby island carved on a tree.

Thus, England's first attempt to plant a permanent settlement on the North American coast failed, as had similar efforts by Portugal on Cape Breton Is-

land (in the early 1520s) and France in northern Florida (in the mid-1560s). All three enterprises collapsed because of the hostility of their neighbors and their inability to be self-sustaining in food.

The explanation for such failures becomes clear in Thomas Harriot's *A Briefe and True Report of the*

HARRIOT'S BRIEFE AND TRUE REPORT

New Found Land of Virginia, published in 1588 to publicize Raleigh's colony. Harriot, a noted scientist who sailed with the second of the preliminary voyages to Roanoke, described the animals, plants, and people of the region for an English readership. His account revealed that although the explorers depended on nearby villagers for most of their food, they needlessly antagonized their neighbors by killing some of them for what Harriot himself admitted were unjustifiable reasons. The scientist advised later colonizers to deal with the native peoples of America more humanely than his comrades had.

Harriot's *Briefe and True Report* depicted for his English readers a bountiful land full of opportunities for quick profit. The people already residing there would, he thought, "in a short time be brought to civilitie" through conversion to Christianity, admiration for European superiority, or conquest—if they did not die from disease, the ravages of which he witnessed. Thomas Harriot's prediction was far off the mark: European dominance of North America would be difficult to achieve.

Summary *Online Study Center* ACE the Test

*T*he process of initial contact between Europeans and Americans that ended near the close of the sixteenth century began approximately 250 years earlier when Portuguese sailors first set out to explore the Mediterranean Atlantic and settle its islands. That region of the Atlantic so close to European and African shores nurtured mariners who, like Christopher Columbus, ventured into previously unknown waters. When Columbus first reached the Americas, he thought he had found Asia, his intended destination. Later explorers knew better but, except for the Spanish, regarded the Americas primarily as a barrier to their long-sought goal of an oceanic route to the riches of China and the Moluccas. Ordinary European fishermen were the first to realize that the northern coasts had valuable products to offer: fish and furs, both much in demand in their homelands.

The wealth of the north could not compare to that of Mesoamerica. The Aztec Empire, heir to the trading networks of Teotihuacán as well as to the intellectual sophistication of the Mayas, dazzled the conquistadors with the magnificence of its buildings and its seemingly unlimited wealth. The Aztecs believed that their Fifth Sun would end in earthquakes and hunger. Hunger they surely experienced after Cortés's invasion; and if there were no earthquakes, the great temples tumbled to the ground nevertheless, as the Spaniards used their stones (and Indian laborers) to construct cathedrals honoring their God and his son, Jesus, rather than Huitzilopochtli. The conquerors employed first American and later enslaved African workers to till the fields, mine the precious metals, and herd the livestock that earned immense profits for themselves and their mother country.

The initial impact of Europeans on the Americas proved devastating. Flourishing civilizations were, if not entirely destroyed, markedly altered in just a few decades. By the end of the sixteenth century, fewer people resided in North America than had lived there before Columbus's arrival, even taking into account the arrival of many Europeans and Africans. And the people who did live there—Indian, African, and European—resided in a world that was indeed new—a world engaged in the unprecedented process of combining foods, religions, economies, styles of life, and political systems that had developed separately for millennia. Understandably, conflict and dissension permeated that process.

LEGACY FOR A PEOPLE AND A NATION
Columbus Day

Each year, the United States celebrates the second Monday in October as a tribute to Christopher Columbus's landing in the Bahamas in 1492. The first known U.S. celebration of Columbus's voyage occurred in New York City on October 12, 1792, when a men's social club gave a dinner to mark its three hundredth anniversary. In the late 1860s, Italian American communities in New York City and San Francisco began to celebrate October 12, but not until 1892 did a congressional resolution order a one-time national commemoration. Columbus Day was first observed as a national holiday in 1971.

Today, the annual observances can arouse strong emotions. The American Indian Movement, founded in 1968, has declared that "from an indigenous vantage point, Columbus' arrival was a disaster" and that he "deserves no recognition or accolades." At the same time, people of Hispanic descent have claimed Columbus as their own, insisting that his voyage was "a thoroughly Spanish event." In some cities, most notably New York, their celebrations rival those long organized by Italian Americans; in others, such as Miami, Hispanics control the official commemorations. Still other Latinos, especially those of Mexican descent living in Los Angeles, call October 12 Día de la Raza and use it as an occasion to protest current U.S. immigration policy.

As ethnic diversity has increased in the nation and as peoples of different origins have sought to claim a share of the American heritage, holidays have unsurprisingly become the occasion for heated contests. Each fall, the American people and nation continue to confront the controversial legacy of Columbus's 1492 voyage.

EUROPEANS COLONIZE NORTH AMERICA 1600–1640

Captain William Rudyerd seemed like a man any Puritan colony in the Americas would prize, so when his older brother urged the planners of the new settlement to appoint him muster master general, they readily agreed. Rudyerd, a veteran of European wars, followed the new dissenting English faith, as did the planners and many of the settlers. In the colony's first years, Rudyerd proved to be a vigorous soldier who worked hard to train the settlers to defend themselves. But he also proved to be a vigorous defender of his own status, and his actions wreaked havoc in the fragile community. The captain beat to death a servant suffering from scurvy (thinking the servant merely lazy), and he also quarreled continually with other settlers, believing they failed to show the proper respect to a gentleman of noble birth.

Similar conflicts occurred in all the Anglo-American settlements, as gentlemen accustomed to unquestioning deference from their inferiors learned that in a colonial setting, their inherited social standing could be challenged. But in Rudyerd's colony, the disputes were especially dangerous, because the settlers lived on Providence Island, an isolated Puritan outpost off the coast of modern Nicaragua.

Providence Island, founded by a company of Puritan adventurers in 1630, sought to establish an English beachhead that could lead to successful colonization of the Central American mainland. Yet the outpost's failure to establish a viable economy and, ultimately, its desperate attempts to stay afloat financially by serving as a base for English privateers caused its downfall. That decision led the Spaniards to conclude that the Puritans must be removed. In May 1641, a large Spanish fleet captured the island, and the English survivors scattered to other Caribbean settlements or returned to England.

By this time, though, Spain no longer predominated in the Americas. France, the Netherlands, and England all had permanent colonies in North America by the 1640s. The French and Dutch colonies, like the Spanish out-

New Spain, New France, and New Netherland

The Caribbean

English Interest in Colonization

LINKS TO THE WORLD
Wampum

The Founding of Virginia

Life in the Chesapeake

The Founding of New England

Life in New England

LEGACY FOR A PEOPLE AND A NATION
The Foxwoods Casino and the Mashantucket Pequot Museum

Online Study Center
This icon will direct you to interactive map and primary source activities on the website
http://college.hmco.com/pic/nortonbrief7e

CHRONOLOGY

1533 • Henry VIII divorces Catherine of Aragon; English Reformation begins

1558 • Elizabeth I becomes queen

1565 • Founding of St. Augustine (Florida), oldest permanent European settlement in present-day United States

1598 • Oñate conquers Pueblos in New Mexico for Spain

1603 • James I becomes king

1607 • Jamestown founded, first permanent English settlement in North America

1608 • Quebec founded by the French

1610 • Founding of Santa Fe, New Mexico

1611 • First Virginia tobacco crop

1614 • Fort Orange (Albany) founded by the Dutch

1619 • Virginia House of Burgesses established, first representative assembly in the English colonies

1620 • Plymouth colony founded, first permanent English settlement in New England

1622 • Powhatan Confederacy attacks Virginia

1624 • Dutch settle on Manhattan Island (New Amsterdam)
• English colonize St. Kitts, first island in Lesser Antilles to be settled by Europeans
• James I revokes Virginia Company's charter

1625 • Charles I becomes king

1630 • Massachusetts Bay colony founded

1634 • Maryland founded

1636 • Williams expelled from Massachusetts Bay, founds Providence, Rhode Island
• Connecticut founded

1637 • Pequot War in New England

1638 • Hutchinson expelled from Massachusetts Bay colony, goes to Rhode Island

c. 1640 • Sugar cultivation begins on Barbados

1642 • Montreal founded by the French

1646 • Treaty ends hostilities between Virginia and Powhatan Confederacy

posts, were settled largely by European men who interacted regularly with indigenous peoples, using their labor or seeking to convert them to Christianity. Like the conquistadors, French and Dutch merchants and planters hoped to make a quick profit and then perhaps return to their homelands. The English, as Thomas Harriot had made clear in the 1580s, were just as interested in profiting from North America. But they pursued those profits in a different way.

In contrast to other Europeans, most of the English settlers, including those of the failed Providence Island colony, came to America intending to stay. Especially in the area that came to be known as New England, they arrived in family groups. They re-created European society and family life to an extent not possible in the other colonies, where migrant men found their sexual partners within the Indian or African populations. Among the English colonies, those in the Chesapeake region and on the Caribbean islands most closely resembled colonies founded by other nations with economies, like those of Hispaniola or Brazil, based on large-scale production for the international market by a labor force composed of bonded servants and slaves.

Wherever they settled, the English, like other Europeans, prospered only after they learned to adapt to the alien environment. The first permanent English colonies survived because nearby Indians assisted the newcomers. The settlers had to learn to grow unfamiliar American crops. They also had to develop extensive trading relationships with Native Americans and with colonies established by other European countries. Needing laborers for their fields, they first used English indentured servants, then later began to import African slaves. Thus, the early history of the region that became the United States and the English Caribbean is best understood not as an isolated story of English colonization, but rather as a series of complex interactions among a variety of European, African, and American peoples and environments. ■

New Spain, New France, and New Netherland

Spaniards established the first permanent European settlement within the boundaries of the modern United States, but others initially attempted that feat. Twice in the 1560s, groups of French Protestants (Huguenots) sought to escape from persecution in their homeland by planting colonies on the south Atlantic coast. A passing ship rescued the starving survivors of the first, in present-day South Carolina. The second, near modern Jacksonville, Florida, was destroyed in 1565 by a Spanish expedition under the command of Pedro Menéndez de Avilés. To ensure Spanish domination of the strategically important region (located near sea-lanes used by Spanish treasure ships bound for Europe), Menéndez set up a small fortified outpost, which he named St. Augustine—now the oldest continuously inhabited European settlement in the United States. Franciscan missionaries soon followed, and by the end of the sixteenth century, a chain of Franciscan missions stretched across northern Florida.

More than thirty years after the founding of St. Augustine, in 1598, Juan de Oñate, a Mexican-born adventurer, led a group of about five hundred soldiers and settlers to New Mexico. At first the Pueblos greeted the newcomers cordially.

NEW MEXICO

When the Spaniards began to torture, murder, and rape the villagers to extort food and clothing, however, the residents of Acoma killed several soldiers. The invaders responded ferociously, killing more than eight hundred people and capturing the remainder. Not surprisingly, the other Pueblo villages surrendered.

Because New Mexico held little wealth and was too far from the Pacific coast to assist in protecting Spanish sea-lanes, many of the Spaniards returned to Mexico, and officials considered abandoning the isolated colony. Instead, in 1609, the authorities decided to maintain a small military outpost and a few Christian missions in the area, with the capital at Santa Fe (founded in 1610). Here too, Spanish leaders were granted *encomiendas*, but the absence of mines or fertile agricultural lands made for small profit.

After Spain's destruction of France's Florida settlement in 1565, the French turned their attention northward. In 1608 Samuel de Champlain set up a trading post at an interior site the local Iroquois had called Stadacona; Champlain renamed it Quebec. He had chosen well: Quebec was the most easily defended spot in the entire St. Lawrence River valley and controlled access to the heartland of the continent. In 1642 the French established a second post, Montreal, at the falls of the St. Lawrence (and thus at the end of navigation by oceangoing vessels).

QUEBEC AND MONTREAL

Before the founding of these settlements, fishermen served as the major transporters of North American beaver pelts to France, but the new posts quickly took over control of the lucrative trade in furs (see Table 2.1). In the hope of attracting settlers, the colony's leaders gave land grants along the river to wealthy seigneurs (nobles), who then imported tenants to work their farms. Even so, more than twenty-five years after Quebec's founding, it had just sixty-four resident families, along with traders and soldiers. With respect to territory occupied and farmed, northern New France never grew much beyond the confines of the river valley between Quebec and Montreal (see Map 2.1). Thus, it differed significantly from New Spain, where Europeans resided in widely scattered locations and Spanish men sometimes directly supervised Indian laborers.

Missionaries of the Society of Jesus (Jesuits), a Roman Catholic order dedicated to converting non-

TABLE 2.1

The Founding of Permanent European Colonies in North America, 1565–1640

Colony	Founder(s)	Date	Basis of Economy
Florida	Pedro Menéndez de Avilés	1565	Farming
New Mexico	Juan de Oñate	1598	Livestock
Virginia	Virginia Company	1607	Tobacco
New France	France	1608	Fur trading
New Netherland	Dutch West India Company	1614	Fur trading
Plymouth	Pilgrims	1620	Farming, fishing
Maine	Sir Ferdinando Gorges	1622	Fishing
St. Kitts, Barbados, et al.	European immigrants	1624	Sugar
Massachusetts Bay	Massachusetts Bay Company	1630	Farming, fishing, fur trading
Maryland	Cecilius Calvert	1634	Tobacco
Rhode Island	Roger Williams	1636	Farming
Connecticut	Thomas Hooker	1636	Farming, fur trading
New Haven	Massachusetts migrants	1638	Farming
New Hampshire	Massachusetts migrants	1638	Farming, fishing

JESUIT MISSIONS IN NEW FRANCE believers to Christianity, also came to New France. First arriving in Quebec in 1625, the Jesuits, whom the Indians called Black Robes, initially tried to persuade indigenous peoples to live near French settlements and adopt European agricultural methods. When that effort failed, the Black Robes learned Indian languages and traveled to remote regions of the interior, where they lived in twos and threes among hundreds of potential converts.

Using a variety of strategies, Jesuits sought to undermine the authority of village shamans (the traditional religious leaders) and to gain the confidence of leaders who could influence others. Trained in rhetoric, they won admirers by their eloquence. Immune to smallpox (for all had survived the disease already), they explained epidemics among the Indians as God's punishment for sin. Perhaps most important, they amazed the villagers by communicating with each other over long distances through marks on paper. The Indians' desire to learn how to harness the extraordinary power of literacy was one of the critical factors making them receptive to the missionaries' spiritual message.

The Jesuits slowly gained thousands of converts, some of whom moved to reserves set aside for Christian Indians. In those communities, the converts replaced their own culture's traditional equal treatment of men and women with notions more congenial to the Europeans' insistence on male dominance and female subordination. They also altered their practice of allowing premarital sexual relationships and easy divorce, customs that Catholic doctrine prohibited.

Online Study Center
Improve Your Grade
Primary Source: Jesuits' Interpretation of Gender Roles

Jesuit missionaries faced little competition from other Europeans for native peoples' souls, but French fur traders had to confront a direct challenge. In 1614, five years after Henry Hudson explored the river that bears his name, his sponsor, the Dutch West India Company, established an outpost (Fort Orange) on that river at the site of present-day Albany, New York. Like the French, the Dutch sought beaver pelts. Because the Dutch were interested primarily in trade rather than colonization,

NEW NETHERLAND

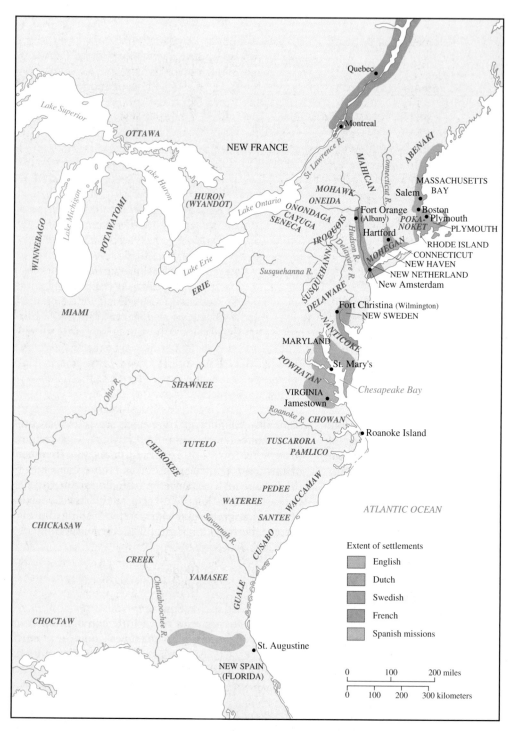

Map 2.1 European Settlements and Indians in Eastern North America, 1650

Note the widely scattered European settlements along the ocean and riverbanks, while America's native inhabitants controlled the vast interior.

New Netherland remained small. The colony's southern anchor was New Amsterdam (see Map 2.1), a town founded in 1624 on Manhattan Island.

As the Dutch West India Company's colony in North America, New Netherland was an unimportant part of a vast commercial empire. The colony was ruled autocratically, and settlers felt little loyalty to their nominal leaders. Few migrants arrived. Even a company policy of 1629 that offered a large land grant, or patroonship, to anyone who would bring fifty settlers to the province failed to attract takers. As late as the mid-1660s, New Netherland had only about five thousand inhabitants. Some of those were Swedes and Finns, who resided in the former colony of New Sweden (founded in 1638 on the Delaware River), which was taken over by the Dutch in 1655.

The American Indian allies of New France and New Netherland clashed with each other in part because of fur trade rivalries. In the 1640s, the Iroquois, who traded chiefly with the Dutch and lived in modern upstate New York, went to war against the Hurons, who traded primarily with the French and lived in present-day Ontario. Using guns supplied by the Dutch, the Iroquois largely exterminated the Hurons, whose population had already been decimated by a smallpox epidemic. The Iroquois thus established themselves as a major force in the region, one that Europeans could ignore only at their peril. And the European demand for beaver pelts had disastrously affected native communities and their interactions.

The Caribbean

n the Caribbean, France, the Netherlands, and England fought openly in the first half of the seventeenth century. The Spanish concentrated their efforts on colonizing the Greater Antilles: Cuba, Hispaniola, Jamaica, and Puerto Rico. They left many smaller islands alone. But other European nations saw the tiny islands as both bases from which to attack Spanish vessels loaded with American gold and silver and sources of valuable tropical products such as spices, dyes, and fruits.

England was the first northern European nation to establish a permanent foothold in the smaller West Indian islands (the Lesser Antilles). English people settled on St. Christopher (St. Kitts) in 1624, then later on other islands such as Barbados (1627) and

Providence. France colonized Guadeloupe and Martinique, and the Dutch gained control of St. Eustatius (strategically located near St. Kitts). Because of conflict among the European powers, most of the islands were attacked at least once during the course of the century, and some, like Providence, changed hands.

Why did other Europeans devote so much energy to gaining control of these small volcanic islands that Spain had neglected? The primary answer to that question is sugar. Europeans loved sugar; it gave them a quick energy boost and served as a sweetener for two stimulating, addictive, and bitter Asian drinks: coffee and tea.

SUGAR CULTIVATION

Early in the 1640s, English residents of Barbados discovered that the island's soil and climate were ideally suited for cultivating sugar cane. At the time, a major supplier of the world's sugar was Brazil, where numerous small farmers grew much of the crop and took their cane to central mills. To pay for processing, they turned a large proportion of their crop over to the mill owners, who could not coordinate the actions of the independent farmers. This production method was highly inefficient.

That changed in Barbados. Between 1630 and 1654, the Dutch took control of northeastern Brazil, where they learned Portuguese techniques for growing and processing the crop. Dutch merchants taught those skills to Barbadians, expecting to sell them African slaves and to transport barrels of sugar products to Europe. The results must have exceeded their wildest dreams. In the explosive Barbados sugar boom that began in the 1640s, planters increased the size of their landholdings, adopted large-scale gang labor by bondspeople, and built their own sugar mills that could operate with great efficiency. Planters, slave traders, and Dutch shipping interests alike earned immense profits from introducing economies of scale into sugar production. Sugar remained the most valuable American commodity for more than one hundred years. Yet in the long run, the future economic importance of the Europeans' American colonies lay on the mainland rather than in the Caribbean.

English Interest in Colonization

he failure of Raleigh's Roanoke colony ended English efforts to settle in North America for nearly two decades. When the English decided

Wampum

When Europeans first came to North America, they quickly learned that native peoples highly valued small cylindrical beads made from whelk and quahog shells, known collectively as wampum. The white and purple beads had been strung on fibers for centuries to make necklaces and ornamental belts, but with the Europeans' arrival, wampum changed its character, becoming a currency widely employed by both groups.

The transformation of wampum occurred not only because the Indians prized it and would trade deerskins and beaver pelts to acquire the beads, but also because Dutch and English settlers lacked an equally handy medium of exchange. These settlers had limited access to coins and currency from their homelands, yet they needed to do business with each other and with their native neighbors. Wampum filled a key need, especially in the first decades of settlement.

Whelk (white) and quahog (purple) shells were found primarily along the shores of Long Island Sound. Narragansetts, Montauks, Niantics, and other local peoples had long gathered the shells during the summers; women then fashioned the beads during the long northeastern winters. The shells were hard and brittle, so shaping them into hollow beads was a time-consuming task involving considerable skill. But Europeans' metal tools, including fine drills, allowed a rapid increase in the quantity and quality of wampum. Some villages gave up their hunter-gatherer modes of subsistence and settled permanently in shell-rich areas, where they focused almost exclusively on the manufacture of wampum.

Wampum played a key role in the early economy of both New Netherland and New England. Dutch settlers in Manhattan traded such manufactured goods as guns and kettles, axes, or knives with the wampum makers, then transported wampum up the Hudson River to Fort Orange, where they used it to purchase furs and skins from the Iroquois. In 1627, Isaac de Rasière, a Dutch trader, introduced wampum to the English colonists at Plymouth when he offered it in exchange for corn. Ten years later, the Massachusetts Bay colony made wampum legal tender for the payment of debts under 12 pennies, at a rate of 6 white beads or 3 purple beads (which were

rarer) to 1 penny. Wampum beads could be traded in loose handfuls but more often were strung on thin cords in set amounts worth English equivalents. People trading larger sums measured in wampum always feared being shortchanged. In 1660, one resident of New Netherland agreed to accept payment of a substantial debt in wampum only if his wife personally counted all the beads.

Wampum—originally with purely ornamental significance for its Indian makers—became an initial, indispensable link in the commerce between Europe and North America.

Before Europeans arrived in North America, wampum served primarily ceremonial purposes for native peoples, as in this wampum belt depicting the six nations of the Iroquois and the thirteen American colonies. But several decades later, after Dutch and English colonists came to rely on it as a medium of exchange and European tools made it easier to manufacture, wampum became far more utilitarian in design and appearance.   (Right: Photo by MPI/Hulton Archives/Getty Images; below: Image #18491 Wampum Beads by Craig Chesek, courtesy the Library, American Museum of Natural History

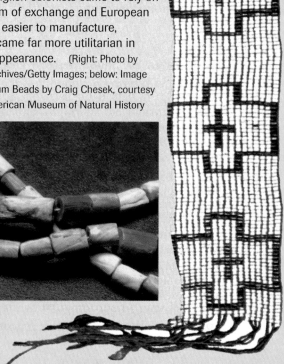

in 1606 to try once more, they again planned colonies that imitated the Spanish model. Yet their success came when they abandoned that model and sent large numbers of men and women to set up agriculturally based colonies on the mainland. Two major developments prompted approximately 200,000 ordinary English men and women to move to North America in the seventeenth century and led their government to encourage their emigration.

The onset of dramatic social and economic change stimulated many English to move to North

SOCIAL CHANGE IN ENGLAND

America. In the 150 years after 1530, largely as a result of the introduction of nutritious American crops into Europe, England's population doubled. All those additional people needed food, clothing, and other goods. The competition for goods led to high inflation, coupled with a fall in real wages as the number of workers increased. The enhanced demand for food and wool for clothing benefited those with sizable landholdings, but drove landless peasants and those with small amounts of land into unremitting poverty.

Well-to-do English people reacted with alarm as they saw landless and homeless people fill the streets and highways. Obsessed with the problem of maintaining order, officials came to believe that England was overcrowded. They concluded that colonies established in North America could siphon off England's "surplus population," thus easing social strains at home. For similar reasons, many English people decided that they could improve their circumstances by migrating to a large, land-rich, apparently empty continent. Such economic considerations were rendered even more significant in light of the second development, a major change in English religious practice.

The sixteenth century witnessed a religious transformation that eventually led large numbers of English

ENGLISH REFORMATION

dissenters to leave their homeland. In 1533 Henry VIII, wanting a male heir and infatuated with Anne Boleyn, sought to annul his marriage to his Spanish-born queen, Catherine of Aragon. When the pope refused to approve the annulment, Henry left the Roman Catholic Church. He founded the Church of England and—with Parliament's concurrence—proclaimed himself its head. At first the reformed Church of England differed little from Catholicism in its practices, but under Henry's

daughter Elizabeth I (the child of his marriage to Anne Boleyn), new currents of religious belief that had originated on the European continent early in the sixteenth century dramatically affected the English church.

This Protestant Reformation was led by Martin Luther, a German monk, and John Calvin, a French cleric and lawyer. Challenging the Catholic doctrine that priests must serve as intermediaries between laypeople and God, Luther and Calvin insisted that people could interpret the Bible for themselves. Both Luther and Calvin rejected Catholic rituals, denying the need for an elaborate church hierarchy. They also asserted that faith in God was the key to salvation, rather than—as Catholic teaching had it—a combination of faith and good works. Calvin went further than Luther, stressing God's omnipotence and emphasizing the need for people to submit totally to God's will.

During her long reign (1558–1603), Elizabeth I tolerated religious diversity as long as her subjects

PURITANS AND SEPARATISTS

acknowledged her authority as head of the Church of England. By the late sixteenth century, many English Calvinists—those who came to be called Puritans because they wanted to purify the Church of England or Separatists because they wanted to leave it entirely—believed that the English Reformation had not gone far enough. Henry had simplified the church hierarchy; they wanted to abolish it altogether. Henry had subordinated the church to the interests of the state; they wanted a church free from political interference. And whereas the Church of England continued to include all English people, Puritans and Separatists wanted to confine church membership to the "saved"—those God had selected for salvation before birth.

Paradoxically a key article of their faith insisted that people could not know for certain if they were "saved" because mortals could not comprehend or affect their predestination to heaven or hell. Thus, pious Puritans and Separatists confronted a serious dilemma: if one was predestined for heaven or hell and could not alter one's fate, why should one attend church or do good works? They resolved this conundrum by reasoning that God gave the elect the ability to accept salvation and to lead a good life. Although piety and good works could not earn a place in heaven, they could indicate one's place in the ranks of the saved.

Elizabeth I's Stuart successors, her cousin James I (1603–1625) and his son Charles I (1625–1649), were less tolerant of religious dissent.

THE STUART MONARCHS

As Scots, they also had little respect for the traditions of representative government that had developed in England. They insisted on the divine right of kings—that a monarch's power came directly from God and that his subjects had a duty to obey him. A king's authority was absolute, they held.

Both James I and Charles I believed that their authority empowered them to enforce religious conformity. Because Puritans and Separatists—and the remaining English Catholics—challenged many important precepts of the English church, the monarchs authorized the removal of dissenting clergymen from their pulpits. In the 1620s and 1630s, a number of English dissenters moved to America, where they hoped to put their religious beliefs into practice unmolested by the Stuarts or the church hierarchy.

Unlike other Europeans, whose governments helped fund their migrations, many of the dissenters and other English people who migrated to North America and the Caribbean were financed by joint-stock companies. Stock sales funded these forerunners of modern corporations, which had been developed decades earlier to pool the resources of many small investors in trading voyages. They worked well for that purpose: no one risked too much money, and investors usually received quick returns. But joint-stock companies turned out to be a poor way to finance colonies because the early settlements required enormous amounts of capital and, with rare exceptions, failed to return much immediate profit. Colonies founded by joint-stock companies consequently suffered from a chronic lack of capital.

JOINT-STOCK COMPANIES

The Founding of Virginia

In 1606, envisioning the possibility of earning great profits by finding precious metals and opening new trade routes, a group of merchants and wealthy gentry established a joint-stock venture, the Virginia Company, and obtained a charter from King James I. A settlement they financed in present-day Maine soon collapsed, but a second enterprise would become England's first permanent colony in the Western Hemisphere.

In 1607, the Virginia Company sent 104 men and boys to a region near Chesapeake Bay. They arrived in May and established the settlement called Jamestown. Ill equipped for survival in the unfamiliar environment, the colonists were afflicted by dissension and disease. Moreover, through sheer bad luck, they arrived in the midst of a severe drought (now known to be the worst in the region for 1,700 years). The lack of rainfall not only made it difficult for them to cultivate crops but also polluted their drinking water.

JAMESTOWN

By January 1608, only thirty-eight of the original colonists remained alive. Many of the first immigrants were gentlemen or soldiers who resisted hard labor, tried to maintain traditional social hierarchies, and retained elaborate English dress and casual work habits despite their desperate circumstances. Such attitudes, combined with the effects of chronic malnutrition and epidemic disease, took a terrible toll. Only when Captain John Smith, one of the colony's lower-status founders, imposed military discipline in 1608 was Jamestown saved from collapse. But after Smith's departure the settlement experienced a severe "starving time" (the winter of 1609–1610). Although more settlers (including a few women and children) arrived in 1608 and 1609 and living conditions slowly improved, as late as 1624 only 1,300 of approximately 8,000 English immigrants to Virginia remained alive.

Jamestown owed its survival to a group of six Algonquian tribes known as the Powhatan Confederacy (see Map 2.1). Powhatan was aggressively consolidating his authority over some twenty-five smaller bands when the Europeans arrived. Fortunately for the colonists, Powhatan at first viewed them as potential allies and a reliable source of useful items such as knives and guns. In return, Powhatan's people traded their excess corn and other foodstuffs to the starving settlers. But the initially cordial relationship soon deteriorated. Drought reduced the Indians' crops, and they could no longer exchange food. Suspecting duplicity, English colonists kidnapped Powhatan's daughter, Pocahontas, holding her as a hostage. In captivity, she agreed in 1614 to marry a colonist, John Rolfe, perhaps as a form of diplomacy.

THE POWHATAN CONFEDERACY

English and Algonquian peoples had much in common: deep religious beliefs, a lifestyle oriented around agriculture, clear political and social hierarchies, and sharply defined gender roles. Yet the two groups focused on their cultural differences. English men regarded Indian men as lazy because they did not cultivate crops and spent much of their time hunting (a sport, not work, in English eyes). Indian men thought English men effeminate because they did "women's work" of cultivation.

ALGONQUIAN AND ENGLISH CULTURAL DIFFERENCES

Other differences between the two cultures caused serious misunderstandings. Among East Coast Algonquians, political power and social status were not necessarily passed down through the male line. Members of the English gentry inherited their position from their fathers, and English leaders tended to rule autocratically. By contrast, the authority of Algonquian leaders rested on consensus. Accustomed to the European concept of powerful kings, the English sought such figures in native villages. Often (for example, when negotiating treaties) they willfully overestimated the ability of chiefs to make independent decisions for their people.

Furthermore, Algonquians and English had very different notions of property ownership. Most Algonquian villages held their land communally. It could not be bought or sold absolutely, although certain rights to use the land (for example, for hunting or fishing) could be transferred. English people, in contrast, were accustomed to individual farms and to buying and selling land. The English also refused to accept Indians' claims to traditional hunting territories, insisting that only land intensively cultivated could be regarded as owned or occupied. Above all, the English settlers believed unwaveringly in the superiority of their civilization.

The spread of tobacco cultivation upset the balance of power in early Virginia. In tobacco, the settlers and the Virginia Company found the salable commodity for which they had been searching. John Rolfe planted the first crop in 1611. By the late 1620s, shipments totaled 1.5 million pounds. The great tobacco boom had begun, fueled by high prices and substantial profits for planters, who were meeting the escalating demand in Europe and Africa. Although the price of tobacco fluctuated wildly from year to year, the crop made Virginia

TOBACCO CULTIVATION

prosper. Soon the once-all-male outpost was an agricultural settlement inhabited by both men and women.

Farmers learned quickly that successful tobacco cultivation required abundant land, since a field could produce only about three satisfactory crops before it had to lie fallow for several years to regain its fertility. Thus, the small English settlements began to expand rapidly: eager applicants asked the Virginia Company for large land grants on both sides of the James River and its tributary streams.

To attract more settlers to the colony, the Virginia Company in 1617 developed the "headright" system: every new arrival paying his or her own way was promised a land grant of fifty acres; those who financed the passage of others received similar headrights for each person. To ordinary English farmers, many of whom owned little or no land, the headright system offered a powerful incentive to move to Virginia. To wealthy gentry, it promised the possibility of establishing vast agricultural enterprises worked by large numbers of laborers. Two years later, the company introduced a second reform, authorizing the landowning men of the major Virginia settlements to elect representatives to an assembly called the House of Burgesses. English landholders had long been accustomed to electing members of Parliament and controlling their own local governments, and they expected the same privilege in the nation's colonies.

VIRGINIA COMPANY POLICIES

Opechancanough, Powhatan's brother and successor, watched the English colonists steadily encroaching on the confederacy's lands and attempting to convert its members to Christianity. Recognizing the danger his brother had overlooked, the war leader launched coordinated attacks all along the James River on March 22, 1622. By the end of the day, 347 colonists (about one-quarter of the total) lay dead. Virginia reeled from the blow but did not collapse, and an uneasy peace prevailed. Two decades later, Opechancanough tried one last time to repel the invaders. He failed, losing his life in the war that ensued. After this defeat and a 1646 treaty subordinating the Powhatan Confederacy to English authority, the Indians' efforts to resist the spread of European settlement ended.

INDIAN UPRISINGS

The 1622 Powhatan uprising that failed to destroy the colony succeeded in killing its parent. The

A comparison of the portrait of Sir Walter Raleigh and his son (left), with that of an Algonquian Indian drawn by John White, from Raleigh's Roanoke expedition (right), shows a dramatic difference in standard dress styles that, for many, must have symbolized the apparent cultural gap between Europeans and Americans. Yet that both men (and the young boy) were portrayed in similar stances, with "arms akimbo," demonstrated that all were high-status individuals. In Europe, only aristocrats were represented in such an aggressive pose.   (Left: National Portrait Gallery, London; right: © Trustees of the British Museum)

Virginia Company never made any profits, for internal corruption and the heavy cost of supporting the settlers offset all its earnings. In 1624 James I revoked the charter, transforming Virginia into a royal colony ruled by officials he appointed. James continued the headright policy but abolished the assembly. Virginians protested so vigorously, however, that by 1629 the House of Burgesses was functioning once again. Because Virginians successfully insisted on governing themselves at the local level, the political structure of England's American possessions came to differ from that of New Spain, New France, and New Netherland, all of which were ruled autocratically.

Life in the Chesapeake

y the 1630s, tobacco was firmly established as the staple crop and chief source of revenue in Virginia. It quickly became just as important in the second English colony planted on Chesapeake Bay: Maryland, given by Charles I to George Calvert, first Lord Baltimore, as a personal possession (proprietorship) and settled in 1634. The Calverts intended the colony to serve as a haven for their persecuted fellow Catholics. Cecilius Calvert, second Lord Baltimore, became the first colonizer to offer freedom of religion to all Christian settlers; he understood that protecting the Protestant majority could also ensure Catholics' rights.

In everything but religion, the two Chesapeake colonies resembled each other. In Maryland as in Virginia, tobacco planters spread out along the river banks, establishing isolated farms instead of towns. The region's deep, wide rivers offered dependable water transportation, and each farm or group of farms had its own wharf, where oceangoing vessels could take on or discharge cargo. As a result, Virginia and Maryland had few towns, for their residents did not need commercial centers in which to buy and sell goods.

Online Study Center **Improve Your Grade**
Interactive Map: Patterns of Settlement in Surry County, Virginia, 1620–1660

Because the planting, cultivation, and harvesting of tobacco were labor intensive, successful Chesapeake tobacco farms required laborers. Nearby Indians, their numbers reduced by war and disease, could not supply the needed workers. Nor were enslaved Africans available: merchants could more easily and profitably sell slaves to Caribbean sugar planters. By 1650 only about three hundred blacks, some of them free, lived in Virginia—a tiny fraction of the population.

DEMAND FOR LABORERS

Chesapeake tobacco farmers thus looked primarily to England to supply their labor needs. Under the headright system (which Maryland also adopted in 1640), a tobacco farmer anywhere in the Chesapeake could simultaneously obtain both land and labor by importing workers from England. Good management would make the process self-perpetuating: a farmer could use his profits to pay for the passage of more workers and thereby gain title to more land.

Because men did the agricultural work in European societies, colonists assumed that field laborers should be men. Such male laborers, along with a few women, immigrated to America as indentured servants: in return for their passage, they contracted to work for periods ranging from four to seven years. Indentured servants accounted for 75 to 85 percent of the approximately 130,000 English immigrants to Virginia and Maryland during the seventeenth century.

Males between the ages of fifteen and twenty-four composed roughly three-quarters of these servants; only one immigrant in five or six was female. Most of these young men came from farming or laboring families and were what their contemporaries called the "common sort."

For such people, the Chesapeake appeared to offer good prospects. Servants who completed their indentures earned "freedom dues" consisting of clothes, tools, livestock, casks of corn and tobacco, and sometimes even land. Yet immigrants' lives were difficult. Servants typically worked six days a week, ten to fourteen hours a day. Their masters could discipline or sell them, and they faced severe penalties for running away. Even so, the laws did offer them some protection. For example, their masters were supposed to supply them with sufficient food, clothing, and shelter, and cruelly treated servants could turn to the courts for assistance.

CONDITIONS OF SERVITUDE

Servants and their masters alike contended with epidemic disease. Immigrants first had to survive the process the colonists called "seasoning"—a bout with disease (probably malaria) that usually occurred during their first Chesapeake summer. They then often endured recurrences of malaria, along with dysentery, typhoid fever, and other diseases. Consequently, about 40 percent of male servants did not survive long enough to become freedmen.

For those who survived their indentures, however, the opportunities for advancement were real. Until the last decades of the seventeenth century, former servants often became independent farmers ("freeholders"), living a modest but comfortable existence. Some even assumed positions of political prominence. But after 1670, tobacco prices declined, and good land grew increasingly scarce and expensive, and in 1681 Maryland dropped its legal requirement that servants receive land as part of their freedom dues. By 1700 the Chesapeake was no longer the land of opportunity it once had been.

Life in the early Chesapeake was hard for everyone, regardless of sex or status. Farmers (and sometimes

STANDARD
OF LIVING

their wives) toiled in the fields alongside servants. Most people rose and went to bed with the sun, lived in one- or two-room ramshackle houses, and consumed a filling but not especially nutritious diet based on pork and corn. Colonists devoted their income to improving their farms, buying livestock, and purchasing more laborers rather than to improving their standard of living.

The predominance of males, the incidence of servitude, and the high mortality rates combined to produce unusual patterns of family life.

CHESAPEAKE
FAMILIES

Female servants normally could not marry during their terms of indenture because masters did not want pregnancies to deprive them of workers. Many male ex-servants could not marry at all because of the scarcity of women. In contrast, nearly every adult free woman in the Chesapeake married. Yet because of high infant mortality and because almost all marriages were delayed by servitude or broken by death, Chesapeake women commonly reared only one to three healthy children, in contrast to English women, who normally had at least five.

Thus, Chesapeake families were few, small, and short-lived. Parents often died while their children were still young. In one Virginia county, for example, more than three-quarters of the children had lost at least one parent by the time they either married or reached age twenty-one. Indeed, the large number of orphaned children prompted a legal innovation: the establishment of orphans' courts to oversee the management of orphans' property.

Because of the low rate of natural increase, immigrants composed a majority of the Chesapeake population throughout the seventeenth century.

CHESAPEAKE
POLITICS

Thus, most members of Virginia's House of Burgesses and Maryland's House of Delegates (established in 1635) were immigrants; they also dominated the governor's council, which simultaneously served as each colony's highest court, part of the legislature, and executive adviser to the governor. A native-born ruling elite emerged only in the early eighteenth century. Until then, the Chesapeake's leaders, as immigrants lacking strong ties to one another or to the colonies, made for contentious politics rather than stability.

The Founding of New England

*T*he economic motives that prompted English people to move to the Chesapeake and Caribbean colonies also drew men and women to New England. But because Puritans organized the New England colonies and also because of environmental factors, the northern settlements turned out very differently from those in the South.

Hoping to exert control over a migration that appeared disorderly, royal bureaucrats in late 1634 ordered port officials in London to collect information on all travelers departing for the colonies. The resulting records for the year 1635 document the departure of 53 vessels in that year alone. On those ships sailed almost 5,000 people, with 2,000 departing for Virginia, about 1,200 for New England, and the rest for island destinations. Nearly three-fifths of all the passengers were between 15 and 24 years old, reflecting the predominance of young male servants among migrants to America. But among those bound for New England, such youths constituted less than one-third of the total; nearly 40 percent were between ages 25 and 50, and another third were aged 14 and below. Whereas women made up just 14 percent of those going to Virginia, they composed almost 40 percent of the passengers to New England. It is therefore evident that New Englanders often traveled in family groups. They also brought more goods and livestock with them and tended to travel with other people from the same regions. In short, although migrants to the Chesapeake and the islands most commonly left friends and families behind, those who moved to New England came in concert with their close associates, which must have made for a more comfortable and less lonely life.

CONTRASTING
REGIONAL
DEMOGRAPHIC
PATTERNS

Among Chesapeake migrants, only the Catholics who moved to Maryland seem to have been motivated by religious concerns, and neither the Church of England nor the Catholic Church much affected the settlers. Yet religion inspired many of the people who colonized New England, and Puritan congregations quickly became key institutions.

CONTRASTING
REGIONAL
RELIGIOUS
PATTERNS

Religion constantly affected the lives of pious Puritans, who regularly reassessed the state of their souls. Many devoted themselves to self-examination and Bible study, and families prayed together each day under the guidance of the husband and father. Yet because even the most pious could never be certain that they were numbered among the elect, anxiety about their spiritual state troubled devout Puritans.

Separatists who thought the Church of England too corrupt to be salvaged were the first to move to

SEPARATISTS

New England, hoping to isolate themselves and their children from the corrupting influence of worldly temptations. In 1620, some Separatists, many of whom had earlier migrated to Holland in quest of the right to freely practice their religion, received permission from the Virginia Company to colonize the northern part of its territory. That September more than one hundred people, only thirty of them Separatists, set sail from England on the old and crowded *Mayflower*. Two months later, they landed in America, but farther north than they had intended. Given the lateness of the season, they decided to stay where they were. They established their settlement on a fine harbor and named it Plymouth.

Even before they landed, the Pilgrims had to surmount their first challenge—from the "strangers," or non-Separatists, who sailed with them to America. Because they landed outside the jurisdiction of the Virginia Company, some of the strangers questioned the authority of the colony's leaders. In response, the Mayflower Compact, signed in November 1620 on board the ship, established a "Civil Body Politic" and a rudimentary legal authority for the colony. The male settlers elected a governor and at first made all decisions for the colony at town meetings. Later, after more towns had been founded, Plymouth, like Virginia and Maryland, created an assembly to which the landowning male settlers elected representatives.

Survival also challenged the Pilgrims. Like the Jamestown settlers before them, they were poorly

INDIAN
RELATIONS

prepared for their new environment. Winter quickly descended, compounding their difficulties. Only half the *Mayflower*'s passengers lived to see spring. But, again like the Virginians, the Pilgrims benefited from the political circumstances of nearby Indians.

The Pokanokets (a branch of the Wampanoags) controlled the area in which the Pilgrims settled and decided to ally with the newcomers to protect themselves from the powerful Narragansetts of the southern New England coast. In the spring of 1621, their leader, Massasoit, signed a treaty with the Pilgrims, and during the colony's first difficult years, the Pokanokets supplied the English with essential foodstuffs. The settlers were also assisted by Squanto, an Indian who had earlier been captured by fishermen and taken to Europe, where he learned to speak English. Squanto became the Pilgrims' interpreter and a major source of information about the unfamiliar environment.

Before the 1620s ended, a group of Puritan Congregationalists (who hoped to reform the Church of

MASSACHUSETTS
BAY COMPANY

England from within) launched the colonial enterprise that would come to dominate New England. Charles I, who became king in 1625, was more hostile to Puritans than his father had been. In response to Charles's attempts to suppress Puritanism, some Congregationalist merchants, concerned about their long-term prospects in England, sent a body of colonists to Cape Ann (north of Cape Cod) in 1628. The following year the merchants obtained a royal charter, constituting themselves as the Massachusetts Bay Company.

The new joint-stock company quickly attracted the attention of Puritans of the "middling sort," who remained committed to the goal of reforming the Church of England but concluded that they should pursue that aim in America. In a dramatic move, the Congregationalist merchants boldly decided to transfer the Massachusetts Bay Company's headquarters to New England. The settlers would then be answerable to no one in the mother country and would be able to handle their affairs as they pleased.

The most important recruit to the new venture was John Winthrop. In October 1629, the Massachusetts

GOVERNOR JOHN
WINTHROP

Bay Company elected Winthrop its governor, and he organized the initial segment of the great Puritan migration to America. In 1630 more than one thousand English men and women moved to Massachusetts—most of them to Boston, which soon became the largest town in English North America. By 1643 nearly twenty thousand compatriots had followed them.

■ Some scholars now believe that this 1638 painting by the Dutch artist Adam Willaerts depicts the Plymouth colony about fifteen years after its founding. The shape of the harbor, the wooden gate, and the houses straggling up the hill all coincide with contemporary accounts of the settlement. No one believes that Willaerts himself visited Plymouth, but people returning from the colony to Holland, where the Pilgrims had lived for years before emigrating, could well have described Plymouth to him.   (© J. D. Bangs, Courtesy of Leiden American Pilgrim Museum, The Netherlands)

Winthrop's was a transcendent vision. He foresaw in Puritan America a true commonwealth, a community in which each person put the good of the whole ahead of private concerns. "In America we shall be as a city upon a hill," he asserted, "the eyes of all people are upon us." Although, as in England, this society would be characterized by social inequality and clear hierarchies of status and power, Winthrop hoped that its members would live according to the precepts of Christian love. Such an ideal was beyond human reach, but it persisted well into the third and fourth generations of the immigrants' descendants.

The Puritans expressed their communal ideal chiefly in the doctrine of the covenant. They believed God had made a covenant—that is, an agreement or contract—with them when they were chosen for the special mission to America. In turn,

COVENANT
IDEAL

they covenanted with one another, promising to work together toward their goals. The founders of churches, towns, and even colonies in Anglo-America often drafted formal documents setting forth the principles on which their institutions would be based. The Mayflower Compact was a such a covenant.

The leaders of Massachusetts Bay likewise transformed their original joint-stock company charter into the basis for a covenanted community based on mutual consent. Under pressure from landowning male settlers, they gradually changed the General Court—officially the company's small governing body—into a colonial legislature. They also granted the status of freeman, or voting member of the company, to all property-owning adult male church members. Less than two decades after the first large group of Puritans arrived in Massachusetts Bay, the colony had a functioning system of self-government composed of a governor and a two-house legislature. The General Court also established a judicial system modeled on England's.

The colony's method of distributing land helped further the communal ideal. Groups of men applied

NEW ENGLAND TOWNS

together to the General Court for grants of land on which to establish towns (novel governance units that did not exist in England). The men receiving such a grant determined how the land would be distributed. First they laid out lots for houses and a church. Then they gave each family parcels of land scattered around the town center: a pasture here, a woodlot there, an arable field elsewhere. Every man obtained land, but the best and largest plots went to the most distinguished among them (including the minister).

Thus, New England settlements initially tended to be more compact than those of the Chesapeake. Town centers developed quickly, evolving in three distinctly different ways. Some, chiefly isolated settlements in the interior, tried to sustain Winthrop's vision of harmonious community life based on diversified family farms. A second group, the coastal towns like Boston and Salem, became bustling seaports. The third category, commercialized agricultural towns, grew up in the Connecticut River valley, where easy water transportation enabled farmers to sell surplus goods readily.

When migrants began to move beyond the territorial limits of the Massachusetts Bay colony into

INTERNAL MIGRATION

Connecticut (1636), New Haven (1638), and New Hampshire (1638), the same pattern of land grants persisted. (Only Maine, thinly populated by coastal fishing families, deviated.) The migration to the Connecticut Valley ended the Puritans' relative freedom from clashes with nearby Indians. The first English people in the valley moved there from Massachusetts Bay under the direction of their minister, Thomas Hooker. Although remote from other English towns, the wide river promised ready access to the ocean. The site had just one problem: it fell within the territory controlled by the powerful Pequots.

The Pequots' dominance stemmed from their role as primary middlemen in the trade between New

PEQUOT WAR

England Indians and the Dutch in New Netherland. The arrival of English settlers signaled the end of this power, for previously subordinate bands could now trade directly with Europeans. Pequots and English colonists clashed even before the establishment of settlements in the Connecticut Valley, but their founding tipped the balance toward war. After two English traders were killed (not by Pequots), the English raided a Pequot village. In return, the Pequots attacked the new town of Wethersfield in April 1637, killing nine and capturing two. To retaliate, a Massachusetts Bay expedition the following month attacked and burned the main Pequot town on the Mystic River. The English and their Narragansett allies slaughtered at least four hundred Pequots, mostly women and children.

For the next thirty years, the New England Indians accommodated themselves to the spread of European settlement. They traded with the newcomers and sometimes worked for them, but for the most part they resisted acculturation or incorporation into English society. Native Americans persisted in using traditional farming methods, without plows or fences. The one European practice they adopted was keeping livestock: domesticated animals provided excellent sources of meat now that their hunting territories had been turned into English farms and game had disappeared.

Although the official seal of the Massachusetts Bay colony showed an Indian crying, "Come over

JOHN ELIOT'S PRAYING TOWNS

and help us," most colonists showed little interest in converting the Algonquians to Christianity. Only a few Massachusetts clerics, most notably John Eliot, seriously undertook missionary activities. Eliot insisted that converts reside in towns, farm the land in English fashion, assume English names, wear European-style clothing and shoes, cut their hair, and stop observing a wide range of their own customs. He understandably met with little success. At the peak of Eliot's efforts, only eleven hundred Indians lived in the fourteen "Praying Towns" he established.

The Jesuits' successful missions in New France contrasted sharply with the Puritans' failure to win

MISSIONARY ACTIVITIES COMPARED

many converts. Catholicism had several advantages over Puritanism. The Catholic Church employed beautiful ceremonies, instructed converts that through good works they could help to earn their own salvation, and offered Indian women an inspiring role model: the Virgin Mary. In Montreal and Quebec, communities of nuns taught Indian women and children and ministered to their needs. Furthermore, the few French colonists on the St. Lawrence did not alienate potential converts by encroaching steadily on their lands (as did New Englanders). Perhaps most important, the Jesuits understood that Christian beliefs could be compatible with Native American culture. Unlike Puritans, Jesuits accepted converts who did not wholly adopt European styles of life.

What attracted Indians to these religious ideas? Conversion often alienated new Christians (both Catholic and Puritan) from their relatives and traditions—a likely outcome that must have caused many potential converts to think twice about making such a commitment. But surely many hoped to use the Europeans' religion as a way to cope with the dramatic changes the intruders had wrought. The combination of disease, alcohol, new trading patterns, and loss of territory disrupted customary patterns of life to an unprecedented extent. Shamans had little success in restoring traditional ways. Many Indians must have concluded that the Europeans' own ideas could provide the key to survival in the new circumstances.

Life in New England

*N*ew England's colonizers adopted lifestyles that differed considerably from those of both their Indian neighbors and their counterparts in the Chesapeake. Unlike the Algonquian bands, who usually moved four or five times each year to take full advantage of their environment, English people lived in the same location year-round. And unlike residents of the Chesapeake, New Englanders constructed sturdy dwellings intended to last. They used the same fields again and again, fertilizing with manure rather than clearing new fields every few years. And they fenced their croplands to prevent them from being overrun by the cattle, sheep, and hogs that were their chief sources of meat.

Because Puritans commonly moved to America in family groups, the age range in early New England

NEW ENGLAND FAMILIES

was wide; and because many more women went to New England than to the tobacco colonies, the population could immediately begin to reproduce. Also, New England was

much healthier than the Chesapeake. Once Puritan settlements had survived the difficult first few years, New England proved to be even healthier than the mother country. Adult male migrants to the Chesapeake lost about ten years from their English life expectancy of fifty to fifty-five years; their Massachusetts counterparts gained five or more years. Consequently, while Chesapeake families were few in number and small in size, New England families were numerous and large. If seventeenth-century Chesapeake women could expect to rear one to three healthy children, New England women could anticipate raising five to seven.

The nature of the population had other major implications for family life. New England in effect created grandparents, since in England people rarely lived long enough to know their children's children. And whereas early Chesapeake parents commonly died before their children married, New England parents exercised a good deal of control over their adult offspring. Young men could not marry without acreage to cultivate, and because of the communal land-grant system, they had to depend on their fathers to give them that land. Daughters too needed a dowry of household goods supplied by their parents. Yet parents relied on their children's labor and often seemed reluctant to see them marry and start their own households. These needs at times led to considerable conflict between the generations.

Another important difference lay in the influence of religion on New Englanders' lives. Puritans controlled

IMPACT OF RELIGION

their governments. Congregationalism was the only officially recognized religion; except in Rhode Island, founded by dissenters from Massachusetts, members of other sects had no freedom of worship. Some non-Puritans voted in town meetings, but in Massachusetts Bay and New Haven, church membership was a prerequisite for voting in colony elections. All the early colonies taxed residents to build meetinghouses and pay ministers' salaries, but Puritan colonies in particular attempted to enforce strict codes of moral conduct. Colonists there were frequently tried for drunkenness, card playing, even idleness. Couples who had sex during their engagement—as revealed by the birth of a baby less than nine months after their wedding—were fined and publicly humiliated. More harshly treated were men—and a handful of women—who engaged in behaviors that today would be called homosexual. (The term did not then exist.) Several men who had consenting same-sex relationships were hanged.

Puritans objected to secular interference in religious affairs but at the same time expected the church to influence the conduct of politics and the affairs of society. They also believed that the state was obliged to support and protect the one true church—theirs. As a result, although they came to America seeking freedom to worship as they pleased, they saw no contradiction in refusing to grant that freedom to others.

Roger Williams, a Separatist who immigrated to Massachusetts Bay in 1631, quickly ran afoul of that

ROGER WILLIAMS

Puritan orthodoxy. He told his fellow settlers that the king of England had no right to grant them land already occupied by Indians, that church and state should be kept entirely separate, and that Puritans should not impose their religious beliefs on others. Because Puritan leaders placed a heavy emphasis on achieving consensus in both religion and politics, they could not long tolerate significant dissent.

Banished from Massachusetts, Williams journeyed in early 1636 to the head of Narragansett Bay, where he founded the town of Providence. Because Williams believed that government should not interfere with religion in any way, Providence and other towns in what became Rhode Island adopted a policy of tolerating all religions, including Judaism. Along with Maryland, the tiny colony that Williams founded presaged the religious freedom that eventually became one of the hallmarks of the United States.

A dissenter who presented a more sustained challenge to Massachusetts Bay colony leaders was Mistress

ANNE HUTCHINSON

Anne Marbury Hutchinson. A skilled medical practitioner who was popular with the women of Boston, she greatly admired John Cotton, a minister who stressed the covenant of grace, or God's free gift of salvation to unworthy human beings. By contrast, most Massachusetts clerics emphasized the need for Puritans to engage in good works, study, and reflection in preparation for receiving God's grace. After spreading her ideas for months in the context of childbirth gatherings—when no men were present—Hutchinson began holding women's meetings in her home to discuss Cotton's sermons. She emphasized the covenant of grace more than did Cotton himself, and she even adopted the belief that the

elect could be assured of salvation and communicate directly with God. Such ideas had an immense appeal for Puritans. Anne Hutchinson offered them certainty of salvation instead of a state of constant anxiety.

Hutchinson's ideas posed a dangerous threat to Puritan orthodoxy. So in November 1637, officials charged her with having maligned the colony's ministers. For two days she defended herself cleverly, but then she boldly declared that God had spoken to her directly, explaining that he would curse the Puritans' descendants for generations if they harmed her. That assertion ensured her banishment to Rhode Island in 1638.

The authorities in Massachusetts Bay perceived Anne Hutchinson as doubly dangerous to the existing order: she threatened not only religious orthodoxy but also traditional gender roles. Puritans believed in the equality before God of all souls, including those of women, but they considered actual women (as distinct from their spiritual selves) inferior to men. Christians had long followed Saint Paul's dictum that women should keep silent in church and submit to their husbands. Hutchinson did neither. A minister told her bluntly: "You have stept out of your place, you have rather bine a Husband than a Wife and a preacher than a Hearer; and a Magistrate than a Subject."

The New England authorities' reaction to Anne Hutchinson reveals the depth of their adherence to European gender-role concepts. To them, an orderly society required the submission of wives to husbands as well as the obedience of subjects to rulers.

Summary *Online Study Center* ACE the Test

By the middle of the seventeenth century, Europeans had come to North America to stay, signaling major changes for the peoples of both hemispheres. Europeans killed Indians with their weapons and diseases and had but limited success in converting them to Christian sects. Contacts with indigenous peoples taught Europeans to eat new foods, speak new languages, and recognize, however reluctantly, the persistence of other cultural patterns. The prosperity and even survival of many of the European colonies depended heavily on the cultivation of American crops (maize and tobacco) and an Asian crop (sugar), thus attesting to the importance of post-Columbian ecological change.

In America, Spaniards reaped the benefits of their South and Central American gold and silver mines, while French people earned their primary profits from Indian trade (in Canada) and cultivating sugar cane (in the Caribbean). Sugar also enriched the Portuguese. The Dutch concentrated on commerce—trading in furs and sugar as well as carrying human cargoes of enslaved Africans to South America and the Caribbean.

Although the English colonies, too, at first sought to rely on trade, they quickly took another road altogether when many English people of the "middling sort" decided to migrate to North America. To a greater extent than their European counterparts, the English transferred the society and politics of their homeland to a new environment. Their sheer numbers, coupled with their need for vast quantities of land on which to grow their crops and raise their livestock, inevitably brought them into conflict with their Indian neighbors. Ultimately New England and the Chesapeake would also be drawn into the increasingly fierce rivalries besetting the European powers. Those rivalries would continue to affect Americans of all races until after the mid-eighteenth century, when France and England fought the greatest war yet known, and the Anglo-American colonies had won their independence.

LEGACY FOR A PEOPLE AND A NATION

The Foxwoods Casino and the Mashantucket Pequot Museum

In 1992 the Mashantucket Pequots opened the enormously successful Foxwoods Resort Casino on their small reservation in southeastern Connecticut. Just six years later, in August 1998, the Pequots proudly inaugurated a new museum (built with some of their substantial profits) presenting their people's story. Both developments surprised many Americans, who did not realize that Native Americans still lived in New England. The existence of the Pequots was particularly startling, because histories had long recorded that the nation was destroyed in the Pequot War of 1637.

Survivors of the Mystic River massacre had regrouped in the Mashantucket swamps, building lives as farmers, laborers, and craftspeople. Some left the area, but a few Pequots remained: the 1910 census, the source today for determining Pequot tribal membership, counted sixty-six residents of a reservation just 213 acres in size. By the 1970s, the residents had been reduced to two, and the state of Connecticut threatened to turn the reservation into a park. But an elder, Elizabeth George, persuaded several hundred people tracing descent from those listed in 1910 to return to live on the reservation. In 1983 the determined Pequots won formal federal recognition, which in turn allowed them to build the profitable casino, a hotel, and several restaurants, and to begin purchasing more land.

Now the museum introduces the history of the Pequots and of eastern Algonquian peoples to hundreds of thousands of visitors each year. At its heart is a re-creation of a Pequot village as it would have looked shortly before Europeans first arrived on Connecticut's shores, complete with sounds and smells controlled by state-of-the-art computers. Exhibits detail the origins of the Pequot War, and a film narrates the tale of the massacre.

The Pequots' success has helped to embolden other eastern Algonquian nations to reassert publicly their long-suppressed Indian identities. The Pequot people's dedication to preserving their culture and reaffirming their history has created a remarkable legacy for the nation.

NORTH AMERICA IN THE ATLANTIC WORLD 1640–1720

*T*he *Seaflower*, Captain Thomas Smith, master, lay at anchor in Boston harbor in early September 1676, awaiting official documents signed by the governors of Massachusetts and Plymouth. Smith expected to sell the cargo in his hold when he got to the West Indies. But that cargo differed from most: it comprised human beings, nearly two hundred "heathen Malefactors—men, women, and Children." The certificates from the governors explained "To all People" the origins of Captain Smith's human cargo: "Philip an heathen Sachem . . . with others his wicked complices and abettors have treacherously and perfidiously rebelled against" these colonies. "By due and legall procedure," the captives on board the *Seaflower* were "Sentenced & condemned to perpetuall Servitude." The Pokanoket leader, King Philip (called Metacom at birth and later renamed "Philip" by New Englanders), had been killed a month earlier in the war that bore his name. His young son seems to have been sold into slavery, along with many shiploads of Philip's followers.

Only one prominent New Englander objected on moral grounds to the policy of selling the vanquished Algonquians into West Indian slavery. The Reverend John Eliot reminded the authorities that the colonists had a solemn duty to "inlarge the kingdom of Jesus Christ"; "to sell [the Indians] away for slaves, is to hinder the inlargement of his kingdom." If the Indians deserved to die, then "godly governors" should ensure that they died "penitently," rather than depriving them of "all meanes of grace" by selling them as slaves. It was the subversion of God's plan for Massachusetts, not enslavement itself, that concerned Eliot.

The tale of Thomas Smith and the *Seaflower*'s human cargo illustrates not only the English colonists' willingness to enslave "heathen" peoples and their increasingly contentious relationship with Native Americans, but also the participation of the mainland colonies in a growing international network. North America, like England itself, was becoming embedded in a worldwide matrix of trade and warfare. The web woven by oceangoing

Growth of Anglo-American Settlements

A Decade of Imperial Crises: The 1670s

African Slavery on the Mainland

The Web of Empire and the Atlantic Slave Trade

LINKS TO THE WORLD
International Piracy

Enslavement of Africans and Indians

Imperial Reorganization and the Witchcraft Crisis

LEGACY FOR A PEOPLE AND A NATION
Americans of African Descent

Online Study Center
This icon will direct you to interactive map and primary source activities on the website http://college.hmco.com/pic/nortonbrief7e

CHRONOLOGY

1642–46 • English Civil War

1649 • Charles I executed

1651 • First Navigation Act passed to regulate colonial trade

1660 • Stuarts restored to throne
• Charles II becomes king

1663 • Carolina chartered

1664 • English conquer New Netherland
• New York founded
• New Jersey established

1670s • Marquette, Jolliet, and La Salle explore the Great Lakes and Mississippi valley for France

1675–76 • King Philip's War devastates New England

1676 • Bacon's Rebellion disrupts Virginia government
• Jamestown destroyed

1680–1700 • Pueblo revolt temporarily drives Spaniards from New Mexico

1681 • Pennsylvania chartered

1685 • James II becomes king

1686–89 • Dominion of New England established, superseding all charters of colonies from Maine to New Jersey

1688–89 • James II deposed in Glorious Revolution
• William and Mary ascend throne

1688–99 • King William's War fought on northern New England frontier

1692 • Witchcraft crisis in Salem; nineteen executions result

1696 • Board of Trade and Plantations established to coordinate English colonial administration

1701 • Iroquois adopt neutrality policy toward France and England

1702–13 • Queen Anne's War fought by French and English

1711–13 • Tuscarora War (North Carolina) leads to capture or migration of most Tuscaroras

1715 • Yamasee War nearly destroys South Carolina

1718 • New Orleans founded in French Louisiana

vessels now crisscrossed the globe, carrying European goods to America and Africa, West Indian sugar to New England and Europe, Africans to the Americas, and New England fish and wood products—and occasionally Indian slaves—to the Caribbean.

Three developments shaped life in the mainland English colonies between 1640 and 1720: the expansion of slavery, changes in the colonies' political and economic relationships with England, and escalating conflicts with Indians and other European colonies in North America.

The explosive growth of the slave trade significantly altered the Anglo-American economy. Carrying human cargoes paid off handsomely. At first primarily encompassing Indians and already enslaved Africans from the Caribbean, the trade soon came to focus on cargoes brought to the Americas directly from Africa. The arrival of large numbers of West African peoples dramatically reshaped colonial society and fueled the international trading system. Moreover, the burgeoning North American economy attracted new attention from colonial administrators in London, who attempted to supervise the American settlements more effectively to ensure that the mother country benefited from their economic growth.

Neither English colonists nor London administrators could ignore other peoples living on the North American continent. As the English settlements expanded, they came into violent conflict not only with powerful Indian nations but also with the Dutch, the Spanish, and especially the French. By 1720, war had become an all-too-familiar feature of American life. No longer isolated from each other or from Europe, the people and products of the North American colonies had become integral to the world trading system and inextricably enmeshed in its conflicts. ■

Growth of Anglo-American Settlements

Between 1642 and 1646, civil war between supporters of King Charles I and the Puritan-dominated Parliament engulfed the colonists' English homeland. Parliament triumphed, leading to the execution of the king in 1649 and interim rule by the parliamentary army's leader, Oliver Cromwell. But after Cromwell's death, Parliament decided to restore the monarchy if Charles I's son and heir agreed to restrictions on his authority. Charles II did so, and the Stuarts returned to the throne in 1660. The new king subsequently rewarded nobles and others who had supported him during the Civil War with huge tracts of land on the North American mainland. The colonies so established made up six of the thirteen polities that eventually would form the American nation: New York, New Jersey, Pennsylvania (including Delaware), and North and South Carolina. Collectively, these became known as the Restoration colonies because they were created by the restored Stuart monarchy. All were proprietorships; in each of them, as in Maryland, one man or several men held title to the soil and controlled the government.

In 1664, Charles II gave his younger brother James, the duke of York, the region between the

NEW YORK Connecticut and Delaware Rivers, including the Hudson valley and Long Island. James immediately organized an invasion fleet. In August James's warships anchored off Manhattan Island and demanded New Netherland's surrender. The colony complied without resistance.

Thus James acquired a heterogeneous possession, which he renamed New York (see Table 3.1). An appreciable minority of English people already lived there, along with sizable numbers of Indians, Africans, and Germans and a smattering of other European peoples. The Dutch West India Company had actively imported slaves into the colony. Indeed, almost one-fifth of Manhattan's approximately fifteen hundred inhabitants were of African descent.

Recognizing the population's diversity, James's representatives moved cautiously in their efforts to establish English authority. The Duke's Laws, a legal code proclaimed in 1665, applied solely to the English settlements on Long Island, only later being extended to the rest of the colony. James's policies initially maintained Dutch forms of local government, confirmed Dutch land titles, and allowed Dutch residents to maintain customary legal practices. Each town was permitted to decide which church (Dutch Reformed, Congregational, or Church of England) to support with its tax revenues. Much to the dismay of English residents, the Duke's Laws made no provision for a representative assembly. Like other Stuarts, James distrusted legislative bodies, and not until 1683 did he agree to the colonists' requests for an elected legislature. The English takeover thus had little immediate effect on the colony. Its population grew slowly, barely reaching eighteen thousand by the time of the first English census in 1698.

A primary reason for New York's slow growth was that in 1664 the duke of York regranted the land

NEW JERSEY between the Hudson and Delaware Rivers—East and West Jersey—to his friends Sir George Carteret and John Lord Berkeley. That grant deprived New York of much fertile land and hindered its economic growth. Meanwhile, the Jersey proprietors acted rapidly to attract settlers, promising generous land grants, limited freedom of religion, and—without authorization from the Crown—a representative assembly. As a result, New Jersey grew quickly; in 1726, at the time of its first census as a united colony, it had 32,500 inhabitants, only 8,000 fewer than New York.

Within twenty years, Berkeley and Carteret sold their interests in the Jerseys to separate groups of investors. The purchasers of all of Carteret's share (West Jersey) and portions of Berkeley's (East Jersey) were members of the Society of Friends, also called Quakers, who rejected earthly and religious hierarchies. Quakers believed that anyone could be saved by directly receiving God's "inner light" and that all people

TABLE 3.2

The Founding of English Colonies in North America, 1664–1681

Colony	Founder(s)	Date	Basis of Economy
New York (formerly New Netherland)	James, duke of York	1664	Farming, fur trading
New Jersey	Sir George Carteret John Lord Berkeley	1664	Farming
North Carolina	Carolina proprietors	1665	Tobacco, forest products
South Carolina	Carolina proprietors	1670	Rice, indigo
Pennsylvania (incl. Delaware)	William Penn	1681	Farming

were equal in God's sight. With no formally trained clergy, Quakers allowed anyone, male or female, to speak in meetings or spread God's word. The Quaker message of radical egalitarianism was unwelcome in the hierarchical society of England and the colonies, and Quakers encountered persecution everywhere.

The Quakers obtained their own colony in 1681, when Charles II granted the region between Maryland and New York to his close friend William Penn, a prominent member of the sect. Although Penn held the colony as a personal proprietorship, he saw his province not merely as a source of revenue but also as a haven for persecuted coreligionists. Penn offered land to all comers on liberal terms, promised toleration of all religions (although only Christians were given the vote), guaranteed English liberties such as the right to bail and trial by jury, and pledged to establish a representative assembly. He also publicized the ready availability of land in Pennsylvania throughout Europe.

PENNSYLVANIA

Penn's activities and the Quakers' attraction to his lands gave rise to a migration rivaling the Puritan exodus to New England in the 1630s. By mid-1683, more than three thousand people—among them Welsh, Irish, Dutch, and Germans—had moved to Pennsylvania, and within five years the population reached twelve thousand. Philadelphia, carefully planned on the navigable Delaware River to be the major city in the province, drew merchants and artisans from throughout the English-speaking world. Pennsylvania's plentiful and fertile lands soon enabled its residents to begin exporting surplus flour and other foodstuffs to the West Indies. Practically

overnight Philadelphia acquired more than two thousand citizens and started to challenge Boston's commercial dominance.

A pacifist with egalitarian principles, Penn attempted to treat native peoples fairly. He learned to speak the language of the Delawares (or Lenapes), from whom he purchased tracts of land to sell to European settlers. Penn also established strict regulations for trade and forbade the sale of alcohol to Indians. His policies attracted native peoples, who moved to Pennsylvania near the end of the seventeenth century to escape repeated clashes with English colonists in other colonies. Most important were the Tuscaroras, Shawnees, and Miamis. By a supreme irony, however, the same toleration that attracted Native Americans also brought non-Quaker Europeans, who showed little respect for Indian claims. In effect, Penn's policy was so successful that it caused its own downfall.

The southernmost proprietary colony, granted by Charles II in 1663, encompassed a huge tract of land stretching from the southern boundary of Virginia to Spanish Florida. The area had great strategic importance: a successful English settlement there would prevent the Spaniards from pushing farther north. The proprietors named their new province Carolina in honor of Charles (*Carolus* in Latin). The "Fundamental Constitutions of Carolina," which they asked the political philosopher John Locke to draft for them, set forth an elaborate plan for a colony governed by a hierarchy of landholding aristocrats, with a carefully structured distribution of political and economic power.

CAROLINA

However, Carolina quickly developed two distinct population centers, which in 1729 split into separate colonies. Virginia planters settled the Albemarle region that became North Carolina. They established a society much like their own, with an economy based on cultivating tobacco and exporting such forest products as pitch, tar, and timber. Because North Carolina lacked a satisfactory harbor, its planters relied on Virginia's ports and merchants to conduct their trade, and the colonies remained tightly linked. The other population center, which eventually formed the core of South Carolina, developed at Charles Town, founded in 1670 near the juncture of the Ashley and Cooper Rivers. Many of its early residents had migrated from Barbados and expected to establish plantation agriculture.

But after unsuccessfully attempting to grow tropical plants (including sugar), the Carolinians began to raise corn and herds of cattle, which they sold to Caribbean sugar planters hungry for foodstuffs. They also depended on trade with nearby Indians to supply commodities they could sell elsewhere: deerskins, almost as valuable as beaver pelts, and Indian slaves. During the first decade of the eighteenth century, Carolinians exported an average of 54,000 skins annually. Before 1715 they exported an estimated 30,000 to 50,000 Indian slaves.

The English Civil War also affected the earlier English settlements, retarding their development. In

THE CHESAPEAKE AND NEW ENGLAND the Chesapeake, struggles between supporters of the king and of Parliament caused military clashes in Maryland and political upheavals in Virginia. But once the war ended and immigration resumed, the colonies expanded once again. Wealthy Chesapeake tobacco growers imported increasing numbers of English indentured servants to work on what were developing into large plantations.

In New England, migration essentially ceased after the Civil War began in 1642, and few Puritans migrated after the Restoration. Yet the Puritan colonies' population continued to grow dramatically because of natural increase. By the 1670s, New England's population had more than tripled, reaching approximately seventy thousand. Such a rapid expansion placed great pressure on available land. Many members of the third and fourth generations had to migrate—north to New Hampshire or Maine, south to New York or

New Jersey, west beyond the Connecticut River—to find sufficient farmland. Others abandoned agriculture and learned such skills as blacksmithing or carpentry to support themselves in the growing towns.

Online Study Center **Improve Your Grade**
Interactive Map: English Migration, 1610–1660

The people who remained behind in the small yet densely populated New England communities

WITCHCRAFT experienced a new phenomenon after approximately 1650: burgeoning witchcraft accusations and trials. Most people in the seventeenth century believed that witches existed. These allies of the Devil were thought to harness invisible spirits for good or evil purposes. For example, a witch might engage in fortunetelling or cause the death of a child or valuable animals. Yet among English mainland colonies, only New England witnessed many trials of accused witches (about one hundred in all before 1690). Most, though not all, of the accused were middle-aged women who had angered their neighbors. Historians have concluded that day-to-day interaction in the closely knit communities bred long-standing quarrels that led to such accusations. Even so, only a few of the accused were convicted, and fewer still were executed.

That New England courts halted questionable prosecutions suggests that well-established political and judicial structures were present

COLONIAL POLITICAL STRUCTURES in almost all the Anglo-American colonies by the last quarter of the seventeenth century. In New England, property-holding men or the legislature elected the governors; in other regions, the king or the proprietor appointed such leaders. A council, either elected or appointed, advised the governor on matters of policy and served as the upper house of the legislature. Each colony had a judiciary with local justices of the peace, county courts, and, usually, an appeals court composed of the councilors.

Local political institutions also developed. In New England, elected selectmen initially governed the towns, but by the end of the seventeenth century, town meetings, held at least annually and attended by most free adult male residents, handled matters of local concern. In the Chesapeake colonies and both of the Carolinas, appointed magistrates ran local governments. At first, the same was true in Pennsylvania, but by the early eighteenth century, elected county officials began to take over some government functions. And in New York, local elections were the rule even before the establishment of the colonial assembly in 1683.

A Decade of Imperial Crises: The 1670s

*a*s the Restoration colonies were extending the range of English settlement in North America, the first English colonies and French and Spanish settlements faced new crises caused primarily by their changing relationships with indigenous peoples. Between 1670 and 1680, New England, Virginia, New France, and New Mexico experienced bitter conflicts as their interests collided with those of America's original inhabitants.

In the mid-1670s, Louis de Buade de Frontenac, the governor-general of Canada, decided to expand

NEW FRANCE AND THE IROQUOIS

New France's reach to the south and west, hoping to establish a trade route to Mexico and gain direct control of the valuable fur trade on which the colony's prosperity rested. Accordingly, he encouraged the explorations of Father Jacques Marquette, Louis Jolliet, and Robert Cavelier de La Salle in the Great Lakes and Mississippi valley regions. His goal, however, brought him into conflict with the powerful Iroquois Confederacy, comprising five Indian nations: the Mohawks, Oneidas, Onondagas, Cayugas, and Senecas. (In 1722 the Tuscaroras became the sixth.)

Under the terms of a unique defensive alliance forged early in the sixteenth century, a representative council made decisions of war and peace for the entire Iroquois Confederacy, although each nation still retained some autonomy and could not be forced to comply with a council directive. Before the arrival of Europeans, the Iroquois waged wars primarily to acquire captives to replenish their population. The Europeans' presence created an economic motive: the desire to dominate the fur trade and gain unimpeded access to European goods. The war with the Hurons in the 1640s initiated a series of conflicts with other Indians known as the Beaver Wars, in which the Iro-

■ Contemporary engraving of John Verelst's 1710 portrait of the Mohawk chief known as Hendrick to Europeans (his Indian name was rendered as "Dyionoagon" or "Tee Yee Neen Ho Ga Row"). Hendrick and three other Iroquois leaders visited London in 1710, symbolically cementing the Covenant Chain negotiated in 1677. His primarily European dress and the wampum belt in his hand accentuate his identity as a cross-cultural diplomatic emissary.
(Anne S. K. Brown Military Collection, Brown University Library)

quois fought to achieve control of the lucrative peltry trade.

In the mid-1670s, as Iroquois dominance grew, the French intervened, for an Iroquois triumph would have destroyed France's plans to trade directly with western Indians. Over the next twenty years, the French launched repeated attacks on Iroquois villages. The English offered little assistance other than weapons to their trading partners. Its people and resources depleted by constant warfare, the confederacy in 1701 negotiated a neutrality treaty with France and other Indians. For the next half-century, the Iroquois nations maintained their power through trade and skillful diplomacy rather than warfare.

The wars against the Iroquois were crucial components of French Canada's plan to penetrate the heartland of North America. Unlike the Spaniards, French adventurers did not attempt to subjugate the Indians they encountered or formally claim large territories for France. And by tolerating the French presence, Indians gained access to European goods.

FRENCH EXPANSION

When France decided to strengthen its presence near the Gulf of Mexico by founding New Orleans in 1718—to counter westward thrusts of the English colonies and eastward moves of the Spanish—the Mississippi posts became the glue of empire. *Coureurs de bois* (literally, "forest runners") traveled regularly between Quebec and Louisiana, using the rivers and lakes of the interior to carry trade goods to French outposts. At most such sites lived a small military garrison and a priest, surrounded by powerful nations such as the Choctaws, Chickasaws, and Osages. In all the French outposts, the shortage of European women led to unions between French men and Indian women and to the creation of mixed-race people known as *métis*.

In New Mexico, too, a crisis in the 1670s led to long-term consequences. Under Spanish domination, the Pueblo peoples had added Christianity to their religious beliefs while retaining traditional rituals. But as decades passed, Franciscans adopted increasingly brutal tactics to erase all traces of the native religion. Those who held *encomiendas* also placed heavy labor demands on the population. In 1680, Pueblos under the leadership of Popé, a respected shaman, successfully revolted, driving the Spaniards out of New Mexico. Spanish authority was restored by 1700, but Spanish governors no longer attempted to reduce the Pueblos to bondage or to violate their cultural integrity. The Pueblo revolt was the most successful and sustained Indian resistance movement in colonial North America.

POPÉ AND THE PUEBLO REVOLT

When the Spanish expanded their territorial claims to the east and north, they followed the same strategy they had adopted in New Mexico, establishing their presence through military outposts and Franciscan missions. The army maintained order among the subject Indians and guarded the boundaries of New Spain. The friars concentrated on conversions. By the late eighteenth century, Spain claimed a vast territory that stretched from California (first colonized in 1769) through Texas (settled after 1700) to the Gulf Coast.

SPAIN'S NORTH AMERICAN POSSESSIONS

In the more densely settled English colonies, hostilities developed in the 1670s over land. In both New England and Virginia—though for different reasons—settlers began to encroach on territories that until then had remained in the hands of Native Americans.

By the early 1670s, the growing settlements in southern New England surrounded Wampanoag ancestral lands on Narragansett Bay. The local chief, King Philip, troubled by the loss of territory and concerned about the impact of European culture and Christianity on his people, led his warriors in attacks on nearby communities in June 1675. Other Algonquian peoples, among them Nipmucks and Narragansetts, soon joined King Philip's forces. In the fall, the Indian nations jointly attacked settlements in the northern Connecticut River valley, and the war spread to Maine when the Abenakis entered the conflict. In early 1676, the Indians devastated well-established villages and even attacked Plymouth and Providence. Altogether, the alliance wholly or partially destroyed twenty-five of ninety-two northern towns and attacked forty others.

KING PHILIP'S WAR

The tide turned in southern New England in the summer of 1676. The Indian coalition ran short of food and ammunition, and after King Philip was killed that August, the southern alliance crumbled. Nevertheless, fighting continued on the Maine frontier for another two years until both sides agreed to end the conflict. Many surviving Pokanokets, Nipmucks, and Narragansetts were captured and sold into slavery, and still more died of starvation and disease. New Englanders had broken the power of the southern coastal native peoples. Thereafter, the Indians lived in small clusters, subordinated to the colonists and often working as servants or sailors. But the settlers had paid a terrible price for their victory: an estimated one-tenth of the able-bodied adult male population was killed or wounded. Proportional to population, it was the most costly conflict in American history.

Not coincidentally, conflict with Indians simultaneously wracked Virginia. In the early 1670s, Virginians avidly eyed the rich lands north of the York River reserved for native peoples by early treaties. When some Doeg Indians killed an English servant in July 1675, settlers attacked not only the Doegs but also the powerful Susquehannocks. In retaliation, Susquehannock bands raided outlying farms early in 1676. When Governor William Berkeley resisted starting a major war, dissatisfied land-hungry colonists rallied behind the leadership of a recent immigrant, the wealthy Nathaniel Bacon, who like other new arrivals had found all the desirable land in settled areas already occupied.

BACON'S REBELLION

After Bacon held members of the House of Burgesses hostage until they authorized him to attack the Indians, Berkeley declared Bacon and his men to be in rebellion. As the chaotic summer of 1676 wore on, Bacon alternately pursued Indians and battled the governor's supporters. In September he marched on Jamestown itself, burning the capital to the ground. But when Bacon died the following month, the rebellion began to collapse. Even so, a new treaty signed in 1677 opened much of the disputed territory to English settlement.

The war, a turning point in Virginia's relationship with nearby Indians, also marked a turning point in the colony's internal race relations. After Bacon's Rebellion, Virginia landowners for the first time began to purchase large numbers of imported African slaves. By 1700 Anglo-Americans in the Chesapeake had irrevocably altered the racial composition of their labor force.

African Slavery on the Mainland

In the 1670s and 1680s, the prosperity of the Chesapeake rested on tobacco, and successful tobacco cultivation depended on an ample labor supply. But fewer and fewer English men and women proved willing to indenture themselves for long terms of service in Maryland and Virginia. To obtain the workers they needed, wealthy Chesapeake tobacco growers looked to the Caribbean sugar islands, where planters had eagerly purchased African slaves since the 1640s.

Slavery had been practiced in Europe (although not in England) for centuries. European Christians, both Catholics and Protestants, believed that enslaving heathen peoples was justifiable in religious terms. Consequently, when Portuguese mariners reached the sub-Saharan African coast and encountered non-Christian societies holding slaves, they purchased bondspeople as part of the exchange of many items.

WHY AFRICAN SLAVERY?

Some slaves were taken to the Iberian Peninsula; others to the Wine Islands. Iberians then exported African slavery to their American possessions, New Spain and Brazil. Because the Catholic Church prevented the formal enslavement of Indians in those domains and free laborers could find better work than enduring the mines or sugar plantations, African bondspeople became mainstays of the Caribbean and Brazilian economies. Sugar planters on English islands, who had the same problems of labor supply, also purchased slaves.

The slave system that was well established in the Caribbean by the mid-1650s did not immediately take root in the English mainland colonies. Before the 1660s, the few residents of African descent on the mainland varied in status: some were free, some indentured, some enslaved. All came from a population that the historian Ira Berlin has termed Atlantic creoles. Often of mixed race, many came to the English colonies from elsewhere in the Americas. Already familiar with Europeans, the Atlantic creoles fit easily into established niches in the hierarchical social structures of the early colonies. Berlin has characterized all the early mainland colonies as "societies with slaves": some people were held in perpetual bondage, but the societies did not rely wholly on slave labor. He usefully contrasts such communities with "slave societies," in which slavery served as the fundamental basis of the economy.

ATLANTIC CREOLES IN SOCIETIES WITH SLAVES

The many ambiguities of status in societies with slaves are evident in early laws in which Virginians and Marylanders revealed initial difficulty in developing a definition of enslavement. Several Virginia statutes used the term *Christian* to mean "free person"; when at least one slave converted and therefore claimed freedom, the House of Burgesses provided (in 1667) that "the blessed sacrament of baptism" would not liberate bondspeople from perpetual servitude. And in 1670 the House of Burgesses declared that "all servants not being christians imported into this colony by shipping shalbe slaves for their lives," but similar servants that "shall come by land" would serve only for a term of years. The awkward phrases attempted to differentiate Africans from Indians; Virginians saw both groups as distinguishable from English people, but expressed those distinctions in terms of religion and geography rather than race.

Just a few years later, Chesapeake legislators started to employ racial terminology, as increasing numbers of slaves arrived each year, first from the Caribbean and then directly from Africa. Virginia in 1682 altered its definition of who could be enslaved, declaring bluntly that "Negroes, Moors, Mollatoes or Indians" arriving "by sea or land" could all be held in bondage for life if their "parentage and native country are not christian." Most of the English colonies, even those without many bondspeople, adopted detailed codes to govern slaves' behavior. By 1700 African slavery was firmly established as the basis of the economy in the Chesapeake and South Carolina as well as in the Caribbean. Under Berlin's definition, those colonies had become "slave societies."

MAINLAND SLAVE SOCIETIES

English enslavers evidently had few moral qualms about these actions. Few at the time questioned the decision to hold Africans and their descendants in perpetual bondage. Initially the colonists lacked clear conceptual categories defining both "race" and "slave." They developed such categories and their meanings over time, through their experience with the institution of African (and Indian) slavery, originally adopted for economic reasons.

Between 1492 and 1770 more Africans than Europeans came to the Americas. Most went to Brazil or the Caribbean: of at least 10 million enslaved people brought to the Americas during the existence of slavery, only about 260,000 by 1775 were imported into what would become the United States. This massive trade in human beings is best understood within the context of the Atlantic trading system that developed during the middle years of the seventeenth century.

The Web of Empire and the Atlantic Slave Trade

*T*he elaborate Atlantic economic system is commonly called the triangular trade, with the slave traffic viewed as the triangle's middle leg and therefore called the middle passage. But *triangular trade* fails to convey the complexities of the Atlantic world's late-seventeenth-century commercial relationships. Trade involving Europe, Africa, and the Americas moved across the ocean not in easily diagrammed patterns but in a complicated and inextricably linked web of people and products (see Map 3.1).

Although slavery had long been practiced, the oceanic slave trade was entirely new and was the linchpin of the Atlantic system. The expanding network of commerce between Europe and its colonies was fueled by the sale and transport of slaves, the exchange of commodities produced by slave labor, and the need to feed and clothe so many bound laborers. The profits from Chesapeake tobacco and Caribbean and Brazilian sugar sold in Europe paid for both the African laborers who grew these crops and European manufactured goods. Europeans purchased slaves from African coastal rulers for resale in their colonies and acquired sugar and tobacco from America for sale in Europe, in exchange dispatching their manufactures everywhere.

ATLANTIC TRADING SYSTEM

New England had the most complex relationship to the trading system. The region produced only one item England wanted: tall trees to serve as masts for sailing vessels. To buy English manufactures, New Englanders therefore needed profits earned elsewhere: the Wine Islands and the Caribbean. Those islands lacked precisely the items that New England could produce in abundance: cheap food (corn and salt fish) to feed the slaves and wood for barrels to hold wine, sugar, and molasses. By the late 1640s, New England's economy rested on consumption by slaves and their owners. After the founding of Pennsylvania, New York, and New Jersey, those colonies too participated in the lucrative West Indian trade.

NEW ENGLAND AND THE CARIBBEAN

Shopkeepers in the interior of New England and the middle colonies bartered with local farmers for grains, livestock, and barrel staves, then traded those

International Piracy

The web of commerce across the Atlantic drove trade—and theft—to new levels. The last decades of the seventeenth century were the heyday of pirates, who, from bases in North America and the Caribbean, ranged the world. In New York and Charles Town, merchants asked few questions about the origins of valuable goods, and the solitary ocean voyages of merchant and slaving vessels were easy prey for resourceful marauders. The cargoes of precious metals, slaves, and luxury goods such as fine wines and silks made the return worth the risk.

As early as the sixteenth century, European kingdoms encouraged attacks on the commerce of rivals. Queen Elizabeth knighted Francis Drake for the treasure he stole from Spain. Though in wartime, letters of marque could transform law-breaking pirates into legal privateers, authorized to prey on the enemy, the line between pirates and privateers was easily breached. Privateers could keep most of their booty, and the crews, with sailors of many nations, were loyal primarily to themselves.

The infamous Captain William Kidd (c. 1645–1701) was both pirate and privateer. Probably Scots by birth, he plundered in the Caribbean before settling in New York, where he married a rich widow and cultivated local politicians. In 1696 he returned to sea with new privateering credentials, issued in London. With a crew recruited in England and New York, he sailed to the In-

dian Ocean, picking up other mariners along the way. Kidd encountered no vessels he could legally capture, and his crew, composed largely of pirates, became restive, so he resumed marauding. Over the next months, Kidd and his men seized Dutch and Portuguese ships and eventually a freighter sailing from India to the Moluccas. In late 1698, they headed for the Americas with a booty of valuable textiles. But in Boston, Kidd was arrested for piracy and murder. The English and colonial governments, he discovered, were newly committed to stamping out piracy. Sent to London for trial, he was convicted and hanged in May 1701.

Captain Kidd's exploits were a product of his time and place. In the 1690s, international crews of buccaneers sailed from the Americas to wherever in the world they thought they would find rich prizes. The rapidly developing web of international commerce that linked the Western Hemisphere to Africa, Asia, and Europe also spawned the legendary thieves who preyed on it.

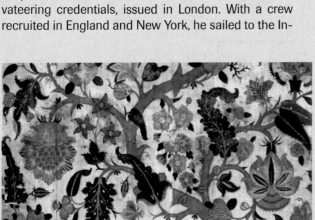

The sorts of valuable, exotic items pictured here were among the cargoes pirates sought. Fine ceramics and textiles from Asia commanded high prices from American and European purchasers who did not concern themselves with the origins of these desirable consumer goods. (Left: V&A Image, The Victoria and Albert Museum, London; right: The Metropolitan Museum of Art, purchased by subscription, 1879. [79.2.311] Photograph © 1995 The Metropolitan Museum of Art)

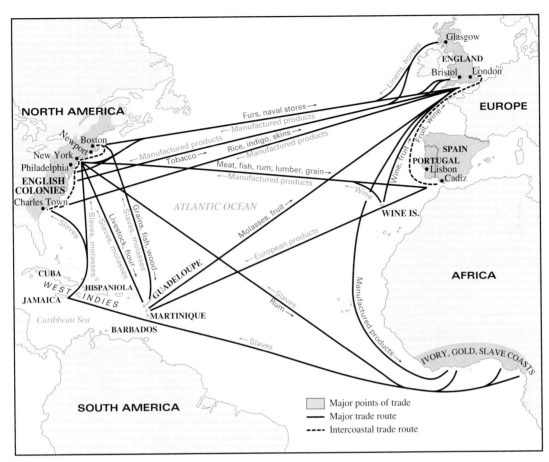

Map 3.1   Atlantic Trade Routes

By the late seventeenth century, an elaborate trade network linked the countries and colonies bordering the Atlantic Ocean. The most valuable commodities exchanged were enslaved people and the products of slave labor.

items to merchants in port towns. Such merchants dispatched ships to the Caribbean, where they sailed from island to island, exchanging their cargoes for molasses, fruit, spices, and slaves. Once they had a full load, the ships returned to Boston, Newport, New York, or Philadelphia to dispose of their cargoes. Americans began to distill molasses into rum, which was shipped to Africa and traded for slaves.

Tying the system together was the voyage that brought Africans to the Americas. That voyage was always traumatic and sometimes fatal. An average of 10 to 20 percent of the newly enslaved died en route. In addition, another 20 percent or so of slaves died ei-

ther before the ships left Africa or shortly after their arrival in the Americas. Their European captors also died at high rates, chiefly of diseases endemic to Africa. Just 10 percent of the men sent to run the Royal African Company's forts in Lower Guinea lived to return home to England.

Most of the enslaved people carried to North America originated in West Africa. Certain coastal rulers served as middlemen, allowing the establishment of permanent slave-trading posts in their territories and supplying resident Europeans with slaves to fill their ships.

West Africa and the Slave Trade

Such rulers controlled both European traders' access to slaves and inland peoples' access to desirable European goods. The slave trade had varying political and economic consequences for the nations of West Africa. The trade's centralizing tendencies helped create such powerful eighteenth-century kingdoms as Dahomey and Asante. Furthermore, the extent of nations' participation in the trade varied according to their involvement in warfare. And because prisoners of war constituted the bulk of the slaves shipped to the Americas, the most active traders were also the most successful in battle.

The trade in human beings did not uniformly depopulate West Africa, a fertile and densely inhabited region. Instead, the slave trade affected African societies unevenly. For example, rulers in parts of Upper Guinea, especially modern Gambia and Senegal, largely resisted involvement with the trade. Despite planters' preference for male slaves, women predominated in cargoes originating in the Bight of Biafra (modern Cameroon, Gabon, and southeastern Nigeria). And in such regions as the Gold Coast, the trade had a significant impact on the sex ratio of the remaining population. There, a relative shortage of men increased work demands on women, encouraged polygyny, and opened new avenues for advancement to women and their children.

By the late seventeenth century, the Atlantic commerce in slaves and the products of slave labor

EUROPEAN RIVALRIES AND THE SLAVE TRADE

constituted the basis of the European economic system, previously oriented toward the Mediterranean and Asia. Thus Columbus, seeking the wealth of Asia, instead found the lands that—along with Africa—ultimately replaced Asia as the source of European prosperity.

European nations fought bitterly to control the slave trade. The Portuguese, who at first dominated the trade, were supplanted by the Dutch in the 1630s. The Dutch, in turn, lost out to the English, who by the 1670s controlled the trade through the Royal African Company. Holding a monopoly on all English trade with sub-Saharan Africa, this company transported about 100,000 slaves to England's Caribbean colonies. Yet even before the company's monopoly expired in 1712, many individual English traders had illegally entered the market for slaves, and by the early eighteenth century they carried most of the Africans imported into the colonies, earning huge profits from successful voyages.

English officials decided to tap into the profits produced by the expanding Atlantic trading system. Chesapeake tobacco and Caribbean sugar had obvious value, but other colonial products also had considerable potential. Additional tax revenues could put England back on a sound financial footing after the disruptions of the Civil War, and English merchants wanted to ensure that they—not their Dutch rivals—reaped the benefits of trading with English colonies. Parliament accordingly began to draft laws designed to confine the proceeds of the English imperial web of trade primarily to the mother country.

Like other European nations, England based its commercial policy on a series of assumptions about

MERCANTILISM

the world's economic system. Collectively called mercantilism, these assumptions viewed the economic world as a collection of national states, whose governments competed for shares of a finite amount of wealth. Each nation sought to become as economically self-sufficient as possible while maintaining a favorable balance of trade by exporting more than it imported. Colonies were important because they could supply valuable raw materials and serve as a market for the mother country's manufactured goods.

Parliament applied mercantilist thinking to the American colonies in laws known as the Navigation

NAVIGATION ACTS

Acts. The major acts—passed between 1651 and 1673—established three main principles. First, only English or colonial merchants and ships could engage in trade in the colonies. Second, certain valuable American products could be sold only in England or in English colonies. At first, these "enumerated" goods included wool, sugar, tobacco, indigo, ginger, and dyes; later acts added rice, naval stores (spars, pitch, tar, and turpentine), copper, and furs to the list. Third, all foreign goods destined for sale in the colonies had to be shipped by way of England and English import duties paid. Some years later, a new series of laws established a fourth principle: the colonies could not export items (such as wool clothing, hats, or iron) that competed with English products.

The Navigation Acts aimed at forcing American trade to center on England. The mother country would benefit from both colonial imports and exports. The laws adversely affected some colonies, like those in the Caribbean and the Chesapeake, because planters there could not seek new markets for their staple crops. In others, the impact was minimal or even positive. Builders and owners of ships benefited from the monopoly on American trade given to English and colonial merchants. And the northern and middle colonies produced many unenumerated goods (fish and flour, for example) that could be traded directly to foreign buyers as long as the goods were carried in English or American ships.

The English authorities soon learned that writing mercantilist legislation was far easier than enforcing it. The many harbors of the American coast provided ready havens for smugglers, and colonial officials often looked the other way when illegally imported goods were offered for sale. Consequently, Parliament in 1696 enacted another Navigation Act, establishing in America a number of vice-admiralty courts, which operated without juries. Because American juries tended to favor local smugglers over customs officers, Parliament decided to remove Navigation Act cases from the regular colonial courts.

Enslavement of Africans and Indians

*F*ollowing Bacon's Rebellion, so many Africans were imported into Virginia and Maryland so rapidly that by 1710, people of African descent composed one-fifth of the region's population. Even so, a decade later, American-born slaves already outnumbered their African-born counterparts in the Chesapeake, and the native-born proportion continued to grow.

Slaves brought from Africa tended to be assigned to outlying parts of the plantations (called quarters),

African Enslavement in the Chesapeake

at least until they learned some English and the routines of tobacco cultivation. Mostly men, they often lived in quarters of ten to fifteen workers housed together in one or two buildings and supervised by an Anglo-American overseer. Each man was expected to cultivate about two acres of tobacco a year. Planters allowed them Sunday off. Many used that time to

cultivate their own gardens or to hunt or fish to supplement their meager diets. Only rarely could they form families because there were so few women among newly imported Africans.

Slaves usually cost about two and a half times as much as indentured servants, but they repaid the greater investment with a lifetime of service. Planters with enough money could acquire slaves, accumulate wealth, and establish large plantations. Other planters could afford neither slaves nor indentured servants, whose cost had risen because of their scarcity. Anglo-American society in the Chesapeake thus became more and more stratified—that is, the gap between rich and poor steadily widened. The introduction of large numbers of African slaves contributed to this outcome.

Africans who had lived in the Caribbean came with their masters to South Carolina from Barbados

African Enslavement in South Carolina

in 1670, composing one-quarter to one-third of the early population. The Barbadian slaveowners quickly discovered that African-born slaves had a variety of skills well suited to South Carolina. African-style dugout canoes became the chief means of transportation in the colony, which was crossed by rivers and included large islands just offshore. Fishing nets copied from African models proved more efficient than those of English origin. Africans' skill at killing crocodiles in their native country equipped them to handle alligators in America. Finally, Africans adapted their traditional techniques of cattle herding for use in America. Since meat and hides numbered among the colony's chief exports in its earliest years, Africans contributed significantly to South Carolina's prosperity.

After 1700, South Carolinians began to import slaves directly from Africa. From 1710 to midcentury, African-born slaves constituted a majority of the slave population there, which, coupled with the similarity of the semitropical South Carolinian and West African environments, ensured that more aspects of West African culture survived in that colony than elsewhere on the North American mainland. Only in South Carolina did enslaved parents continue to give their children African names; only there did a dialect develop that combined English words with African terms. (Known as Gullah, it has survived to the present day in isolated areas.) African skills remained useful, so techniques lost in other regions when the migrant generation died were passed down to the migrants' children. And in South Carolina African women became the primary petty traders, dominating the markets of Charles Town as they did those of Guinea.

The importation of large numbers of Africans coincided with the successful introduction of rice in

RICE AND INDIGO

South Carolina. English people knew little about the techniques of growing and processing rice, but people from Africa's Rice Coast had spent their lives working with the crop. The Africans almost certainly assisted their English masters in cultivating the crop profitably. Every slave on a rice plantation was expected to cultivate three to four acres of rice a year and to grow part of their own food. In a universally adopted system of predefined work assignments, after bondspeople had finished their set "tasks" for the day, they could rest or work in their own garden plots or on other projects. Experienced slaves could often complete their tasks by early afternoon; after that, as on Sundays, their masters had no legitimate claim on their time.

Developers of South Carolina's second cash crop also used the task system and drew on slaves' specialized skills. Indigo, the only source of blue dye for England's textile industry, was much prized. In the early 1740s, Eliza Lucas, a young woman managing her father's plantations, began to experiment with indigo cultivation. Drawing on the knowledge of slaves and overseers from the Caribbean, she developed the planting and processing techniques later adopted throughout the colony. Indigo grew on high ground, and rice was planted in low-lying swamps; rice and indigo also had different growing seasons. Thus, the two crops complemented each other.

Among the people held in slavery in both Carolinas were Indian captives who had been retained

INDIAN ENSLAVEMENT IN NORTH AND SOUTH CAROLINA

rather than exported. In 1708, enslaved Indians composed as much as 14 percent of the South Carolina population. The widespread traffic in Indian slaves significantly affected South Carolina's relationship with its indigenous neighbors. Native Americans used the ready market for captive enemies to rid themselves of real or potential rivals. Yet native groups soon learned that Carolinians could not be trusted. As settlers and

traders shifted their priorities, first one set of former allies and then another found themselves the enslaved rather than the enslavers.

At first the Carolinians themselves did not engage directly in conflicts with neighboring native groups. But in 1711 the Tuscaroras, an Iroquoian people, attacked a Swiss-German settlement at New Bern that had expropriated their lands. South Carolinians and their Indian allies then combined to defeat the Tuscaroras in a bloody war in 1713. Afterward, more than a thousand Tuscaroras were enslaved, and the remnants of the group drifted northward, where they joined the Iroquois Confederacy.

Four years later, the Yamasees, who had helped overcome the Tuscaroras, turned on their English allies. In what seems to have been long-planned retaliation for multiple abuses by traders as well as threats to their own lands, the Yamasees enlisted the Creeks and other Muskogean peoples in coordinated attacks on outlying English settlements. In the spring and summer of 1715, English and African refugees by the hundreds streamed into Charles Town. The Creek-Yamasee offensive was eventually thwarted when reinforcements arrived from the north, colonists hastily armed their African slaves, and Cherokees joined the fight against the Creeks, their ancient foes. After the war, Carolinian involvement in the Indian slave trade essentially ceased, for all their native neighbors moved away for self-protection: Creeks migrated west, Yamasees went south, and other groups moved north.

Indian or African slavery was never of great importance to Spain's North American territories,

SLAVES IN SPANISH AND FRENCH NORTH AMERICA

which had no plantations or cash crops. As slavery took deeper root in South Carolina, Florida officials in 1693 offered freedom to fugitives who would convert to Catholicism. Hundreds of South Carolina runaways took advantage of the offer. Many settled in a town founded for them near St. Augustine, Gracia Real de Santa Teresa de Mose, headed by a former slave and militia captain.

In early Louisiana, too, slaves—some Indians, some Atlantic creoles—at first composed only a tiny proportion of the residents. But a growing European population demanded that the French government supply them with slaves, and in 1719 officials finally acquiesced, dispatching more than six thousand Africans (most from Senegal) over the next decade.

The residents failed to develop a successful plantation economy, but they did anger the Natchez Indians, whose lands they had usurped. In 1729 the Natchez, assisted by newly arrived slaves, attacked northern reaches of the colony, killing more than 10 percent of its European people. The French struck back, slaughtering the Natchez and their enslaved allies.

Atlantic creoles from the Caribbean and Indians from the Carolinas and Florida composed almost all

ENSLAVEMENT IN THE NORTH

the bondspeople in the northern mainland colonies. Some bondspeople resided in urban areas, especially New York, which in 1700 had a larger black population than any other mainland city. Women tended to work as domestic servants, men as unskilled laborers. Yet most bondspeople worked in rural agriculture. Some slaves also worked for iron-masters at forges and foundries. Although relatively few northern colonists owned slaves, those who did relied heavily on their labor and had good reason to want to preserve the institution.

Imperial Reorganization and the Witchcraft Crisis

In the early 1680s, London administrators confronted a bewildering array of colonial governments. Massachusetts Bay (including Maine) functioned under its original charter. Neighboring Connecticut (having absorbed New Haven) and Rhode Island were granted charters by Charles II in 1662 and 1663, respectively, but Plymouth remained autonomous. Virginia, a royal colony, was joined in that status by New Hampshire in 1679 and New York in 1685 when its proprietor ascended the throne as James II. All the other mainland settlements were proprietorships.

By the 1670s, these colonial governments and their residents had become accustomed to considerable

COLONIAL AUTONOMY CHALLENGED

local political autonomy. Free adult men who owned more than a minimum amount of property (which varied from place to place) expected to have an influential voice in their governments, especially in decisions concerning taxation. After James II became king in 1685, such expectations clashed with those of the

monarch. James and his successors sought to bring more order to colonial administration by tightening the reins of government and reducing the colonies' political autonomy. Administrators began to chip away at the privileges granted in colonial charters and to reclaim proprietorships for the Crown. Massachusetts (1691), New Jersey (1702), and the Carolinas (1729) all became royal colonies. The charters of Rhode Island, Connecticut, Maryland, and Pennsylvania were temporarily suspended but ultimately restored to their original status.

The most drastic reordering of colonial administration targeted Puritan New England, which English

DOMINION OF NEW ENGLAND

officials saw as a hotbed of smuggling. Moreover, Puritans refused to allow freedom of religion to non-Congregationalists and insisted on maintaining laws incompatible with English practice. New England thus seemed an appropriate place to exert English authority with greater vigor. The Crown revoked the charters of all the colonies from New Jersey to Maine and established the Dominion of New England in 1686. Sir Edmund Andros, the governor, had immense power: Parliament dissolved all the assemblies, and Andros needed only the consent of an appointed council to make laws and levy taxes.

New Englanders endured Andros's autocratic rule for more than two years. Then they learned that

GLORIOUS REVOLUTION IN AMERICA

James II's hold on power was crumbling amid anger at taxes he had levied without parliamentary approval and his announcement that he had converted to Catholicism. In April 1689, Boston's leaders jailed Andros and his associates. The following month they received definite news that in 1688, Parliament had deposed James and offered the throne to his daughter Mary and her husband, the Dutch prince William of Orange, both Protestants. Called the Glorious Revolution, this bloodless coup affirmed the supremacy of both Parliament and Protestantism.

Bostonians quickly proclaimed their loyalty to William and Mary, writing to England for instructions about the form of government they should now adopt. In other colonies, too, the Glorious Revolution emboldened people for revolt. In Maryland the Protestant Association overturned the government of the Catholic proprietor, and in New York a militia officer of German origin, Jacob Leisler, assumed control of the government. Like the New Englanders, the Maryland and New York rebels supported William and Mary and saw themselves as carrying out the colonial phase of the English revolt against Stuart absolutism.

But, like James II, William and Mary believed that England should exercise tighter control over its unruly American possessions. Consequently, only the Maryland rebellion received royal sanction, primarily because of its anti-Catholic thrust. In New York, Jacob Leisler was hanged for treason, and Massachusetts (including the formerly independent jurisdiction of Plymouth) became a royal colony with an appointed governor. The province retained its town meeting system of local government and continued to elect its council, but the new 1691 charter eliminated the traditional religious test for voting and office-holding. A parish of the Church of England appeared in the heart of Boston.

A war with the French and their Algonquian allies compounded New England's difficulties. King

KING WILLIAM'S WAR

Louis XIV of France allied himself with the deposed James II, and England declared war on France in 1689. In Europe, this conflict was known as the War of the League of Augsburg, but the colonists called it King William's War. Indian attacks wholly or partially destroyed several English settlements in New York, Maine, and New Hampshire. Even the Peace of Ryswick (1697), which formally ended the war in Europe, failed to bring much of a respite from warfare to the northern frontiers. Maine could not be fully resettled for several decades because of the continuing conflict.

During the hostilities, New Englanders understandably feared a repetition of the devastation of

THE 1692 WITCHCRAFT CRISIS

King Philip's War. For eight months in 1692, witchcraft accusations spread like wildfire through the rural communities of Essex County, Massachusetts—precisely the area most threatened by the Indian attacks in southern Maine and New Hampshire. Earlier incidents in which personal disputes occasionally led to isolated witchcraft charges bore little relationship to the witch fears that convulsed the region in 1692. Before the crisis ended, 14 women and 5 men were hanged, 1 man was pressed to death with heavy

stones, 54 people confessed to being witches, and more than 140 people were jailed, some for many months.

The crisis began in late February 1692 when several young women in Salem Village (an outlying precinct of the bustling port of Salem) formally charged some older female neighbors with having tortured them in spectral form. Soon other accusers and confessors chimed in, some of them female domestic servants who had been orphaned in the Indian attacks on Maine. One had lost her grandparents in King Philip's War and her parents in King William's War. These young women, perhaps the most powerless people in a region apparently powerless to affect its fate, offered their fellow New Englanders a compelling explanation for the seemingly endless chain of troubles afflicting them: their province was under direct attack not only by the Indians but also by the Devil and his allied witches. The so-called afflicted girls accused not just the older women, but also prominent men from the Maine frontier who had traded with or failed to defeat the Indians. The colony's magistrates, who were also its political and military leaders, were all too willing to believe such accusations, because if the Devil had caused New England's current troubles, they personally bore no responsibility.

In October, the worst phase of the crisis ended when the governor, supported by several prominent clergymen, dissolved the special court established to try the suspects. Most critics of the trials did not think the girls were faking, nor did they conclude that witches did not exist or that confessions were false. Rather, they questioned whether the guilt of the accused could be legally established by the evidence presented in court. During the final trials in regular courts, almost all the defendants were acquitted, and the governor reprieved the few found guilty.

Online Study Center
Improve Your Grade
Primary Source: Ann Putnam's Deposition

In 1696, England took a major step in colonial administration by creating the fifteen-member Board

NEW IMPERIAL MEASURES

of Trade and Plantations, which thereafter served as the chief organ of government concerned with the American colonies. Previously, no single body had that responsibility. The board gathered information, reviewed Crown

The Wonders of the Invisible World.

OBSERVATIONS

As well *Historical* as *Theological*, upon the NATURE, the NUMBER, and the OPERATIONS of the

DEVILS.

Accompany'd with,

I. Some Accounts of the Grievous Molestations, by DÆMONS and WITCHCRAFTS, which have lately annoy'd the Countrey; and the Trials of some eminent *Malefactors* Executed upon occasion thereof : with several Remarkable *Curiosities* therein occurring.

II. Some Counsils, Directing a due Improvement of the terrible things, lately done, by the Unusual & Amazing Range of EVIL SPIRITS, in Our Neighbourhood : & the methods to prevent the *Wrongs* which those *Evil Angels* may intend against all sorts of people among us ; especially in Accusations of the Innocent.

III. Some Conjectures upon the great EVENTS, likely to befall, the WORLD in General, and NEW-ENGLAND in Particular ; as also upon the Advances of the TIME, when we shall see BETTER DAYES.

IV A short Narrative of a late Outrage committed by a knot of WITCHES in *Swedeland*, very much Resembling, and so far Explaining, *That* under which our parts of *America* have laboured !

V. THE DEVIL DISCOVERED : In a Brief Discourse upon those TEMPTATIONS, which are the more Ordinary *Devices* of the Wicked One.

By **Cotton Mather.**

Boston Printed by *Benj. Harris* for *Sam. Phillips*. **1693.**

■ The Reverend Cotton Mather of Boston, twenty-nine years old in 1692 at the time of the Salem witchcraft crisis, rushed this book—*The Wonders of the Invisible World*—into print shortly after the trials ended. He tried to explain to his fellow New Englanders the "Grievous Molestations, by Daemons and Witchcrafts, which have lately annoy'd the Countrey" by providing both brief trial narratives and examples of similar recent occurrences elsewhere, most notably in Mohra, Sweden.   (Image courtesy of The Massachusetts Historical Society)

appointments in America, scrutinized legislation passed by colonial assemblies, supervised trade policies, and advised successive ministries on colonial issues. Still, the Board of Trade did not have any direct powers of enforcement. It also shared jurisdiction over American affairs not only with the customs ser-

vice but also with a member of the ministry. In short, supervision of the American provinces remained decentralized and haphazard.

That surely made it easier for Massachusetts and the rest of the English colonies in America to accommodate themselves to the new imperial order. Most colonists resented alien officials who arrived in America determined to implement the policies of king and Parliament, but they adjusted to their demands and to the trade restrictions imposed by the Navigation Acts. They fought another of Europe's wars—the War of the Spanish Succession, or Queen Anne's War in the colonies—from 1702 to 1713 without enduring the stresses of the first. Colonists who allied themselves with royal government received patronage in the form of offices and land grants and composed "court parties" that supported English officials. Others, who were either less fortunate in their friends or more principled in defense of colonial autonomy, made up the opposition, or "country" interest. By the end of the first quarter of the eighteenth century, most men in both groups had been born in America and were members of elite families.

Summary   *Online Study Center*   **ACE the Test**

*T*he eighty years from 1640 to 1720 established the basic economic and political patterns that were to structure mainland colonial society. By 1720, nearly the entire east coast of North America was in English hands, and Indian control east of the Appalachian Mountains had largely been broken. What had been an immigrant population was now mostly American-born, except for the many African-born people in South Carolina; economies originally based on trade in fur and skins had become far more complex and more closely linked with the mother country; and a wide variety of political structures had been reshaped into a more uniform pattern. Yet at the same time, the introduction of large-scale slavery into the Chesapeake and the Carolinas differentiated their societies from those of the colonies to the north. They had become true slave societies, heavily reliant on a system of perpetual servitude. Although the northern colonies were not slave societies, their economies rested on profits derived from the Atlantic trading system, the key element of which was traffic in enslaved humans.

Meanwhile, from a small outpost in Santa Fe, New Mexico, and missions in Florida, the Spanish had expanded their influence throughout the Gulf Coast region and as far north as California. The French had come to dominate the length of the Mississippi River and the entire Great Lakes region. Both groups of colonists lived near Indian nations and depended on the indigenous people's labor and goodwill. The extensive Spanish and French presence to the south and west of the English settlements made future conflicts among the European powers in North America nearly inevitable.

By 1720, the essential elements of the imperial administrative structure that would govern the English colonies until 1775 had been put firmly in place. The regional economic systems originating in the late seventeenth and early eighteenth centuries also continued to dominate North American life until after independence. And Anglo-Americans had developed the commitment to autonomous local government that later would lead them into conflict with Parliament and the king.

LEGACY FOR A PEOPLE AND A NATION
Americans of African Descent

After the 1670s, the rise of southern economies based largely on the enslavement of Africans, and the widespread employment of enslaved Africans in northern colonies, dramatically altered the American population. By 1775, more than a quarter million Africans had been imported into the territory that later became the United States, constituting about 20 percent of the population at the time of the Revolution.

According to the 2000 census, 12.5 percent of the American people now claim descent from African ancestors. Because the legal importation of African slaves ended in 1808 and the United States attracted relatively few voluntary migrants of African descent until the late twentieth century, most of today's African Americans have colonial ancestors, a claim few Americans of European descent can make.

The modern African American population reflects the large number of interracial sexual relationships (both coerced and voluntary) during the long African residence in mainland North America. African Americans, both free and enslaved, have had children with both Europeans and Indians since the colonial period; more recently, they have intermarried with Asian immigrants. In large part the mingling of different peoples of color resulted from state miscegenation laws, which from the early years of the American republic until 1967—when the Supreme Court struck them down—forbade legal marriages between people of European descent and those of other races. That forced the non-European groups to seek partners only among themselves. And other state and federal laws then defined people with any appreciable African ancestry as "black."

Recently, increasing numbers of interracial unions have produced multiracial children. The 2000 census for the first time allowed Americans to define themselves as members of more than one race. Opposition to this change came largely from leaders of the African American community, and on census forms, people of African descent proved less willing to define themselves as multiracial than did people with other origins. The racial self-definition of this large component of the American people thus continues to be influenced by a legacy of discrimination.

*A*MERICAN SOCIETY TRANSFORMED 1720–1770

"*W*as I in that Country I would not Stay one day longer in it," Alexander McAllister wrote to his cousin in Scotland in late 1770. "If god Spers [spares] you in this Cuntrie but a few years you will blis [bless] the day you left." As a youth, McAllister had moved from the Scottish Highlands to North Carolina with his parents. In many letters to friends and family back in Argyleshire, he elaborated on the attractions of his adopted home at Cross Creek. Anyone could easily grow corn, wheat, barley, rye, oats, potatoes, and tobacco, he wrote: "In truth it is the Best poor mans Cuntry I Ever heard of." McAllister assured his correspondents that all immigrants were doing well, insisting that "ther is non but what is in a good way."

One historian has estimated that McAllister's network of correspondence brought about five thousand of his countrymen to North America in the two decades after the mid-1750s. When Scots arrived in North Carolina with letters of introduction from people McAllister knew, he helped them find land and supplies. Although he understood that, as he told one correspondent, "the best [land] is taken up many years ago," and that newcomers' first few years would be hard, he never altered his recommendations. Certainly McAllister himself thrived in his new homeland; by the late 1780s, having fathered numerous children by two wives, he owned forty slaves and more than 2,500 acres of land. He served as an elder of the Presbyterian church, a member of the colonial assembly, and a state senator after independence was won. Although he was more successful than most migrants, his prosperity showed what some could achieve.

Alexander McAllister and other Highland Scots took part in a massive eighteenth-century migration of European and African peoples that by 1770 had changed the nature of the American population and the look of the American landscape. Ethnic diversity was especially pronounced in the small colonial cities, but the countryside too attracted settlers from many European nations. The British colonies south of New England drew by far the largest number of newcomers. Their arrival not only swelled the population but also

Population Growth and Ethnic Diversity

Economic Growth and Development

Colonial Cultures

LINKS TO THE WORLD
Exotic Beverages

Colonial Families

Politics: Stability and Crisis in British America

A Crisis in Religion

LEGACY FOR A PEOPLE AND A NATION
"Self-Made Men"

Online Study Center
This icon will direct you to interactive map and primary source activities on the website
http://college.hmco.com/pic/nortonbrief7e

C H R O N O L O G Y

1691 • Locke's *Two Treatises of Government* published, a key example of Enlightenment political thought

1732 • Founding of Georgia

1739 • Stono Rebellion (South Carolina) leads to increased white fears of slave revolts
   • George Whitefield arrives in America; Great Awakening broadens

1739–48 • King George's War disrupts American economy

1740s • Black population of the Chesapeake begins to grow by natural increase, contributing to rise of large plantations

1741 • New York City "conspiracy" reflects whites' continuing fears of slave revolts

1760s • Baptist congregations take root in Virginia

1760–75 • Peak of eighteenth-century European and African migration to English colonies

1765–66 • Hudson River land riots pit tenants and squatters against large landlords

1767–69 • Regulator movement (South Carolina) tries to establish order in backcountry

1771 • North Carolina Regulators defeated by eastern militia at Battle of Alamance

altered political balances and affected the religious climate by introducing new sects.

Along with population growth and the new ethnic diversity, several other key themes marked colonial development in the mid-eighteenth century: the increasing importance of colonial urban centers, the creation of a prosperous urban elite, rising levels of consumption for all social ranks, and the new significance of internal markets. In the French and British mainland colonies, exports continued to dominate the economy in an international commercial system that fluctuated wildly. Yet expanding local populations demanded greater quantities and types of goods, and Europe could not supply all those needs. Therefore, colonists came to depend more on exploiting and consuming their own resources.

Intermarried networks of wealthy families developed in each of Europe's American possessions by the 1760s. These well-off, educated colonists participated in transatlantic intellectual life, such as the movement known as the Enlightenment, whereas many colonists of the "lesser sort" could neither read nor write. The elites lived in comfortable houses and enjoyed leisure-time activities. Most colonists, whether free or enslaved, worked with their hands from dawn to dark. Such divisions were most pronounced in British America, where the social and economic distance among different ranks of Anglo-Americans had widened noticeably by 1750.

In 1720, much of North America was still under Indian control. By 1770, settlements of Europeans and Africans ruled by Great Britain filled almost all of the region between the Appalachian Mountains and the Atlantic Ocean; and the British, as discussed in the next chapter, had come to dominate the extensive system of rivers and lakes running through the heart of the continent. Spanish missions extended in a great arc from present-day northern California to the Gulf Coast. Immigration, population growth, geographical expansion, new economic activity, and social change had transformed the character of Europe's North American possessions. ■

Population Growth and Ethnic Diversity

*O*nly about 250,000 European and African Americans resided in the colonies in 1700; by 1775, 2.5 million lived there. Such rapid expansion appears even more remarkable when it is compared with the modest changes that occurred in French and Spanish North America. At the end of the eighteenth century, Texas had only about 2,500 Spanish residents and California even fewer; the largest Spanish colony, New Mexico, included just 20,000 or so. The total European population of New France was about 70,000 in the 1760s.

Although migration accounted for a considerable share, most of the growth in Anglo America resulted from natural increase. Once the difficult early decades of settlement had passed and the sex ratio evened out in the South (after 1700), the American population doubled approximately every twenty-five years. Such a rate of growth, unparalleled in human history until very recent times, had a variety of causes, chief among them women's youthful age at the onset of childbearing, from late teens to early twenties. Since married women became pregnant every two or three years, women normally bore five to ten children. Because the colonies were relatively healthful places to live, especially north of Virginia, a large proportion of children who survived infancy reached maturity and began families of their own. Consequently, about half of the American population was under sixteen years old in 1775.

The height of the slave trade occurred in the eighteenth century, when about two-thirds of all slaves were carried across the Atlantic as rice, indigo, tobacco, and sugar plantations expanded rapidly. In the slaveholding societies of South America and the Caribbean, a surplus of males over females and appallingly high mortality rates meant that only a large, continuing influx of slaves could maintain the work force. South Carolina, where rice cultivation was difficult and unhealthful and planters preferred to purchase men, also required an inflow of Africans. But in the Chesapeake the number of bondspeople grew especially rapidly because imports were added to an enslaved population that, with tobacco's easier work

INVOLUNTARY MIGRANTS FROM AFRICA

routines and a roughly equal sex ratio, began to sustain itself through natural increase after 1740.

The involuntary migrants came from many different ethnic groups and regions of Africa (see Map 4.1), and people from the same area (enemies as well as allies) tended to be taken to the Americas together. That tendency was heightened by planter partiality for slaves of particular ethnic groups. Virginians, for example, evidently preferred to purchase Igbos from the Bight of Biafra (modern Cameroon, Gabon, and southeastern Nigeria), whereas South Carolinians and Georgians selected Senegambians and people from West Central Africa (modern Congo and Angola). Rice planters' desire to purchase Senegambians, who had cultivated rice in their homeland, is easily explained, but historians disagree about the reasons for the other preferences.

Thousands, possibly tens of thousands, of these enslaved Africans were Muslims. Some were literate in Arabic, and several came from aristocratic families. The discovery of noble birth could lead to a slave's being freed to return home. Job Ben Solomon, for example, arrived in Maryland in 1732. Himself a slave trader from Senegal, he had been captured by raiders while selling bondspeople in Gambia. A letter he wrote in Arabic so impressed his owners that he was liberated the next year.

Despite the approximately 280,000 slaves brought to the mainland, American-born people of African descent soon numerically dominated the enslaved population because of high natural increase. A planter who owned adult female slaves could watch the size of his labor force expand steadily. The slaveholder Thomas Jefferson indicated that he fully understood the connections when he observed, "I consider a woman who brings a child every two years more profitable than the best man of the farm. What she produces is an addition to the capital, while his labors disappear in mere consumption."

In addition to the new group of Africans, about 585,000 Europeans moved to North America during the eighteenth century, most of them after 1730. Late in the seventeenth century, English officials decided to recruit German and French Protestants to prevent further large-scale emigration from England itself. Influenced by mercantilist thought, they had come to regard a large, industrious population at home as an asset rather

NEWCOMERS FROM EUROPE

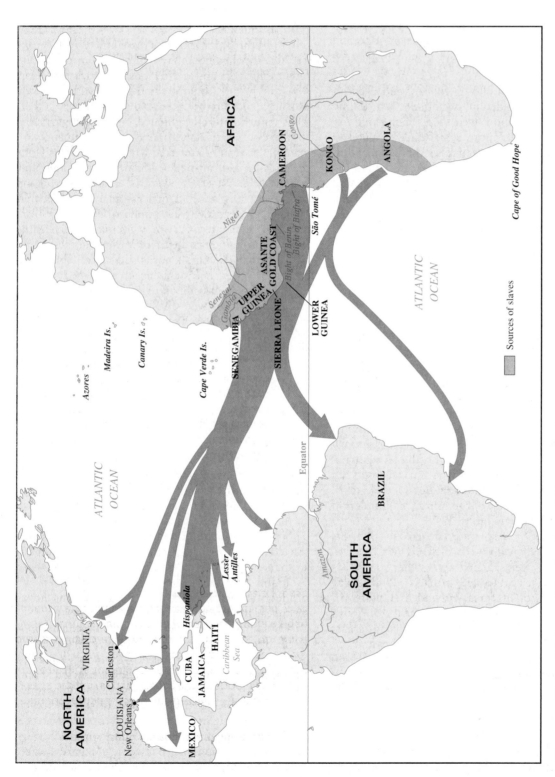

Map 4.1 Major Origins and Destinations of Africans Enslaved in the Americas

Enslaved Africans were drawn from many regions of western Africa (with some coming from the interior of the continent) and were shipped to areas throughout the Americas.

than a liability. Thus, they deported to the colonies "undesirables"—convicts and Jacobite rebels (supporters of the deposed Stuart monarchs)—but otherwise discouraged emigration. They offered foreign Protestants free lands and religious toleration.

The patterns evident in the chapter-opening vignette applied generally to all the voluntary eighteenth-century European migrants. Early arrivals wrote home, starting chains of migration from particular regions. The most successful migrants came well prepared, having learned from their American correspondents that land and resources were abundant, especially in the backcountry, but that they would need capital to take full advantage of the new opportunities. People who arrived penniless did less well.

Online Study Center **Improve Your Grade**
Interactive Map: Immigration and Frontier Expansion to 1755

SCOTS-IRISH, GERMANS, AND SCOTS

One of the largest groups of immigrants—nearly 150,000—came from Ireland or Scotland. About 66,000 Scots-Irish descendants of Presbyterian Scots who had settled in the north of Ireland during the seventeenth century joined some 35,000 people who came directly to America from Scotland. Another 43,000 migrated from southern Ireland. High rents, poor harvests, and religious discrimination (in Ireland) combined to push people toward North America. Vessels engaged in the linen trade with Pennsylvania regularly left Ireland with plenty of room for passengers. By the 1720s, the migration route was well established, fueled by positive reports of prospects for advancement in North America.

Such immigrants usually landed in Philadelphia or New Castle, Delaware. They moved into the backcountry of western Pennsylvania along the Susquehanna River, where the colonial government created a county named Donegal for them. Later migrants moved farther west and south, to the backcountry of Maryland, Virginia, and the Carolinas. Frequently unable to afford any acreage, they settled illegally on land belonging to Indians, land speculators, or colonial governments. In the frontier setting, they gained a reputation for lawlessness, hard drinking, and ferocious fighting.

Migrants from Germany numbered about 85,000. Most emigrated between 1730 and 1755, also usually arriving in Philadelphia. Late in the century, they and their descendants accounted for one-third of Pennsylvania's residents. But many Germans moved west and then south into the backcountry of Maryland and Virginia. Others landed in Charles Town and settled in the southern interior. The Germans belonged to a wide variety of Protestant sects and in Pennsylvania added to the colony's substantial religious diversity.

The most concentrated period of immigration to the colonies fell between 1760 and 1775. Tough economic times in Germany and the British Isles led many to seek a better life in America; simultaneously, the slave trade burgeoned. In those fifteen years more than 220,000 persons arrived—nearly 10 percent of the entire population of British North America in 1775. Late-arriving free immigrants had little choice but to remain in the cities or move to the edges of settlement; land elsewhere was fully occupied.

MAINTAINING ETHNIC AND RELIGIOUS IDENTITIES

Because of these migration patterns and the concentration of slaveholding in the South, half the colonial population south of New England had non-English origins by 1775. Whether the migrants assimilated readily into Anglo-American culture depended on patterns of settlement, the size of the group, and the strength of the migrants' ties to their common culture. For example, the Huguenots—French Protestants who fled religious persecution in their homeland after 1685—settled in tiny enclaves in American cities but were unable to sustain either their language or their religious practices. By contrast, the colonial Jews, an equally small group, maintained a distinct identity. In places like New York and Newport, Rhode Island, they established synagogues and worked actively to preserve their religion. As a general rule, members of the larger groups of migrants (Germans, Irish, and Scots) found it easier to sustain their Old World ways.

Where migrants from different countries settled in the same region, ethnic antagonisms often surfaced. Anglo-American elites fostered such antagonisms to maintain their political and economic power, and they frequently subverted the colonies' generous naturalization laws, thus depriving even long-resident immigrants of a voice in government. The elites probably would have preferred to ignore the English colonies' growing racial and ethnic diversity, but ultimately they could not do so. When they moved toward revolution in the 1770s, they recognized that they needed the support of non-English Americans. Quite deliberately, they began to speak of "the rights of man," rather than "English liberties," when they sought recruits for their cause.

Economic Growth and Development

*T*he dramatic increase in the population of Anglo America served as one of the few sources of stability for the colonial economy, which was driven primarily by the vagaries of international markets. A comparison to French and Spanish America reveals significant differences. The population and economy of New Spain's Borderlands stagnated. The isolated settlements produced few items for export. French Canada exported large quantities of furs and fish, but monopolistic trade practices ensured that most of the profits ended up in the home country. The Louisiana colony required substantial government subsidies to survive. Of France's American possessions, only the Caribbean islands flourished economically.

In British North America, by contrast, the rising population generated ever-greater demands for goods

OVERVIEW OF THE ANGLO-AMERICAN ECONOMY

and services, leading to the development of small-scale colonial manufacturing and a complex network of internal trade. Roads, bridges, mills, and stores were built to serve the many new settlements. A lively coastal trade developed, and its ships not only collected goods for export and distributed imports but also sold items made in America. The colonies thus began to move away from their earlier pattern of dependence on European manufactured goods. Iron making became the largest indigenous industry; by 1775, Anglo America's iron production surpassed England's.

The major energizing, yet destabilizing, influence on the colonial economy nevertheless remained foreign trade. Colonial prosperity still depended heavily on overseas demand for American products like tobacco, rice, indigo, fish, and barrel staves, which earned the colonists the credit they needed to purchase English and European imports. If demand for

American exports slowed, the colonists' income dropped, as did their ability to buy imported goods.

Despite fluctuations, the economy slowly grew during the eighteenth century. That growth produced

WEALTH AND POVERTY

better standards of living for all property-owning Americans. Early in the century, households began to acquire amenities such as chairs and earthenware dishes. Diet also improved as trading networks brought access to more varied foods. Thus, the colonists became consumers, in the sense that for the first time they could make choices among a variety of products and could afford to buy items not essential for subsistence.

Yet the benefits of economic growth were unevenly distributed: wealthy Americans improved their position relative to other colonists. The native-born elite families who dominated American political, economic, and social life by 1750 had begun the century with sufficient capital to take advantage of the changes caused by population growth. They were the urban merchants, the large landowners, the slave traders, and the owners of rum distilleries. Their rise helped make the social and economic structure of mid-eighteenth-century America more stratified than before.

New arrivals did not have the opportunities for advancement that had greeted their predecessors. Even so, few free settlers in rural areas (where about 95 percent of colonists lived) appear to have been truly poor. But in the cities, families of urban laborers lived on the edge of destitution. In Philadelphia, for instance, a male laborer's average annual earnings fell short of the amount needed to supply his family with the bare necessities. Even in a good year, his wife or children had to do wage work; a bad year could reduce the family to beggary. By the 1760s, applicants for assistance overwhelmed public urban poor-relief systems, and some cities began to build workhouses or almshouses to shelter the growing number of poor people.

Within this overall picture were different regional patterns: New England, the middle colonies (Pennsylvania, New York, and New Jersey), the Chesapeake (including North Carolina), and the Lower South (South Carolina and Georgia) each had its own economic rhythm derived from the nature of its export trade.

In New England, three elements combined to influence economic development: the nature of the landscape, New England's leadership in shipping, and the impact of imperial wars. Wood products constituted important salable commodities because farms did not produce surpluses other than livestock. They were worked primarily by family members; the region had relatively few hired laborers. It also had the lowest average wealth per freeholder in the colonies. But New England had many wealthy merchants and professionals who profited substantially from trade with the Caribbean.

NEW ENGLAND AND KING GEORGE'S WAR

Boston, by the 1730s a major shipbuilding center, soon felt the impact when warfare between European powers resumed in 1739. British vessels clashed with Spanish ships in the Caribbean, sparking a conflict known in America as King George's War (called the War of the Austrian Succession in Europe). The war initially energized Boston's economy. New England privateers seized enemy shipping, and area merchants profited from military supply contracts. But then New Englanders suffered major losses in Caribbean battles and forays against Canada. In 1745 a New England expedition captured the French fortress of Louisbourg (in modern Nova Scotia), but the expensive victory led to heavy taxation of Massachusetts residents, and after the war, unprecedented numbers of widows and children crowded Boston's relief rolls. The shipbuilding boom ended when the war did, the economy stagnated, and taxes remained high. Britain even returned Louisbourg to France in the Treaty of Aix-la-Chapelle (1748).

King George's War and its aftermath affected the middle colonies more positively because of the greater fertility of the soil in those regions, where commercial farming prevailed. With the outbreak of hostilities, the middle colonies were able to profit from the wartime demand for grain and flour, especially in the Caribbean. After the war, poor grain harvests in Europe caused flour prices to rise rapidly. Philadelphia and New York became leaders in the foodstuffs trade.

MIDDLE COLONIES AND THE CHESAPEAKE

Increased European demand for grain had a significant impact on the Chesapeake as well. After 1745, some Chesapeake planters began to convert tobacco fields to wheat and corn. By diversifying their crops, they could avoid dependency on one product for their income. Tobacco still ruled, but the conversion to grain brought about the first significant change in Chesapeake settlement patterns by encouraging the development of port towns (like Baltimore) to house the merchants who marketed the new products.

The Lower South too depended on staple crops and an enslaved labor force, but after Parliament in 1730 removed rice from the list of enumerated products, South Carolinians could trade directly with continental Europe. Rice prices thereafter climbed steeply, doubling by the late 1730s. Dependence on European sales had its drawbacks, however. King George's War in 1739 disrupted trade, causing a decade-long depression in South Carolina. Still, prosperity returned by the 1760s. Indeed, the Lower South experienced more rapid economic growth in that period than did the other colonial regions. Partly as a result, it had the highest average wealth per freeholder in Anglo America by the time of the American Revolution.

THE LOWER SOUTH

Closely linked to South Carolina geographically, demographically, and economically was the mainland's newest colony, Georgia, chartered in 1732 as a haven for English debtors released from confinement to settle the colony. Its founder, James Oglethorpe, envisioned Georgia as a garrison province peopled by sturdy farmers who would defend the southern flank of English settlement against Spanish Florida. Thus, its charter prohibited slavery. But Carolina rice planters won removal of the restriction in 1751. Thereafter, they essentially invaded Georgia, which—despite remaining politically independent and becoming a royal colony in 1752—developed into a rice-planting slave society resembling South Carolina.

GEORGIA

The differing economic impacts of King George's War on the British mainland colonies highlight a crucial fact: those colonies did not compose a unified whole. Although linked economically into regions, they had few political or social ties beyond or even within those regions. Despite the growing coastal trade, the individual colonies' economic fortunes depended not on their neighbors in America but rather on the shifting markets of Europe and the Caribbean.

Colonial Cultures

a seventeenth-century resident of England's American possessions miraculously transported to 1750 would have been surprised by what one historian has termed "the refinement of America." Native-born colonial elites sought to distinguish themselves from ordinary folk in a variety of ways as they consolidated their hold on the local economy and political power.

Wealthy colonists spent their money ostentatiously. Most notably, they built large houses with rooms specifically designed for such forms of socializing as dancing, card playing, or drinking tea. Sufficiently well-off to enjoy "leisure" time, they attended concerts and the theater, gambled at horse races, and played billiards and other games. They also cultivated polite manners. Elite families in New Mexico, Louisiana, and Quebec also set themselves off from the "lesser sort."

GENTEEL CULTURE

Online Study Center
Improve Your Grade
Primary Source: Virginia Gentleman Weighs "a Frail Woman's" Class

Men from such families prided themselves not only on their possessions and positions, but also on their level of education and their intellectual connections to Europe. Many had been tutored by private teachers; some even attended college in Europe or America. (Harvard, the first colonial college, was founded in 1636.) From a seventeenth-century focus on ancient languages and theology, colleges by the mid-eighteenth century broadened their curricula to include courses on mathematics, the natural sciences, law, and medicine. Accordingly, a very few young men from elite or upwardly mobile families enrolled in college to study for careers other than the ministry. American women were mostly excluded from advanced education.

The intellectual current known as the Enlightenment deeply affected the learned clergymen who headed colonial colleges and their students. In the mid-seventeenth century, some European thinkers began to analyze nature in an effort to determine the laws that govern the universe. They employed experimentation and

THE ENLIGHTENMENT

■ Elizabeth Murray, the subject of this 1769 painting by John Singleton Copley, was the wife of James Smith, a wealthy rum distiller. Her fashionable dress and pose would seem to mark her as a lady of leisure, yet both before and during her marriage, this Scottish immigrant ran a successful dry goods shop in Boston. She thus simultaneously catered to and participated in the new culture of consumption. (Gift of Joseph W. R. Rogers and Mary C. Rogers. Museum of Fine Arts, Boston. Reproduced with permission. © Museum of Fine Arts, Boston)

abstract reasoning to discover general principles behind phenomena such as the motions of planets and stars and the characteristics of light and sound. Above all, Enlightenment philosophers emphasized acquiring knowledge through reason. Belief in such phenomena as witchcraft and astrology thus came under attack.

The Enlightenment supplied educated, well-to-do people in Europe and America with a common vocabulary and a unified view of the world, through which they endeavored to make sense of God's orderly creation. American naturalists like John and William Bartram supplied European scientists with information about New World plants and animals so that they could be included in universal classification systems. A notable American participant in the Enlightenment was Benjamin Franklin, who retired from a successful printing business in 1748 when he was just forty-two, thereafter devoting himself to scientific experimentation and public service. His *Experiments and Observations on Electricity* (1751) established the terminology and basic theory of electricity still used today.

The Enlightenment spirit of experimentation affected the lives of ordinary Americans most dramatically through advances in medicine—specifically, the treatment of smallpox. The Reverend Cotton Mather, a prominent Puritan cleric, learned from his African-born slave about inoculation (deliberately infecting a person with a mild case of a disease) as a protection against smallpox. When Boston in 1720–1721 suffered a major smallpox epidemic, Mather urged the adoption of inoculation despite fierce opposition from the city's leading physician. Mortality rates eventually supported Mather: of those inoculated, just 3 percent died; of others, 15 percent.

Enlightenment rationalism affected politics as well as science. John Locke's *Two Treatises of Government* (1691) challenged previous concepts of a divinely sanctioned political order. Men created governments and so could alter them, Locke declared. A ruler who broke his contract with the people and failed to protect their rights could legitimately be ousted from power by peaceful—or even violent—means. A proper political order could prevent the rise of tyrants; God's natural laws governed even the power of monarchs.

The world in which such ideas were discussed was that of the few, not the many. Most residents of

ORAL CULTURES

North America did not know how to read or write, and books were scarce and expensive. No colony required children to attend school; European American youngsters who learned to read usually did so in their own homes. A few months at a private "dame school" run by a literate local widow might teach them the basics of writing and simple arithmetic. Few Americans tried to instruct enslaved children. And only the most zealous Indian converts learned Europeans' literacy skills.

Thus, the cultures of colonial North America were primarily oral, communal, and—at least

through the first half of the eighteenth century— intensely local. Different areas developed divergent cultural traditions, and racial and ethnic variations heightened those differences. Public rituals served as the chief means through which the colonists forged their cultural identities.

Attendance at church was perhaps the most important such ritual. In Congregational (Puritan)

RELIGIOUS AND CIVIC RITUALS

churches, church leaders assigned seating to reflect position in the community. By the mid-eighteenth century, wealthy men and their wives sat in privately owned pews; their children and servants, and the less fortunate members of the community, sat in sex-segregated fashion at the rear or sides of the church. In eighteenth-century Virginia, seating in Church of England parishes also conformed to the local status hierarchy. In Quebec city, formal processions of men into the parish church celebrated Catholic feast days; each participant's rank determined his placement in the procession. By contrast, Quaker meetinghouses in Pennsylvania and elsewhere used an egalitarian, though also sex-segregated, seating system.

Communal culture also centered on the civic sphere. In New England, colonial governments proclaimed official days of thanksgiving and days of fasting and prayer. Everyone was expected to participate in the public rituals held in churches on such occasions. Monthly militia musters of all able-bodied men (known as training days) also brought the community together. In the Chesapeake, important cultural rituals occurred on court and election days. When the county court met, men came from miles around to file suits, appear as witnesses, or serve as jurors. Attendance at court functioned as a method of civic education; from watching the proceedings, men learned what behavior their neighbors expected of them.

Everywhere in colonial North America, the public punishment of criminals, including hangings and whippings, served not just to humiliate the offender and express community outrage but also to remind the community of proper standards of behavior. Penalties often shamed miscreants in especially appropriate ways. When a New Mexico man assaulted his father-in-law, he was directed to kneel before him and beg his forgiveness in front of the entire community.

The wide availability of consumer goods after the early years of the eighteenth century fostered new

Exotic Beverages

As colonists became consumers, they developed a taste not only for tea (from China) but for coffee (from Arabia), chocolate (from Mesoamerica), and rum (distilled from sugar, which also sweetened the bitter taste of the other three). The demand for these once-exotic beverages in America and Europe helped reshape the world economy after the mid-seventeenth century. Indeed, one historian has estimated that approximately two-thirds of the people who migrated across the Atlantic before 1776 were involved in one way or another, primarily as slaves, in the production of tobacco, calico, and these four drinks for the world market. The exotic beverages had a profound impact, too, on custom and culture, as they moved swiftly from luxury to necessity.

Each beverage had its own pattern of consumption. Chocolate, brought to Spain from Mexico and enjoyed there for a century before spreading more widely throughout Europe, became the preferred drink of aristocrats, consumed hot at intimate gatherings in palaces and mansions. Coffee, by contrast, became the preeminent morning beverage of English and colonial businessmen, who praised its caffeine for keeping drinkers sober and focused. Coffee was served in new public coffeehouses, patronized only by men, where politics and business were the topics of conversation. The first coffeehouse opened in London in the late 1660s; Boston had several by the 1690s. By the mid-eighteenth century, though, tea had supplanted coffee as the preferred hot, caffeinated beverage in England and America. It was consumed in the afternoons, in private homes at tea tables presided over by women. Tea embodied genteel status and polite conversation. In contrast, rum was the drink of the masses. This inexpensive, potent distilled spirit, made possible by new technology and the increasing production of sugar, was devoured by free working people everywhere in the Atlantic world.

The American colonies played a vital role in the production, distribution, and consumption of each of these beverages. Chocolate, most obviously, originated in America, and cacao plantations in the South American tropics multiplied in size and number to meet the rising demand. Coffee and tea (particularly the latter) were as avidly consumed in the colonies as in England. And rum involved Americans in every phase of its production and consumption. The sugar grown on French and English Caribbean plantations was transported to the mainland in barrels and ships made from North American wood. There the syrup was turned into rum at 140 distilleries. The Americans themselves drank a substantial share of the distilleries' output—an estimated four gallons per person annually—but exported much of it to Africa. There the rum purchased more slaves to produce more sugar to make still more rum, and the cycle began again.

Thus new tastes and customs connected to four different beverages linked the colonies to the rest of the world and altered their economic and social development.

The frontispiece of Peter Muguet, *Tractatus De Poto Caphe, Chinesium The et de Chocolata,* 1685. Muguet's treatise visually linked the three hot, exotic beverages recently introduced to Europeans. The drinks are being consumed by representatives of the cultures in which they originated: a turbaned Turk (with coffeepot in the foreground), a Chinese man (with teapot on the table), and an Indian drinking from a hollowed, handled gourd (with a chocolate pot and ladle on the floor in front of him). (Library of Congress)

RITUALS OF
CONSUMPTION rituals centered on consumption. First came the acquisition of desirable items. By 1750 specialized shops selling nonessentials had proliferated in cities such as Boston, New York, Philadelphia, and New Orleans, and even small and medium-size towns had one or two retail establishments. A colonist with money to spend would set aside time to "go shopping," a novel and pleasurable activity. The purchase of a desired object—for example, a ceramic bowl or a mirror—marked only the beginning of consumption rituals.

Consumers would then deploy their purchases in an appropriate manner: hanging the mirror prominently on a wall, displaying the bowl on a table or sideboard. Individual colonists took pleasure in owning lovely objects, but they also proudly displayed their acquisitions publicly for kin and neighbors to admire.

Tea drinking, a consumption ritual dominated and controlled by women, played an especially important role in Anglo-American consumption rituals. From early in the eighteenth century, households with aspirations to genteel status sought to acquire proper tea accouterments: not just pots and cups but also strainers, sugar tongs, bowls, and even special tables. Because of its cost, tea served as a crucial marker of status. Although poor households also consumed tea, they could not afford the fancy equipment that their better-off neighbors used.

Other sorts of rituals allowed the disparate cultures of colonial North America to interact with one another. Particularly important

RITUALS ON THE "MIDDLE GROUND" rituals developed on what the historian Richard White has termed the "middle ground"—that is, the psychological and geographical space in which Indians and Europeans encountered each other.

When Europeans sought to trade with Indians, they encountered an indigenous system of exchange that stressed gift giving rather than formalized buying and selling. Although French and English traders complained constantly about the need to present Indians with gifts prior to negotiating for pelts and skins, successful bargaining required such a step. Over time, an appropriate ritual developed. A European trader arriving at a village would give gifts (cloth, rum, gunpowder, and other items) to Indian

hunters. Eventually those gifts would be reciprocated, and formal trading could begin. To the detriment of Indian societies, rum became a crucial component of these intercultural trading rituals. Traders soon concluded that drunken Indians would sell their furs more cheaply.

Intercultural rituals also developed to deal with murders. Europeans sought to identify and punish a murderer. To Indians, such "eye for an eye" revenge was just one of many possible responses to murder. Compensation could also be accomplished by capturing an Indian or colonist who could take the dead person's place or by "covering the dead"—providing the family of the deceased with compensatory goods. Eventually, the French and the Algonquians evolved an elaborate ritual that encompassed elements of both societies' traditions: murders were investigated and murderers identified, but by mutual agreement deaths were usually "covered" by trade goods rather than by blood revenge.

Colonial Families

*F*amilies (rather than individuals) constituted the basic units of colonial society. People living together as families, commonly under the direction of a marital pair, were everywhere the chief mechanisms for both production and consumption. Yet family forms and structures varied widely in the mainland colonies, and not all were headed by couples.

As Europeans consolidated their hold on North America during the first three-quarters of the eighteenth

INDIAN FAMILIES century, Native Americans had to adapt. Bands reduced in numbers by disease and warfare recombined into new units; for example, the group later known as the Catawbas emerged in the 1730s in the western Carolinas from the fragmentary remains of several earlier Indian nations. Likewise, pressure from European secular and religious authorities reshaped Indian family forms. Whereas many Indian societies had permitted easy divorce, Christian missionaries frowned on such practices; and societies that had allowed polygynous marriages (including New England Algonquians) redefined such relationships, designating one wife as "legitimate" and others as "concubines."

Continued high mortality rates created Indian societies in which extended kin took on new importance, for when parents died, relatives assumed child-rearing responsibilities. Furthermore, European dominance in a region meant that Indians could no longer pursue traditional modes of subsistence. That in turn altered family life. In New England, for instance, Algonquian husbands and wives often could not live together, for adults supported themselves by working separately (perhaps wives as domestic servants, husbands as sailors). And in New Mexico, detribalized Navajos, Pueblos, and Apaches employed as servants by Spanish settlers clustered in the small towns of the Borderlands. Known collectively as *genizaros*, they lost contact with Indian cultures.

Wherever the population contained relatively few European women, sexual liaisons occurred between

MIXED-RACE
FAMILIES

European men and Indian women. The resulting mixed-race population of *mestizos* and *métis* worked as a familial "middle ground" to ease other cultural interactions. In New France and the Anglo-American backcountry, such families frequently resided in Indian villages and were enmeshed in trading networks; often, children of these unions became prominent leaders of Native American societies. By contrast, in the Spanish Borderlands, the offspring of Europeans and *genizaros* were treated as degraded individuals.

Eighteenth-century Anglo-Americans used the word *family* to mean all the people who occupied one

EUROPEAN
AMERICAN
FAMILIES

household (including any resident servants or slaves). European migrants to North America had far more stable family lives than did Indian and *mestizo* peoples. European men or their widows headed households considerably larger than American families today. Typical households were nuclear—that is, they included only parents and children. The head of the household represented it to the outside world, managing the finances and holding legal authority over the rest of the family, including his servants or slaves.

In English, French, and Spanish America alike, the vast majority of European families supported themselves through agriculture. The scale and nature of the work varied: the production of indigo in Louisiana required different sorts of labor from subsistence farming in New England or cattle ranching in

Texas. As in other societies, household tasks were allocated by sex.

The mistress took responsibility for what Anglo-Americans called "indoor affairs." She and her female helpers prepared food, cleaned the house, did laundry, and often made clothing. Preparing food alone involved planting and cultivating a garden, harvesting and preserving fruits and vegetables, salting and smoking meat, milking cows and making butter and cheese, not to mention cooking and baking. The head of the household and his male helpers were responsible for "outdoor affairs." They planted and cultivated the fields, built fences, chopped wood for the fireplace, harvested and marketed crops, cared for livestock, and butchered cattle and hogs to provide meat.

Most African American families lived as components of European American households. More than

AFRICAN
AMERICAN
FAMILIES

95 percent of colonial African Americans were held in perpetual bondage. Although many African Americans lived on farms with only one or two other slaves, others had the experience of living and working in a largely black setting. In South Carolina, a majority of the population was of African origin; in Georgia, about half; and in the Chesapeake, 40 percent.

The setting in which African Americans lived determined the shape of their family lives, yet wherever possible, slaves established strong family structures in which youngsters carried relatives' names. In the North, the scarcity of other blacks often made it difficult for bondspeople to form stable households. In the Chesapeake, men and women who regarded themselves as married (slaves could not legally wed) frequently lived in different quarters or even on different plantations. Children generally resided with their mothers, seeing their fathers only on Sundays. On large Carolina and Georgia rice plantations, however, enslaved couples usually lived together with their children.

Because all the English colonies legally permitted slavery, bondspeople had few options for escape.

FORMS OF
RESISTANCE

Some recently arrived Africans stole boats to try to return home or ran off in groups to frontier regions to join the Indians or establish independent communities. Among American-born slaves, family ties strongly affected such decisions. South Carolina planters soon learned, as one wrote, that slaves "love their families dearly and none runs away from the other." Thus, many owners sought to keep families together for purely practical reasons.

Although colonial slaves rarely rebelled collectively, they often resisted enslavement in other ways. Bondspeople uniformly rejected attempts by their owners to commandeer their labor on Sundays without compensation. Extended-kin groups protested excessive punishment of relatives and sought to live near each other. Among African American families who had lived on the same plantation for several generations, relatives could help with child rearing and similar tasks, providing a kind of insurance if parents and children were separated by sale. Among African Americans, just as among Indians, the extended family served a more important function than it did among European Americans.

Most slave families managed to carve out a small measure of autonomy, especially in their working and spiritual lives. Enslaved Muslims often clung to their faith. Some African Americans preserved traditional beliefs; others converted to Christianity (often retaining some African elements), finding comfort in the assurance that all people would be free and equal in heaven. South Carolina and Georgia slaves jealously guarded their customary ability to control their own time after the completion of their "tasks." Late in the century, some Chesapeake planters with a surplus of laborers began to hire out slaves to others, often allowing the workers to keep a small part of their earnings. Such accumulated property could buy desired goods or serve as a legacy for children.

Just as African and European Americans lived together on plantations, so too they lived in unsegregated urban neighborhoods. In 1760s Philadelphia, one-fifth of the work force was enslaved, and by 1775, blacks composed nearly 15 percent of the population of New York City. Such cities were nothing but large towns by today's standards. In 1750, the largest, Boston, had just seventeen thousand inhabitants. Life in the cities nonetheless differed considerably from that in rural areas. City dwellers everywhere purchased food and wood at markets. They also had much more contact with the world beyond their own homes than did their rural counterparts.

By the 1750s, most major cities had at least one weekly newspaper that printed the latest "advices

LIFE IN THE CITIES

from London," news from other English colonies, and local reports. Newspapers were available at taverns and inns, so people who could not afford to buy them could catch up on the news. Even illiterates could do so, since literate customers often read the papers aloud. Contact with the outside world, however, had its drawbacks. Sailors sometimes brought deadly diseases into port.

Politics: Stability and Crisis in British America

*E*arly in the eighteenth century, Anglo-American political life exhibited a new stability. By then, most residents had been born in America. Men from genteel families dominated the political structures in each province, for voters (free male property holders) tended to defer to their well-educated "betters."

Throughout the Anglo-American colonies, political leaders sought to increase the powers of elected assemblies. Assemblies began to claim privileges associated with the British House of Commons, such as the rights to initiate all tax legislation and to control the militia. The assemblies also developed ways to influence British appointees, especially by threatening to withhold their salaries. In some colonies (Virginia and South Carolina, for example), elite members of the assemblies usually presented a united front to royal officials, but in others (such as New York), they fought among themselves long and bitterly. To win hotly contested elections, New York's genteel leaders began to appeal to "the people" and compete openly for their votes. Yet in 1733, that same New York government imprisoned a newspaper editor, John Peter Zenger, who had too vigorously criticized its actions. Defending Zenger against the charge of "seditious libel," his lawyer argued that the truth could not be defamatory, thus helping to establish a free-press principle now found in American law.

RISE OF THE ASSEMBLIES

Much of the business of colonial assemblies would today be termed administrative. Only rarely did they formulate new policies or pass significant laws. Assemblymen saw themselves as acting defensively to prevent encroachments on the colonists' liberties— for example, by preventing governors from imposing oppressive taxes. By midcentury, they were comparing the structure of their governments to Britain's balanced combination of monarchy, aristocracy, and democracy. Drawing rough analogies, political leaders equated their governors with the monarch, their councils with the aristocracy, and their assemblies with the House of Commons. All three elements were believed essential to good government, but Anglo-Americans viewed governors and appointed councils as potential threats to customary colonial ways of life, since they primarily represented Britain. Many colonists saw the assemblies, however, as the people's representatives and protectors.

Yet the colonial ideal of the assembly as the defender of the people's liberties differed from the colonial reality. The assemblies, firmly controlled by dominant families, rarely responded to the concerns of their poorer constituents. Although settlements continually expanded, assemblies failed to reapportion themselves to provide adequate representation for newer communities, leading to serious grievances among frontier dwellers. In reality, the assemblies most dearly defended wealthy colonists, particularly the assembly members themselves.

At midcentury, the political structures that had stabilized in a period of relative calm confronted a series of crises. The crises of various descriptions exposed the internal tensions building in the pluralistic American society. Most important, they demonstrated that the political accommodations arrived at in the aftermath of the Glorious Revolution were no longer adequate to govern Britain's American empire.

One of the first and greatest crises occurred in South Carolina. Early one morning in September 1739, about twenty South Carolina slaves gathered near the Stono River south of Charles Town. Seizing guns and ammunition from a store, they killed the storekeepers and some nearby planter families. Then, joined by other local slaves, they headed toward Florida in hopes of finding refuge. Later that day, however, a troop of militia attacked the fugitives, who then numbered about a hundred, killing some and dispersing the rest. More than a week later, most of the remaining conspirators were captured. Those not killed on the spot were later executed.

STONO REBELLION

The Stono Rebellion shocked residents of other colonies as well as South Carolinians. Throughout

NEW YORK CONSPIRACY

British America, laws governing the behavior of African Americans were stiffened. In New York City, the news from the South, coupled with fears of Spain generated by the outbreak of King George's War, set off a reign of terror in the summer of 1741. Hysterical whites suspected a biracial gang of conspiring to foment a slave uprising under the guidance of a supposed priest in the pay of Spain. By summer's end, thirty-one blacks and four whites had been executed for participating in the alleged plot. The Stono Rebellion and the New York "conspiracy" not only exposed and confirmed Anglo-Americans' deepest fears about the dangers of slaveholding but also revealed the assemblies' inability to prevent serious internal disorder. Events of the next two decades confirmed that pattern.

By midcentury most of the fertile land east of the Appalachians had been purchased or occupied. Consequently, conflicts over land titles and conditions of landholding multiplied. In 1746, for example, some New Jersey farmers clashed violently with agents of the East Jersey proprietors, who claimed the farmers' land as theirs and demanded annual payments, called quit-rents, for the use of the property.

LAND RIOTS

The most serious land riots of the period took place in the lower Hudson River valley in 1765–1766. Late in the seventeenth century, the governor of New York had granted huge tracts there to prominent colonial families. The proprietors divided these estates into small farms, which they rented chiefly to poor Dutch and German migrants. After 1740, though, increasing numbers of migrants from New England resisted tenancy on the great New York estates. Many squatted on vacant portions of the manors, and they rebelled violently when proprietors tried to evict them in the mid-1760s, resisting successfully until British troops finally captured their leaders.

Violent conflicts of a different sort erupted in the late 1760s in South Carolina and the early 1770s in North Carolina, pitting backcountry farmers against wealthy eastern planters who controlled the provincial governments. Frontier dwellers, most of Scots-Irish origin, protested their lack of an adequate voice in colonial political affairs. South Carolinians for months policed the coun-

REGULATORS IN THE CAROLINAS

tryside in vigilante bands known as Regulators, complaining of lax and biased law enforcement. North Carolina Regulators, who primarily objected to heavy taxation, fought and lost a battle with eastern militiamen at Alamance in 1771.

A Crisis in Religion

*T*he most widespread crisis of this period was religious. From the mid-1730s through the 1760s, waves of religious revivalism—today known collectively as the First Great Awakening—swept over various colonies, primarily New England (1735–1745) and Virginia (1750s and 1760s). Orthodox Calvinists sought to combat Enlightenment rationalism, which denied innate human depravity. In addition, many recent immigrants and residents of the backcountry had no prior religious affiliation and were potential converts for evangelists.

The Great Awakening began in New England, where descendants of the Puritan founding generation still composed the membership of Congregational churches. During 1734 and 1735, Reverend Jonathan Edwards, a noted preacher and theologian, noticed a remarkable reaction among the youthful members of his church in Northampton, Massachusetts, to a message based squarely on Calvinist principles. Individuals could attain salvation, Edwards contended, only through recognition of their own depraved natures and the need to surrender completely to God's will. Such intensely emotional surrender came to be seen as a single identifiable moment of conversion.

The effects of such conversions remained isolated until 1739, when George Whitefield, a Church of England clergyman, arrived in America. For fifteen months, he toured the British colonies preaching to large audiences from Georgia to New England. A gripping orator, Whitefield in effect generated the Great Awakening. Everywhere he traveled, his fame preceded him. Thousands of free and enslaved folk turned out to listen and to experience conversion. Regular clerics initially welcomed Whitefield and the American-born itinerant evangelist preachers, who quickly imitated him. Soon, however, many clergymen began to realize that although "revived" religion filled their churches,

GEORGE WHITEFIELD

it ran counter to their own approach to doctrine and matters of faith. They disliked the emotional style of the itinerant revivalists and the disruption of normal church attendance patterns. Particularly troublesome were female exhorters who proclaimed their right to expound God's word.

Opposition to the Awakening heightened rapidly, causing congregations to splinter. "Old Lights"—traditional clerics and their followers—engaged in bitter disputes with the "New Light" evangelicals. Already characterized by numerous sects, American Protestantism fragmented further as the major denominations split into Old Light and New Light factions and as new evangelical sects—Methodists and Baptists—gained adherents. Paradoxically, the angry fights and the rapid rise in the number of distinct denominations eventually led to an American willingness to tolerate religious diversity.

IMPACT OF THE AWAKENING

Most significant, the Awakening challenged traditional modes of thought, for the revivalists' message directly contested the colonial tradition of deference. Itinerant preachers, only a few of whom were ordained clergymen, claimed they understood the will of God better than did elite college-educated clerics. The Awakening's emphasis on emotion rather than learning undermined the validity of received wisdom, and New Lights questioned not only religious but also social and political orthodoxy.

Nowhere was this trend more evident than in Virginia, where taxes supported the established Church of England. By the 1760s, Baptists had gained a secure foothold in Virginia; inevitably, their beliefs and behavior clashed with the way most genteel families lived. They rejected as sinful the horseracing, gambling, and dancing that occupied much of the gentry's leisure time. They addressed one another as "Brother" and "Sister" regardless of social status, and they elected the leaders of their congregations.

VIRGINIA BAPTISTS

Strikingly, almost all the Virginia Baptist congregations included both free and slave members. Church rules applied equally to all members; interracial sexual relationships, divorce, and adultery were forbidden to all. In addition, congregations forbade masters from breaking up slave couples through sale. Biracial committees investigated complaints about church members' misbehavior. Churches excommunicated slaves for stealing from their masters, but they also excommunicated masters for physically abusing their slaves. Some Baptists decided that owning slaves was "unrighteous" and freed their bondspeople.

Summary   *Online Study Center*   ACE the Test

*T*he Great Awakening injected an egalitarian strain into Anglo-American life at midcentury. Although primarily a religious movement, the Awakening had important social and political consequences, calling into question habitual modes of behavior in the secular as well as the religious realm. In short, the Great Awakening helped break Anglo-Americans' ties to their seventeenth-century origins. So too did the newcomers from Germany, Scotland, Ireland, and Africa, who brought with them their languages, customs, and religions.

The economic life of all Europe's North American colonies proceeded simultaneously on two levels. On the farms, plantations, and ranches on which most colonists resided, chores dominated people's lives while providing the goods consumed by households and sold in the markets. Simultaneously, an intricate international trade network affected the economies of the European colonies. The bitter wars fought by European nations during the eighteenth century inevitably involved the colonists by creating new opportunities for overseas sales or by disrupting their traditional markets. The volatile colonial economy fluctuated for reasons beyond Americans' control.

A century and a half after European peoples first settled in North America, the colonies mixed diverse European, American, and African traditions into a novel cultural blend that owed much to Europe but just as much to North America itself. Europeans who interacted regularly with peoples of African and American origin—and with Europeans who came from nations other than their own—had to develop new identities and new methods of accommodating intercultural differences in addition to creating ties within their own potentially fragmenting communities. Yet at the same time, the dominant colonists continued to identify themselves as French, Spanish, or British rather than as Americans. In the 1760s, how-

ever, some Anglo-Americans began to realize that their interests did not necessarily coincide with those of Great Britain or its monarch. For the first time, they offered a direct challenge to British authority.

LEGACY FOR A PEOPLE AND A NATION
"Self-Made Men"

One of the most common American themes celebrates the "self-made man" (always someone explicitly male) of humble origins who gains wealth and/or prominence through his own extraordinary effort and talent. The initial exemplars of this tradition lived in eighteenth-century America and the wider Atlantic world. Benjamin Franklin's *Autobiography* chronicled his method for achieving success as a printer after beginning life as the seventeenth child of a Boston candlemaker. From such humble origins, Franklin became a wealthy, influential man.

Franklin's tale is rivaled by that of a man apparently born a slave in South Carolina. Having worked for years as a sailor, he purchased his freedom, learned to read and write, held an important administrative post, married a wealthy young English woman, became an influential abolitionist, and eventually published a popular autobiography. His first master called him Gustavus Vassa, but when publishing his *Interesting Narrative* in 1789, he called himself Olaudah Equiano.

In that *Narrative,* Equiano claimed to have been born in Africa in 1745, kidnapped at the age of eleven, and carried first to Barbados, then to Virginia, where a British naval officer purchased him and introduced him to a maritime life. For years, scholars and students have relied on that account for its insights into the middle passage. But evidence recently uncovered by Vincent Carretta, while confirming the accuracy of much of Equiano's autobiography, shows that Equiano twice publicly identified his birthplace as Carolina. Why would Equiano conceal his origins? Carretta speculates that the *Narrative* gained part of its credibility from Equiano's African birth.

Equiano, or Vassa, thus truly "made himself." Equiano used information undoubtedly gleaned from acquaintances who *had* experienced the middle passage to accurately depict the horrors of the slave trade. In the process he became one of the first Americans to explicitly reinvent himself.

SEVERING THE BONDS OF EMPIRE 1754–1774

*T*he two men must have found the occasion remarkable. The artist customarily painted portraits of the wealthy and high born, not of artisans. Moreover, the political sympathies of the artist, John Singleton Copley, lay primarily with Boston's conservatives, whereas the sitter, Paul Revere, was a noted leader of resistance to British policies. Yet sometime in 1768, Revere commissioned Copley to paint his portrait, and the result is one of the greatest works of American art.

Copley portrayed Revere, a silversmith, surrounded by the tools of his trade and contemplating a teapot he was crafting. Revere's pose and apparel convey an impression of thoughtfulness, virtuous labor, and solidity. The teapot too carries a message, especially in the year 1768. Simultaneously a reflection of a craftsman's skills and a prominent emblem of the new "empire of goods" in British America, it resonated with symbolism because, as shall be seen later in this chapter, tea boycotts were an important component of colonial resistance to Great Britain.

In retrospect, John Adams identified the years between 1760 and 1775 as the era of the true American Revolution. The Revolution, Adams declared, ended before the fighting started, for it was "in the Minds of the people," involving not the actual winning of independence but a fundamental shift of allegiance from Britain to America. Today, not all historians would concur that the shift Adams identified constituted the Revolution. But none would deny the importance of those crucial years.

The story of the 1760s and early 1770s describes an ever-widening split between Great Britain and Anglo America. In the long history of British settlement in the Western Hemisphere, considerable tension had occasionally marred the relationship between individual provinces and the mother country. Still, that tension had rarely persisted for long and had not been widespread, except during the crisis following the Glorious Revolution in 1689. In the 1750s, however, a series of events caused the colonists to examine

Renewed Warfare Among Europeans and Indians

LINKS TO THE WORLD
The First Worldwide War

1763: A Turning Point

The Stamp Act Crisis

Resistance to the Townshend Acts

Confrontations in Boston

Tea and Turmoil

LEGACY FOR A PEOPLE AND A NATION
The Census and Reapportionment

Online Study Center
This icon will direct you to interactive map and primary source activities on the website http://college.hmco.com/pic/nortonbrief7e

CHRONOLOGY

1754 • Albany Congress meets to try to forge colonial unity
 • Fighting breaks out with Washington's defeat at Fort Necessity

1756 • Britain declares war on France; Seven Years War officially begins

1759 • British forces take Quebec

1760 • American phase of war ends with fall of Montreal to British troops
 • George III becomes king

1763 • Treaty of Paris ends Seven Years War
 • Pontiac's allies attack British forts in West
 • Proclamation of 1763 attempts to close land west of Appalachians to English settlement

1764 • Sugar Act lays new duties on molasses, tightens customs regulations
 • Currency Act outlaws paper money issued by the colonies

1765 • Stamp Act requires stamps on all printed materials in colonies
 • Sons of Liberty formed

1766 • Stamp Act repealed
 • Declaratory Act insists that Parliament can tax the colonies

1767 • Townshend Acts lay duties on trade within the empire, send new officials to America

1768–70 • Townshend duties resisted; boycotts and public demonstrations divide merchants and urban artisans

1770 • Lord North becomes prime minister
 • Townshend duties repealed, except for tea tax
 • Boston Massacre kills five colonial rioters

1772 • Boston Committee of Correspondence formed

1773 • Tea Act aids East India Company
 • Boston Tea Party protests the Tea Act

1774 • Coercive Acts punish Boston and Massachusetts as a whole
 • Quebec Act reforms government of Quebec
 • First Continental Congress called

their relations with Great Britain. It all started with the Seven Years War.

Britain's overwhelming victory in that war, confirmed by treaty in 1763, forever altered the balance of power in North America. France was ousted from the continent and Spain from Florida, events with major consequences for both the indigenous peoples of the interior and the residents of the British colonies. Indians could no longer play off European powers against one another and so lost one of their major diplomatic tools. Anglo-Americans no longer had to fear the French threat on their northern and western borders or the Spanish in the Southeast.

The British victory in 1763 had a significant impact on Great Britain. Britain's massive war-related debt needed to be paid, and so Parliament for the first time imposed revenue-raising taxes on the colonies in addition to the customs duties that had long regulated trade. That decision exposed differences in the political thinking of Americans and Britons.

During the 1760s and early 1770s, a broad coalition of the residents of Anglo America resisted new tax levies and attempts by British officials to tighten control over provincial governments. The colonies' elected leaders became ever more suspicious of Britain's motives as the years passed. They laid aside old antagonisms to coordinate their responses to the new measures, and they slowly began to reorient their political thinking. As late as the summer of 1774, though, few harbored thoughts of independence. ∎

Renewed Warfare Among Europeans and Indians

*I*n the mid-eighteenth century, the English colonies along the Atlantic seaboard were surrounded by hostile, or potentially hostile, neighbors: Indians everywhere, the Spanish in Florida and along the coast of the Gulf of Mexico, the French along the great inland system of rivers and lakes that stretched from the St. Lawrence to the Mississippi. The Spanish outposts posed little direct threat, for Spain's days as a major power had passed. But the long chain of French forts and settlements dominated the North American interior, facilitating trading partnerships and alliances with the Indians. In none of the three wars fought between 1689 and 1748 was England able to shake France's hold on the American frontier, although the Peace of Utrecht, which ended Queen Anne's War in 1713, gave the English control of such peripheral northern areas as Newfoundland, Hudson's Bay, and Acadia (Nova Scotia) (see Table 5.1).

During both Queen Anne's War and King George's War, the Iroquois Confederacy maintained

IROQUOIS NEUTRALITY

the policy of neutrality it had first developed in 1701, skillfully manipulating the Europeans while refusing to commit warriors fully to either side. The Iroquois continued a long-standing conflict with Cherokees and Catawbas in the South, thus giving their young warriors combat experience and acquiring new captives to replace population losses. They also cultivated peaceful relationships with Pennsylvania and Virginia, in part so the colonists would endorse their domination of the Shawnees and Delawares. And they forged friendly ties with Algonquians of the Great Lakes region, thereby avoiding potential assaults from those allies of the French and also making themselves indispensable middlemen for commerce and communication between the Atlantic coast and the West. Thus, the Iroquois consolidated their control over the entire American interior north of Virginia and south of the Great Lakes.

But even the Iroquois could not prevent the region inhabited by the Shawnees and Delawares (now western Pennsylvania and eastern Ohio) from providing the spark that set off a major war. That conflict spread from America to Europe, decisively resolving

the contest for North America. Trouble began in the mid-1740s, when Iroquois negotiators, claiming to speak for Delawares and Shawnees, ceded large tracts of the subordinate tribes' land to English colonists. Disgruntled Delawares and Shawnees migrated west, and Virginia land speculators began pressing to develop the ceded territory, focusing first on the area where the Allegheny and Monongahela Rivers join to form the Ohio (see Map 5.1).

That region, also claimed by Pennsylvania, was vital to the French, for the Ohio River offered direct access to French posts on the Mississippi. A permanent British presence in the Ohio country would threaten France's control of the western fur trade and its prominence in the Mississippi valley. A devastating 1752 raid by the French and Indians on a trading outpost at the site of modern Cleveland rid the region of Pennsylvanians, but the speculators of Virginia posed a more serious challenge. Accordingly, in 1753, the French pushed southward from Lake Erie, building fortified outposts at strategic points.

In response to the French threat, delegates from seven northern and middle colonies gathered in

ALBANY CONGRESS

Albany, New York, in June 1754. Backed by administrators in London, they sought two goals: to persuade the Iroquois to abandon their traditional neutrality and to coordinate the defenses of the colonies. They succeeded in neither. The Iroquois saw no reason to change a policy that had served them well for half a century. And although the Albany Congress delegates adopted a Plan of Union (which would have established an elected intercolonial legislature with the power to tax), their provincial governments uniformly rejected the plan—primarily because those governments feared a loss of autonomy.

While the Albany Congress delegates deliberated, the war they sought to prepare for was already beginning. The governor of Virginia sent a small militia troop to the forks of the Ohio, then later dispatched reinforcements. When a substantial French force arrived at the forks, the first contingent of Virginia militia surrendered peacefully, and the French then began to construct Fort Duquesne. Learning of the confrontation, the inexperienced young officer leading the Virginia reinforcements pressed onward, attacked a French detachment, and then allowed himself to be trapped in his crudely built Fort Necessity at Great

TABLE 5.1

The Colonial Wars, 1689–1763

American Name	European Name	Dates	Participants	American Sites	Dispute
King William's War	War of the League of Augsburg	1689–97	England, Holland versus France, Spain	New England, New York, Canada	French power
Queen Anne's War	War of Spanish Succession	1702–13	England, Holland, Austria versus France, Spain	Florida, New England	Throne of Spain
King George's War	War of Austrian Succession	1739–48	England, Holland, Austria versus France, Spain, Prussia	West Indies, New England, Canada	Throne of Austria
French and Indian War	Seven Years War	1756–63	England versus France, Spain	Ohio country, Canada	Possession of Ohio country

Meadows, Pennsylvania. After a day-long battle (on July 3, 1754), during which more than one-third of his men were killed or wounded, twenty-two-year-old George Washington surrendered. He and his men were allowed to return to Virginia.

Washington's grievous blunder helped ignite a war that eventually would encompass nearly the entire world. He also ensured that the Ohio Indians would support France. In July 1755, a few miles south of Fort Duquesne, a combined force of French and Indians ambushed British and colonial troops led by General Edward Braddock, killing Braddock and demoralizing his surviving soldiers. After news of the debacle reached London, Britain declared war on France in 1756, formally beginning the conflict known as the Seven Years War.

SEVEN YEARS WAR

For three more years, one British disaster followed another. British officers tried, without much success, to coerce the colonies into supplying men and materiel to the army. The war went so badly that Britain began to fear France would try to retake Nova Scotia. Afraid the approximately twelve thousand French residents of Nova Scotia might break their pledges of neutrality, Britain forced about half of them from their homeland—the first large-scale modern deportation. Ships crammed with Acadians sailed to each of the mainland colonies, where the dispirited exiles encountered hostility and discrimination.

In 1757, William Pitt, a civilian official, was placed in charge of the war effort. Pitt agreed to reimburse the colonies for their wartime expenditures and placed troop recruitment wholly in local hands, thereby gaining greater American support for the war. In July 1758, British forces recaptured the fortress at Louisbourg controlling the entrance to the St. Lawrence River, thus cutting the major French supply route. Then, in September 1759, General James Wolfe's troops took Quebec. Sensing a British victory, the Iroquois abandoned their traditional neutrality and allied with Britain. A year later, the British captured Montreal, and the American phase of the war ended.

In the Treaty of Paris (1763), France ceded its major North American holdings to Britain. Spain, an ally of France toward the end of the war, gave Florida to the victors. France, meanwhile, ceded Louisiana west of the Mississippi to its ally Spain. The British thus gained control of the continent's fur trade. No longer would the English seacoast colonies have to worry about the threat to their existence posed by the French presence.

Map 5.1   European Settlements and Indians, 1754

By 1754, Europeans had expanded the limits of the English colonies to the
eastern slopes of the Appalachian Mountains.

The First Worldwide War

Today we call two twentieth-century conflicts "world wars," but the first worldwide war predated them by more than a century. The contest began in the backwoods of southwestern Pennsylvania in the spring of 1754, over a seemingly local quarrel: whether Britain or France would build a fort at the forks of the Ohio. That it eventually involved combatants around the world attests not only to the growing importance of European nations' overseas empires but also to the increasing centrality of North America in their struggles for dominance.

Previous wars among Europeans had taken place mostly in Europe, though overseas colonies occasionally got involved. But the contest at the forks of the Ohio helped to reinvigorate a conflict between Austria and Prussia that sent the nations of Europe scrambling for allies. Eventually England, Hanover, and Prussia lined up against France, Austria, and Russia, joined by Sweden, Saxony, and, later, Spain. The war in Europe would last seven years. In 1763 these nations signed a peace treaty that returned the continent to the status quo before the war, but elsewhere, in the rest of the world, Britain had decisively vanquished both France and Spain.

"Elsewhere" included a mind-boggling list of battles. In the Caribbean, Britain seized the French islands of Guadeloupe and Martinique and took Havana, Cuba, from Spain. In North America, the British recaptured the French fortress of Louisbourg and conquered the capital of New France, Quebec. In Africa, the British overwhelmed France's slave-trading posts in Senegambia. In India, British forces won control of Bengal by defeating both a local ruler and French soldiers stationed there. Three years later, the British beat a French army at Pondicherry. So four months after France lost Canada, its influence in India was also extinguished. At the very end of the war, a British expedition took Manila in the Philippines from Spain. The commander there had not yet learned that his nation had declared war on Britain, so the assault caught him unaware.

Thus, the war that started in the American backcountry revealed the steadily growing links between North America and the rest of the world. And the aftermath exposed an unexpected further link. Both winners and losers had to pay for this first worldwide war. Financial struggles in Britain and France, though separate, ultimately produced similar outcomes: revolutions abroad (for Britain, in America) and at home (for France).

In 1771 the artist Dominic Serres, the Elder, depicted British naval vessels attacking the French fortress at Chandernagore in India in 1757 (at left in background). Cannon fire from the warships was critical to the British victory, one of the keys to the conquest of India during the Seven Years War.
(National Maritime Museum, London)

Online Study Center **Improve Your Grade**
Interactive Map: European Claims in North America

The overwhelming British triumph stimulated some Americans to think expansively. People like the Philadelphia printer Benjamin Franklin, who had long touted the colonies' wealth and potential, predicted a glorious new future for British North America. Such individuals uniformly opposed any laws that would retard America's growth and persistently supported steps to increase Americans' control over their own destiny. Many of them also invested heavily in western land speculations.

1763: A Turning Point

he great victory over France had an irreversible impact on North America, felt first by the indigenous peoples of the interior. With France excluded from the continent altogether and Spanish territory confined to west of the Mississippi, the diplomatic strategy that had served the Indians well for so long was now obsolete. The consequences were immediate and devastating.

Even before the Treaty of Paris, British advances in the American war in 1758 denied the Creeks and Cherokees in the South of their ability to force concessions by threatening to turn instead to France or Spain. In desperation, and in retaliation for British atrocities, Cherokees attacked the Carolina and Virginia frontiers in 1760. The Indians were defeated the following year and late in 1761 agreed to a treaty allowing the construction of British forts in their territories and opening a large tract of land to European settlement.

In the Ohio country, the Ottawas, Chippewas, and Potawatomis reacted angrily when Great Britain,

NEOLIN AND PONTIAC

no longer facing French competition, raised the price of trade goods and ended traditional gift-giving practices. Settlers rapidly moved into the Monongahela and Susquehanna valleys. A shaman named Neolin (also known as the Delaware Prophet) urged Indians to both resist British incursions and throw off dependence on European goods (especially alcohol). If all Indians west of the mountains united to reject the invaders, Neolin declared, the Master of Life would replenish the depleted

■ Benjamin West, the first well-known American artist, engraved this picture of a prisoner exchange at the end of Pontiac's Uprising, showing the return of settlers abducted during the war. In the foreground, a child resists leaving the Indian parents he had grown to love. Many colonists were fascinated by the phenomenon West depicted: the reluctance of captives to abandon their adoptive Indian families. (Ohio Historical Society)

deer herds and once again look kindly on his people. Yet ironically, Neolin's call for a return to native traditions, in its reference to a single Master of Life, itself showed the influence of Europeans' Christianity.

Pontiac, the war chief of an Ottawa village near Detroit, became the leader of a movement based on Neolin's precepts. In the spring of 1763, Pontiac forged an unprecedented alliance among many Indian nations. He then laid siege to Fort Detroit while war parties attacked other British outposts in the Great Lakes. Detroit withstood the siege, but by late June, all the other forts west of Niagara and north of Fort Pitt (formerly Fort Duquesne) had fallen to the alliance. Indians then raided the Virginia and Pennsylvania frontiers at will throughout the summer, killing at least two thousand settlers. Still, they failed to take the strongholds of Niagara, Fort Pitt, or Detroit. In early August, colonial militiamen soundly defeated a combined Indian force at Bushy Run, Pennsylvania. A treaty ending the war was finally negotiated three years later.

The uprising showed that the huge territory Britain had acquired from France would be difficult

PROCLAMATION OF 1763

to govern. In October, the governing ministry issued the Proclamation of 1763, which designated the headwaters of rivers flowing into the Atlantic from the Appalachian

Mountains as the temporary western boundary for colonial settlement (see Map 5.1). Its promulgators expected the proclamation to prevent clashes by keeping colonists off Indian lands until tribes had given up their territory by treaty. But it infuriated those who had already squatted on lands west of the line, as well as land speculation companies from Pennsylvania and Virginia. Though the latter group negotiated with the Iroquois to push the boundary farther west and south, they could not convince administrators in London to validate their speculations. Significant western expansion, the British realized, would require the expenditure of funds they did not have.

The hard-won victory in the Seven Years War had cost Britain millions of pounds and created an

GEORGE III

immense war debt. The problem of paying this debt and funding the defense of the newly acquired territories bedeviled George III, who in

1760 had succeeded his grandfather, George II. The twenty-two-year-old king, an intelligent, passionate man with a mediocre education, was an erratic judge of character. During the crucial years between 1763 and 1770, when the rift with the colonies grew ever wider and a series of political crises beset England, the king replaced ministers with bewildering rapidity. Determined to assert the monarchy's power, but immature and unsure of himself, he often substituted stubbornness for cleverness, and he regarded adherence to the status quo as the hallmark of patriotism.

The man he selected as prime minister in 1763, George Grenville, confronted a financial crisis: England's burden of indebtedness had nearly doubled since 1754. Grenville's ministry had to find new sources of funds, and the British people themselves

were already heavily taxed. Since the colonists had benefited greatly from the wartime expenditures, Grenville concluded that Anglo-Americans should be asked to pay a larger share of the cost of running the empire.

Grenville did not question Great Britain's right to levy taxes on the colonies. Like all his countrymen, he

THEORIES OF REPRESENTATION

believed that the government's legitimacy derived ultimately from the consent of the people, but he defined consent differently from the colonists. Americans had come to

believe that they could be represented only by men who lived nearby and for whom they or their property-holding neighbors had voted. Grenville and his English contemporaries, however, believed that Parliament—king, lords, and commons acting together—by definition represented all British subjects, even colonists, who could not vote.

Parliament saw itself as collectively representing the entire nation; the particular constituency that chose a member of the House of Commons had no special claim on that member's vote, nor did he have to live near his constituents. According to this theory of government, called *virtual representation*, the colonists were seen as virtually, if not actually, represented in Parliament. Thus, their consent to acts of Parliament could be presumed. In the colonies, by contrast, members of the lower houses of the assemblies were viewed as specifically representing the regions that had elected them. Before Grenville proposed to tax the colonists, the two notions had coexisted because no conflict exposed the central contradiction.

Events in the 1760s threw into sharp relief Americans' attitudes toward political power. The colonists had become accustomed to a central

REAL WHIGS

government that wielded only limited authority over them, affecting their daily lives very little. Consequently, they believed that a good government was one that largely left them alone, a view in keeping with the theories of a group of British writers known as the Real Whigs. These writers stressed the danger inherent in a powerful government, particularly one headed by a monarch. They warned the people to guard constantly against government attempts to encroach on their liberty and seize their property. Political power, they wrote, was always to be feared. Only perpetual vigilance could preserve the people's precious yet fragile liberty, which was closely tied to their right to private property.

Britain's attempts to tighten the reins of government and raise revenues from the colonies convinced many Americans to interpret British measures in light of the Real Whigs' warnings, especially because of the link between liberty and property rights. Excessive and unjust taxation, they believed, could destroy their freedoms. In time they began to see oppressive designs behind the actions of Grenville and his successors. In the mid-1760s, however, colonial leaders did not immediately accuse Grenville of conspiring to oppress them. They at first merely questioned the wisdom of the laws he proposed.

Parliament passed the first such measures, the Sugar and Currency Acts, in 1764. The Sugar Act
revised existing customs regulations

SUGAR AND
CURRENCY ACTS

and laid new duties on some foreign imports into the colonies. Its most important provisions, strongly advocated by influential planters of the British Caribbean wishing to increase demand for their sugar, aimed to discourage American rum distillers from smuggling French West Indian molasses. It also established a vice-admiralty court at Halifax, Nova Scotia. (Vice-admiralty courts operated without juries.) Although the Sugar Act appeared to resemble the Navigation Acts, which the colonies had long accepted as legitimate, it broke with tradition in being explicitly designed to raise revenue, not to channel American trade through Britain. The Currency Act effectively outlawed colonial issues of paper money because British merchants had long complained that Americans were paying their debts in inflated local currencies. Americans could accumulate little sterling, since they imported more than they exported; thus, the act seemed to the colonists to deprive them of a useful medium of exchange.

The Sugar and Currency Acts were imposed on an economy already hit hard by a depression that followed when the Seven Years War shifted overseas. Individual American essayists and incensed colonial governments protested the new policies. But, lacking any precedent for a united campaign against acts of Parliament, Americans in 1764 took only hesitant and uncoordinated steps. Eight colonial legislatures sent separate petitions to Parliament requesting the Sugar Act's repeal, arguing that its commercial re-

strictions would hurt Britain as well as the colonies and that they had not consented to its passage. The protests had no effect, and Grenville proceeded with another revenue plan.

The Stamp Act Crisis

The Stamp Act (1765), Grenville's most important proposal, was modeled on a law that had been in effect in Great Britain for almost a century. It touched nearly every colonist by requiring tax stamps on most printed materials, but it fell heaviest on merchants and others of the colonial elite, who used printed matter more frequently than did ordinary folk. Anyone who purchased a newspaper, made a will, transferred land, bought dice or playing cards, applied for a liquor license, or borrowed money would have to pay the tax. The act also required that tax stamps be paid for with scarce sterling and that violators be tried in vice-admiralty courts. Finally, such a law would break decisively with the colonial tradition of self-imposed taxation.

The most important colonial pamphlet protesting the Sugar Act and the proposed Stamp Act was
The Rights of the British Colonies

JAMES OTIS'S
RIGHTS OF
THE BRITISH
COLONIES

Asserted and Proved, by James Otis Jr., a brilliant young Massachusetts attorney. Otis starkly exposed the ideological dilemma that confounded the colonists for the next decade. How could they justify their opposition to certain acts of Parliament without questioning Parliament's authority over them? On the one hand, Otis asserted, Americans were "entitled to all the natural, essential, inherent, and inseparable rights" of Britons, including the right not to be taxed without their consent. On the other hand, Otis admitted that under the British system, "the power of parliament is uncontrollable but by themselves, and we must obey."

Otis's first contention implied that Parliament could not constitutionally tax the colonies because Americans were not represented in its ranks. Yet his second point both acknowledged political reality and accepted the prevailing theory of British government: that Parliament was the sole, supreme authority in the empire. Even unconstitutional laws enacted by Parliament had to be obeyed until Parliament decided to repeal them. Otis tried to find a middle ground by proposing colonial representation in Parliament, but his idea was never taken seriously on either side of the Atlantic. The British believed that the colonists were already virtually represented in Parliament, and Anglo-Americans quickly realized that a handful of colonial delegates to London would simply be outvoted.

Otis published his pamphlet before the Stamp Act was passed. When Americans first learned of the act's adoption in the spring of 1765, they reacted indecisively. Few colonists publicly favored the law, but colonial petitions had already failed to prevent its adoption, and further lobbying appeared futile. Perhaps Otis was correct: the only course open to Americans was to pay the stamp tax, reluctantly but loyally.

Not all the colonists shared Otis's view. One twenty-nine-year-old lawyer serving his first term in the Virginia House of Burgesses was

PATRICK HENRY AND THE VIRGINIA STAMP ACT RESOLVES

appalled by his fellow legislators' unwillingness to oppose the Stamp Act. "Alone, unadvised, and unassisted," Patrick Henry decided to act. "On a blank leaf of an old law book," he wrote the Virginia Stamp Act Resolves.

Henry introduced his seven proposals near the end of the 1765 legislative session, when many burgesses had already departed for home. His fiery speech led the Speaker of the House to accuse him of treason. (Henry denied the charge, contrary to the nineteenth-century myth that he exclaimed, "If this be treason, make the most of it!") The few burgesses remaining adopted five of Henry's resolutions by a bare majority. Although they repealed the most radical of the five the next day, their action had far-reaching effects.

The four propositions that the burgesses adopted repeated Otis's arguments, asserting that the colonists had never forfeited the rights of British subjects, among which was consent to taxation. The other three resolutions went much further. The one that was repealed claimed for the burgesses "the only exclusive right" to tax Virginians, and the final two (those never considered) asserted that residents of Virginia need not obey tax laws passed by other legislative bodies (namely, Parliament).

The burgesses' decision to accept only the first four of Henry's resolutions anticipated the position

CONTINUING LOYALTY TO BRITAIN

most Americans would adopt throughout the following decade. Though willing to contend for their rights, the colonists did not seek independence. Rather, they wanted some measure of self-government. Accordingly, they backed away from the assertions that they owed Parliament no obedience and that only their own assemblies could tax them.

Over the next ten years, America's political leaders searched for a formula that would enable them to control their internal affairs, especially taxation, but remain under British rule. The chief difficulty lay in British officials' inability to compromise on the issue of parliamentary power. The notion that Parliament could exercise absolute authority over all colonial possessions was inherent in the British theory of government. In effect, the Americans wanted British leaders to revise their fundamental understanding of the workings of their government. And that was simply too much to expect.

The ultimate effectiveness of Americans' opposition to the Stamp Act derived not from ideological arguments over parliamentary power but from the decisive and inventive actions of some colonists. In August 1765 the Loyal Nine, a Boston social club of printers, distillers, and other artisans, organized a demonstration against the Stamp Act. Hoping to show that people of all ranks opposed the act, they approached the leaders of the city's rival laborers' associations, based in Boston's North End and South End neighborhoods. The two gangs often clashed, but the Loyal Nine convinced them to lay aside their differences to participate in the demonstration.

Early on August 14, the demonstrators hung an effigy of Andrew Oliver, the province's stamp distributor,

ANTI–STAMP ACT DEMONSTRATIONS

from a tree on Boston Common. That night a large crowd led by a group of about fifty well-dressed tradesmen paraded the effigy around the city and threw stones at officials who tried to disperse them. In the midst of the melee, the North End and South End leaders drank a toast to their successful union. Oliver publicly promised not to fulfill the duties of his office. Twelve days later, a mob reportedly led by the South End leader Ebenezer MacIntosh attacked the homes of several customs officers. The crowd then destroyed Lieutenant Governor Thomas Hutchinson's elaborately furnished townhouse, an action that drew no praise from Boston's respectable citizens.

The differences between the two Boston mobs of August 1765 exposed divisions that would continue to characterize colonial protests. Few residents of the colonies sided with Great Britain during the 1760s, but various colonial groups had divergent goals. The skilled craftsmen who composed the Loyal Nine and merchants, lawyers, and others of the educated elite preferred orderly demonstrations confined to political issues. For the city's laborers, by contrast, economic grievances may have been paramount. Certainly, their wrecking of Hutchinson's house suggests resentment against the lieutenant governor's ostentatious display of wealth.

AMERICANS'
DIVERGENT
INTERESTS

Colonists, like Britons, had a long tradition of crowd action in which disfranchised people took to the streets to redress deeply felt local grievances. But the Stamp Act controversy drew ordinary urban folk into the vortex of transatlantic politics for the first time. Matters that previously had been of concern only to the gentry or to members of colonial legislatures were now discussed on every street corner.

The entry of unskilled workers, slaves, and women into imperial politics both threatened and aided the elite men who wanted to mount effective opposition to British measures. To be sure, crowd action could have a stunning impact. Anti–Stamp Act demonstrations occurred in cities and towns stretching from Halifax in the north to the Caribbean island of Antigua in the south, and by November 1, when the law was scheduled to take effect, not one stamp distributor was willing to carry out his duties. Thus, the act could not be enforced. But wealthy men also recognized that mobs composed of the formerly powerless could endanger their own dominance. What would happen, they wondered, if the crowd turned against them?

Elite men therefore attempted to channel resistance into acceptable forms by creating an intercolonial association, the Sons of Liberty. New Yorkers organized the first such group in early November, and branches spread rapidly through the coastal cities. Composed of merchants, lawyers, and prosperous tradesmen, the Sons of Liberty by early 1766 linked protest leaders from Charleston, South Carolina, to Portsmouth, New Hampshire.

SONS OF LIBERTY

The Sons of Liberty could influence events but could not control them. In Charleston in October 1765, an informally organized crowd forced the resignation of the South Carolina stamp distributor. But the new Charleston chapter of the Sons of Liberty was horrified when in January 1766, local slaves paraded through the streets crying, "Liberty!" Freedom from slavery was not the sort of liberty elite slaveowners had in mind.

In Philadelphia, too, resistance leaders were dismayed when an angry mob threatened to attack Benjamin Franklin's house. The city's laborers believed Franklin was partly responsible for the Stamp Act, since he had obtained the post of stamp distributor for a close friend. But Philadelphia's artisans—the backbone of the opposition movement there and elsewhere—were fiercely loyal to Franklin and gathered to protect his home and family from the crowd. The resulting split between the better-off tradesmen and the common laborers prevented the establishment of a successful workingmen's alliance like that of Boston.

During the fall and winter of 1765–1766, opposition to the Stamp Act proceeded on three separate fronts. Colonial legislatures petitioned Parliament to repeal the hated law, and courts closed because they could not obtain the stamps now required for all legal documents. In October nine colonies sent delegates to a general congress. The Stamp Act Congress met in New York to draft a unified but conservative statement of protest, stressing economic considerations rather than issues of American rights. At the same time, the Sons of Liberty held mass meetings to rally public support for resistance. Finally, American merchants organized nonimportation associations to pressure British exporters. By the 1760s, one-quarter of all British exports went to the colonies, and American merchants reasoned that London merchants whose sales suffered severely would lobby for repeal. Since times were bad, American merchants believed that nonimportation would also help reduce their bloated inventories.

OPPOSITION
AND REPEAL

In March 1766, Parliament repealed the Stamp Act. The nonimportation agreements had had the anticipated effect among wealthy London merchants. But boycotts, formal protests, and crowd actions were less important in winning repeal than was the appointment of a new prime minister. Lord Rockingham, who replaced Grenville in the summer of 1765, had opposed the Stamp Act, not because he believed Parliament lacked the power to tax the colonies but because he thought the law unwise and divisive. Thus, although Rockingham proposed repeal, he linked it to passage of a Declaratory Act, which asserted Parliament's authority to tax and legislate for Britain's American possessions "in all cases whatsoever." Colonists welcomed the Stamp Act's repeal with celebrations stressing their unwavering loyalty to Great Britain; few of them saw the implications of the Declaratory Act.

Resistance to the Townshend Acts

In the summer of 1766, another change in the ministry in London revealed how fragile the colonists' victory had been. The new prime minister, William Pitt, was often ill, and another minister, Charles Townshend, became the dominant force in the ministry. An ally of Grenville, Townshend decided to renew the attempt to obtain additional funds from Britain's American possessions.

The duties Townshend proposed in 1767, to be levied on trade goods like paper, glass, and tea, seemed to be nothing more than extensions of the existing Navigation Acts. But the Townshend duties differed from previous customs levies in two ways. First, they applied to items imported into the colonies from Britain, not from foreign countries. Thus, they violated mercantilist theory (see Chapter 3). Second, the revenues were to fund the salaries of some royal officials in the colonies. Previously those men were paid from local taxation, and assemblies could ensure their cooperation by threatening to withhold their salaries. Now assemblies would lose some of that leverage. In addition, Townshend's scheme would create an American Board of Customs Commissioners and vice-admiralty courts at Boston, Philadelphia, and Charleston. These moves angered merchants because more vigorous enforcement of the Navigation Acts would threaten their profits.

Online Study Center **Improve Your Grade**
Primary Source: William Shepherd Attempts to Collect Customs Duties

The passage of the Townshend Acts drew a quick response. One series of essays in particular, *Letters*

JOHN DICKINSON'S FARMER'S LETTERS

from a Farmer in Pennsylvania, by the prominent lawyer John Dickinson, expressed a broad consensus. Dickinson contended that Parliament could regulate colonial trade but could not exercise that power to raise revenue. By distinguishing between trade regulation and unacceptable commercial taxation, Dickinson avoided the sticky issue of consent and how it affected colonial subordination to Parliament. But his argument created a different, and equally knotty, problem. In effect, it obligated the colonies to assess Parliament's motives in passing any law pertaining to trade before deciding whether to obey it. That was an unworkable position in the long run.

The Massachusetts assembly responded to the Townshend Acts by drafting a letter to circulate among the other colonial legislatures, calling for unity and suggesting a joint petition of protest. Not the letter itself but the ministry's reaction to it united the colonies. When Lord Hillsborough, the first secretary of state for America, learned of the circular letter, he ordered Governor Francis Bernard of Massachusetts to insist that the assembly recall it. He also directed other governors to prevent their assemblies from discussing the letter. Hillsborough's order gave colonial assemblies the incentive to join forces against this new threat to their prerogatives. In late 1768 the Massachusetts legislature met, debated, and resoundingly rejected recall. Bernard immediately dissolved the assembly, and other governors followed suit when their legislatures debated the circular letter.

Like other formal assertions of colonial rights, the vote against recalling the circular letter provided a symbol to be commemorated in the public rituals organized by supporters of the resistance. Such rituals, as when legislators drank mass public toasts or Boston's Sons of Liberty invited hundreds to dine with them, served important educational and unifying functions. As pamphlets did for the literate, public processions, celebrations, and song fests taught illiterate Americans about the reasons for resistance and encouraged their commitment to the cause.

During the campaign against the Townshend duties, the Sons of Liberty and other American leaders stepped up the deliberate effort to involve ordinary folk in the resistance movement. Most important, they urged colonists of all ranks and both sexes to sign agreements not to purchase or consume British products. The new consumerism that previously had linked the colonists economically now linked them politically as well, offering a ready method of displaying their allegiance.

As the primary purchasers of textiles and household goods, women played a central role in the nonconsumption movement and introduced public rituals of their own. In Boston more than three hundred matrons publicly promised not to buy or drink tea, "Sickness excepted." The women of Wilmington, North Carolina, burned their tea after walking through town in a solemn procession. The best known of the protests, the so-called Edenton Ladies Tea Party, actually was a meeting of prominent North Carolina women who pledged formally to work for the public good and support resistance to British measures.

DAUGHTERS OF LIBERTY

Women also encouraged home manufacturing. In many towns, young women calling themselves Daughters of Liberty met to spin in public in an effort to persuade other women to make homespun, thereby ending the colonies' dependence on British cloth. When young ladies from well-to-do families sat publicly at spinning wheels all day, eating only American food and drinking local herbal tea, they were serving as political instructors. Many women took great satisfaction in their newfound role.

But the colonists were by no means united in support of nonimportation and nonconsumption. If the Stamp Act protests had occasionally revealed a division between artisans and merchants on one side and common laborers on the other, resistance to the Townshend Acts exposed new splits in American ranks. The most significant—which arose from a change in economic circumstances—divided urban artisans and merchants, allies in 1765 and 1766.

DIVIDED OPINION OVER BOYCOTTS

The Stamp Act boycotts had helped revive a depressed economy by creating a demand for local products and reducing merchants' inventories. But in 1768 and 1769, merchants were enjoying boom times and had no financial incentive to support a boycott. They signed the agreements only reluctantly. In contrast, artisans supported nonimportation enthusiastically, recognizing that the absence of British goods would create a ready market for their own manufactures. Tradesmen also used coercion, sometimes destroying property, to enforce boycotts.

Such tactics were effective: colonial imports from England dropped dramatically in 1769. But they also aroused heated opposition. Some Americans who supported resistance to British measures began to question the use of violence to force others to join the boycott. In addition, wealthier and more conservative colonists were frightened by the threat to private property inherent in the campaign. Political activism by ordinary colonists challenged the ruling elite's domination.

Americans were relieved when news arrived in April 1770 that the Townshend duties had been repealed, with the exception of the tea tax. A new prime minister, Lord North, persuaded Parliament that duties on trade within the empire were ill advised. Although some colonial leaders argued that nonimportation should continue until the tea tax was repealed, merchants quickly resumed importing. The rest of the Townshend Acts remained in force, but repealing the duties made the other provisions appear less objectionable.

TOWNSHEND DUTIES REPEALED

Confrontations in Boston

On the very day Lord North proposed repeal of the Townshend duties, a confrontation between civilians and soldiers in Boston led to the death of five Americans. The origins of the event that patriots called the Boston Massacre lay in repeated clashes between customs officers and the people of Massachusetts. The decision to base the American Board of Customs Commissioners in Boston was the source of the problem.

Mobs targeted the customs commissioners from the day they arrived in November 1767. In June 1768 their seizure of the patriot leader John Hancock's sloop *Liberty* on suspicion of smuggling caused a riot in which customs officers' property was destroyed. The riot in turn helped convince the British that troops were needed to maintain order in the unruly port. The troops constantly reminded Bostonians of the oppressive potential of British power. Redcoat patrols roamed the city day and night, questioning and sometimes harassing passersby. Parents began to fear for the safety of their daughters, who were subjected to soldiers' coarse sexual insults. But the greatest potential for violence lay in the uneasy relationship between the soldiers, many of whom competed for unskilled jobs in their off-duty hours, and Boston laborers. The two groups brawled repeatedly.

Early on the evening of March 5, 1770, a crowd of laborers began throwing hard-packed snowballs at soldiers guarding the Customs House. Goaded beyond endurance, the sentries acted against express orders and fired on the crowd, killing four and wounding eight, one mortally. Resistance leaders idealized the dead rioters as martyrs for the cause of liberty, holding a solemn funeral and later commemorating March 5 annually with patriotic orations.

BOSTON MASSACRE

Leading patriots wanted to ensure that the soldiers did not become martyrs as well. Thus, when the soldiers were tried for the killings in November, John Adams and Josiah Quincy Jr., both unwavering patriots, acted as their defense attorneys and won

■ Shortly after the Boston Massacre, Paul Revere printed this illustration of the confrontation near the Customs House on March 5, 1770. Offering visual support for the patriots' version of events, it showed the British soldiers firing on an unresisting crowd (instead of the aggressive mob described at the soldiers' trial) and—even worse—a gun firing from the building itself, which has been labeled "Butcher's Hall." (Photo: Anne S. K. Brown Military Collection, Brown University Library)

acquittal of all but two, who were released after being branded on the thumb. Undoubtedly the favorable outcome of the trials persuaded London officials not to retaliate against the city.

For the next few years, amid a superficial calm, the most outspoken colonial newspapers published

A BRITISH PLOT?

essays drawing on Real Whig ideology and accusing Great Britain of deliberately scheming to oppress the colonies. After the Stamp Act's repeal, the patriots had praised Parliament; following repeal of the Townshend duties, they warned of impending tyranny. Formerly viewed as an isolated mistake, the stamp tax now appeared to be part of a plot against American liberties. Essayists pointed to the stationing of troops in Boston and the growing number of vice-admiralty courts as evidence of plans to "enslave" the colonists.

Still, no one yet advocated complete independence from the mother country. Although the patriots were becoming increasingly convinced that they should seek freedom from parliamentary authority, they continued to acknowledge their British identity and their allegiance to George III. They therefore began to envision a system that would enable them to be ruled by their own elected legislatures while remaining loyal to the king. But any such scheme violated Britons' conception of Parliament's sole undivided sovereignty over the empire.

Then, in the fall of 1772, the North ministry began to implement the Townshend Act that provided for governors and judges to be paid from customs revenues. In early November, voters at a Boston town meeting established a Committee of Correspondence to publicize the decision by exchanging letters with other Massachusetts towns. Heading the committee was the man who had proposed its formation, Samuel Adams.

Fifty-one in 1772, Samuel Adams had been a Boston tax collector, a member and clerk of the

SAMUEL ADAMS AND COMMITTEES OF CORRESPONDENCE

Massachusetts assembly, an ally of the Loyal Nine, and a member of the Sons of Liberty. An experienced political organizer, he continually stressed the need for prudent collective action. His Committee of Correspondence thus undertook the task of creating an informed consensus among all the residents of Massachusetts.

Such committees, which were eventually established throughout the colonies, represented the next logical step in the organization of American resistance. Until 1772, the protest movement was largely confined to the seacoast and primarily to major cities and towns. Adams realized that the time had come to involve more colonists in the struggle. Accordingly, the Boston town meeting directed the Committee of Correspondence "to state the Rights of the Colonists and of this Province in particular," to list "the Infringements and Violations thereof that have been, or from time to time may be made," and to send copies to the other towns throughout the province.

The statement of colonial rights declared that Americans had absolute rights to life, liberty, and property. The idea that "a British house of commons, should have a right, at pleasure, to give and grant the property of the colonists" was "irreconcileable" with "the first principles of natural law and Justice . . . and of the British Constitution in particular." The list of grievances complained of taxation without representation, the presence of unnecessary troops and customs officers on American soil, the use of imperial revenues to pay colonial officials, the expanded jurisdiction of vice-admiralty courts, and even the nature of the instructions given to American governors by their superiors in London. No mention was made of obedience to Parliament. Patriots—at least in Boston—placed American rights first, loyalty to Great Britain a distant second.

In their response, most towns aligned themselves with the city. From Braintree came the assertion that "all civil officers are or ought to be Servants to the people and dependent upon them for their official Support, and every instance to the Contrary from the Governor downwards tends to crush and destroy civil liberty." The town of Holden declared that "the People of New England have never given the People of Britain any Right of Jurisdiction over us." And the citizens of Petersham commented that resistance to tyranny was "the first and highest social Duty of this people." Beliefs like these made the next crisis in Anglo-American affairs the final one.

Tea and Turmoil

he tea tax was the only Townshend duty still in effect by 1773. In the years after 1770, some Americans continued to boycott English tea, while others resumed drinking it. Tea figured prominently in the colonists' social lives, so observing the boycott required them not only to forgo a favorite beverage but also to alter habitual forms of socializing. Tea thus retained an explosively symbolic character even though the boycott began to fall apart after 1770.

In May 1773, Parliament passed an act designed to save the East India Company from bankruptcy.

TEA ACT

The company, which held a monopoly on British trade with the East Indies, was critically important to the British economy. According to the Tea Act, legal tea would henceforth be sold in America only by the East India Company's designated agents, which would enable the company to avoid middlemen in both England and the colonies and to price its product competitively with smuggled tea. The net result would be cheaper tea for American consumers, but tea that still would be taxed under the Townshend law. Resistance leaders interpreted the new measure as a pernicious device to make them admit Parliament's right to tax them. Others saw the Tea Act as the first step in establishing an East India Company monopoly of all colonial trade. Residents of the four cities designated to receive the first shipments of tea prepared to respond to what they perceived as a new threat to their freedom.

In New York City, the tea ships failed to arrive on schedule. In Philadelphia, Pennsylvania's governor persuaded the captain to turn around and sail back to Britain. In Charleston, the tea was unloaded and stored; some was destroyed and the rest sold in 1776 by the new state government. The only confrontation occurred in Boston, where both the town meeting and Governor Thomas Hutchinson rejected compromise.

The first of three tea ships entered Boston harbor on November 28. After a series of mass meetings,

THE BOSTON
TEA PARTY

Bostonians voted to post guards on the wharf to prevent the tea from being unloaded. Hutchinson refused to permit the vessels to leave the harbor.

On December 16, more than five thousand people (nearly a third of the city's population) crowded into Old South Church. The meeting, chaired by Samuel Adams, made a final attempt to persuade Hutchinson to send the tea back to England. But the governor remained adamant. In the early evening, Adams reportedly announced "that he could think of nothing further to be done—that they had now done all they could for the Salvation of their Country." Cries then rang out from the back of the crowd: "Boston harbor a tea-pot tonight! The Mohawks are come!" Within a few minutes, about sixty men of all social ranks crudely disguised as Indians assembled at the wharf, boarded the three ships, and dumped the cargo into the harbor. By 9:00 P.M. their work was done: 342 chests of tea worth approximately £10,000 floated in splinters on the water.

While resistance leaders rejoiced, the North administration reacted with considerably less enthusiasm. In

COERCIVE AND
QUEBEC ACTS

March 1774, Parliament adopted the first of four laws that became known as the Coercive, or Intolerable, Acts. It ordered the port of Boston closed until the tea was paid for, prohibiting all but coastal trade in food and firewood. Passed later in the spring, the Massachusetts Government Act altered the province's charter, substituting an appointed council for the elected one, increasing the governor's powers, and forbidding most town meetings; the Justice Act provided that a person accused of committing murder while suppressing a riot or enforcing the laws could be tried outside the colony where the incident occurred; and the Quartering Act allowed military officers to commandeer privately owned buildings to house their troops. Thus, the Coercive Acts punished not just Boston but all of Massachusetts, alerting other colonies that their residents too could be subject to retaliation if they opposed British authority.

After passing the last of the Coercive Acts, Parliament turned its attention to reforming the government of Quebec. The 1774 Quebec Act granted greater religious freedom to Catholics—alarming Protestant colonists—and reinstated French civil law. Most important, the act annexed to Quebec the area east of the Mississippi River and north of the Ohio River. It thus removed that region from the jurisdiction of seacoast colonies that claimed parts of it—and made the task of wealthy colonists who hoped to develop the Ohio country much more difficult.

Members of Parliament who voted for the punitive legislation believed that the acts would be obeyed. But to patriots, the Coercive Acts and the Quebec Act proved what they had feared since 1768: that Great Britain had embarked on a deliberate plan to oppress them. If the port of Boston could be closed, why not the ports of Philadelphia or New York? If the royal charter of Massachusetts could be changed, why not the charter of South Carolina? If troops could be forcibly quartered in private houses, did not that action pave the way for the occupation of all of America?

The Boston Committee of Correspondence urged all the colonies to join in an immediate boycott of British goods. But the other provinces hesitated. Rhode Island, Virginia, and Pennsylvania each suggested that another intercolonial congress be convened to consider an appropriate response. Few people wanted to take hasty action; even the most ardent patriots remained loyal to Britain and hoped for reconciliation with its leaders. So the colonies agreed to send delegates to Philadelphia in September to attend a Continental Congress.

Summary *Online Study Center* ACE the Test

Just twenty years earlier, at the outbreak of the Seven Years War in the wilderness of western Pennsylvania, no one could have predicted that the future would bring such swift and dramatic change to Britain's mainland colonies. Yet that conflict—which simultaneously removed France from North America and created a huge war debt Britain had to find ways to pay—set in motion the process leading to the convening of the First Continental Congress.

In the years after the war ended in 1763, momentous changes occurred in the ways colonists thought about themselves and their allegiances. Once linked unquestioningly to Great Britain, they began to develop a sense of their own identity as Americans, including a recognition of the cultural and social gulf that separated them from Britons. They started to realize that their concept of the political process differed from that held by people in the mother country. They also came to understand that their economic interests did not necessarily coincide with those of Great Britain. Colonial political leaders reached such conclusions only after a long train of events.

By the late summer of 1774, Americans were committed to resistance but not to independence. Even so, they had started to sever the bonds of empire. During the next decade, they would forge the bonds of a new American nationality to replace those rejected Anglo-American ties.

LEGACY FOR A PEOPLE AND A NATION
The Census and Reapportionment

When in the prerevolutionary years American colonists argued that "they were not represented in" Parliament, they developed a definition of *representation* very different from the understanding traditionally accepted in Great Britain. There, numbers did not matter: the entire British population was seen as being "virtually" represented in Parliament.

Americans, by contrast, placed great emphasis on being represented in government by someone for whom they—or at least their better-off male neighbors—had actually voted. And that carried with it the related desire for election districts that were regularly reapportioned in accordance with the movements and increase of the population. Article 1, Section 2, of the U.S. Constitution thus provides for an "actual enumeration" of the nation's residents every ten years so that "representatives . . . shall be apportioned among the several States . . . according to their respective numbers." Each decade, from 1790 to 2000, the government has tried to count the nation's residents accurately—although, according to historians and demographers, it has often failed to achieve that goal.

The 2000 census, the planning for which Congress debated heatedly, turned out to be the most accurate in recent decades. It also led to two Supreme Court decisions: one outlining appropriate techniques for conducting the mandated "actual enumeration" of the American population, and another rejecting Utah's challenge to the final count. (Utah, which has only one member of the House and hoped to obtain a second, charged that the Census Bureau had improperly awarded a seat to North Carolina.) In other years too, especially

1920, near the close of an era of dramatic demographic change, planning and conducting the census proved extremely contentious. The commonly unacknowledged origin of such contests lies in Americans' prerevolutionary experience.

Thus, every ten years, the nation must still wrestle with an enduring legacy of the colonial period: the need to enumerate the American people and alter the boundaries of electoral districts according to the results.

a REVOLUTION, INDEED 1774–1783

The Shawnee chief Blackfish named his new captive Sheltowee, or Big Turtle, and adopted him as his son. Blackfish's warriors had easily caught the lone hunter, who was returning with a slaughtered buffalo to an encampment of men. The captive then persuaded his fellow frontiersmen to surrender. It was February 1778. The hunter was Daniel Boone, who recently had moved his family from North Carolina to the western region of Virginia known as Kentucky. Some historians have wondered about Boone's allegiance during the American Revolution, for he moved to the frontier just as the war began. His encounter with the Shawnees highlights many ambiguities of revolutionary era loyalties.

The Shawnees were seeking captives to compensate for the death of their chief Cornstalk. Of the twenty-six men taken with Boone, about half were adopted into Shawnee families; the others were dispatched as prisoners to the Shawnees' British allies. Boone, who assured Blackfish that he would later negotiate the surrender of the women and children remaining at his home settlement of Boonesborough, watched and waited. In June 1778 he escaped, hurrying home to warn the Kentuckians of impending attack. When Blackfish's Shawnees and their British allies appeared outside the Boonesborough stockade in mid-September, Boone proved amenable to negotiations. Fragmentary evidence suggests the settlers agreed to swear allegiance to the British in order to avert a bloody battle. But the discussions dissolved into a melee, and the Indians then besieged the fort for a week before withdrawing. With that threat gone, Boone was charged with treason and court-martialed by Kentucky militia. Although he was cleared, questions haunted him for the rest of his life.

Where did Daniel Boone's loyalties lie? Had he betrayed the settlers to the Shawnees and sought to establish British authority in Kentucky? Had he—as he later claimed—deceived the Shawnees? Or had he made the survival of the fragile settlements his highest priority?

Government by Congress and Committee

Contest in the Backcountry

Choosing Sides

LINKS TO THE WORLD
New Nations

War and Independence

The Struggle in the North

Life in the Army and on the Home Front

Victory in the South

Surrender at Yorktown

LEGACY FOR A PEOPLE AND A NATION
Revolutionary Origins

Online Study Center
This icon will direct you to interactive map and primary source activities on the website http://college.hmco.com/pic/nortonbrief7e

CHRONOLOGY

1774 • First Continental Congress meets in Philadelphia, adopts Declaration of Rights and Grievances
  • Continental Association implements economic boycott of Britain; committees of observation established to oversee boycott

1774–75 • Provincial conventions replace collapsing colonial governments

1775 • Battles of Lexington and Concord; first shots of war fired
  • Second Continental Congress begins
  • Washington named commander-in-chief
  • Dunmore's proclamation offers freedom to patriots' slaves who join British forces

1776 • Paine publishes *Common Sense,* advocating independence
  • British evacuate Boston
  • Declaration of Independence adopted
  • New York City falls to British

1777 • British take Philadelphia
  • Burgoyne surrenders at Saratoga

1778 • French alliance brings vital assistance to the United States
  • British evacuate Philadelphia

1779 • Sullivan expedition destroys Iroquois villages

1780 • British take Charleston

1781 • Cornwallis surrenders at Yorktown

1782 • Peace negotiations begin

1783 • Treaty of Paris signed, granting independence to the United States

Daniel Boone was not the only American of uncertain or shifting allegiance in the 1770s. As a civil war, the American Revolution uprooted thousands of families, disrupted the economy, and forced many colonists into permanent exile; it also led Americans to develop new conceptions of politics, and it created a nation from thirteen separate colonies.

The struggle for independence required revolutionary leaders to accomplish three separate but closely related tasks. The first was political and ideological: transforming a consensus favoring loyal resistance into a coalition supporting independence, a task the colonies' leaders pursued using various measures, from persuasion to coercion.

The second involved foreign relations. To win independence, patriot leaders knew they needed international recognition and aid, particularly from France. Thus, they dispatched to Paris the most experienced American diplomat, Benjamin Franklin.

Only the third task directly involved the British. George Washington, commander-in-chief of the American army, soon recognized that his primary goal should be not to win battles but to avoid losing them decisively. The outcome of any one battle was less important than ensuring that his army survived to fight another day. The American war effort was aided by Britain's focus on military victories rather than on the primary goal of retaining the colonies' allegiance. In the end, British mistakes and American endurance, more than military prowess, decided the outcome. ■

Government by Congress and Committee

*W*hen the fifty-five delegates to the First Continental Congress convened in Philadelphia in September 1774, they knew that many Americans would support any measures they adopted. That summer, open meetings held throughout the colonies had endorsed the idea of another nonimportation pact. Committees of correspondence publicized these meetings so effectively that Americans everywhere knew about them. Most of the congressional delegates were selected by extralegal provincial conventions, since governors had forbidden regular assemblies to conduct formal elections. Thus, the very act of designating delegates to attend the Congress involved Americans in open defiance of British authority.

The colonies' leading political figures—most of them lawyers, merchants, and planters—attended the

FIRST CONTINENTAL CONGRESS

Philadelphia Congress, representing every colony but Georgia. The Massachusetts delegation included both Samuel Adams and his younger cousin John, an ambitious lawyer. Among others, New York sent John Jay, a talented young attorney. From Pennsylvania came the conservative Joseph Galloway and his long-time rival, John Dickinson. Virginia elected patriot zealots Richard Henry Lee and Patrick Henry, as well as George Washington.

The congressmen faced three tasks when they convened on September 5, 1774. The first two were explicit: defining American grievances and developing a plan for resistance. The third—articulating their constitutional relationship with Great Britain—proved troublesome. The most radical congressmen, like Lee of Virginia, argued that the colonists owed allegiance only to George III and that Parliament was nothing more than a legislature for Britain, with no authority over the colonies. The conservatives—Joseph Galloway and his allies—proposed a formal plan of union that would have required Parliament and a new American legislature to consent jointly to all laws pertaining to the colonies. The delegates narrowly rejected Galloway's proposal but also refused to embrace the radicals' position.

Finally, they accepted a compromise position worked out by John Adams. The crucial clauses in the Congress's Declaration of Rights and Grievances declared that Americans would obey Parliament, but only because that action was in everyone's best interest, and asserted that colonists would resist all taxes in disguise, like the Townshend duties. Remarkably, such a position—which only a few years before would have been regarded as extreme—represented a compromise in the fall of 1774.

With the constitutional issue resolved, the delegates readily agreed on the laws they wanted repealed

CONTINENTAL ASSOCIATION

(notably the Coercive Acts) and decided to implement an economic boycott while petitioning the king for relief. They adopted the Continental Association, which called for nonimportation of British goods (effective December 1, 1774), nonconsumption of British products (effective March 1, 1775), and nonexportation of American goods to Britain and the British West Indies (effective September 10, 1775).

The provisions of the Association were carefully designed to appeal to different groups and regions. For example, the delay of the nonconsumption agreement until three months after nonimportation took effect would allow northern urban merchants to sell items they already had. And the postponement of nonexportation for nearly a year gave small farmers in Virginia time to dry and cure their tobacco crop and northern exporters of wood products and foodstuffs to the Caribbean a final season of sales before the embargo began.

To enforce the Continental Association, Congress recommended the election of local committees

COMMITTEES OF OBSERVATION

of observation and inspection. By specifying that committee members be chosen by all men qualified to vote for members of the lower house of the colonial legislatures, Congress guaranteed the committees a broad popular base. The seven to eight thousand committeemen became the local leaders of American resistance.

Though officially charged only with overseeing implementation of the boycott, the committees soon became de facto governments. They examined merchants' records and published the names of those who continued to import British goods. They promoted home manufactures, encouraging Americans to adopt simple modes of dress and behavior to symbolize their commitment to liberty and virtuous conduct. Since expensive leisure-time activities were believed to reflect vice and corruption, Congress urged Americans to forgo dancing, gambling, horseracing, cockfighting, and other forms of "extravagance and dissipation." Thus, private activities acquired public significance.

The committees gradually extended their authority over many aspects of American life. They attempted to identify opponents of American resistance, developing elaborate spy networks and investigating reports of questionable remarks and activities. Suspected dissenters were urged to support the colonial cause; if they refused, the committees had them watched, restricted their movements, or tried to force them to leave the area. People engaging in casual political exchanges with friends one day could find themselves charged with "treasonable conversation" the next.

While the committees of observation were expanding their power during the winter and early spring of 1775, the regular colonial governments were collapsing. Only a few legislatures continued to meet without encountering patriot challenges to their authority. In most colonies, popularly elected provincial conventions took over the task of running the government. In late 1774 and early 1775, these conventions approved the Continental Association, elected delegates to the Second Continental Congress (scheduled for May), organized militia units, and gathered arms and ammunition.

PROVINCIAL CONVENTIONS

Unable to stem the tide of resistance, the British-appointed governors and councils watched helplessly as their authority crumbled. Courts were prevented from holding sessions, taxes were paid to the conventions' agents rather than to provincial tax collectors, sheriffs' powers were challenged, and militiamen would muster only when committees ordered. In short, during the six months preceding the battles at Lexington and Concord, independence was being won at the local level. Not many Americans fully realized what was happening. The vast majority still proclaimed their loyalty to Great Britain, denying that they sought to leave the empire.

Contest in the Backcountry

*A*fter the mid-1760s, land-hungry folk, ignoring the Proclamation of 1763, pronouncements by colonial governors, and the threat of Indian attacks, swarmed onto lands along the Ohio River and its tributaries. Sometimes they purchased property from opportunistic speculators; often they simply squatted on land in hopes that their titles would eventually be honored. By late 1775, thousands of new homesteads dotted the backcountry from western Pennsylvania south through Virginia and eastern Kentucky into western North Carolina.

Few of the backcountry folk saw the region's native peoples in a positive light. The frontier dwellers had little interest in the small-scale trade that had once helped to sustain an uneasy peace in the region; they only wanted land on which to grow crops and pasture their livestock. They interpreted Pontiac's uprising as a sign that no Indian—regardless of religion or tribal affiliation—could be trusted. That widely held opinion was first publicly exhibited in December 1763 when a group of fifty Scots-Irish men from Paxton Township, Pennsylvania, massacred twenty peaceful Christian Conestoga Indians.

DISTRUST AND WARFARE

In 1774, Virginia, headed by a new governor, Lord Dunmore, moved vigorously to assert its title to the rapidly developing backcountry. During the spring and early summer, tensions mounted as Virginians surveyed land in Kentucky in territory still claimed by the Shawnees. "Lord Dunmore's war" consisted of one large-scale confrontation between Virginia militia and some Shawnee warriors. Neither side won a clear-cut victory, but in the immediate aftermath, thousands of settlers—including Daniel Boone and his associates—flooded across the mountains.

When the Revolutionary War began just as large numbers of people were migrating into Kentucky, the loyalties of all Indians and settlers in the backcountry remained, like Boone's, fluid and uncertain. They were more or less at war with each other, and which side each would take in the imperial struggle might well depend on which could better serve their interests. Understanding that, the Continental Congress moved to establish garrisons in the Ohio country. Relying on such protection, as many as twenty thousand settlers poured into Kentucky by 1780. Yet frontier affiliations were not clear: the growing town of Pittsburgh, for example, harbored many active loyalists.

The native peoples' grievances against the European American newcomers predisposed many toward an alliance with Great Britain. Yet some chiefs urged caution: after all, the failure to enforce the Proclamation of 1763 suggested that Britain lacked the will and ability to protect them in the future. Furthermore, British officials

INDIANS' CHOICES

hesitated to make use of their potential native allies, realizing that neither the Indians' style of fighting nor their war aims necessarily coincided with British goals and methods. Accordingly, they at first sought from Indians only a promise of neutrality.

Recognizing that their standing with native peoples was poor, the patriots also sought the Indians' neutrality. In 1775, the Second Continental Congress sent a general message to Indian communities describing the war as "a family quarrel between us and Old England" and requesting that they "not join on either side." A group of Cherokees led by Chief Dragging Canoe nevertheless decided to take advantage of the "family quarrel" to regain some land. They attacked settlements along the western borders of the Carolinas and Virginia in the summer of 1776. But a militia campaign destroyed many Cherokee towns. Dragging Canoe and his diehard followers fled to the west; the rest of the Cherokees agreed to a treaty that ceded still more of their land.

Bands of Shawnees and Cherokees continued to attack frontier settlements in the backcountry throughout the war, but dissent in their own ranks crippled their efforts. The British victory over France had destroyed the Indian nations' most effective means of maintaining their independence: playing European powers off against one another. Successful strategies were difficult to envision under these new circumstances, and Indian communities split asunder as older and younger men, or civil and war leaders, disagreed vehemently over what policy to adopt. Only a few communities unwaveringly supported the American revolt; most other native villages either tried to remain neutral or hesitantly aligned with the British. And the settlers fought back: in 1778 and early 1779, a frontier militia force under George Rogers Clark captured British posts in modern Illinois (Kaskaskia) and Indiana (Vincennes), but the Anglo-Americans could never take the redcoats' major stronghold at Detroit.

INDIANS DURING THE REVOLUTION

Warfare between settlers and Indian bands persisted in the backcountry long after fighting between the patriots and redcoats had ceased. Indeed, the Revolutionary War itself constituted a brief chapter in the ongoing struggle for control of the region west of the Appalachians that began in 1763 and continued into the next century.

Choosing Sides

In 1765, protests against the Stamp Act had won the support of most colonists in the Caribbean and Nova Scotia as well as in the future United States. Demonstrations occurred in Halifax and Britain's Caribbean possessions as well as in Boston, New York, and Charleston. When the act went into effect, though, islanders loyally paid the stamp duties until repeal. And eventually a significant number of colonists in North America and the West Indies began to question both the aims and the tactics of the resistance movement. Doubts arose with particular urgency in Nova Scotia and the Caribbean.

Both the northern mainland and southern island colonies depended heavily on Great Britain militarily and economically. Despite the overwhelming British victory in the Seven Years War, they believed themselves vulnerable to French counterattack and were eager to have regular troops and naval vessels stationed within their borders. Additionally, sugar planters—on some islands outnumbered by their bondspeople twenty-five to one—feared the potential for slave revolts in the absence of British troops.

NOVA SCOTIA AND THE CARIBBEAN

Economically, Nova Scotians and West Indians had major reasons for choosing to support the mother country. In the mid-1770s, the northerners began to reduce New England's domination of the Caribbean and northern coastal trade, and once the shooting started, they benefited greatly from Britain's retaliatory measures against the rebels' commerce. British sugar producers relied for their profits primarily on their monopoly of trade within the empire, for more efficient French planters were able to sell their sugar for one-third less. Neither islanders nor Nova Scotians had reason to believe that they would be better off independent.

In the thirteen colonies, active revolutionaries accounted for about two-fifths of the European American population. Among them were yeoman farmers, members of dominant Protestant sects, Chesapeake gentry, merchants dealing mainly in American commodities, city artisans, elected officeholders, and people of English descent. Wives usually, but not always, adopted their husbands' political beliefs. Although all these patriots supported the

PATRIOTS

Revolution, they pursued divergent goals within the broader coalition, as they had in the 1760s. Some sought limited political reform, others extensive political change, and still others social and economic reforms.

Some colonists, though, found that they could not in good conscience endorse independence. Most objected to parliamentary policies, but they preferred the remedy of imperial constitutional reform. Their objections to violent protest, their desire to uphold legally constituted government, and their fears of anarchy combined to make them sensitive to the dangers of resistance.

About one-fifth of the European American population remained loyal to Great Britain, firmly rejecting independence. Most loyalists had *LOYALISTS* long opposed the men who became patriot leaders, though for varying reasons. British-appointed government officials; Anglican clergy everywhere and lay Anglicans in the North, where they were in the minority; tenant farmers, particularly those with patriot landlords; members of persecuted religious sects; many veterans of backcountry southern rebellion against eastern rule; and non-English ethnic minorities, especially Scots: past experience led all these groups to fear the power wielded by those who controlled the colonial assemblies. Joined by merchants whose trade depended on imperial connections and by former British soldiers who had settled in America after 1763, they formed a loyalist core. As the British army evacuated American posts during and after the war, many loyalists followed and scattered to different parts of the British Empire—Britain, the Bahamas, and especially Canada. All told, perhaps as many as 100,000 Americans preferred exile to life in a nation independent of British rule.

Between the patriots and the loyalists, perhaps two-fifths of European Americans tried to avoid taking sides. Some were sincere *NEUTRALS* pacifists, such as Quakers. Others opportunistically shifted their allegiance to whatever side happened to be winning currently. Still others simply wanted to be left alone. The last group included large numbers in the southern backcountry (including Boone's Kentucky), where Scots-Irish settlers had little love for either the patriot gentry or the English authorities.

To patriots, apathy or neutrality was as heinous as loyalism. By the winter of 1775–1776, the Second Continental Congress was recommending that all "disaffected" persons be disarmed and arrested. State legislatures passed laws severely penalizing suspected loyalists or neutrals. Many began to require all voters (or, in some cases, all free adult men) to take oaths of allegiance; the penalty for refusal was usually banishment to England or extra taxes. After 1777, many states confiscated the property of banished persons, using the proceeds for the war effort.

Online Study Center **Improve Your Grade**
Primary Source:
  Pennsylvania Radicals Attack Loyalism

The patriots' policies helped ensure that their scattered and persecuted opponents could not band together to threaten the revolution-*SLAVERY AND* ary cause. But loyalists and neutrals *REVOLUTIONARY* were not the patriots' only worry, *FERVOR* for revolutionaries could not assume that their slaves would support them.

In New England, with few resident bondspeople, revolutionary fervor was widespread, and free African Americans enlisted in local patriot militias. The middle colonies and Virginia and Maryland were more divided but still largely revolutionary. In contrast, South Carolina and Georgia, where slaves composed more than half the population, were noticeably less enthusiastic about resistance. Georgia sent no delegates to the First Continental Congress and reminded its representatives at the second one to consider its circumstances, "with our blacks and tories [loyalists] within us," when voting on the question of independence. On the mainland as well as in the Caribbean islands, colonists feared the potential enemy in their midst.

Bondspeople faced a dilemma. Their goal was *personal* independence. But how best could they escape from slavery? Should they fight with *SLAVES'* or against their masters? African *DILEMMA* Americans made different decisions, but to most slaves, supporting the British appeared the more promising choice. In late 1774 and early 1775, groups of slaves began to offer to assist the British army in return for freedom. Some bondspeople futilely petitioned General Thomas Gage, who commanded British forces in Boston, promising to fight for the redcoats if he would liberate them. The most serious incident occurred in

New Nations

In northern North America before the Revolution, only Nova Scotia had a sizable number of English-speaking settlers. During and after the Revolution, however, many loyalist families, especially those from the northern and middle colonies, moved to the region that is now Canada, which remained under British rule. The provinces of New Brunswick and Upper Canada (later Ontario) were established to accommodate them, and some exiles settled in Quebec as well, laying the foundation of the modern bilingual (but majority English-speaking) Canadian nation.

Sierra Leone too was founded by colonial exiles: African Americans who had fled to the British army during the war, many of whom ended up in London. Seeing the refugees' poverty, a group of charitable merchants—calling themselves the Committee to Aid the Black Poor—developed a plan to resettle the African Americans elsewhere. The refugees concurred in a scheme to return them to the land of their ancestors. In early 1787, vessels carrying about four hundred settlers reached Sierra Leone in West Africa. In 1792, they were joined by several thousand other loyalist African Americans who had originally moved to Nova Scotia. The influx ensured the colony's survival; it remained part of the British Empire until achieving its independence in 1961.

While the Sierra Leone migrants were preparing to sail from London in late 1786, the first prison ships were simultaneously being readied for Australia. Unable to use the United States as a dumping ground for convicts, as it had the colonies throughout the eighteenth century, the British needed another destination for convicts sentenced to transportation for crimes such as theft, assault, and manslaughter. It decided to send them halfway around the world, to the continent Captain James Cook had explored and claimed in 1770. Long before 1868, when Britain stopped sending convicts to Australia, voluntary migrants had begun to arrive. The modern nation was created on January 1, 1901.

Thus, the founding event in the history of the United States links the nation to the formation of its northern neighbor and to new nations in West Africa and the Asian Pacific.

An early view of the settlement of black loyalists in West Africa, the foundation of the modern nation of Sierra Leone. (Manuscripts, Archives and Rare Books Division, Schomburg Center for Research in Black Culture, The New York Public Library, Astor, Lenox and Tilden Foundations.)

Thomas Rowlandson, an English artist, sketched the boatloads of male and female convicts as they were being ferried to the ships that would take them to their new lives in the prison colony of Australia. Note the gibbet on the shore with two hanging bodies—symbolizing the fate these people were escaping. (By permission of the National Library of Australia)

1775 in Charleston, where Thomas Jeremiah, a free black harbor pilot, was brutally executed after being convicted of attempting to foment a slave revolt.

The slaveowners' worst fears were realized in November 1775, when Virginia's royal governor, Lord Dunmore, offered to free any slaves and indentured servants who would leave their patriot masters to join the British forces. In addition to obtaining added manpower, Dunmore hoped to disrupt the economy by depriving planters of their labor force. But only about one thousand African Americans rallied to the British standard. Even so, Dunmore's proclamation led Congress in January 1776 to modify a policy that had prohibited the enlistment of African Americans in the regular American army.

The patriots sometimes turned rumors of slave uprisings to their own advantage. In South Carolina, resistance leaders argued that unity under the Continental Association would protect masters from their slaves at a time when royal government was unable to muster adequate defense forces. The strategy drew many fearful whites into the patriot camp.

Patriots could never completely ignore the threats posed by loyalists, neutrals, slaves, and Indians, but fear of these groups rarely hampered the revolutionary movement. In general, the practical impossibility of a large-scale slave revolt, the dissension in Indian communities, and the patriots' successful campaign to disarm and neutralize loyalists ensured that the revolutionaries would by and large remain firmly in control of the countryside.

War and Independence

*O*n January 27, 1775, Lord Dartmouth, secretary of state for America, addressed a fateful letter to General Thomas Gage in Boston, urging him to take a decisive step. Opposition could not be "very formidable," Dartmouth wrote, and it would be better to bring on conflict now than "in a riper state of Rebellion."

After Gage received Dartmouth's letter on April 14, he sent an expedition to confiscate colonial military

Battles of Lexington and Concord

supplies stockpiled at Concord, some 20 miles away. Bostonians dispatched two messengers, William Dawes and Paul Revere (later joined by Dr. Samuel Prescott), to rouse

the countryside. So when the British vanguard of several hundred men approached Lexington at dawn on April 19, they found a ragtag group of seventy militiamen. The Americans' commander ordered his men to withdraw, realizing they could not halt the redcoats. But as they began to disperse, a shot rang out; the British soldiers then fired several volleys. When they stopped, eight Americans lay dead. The British moved on to Concord, 5 miles away.

There the contingents of militia were larger. An exchange of gunfire at the North Bridge left three redcoats dead. Thousands of militiamen then fired from houses and from behind trees and bushes as the British retreated to Boston. By the end of the day, the redcoats had suffered 272 casualties, including 70 deaths. The patriots suffered just 93 casualties.

By the evening of April 20, perhaps twenty thousand American militiamen had gathered around Boston. Many, needed at home for

First Year of War

spring planting, did not stay long, but those who remained dug in along siege lines encircling the city. For nearly a year, the two armies sat and stared at each other. The redcoats attacked their besiegers only once, on June 17, when they advanced against trenches atop Breed's Hill in Charlestown. In that misnamed Battle of Bunker Hill, the British incurred their greatest losses of the entire war: over 800 wounded and 228 killed. The Americans, though forced to abandon their position, lost less than half that number.

During the same eleven-month period, patriots captured Fort Ticonderoga, a British fort on Lake Champlain, acquiring much-needed cannon. Trying to bring Canada into the war on the American side, they also mounted a northern campaign that ended in disaster, with their troops ravaged by smallpox, at Quebec in early 1776. Most significant, the lull in the fighting at Boston gave both sides a chance to regroup, organize, and plan their strategies.

Online Study Center Improve Your Grade
Interactive Map:
  The First Battles in the War for Independence, 1775

Lord North and his new American secretary, Lord George Germain, made three central assumptions

British Strategy

about the war they faced. First, they concluded that patriot forces could not withstand the assaults of trained

British regulars. Accordingly, they dispatched to America the largest force Great Britain had ever assembled anywhere: 32,000 troops, accompanied by tons of supplies and supporting naval vessels and sailors. Such an extraordinary effort, they thought, would ensure a quick victory. In a common eighteenth-century practice, included among the troops were mercenaries from the German state of Hesse.

Second, British officials and army officers treated this war as comparable to wars in Europe. They adopted a conventional strategy of capturing major American cities and defeating the rebel army decisively without suffering serious casualties themselves. Third, they assumed that a clear-cut military victory would automatically restore the colonies' allegiance.

All these assumptions proved false. North and Germain vastly underestimated Americans' commitment to armed resistance. Battlefield defeats did not lead patriots to sue for peace. London officials also failed to recognize the significance of the American population's dispersal over an area 1,500 miles long. Although Britain would control each of the largest American ports at some time during the war, less than 5 percent of the population lived in those cities. Furthermore, the coast offered so many excellent harbors that essential commerce was easily rerouted.

Most of all, British officials did not at first understand that military triumph would not necessarily lead to political victory. Securing the colonies permanently would require hundreds of thousands of Americans to return to their original allegiance. After 1778, the ministry adopted a strategy designed to achieve that goal through the expanded use of loyalist forces and the restoration of civilian authority in occupied areas. But the new policy came too late. Britain's leaders never fully realized that they were fighting an entirely new kind of conflict: the first modern war of national liberation.

Great Britain at least had a bureaucracy ready to supervise the war effort. The Americans had only the

SECOND CONTINENTAL CONGRESS

Second Continental Congress, originally intended simply to consider the ministry's response to the Continental Association. Instead, the delegates who convened in Philadelphia on May 10, 1775, had to assume the mantle of intercolonial government. As the summer passed, Congress authorized the printing of money, established a committee to supervise relations

with foreign countries, and took steps to strengthen the militia. Most important, it created the Continental Army and appointed its generals.

Until Congress met, the Massachusetts provincial congress had taken responsibility for organizing the militiamen encamped at Boston. However, the cost of maintaining that army was a burden, so Massachusetts asked the Continental Congress to assume the task of directing it. As a first step, Congress had to choose a commander-in-chief, and many delegates recognized the importance of naming someone who was not a New Englander. John Adams proposed the appointment of a Virginian whose military experience and excellent character "would command the Approbation of all America": George Washington. The Congress unanimously concurred.

Washington was no fiery radical and had not played a prominent role in the prerevolutionary

WASHINGTON AS LEADER

agitation. Devoted to the American cause, he was dignified, conservative, and respectable—a man of unimpeachable integrity. Though unmistakably an aristocrat, he was unswervingly committed to representative government. His stamina was remarkable, and he both looked and acted like a leader.

Washington needed all the coolness and caution he could muster when he took command of the army

BRITISH EVACUATION OF BOSTON

outside Boston in July 1775. It took him months, but he imposed hierarchy and discipline on the unruly troops and brought order to the supply system. In March 1776, the arrival of cannon from Ticonderoga finally enabled him to put direct pressure on the redcoats in the city. Sir William Howe, who had replaced Gage, wanted to transfer his troops to New York City anyway, and the patriots' new cannon decided the matter. On March 17, the British and more than a thousand of their loyalist allies abandoned Boston forever.

That spring of 1776, as the British fleet left Boston for the temporary haven of Halifax, the colonies were moving inexorably toward a declaration of independence. Even months after fighting began, American leaders had still denied seeking a break with Great Britain until a pamphlet published in January 1776 advocated such a step.

Thomas Paine's *Common Sense* exploded on the American scene, quickly selling tens of thousands of

■ George Washington at Princeton, 1779, by Charles Willson Peale. Two years after the battle, Peale created this heroic image of the Continental Army's commander, intended (as were all his portraits of revolutionary leaders) to instill patriotic sentiments and pride in its viewers. (Courtesy of the Pennsylvania Academy of the Fine Arts, Philadelphia. Gift of Maria McKean Allen and Phoebe Warren Downes through the bequest of their mother, Elizabeth Wharton McKean)

that only a balance of monarchy, aristocracy, and democracy could preserve freedom, he advocated establishing a republic, a government by the people with no king or nobility. Instead of acknowledging the benefits of links to the mother country, Paine insisted that Britain had exploited the colonies unmercifully. And for the frequently heard assertion that an independent America would be weak and divided, he substituted an unlimited confidence in America's strength once freed from European control.

It is unclear how many people were converted to the cause of independence by reading *Common Sense*. But by late spring, independence had become inevitable. On May 10, the Second Continental Congress formally recommended that individual colonies form new governments, replacing their colonial charters with state constitutions.

Then on June 7, Richard Henry Lee of Virginia, seconded by John Adams of Massachusetts, introduced the crucial resolution: "that these United Colonies are, and of right ought to be, free and independent States, . . . absolved of all allegiance to the British Crown." Congress debated Lee's resolution but postponed a vote on adopting it until early July and appointed a five-man committee—including Thomas Jefferson, John Adams, and Benjamin Franklin—to draft a declaration of independence. The committee assigned primary responsibility for writing the declaration to Jefferson, who was well known for his eloquent style.

The thirty-four-year-old Thomas Jefferson, a Virginia lawyer and member of the House of Burgesses, had read widely in history and political theory. That broad knowledge was evident in both the declaration and his draft of the Virginia state constitution, completed a few days before his appointment to the committee.

JEFFERSON AND THE DECLARATION OF INDEPENDENCE

The draft of the declaration was laid before Congress on June 28, 1776. The delegates officially voted for independence four days later, then debated the wording of the declaration for two more days, adopting it with some changes on July 4. Since Americans had long ago ceased to see themselves as legitimate subjects of Parliament, the Declaration of Independence concentrated on George III (see the appendix). The document accused the king of attempting to destroy representative government in the colonies and

COMMON SENSE copies. The author, a radical English printer who had lived in America only since 1774, called stridently for independence. Paine also challenged many common American assumptions. Rejecting the notion of oppressing Americans through the unjustified use of excessive force.

The declaration's chief long-term importance, however, did not lie in its lengthy catalogue of grievances against George III. It lay in the ringing statements of principle that have served ever since as the ideal to which Americans aspire: "We hold these truths to be self-evident: That all men are created equal; that they are endowed by their Creator with certain unalienable rights; that among these are life, liberty and the pursuit of happiness; that, to secure these rights, governments are instituted among men, deriving their just powers from the consent of the governed." These phrases have echoed down through American history like no others.

When the delegates in Philadelphia adopted the declaration, they were committing treason. Therefore, when they concluded the declaration with the assertion that they "mutually pledge[d] to each other our lives, our fortunes, and our sacred honor," they spoke no less than the truth. The real struggle still lay ahead.

The Struggle in the North

*O*n July 2, the day Congress voted for independence, redcoats landed on Staten Island, having returned south from Halifax (see Map 6.1). Washington marched his army of seventeen thousand from Boston to defend Manhattan. Because Sir William Howe waited until more troops arrived from England before attacking, the American army was able to prepare defenses.

But Washington and his men, still inexperienced in fighting and maneuvering, made major mistakes,

NEW YORK AND NEW JERSEY

losing battles at Brooklyn Heights and on Manhattan Island. The city fell to the British, who captured nearly three thousand American soldiers. Washington then slowly retreated across New Jersey, and British forces took control behind him. Occupying troops met little opposition; the revolutionary cause appeared to be in disarray. "These are the times that try men's souls," wrote Thomas Paine in his pamphlet *The Crisis*.

The British forfeited their advantage, however, as redcoats stationed in New Jersey went on a rampage of rape and plunder. Washington determined to strike

Map 6.1   The War in the North, 1775–1777

The early phase of the Revolutionary War was dominated by British troop movements in the Boston area, the redcoats' evacuation to Nova Scotia in the spring of 1776, and the subsequent British invasion of New York and New Jersey.

back. Moving quickly under cover of a nasty winter storm, he crossed the ice-choked Delaware River at night to attack a Hessian encampment at Trenton early on the morning of December 26. The patriots captured more than nine hundred Hessians and killed thirty; only three Americans were wounded. A few days later, Washington attacked again at Princeton. Having gained command of the field and buoyed American spirits, he set up winter quarters at Morristown, New Jersey.

British strategy for 1777, sketched in London over the winter, aimed to cut New England off from

CAMPAIGN OF 1777

the other colonies. General John Burgoyne, a subordinate of Howe and one of the planners, would lead an invading force of redcoats and Indians down the Hudson River from Canada to rendezvous near Albany with a similar force that would move east along the Mohawk River valley. The combined forces would then presumably link up with Howe's troops in New York City. But in New York, Howe simultaneously prepared his own plan to capture Philadelphia. Consequently, in 1777, the British armies in America would operate independently. The result would be disaster.

Howe took Philadelphia, but inexplicably he spent six weeks transporting his troops by sea instead of marching them overland and ended up only 40 miles closer to his goal than when he started. By the time he advanced on the city, Washington had had time to prepare its defenses. Twice, at Brandywine Creek and again at Germantown, the two armies clashed near the patriot capital. Although the British won both engagements, the Americans handled themselves well. The redcoats took Philadelphia in late September, but to little effect. The campaign season was nearly over, and far to the north Burgoyne was going down to defeat.

Burgoyne and his men had set out from Montreal in mid-June, traveling first by boat on Lake Champlain, then later marching slowly overland toward the Hudson, forced as they went to clear giant trees felled across their path by patriot militiamen. An easy triumph at Fort Ticonderoga in July was followed in August by two setbacks—the redcoats and Indians marching east along the Mohawk River turned back after a battle at Oriskany, New York; and in a clash near Bennington, Vermont, American militiamen nearly wiped out eight hundred of Burgoyne's German mercenaries. Then, after several skirmishes with an American army commanded by General Horatio Gates, Burgoyne was surrounded near Saratoga, New York. On October 17, 1777, he surrendered his entire force of more than six thousand men.

The August 1777 battle at Oriskany divided the Iroquois Confederacy. The Six Nations had formally pledged to remain neutral in the war.

IROQUOIS CONFEDERACY SPLINTERS

But two influential Mohawk leaders, the siblings Mary and Joseph Brant, believed that the Iroquois should ally with the British to protect their territory from land-hungry colonists. The Brants won over to the British the Senecas, Cayugas, and Mohawks. But the Oneidas preferred the American side and brought the Tuscaroras with them. The Onondagas split into three factions, one on each side and one supporting neutrality. The wartime division shattered the Iroquois' three-hundred-year league of friendship.

Disunion and the confederacy's abandonment of neutrality had significant consequences. In 1778 Iroquois warriors allied with the British raided frontier villages in Pennsylvania and New York. To retaliate, an American expedition under General John Sullivan burned Iroquois crops, orchards, and settlements. The resulting devastation led many bands to seek food and shelter north of the Great Lakes. A large number of Iroquois settled permanently in Canada. Burgoyne's surrender at Saratoga brought joy to patriots, discouragement to loyalists and Britons. It also prompted Lord North to authorize a peace commission to offer the Americans what they had requested in 1774—in effect, a return to the imperial system of 1763. That proposal came far too late: the patriots rejected the overture.

Most important, the American victory at Saratoga drew France formally into the conflict. Ever since 1763, the French had sought to avenge their defeat in the Seven Years War, and the American Revolution gave them that opportunity. Even before Benjamin Franklin arrived in Paris in late 1776, France covertly supplied the revolutionaries with military necessities.

Franklin worked tirelessly to strengthen ties between the two nations. Adopting a plain style of dress

FRANCO-AMERICAN ALLIANCE OF 1778

and presenting himself as a representative of American simplicity, he played on the French image of Americans as virtuous farmers.

His efforts culminated in 1778 when the countries signed two treaties. In the Treaty of Amity and Commerce, France recognized American independence, establishing trade ties with the new nation. In the Treaty of Alliance, France and the United States promised—assuming that France would declare war on Britain, which it soon did—that neither would negotiate peace without consulting the other. France also formally abandoned any claim to Canada and to North American territory east of the Mississippi River.

The French alliance had two major benefits for the patriot cause. First, France began to aid the Americans openly, sending troops and naval vessels in addition to arms, ammunition, clothing, and blankets. Second, Britain could no longer focus solely on the American mainland, for it had to fight France in the Caribbean and elsewhere. Spain's entry into the war in 1779 as an ally of France (but not of the United States) further magnified Britain's problems, for the Revolution then became a global war.

Life in the Army and on the Home Front

*O*nly in the first months of the war was the revolutionaries' army manned primarily by the semi-mythical "citizen soldier" militiaman. After a few months or at most a year, the early arrivals went home. They reenlisted, if at all, only briefly and only if the contending armies came close to their farms and towns.

After 1776 the ranks of the Continental Army—those who enlisted for long periods or for the war's duration—were filled primarily by young, single, or propertyless men who signed up to earn monetary bonuses or allotments of land after the war. As the fighting dragged on, those bonuses and land grants grew larger. To meet their quotas of enlistees, towns and states eagerly signed up everyone they could, including slaves and indentured servants (who were promised freedom after the war) and recent immigrants.

DIVERSITY IN THE RANKS

Recruiters in northern states turned increasingly to African Americans, both slave and free. Southern states initially resisted the trend, but later all but Georgia and South Carolina also enlisted black soldiers. Approximately five thousand African Americans eventually served in the Continental Army, most winning their freedom as a result. They commonly served in racially integrated units but were assigned tasks that others shunned, such as cooking and driving wagons.

Also attached to the American forces were a number of women, the wives and widows of poor soldiers, who came to the army with their menfolk because they were too impoverished to survive alone. Such camp followers—estimated overall to be about 3 percent of the number of troops—worked as cooks, nurses, and launderers in return for rations and low wages.

The officers of the Continental Army developed an intense sense of pride and commitment to the revolutionary cause that helped to forge an esprit de corps that outlasted the war. The realities of warfare were often dirty, messy, and corrupt, but the officers drew strength from a developing image of themselves as professionals who sacrificed personal gain for the good of the entire nation.

OFFICER CORPS

■ Barzillai Lew, a free African American born in Groton, Massachusetts, in 1743, served in the Seven Years War before enlisting with patriot troops in the American Revolution. An accomplished fifer, Lew fought at the Battle of Bunker Hill. Like other freemen in the North, he cast his lot with the revolutionaries, in contrast to southern bondspeople, who tended to favor the British.   (Courtesy of Mae Theresa Bonitto)

The officers' wives too prided themselves on their and their husbands' service to the nation. Unlike poor women, they did not travel with the army but instead came for extended visits while the troops were in camp. They brought with them food, clothing, and household furnishings to make their stay more comfortable, and they entertained each other and their menfolk at teas, dinners, and dances. Socializing and discussing current events created friendships later renewed in civilian life when some of their husbands became the new nation's leaders.

Life in the American army was difficult for everyone, although ordinary soldiers endured more hardships than their officers. Wages, even when paid, were small. Rations (a daily standard allotment of bread, meat, vegetables, milk, and beer) did not always appear, and men had to forage for their food. Clothing and shoes the army supplied were often of poor quality; soldiers had to make do or find their own. When conditions deteriorated, troops threatened mutiny (though only a few carried out that threat) or, more often, simply deserted.

HARDSHIP AND DISEASE

Endemic disease in the camps—especially dysentery, various fevers, and, early in the war, smallpox—made matters worse. Unlike British soldiers, most native-born colonists had not been exposed to smallpox, so soldiers and civilians were vulnerable when smallpox spread through the northern countryside after the early months of 1774.

Washington recognized that smallpox could potentially decimate the revolutionaries' ranks, especially after it helped cause the failure of the 1775 Quebec expedition. Thus, in Morristown in early 1777, he ordered that the entire regular army and all new recruits be inoculated, although some would die from the risky procedure and survivors would be incapacitated for weeks. Washington's dramatic measures helped protect Continental soldiers later in the war, contributing significantly to the eventual American victory.

Men who enlisted in the army or served in Congress were away from home for long periods of time. In their absence, their womenfolk, who previously had handled only the "indoor affairs" of the household, shouldered the responsibility for "outdoor affairs" as well. John and Abigail Adams took great pride in Abigail's developing skills as a "farmeress." Like other female contemporaries, Abigail Adams stopped calling the farm "yours" in letters to her husband and began referring to it as "ours." Most women did not work in the fields themselves, but they supervised field workers and managed their families' resources.

HOME FRONT

Wartime disruptions affected all Americans. Even far from the battlefields, people suffered from shortages of necessities like salt, soap, and flour. Small luxuries like new clothing or even ribbons or gloves were essentially unavailable. Severe inflation added to the country's woes. For those who lived near the armies' camps or lines of march, difficulties were compounded. Soldiers of both sides plundered farms and houses, looking for food or salable items—and they carried disease with them wherever they went.

Victory in the South

In the aftermath of the Saratoga disaster, Lord George Germain and British military officials reassessed their strategy. Loyalist exiles in London persuaded them to shift the field of battle southward, contending that loyal southerners would welcome the redcoat army as liberators.

Sir Henry Clinton, Howe's replacement, oversaw the regrouping of British forces in America. In 1778 he sent a convoy that successfully captured the French Caribbean island of St. Lucia, which thereafter served as a key base for Britain. In late 1779, Clinton sailed down the coast from New York to besiege Charleston (formerly Charles Town), the most important city in the South (see Map 6.2). The Americans held out for months, but on May 12, 1780, General Benjamin Lincoln surrendered the entire southern army. The redcoats then spread throughout South Carolina, organizing loyalist regiments.

SOUTH CAROLINA AND THE CARIBBEAN

Yet the triumph was less complete than it appeared. The success of the southern campaign depended on control of the seas, so that the widely dispersed British armies could coordinate their efforts. For the moment, the Royal Navy safely dominated the American coastline, but French naval power posed a threat to the entire southern enterprise. American privateers infested Caribbean waters, seizing valuable cargoes bound to and from the British West Indies. And after late 1778, France picked off British islands one by one.

Then, too, the redcoats never managed to establish full control of the areas they seized in South Carolina. Patriot bands operated freely, and loyalists could not be protected. In fact, the fall of Charleston spurred the patriots to greater exertions. The outcome was vicious guerrilla warfare.

Nevertheless, the war in South Carolina went badly for the patriots throughout most of 1780. At

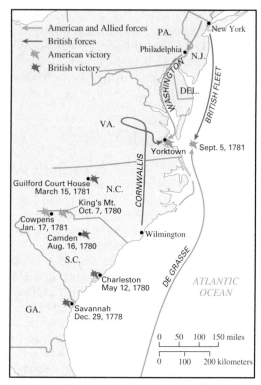

Map 6.2   The War in the South

The southern war—after the British invasion of Georgia in late 1778—was characterized by a series of British thrusts into the interior, leading to battles with American defenders in both North and South Carolina. Finally, after promising beginnings, Cornwallis's foray into Virginia ended with disaster at Yorktown in October 1781.

Camden in August, forces under Lord Cornwallis, the new British commander in the South, crushed a reorganized southern army led by Horatio Gates. Thousands of enslaved African Americans joined the redcoats, seeking promised freedom. Their actions disrupted planting and harvesting in the Carolinas, as the British had hoped.

After the Camden defeat, Washington appointed General Nathanael Greene to command the southern campaign. In the dire circumstances that he faced, Greene recognized that the patriots could win only by convincing the populace that they could bring stability to the region.

GREENE AND THE SOUTHERN CAMPAIGN

He adopted a conciliatory policy toward loyalists and neutrals, persuading South Carolina to pardon those who had fought for the British if they would now join patriot militias. He also ordered his troops to treat captives fairly and not to loot loyalist property.

Since he had so few regulars (only sixteen hundred when he took command), Greene had to rely on western volunteers and could not afford to have frontier militia companies occupied in defending their homes from Indian attack. He accordingly pursued diplomacy aimed at keeping the Indians out of the war. His policy worked: by war's end, only the Creeks remained allied with Great Britain.

Even before Greene took command of the southern army in December 1780, the tide had begun to turn. In October, at King's Mountain, a force from the backcountry defeated a large party of redcoats and loyalists. Then in January 1781, Greene's trusted aide Daniel Morgan brilliantly routed the crack British regiment Tarleton's Legion at Cowpens. Greene himself confronted the main body of British troops under Lord Cornwallis at Guilford Court House, North Carolina, in March. Although Cornwallis controlled the field at the end of the day, most of his army had been destroyed. He had to retreat to the coast to receive supplies and fresh troops from New York.

Surrender at Yorktown

Cornwallis headed north into Virginia, where he joined forces with a detachment of redcoats commanded by the American traitor Benedict Arnold. Instead of acting decisively with his new army of 7,200 men, Cornwallis withdrew to the peninsula between the York and James Rivers, where he fortified Yorktown and awaited supplies and reinforcements. Seizing the opportunity, Washington quickly moved more than 7,000 troops south from New York City. When a French fleet defeated the Royal Navy vessels sent to relieve Cornwallis, the British general was trapped. On October 19, 1781, Cornwallis surrendered. When news of the defeat reached London, Lord North's ministry fell. Parliament voted to cease offensive operations in America, authorizing peace negotiations. Washington returned with the main army to the environs of New York, where his underpaid—and, they thought, underappreciated—

officers grew restive; in March 1783, they threatened to mutiny unless Congress compensated them adequately. Washington, warned in advance of the so-called Newburgh Conspiracy, met the challenge brilliantly. Summoning his officers, he defused the crisis with a well-reasoned but emotional speech drawing on their patriotism. When, fumbling for glasses, he remarked that "I have grown gray in your service and now find myself growing blind," eyewitnesses reported that many of the rebellious officers began to cry. At the end of the year, Washington stood before Congress and formally resigned his commission as commander-in-chief. Through this action, Washington established an enduring precedent: civilian control of the American military.

The war had been won, but at terrible cost. More than twenty-five thousand American men had died.

The Cost of Victory

In the South, years of guerrilla warfare and the loss of thousands of runaway slaves shattered the economy. Indebtedness soared, and local governments were crippled for lack of funds, since few people could afford to pay their taxes.

Americans rejoiced when they learned of the preliminary peace treaty signed at Paris in November 1782. The American diplomats—

Treaty of Paris

Benjamin Franklin, John Jay, and John Adams—ignored their instructions from Congress to be guided by France and instead negotiated directly with Great Britain. Their instincts were sound: the French government was more an enemy to Britain than a friend to the United States. In fact, French ministers worked secretly behind the scenes to try to prevent the establishment of a strong and unified government in America. But the American delegates proved adept at power politics, and, weary of war, the new British ministry, headed by Lord Shelburne, made numerous concessions.

The treaty, signed formally on September 3, 1783, granted the Americans unconditional independence. Generous boundaries delineated the new nation: to the north, approximately the present-day boundary with Canada; to the south, the 31st parallel (about the modern northern border of Florida); to the west, the Mississippi River. Florida, which Britain had acquired in 1763, reverted to Spain. The Americans also gained unlimited fishing rights off Newfoundland. In ceding so much land to the United States, Great Britain ignored the territorial rights of its Indian allies. British diplomats also poorly served loyalists and British merchants. The treaty's ambiguously worded clauses pertaining to the payment of prewar debts and the postwar treatment of loyalists caused trouble for years to come.

Summary *Online Study Center* ACE the Test

The long war finally over, the victorious Americans could look back on their achievement with satisfaction and awe. They had taken on the greatest military power in the world and won. In the process, they reshaped the physical and mental landscapes in which they lived. They abandoned the British identity once so important to them and began creating loyalty to a new nation. They also laid claim to most of the territory east of the Mississippi River and south of the Great Lakes, thereby greatly expanding the land potentially open to their settlements and threatening Indian dominance of the interior.

In achieving independence, Americans surmounted formidable challenges. But in the future they faced perhaps even greater ones: establishing stable republican governments at the state and national levels and ensuring their government's continued existence in a world of bitter rivalries among the major powers—Britain, France, and Spain.

LEGACY FOR A PEOPLE AND A NATION
Revolutionary Origins

The United States was created in an event termed the "American Revolution." Yet many historians would contend today that it was not truly "revolutionary," if a revolution means overturning an earlier power structure. The nation won its independence and established a republic, but essentially the same men who had led the colonies also led the new country (with the exception of British officials and appointees). In sharp contrast, the French Revolution witnessed the execution of the monarch and many aristocrats, and a consequent redistribution of authority. So the legacy of the "American Revolution" appears ambiguous.

Since the "revolution," groups of widely varying political views, from far left to far right, have claimed to represent its true meaning. Acting "in the spirit of the Revolution," people protesting discriminatory policies against women and minorities (usually "liberals") invoke the "created equal" language of the Declaration of Independence; left-wing organizations rail against concentrations of wealth and power in the hands of a few. Those protesting higher taxes (usually "conservatives" wanting a reduced role for government) often adopt the symbolism of the Boston Tea Party. Right-wing militias arm themselves against what they believe is a malevolent government, just as they believe the minutemen did in 1775. The message of the Revolution can be evoked to support extralegal demonstrations of any description, from invasions of military bases by antiwar protesters to demonstrations outside abortion clinics, all of which may be analogized to the demonstrations against British policies in the 1760s. But the Revolution can also be evoked to oppose such street protests, because—some would argue—in a republic change should come peacefully, via the ballot box, not the streets.

Just as Americans in the eighteenth century disagreed over the meaning of their struggle against the mother country, so the legacy of revolution remains contested in the first decade of the twenty-first century, for both the nation and today's American people.

FORGING A NATIONAL REPUBLIC 1776–1789

On December 26, 1787, a group of Federalists—supporters of the proposed Constitution—gathered in Carlisle, a town on the Pennsylvania frontier. The men planned to fire a cannon to celebrate their state convention's ratification vote two weeks earlier, but a large crowd of Antifederalists prevented them from doing so. After forcing the Federalists to flee, the angry Antis publicly burned a copy of the Constitution.

The next day, the Federalists returned in force to fire their cannon and read the convention's ratification proclamation. Deciding against another violent confrontation, Antifederalists instead paraded around the town effigies of two supporters of the Constitution, then burned them. When Federalist officials later arrested several Antifederalists on riot charges, the Antifederalist-dominated militia mustered to break the men out of jail. Only a flaw in the warrant—which freed the arrestees legally—prevented another bloody brawl.

The Carlisle riots presaged violent disputes over the new Constitution in Albany (New York), Providence (Rhode Island), and other cities. These incidents manifested an ongoing struggle that began in 1775 and continued until the end of the century. In that contest, Americans argued continually over how to implement republican principles and who represented the people's will. Easterners debated with westerners; elites contended with ordinary folk. Public celebrations played an important part in the struggle, because in a world in which only relatively few property-holding men had the right to vote, other people expressed their political opinions in the streets.

Republicanism—the idea that governments should be based wholly on the consent of the people—originated with political theorists in ancient Greece and Rome. Republics, theorists declared, were desirable yet fragile forms of government. Unless their citizens were especially virtuous—that is, sober, moral, and industrious—and largely in agreement on key issues, republics were doomed to failure. When Americans left the British Empire, they abandoned the idea that the best system of government required participation by

Creating a Virtuous Republic

LINKS TO THE WORLD
Novels

The First Emancipation and the Growth of Racism

Designing Republican Governments

Trials of the Confederation

Order and Disorder in the West

From Crisis to the Constitution

Opposition and Ratification

LEGACY FOR A PEOPLE AND A NATION
Women's Education

Online Study Center
This icon will direct you to interactive map and primary source activities on the website
http://college.hmco.com/pic/nortonbrief7e

CHRONOLOGY

1776 • Second Continental Congress directs states to draft constitutions

1777 • Articles of Confederation sent to states for ratification
• Vermont becomes first state to abolish slavery

1781 • Articles of Confederation ratified

1786 • Annapolis Convention meets, discusses reforming government

1786–87 • Shays's Rebellion in western Massachusetts raises questions about future of the republic

1787 • Northwest Ordinance organizes territory north of Ohio River and east of Mississippi River
• Constitutional Convention

1788 • Hamilton, Jay, and Madison write *The Federalist*
• Constitution ratified

1794 • Wayne defeats Miami Confederacy at Fallen Timbers

1795 • Treaty of Greenville opens Ohio to settlement

1800 • Weems publishes his *Life of Washington*

a king, the nobility, and the people. They substituted a belief in the superiority of republicanism, in which the people, not Parliament, were sovereign. That decision raised several interrelated questions. How could Americans ensure political stability? How could they foster consensus among the populace? How could they create and sustain a virtuous republic?

America's political and intellectual leaders worked hard to inculcate virtue in their fellow countrymen and countrywomen. After 1776, American literature, theater, art, architecture, and education all pursued explicitly moral goals. The education of women was considered particularly important, for as the mothers of the republic's children, they were primarily responsible for ensuring the nation's future. On such matters, Americans could agree, but they disagreed on many other critical issues. Almost all white men assumed that women, Indians, and African Americans should have no formal role in politics, but they found it difficult to reach a consensus on how many of their own number should be included, how often elections should be held, or how their new governments should be structured.

Especially troublesome were Thomas Jefferson's words in the Declaration of Independence: "all men are created equal." Given that bold statement of principle, how could white republicans justify holding African Americans in perpetual bondage? Some answered that question by freeing their slaves or by voting for state laws that abolished slavery. Others responded by denying that blacks were "men" in the same sense as whites.

The most important task facing Americans in these years was the construction of a genuinely national government. Before 1765 the British mainland colonies had rarely cooperated on common endeavors, but fighting the Revolutionary War brought them together and created a new nationalistic spirit. During the war, Americans began the process of replacing loyalties to state and region with loyalties to the nation.

Still, forging a national republic was neither easy nor simple. America's first such government, under the Articles of Confederation, proved too weak and decentralized. But some of the nation's political leaders learned from their experiences and tried another approach when they drafted the Constitution in 1787. Although some historians have argued that the Constitution represents an "aristocratic" counterrevolution against the "democratic" Articles, the two documents are more accurately viewed as successive attempts to solve the same problems—for instance, the relationship of states and nation and the extent to which authority should be centralized. ■

Creating a Virtuous Republic

*W*hen the colonies declared their independence from Great Britain, John Dickinson recalled many years later, "there was no question concerning forms of Government, no enquiry whether a Republic or a limited Monarchy was best. . . . We knew that the people of this country must unite themselves under some form of Government and that this could be no other than the republican form." But how should that goal be implemented?

Three different definitions of republicanism emerged in the new United States. Ancient history and political theory informed the first, held chiefly by members of the educated elite. The histories of popular governments in Greece and Rome suggested that republics could succeed only if they were small in size and homogeneous in population. Unless a republic's citizens were willing to sacrifice their own private interests for the good of the whole, the government would collapse. In return for sacrifices, though, a republic offered its citizens equality of opportunity. A republic's government would be in the hands of a "natural aristocracy" of men whose rank had been attained by merit rather than inheritance.

VARIETIES OF REPUBLICANISM

A second definition, advanced by other members of the elite but also by some skilled craftsmen, drew more on economic theory than on political thought. Instead of perceiving the nation as an organic whole composed of people nobly sacrificing for the common good, this version of republicanism followed the Scottish theorist Adam Smith in emphasizing individuals' pursuit of rational self-interest. When republican men sought to improve their own economic and social circumstances, the entire nation would benefit. Republican virtue would be achieved through the pursuit of private interests rather than through subordination to some communal ideal.

The third notion of republicanism was less influential but more egalitarian than the other two. Many of its illiterate or barely literate proponents could write little to promote their beliefs. Men who advanced the third version of republicanism called for widening men's participation in the political process. They also wanted government to respond directly to the needs of ordinary folk, rejecting any notion that the "lesser sort" should automatically defer to their "betters." They were indeed democrats in more or less the modern sense.

Despite their differences, the three strands of republicanism shared many of the same assumptions. All three contrasted the industrious virtue of America to the corruption of Britain and Europe. In the first version, that virtue manifested itself in frugality and self-sacrifice; in the second, it would prevent self-interest from becoming vice; in the third, it justified including even propertyless free men in the ranks of voters.

As citizens of the United States set out to construct their republic, they believed they were embarking on an unprecedented enterprise. With great pride in their new nation, they expected to replace the vices of monarchical Europe—immorality, selfishness, and lack of public spirit—with the sober virtues of republican America. They wanted to embody republican principles not only in their governments but also in their society and culture. They looked to painting, literature, drama, and architecture to convey messages of nationalism and virtue to the public.

VIRTUE AND THE ARTS

Americans faced a crucial contradiction at the very outset of their efforts. To some republicans, the fine arts themselves represented vice. What need did a frugal yeoman have for a painting—or, worse yet, a novel? The first American artists, playwrights, and authors thus confronted an impossible dilemma: they wanted to produce works embodying virtue, but those very works were viewed by many as corrupting.

Still, they tried. William Hill Brown's *The Power of Sympathy* (1789), the first novel written in the United States, was a lurid tale of seduction intended as a warning to young women. In Royall Tyler's *The Contrast* (1787), the first successful American play, the virtuous conduct of Colonel Manly was "contrasted" with the reprehensible behavior of the fop Billy Dimple. The most popular book of the era, Mason Locke Weems's *Life of Washington* (1800), was intended by its author to "hold up his great Virtues . . . to the imitation of Our Youth."

Painting and architecture, too, were expected to embody high moral standards. Two of the most prominent artists of the period, Gilbert Stuart and Charles Willson Peale, painted innumerable portraits of upstanding republican citizens. John Trumbull's vast canvases depicting milestones of American history such as Cornwallis's capitulation at Yorktown were intended to instill patriotic sentiments in their viewers. Architects likewise hoped to convey in their buildings a sense of the young republic's ideals. When the Virginia government asked Thomas Jefferson for advice on the design of the state capitol in Richmond, Jefferson unhesitatingly recommended copying a Roman building. Jefferson set forth ideals that would guide American architecture for a generation to come: simplicity of line, harmonious proportions, a feeling of grandeur.

Despite the artists' efforts, some Americans began to detect signs of luxury and corruption by the mid-1780s. The resumption of European trade after the war brought a return to fashionable clothing and abandonment of the simpler homespun garments patriots had once worn with pride. Elite families again attended balls and concerts. Parties no longer seemed complete without gambling and cardplaying. Especially alarming to fervent republicans was the establishment in 1783 of the Society of the Cincinnati, a hereditary association for Revolutionary War officers and their male descendants. Opponents feared the group would become the nucleus of a native-born aristocracy.

Americans' deep-seated concern for the future of the republic focused their attention on their children,

EDUCATIONAL REFORM

the "rising generation." Education had previously been seen as a private means to personal advancement, a concern only for individual families. Now, schooling would serve a public purpose. If young people were to become useful citizens prepared for self-government, they would need a good education. The very survival of the nation depended on it. The 1780s and 1790s thus witnessed two major changes in educational practice.

First, some northern states began to use tax money to support public elementary schools. In 1789 Massachusetts became one of the first states to require towns to offer free public elementary education. Second, schooling for girls was improved. Americans realized that mothers would have to be properly educated if they were to instruct their children adequately for republican citizenship. Therefore, Massa-

chusetts insisted in its 1789 law that town elementary schools be open to girls as well as boys. Throughout the United States, private academies were founded to give teenage girls from well-to-do families an opportunity for advanced schooling. No one yet proposed opening colleges to women, but a few fortunate girls could study history, geography, rhetoric, and mathematics.

The chief theorist of women's education in the early republic was Judith Sargent Murray of Massa-

JUDITH SARGENT MURRAY

chusetts. In a series of essays published in the 1780s and 1790s, Murray argued that women and men had equal intellectual capacities,

■ Judith Sargent Stevens (later Murray), by John Singleton Copley, c. 1770–1772. The eventual author of tracts advocating improvements in women's education sat for this portrait two decades earlier, during her first marriage. Her clear-eyed gaze suggests both her intelligence and her seriousness of purpose. (Terra Foundation for the American Art, Chicago/Art Resource, NY)

Novels

The citizens of the United States, fiercely patriotic and proud of achieving political independence from Great Britain, also sought intellectual and cultural independence. In novels, poems, paintings, plays, and histories, they explored aspects of their new national identity. Ironically, though, the standards against which they measured themselves and the models they followed were European, primarily British.

That was especially true of the most widely read form of literature in the new United States, the novel. Susanna Haswell Rowson's *Charlotte: A Tale of Truth,* the most popular early "American" novel, was actually composed in England, where the novel, as a literary form, originated. In the mid-eighteenth century Samuel Richardson had composed the first works of fiction that today are called novels, the very name revealing their "newness," or novelty. Written in epistolary style (that is, through letters drafted by the various characters), Richardson's novels—*Pamela* (1740), *Clarissa* (1748), and *Sir Charles Grandison* (1753)—all revolved around the courtship and sexual relationships of young adults. The same themes permeated *Charlotte* and Richardson's other American imitators, and for good reason. Changing social mores in the late eighteenth century largely freed English and American young people from parental supervision of their marital decisions. While giving them greater individual choice, that freedom also rendered girls particularly vulnerable to new dangers of deception and seduction by unscrupulous suitors. And these same young women, as a group, were the most avid readers of novels, especially as expanded women's education increased female literacy rates.

William Hill Brown's *Power of Sympathy* (1789) and Hannah Foster's *Coquette* (1797), fictional versions of true "seduction and abandonment" tales, had avid reader-

ships, but neither matched the sales of *Charlotte,* which despite its subtitle, *A Tale of Truth,* had no known factual basis. Rowson, born in England but raised in Massachusetts as the daughter of a customs officer in the British service, lived with her family in England during the Revolution but permanently returned to the United States in 1793. Her popular novel, first published in London in 1791, was reprinted in Philadelphia three years later and eventually went through more than 160 editions. *Charlotte* (later titled *Charlotte Temple*) narrates the story of a naive young woman who elopes, pregnant and unmarried, with her seducer, only to be deserted when a beautiful, rich, and virtuous rival appears on the scene. After giving birth to her baby, Charlotte dies in her father's arms, with her last breath directing him to care for the child. "Oh my dear girls," Rowson cautions her readers, "pray for fortitude to resist the impulses of inclination, when it runs counter to the precepts of religion and virtue."

Generations of young American women sobbed over Charlotte's fate, visiting Trinity churchyard in lower Manhattan, where a real-life counterpart of the fictional heroine was reputed to be buried. Their tears and women's preference on both sides of the Atlantic for such sentimental novels linked the young readers and their nation to the former mother country from which they were nominally so eager to separate.

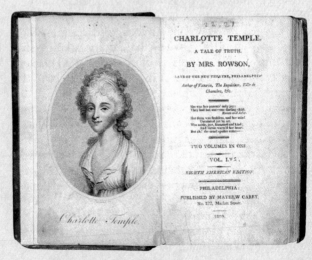

This "Eighth American Edition" (such statements on the title pages of early novels can rarely be trusted because some printings were pirated) of Susanna Rowson's *Charlotte Temple* included a "portrait" of its entirely fictional heroine. That engraving thus reinforced the subtitle, *A Tale of Truth.* *(AC7.R7997.791c 1809, Houghton Library, Harvard College Library)*

113

that boys and girls should be offered equivalent scholastic training, and that girls should be taught to support themselves by their own efforts.

Murray's theories were part of a general rethinking of women's position that occurred as a result of the Revolution. Both men and women realized that female patriots had made vital contributions to winning the war through their work at home and that their notions of proper gender roles had to be rethought. Americans began to develop new ideas about the role women should play in a republican society.

The best-known expression of those new ideas appears in a letter Abigail Adams addressed to her

WOMEN AND THE REPUBLIC

husband, John, in March 1776. "In the new Code of Laws which I suppose it will be necessary for you to make I desire you would Remember the Ladies," she wrote. "If perticuliar care and attention is not paid to the Laidies we are determined to foment a Rebellion, and will not hold ourselves bound by any Laws in which we have no voice, or Representation." With these words, Abigail Adams took a step soon to be duplicated by other disfranchised Americans: she deliberately applied the ideology developed to combat parliamentary supremacy to purposes that revolutionary leaders had never intended.

Abigail Adams did not ask that women be allowed to vote, but others claimed that right. The men who drafted the New Jersey state constitution in 1776 defined voters carelessly as "all free inhabitants" who met certain property qualifications. They thereby unintentionally gave the vote to property-holding white spinsters and widows, as well as free black landowners. Qualified women and African Americans regularly voted in New Jersey's local and congressional elections until 1807, when the state legislature disfranchised them. Yet that women voted at all was evidence of their altered perception of their place in the country's political life.

Such dramatic episodes were unusual. After the war, European Americans continued to believe that a woman's primary function was to be a good wife, mother, and mistress of the household. They perceived significant differences between the male and female characters. That distinction eventually enabled Americans to resolve the conflict between the two most influential strands of republican thought. Because wives could not own property or participate directly in economic life, women in general came to be seen as the embodiment of self-sacrificing, disinterested republicanism. Through new female-run charitable associations founded after the war, better-off women assumed public responsibilities, in particular by caring for poor widows and orphaned children. This freed men to pursue economic self-interest (that other republican virtue), secure in the knowledge that their wives and daughters were fulfilling the family's obligation to the common good. The ideal republican man therefore was an individualist, seeking advancement for himself and his family. The ideal republican woman, by contrast, always put the well-being of others ahead of her own.

Together European American men and women established the context for the creation of a virtuous republic. But how did approximately 700,000 African Americans fit into the developing national plan?

The First Emancipation and the Growth of Racism

R evolutionary ideology exposed one of the primary contradictions in American society. Both European and African Americans saw the irony in slaveholders' claims that they sought to prevent Britain from "enslaving" them. In 1773 Dr. Benjamin Rush of Philadelphia, an ardent patriot, warned that liberty "cannot thrive long in the neighborhood of slavery."

African Americans did not need revolutionary ideology to tell them that slavery was wrong, but they quickly took advantage of that ideology. In 1779 a group of slaves from Portsmouth, New Hampshire, asked the state legislature "from what authority [our masters] assume to dispose of our lives, freedom and property." The same year several bondspeople in Fairfield, Connecticut, petitioned the legislature for their freedom, characterizing slavery as a "dreadful Evil" and "flagrant Injustice."

Both legislatures responded negatively, but the postwar years witnessed the gradual abolition of

EMANCIPATION AND MANUMISSION

slavery in the North, a process that has become known as "the first emancipation." Vermont banned slavery in its 1777 constitution. Massachusetts courts decided in the 1780s that a clause in the state constitution prohibited slavery. Most of the other states north of Maryland adopted gradual emancipation laws between 1780 (Pennsylvania) and 1804 (New Jersey). No southern state adopted similar general emancipation laws, but the legislatures of Virginia (1782), Delaware (1787), and Maryland (1790 and 1796) altered laws that had restricted slaveowners' ability to free their bondspeople. South Carolina and Georgia never considered adopting such acts, and North Carolina insisted that all manumissions (emancipations of individual slaves) be approved by county courts.

Revolutionary ideology thus had limited impact on the well-entrenched economic interests of large slaveholders. Only in the North, where slaves were relatively few, could state legislatures vote to abolish slavery. Even there, legislators' concern for property rights led them to favor gradual emancipation. For example, New York's law freed children born into slavery after July 4, 1799, but only after they had reached their mid-twenties (and provided their masters with labor until then). Thus, the owners' current human property remained largely intact. For decades, then, African Americans in the North lived in an intermediate stage between slavery and freedom. Although the emancipation laws forbade the sale of slaves to jurisdictions in which the institution remained legal, slaveowners regularly circumvented such provisions. The 1840 census still recorded the presence of slaves in several northern states; not until later that decade did Rhode Island and Connecticut, for instance, abolish all vestiges of slavery.

Despite the slow progress of abolition, the ranks of free people of African descent in the United States,

GROWTH OF FREE BLACK POPULATION

few in number before the war, grew dramatically in the first years after the Revolution. Wartime disruptions radically augmented the freed population, adding slaves who had escaped from plantations during the war, others who had served in the American army, and still others who had been emancipated by their owners or by state laws. By 1790 nearly 60,000 free people of color lived in the United States; ten years later, they numbered more than 108,000, nearly 11 percent of the total African American population.

In the Chesapeake, economic changes and the rising influence of antislavery Baptists and Methodists accelerated manumissions. With declining soil fertility and the shift from tobacco growing to less labor-intensive grain cultivation, planters began to complain about "excess" slaves. They occasionally solved that problem by freeing some of their less productive or more favored bondspeople or agreeing to allow slaves to work independently and purchase their freedom.

In the 1780s and thereafter, freed people from rural areas often made their way to northern port cities.

MIGRATION TO NORTHERN CITIES

Boston and Philadelphia, where slavery was abolished sooner than in New York City, were popular destinations. Women outnumbered men among the migrants by a margin of three to two, for they had better employment opportunities in the cities, especially in domestic service. Some freedmen also worked in domestic service, but larger numbers were employed as unskilled laborers and sailors. A few women and a sizable proportion of men were skilled workers or retailers. As soon as possible, freed people established independent two-parent nuclear families instead of continuing to live in their employers' households. They also began to occupy distinct neighborhoods, probably as a result of discrimination.

Both communities and laws discriminated against freed people as against slaves. South Carolina, for example, did not permit free blacks to testify against whites in court. New Englanders tried to use indenture contracts to control freed youths. Public schools often refused to educate children of color. Freedmen found it difficult to purchase property and find good jobs. And though in many areas African Americans were accepted as members—even ministers—of evangelical churches, they were rarely allowed an equal voice in church affairs.

Gradually freed people developed their own institutions. In Charleston mulattos formed the Brown

FREED PEOPLE'S INSTITUTIONS

Fellowship Society, which provided insurance coverage for its members, financed a school, and helped support orphans. In 1794 former slaves in Philadelphia and Baltimore founded societies that eventually became the African Methodist Episcopal (AME) denomination. AME churches later sponsored schools in a number of cities and, along with African Baptist, African Episcopal, and African Presbyterian churches, became cultural centers of the free black community.

Their endeavors were all the more important because in the postrevolutionary years, a formal racist theory developed in the United States. European Americans had long regarded their slaves as inferior, but the most influential writers had argued that African slaves' seemingly debased character derived from their enslavement, rather than enslavement being the consequence of inherited inferiority. In the Revolution's aftermath, though, slaveowners needed to defend holding other human beings in bondage against the notion that "all men are created equal." Consequently, they began to argue that people of African descent were less than fully human and that the principles of republican equality applied only to European Americans. To avoid having to confront the contradiction between their practice and the egalitarian implications of revolutionary theory, they redefined the theory.

Simultaneously, the notion of "race" appeared in coherent form, applied to groups defined by skin color as "whites" and "blacks." The rise of egalitarian thinking among European Americans both downplayed status distinctions within their own group and differentiated all "whites" from people of color. (That differentiation soon manifested itself in new miscegenation laws adopted in both northern and southern states to forbid intermarriage among whites and blacks or Indians.) Meanwhile, a generation or two as slaves on American soil forged the identity "African" or "black" from the various ethnic and national affiliations of people who had survived the transatlantic crossing. Strikingly, among the first to term themselves "Africans" were oceanic sailors: men whose wide-ranging contacts with Europeans caused them to construct a separate, unified identity. Thus, in the revolutionary era, *whiteness* and *blackness*—along with the superiority of the former—developed as contrasting terms in tandem with each other.

Such racism had several intertwined elements. First came the assertion that, as Thomas Jefferson insisted in 1781, blacks were "inferior to the whites in the endowments both of body and mind." There followed the belief that blacks were congenitally lazy and disorderly, even though owners had often argued, conversely, that slaves were "natural" workers. Third was the notion that all blacks were sexually promiscuous and that African American men lusted after European American women. The specter of interracial sexual intercourse involving black men and white women haunted early American racist thought. Significantly, the more common reverse circumstance—the sexual exploitation of enslaved women by their masters—aroused little comment or concern.

African Americans did not allow these developing racist notions to go unchallenged. Benjamin Banneker, a free black surveyor, astronomer, and mathematical genius, directly disputed Thomas Jefferson's belief in Africans' intellectual inferiority. In 1791 Banneker sent Jefferson a copy of his latest almanac (which included his astronomical calculations) as an example of blacks' mental powers. Jefferson's response admitted Banneker's intelligence but indicated that he regarded Banneker as an exception.

At its birth, then, the republic was defined by its leaders as an exclusively white male enterprise. Indeed,
some historians have argued that the subjugation of blacks and women was necessary for theoretical equality among white men. They suggest that identifying a common racial antagonist helped create white solidarity and lessen the threat to gentry power posed by the enfranchisement of poorer white men. Some scholars have pointed out that it was less dangerous to allow white men with little property to participate formally in politics than to open the possibility that they might join with former slaves to question the rule of elites. That was perhaps one reason why after the Revolution, the division of American society between slave and free was transformed into a division between blacks—some of whom were free—and whites. The white males wielding power ensured their continued dominance in part by substituting race for enslavement as the primary determinant of African Americans' status.

Designing Republican Governments

*I*n May 1776, the Second Continental Congress directed states to devise new republican governments to replace the provincial congresses and committees that had met since 1774. Thus, American men initially concentrated on drafting state constitutions and devoted little attention to their national government.

They immediately faced the problem of defining a "constitution." Americans wanted to create tangible documents specifying the fundamental structures of government. Beginning with Vermont in 1777 and Massachusetts in 1780, the states decided that specially elected conventions—not their regular legislative bodies—should draft the constitutions. Then, seeking direct authorization from the people—the theoretical sovereigns in a republic—delegates submitted the new constitutions to voters for ratification.

STATE CONSTITUTIONS

The framers of state constitutions concerned themselves primarily with outlining the distribution of and limitations on government power. Through their experience under British rule, Americans had learned to fear the power of the governor and see the legislature as their defender. Accordingly, the first state constitutions typically provided for the governor to be elected annually (commonly by the legislature), limited the number of terms he could serve, and gave him little independent authority. Simultaneously, the constitutions expanded the legislature's powers. Every state except Pennsylvania and Vermont retained a two-house structure, with members of the upper house having longer terms and being required to meet higher property-holding standards. But they also redrew electoral districts to reflect population patterns more accurately, and they increased the number of members in both houses. Finally, most states lowered property qualifications for voting. Thus, the revolutionary era witnessed the first deliberate attempt to broaden the base of American government, a process that has continued into our own day.

The constitutions also included explicit limitations on government authority. To protect what their authors regarded as the inalienable rights of individual citizens, seven of the constitutions contained formal bills of rights, and the others had similar clauses. Most guaranteed citizens freedom of the press, the right to a fair trial, the right of consent to taxation, and protection against general search warrants. An independent judiciary was charged with upholding such rights. Most states also guaranteed freedom of religion, but with restrictions. For example, seven states required that all officeholders be Christians, and some continued to support churches with tax money.

LIMITING STATE GOVERNMENTS

In general, the constitution makers put far greater emphasis on preventing state governments from becoming tyrannical than on making them effective in wielding political authority. This approach to shaping governments was understandable, given the American experience with Great Britain. But establishing such weak political units, especially in wartime, practically ensured that the constitutions soon would need revision.

Invariably, the revised versions increased the powers of the governor and reduced the legislature's authority. In the mid-1780s, some American political leaders started to develop a theory of checks and balances. To control government power, they sought to balance the powers of the legislative, executive, and judicial branches against one another.

REVISING THE STATE CONSTITUTIONS

The constitutional theories Americans applied at the state level did not at first influence their conception of national government. Since American officials initially focused on organizing the military struggle against Britain, the powers and structure of the Continental Congress evolved by default early in the war. Not until late 1777 did Congress send the Articles of Confederation to the states for ratification.

The chief organ of national government was a unicameral (one-house) legislature in which each state had one vote. Its powers included conducting foreign relations, mediating disputes between states, controlling maritime affairs, regulating Indian trade, and valuing state and national coinage. The Articles did not give the national government the ability to raise revenue effectively to enforce a uniform commercial policy. The United States of America was described as "a firm league of friendship" in which each state "retains its sovereignty, freedom and independence, and every Power, Jurisdiction and right, which is not by this confederation expressly delegated to the United States, in Congress assembled."

ARTICLES OF CONFEDERATION

The Articles required unanimous consent of state legislatures for ratification or amendment, and a clause concerning western lands proved troublesome. The draft accepted by Congress allowed states to retain all land claims derived from their original charters. Maryland, whose charter specified no western land claims, feared being overpowered by states that could

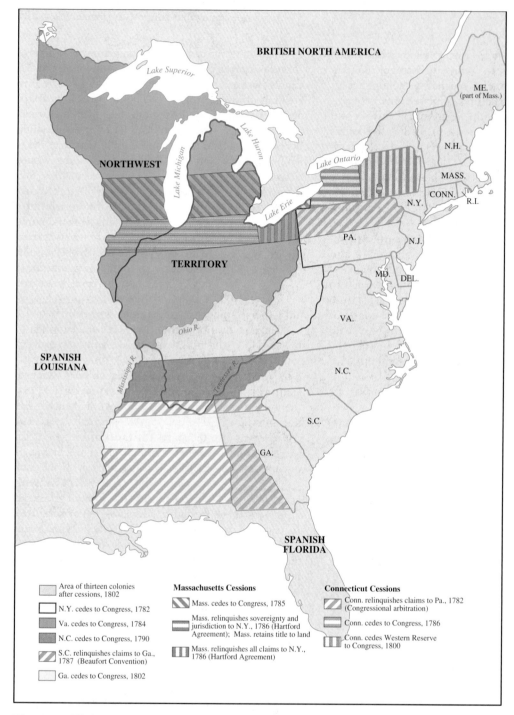

Map 7.1   Western Land Claims and Cessions, 1782–1802

After the United States achieved independence, states competed with each other for control of valuable lands to which they had possible claims under their original charters. That competition led to a series of compromises among the states or between individual states and the new nation, which are indicated on this map.

grow in size and power through land claims beyond the Appalachians. It therefore refused to accept the Articles until 1781, when Virginia finally promised to surrender its western holdings to national jurisdiction (see Map 7.1). Other states followed suit, establishing the principle that unorganized lands would be held by the nation as a whole.

The capacity of a single state to delay ratification for three years portended the fate of American government under the Articles of Confederation. The Articles' authors had not given adequate thought to the distribution of power within the national government or to the relationship between the Confederation and the states. The Congress they created was simultaneously a legislative body and a collective executive (there was no judiciary), but it had no independent income and no authority to compel the states to accept its rulings.

Trials of the Confederation

*Fi*nance posed the most persistent problem that both state and national governments faced. Because legislators at all levels levied taxes only reluctantly, both Congress and the states at first tried to finance the war simply by printing currency. Although the money was backed by nothing but good faith, it circulated freely and without excessive depreciation during 1775 and most of 1776.

But in late 1776, as the American army suffered reverses in New York and New Jersey, prices began to rise, and inflation set in. The currency's value rested on Americans' faith in their government, a faith that was sorely tested during the dark days of early British triumphs in the South (1779 and 1780). By early 1780, it took forty paper dollars to purchase one silver dollar. Soon, Continental currency was worthless.

FINANCIAL AFFAIRS

In 1781, faced with total collapse of the monetary system, the congressmen undertook ambitious reforms. After establishing a department of finance under the wealthy Philadelphia merchant Robert Morris, they asked the states to amend the Articles of Confederation to allow Congress to levy a duty of 5 percent on imported goods. Morris put national finances on a solid footing, but the customs duty was never adopted. First Rhode Island and then New

York refused to agree to the tax. The states' resistance reflected fear of a too-powerful central government.

Because the Articles denied Congress the power to establish a national commercial policy, the realm of foreign trade also exposed the new government's weaknesses. Immediately after the war, Britain, France, and Spain restricted American trade with their colonies. Congress watched helplessly as British manufactured goods flooded the United States while American produce could no longer be sold in the British West Indies, once its prime market. Although Americans reopened commerce with other European countries and started a profitable trade with China in 1784, neither substituted for access to closer and larger markets.

FOREIGN AFFAIRS

Congress furthermore had difficulty dealing with the Spanish presence on the nation's southern and western borders. Determined to prevent the republic's expansion, Spain in 1784 closed the Mississippi River to American navigation, thereby depriving the growing settlements west of the Appalachians of their access to the Gulf of Mexico. Congress opened negotiations with Spain in 1785, but the talks collapsed the following year after Congress divided sharply: southerners and westerners insisted on navigation rights on the Mississippi, whereas northerners were willing to abandon that claim in order to win commercial concessions in the West Indies. To some congressmen, a national consensus on foreign affairs seemed unreachable.

Two provisions of the 1783 Treaty of Paris also aroused considerable opposition: Article Four, which promised the repayment of prewar debts (most of them owed by Americans to British merchants), and Article Five, which recommended that states allow loyalists to recover their confiscated property. States passed laws denying British subjects the right to sue for recovery of debts or property in American courts, and town meetings decried the loyalists' return.

PEACE TREATY PROVISIONS

Online Study Center **Improve Your Grade**
Primary Source: Loyalist Widow Decries the Fate of Tory Exiles in Canada

The refusal of state and local governments to comply with Articles Four and Five gave Britain an excuse to maintain military posts on the Great Lakes long after its troops were supposed to have withdrawn. Furthermore, Congress's inability to convince the states to implement the treaty disclosed its lack of power. Concerned nationalists argued publicly that enforcement of the treaty, however unpopular, was a crucial test of the republic's credibility in foreign affairs.

Order and Disorder in the West

Congressmen also confronted knotty problems when they considered the status of land beyond the Appalachians. Although British and American diplomats did not discuss tribal claims, the United States assumed that the Treaty of Paris cleared its title to all land east of the Mississippi except the area still held by Spain. Still, recognizing that land cessions should be obtained from the most powerful tribes, Congress initiated negotiations with both northern and southern Indians.

At Fort Stanwix, New York, in 1784, American diplomats negotiated a treaty with chiefs who said they represented the Iroquois; and at Hopewell, South Carolina, in late 1785 and early 1786, they did the same with emissaries from the Choctaw, Chickasaw, and Cherokee nations. In 1786 the Iroquois formally repudiated the Fort Stanwix treaty, denying that the men who attended the negotiations had been authorized to speak for the Six Nations. The confederacy threatened new attacks on frontier settlements, but everyone knew the threat was empty; the flawed treaty stood by default. Thereafter, New York State purchased large tracts of land from individual Iroquois nations, and by 1790 the once-dominant confederacy was confined to a few scattered reservations. In the South too, the United States took the treaties as confirmation of its sovereignty, authorizing settlers to move onto the territories in question. European Americans poured over the southern Appalachians, provoking the Creeks—who had not agreed to the Hopewell treaties—to defend their territory by declaring war. Only in 1790 did they come to terms with the United States.

After the collapse of Iroquois power, once-subordinate western nations such as the Shawnees, Chippewas, Ottawas, and Potawatomis formed their own confederacy and demanded direct negotiations

INDIAN RELATIONS

with the United States. They intended to present a united front so as to avoid the piecemeal surrender of land by individual bands and villages.

At first the national government ignored the western confederacy. Shortly after state land cessions were completed, Congress began to organize the Northwest Territory, bounded by the Mississippi River, the Great Lakes, and the Ohio River. Ordinances passed in 1784, 1785, and 1787 outlined the process through which the land could be sold to settlers and formal governments organized.

ORDINANCES OF 1784 AND 1785

In 1785, Congress directed that the land be surveyed into townships 6 miles square, each divided into thirty-six sections of 640 acres (1 square mile). Revenue from the sale of the sixteenth section of each township was to be reserved for the support of public schools—the first instance of federal aid to education in American history. One dollar was the minimum price per acre; the minimum sale was one section. The resulting $640 minimum outlay was beyond the reach of ordinary Americans. Proceeds from western land sales constituted the first independent revenues available to the national government.

The most important of the three land policies—the Northwest Ordinance of 1787—contained a bill of rights guaranteeing settlers freedom of religion and the right to a jury trial, forbidding cruel and unusual punishments, and nominally prohibiting slavery. Eventually that prohibition became an important symbol for antislavery northerners, but at the time it had little effect. Some residents of the territory already had slaves, and Congress did not intend to deprive them of their property. Moreover, the ordinance allowed slaveowners to "lawfully reclaim" runaway bondspeople who took refuge in the territory—the first national fugitive slave law. Not until 1848 was enslavement abolished throughout the region, now known as the Old Northwest. And by omission Congress implied that slavery would be legal in the territories south of the Ohio River.

NORTHWEST ORDINANCE

The ordinance of 1787 also specified the process by which residents of the territory could organize state governments and seek admission to the Union "on an equal footing with the original States." Early in the nation's history, therefore, Congress laid down

■ The two chief antagonists at the Battle of Fallen Timbers and negotiators of the Treaty of Greenville (1795). On the left, Little Turtle, the leader of the Miami Confederacy; on the right, General Anthony Wayne. Little Turtle, in a copy of a portrait painted two years later, appears to be wearing a miniature of Wayne on a bear-claw necklace.
(Left: Chicago Historical Society/Neg #ICHi–35980/Painter–Ralph Dille; right: Independence National Historic Park)

a policy of admitting new states and ensuring their residents the same rights held by citizens of the original states.

In a sense, though, in 1787 the ordinance was purely theoretical. Miamis, Shawnees, and Delawares refused to acknowledge American sovereignty and attacked unwary pioneers who ventured too far north of the Ohio River. In 1788 the Ohio Company, to which Congress had sold a large tract of land at reduced rates, established the town of Marietta at the juncture of the Ohio and Muskingum Rivers. But Indians prevented the company from extending settlement very far into the interior. After General Arthur St. Clair, the Northwest Territory's first governor, failed to negotiate a meaningful treaty with the Indians in early 1789, the United States could not avoid clashing with the Miami-led western confederacy.

Little Turtle, the able war chief of the Miami Confederacy, defeated first General Josiah Harmar (1790) and then St. Clair himself (1791) in major battles near the present border between Indiana and Ohio. More than six hundred of St. Clair's men died, and scores more were wounded, in the United States's worst defeat in the entire history of the American frontier. In 1793 the Miami Confederacy declared that peace could be achieved only if the United States recognized the Ohio River as its northwestern boundary. But the national government refused, and a new army under General Anthony Wayne, a Revolutionary War hero, attacked and defeated the confederacy in August 1794 at the Battle of Fallen Timbers. Peace negotiations began after the victory.

WAR IN THE OLD NORTHWEST

The Treaty of Greenville (1795) gave each side a portion of what it wanted. The United States gained the right to settle much of what was to become Ohio, and Indians received the acknowledgment they had long sought. At Greenville, the United States formally accepted the principle of Indian sovereignty, by virtue of residence, over all lands the native peoples had not ceded. Never again would the U.S. government claim that it had acquired Indian territory solely through negotiation with a European or North American country.

The problems the United States encountered in ensuring safe settlement of the Northwest Territory revealed the basic weakness of the Confederation government. Not until after the Articles of Confederation were replaced with a new constitution could the United States muster sufficient force to implement the Northwest Ordinance.

From Crisis to the Constitution

The most obvious deficiencies of the Articles concerned finance, overseas trade, and foreign affairs. Congress could not levy taxes or impose its will on the states to establish a uniform commercial policy or ensure the enforcement of treaties. Partly as a result, the American economy slid into a depression less than a year after war's end. Exporters of staple crops (especially tobacco and rice) and importers of manufactured goods suffered from the postwar restrictions European powers imposed on American commerce. Although recovery began by 1786, the war's effects proved impossible to erase.

The war wrought permanent change in the American economy. The near total cessation of foreign commerce in nonmilitary items during the war stimulated domestic manufacturing. Consequently, despite the influx of European goods after 1783, the postwar period witnessed the stirrings of American industrial development. For example, the first American textile mill began production in Pawtucket, Rhode Island, in 1793. Moreover, foreign trade patterns continued to shift from Europe toward the West Indies. Foodstuffs shipped to the French and Dutch Caribbean islands became America's largest single export.

ECONOMIC CHANGE AND COMMERCIAL REFORM

Recognizing the Confederation Congress's inability to deal with commercial matters, representatives of Virginia and Maryland met in March 1785 to negotiate an agreement about trade on the Potomac River, which formed part of their border. The successful meeting led to an invitation to other states to discuss trade policy at a convention in Annapolis, Maryland. Although nine states named representatives to the meeting in September 1786, only five delegations attended, too few to have any significant impact on the political system. Those present issued a call for another convention, to be held in Philadelphia nine months later, "to devise such further provisions as shall . . . appear necessary to render the constitution of the federal government adequate to the exigencies of the Union."

The other states did not respond immediately. But then an armed rebellion in Massachusetts convinced doubters that reform was needed. Farmers from the western part of the state, many of them veterans, violently opposed the high taxes levied by the eastern-dominated legislature to pay off war debts. Courts had also begun to foreclose on the lands of tax defaulters. On January 25, 1787, about 1,500 men nominally led by Daniel Shays, a former officer in the Continental Army, assaulted the federal armory at Springfield. The militiamen mustered to defend the armory fired on their former comrades in arms, who then withdrew. But in challenging the legitimacy of a government controlled by eastern merchants, the westerners termed Massachusetts "tyrannical" and insisted that "whenever any encroachments are made either upon the liberties or properties of the people, if redress cannot be had without, it is virtue in them to disturb government." They thereby explicitly linked their rebellion to the earlier independence struggle.

SHAYS'S REBELLION

To some, the rebellion confirmed the need for a much stronger federal government. After most of the states had already appointed delegates, the Confederation Congress belatedly endorsed the proposed convention, "for the sole and express purpose of revising the Articles of Confederation." In mid-May 1787, fifty-five men, representing all the states but Rhode Island, assembled in Philadelphia.

CONSTITUTIONAL CONVENTION

The vast majority of delegates to the Constitutional Convention were men of property and substance. Their ranks included merchants, planters, physicians, generals, governors, and especially lawyers—twenty-three had studied the law. Most had been born in America. Most were Congregationalists, Presbyterians, or Anglicans. In an era when only a tiny proportion of the population had any advanced education, more than half of the delegates had attended college. A few had been educated in Britain, but most had graduated from American institutions. The youngest delegate was twenty-six, the oldest—Benjamin Franklin—eighty-one. Like George Washington, whom they elected their presiding officer, most were in their vigorous middle years. A dozen men did the bulk of the convention's work. Of these, James Madison of Virginia was by far the most important; he deserves the title "Father of the Constitution."

Madison stood out among the delegates for his systematic preparation for the Philadelphia meeting.

MADISON AND THE CONSTITUTION

Through Jefferson in Paris, he bought more than two hundred books on history and government, carefully analyzing their accounts of past confederacies and republics. A month before the Constitutional Convention began, he summed up the results of his research in a lengthy paper entitled "Vices of the Political System of the United States." In this paper, Madison set forth the principle of checks and balances. The government, he believed, had to be constructed in such a way that it could not become tyrannical or fall wholly under the influence of a particular faction. He regarded the large size of a potential national republic as an advantage in that respect, rejecting the common assertion that republics had to be small to survive. Because the large, diverse nation would include many different factions, no one of them would be able to control the government. Political stability would result from compromises among the contending parties.

The so-called Virginia Plan, introduced on May 29 by Edmund Randolph, embodied Madison's

VIRGINIA AND NEW JERSEY PLANS

conception of national government. The plan provided for a two-house legislature, the lower house elected directly by the people and the upper house selected by the lower; representation in both houses proportional to property or population; an executive elected by Congress; a national judiciary; and congressional veto over state laws. The Virginia Plan gave Congress the broad power to legislate "in all cases to which the separate states are incompetent." Had it been adopted

intact, it would have created a government in which national authority reigned unchallenged and state power was greatly diminished. Proportional representation in both houses would also have given large states a dominant voice in the national government.

The convention included many delegates who recognized the need for change but believed the Virginia Plan went too far in the direction of national consolidation. Disaffected delegates—particularly those from small states—united under the leadership of William Paterson of New Jersey, who presented an alternative scheme; the New Jersey Plan called for strengthening the Articles rather than completely overhauling the government. Although the convention initially rejected Paterson's position, he and his allies won a number of victories in the months that followed.

The delegates began their work by discussing the structure and functions of Congress. They readily

DEBATES OVER CONGRESS

agreed that the new national government should have a two-house (bicameral) legislature. But they discovered that they differed widely in their answers to three key questions: Should representation in *both* houses of Congress be proportional to population? How was representation in either or both houses to be apportioned among the states? And, finally, how were the members of the two houses to be elected?

The last issue proved the easiest to resolve. To quote John Dickinson, the delegates thought it "essential" that members of the lower branch of Congress be elected directly by the people and "expedient" that members of the upper house be chosen by state legislatures. Since legislatures had selected delegates to the Confederation Congress, they would expect a similar privilege in the new government. Disappointing them might create significant opposition to the Constitution among state political leaders.

The method of representation in the Senate caused considerably greater disagreement. The delegates accepted without much debate the principle of proportional representation in the House of Representatives. But small states argued for equal representation in the Senate, while large states supported a proportional plan for the upper house. For weeks the convention deadlocked. A committee appointed to work out a compromise recommended equal representation in the Senate, coupled with a proviso that all appropriation bills originate in the lower house.

But not until the convention accepted a suggestion that a state's two senators vote as individuals rather than as a unit was a breakdown averted.

One critical question remained: How was representation in the lower house to be apportioned among states? Delegates concurred

SLAVERY AND THE CONSTITUTION

that a census should be conducted every ten years to determine the nation's actual population, and they agreed that Indians who paid no taxes should be excluded for purposes of representation. Delegates from states with large numbers of slaves wanted African and European inhabitants to be counted equally; delegates from states with few slaves wanted only free people to be counted. The convention resolved the dispute by using a formula developed by the Confederation Congress in 1783 to allocate financial assessments among states: three-fifths of slaves would be included in population totals. (The formula reflected the delegates' judgment that slaves were less efficient producers of wealth than free people, not that they were 60 percent human and 40 percent property.) The three-fifths compromise on representation won unanimous approval.

Although the words *slave* and *slavery* do not appear in the Constitution (the framers used euphemisms such as "other persons"), the document contained both direct and indirect protections for slavery. The three-fifths clause, for example, ensured white southern male voters not only congressional representation out of proportion to their numbers but also a disproportionate influence on the selection of the president, since the number of each state's electoral votes was determined by the size of its congressional delegation. The Constitution prohibited Congress from outlawing the slave trade for at least twenty years, and the fugitive slave clause required all states to return runaways to their masters. By guaranteeing that the national government would aid any states threatened with "domestic violence," the Constitution promised aid in putting down future slave revolts.

Once delegates reached agreement on the problems of slavery and representation, they readily achieved consensus on the other

CONGRESSIONAL AND PRESIDENTIAL POWERS

issues. All agreed that the national government needed the authority to tax and regulate commerce. And while delegates enumerated congressional powers, they then provided for flexibil-

ity by granting Congress all authority "necessary and proper" to carry out those powers. They further provided that the Constitution plus national laws and treaties would constitute "the supreme law of the land; and the judges in every state shall be bound thereby." As another means of circumscribing state powers, delegates drafted a long list of actions forbidden to states. The also provided that religious tests could never be required of U.S. officeholders. Finally, the convention established the electoral college and a four-year term for the chief executive, who could seek reelection. Foreign affairs were placed in the hands of the president, who was also made the commander-in-chief of the armed forces. (The text of the Constitution appears in the appendix.)

The key to the Constitution was the distribution of political authority—that is, separation of powers among executive, legislative, and judicial branches of the national government and division of powers between states and nation. The systems of checks and balances would make it difficult for the government to become tyrannical. At the same time, though, the elaborate system would sometimes prevent the government from acting quickly and decisively. Furthermore, the Constitution drew such a vague line between state and national powers that the United States fought a civil war in the next century over that very issue.

The convention held its last session on September 17, 1787. Of the forty-two delegates still present, only three refused to sign the Constitution, two of them in part because of the lack of a bill of rights. Although the delegates had accepted the Constitution, a key question remained: Would the states ratify it?

Opposition and Ratification

The ratification clause provided for the new system to take effect once it was approved by special conventions in at least nine states, with delegates being elected by qualified voters. Thus, the national Constitution, unlike the Articles of Confederation, would rest directly on popular authority.

As states began to elect delegates to the special conventions, discussion of the proposed government grew more heated. Newspaper essays and pamphlets vigorously defended or attacked the Philadelphia convention's decisions. The extent of the debate was unprecedented, and it quickly became apparent that disputes within the Constitutional Convention had been mild compared to the divisions of opinion within the populace as a whole.

Those supporting the proposed Constitution called themselves Federalists. They argued that the

FEDERALISTS AND ANTIFEDERALISTS

carefully structured government would preclude the possibility of tyranny. A republic could be large, they declared, if the government's design prevented any one group from controlling it. The separation of powers, and the division of powers between states and nation, would accomplish that goal. People did not need to be protected from the powers of the new government in a formal way. Instead, their liberties would be guarded by elected officials of the "better sort" whose only goal (said George Washington) was "to merit the approbation of good and virtuous men."

The Federalists termed those who opposed the Constitution Antifederalists. Antifederalists feared a too-powerful central government. They saw the states as the chief protectors of individual rights; consequently, weakening the states could bring the onset of arbitrary power. Heirs of the Real Whig ideology of the late 1760s and early 1770s, Antifederalists stressed the need for constant popular vigilance to avert oppression. Indeed, some of them had originally promulgated those ideas—Samuel Adams, Patrick Henry, and Richard Henry Lee led the opposition to the Constitution. Joining them were small farmers preoccupied with guarding their property against excessive taxation, backcountry Baptists and Presbyterians, and ambitious, upwardly mobile men who would benefit from an economic and political system less tightly controlled than that the Constitution envisioned. Federalists denigrated such men as disorderly, licentious, and even "unmanly" and "boyish" because they would not follow the elites' lead in supporting the Constitution.

Online Study Center **Improve Your Grade**
Interactive Map: Federalist and Antifederalist Strongholds, 1787–1790

As public debate continued, Antifederalists focused on the Constitution's lack of a bill of rights.

BILL OF RIGHTS

Even if the new system weakened the states, critics believed, specific guarantees of rights could still protect people from tyranny. *Letters of a Federal Farmer,* perhaps the most widely read Antifederalist pamphlet, listed the rights that should be protected: freedom of the press and religion, trial by jury, and guarantees against unreasonable searches.

As state conventions considered ratification, the lack of a bill of rights loomed ever larger. Four of the

RATIFICATION

first five states to ratify did so unanimously, but serious disagreements then surfaced. Massachusetts, in which Antifederalist forces had been bolstered by a backlash against the state government's heavy-handed treatment of the Shays rebels, ratified by a majority of only 19 votes out of 355 cast. In June 1788, when New Hampshire ratified, the requirement of nine states was satisfied. But New York and Virginia had not yet voted, and everyone realized the new Constitution could not succeed unless those key states accepted it.

Despite a valiant effort by the Antifederalist Patrick Henry, pro-Constitution forces won by 10 votes in the Virginia convention. In New York, James Madison, John Jay, and Alexander Hamilton campaigned for ratification by publishing *The Federalist,* a political tract that explained the theory behind the Constitution and masterfully answered its critics. Their reasoned arguments, coupled with Federalists' promise to add a bill of rights to the Constitution, helped win the battle. On July 26, 1788, New York ratified the Constitution by the slim margin of 3 votes. Although the last states—North Carolina and Rhode Island—did not join the Union until November 1789 and May 1790, respectively, the new government was a reality.

Americans in many cities celebrated ratification (somewhat prematurely) with a series of parades on

CELEBRATING RATIFICATION

July 4, 1788. The carefully planned processions dramatized the history and symbolized the unity of the new nation, seeking to counteract memories of the dissent that had so recently engulfed such towns as Carlisle, Pennsylvania. Like pre-Revolution protest meetings, the parades served as political lessons for literate and illiterate Americans alike. The processions aimed to educate men and women about the significance of the new Constitution and instruct them about political leaders' hopes for industry and frugality on the part of a virtuous American public.

Summary ☼ *Online Study Center* ACE the Test

During the 1770s and 1780s, the nation took shape as a political union. It began to develop an economy independent of the British Empire and attempted to chart its own course in the world to protect the national interest. Some Americans outlined cultural and intellectual goals for a properly virtuous republic. An integral part of the formation of the Union was the systematic formulation of American racist thought. Emphasizing race as a determinant of African Americans' standing in the nation, and defining women as nonpolitical, allowed men who now termed themselves "white" to define *republicanism* to exclude all people but themselves and ensure their control of the country.

The experience of fighting a war and struggling for survival as an independent nation altered the political context of American life in the 1780s. At the outset of the war, most Americans believed that "that government which governs best governs least," but by the late 1780s, many had changed their minds. They were the drafters and supporters of the Constitution, who concluded from the republic's vicissitudes under the Articles of Confederation that a more powerful central government was needed. During ratification debates, they contended that their proposals were just as "republican" in conception as the Articles (if not more so). Ratification created the constitutional republic; the decade of the 1790s would witness the first hesitant steps toward the creation of a true nation, the United States of America.

LEGACY FOR A PEOPLE AND A NATION
Women's Education

Women today constitute a majority of students enrolled in U.S. colleges and universities. Because women were denied all access to collegiate education in this country until the mid-nineteenth century, that is a remarkable development. Moreover, it differentiates the United States from other nations, where the majority of university students are male. The origins of women's higher education lie deep, in the republican ideology of the 1770s and 1780s.

Once the United States had established republican forms of government, its citizens began to worry about sustaining those governments. The future, everyone knew, lay in the hands of the nation's children, especially its sons. And theorists concluded that those sons could successfully perpetuate the republic only if they learned the lessons of patriotism from their mothers. Male and female reformers therefore began to argue that women in the United States should be better educated than those who lived under other forms of government.

Some American reformers founded private academies (roughly equivalent to modern high schools) to teach young women from leading families such subjects as history, geography, mathematics, and languages. Some of the women who attended those academies later started educational establishments of their own—including Mary Lyon, who in 1837 founded Mt. Holyoke College in western Massachusetts, the first institution of higher education for women in the United States. A few years later, some colleges for men (such as Oberlin, in Ohio) and state universities (for example, Michigan) admitted women, and a number of women's colleges were established. Not until the second half of the twentieth century, however, did American women gain truly equal access to higher education. In the 1970s, such Ivy League universities as Yale and Princeton finally opened their doors to women students, and others (such as Cornell) that had restricted women's enrollment through quotas removed all constraints. Along with the existence of the nation itself, increased educational opportunity for women is therefore one of the most important legacies of the revolutionary era for the American people.

THE EARLY REPUBLIC: CONFLICTS AT HOME AND ABROAD 1789–1800

*I*n the last months of 1798, the wealthy Philadelphia matron Deborah Norris Logan met with widespread public criticism. Her husband, the Jefferson supporter Dr. George Logan, had undertaken a personal peace mission to France, fearing the prospect of war between the United States and its former ally. In his absence, his wife loyally defended her husband's actions, and she in turn had to endure a campaign unlike any an American woman had ever experienced. That such an episode could occur suggested the political symbolism now embodied by women, the growing division between the factions known as Federalists and Democratic-Republicans, and the significance of foreign affairs in the early republic.

First to attack was "Peter Porcupine," the Federalist newspaper editor William Cobbett, who observed with sly sexual innuendo in his *Porcupine's Gazette* in July that "it is said that JEFFERSON went to his friend Doctor Logan's farm and spent three days there, soon after the Doctor's departure for France. *Query:* What did he do there? Was it to arrange the Doctor's *valuable manuscripts?*" Later Cobbett suggested that both George and Deborah Logan should be pilloried for their actions—him, presumably, for treason and her, Cobbett implied, for adultery. Understanding the symbolic significance of women's virtuous conduct in the fragile young republic, Democratic-Republican newspapers leaped to Deborah's defense, attacking Cobbett's vulgarity and insisting that not even a corrupt Londoner could have written "a greater libel upon public virtue or national morals."

Deborah Logan remained resolute. As reports emerged that her husband had had some success in quelling hostilities, she reveled in the praise subsequently showered on him. George Logan was enthusiastically welcomed home, at least by Jeffersonian partisans. Congress, controlled by Federalists, was less impressed. In January 1799 it adopted the so-called Logan Act, still

Building a Workable Government

Domestic Policy Under Washington and Hamilton

The French Revolution and the Development of Partisan Politics

Partisan Politics and Relations with Great Britain

John Adams and Political Dissent

Indians and African Americans at the End of the Century

LINKS TO THE WORLD
Haitian Refugees

LEGACY FOR A PEOPLE AND A NATION
Dissent During Wartime

Online Study Center
This icon will direct you to interactive map and primary source activities on the website http://college.hmco.com/pic/nortonbrief7e

CHRONOLOGY

1789 • Washington inaugurated as first president
• Judiciary Act of 1789 organizes federal court system
• French Revolution begins

1790 • Hamilton's *Report on Public Credit* proposes assumption of state debts

1791 • First ten amendments (Bill of Rights) ratified
• First national bank chartered

1793 • France declares war on Britain, Spain, and the Netherlands
• Washington's neutrality proclamation
• Democratic-Republican societies founded

1794 • Whiskey Rebellion in western Pennsylvania

1795 • Jay Treaty with England
• Pinckney's Treaty with Spain

1796 • First contested presidential election: Adams elected president, Jefferson vice president

1798 • XYZ affair
• Sedition Act penalizes dissent
• Virginia and Kentucky resolutions

1798–99 • Quasi-War with France

1800 • Franco-American Convention
• Gabriel's Rebellion

in effect, which forbids private citizens from undertaking diplomatic missions.

The controversy caused by the Logans' actions was but one of many such battles in the 1790s. The fight over ratifying the Constitution turned out to presage an even wider division over the major political, economic, and diplomatic questions confronting the young republic: the extent to which authority should be centralized in the national government; the relationship of national power and states' rights; the formulation of foreign policy in an era of continual warfare in Europe; and the limits of dissent. Americans did not anticipate the acrimonious disagreements that rocked the 1790s. And no one predicted the difficulties that would develop as the United States attempted to deal with Indian nations now wholly encompassed within its borders.

Most important of all, perhaps, Americans could not understand or fully accept the division of the country's political leaders into two factions (not yet political parties), believing that only monarchies should experience such factional disputes. In republics, they believed, the rise of factions signified decay and corruption. ■

Building a Workable Government

*T*he nationalistic spirit expressed in the processions celebrating ratification of the Constitution carried over to the first session of Congress. Only a few Antifederalists ran for office in the congressional elections held late in 1788, and even fewer were elected. Thus, the First Congress consisted chiefly of men who supported a strong national government. The drafters of the Constitution had deliberately left many key issues undecided, so the nationalists' domination of Congress meant that their views on those points quickly prevailed.

Congress faced four immediate tasks when it convened in April 1789: raising revenue to support the new government, responding to states' calls for a bill of rights, setting up executive departments, and organizing the federal judiciary. The last task was especially important. The Constitution had established a Supreme Court but left it to Congress to decide whether to have other federal courts as well.

FIRST CONGRESS

James Madison, who had been elected to the House of Representatives, soon became as influential in Congress as he had been at the Constitutional Convention. A few months into the first session, he persuaded Congress to adopt the Revenue Act of 1789, imposing a 5 percent tariff on certain imports. Thus, the First Congress quickly achieved what the Confederation Congress never had: an effective national tax law. The new government would have problems in its first years, but lack of revenue was not one of them.

Madison also took the lead with respect to constitutional amendments. He placed nineteen proposed amendments before the House. The

BILL OF RIGHTS

states soon ratified ten, which officially became part of the Constitution on December 15, 1791. Their adoption defused Antifederalist opposition and rallied support for the new government.

The First Amendment specifically prohibited Congress from passing any law restricting the right to freedom of religion, speech, press, peaceable assembly, or petition. The Second Amendment guaranteed the right "to keep and bear arms" because of the need for a "well-regulated Militia." Thus, the constitutional right to bear arms was based on the expectation that most able-bodied men would serve the nation as citizen-soldiers, and there would be little need for a standing army, which former colonists feared as a threat to freedom. The Third Amendment limited the conditions under which troops could be quartered in private homes. The Fourth Amendment prohibited "unreasonable searches and seizures"; the Fifth and Sixth established the rights of accused persons; the Seventh specified the conditions for jury trials in civil (as opposed to criminal) cases; and the Eighth forbade "cruel and unusual punishments." The Ninth and Tenth Amendments reserved to the people and the states other unspecified rights and powers. In short, the amendments' authors made it clear that in listing some rights, they did not mean to preclude the exercise of others.

Congress also considered the organization of the executive branch. It readily agreed to continue the

EXECUTIVE AND JUDICIARY

three administrative departments established under the Articles of Confederation: War, Foreign Affairs (renamed State), and Treasury. Congress instituted two lesser posts: the attorney general—the nation's official lawyer—and the postmaster general. And by agreeing that the president alone could dismiss officials he had originally appointed with the consent of the Senate, Congress established the principle that the heads of

executive departments are accountable solely to the president. Aside from constitutional amendments, the most far-reaching piece of legislation enacted by the First Congress was the Judiciary Act of 1789, which defined the jurisdiction of the federal judiciary and established a six-member Supreme Court, thirteen district courts, and three circuit courts of appeal. Its most important provision, Section 25, allowed appeals from state courts to federal courts when cases raised certain types of constitutional issues. Section 25 thus implemented Article VI of the Constitution, which stated that federal laws and treaties were to be "the supreme Law of the Land." The Judiciary Act of 1789 presumed that the wording of Article VI implied the right of appeal from state to federal courts, although the Constitution did not explicitly permit such action. Nineteenth-century states' rights advocates would challenge this interpretation.

In a significant 1796 decision, *Ware v. Hylton,* the Court for the first time declared a state law unconstitutional. That same year it also reviewed the constitutionality of an act of Congress, upholding it in the case of *Hylton v. U.S.* The most important case of the decade, *Chisholm v. Georgia* (1793), established that states could be sued in federal courts by citizens of other states. The Eleventh Amendment to the Constitution overruled this decision, which was unpopular with state governments, five years later.

In early 1790, three groups of Quakers petitioned Congress to end the foreign slave trade, despite the

DEBATE OVER SLAVERY

constitutional provisions forbidding such action before 1808. The ensuing debates directly addressed the questions suppressed in euphemisms in the Constitution itself. Southerners vigorously asserted that Congress not only should reject the petitions but should not even discuss them seriously. The legislators went on to develop a positive defense of slavery, insisting that abolition would cause more problems than it solved, primarily by confronting the nation with how to deal with a sizable population of freed people. Some northern congressmen contested the southerners' position, but a consensus soon emerged to quash such discussions in the future. Congress accepted a committee report denying it the power to halt the slave trade before 1808 or effect the emancipation of any slaves at any time, that authority "remaining with the several States alone."

Domestic Policy Under Washington and Hamilton

*I*n 1783 George Washington returned to Mount Vernon eager for the peaceful life of a Virginia planter. But his fellow countrymen never regarded Washington as just another private citizen. When the new Constitution was adopted, Americans concurred that only George Washington had sufficient stature to serve as the republic's first president. The unanimous vote of the electoral college merely formalized that consensus.

Washington acted cautiously during his first months in office in 1789, knowing that whatever he

WASHINGTON'S FIRST STEPS

did would set precedents for the future. When the title by which he should be addressed aroused controversy, Washington said nothing. The accepted title soon became a plain "Mr. President." By using the heads of the executive departments collectively as his chief advisers, he created the cabinet. As the Constitution required, he sent Congress an annual State of the Union message. Washington also concluded that he should exercise his veto power over congressional legislation very sparingly—only, indeed, if he became convinced a bill was unconstitutional.

Early in his term, Washington undertook elaborately organized journeys to all the states. At each stop, he was ritually welcomed by uniformed militia units, young women strewing flowers in his path, local leaders, groups of Revolutionary War veterans, and respectable citizens who gave formal addresses reaffirming their loyalty to the United States. The president thus personally came to embody national unity, simultaneously drawing ordinary folk into the sphere of national politics.

Washington's first major task as president was to choose the heads of the executive departments. For the War Department he selected Henry Knox of Massachusetts, his reliable general of artillery during the Revolution. His choice for the State Department was his fellow Virginian Thomas Jefferson, just returned from his post as minister to France. And for the crucial position of secretary of the treasury, the president chose the brilliant, intensely ambitious Alexander Hamilton.

Two traits distinguished Hamilton from most of his contemporaries. First, he displayed an undivided

ALEXANDER HAMILTON

loyalty to the nation as a whole. The illegitimate son of an aristocrat, Hamilton had grown up in poverty in the West Indies and had lived on the mainland only briefly before the war. He had no ties to a particular state, and he showed little sympathy for, or understanding of, demands for local autonomy. Thus, the aim of his fiscal policies was always to consolidate power at the national level. Furthermore, he never feared the exercise of centralized executive authority, as did older counterparts who had clashed repeatedly with colonial governors, and he was not afraid of maintaining close political and economic ties with Britain.

Second, Hamilton regarded his fellow human beings with unvarnished cynicism. Perhaps because of his difficult early life and his own overriding ambition, Hamilton believed people are motivated primarily by self-interest—particularly economic self-interest. He placed no reliance on people's capacity for virtuous and self-sacrificing behavior and could not envision that public-spirited citizens would pursue the common good rather than their own private advantage.

In 1789, Congress ordered the new secretary of the treasury to assess the public debt and submit

NATIONAL AND STATE DEBTS

recommendations for supporting the government's credit. Hamilton found that the country's remaining war debts fell into three categories: those owed by the nation to foreign governments and investors, mostly to France (about $11 million); those owed by the national government to merchants, former soldiers, holders of revolutionary bonds, and the like (about $27 million); and, finally, similar debts owed by state governments (roughly $25 million). With respect to the national debt, few disagreed: Americans recognized that if their new government was to succeed, it would have to repay at full face value those financial obligations incurred by the nation while winning independence.

The state debts were another matter. Some states—notably Virginia, Maryland, North Carolina, and Georgia—already had paid off most of their war debts. They would oppose the national government's assumption of responsibility for other states' debts. Massachusetts, Connecticut, and South Carolina, by contrast, still had sizable unpaid debts and would welcome a system of national assumption. The possible assumption of state debts also had political implications. Consolidating the debt in the hands of the national government would help to concentrate economic and political power at the national level. A contrary policy would reserve greater independence of action for the states.

Hamilton's first *Report on Public Credit,* sent to Congress in January 1790, proposed that Congress

HAMILTON'S FINANCIAL PLAN

assume outstanding state debts, combine them with national obligations, and issue new securities covering both principal and accumulated unpaid interest. Hamilton thereby hoped to ensure that holders of the public debt— many of them wealthy merchants and speculators— had a significant financial stake in the new government's survival. The opposition coalesced around James Madison, who was against the assumption of state debts for two reasons: first, his state had already paid off most of its obligations, and second, he wanted to avoid rewarding wealthy speculators who had purchased debt certificates at a small fraction of their face value from needy veterans and farmers.

The House initially rejected the assumption of state debts. The Senate, however, adopted Hamilton's plan largely intact. A series of compromises followed, in which the assumption bill became linked with another controversial issue: the location of the permanent national capital. Several related political deals were struck. A southern site—on the Potomac River— was selected for the capital, and the first part of Hamilton's financial program became law in August 1790.

Four months later, Hamilton submitted to Congress a second report on public credit, recommending

FIRST BANK OF THE UNITED STATES

the chartering of a national bank. The Bank of the United States, to be chartered for twenty years, was to be capitalized at $10 million. Just $2 million would come from public funds. Private investors would supply the rest. The bank would also act as collecting and disbursing agent for the Treasury, and its notes would circulate as the nation's currency, providing a dependable medium of exchange. Most political leaders recognized that such an institution would be beneficial, but asked whether the Constitution gave Congress the power to establish such a bank.

James Madison answered that question with a resounding no. He pointed out that Constitutional

INTERPRETING THE CONSTITUTION

Convention delegates had specifically rejected a clause authorizing Congress to issue corporate charters. Consequently, he argued, the power to do so could not be inferred from other parts of the Constitution. Thomas Jefferson, the secretary of state, agreed with Madison. Jefferson referred to Article I, Section 8, of the Constitution, which gave Congress the power "to make all Laws which shall be necessary and proper for carrying into Execution the foregoing Powers." The key word, Jefferson argued, was *necessary:* Congress could do what was needed, but without specific constitutional authorization, it could not do what was merely desirable. Thus, Jefferson formulated the strict-constructionist interpretation of the Constitution.

Washington asked Hamilton to reply to the negative assessments of his proposal. Hamilton's *Defense of the Constitutionality of the Bank* (1791) brilliantly expounded a broad-constructionist view of the Constitution. Hamilton argued forcefully that Congress could choose any means not specifically prohibited by the Constitution to achieve a constitutional end. He reasoned thus: if the end was constitutional and the means was not unconstitutional, then the means was constitutional. Washington concurred, and the bill became law. Both the bank and the debt-funding scheme proved successful. The new nation's securities became desirable investments, and the capital they attracted contributed to a new prosperity.

In December 1791, Hamilton presented to Congress his *Report on Manufactures,* outlining an

HAMILTON'S REPORT ON MANUFACTURES

ambitious plan for encouraging and protecting the United States's infant industries. Hamilton argued that the nation could never be truly independent as long as it relied heavily on Europe for manufactured goods. He thus urged Congress to promote the immigration of technicians and laborers and to support industrial development through a limited use of protective tariffs. Many of Hamilton's ideas were implemented in later decades, but in 1791 most congressmen firmly believed that America's future lay in agriculture and the carrying trade and that the mainstay of the republic was the virtuous small farmer. Therefore, Congress rejected the report.

That same year, Congress accepted Hamilton's proposed tax on whiskey produced within the United

States. Although proceeds from the Revenue Act of 1789 covered the interest on the national debt, the decision to fund state debts meant that the national government required additional income. A tax on whiskey affected relatively few farmers—those west of the mountains who sold their grain in the form of distilled spirits to avoid the high cost of transportation. Moreover, Hamilton knew that those western farmers were Jefferson's supporters, and he saw the benefits of taxing them rather than the merchants who supported his own policies.

News of the tax set off protests in frontier areas of Pennsylvania. Unrest continued for two years on

WHISKEY REBELLION

the frontiers of Pennsylvania, Maryland, and Virginia. President Washington responded with restraint until violence erupted in July 1794, when western Pennsylvania farmers resisted a federal marshal and a tax collector trying to enforce the law. Three rioters were killed and several militiamen wounded. About seven thousand rebels convened on August 1 to plot the destruction of Pittsburgh but decided not to face the heavy guns of the fort guarding the town. Washington then took decisive action to prevent a crisis reminiscent of Shays's Rebellion. On August 7, he called on the insurgents to disperse and summoned almost thirteen thousand militia from Pennsylvania and neighboring states. By the time federal forces marched westward in October and November, the disturbances had ceased.

The chief importance of the Whiskey Rebellion's suppression lay in the message it conveyed to the American people. The national government, Washington had demonstrated, would not allow violent resistance to its laws. In the republic, change would be effected peacefully, by legal means.

The French Revolution and the Development of Partisan Politics

By 1794, some Americans were already beginning to seek change systematically through electoral politics, even though traditional political theory regarded organized opposition as illegitimate. In a republic, serious and sustained disagreement was taken as a sign of corruption and subversion.

Jefferson and Madison became convinced as early as 1792 that Hamilton's policy of favoring

DEMOCRATIC-REPUBLICANS AND FEDERALISTS

wealthy commercial interests at the expense of agriculture aimed at imposing a corrupt, aristocratic government on the United States. Characterizing themselves as the true heirs of the Revolution, Jefferson, Madison, and their followers in Congress began calling themselves Democratic-Republicans. Hamilton likewise accused Jefferson and Madison of plot-

MAD TOM in A RAGE

■ A Federalist political cartoon from the 1790s shows "Mad Tom" Paine "in a rage," trying to destroy the federal government as carefully constructed (in classical style) by President Washington and Vice President Adams. That Paine is being aided by the Devil underscores the hostility to partisanship common in the era.   (The Huntington Library, Art Collections, and Botanical Gardens, San Marino, California/Superstock)

ting to destroy the republic. He and his supporters began calling themselves Federalists, to legitimize their claims and link themselves with the Constitution. Each group accused the other of being an illicit faction working to sabotage the republican principles of the Revolution. (By traditional definition, a faction was opposed to the public good.) Newspapers aligned with the two sides fueled partisanship, publishing virulent attacks on their political opponents.

At first, President Washington tried to remain aloof from the political dispute that divided Hamilton and Jefferson, his chief advisers. Yet the growing controversy helped persuade him to seek a second term of office in 1792 in hopes of promoting political unity. But in 1793 and thereafter, developments in foreign affairs magnified the disagreements.

In 1789 Americans welcomed the news of the French Revolution and France's move toward republicanism. But by the early 1790s, the

THE FRENCH REVOLUTION

reports from France were disquieting. Outbreaks of violence continued, ministries succeeded each other with bewildering rapidity, and executions mounted—the king himself was beheaded. Although many Americans, including Jefferson and Madison, retained a sympathetic view of the revolution, Hamilton and others began to cite France as a prime example of the perversion of republicanism.

Debates within the United States intensified when the newly republican France, fearing that neighboring monarchies would crush the revolution and seeking to spread republicanism throughout the continent, declared war first on Austria and then, in 1793, on Britain, Spain, and Holland. Americans faced a dilemma. The 1778 Treaty of Alliance with France bound them to that nation "forever," and a mutual commitment to republicanism created ideological bonds. Yet the United States was connected to Great Britain as well. Beyond the shared history and language, Great Britain was America's most important trading partner. Indeed, the financial system of the United States depended heavily on import tariffs levied on goods from the former mother country.

The political and diplomatic climate grew even more complicated in April 1793, when Citizen Edmond

CITIZEN GENÊT

Genêt, a representative of the French government, landed in Charleston, South Carolina. As Genêt made his way north to New York City, he re-cruited Americans for expeditions against British and Spanish colonies in the Western Hemisphere, freely distributing privateering commissions. Genêt's arrival raised troubling questions for President Washington. Should he receive Genêt, thus officially recognizing the French revolutionary government? Should he acknowledge an obligation to aid France under the terms of the 1778 Treaty of Alliance? Or should he proclaim American neutrality?

For once, Hamilton and Jefferson saw eye to eye. Both told Washington that the United States could not afford to ally itself with either side. Washington concurred. He received Genêt but also issued a proclamation informing the world that the United States would adopt "a conduct friendly and impartial toward the belligerent powers."

Genêt himself disappeared from the diplomatic scene when his faction fell from power in Paris, but the domestic divisions he helped to widen were perpetuated by clubs called Democratic-Republican societies. These activist organizations were formed by Americans sympathetic to the French Revolution and worried about the policies of the Washington administration.

More than forty Democratic-Republican societies were organized between 1793 and 1800. Their

DEMOCRATIC-REPUBLICAN SOCIETIES

members saw themselves as heirs of the Sons of Liberty, seeking the same goal as their predecessors: protection of people's liberties against encroachments by corrupt and self-serving rulers. To that end, they publicly protested the Washington administration's fiscal and foreign policy and repeatedly proclaimed their belief in the rights to free speech, free press, and assembly. Like the Sons of Liberty, the Democratic-Republican societies chiefly comprised artisans and craftsmen, although professionals, farmers, and merchants also joined.

The rapid growth of such groups deeply disturbed Hamilton and eventually Washington himself. Some newspapers charged that the societies were subversive agents of a foreign power. The counterattack climaxed in the fall of 1794, when Washington accused the societies of having fomented the Whiskey Rebellion.

In retrospect, Washington and Hamilton's reaction to the Democratic-Republican societies seems disproportionately hostile. But at the time, factions were seen as dangerous, and the idea that a loyal opposition was part of a free government had not yet been accepted.

Partisan Politics and Relations with Great Britain

I n 1794 George Washington dispatched Chief Justice John Jay to London to negotiate four unresolved questions in Anglo-American relations. The first point at issue was recent British seizures of American merchant ships trading in the French West Indies. The United States wanted to establish the principle of freedom of the seas and assert its right, as a neutral nation, to trade freely with both combatants. Second, in violation of the 1783 peace treaty, Great Britain had not yet evacuated its posts in the American Northwest. The Americans also hoped for a commercial treaty and sought compensation for the slaves who left with the British army at the end of the war.

The negotiations in London proved difficult, since Jay had little to offer in exchange for the concessions

JAY TREATY

he sought. Britain did agree to evacuate the western forts and ease restrictions on American trade with England and the West Indies. The treaty established two arbitration commissions—one to deal with prewar debts Americans owed to British creditors and the other to hear claims for captured American merchant ships—but Britain adamantly refused to compensate slaveowners for their lost bondspeople. Under the circumstances, Jay did remarkably well: the treaty averted a war with England that the United States could not have won at the time. Nevertheless, most Americans, including the president, were dissatisfied.

The Senate debated the Jay Treaty in secret, so members of the public did not learn its provisions until after Senate ratification in June 1795. The Democratic-Republican societies led protests against the treaty. Especially vehement opposition arose in the South over the failure to obtain compensation for runaway slaves and against the commission on prewar debts, which might require planters to pay off sizable obligations to British merchants. Once President Washington had signed the treaty, though, there seemed little the Democratic-Republicans could do to

prevent it from taking effect. Just one opportunity remained: Congress had to appropriate funds to carry out the treaty provisions.

When the House debated the issue in March 1796, members opposing the treaty tried to prevent approval of the appropriations. To that end, they asked Washington to submit to the House all documents pertinent to the negotiations. In successfully resisting the House's request, Washington established the doctrine of executive privilege: the power of the president to withhold information from Congress if he believes circumstances warrant doing so.

In the end, the House appropriated the money for the Jay Treaty. In 1795 Thomas Pinckney of South Carolina had negotiated a treaty with Spain giving the United States navigation privileges on the Mississippi River, a boon to the South and West. Regional interests and the popularity of Pinckney's Treaty helped overcome opposition to the Jay Treaty.

Analysis of the vote reveals both the regional nature of divisions and the growing cohesion of the

PARTISAN DIVISIONS IN CONGRESS

Democratic-Republican and Federalist factions in Congress. Voting for the appropriations were 44 Federalists and 7 Democratic-Republicans; voting against were 45 Democratic-Republicans and 3 Federalists. The final tally also divided by region: southerners cast the vast majority of votes against the bill.

The small number of defectors on both sides reveals a new force at work in American politics: partisanship. Voting statistics from the first four Congresses show the ever-increasing tendency of members of the House of Representatives to vote as cohesive groups rather than as individuals. The growing division cannot be explained in the terms used by Jefferson and Madison (aristocrats versus the people) or by Hamilton and Washington (true patriots versus subversive rabble). Simple economic differences between agrarian and commercial interests do not provide the answer either.

Nevertheless, certain distinctions can be made. Democratic-Republicans, especially prominent in the

BASES OF PARTISANSHIP

southern and middle states, tended to be self-assured, confident, and optimistic about both politics and the economy. Southern planters, firmly in control of their region and of a class of enslaved laborers, foresaw a prosperous future based partly on continued westward expansion, a movement they expected to dominate. Democratic-Republicans employed democratic rhetoric to win the allegiance of small farmers south of New England. Members of non-English ethnic groups—especially Irish, Scots, and Germans—found Democratic-Republicans' words attractive. Democratic-Republicans of all descriptions emphasized developing America's own resources, worrying less than Federalists did about the nation's place in the world. Democratic-Republicans also remained sympathetic to France in international affairs.

By contrast, Federalists, concentrated in New England, came mostly from English stock. Insecure and uncertain of the future, they stressed the need for order, authority, and regularity in the political world. Federalists had no grassroots political organization and put little emphasis on involving ordinary people in government. Wealthy New England merchants aligned themselves with the Federalists, but so too did the region's farmers who, prevented from expanding agricultural production because of New England's poor soil, gravitated toward the more conservative party. Federalists, like Democratic-Republicans, assumed that southern and middle-state interests would dominate the land west of the mountains, so they had little incentive to work actively to develop that potentially rich territory. In Federalist eyes, potential enemies—both internal and external—perpetually threatened the nation, which required a continuing alliance with Great Britain for its own protection. Overall, their vision proved narrow and unattractive, holding out little hope for a better future for residents of any particular region.

The presence of the two organized groups made the presidential election of 1796 the first serious contest for the position. Wearied by criticism, George Washington decided to retire. In September Washington published his Farewell Address. In it he outlined two principles that guided American foreign policy at least until the late 1940s: to maintain commercial but not political ties to other nations and to enter no permanent alliances. He thus encouraged the nation to follow the path of independent action in foreign affairs, today called unilateralism.

WASHINGTON'S FAREWELL ADDRESS

Washington also lamented the existence of factional divisions, and historians have often interpreted this as a call to end partisanship for the good of the whole. But in the context of the impending presidential election, the Farewell Address appears rather as an attack on the legitimacy of the Democratic-Republican opposition. Washington advocated unity behind the Federalist banner, while both sides perceived their opponents as misguided, unpatriotic troublemakers who sought to undermine revolutionary ideals.

Online Study Center **Improve Your Grade**
Primary Source: Washington's Farewell Address

To succeed Washington, the Federalists in Congress put forward Vice President John Adams, with the diplomat Thomas Pinckney as his running mate. Congressional Democratic-Republicans chose Thomas Jefferson as their presidential candidate; Aaron Burr of New York agreed to run for vice president.

ELECTION OF 1796

That the election was contested does not mean that the people decided its outcome. Voters could cast their ballots only for electors, not for the candidates themselves, and not all electors publicly declared their preferences. State legislatures, not a popular vote, selected more than 40 percent of the members of the electoral college. Moreover, the Constitution's drafters had not foreseen the development of competing national political organizations, so the Constitution provided no way to express support for one person for president and another for vice president. The electors simply voted for two people. The man with the highest total became president; the one with the second highest, vice president. Thus, Adams, the Federalist, won the presidency with 71 votes, and Jefferson, the Democratic-Republican, with 68 votes, became the vice president.

John Adams and Political Dissent

John Adams took over the presidency peculiarly blind to the partisan developments of the previous four years. As president, he never abandoned an outdated notion discarded by George Washington as early as 1794: that the president should be above politics, an independent and dignified

■ John Adams, painted in 1798 by the English artist William Winstanley. Adams wears the same suit and sword he donned for his inauguration as the second president in March 1797. The open books and quill pen on the table suggest his lifelong love of reading and writing. (U.S. Department of the Interior, National Park Service, Adams National Historic Site)

figure. Thus, Adams kept Washington's cabinet intact, despite its key members' allegiance to his chief rival, Alexander Hamilton. Adams often adopted a passive posture, letting others (usually Hamilton) take the lead when he as president should have acted decisively. As a result, his administration gained a reputation for inconsistency. When Adams's term ended, the Federalists were severely divided. But Adams's detachment from Hamilton's maneuverings did enable him to weather the greatest international crisis the republic had yet faced: the Quasi-War with France.

The Jay Treaty improved America's relationship with Great Britain, but it provoked the French

XYZ AFFAIR

government to retaliate by ordering its ships to seize American vessels carrying British goods. In response, Congress increased military spending, and President Adams sent three commissioners to Paris to negotiate a settlement. For months, the American commissioners sought talks with Talleyrand, the French foreign minister, but Talleyrand's agents demanded a bribe of $250,000 before negotiations could begin. The Americans reported the incident in dispatches that the president received in early March 1798. Adams informed Congress of the impasse and recommended further increases in defense appropriations.

Convinced that Adams had deliberately sabotaged the negotiations, congressional Democratic-Republicans insisted that the dispatches be turned over to Congress. Adams complied, aware that releasing the reports would work to his advantage. He withheld only the names of the French agents, referring to them as X, Y, and Z. The revelation that the Americans had been treated with contempt stimulated a wave of anti-French sentiment. Cries for war filled the air. Congress formally abrogated the Treaty of Alliance and authorized American ships to seize French vessels.

Thus began an undeclared war with France. U.S. warships and French privateers seeking to capture

QUASI-WAR WITH FRANCE

American merchant vessels fought the Quasi-War in Caribbean waters. Although Americans initially suffered heavy losses of merchant shipping, by early 1799 the U.S. Navy had established its superiority in the West Indies, easing the threat to America's vital trade in that region.

The Democratic-Republicans, who opposed war and continued to sympathize with France, could do

ALIEN AND SEDITION ACTS

little to stem the tide of anti-French feelings. Since Agent Y had boasted of the existence of a "French party in America," Federalists flatly accused Democratic-Republicans (including George Logan) of traitorous designs. And Federalists saw the climate of opinion as an opportunity to deal a death blow to their opponents. Now that the country seemed to see the truth of what they had been saying ever since the Whiskey Rebellion in 1794—that Democratic-Republicans were subversive foreign agents—Federalists sought to codify that belief into law. In 1798 the Federalist-controlled Congress adopted a set of four laws known as the Alien and Sedition Acts, intended to suppress dissent and prevent further growth of the Democratic-Republican faction.

Three of the acts targeted recently arrived immigrants, whom Federalists accurately suspected of being Democratic-Republican in their sympathies. The Naturalization Act lengthened the residency period required for citizenship and ordered all resident aliens to register with the federal government. The two Alien Acts, though not immediately implemented, provided for the detention of enemy aliens in time of war and gave the president authority to deport any alien he deemed dangerous to the nation's security.

The fourth statute, the Sedition Act, sought to control both citizens and aliens. It outlawed conspiracies to prevent the enforcement of federal laws, setting the maximum punishment for such offenses at five years in prison and a $5,000 fine. The act also tried to control speech. Writing, printing, or uttering "false, scandalous and malicious" statements against the government or the president became a crime punishable by as much as two years' imprisonment and a fine of $2,000.

The Sedition Act led to fifteen indictments and ten convictions. Most of the accused were outspoken Democratic-Republican newspaper editors. But the first victim was a hot-tempered Democratic-Republican congressman from Vermont, Matthew Lyon. The Irish-born Lyon was convicted, fined $1,000, and sent to prison for four months for declaring in print that John Adams had displayed "a continual grasp for power" and "an unbounded thirst for ridiculous pomp, foolish adulation, and selfish avarice." Lyon was reelected while serving his jail term.

Faced with prosecutions of their supporters, Jefferson and Madison sought an effective way to

Virginia and Kentucky Resolutions

combat the acts. In doing so, they turned to the state legislatures. Carefully concealing their own role to avoid being indicted for sedition, Jefferson and Madison each drafted a set of resolutions that were introduced into the Kentucky and Virginia legislatures, respectively, in the fall of 1798. Since a compact among the states created the Constitution, they contended, people speaking through their states had a legitimate right to judge the constitutionality of actions taken by the federal government. Both sets of resolutions pronounced the Alien and Sedition Acts unconstitutional and asked other states to join in a concerted protest against them.

Although no other state endorsed them, the Virginia and Kentucky resolutions nevertheless had considerable influence. First, they constituted superb political propaganda, rallying Democratic-Republican opinion throughout the country and placing the party in the revolutionary tradition of resistance to tyrannical authority. Second, the theory of union they proposed inspired southern states' rights advocates in the 1830s and thereafter. Jefferson and Madison had identified a key constitutional issue: How far could states go in opposing the national government? How could a conflict between the two be resolved?

Meanwhile, the Federalists split over the course of action the United States should take toward

Convention of 1800

France. Hamilton and his supporters called for a declaration legitimizing the undeclared naval war. But Adams received a number of private signals, among them Logan's report, that the French government regretted its treatment of the American commissioners. Acting on such assurances, he dispatched the envoy William Vans Murray to Paris to negotiate with Napoleon Bonaparte, France's new leader. The United States sought two goals: compensation for ships the French had seized since 1793 and abrogation of the treaty of 1778. The Franco-American Convention of 1800, which ended the Quasi-War, provided for the latter but not the former. The results of the negotiations did not become known in the United States until after the presidential election of 1800. By then, divisions within the Federalist party had already cost Adams the election.

Indians and African Americans at the End of the Century

By the end of the eighteenth century, the nation had added three states (Vermont, Kentucky, and Tennessee) to the original thirteen and more than 1 million people to the nearly 4 million counted by the 1790 census. Nine-tenths of the approximately 1 million resident African Americans— most still enslaved—lived in the Chesapeake or the

Haitian Refugees

Although many European Americans initially welcomed the news of the French Revolution in 1789, few expressed similar sentiments about the slave rebellion that broke out soon after in the French colony of St. Domingue (later Haiti), which shared the island of Hispaniola with Spanish Santo Domingo. The large number of refugees who soon flowed into the new United States from that nearby revolt brought with them consequences deemed undesirable by most political leaders. Less than a decade after winning independence, the new nation confronted its first immigration crisis.

Among the approximately 600,000 residents of St. Domingue in the early 1790s were about 100,000 free people, almost all of them slaveowners; half were whites, the rest mulattos. When, in the wake of the French Revolution, those free mulattos split the slaveholding population by seeking greater social and political equality, the slaves seized the opportunity to revolt. By 1793, they had triumphed under the leadership of a former slave, Toussaint L'Ouverture, and in 1804 they finally ousted the French, thereafter establishing the republic of Haiti. Thousands of whites and mulattos, accompanied by as many slaves as they could readily transport, sought asylum in the United States during those turbulent years.

Although willing to offer shelter to refugees from the violence, American political leaders nonetheless feared the consequences of their arrival. Southern plantation owners shuddered at the thought that slaves so familiar with ideas of freedom and equality would mingle with their own bondspeople. Many were uncomfortable with the immigration of numerous free people of color, even though the immigrants were part of the slaveholding class. Most of the southern states adopted laws forbidding the entry of Haitian slaves and free mulattos, but the laws were difficult, if not impossible, to enforce, as was a later congressional act to the same effect. And so more than 15,000 refugees—white, black, and of mixed race origins—flooded into the United States and Spanish Louisiana. Many ended up in Virginia (which did not pass an exclusion law) or the cities of Charleston, Savannah, and New Orleans.

There they had a considerable impact on the existing population. In both New Orleans and Charleston,

the influx of mulattos gave rise to heightened color consciousness that placed light-skinned people at the top of a hierarchy of people of color. Not coincidentally, the Charleston Brown Fellowship Society, composed exclusively of free mulattos, was founded in 1793. After the United States purchased Louisiana in 1803, the number of free people of color in the territory almost doubled in three years, largely because of a final surge of immigration from the new Haitian republic. And in Virginia, stories of the successful revolt helped to inspire local slaves in 1800 when they planned the action that has become known as Gabriel's Rebellion.

The Haitian refugees thus linked both European and African Americans to current events in the West Indies, indelibly affecting both groups of people.

A free woman of color in Louisiana early in the nineteenth century, possibly one of the refugees from Haiti. Esteban Rodriguez Miró, named governor of Spanish Louisiana in 1782, ordered all slave and free black women to wear head wraps rather than hats— which were reserved for whites—but this woman and many others subverted his order by nominally complying, but nevertheless creating elaborate headdresses. (Louisiana State Museum)

Lower South. And by 1800, all the Indian nations residing in U.S. territory east of the Mississippi River had made peace with the republic.

The new nation's policymakers, all of European American descent, could not ignore such large proportions of the population. How should the republic deal with eastern Indians, who no longer posed a military threat to the country? Did the growing population of bondspeople present new hazards? The second question took on added significance after 1793, when a bloody revolt of mulattos and blacks led by Toussaint L'Ouverture overthrew French rule in St. Domingue (Haiti).

In 1789 Secretary of War Knox proposed that the new national government assume the task of "civilizing" America's indigenous population. The first step in such a project, Knox suggested, should be to introduce to Indian peoples "a love for exclusive property"; to that end, he proposed that the government give livestock to individual Indians. Four years later, the Indian Trade and Intercourse Act of 1793 codified Knox's plan, promising Indians federally supplied animals, agricultural implements, and instructors.

"Civilizing" the Indians

This well-intentioned plan reflected federal officials' blindness to the realities of native peoples' lives. It ignored both the Indians' traditional commitment to communal notions of landowning and the centuries-long agricultural experience of eastern Indian peoples. The policymakers focused only on Indian men: since they hunted, male Indians were "savages" who had to be "civilized" by being taught to farm. That in these societies women traditionally did the farming was irrelevant because in the eyes of the officials, Indian women—like those of European descent—should properly confine themselves to child rearing, household chores, and home manufacturing.

Indian nations at first responded cautiously to the "civilizing" plan. In the 1790s, people of the Iroquois Confederacy lived in what one historian has called "slums in the wilderness," restricted to small reservations amid expanding Anglo-American farmlands and no longer able to hunt. Quaker missionaries started a demonstration farm among the Senecas, intending to teach men to plow, but women showed greater interest in their message. The same was true among the Chero-

Iroquois and Cherokees

kees of Georgia. As their southern hunting territories were reduced, Cherokee men did begin to raise cattle and hogs, but they startled the reformers by treating livestock like wild game, allowing the animals to run free in the woods and simply shooting them when needed. Men also started to plow the fields, although Cherokee women continued to bear primary responsibility for cultivation and harvest.

Iroquois men became more receptive to the Quakers' lessons after the spring of 1799, when a Seneca named Handsome Lake experienced a remarkable series of visions. Like other prophets stretching back to Neolin (see Chapter 5), Handsome Lake preached that Indian peoples should renounce alcohol, gambling, and other destructive European customs. He directed his followers to heed the Quakers' lessons, but in doing so, he aimed above all to preserve Iroquois culture. Handsome Lake recognized that since men could no longer hunt to obtain meat, only by adopting the European sexual division of labor could the Iroquois retain an autonomous existence.

Online Study Center **Improve Your Grade**
Interactive Map: African American Population, 1790

African Americans had long been forced to conform to European American notions of proper gender roles and had embraced Christianity. Yet just as Cherokees and Iroquois adapted the reformers' plans to their own purposes, so too enslaved blacks found new meanings in the dominant society's ideas. African Americans (both slave and free) became familiar with concepts of liberty and equality during the Revolution. They also witnessed the benefits of fighting collectively for freedom rather than resisting individually or running away. And as white evangelicals by the end of the century began to back away from their earlier racial egalitarianism, African Americans increasingly formed their own separate Baptist and Methodist congregations.

Such congregations near Richmond became the seedbeds of revolt. Gabriel, an enslaved blacksmith who argued that African Americans should fight for their freedom, carefully planned a large-scale rebellion. Often accompanied by his brother Martin, a preacher, he visited Sunday church services, where blacks gathered outside the watchful eyes of their owners. Gabriel first recruited to his cause other skilled African Americans

Gabriel's Rebellion

who like himself lived in semifreedom under minimal supervision. Next he enlisted rural slaves. The conspirators planned to attack Richmond on the night of August 30, 1800, set fire to the city, seize the state capitol, and capture the governor. At that point, Gabriel believed, other slaves and sympathetic poor whites would join in.

The plan showed considerable political sophistication, but heavy rain forced a postponement. Several planters then learned of the plan from slave informers and spread the alarm. Gabriel avoided arrest for some weeks, but militia troops quickly apprehended and interrogated most of the other leaders of the rebellion. Twenty-six conspirators, including Gabriel himself, were hanged, but that did not end the unrest among Virginia's slaves.

At his trial, one of Gabriel's followers made explicit the links that so frightened Chesapeake slaveholders. He told his judges that, like George Washington, "I have adventured my life in endeavouring to obtain the liberty of my countrymen, and am a willing sacrifice in their cause." Southern state legislatures responded to such claims by increasing the severity of the laws regulating slavery. Before long, all talk of emancipation ceased in the South, and slavery became even more firmly entrenched as an economic institution and way of life.

Summary *Online Study Center* ACE the Test

*A*s the nineteenth century began, inhabitants of the United States faced changed lives in the new republic. Indian peoples east of the Mississippi River found that they had to give up some parts of their traditional culture to preserve others. Some African Americans struggled unsuccessfully to free themselves from the inhuman bonds of slavery, then subsequently confronted more constraints than ever before because of increasingly restrictive laws.

European Americans too adjusted to changed circumstances. The first eleven years of government under the Constitution established many enduring precedents for congressional, presidential, and judicial action—among them the establishment of the cabinet, interpretations of key clauses of the Constitution, and the stirrings of judicial review of state and federal legislation. Building on successful negotiations with Spain, Britain, and France, the United States developed its diplomatic independence, striving to avoid entanglement with European countries and their wars. The 1790s also spawned vigorous debates over foreign and domestic policy and saw the beginnings of a system of organized political factionalism.

At the end of the 1790s, after more than a decade of struggle, the Jeffersonian view of the future of republicanism prevailed over Hamilton's vision. For decades to come, the country would be characterized by a decentralized economy, minimal government, and maximum freedom of action and mobility for individual white men. Jeffersonians failed to extend to white women, Indian peoples, and African Americans the freedom and individuality they recognized as essential for themselves.

LEGACY FOR A PEOPLE AND A NATION
Dissent During Wartime

The Quasi-War with France in 1798 and 1799, the nation's first overseas conflict, brought the first attempt to suppress dissent. The Sedition Act of 1798 tried to quiet the Democratic-Republicans' criticism of the war and President John Adams. Ten men were fined and jailed after being convicted under the statute's provisions.

Americans might assume that their right to free speech under the First Amendment, more fully accepted now than it was two hundred years ago, today protects dissenters during war, but the history of the nation suggests otherwise. Each major conflict fought under the Constitution—the Civil War, World War I, World War II, and Vietnam—has stimulated efforts by both government and individual citizens to suppress dissenting voices. For example, during the Civil War, the Union jailed civilian Confederate sympathizers, holding them under martial law for long periods. During World War I, a Sedition Act allowed the government to deport immigrant aliens who too vocally criticized the war effort. Moreover, citizens who objected to government policies endured a variety of formal and informal sanctions by their neighbors. During World War II, those who had opposed American entry into the war were denied public outlets for their ideas. The divisions over antiwar protests in the Vietnam era still affect the nation today. Although during the first Persian Gulf war (1991) and the Afghanistan campaign (2001), military officials restricted reporters' access to the battlefront, that policy was reversed during the war against Iraq (2003), with mixed results.

Freedom of speech is never easy to maintain, and wartime conditions make it much more difficult. When the nation comes under attack, many patriotic Americans argue that the time for dissent has ceased. Others contend that if freedom in the nation is to mean anything, people must have the right to speak their minds freely at all times. Events in the United States since the attacks of September 11, 2001, suggest that this legacy remains extremely contentious for the American people.

PARTISAN POLITICS AND WAR: THE DEMOCRATIC-REPUBLICANS IN POWER 1801–1815

*J*ohn Foss, captured by "pirates" off the Barbary Coast of North Africa in the 1790s, wrote of the "hellish tortures and punishments" inflicted "on the unfortunate Christians." Marched through Algiers, the party of nine ragged sailors heard shouts from the Islamic crowds praising victories over "Christian dogs," and in prison they learned of ten other American vessels recently captured. In Algiers they became white slaves under African masters.

In the nineteenth century, the dramatic Barbary captivity stories, in telling of captives beaten as Christians and humiliated as Americans and of white slaves with black masters, turned American assumptions on their heads. Firsthand descriptions of Africa projected images of a despotic, depraved people, so very different from Americans. In the end, the Americans—at least those who survived to tell their stories—prevailed, and so the stories became epic affirmations of western culture over "barbarians."

In reality, the "pirates"—from what Europeans called the Barbary states and Africans the Maghreb—had challenged the United States in a most fundamental way: was this new nation an independent, sovereign state that could protect its citizens and commerce abroad?

The issue was money. In 1801 the *bashaw* of Tripoli, angry over the young nation's refusal to pay tribute for safe passage of its ships through the Mediterranean, declared war on the United States. President Thomas Jefferson responded by sending a naval squadron to protect American ships in the area. After two years of stalemate, Jefferson ordered a blockade of Tripoli, but the American frigate *Philadelphia* ran aground in its harbor, and three hundred American officers and sailors were captured. Jefferson refused to

The Jefferson Presidency and Marshall Court

Louisiana and Lewis and Clark

A New Political Culture

Indian Resistance

American Shipping Imperiled

"Mr. Madison's War"

LINKS TO THE WORLD
Industrial Piracy

Peace and Consequences

LEGACY FOR A PEOPLE AND A NATION
States' Rights and Nullification

Online Study Center
This icon will direct you to interactive map and primary source activities on the website
http://college.hmco.com/pic/nortonbrief7e

C H R O N O L O G Y

1800 • Jefferson elected president, Burr vice president

1801 • Marshall becomes chief justice of the United States
• Jefferson inaugurated as first Democratic-Republican president

1801–05 • United States defeats Barbary pirates in Tripoli War

1803 • *Marbury v. Madison* establishes judicial review
• United States purchases Louisiana Territory from France

1804 • Burr kills Hamilton in a duel
• Jefferson reelected president, Clinton vice president

1804–06 • Lewis and Clark explore Louisiana Territory

1805 • Prophet emerges as Shawnee leader

1807 • *Chesapeake* affair
• Embargo Act halts foreign trade

1808 • Congress bans importation of slaves to the United States

• Madison elected president, Clinton vice president

1808–13 • Prophet and Tecumseh organize Native American tribal resistance

1808–15 • Embargoes and war stimulate domestic manufacturing

1812 • Madison reelected president, Gerry vice president

1812–15 • United States and Great Britain fight the War of 1812

1813 • Death of Tecumseh ends effective pan-Indian resistance

1814 • Jackson's defeat of Creeks at Battle of Horseshoe Bend begins Indian removal from the South
• Treaty of Ghent ends the War of 1812

1814–15 • Hartford Convention undermines Federalists

1815 • Battle of New Orleans makes Jackson a national hero

ransom them. With the blockade still in place, seven marines and four hundred soldiers of fortune marched overland from Egypt to seize the port of Derne, on the shores of Tripoli. Finally, by treaty with Tripoli in 1805, the United States paid $60,000 to free the *Philadelphia* prisoners, and the war was over. But the United States continued to pay tribute to the other three Barbary states until 1815. The question of U.S. independence and sovereignty still rankled.

In replacing John Adams as president, Thomas Jefferson piloted the young nation in new directions at home as well as abroad. In the tradition of the Revolution, Jefferson and his Democratic-Republican successor presidents sought to restrain the national government, believing that limited government would

foster republican virtue. The Federalists advocated a strong national government with centralized authority to promote economic development. In addition to politics, divisions along lines of class, race, ethnicity, gender, religion, and region contributed to factionalism. As the factions competed for popular support, they laid the basis for a national political culture.

Events abroad and in the West both encouraged and threatened Americans. Seizing one opportunity, the United States purchased the Louisiana Territory. But as American interests turned westward, events in Europe and at sea on the Atlantic forced an about-face. Caught between the warring British and French, the United States found its ships seized, its foreign commerce interrupted, its sailors forcibly drafted, and its rights as a neutral and independent nation violated. In what some have called the second war for independence, the United States fought Great Britain to a standoff, while on another front shattering Native American unity and resistance. A peace treaty restored the prewar status quo, but the war and the treaty reaffirmed U.S. sovereignty and strengthened America's determination to steer clear of further European conflicts. The war also stimulated industry and nationalism. ■

The Jefferson Presidency and Marshall Court

*I*n later years, Thomas Jefferson would always refer to his winning the presidency as the "Revolution of 1800." The Democratic-Republicans, he believed, would restore government to its limited role, restrained and frugal. He stressed the republican virtues of independence, self-reliance, and equality, in contrast to the monarchical ambitions of the Federalists. To counter Federalist formality, Jefferson and his fellow Democratic-Republicans promoted simplicity, even in dress. They wore plain trousers instead of the wigs and knee breeches favored by George Washington and John Adams.

Yet in his inaugural address in March 1801, Jefferson reached out to his opponents. Standing in the

JEFFERSON'S INAUGURAL

Senate chamber, he appealed to the electorate not as party members but as citizens sharing common beliefs. "We are all republicans, we are all federalists," Jefferson offered, laying out his vision of a restored republicanism: "A wise and frugal government, which shall restrain men from injuring one another, which shall leave them free to regulate their pursuits of industry and improvement, and shall not take from the mouth of labor the bread it has earned."

But outgoing president John Adams was not there to hear Jefferson's call for unity. He had left Washington before dawn to avoid the Democratic-Republican takeover. He and Jefferson, once close friends, now disliked each other intensely. Despite the spirit of Jefferson's inaugural address, the Democratic-Republicans and Federalists remained bitter opponents.

To implement the restoration of republican values, Jefferson aggressively extended the Democratic-

DEMOCRATIC- REPUBLICAN ASCENDANCY

Republicans' grasp on the national government. Virtually all of the six hundred or so officials appointed during the administrations of Washington and Adams had been loyal Federalists. To bring into his administration men who shared his vision of an agrarian republic and individual liberty, Jefferson refused to recognize appointments Adams had made in the last days of his presidency and dismissed Federalist customs collectors from New England ports. He awarded vacant treasury and judicial offices to Democratic-Republicans. By July 1803, Federalists held only 130 of 316 presidentially controlled offices.

The Democratic-Republican Congress proceeded to affirm its belief in limited government. Albert Gallatin, secretary of the treasury, and Representative John Randolph of Virginia translated ideology into policy, putting the federal government on a diet. Congress repealed all internal taxes, including the whiskey tax. Gallatin cut the army budget in half and reduced the 1802 navy budget by two-thirds. He then moved to reduce the national debt from $83 million to $57 million as part of a plan to retire it altogether by 1817.

More than frugality, however, distinguished Democratic-Republicans from Federalists. Before Jefferson's election, opposition to the Alien and Sedition Acts of 1798 had helped unite Democratic-Republicans. Jefferson now declined to use the acts against his opponents, and Congress let them expire in 1801 and 1802. Congress also repealed the Naturalization Act of 1798, which had required fourteen years of residency for citizenship. The 1802 act that replaced it required only five years of residency, loyalty to the Constitution, and the forsaking of foreign allegiance and titles.

The Democratic-Republicans turned next to the judiciary, the last stronghold of Federalist power.

WAR ON THE JUDICIARY

During the 1790s, not a single Democratic-Republican had occupied the federal bench; thus, the judiciary became a battlefield following the revolution of 1800. The first skirmish erupted over repeal of the Judiciary Act of 1801, which had been passed in the final days of the Adams administration. The act created fifteen new judgeships, which Adams filled by signing "midnight" appointments until his term was just hours from expiring. The act also reduced by attrition the number of justices on the Supreme Court from six to five. Since that reduction would have denied Jefferson a Supreme Court appointment until two vacancies occurred, the new Congress, dominated by the Democratic-Republicans, repealed the 1801 act.

Partisan Democratic-Republicans next targeted opposition judges for removal. Democratic-Republicans were especially infuriated with the Federalist judges who had refused to review the Sedition Act, under which Federalists had prosecuted critics of the Adams administration. At Jefferson's prompting, the House impeached (indicted) Federal District Judge John Pickering of New Hampshire, an emotionally disturbed alcoholic. In 1805 the Senate convicted him, removing him from office.

The day Pickering was ousted, the House impeached Supreme Court Justice Samuel Chase for judicial misconduct. A staunch Federalist, Chase had repeatedly denounced Jefferson's administration from the bench. The Democratic-Republicans, however, failed to muster the two-thirds majority of senators necessary to convict him. Chase's acquittal preserved the Court's independence and established the precedent that criminal actions, not political disagreements, were the only proper grounds for impeachment. In his tenure as president, Jefferson appointed three new Supreme Court justices. Nonetheless, under Chief Justice John Marshall, the Court remained a Federalist stronghold.

In his last weeks as a lame-duck president, Adams, in an act especially galling to Jefferson, appointed

JOHN
MARSHALL

Marshall as chief justice. A Virginia Federalist, Marshall was an autocrat by nature but possessed a grace and openness of manner that complemented the new Republican political style. Under Marshall's domination, the Supreme Court retained a Federalist outlook even after Democratic-Republican justices achieved a majority in 1811. Throughout his tenure (1801–1835), the Court consistently upheld federal supremacy over the states and protected the interests of commerce and capital.

Marshall made the Court an equal branch of government in practice as well as theory. Judicial service, previously regarded lightly, became a coveted honor for ambitious and talented men. Marshall also

■ This portrait of President Thomas Jefferson was painted by Rembrandt Peale in 1805. Charles Willson Peale (Rembrandt's father) and his five sons helped establish the reputation of American art in the new nation. Rembrandt Peale achieved fame for his presidential portraits; here he has captured Jefferson in a noble pose without the usual symbols of office or power, befitting the Republican age.   (© Collection of The New York Historical Society)

unified the Court, influencing the justices to issue joint majority opinions rather than a host of individual concurring judgments. Marshall himself became the voice of the majority: from 1801 through 1810, he wrote 85 percent of the opinions, including every important one.

Marshall significantly increased the Supreme Court's power in the landmark case of *Marbury v.*

MARBURY V.
MADISON

Madison (1803). William Marbury, one of Adams's midnight appointees, had been named a justice of the peace in the District of Columbia.

James Madison, Jefferson's new secretary of state, declined to certify Marbury's appointment so that the president could instead appoint a Democratic-Republican. Marbury sued, requesting a writ of mandamus (a court order forcing the president to appoint him). The case presented a political dilemma. If the Supreme Court ruled in favor of Marbury and issued a writ, the president probably would not comply with it, and the Court had no way to force him to do so. But if the Federalist-dominated bench refused to issue the writ, it would be handing the Democratic-Republicans a victory.

Marshall brilliantly avoided both pitfalls. Speaking for the Court, he ruled that Marbury had a right to his appointment but that the Supreme Court could not compel Madison to honor the appointment because the Constitution did not grant the Court power to issue a writ of mandamus. In the absence of any specific mention in the Constitution, Marshall ruled, the section of the Judiciary Act of 1789 that authorized the Court to issue such writs was unconstitutional. In *Marbury v. Madison*, the Supreme Court denied itself the power to issue writs of mandamus but established its far greater power to judge the constitutionality of laws passed by Congress.

In succeeding years Marshall fashioned the theory of judicial review, the power of the Supreme Court to decide the constitutionality of legislation and presidential acts. Since the Constitution was the supreme law, he reasoned, any federal or state act contrary to the Constitution must be null and void. The Supreme Court, whose duty it was to uphold the law, would decide whether a legislative act contradicted the Constitution. The power of judicial review established in *Marbury v. Madison* permanently enhanced the independence of the judiciary.

Louisiana and Lewis and Clark

*D*emocratic-Republicans and Federalists divided sharply over other issues; the acquisition of the Louisiana Territory in 1803 was another point of contention. Jefferson shared with many other Americans the belief that the United States was destined to expand its "empire of liberty."

By 1800 hundreds of thousands of Americans had settled in the rich Mississippi and Ohio River val-leys, intruding on Indian lands. These settlers floated their farm goods down the Ohio and Mississippi Rivers to New Orleans for export. Whoever controlled the port of New Orleans had a hand on the throat of the American economy. Spain had owned Louisiana since acquiring it from France at the end of the Seven Years War in 1763. Americans preferred Spanish control to control by France, a much stronger power.

In secret pacts with Spain in 1800 and 1801, however, France had reacquired the territory. The United States learned of the transfer only in 1802, when Napoleon seemed poised to rebuild a French empire in the New World. Then, on the eve of ceding control to the French, Spain violated Pinckney's Treaty by denying Americans the privilege of storing their products at New Orleans prior to transshipment to foreign markets. Western farmers and eastern merchants thought a devious Napoleon had closed the port; they grumbled and talked war.

Jefferson personally took charge. To relieve the pressure for war and win western farm support, he prepared for war while sending Virginia governor James Monroe as his personal envoy to join Robert Livingston, the American minister in France. Their mission: to buy the port of New Orleans and as much of the Mississippi valley as possible. Meanwhile, Congress authorized the call-up of eighty thousand militiamen in case war became necessary. Arriving in Paris in April 1803, Monroe was astonished to learn that France already had offered to sell all 827,000 square miles of Louisiana to the United States for a mere $15 million. Napoleon had lost interest in the New World. On April 30 Monroe and Livingston signed a treaty buying the vast territory, whose exact borders and land were uncharted (see Map 9.1).

The Louisiana Purchase doubled the size of the nation and opened the way for continental expansion. But was this most popular achievement of Jefferson's presidency constitutional? The Constitution nowhere authorized the president to acquire new territory and incorporate it into the nation. But Jefferson believed that the president's implied powers to protect the nation justified the purchase. His long-standing interest in Louisiana and the West also allayed his constitutional concerns. As a naturalist and scientist, Jefferson seemed obsessed with the West—its geography, people,

**LOUISIANA
PURCHASE**

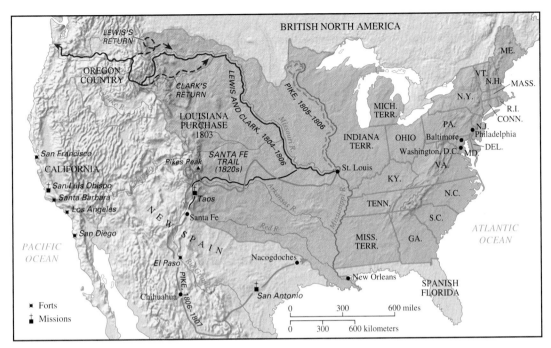

Map 9.1   Louisiana Purchase

The Louisiana Purchase (1803) doubled the area of the United States and opened the trans-Mississippi West for American settlement.

plants, and animals. He was also interested in finding "the shortest & most convenient route of communications between the U.S. & the Pacific Ocean."

In 1803 Jefferson sent an expedition headed by Meriwether Lewis and William Clark to the Pacific coast via the Missouri and Columbia Rivers. The expedition had political as well as scientific import, for British exploration in Canada had raised fears that the British would dominate the West. Lewis and Clark officially started their journey in May 1804. They traveled up the Missouri River and wintered at Fort Mandan in present-day North Dakota. Here they selected their twenty-nine-member corps, called the Corps of Discovery, and were joined by Indian guides. In April 1805 they resumed their journey. At times they lost their way, tumbled down steep mountain trails, and slept in the snow. In November 1805 they reached the Pacific Ocean in present-day Oregon, where they wintered, and the following March they began the re-

Lewis and Clark

turn trek. Lewis and Clark split up to explore alternate routes and reunited in August 1806. They arrived home in St. Louis on September 23, 1806.

Online Study Center **Improve Your Grade**
Primary Source: The President's Instructions to Meriwether Lewis

The original Corps of Discovery reflected American diversity. It included army regulars and young adventurers from Kentucky. Among them were half-French, half-Omaha, and half-Shawnee men. Clark brought his slave, York. Immigrants included an Irishman and a German. Later, at the Mandan villages, Lewis and Clark took on the French Canadian trader Toussaint Charbonneau because they wanted his pregnant fifteen-year-old Shoshone wife, Sacagawea, who knew the languages of the mountain Indians. She proved invaluable as a guide and translator.

Corps of Discovery

Headed by army officers, the expedition followed military rules. At times, however, it was more informal and democratic than army regulations or even civilian society allowed. When trouble arose, Lewis and Clark held courts-martial to discipline corps members for such infractions as drunkenness. Contrary to army rules, enlisted men sat on the court. And in November 1805, to determine where to locate winter quarters on the Pacific coast, all voted, including the slave York and the Indian woman Sacagawea. Yet issues of race and gender were present. At the end of the journey, the names of York and Sacagawea were not on the roster Lewis submitted to the War Department, and neither received pay for their indispensable work.

Although some Americans still believed that the West was uninhabited, Lewis and Clark knew better. They anticipated a crowded wilderness and hoped to cement U.S. relations with Indians. The explorers carried gifts for Native American leaders, both to establish goodwill and to stimulate interest in trading for American manufactured goods. They brought back stories not only of various peoples but also of fauna and flora unknown to the western scientific community. Lewis sent boxes of natural-history specimens to Jefferson, including plant and tree cuttings. The two also mapped the West and, with their reports and specimens, furthered dreams of a continental empire.

Online Study Center **Improve Your Grade**
Interactive Map: Louisiana Purchase and the Lewis and Clark Expedition

Other explorations followed Lewis and Clark's. In 1805 and 1806 Lieutenant Zebulon Pike sought the source of the continent-cutting river and a navigable water route to the Far West. When Pike and his men wandered into Spanish territory to the south, the Spanish held them captive for several months in Mexico. After his release, Pike wrote an account of his experiences that set commercial minds spinning. Over the next few decades, Americans avidly read accounts of western exploration. A road to the Southwest opened with the Santa Fe Trail in the 1820s, and settlement followed the trail.

EXPLORATION OF THE WEST

New Spain's Tejas (Texas) province bordered the Louisiana Territory. Provincial officials welcomed Americans, some of whom fought as volunteers with Indians and Mexican rebels in a twelve-year war with Spain that ended with Mexican independence in 1821. The establishment of an independent Mexico inspired these Americans to dream of an independent Texas nation—a place for white Americans. Envisioning the West as uninhabited, they did not imagine a place for Mexicans or indigenous peoples in the "empire of liberty."

A New Political Culture

Jefferson described his presidency as the beginning of a new era. Although the electorate was limited mostly to white males over age twenty-one who held property, the Democratic-Republicans had taken their appeals to the people in the elections of 1800. While Federalists thought that for candidates to debate their merits in front of voters was demeaning, a subversion of the natural political order, the Democratic-Republicans did not. Now in office, they worked hard to keep public opinion on their side.

One way to control public opinion was through the press. The new president persuaded the *National Intelligencer* to move from Philadelphia to Washington, and during the ensuing Democratic-Republican administrations, it served as the official voice. In 1801 Alexander Hamilton launched the *New-York Evening Post* as the Federalist voice. While boosting Federalists, it often called Jefferson a liar and depicted him as head of a slave harem. Newspapers circulated widely and were often read aloud in taverns, coffeehouses, and hotels. Like the political parties, they helped build a national political culture. In 1800 the nation had 260 newspapers; by 1810 it had 396. Editors were outrageously partisan.

THE PARTISAN PRESS

After the Federalist defeat in 1800, a younger generation of Federalists began to imitate the Democratic-Republicans. Led by such men as Josiah Quincy, a Massachusetts congressman, the Younger Federalists presented their faction as the people's party, portraying Democratic-Republicans as autocratic planters. In attacking frugal government, the Younger Federalists played on fears of a weakened army and navy. Eastern merchants depended on a strong navy to protect ocean trade; westerners looked to the army to defend them as they encroached on Indian territory.

For Democratic-Republicans, distinctive regional interests inspired a new style of campaigning, symbolized by the political barbecue.

GRASSROOTS CAMPAIGNING In New York, campaigners roasted oxen; on the New England coast, they held clambakes. Guests washed down their meals with beer and punch and listened to the lengthy orations of candidates. The speakers attacked their opponents' character, resorting to slander and gossip and often making wild accusations. Some historians have speculated that these developing party rituals helped contain more violent expression.

The Federalists never mastered the art of campaigning. Older Federalists remained opposed to popular appeals. And though strong in Connecticut, Delaware, and a few other states, the Federalists were weak at the national level and could not manage sustained competition. The extremism of some Older Federalists discredited most of the rest. For instance, Timothy Pickering, a Massachusetts congressman and former secretary of state, opposed the Louisiana Purchase, feared Jefferson's reelection, and urged the secession of New England in 1803 and 1804. He won some support, but most Federalists balked at his plan for secession. Ever the opportunist, Vice President Aaron Burr, intrigued with Pickering's idea, fantasized about leading New York into secession, with other states following. But when Burr lost his bid to become governor of New York in 1804, dreams of a northern confederacy evaporated.

The controversies surrounding Burr illustrate the convergence of the political and the personal. In the

BURR AND PERSONAL ANIMOSITY election of 1800, he understood he was the vice-presidential candidate, but when all seventy-three of the Democratic-Republican electors cast ballots for both Jefferson and Burr, Burr challenged Jefferson for the presidency. The Constitution required that because neither had a plurality, the contest be decided in the House of Representatives, with each state's congressmen voting as a unit. It took thirty-five ballots for the House, still with a Federalist majority, to decide that Jefferson would be a lesser evil than Burr. In response

to the tangle, the Twelfth Amendment to the Constitution (1804) changed the method of voting in the electoral college to allow for a party ticket.

For Burr it was a short step from personal animosity into violence. He and the hothead Alexander Hamilton had long despised each other. Hamilton thwarted Burr's attempt to steal the election of 1800 from Jefferson, and in the 1804 mudslinging New York gubernatorial race, he backed Burr's Democratic-Republican rival. When Hamilton accused Burr of being a liar, Burr challenged him to a duel. With his honor at stake, Hamilton accepted even though his son Philip had died in 1801 from dueling wounds. Because New York had outlawed dueling, the two men met across the Hudson River at Weehawken, New Jersey, in July 1804. Hamilton did not fire, and he paid for that decision with his life. Burr was indicted for murder.

His political career in ruins, Burr schemed to create in the Southwest a new empire carved out of the Louisiana Territory. With the collusion of General James Wilkinson, the U.S. commander in the Mississippi valley, Burr planned to raise a private army to grab land from the United States or from Spain (his exact plans remain unknown). Wilkinson switched sides and informed President Jefferson of Burr's devious intention. Jefferson personally assisted the prosecution in Burr's 1807 trial for treason, over which Chief Justice Marshall presided. The jury acquitted Burr, who fled to Europe.

Campaigning for reelection in 1804, Jefferson took credit for the restoration of republican values and

ELECTION OF 1804 the acquisition of the Louisiana Territory. The Democratic-Republicans claimed they ended the Federalist threat to liberty by repealing the Alien and Sedition and Judiciary Acts and boasted of reducing the size of government by cutting spending. American trade with Europe was flourishing, allowing Jefferson to demonstrate support for commerce too.

Jefferson's opponent in 1804 was Charles Cotesworth Pinckney, a wealthy South Carolina lawyer and former Revolutionary War aide to George Washington. As Adams's running mate in 1800, Pinckney had inherited the Federalist leadership. Jefferson and his running mate, George Clinton of New York, easily won the election.

Indian Resistance

Lewis and Clark's account testified to the Indian presence in the West, and most Americans viewed Native Americans, no matter where they lived, as obstacles to American settlement. Violations of treaties and coerced new ones forcing Indians to cede ever more land continually shrank Indian territory.

In the early 1800s two Shawnee brothers, Prophet (1775–1837) and Tecumseh (1768–1813), challenged

THE PROPHET

further American encroachment by fostering a pan-Indian federation that stretched from the Old Northwest to the South. Prophet's early life typified Indians' experiences in the Old Northwest. Born in 1775, Prophet, called Lalawethika ("Noisemaker"), was expelled as a young man to Ohio with other Shawnees under the 1795 Treaty of Greenville (see Chapter 7), and he later moved to Indiana. Within Prophet and Tecumseh's own lifetimes, the Shawnees had lost most of their Ohio land. Displacement left Lalawethika forlorn, and he turned to whiskey for escape. He also turned to traditional folk knowledge and remedies and in 1804 became a tribal medicine man. His medicine, however, could not stop the white man's diseases from ravaging his village.

Lalawethika emerged from his own battle with illness in 1805 as a new man, called Tenskwatawa ("the Open Door"), or "the Prophet." Claiming to have died and been resurrected, he traveled widely in the Ohio River valley, attacking the decline of moral values among Native Americans, warning of damnation for those who drank whiskey, and condemning intertribal battles. He urged Indians to return to the

■ The Shawnee chiefs Tecumseh *(left)* and Prophet *(right).* The two brothers led a revival of traditional Shawnee culture and preached Native American federation against white encroachment. In the War of 1812 they allied themselves with the British, but Tecumseh's death at the Battle of the Thames (1813) and British indifference thereafter caused Native Americans' resistance and unity to collapse.   (Left: MPI/Hulton Archives/Getty Images; Right: © Smithsonian American Art Museum, Washington, D.C./Art Resource, NY)

old ways and abandon white customs. Prophet's outspoken opposition to federal Indian policy drew others into his camp, and as his message spread to southern tribes, the federal government and white settlers became alarmed.

By 1808 Prophet and his older brother, Tecumseh, talked less about spiritual renewal and more about

TECUMSEH resisting American aggression. Together they invited Indians from all nations to settle in pan-Indian towns in Indiana, first at Greenville (1806–1808) on the Wabash, called Prophetstown by whites, and then at Tippecanoe (1808–1812). The new towns challenged the treaty-making process, and the Americans viewed them as places promoting Indian resistance. In effect, Tecumseh was turning Prophet's religious movement into a political one. In repudiating land cessions to the government under the Treaty of Fort Wayne (1809), Tecumseh told Indiana's governor, William Henry Harrison, at Vincennes in 1810 that "the only way to check and stop this evil is, for all the red men to unite in claiming a common and equal right in the land, . . . for it . . . belongs to all, for the use of each. . . . No part has a right to sell, even to each other, much less to strangers."

Tecumseh, a towering six-foot warrior and charismatic orator, sought to unify northern and southern Indians by traveling widely, preaching Indian resistance. And he warned Harrison that Indians would resist white occupation of the 2.5 million acres on the Wabash River that they had ceded in the Treaty of Fort Wayne.

But the Indians could not match the armed might of the United States. In November 1811, while Tecumseh was recruiting support in the South, Harrison moved against the Prophet and his followers. In the Battle of Tippecanoe, the army burned the town and dispersed Prophet's and Tecumseh's supporters. The spiritual and political movement initiated by the brothers began to unravel.

American Shipping Imperiled

" *P* eace, commerce, and honest friendship with all nations, entangling alliance with none," President Jefferson had proclaimed in his first inaugural address. Jefferson's efforts to stand aloof from European conflict were successful until 1805. Thereafter, the United States could not escape the web of European hostilities.

The economy of the early republic relied heavily on shipping, and the commercial fleet extended

U.S. COMMERCE American trade not only to Britain but around the world. American fishermen explored the Atlantic, while whalers hunted in the Atlantic and Pacific. Americans exported cotton, lumber, sugar, and other commodities to Europe, and brought back manufactured goods. The slave trade lured American sailing ships to Africa. Boston, Salem, and Philadelphia merchants opened trade with China, sending cloth and metal to swap for furs with Chinook Indians on the Oregon coast, then sailing to China to trade for porcelain, tea, and silk.

The root of America's problems lay in the May 1803 renewal of the Napoleonic wars between France and Britain. Initially American commerce benefited from the conflict, as the United States became the chief supplier of grain to Europe. American merchants also gained control of most of the West Indian trade. But by 1806, France and Britain, locked in a military stalemate, launched a commercial war, blockading each other's trade. As a trading partner of both countries, the United States paid a high price.

All tension focused on the high seas as Britain suffered a severe shortage of sailors, and those in

IMPRESSMENT OF AMERICAN SAILORS service, demoralized by harsh treatment, frequently deserted. The Royal Navy resorted to stopping American vessels and impressing, or forcibly detaining, British deserters, British-born naturalized American seamen, and other unlucky sailors suspected of being British. Perhaps six to eight thousand Americans were impressed in this way between 1803 and 1812.

Anglo-American relations steadily deteriorated. Then in June 1807, the forty-gun frigate U.S.S.

CHESAPEAKE AFFAIR *Chesapeake* left Norfolk, Virginia, and while still inside American territorial waters met the fifty-gun British frigate *Leopard*. When the *Chesapeake* refused to be searched for deserters, the *Leopard* repeatedly fired its cannon broadside into the American ship. Three Americans were killed and eighteen wounded. The British seized four deserters from the Royal Navy—three of them

American citizens. Damaged and humiliated, the *Chesapeake* returned to port.

Had the United States been better prepared militarily, the ensuing howl of public indignation might have brought about a declaration of war. But the still-fledgling country was no match for the British navy. With Congress in recess, Jefferson was able to avoid hostilities. In July the president closed American waters to British warships and soon after increased military and naval expenditures. In December 1807 Jefferson again put economic pressure on Great Britain by invoking the Non-Importation Act, followed eight days later by a new restriction, the Embargo Act.

The Embargo Act forbade all exports from the United States to any country, an action that Jefferson perceived as a short-term measure

EMBARGO ACT   to avoid war. Exports dropped by some 80 percent in 1808. Mercantile New England, a bastion of Federalist opposition to Jefferson, was especially hard hit, and in the winter of 1808–1809 talk of secession spread from one port to another.

Few American policies were as well intentioned and as unpopular and unsuccessful as Jefferson's embargo. Moreover, the embargo had little impact on Britain, and France used the policy as an excuse to set privateers against American ships that had evaded the embargo. The French cynically claimed that such ships were British vessels in disguise because the embargo prevented American ships from sailing.

Although general unemployment soared, U.S. manufacturers received a boost from the embargo,

DOMESTIC   since the domestic market became
MANUFACTURING   theirs exclusively, and merchants began to shift their capital from shipping to manufacturing. Factories were still new in America. English immigrant Samuel Slater set up the first American textile mill in Rhode Island in the 1790s. It used water-powered spinning machines that he had built from memorized British models. Although Federalists like Alexander Hamilton had pushed the United States to promote manufacturing, Jefferson envisioned an "empire of liberty" that was agricultural and commercial, not industrial. Democratic-Republican policy did not promote industry, but disruption in commerce made domestic manufactures profitable. In 1807 there were

twenty cotton and woolen mills in New England; by 1813 there were more than two hundred.

As the election of 1808 approached, the Democratic-Republicans faced factional dissent and

ELECTION   dissatisfaction in seaboard states
OF 1808   hobbled by the embargo. Jefferson followed Washington's lead in renouncing a third term. He supported James Madison, his secretary of state, as the Democratic-Republican standard-bearer. Madison won the endorsement of the party's congressional caucus and with his running mate, Vice President George Clinton, defeated the Federalist ticket.

Under the pressure of domestic opposition, the embargo eventually collapsed. In its place, the

NON-   Non-Intercourse Act of 1809 re-
INTERCOURSE   opened trade with all nations except
ACT   Britain and France, and it authorized the president to resume trade with Britain or France if either ceased to violate neutral rights. Although the new law solved the problems created by the embargo, it did not prevent further British and French interference with American commerce.

When the Non-Intercourse Act expired in 1810, Congress substituted Macon's Bill Number 2, which reopened trade with both Great Britain and France but provided that when either nation stopped violating American commercial rights, the president could suspend American commerce with the other. Madison, eager to avoid war, fell victim to French duplicity. When Napoleon accepted the offer, Madison declared nonintercourse with Great Britain in 1811. The French, however, continued to seize American ships, and nonintercourse failed a second time. But because the Royal Navy dominated the seas, Britain, not France, became the main focus of American hostility.

"Mr. Madison's War"

*A*lthough unprepared for war in 1812, the United States under President Madison, having exhausted all efforts to alter British policy and fearing for the survival of American independence, seemed unable to avoid it. The Democratic-Republican "War Hawks," elected to Congress in

Although Americans pride themselves on inventiveness and hard work, their start in industrial development depended on importing technology, sometimes by stealth. Great Britain, which in the late eighteenth century had pioneered the invention of mechanical weaving and power looms, knew the value of its head start in the industrial revolution and prohibited the export of textile technology. But the British-born brothers Samuel and John Slater, their Scottish-born power-loom-builder William Gilmore, and Bostonians Francis Cabot Lowell and Nathan Appleton evaded British restrictions and patents to establish America's first textile factories.

As an apprentice and then a supervisor in a British cotton-spinning factory, Samuel Slater had mastered the machinery and the process. Britain forbade the export of textile technology, so Slater emigrated to the United States disguised as a farmer. In 1790 in Pawtucket, Rhode Island, on the Blackstone River, he opened the first water-powered spinning mill in America, rebuilding the complex machines from memory. With his brother John and their Rhode Island partners, Moses and Obadiah Brown and William Almy, Slater later built and oversaw mills in Rhode Island and Massachusetts. In 1815 he hired a recent immigrant, William Gilmore, to build a water-powered loom like those used in Britain. Later in the 1820s, the Slaters introduced British steam-powered looms. Spinning and weaving would now be done in New England factories organized on British models.

In 1810 Francis Cabot Lowell had the same idea as the Slaters: to build modern mills with mechanical, water-powered looms. Lowell took a family vacation to Britain, and, in Edinburgh, Scotland, he met fellow Bostonian Nathan Appleton. Impressed by the textile mills they had seen in Britain, they laid plans to introduce water-powered mechanical weaving into the United States. They knew they had to acquire the "improved manufactures" from Britain that had made Manchester famous as a textile center. Lowell went to Manchester, during the day visiting and observing the factories and meeting the factory managers. At night, he returned to his hotel to sketch from memory the power looms and processes he saw. Back in the United States, he and others formed the Boston Associates, which created the Waltham-Lowell Mills based on Lowell's industrial piracy. The Lowell boarding houses, however, were intended as an alternative to the tenements and slums of Manchester. Within a few years, textiles would be a major American industry, and the Associates would dominate it.

Thus, the modern American industrial revolution began with international links, not homegrown American inventions. Ingenuity and industrial piracy put the United States on the road to industrial advancement.

This contemporary painting shows the Boston Manufacturing Company's 1814 textile factory at Waltham, Massachusetts. All manufacturing processes were brought together under one roof, and the company built its first factories in rural New England to tap roaring rivers as a power source. (Courtesy of Gore Place Society, Waltham, Mass.)

1810, cried loudest for war. Britain's response came too late. In spring 1812, the admiralty ordered British ships not to stop, search, or seize American warships. Then in June, Britain reopened the seas to American shipping. Hard times had hit the British Isles: the Anglo-French conflict had blocked much British commerce to the European continent, and exports to the United States had fallen 80 percent. But two days after the change in British policy and before word of it had crossed the Atlantic, Congress declared war.

In his message to Congress on June 1, 1812, President Madison enumerated familiar grievances: impressment, interference with neutral trading rights, and British alliances with western Indians. More generally, the Democratic-Republicans resolved to defend American independence and honor, but some Americans saw an opportunity to conquer and annex British Canada.

DEBATE ON THE WAR

The war Congress was a partisan one. Most militant were the War Hawks, land-hungry southerners and westerners, all Democratic-Republicans, led by John C. Calhoun of South Carolina and House Speaker Henry Clay of Kentucky. Most representatives from the coastal states opposed war because armed conflict with the Royal Navy would interrupt American shipping. On the vote in Congress, not a single Federalist favored war. However, both houses of Congress voted for war, and President Madison signed the bill on June 19. Critics instantly called it "Mr. Madison's War."

During these years, politics and personal animosities were often so intense that political compromise and cooperation, essential to politics, seemed almost impossible. But social events at the Executive Mansion, dominated by the magnetic Dolley Madison, provided the site for political compromises. She had, said one observer, "the magic power of converting enemies into friends." At state dinners, she sat at the head of the table and made socializing a state craft. Under Dolley Madison, the White House took on its modern role as the focus of presidential politics. Her Wednesday evening socials brought all political factions together, the only place where political enemies talked cordially. James Madison lacked Jefferson's intellect, but with his wife in the lead, he

DOLLEY MADISON AND FEMALE POLITICAL WORK

was a far more successful politician than Jefferson had been.

Jefferson's warning that "our constitution is a peace establishment—it is not calculated for war" proved true. Although the U.S. Navy had a corps of experienced officers who had proved their mettle in the Barbary War, it was no match for the Royal Navy. The U.S. Army had neither an able staff nor an adequate force of enlisted men. Senior army officers were aged Revolutionary War veterans or political hacks. The army depended on political leaders and state militias to recruit volunteers, and not all states cooperated. The government offered enlistees a sign-up bonus of $16, monthly pay of $5, a full set of clothes, and a promise of three months' pay and rights to purchase 160 acres of western land upon discharge. Forty-two percent of the enlistees were illiterate.

RECRUITMENT

Canada was tempting, and Americans expected to take it quickly. The mighty Royal Navy could not reach the Great Lakes because there was no direct access to them from the Atlantic. Canada's population was just 0.5 million, the United States's 7.5 million. Canada had 7,000 regulars in uniform; the United States, 12,000. And Americans hoped that the French in Canada might welcome U.S. forces.

INVASION OF CANADA

Begun with high hopes, the invasion of Canada ended in disaster. The American strategy concentrated on the West, aiming to split Canadian forces and isolate the pro-British Indians. At the outset of the war, Tecumseh joined the British, who promised him in return an Indian nation in the Great Lakes region. U.S. general William Hull, territorial governor of Michigan, marched his troops into Upper Canada, with the goal of conquering Montreal. Hull had surrounded himself with newly minted colonels as politically astute and militarily ignorant as he was. He waged a timid campaign, losing Mackinac Island, Fort Dearborn in Chicago, and Fort Detroit and leaving the entire Midwest exposed to the enemy. By the winter of 1812–1813, the British controlled about half of the Old Northwest.

The United States had no greater success on the Niagara front, where New York borders Canada. At the Battle of Queenstown, Canada, north of Niagara, the U.S. Army met defeat because the New York militia refused to leave New York. This frustrating scenario was repeated near Lake Champlain when the New York militia refused to cross into Canada, and tenacious opposition from British regulars, their Indian allies, and Canadians, many of them loyalists who had fled the American Revolution, foiled American plans to attack Montreal.

The navy provided the only good news in the first year of the war. The U.S.S. *Constitution*, the U.S.S. *Wasp*, and the U.S.S. *United States*

NAVAL BATTLES

all bested British warships on the Atlantic Ocean. However, in the first year of war, the Americans lost 20 percent of their ships, while in defeat the British lost just 1 percent. With only seventeen ships in 1812, the United States could not prevent Britannia from ruling the waves. By 1814, a Royal Navy blockade covered nearly all American ports. After 1811, American trade overseas had declined nearly 90 percent, and the decline in revenues from customs duties threatened to bankrupt the federal government and prostrate New England.

The contest for control of the Great Lakes, the key to the war in the Northwest, evolved as a ship-building race. Under Master Com-

GREAT LAKES
CAMPAIGN

mandant Oliver Hazard Perry and shipbuilder Noah Brown, the United States outbuilt the British on Lake Erie and defeated them at the bloody Battle of Put-in-Bay on September 10, 1813. With this costly victory, the Americans gained control of Lake Erie.

General William Henry Harrison then began what proved to be among the most successful U.S. land campaigns in the war. Harrison's force of forty-five hundred men took Detroit. Then they crossed to Canada, defeating the British, Shawnee, and Chippewa forces on October 5 at the Battle of the Thames. The United States regained control of the Old Northwest. Moreover, Tecumseh died in the battle, and with his death, Native American unity expired.

After defeating Napoleon in Europe in April 1814, the British launched a land counteroffensive against the United States, con-

BURNING OF
WASHINGTON

centrating on the Chesapeake Bay region. Royal troops occupied Washington, D.C., in August and set it ablaze. The attack on the cap-

ital was only a diversion, however. The major battle occurred in September 1814 at Baltimore, where the Americans held firm. Francis Scott Key, detained on a British ship, watched the bombardment of Fort McHenry from Baltimore harbor and the next morning wrote the verses of "The Star-Spangled Banner" (which became the national anthem in 1931). Although the British inflicted heavy damage both materially and psychologically, they achieved little militarily. They halted their offense, and the war was stalemated.

The last campaigns of the war took place in the South, against the Creeks along the Gulf of Mexico and against the British around New

CAMPAIGN
AGAINST THE
CREEKS

Orleans. The Creeks had responded to Tecumseh's call to resist U.S. expansion. In December 1812 General Andrew Jackson raised his Tennessee militia to fight the Creeks. Jackson's men defeated the Creek nation at the Battle of Horseshoe Bend in Mississippi Territory in March 1814. As a result, the Creeks ceded two-thirds of their land and withdrew to the southern and western part of Mississippi Territory (what is now Alabama); the removal of Indians from the South had begun. Jackson became a major general in the regular army and continued south toward the Gulf of Mexico. After seizing Pensacola in Spanish Florida and securing Mobile, he marched to New Orleans.

Early in December, the British fleet landed troops east of the city of New Orleans, hoping to seize the

BATTLE OF
NEW ORLEANS

mouth of the Mississippi River and thus strangle the lifeline of the American West. They faced American regulars, Tennessee and Kentucky volunteers, and two companies of free African American volunteers from New Orleans. On January 8, 1815, after three weeks of cat-and-mouse, the two forces met head-on. Jackson's poorly trained army held its fortified position against a British contingent of six thousand. At day's end, more than two thousand British soldiers lay dead or wounded; Americans suffered only twenty-one casualties. Andrew Jackson emerged a national hero, and Americans memorialized the battle in song and paintings. The Battle of New Orleans actually took place after the end of the war. Unknown to the participants, a treaty had been signed in Ghent, Belgium, two weeks before the battle.

Peace and Consequences

*T*he Treaty of Ghent, ratified by the Senate on February 17, 1815, essentially restored the prewar status quo. It provided for an end to hostilities, release of prisoners, restoration of conquered territory, and arbitration of boundary disputes. It made no mention of impressment, blockades, or other maritime rights for neutrals, nor did it satisfy any British demands.

Why did the negotiators settle for so little? Events in Europe had made peace and the status quo acceptable at the end of 1814, as they had not been in 1812. Napoleon's defeat allowed the United States to abandon its demands, since impressment and interference with American commerce had become moot issues. Similarly, war-weary Britain, its treasury nearly depleted, stopped pressing for a military victory.

The War of 1812 affirmed the independence of the American republic and ensured Canada's inde-

CONSEQUENCES   pendence from the United States. Although conflict with Great Britain over trade and territory continued, it never again led to war. The experience strengthened America's resolve to steer clear of European politics because the Anglo-French conflagration had drawn the United States into war. At the same time, with Indian resistance broken, U.S. expansion would spread south and west, not north to Canada.

Conflict carried disastrous results for most Native Americans. The ninth article of the Treaty of Ghent pledged the United States to end hostilities and restore "all the possessions, rights, and privileges" that Indians had enjoyed before the war. Midwestern Indians signed more than a dozen treaties with the United States in 1815, but they had little meaning. With the death of Tecumseh, the Indians had lost their most powerful political and military leader; with the withdrawal of the British, they had lost their strongest ally. The Shawnees, Potawatomis, Chippewas, and others had lost the means to resist American expansion.

The war exposed contradictions and American fears about the growing African American population. In the Deep South, fear of arming slaves kept them out of the military except in New Orleans, where a free black militia dated back to Spanish control of Louisiana. The British army recruited slaves, offering them freedom in return for joining their side. Thus, the British assault on Washington and Baltimore included former slaves. Ironically, the United States made the same offer to slaves in Canada, and both sides gave freedom to slaves in the Old Northwest who joined the military. New York State offered freedom to slaves who enlisted and compensated their masters. In Philadelphia black leaders formed a "Black Brigade" to defend the city.

The war also exposed weaknesses in defense and transportation at home. American generals had found U.S. roads inadequate to move troops and supplies. Thus, improved transportation and a well-equipped army became national priorities in the postwar years. In 1815 Congress voted a standing army of ten thousand men—three times the size of the army during Jefferson's administration. In 1818 the National Road reached Wheeling, Virginia (now West Virginia), from its Cumberland, Maryland, beginning.

Perhaps most important of all, the war stimulated economic growth. The prewar trade restrictions and the war itself spurred the production of manufactured goods because New England capitalists began to invest in home manufactures and factories. The effects of these changes were far-reaching.

Finally, the conflict sealed the fate of the Federalists. Realizing that they could not win a presidential election in wartime, the Federalists joined renegade Democratic-Republicans in supporting New York City mayor DeWitt Clinton in the election of 1812. Federalist organization peaked at the state level as the Younger Federalists campaigned hard. The Federalists nevertheless lost to President Madison. They gained some congressional seats, but their star was waning.

With the war stalemated and their region's economy shattered, delegates from New England met in

HARTFORD   Hartford, Connecticut, in the winter of 1814–1815 to discuss revising CONVENTION   the national compact or pulling out of the republic. Moderates prevented a resolution of secession, but the convention condemned the war and the embargo and endorsed radical changes in the Constitution, such as restricting the presidency to one term and requiring a two-thirds congressional vote to admit new states to the Union. The delegates plotted to preserve

New England Federalist political power as electoral strength shifted to the South and West.

The timing of the Hartford Convention proved lethal. The victory at New Orleans and news of the peace treaty made the convention look ridiculous, if not treasonous. Although Federalists survived in a handful of states until the 1820s, the faction dissolved.

Summary *Online Study Center*   **ACE the Test**

The 1800 election marked the peaceful transition in power from the Federalists to the opposition Democratic-Republicans. New president Thomas Jefferson sought both to unify the nation and to solidify Democratic-Republican control of the government. Jeffersonians favored frugal government.

The Supreme Court under Chief Justice John Marshall remained a Federalist bastion. Marshall would ensure, until 1835, the dominance of Federalist principle: federal supremacy over the states and the protection of commerce and capital. In *Marbury v. Madison* (1803), the Supreme Court established its power of judicial review.

With the acquisition of Louisiana Territory, the United States doubled its size. Lewis and Clark's Corps of Discovery practiced "buckskin diplomacy" while exploring the land, flora, fauna, and people west of the Mississippi. Increasingly Americans looked westward.

Both the Federalists and the Democratic-Republicans competed at the grassroots level for popular support. Political conflict was bitter, and, assisted by the partisan press, political intensity began to build a national political culture.

Despite internal divisions, the greatest threats came from abroad. In both the war with the Barbary states and the War of 1812, the United States sought to guard its commerce and ships on the high seas. The Treaty of Ghent, ending the War of 1812, reaffirmed American independence. The war also broke Indian resistance in the West and South. At the same time, embargoes and war forced Americans to look toward domestic markets and jump-started American manufacturing.

LEGACY FOR A PEOPLE AND A NATION
States' Rights and Nullification

When the Constitution replaced the Articles of Confederation, the United States had a much stronger central government, but its exact relationship with the states was ambiguous because Constitutional Convention delegates could not agree on whether states or nation should prevail in the event of irreconcilable conflict. The Tenth Amendment to the Constitution offered only a slight clarification: powers not delegated to the central government, it said, were reserved to the states or to the people. Who would determine which powers had been delegated to which authority remained to be defined.

When New England Federalists met in Hartford at the end of 1814, they drew on the doctrine of nullification, first announced sixteen years earlier in Jefferson's Kentucky Resolution and Madison's Virginia Resolution. Opposing the Alien and Sedition Acts, these resolutions had asserted that if the national government assumed powers not delegated to it by the Constitution, states could nullify federal actions—that is, declare them inoperative within state borders. At Hartford, Federalist representatives of New England states discussed taking nullification a step further by seceding, or withdrawing from the Union. They backed away from this extreme step, but their formulation of the rights of states to evaluate and nullify federal authority left a legacy for dissent that would be played out in crises to the present day.

In the following decade, South Carolina nullified federal tariffs that it opposed, and in 1861 southern states threatened by Abraham Lincoln's election to the presidency claimed the right of secession. Although the Civil War supposedly settled the issue—states could neither nullify federal law nor secede—southern states opposing the Supreme Court's 1954 ruling in favor of school integration again claimed the right to nullify "unauthorized" federal policy within their borders. In the 1990s, some western states sought to nullify federal envi-ronmental laws. The Hartford Convention's legacy for a people and a nation provides Americans who dissent from national policy a model for using state governments as vehicles for their protests.

*N*ATIONALISM, EXPANSION, AND THE MARKET ECONOMY 1816–1845

*T*he Hutchinson Family from rural New Hampshire was the most popular singing group in nineteenth-century America. Abby, Asa, Jesse, John, and Judson Hutchinson performed the patriotic, religious, and sentimental songs that had dominated popular music since the Revolution. Unlike most other musical groups, the Hutchinsons not only sang but also presented well-rehearsed and elaborately produced performances. They used folk tunes, but their lyrics explored controversial topics such as abolition and temperance.

The Hutchinson Family traveled by rail, performing across the expanding United States, but drawing their largest audiences in the growing cities of the North. The family's fee for a single night in the 1840s reached $1,000, about four hundred times a worker's daily wage. They had an entourage of managers, agents, and publishers. Hawkers sold sheet music, portraits, and songbooks at the Hutchinsons' concerts. The Hutchinson Family made a business of music and entertainment, selling nostalgia and reform.

The Hutchinsons' concert tours exemplified the market economy, in which goods and services sold in cash or credit transactions created a network of exchange that bound distant enterprises together. The family performed in western areas in the 1840s that had had no American settlements twenty years before. The canals and railroads that carried them increasingly linked the nation's regions after the War of 1812. People moved inland from the seacoast. Grain went east to coastal cities, slave-grown cotton went to Europe, and ready-made men's garments from New York and Cincinnati sold across the nation. Increasingly, farmers turned to staple-crop agriculture, and city people worked not for themselves but for others, for wages. These large-scale enterprises needed capital, and new financial institutions amassed and loaned it. Mechanization took hold; factories and precision-made machinery put home workshops and handcrafters out of business. In turn, the increased specialization

Postwar Nationalism

The Market Economy and Government's Role

Transportation Links

LINKS TO THE WORLD
The United States as a Developing Nation

Commercial Farming

The Rise of Manufacturing and Commerce

Workers and the Workplace

Americans on the Move

Native American Resistance and Removal

LEGACY FOR A PEOPLE AND A NATION
A Mixed Economy

Online Study Center
This icon will direct you to interactive map and primary source activities on the website
http://college.hmco.com/pic/nortonbrief7e

CHRONOLOGY

1815 • Madison proposes internal improvements

1816 • Second Bank of the United States chartered
• Tariff of 1816 imposes first substantial duties
• Monroe elected president

1817 • Rush-Bagot Treaty limits British and American naval forces on Lake Champlain and Great Lakes

1819 • *McCulloch v. Maryland* establishes supremacy of federal over state law
• Adams-Onís Treaty with Spain gives Florida to U.S. and defines Louisiana territorial border

1819–23 • Hard times bring unemployment

1820 • Missouri Compromise creates formula for admitting slave and free states
• Monroe reelected

1820s • New England textile mills expand

1823 • Monroe Doctrine closes Western Hemisphere to European intervention

1824 • *Gibbons v. Ogden* affirms federal over state authority in interstate commerce
• Monroe proposes Indian removal

1825 • Erie Canal completed

1830 • Railroad era begins
• Congress passes Indian Removal Act

1830s • McCormick reaper, Deere steel plow patented

1830s–40s • Cotton production shifts to Mississippi valley

1831 • Trail of Tears begins with the forced removal of the Choctaws
• Cherokees turn to courts to defend treaty rights in *Cherokee Nation v. Georgia*

1832 • Marshall declares Cherokee nation a distinct political community in *Worcester v. Georgia*

1834 • Women workers strike at Lowell textile mills

1835–42 • Seminoles successfully resist removal in Second Seminole War

1836 • Second Bank of the United States closes

1837 • *Charles River Bridge v. Warren Bridge* encourages new enterprises
• Panic of 1837 begins economic downturn

1839–43 • Hard times strike again

1842 • *Commonwealth v. Hunt* declares strikes lawful

1844 • Government grant sponsors first telegraph line

in agriculture, manufacturing, transportation, and finance further fired the engines of the new nationwide, capitalist, market-oriented economy.

The end of the War of 1812 unleashed this growth. A new nationalist spirit encouraged the economy and promoted western expansion at home, trade abroad, and assertiveness throughout the Western Hemisphere. Economic growth and territorial expansion, however, generated sectional conflicts over slavery and economic development. Migration and changes in the ways people worked also created new tensions. Journeyman tailors, displaced by retailers and cheaper labor, found their trades disappearing. New England farm daughters who became wage workers found their

world changing no less radically. Moreover, nationwide boom-and-bust cycles wrenched livelihoods and lives. Mills, factories, roads, canals, and railroads altered or destroyed the landscape.

Everywhere Americans were on the move. Settlement moved to the interior, and farms and cities, linked first by rivers, then by roads, canals, and railroads, stretched to the Ohio and Mississippi River valleys and beyond. The Indian inhabitants attempted to hold their ground but were in the end removed to the West, pushed off their lands by the same drive for profit—a nationalist spirit reshaping national politics and the dynamic American economy. ■

Postwar Nationalism

*N*ationalism surged after the War of 1812. Self-confident, Americans asserted themselves at home and abroad as Democratic-Republicans borrowed from the Federalists' agenda and encouraged economic growth. In his December 1815 message to Congress, James Madison recommended economic development and military expansion. His agenda included a national bank (the charter of the first bank had expired in 1811) and improved transportation. To raise government revenues and foster manufacturing, Madison called for a protective tariff—a tax on imported goods designed to protect American manufactures. Yet his program acknowledged Jeffersonian republicanism: only a constitutional amendment, Madison argued, could authorize the federal government to build local roads and canals.

A new generation of congressional leaders, with a new national outlook, saw Madison's program as a way of unifying the country. **NATIONALIST PROGRAM** Democratic-Republican John C. Calhoun of South Carolina and House Speaker Henry Clay of Kentucky believed that the tariff would stimulate industry. The agricultural South and West would sell cotton to the churning mills of New England and food to its millworkers. Goods would move on roads and canals, and tariff revenues would provide money to build them. A national bank would handle the transactions.

In 1816 Congress enacted much of the nationalist program. It chartered the Second Bank of the United States, which, like its predecessor, mixed public and private ownership: the government provided one-fifth of the bank's capital and appointed one-fifth of its directors. Congress also passed a protective tariff to aid industries. The Tariff of 1816 levied taxes on imported woolens and cottons and on iron, leather, hats, paper, and sugar, in effect raising their prices in the United States. Foreshadowing a growing trend, support for the tariff divided along sectional lines: New England and the western and Middle Atlantic states stood to benefit and applauded it, but the South did not.

The South did press for better transportation. It was Calhoun who promoted roads and canals to "bind the republic together." However, Madison vetoed Calhoun's internal improvements (public works) bill as unconstitutional. The president did approve funds for extending the National Road to Ohio, deeming it a military necessity.

James Monroe, Madison's successor and the last president to have attended the Constitutional Convention, continued Madison's domestic program, supporting tariffs and vetoing internal improvements. **JAMES MONROE** Monroe was a most ordinary and colorless man who rarely had an original idea. But in 1816 he easily defeated the last Federalist presidential nominee, Rufus King. A Boston newspaper dubbed this one-party period the "Era of Good Feelings."

Led by Federalist chief justice John Marshall, the Supreme Court became the bulwark of a nationalist point of view. In *McCulloch v. Maryland* (1819), the Court struck down a Maryland law taxing banks within the state that were not chartered by the Maryland legislature— **MCCULLOCH V. MARYLAND** a law aimed at hindering the Baltimore branch of the federally chartered Second Bank of the United States, which had refused to pay the tax and sued. At issue was state versus federal jurisdiction. Speaking for a unanimous Court, Marshall asserted the supremacy of the federal government over the states.

In his opinion, Marshall went on to consider whether Congress could issue a bank charter. The Constitution did not spell out such power, but Marshall noted that Congress had the authority to pass "all laws which shall be necessary and proper for carrying into execution" the enumerated powers of the government. Marshall ruled that Congress could legally exercise "those great powers on which the welfare of the nation essentially depends." The bank charter was declared legal. *McCulloch v. Maryland* thus joined nationalism and economics. By asserting federal supremacy, Marshall protected the commercial and industrial interests that favored a national bank. The decision was only one in a series of rulings that cemented the federalist view.

Monroe's secretary of state, John Quincy Adams, matched the self-confident Marshall Court in assertiveness and nationalism. From 1817 to **JOHN QUINCY ADAMS** 1825 he brilliantly managed the nation's foreign policy, stubbornly pushing for expansion, fishing rights for Americans in Atlantic waters, political distance from the Old World, and peace. An ardent expansionist, he nonetheless believed that expansion must come about through negotiations, not war, and that newly acquired territories must bar slavery.

Adams faced major diplomatic challenges. U.S. northern and southern borders were not clearly defined and were a potential source of conflict with Great Britain and Spain. Still, Great Britain was the largest buyer of American exports, and British textile mills depended on American cotton; both sides looked to commerce to cement better relations. The United States also sought to prevent European conflicts from spilling over into the New World.

Although an Anglophobe, Adams worked to strengthen the peace with Great Britain negotiated at Ghent (1814). In 1817 the two nations agreed in the Rush-Bagot Treaty to sharply limit their naval forces on Lake Champlain and the Great Lakes. This first disarmament treaty of modern times led to the demilitarization of the border between the United States and Canada. Adams then pushed for the Convention of 1818, which fixed the United States–Canadian border from Lake of the Woods in Minnesota westward to the Rockies along the 49th parallel (see Map 10.1). When they could not agree on the boundary west of the Rockies, Britain and the United States settled on joint occupation of Oregon for ten years (renewed indefinitely in 1827).

Adams next moved to settle long-term disputes with Spain. During the War of 1812 the United States had seized Mobile and the remainder of West Florida. After the war, Adams took advantage of Spain's preoccupation with domestic and colonial troubles to

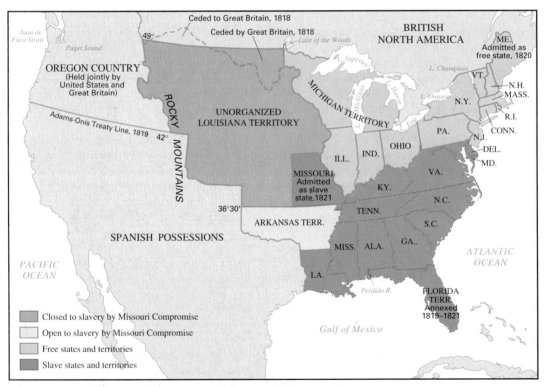

Map 10.1   Missouri Compromise and the State of the Union, 1820

The compromise worked out by House Speaker Henry Clay established a formula that avoided debate over whether new states would allow or prohibit slavery. In the process, it divided the United States into northern and southern regions.

negotiate for the purchase of East Florida. During the 1818 talks, General Andrew Jackson occupied much of present-day Florida on the pretext of suppressing Seminole raids against American settlements across the border. Adams was furious with Jackson but defended his brazen act.

The following year, Don Luís de Onís, the Spanish minister to the United States, agreed to cede Florida to the United States without payment, while the United States agreed to renounce its dubious claims to northern Mexico (Texas) and assume $5 million of claims by American citizens against Spain. The Adams-Onís, or Transcontinental, Treaty also defined the southwestern boundary of the Louisiana Purchase and set the southern border of Oregon at the 42nd parallel (see Map 10.1). Expansion was achieved at little cost and without war. In Florida, some planter-slaveholders and traders welcomed the American flag. Creeks and Seminoles, free blacks, runaway slaves, and Spanish-speaking town dwellers did not.

John Quincy Adams's desire to insulate the United States and the Western Hemisphere from European conflict brought about his greatest achievement: the Monroe Doctrine. Between 1808 and 1822, the United Provinces of the Río de la Plata (present-day northern Argentina, Paraguay, and Uruguay), Chile, Peru, Colombia, and Mexico all broke free from Spain. Monroe and Adams moved cautiously, seeking to avoid conflict with Spain and to be assured of the stability of the new regimes. But in 1822 the United States became the first nation outside Latin America to recognize the new states.

INDEPENDENT STATES IN LATIN AMERICA

To the United States, Europe again offered potential threats to the stability of the New World. After France, to bolster the weak Spanish monarchy against domestic rebellion, occupied Spain, the United States feared that France would return the new Latin American states to colonial rule. Great Britain, similarly distrustful of France, proposed a joint United States–British declaration against European intervention in the Western Hemisphere and a joint disavowal of territorial ambitions in the region. Adams rejected the British overture, following George Washington's admonition to avoid foreign entanglements. He also interpreted Britain's proposal to disavow territorial ambitions as an attempt to thwart American expansion.

President Monroe presented the American position—the Monroe Doctrine—to Congress in December 1823. His message called for noncolonization of the Western Hemisphere by European nations, a principle that addressed American anxiety not only about Latin America but also about Russian expansion beyond Alaska and settlements in California. He also demanded nonintervention by Europe in the affairs of independent New World nations, and he pledged noninterference by the United States in European affairs, including those of Europe's existing New World colonies.

MONROE DOCTRINE

Monroe's words, however, carried no force. Indeed, the policy depended on the support of the British, who wanted to keep other European nations out of the hemisphere to protect their dominance in the Atlantic trade. Europeans ignored the Monroe Doctrine; it was the Royal Navy they respected, not American policy.

Online Study Center **Improve Your Grade**
Primary Source: Monroe Doctrine

While nationalism brought Americans together, slavery divided them. Since the drafting of the Constitution, political leaders had tried to avoid the issue. The one exception was an act ending the foreign slave trade after January 1, 1808, which passed without much opposition. Slavery was dying out in the North, but not in border and southern states. In 1819 the question crept onto the political agenda when Missouri residents petitioned Congress for admission to the Union as a slave state. For two and a half years, the issue dominated Congress. "This momentous question," wrote Thomas Jefferson, "like a fire bell in the night, awakened and filled me with terror."

"FIRE BELL IN THE NIGHT"

The debate transcended slavery in Missouri. Five new states had joined the Union since 1812: Louisiana, Indiana, Mississippi, Illinois, and Alabama. Of these, Louisiana, Mississippi, and Alabama permitted slavery. Because Missouri was on the same latitude as free Illinois, Indiana, and Ohio (a state since 1803), its admission as a slave state would thrust slavery farther northward. It would also tilt the uneasy political balance in the Senate toward the slave states. In 1819 the Union consisted of eleven slave and eleven free states.

Some considered this process beneficial—a self-adjusting cycle that eliminated unprofitable economic ventures. In theory, people concentrated on the activities they did best, and the economy as a whole became more efficient. Believers in the system also argued that it enhanced individual freedom, since theoretically each seller, whether of goods or of labor, determined the price. But in fact, the system tied workers to a perpetual roller coaster; they became dependent on wages—and on the availability of jobs—for their very survival.

The market economy also ushered in another type of boom-and-bust cycle: harvest and destruction. Canals and railroads spurred demand for distant resources, then accelerated the destruction of forests, natural waterways, and landscape features. Railroads made possible large-scale lumbering of pinewood forests in Michigan and Wisconsin. During the 1840s, lumber companies deforested millions of acres, leaving most of that land unfit even for agriculture. The process of harvest and destruction would eventually change the ecology of the United States.

The idea of a market economy drew on eighteenth-century republicanism. It emphasized economic liberty and individualism. Limited

GOVERNMENT'S ECONOMIC ROLE

government, adherents argued, fostered economic expansion as individuals pursuing their private interests benefited the nation as a whole. Nonetheless, the federal government played an active role in technological and industrial growth. Federal arsenals pioneered new manufacturing techniques that helped develop the machine-tool industry. The U.S. Post Office fostered the circulation of information, a critical element in a market economy. The post office also played a brief but crucial role in the development of the telegraph, financing the first telegraph line, from Washington to Baltimore, in 1844. The government protected inventions and domestic industries. Patent laws gave inventors a seventeen-year monopoly on their inventions, and tariffs protected American industry from foreign competition.

Government policy also fostered farm life. Republicanism associated farming with virtue, independence, and productivity, essential values in the new republic, and the federal government surveyed public land and opened it to settlement. Internal improvements such as harbors, roads, and canals—some underwritten by government—linked new farms in the West to markets in the East. When Indians got in the way of expansion, the federal government moved them across the Mississippi River.

The federal judiciary validated government promotion of the economy and encouraged business enterprise and risk taking. In *Gibbons*

LEGAL FOUNDATIONS OF COMMERCE

v. Ogden (1824), the Supreme Court overturned a New York State law that gave Robert Fulton and Robert Livingston a monopoly on the New York–New Jersey steamboat trade. Aaron Ogden, their successor, lost the monopoly when Chief Justice John Marshall ruled that the congressional power to license new enterprises took precedence over New York's grant of monopoly rights to Fulton and Livingston. Marshall declared that Congress's power under the commerce clause of the Constitution extended to "every species of commercial intercourse," including transportation. In defining interstate commerce broadly, the Marshall Court expanded federal powers over the economy while restricting the ability of states to control economic activity within their borders.

Federal and state courts, in conjunction with state legislatures, also encouraged the proliferation of corporations—organizations entitled

CORPORATIONS

to hold property and transact business as if they were individuals. Corporation owners, called shareholders, were granted *limited liability,* or freedom from responsibility for the company's debts beyond their original investments. In 1800 the United States had three hundred incorporated firms; by 1830, the New England states alone had issued nineteen hundred charters.

Legislative action allowed the creation of corporations, but the courts played a crucial role in extending their powers and protecting

CHARLES RIVER BRIDGE CASE

them. Two Massachusetts cases in 1819, for instance, upheld the limited liability of stockholders. And the U.S. Supreme Court in *Charles River Bridge v. Warren Bridge* (1837) paved the way for new enterprises and technologies, favoring competition over monopoly and the public interest over implied privileges in old contracts.

The Massachusetts legislature had chartered the Charles River Bridge Company in 1785 and six years later extended its charter for seventy years. In return for building a bridge between Charlestown and Boston, the owners received the right to collect tolls. In 1828 the legislature chartered another company to build the Warren Bridge across the Charles nearby; the new bridge could collect tolls for six years, after which the bridge would be turned over to the state and be free of tolls. The Charles River Bridge Company sued in 1829, claiming that the new bridge breached the earlier charter.

Speaking for a 4-to-3 majority, Marshall's successor, Roger Taney, declared that the original charter did not confer the privilege of monopoly and that exclusivity could not therefore be implied. Taney ruled that charter grants should be interpreted narrowly and that ambiguities would be decided in favor of the public interest. New enterprises should not be restricted by old charters.

In promoting the economy, state governments far surpassed the federal government. From 1815 through
STATES' SUPPORT FOR THE ECONOMY the 1840s, for example, government money, mostly from the states, financed three-fourths of the nearly $200 million invested in canals. In the 1830s the states started to invest in rail construction. Although the federal government played a larger role in constructing railroads than in building canals, state and local governments provided more than half of the capital for southern rail lines. State governments also invested in corporate and bank stocks, providing much-needed capital. In fact, states' investments equaled or exceeded those of private enterprise.

Political controversy raged over questions of state versus federal activity, but all parties agreed on the general goal of economic expansion. Indeed, during these years, the major restraint on government action was not philosophical but financial: the public purse was small. As the private sector grew more vigorous, entrepreneurs looked less to government for financial support, and the states played less of a role in investment.

Transportation Links

Improved transportation facilitated economic growth. Outside the South states invested heavily in roads, canals, and railroads, with much of the financing borrowed from Europe. With regional and national financial institutions increasingly concentrated in New York, Boston, and Philadelphia, northeastern seaboard cities became the center of American commerce. New York financial and commercial houses dominated the American export trade, not only of New England textiles but also of southern cotton. The Deep South, with most of its capital invested in slave labor and land, built fewer canals, railroads, and factories and remained mostly rural.

Water routes provided the cheapest and most available transportation. However, as settlement extended beyond the river links, the federal and state governments, followed by private corporations, invested heavily in alternative transportation modes.

In the 1820s new arteries opened up east-west travel. The National Road, which originated in
EAST-WEST LINKS Cumberland, Maryland, reached Columbus, Ohio, in 1833. More important, the Erie Canal, completed in 1825, linked the Great Lakes with New York City and the Atlantic Ocean. Railroads and later the telegraph would solidify these east-west links. Other than the coastal trade, links between the Deep South and the North were rare.

The 363-mile-long Erie Canal was a visionary enterprise. When the state of New York authorized its
CANALS construction in 1817, the longest American canal was only 28 miles long. Vigorously promoted by Governor DeWitt Clinton, the Erie shortened the journey between Buffalo and New York City from twenty to six days and reduced freight charges from $100 to $5 a ton.

The success of the Erie Canal triggered an explosion of canal building. By 1840 canals crisscrossed the Northeast and Midwest, and total canal mileage reached 3,300. None of these canals enjoyed the financial success of the Erie. As the high cost of construction combined with an economic contraction, investment in canals began to slump in the 1830s. By midcentury more miles were being abandoned than built. The canal era had ended.

Meanwhile, railroad construction boomed. The railroad era in the United States began in 1830 when
RAILROADS Peter Cooper's locomotive, "Tom Thumb," first steamed along 13 miles of Baltimore and Ohio Rail-

The United States as a Developing Nation

In the early nineteenth century, the United States was a "developing nation" as its economy slowly shifted from dependence on agriculture and raw materials to producing manufactured goods. In order to develop economically, the United States imported capital to finance international trade, internal improvements, and early factories.

American political and economic leaders in the early part of the nineteenth century talked as if they were masters of their own fate. In many ways, however, the United States remained economically dependent on its former mother country, Great Britain. The political independence that the United States won in the Revolutionary War and affirmed in the War of 1812 was not matched in the economic sphere.

Following the War of 1812, Americans depended on Britain for capital investment. Ninety percent of all U.S. foreign capital came from Britain, and around 60 percent of all British capital exports flowed to the United States. Americans used British capital to develop first the canals, then the railroads that facilitated American industrial development. For instance, from 1817 to 1825 the British invested $7 million in New York State bonds to finance the Erie Canal. Altogether, European investors provided 80 percent of the money to build the Erie, and the United States depended on mostly British capital to finance America's internal improvements.

As a developing nation, the United States imported more goods than it exported. In other words, Americans consumed more than they produced. It was able to do so because imported capital balanced the trade deficit. As in most developing countries, exports were concentrated in agricultural commodities; 50 percent of the value of all exports was in cotton. And British credit financed cotton sales.

As a developing nation, U.S. dependency on international capital was highlighted when imported capital was interrupted, as in the Panics of 1819 and 1837. Though the financial crises began in the United States, the hard times were made worse in both cases when British investors and creditors squeezed Americans. Economic crises in England led investors to pull out capital from the United States while merchants demanded that Americans pay what they owed to British creditors. Money became tight, and the economy declined.

Thus both economic development and hard times revealed the significance of international capital links to the United States, a developing nation.

In the 1820s, canals like the Erie linked the West with eastern cities and the Atlantic Ocean, and thus world trade. U.S. exports were concentrated in agriculture, and the Erie and other canals carried grain to the world market. Charles Klackner published this view of a canal boat and its passengers, based on a contemporary painting by Edward Lamson Henry. Canal boats carried gentlemen and ladies as well as more modest citizens, many of them immigrants on their way to settling western lands.
(Chicago Historical Society Neg #ICHi-35979/Painter–Ralph Dille)

road track. By 1850 the United States had nearly 9,000 miles of track.

The earliest railroads connected nearby cities; not until the 1850s did railroads offer long-distance service at reasonable rates. The early lines had to overcome technical problems. In addition, the lack of a common standard for the width of track thwarted development of a national system. A journey from Philadelphia to Charleston, South Carolina, involved eight different track widths (called gauges), which meant that passengers and freight had to change trains seven times.

Technology and investments in transportation dramatically reduced travel time and shipping cost.

REDUCTION IN TRAVEL TIME AND COST Before 1815 river transportation was the only feasible route for long-distance journeys. In 1815 a traveler took four days to go by stagecoach from New York City to Baltimore. By 1830 the journey took a day and a half, while the Erie Canal reduced the New York–Detroit journey from four weeks to two. Before the War of 1812, wagon transportation cost 30 to 70 cents per ton per mile. By midcentury, railroads had brought the cost of land transportation down 95 percent and reduced the journey to one-fifth the time.

Commercial Farming

*a*lthough manufacturing increased steadily, agriculture remained the backbone of the economy and American exports. But increasingly the market economy altered farming. Although the plantation system had always been market oriented, self-sufficient farm households were becoming market oriented too. Equally important, the center of commercial farming moved westward. In the 1830s and after, the plantation South shifted toward the Mississippi River valley, while commercial farming came to dominate the Old Northwest and the Ohio River valley, then moved even farther westward to the prairies.

After the 1820s, northeastern agriculture began to decline. Eastern farmers had cultivated all the land

NORTHEASTERN AGRICULTURE available to them. Moreover, small New England farms, with their uneven terrains, did not lend themselves to the new labor-saving farm implements introduced in the 1830s—mechanical sowers, reapers, and threshers.

As a result, many northern farmers either moved west or gave up farming for jobs in the merchant houses and factories.

The farmers who remained in New England, as well as those in the Middle Atlantic, adapted to the changed environment. By the 1850s, many of these farm families had abandoned the commercial production of wheat and corn. Instead, they improved their livestock, especially cattle, and specialized in vegetable and fruit production and dairy farming. They financed these initiatives through land sales and debt. Indeed, increasing land values, not farming, promised the greatest profit.

Farm women had a distinctive role in the market economy. Many sold eggs, dairy products, and garden

WOMEN'S PAID LABOR produce in local markets, and their earnings became essential to household incomes. Butter and cheese making replaced spinning and weaving; farm women now sold commodities and bought cloth. The work was physically demanding and added to regular home and farm chores. Yet women took pride in their work, often gaining from it a sense of independence that was as valuable as their profits.

Women's success at butter and cheese making led some farms to specialize in dairy production. After the Erie Canal opened, Ohio dairy farms had access to New York's export trade. Ohio entrepreneurs put cheese into factory production in the 1840s. Canals and railroads took the cheese to eastern ports, where wholesalers sold it around the world.

Individually and collectively, Americans still valued agrarian life. State governments energetically promoted commercial agriculture to spur economic growth and sustain the values of an agrarian-based republic. Massachusetts in 1817 and New York in 1819 began to subsidize agricultural prizes and county fairs. New York required contestants to submit written descriptions of how they grew their prize crops; the state then published the essays to encourage new methods and specialization. The post office circulated farm journals that helped familiarize farmers with developments in agriculture.

Gradually the Old Northwest replaced the Northeast as the center of American family agriculture.

MECHANIZATION OF AGRICULTURE Farms in the Old Northwest were large, flat, and suited to the new mechanized farming implements.

Cyrus McCormick had invented the horse-drawn mechanical reaper in 1831. He built a factory in Chicago that by 1847 sold a thousand reapers a year. Midwestern farmers bought reapers on credit and paid for them with the profits from their high yields. Similarly, John Deere's steel plow, invented in 1837, replaced the traditional iron plow; steel blades kept the soil from sticking and were tough enough to break the roots of prairie grass.

And just in time. The Midwest was becoming one of the leading agricultural regions of the world. Midwestern farms fed the cities in the East, bursting with growing immigrant populations, and still produced enough to export to Europe.

At the end of the eighteenth century, southern agriculture was diverse. Indeed, cotton was profitable only for planters in the Sea Islands of South Carolina and Georgia, where slaves grew the long, silky variety. Then Whitney's cotton gin (1793), by efficiently removing the seeds from the short-staple cotton that would grow in the interior, transformed southern agriculture, revived and expanded slavery, and boosted export of both cotton and cloth.

THE COTTON SOUTH

After 1800 the cultivation of short-staple cotton spread rapidly. By the 1820s there were cotton plantations in the fertile lands of Louisiana, Mississippi, Alabama, Arkansas, and Tennessee. Each decade after 1820, the total crop doubled. By 1825 the slave South was the world's dominant supplier of cotton, and the white fibers were America's largest export. Southerners with capital bought more land and more slaves and planted ever more cotton.

No other region was more tied to international markets than the South, yet the region seemed immune to the transforming potential of foreign trade. Most southern capital remained concentrated in land and slaves. It could not shift easily to support manufacturing and commerce. In many ways, the cotton economy resembled a colonial economy. Planters depended on distant agents to represent them and handle their finances, which often included loans. Thus, critical market decisions were made by bankers, financiers, and brokers, all outside the South. The South was engaged in the new market economy, but at a distance.

The cotton boom, dependent on slave labor, defined the South's economy and society as it moved westward. Slaveholders were oriented to the market economy, like commercial farmers, merchants, and entrepreneurs in the North. But they did not pay wages for labor; they bought laborers. Ultimately this distinctive system (see Chapter 13) would separate the South from the national economy and the nation.

The Rise of Manufacturing and Commerce

British visitors to the 1851 London Crystal Palace Exhibition, the first modern world's fair, were impressed by American design and fine tooling of working parts. American companies displayed hundreds of American machines and wares. Most impressive to the Europeans were Alfred C. Hobb's unpickable padlocks, Samuel Colt's revolvers, and Robbins and Lawrence's rifles. All were machine-tooled rather than handmade, products of what the British called the American system of manufacturing.

The American system of manufacturing used precision machinery to produce interchangeable parts that did not require individual adjustment to fit. Eli Whitney had promoted the idea of interchangeable parts in 1798 when he contracted with the federal government to make ten thousand rifles in twenty-eight months. By the 1820s the U.S. Ordnance Department had contracted with private firms to introduce machine-made interchangeable parts for firearms. The American system quickly spread beyond the arsenals, creating the machine-tool industry—the manufacture of machines for purposes of mass production. One outcome was an explosion in consumer goods that were inexpensive yet of uniformly high quality.

AMERICAN SYSTEM OF MANUFACTURING

Even larger than the machine-tool industry was the textile industry. New England mills began processing and weaving slave-grown cotton in the same decade that Whitney patented his gin. Boosted by embargo and war, then protected by the tariff, the textile industry boomed with the expansion of cotton cultivation after the war.

TEXTILE MILLS

The Boston Manufacturing Company, chartered in 1813, radically transformed textile manufacturing. The owners, Francis Cabot Lowell and other Boston merchants, erected their factories in Waltham, Massachusetts, bringing all the manufacturing processes to a single location. They employed a resident manager to run the mill, thus separating ownership from management. By the 1840s a cotton mill resembled a modern factory, and textiles were the most important industry in the nation. Cotton cloth production rose from 4 million yards in 1817 to 323 million in 1840. The industry employed around eighty thousand workers in the mid-1840s, more than half of them women.

The early mills, dependent on waterpower, sprung up in rural areas. By erecting dams and watercourses, mill owners diverted water from farmers and destroyed fishing, an important resource in rural and village America. To protect their customary rights, fishermen and farmers fought the manufacturers in New England state legislatures, but petitions from job seekers in the mill environs supported the manufacturers. The ensuing compromises promoted mill development.

Textile manufacturing changed New England and had its greatest impact on Lowell, Massachusetts. The population of Lowell, the "city of spindles" and the prototype of early American industrialization, grew from twenty-five hundred to thirty-three thousand between 1826 and midcentury. The largest of the cotton-mill towns and the front runner in technological change, Lowell boasted the biggest work force, the greatest output, and the most capital invested.

In addition to leading many women to begin purchasing inexpensive cloth rather than making their own, the success of the textile factories spawned the ready-made clothing industry. Before the 1820s, women sewed most clothing at home. Some people purchased used clothing, and tailors and seamstresses made wealthy men's and women's clothing to order. By the 1820s and 1830s, much clothing was mass-produced. Manufacturers used two methods. In one, the clothing was made in a factory; in the other, at home, through the putting-out system. In this arrangement, a journeyman tailor—a trained craftsman employed by a master tailor who owned the workshop—cut the fabric panels in the factory, and the masters "put out" the sewing at piece rates to women working in their own homes. The work itself was familiar, but the change was significant: women were producing goods

READY-MADE CLOTHING

for wages and for the market, not primarily for their families.

Most of the early mass-produced clothes, crude and loose fitting, were made for men who lived in city boarding and rooming houses. Improvements in fit and changes in men's fashion eventually made ready-to-wear apparel more acceptable to clerks and professional men. In the 1840s, men began wearing the short sack coat. This forerunner of the modern suit jacket fit loosely and needed little custom tailoring. Now even upper-class men were willing to consider ready-made apparel. Most women made their own clothes, but those who could afford to do so employed seamstresses.

Retail clothing stores began to stock ready-made clothes in the 1820s. Their owners often bought goods wholesale, though many manufactured shirts and trousers in their own factories. Lewis and Hanford of New York City boasted of cutting more than 100,000 garments in the winter of 1848–1849. The firm sold most of its clothing in the South and owned its own retail outlet in New Orleans. In the West, Cincinnati became the center of the new men's clothing industry, which employed fifteen hundred men and ten thousand women by midcentury.

RETAIL MERCHANTS

Commerce expanded hand in hand with manufacturing. Cotton, for instance, had once been traded by plantation agents, who sold the raw cotton and bought manufactured goods that they then sold to plantation owners, extending them credit when necessary. Cotton exports rose from 83 million pounds in 1815 to more than 1 billion pounds in 1849. Gradually some agents came to specialize in finance alone: they were cotton brokers, who for a commission brought together buyers and sellers. Similarly, wheat and hog brokers sprang up in the West—in Cincinnati, Louisville, and St. Louis. The distribution of finished goods also became more specialized as wholesalers bought large quantities of particular items from manufacturers, and jobbers broke down the wholesale lots for retail stores and country merchants.

SPECIALIZATION OF COMMERCE

Commercial specialization transformed some traders in big cities, especially New York, into virtual merchant princes. After the Erie Canal opened, New York City became a stop on every major trade route from Europe, the southern ports, and the West. New

York traders were the middlemen for southern cotton and western grain. Merchants in other cities played a similar role within their own regions. Some traders invested their profits in factories, further stimulating urban manufacturing. Some cities specialized: Rochester became a milling center, and Cincinnati—"Porkopolis"—became the first meatpacking center.

Financial institutions played a significant role in the expansion of manufacturing and commerce. **BANKING AND CREDIT SYSTEMS** Banks, insurance companies, and corporations linked savers—those who deposited money in banks—with producers and speculators who wished to borrow money. After 1816, the Second Bank of the United States injected a national perspective into finance, but many farmers, local bankers, and politicians denounced the bank as a monster serving national, not local, interests. Western landowners suffered severe losses when the Second Bank reduced loans in the western states during the Panic of 1819. In 1836 critics finally succeeded in killing the bank (discussed in Chapter 11).

The closing of the Second Bank in 1836 caused a nationwide credit shortage, which, in conjunction with the Panic of 1837, led to fundamental reforms in banking. Michigan and New York, and soon other states, introduced charter laws promoting what was called free banking. Previously every new bank had needed a special legislative charter to operate; thus, each bank incorporation involved a political process. Under the new laws, any proposed bank that met certain minimum conditions—amount of capital invested, number of notes issued, and types of loans offered—would receive a state charter automatically, allowing banks to incorporate more easily.

Free banking proved to be a significant stimulus to the economy in the late 1840s and 1850s. New banks sprang up everywhere, providing merchants and manufacturers with the credit they needed. Free-banking laws also served as a precedent for general incorporation statutes that allowed manufacturing firms to receive state charters without special legislative acts.

Workers and the Workplace

Loud the morning bell is ringing,
   Up, up sleepers, haste away;

Yonder sits the redbreast singing,
   But to list we must not stay.

. . . .

Sisters, haste, the bell is tolling,
   Soon will close the dreadful gate;
Then, alas! We must go strolling,
   Through the counting-room too late.

. . . .

Now the sun is upward climbing,
   And the breakfast hour has come;
Ding, dong, ding, the bell is chiming,
   Hasten, sisters, hasten home.

The poet, writing in 1844 in the *Factory Girl's Garland,* uses the sound of the factory bell as a refrain to emphasize its incessant control, announcing when the workers are to wake, eat, begin work, stop work, and go to sleep. Night and day, the millworkers felt the stress of factory schedules.

The first generation of young single women who left New England villages and farms to work in the mills arrived with great optimism. The mills offered steady work and good pay, plus airy boarding houses, prepared meals, and cultural activities such as evening lectures. Sisters and cousins often worked and lived in the same mill and boarding house. They helped each other adjust, and their letters home drew kin to the mills. Most arrivals were sixteen and stayed only about five years. When they left the mills to marry, other younger women took their places.

In the hard times from 1837 to 1842, most mills ran only part time. Subsequently, managers pressured **BOOM AND BUST IN THE TEXTILE MILLS** workers by means of the speed-up, the stretch-out, and the premium system. The speed-up increased the speed of the machines, the stretch-out increased the number of machines each worker had to operate, and premiums paid to the overseers whose departments produced the most cloth encouraged them to pressure workers for greater output. In the race for profits, owners lengthened hours, cut wages, tightened discipline, and packed the boarding houses. Some mill workers began to think of themselves as slaves.

New England mill workers responded to their deteriorating working conditions by organizing and **PROTESTS** striking. In 1834, in reaction to a 25 percent wage cut, they unsuccessfully "turned out" (struck) against the

Lowell mills. Two years later, when boarding house fees increased, they turned out again. In the 1840s, Massachusetts mill women joined other workers to press for state legislation mandating a ten-hour day. They also aired their complaints in worker-run newspapers.

The women's labor organizations were weakened by worker turnover. Few of the militant native-born mill workers stayed on to fight the managers and owners, and gradually fewer New England daughters entered the mills. In the 1850s, Irish immigrant women who lived at home replaced them. Technological improvements in the looms and other machinery had made the work less skilled and more routine. The mills could thus pay lower wages and draw from a reservoir of unskilled labor.

A growing gender division in the workplace, especially in the textile, clothing, and shoemaking industries, was one important out-

GENDER DIVISIONS IN WORK

come of large-scale manufacturing. Although women and men in traditional agricultural and artisan households tended to perform different tasks, they worked as a family unit. As wage work spread, however, men's and women's work cultures became increasingly separate. The women and girls who left home for jobs in textile mills worked and lived in a mostly female world. In the clothing and shoemaking industries, whose male artisans had once worked at home assisted by unpaid family labor, men began working outside the home while women continued to work at home through the putting-out system. Tasks and wages too became rigidly differentiated: women sewed, whereas men shaped materials and finished products, receiving higher wages in shops employing men only.

The market economy had an impact on unpaid household labor as well. As home and workplace became separate and labor came to be defined in terms of wages (what could be sold in the marketplace) rather than production (what could be made by hand), the unpaid labor of women was devalued. Yet the family depended on women's work within the household, ever more so as sons and even daughters sought wage work outside the home and had less time for household tasks. Thus, gender defined household labor, and in the market economy, it went unrecorded, seemed to be worth little, and was taken for granted.

The new textile mills, shoe factories, iron mills, and railroads were the antithesis of traditional work-

shop and household production. In factories, authority was hierarchically organized. Factory workers lost

CHANGES IN THE WORKPLACE

their sense of autonomy as impersonal market forces seemed to dominate their lives. Their jobs were insecure, as competition frequently led to layoffs and new machines and division of labor allowed replacement by cheaper, less-skilled workers or even children. Moreover, the formal rules of the factory contrasted sharply with the informal atmosphere of artisan shops and farm households. When master craftsmen turned their workshops into small factories and became managers, journeymen became factory operatives. In large factories, paid supervisors directed the workers, who never saw the owners. Mill workers had to tolerate the roar of the looms, and all workers on power machines risked accidents that could maim or even kill. Perhaps most demoralizing, opportunities for advancement in the new system were virtually nil.

Wage workers felt distanced from traditional culture as well. As wage work became common, the republican virtues associated with independent craft traditions eroded. The rigid rules of factory work and the swings in employment brought on by boom-and-bust cycles restricted individual freedom.

In response, some workers organized to resist the changes wrought by the market economy and factories and to regain control of their work and their lives. Women textile workers organized into unions

LABOR PARTIES

and demonstrated for better wages and conditions or lobbied legislatures for relief. Male workers also organized and protested, but because they were eligible to vote, they also organized political parties. Labor parties first formed in Pennsylvania, New York, and Massachusetts in the 1820s and then spread elsewhere; they advocated free public education and abolishing imprisonment for debt and opposed banks and monopolies.

Organized labor's greatest achievement during this period was to gain relief from the threat of conspiracy laws. When journeyman shoemakers organized during the first decade of the century, their

EMERGENCE OF A LABOR MOVEMENT

employers accused them of criminal conspiracy. Although the courts acknowledged the journeymen's right to organize, judges viewed strikes as illegal until a Massachusetts case, *Commonwealth v. Hunt* (1842), ruled that Boston journeyman bootmakers could strike "in such manner as best to subserve their own interests."

Yet permanent labor organizations were difficult to sustain. Most workers outside the crafts were unskilled or semiskilled at best. Moreover, religion, race, ethnicity, and gender divided workers, and labor organizations excluded African Americans and women. (Massachusetts mill women organized their own unions.) The first unions arose among urban journeymen in printing, woodworking, shoemaking, and tailoring. They tended to be local; the strongest resembled medieval guilds in that members sought to protect themselves against the competition of inferior workmen by regulating apprenticeship and establishing minimum wages. Umbrella organizations composed of individual craft unions, like the National Trades Union (1834), arose in several cities in the 1820s and 1830s, but they failed during hard times. Labor organizations remained weak, and after 1830 workers' share of the national wealth declined.

Americans on the Move

*a*fter the War of 1812, the United States grew in size and population. The Louisiana Purchase (1803) had doubled the land area of the United States, and acquisitions in the 1840s nearly doubled it again. Throughout the Atlantic world, population soared, and that of the United States grew by a third in each decade. Between 1820 and 1845, the U.S. population increased from 9.6 million to 20.2 million.

The United States expanded outward, mostly westward, from its original seaboard base. The admission of new states tells the

WESTWARD MOVEMENT

story: Indiana, Mississippi, Illinois, Alabama, Maine, and Missouri brought the Union to twenty-four states by the 1820s. Arkansas and Michigan followed in the 1830s, as did Florida, Texas, Iowa, and Wisconsin in the following decade.

During the first two decades of the century, Americans poured into the Ohio River valley; starting in the 1820s, they moved into the Mississippi River valley and beyond. By midcentury, two-thirds of Americans lived west of the Appalachians. Mostly young and hard working, they had visions of establishing family farms and achieving economic security.

Some 5 to 10 percent of Americans moved each year. Restless, they settled only temporarily and then moved on. Although most people lived on farms, there was also a steady rural-to-urban migration.

After the 1820s, the heart of cotton cultivation and the plantation system shifted from the coastal states to Alabama and the newly settled Mississippi valley—Tennessee, Louisiana, Arkansas, and Mississippi. Southerners brought their in-

THE SOUTH

stitutions; they forced slaves to move with them, and yeoman farmers followed.

The shift was dramatic. The population of Mississippi soared from 73,000 in 1820 to 607,000 in 1850, with African American slaves in the majority. Across the Mississippi River, the population of Arkansas went from 14,000 in 1820 to 210,000 in 1850. Indian removal made this expansion possible. After the United States acquired Florida and attempted to colonize and suppress the Indian peoples there, southerners poured into the new territory. And while Texas was still part of Mexico in 1835, 35,000 Americans, including 3,000 slaves, lived there. Texas independence in 1836 spurred further American immigration. By 1845 the Anglo population was 125,000. Statehood that year opened the floodgates.

Not all moves were westward. A steady stream drifted from the Upper South to the Ohio valley, from slave to free states. Though northern black people moved westward as well, thousands of free people of

MOVES NORTH

color moved to northern states and Canada in the 1830s following the adoption of black codes and mob violence in the South. Fugitives from slavery too went north. In the Southwest, when the U.S. Army suppressed the Comanches, Apaches, Navajos, and Utes, Hispanic migration accelerated north into areas of Texas and present-day New Mexico and Utah.

Online Study Center **Improve Your Grade**
Interactive Map: Settled Areas of the United States, 1820 and 1840

Settlers needed land and credit. Reflecting the nationalist outlook, the federal government hoped to fill the West with non-Indian peoples

LAND GRANTS TO STATES

and thus promote republican virtue. Some public lands were granted as rewards for military service: veterans of the War of 1812 received 160 acres. After 1819 the government reduced the price of public land to an affordable $1.25 an acre, with a minimum purchase of 80 acres.

Some eager pioneers settled land before it had been surveyed and offered for sale. Such illegal settlers, or squatters, then had to buy the land at auction and faced the risk of being unable to purchase it. In 1841, to facilitate settlement and end property disputes, Congress passed the Pre-emption Act, which legalized settlement prior to surveying.

Since most settlers needed to borrow money, private credit systems arose. Nearly all economic activity in the West involved credit, from *CREDIT* land sales to produce shipments to railroad construction. In 1816 and 1836 easy credit boosted land prices. When tight credit, high interest, low prices, or destructive weather squeezed farmers' income, land values collapsed, ending the speculative bubble. Mortgage bankers and speculators then purchased land cheaply. As a consequence, many farmers became renters instead of owners of land. Tenancy became more common in the West than it had been in New England.

From the start, newly settled western areas depended on their links with towns and cities. Ohio River cities—Louisville and Cincinnati— *FRONTIER CITIES* and the old French settlements— Detroit on the Great Lakes, St. Louis on the Mississippi River—predated and promoted the earliest western settlements. So too in the South, from New Orleans to Natchez to Memphis, towns spearheaded settlement and economic growth. Steamboats connected the river cities with eastern markets and ports, carrying grain east and returning with finished goods. Like cities in the Northeast, these western cities eventually developed into manufacturing centers.

Native American Resistance and Removal

Indians were also on the move, but in forced migrations. To make way for white expansion, the indigenous cultures of the eastern and southern woodlands were uprooted. Perhaps 100,000 eastern and southern Indian people were removed between

1820 and 1850; about 30,000 died in the process. Those who remained became virtually invisible.

In theory, under the U.S. Constitution, the federal government recognized and treated Indian nations as sovereign foreign nations. Indeed *TREATY MAKING* the United States received Indian delegations with pomp and ceremony. Agreements between Indian nations and the United States were signed, sealed, and ratified like other international treaties. In practice, however, treaty making and Indian sovereignty were fictions. The United States imposed conditions on Indian representatives, and as the nation expanded, new treaties replaced old ones, shrinking Indian landholdings. Eventually, under President Andrew Jackson, wholesale removal would be the order of the day.

To maintain independence and preserve traditional ways, many Indian nations tried to accommodate to the expanding market economy. In *INDIANS IN THE* the first three decades of the century, *MARKET* the Choctaw, Chickasaw, and Creek *ECONOMY* peoples in the lower Mississippi became suppliers and traders. Under treaty provisions, Indian commerce took place through trading posts and stores that provided Indians with supplies and purchased or bartered Indian-produced goods. The trading posts extended credit to chiefs, who fell into debt. With pelt prices falling, the debts grew enormously and often could be paid off only by selling land to the federal government. By 1822 the Choctaw nation had sold 13 million acres but still carried a debt of $13,000. The Indians struggled to adjust, but with the loss of land came dependency. The Choctaws came to rely on white Americans not only for manufactured goods but also for food.

Dependency facilitated removal of American Indian peoples to western lands. While the population of other groups increased greatly, the Indian population fell. War, forced removal, disease (especially smallpox), and malnutrition reduced many Indian nations by 50 percent. More than half of the Pawnees, Omahas, Otoes, Missouris, and Kansas died in the 1830s alone.

The wanderings of the Shawnees illustrate the uprooting of Indian people. After giving up 17 million acres in Ohio in the 1795 Treaty of *SHAWNEES* Greenville, the Shawnees scattered to Indiana and eastern Missouri. After the War of 1812, Prophet's Indiana group withdrew to Canada under British protection. In 1822 other Shawnees sought Mexican protection and moved from Missouri to present-day eastern Texas. As the U.S. government promoted removal to Kansas, Prophet returned from Canada to lead a group to the new Shawnee lands in eastern Kansas in 1825. When Missouri achieved statehood in 1821, Shawnees living there were also forced to move to Kansas, where in the 1830s other Shawnees removed from Ohio or expelled from Texas joined them. By 1854, however, Kansas was open to white settlement, and the Shawnees had to cede seven-eighths of their land, or 1.4 million acres.

Removal had a profound impact on all Shawnees. The men lost their traditional role as providers; their methods of hunting woodland animals were useless on the prairies of Kansas. As grain became the tribe's dietary staple, Shawnee women played a greater role as providers, supplemented by government aid under treaty provisions. Remarkably, the Shawnees preserved their language and culture in the face of these drastic changes.

Ever since the early days of European colonization, whites had sought to assimilate American Indians through education and Christianity.

ASSIMILATION AND EDUCATION Westward expansion reinvigorated this goal. In 1819, in response to missionary lobbying, Congress appropriated $10,000 annually for "civilization of the tribes adjoining the frontier settlements." Protestant missionaries administered the "civilizing fund" and established mission schools. Catholic missions were already established in the Southwest and California.

Within five years, thirty-two boarding schools enrolled Indian students. They substituted English for American Indian languages and taught agriculture alongside the Christian Gospel. But at the program's peak, schools across the United States enrolled fewer than fifteen hundred students, and to settlers eyeing Indian land, assimilation through education seemed too slow a process. Thus, wherever native peoples lived, illegal settlers disrupted their lives. Although obligated to protect the integrity of treaty lands, the federal government did so only halfheartedly. With government supporting westward expansion, legitimate Indian claims had to give way to the advance of white civilization. In the 1820s, it became apparent

that Indians could not be persuaded to cede enough acreage to satisfy land-hungry whites.

In late 1824, President James Monroe proposed to Congress that Indians be moved beyond the Mississippi River. Monroe's proposition

INDIAN REMOVAL AS FEDERAL POLICY targeted the Cherokees, Creeks, Choctaws, and Chickasaws, who unanimously rejected it.

Pressure from Georgia had prompted Monroe's policy. Cherokees and Creeks lived in northwestern Georgia, and in the 1820s the state accused the federal government of not fulfilling its 1802 promise to remove the Indians in return for the state's renunciation of its claim to western lands. Neither Monroe's removal messages nor further cessions by the Creeks satisfied Georgia. In 1826, under federal pressure, the Creek nation ceded all but a small strip of its Georgia acreage. Georgians were unmoved: only the removal of the Georgia Creeks to the West could resolve the conflict between the state and the federal government.

Adapting to American ways could not forestall removal. No people met the challenge of assimilating more thoroughly than the

CHEROKEES Cherokees. Between 1819 and 1829 the tribe became economically self-sufficient and politically self-governing; the twelve to fifteen thousand adult Cherokees came to think of themselves as a nation, not a collection of villages. Sequoyah, a self-educated Cherokee, devised an eighty-six-character alphabet that made possible a Cherokee-language Bible and a bilingual tribal newspaper, *Cherokee Phoenix*. Between 1820 and 1823 the Cherokees created a formal government with a bicameral legislature, a court system, and a salaried bureaucracy. In 1827 they adopted a written constitution, modeled after that of the United States. Cherokee land laws, however, differed from U.S. law. The tribe collectively owned all Cherokee land and forbade land sales to outsiders. Economic change paralleled political adaptation. Many Cherokees became individual farmers and slaveholders in an economy of commodity trade based on barter, cash, and credit. By 1833 they held fifteen hundred black slaves.

But Cherokees' political and economic changes failed to win respect or acceptance from southerners. In the 1820s, Georgia pressed them to sell the 7,200 square miles of land they held in the state. When the

Cherokees declined to negotiate cession, Georgia annulled their constitution, extended the state's sovereignty over them, prohibited the Cherokee National Council from meeting except to cede land, and ordered their lands seized. The discovery of gold on Cherokee land in 1829 whetted Georgia's appetite for Cherokee territory.

Backed by sympathetic whites but not by the new president, Andrew Jackson, the Cherokees under Chief John Ross turned to the federal courts to defend their treaty with the United States and to prevent Georgia from seizing more land. In *Cherokee Nation v. Georgia* (1831), Chief Justice John Marshall ruled that under the federal Constitution, an Indian tribe was neither a foreign nation nor a state and therefore had no standing in federal courts. Nonethe-

CHEROKEE NATION V. GEORGIA

less, said Marshall, the Indians had an unquestionable right to their lands; they could lose title only by voluntarily giving it up. A year later, in *Worcester v. Georgia*, Marshall defined the Cherokee position more clearly. The Indian nation was, he declared, a distinct political community in which "the laws of Georgia can have no force" and into which Georgians could not enter without permission or treaty privilege. Georgia refused to comply.

President Andrew Jackson refused to interfere because the case involved a state action. Keen to open up new lands for settlement, Jackson favored expelling the Cherokees. In the Removal Act of 1830, Congress had provided Jackson with the funds he needed to negotiate new treaties and resettle the resistant tribes west of the Mississippi (see Map 10.2).

The Choctaws went first; they made the forced journey from Mississippi and Alabama to the West

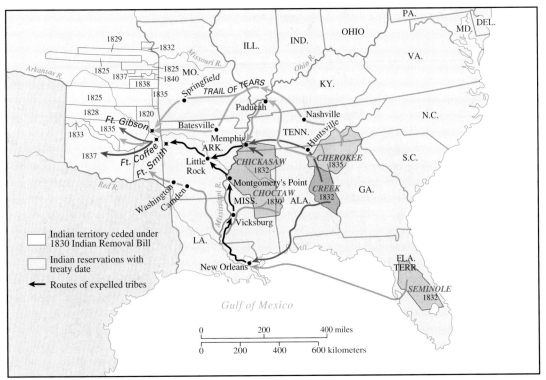

Map 10.2   Removal of Native Americans from the South, 1820–1840

Over a twenty-year period, the federal government and southern states forced Native Americans to exchange their traditional homes for western land. Some tribal groups remained in the South, but most settled in the alien western environment.

in the winter of 1831 and 1832. The Creeks in Alabama resisted removal until 1836, when the army pushed them westward. A year later, the Chickasaws followed.

Having fought removal in the courts, the Cherokees were divided. Some believed that further resistance was hopeless and accepted removal as the only chance to preserve their civilization. The leaders of this minority agreed in 1835 to exchange their southern home for western land in the Treaty of New Echota. Most, though, wanted to stand firm. John Ross, with petitions signed by fifteen thousand Cherokees, lobbied the Senate against ratification of the treaty. They lost. But when the time for evacuation came in 1838, most Cherokees refused to move. President Martin Van Buren sent federal troops to round them up. About twenty thousand Cherokees were evicted, held in detention camps, and marched to Indian Territory in present-day Oklahoma under military escort. Nearly one-quarter of them died of disease and exhaustion on what came to be known as the Trail of Tears.

When the forced march to the West ended, the Indians had traded about 100 million acres east of the Mississippi for 32 million acres west of the river plus $68 million. Only a few scattered remnants, among them the Seminoles in Florida and the Cherokees in the southern Appalachian Mountains, remained in the East and South.

Forced removal had a disastrous impact on the displaced tribes. In the West they encountered an alien environment; lacking traditional ties, few felt at peace with the land. The animals and plants they found were unfamiliar. Unable to live off the land, many became dependent on government payments for survival. Removal also brought new internal conflicts. The Cherokees in particular experienced violence between pro- and antitreaty factions. Moreover, conflict arose between Native American groups migrating from the South and East and Indians already living in the West, as they were forced to share land and scarce resources.

In Florida a small band of Seminoles continued to resist. Some Seminole leaders agreed in the Treaty of Payne's Landing to relocate to the West within three years, but others opposed the treaty. A minority under Osceola, a charismatic leader,

SECOND SEMINOLE WAR

■ *The Trail of Tears,* by twentieth-century Pawnee artist Brummet Echohawk. About twenty thousand Cherokees were evicted in 1838–1839, and about one-quarter of them died on the forced march to present-day Oklahoma. (Gilcrease Museum, Tulsa, OK)

refused to vacate their homes and fought the pro-treaty group. When federal troops were sent to impose removal in 1835, Osceola waged a fierce guerrilla war against them. Osceola was captured under a white flag of truce and died in an army prison in 1838, but the Seminoles continued the fight. In 1842 the United States abandoned the removal effort. Most of Osceola's followers agreed to move west to Indian Territory in 1858, but many Seminoles remained in the Florida Everglades, proud of having resisted conquest.

Summary   *Online Study Center*   ACE the Test

Nationalism and self-confidence accompanied the end of the War of 1812. Under the Democratic-Republicans the federal government fostered expansion and economic growth through internal improvements, tariffs, the Second Bank of the United States, land sales, and Indian removal. The Supreme Court and American diplomats, too, asserted nationalism. John Quincy Adams negotiated peace and secure borders with Great Britain and Spain, and through the Monroe Doctrine insulated the Western Hemisphere from European conflict.

But sectionalism accompanied nationalism and geographical expansion. Conflicts over tariffs, economic hard times, and slavery brought discord. The Missouri Compromise was a stopgap measure to avoid the explosive issue of slavery.

From 1816 through 1845, the United States experienced explosive growth. Population increased sixfold and moved westward. New farms grew cotton and grain for the market, and cities followed. In the process, Indians were pushed aside.

Agriculture remained the dominant industry, though by midcentury a booming manufacturing sector challenged farming. And agriculture itself was becoming market oriented and mechanized. The market economy brought sustained growth; it also ushered in cycles of boom and bust that brought hard times and unemployment. The growing economy also meant growing destruction of the environment.

Large-scale manufacturing altered traditional patterns of production and consumption. Farm families began to purchase goods formerly made at home, and geared production to faraway markets. Farm women increasingly contributed income from market sales to the household purse. In New England many young women left the family farm to become the first factory workers in the new textile industry. In the new mills and factories, workplace relations became more impersonal, working conditions grew harsher, and men's and women's work became increasingly dissimilar. Industrial jobs began to attract large numbers of immigrants, and some workers organized labor unions.

LEGACY FOR A PEOPLE AND A NATION
A Mixed Economy

How active should the U.S. government be? Should it run, regulate, or leave to the market system health care, Social Security and private pensions, corporate concentration, and stock trading and investments? In other words, to what degree should the government be responsible for the well-being of the economy and individuals?

The Articles of Confederation limited government, the Constitution empowered it, and the Bill of Rights restricted it in specific areas. While Americans have continuously debated the appropriate role of government, the United States has generally occupied a middle ground: a mixed economy.

In the early nineteenth century, government played an active role in economic and social expansion. Federal and state governments built roads and canals, developed harbors, and operated post offices and the early telegraph. More commonly the government intervened to stimulate and regulate the private sector.

In the late nineteenth century, advocates of laissez-faire, or hands-off, government, challenged the pre–Civil War tradition of active government. Laissez faire dominated briefly until the 1880s and 1890s, when large corporations and trusts accumulated so much power that governments stepped in to regulate railroads and business concentration.

After the turn of the century, the federal government extended regulation to food, drugs, the environment, working conditions, and fair business practices. In the 1930s, the crisis of the Great Depression, followed in the 1940s by World War II, would lead the federal government to establish the modern welfare state, which operates through a mixed public-private structure.

Early in the twenty-first century, Americans again debate the appropriate role of government. Conservatives view government as the problem rather than the solution, arguing that government regulation hampers individual freedom and distorts the law of supply and demand. Advocates of an activist government argue that only the government has the power and resources to check economic concentration and to protect health, safety, and the environment. The framework of this debate is a legacy from before the Civil War.

REFORM AND POLITICS IN THE AGE OF JACKSON 1824–1845

"**I** proceed, Gentlemen, briefly to call your attention to the present state of Insane persons confined within this Commonwealth," Dorothea Dix petitioned the 1843 Massachusetts legislature, "in cages, closets, stalls, pens! Chained, naked, beaten with rods and lashed into obedience."

A year earlier, in a visit to a Newburyport almshouse, Dix had discovered one man residing in a shed whose door opened to the local "dead room," or morgue; his only companions were corpses. Shocked, she heard from an attendant about another insane inmate: "a woman in a cellar." Dix asked to see her. The superintendent warned Dix that the woman "was dangerous to be approached." Dix pressed on. They unlocked the doors and entered an underground cell. In the shadows Dix saw "a female apparently wasted to a skeleton, partially wrapped in blankets." She was withered, wrote Dix, "not by age, but by suffering." When the inmate saw the visitors, she wailed with despair: "Why am I consigned to hell? . . . I used to pray, I used to read the Bible. . . . I had friends; why have all forsaken me!—my God! my God! why hast thou forsaken me?"

Dix described in the most personal and vivid terms her visits to jails, almshouses, and private homes, and the cruel treatment of the insane. Her petition to the General Court of Massachusetts was so graphic and shocking that the legislature voted to reprint it as a government pamphlet. Part petition, part sermon, and part autobiography, it made riveting reading.

Dix epitomized much of early-nineteenth-century reform. She started with a religious belief in individual self-improvement and human perfectibility that led her to advocate collective responsibility. She made reform her career, fearlessly entering the public arena. Investigating asylums, petitioning the Massachusetts legislature, and lobbying other states and Congress, Dix moved from reform to politics, and she helped create a new public role for women, in the process broadening the base of political participation.

From Revival to Reform

Abolitionism and the Women's Movement

LINKS TO THE WORLD
The International Antislavery Movement

Jacksonianism and Party Politics

Federalism at Issue: The Nullification and Bank Controversies

The Whig Challenge and the Second Party System

Manifest Destiny and Expansionism

LEGACY FOR A PEOPLE AND A NATION
The Bible Belt

Online Study Center
This icon will direct you to interactive map and primary source activities on the website
http://college.hmco.com/pic/nortonbrief7e

181

CHRONOLOGY

1790s–1840s • Second Great Awakening spreads religious fervor

1820s • Reformers in New York and Pennsylvania establish model penitentiaries

1824 • No presidential candidate wins a majority in the electoral college

1825 • House of Representatives elects Adams president

1826 • American Society for the Promotion of Temperance founded
• Morgan affair is catalyst for Antimasonry movement

1828 • Tariff of Abominations passed
• Jackson elected president

1830 • Webster-Hayne debate explores the nature of the Union

1830s–40s • Democratic-Whig competition gels in second party system

1831 • Garrison begins abolitionist newspaper *The Liberator*
• First national Antimason convention

1832 • Jackson vetoes rechartering of the Second Bank of the United States
• Jackson reelected president

1832–33 • South Carolina nullifies tariffs of 1828 and 1832, prompting nullification crisis

1836 • Republic of Texas established after breaking from Mexico
• Specie Circular ends credit purchase of public lands
• Van Buren elected president

1837 • Financial panic ends boom of the 1830s

1838–39 • United States and Canada mobilize their militias over Maine–New Brunswick border dispute

1839–43 • Hard times spread unemployment and deflation

1840 • Whigs win presidency under Harrison

1841 • Tyler assumes the presidency after Harrison's death
• "Oregon fever" attracts settlers to the Northwest and intensifies expansionism

1843 • Dix petitions Massachusetts legislature regarding deplorable condition of insane asylums

1844 • Polk elected president

1845 • Texas admitted to the Union

1848 • Woman's Rights Convention at Seneca Falls, New York, calls for women's suffrage

The religious and reform fervor of the period arose both as part of the spiritual renewal known as the Second Great Awakening and as a response to the enormous transformation the United States experienced after the War of 1812. Immigration, the spread of a market economy, growing inequality, the westward advance of settlement, and territorial expansion all contributed to remaking the United States.

Anxieties wrought by rapid change drove the impulse to reform society. Men and women organized to end the abuses of alcohol and prostitution, improve conditions in prisons and asylums, oppose secret and antidemocratic societies, end slavery, and achieve equal rights for women. Inevitably reform movements pushed men and women into politics, though only men voted. Opponents of reform were equally concerned about social problems. They were, however, skeptical about human perfectibility, and they distrusted the exercise of power.

Two issues in particular bridged reform and politics: the short-lived Antimasonry frenzy against secret societies and the intense, uncompromising crusade for an immediate end to slavery. Though Antimasons organized the first third-party movement, abolition eventually overrode all other concerns.

The Jacksonians too saw themselves as reformers. They opposed special privileges and the Second Bank of the United States. President Andrew Jackson believed that a strong federal government restricted individual freedom by favoring one group over another. Social and religious reformers disagreed. Wanting a more active federal role, they rallied around the new Whig Party. Democrats and Whigs constituted a new party system, characterized by strong organizations, intense loyalty, and energetic religious and ethnic competition.

Both parties eagerly promoted expansionism during the prosperous 1840s. Democrats saw the agrarian West as an antidote to urbanization and industrialization; Whigs focused on the new commercial opportunities it offered. Expanding the nation to the Pacific seemed to be the manifest destiny of the United States. ■

From Revival to Reform

*R*eligion was probably the strongest motivation behind organized benevolence and reform. Beginning in the late 1790s religious revivals galvanized Protestants, especially women, into social action. At camp meetings, sometimes lasting a week with thousands in attendance, preachers exhorted sinners to repent and become genuine Christians. They offered salvation to all through personal conversion. At a time when only a minority could read and write, itinerant evangelists were democratizing American religion, making it available to all.

Resembling the Great Awakening of the eighteenth century (see Chapter 4), the movement came to

SECOND GREAT AWAKENING

be called the Second Great Awakening. It raised hopes for the Second Coming of the Christian messiah and the establishment of God's Kingdom on earth. Revivalists resolved to speed the Second Coming by combating the forces of evil and darkness. Some believed that the United States had a special mission in God's design and a special role in eliminating evil. Under revivalist influence, the role of churches and ministers in community life diminished as lay participation increased, and evangelical Christians across the country tried to right the wrongs of the world.

In the South, huge numbers of people regularly attended revivals, but they especially drew women and African Americans, free and slave. The call to personal repentance and conversion invigorated Protestantism, giving southern churches an evangelical base and evangelicalism a southern accent. In essence, the Second Great Awakening turned the South into the Bible belt. It also mostly ignored slavery, thus accommodating to it.

In the North, New York lawyer Charles G. Finney led the revival movement. After his 1821 soul-shaking conversion, Finney abandoned the law to convert souls. Salvation could be achieved, Finney preached, through spontaneous conversion like his own. He mesmerized his audiences and in everyday language preached that "God has made man a moral free agent." In other words, evil was avoidable: Christians were not doomed by original sin, and anyone could achieve salvation.

Revivalism had a particularly strong base among Methodists and Baptists, and these denominations grew the most because their structure maximized democratic participation and drew their ministers from ordinary folk. As Methodists and Baptists moved west, migration patterns spread not only religion but also the impulse for moral reform. All revivalists shared a belief in individual self-improvement, and the doctrine of perfectibility demanded that Christians actively organize and convert others. Thus, the Second Great Awakening bred reform, and evangelical Protestants became missionaries for both religious and secular salvation, generating new religious groups and voluntary reform societies. New sects like the

Mormons arose out of this ferment. So did associations that addressed the pressing issues of the day: temperance, education, Sabbath observance, dueling, and later slavery.

More women than men answered the call of Christianity, sustaining the Second Great Awakening and invigorating local churches.

EVANGELICAL WOMEN

Gradually women brought their families and sometimes their husbands into church and reform. Women, more than men, tended to feel personally responsible for counteracting the secular orientation of the expanding market economy. Emotionally charged conversion could return women to what they believed was the right path. It also offered them communal ties with other women.

Female missionary societies motivated organized religious and benevolent activity on an unprecedented scale. For women and some men, reform represented their first political involvement at a time when women did not vote. In reform organizations, women represented themselves; by participating directly in service activities, they pioneered new, visible, public roles for women.

An exposé of prostitution in New York City illustrates how reform led to political action. In response to an 1830 report documenting widespread prostitution in the city,

FEMALE REFORM SOCIETIES

New York businessmen and politicians defended the city's good name against "those base slanders." Women, moved by the plight of "fallen women," organized to fight prostitution. But whereas male reformers targeted the prostitutes, the newly organized Female Moral Reform Society focused on the men who victimized young women, publicizing the names of brothel clients.

During the 1830s, the New York society expanded. Calling itself the American Female Moral Reform Society, by 1840 it had 555 affiliated chapters across the nation. The society also entered the political sphere. In New York State in the 1840s, it successfully lobbied for criminal sanctions against men who seduced women into prostitution, as well as against prostitutes themselves.

One of the most successful reform efforts was the campaign against alcohol. Americans in 1800 consumed alcohol at the formidable annual rate of 5 gallons per capita,

TEMPERANCE

and alcohol played a significant role in men's social lives. Why then did temperance become such a vital issue? Like all nineteenth-century reform, temperance had a strong religious foundation.

Evangelicals considered drinking sinful, and forsaking alcohol was frequently part of conversion. The sale of whiskey often violated the Sabbath; many workers labored for six days and spent Sunday at the public house drinking and socializing. Alcoholism also destroyed families and caused poverty and crime. In the early 1840s, thousands of ordinary women formed Martha Washington societies to protect families by reforming alcoholics, raising children as teetotalers, and spreading the temperance message. Employers complained that drinkers took "St. Monday" as a holiday to recover from Sunday. In the new world of the factory, drinking was unacceptable.

As the temperance movement gained momentum, its goal shifted from moderation to voluntary abstinence and finally to prohibition. The American Society for the Promotion of Temperance, organized in 1826 to promote pledges of abstinence, became a pressure group for state prohibition legislation. By the mid-1830s five thousand state and local temperance societies touted teetotalism, and more than 1 million people had taken the pledge. As the movement spread, per capita consumption of alcohol fell from 5 gallons to below 2 gallons in the 1840s. Moreover, a number of northern states followed Maine in outlawing the sale of alcohol except for medicinal purpose.

From the 1820s on, many reformers expressed their prejudices by regarding alcohol as an evil introduced by Catholic immigrants. Rum and immigrants, they claimed, defiled the Sabbath, brought poverty, and supported the feared papacy. In fact, many Catholics took the pledge of abstinence. But even Catholic teetotalers tended to oppose state regulation of drinking. They favored self-control, not state coercion.

As Dorothea Dix urged, moral reform also stimulated the construction of institutions to house prisoners, the mentally ill, orphans,

PENITENTIARIES AND ASYLUMS

delinquent children, and the poor. Such institutions were needed, reformers argued, to shelter victims of society's turbulence and impose on them familial discipline. Through discipline and the banning of idleness, inmates might become self-reliant and responsible.

■ As the temperance movement spread, the evils of alcohol became a major theme in popular culture. This 1830s lithograph, *Mortgaging the Farm,* hints at drinking's potential destructiveness. Drunken, idle farmers sit in the shadow of the gallows holding the tavern's signboard.   (Old Sturbridge Village)

In the 1820s New York and Pennsylvania rejected incarceration to punish criminals or remove them from society, introducing instead regimens to rehabilitate them. New York's Auburn prison placed prisoners in individual cells but brought them together in common workshops. Pennsylvania's prisons isolated prisoners completely, forcing them to eat, sleep, and work in their individual cells and allowing them contact only with guards and visitors.

Insane asylums, hospitals, and orphanages instituted similar approaches. Formerly the prescribed treatment had removed disturbed individuals from society and isolated them among strangers, many with criminals. The new asylums were clean and orderly. In response to Dorothea Dix's crusade and reform societies, twenty-eight of the thirty-three states had public institutions for the mentally ill by 1860.

Critical to reform movements was building networks. Reform and literary societies brought national speakers like Dorothea Dix, abolitionist Frederick Douglass, and hundreds of others to cities and towns to preach reform. Annual conventions increased personal contacts and motivated supporters. Reformers made use of new technology, such as the new steam presses that permitted mass publication of their newspapers and pamphlets, to spread their word.

More intense than the asylum movement was the briefer crusade against Freemasonry, a secret fraternity that had come to the United States from England in the eighteenth century. Sons of the Enlightenment such as Benjamin Franklin and George Washington were attracted to Masonry, because it emphasized individual belief in a deity (as opposed to organized religion or a single church's doctrine). In the early nineteenth century Freemasonry attracted men prominent in commerce and civic affairs.

ANTIMASONRY

Opponents of Masonry believed that its secrecy and appeal to elites were antidemocratic and antirepublican. Publications such as the *Anti Masonic Almanac* attacked Masonic initiation rites. Evangelicals labeled the order satanic. Antimasons argued that Masonry threatened the family because it excluded women and encouraged men to neglect their families for alcohol and ribald entertainments at Masonic lodges. The political arena quickly absorbed Antimasonry, and its short life illustrates the close association of politics and reform in the 1820s and after.

The catalyst for Antimasonry as an organized movement was the suspected murder of William Morgan, a disillusioned Mason who published an exposé in 1826. Even before the book appeared, a group of Masons abducted Morgan in Canandaigua, New York. It was widely believed that his kidnappers murdered him, though his body was never found.

MORGAN AFFAIR

Events seemed to confirm Masonry's antidemocratic character. Prosecutors who were Masons appeared to obstruct the investigation of Morgan's abduction. The public pressed for justice, and a series of notorious trials from 1827 through 1831 led many to suspect a cover-up. Antimasonry coalesced overnight in western New York, and it quickly became a political movement that spread to other states.

With growing popular support, the Antimasons held conventions in 1827 to select candidates to oppose Masons running for office. The next year, the conventions supported John Quincy Adams for president

CONVENTION SYSTEM

and opposed Andrew Jackson because he was a Mason. The Antimasons held the first national political convention in Baltimore in 1831, and a year later they nominated William Wirt as their presidential candidate. Thus, the Antimasons became a rallying point for anti-Jacksonians. Their electoral strength lay in New England and New York. Antimasonry found little support in the slave South.

By the mid-1830s, Antimasonry had lost momentum. A single-issue party, the Antimasons declined along with Freemasonry. Yet the movement left its mark on the politics of the era. As a moral crusade focused on public officeholders, it inspired broad participation in the political process. The Antimasons also changed party organization by pioneering the convention, rather than the caucus, for nominating candidates for office and by introducing the party platform.

Abolitionism and the Women's Movement

*a*ntimasonry foreshadowed and had much in common with abolitionism. To abolitionist William Lloyd Garrison, both slavery and Masonry undermined republican values. Eventually the issue of slavery consumed all other reforms and threatened the nation itself. Those who advocated immediate emancipation saw slavery as, above all, a moral issue—the ultimate sin.

Free blacks in the North had demanded an end to slavery since the Revolution. In 1800 Richard Allen, the first bishop of the African Methodist Episcopal (AME) Church, eulogized former president George Washington for freeing his slaves, and his sermon on immediatism— an immediate end to slavery—was widely circulated as a pamphlet. To free blacks, slavery was both a moral issue and a personal one; while slavery was legal, they were always at risk of being seized as fugitives. David Walker's *Appeal . . . to the Colored Citizens* (1829) was a clarion call for immediatism and helped politicize many abolitionists. Walker, a southern-born free black, was Boston's leading abolitionist until his death in 1830. By then fifty black abolitionist societies in the United States were assisting fugitive slaves, lobbying for emancipa-

AFRICAN AMERICAN ABOLITIONISTS

■ Women played an activist role in reform, especially in abolitionism. A rare daguerreotype from August 1850 shows women and men, including Frederick Douglass, on the podium at an abolitionist rally in Cazenovia, New York.   (Collection of J. Paul Getty Museum, Los Angeles, California)

tion, and exposing slavery's evils. A free black press spread the word.

Few whites, however, advocated the abolition of slavery before the 1830s. In the North, where by 1820 slavery had been virtually abolished, whites took little interest in the issue. Antislavery sentiment appeared strongest in the Upper South. The American Colonization Society, founded in 1816, advocated gradual, voluntary emancipation and resettlement of former slaves in Africa, establishing the colony of Liberia for that purpose in the 1820s. Society members did not believe that free blacks had a place in the United States, and they included Jefferson and other slaveholders, some evangelicals and Quakers, and (briefly) a few blacks.

During the 1830s, however, a small number of white reformers, driven by moral urgency, joined the

GRADUAL EMANCIPATION

The International Antislavery Movement

The heart of the international antislavery movement had been in Great Britain, but in the 1830s, many of Britain's local antislavery societies thought they had accomplished their mission and disbanded. In 1833 Parliament ended slavery in the British Empire, and over the previous three decades, the international slave trade had greatly diminished. At the same time, however, abolitionism in the United States was on the rise, and now militant American black abolitionists revived the international movement to end slavery where it still existed: in Spanish possessions like Cuba, in independent and colonial South America, in Africa and Asia, and in the United States.

Seeking to raise money and put international pressure on the United States to abolish slavery, African American abolitionists in the 1840s toured Britain regularly to appeal for support. Especially effective were ex-slaves, who recounted their firsthand experiences of slavery and bared their scarred bodies. In 1845 Frederick Douglass began a nineteen-month tour, giving three hundred lectures in Britain.

In 1849 black abolitionists William Wells Brown, Alexander Crummell, and J. W. C. Pennington were among the twenty American delegates at the international Paris Peace Conference. There, Brown likened war and slavery, telling the eight hundred delegates from western Europe and the United States that "it is impossible to maintain slavery without maintaining war." His scheduled brief lecture tour in Britain turned into a five-year exile because, after passage of the 1850 Fugitive Slave Law, he feared being seized and sent back to slavery if he returned to the United States. In 1854 British abolitionists purchased his freedom from his former master.

Gandy, Douglass, Brown, and dozens of other former slaves helped revive abolitionism as an international issue. They energized the British and Foreign Anti-Slavery Society, founded in 1839, and hundreds of more militant, local societies. By the early 1850s national abolitionist movements succeeded in abolishing slavery in Colombia, Argentina, Venezuela, and Peru. As advocates of women's rights, international peace, temperance, and other reforms, the United States's black abolitionists also linked Americans to reform movements around the world.

William Wells Brown's autobiography stirred abolitionists in the United States and England. In 1849 Brown was among the American delegates to the Paris Peace Conference, then spent the next five years as an exile in Britain, fearing being sent back to slavery under the 1850 Fugitive Slave Act. He returned to the United States only after British abolitionists purchased his freedom from his former master. (Documenting the American South [http://docsouth.unc.edu], The University of North Carolina at Chapel Hill Libraries)

black crusade for immediate emancipation. Soon the immediatists, who demanded immediate, complete, and uncompensated emancipation, surpassed the gradualists as the dominant strand of abolitionism. The most prominent and uncompromising immediatist was the incendiary William Lloyd Garrison. In 1831 Garrison began publishing *The Liberator,* in whose first issue he declared, "I am in earnest—I will not equivocate—I will not excuse—I will not retreat a single inch—and *I will be heard.*"

Garrison's refusal to work with anyone who tolerated the delay of emancipation isolated him from other white opponents of slavery. Still, by his actions and rhetorical power, Garrison helped to push antislavery onto the national agenda, though he had no specific plan for abolishing slavery.

It is difficult to differentiate between those who became immediatists and those who did not. Immediatists were often young evangelicals active in benevolent societies in the 1820s; many became ordained ministers; and many had personal contact with free blacks. They were convinced that slaveholding was a sin. They also shared great moral intensity and were unwilling to compromise.

IMMEDIATISTS

In the 1840s escaped slaves Frederick Douglass and Harriet Tubman joined forces with white reformers in the American Anti-Slavery Society. Those who had experienced slavery firsthand, like Douglass and Sojourner Truth, wrote personal narratives that mobilized northerners. Most benevolent workers and reformers, however, kept their distance from the immediatists. They shared the view that slavery was a sin but believed in gradual emancipation. They feared that if they moved too fast or attacked sinners too harshly, they would destroy the harmony and order they sought.

Immediatists' greatest recruitment successes resulted from defending their own constitutional rights, not the rights of slaves. Wherever they went, immediatists found their free speech threatened by hostile crowds. Mob violence peaked in 1835 with more than fifty riots aimed at abolitionists or African Americans. In 1837 in Alton, Illinois, a mob murdered abolitionist editor Elijah P. Lovejoy. Public outrage at Lovejoy's murder increased antislavery support in the North.

OPPOSITION TO ABOLITIONISTS

In the South, mobs blocked the distribution of antislavery tracts. Steam-powered presses and technological developments in papermaking in the 1830s enabled the American Anti-Slavery Society to publish millions of pamphlets. The state of South Carolina intercepted and burned abolitionist literature. In 1835 proslavery assailants killed four abolitionists in South Carolina and Louisiana and forty supposed insurrectionists in Mississippi and Louisiana.

At a rally in Boston in 1835, former Federalist Harrison Gray Otis portrayed abolitionists as subversives. Abolitionists, he predicted, would turn to politics, causing unforeseeable calamity. "What will become of the Union?" Otis asked.

Abolitionists were already bombarding Congress with petitions to abolish slavery and the slave trade in the District of Columbia, which Congress governed. The House in 1836 adopted what abolitionists labeled the "gag rule," which automatically tabled abolitionist petitions, effectively preventing debate on them. In a dramatic defense of the right of petition, former president John Quincy Adams, now a representative from Massachusetts, took to the floor again and again to speak against the gag rule. (Its repeal in 1844 was anticlimactic.)

GAG RULE

The Missouri Compromise, censorship of the mails, and the gag rule represented attempts to keep the issue of slavery out of the political arena. Yet the more that national leaders, especially Democrats, worked to avoid the matter, the more antislavery forces hardened their resolve.

Abolitionism was highly factionalized, and its adherents fought one another as often as they fought the defenders of slavery. They were divided between Garrison's emphasis on "moral suasion"—winning over the hearts of slaveowners rather than coercing them—and the practical politics of James G. Birney, the Liberty Party's candidate for president in 1840 and 1844. They also disagreed about the place of free blacks in American society. And the movement split over other reforms, especially the roles and rights of women.

Women had been prominent in the antislavery movement from the start, in many cases as active and politically involved as men. Lydia Maria Child, Maria Chapman, and Lucretia Mott served on the American Anti-Slavery Society's executive committee; Child and Chapman served as editors of its official paper, the *National Anti-Slavery Standard.* Garrison's moral suasion at-

WOMEN ABOLITIONISTS

tracted many women because it gave them a platform from which to oppose slavery. Yet some politically active societies excluded women because they could not vote and opposed women's roles in reform.

In the 1830s abolitionists Angelina and Sarah Grimké were attacked for speaking to mixed audiences. One pastoral letter declared that women should obey, not lecture, men. This reaction turned the Grimkés' attention from the condition of slaves to the condition of women. Born into a Charleston, South Carolina, slaveholding family, both sisters had experienced conversion, became outspoken abolitionists, moved north, and found a home in Garrison's immediatism. Now they confronted the concept of "subordination to man," insisting that men and women had the "same rights and same duties." Together the Grimkés initiated a new reform movement to secure legal and social equality of women.

〰️ *Online Study Center*
Improve Your Grade
Primary Source: Rules for Husbands and Wives

Public participation in religious revival and 25p10.5-reform had led some women to reexamine

WOMEN'S RIGHTS	their positions in society. As the predominant group in the Second Great Awakening, women began to challenge male domination in religion.

Revivals brought ordinary women into the public sphere. Female societies and reform networks, convention participation, and advocacy opened new roles to women. The market economy also created new occupations for women outside their homes.

Women abolitionists were among the leaders on behalf of women's rights. In July 1848 Elizabeth Cady Stanton, Lucretia Mott, and Lucy Stone organized the Woman's Rights Convention at Seneca Falls, New York. Three hundred women and men reformers gathered to demand political, social, and economic equality for women. They protested women's legal disabilities—inability to vote, limited property rights—and their social restrictions—exclusion from advanced schooling and from most occupations. Their Declaration of Sentiments indicted the injustices suffered by women and launched the women's rights movement. "All men and women are created equal," the declaration proclaimed. If women had the vote, participants argued, they could protect themselves and realize their full potential as moral and spiritual leaders.

Advocates of women's rights were slow to garner support, especially from men, who held most of the political and legal power. In the 1840s the question of women's suffrage split the antislavery movement. Some men joined the ranks, notably Garrison and Frederick Douglass, but most men actively opposed a vote for women.

Jacksonianism and Party Politics

In the 1820s, reform pushed its way into politics. No less than reformers, politicians sought to control the direction of change in the expanding nation. The 1824 presidential election ignited a political fire that reformers, abolitionists, and expansionists would continuously stoke. By the 1830s, politics had become the great American pastime.

The election of 1824, in which John Quincy Adams and Andrew Jackson faced off for the first time, heralded a more open political system. From 1800 through 1820 the system in which a congressional caucus chose the Democratic-Republican nominees (Jefferson, Madison, and Monroe) had worked well. That it limited voters' involvement in choosing candidates was not an anomaly because in 1800, only five of the sixteen states selected presidential electors by popular vote. In most of the others, state legislatures selected the electors. By 1824, however, eighteen of twenty-four states chose electors by popular vote.

The Democratic-Republican caucus in 1824 chose William H. Crawford of Georgia, secretary of the

ELECTION OF 1824	treasury, as its presidential candidate. But other Democratic-Republicans, emboldened by the chance to appeal directly to voters, put themselves forward as sectional candidates. John

Quincy Adams drew support from New England, while westerners backed House Speaker Henry Clay of Kentucky. Secretary of War John C. Calhoun hoped for support from the South and from Pennsylvania. The Tennessee legislature nominated Andrew Jackson, a popular military hero of unknown political views. Jackson had the most widespread support. By boycotting the caucus and attacking it as undemocratic, these men and their supporters ended the role of Congress in nominating presidential candidates.

In the four-way presidential election of 1824, Andrew Jackson led in both electoral and popular votes, but no candidate received a majority in the electoral college. Adams finished second, and Crawford and Clay trailed far behind (Calhoun had dropped out of the race before the election). Under the Constitution, the House of Representatives, voting by state delegation, one vote to a state, selected the next president from among the candidates. Clay, who had received the fewest votes, was dropped. Crawford, a stroke victim, never received serious consideration. The influential Clay backed Adams, who received the votes of thirteen of the twenty-four state delegations to win. Clay then became Adams's secretary of state, the traditional steppingstone to the presidency.

Angry Jacksonians denounced the outcome as a "corrupt bargain." The Democratic-Republican Party split. The Adams wing emerged as the National Republicans; the Jacksonians became the Democrats and immediately began planning for 1828.

After taking the oath of office, Adams proposed a strong nationalist policy incorporating Henry Clay's "American System," a program of protective tariffs, a national bank, and internal improvements. Brilliant as a diplomat and secretary of state, Adams was an inept president. He underestimated the lingering effects of the Panic of 1819 and the resulting staunch opposition to a national bank and protective tariffs. Meanwhile, supporters of Andrew Jackson sabotaged Adams's administration at every opportunity.

THE ELECTION OF 1828

The 1828 election campaign, pitting Adams against Jackson, was rowdy and intensely personal. Jackson's supporters accused Adams, when he was envoy to Russia, of having secured prostitutes for the czar. Anti-Jacksonians published reports that Rachel Jackson had had an affair with and married Jackson before her first husband divorced her. After the election, Rachel Jackson discovered a pamphlet defending her, and she was shocked by the extent of the charges. When she died of a heart attack in December 1828, Jacksonians charged that she was "murdered."

Jackson swamped Adams, carrying 56 percent of the popular vote and winning in the electoral college by 178 to 83 votes. He and his supporters believed that the will of the people had finally been served. Through a lavishly financed coalition of state parties, political leaders, and newspaper editors, a popular movement had elected the president, and a new era had begun. The Democratic Party became the first well-organized national political party in the United States, and tight party organization became the hallmark of nineteenth-century American politics.

ANDREW JACKSON AND THE DEMOCRATS

Nicknamed "Old Hickory" after the toughest of American hardwoods, Andrew Jackson was a rough-and-tumble, ambitious man. He rose from humble beginnings to become a wealthy planter and slaveholder and the first president from the West. He had an instinct for politics and picked both issues and supporters shrewdly.

Jackson and his supporters viewed the strong federal government advocated by John Quincy Adams as the enemy of individual liberty. The Democrats represented a wide range of views but shared a fundamental commitment to the Jeffersonian concept of an agrarian society.

Jacksonians feared the concentration of economic and political power. They believed that government intervention in the economy benefited special-interest groups and created corporate monopolies that favored the rich. They sought to restore the independence of the individual—the artisan and the ordinary farmer—by ending federal support of banks and corporations and restricting the use of paper currency, which they distrusted.

Jackson and his supporters opposed reform as a movement. Reformers eager to turn their programs into legislation called for a more activist government. But Democrats tended to oppose programs like educational reform and a public education system. They believed, for instance, that public schools restricted individual liberty by interfering with parental responsibility and undermined freedom of religion by replacing church schools. Nor did Jackson share reformers' humanitarian concerns.

JACKSONIANS AS REFORMERS

Jacksonians considered themselves reformers in a different way. By restraining government and emphasizing individualism, they sought to restore traditional republican virtues, such as prudence and economy. Jackson sought to encourage self-discipline and self-reliance, traits undermined by economic and social change.

Like Jefferson, Jackson strengthened the executive branch of government even as he weakened the federal role. In combining the roles of party leader and chief of state, he centralized power in the White

House. Jackson relied on political friends, his "Kitchen Cabinet," for advice; he rarely consulted his official cabinet. By rotating officeholders, Jackson introduced a spoils system that rewarded his followers handsomely and thereby strengthened party organization and loyalty.

Jackson rejected elitism and special favors and stressed popular government. Time and again he declared that sovereignty resided with the people, not with the states or the courts. In this respect, Jackson was a reformer; he returned government to majority rule. Yet it is hard to distinguish between Jackson's belief in himself as the instrument of the people and demagogic arrogance.

Animosity between Jackson's supporters and opponents grew year by year. Massachusetts senator Daniel Webster feared the men around the president; Henry Clay most feared Jackson himself. They contended that rotation in office, with appointments based on loyalty rather than competence, corrupted government. Opponents mocked Jackson as "King Andrew I," charging him with abuse of power by ignoring the Supreme Court's ruling on Cherokee rights, using the spoils system, and consulting his Kitchen Cabinet. Critics also accused him of recklessly destroying the economy.

Amid this agitation, Jackson invigorated the philosophy of limited government. In 1830 he vetoed the Maysville Road bill, which would have funded construction of a 60-mile turnpike from Maysville to Lexington, Kentucky. A federally subsidized internal improvement confined to one state was unconstitutional, he charged; such projects were properly a state responsibility. The veto undermined Henry Clay's nationalist program and personally embarrassed Clay because the project was in his home district.

Federalism at Issue: The Nullification and Bank Controversies

Soon Jackson had to face directly the question of the proper division of sovereignty between state and central governments. The slave South feared federal power, no state more so than South Carolina. Southerners also resented protectionist tariffs, one of the foundations of Clay's American System, which in 1824 and 1828 protected northern factories by imposing import duties on manufactured cloth and iron. But the tariff raised the costs of these goods to southerners, who labeled the high tariff of 1828 the Tariff of Abominations.

South Carolina's political leaders went so far as to reject the 1828 tariff, invoking the doctrine of nullification, according to which a state had the right to overrule, or nullify, federal legislation. Nullification was based on the idea expressed in the Virginia and Kentucky resolutions of 1798 (see Chapter 8)—that the states, representing the people, have a right to judge the constitutionality of federal actions. Jackson's vice president, John C. Calhoun of South Carolina, argued in his unsigned *Exposition and Protest* that in any disagreement between the federal government and a state, a special state convention—like the conventions called to ratify the Constitution—should decide the conflict by either nullifying or affirming the federal law. Only the power of nullification, Calhoun asserted, could protect the minority against the tyranny of the majority.

NULLIFICATION

In public, Calhoun let others advance nullification. He hoped to avoid embarrassing the Democratic ticket and to win Jackson's support as the Democratic presidential heir apparent. Thus, in early 1830, Calhoun presided silently over the Senate and its packed galleries when Senator Daniel Webster of Massachusetts and Senator Robert Y. Hayne of South Carolina debated states' rights and the nature of the Union, with nullification a subtext. At the climax of the debate, Webster invoked two powerful images. One was the outcome of nullification: "states dissevered, discordant, belligerent; on a land rent with civil feuds, or drenched . . . in fraternal blood!" The other was a patriotic vision of a great nation flourishing under the motto "Liberty and Union, now and forever, one and inseparable."

WEBSTER-HAYNE DEBATE

Though sympathetic to states' rights and distrustful of the federal government, Jackson rejected the idea of state sovereignty. Believing deeply in the Union, he shared Webster's dread of nullification. Soon after the Webster-Hayne debate, the president made his position clear at a Jefferson Day dinner with the toast "Our Federal Union, it must and shall be preserved." Vice President Calhoun, when his turn came, toasted, "The Federal Union—next to our liberty the most dear." Calhoun thus revealed his adherence to states' rights.

Tension resumed when Congress passed a new tariff in 1832 reducing some duties but retaining high taxes on imported iron, cottons, and woolens. Though a majority of southern representatives supported the new tariff, South Carolinians refused to go along. More than the duties, they feared that the act could set a precedent for congressional legislation on slavery. In November 1832 a South Carolina state convention nullified both tariffs, making it unlawful for federal officials to collect duties in the state.

NULLIFICATION CRISIS

Old Hickory responded quickly. In December he issued a proclamation opposing nullification. He moved troops to federal forts in South Carolina and prepared U.S. marshals to collect the required duties. At Jackson's request, Congress passed the Force Act, which authorized the president to call up troops but also offered a way to avoid force by collecting duties before foreign ships reached Charleston's harbor. At the same time, Jackson extended an olive branch by recommending tariff reductions.

Calhoun, disturbed by South Carolina's drift toward separatism, resigned as vice president and soon won election to represent South Carolina in the U.S. Senate. There he worked with Henry Clay to draw up the compromise Tariff of 1833. Quickly passed by Congress and signed by the president, the new tariff lengthened the list of duty-free items and reduced duties over nine years. Satisfied, South Carolina's convention repealed its nullification law. In a final salvo, it also nullified Jackson's Force Act. Jackson ignored the gesture.

Nullification offered a genuine debate on the nature and principles of the republic. Each side believed it was upholding the Constitution. Neither side won a clear victory, though both claimed to have done so. It took another crisis, over a central bank, to define the powers of the federal government more clearly.

The Second Bank of the United States, whose twenty-year charter was scheduled to expire in 1836, served as a depository for federal funds, its notes circulating as reliable currency that could be exchanged for gold; it kept state banks honest

SECOND BANK OF THE UNITED STATES

by refusing to accept the bank notes of any bank lacking sufficient gold reserves. Most state banks resented the central bank's police role: by presenting a state bank's notes for redemption all at once, the Second Bank could easily ruin a bank. Moreover, with less money in reserve, state banks found themselves unable to compete on an equal footing with the Second Bank.

Many state governments also regarded the national bank as unresponsive to local needs. Westerners and urban workers remembered with bitterness the bank's conservative credit policies during the Panic of 1819. As a private, profit-making institution, its policies reflected the interest of its owners. Its president, Nicholas Biddle, was an eastern patrician who symbolized all that westerners found wrong with the bank.

The bank's charter was valid until 1836, but with the 1832 presidential campaign in view, Henry Clay, the National Republican presidential candidate, persuaded Biddle to ask Congress to approve an early rechartering. Clay intended to pressure Jackson to sign the rechartering bill or to face an override of his veto. The plan backfired, however, when the Senate failed to override the president's veto. Jackson's veto message was an emotional attack on the undemocratic nature of the bank. With the bank the prime issue in the 1832 campaign, and with Jackson denouncing special privilege and economic power, he won reelection easily.

In 1833 Jackson moved to dismantle the Second Bank of the United States. He deposited federal funds in state-chartered banks (critics called them his "pet banks"). Without federal money, the Second Bank shriveled. When its federal charter expired in 1836, it became just another Pennsylvania-chartered private bank. Five years later, it closed its doors.

JACKSON'S SECOND TERM

As the bank died, Congress passed the Deposit Act of 1836. The act authorized the secretary of the treasury to designate one bank in each state and territory to provide the services formerly performed by the Bank of the United States. The act provided that the federal surplus in excess of $5 million be distributed to the states as interest-free loans beginning in 1837.

The surplus had derived from wholesale speculation in public lands: speculators borrowed money to purchase public land, used the land as collateral for credit to buy additional acreage, and repeated the cy-

SPECIE CIRCULAR

1836, only specie—gold or silver—or Virginia scrip (paper money) would be accepted as payment for land. By ending credit sales, it significantly reduced purchases of public land and the federal budget surplus. As a result, the government suspended payments to the states soon after they began.

The policy was a disaster. The increased demand for specie squeezed banks. Credit contracted as banks issued fewer notes and loans. In the waning days of Jackson's administration, Congress voted to repeal the circular, but the president pocket-vetoed the bill by holding it unsigned until Congress adjourned. Finally in May 1838, a joint resolution of Congress overturned the circular.

The first six presidents had vetoed nine bills; Jackson alone vetoed twelve. Previous presidents had

USE OF THE VETO

believed that vetoes were justified only on constitutional grounds, but Jackson considered policy disagreement legitimate grounds as well. Using the veto to control Congress, in effect, Jackson made the executive for the first time a rival branch of government, equal in power to Congress.

The Whig Challenge and the Second Party System

*M*ost historians view the 1830s and 1840s as an age of reform and popularly based political parties. As the passions of reformers and abolitionists spilled over into politics, party differences became paramount, and party loyalties solidified. For the first time in American history, grassroots political groups, organized from the bottom up, set the tone of political life.

Opponents of the Democrats found shelter under a common umbrella, the Whig Party, in the 1830s.

WHIG PARTY

From 1834 through the 1840s, the Whigs and the Democrats competed on a nearly equal footing at local and national levels and achieved a stability previously unknown in American politics. The political competition of this period—known as the second party system—was more intense and well organized than the first party system of Democratic-Republicans versus Federalists. As political interest

■ This 1830 Ralph E. W. Earl oil painting of President Andrew Jackson, entitled *Tennessee Gentleman*, captures the complexity of Jackson's image. The first president from the West and the first born in a log cabin, Jackson nonetheless poses as an aristocrat with his plantation house, The Hermitage, in the background.   (Courtesy, The Hermitage—The Home of Andrew Jackson)

cle. The state banks providing the loans issued bank notes. Jackson, who opposed paper money, feared that the speculative craze threatened the stability of state banks and undermined the interests of settlers, who could not compete with speculators in bidding for the best land.

Reflecting his hard-money instincts, the president ordered Treasury Secretary Levi Woodbury to issue the Specie Circular. It provided that after August broadened, states expanded white male voting. By 1840 only seven of twenty-six states had property restrictions for male suffrage.

Increasingly the parties diverged. Whigs favored economic expansion through an activist government,

WHIGS AND REFORMERS

Democrats through limited central government. Whigs supported corporate charters, a national bank, and paper currency; Democrats were opposed to all three. Whigs also favored more humanitarian reforms than did Democrats, including public schools, abolition of capital punishment, prison and asylum reform, and temperance. Whigs were generally more optimistic than Democrats and more enterprising. The chartering of corporations, they argued, expanded economic opportunity for everyone, laborers and farmers alike. Democrats, distrustful of concentrated economic power and moral and economic coercion, held fast to the Jeffersonian principle of limited government.

Religion and ethnicity, not economics and class, most influenced party affiliation. The Whig Party won the favor of evangelical Protestants and the small number of free black voters and was the vehicle of revivalist Protestantism. Indeed, Whigs practiced a kind of political revivalism. Their rallies resembled camp meetings; in their speeches, they employed pulpit rhetoric, and their programs embodied the perfectionist beliefs of reformers.

In their appeal to evangelicals, Whigs alienated members of other faiths. The evangelicals' ideal Christian state had no room for Catholics, Mormons, Unitarians, Universalists, or religious freethinkers. Those groups opposed Sabbath laws and temperance legislation in particular and state interference in moral and religious questions in general. As a result, more than 95 percent of Irish Catholics, 90 percent of Reformed Dutch, and 80 percent of German Catholics voted Democratic.

Jackson handpicked Vice President Martin Van Buren to head the Democratic ticket in the 1836 presidential election. The Whigs, not

ELECTION OF 1836

yet organized into a national party, entered three sectional candidates: Daniel Webster of New England, Hugh White of the South, and William Henry Harrison of the West. By splintering the vote, they hoped to throw the election into the House of Representatives. Van Buren, however, comfortably captured the electoral college despite an edge of only 25,000 votes out of 1.5 million cast.

Van Buren took office just weeks before the American credit system collapsed. In response to the

VAN BUREN AND HARD TIMES

impact of the Specie Circular, New York banks stopped redeeming paper currency with gold in mid-1837. Soon all banks suspended payments in hard coin. Thus began a downward economic spiral that curtailed bank loans and strangled business confidence. Hard times persisted from 1839 until 1843.

Ill-advisedly, Van Buren followed Jackson's hard-money policies. He cut federal spending, which caused prices to drop further, and he opposed a national bank, which would have expanded credit. Even worse, the president proposed a new regional treasury system for government deposits. The treasury branches would accept and pay out only gold and silver coin; they would not accept paper currency or checks drawn on state banks. Van Buren's independent treasury bill became law in 1840. By increasing the demand for hard coin, it deprived banks of gold and further accelerated price deflation.

With the nation in the grip of hard times, the Whig strategy for the election of 1840 was simple: hold on to

WILLIAM HENRY HARRISON AND THE ELECTION OF 1840

loyal supporters and win over independents by blaming hard times on the Democrats. The Whigs rallied behind a military hero, General William Henry Harrison, conqueror of the Shawnees at Tippecanoe Creek in 1811. The Democrats renominated President Van Buren.

Harrison, or "Old Tippecanoe," and his running mate, John Tyler of Virginia, ran a "log cabin and hard cider" campaign—a people's crusade—against the aristocratic president in "the Palace." In a huge turnout, 80 percent of eligible voters cast ballots. Harrison won the popular vote by a narrow margin but swept the electoral college by 234 to 60.

Within a month of his inauguration, Harrison died of pneumonia. His successor, John Tyler, had

PRESIDENT TYLER

left the Democratic Party to protest Jackson's nullification proclamation. Tyler turned out to be more Democrat than Whig. He repeatedly vetoed

Henry Clay's protective tariffs, internal improvements, and bills to revive the Bank of the United States. Two days after Tyler's second veto of a bank bill, the entire cabinet resigned except Secretary of State Daniel Webster, who was busy with treaty negotiations; he left shortly after. Tyler became a president without a party, and the Whigs lost the presidency without losing an election.

Hard times in the late 1830s and early 1840s deflected attention from a renewal of Anglo-American tensions that had multiple sources:

ANGLO-AMERICAN TENSIONS northern commercial rivalry with Britain, the default of state governments and corporations on British-held debts during the Panic of 1837, rebellion in Canada, boundary disputes, southern alarm over West Indian emancipation, and American expansionism.

One problem disrupting Anglo-American relations was an old border dispute between Maine and New Brunswick. When Canadian lumbermen cut trees in the disputed region in the winter of 1838–1839, the citizens of Maine attempted to expel them. The lumbermen captured a Maine land agent and posse, both sides mobilized their militias, and Congress authorized a call-up of fifty thousand men. Ultimately, a truce was arranged, and no blood was spilled. The two sides compromised on their conflicting land claims in the Webster-Ashburton Treaty (1842).

The border dispute with Great Britain prefigured conflicts that were to erupt in the 1840s over the expansion of the United States. With Tyler's succession to power in 1841 and James K. Polk's Democratic victory in the presidential election of 1844, federal activism in the domestic sphere ended for the rest of the decade, as attention turned to territorial expansion.

Manifest Destiny and Expansionism

*T*he belief that American expansion westward and southward was inevitable, just, and divinely ordained was first labeled "manifest destiny" in 1845 by John L. O'Sullivan, editor of the *United States Magazine and Domestic Review*. The annexation of Texas, O'Sullivan wrote, was "the fulfillment of our manifest destiny to overspread the continent allotted by Providence for the free development of our yearly multiplying millions."

As the proportion of Americans living west of the Appalachians grew, both national parties joined the popular clamor for expansion. Agrarian Democrats sought western land to balance urbanization. Enterprising Whigs looked to the new commercial opportunities the West offered. Southerners envisioned the extension of slavery and more slave states.

Fierce national pride spurred the quest for land. Americans were convinced that theirs was the greatest country on earth, with a special role to play in the world. To Americans, expansion promised to extend the benefits of a republican system of government to the unfortunate and the inferior.

In part, racism contributed to manifest destiny. The impulse to colonize and develop the West was based on the belief that Euro-Americans could use the land more productively than American Indians or Hispanics. Euro-Americans viewed these peoples as inferior, best controlled or conquered. Thus, the same racial attitudes that justified slavery and discrimination against black people supported expansion in the West.

Among the long-standing objectives of expansionists was Texas, which in addition to present-day

REPUBLIC OF TEXAS Texas included parts of Oklahoma, Kansas, Colorado, Wyoming, and New Mexico (see Map 11.1). After winning independence from Spain in 1821, Mexico encouraged the development of its remote northern province, offering large tracts of land virtually free to U.S. settlers called *empresarios*. The settlers in turn agreed to become Mexican citizens, adopt Catholicism, and bring hundreds of American families into the area.

By 1835 thirty-five thousand Americans, including many slaveholders, lived in Texas. As the new settlers' numbers and power grew, they tended to ignore their commitments to the Mexican government. In response, dictator General Antonio López de Santa Anna tightened control over the region. In turn, the Anglo immigrants and *Tejanos*—Mexicans living in Texas—rebelled. At the Alamo mission in San Antonio in 1836, fewer than two hundred Texans made a heroic but unsuccessful stand against three thousand Mexicans under General Santa Anna. With

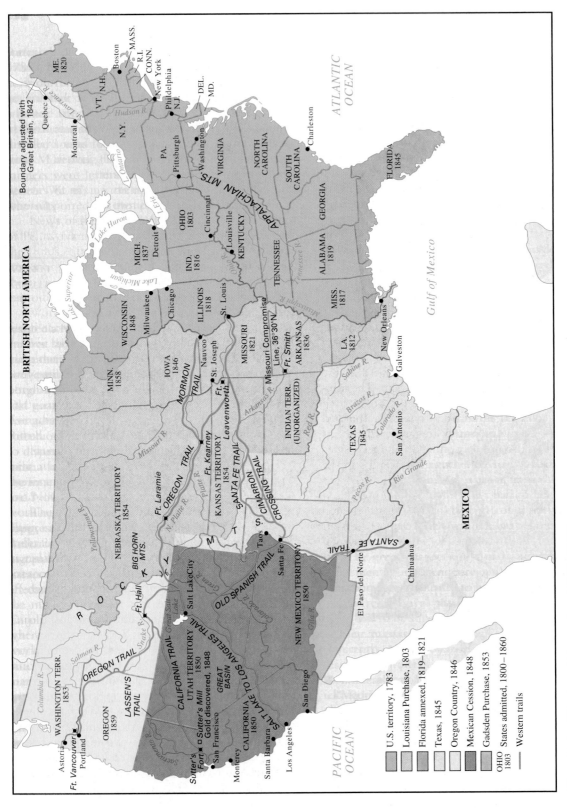

Map 11.1　Westward Expansion, 1800–1860

Through exploration, purchase, war, and treaty, the United States became a continental nation, stretching from the Atlantic to the Pacific.

Legend:
- U.S. territory, 1783
- Louisiana Purchase, 1803
- Florida annexed, 1819–1821
- Texas, 1845
- Oregon Country, 1846
- Mexican Cession, 1848
- Gadsden Purchase, 1853
- OHIO 1803 States admitted, 1800–1860
- —— Western trails

Map labels:

BRITISH NORTH AMERICA

Boundary adjusted with Great Britain, 1842

Quebec
Montreal
St. Lawrence R.
Hudson R.
L. Ontario
L. Erie
Lake Huron
Lake Michigan
Lake Superior

ME. 1820
VT. N.H.
Boston
MASS.
R.I.
CONN.
New York
Philadelphia
N.J.
DEL.
MD.
N.Y.
PA.
Pittsburgh
Washington
VIRGINIA
NORTH CAROLINA
SOUTH CAROLINA
Charleston
GEORGIA
FLORIDA 1845
ATLANTIC OCEAN

APPALACHIAN MTS.
OHIO 1803
Cincinnati
Louisville
KENTUCKY
TENNESSEE
ALABAMA 1819
MICH. 1837
Detroit
IND. 1816
ILLINOIS 1818
Chicago
Milwaukee
WISCONSIN 1848
St. Louis
MISS. 1817
Ohio R.
Tennessee R.
Mississippi R.

MINN. 1858
IOWA 1846
Nauvoo
St. Joseph
MORMON TRAIL
MISSOURI 1821
Missouri Compromise Line, 36°30′N.
Ft. Smith
ARKANSAS 1836
INDIAN TERR. (UNORGANIZED)
LA. 1812
New Orleans
Galveston
Gulf of Mexico

NEBRASKA TERRITORY 1854
Ft. Laramie
OREGON TRAIL
Ft. Kearney
Leavenworth
Ft. Leavenworth
KANSAS TERRITORY 1854
SANTA FE TRAIL
Missouri R.
N. Platte R.
Platte R.
Arkansas R.
Red R.
Sabine R.
Brazos R.
Colorado R.
TEXAS 1845
San Antonio
Pecos R.
Rio Grande
MEXICO

BIG HORN MTS.
ROCKY MTS.
Yellowstone R.
S. CIMARRON CROSSING TRAIL
Taos
Santa Fe
NEW MEXICO TERRITORY 1850
OLD SPANISH TRAIL
El Paso del Norte
Chihuahua
SANTA FE TRAIL

Columbia R.
Salmon R.
Snake R.
Ft. Hall
LASSEN'S TRAIL
OREGON TRAIL
WASHINGTON TERR. 1853
OREGON 1859
Astoria
Ft. Vancouver
Portland

UTAH TERRITORY 1850
Salt Lake City
Great Salt Lake
Green R.
GREAT BASIN
CALIFORNIA TRAIL
LOS ANGELES TRAIL
SALT LAKE TO LOS ANGELES
Colorado R.
Gila R.

CALIFORNIA 1850
Sutter's Fort
Sutter's Mill
Gold discovered, 1848
Sacramento R.
San Francisco
Monterey
Santa Barbara
Los Angeles
San Diego
PACIFIC OCEAN

"Remember the Alamo" as their rallying cry, the Texans won independence by the end of the year.

Texas established the independent Lone Star Republic but soon sought annexation to the United States. The issue quickly became politically explosive. Southerners favored annexing proslavery Texas; abolitionists, many northerners, and most Whigs opposed annexation. In recognition of the political dangers, President Jackson reneged on his promise to recognize Texas, and President Van Buren ignored annexation. Texans then talked about closer ties with the British and extending their republic to the Pacific coast. President Tyler, concerned that a Texas alliance with Britain might threaten American independence and also hoping to gain southern support for an 1844 election bid, pressed for annexation.

OREGON FEVER

As southerners sought expansion to the Southwest, northerners looked to the Northwest. In 1841 "Oregon fever" struck thousands who, lured by the glowing reports of missionaries, took to the Oregon Trail. The 2,000-mile journey took six months or more, but within a few years, five thousand settlers had arrived in the fertile Willamette valley.

Britain and the United States had jointly occupied the disputed Oregon Territory since the Convention of 1818. Beginning with the administration of President John Quincy Adams, the United States had tried to fix the boundary at the 49th parallel, but Britain had refused. In 1843 a Cincinnati convention of expansionists demanded the entire Oregon Country for the United States, up to its northernmost border at latitude 54°40'. Soon "Fifty-four Forty or Fight" became the rallying cry of American expansionists.

POLK AND THE ELECTION OF 1844

With antislavery forces favoring both expansion into Oregon and rejection of annexing Texas, anxious southern leaders persuaded the 1844 Democratic convention to adopt a rule requiring the presidential nominee to receive two-thirds of the convention votes. In effect, the southern states acquired a veto, which they wielded to block Van Buren's nomination because of his opposition to slavery and Texas an-nexation. Instead, the party chose House Speaker James K. Polk, a hard-money Jacksonian, avid expansionist, and slaveholding cotton planter from Tennessee. The Whigs and their nominee, Henry Clay, argued that the Democrats' belligerent nationalism would lead the nation into war with Great Britain or Mexico, or both. Clay favored expansion through negotiation.

With a well-organized campaign, Polk won the election by 170 electoral votes to 105. He won the popular vote by just 38,000 out of 2.7 million votes cast and New York's 36 electoral votes by only 6,000 popular votes. Abolitionist James G. Birney, the Liberty Party candidate, had drawn almost 16,000 votes away from Clay, handing New York and the election to Polk.

ANNEXATION OF TEXAS

Interpreting Polk's victory as a mandate for annexation, President Tyler proposed that Texas be admitted by joint resolution of Congress. The resolution passed, and three days before leaving office, Tyler signed it. Mexico, which did not recognize Texas independence, immediately broke relations with the United States. In October the citizens of Texas ratified annexation, and Texas joined the Union in December 1845.

Summary   **Online Study Center**   ACE the Test

Religion, reform, and expansionism shaped politics from 1824 through the 1840s. As the Second Great Awakening spread through villages and towns, the converts, especially women, organized to reform a rapidly changing society. Religion imbued men and women with zeal to right the wrongs of American society and the world. Reformers pursued perfectionism and republican virtue by battling with the evils of slavery, prostitution, and alcohol. In the process, women entered the public sphere as advocates of reform. Two issues in particular—the comet of Antimasonry and the smoldering fire of abolitionism—aroused passions that transformed moral crusades into political movements. With women's rights and nationalism contributing, the mix of issues made politics far more critical and engaging than just voting at elections.

The organized parties of the 1820s and the struggles between the National Republicans and the Democrats, then between the Democrats and the Whigs, stimulated even greater interest in campaigns and political issues. The Democrats, who rallied around Andrew Jackson, and Jackson's opponents, who came together under the Whig tent, competed almost equally for the loyalty of voters. Both parties favored economic expansion. Their worldviews, however, differed fundamentally. Whigs were more optimistic and favored greater centralized government initiative. Democrats harbored a deep-seated belief in limited government. The controversies over the Second Bank of the United States and nullification allowed Americans to debate the principles of the republic.

Many Americans caught the fever of expansionism. Euro-American farmers sought land, slaveholders wished to extend slavery, and millions itched to move westward. The admission of Texas into the Union in 1845 served one destiny—expansion—but also sharpened the nation's increasing divisions over slavery.

LEGACY FOR A PEOPLE AND A NATION
The Bible Belt

Had an eighteenth-century visitor to North America asked for the Bible belt, she would have been directed to New England. By the 1830s, however, the South was the most churched region. The Second Great Awakening spread like wildfire through the South. By the 1830s, more than half of white and one-quarter of black southerners had undergone a conversion experience, and religion and the South formed a common identity.

Religion helped define southern distinctiveness. Southern Protestant liturgy and cadences were as much African as European; thus, southern and northern denominations grew apart. They formally separated in the 1840s when Southern Baptists and Methodists withdrew from the national organizations that had barred slaveowners from church offices. Presbyterians withdrew later. After the Civil War, evangelical denominations remained divided into northern and southern organizations.

Southern religion maintained tradition and resisted modern ways. Mostly evangelical, it emphasized conversion and a personal battle against sin. By the twentieth century, fundamentalism, which stressed a literal reading of the Bible, reinforced resistance to modernism. Yet southern Protestantism lost ground as a political force in opposing evolution and in alliances with nativist, anti-immigrant groups.

But evangelicalism rose again in the 1960s, especially after a Catholic—John F. Kennedy—won the Democratic nomination for president. Many evangelicals began to vote their religion, moving to the Republican Party, and in 1964 Republican Barry Goldwater won the Bible belt states, breaking up the solid Democratic block. His conservative rhetoric resonated with southerners concerned about desegregation and erosion of religious values.

In the 1980s and 1990s, the Bible belt became the base of mobilized evangelical political action led by the Moral Majority. Religious and cultural issues rallied southern evangelicals: defending the traditional family, advocating prayer in schools, and opposing abortion, the Equal Rights Amendment, and gay rights legislation. In their own eyes, fundamentalist evangelical Protestants were defending biblical principles.

Thus, the revivals that began in the early 1800s have rippled in ever wider circles across the South for two centuries, shaping the distinctive southern blend of culture and politics.

PEOPLE AND COMMUNITIES IN THE NORTH AND WEST 1830–1860

*a*t eight o'clock on a snowy St. Patrick's Day morning in Lowell, Massachusetts, in 1841, more than one hundred members of the Irish Benevolent Society prepared to march through the mill town with a brass band. Each year, across the United States and around the world, Irish settlers and their descendants expressed their Irish pride by celebrating St. Patrick's Day. In colonial America, mostly Scots-Irish Protestants toasted Ireland and Britain at banquets. After the War of 1812, the banqueters and marchers, mostly middle-class Irish, represented charities and raised money to assist immigrants. New arrivals were mostly Catholic, and the parades and banquets brought together Catholics and Protestants.

But events in Ireland made the American Irish community increasingly Catholic. After a failed revolution against Britain in 1798, the 1800 Act of Union merged Ireland into the United Kingdom, eliminated the Irish Parliament, and disfranchised Catholics, making them powerless. Declining farm sizes and a population explosion impoverished them. Visiting Ireland in 1835, a stunned Alexis de Tocqueville wrote to his father, "You cannot imagine what a complexity of miseries five centuries of oppression and disorders and religious hostility have piled up on this poor people."

While many struggled in Ireland, others left their country. In England, industrial Manchester and London offered jobs, but more distant America offered political and religious freedom as well as economic opportunities. Thus, in the 1820s and 1830s, St. Patrick's Day increasingly became identified with Irish Catholics. Recent immigrants were poorer, and they could not pay for banquets. But parades were an opportunity to express their solidarity as well as their appreciation for America. They marched against the British and for equal rights in Ireland, often wearing red, white, and blue as well as green, to demonstrate their identity. Both Americans and the Irish had suffered, they

Country Life

The West

LINKS TO THE WORLD
Gold in California

City Life

Extremes of Wealth

Family Life

Immigrant Lives in America

Free People of Color

LEGACY FOR A PEOPLE AND A NATION
White Fascination with and Appropriation of Black Culture

Online Study Center
This icon will direct you to interactive map and primary source activities on the website
http://college.hmco.com/pic/nortonbrief7e

C H R O N O L O G Y

1830 • Smith founds Mormon Church
    • First National Negro Convention

1830s–50s • Urban riots commonplace

1832 • Rice debuts in New York minstrel show

1835 • Arkansas passes first women's property law

1837 • Boston employs paid policemen

1837–48 • Mann heads the Massachusetts Board of Education

1838 • Mormons driven out of Missouri

1841–47 • Brook Farm combines spirituality, work, and play in a utopian rural community

1842 • Knickerbocker baseball club formed

1844 • Nativist riots peak in Philadelphia
    • Smith brothers murdered in Illinois

1845 • Irish potato blight begins
    • *Narrative of the Life of Frederick Douglass* appears

1846–47 • Mormon trek to the Great Salt Lake

1847–57 • Immigration at peak pre–Civil War levels

1848 • Abortive revolution in German states
    • U.S. acquires Alta California in Treaty of Guadalupe Hidalgo
    • Gold discovered in California

1849 • California gold rush transforms the West Coast

1852 • Stowe's *Uncle Tom's Cabin* published

1854 • Large-scale Chinese immigration begins
    • Germans replace Irish as largest group of new arrivals

1855 • New York establishes Castle Garden as immigrant center

pointed out, from British tyranny. St. Patrick's Day speakers reminded audiences that "republicanism" was both an American and Irish principle. Editor Thomas O'Connor, who described himself as an "Irishman by birth" and an "American by adoption," toasted "America as she is, Ireland as she ought to be." St. Patrick's Day linked American and Irish causes.

But increasingly American Irish Protestants stayed away from such events. They identified with Britain, not the Irish opposition. In the 1820s, they began to skip St. Patrick's Day parades and march instead on July 12, commemorating the English victory of William of Orange in the Battle of the Boyne in 1690. They purposefully distanced themselves from the new immigrants, becoming Whigs while the new immigrants gravitated to Andrew Jackson. Then, in

the 1840s and 1850s, as potato blight and famine stalked Ireland, nearly 2 million Irish immigrants—almost all Catholics—arrived in the United States. Now St. Patrick's Day marches attracted not hundreds but thousands, and nativists jeered the marchers, occasionally assaulting them.

The huge Irish immigration was only part of a worldwide population movement. From the 1830s through the 1850s, millions of Europeans arrived on America's shores, transforming the American nation. Within large cities and in the countryside, whole districts became ethnic and religious enclaves.

The cultural traditions of European immigrants differed from those in the American colonial past, and some white Americans came to see the differences as racial rather than cultural. Black Americans became racial outsiders, as did Hispanics in the Southwest. In a society growing ever more diverse and complex, conflict became common.

The market economy both energized and accentuated the differences among Americans. In the nation's cities, both wealth and poverty reached extremes unknown in the countryside. Ethnicity, race, religion, and class divided Americans as well. Farm families attempted to maintain cohesive, rural villages, while utopians and groups like the Mormons sought to create self-governing communal havens.

The market economy altered family life too. As commerce and industry grew, the home lost its function as a workplace. Goods formerly made at home were now mass-manufactured in factories and bought in stores. Public schools took over much of the family's traditional role as prime educator. Leisure became a commodity to be purchased by those who could afford it. Families shrank in size, and more people lived outside family units. ◼

Country Life

Rural life changed significantly in the first half of the nineteenth century. Farm population in the coastal states declined as towns grew and manufacturing expanded. Farm families sought more fertile and cheaper land in the West. Market-oriented communities arose there, linked to eastern markets by the new transportation networks.

The railroad depot and post office in the farm village linked farmers with the rest of the world. But in

FARM
COMMUNITIES

these villages, with their churches, general stores, and taverns, communal values still ruled. Families gathered on one another's farms to accomplish as a community what they could not manage individually. Barn-raisings regularly brought people together. The neighbors came by buggy to help a farm family raise the walls and build a roof. Afterward everyone celebrated with a hearty communal feast and singing, dancing, and

games. Similar gatherings took place at harvest time and on special occasions.

Farm men and women had active social lives. Men met frequently at general stores, weekly markets, and taverns, and they hunted and fished together. Some women also attended market. More typically they met at after-church dinners, prayer groups, sewing and corn-husking bees, and quilting parties. These were cherished opportunities to exchange experiences, thoughts, and spiritual support and to swap letters, books, and news.

Traditional country bees had their town counterparts. Fredrika Bremer, a Swedish visitor, described

BEES

a sewing bee in Cambridge, Massachusetts, in 1849, at which neighborhood women made clothes for "a family who had lost all their clothing by fire." Yet town bees were not the all-day family affairs of the countryside, and those who moved from farm to town missed the country gatherings. In town, people were wage earners and consumers, and the market economy shaped and controlled their daily lives.

Most Americans came to accept these changes, but some tried to resist. One opposition path was to restore traditional work and social cohesion by living in rural utopian communities. Some groups, like the Shakers, had originated in eighteenth-century Europe, while others, like the Mormons, arose out of the religious ferment of the Second Great Awakening. What they shared in common was a commitment to rural communal living as members experimented with innovative (sometimes shocking) family arrangements and more egalitarian gender roles in a cooperative rather than competitive environment.

Online Study Center
Improve Your Grade
Primary Source: Oneida Sisters Comment on Love and Labor

The Shakers, the largest of the communal utopian experiments, reached their peak between 1820 and

SHAKERS

1860 when six thousand members lived in twenty settlements in eight states. Founder Ann Lee, who advocated celibacy, had brought the sect to America in 1774. Shakers got their name from the singing and dancing in their worship service.

In religious practice and social relations, Shakers offered an alternative to changing urban and rural life.

■ *The Lackawanna Valley* (1855) by George Inness. Hired by the Lackawanna Railroad to paint a picture showing the company's new roundhouse at Scranton, in northeastern Pennsylvania, Inness combined landscape and locomotive technology into an organic whole. Industrialism, Inness seems to say, belonged to the American landscape; it would neither overpower nor obliterate the land.   (Gift of Mrs. Huttleston Rogers, © 1996 Board of Trustees, National Gallery of Art, Washington, D.C.)

They lived communally, abolishing individual families. Leaders tended to be women. However, the settlements depended on constant recruitment. In addition to their celibacy, most members stayed only a short time, being temporary refugees from hardship or abuse, or families who found themselves unsuited to communal living. In the middle of the nineteenth century, Shaker communities began a slow but steady decline.

The Church of Jesus Christ of Latter-Day Saints, known as the Mormons, was the most successful com-

MORMON
COMMUNITY OF
SAINTS

munitarian experiment and, like the Shakers, restructured family life. During the religious ferment of the 1820s in western New York, Joseph Smith,

a young farmer, reported that an angel called Moroni had given him engraved divine gold plates. Smith published his revelations as the *Book of Mormon* and organized a church in 1830. The next year the community moved west to Ohio to await the second coming of Jesus. Angry mobs drove them from Ohio to Missouri, where in 1838 the governor gathered evidence to indict Smith and other Mormon leaders for treason.

Smith and his followers resettled in Nauvoo, Illinois. The state legislature gave them a city charter that made them self-governing and authorized a local militia. But hostility arose again, especially after Smith introduced the practice of polygamy in 1841. In 1842 Smith became mayor, and Nauvoo petitioned the federal government to be a self-governing territory, further antagonizing opponents. After Smith and his brother were charged with treason, jailed, and then murdered in 1844, the Mormons left Illinois to seek security in the wilderness. In 1847 they arrived in the Great Salt Lake valley, in the unorganized territory of Utah, and established a patriarchal, cooperative "community of saints." Now led by Brigham Young, they achieved religious freedom and political autonomy.

In Utah the Mormons distributed agricultural land according to family size. An extensive irrigation system, constructed cooperatively, transformed the arid valley into a rich oasis. As the colony developed, the church elders gained control of water, trade, industry, and eventually the territorial government of Utah.

Though short-lived (1841–1847), the Brook Farm cooperative near Boston played a significant role in the flowering of a national literature. Its members were inspired by transcendentalism—the belief that the physical world is secondary to the spiritual realm, which can be reached only by intuition. During these years Nathaniel Hawthorne, Ralph Waldo Emerson, and Margaret Fuller (editor of the leading transcendentalist journal, *Dial*) joined Henry David Thoreau, Herman Melville, and others in a literary outpouring known today as the American Renaissance. In philosophical intensity and moral idealism, their work was both distinctively American and an outgrowth of the European romantic movement. Their themes were universal, their settings and characters American.

AMERICAN RENAISSANCE

The essayist Ralph Waldo Emerson was the prime mover of the American Renaissance and a pillar of the transcendental movement. "We live in succession, in division, in parts, in particles," Emerson wrote. "We see the world piece by piece, as the sun, the moon, the animal, the tree; but the whole, of which these are the shining parts, is the soul." Intuitive experience of God is attainable, insisted Emerson, because "the Highest dwells" within every individual in the form of the "Over-Soul."

The West

*I*n the 1840s a trickling stream of migrants followed the Oregon Trail to the West Coast. Then, in 1848, gold was discovered in California. The next year a pioneer observed that the Oregon Trail "bore no evidence of having been much traveled." Traffic flowed south instead, and California drew population to the Pacific slope.

When the United States acquired Alta California from Mexico in the 1848 Treaty of Guadalupe Hidalgo (covered in Chapter 14), the province was inhabited mostly by Indians, with some Mexicans living on large estates. A chain of small settlements surrounded military forts (*presidios*) and missions. That changed almost overnight after James Marshall, a carpenter, spotted gold particles in the millrace at Sutter's Mill (northwest of Sacramento) in January 1848. Word of the discovery spread, and Californians rushed to scrabble for instant fortunes.

GOLD RUSH

By 1849 the news had sped around the world, and hundreds of thousands of fortune seekers, mostly young men, streamed into California. Gold mining seemed to offer instant riches, and indeed, some did make fortunes. Most "forty-niners," however, never found enough gold to pay their expenses. "The stories you hear frequently in the States," one gold seeker wrote home, "are the most extravagant lies imaginable—the mines are a humbug." Many found work in California's cities and agricultural districts more profitable. Meanwhile, enterprising merchants rushed to supply, feed, and clothe the new settlers. One such merchant was Levi Strauss, a German Jewish immigrant, whose tough mining pants found a ready market among the prospectors.

The forty-niners had to be fed. Thus began the great California agricultural boom. Farmers preferred wheat for its minimal investment and quick return at the end of a relatively short growing season. California farmers eagerly imported horse-drawn machines, since labor was scarce (and expensive). By the mid-1850s, California exported wheat and had become firmly linked, through commerce, to the rest of the United States. Farmers on the West Coast cleared the land and, because success often depended on their access to water, sought to divert streams and rivers to irrigate their land.

FARMING

Most men in California came alone, drawn by a sense of adventure and personal opportunity. Women who accompanied their husbands—only one-seventh of the travelers on the overland trails were women—experienced migration differently. Their lives drastically

Gold in California

When James Marshall discovered gold in Sutter's Mill, California, in January 1848, word spread quickly—and quite literally around the world. Within a year, tens of thousands of adventurers from other countries had rushed to California, the new "land of opportunity." Soon it was as cosmopolitan as any other American place.

In an era before the telegraph crossed the oceans, it is surprising how fast the news traveled. Mexicans heard of the gold strike first. Overland travelers brought the news south to Baja California and Sonora in Mexico. By spring 1849 some six thousand Mexicans were panning for gold in California.

Sailing ships brought news of California gold to Hawai'i. "Honolulu has never before witnessed such an excitement as the gold fever has created," the newspaper *Honolulu Polynesian* reported in the summer of 1848. Gold seekers and merchants sailed from Hawai'i to California, and their letters home recruited others to come.

A ship brought news of California gold discoveries to Valparaiso, Chile, in August 1848. More dramatically, a few weeks later, another sailing vessel landed with $2,500 in gold dust aboard. Before the end of the year, two thousand Chileans had left for California, and many Chilean merchants opened branch stores in San Francisco.

Word of gold reached Australia in December 1848, and by 1850 every ship in Sydney harbor was destined for California. News had already reached China in mid-1848. A San Francisco merchant headed for the gold fields, Chum Ming, had written a cousin about his hopes for wealth. Four months later, the cousin arrived in San Francisco, with fellow villagers he had recruited. After the upheavals of the Taiping Revolution in 1850, Chinese migration soared. By the mid-1850s, one in five gold miners was Chinese.

Californians, new and old, foreign and native-born, expressed amazement at the ethnic variety. One described it as "the most curious Babel of a place imaginable." In 1850 the new state of California had nearly 40 percent foreign-born inhabitants, the majority non-European. Through word of mouth, rumor, letters home, and newspaper reports, the discovery of gold in 1848 linked California to millions of ordinary people around the globe.

This 1855 Frank Marryat drawing of a San Francisco saloon dramatizes the international nature of the California gold rush. Like theater performers, the patrons of the saloon dress their parts as Yankees, Mexicans, Asians, and South Americans. (© Collection of the New York Historical Society)

changed as they left behind networks of friends and kin to journey, often with children, along an unknown and hazardous path to a strange environment. Yet in the West, their domestic skills were in great demand. They received high fees for cooking, laundering, and sewing, and they ran boarding houses and hotels.

City Life

*I*rish and other European immigrants and rural migrants made cities, especially northern ones, expand geometrically. Europeans spread westward, and small rural settlements quickly became towns. In 1830 the nation had only 23 cities with 10,000 or more people and only 7 with more than 25,000. By 1860, 93 towns exceeded 10,000, 35 towns had more than 25,000, and 9 exceeded 100,000 (see Map 12.1).

Some cities became great metropolitan centers. By 1830 New York City had been the nation's most populous city and major commercial center for twenty years. At midcentury, Baltimore and New Orleans dominated the South, and San Francisco was the leading West Coast city. In the Midwest, the new lake cities (Chicago, Detroit, and Cleveland) began to pass the frontier river cities (Cincinnati, Louisville, and Pittsburgh) founded a generation earlier.

As the nation's premier city, New York grew from 202,000 people in 1830 to over 814,000 in 1860. The immigrant port city was mostly Irish and Ger-

NEW YORK CITY

man by the 1850s. Across the East River, Brooklyn tripled in size between 1850 and 1860, becoming the nation's third-largest city, with a population of 279,000. Many people were short-term residents of the two cities; the majority did not stay ten years. Thus, New York was ever changing, full of energy, reeking of sweat, horse dung, and garbage—and above all, teeming with people.

By modern standards, nineteenth-century cities were disorderly, unsafe, and unhealthy. Expansion occurred so rapidly that few cities could handle the

URBAN PROBLEMS

problems it brought. For example, migrants from rural areas were accustomed to relieving themselves outside and throwing refuse in vacant areas. In the city, such waste

smelled, spread disease, and polluted water. New York City partially solved the problem in the 1840s by abandoning wells in favor of reservoir water piped into buildings and outdoor fountains. In some districts, scavengers and refuse collectors carted away garbage and human waste, but in much of the city, it just rotted on the ground. Only one-quarter of New York City's streets had sewers by 1857.

Cities lacked adequate taxing power to provide services for all. The best the city could do was to tax property adjoining new sewers, paved streets, and water mains. Thus, basic services depended on residents' ability to pay. As a result, those most in need of services got them last. Private companies could be chartered to sell basic services. This plan worked well for gas lighting. Baltimore first chartered a private gas company in 1816; by midcentury, every major city was lit by a private gas supplier. The private sector, however, lacked the capital to build adequate citywide water systems. City governments therefore had to assume that responsibility.

Cities led in offering public education. In 1800 only New England had public schools; by 1860 every state offered some public education to whites. Under

HORACE MANN AND PUBLIC SCHOOLS

Horace Mann, secretary of the state board of education from 1837 to 1848, Massachusetts established a minimum school year of six months and formalized the training of teachers.

Mann advocated free, state-sponsored education. "If we do not prepare children to become good citizens," Mann argued, "if we do not develop their capacities, . . . then our republic must go down to destruction." Universal education, Mann proposed, would end misery and crime. Mann and others responded to the changes wrought by the market economy, urbanization, and immigration. The typical city dweller was a newcomer, from abroad or from the country. Public schools would take the children of strangers and give them shared values. Few states, however, included free black children in public schools.

Free public schools altered the scope of education. Schooling previously had focused on literacy, religious training, and discipline. Under Mann's leadership, the curriculum became more secular and appropriate for America's future clerks, farmers, and workers. Students studied geography, American

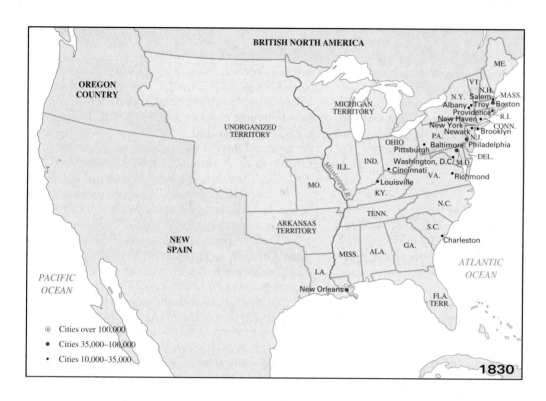

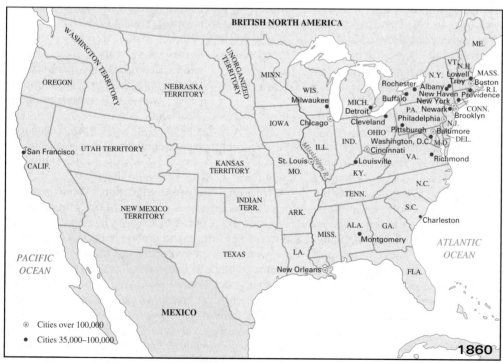

Map 12.1 Major American Cities in 1830 and 1860

The number of Americans who lived in cities increased rapidly between 1830 and 1860, and the number of large cities grew as well. In 1830 only New York City had a population exceeding 100,000; thirty years later, eight more cities had surpassed that level.

history, arithmetic, and science. Schools retained moral education, but they dropped direct religious indoctrination.

Catholics, immigrants, blacks, and workers sought to control their own schools, but the state legislatures established secular statewide standards under Protestant educators. Catholics in New York responded by building their own educational system over the next half-century. When Los Angeles became a city in 1850, it attempted to establish bilingual Spanish-English instruction, but the idea was dropped because trained bilingual teachers could not be found.

Towns and cities created new patterns of leisure as well as work. In rural society, social activities and work often took place at home. But in cities, dedicated spaces—streets, theaters, sports fields—constituted a public sphere where people could socialize. Through the sale of admission tickets or membership in associations, leisure became a commodity to be purchased and reflected ethnic, racial, and class divisions. Even in cities, however, some traditional rural pursuits continued. Fishing remained popular, men played games of strength and skill in taverns, and churches served as social centers.

LEISURE

Americans read more too. Thanks to the expansion of public education, the vast majority of native-born white Americans were literate by the 1850s. For the reading public, fiction and autobiographies competed with religious tracts as popular literature. Newspapers and magazines printed fiction, and bookstores in large cities sold novels and autobiographies. Frederick Douglass's powerful attack on slavery in his 1845 autobiography sold widely. Many popular novels, some written by women, often for women, were set in the home and upheld Christian values. Yet they also can be read as a challenge to prevailing values. Although Susan Warner's *The Wide, Wide, Wide World* (1850), Nathaniel Hawthorne's *The House of the Seven Gables* (1851), and Fanny Fern's *Ruth Hall* (1855) did not challenge women's traditional domestic roles, they accorded women a special moral bearing. In giving a positive cast to notions of community and republican virtue, they implicitly criticized the growing market economy. By the 1850s popular fiction circulated widely. Harriet Beecher Stowe's antislavery novel, *Uncle Tom's Cabin,*

READING

or Life Among the Lowly (1852), sold 300,000 copies in book form in its first year.

A theater was often the second public building constructed in a town—after a church. Large cities boasted two or more theaters catering to different classes. Some plays cut across class lines. Shakespeare was performed so often and appreciated so widely that even illiterate theatergoers knew his plays well. In the 1840s, musical and dramatic presentations took on a more professional tone; newly popular minstrel shows and traveling circuses offered carefully rehearsed routines including dancing and music.

THEATER

By the 1840s, hundreds of traveling minstrel troupes presented a European version of African American culture. Minstrel acts had first appeared twenty or thirty years earlier, when white men, in burned cork makeup, imitated African Americans in song, dance, and patter. In the early 1830s, Thomas D. Rice of New York became famous for his role as Jim Crow, an old southern slave. In ill-fitting patched clothing and torn shoes, the blackface Rice shuffled, danced, and sang on stage.

MINSTREL SHOWS

Minstrelsy stereotyped black people by exaggerating physical features. It also portrayed African Americans as being sensual and lazy. The fictional representation of blacks on stage defined not only "blackness" but also "whiteness." Whiteness as a racial category took on meaning as laughing white audiences distinguished themselves from the black characters. The net effect was to stoke the fires of racism and thereby further the growing racial tensions in the United States.

Increasingly, urban recreation and sports became formal commodities to be purchased. One had to buy a ticket to go to the theater, the circus, the racetrack, or the ballpark.

SPORTS

Spectator sports surged. In addition to horseracing, boxing and baseball attracted large, urban male crowds. News of an 1849 Maryland boxing match was so much in demand that a round-by-round account of the fight was telegraphed throughout the East. In baseball, organized leagues replaced spontaneity, and in 1845 the Knickerbocker Club, which had been formed in 1842, drew up rules for the game.

■ Thomas D. Rice playing Jim Crow in blackface at the Bowery Theater in New York City, 1833. The rowdy audience climbed on the stage, leaving Rice little room to perform. In representing African Americans on stage, Rice and other minstrels contributed to establishing black and white as racial categories. (© Collection of the New York Historical Society)

Ironically, public leisure soon developed a private dimension. Exclusive private associations provided

CITY CULTURE

space and occasions for leisure apart from crowds and rowdiness. While old-stock middle- and upper-class Americans were isolating themselves, members of various ethnic, racial, and religious groups formed their own associations. The Irish formed the Hibernian Society, the Germans brought Turnvereine physical-cultural clubs across the Atlantic, Jews founded B'nai B'rith, and African Americans started chapters of the Prince Hall Masons in their communities. Women too organized their own associations, ranging from literary clubs to benevolent societies. Associations brought together like people, but they also formalized divisions.

A youth culture emerged on New York's Bowery, an entertainment strip, in the 1840s. Older New

Yorkers feared the "Bowery boys and gals," whose ostentatious dress and behavior seemed threatening to them. A Bowery boy had long hair, often greased into a roll. He wore a broad-brimmed black hat and as much jewelry as he could afford. His swaggering gait frightened many in the middle class. Equally disturbing to old New Yorkers were the young working women who strolled the Bowery. Unlike more genteel ladies, who wore modest veils or bonnets, Bowery "gals" flaunted outlandish costumes and ornate hats.

Most working people spent much of their lives outdoors; they worked in the streets as laborers, shopped in open markets, paraded, and socialized on sidewalks; they courted, argued, and defended their turf in public places. Increasingly, urban streets served as a political arena as crowds formed to listen to speakers, respond and demonstrate, and sometimes take mob action.

In the 1830s riots became commonplace as professionals, merchants, craftsmen, and laborers vented their rage against political and economic rivals. "Gentlemen of property and standing," unnerved by antislavery proponents, sacked abolitionist and antislavery organizations, even murdering newspaper editor Elijah Lovejoy in Alton, Illinois, in 1837. In the 1840s "respectable" citizens drove the Mormons out of Missouri and Illinois. In Philadelphia ongoing racial and ethnic conflict came to a head in 1844 when Protestant skilled workers attacked Irish Catholics. Smaller cities too became battlegrounds as nativist riots peaked in the 1850s. By 1860 more than 1,000 people had died in urban riots.

URBAN RIOTS

As public disorder spread, Boston hired uniformed policemen in 1837 to supplement its part-time watchmen and constables, and New York in 1845 established a uniformed force. Nonetheless, middle-class city dwellers did not venture out alone at night. In the midst of so much noise, crime, and conflict, the lavish uptown residences of the very rich rose like an affront to those struggling to survive.

Extremes of Wealth

*a*fter visiting America in 1831 and 1832, Alexis de Tocqueville characterized the United States as primarily a place of equality and opportunity for white males. Tocqueville attributed American equality—the relative fluidity of the social order—to Americans' mobility and restlessness. Geographic mobility, he felt, offered people a chance to start anew regardless of where they came from or who they were.

Others disagreed with this egalitarian view of American life. *New York Sun* publisher Moses Yale Beach believed a new aristocracy based on wealth and power was forming. Beach listed 750 New Yorkers with assets of $100,000 or more in 1845. John Jacob Astor, with a fortune of $25 million, led the list of 19 millionaires. Ten years later, Beach reported more than 1,000 New Yorkers worth $100,000, among them 28 millionaires. Tocqueville himself, sensitive to conflicting trends in American life, had described the new industrial wealth. The rich and well educated

GREAT FORTUNES

"come forward to exploit industries," Tocqueville wrote, and become "more and more like the administrators of a huge empire. . . . What is this if not an aristocracy?"

Wealth throughout the United States was becoming concentrated in the hands of a relatively small number of people. In New York City between 1828 and 1845, the richest 4 percent of the city's population increased their holdings from an estimated 63 percent to 80 percent of all individual wealth. By 1860 the top 5 percent of American families owned more than half of the nation's wealth.

From 1826 until his death in 1851, Philip Hone, one-time mayor of New York, kept a diary, meticulously recording the life of an American aristocrat. On February 28, 1840, for instance, Hone attended a masked ball at the Fifth Avenue mansion of Henry Breevoort Jr. and Laura Carson Breevoort. The five hundred invited ladies and gentlemen wore costumes adorned with ermine and gold. Like their counterparts in Boston, Philadelphia, Baltimore, and Charleston, the New York elite lived in mansions attended by servants and could escape the city for country estates or grand tours of Europe.

URBAN ELITE

Much of this wealth was inherited. For every John Jacob Astor who made millions in the western fur trade, ten others had inherited or married money. Many of the wealthiest New Yorkers bore the names of the colonial commercial elite: Breevoort, Roosevelt, Van Rensselaer, and Whitney. These rich New Yorkers were not idle; they worked at increasing their fortunes and power by investing in commerce and manufacturing. Wealth begat wealth, and marriage cemented family ties.

But just a short walk from this wealth, native-born working poor, newly arrived immigrants, and free blacks jostled in crowded streets with thieves, beggars, and prostitutes. Poor working men and women fretted continually that hard times were imminent. They dreaded poverty, chronic illness, disability, and old age. With good reason, women feared raising children without a spouse, as few women's jobs paid enough to support a family.

New York City's Five Points section, a few blocks from City Hall, lacked running water and sewers and was notorious for its physical and moral squalor. Dominated by the

URBAN SLUMS

Old Brewery, converted to housing, the neighborhood was predominantly Irish but also home to a few free black people. Contemporaries estimated that more than a thousand people lived in the Old Brewery's rooms and cellars. Throughout the city, workers' housing was at a premium. Houses built for two families often held four; tenements built for six families held twelve. Families took in lodgers to help pay the rent.

Meanwhile, a small but distinct middle class appeared on the urban scene—city businessmen, traders, and professionals serving the growth and specialization of trade. Middle-class families enjoyed new consumer items: wool carpeting, fine wallpaper, rooms full of furniture, and indoor toilets. They filled the family pews in church on Sundays; their male children went to college. They were as distant from Philip Hone's world as from that of the working class and the poor. Increasingly they looked to the family and home as the core of middle-class life.

THE MIDDLE CLASS

Family Life

As urban families in the nineteenth-century market economy began to lose their role as producers, the result was sweeping change in the household economy as men increasingly worked for wages outside the home, and so did their offspring.

English common law gave husbands absolute control over the family. Men owned their wives' personal property, they were legal guardians of the children, and they owned whatever family members produced or earned. A father still had the legal authority to oppose his daughter's choice of husband. Nonetheless, most American women, with their parents' blessing, chose their own marriage partners.

LEGAL RIGHTS

Married women made modest gains in property and spousal rights from the 1830s on. Arkansas in 1835 passed the first married women's property law, and by 1860 sixteen more states had followed suit. In those states, when a wife inherited, earned, or acquired property, it was hers, not her husband's, and she could write a will. In the 1830s states began to liberalize divorce, adding cruelty and desertion as grounds for divorce. Nonetheless, divorce was rare.

In working-class families, women left their parental homes as early as age twelve, earning wages most of their lives, with only short respites for bearing and rearing children. Primarily unmarried girls and women worked as domestic servants in other women's homes; married and widowed women worked as laundresses, seamstresses, and cooks. Some hawked food and wares on city streets; others did piecework sewing at home in the putting-out system; and some became prostitutes. Few of these occupations enabled women to support themselves, let alone a family, at a respectable level.

WORKING WOMEN

Middle-class Americans, however, sought to keep women close to home. They idealized the family as a moral institution characterized by selflessness and cooperation. The world of work—the market economy—was seen as an arena of conflict identified with men and dominated by base self-interest. If young girls left home to work—in New England's textile mills, in new urban stores as clerks—it was only for a brief interval before marriage.

The domestic ideal restricted the paying jobs available to middle-class women, but one occupation was considered consistent with genteel femininity: teaching. In 1823 the Beecher sisters, Catharine and Mary, established the Hartford Female Seminary and offered history and science to the traditional women's curriculum of domestic arts and religion. A decade later Catharine Beecher successfully campaigned for teacher-training schools for women. By 1850 many women worked for a time as teachers, usually for two to five years. Unmarried women earned about half the salary of male teachers.

TEACHERS

The market economy brought economic insecurity and altered family life. As the American population moved west, kin became separated, and multigenerational families in the same household became less common. And all families, regardless of class or region, were shrinking in size. In 1830 American women bore an average of five or six children; by 1860 the figure had dropped to five. This decline occurred despite the arrival of many immigrants with large-family traditions; thus, the birth rate among native-born women declined even more steeply.

FAMILY SIZE

A number of factors account for reduced family size. Small families were viewed as increasingly desirable in an economy in which the family was a unit of consumption rather than production. In smaller families, parents could give children more attention, better education, and more financial help. Evidence suggests many wives and husbands deliberately limited the size of families.

The demographic data suggest that changes in childbearing reduced family size. Average age at marriage rose, thus shortening the period of potential childbearing. The age at which women bore their last child dropped from around forty in the mid-eighteenth century to around thirty-five in the mid-nineteenth.

But couples also limited family size through birth control. Traditional practices continued—coitus interruptus (withdrawal of the male before completion of the sexual act), breast-feeding to prolong infertile periods, and rhythm methods. Traditional remedies from American Indian to African folk medicine spread as well. Cheap rubber condoms became available in the 1850s. Douching after intercourse was also practiced. None of the methods was particularly reliable.

ABORTION   As formerly private concerns began to be discussed publicly, women shared and purchased information on limiting reproduction. If all else failed, women resorted to abortions, especially after 1830. Ineffective folk methods of self-induced abortion had been around for centuries, but in the 1830s abortionists, mostly women, advertised surgical services in large cities. To protect women from unqualified abortionists, and in response to reformers opposed to abortion, states began to regulate the procedure. By 1860 twenty states had either restricted late-term abortions or prohibited abortion altogether.

Smaller size and fewer births changed the family. At one time, birth and infant care had occupied nearly the entire span of women's adult lives. In smaller families, individual children received greater attention, and childhood gradually came to be perceived as a distinct period in the life span.

SINGLE MEN AND WOMEN   Many single men lived and worked outside traditional families. In urban areas, rooming and boarding houses provided them with places to sleep and eat. The expansion of cities and the market economy led more women to live outside families as well. Women like Louisa May Alcott (1832–1888), author of *Little Women* (1868), who lived most of her life in Massachusetts, followed an independent path. Her father never adequately provided for his family. Louisa May Alcott supported the family by working as a seamstress, governess, teacher, and housemaid before her writing brought her success. "I think I shall come out right, and prove that . . . I can support myself," she wrote her father in 1856. "I like the independent feeling; and though not an easy life, it is a free one, and I enjoy it."

To foreswear marriage and a family was not easy in a society that considered family the appropriate foundation of a moral life for women. But Alcott and other unmarried women managed to pursue careers and lives defined by female relationships. Given the difficulty women had finding ways to support themselves, they undertook independence at great risk. Nonetheless, the proportion of single women in the population increased significantly in the nineteenth century. Independent white women, in sum, were taking advantage of new opportunities offered by the market economy and urban expansion. At the same time communitarian ventures in rural America, like the Shakers and Mormons, offered experimentation in new family relationships.

Immigrant Lives in America

The 5 million immigrants who came to the United States between 1830 and 1860 outnumbered the entire population of the country recorded in the first census in 1790. The vast majority were European (see Figure 12.1). During the peak period of pre–Civil War immigration, from 1847 through 1857, 3.3 million immigrants entered the United States; 1.3 million were from Ireland and 1.1 million from the German states. By 1860, 15 percent of the white population was foreign-born.

This massive migration had been set in motion decades earlier. At the turn of the nineteenth century, the Napoleonic wars gave rise to one of the greatest population shifts in history; ultimately it lasted more than a century. War, revolution, famine, religious persecution, and the lure of industrialization led many Europeans to leave home. From the other side of the world, 41,000 Chinese, nearly all men, entered the United States from 1854 through 1860. The United States attracted immigrants as its economy offered jobs and its

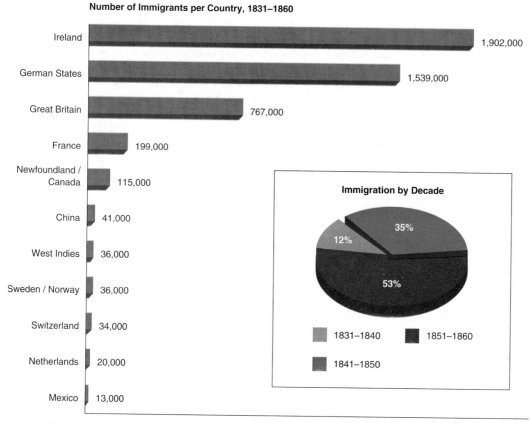

Figure 12.1 **Major Sources of Immigration to the United States, 1831–1860**

Most immigrants came from two areas: Great Britain, of which Ireland was a part, and the German states. These two areas sent more immigrants between 1830 and 1860 than the inhabitants of the United States enumerated at the first census in 1790. By 1860, 15 percent of the white population was of foreign birth. (Source: Data from Stephan Thernstrom, ed., *Harvard Encyclopedia of American Ethnic Groups* [Cambridge, Mass., and London: Harvard University Press, 1980], 1047.)

Constitution protected religious freedom. Not all planned to stay permanently, and many, like the Irish, saw themselves as exiles from their homeland.

Online Study Center **Improve Your Grade**
Interactive Map:
Origin and Settlement of Immigrants, 1820–1850

The market economy needed workers. Large construction projects and mining operations sought

PROMOTION OF IMMIGRATION
strong young men, and textile mills sought young women. Both private firms and governments recruited

European immigrants. Midwestern and western states lured potential settlers to promote economic growth. In the 1850s Wisconsin, for instance, appointed a commissioner of emigration, who advertised the state's advantages in European newspapers. Europeans' awareness of the United States grew as employers, states, and shipping companies promoted opportunities across the Atlantic. Often the message was stark: work and prosper in America, or starve in Europe. The price of passage across the ocean after 1848 was within easy reach of millions of Europeans.

Immigrants endured the hardships of travel and of living in a strange land. The average transatlantic crossing took six weeks; in bad weather, it could take three months. Disease spread unchecked among people packed together like cattle in steerage. More than seventeen thousand immigrants, mostly Irish, died from "ship fever" in 1847. On arrival, con artists and swindlers preyed on newcomers. In response, New York State established Castle Garden as an immigrant center in 1855. There, at the tip of Manhattan Island, the major port for European entry, immigrants were somewhat sheltered from fraud. Authorized transportation companies maintained offices in the large rotunda and assisted new arrivals with their travel plans.

Settling In   Most immigrants gravitated toward cities, and many stayed in New York City itself. By 1855, 52 percent of its 623,000 inhabitants were immigrants—28 percent from Ireland and 16 percent from the German states. Boston also took on a European tone; throughout the 1850s the city was about 35 percent foreign born, of whom more than two-thirds were Irish. In the West, St. Louis and San Francisco had foreign-born majorities. Southern cities like Charleston and Savannah had significant Irish settlements.

Some immigrants settled in rural areas, though they tended to avoid the rural South, with its predominance of slave labor. German, Dutch, and Scandinavian farmers, in particular, headed toward the Midwest. Greater percentages of Scandinavians and Netherlanders took up farming than did other nationalities; both groups came mostly as religious dissenters and migrated in family units.

Immigrant Disenchantment   Not all arrivals found success in the United States; hundreds of thousands returned to their homelands disappointed. Before the famines of the late 1840s hit Ireland, American recruiters had lured many Irish to work on American canals and railroads and in construction. The promise that "he should soon become a wealthy man" lured Michael Gaugin, who had worked for thirteen years as an assistant engineer in the construction of a Dublin canal. The Irish agent for a New York firm convinced him to quit his job to come to America. But Gaugin landed in New York City during the financial panic of 1837. He could not find work, and within two months he was broke, struggling to find the means to return to Ireland.

Irish Immigrants   Before the great famine, caused by a blight that ruined the potato crop, Ireland's food staple, there had been a substantial outmigration from Ireland, mostly to English cities, but also a steady stream to the United States. From 1845 to 1849, death from starvation, malnutrition, and typhus spread in Ireland. In all, 1 million died and about 1.5 million scattered around the world, two-thirds of them to the United States. In every year but one between 1830 and 1854, the Irish constituted the largest group of immigrants.

Although most Irish made an economic decision to leave their homeland, they often viewed themselves as political exiles, forced to flee because of British tyranny. While nature caused the potato blight, they blamed British misrule for the events that led to famine. Thus, settlers of the Irish diaspora—in the United States, Canada, Australia, South Africa, Argentina, and even England—tended to be politically active. In the United States especially, as in St. Patrick's Day parades, they displayed their two national identities.

Most of the new immigrants from Ireland were young, female, poor, from rural counties, and Roman Catholic. In America, these women found work in textile mills and households. Young Irishmen worked in transportation and construction. The Irish supported their families back home and in Irish enclaves in cities, built Catholic churches and schools, and established networks of charitable and social organizations.

Racial Ideas   This wave of Irish immigrants, descended from the ancient Celts who spoke Gaelic, differed greatly from the Protestant Scots-Irish who had migrated earlier to the American colonies. Many considered the Celts inferior. The British had thought them barbaric, and colonists carried those views to America. Dr. Robert Knox of the Edinburgh College of Surgeons believed "the source of all evil lies in the race, the Celtic race of Ireland." Many Americans agreed. They talked about Celtic racial characteristics: a small, upturned nose, high forehead, and black tint of skin. As scientists like Knox began to classify peoples into biological types, scientific theory buttressed the developing notion of race.

With the immigration of new groups to the United States—Celts, Jews, and Catholics, for instance—with the black population expanding, and with territorial expansion bringing in Hispanics and more Indians, native-born white Americans were increasingly confronted with people who did not look like them. Many considered these non-British, non-European, non-Protestant people separate races. Ralph Waldo Emerson asserted the importance of race in *English Traits* (1856). To Emerson, a race passes on to its members its physical, intellectual, and moral characteristics. "Race avails . . . that all Celts are Catholics," Emerson wrote. "Race is a controlling influence in the Jew. . . . Race in the negro (sic) is of appalling importance."

Closely related to racial stereotyping in its causes and nasty effects was anti-Catholicism, which became

ANTI-
CATHOLICISM

strident in the 1830s and was most overt and cruel in Boston with its many Irish. Anti-Catholic riots were almost commonplace. In Lawrence, Massachusetts, for instance, a mob leveled the Irish neighborhood in 1854.

The native-born whites who rejected the Irish and hated Catholics were motivated in part by economic competition and anxiety. Competition was stiffest among the lowest paid and least desirable jobs. To apprehensive workers, racializing the Irish as Celts was a way to keep them out of the running. Irish Catholics were also blamed for nearly every social problem, from immorality and alcoholism to poverty and economic upheaval. Impoverished native-born workers complained to the Massachusetts legislature in 1845 that the Irish displaced "the honest and respectable laborers of the State." American workers, they claimed, "not only labor for the body but for the mind, the soul, and the State."

In emphasizing "the soul, and the State," native-born workers added a political dimension to their racial expression. Republicanism depended on broad participation and the consent of the governed, and it seemed to American nativists that the Irish, a non-white, non-British "race," were not fit to participate.

By and large Americans viewed most Germans, unlike the Irish, as white, especially the majority

GERMAN
IMMIGRANTS

Protestant group. They shared a racial stock with the English. Americans stereotyped Germans as hard working, self-reliant, and intelligent, attributes also applied to white

people. Many believed that Germans fit more easily than the Irish into American culture.

In 1854 Germans replaced the Irish as the largest group of new arrivals. Potato blight also prompted emigration from the German states in the 1840s, as did other hardships. Many came from regions where small landholdings made it hard to eke out a living. Craftsmen displaced by the industrial revolution sought jobs in America's expanding market economy. Political refugees—liberals, freethinkers, socialists, communists, and anarchists—fled to the United States after the abortive revolutions of 1848.

In the South, Germans were peddlers and merchants; in the North and West, they worked as farmers, urban laborers, and businessmen. Their tendency to migrate as families and groups helped them maintain German customs and institutions. Many settled in small towns and rural areas, where they could preserve their language and regional German cultures. In larger cities, their tendency to cluster together transformed the tone of communities like Cincinnati and Milwaukee.

Non-Protestant Germans did not fare so well. A significant number of German immigrants were Jewish, and Jews were considered a separate race. Anti-Catholics attacked German immigrants who were Catholic. The Sunday tradition of urban German families gathering at beer gardens to eat and drink, dance and sing, and sometimes play cards outraged Protestants, who viewed this behavior as violating the sanctity of the Lord's day.

From Florida to Texas and the Southwest to California, Hispanic inhabitants of the borderlands became "immigrants" without actually moving; treaties

HISPANICS

placed them in the United States. Some Mexicans were unhappy to find themselves in a new country, while others welcomed the political self-government the United States seemed to promise.

But reality denied promise. In Nueces County, Texas, at the time of the Texas Revolution (1836), Mexicans held all the land; twenty years later, they had lost it. The new Anglo owners produced crops for the market economy; *rancheros* and *vaqueros*—cowboys—became obsolete. Although many Mexicans, called *Tejanos*, had fought for Texas's independence, new Anglo settlers tended to treat them as inferiors and foreigners. They became second-class citizens on land where they had lived for generations. Still, they retained their culture. They held fast to their language, Roman Catholic religion, and cultural traditions.

In California—unlike in Texas, New Mexico, and Arizona—Hispanic society and political power quickly gave way to American and European culture. *Californios,* the Mexican population, numbered 10,000 in 1848, or two-thirds of the non-Indian population. By the end of the century, the Hispanic population was 15,000 out of 1.5 million, and Hispanic culture was only a remnant.

White Americans considered Hispanics, a group descended from Indians and Spaniards, as a separate, nonwhite race. Anglo-Americans also inherited the British view of Spaniards as inferior, lazy, and decadent, stereotypes they applied to Hispanics. Racializing Hispanics helped to justify the attitudes and actions of aggressive whites.

Free People of Color

*B*lacks, slave and free, were the most visible nonwhite group in the early nineteenth century. As their numbers grew, from 2.3 million in 1830 to 4.4 million in 1860, whites increasingly viewed them as a racial group, a people apart. In law and society, most black people found themselves outsiders in the land of their birth.

GROWTH OF THE BLACK POPULATION

The free African American population grew from 320,000 in 1820 to almost 500,000 in 1860. Nearly half lived in the urban North and almost an equal number in the Upper South, where, outside of Baltimore—the nation's largest black community—most were rural. A scattering of free people of color lived in the Deep South. Despite differences in occupation, wealth, education, religion, and social status, the necessity of self-defense promoted solidarity among free blacks.

Ex-slaves constantly increased the ranks of free people of color in the North. Some, like Frederick Douglass and Harriet Tubman, were fugitives. Tubman, a slave in Maryland, escaped to Philadelphia in 1849. Over the next two years, she returned twice to free her two children, her sister, her mother, and her brother and his family. Some slaves received freedom in owners' wills. And some owners freed their children born of liaisons or forced relations with slaves or released elderly slaves rather than support them in old age.

AFRICAN AMERICAN COMMUNITIES

Black people, free and slave, forged their own communities and culture. Swept up by the Second Great Awakening, blacks turned increasingly to religion, most often to Christianity. But as they founded their own churches and denominations, like the African Methodist Episcopal (AME) Church (1816), they reshaped ritual and practice. Services reflected black musical traditions, and they gave theological prominence to themes of equality, exodus, and freedom. Black churches and preachers, both male and female, played central roles in their communities. Ministers were political leaders and abolitionists, united in their opposition to the enslavement of other black people, sometimes their own kin.

A network of voluntary associations became the hallmark of black communities. Besides the churches, men and women organized reform societies, fraternal and benevolent associations, literary societies, and schools. In Philadelphia in the 1840s, more than half of the black population belonged to mutual beneficiary societies. Many black leaders believed these mutual aid societies would encourage thrift, industry, and morality, thus assisting their members in improving themselves. But no amount of effort could completely counteract the burden of white racism, which impinged on every aspect of their lives.

POLITICAL ACTIVISM

In the majority of states where free blacks were excluded from the ballot, they formed organizations to fight for equal rights. Among the early efforts was the Negro Convention movement. From 1830 to 1835, and irregularly thereafter, free blacks held national conventions with delegates drawn from city and state organizations. Under middle-class leadership, the convention movement served as a forum to attack slavery and agitate for equal rights. Militant new black newspapers joined the struggle.

DISCRIMINATION AND EXCLUSION

Activists fought their second-class status and the continuation of slavery. Although the Bill of Rights and the Constitution promised protection of civil rights, eighteenth-century political theory had defined the republic as being for whites only (see Chapter 7), and early federal legislation excluded blacks from common rights. The first naturalization law in 1790 limited citizenship to "free white persons." And after 1821, every new state admitted until the Civil War, free and slave, banned blacks from voting. Finally, when Congress organized the Oregon and New Mexico Territories, it reserved public land grants for whites. Clearly free people of color were defined as an alien race.

Even in the North, states attempted to exclude African Americans. Many states barred free blacks or required them to post bonds ranging from $500 to $1,000 to guarantee their good conduct. Only in Massachusetts, New Hampshire, Vermont, and Maine could blacks vote on an equal basis with whites throughout the early nineteenth century. In 1842 African Americans gained the right to vote in Rhode Island, but they had lost it earlier in Pennsylvania and Connecticut. Only Massachusetts permitted blacks to serve on juries. Four midwestern states and California did not allow African Americans to testify against whites. In Oregon blacks could not own real estate, make contracts, or sue in court.

Black people also faced economic restrictions. They were excluded from the new factory and clerical jobs of the expanding market economy. In the North and Upper South, black women, who were more likely to work for wages than white women, whether married or single, worked as house servants, cooks, washerwomen, and child nurses. Most black men were construction workers, porters, longshoremen, and day laborers. All suffered frequent unemployment.

Some black men and women turned service occupations into businesses. In the growing cities, blacks opened restaurants, taverns, hotels, barber shops, and employment agencies for domestic servants. A few became very successful economically, like sail maker James Forten (Philadelphia), barber Samuel Mordechai (St. Louis), and ship captain Paul Cuffee. With professionals—ministers, teachers, physicians and dentists, lawyers, and newspaper editors—they formed a growing black middle class.

While free people of color sought economic and political security, they forged their own cultural identity. They began to call themselves "Colored Americans" rather than "Africans." Like the Irish on St. Patrick's Day, they acknowledged a dual identity as African descendants and as Americans. There is much

AFRICAN
AMERICAN
CULTURE

evidence that they mixed African and American cultures in distinct ways. They dressed up for church, wearing their "Sunday go-to-meetin' clothes." They modified African hairstyles in cutting, wrapping, and braiding their hair. Africans brought the banjo and drum to the New World, introducing new rhythms to Europeans. Black brass bands created what Walt Whitman called "grand American opera."

Most expressive was African American dance. From Congo Square in New Orleans on Sundays to the integrated "dives" in Five Points, New York, visitors observed African-based dance movements unknown to Europeans. Frederick Bremer in South Carolina in 1850 described such movements in a black church. They sang "with all their souls and with all their bodies in unison, for their bodies wagged, their heads nodded, their feet stamped, their knees shook, their elbows and their hands beat time to the tune." Here were the African traditions of polyrhythms, improvisation, and intensive physicality.

In the late 1840s and 1850s the mood of many free blacks turned pessimistic. They felt frustrated by the failure of the abolitionist movement and angered by the passage of the stringent Fugitive Slave Act of 1850 (discussed in Chapter 14). Some fled to Canada. Many more were swept up in a wave of black nationalism that stressed racial solidarity, self-help, and a growing interest in Africa. Before this time, efforts to send African Americans "back to Africa" had originated with whites seeking to rid the United States of blacks, and nearly all African American leaders had been opposed. But in the 1850s, some participated in emigrationist conventions led by abolitionists Henry Bibb and Martin Delany. With the coming of the Civil War, the status of blacks would move onto the national political agenda.

Summary ⟿ *Online Study Center* ACE the Test

The American people and communities in the North and West were far more diverse and turbulent in the 1850s than they had been in the 1820s. The market economy and westward movement altered rural and urban life and class structure; heavy immigration, growing racial ideas, and the anguished position of free people of color added to the tensions. Inequality increased, as did the gap between the haves and the have-nots. As the nation grew more populous and the market economy upset work and social relations, many felt a loss of tradition and community. Some longed to return to old values. Utopians like the Shakers, Mormons, and Brook Farmers sought to counter isolation and individualism.

Increasingly cities became the center of American life, with New York the predominant metropolis. Growing populations brought new problems, however, and cities struggled to provide adequate public health, safety, and education for their residents. Large cities offered rich leisure activities, but people divided along class, ethnic, and racial lines.

In the midst of these changes, families adapted to the urban, market economy. They became consumers rather than producers, and they shrank in size as women had fewer children. Middle-class families sought to insulate their homes from the competition of the market economy. Increasingly cities offered opportunities for people to live outside of families.

Famine and oppression in Europe propelled millions of people across the Atlantic. American expansion added Hispanics to the nation. Diversity, competition, and religious and scientific thought fueled racial ideas. Many European descendants began to view the Irish, Hispanics, and African Americans as inferior races.

LEGACY FOR A PEOPLE AND A NATION
White Fascination with and Appropriation of Black Culture

White Americans' fascination with and appropriation of black culture blossomed in the early nineteenth century. Whites performed songs and dances from blackface minstrel reviews, while urban young people imitated black language, dress, and hairstyles. In the 1850s white songwriter Stephen Foster's "Old Folks at Home," "Susanna," and "Camptown Races" were enormously popular.

American popular culture combined African, European, and African American traditions. Its emphasis on performance, improvisation, strong rhythms, vernacular language, multiple meanings, and integration into everyday life is evidence of strong African ties. These elements appealed to whites because of their expressive power. Whites also believed that black cultural forms were "exotic" and offered "natural" forms of expression.

Black traditions continue to influence popular culture today. Minstrelsy turned into vaudeville and Broadway theater. Popular dance and music, performed mostly by whites, drew heavily on black gospel, slave spirituals, the blues, and jazz. Black traditions influenced the swing bands of the 1930s, and after World War II, they shaped rhythm and blues, rock 'n' roll, and, later, rap, hip-hop, and ska.

Until recently, most whites experienced black culture as appropriated by whites. But in the late twentieth century, a synthesis of black and white traditions became notable. In the early 1950s Bill Haley and the Comets, a white group, combined black rhythm and blues with white country and western music. Their 1954 sensation, "Shake, Rattle & Roll," for instance, was a sanitized version of Big Joe Turner's rhythm and blues hit. White audiences responded enthusiastically, and when Haley and the Comets played "Rock Around the Clock" in the 1955 movie *Blackboard Jungle*, rock 'n' roll took off. Elvis Presley too synthesized rhythm and blues and gospel with country music and middle-of-the-road popular music. Rap and hip-hop built on the talking blues, call and response, and urban black and Chicano/a dance styles of the 1970s. White suburban youth made them dominant popular forms.

Popular music and dance, with its African American roots, is uniquely American. Young people fostered this popular culture and used its expressive elements to define themselves. Thus, African American culture has given the people and the nation a unique cultural legacy.

$\mathcal{P}$EOPLE AND COMMUNITIES IN A SLAVE SOCIETY: THE SOUTH 1830–1860

$\mathcal{P}$ierce Butler was broke. It was late winter 1859, fear of disunion dominated national life, and Butler's slave auction had all of coastal Georgia and South Carolina talking. Butler had divided his time between the family's ostentatious home in Philadelphia and 1,500 acres of cotton plantations in Georgia, worked by eight hundred slaves. By 1859 Butler had squandered a fortune of $700,000 through speculation and gambling.

Most of Butler's properties and possessions in Philadelphia were sold to satisfy his creditors. Then came the largest slave auction in American history. In the last week of February, 436 Butler slaves were taken to Savannah by railroad and steamboat. People of all ages—infants, husbands, wives, children, grandparents—huddled in fearful expectation. The auction lasted an agonizing two days in a driving rainstorm.

If possible, families were sold intact for group prices; thus, the old and infirm could still be liquidated, while the closest kin stayed together. A seventeen-year-old "Prime woman" and her three-month-old son went for $2,200. A nineteen-year-old "prime young man" netted $1,295. Some families of four brought only $1,600 together. At the end of the second day of what blacks in the region called the "weeping time," Butler had amassed $303,850 by selling 436 human beings.

As long as slavery was perceived as a peculiarly southern institution, it did not seem to bother many northerners at first glance. But as slavery spread westward, its worst elements, such as the Butler auction, threatened and disturbed growing numbers of restless Americans. And on the ground in the South, slaves struggled to survive and resist.

By the 1830s, the North was an emerging market economy embarking on an industrial revolution. The South, with a different kind of growth and pros-

The Distinctive South?

Free Southerners: Farmers, Free Blacks, and Planters

LINKS TO THE WORLD
"King Cotton" in the World Economy

Slave Life and Labor

Slave Culture

Slave Resistance and Rebellion

Harmony and Tension in a Slave Society

LEGACY FOR A PEOPLE AND A NATION
Reparations for Slavery

Online Study Center
This icon will direct you to interactive map and primary source activities on the website http://college.hmco.com/pic/nortonbrief7e

CHRONOLOGY

1810–20 • 137,000 slaves are forced to move from North Carolina and the Chesapeake to Alabama, Mississippi, and other western regions

1822 • Vesey's insurrection plot is discovered in South Carolina

1830s • Vast majority of African American slaves are native-born in America

1830s–40s • Cotton trade grows into largest source of commercial wealth and America's leading export

1831 • Turner leads a violent slave rebellion in Virginia

1832 • Virginia holds the last serious debate in the South about the future of slavery; gradual abolition is voted down
• Publication of Dew's proslavery tract, *Abolition of Negro Slavery*

1836 • Arkansas gains admission to the Union as a slave state

1845 • Florida and Texas gain admission to the Union as slave states
• Publication of Douglass's *Narrative of the Life of Frederick Douglass, An American Slave*

1850 • Planters' share of agricultural wealth in the South is 90 to 95 percent

1850–60 • Of some 300,000 slaves who migrate from Upper to Lower South, 60 to 70 percent go by outright sale

1857 • Publication of Helper's *The Impending Crisis*, denouncing the slave system

1860 • 405,751 mulattos in the United States, 12.5 percent of the African American population
• Three-quarters of all southern white families own no slaves

1861 • South produces largest cotton crop ever

perity, also participated in the market revolution. New lands were settled and new states peopled, and steadily the South emerged as the world's most extensive and vigorous slave economy, linked to an international cotton trade and textile industry. Slavery had a far-reaching influence on all of southern society. The Old South's wealth came from export crops, land, and slaves, and its population was almost wholly rural. ■

The Distinctive South?

Certain American values such as materialism, individualism, and faith in progress have been associated with the North in the nineteenth century, and values such as tradition, intolerance, and family loyalty with the South. The South, so the stereotype has it, was static, and the North dynamic. There are many measures of just how different the South was from the North in the antebellum era, and at the same time there were many Souths: low-country rice and cotton regions with dense slave populations; mountainous regions of small farmers, plantation culture, and subsistence agriculture; Texas grasslands; cities with bustling ports and merchants.

The South was distinctive because of its commitment to slavery, but it was also much like the rest of the nation. The South and the North were roughly the same size geographically. By the 1830s, white southerners shared a heritage from the era of the American Revolution with their fellow free citizens in the North. Southerners spoke the same language, worshiped the same Protestant God, and lived under the same cherished

SOUTH-NORTH SIMILARITY

Constitution as northerners, and they shared common attitudes toward government. Down to the 1840s, northerners and southerners both invoked the doctrine of states' rights against federal authority. A faith in the future fueled by a sense of American mission and the dreams inspired by westward movement were as much a part of southern as of northern experience. But as slavery and the plantation economy expanded, the South did not become a land of individual opportunity in quite the same manner as the North.

Research has shown that slavery was a profitable labor system for planters. As it grew, the slave-based economy of money-crop agriculture reflected planters' rational choices. More land and more slaves generally converted into more wealth. By the eve of the Civil War in 1860, the distribution of wealth and property in the two sections was almost identical: 50 percent of free adult males owned only 1 percent of real and personal property, while the richest 1 percent owned 27 percent of the wealth. Both North and South had ruling classes, and entrepreneurs in both sections, whether planters in the Mississippi Delta or factory owners in New England, sought their fortunes in a shared and expanding market economy.

But there were also important differences between the North and the South. The South's climate

SOUTH-NORTH DISSIMILARITY

and longer growing season gave it an unmistakable rural and agricultural destiny. Its people, white and black, developed an intense attachment to place, to the ways people were related to the land and to one another. It developed as a biracial society of brutal inequality, where the liberty of one race directly depended on the enslavement of another.

Cotton growers spread out over as large an area as possible to maximize production and income. Population density was low; by 1860, there were only 2.3 people per square mile in vast and largely unsettled Texas and 18.0 in Georgia. Population density in the nonslaveholding states east of the Mississippi River was almost three times higher. The Northeast had an average of 65.4 people per square mile, Massachusetts 153.1, and New York City 86,400.

Where people were scarce, it was difficult to finance and operate schools, churches, libraries, or even inns and restaurants. Southerners were strongly committed to their churches, and some believed in the importance of universities, but all such institutions were

far less developed than those in the North. Factories were rare because planters invested most of their capital in slaves. And despite concerted efforts, the South had only 35 percent of the nation's railroad mileage in 1860.

The South did have urban centers, especially ports like New Orleans and Charleston, which became bustling crossroads of commerce and small-scale manufacturing. But slavery slowed urban growth. And because of the lack of jobs, the South did not attract immigrants as readily as the North did.

Like most northerners, antebellum southerners practiced evangelical Christianity. But southern evangelicalism was distinct from northern practice. In the South, Baptists and Methodists concentrated on personal rather than social improvement. By the 1830s in the North, evangelicalism was a major wellspring of reform movements; but in the states where blacks were so numerous and unfree, religion, as one scholar has written, preached "a hands-off policy concerning slavery." The only reform movements that did take hold in the South, such as temperance, focused on personal behavior, not social reform.

Perhaps in no other way was the South more distinctive than in its embrace of a particular worldview,

A SOUTHERN WORLDVIEW AND THE PROSLAVERY ARGUMENT

a system of thought and meaning held especially by the planter class but influencing all groups of whites. At the heart of the proslavery argument was a deep and abiding racism. The persistence of modern racism in all sections of the United States is all

the more reason to comprehend antebellum southerners' justifications for human slavery.

By 1830, white southerners defended slavery as a "positive good," not merely a "necessary evil." They used the Bible and its many references to slaveholding, as well as the ancient roots of slavery, to foster a historical argument for bondage. Slavery, they deemed, was the natural status of blacks. Whites were the more intellectual race, in this view, and blacks the more inherently physical, and therefore destined for labor.

Some southerners defended slavery in practical terms; they saw their bondsmen as an economic necessity in their quest for prosperity. Others argued that slaveholding was essentially a matter of property rights. James Henry Hammond of South Carolina spoke for many southerners in his unwillingness to "deal in abstractions" about the "right and wrong" of slavery: property was sacred, and slaves were legal property—end of argument.

The deepest root of the proslavery argument was a hierarchical view of the social order as slavery's defenders believed God or nature had prescribed it. Southerners cherished stability, duty, and honor, believing social change should come in slow increments, if at all. When the Virginia legislature debated the gradual abolition of slavery in 1831–1832, Thomas R. Dew, a slaveholder and professor of law and history, contended, "There is a time for all things, and nothing in this world should be done before its time." Dew's widely read work, *Abolition of Negro Slavery* (1832), ushered in an outpouring of proslavery writing that would intensify over the next thirty years. Dew declared black slavery part of the "order of nature," indispensable to the "deep and solid foundations of society," and the basis of the "well-ordered, well-established liberty" of white Americans. Dew's well-ordered society also included his conception of the proper division of men and women into separate spheres and functions.

Proslavery advocates held very different views from those of northern reformers on the concepts of freedom, progress, and equality. They turned natural-law doctrine to their favor, arguing that the natural state of mankind was inequality of ability and condition, not equality. Proslavery writers believed that people were born to certain stations in life; they stressed dependence over autonomy, and duty over rights, as the human condition.

Hence, many slaveholders believed that their ownership of people bound them to a set of paternal obligations in a familial relationship between masters and slaves. Although contradicted by countless examples of slave resistance and escape, planters needed to believe in, and exerted great energy in constructing, the idea of the contented slave. Slaveholders needed to justify endlessly how much the freedom and profits of whites depended on the bondage of blacks.

What the South had become by the 1830s, and grew even more fully into by 1860, was not merely a society with slaves, but a *slave society* (see Chapter 3). Slavery and race affected everything in the Old South. Whites, slaveholding or not, and blacks, slave or free, all grew up, were socialized, married, reared children, and honed their most basic habits of behavior under the

A Slave Society

influence of slavery. Slavery shaped the social structure of the South, fueled almost anything meaningful in its economy, and came to dominate its politics.

The South was interdependent with the North and the West and even with Europe in a growing capitalist market system. Southerners relied on northern banks, northern steamship companies, and northern merchants to keep the cotton trade flowing. But there were elements of that system that southerners increasingly rejected during the antebellum era, especially urbanism, the wage labor system, a broadening right to vote, and any threats to the racial and class order on which they so depended.

Just how distinctive the South was will always be debated. Culturally, the South developed a proclivity to tell its own story. Its ruralness and its sense of tradition may have given southerners a special habit of telling tales. "Southerners . . . love a good tale," said Mississippi writer Eudora Welty. The South's tragic and distinct story begins in the Old South. The story was distinctive and national all at once.

Free Southerners: Farmers, Free Blacks, and Planters

a large majority of white southern families (three-quarters in 1860) owned no slaves. Some lived in towns, but most were yeoman farmers who owned their own land and grew their own food. The social distance between different groups of whites was great. Still greater was the distance between whites and blacks.

Yeoman farmers were individualistic and hard working, but their status as a numerical majority did

Yeoman Farmers

not mean that they set the political or economic direction of the slave society. Self-reliant and often isolated, always absorbed in the work of their farms, they operated both apart from and within the slave-based staple-crop economy.

Yeomen pioneered the southern wilderness, moving into undeveloped regions—or Indian land after removal—and building log cabins. After the War of 1812, they moved in successive waves down the southern Appalachians into the Gulf lands. In large sections of the South, small, self-sufficient farms were

■ Eastman Johnson's *Fiddling His Way* (1866) depicts rural life by representing the visit of an itinerant black musician to a farm family. Expressions and gestures suggest remarkable ease between the races at the yeoman level of southern society.   (Eastman Johnson [American, 1824–1906] *Fiddling His Way*, 1866, oil on canvas, 24¼ x 36½ inches. Bequest of Walter P. Chrysler, Jr., Chrysler Museum of Art, Norfolk, VA 89.60)

the norm. Lured by stories of good land, many men uprooted their wives and children repeatedly.

On the southern frontier, men worked hard to fields and establish farms, while their wives labored in the household economy and patiently re-created the social ties—to relatives, neighbors, fellow churchgoers—that enriched everyone's experience. Women seldom shared the men's excitement about moving. They dreaded the isolation and loneliness of the frontier.

Some yeomen acquired large tracts of level land, purchased slaves, and became planters. They forged part of the new wealth of the boom states of Mississippi and Louisiana, the region to which the southern political power base shifted by the 1840s and 1850s. Others clung to familiar mountainous areas or kept moving as independent farmers.

The yeomen enjoyed a folk culture based on family, church, and local region. They flocked to religious revivals called camp meetings, and in between got together for house-raisings, logrollings, quilting bees, corn-shuckings, and hunting for both food and sport. Such occasions combined work with fun and fellowship.

YEOMAN FOLK CULTURE

A demanding round of work and family responsibilities shaped women's lives in the home. In addition to preparing and preserving food, they worked in the fields to an extent that astonished travelers such as Frances Trollope, who believed yeomen had rendered their wives "slaves of the soil." Household tasks continued during frequent pregnancies and childcare. Primary nursing and medical care also fell to mothers, who often relied on folk wisdom.

Among the men were many who aspired to wealth, eager to join the race for slaves and cotton profits. Others were content with their independence, family, religion, and recreation. All worked hard.

YEOMAN LIVELIHOODS

North Carolinian Ferdinand L. Steel, who took up farming in Mississippi, was a typical yeoman. Steel rose every day at five and worked until sundown. With the help of his family, he raised corn, wheat, pork, and vegetables. Cotton was his cash crop: he sold five or six bales (about 2,000 pounds) a year to obtain money for sugar, coffee, salt, calico, gunpowder, and a few other store-bought goods.

Thus, Steel entered the market economy as a small farmer, but with mixed results. He complained that cotton cultivation was brutal work and not profitable. He felt like a serf in cotton's kingdom. When cotton prices fell, a small grower like Steel could be driven into debt and lose his farm.

Steel's life in Mississippi in the 1840s retained much of the flavor of the frontier. He made all the family's shoes; his wife and sister sewed dresses, shirts, and "pantaloons." The Steel women also rendered their own soap and spun and wove cotton into cloth; the men hunted game. As the nation fell deeper into crisis over the future of slave labor, this independent southern farmer never came close to owning a slave.

The focus of Steel's life was family and religion. Family members prayed together daily, and Steel studied Scripture for an hour after lunch. He borrowed histories and religious books from his church. Eventually he became a traveling Methodist minister. "My life is one of toil," he reflected, "but blessed be God that it is as well with me as it is."

Toil with even less security was the lot of two other groups of free southerners: landless whites and free blacks. A sizable minority of white southern workers—from 25 to 40 percent—were unskilled laborers who owned no land and worked for others in the countryside and towns. Their property consisted of a few household items and some animals—usually pigs—that could feed themselves on the open range. The landless included some immigrants, especially Irish, who did heavy and dangerous work such as building railroads and digging ditches.

LANDLESS WHITES

In the countryside, white farm laborers struggled to purchase land in the face of low wages or, if they rented, unpredictable market prices for their crops. By scrimping and saving and finding odd jobs, some managed to climb into the ranks of yeomen. When James and Nancy Bennitt of North Carolina succeeded in their ten-year struggle to buy land, they decided to avoid the unstable market in cotton and raised extra corn and wheat as sources of cash.

By 1860, as the South anticipated war to preserve its society, between 300,000 and 400,000 white people in the four states of Virginia, North and South Carolina, and Georgia lived in genuine poverty, approximately one-fifth of the total white population. Their lives were harsh to say the least.

For the nearly quarter-million free blacks in the South in 1860, conditions were often little better than the slaves'. They usually did not own land and had to labor in someone else's fields, often beside slaves. By law, free blacks could not own a gun, buy liquor, violate curfew, assemble except in church, testify in court, or (throughout the South after 1835) vote. Despite these obstacles, a minority bought land, and others found jobs as skilled craftsmen.

FREE BLACKS

A few free blacks prospered and bought slaves, most of them purchasing their own wives and children (whom they could not free, since laws required newly emancipated blacks to leave their states). In 1830 there were 3,775 free black slaveholders in the South; 80 percent lived in the four states of Louisiana, South Carolina, Virginia, and Maryland, and approximately half of the total lived in the two cities of New Orleans and Charleston.

Online Study Center
Improve Your Grade
Primary Source: Black Recollections of Freedom's Impact

In the cotton and Gulf regions, a large proportion of free blacks were mulattos, the privileged offspring of wealthy white planters. Not all planters freed their mixed-race offspring, but those who did often recognized a moral obligation and gave their children a good education and financial backing. In a few cities like New Orleans, Charleston, and Mobile, extensive interracial sex, as well as migrations from the Caribbean, had produced a mulatto population that was recognized as a distinct class.

FREE BLACK COMMUNITIES

In many southern cities by the 1840s, free black communities formed, especially around an expanding number of churches. By the late 1850s, Baltimore had fifteen churches, Louisville nine, and Nashville and St. Louis four each, and most of them were African Methodist Episcopal. Class and race distinctions were important to southern free blacks, but outside a few cities, which developed fraternal orders of skilled craftsmen and fellowships of light-skinned people, most mulattos experienced hardship. In the United States, "one drop" of black "blood" made them black, and potentially enslaveable.

At the top of the southern social pyramid were slaveholding planters. As a group they lived well, but most lived in comfortable farmhouses, not on the opulent scale that legend suggests. A few statistics tell the story: in 1850, 50 percent of southern slaveholders had fewer than five slaves; 72 percent had fewer than ten; 88 percent had fewer than twenty. Thus, the average slaveholder was not a wealthy aristocrat but an aspiring farmer, and usually of humble origins.

PLANTERS

The richest planters used their wealth to model genteel sophistication. Extended visits, parties, and balls to which women wore the latest fashions provided opportunities for friendship, courtship, and display. These entertainments were especially important as diversions for plantation women, and at the same time they sustained a rigidly gendered society. Young women relished social events to break the monotony of their domestic lives.

Most of the planters in the cotton-boom states of Alabama and Mississippi were newly rich by the 1840s. As one historian put it, "a number of men mounted from log cabin to plantation mansion on a stairway of cotton bales, accumulating slaves as they climbed." And many did not live like rich men. They put their new wealth into cotton acreage and slaves even as they sought refinement and high social status.

Slaveholding men dominated society and, especially among the wealthiest and oldest families, justified their dominance over white women and black slaves through a paternalistic ideology. Instead of stressing the profitable aspects of commercial agriculture, they focused on their obligations, viewing themselves as custodians of the

SOUTHERN PATERNALISM

welfare of society in general and of the black families they owned in particular. The paternalistic planter saw himself not as an oppressor but as the benevolent guardian of an inferior race.

Paul Carrington Cameron, North Carolina's largest slaveholder, exemplifies this mentality. After a period of sickness among his one thousand North Carolina slaves (he had hundreds more in Alabama and Mississippi), Cameron wrote, "I fear the Negroes have suffered much from the want of proper attention and kindness under this late distemper . . . no love of lucre shall ever induce me to be cruel."

It was comforting to rich planters to see themselves in this way, and slaves—accommodating to the realities of power—encouraged their masters to think their benevolence was appreciated. Paternalism also served as a defense against abolitionist criticism. Still, paternalism often covered harsher assumptions. As talk of paternalistic duties increased, theories about the complete and permanent inferiority of blacks multiplied. In reality, paternalism grew as a give-and-take relationship between masters and slaves, each extracting from the other what they desired: owners took labor from the bondsmen, while slaves expected from masters a measure of autonomy and living space. But it also evolved as a theory of black slavery and white dominance.

Even Paul Cameron's benevolence vanished with changed circumstances. After the Civil War, he bristled at African Americans' efforts to be free. Writing on Christmas Day 1865, Cameron showed little Christian charity (but a healthy profit motive) when he declared, "I am convinced that the people who gets rid of the free negro first will be the first to advance in improved agriculture. Have made no effort to retain any of mine [and] will not attempt a crop beyond the capacity of 30 hands." With that he turned off his land nearly a thousand black people, rented his fields to several white farmers, and invested in industry.

Relations between men and women in the planter class were similarly paternalistic. The upper-class southern woman was raised and educated to be a wife, mother, and subordinate companion to men. South Carolina's Mary Boykin Chesnut wrote of her husband, "He is master of the house. To hear is to obey. . . . All the comfort of my life depends upon his being in a good humor." In a social system based on the coercion of an entire race, women were not allowed to challenge society's rules on sexual or racial relations.

"King Cotton" in the World Economy

The economy of the Old South was deeply intertwined with international trade. Cash crops such as cotton were exported, and the fate of this slave society depended on world trade, especially with Europe.

The American South so dominated the world's supply of cotton that the size of the U.S. crop normally determined the price in an international market where demand continued to skyrocket. This circumstance gave southern planters enormous confidence that the cotton boom was permanent and that the industrializing nations of England and France in particular would always bow to "King Cotton."

American cotton doubled in yield each decade after 1800 and provided three-fourths of the world's supply by the 1840s. Southern staple crops were fully three-fifths of all American exports by 1850, and one of every seven workers in England depended on American cotton for a job. Indeed, cotton production made slaves the single most valuable financial asset in the United States—greater in dollar value than all of America's banks, railroads, and manufacturing combined.

The Old South never developed its own banking and shipping capacity to any degree. If it had, its effort to be an international cartel might have succeeded longer. Most southern bank deposits were in the North, and southern cotton planters became ever more dependent on New York for shipping.

Until 1840 the cotton trade furnished much of the export capital to finance northern economic growth. After that date, however, the northern economy expanded without dependence on cotton profits. Nevertheless, southern planters and politicians continued to boast of King Cotton's supremacy. "No power on earth dares . . . to make war on cotton," James Hammond lec-

tured the U.S. Senate in 1858. "Cotton is king." Although the South produced 4.5 million bales in 1861, its greatest cotton crop ever, this link to the world was about to collapse in a civil war. Thereafter, cotton was more a shackle to the South than a king.

Cotton traded to England would be returned to the United States in fabric collections called sample books, such as this Norwich Textile Sample Book. Orders were placed and then shipped to Americans. (Courtesy, The Henry Francis du Pont Winterthur Library: Joseph Downs Collection of Manuscripts & Printed Ephemera)

225

Planters' daughters usually attended one of the South's rapidly multiplying boarding schools. There they formed friendships with other girls and received an education. Typically the young woman could entertain suitors whom her parents approved. But very soon she had to choose a husband and commit herself for life to a man whom she generally had known only briefly. Young women were often alienated and emotionally unfulfilled. They had to follow the wishes of their families, especially fathers. "It was for me best that I yielded to the wishes of papa," wrote a young North Carolinian in 1823. "I wonder when my best will cease to be painful and when I shall begin to enjoy life instead of enduring it."

Upon marriage, a planter class woman ceded to her husband most of her legal rights, becoming part

Marriage and Family Among the Planter Class

of his family. Most of the year she was isolated on a large plantation, where she had to oversee the cooking and preserving of food, manage the house, supervise care of the children, and attend sick slaves. It is not surprising that a perceptive young white woman sometimes approached marriage with anxiety.

Childbearing often involved grief, poor health, and death. In 1840 the birth rate for white southern women in their childbearing years was almost 30 percent higher than the national average. By 1860 the average southern white woman could expect to bear six children, with one or more miscarriages likely. For women who wanted to plan their families, methods of contraception and medical care were uncertain. Complications of childbirth were a major cause of death, occurring twice as often in the hot, humid South as in the Northeast.

Sexual relations between planters and slaves were another source of problems that white women had to endure but were not supposed to notice. "Violations of the moral law . . . made mulattoes as common as blackberries," protested a woman in Georgia, but wives had to play "the ostrich game." "A magnate who runs a hideous black harem," wrote Mrs. Chesnut, ". . . poses as the model of all human virtues to these poor women whom God and the laws have given him."

Southern men tolerated little discussion by women of the slavery issue. In the 1840s and 1850s, as abolitionist attacks on slavery increased, southern men published a barrage of articles stressing that women should restrict their concerns to the home. The *Southern Quarterly Review* declared, "The proper place for a woman is at home. One of her highest privileges, to be politically merged in the existence of her husband."

But some southern women were beginning to seek a larger role. A study of women in Petersburg, Virginia, revealed behavior that valued financial autonomy. Over several decades before 1860, the proportion of women who never married, or did not remarry after the death of a spouse, grew to exceed 33 percent. Likewise, the number of women who worked for wages, controlled their own property, and ran millinery or dressmaking businesses increased. In managing property, these and other women benefited from legal changes; to protect families from the husband's indebtedness during business panics and recessions, reforms gave married women some property rights.

Slave Life and Labor

For African Americans, slavery was a burden that destroyed some people and forced others to develop modes of survival. Slaves knew a life of poverty, coercion, toil, and resentment. They provided the physical strength, and much of the know-how, to build an agricultural empire. But their daily lives embodied the nation's most basic contradiction in the world's model republic: they were on the wrong side of a brutally unequal power relationship.

Southern slaves enjoyed few material comforts beyond the bare necessities. Although they generally

Slaves' Everyday Conditions

had enough to eat, their diet was plain and monotonous and lacking in nutrition. Clothing was plain, coarse, and inexpensive. Few slaves received more than one or two changes of clothing for hot and cold seasons and one blanket each winter. Children of both sexes ran naked in hot weather and wore long cotton shirts in winter. Many slaves had to go without shoes until December. Their bare feet were often symbolic of their status—one reason why, after freedom, many black parents were so anxious to provide their children with shoes.

Some of the richer plantations provided substantial houses, but the average slave lived in crude ac-

■ Thomas S. Noble's painting *The Last Sale of Slaves* depicts the public drama and family horror of slave auctions. Noble's work stimulated a heated newspaper debate in St. Louis over its abolitionist message. The sight of people treated as property and bills of sale signed on the table leave slavery's most haunting images.   (Missouri Historical Society, St. Louis)

commodations, usually one-room cabins. The gravest drawback of slave cabins was their unhealthfulness. Each dwelling housed one or two families. Crowding and lack of sanitation fostered the spread of infection and contagious diseases such as typhoid fever, malaria, and dysentery.

Hard work was the central fact of slaves' existence. The long hours and large work gangs that characterized Gulf Coast cotton districts operated almost like factories in the field. Overseers rang the morning bell before dawn. And as one woman recalled when interviewed in the 1930s, "it was way after sundown fore they could stop that field work. Then they had to hustle to finish their night work [such as watering livestock or cleaning cotton] in time for supper, or go to bed without it."

SLAVES' WORK ROUTINES

Working "from sun to sun" became a norm in much of the South. As one planter put it, slaves were the best labor because "you could command them and make them do what was right." Profit took precedence over paternalism. Slave women did heavy fieldwork, often as much as the men and even during pregnancy. Old people were kept busy caring for young children, doing light chores, or carding, ginning, and spinning cotton.

Slave children were the future of the system and were widely valued. In 1858 an unidentified slaveowner calculated that a slave girl he purchased in 1827 for $400 had three sons now worth $3,000 as his working field hands. Slave children gathered kindling, carried water to the fields, lifted cut sugar-cane stalks into carts, chased birds away from sprouting rice plants, and labored at many levels of cotton and tobacco production.

Incentives too were part of the labor regime and the master-slave relationship. Planters in the South Carolina and Georgia low country used a task system whereby slaves were assigned measured amounts of work to be performed in a given amount of time. So much cotton on a daily basis was to be picked or so many rows hoed or plowed in a particular slave's specified section. When their task and "clock time" was up, slaves' time was their own, for working in garden plots, tending to hogs, or even hiring out their own extra labor. The system's incentives afforded many slave families life-sustaining material benefits and personal space. From this experience, slaves often developed their own sense of property ownership.

Incentives notwithstanding, the slaveowner enjoyed a monopoly on force and violence. Whites throughout the South believed that slaves "can't be governed except with the whip." Evidence suggests that whippings were less frequent on small farms than on large plantations. But beatings symbolized authority to the master and tyranny to the slaves, who made them a benchmark for evaluating a master. In the words of former slaves, a good owner was one who did not "whip too much"; a bad owner "whipped till he's bloodied you and blistered you."

VIOLENCE AGAINST SLAVES

The master wielded virtually absolute authority on his plantation, and terrible abuses could and did occur. Courts did not recognize the word of chattel. Pregnant women were whipped, and there were burnings, mutilations, tortures, and murders. Yet physical cruelty may have been less prevalent in the United States than in other slaveholding parts of the New World. Especially in some of the sugar islands of the Caribbean, treatment was so poor and death rates so high that the heavily male slave population shrank. In the United States, by contrast, the slave population experienced a steady natural increase as births exceeded deaths.

The worst evil of American slavery was not its physical cruelty but the nature of slavery itself: coercion, belonging to another person, virtually no hope for mobility or change. A woman named Delia Garlic made the essential point: "It's bad to belong to folks that own you soul an' body. I could tell you 'bout it all day, but even then you couldn't guess the awfulness of it."

The great majority of American slaves retained their mental independence and self-respect despite their bondage. Contrary to popular belief at the time, they were not loyal partners in their own oppression. They had to be subservient and speak honeyed words to their masters, but they talked and behaved quite differently among themselves. The evidence of their resistant attitudes comes from their actions and their own life stories. In his autobiography (1845), Frederick Douglass wrote that most slaves, when asked about "their condition and the character of their masters, almost universally say they are contented, and that their masters are kind." Slaves did this, said Douglass, because they were governed by the maxim that "a still tongue makes a wise head," especially in the presence of unfamiliar people.

Some former slaves remembered warm feelings between masters and slaves, but the prevailing attitudes were distrust and antagonism.

SLAVE-MASTER RELATIONSHIPS

Slaves saw through acts of kindness. One woman said her mistress was "a mighty good somebody to belong to" but only "'cause she was raisin' us to work for her." Another observed that his master "fed us reg'lar on good, 'stantial food, just like you'd tend to your horse, if you had a real good one."

Slaves were alert to the thousand daily signs of their degraded status. One man recalled the general rule that slaves ate cornbread and owners ate biscuits. A former slave recalled, "Us catch lots of 'possums," but "the white folks at 'em." If the owner took his slaves' garden produce to town and sold it for them, the slaves often suspected him of pocketing part of the profits.

Suspicion often grew into hatred. When a yellow fever epidemic struck in 1852, many slaves saw it as God's retribution. An elderly ex-slave named Minnie Fulkes cherished the conviction that God was going to punish white people for their cruelty to blacks. She described the whippings that her mother had to endure, and then she exclaimed, "Lord, Lord, I hate white people and the flood waters goin' to drown some more."

Slave Culture

a people is always "more than the sum of its brutalization," wrote the African American novelist Ralph Ellison in 1967. The resource that enabled slaves to maintain hope and defiance was their culture: a body of beliefs, values, and practices born of their past and maintained in the present. As best they could, they built a community knitted together by stories, music, a religious worldview, leadership, the smells of their cooking, the sounds of their voices, and the tapping of their feet. Thus slaves endured and found loyalty and strength among themselves.

Slave culture changed significantly after 1800, as fewer and fewer slaves were African-born. By

AFRICAN CULTURAL SURVIVAL

the 1830s, the vast majority of slaves in the South were native-born Americans.

Despite lack of firsthand memory, African influences remained strong, especially in appearance and forms of expression. Some slave men plaited their hair into rows and fancy designs; slave women often wore their hair "in string"—tied in small bunches with a string or piece of cloth. A few men and many women wrapped their heads in kerchiefs of West African styles and colors.

Music, religion, and folktales were parts of daily life for most slaves. Borrowing partly from their African background, as well as forging new American folkways, they developed what scholars have called a "sacred world-view" that affected all aspects of work, leisure, and self-understanding. Slaves made musical instruments with carved motifs that resembled African stringed instruments. Their drumming and dancing followed African patterns that made whites marvel. One visitor to Georgia in the 1860s described a ritual dance of African origin: "A ring of singers is formed. . . . They then utter a kind of melodious chant, which gradually increases in strength, and in noise, until it fairly shakes the house."

Many slaves continued to believe in spirit possession. Their belief resembled the African concept of the living dead—the idea that deceased relatives visit the earth for many years until the process of dying is complete. Slaves also practiced conjuration and quasi-magical root medicine. By the 1850s, the most notable conjurers and root doctors were reputed to live in South Carolina, Georgia, Louisiana, and other isolated coastal areas with high slave populations.

These cultural survivals provided slaves with a sense of their separate past and special ways. Such practices and beliefs were not static "Africanisms" or mere "retentions." They were cultural adaptations, living traditions re-formed in the Americas in response to new experience. African American slaves in the Old South were a people forged by two centuries of cultural mixture in the Atlantic world, and the South itself melded many African and European cultural forces.

As they became African Americans, slaves also developed a sense of racial identity. In the colonial period, Africans had arrived in America from many different states and kingdoms, represented by distinctive languages, body markings, and traditions. Planters had used ethnic differences to create occupational hierarchies. By the early antebellum period, however, old ethnic identities were giving way as American slaves increasingly saw themselves as a single group unified by race. Africans had arrived in the

New World with virtually no concept of "race"; by the antebellum era, their descendants had learned that race was now the defining feature of their lives.

With the maturing of African American culture, more and more slaves adopted Christianity. But they fashioned Christianity into an instrument of support and resistance. Theirs was a religion of justice and deliverance, quite unlike the religious propaganda their masters directed at them. "You ought to have heard that preachin'," said one man. "'Obey your master and mistress, don't steal chickens and eggs and meat,' but nary a word about havin' a soul to save." Slaves believed that Jesus cared about their souls and their plight. For them, Christianity was a religion of personal and group salvation. Many slaves nurtured an unshakable belief that God would enter history and end their bondage. This faith—and the joy and emotional release that accompanied worship—sustained them.

Slaves' Religion and Music

Slaves also adapted Christianity to African practices. In West African belief, devotees are possessed by a god so thoroughly that the god's own personality replaces the human personality. In the late antebellum era, Christian slaves experienced possession by the Protestant "Holy Spirit." The combination of shouting, singing, and dancing that seemed to overtake black worshipers formed the heart of their religious faith. "The old meeting house caught fire," recalled an ex-slave preacher. "The spirit was there. . . . God saw our need and came to us." And out in brush arbors or in meetinghouses, slaves took in the presence of God and sang away their woes.

Rhythm and physical movement were crucial to slaves' religious experience. In their own preachers' chanted sermons, which reached out to gather the sinner into a narrative of meanings and cadences along the way to conversion, an American tradition was born. The chanted sermon was both a message from Scripture and a patterned form that required audience response punctuated by "yes sirs!" and "amens!" But it was in song that the slaves left their most sublime gift to American culture.

Tension and sudden change between sorrow and joy animates many of the slave songs: "Sometimes I feel like a motherless chile . . . / Sometimes I feel like an eagle in the air, / Spread my wings and fly, fly, fly!" Many songs also express a sense of intimacy and closeness with God. Some songs display an unmistak-

able rebelliousness, such as the enduring, "He said, and if I had my way / If I had my way, if I had my way, / I'd tear this building down!" And some spirituals reached for a collective sense of hope in the black community as a whole:

> O, gracious Lord! When shall it be,
> That we poor souls shall all be free;
> Lord, break them slavery powers—
> Will you go along with me?
> Lord break them slavery powers,
> Go sound the jubilee!

In many ways, American slaves converted the Christian God to themselves. They sought an alternative world in which they could live. In a thousand variations on the Br'er Rabbit folktales in which the weak survive by wit and power is reversed, and in the countless refrains of their songs, they fashioned survival and resistance out of their cultural imagination.

American slaves clung tenaciously to the personal relationships that gave meaning to life. Although American law did not recognize slave families, masters permitted them; in fact, slaveowners expected slaves to form families and have children. As a result, even along the rapidly expanding edge of the cotton kingdom, there was a normal ratio of men to women, young to old.

The Black Family in Slavery

Following African kinship traditions, African Americans avoided marriage between cousins. By naming their children after relatives of past generations, African Americans emphasized their family histories. If they chose to bear the surname of a slaveowner, it was often the name of the owner under whom their family had begun their bondage in America.

For slave women, sexual abuse and rape by white masters were ever-present threats. By 1860 there were 405,751 mulattos in the United States, 12.5 percent of the African American population, and the majority were the offspring of involuntary relationships. Buying slaves for sex was all too common at the New Orleans slave market. In what was called the "fancy trade" (a "fancy" was a young attractive slave girl or woman), females were often sold for prices as much as 300 percent higher than the average. At such auctions for young women, slaveholders exhibited some of the ugliest values at the heart of the slave system.

Slave women had to negotiate this confused world of desire, threat, and shame. Harriet Jacobs spent much of her youth and early adult years dodging her owner's relentless sexual pursuit. In recollecting her desperate effort to protect her children, Jacobs asked a haunting question that many slave women carried with them to their graves: "Why does the slave ever love? Why allow the tendrils of the heart to twine around objects which may at any moment be wrenched away by the hand of violence?"

Separation from those they loved by violence, sexual appropriation, and sale was what slave families feared and hated most. Many

THE DOMESTIC SLAVE TRADE

struggled for years to keep their children together and, after emancipation, to reestablish contact with loved ones lost by forced migration and sale. Between 1820 and 1860, an estimated 2 million slaves were moved into the region extending from western Georgia to eastern Texas. When the Union Army registered thousands of black marriages in Mississippi and Louisiana in 1864 and 1865, fully 25 percent of the men over age forty reported that they had been forcibly separated from a previous wife.

Many antebellum white southerners made their living from the slave trade. In South Carolina alone, by the 1850s there were over one hundred slave-trading firms selling an annual average of approximately 6,500 slaves to southwestern states. Although southerners often denied it, vast numbers of slaves moved west by outright sale, not by migrating with their owners.

Slave traders were practical, roving businessmen. They were sometimes considered degraded by white planters, but many slaveowners did business with them. Traders did their utmost to make their slaves appear young, healthy, and happy, cutting gray whiskers off men and forcing people to dance and sing as buyers arrived for an auction. When transported to the southwestern markets, slaves were often chained together in "coffles," which made journeys of 500 miles or more on foot.

The complacent mixture of racism and business among traders is evident in their own language. "I refused a girl 20 year[s] old at 700 yesterday," one trader wrote to another in 1853. "If you think best to take her at 700 I can still get her. She is very badly whipped but good teeth." Some sales were transacted at owners' requests. "Bought a cook yesterday that was to go out of state," wrote a trader; "she just made the people mad that was all."

Slave Resistance and Rebellion

 laves brought to their efforts at resistance the same common sense and determination that characterized their struggle to secure their family lives. The scales were weighted heavily against overt revolution, and the slaves knew it. But they seized opportunities to alter their work and life conditions.

Sometimes slaves slacked off work when they were not being watched. Sometimes they manifested

STRATEGIES OF RESISTANCE

their discontent by sabotaging equipment, stealing food, or being wantonly careless about work. Many male, and some female, slaves acted out their defiance by violently attacking overseers or even their owners. Southern court records and newspapers are full of accounts of these resistant slaves who gave the lie to the image of docile bondsmen. The price they paid was high. Such lonely rebels were customarily secured and flogged, sold away, or hanged.

Many individual slaves attempted to run away to the North, and some received assistance from the loose network known as the Underground Railroad (discussed in the next chapter). But it was more common for slaves to run off temporarily and hide in the woods. Approximately 80 percent of runaways were male; women could not flee as readily because of their responsibility for children. Fear, disgruntlement over treatment, or family separation might motivate slaves to risk all in flight. Only a minority of those who tried such escapes ever made it to freedom in the North or Canada.

American slavery produced some fearless revolutionaries. Gabriel's Rebellion involved as many as a thousand slaves when it was discovered in 1800 (see Chapter 8). According to controversial court testimony, a similar conspiracy existed in Charleston in 1822, led by a free black named Denmark Vesey. According to one long-argued interpretation, Vesey was a heroic revolutionary determined to free his people or die trying. But in a recent challenge, historian Michael Johnson points out that the court testimony is the only reliable source on the alleged insurrection. The court, says Johnson, built its case on rumors and intimidated witnesses, and "conjured into being" an insurrection not about to occur in reality. Whatever the facts, when the arrests and trials were over, thirty-seven "conspirators" were executed, and more than three dozen others were banished from the state.

Online Study Center   Improve Your Grade
Interactive Map: Escaping from Slavery

The most famous rebel of all, Nat Turner, struck for freedom in Southampton County, Virginia, in

NAT TURNER'S
INSURRECTION

1831. The son of an African woman who passionately hated her enslavement, Nat Turner was a precocious child who learned to read when he was very young. Encouraged by his first owner to study the Bible, he enjoyed certain privileges but also endured hard work and changes of masters. His father successfully escaped to freedom.

Eventually young Nat became a preacher with a reputation for eloquence and mysticism. After nurturing his plan for several years, Turner led a band of rebels from farm to farm in the predawn darkness of August 22, 1831. The group severed limbs and crushed skulls with axes or killed their victims with guns. Before they were stopped, Turner and his followers had slaughtered sixty whites of both sexes and all ages in forty-eight hours. The rebellion was put down, Turner hanged, and an estimated two hundred African Americans, including innocent victims, killed by vengeful whites. In the wake of the insurrection, many states stiffened legal codes against black education and religious practices.

Harmony and Tension in a Slave Society

From 1830 to 1860, slavery impinged on laws and customs, individual values, and, increasingly, every aspect of southern politics. In all things, from their workaday movements to Sunday worship, slaves fell under the supervision of whites. State courts held that a slave "has no civil right" and could not hold property "except at the will and pleasure of his master." Revolts like Nat Turner's tightened the legal straitjacket even more. As political conflicts between North and South deepened, fears of slave re-

volt grew, and restrictions on slaves increased accordingly.

State and federal laws aided the capture of fugitive slaves and required nonslaveholders to support the slave system. All white male citizens had a legal duty to participate in slave patrols. Ship captains, harbor masters, and other whites were required to scrutinize the papers of African Americans who might be attempting to escape bondage.

Slavery deeply affected southern values precisely because it was the main determinant of wealth. Own-

SLAVERY,
WEALTH, AND
SOCIAL
STANDING

ership of slaves guaranteed the labor to produce cotton and other crops on a large scale. Slaves were a commodity and an investment, much like gold; people bought them on speculation, hoping for a steady rise in their market values. Wealth in slaves also translated into political power: a solid majority of political officeholders were slaveholders, and the most powerful were usually large-scale planters.

Slavery's influence spread throughout the social system until even the values and mores of nonslaveholders bore its imprint. The availability of slave labor tended to devalue free labor: where strenuous work under supervision was reserved for an enslaved race, few free people relished it. When Alexis de Tocqueville crossed from Ohio into Kentucky in his travels in 1831, he observed that on "the right bank of the Ohio [River] everything is activity, industry; labor is honoured; there are no slaves. Pass to the left bank and . . . the enterprising spirit is gone. There, work is not only painful; it is shameful." Tocqueville's own class impulses, however, were at home in the South, where he found a "veritable aristocracy."

The values of the aristocrat—lineage, privilege, pride, and refinement of person and manner—com-

ARISTOCRATIC
VALUES AND
FRONTIER
INDIVIDUALISM

manded respect throughout the South. Many of those qualities were in short supply, however, in the recently settled portions of the cotton kingdom, where the frontier values of courage and self-reliance ruled. Independence and defense of one's honor became highly valued traits for planter and frontier farmer alike. Thus, instead of gradually disappearing, as it did in the North, dueling, which required men to defend their honor through violence, lasted much longer in the South.

Other aristocratic values of the planter class were less acceptable to less wealthy whites. In their pride, planters expected not only to wield power but to receive deference from poorer whites. But the sternly independent yeoman class resented infringements of their rights. Also conscious of national democratic ideals, yeomen sometimes challenged or rejected the political pretensions of planters, whose claims to a republican ideal of white men leading other white men was built on a foundation of black slave labor.

Class tensions emerged in the western, nonslaveholding parts of the seaboard states by the 1830s.

YEOMAN DEMANDS AND WHITE CLASS RELATIONS

There, yeoman farmers resented their underrepresentation in state legislatures and the corruption in local government. After vigorous debate, the reformers won many battles. Voters in more recently settled states of the Old Southwest adopted white manhood suffrage and other electoral reforms, including popular election of governors, legislative apportionment based on white population only, and locally chosen county government.

Slaveowners knew that a more open government structure could permit troubling issues to arise. In Virginia, it was nonslaveholding westerners who petitioned and initiated the 1831–1832 debate over the gradual abolition of slavery in the wake of Nat Turner's Rebellion.

Given such tensions, why were class confrontations among whites so infrequent? One of the most important factors was race. The South's racial ideology stressed the superiority of all whites to blacks. Thus, slavery became the basis of equality among whites, and racism inflated the status of poor whites and gave them a common interest with the rich. Family ties also linked some nonslaveholders to wealthy planters, especially on the expanding frontier. And the Old South was a fluid society in which constant mobility and the westward-expanding cotton kingdom gave yeomen the hope of rising in status by acquiring land and slaves.

Most important, in their daily lives, yeomen and slaveholders were seldom in conflict. Before the Civil War, most yeomen were able to pursue their independent lifestyle unhindered. They worked their farms, avoided debt, and marked progress for their families that in their rural habitats was unrelated to slaveholding. Likewise, slaveholders pursued their goals quite independent of yeomen.

Suppression of dissent also played an increasing role. After 1830, white southerners who criticized the slave system out of moral conviction or class resentment were intimidated, attacked, or legally prosecuted. By the 1850s, the defense of slavery's interests exerted an ever more powerful influence on southern politics and society.

Still, there were signs that the relative lack of conflict between slaveholders and nonslaveholders

HARDENING OF CLASS LINES

was coming to an end in the late antebellum period. As cotton lands filled up, nonslaveholders saw their opportunities beginning to narrow; meanwhile, wealthy planters enjoyed expanding profits. The risks of entering cotton production were becoming too great and the cost of slaves too high for many yeomen to rise in society. From 1830 to 1860, the percentage of white southern families holding slaves declined steadily from 36 to 25 percent. Yet with slaveowners a smaller portion of the population, planters continued to own 90 to 95 percent of the South's agricultural wealth.

Urban artisans and mechanics felt the pinch acutely. Their numbers were few, and in bad times, they were often the first to lose work as markets collapsed. Moreover, they faced stiff competition from urban slaves, whose masters wanted to hire them out to practice trades. White workers protested, demanding that economic competition from slaves be forbidden, but they were ignored. However, their angry protests resulted in harsh restrictions on free African American laborers and craftsmen. Pre–Civil War politics reflected these tensions as well. Anticipating possible secession and the prospect of a war to defend slavery, slaveowners expressed growing fear about the loyalty of nonslaveholders. Schemes to widen the ownership of slaves were discussed, including reopening the African slave trade. In North Carolina, a bitter controversy erupted over the combination of high taxes on land and low taxes on slaves. When nonslaveholder Hinton R. Helper denounced the slave system in *The Impending Crisis*, published in 1857, discerning planters feared the eruption of such controversies in every southern state.

But for the moment slaveowners stood secure. In the 1850s, they occupied from 50 to 85 percent of the seats in state legislatures and a similarly high percentage of the South's congressional seats. Planters' interests controlled all the other major social institutions. Professors who criticized slavery had been dismissed; schoolbooks that contained "unsound" ideas had been replaced. And almost all the Methodist and Baptist clergy had become slavery's most vocal defenders.

Summary *Online Study Center* ACE the Test

During the thirty years before the Civil War, the South grew as part of America's westward expansion. Ideologically and economically, the southern states developed in many distinctive ways; at the same time, they were also deeply enmeshed in the nation's heritage and political economy. Far more than the North, the antebellum South was a biracial society; whites grew up directly influenced by black folkways and culture, and blacks, the vast majority of whom were slaves, became predominantly native-born Americans and the cobuilders with whites of a rural, agricultural society. From the Old South on to modern times, white and black southerners have always shared a tragic, mutual history.

With the sustained cotton boom, the South grew fatefully into a much larger slave society than it had been early in the century. The coercive influence of slavery affected virtually every element of southern life and politics. Despite the white supremacy that united them, the democratic values of yeomen often clashed with the profit motives of aristocratic planters. The benevolent self-image and paternalistic ideology of slaveholders ultimately had to stand the test of the slaves' own judgments. African American slaves responded by fashioning over time a rich, expressive folk culture and a religion of personal and group deliverance.

By 1850, through their own wits and on the backs of African labor, white southerners had aggressively built one of the last profitable, expanding slave societies on earth. North of them, deeply intertwined with them in the same nation, market economy, constitutional system, and history, a different kind of society had grown even faster—one driven by industrialism and free labor. The clash of these two deeply connected yet divided societies was about to explode in political storms over how the nation would define its future.

LEGACY FOR A PEOPLE AND A NATION
Reparations for Slavery

How should the United States come to terms with 250 years of racial slavery? Does the nation owe a long-overdue debt to black people for their oppression?

In the wake of emancipation in 1865 and rooted in vague federal promises, many former slaves believed they were entitled to "forty acres and a mule," but these never materialized. As the leader of a planters' association put it in 1865, "The emancipated slaves own nothing, because nothing but freedom has been given to them."

Recently a widespread debate over "reparations" for slavery has emerged. Since the 1960s, Americans have learned a great deal about how slave labor created American wealth: how insurance companies insured slaves, how complicitous the U.S. government was in slavery's defense and expansion, and how slaves built the U.S. Capitol while their owners received $5 a month for their labor.

The debate is fueled by a wealth of analogies: the reparations paid to Japanese Americans interned in World War II, the reparations paid to several Native American tribes for their stolen land, and a suit settled in 1999 that will pay an estimated $2 billion to some twenty thousand black farmers for discrimination practiced by the Agriculture Department in the early twentieth century.

On the other side, some argue that because there are no living former slaves or slaveholders, reparations for slavery can never take the form of money. But in 2002, a lawsuit was filed against three major corporations that allegedly profited from slavery, and the National Reparations Coordinating Committee promises a suit against the

U.S. government itself. Critics argue that resources would be better spent "making sure black kids have a credible education" and in rebuilding inner cities. The movement for reparations has strong support in grassroots black communities, and the issue has become the subject of a broad public debate. The legacy of slavery for a people and a nation promises to become America's most traumatic test of how to reconcile its history with justice.

SLAVERY AND AMERICA'S FUTURE: THE ROAD TO WAR 1845–1861

*T*he delegates who filed into the Musical Fund Hall in Philadelphia on June 17, 1856, knew they had created something special in American politics. The first national nominating convention of the Republican Party met to approve a platform and select their presidential ticket. Formed just two years earlier, in 1854, the party drew together a broad coalition of northern politicians who opposed the expansion of slavery and the growing power of the South in the federal government. Republicans had come to Philadelphia to offer the American electorate a genuinely antislavery future.

Their coalition combined former Democrats; former founding members of the American Party, a group that wanted to prohibit foreigners, especially Catholics, from settling in the United States; and many former Whigs, whose party had been shattered by the crisis over slavery and its expansion. They consisted of conservatives, moderates, and radicals; some believed slavery a moral evil, while others saw it as a political problem.

At this convention, a radical temper prevailed. The convention was only minutes old when the temporary chairman used the Declaration of Independence to label slavery a great political danger to the nation's future. Speaker after speaker declared that their party would render "freedom national" and "slavery sectional" by using the power of Congress to outlaw human bondage in all western territories.

The convention's platform committee was chaired by David Wilmot, a former Democrat who was no friend of black civil and political rights. But Wilmot, like the others, was firmly opposed to slavery's expansion and endorsed the protection of free white men's labor and landownership across the continent. At the heart of the platform was the short, direct credo calling on Congress to "prohibit in the territories those twin relics of barbarism—polygamy and slavery." The Republicans nominated John C. Frémont, the

The War with Mexico and Its Consequences

1850: Compromise or Armistice?

Slavery Expansion and Collapse of the Party System

LINKS TO THE WORLD Annexation of Cuba

Slavery and the Nation's Future

Disunion

LEGACY FOR A PEOPLE AND A NATION *Terrorist or Freedom Fighter?*

Online Study Center
This icon will direct you to interactive map and primary source activities on the website http://college.hmco.com/ pic/nortonbrief7e

C H R O N O L O G Y

1846 • War with Mexico begins
• Oregon Treaty negotiated
• Wilmot Proviso inflames sectional divisions

1847 • Cass proposes idea of popular sovereignty

1848 • Treaty of Guadalupe Hidalgo gives United States new territory in the Southwest
• Free-Soil Party formed
• Taylor elected president

1849 • Gold discovered in California, which applies for admission to Union as free state

1850 • Compromise of 1850 passed in separate bills

1852 • Stowe publishes *Uncle Tom's Cabin*
• Pierce elected president

1854 • Kansas-Nebraska Act wins approval and ignites controversy
• Republican Party formed
• Return of fugitive Burns from Boston to slavery in Virginia

1856 • Bleeding Kansas troubles nation
• Brooks attacks Sumner in Senate chamber

• Buchanan elected president, but Republican Frémont wins most northern states

1857 • *Dred Scott v. Sandford* endorses southern views on black citizenship and slavery in territories
• Economic panic and widespread unemployment begins

1858 • Kansas voters reject Lecompton Constitution

1859 • Brown raids Harpers Ferry

1860 • Democratic Party splits in two; southern Democrats demand "Slave Code for the Territories"
• Lincoln elected president
• Crittenden Compromise fails
• South Carolina secedes from Union

1861 • Six more Deep South states secede
• Confederacy established at Montgomery, Alabama
• Attack on Fort Sumter begins Civil War
• Four states in the Upper South join the Confederacy

famous western explorer and former California senator, for president. In the election that followed, Americans began to vote by section and not by party as never before. The Republican coalition began to unify the North around keeping the West free and alarmed the South, which now saw the future of its slave society endangered by a political movement determined to limit, if not destroy, slavery. Frémont lost the 1856 election, but the Republicans made the best showing a newly born party ever had in its first presidential bid.

Meanwhile, in Kansas territory, open warfare had exploded between proslavery and antislavery settlers. On the floor of the U.S. Senate, a southern representative beat a northern senator senseless. A new fugitive slave law sent thousands of blacks, fearing for their liberty and their lives, fleeing to Canada. The tradition of compromise on political problems related to slavery teetered on the brink of complete collapse. Within a year the Supreme Court had issued a dramatic decision about slavery, its constitutionality in westward expansion, and the status of African American citizenship—to the delight of most southerners and the dread of most northerners. And abolitionist John Brown was planning a raid into Virginia to start a slave rebellion.

The political culture of the American republic was disintegrating. As the 1850s advanced, slavery pulled Americans, North and South, into a maelstrom that its best statesmen ultimately could not subdue. A prosperous nation, riven by stark contradictions, was on the road to a terrible war.

Slavery had aroused passions that could be neither contained nor resolved. What began as a dark cloud over the territories became a storm engulfing the nation. Between 1845 and 1853, the United States added Texas, California, Oregon Country, and the Southwest to its domain and launched the settlement of the Great Plains. Each time the nation expanded, it confronted a thorny issue: should new territories and states be slave or free?

The ensuing political storms gave rise to a feeling in both North and South that America's future was at stake. The new Republican Party believed that America's future depended on the unbound labor of free men. They charged southerners with using the power of the federal government to make slavery legal throughout the Union. Southern leaders defended slavery and charged the North with unconstitutional efforts to destroy it. For blacks, the growing dispute brought hope and despair. They could take heart that the country's political strife over slavery might somehow lead to their liberation. But in a nation now trying to define its future, blacks had to wonder whether they had a future at all in America. ■

The War with Mexico and Its Consequences

In the 1840s, territorial expansion surged forward under the leadership of President James K. Polk. The annexation of Texas just before his inauguration did not necessarily make war with Mexico inevitable, but by design and through a series of calculated decisions, Polk brought the conflict on. Polk was determined to fulfill the nation's "manifest destiny" to rule the continent. He wanted Mexico's territory all the way to the Pacific, and all of Oregon Country as well.

During the 1844 campaign, Polk's supporters had threatened war with Great Britain to gain all of

OREGON

Oregon. As president, however, Polk turned first to diplomacy. Not wanting to fight Mexico and Great Britain at the same time, he tried to avoid bloodshed in the Northwest, where America and Britain had jointly occupied disputed territory since 1818. Dropping the demand for a boundary at latitude 54°40', he pressured the British to accept the 49th parallel. In 1846 Great Britain agreed. The Oregon Treaty gave the United States all of present-day Oregon, Washington, and Idaho and parts of Wyoming and Montana.

Toward Mexico, Polk was more aggressive. In early 1846, he ordered American troops to march

"MR. POLK'S WAR"

south and defend the contested border of the Rio Grande. Polk had earlier encouraged Texas to claim the Rio Grande as its southern and western border. He especially desired California as the prize in his expansionist strategy, and he attempted to buy from Mexico a huge tract of land extending to the Pacific. When that effort failed, Polk waited for war. Negotiations between troops on the Rio Grande proved fruitless. The situation became increasingly tense, and on April 24, 1846, Mexican cavalry ambushed a U.S. cavalry unit on the north side of the river; eleven Americans were killed and sixty-three taken captive.

Polk now drafted a message to Congress: Mexico had "passed the boundary of the United States, had invaded our territory and shed American blood on American soil." Polk deceptively declared that "war exists by the act of Mexico itself" and summoned the nation to arms. Two days later, on May 13, the House recognized a state of war with Mexico by a vote of 174 to 14, and the Senate by 40 to 2, with numerous abstentions. Some antislavery Whigs in Congress had tried to oppose the war but were barely allowed to speak. Since Polk withheld key facts, what had happened on the distant Rio Grande was not fully known. But the theory and practice of manifest destiny had launched the United States into its first major war on foreign territory.

The idea of war unleashed great public celebrations. Huge crowds gathered in southern cities to voice

FOREIGN WAR AND THE POPULAR IMAGINATION

support for the war effort. Twenty thousand Philadelphians and even more New Yorkers rallied in the same spirit. After news came of General Zachary Taylor's first two battlefield victories at Palo Alto and Resaca de la Palma, volunteers swarmed recruiting stations. The advent of daily newspapers, printed on new rotary presses, boosted sales by giving the war a romantic appeal.

Here was an adventurous war of conquest in a far-off, exotic land. Here was the fulfillment of Anglo-Saxon–Christian destiny to possess the North American continent and to take "civilization" to the "semi-Indian" Mexicans. For many, racism fueled the expansionist spirit. In 1846 an Illinois newspaper justified the war on the basis that Mexicans were "reptiles in the path of progressive democracy."

The war spawned an outpouring of poetry, song, drama, and lithographs that captured the popular imagination and glorified the conflict. Most of the war-inspired flowering in the popular arts was patriotic. But not everyone cheered. The abolitionist James Russell Lowell considered the war a "national crime committed in behoof of slavery, our common sin." Even proslavery spokesman John C. Calhoun saw the

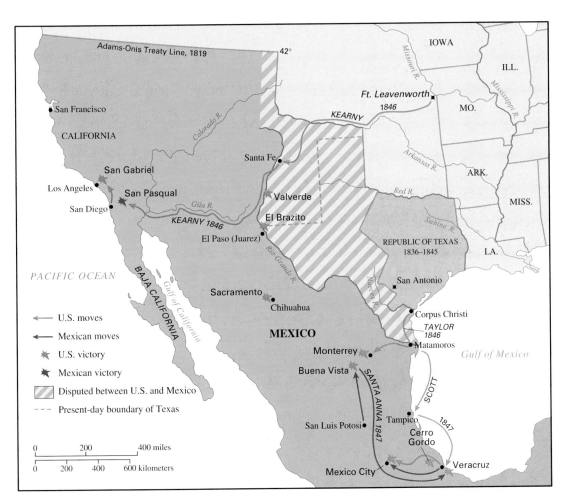

Map 14.1   The War with Mexico

This map shows the territory disputed between the United States and Mexico. After U.S. gains in northeastern Mexico and in New Mexico and California, General Winfield Scott captured Mexico City in the decisive campaign of the war.

perils of expansionism. Mexico, he said, was "the forbidden fruit; the penalty of eating it would be to subject our institutions to political death."

U.S. forces made significant gains early in the war. In May 1846 Colonel Stephen Kearny and a

CONQUEST

small detachment invaded the remote and thinly populated provinces of New Mexico and California. Taking Santa Fe without opposition, Kearny pushed into California, where he joined forces with rebellious American settlers led by Captain John C. Frémont and with a couple of U.S. naval units. General Zachary Taylor's forces attacked and occupied Monterrey, which surrendered in September, securing northeastern Mexico (see Map 14.1). American soldiers established dominion over distant California before the end of 1846. General Winfield Scott now carried the war to the enemy's heartland. Landing at Veracruz, he led fourteen thousand men toward Mexico City. After a series of hard-fought battles, U.S. troops captured the Mexican capital.

Representatives of both countries signed the Treaty of Guadalupe Hidalgo in February 1848. The

TREATY OF GUADALUPE HIDALGO

United States gained California and New Mexico (including present-day Nevada, Utah, and Arizona and parts of Colorado and Wyoming) and recognition of the Rio Grande as the southern boundary of Texas. In return, the American government agreed to settle the claims of its citizens against Mexico ($3.2 million) and pay Mexico a mere $15 million. On the day Polk received the treaty from the Senate, a mob in Paris forced Louis Philippe to abdicate the throne of France. As the 1848 nationalistic revolutions against monarchy spread to Italy, Austria, Hungary, and Germany, republican America seized an empire.

The costs of the war included the deaths of thirteen thousand Americans and fifty thousand Mexicans and U.S.-Mexican enmity that endured into the twentieth century. The war also sharply divided public opinion in the United States. Southwesterners were enthusiastic, as were most southern planters; New Englanders strenuously opposed the war. Whigs in Congress charged that Polk, a Democrat, had "provoked" an unnecessary war and "usurped the power of Congress." An Illinois Whig named Abraham Lincoln called Polk's justifications the "half insane mumbling of a fever-dream."

These charges fed northern fear of the so-called Slave Power. Abolitionists had long warned of a slave-

"SLAVE POWER CONSPIRACY"

holding oligarchy that controlled the South and intended to dominate the nation through its hold on federal power. These dangerous aristocrats had forced the gag rule on Congress in 1836 and threatened northern liberties. To many white northerners, even those who saw nothing wrong with slavery, it was the battle over free speech that first made the idea of a Slave Power credible. The War with Mexico deepened such fears. Had this questionable war, asked antislavery northerners, not been launched for vast, new slave territory?

Northern opinion on the expansion of slavery began to shift, but the impact of the war on southern opinion was even more dramatic. At first some southern leaders criticized the War with Mexico, and few southern congressmen saw slavery as the paramount issue. Many whites in both North and South feared that large land seizures would bring thousands of nonwhite Mexicans into the United States and upset the racial order. An Indiana politician did not want "any mixed races in our Union, nor men of any color except white, unless they be slaves." Despite their racism, however, many statesmen soon saw other prospects in the outcomes of the war.

In August 1846, David Wilmot, a Pennsylvania Democrat, proposed an amendment, or proviso, to

WILMOT PROVISO

a military appropriations bill: that "neither slavery nor involuntary servitude shall ever exist" in any territory gained from Mexico. Although the proviso never passed both houses of Congress, it transformed the debate. Southerners suddenly circled their wagons to protect the future of a slave society. John C. Calhoun asserted a radical new southern position. The territories, Calhoun insisted, belonged to all the states, and the federal government could do nothing to limit the spread of slavery there. Southern slaveholders had a constitutional right rooted in the Fifth Amendment, Calhoun claimed, to take their slaves (as property) anywhere in the territories.

This position, often called "state sovereignty," was a radical reversal of history. In 1787 the Confederation Congress had excluded slavery from the Northwest Territory; Article IV of the federal Constitution had authorized Congress to make "all needful rules and regulations" for the territories, and the Missouri Compromise had barred slavery from most of the Louisiana Purchase. Now, however, southern leaders demanded protection and future guarantees for slavery.

In the North, the Wilmot Proviso became a rallying cry for abolitionists. Eventually the legislatures of fourteen northern states endorsed it—and not because all its supporters were abolitionists. David Wilmot, significantly, was neither an abolitionist nor an antislavery Whig. His goal was to defend "the rights of white freemen" and to obtain California "for free white labor."

Fear of the Slave Power, however, was building a potent antislavery movement that united abolitionists and antiblack voters. At stake was an abiding version of the American Dream: the free individual's access to social mobility through opportunities in the West and the sacred ideal of free labor. Slave labor, thousands of northerners had come to believe, would degrade the honest toil of free men and render them unemployed and propertyless. The West must therefore be kept free of slaves and open to free white men.

The slavery question could not be kept out of national politics. After Polk renounced a second term as

THE ELECTION OF 1848 AND POPULAR SOVEREIGNTY

president, the Democrats nominated Senator Lewis Cass of Michigan for president. Cass, a party loyalist, had devised in 1847 the idea of "popular sovereignty" for the territories—letting residents in the territories decide the question of slavery for themselves. His party's platform declared that Congress lacked the power to interfere with slavery. The Whigs nominated General Zachary Taylor, a southern slaveholder and war hero. The Whig convention similarly refused to assert that Congress had power over slavery in the territories.

New York Democrats committed to the Wilmot Proviso rebelled against Cass and nominated former president Martin Van Buren. Antislavery Whigs and former supporters of the Liberty Party then joined them to organize the Free-Soil Party, with Van Buren as its candidate. This party, whose slogan was "Free Soil, Free Speech, Free Labor, and Free Men," won almost 300,000 northern votes. Taylor polled 1.4 million votes to Cass's 1.2 million and won the White House, but the results were more ominous than decisive. The war with Mexico turned the political issue of slavery expansion into a moral issue. Politics had split along sectional lines as never before. Religious denominations too were splitting into northern and southern wings. As the 1850s dawned, the legacies of the Mexican War and the conflicts of 1848 dominated national life and threatened the nature of the Union itself.

1850: Compromise or Armistice?

The first sectional battle of the new decade involved California. More than eighty thousand Americans flooded into California during the gold rush of 1849. With Congress unable to agree on a formula to govern the territories, President Taylor urged these settlers to apply directly for admission to the Union. They promptly did so, proposing a state constitution that banned slavery. Southern politicians objected because California's admission as a free state would upset the equal balance of fifteen free and fifteen slave states in the Senate. At a minimum, southerners wanted the Missouri Compromise line extended to the Pacific.

Henry Clay, the venerable Whig leader, sensed that the Union was in peril. Twice before—in 1820

DEBATE OVER SLAVERY IN THE TERRITORIES

and 1833—Clay had taken the lead in shaping sectional compromise; now he struggled one last time to preserve the nation. Clay presented a series of compromise measures in the winter of 1850. Over the weeks that followed, he and Senator Stephen A. Douglas of Illinois steered their omnibus bill, or compromise package, through debate and amendment.

The package addressed difficult problems. Would California, or part of it, become a free state? How should the territory acquired from Mexico be organized? Texas, a slave state, claimed large portions of it as far west as Santa Fe. Southerners complained that fugitive slaves were not being returned as the Constitution required, and northerners objected to the sale of human beings in the nation's capital. Most troublesome of all was the status of slavery in the territories.

In Lewis Cass's idea of popular sovereignty Clay and Douglas discovered what one historian called a "charm of ambiguity" that appealed to practical politicians. Ultimately Congress would have to approve statehood for a territory, but "in the meantime," said Cass, it should allow the people living there "to regulate their own concerns in their own way."

Those simple words proved all but unenforceable. When could settlers prohibit slavery? To avoid dissension within their party, northern and southern Democrats explained Cass's statement to their constituents in two incompatible ways. Southerners claimed that neither Congress nor a territorial legislature could bar slavery. Only late in the territorial process, when settlers were ready to draft a state constitution, could they take that step. Northerners, however, insisted that Americans living in a territory were entitled to local self-government and thus could outlaw slavery at any time.

The cause of compromise gained a powerful supporter when Senator Daniel Webster committed his prestige and eloquence to Clay's bill. "I wish to speak today," Webster declaimed on March 7, "not as a Massachusetts man, nor as a Northern man, but as an American. I speak today for the preservation of the Union." When, after months of labor, Clay and Douglas finally brought their legislative package to a vote, they lost. With Clay sick and absent from Washington, Douglas reintroduced the compromise measures one at a time. Although there was no majority for compromise, Douglas shrewdly realized that different majorities might be created for the separate measures. The strategy worked, and the Compromise of 1850 became law.

The compromise had five essential measures: California became a free state; the Texas boundary

COMPROMISE OF 1850 — was set at its present limits (see Map 14.2) and the United States paid Texas $10 million for the loss of New Mexico territory; the territories of New Mexico and Utah were organized on a basis of popular sovereignty; the fugitive slave law was strengthened; and the slave trade was abolished in the District of Columbia. Jubilation greeted passage of the compromise; crowds in Washington and other cities celebrated the happy news.

In reality, there was less cause for celebration than people hoped. As one historian has argued, the Compromise of 1850 was more an "armistice," delaying greater conflict, than a compromise. It had two basic flaws. The first concerned the ambiguity of ter-

ritorial legislation: how exactly was popular sovereignty to be enforced? Southerners insisted there would be no prohibition of slavery during the territorial stage, and northerners declared that settlers could bar slavery whenever they wished. The compromise even allowed the appeal of a territorial legislature's action to the Supreme Court.

The second flaw lay in the Fugitive Slave Act, which gave new—and controversial—protection to

FUGITIVE SLAVE ACT — slavery. The law empowered slaveowners to go into court in their own states to present evidence that a slave who owed them service had escaped. The resulting transcript and a description of the fugitive would then serve as legal proof of a person's slave status, even in free states and territories. Penalties made it a felony to harbor fugitives. And the fees paid to U.S. marshals favored slaveholders: $10 if the alleged fugitive was returned to the slaveowner, $5 if not returned.

Abolitionist newspapers quickly attacked the Fugitive Slave Act as a violation of fundamental American rights. Why were alleged fugitives denied a trial by jury? Why were they given no chance to present evidence or cross-examine witnesses? Why did the law give authorities a financial incentive to send suspected fugitives into bondage? These arguments led to protest meetings all over the North.

Between 1850 and 1854, violent resistance to slave catchers occurred in dozens of northern towns. Sometimes a captured fugitive was broken out of jail or taken from slave agents by abolitionists, as in the case of Shadrach Minkins in 1851 in Boston, who was spirited by a series of wagons and trains across Massachusetts, up through Vermont, to Montreal, Canada. Also in 1851, the small black community in Lancaster County, Pennsylvania, rose up in arms to defend four escaped slaves from a federal posse charged with reenslaving them. At this "Christiana riot," the fugitives shot and killed Edward Gorsuch, the Maryland slaveowner who sought the return of his "property."

At this point, a novel portrayed the humanity and suffering of slaves in a way that touched millions

UNCLE TOM'S CABIN — of northerners. Harriet Beecher Stowe, whose New England family had produced many prominent ministers, wrote *Uncle Tom's Cabin* out of deep moral conviction. Her story, serialized in 1851 and published as a book in 1852, conveyed the agonies that slave families faced. Stowe also portrayed slavery's evil effects on slaveholders, indicting the institution itself more harshly than she indicted the southerners caught in its web. By mid-1853, *Uncle Tom's Cabin* had sold over 1 million copies. Through her book, Stowe brought home the evil of slavery to many who had never before given it much thought.

The popularity of *Uncle Tom's Cabin* alarmed anxious southern whites. In politics and now in popular literature, they saw threats to their way of life. Behind the South's aggressive claims about territorial rights lay the fear that if nearby areas outlawed slavery, they would be used as bases from which to spread abolitionism into the slave states.

Slaveholders were especially disturbed by the 1850s over what was widely called the Underground

THE
UNDERGROUND
RAILROAD

Railroad. This loose, illegal network of civil disobedience, spiriting runaways to freedom in safe houses, had never been very organized. Thousands of slaves did escape by these routes, but largely through their own wits and courage and through the assistance of black vigilance committees in some northern cities.

Online Study Center

Improve Your Grade
Primary Source: Levi Coffin Remembers the Underground Railroad

Moreover, Harriet Tubman, herself an escapee in 1848, returned to her native Maryland and to Virginia nearly twenty times, and through clandestine measures helped as many as three hundred slaves to freedom. Maryland planters were so outraged at her heroic success that they offered a $40,000 reward for her capture.

In Ohio numerous white abolitionists joined with blacks as agents of slave liberation at various points along the river border between slavery and freedom. The Underground Railroad also had numerous maritime routes out of Virginia and the Carolinas and from New Orleans. Some slaves who escaped by sea went to the Caribbean or to England. Many had escaped over the decades to Florida and across the Mexican border. In Mexico they entered a country that had abolished slavery; in Florida many were fully assimilated into the Seminole communities. This constant, dangerous flow of humanity was a testament to

■ In *Still Life of Harriet Tubman with Bible and Candle*, we see the youthful, calm, determined leader of the Underground Railroad. Appearing gentle, Tubman was in her own way a revolutionary who liberated nearly three hundred of her people.   (© psihoyos.com)

human courage and the will for freedom. It never reached the scale that some angry slaveholders believed or that of the countless safe houses and hideaways claimed by hundreds of northern towns and local historical societies today. But in reality and in legend, the Underground Railroad emphasized the slavery crisis and provided slaves with a focus for hope.

The 1852 election gave southern leaders hope for the security of slavery. Franklin Pierce, a Democrat from New Hampshire, handily de-

ELECTION OF
1852 AND THE
COLLAPSE OF
COMPROMISE

feated the Whig nominee, General Winfield Scott. Pierce defended each section's rights as essential to the nation's unity, and southerners hoped that his firm support for the

Compromise of 1850 might end the season of crisis. His easy victory suggested widespread support for the compromise.

Pierce's victory, however, derived less from his strengths than from the Whig Party's weakness. The Whigs were a congressional and state-based party that never had achieved much success in presidential politics. By 1852 sectional discord had rendered the Whig Party all but dead.

President Pierce's embrace of the compromise appalled many northerners. His actions in a fugitive slave case provoked outrage and fear of the Slave Power. The slave Anthony Burns had fled Virginia by stowing away on a ship in 1852. In heavily abolitionist Boston, Burns began a new life. But in 1854 federal marshals found and placed him under guard in Boston's courthouse. An interracial crowd of abolitionists attacked the courthouse, killing a jailer, in an unsuccessful attempt to free Burns.

Pierce moved decisively to enforce the Fugitive Slave Act. He telegraphed local officials to "incur any expense to insure the execution of the law" and sent federal forces to Boston. U.S. troops marched Burns to Boston harbor through streets draped in black. At a cost of $100,000, a single black man was returned to slavery through the power of federal law.

This demonstration of federal support for slavery radicalized opinion. Textile manufacturer Amos A. Lawrence observed that "we went to bed one night old fashioned, conservative, Compromise Union Whigs & waked up stark mad Abolitionists." In New England, states began to pass personal-liberty laws absolving local judges from enforcing the Fugitive Slave Act, in effect nullifying federal authority. What northerners now saw as evidence of a dominating Slave Power, outraged slaveholders saw as the legal defense of their rights.

Pierce seemed unable to avoid sectional conflict in other arenas as well. His proposal for a transcontinental railroad derailed when congressmen fought over its location, North or South. His attempts to acquire foreign territory stirred more trouble. An annexation treaty with Hawai'i failed because southern senators would not vote for another free state, and efforts to acquire slaveholding Cuba angered northerners. In the Pacific, Commodore Matthew Perry's mission to establish trade relations with the Japanese also caused division at home over just how far American expansion should extend. In 1854 Perry negotiated two

ports as coaling stations for American ships, but trading arrangements were slow in coming. Then another territorial bill embroiled Congress and the nation, and the Compromise of 1850 fell into complete collapse.

Slavery Expansion and Collapse of the Party System

The new controversy began in a surprising way. Stephen A. Douglas, one of the architects of the Compromise of 1850, introduced a bill to establish the Kansas and Nebraska Territories. Talented and ambitious for the presidency, Douglas was known for compromise, but he was willing to risk some controversy to benefit Illinois, his home state. A transcontinental railroad would encourage settlement of the Great Plains and stimulate the economy of Illinois, but no company would build it before Congress organized the territories it would cross. To promote the construction of such a railroad, Douglas introduced a bill that inflamed sectional passions.

The Kansas-Nebraska bill exposed the conflicting interpretations of popular sovereignty. Douglas's bill left "all questions pertaining to slavery in the Territories . . . to the people residing therein." Northerners and southerners, however, still disagreed violently over what territorial settlers could constitutionally do. Moreover, the Kansas and Nebraska Territories lay north of latitude 36°30', where the Missouri Compromise prohibited slavery (see Map 14.2). If popular sovereignty were to mean anything in Kansas and Nebraska, it had to mean that the Missouri Compromise was no longer in effect and that settlers could establish slavery there.

THE KANSAS-NEBRASKA BILL

Southern congressmen, anxious to establish slaveholders' right to take slaves into any territory, demanded an explicit repeal of the 36°30' limitation as the price of their support. During a carriage ride with Senator Archibald Dixon of Kentucky, Douglas debated the point at length. Finally he made an impulsive decision: "By God, Sir, you are right. I will incorporate it in my bill, though I know it will raise a hell of a storm."

His bill thus threw open to slavery land from which it had been prohibited for thirty-four years. Opposition from Free-Soilers and antislavery forces

Annexation of Cuba

One of the most contentious issues in antebellum American foreign relations was the annexation of Cuba. As a strategic bulwark against Britain and France in the Western Hemisphere, for its massive sugar wealth, and as a slave society that might reinforce the security of southern slavery, the Spanish-controlled island fired the imagination of manifest destiny.

In the early republic, Presidents Jefferson and Madison had explored acquisition. But until the 1840s, the United States officially supported Spanish rule for stability and the preservation of slavery. The prospect

This cartoon portrays Sam Houston, the famed Texan and proponent of American expansion, rowing the boat for a harpoonist in quest of the whale, Cuba. The dream of appropriating Cuba to the United States died very hard in the antebellum era. *Vanity Fair,* New York, June 1860. (© Bettmann/Corbis)

of slave insurrection and the spread of abolitionism drove many southerners and three Democratic administrations to shift course and pursue acquisition of Cuba. Slaveholding politicians viewed Cuba as critical to expansion; human bondage, they believed, had to expand southward and westward, or it might die.

In 1848 President Polk authorized $100 million to purchase Cuba. The Spanish foreign minister, however, bluntly refused. During the crisis over the Kansas-Nebraska Act in 1854, some southerners planned to seize Cuba by force. Although the expedition never embarked, its prospect outraged antislavery Republicans eager to halt slavery's expansion.

So did the Ostend Manifesto of October 1854. Written after a meeting among the American foreign ministers to Britain, France, and Spain, the document advocated conquest of Cuba if it could not be purchased. The ministers predicted that Cuba "would be Africanized and become a second St. Domingo, with all its attendant horrors to the white race." But antislavery northerners saw schemes of the "Slave Power." The Ostend controversy forced temporary abandonment of annexation efforts, but in 1858, President Buchanan reignited Cuba fever. A fierce Senate debate over yet another purchase offer in early 1859 ended in bitter division over the extension of slavery's domain.

"I want Cuba, and I know that sooner or later we must have it . . . for the planting or spreading of slavery," said Mississippian Albert G. Brown in 1858. Too many northerners, however, understood Brown's intentions. In America's links to the world, in this case only 90 miles from the Florida coast, just as in domestic affairs, the expansion of slavery poisoned the body politic.

was immediate and enduring. The titanic struggle in Congress lasted three and a half months. Douglas eventually prevailed: the bill became law in May 1854 by a vote that demonstrated the dangerous sectionalization of American politics.

But the storm was just beginning. Abolitionists charged sinister aggression by the Slave Power, and northern fears of slavery's influence deepened. Opposition to the Fugitive Slave Act grew dramatically; between 1855 and 1859, Connecticut, Rhode Island, Massachusetts, Michigan, Maine, Ohio, and Wisconsin passed personal-liberty laws. These laws enraged southern leaders by providing counsel for alleged fugitives and requiring trial by jury. More important was the devastating impact of the Kansas-Nebraska Act on political parties. The weakened Whig Party broke apart into northern and southern wings that could no longer cooperate nationally. The Democrats

survived, but their support in the North fell drastically in the 1854 elections.

Online Study Center **Improve Your Grade**
Interactive Map: The Kansas-Nebraska Act and Slavery Expansion, 1854

The beneficiary of northern voters' wrath was a new political party. During the summer and fall of 1854, antislavery Whigs and Democrats, Free-Soilers, and other reformers throughout the Old Northwest met to form the new Republican Party, dedicated to keeping slavery out of the territories. The influence of the Republicans rapidly spread to the East, and they won a stunning victory in the 1854 elections: in their first appearance on the ballot, Republicans captured a majority of northern House

BIRTH OF THE
REPUBLICAN
PARTY

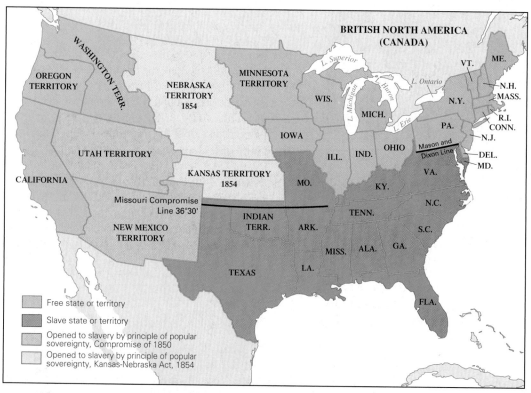

Map 14.2   The Kansas-Nebraska Act and Slavery Expansion, 1854

The vote on the Kansas-Nebraska Act in the House of Representatives demonstrates the sectionalization of American politics due to the slavery question.

seats. Antislavery sentiment had created a new party and caused roughly a quarter of northern Democrats to desert their party. For the first time, too, a sectional party had gained significant power in the political system. Now the Whigs were gone, and only the Democrats struggled to maintain national membership. The Republicans absorbed the Free-Soil Party and grew rapidly in the North. Indeed, the emergence of the Republican coalition of antislavery interests is the most rapid transformation in party allegiance and voter behavior in American history. This fact alone attests to the centrality of slavery expansion in the causation of the Civil War.

Republicans also drew into their coalition a fast-growing nativist movement that called itself the

KNOW-NOTHINGS American Party, or Know-Nothings (because its first members kept their purposes secret, answering, "I know nothing," to all questions). This group exploited nativist fear of foreigners and Catholics. Between 1848 and 1860, nearly 3.5 million immigrants entered the United States—proportionally the heaviest inflow of foreigners ever in American history.

In 1854 anti-immigrant fears gave the Know-Nothings spectacular success in some northern states. They triumphed especially in Massachusetts, electing 11 congressmen, a governor, all state officers, all state senators, and all but 2 of 378 state representatives. The temperance movement also gained new strength early in the 1850s with its promises to stamp out the evils associated with liquor and immigrants (a particularly anti-Irish campaign). In this context, the Know-Nothings strove to reinforce Protestant morality and restrict voting and officeholding to the native-born. But like the Whigs, the Know-Nothings could not keep their northern and southern wings together, and they dissolved after 1856.

With nearly half of the old electorate up for grabs, the demise of the Whig Party ensured a major realignment of the political system.

PARTY REALIGNMENT AND THE REPUBLICANS' APPEAL The remaining parties made appeals to various segments of the electorate. Immigration, temperance, homestead bills, the tariff, and internal improvements all played important roles in attracting voters during the 1850s. The Republicans appealed strongly to those interested in the economic development of the West. Commercial agriculture was booming in the Ohio–Mississippi–Great Lakes area, and residents of that region desired more canals, roads, and river and harbor improvements. They also favored a homestead program through which western land would be made available free to individual farmers. The Republicans seized on these political desires, promising internal improvements and land grants as well as backing higher tariffs for industrialists.

Partisan ideological appeals became the currency of the realigned political system. As Republicans preached "Free Soil, Free Labor, Free Men," they captured a self-image of many northerners. These phrases resonated with traditional ideals of equality, liberty, and opportunity.

"Free Soil, Free Labor, Free Men" seemed an appropriate motto for a northern economy that was energetic, expanding, and prosperous.

REPUBLICAN IDEOLOGY The key to progress appeared to many people to be free labor—the dignity of work and the incentive of opportunity. Any hard-working and virtuous man, it was thought, could improve his condition and achieve economic independence by seizing opportunities that the country had to offer. Republicans argued that the South, with little industry and slave labor, was backward and retrograde by comparison. Their arguments captured much of the spirit of the age in the North. Traditional republicanism hailed the virtuous common man as the backbone of the country. Republicans portrayed their party as the guardian of economic opportunity, giving individuals a chance to work, acquire land, and attain success.

At stake in the enveloping crises of the 1850s were thus two competing definitions of "liberty": southern planters' claims to protection of their liberty in the possession and transport of their slaves anywhere in the land, and northern workers' and farmers' claims to protection of their liberty to seek a new start on free land, unimpeded by a system that defined labor as slave and black. Thus, a growing number of northerners expressed the fear that the rising political storm was an "irrepressible conflict."

Opposition to the extension of slavery had brought the Republicans into being, but party members carefully broadened their appeal by adopting the causes of other groups. As the editor Horace Greeley wrote in 1860, "an Anti-Slavery man per se cannot be elected." But, he added, "a Tariff, River-and-Harbor,

Pacific Railroad, Free Homestead man, may succeed although he is Anti-Slavery." As these elements joined the Republican Party, they also grew to fear slavery even more.

In the South, the disintegration of the Whig Party had left many southerners at loose ends politi-

SOUTHERN
DEMOCRATS

cally. Some gravitated to the American Party, but not for long. In the increasingly tense atmosphere of sectional crisis, these people were highly susceptible to strong states' rights positions and defense of slavery. In the 1850s, most formerly Whig slaveholders converted to the Democrats.

Since Andrew Jackson's day, however, nonslave-holding small farmers had been the heart of the Democratic Party. Democratic politicians, though often slaveowners themselves, lauded the common man and argued that their policies advanced his interests. According to the southern version of republicanism, white citizens in a slave society enjoyed liberty and social equality because black people were enslaved. As Jefferson Davis put it in 1851, slavery elevated every white person's status and allowed the nonslave-holder to "stand upon the broad level of equality with the rich man." Southern Democrats warned that the issue was, "Shall negroes govern white men, or white men govern negroes?" They also portrayed the well-ordered South as the true defender of constitutional principles.

Racial fears and traditional political loyalties helped keep the political alliance between yeoman farmers and planters largely intact through the 1850s. Across class lines, white southerners joined together against what they perceived as the Republican Party's capacity to cause slave unrest in their midst. In the South, no viable party emerged to replace the Whigs. The result was a one-party system that emphasized sectional issues and loyalty. In the South as in the North, political realignment sharpened sectional identities.

Political leaders of both sections used race in their arguments about opportunity. The *Montgomery (Alabama) Mail* warned southern whites in 1860 that the Republicans intended "to free the negroes and force amalgamation between them and the children of the poor men of the South." Republicans warned northern workers that if slavery entered the territo-

ries, the great reservoir of opportunity for ordinary citizens would be poisoned.

In the territory of Kansas, the Kansas-Nebraska Act spawned hatred and violence. Abolitionists and religious groups sent in armed Free-Soil settlers; southerners sent in their reinforcements to establish slavery and prevent "northern hordes" from stealing Kansas away. Conflicts led to bloodshed, and soon the whole nation was talking about "Bleeding Kansas."

Politics in the territory resembled war more than democracy. During elections for a territorial legisla-

BLEEDING
KANSAS

ture in 1855, thousands of proslavery Missourians invaded the polls and ran up a large fraudulent majority for slavery candidates. The resulting legislature legalized slavery, and in response Free-Soilers held an unauthorized convention at which they created their own government and constitution. In the spring of 1856, a proslavery posse sent to arrest the Free-Soil leaders sacked the Kansas town of Lawrence, killing several people. In revenge, John Brown, a radical abolitionist, and some followers murdered five proslavery settlers living along Pottawatomie Creek. Soon, armed bands of guerrillas roamed the territory.

These passions brought violence to the U.S. Senate in May 1856, when Charles Sumner of Massachusetts denounced "the Crime against Kansas." Radical in his antislavery views, Sumner bitterly assailed the president, the South, and Senator Andrew P. Butler of South Carolina. Soon after, Butler's cousin, Representative Preston Brooks, approached Sumner at the latter's Senate desk, raised his cane, and beat Sumner on the head until he collapsed, bleeding, to the floor.

Shocked northerners recoiled from what they saw as another southern assault on free speech and proof of southerners' readiness to use violence. Popular opinion in Massachusetts supported Sumner; voters in South Carolina reelected Brooks and sent him dozens of commemorative canes. The country was becoming polarized.

The election of 1856 showed how extreme that polarization had become. The Democrats chose James Buchanan of Pennsylvania, whose chief virtue was that for the past four years, he had been ambassador to Britain and uninvolved in territorial controversies. Superior party organization helped Buchanan win the election, but he owed his victory to southern support. The Republican candidate, John C. Frémont, won eleven of sixteen free states; Republicans had become the dominant party in the North. The Know-Nothing candidate, Millard Fillmore, won almost 1 million votes in that party's last hurrah. The coming battle, with voter turnouts as high as 75 to 80 percent in many states, would pit a sectional Republican Party against an increasingly divided Democratic Party.

Slavery and the Nation's Future

For years the issue of slavery in the territories had convulsed Congress, which had tried to settle the issue with vague formulas. In 1857 a different branch of government, the Supreme Court, stepped into the fray and attempted to silence controversy with a definitive verdict.

A Missouri slave named Dred Scott had sued his owner for his freedom. Scott based his claim on the fact that his former owner, an army surgeon, had taken him for several years into Illinois, a free state, and into the Wisconsin Territory, from which slavery had been barred by the Missouri Compromise. Scott first won but then lost his case as it moved on appeal through the state courts, into the federal system, and finally to the Supreme Court.

DRED SCOTT CASE

This case involved substantive issues related to slavery and its extension in the territories, which Chief Justice Roger B. Taney of Maryland addressed when, in March 1857, he delivered the majority opinion of a divided Court. Taney declared that as a black slave, Scott was not a citizen of either the United States or Missouri and so was ineligible to sue in federal court; that residence in free territory did not make Scott free; and that Congress had no power to bar slavery from any territory. The decision not only overturned a sectional compromise (the Missouri Compromise of 1820) that had been honored for thirty-seven years; it also invalidated the basic ideas of the Wilmot Proviso and popular sovereignty.

The Slave Power seemed to have won a major constitutional victory. African Americans were especially dismayed, for Taney's decision asserted that the nation's founders had never intended for black people to be citizens, regarding them, the chief justice

wrote, "as beings of an inferior order" with "no rights which the white man was bound to respect." Taney was mistaken; African Americans had been citizens in several of the original states and had voted.

Nevertheless, the ruling seemed to shut the door permanently on black hopes for justice and equal rights. In northern black communities, rage and despair prevailed. Many who were still fugitive slaves sought refuge in emigration to Canada, the Caribbean, or even Africa. One black abolitionist said the *Dred Scott* decision had made slavery "the supreme law of the land and all descendants of the African race denationalized." Uncertain and fearful, blacks contemplated whether they had any future in America.

A storm of angry reaction broke in the North. The decision seemed to confirm every charge against the aggressive Slave Power. "There is such a thing as the slave power," warned the *Cincinnati Daily Commercial*. "It has marched over and annihilated the boundaries of the states." The economic and racial anxieties of poor northern whites reached a peak. The *Cincinnati Freeman* asked, "What security have the Germans and the Irish that their children will not, within a hundred years, be reduced to slavery in this land of their adoption?"

To Abraham Lincoln, the territorial question affected every citizen. "The whole nation," he had declared as early as 1854, "is interested that the best use shall be made of these Territories. We want them for homes of free white people. This they cannot be, to any considerable extent, if slavery shall be planted within them." The territories must be reserved, he insisted, "as an outlet for free white people everywhere."

ABRAHAM LINCOLN AND THE SLAVE POWER

More important, Lincoln warned of slavery's increasing control over the nation. The founders had created a government dedicated to freedom, Lincoln insisted. Admittedly they had recognized slavery's existence, but the public mind, he argued in 1858, had always rested in the belief that slavery would die either naturally or by legislation. The next step in the unfolding Slave Power conspiracy, Lincoln alleged, would be a Supreme Court decision "declaring that the Constitution does not permit a State to exclude slavery from its limits." This charge was not pure hyperbole, for lawsuits soon challenged state laws that freed slaves brought within their borders.

Lincoln's most eloquent statement against the Slave Power was his famous "House Divided" speech, in which he declared:

> "A house divided against itself cannot stand." I believe this government cannot endure, permanently half slave and half free. I do not expect the Union to be dissolved—I do not expect the House to fall—but I do expect it to cease to be divided. It will become all one thing or all the other. Either the opponents of slavery will arrest the further spread of it, and place it where the public mind shall rest in the belief that it is in the course of ultimate extinction; or its advocates will push it forward, till it shall become alike lawful in all the States, old as well as new, North as well as South.

Politically, these forceful Republican arguments offset the difficulties that the *Dred Scott* decision posed. By endorsing the South's doctrine of state sovereignty, the Court had in effect declared that the Republican Party's central position—no extension of slavery—was unconstitutional. Republicans could only repudiate the decision, appealing to a "higher law," or hope to change the personnel of the Court. They did both and gained politically.

For northern Democrats like Stephen Douglas, the Court's decision posed an awful dilemma. Northern voters were alarmed by the prospect that the territories would be opened to slavery. To retain their support, Douglas had to find some way to reassure them. Yet, given his ambitions to lead the national Democratic Party and become president, Douglas could not afford to alienate southern Democrats.

THE LECOMPTON CONSTITUTION AND SECTIONAL DISHARMONY AMONG DEMOCRATS

Douglas chose to stand by his principle of popular sovereignty, even if the result angered southerners. In 1857 Kansans voted on a proslavery constitution that had been drafted at Lecompton. It was defeated by more than ten thousand votes in a referendum boycotted by most proslavery voters. The evidence was overwhelming that Kansans did not want slavery, yet President Buchanan tried to force the Lecompton Constitution through Congress. Breaking with the administration, Douglas threw his weight against the Lecompton Constitution. He gauged opinion in Kansas correctly, for in 1858 voters there rejected the constitution again. But his action infuriated southern Democrats. Increasingly, many southerners believed their sectional rights and slavery would be safe only in a separate nation.

Meanwhile, as the territorial process floundered in Kansas, it also collapsed in Utah. For their practice of polygamy and their theocratic government, the Mormons who settled Utah were among the most persecuted peoples in America. Under the church-centered leadership of seer and prophet Brigham Young, the Mormons claimed the doctrine of popular sovereignty as their basis of independent rule while seeking recognition from Congress of territorial status and polygamy. But a series of corrupt territorial court justices appointed by Presidents Pierce and Buchanan failed to rein in the frontier society.

THE "MORMON WAR" IN UTAH

In 1857 Buchanan dispatched 2,500 troops, one-sixth of the U.S. Army, to suppress Young, who as one historian describes him, ruled "like a traitor in rebellion against the United States." Blocked by winter in the Rockies, the army never reached Utah. The massacre of a wagon train of 120 settlers by the Mormons and Indian allies notwithstanding, the "Mormon War" ended in Young's withdrawing his forces and Buchanan sending peace commissioners and offering amnesty in 1858. The struggle over federal authority, as well as the Mormons' own "peculiar institution" in Utah, would continue for years.

Disunion

I t is worth remembering that in the late 1850s, most Americans were not caught up daily in the slavery crisis. They were preoccupied with personal affairs, especially coping with the effects of the economic panic that began in the spring of 1857. They were worried about widespread unemployment, the plummeting price of wheat, declining wages at a textile mill, or sons who needed land.

The panic had been caused by shortcomings of the unregulated American banking system, frenzied speculation in western lands and railroads, and a weak and overburdened credit system. By 1858 Philadelphia had 40,000 unemployed workers, and New York

City nearly 100,000. Fear of bread riots and class warfare gripped many cities in the North. True to form, blame for such economic woe became sectionalized, as southerners saw their system justified by the temporary collapse of industrial prosperity, and northerners feared even more the incursions of the Slave Power on an insecure future.

Soon, however, the entire nation's focus would be thrown on a new dimension of the slavery question: armed rebellion. John Brown had been raised by staunchly religious and antislavery parents. He relied on an Old Testament conception of justice—"an eye for an eye"—and he had a puritanical obsession with the wickedness of others, especially southern slaveowners. Brown believed that violence in a righteous cause was a holy act. To Brown, the destruction of slavery in America required revolutionary ideology and revolutionary acts.

JOHN BROWN'S RAID ON HARPERS FERRY

On October 16, 1859, Brown led a small band of eighteen whites and blacks in an attack on the federal arsenal at Harpers Ferry, Virginia. Hoping to trigger a slave rebellion, Brown failed miserably and was quickly captured, tried, and executed. Yet his attempted insurrection struck fear into the South. Then it became known that Brown had received financial backing from several prominent abolitionists. When northern intellectuals such as Ralph Waldo Emerson and Henry David Thoreau praised Brown as a holy warrior who "would make the gallows as glorious as the cross," white southerners' outrage multiplied. Most troubling to southerners, perhaps, was that while Republican politicians condemned Brown's crimes, they did so in a way that deflected attention onto the still greater crime of slavery.

Many Americans believed that the election of 1860 would decide the fate of the Union. The Democratic Party was the only party truly national in scope. But at its 1860 convention in Charleston, South Carolina, the Democratic Party split.

ELECTION OF 1860

Stephen A. Douglas wanted his party's presidential nomination, but he could not afford to alienate northern voters by accepting the southern position on the territories. Southern Democrats, however, insisted on recognition of their rights and moved to block Douglas's nomination. When Douglas obtained a majority for his version of the platform, delegates from the Deep South walked out of the convention. After efforts at compromise failed, the Democrats presented two nominees: Douglas for the northern wing, and Vice President John C. Breckinridge of Kentucky for the southern. The Republicans nominated Abraham Lincoln, and a Constitutional Union Party, formed to preserve the nation but strong only in the Upper South, nominated John Bell of Tennessee.

Bell's only issue in the ensuing campaign was the urgency of preserving the Union. Douglas desperately sought to unite his northern and southern supporters, while Breckinridge quickly backed away from the appearance of extremism, and his supporters in several states stressed his unionism. Although Lincoln and the Republicans denied any intent to interfere with slavery in the states where it existed, they stood firm against the extension of slavery into the territories.

The election of 1860 was sectional in character. Lincoln won, but Douglas, Breckinridge, and Bell together received a majority of the votes. Douglas had broad-based support but won few states. Breckinridge carried nine states, all in the Deep South. Bell won pluralities in Virginia, Kentucky, and Tennessee. Lincoln prevailed in the North, but in the four border states that ultimately remained loyal to the Union (Missouri, Kentucky, Maryland, and Delaware), he gained only a plurality, not a majority. Lincoln's victory was won in the electoral college.

Opposition to slavery's extension was the core issue of the Republican Party, and Lincoln's alarm over slavery's growing political power was genuine. Moreover, abolitionists and supporters of free soil in the North worked to keep the Republicans from compromising on their territorial stand. Meanwhile, proslavery advocates and secessionists in the South whipped up public opinion and demanded that state conventions assemble to consider secession.

Lincoln made the crucial decision not to soften his party's position on the territories. He wrote of the need to maintain the bond of faith between voter and candidate and of declining to set "the minority over the majority." Although many conservative Republicans—eastern businessmen and former Whigs who did not feel strongly about slavery—hoped for a compromise, the original and most committed Republicans—old Free-Soilers and antislavery Whigs—were adamant about stopping the expansion of the peculiar institution.

Senator John J. Crittenden of Kentucky tried to craft a late-hour compromise. The Crittenden Compromise proposed that the two sections divide the territories between them at latitude 36°30'. But the southerners would agree to this only if the Republicans did too. When Lincoln ruled out concessions on the territorial issue, Crittenden's peacemaking effort collapsed.

Meanwhile, the Union was being destroyed. On December 20, 1860, South Carolina passed an ordinance of secession. This step marked the inauguration of the secessionist strategy of separate-state secession. Secessionists concentrated their efforts on the most extreme proslavery state, hoping South Carolina's bold act would induce other states

SECESSION AND THE CONFEDERATE STATES OF AMERICA

to follow, with each decision building momentum for disunion.

Southern extremists soon got their way in the Deep South. They called separate state conventions and passed secession ordinances in Mississippi, Florida, Alabama, Georgia, Louisiana, and Texas. By February 1861 these states had joined South Carolina to form a new government in Montgomery, Alabama: the Confederate States of America. The delegates at Montgomery chose Jefferson Davis as their president, and the Confederacy began to function independently of the United States.

This apparent unanimity was deceiving. Confused and dissatisfied with the alternatives, many southerners who in 1860 had voted in the U.S. presidential election stayed home a few months later rather than vote for delegates who would decide on

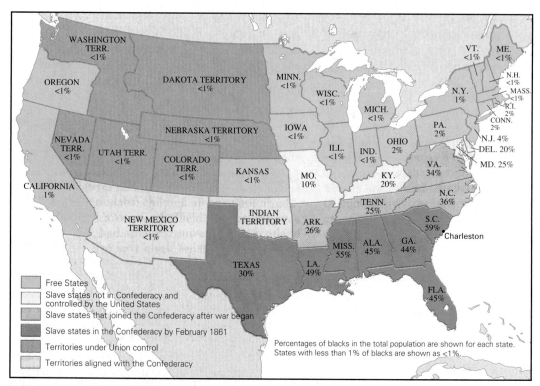

Map 14.3   The Divided Nation—Slave and Free Areas, 1861

After fighting began, the Upper South joined the Deep South in the Confederacy. How does the nation's pattern of division correspond to the distribution of slavery and the percentage of blacks in the population?

secession. Even so, in some state conventions, the vote to secede was close, with secession decided by overrepresentation of plantation districts. Furthermore, the conventions were noticeably unwilling to let voters ratify their acts. Four states in the Upper South—Virginia, North Carolina, Tennessee, and Arkansas—flatly rejected secession and did not join the Confederacy until 1861, after fighting had begun. In the border states, popular sentiment was deeply divided; minorities in Kentucky and Missouri tried to secede, but these slave states ultimately came under Union control, along with Maryland and Delaware (see Map 14.3).

Such misgivings were not surprising. Secession raised the possibility of war and the question of where it would be fought and who would die. Analysis of election returns from 1860 and 1861 indicates that slaveholders and nonslaveholders were beginning to part company politically. Heavily slaveholding counties strongly supported secession, but most counties with few slaves took an antisecession stance (see Figure 14.1). With war on the horizon, yeomen were beginning to consider their class interests and ask themselves how far they would go to support slavery and slaveowners.

As for why the Deep South bolted, we can look to the entreaties of the secession commissioners sent out by the seven seceded states to try to convince the other slave states to join them. Repeatedly they stressed independence as the only way to preserve white racial security and the slave system. Only secession, contended the Alabama commissioner, Stephen Hale, could sustain the "heaven-ordained superiority of the white over the black race."

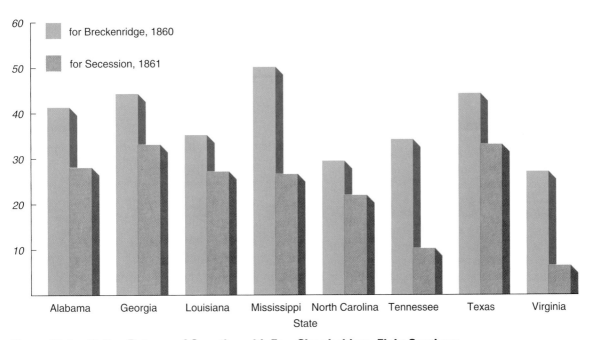

Figure 14.1 Voting Returns of Counties with Few Slaveholders, Eight Southern States, 1860 and 1861

This graph depicts voting in counties whose percentage of slaveholders ranked them among the lower half of the counties in their state. How does voters' support for secession in 1861 compare with support for John Breckinridge, the southern Democratic candidate in 1860? Why was their support for secession so weak? At this time counties with many slaveholders were giving increased support to secession.

The dilemma facing President Lincoln on inauguration day in March 1861 was how to maintain the federal government's authority without provoking war. Proceeding cautiously, he sought only to hold on to forts in the states that had left the Union, reasoning that he could thus assert federal sovereignty while waiting for a restoration. But Jefferson Davis, who could not claim to lead a sovereign nation if the Confederate ports were under foreign (that is, U.S.) control, was unwilling to be so patient. A collision was inevitable.

FORT SUMTER AND OUTBREAK OF WAR

It arrived in the early morning hours of April 12, 1861, at Fort Sumter in Charleston harbor. A federal garrison there ran low on food, and Lincoln notified the South Carolinians that he was sending a ship to resupply the fort. The Montgomery government, facing the choice of attacking the fort or acquiescing to Lincoln's authority, ordered local commanders to obtain a surrender or attack. After two days of heavy bombardment, the federal garrison finally surrendered. Confederates permitted the U.S. troops to sail away on unarmed vessels while Charlestonians celebrated wildly. The Civil War had begun.

Summary *Online Study Center* ACE the Test

Throughout the 1840s and 1850s, most people, North and South, had hoped to keep the nation together. As late as 1858, even Jefferson Davis had declared, "This great country will continue united," saying that "to the innermost fibers of my heart I love it all, and every part."

Why had all efforts to prevent war failed? The conflict that slavery generated was fundamental. The emotions bound up in attacking and defending slavery's future were too powerful, and the interests it affected too vital, for compromise. North and South had fundamentally different attitudes toward the institution. The logic of Republican ideology tended in the direction of abolishing slavery, even though Republicans denied any such intention. The logic of southern arguments led toward establishing slavery everywhere, though southern leaders too denied such a motive. Lincoln put these facts succinctly. In a post-election letter to his old friend Alexander Stephens of Georgia, Lincoln wrote, "You think slavery is right and ought to be expanded; while we think it is wrong and ought to be restricted. That I suppose is the rub."

Territorial expansion generated disputes so frequently that the nation never enjoyed an extended breathing space during the 1850s. Every southern victory increased fear of the Slave Power, and each new expression of Free-Soil sentiment made alarmed slaveholders more insistent in their demands. Eventually even those opposed to war could see no way to avoid it. In the profoundest sense, slavery was the root of the war. But as the fighting began, this, the war's central issue, was shrouded in confusion. How would the Civil War affect slavery, its place in the law, and African Americans' place in society?

LEGACY FOR A PEOPLE AND A NATION
Terrorist or Freedom Fighter?

The greatest significance of John Brown's raid on Harpers Ferry in 1859 rests in its aftermath in American memory. Brown is as important as a symbol as he is for his deeds. He has been one of the most beloved and most loathed figures in American history. In the song that bears his name, "John Brown's Body," a popular marching tune during the Civil War, his "soul goes marching on."

In the wake of his execution, in painting, song, and poetry, people constructed a John Brown mythology. Was he a Christ-like figure who died for the nation's sins? Or was he a terrorist thief who murdered in the name of his own peculiar vision of God's will? Brown can be disturbing and inspiring, majestic and foolish, a monster or a warrior saint. He represented the highest ideals and the most ruthless deeds. He killed for justice.

Over the years, many organizations have adopted John Brown as their justifying symbol, from left-wing students opposing American foreign policy to anti-abortion groups that target clinics and doctors. Today, terrorism and revolutionary violence are often in the news: a federal building explodes in Oklahoma City; suicide bombers attack buses and restaurants in Israel; the Irish Republican Army plants explosives in London subways; and on September 11, 2001, four hijacked passenger airplanes bring terrorism to American soil as never before. The story of John Brown's raid in 1859 forces us to ask when and how revolutionary violence—violence in the name of a political or spiritual end—is justified. That is his legacy for a people and a nation.

TRANSFORMING FIRE: THE CIVIL WAR 1861–1865

*H*e was an ordinary twenty-seven-year-old store clerk from a New England town, who went off to war. In spring 1861, Charles Brewster left his mother and two sisters behind and joined Company C of the Tenth Massachusetts Volunteers. Brewster had no idea of his capacity for leadership or his ability to uphold such values as courage and manliness.

In more than two hundred sometimes lyrical letters to his mother and sisters, Brewster, who rose to lieutenant and adjutant of his regiment, left a trove of commentary on the meaning of war, why slavery had to be destroyed, and, especially, the values of common, mid-nineteenth-century American men. Brewster was as racist as many southerners in his perceptions of blacks. He was no "desperate hero" about battlefield courage, and he nearly died of dysentery twice. He was personally eager for rank and recognition, and eventually held only contempt for civilians who stayed at home. He was often miserably lonely and homesick, and he described battlefield carnage with an honest realism.

Most telling, Brewster's attitudes toward race transformed. In 1862 he defied orders and took in a seventeen-year-old ex-slave as his personal servant. In 1864, after some of the worst battles of the war in Virginia destroyed his regiment, Brewster, frightened of civilian life, reenlisted to be a recruiter of black troops. In this new role, Brewster worked from an office in Norfolk, Virginia, where his principal job was writing "love letters" for illiterate black women to their soldier husbands at the front. In imagining Brewster sitting at a table with a lonely freedwoman, swallowing his prejudices toward blacks and women, and repeatedly writing or reciting the phrases "give my love to . . ." and "your Husband untall Death," we can glimpse the enormous potential for human transformation at work in this war.

The Civil War's astonishing, unexpected changes in North and South obliterated normal patterns of life. Millions of men were swept away into training camps and battle units. Armies of hundreds of thousands marched

America Goes to War, 1861–1862

War Transforms the South

Wartime Northern Economy and Society

The Advent of Emancipation

The Soldiers' War

1863: The Tide of Battle Turns

Disunity, South, North, and West

1864–1865: The Final Test of Wills

LINKS TO THE WORLD
The Civil War in Britain

LEGACY FOR A PEOPLE AND A NATION
The Confederate Battle Flag

Online Study Center
This icon will direct you to interactive map and primary source activities on the website http://college.hmco.com/pic/nortonbrief7e

C H R O N O L O G Y

1861 • Battle of Bull Run
- McClellan organizes Union Army
- Union blockade begins
- U.S. Congress passes first confiscation act
- *Trent* affair

1862 • Union captures Fort Henry and Fort Donelson
- U.S. Navy captures New Orleans
- Battle of Shiloh shows the war's destructiveness
- Confederacy enacts conscription
- McClellan's Peninsula Campaign fails to take Richmond
- U.S. Congress passes second confiscation act, initiating emancipation
- Confederacy mounts offensive in Maryland and Kentucky
- Battle of Antietam ends Lee's drive into Maryland in September
- British intervention in the war on Confederate side is averted

1863 • Emancipation Proclamation takes effect
- U.S. Congress passes National Banking Act
- Union enacts conscription
- African American soldiers join Union Army
- Food riots occur in southern cities
- Battle of Chancellorsville ends in Confederate victory but Jackson's death
- Union wins key victories at Gettysburg and Vicksburg

- Draft riots take place in New York City
- Battle of Chattanooga leaves South vulnerable to Sherman's march into Georgia

1864 • Battles of the Wilderness and Spotsylvania produce heavy casualties on both sides in the effort to capture and defend Richmond
- Battle of Cold Harbor continues carnage in Virginia
- Lincoln requests Republican Party plank abolishing slavery
- Sherman captures Atlanta
- Confederacy begins to collapse on the home front
- Lincoln wins reelection, eliminating any Confederate hopes for a negotiated end to war
- Jefferson Davis proposes emancipation within the Confederacy
- Sherman marches through Georgia to the sea

1865 • Sherman marches through Carolinas
- U.S. Congress approves Thirteenth Amendment
- Lee abandons Richmond and Petersburg
- Lee surrenders at Appomattox Court House
- Lincoln assassinated
- Death toll in war reaches 620,000

over the South, devastating countrysides. Families struggled to survive without their men; businesses tried to cope with the loss of workers. Women in both North and South took on extra responsibilities at home and moved into the work force, some joining the ranks of nurses and hospital workers.

But southern soldiers, and their families, also experienced what few other groups of Americans have— utter defeat. For most of them, hope turned to despair as countless southern farms were ruined. Late

in the war, many southerners yearned only for an end to inflation, shortages, and the death that visited nearly every family.

Northern soldiers, though ultimately victorious, often resented the sacrifices demanded of them. For northern businessmen, however, the conflict ensured vast government expenditures, a heavy demand for goods, and lucrative federal contracts. *Harper's Monthly* reported that an eminent financier expected a long and profitable war, ripe with speculative opportunities. "The battle of Bull Run," predicted the financier, "makes the fortune of every man in Wall Street who is not a natural idiot."

Change was most drastic in the South, where secessionists had launched a conservative revolution for their section's national independence. Born of states' rights doctrine, the Confederacy now had to transform into a centralized nation to fight a vast war. Southern whites had feared that a peacetime government of Republicans would interfere with slavery and upset the routine of plantation life. Instead, their own actions led to a war that turned southern life upside down and imperiled the very existence of slavery.

War altered the North as well, but less sharply. Because most of the fighting took place on southern soil, northern farms and factories remained largely unscathed and busy. Workers lost ground to inflation, but the economy hummed. A new pro-business atmosphere dominated Congress. To the alarm of many, the powers of the federal government and of the president increased during the war.

Ultimately the Civil War forced on the nation a social and political revolution regarding race. Its greatest effect was to compel leaders and citizens to deal directly with the issue they had struggled over but had been unable to resolve: slavery. ■

America Goes to War, 1861–1862

Few Americans understood what they were getting into when the war began. The onset of hostilities sparked patriotic sentiments and joyous ceremonies in both North and South. Northern communities raised companies of volunteers eager to save the Union. In the South, confident recruits boasted of whipping the Yankees and returning home before Christmas.

Through the spring of 1861, both sides scrambled to organize and train their undisciplined armies.

FIRST BATTLE OF BULL RUN

On July 21, 1861, the first battle took place outside Manassas Junction, Virginia, near a stream called Bull Run. General Irvin McDowell and 30,000 Union troops attacked General P. G. T. Beauregard's 22,000 southerners. As raw recruits struggled amid the confusion of their first battle, federal forces began to gain ground. Then they ran into a line of Virginia troops under General Thomas Jackson. "There is Jackson standing like a stone wall," shouted one Confederate. "Stonewall" Jackson's line held, and the arrival of 9,000 Confederate reinforcements won the day for the South. Union troops fled back to Washington.

The unexpected rout at Bull Run gave northerners their first hint that although the United States enjoyed an enormous advantage in resources, victory would not be easy. Pro-Union feeling was growing in western Virginia, and loyalties were divided in the four border slave states: Missouri, Kentucky, Maryland, and Delaware. But the rest of the Upper South—North Carolina, Virginia, Tennessee, and Arkansas—had joined the Confederacy. Moved by an outpouring of regional loyalty, half a million southerners volunteered to fight.

Lincoln gave command of the northern army to General George B. McClellan, an officer who proved to be better at organization and training than at fighting. McClellan devoted the fall and winter of 1861 to readying the Union Army, a formidable force of a quarter-million men whose mission would be to take Richmond, established as the Confederate capital by July 1861.

While McClellan prepared, the Union began to implement other parts of its overall strategy, which

GRAND STRATEGY

called for a blockade of southern ports and eventual capture of the Mississippi River. Like a constricting snake, this "Anaconda plan" would strangle the Confederacy. At first the Union Navy had too few ships to patrol 3,550 miles of coastline effectively. Gradually, however, the navy increased the blockade's effectiveness, though it never stopped southern commerce completely.

Confederate strategy was essentially defensive. A defensive posture not only was consistent with the South's claim of independence, but acknowledged the

Figure 15.1   Comparative Resources, Union and Confederate States, 1861

The North had vastly superior resources. Although the North's advantages in manpower and industrial capacity proved very important, the South still had to be conquered, its society and its will crushed.   (Source: *The Times Atlas of World History.* Time Books, London, 1978. Used with permission.)

North's advantage in resources (see Figure 15.1). But Jefferson Davis called the southern strategy "offensive defensive," taking advantage of opportunities to attack and using its interior lines of transportation to concentrate troops at crucial points.

Strategic thinking on both sides slighted the importance of "the West," that vast expanse of territory between Virginia and the Mississippi River and beyond. Guerrilla warfare broke out in 1861 in the politically divided state of Missouri, and key locations along the Mississippi and other major western rivers would prove to be crucial prizes in the North's eventual victory. Beyond the Mississippi River, the Confederacy hoped to gain an advantage by negotiating treaties with the Cherokees and other Indian tribes. Meanwhile, the Republican U.S. Congress carved the West into territories in anticipation of state making. What began during the Civil War was the start of nearly three decades of offensive warfare against Indians, an enveloping strategy of conquest, relocation, and slaughter.

The last half of 1861 brought no major land battles, but the North made gains by sea. Union naval forces secured vital coastal points in the Carolinas, as well as Fort Pulaski, which defended Savannah. The coastal victories off South Carolina frightened planters, who abandoned their lands and fled. But thousands of slaves greeted

UNION NAVAL CAMPAIGN

what they hoped to be freedom with rejoicing and broke the hated cotton gins. A growing stream of runaways poured into the Union lines. The Union government, unwilling at first to wage a war against slavery, did not acknowledge the slaves' freedom. It began, however, to use their labor in the Union cause.

The coastal incursions worried southerners, but the spring of 1862 confirmed the naval threat. In April Union ships commanded by Admiral David Farragut smashed through log booms blocking the Mississippi River and fought their way upstream to capture New Orleans.

Farther west, three full Confederate regiments were organized, mostly of Cherokees from Indian Territory, but a Union victory at Elkhorn Tavern, Arkansas, shattered southern control of the region. Thereafter, dissension within Native American groups and Union advances reduced Confederate operations in Indian Territory to guerrilla raids.

WAR IN THE FAR WEST

In the westernmost campaign of the war, from February to May 1862, some 3,000 Confederate forces marched north from Texas to fight for control of New Mexico Territory. The military significance of the New Mexico campaign was limited. About 4,000 Colorado and New Mexico Unionists fought for their region, and by May 1 Confederate forces straggled down the Rio Grande River back into Texas, ending their effort.

Meanwhile, in February 1862, land and river forces in northern Tennessee won significant victories for the Union. A Union commander named Ulysses S. Grant captured Fort Henry and Fort Donelson, guarding the Tennessee and Cumberland Rivers. A path into Tennessee, Alabama, and Mississippi now lay open before the Union Army. Grant moved on into southern Tennessee and the first of the war's shockingly bloody encounters, the Battle of Shiloh. Early on April 6, Confederate general Albert Sidney Johnston attacked federal troops caught with their backs to the Tennessee River. Although Johnston was killed, southern forces almost achieved a breakthrough, but Union reinforcements arrived that night. The next day, after ten hours of terrible combat, the Confederates withdrew. Neither side won a victory at Shiloh, yet the losses were staggering. Northern troops lost 13,000 men (killed, wounded, or captured) out of 63,000; southerners sacrificed 11,000 out of 40,000. The true nature of the war was emerging.

GRANT'S TENNESSEE CAMPAIGN AND THE BATTLE OF SHILOH

On the Virginia front, President Lincoln had a different problem. General McClellan was slow to move. Habitually overestimating the size of enemy forces, McClellan called repeatedly for reinforcements and ignored Lincoln's directions to advance. Finally he chose to move by water, sailing his troops down the Chesapeake, landing them on the peninsula between the York and James Rivers, and advancing on Richmond from the east.

MCCLELLAN AND THE PENINSULA CAMPAIGN

After a bloody but indecisive battle at Fair Oaks from May 31 to June 1, the federal armies moved to within 7 miles of the Confederate capital. The Confederate commanding general, Joseph E. Johnston, was badly wounded at Fair Oaks, and President Jefferson Davis placed his chief military adviser, Robert E. Lee, in command. Lee soon foiled McClellan's legions.

First, he sent Stonewall Jackson's corps of 17,000 into the Shenandoah valley behind Union forces, where they threatened Washington, D.C., drawing some federal troops away from Richmond to protect their own capital. Then, in a series of engagements known as the Seven Days Battles, June 26–July 1, Lee forced McClellan to retreat toward the James River. By August 3 McClellan withdrew his army to the Potomac; Richmond remained safe for another two years.

Buoyed by these results, Jefferson Davis conceived an ambitious plan to turn the tide of the war and gain recognition of the Confederacy by European nations. He ordered a general offensive, sending Lee north into Maryland and Generals Kirby Smith and Braxton Bragg into Kentucky. Calling on residents of Maryland and Kentucky (still slave states) to make a separate peace with his government, Davis also invited northwestern states like Indiana, which sent much of their trade down the Mississippi to New Orleans, to leave the Union.

CONFEDERATE OFFENSIVE IN MARYLAND AND KENTUCKY

The plan was promising, but every part of the offensive failed. In the bloodiest day of the entire war, September 17, 1862, McClellan turned Lee back in the Battle of Antietam near Sharpsburg, Maryland. He also, however, indecisively allowed Lee's stricken army to retreat to safety, and Lincoln removed him from command. In Kentucky, Generals Smith and Bragg secured Lexington and Frankfurt, but were then stopped at the Battle of Perryville on October 8. Bragg's army retreated back into Tennessee. Confederate leaders had marshaled all their strength for a breakthrough but had failed. Tenacious defense and stoic endurance now seemed the South's only long-range hope.

But 1862 also brought painful lessons to the North. Confederate general J. E. B. Stuart executed a daring cavalry raid into Pennsylvania in October. Then on December 13, Union general Ambrose Burnside, now in command of the Army of the Potomac, unwisely ordered his soldiers to attack Lee's army, which held fortified positions on high ground at Fredericksburg, Virginia. Lee's men performed so efficiently in killing northerners that Lee was moved to say, "It is well that war is so terrible. We should grow too fond of it."

War Transforms the South

*T*he war caused tremendous disruptions in civilian life and altered southern society beyond all expectations. One of the first traditions to fall was the southern preference for local and limited government. States' rights had been a formative ideology for the Confederacy, but to withstand the massive power of the North, the South needed to centralize, as Jefferson Davis quickly recognized.

Promptly Davis moved to bring all arms, supplies, and troops under his control. But when the states failed to provide sufficient numbers of troops, Davis secured passage in April 1862 of the first national conscription (draft) law in American history. Davis also adopted firm leadership toward the Confederate Congress, which raised taxes and later passed a tax-in-kind—paid in farm products. When opposition arose, the government suspended the writ of habeas corpus (which prevented individuals from being held without trial) and imposed martial law. Despite Davis's unyielding stance, this tax system proved inadequate to the South's war effort.

THE CONFEDERACY AND CENTRALIZATION

Soon the Confederate administration in Richmond gained virtually complete control over the southern economy. Because it controlled the supply of labor through conscription, the administration could compel industry to work on government contracts and supply the military's needs. The Confederate Congress also gave the central government almost complete control of the railroads. A large bureaucracy sprang up to administer these operations. By the war's end, the southern bureaucracy was larger in proportion to population than its northern counterpart.

Historians have long argued over whether the Confederacy was a "rebellion," a "revolution," or the genuine creation of a "nation." Whatever label we apply, Confederates created a culture and an ideology of nationalism. In flags, songs, language, seals, school readers, and

CONFEDERATE NATIONALISM

■ In October 1862 in New York City, photographer Mathew Brady opened an exhibition of photographs from the Battle of Antietam. Although few knew it, Brady's vision was poor, and this photograph of Confederate dead was actually taken by his assistants, Alexander Gardner and James F. Gibson.   (Library of Congress)

other forms of "national characteristics," Confederates created their own story.

In its conservative crusade to preserve the social order and racial slavery and as a bulwark against centralized power, southerners believed the Confederacy was the true legacy of the American Revolution. Also central to Confederate nationalism was a refurbished defense of slavery as a benign, protective institution. And the idea of the "faithful slave" was key to southerners' nationalist cause.

In the face of defeat and devastation, forms of Confederate nationalism collapsed in the final year of the war. But much of the spirit and substance of Confederate nationalism would revive in the postwar period in a new ideology of the Lost Cause.

SOUTHERN CITIES AND INDUSTRY

Clerks and subordinate officials crowded the towns and cities where Confederate departments set up their offices. Clerks had always been males, but now "government girls" staffed the Confederate bureaucracy. The sudden population booms that resulted overwhelmed the housing supply and stimulated new construction. The pressure was especially great in Richmond, whose population increased 250 percent.

As the Union blockade disrupted imports of manufactured products, the traditionally agricultural South forged industries. Many planters shared Davis's hope that industrialization would bring "deliverance, full and unrestricted, from all commercial dependence" on the North or the rest of the world. Indeed, beginning almost from scratch, the Confederacy achieved tremendous feats of industrial development. The government also constructed new railroad lines, in many cases using as laborers slaves who had been relocated from farms and plantations.

CHANGING ROLES OF WOMEN

White women, restricted to narrow roles in antebellum society, gained substantial new responsibilities in wartime. The wives and mothers of soldiers now headed households and performed men's work. Women in nonslaveowning families cultivated fields themselves, while wealthier women suddenly had to perform as overseers and manage field work. In the cities, white women—who had been virtually excluded from the labor force—found a limited number of respectable paying jobs, and female schoolteachers appeared in the South for the first time. Some women gained confidence from their new responsibilities, but others resented their burdens. Many grew angry over shortages and resented cooking and unfamiliar contact with lower-class women.

HUMAN SUFFERING, HOARDING, AND INFLATION

For millions of ordinary southerners, change brought privation and suffering. Mass poverty descended for the first time on many yeoman families that had lost their breadwinners to the army. As a South Carolina newspaper put it, "The duties of war have called away from home the sole supports of many, many families. . . . Help must be given, or the poor will suffer." Women on their own sought help from relatives, neighbors, friends, anyone. Sometimes they pleaded their cases to the Confederate government.

The South was so sparsely populated in many places that the conscription of one skilled craftsman could work a hardship on the people of an entire county. Often they begged in unison for the exemption or discharge of the local miller, a wheelwright, or especially a blacksmith. As a petition from Alabama explained, "Our Section of County [is] left entirely Destitute of any man that is able to keep in order any kind of Farming Tules."

Inflation raged out of control, fueled by the Confederate government's heavy borrowing and inadequate taxes, until prices had increased almost 7,000 percent. Inflation particularly imperiled urban dwellers without their own sources of food. As early as 1861 and 1862, newspapers reported that "want and starvation are staring thousands in the face." Some families came to the aid of their neighbors, and "free markets," which disbursed goods as charity, sprang up in various cities. But hoarding worsened matters, and a rudimentary relief program organized by the Confederacy failed to meet the need.

INEQUITIES OF THE CONFEDERATE DRAFT

As their fortunes declined, people of once-modest means looked around and found abundant evidence that all classes were not sacrificing equally and that Confederate government policies favored the upper class. Until the last year of the war, for example, prosperous southerners could avoid military service by hiring substitutes. Well over 50,000 upper-class southerners did so. In October 1862, when the Confederate Congress exempted from military duty anyone who was supervising at least twenty slaves, protests poured in from every corner of the Confederacy, and North Carolina's legislators formally condemned the law. Its defenders argued, however, that the exemption preserved order and aided food production, and the statute remained on the books.

Dissension spread, and alert politicians and newspaper editors warned of class warfare. The bitterness of letters to Confederate officials suggests the depth of the people's anger. One woman swore to the secretary of war that unless help was provided to poverty-stricken wives and mothers, "an allwise god . . . will send down his fury . . . [on] those that are in power." War magnified existing social tensions in the Confederacy, and created a few new ones.

Wartime Northern Economy and Society

*W*ith the onset of war, change rolled over the North as well. The energies of an industrializing, capitalist society were harnessed to serve the cause of the Union, and the federal government and its executive branch gained new powers. Idealism and greed flourished together, and the northern economy proved its awesome productivity.

At first, the war was a shock to business. Northern firms lost their southern markets, and many

NORTHERN BUSINESS, INDUSTRY, AND AGRICULTURE

companies had to change their products and find new customers to remain open. Southern debts became uncollectible, jeopardizing not only northern merchants but also many western banks. In farming regions, families struggled with a shortage of labor caused by enlistments.

But certain entrepreneurs, such as wool producers, benefited from shortages of competing products, and soaring demand for war-related goods swept some businesses to new success. Secretary of War Edwin M. Stanton's list of the supplies needed by the Ordnance Department indicates the scope of government demand: "7,892 cannon, 11,787 artillery carriages, 4,022,130 small-arms, . . . 1,022,176,474 cartridges for small-arms, 1,220,555,435 percussion caps, . . . 26,440,054 pounds of gunpowder, . . . 90,416,295 pounds of lead." Stanton's list covered

only weapons; the government also purchased huge quantities of uniforms, boots, food, camp equipment, saddles, ships, and other necessities.

War aided some heavy industries in the North, especially iron and steel production. Although new railroad construction slowed, repairs caused increased manufacture of rails. Of considerable significance was the railroad industry's adoption of a standard gauge (width) for track, which eliminated the unloading and reloading of boxcars and created a unified transportation system.

The northern economy also grew because of a complementary relationship between agriculture and industry. Mechanization of agriculture had begun before the war. Wartime recruitment and conscription, however, gave western farmers an added incentive to purchase labor-saving machinery. The shift from human labor to machines created new markets for industry and expanded the food supply for the urban industrial work force. Mechanization in agriculture also meant that northern farm families whose breadwinners went to war did not suffer as much as did their counterparts in the South.

Northern industrial and urban workers did not fare as well. After the initial slump, jobs became plentiful, but inflation ate up much of a

NORTHERN WORKERS' MILITANCY

worker's paycheck. Between 1860 and 1864 consumer prices rose at least 76 percent, while daily wages rose only 42 percent. Workers' families consequently suffered a substantial decline in their standard of living.

As their real wages shrank, industrial workers lost job security. To increase production, some employers replaced workers with labor-saving machines. Other employers urged the government to promote immigration to secure cheap labor. Workers responded by forming unions and sometimes by striking. Skilled craftsmen organized to combat the loss of their jobs and status to machines; women and unskilled workers, who were excluded by the craftsmen, formed their own unions. Indeed, thirteen occupational groups—including tailors, coal miners, and railway engineers—formed national unions during the Civil War.

Hostile employers viewed labor activism as a threat to their freedom of action and accordingly formed statewide or craft-based associations to cooperate and pool information. They shared blacklists of union members and required new workers to sign "yellow dog" contracts (promises not to join a union). To put down strikes, they hired strikebreakers from among blacks, immigrants, and women, and sometimes they used federal troops to break unions.

Labor militance did not prevent employers from making profits or profiteering on government contracts. Unscrupulous businessmen took advantage of the suddenly immense demand for army supplies by selling clothing and blankets made of "shoddy"—wool fibers reclaimed from rags or worn cloth. Shoddy goods often came apart in the rain; most of the shoes purchased in the early months of the war were worthless. Contractors sold inferior guns for double the usual price and passed off tainted meat as good.

Legitimate enterprises also made healthy profits. The output of woolen mills increased so dramatically

ECONOMIC
NATIONALISM
AND
GOVERNMENT-
BUSINESS
PARTNERSHIP

that dividends in the industry nearly tripled. Some cotton mills made record profits on what they sold, even though they reduced their output. Railroads carried immense quantities of freight and passengers, and railroad stocks skyrocketed in value.

Railroads also were a leading beneficiary of government largesse. With southerners absent from Congress, the northern route of the transcontinental railroad quickly prevailed. In 1862 and 1864 Congress chartered two corporations, the Union Pacific Railroad and the Central Pacific Railroad, and assisted them financially in connecting Omaha, Nebraska, with Sacramento, California. Overall, the two corporations gained approximately 20 million acres of land and nearly $60 million in loans.

Other businessmen benefited handsomely from the Morrill Land Grant Act (1862). To promote public education in agriculture, engineering, and military science, Congress granted each state 30,000 acres of federal land for each of its congressional districts. The law eventually fostered sixty-nine colleges and universities, but one of its immediate effects was to enrich a few prominent speculators.

Before the war, there was no adequate national banking, taxation, or currency. Banks operating under state charters issued no fewer than seven thousand different kinds of notes, which were difficult to distinguish from forgeries. During the war, Congress and the Treasury Department established a national banking system empowered to issue national bank notes, and by 1865 most state banks were forced to join the national system. This process created a sounder currency, but also inflexibility in the money supply and an eastern-oriented financial structure.

In response to the war, the Republicans created an activist federal government. Indeed, with agricultural legislation, the land grant colleges, higher tariffs, and railroad subsidies, the federal government entered the economy forever.

Abraham Lincoln, like Jefferson Davis, found that war required active presidential leadership. At

EXPANSION OF
PRESIDENTIAL
POWER

the beginning of the conflict, Lincoln launched a major shipbuilding program without waiting for Congress to assemble. The lawmakers later approved his decision, and Lincoln continued to act in advance of Congress when he deemed such action necessary. In one striking exercise of executive power, Lincoln suspended the writ of habeas corpus for everyone living between Washington, D.C., and Philadelphia. Later in the war, with congressional approval, Lincoln repeatedly suspended habeas corpus and invoked martial law.

On occasion Lincoln used his wartime authority to bolster his own political fortunes. He and his generals proved adept at furloughing soldiers who usually voted Republican so they could vote in close elections.

In thousands of self-governing towns and communities, northern citizens felt a personal connection

THE UNION
CAUSE

to representative government. Secession threatened to destroy their system, and northerners rallied to its defense. Secular and church leaders supported the cause, and in the first two years of the war, northern morale remained remarkably high.

But in the excitement of moneymaking, an eagerness to display one's wealth flourished in the largest cities. *Harper's Monthly* reported that "the suddenly enriched contractors, speculators, and stock-jobbers . . . are spending money with a profusion never before witnessed in our country." The *New York Herald* noted, "This war has entirely changed the American character. . . . The individual who makes the most money—no matter how—and spends the most—no matter for what—is considered the greatest man."

Yet idealism coexisted with ostentation. Abolitionists campaigned to turn the war into a crusade against slavery. Free black communities and churches, both black and white, responded to the needs of slaves who flocked to the Union lines, sending clothing, ministers, and teachers to aid the freed people.

Northern women, like their southern counterparts, took on new roles. Those who stayed home organized over ten thousand soldiers' aid societies, rolled bandages, and raised $3 million to aid injured troops. Women were instrumental in pressing for the first trained ambulance corps in the Union armies, and they formed the backbone of the U.S. Sanitary Commission, which provided crucial nutritional and medical aid to soldiers.

NORTHERN WOMEN ON HOME FRONT AND BATTLEFRONT

Approximately 3,200 women also served as nurses in frontline hospitals, where they pressed for better care of the wounded. Yet women had to fight for a chance to serve at all. The professionalization of medicine since the Revolution had created a medical system dominated by men, and many male physicians did not want women's aid. Even Clara Barton, famous for her persistence in working in the worst hospitals at the front, was ousted from her post in 1863.

The Advent of Emancipation

Despite the sense of loyalty to cause that animated soldiers and civilians on both sides, the governments of the United States and the Confederacy lacked clarity about the purpose of the war. Throughout the first several months of the struggle, both Davis and Lincoln studiously avoided references to slavery. Davis, realizing that emphasis on the issue could increase class conflict, told southerners that they were fighting for constitutional liberty.

Lincoln had his own reasons for not mentioning slavery. It was crucial at first not to antagonize the Union's border slave states, whose loyalty was tenuous. Also for many months, Lincoln hoped that a pro-Union majority would assert itself in the South. It might be possible, he thought, to coax the South back into the Union and stop the fighting. And not all Republicans burned with moral outrage over slavery. A forthright stand by Lincoln on the subject of slavery could split the party. No northern consensus on what to do about slavery existed early in the war.

Lincoln first broached the subject of slavery in a substantive way in March 1862, when he proposed that the states consider emancipation on their own. He asked Congress to promise aid to any state that decided to emancipate, appealing especially to border state representatives. What Lincoln proposed was gradual emancipation, with compensation for slaveholders and colonization of the freed slaves outside the United States. To a delegation of free blacks, he explained that "it is better for us both . . . to be separated."

LINCOLN AND EMANCIPATION

Until well into 1864, Lincoln's administration promoted an impractical scheme to colonize blacks in Central America or the Caribbean. Lincoln saw colonization as one option among others in dealing with the impending freedom of America's 4.2 million slaves.

Other politicians had different ideas. A group of Republicans in Congress, known as the Radicals, dedicated themselves to a war for emancipation. In August 1861, at the Radicals' instigation, Congress passed its first confiscation act. Designed to punish the Confederates, the law confiscated all property used for "insurrectionary purposes." Thus, if the South used slaves in a hostile action, those slaves were declared seized and liberated. A second confiscation act (July 1862) went much further: it confiscated the property of anyone who supported the rebellion, even those who merely resided in the South and paid Confederate taxes. Their slaves were declared "forever free of their servitude." These acts stemmed from the logic that to crush the southern rebellion, the government had to use extraordinary powers.

CONFISCATION ACTS

Lincoln refused to adopt that view in the summer of 1862. He stood by his proposal of voluntary gradual emancipation by the states and made no effort to enforce the second confiscation act. His stance provoked a public protest from Horace Greeley, editor of the powerful *New York Tribune*. In an open letter to the president entitled "The Prayer of Twenty Millions," Greeley pleaded with Lincoln to "execute the laws" and declared, "On the face of this wide earth, Mr. President, there is not one . . . intelligent champion of the Union cause who does not feel that all attempts to put down the Rebellion and at the same time uphold its inciting cause are preposterous and futile." Lincoln's reply was an explicit statement of his calculated approach to the question. "I would save the Union," announced Lincoln. "If I could save the Union without freeing any slave I would do it, and if I could save it by freeing all the slaves I would do it; and if I could save it by freeing some and leaving others alone I would also do that."

When he wrote those words, Lincoln had already decided to boldly issue a presidential Emancipation Proclamation. He was waiting, however, for a Union victory so that it would not appear to be an act of desperation.

On September 22, 1862, shortly after Union success at the Battle of Antietam, Lincoln issued the first part of his two-part proclamation.

EMANCIPATION PROCLAMATION   Invoking his powers as commander-in-chief of the armed forces, he announced that on January 1, 1863, he would emancipate the slaves in the states "in rebellion." Thus, his September proclamation was less a declaration of the right of slaves to be free than a threat to southerners: unless they put down their arms, they would lose their slaves. Lincoln had little expectation that southerners would give up their effort, but he was careful to offer them the option, thus trying to put the onus of emancipation on them.

In the fateful January 1 proclamation, Lincoln excepted (as areas in rebellion) every Confederate county or city that had fallen under Union control. Nor did Lincoln liberate slaves in the border slave states that remained in the Union. "The President has purposely made the proclamation inoperative in all places where . . . the slaves [are] accessible," charged the anti-administration *New York World*. "He has proclaimed emancipation only where he has notoriously no power to execute it."

But if as a legal document the Emancipation Proclamation was wanting, as a moral and political document, it had great meaning. Because the proclamation defined the war as a war against slavery, Radicals could applaud it, even if the president had not gone as far as Congress. Yet at the same time it protected Lincoln's position with conservatives, leaving him room to retreat if he chose and forcing no immediate changes on the border slave states.

Most important, though, thousands of slaves had already reached Union lines in various sections of the South. They had "voted with their feet" for emancipation, as many said, well before the proclamation. And now every advance of federal forces into slave society was a liberating step. This Lincoln knew in taking his own initially tentative, and then forthright, steps toward emancipation.

The need for men soon convinced the administration to recruit northern and southern blacks for the Union Army. By the spring of 1863, African American troops were answering the call of a dozen or more black recruiters barnstorming the cities and towns of the North. Lincoln came to see black soldiers as "the great available and yet unavailed of force for restoring the Union." African American leaders hoped military service would secure equal rights for their people. Once the black soldier had fought for the Union, wrote Frederick Douglass, "there is no power on earth which can deny that he has earned the right of citizenship in the United States."

In June 1864, on the eve of the Republican national convention, Lincoln called the party's chairman to the White House and instructed him to have the party "put into the platform as the keystone, the amendment of the Constitution abolishing and prohibiting slavery forever." The party promptly called for the Thirteenth Amendment. Lincoln demonstrated his commitment by lobbying Congress for quick approval of the measure. The proposed amendment passed in early 1865 and was sent to the states for ratification. The war to save the Union had also become the war to free the slaves.

It has long been debated whether Abraham Lincoln deserves the label "Great Emancipator." Was Lincoln

WHO FREED THE SLAVES?   ultimately a reluctant emancipator, following rather than leading Congress and public opinion? Or did he give essential presidential leadership to the most transformative and sensitive aspect of the war by going slow on emancipation, but once moving, never backpedaling on black freedom? Once Lincoln decided to prosecute the war to the unconditional surrender of the Confederates, he made the destruction of slavery central to the conflict's purpose.

Others have argued, however, that the slaves themselves are the central story in the achievement of their own freedom. When they were near enough to the war zones, they fled for their freedom by the thousands. Some worked as camp laborers for the Union armies, and eventually more than 180,000 black men served in the Union Army and Navy.

However freedom came to individuals, emancipation was a historical confluence of two essential forces: one, a policy directed by and dependent on the military authority of the president in his effort to win the war and two, the will and courage necessary for acts of self-emancipation.

Before the war was over, the Confederacy too addressed the issue of emancipation. Jefferson Davis

A CONFEDERATE PLAN OF EMANCIPATION himself offered a proposal for black freedom of a kind. Late in the war, he was willing to sacrifice slavery to achieve independence. He proposed that the Confederate government purchase forty thousand slaves to work for the army as laborers, with a promise of freedom at the end of their service. Soon Davis upgraded the idea, calling for the recruitment and arming of slaves as soldiers to be freed at war's end. The wives and children of these soldiers, he made plain, must also receive freedom from the states.

Bitter debate over Davis's plan resounded through the Confederacy. When the Confederate Congress approved slave enlistments without the promise of freedom in March 1865, Davis insisted on more. He issued an executive order to guarantee that owners would emancipate slave soldiers and eventually their families.

The war ended before much could come of these desperate Confederate policy initiatives. By contrast, Lincoln's Emancipation Proclamation stimulated a vital infusion of forces into the Union armies. Before the war was over, 134,000 slaves (and 52,000 free blacks) had fought for freedom and the Union. Their participation was pivotal in victory.

The Soldiers' War

*T*he intricacies of policymaking and social revolution were far from the minds of most ordinary soldiers. Military service completely altered their lives. Army life meant tedium, physical hardship, and separation from loved ones. Yet the military experience had powerful attractions as well. It molded men on both sides so thoroughly that they came to resemble one another far more than they resembled civilians back home. Many soldiers forged amid war a bond with their fellows and a connection to a noble purpose that they cherished for years afterward.

Soldiers benefited from certain new products, such as canned condensed milk, but blankets, clothing,

HOSPITALS AND CAMP LIFE and arms were often of poor quality. Hospitals were badly managed at first. Rules of hygiene in large camps were scarcely enforced; latrines were poorly made or carelessly used. Water supplies were unsafe and typhoid epidemics common. About 57,000 men died from dysentery and diarrhea; in fact, 224,000 Union troops died from disease or accidents compared with 140,000 who died as a result of battle.

On both sides, troops quickly learned that soldiering was far from glorious. Before the war, few had seen violent death. Now the war exposed them to the blasted bodies of their friends and comrades. "Any one who goes over a battlefield after a battle," wrote one Confederate, "never cares to go over another. . . . It is a sad sight to see the dead and if possible more sad to see the wounded—shot in every possible way you can imagine." Much of the carnage resulted from tactics that made little sense. Still, Civil War soldiers developed deep commitments to each other and to their task. When at last the war was over, "it seemed like breaking up a family to separate," one man observed.

Online Study Center Improve Your Grade
Primary Source: Heat of Battle from the Southern Soldier's Perspective

Advances in technology made the Civil War particularly deadly. By far the most important were the rifle

THE RIFLED MUSKET and the "minie ball." Bullets fired from a smoothbore musket tumbled and wobbled as they flew through the air and thus were not accurate at distances over 80 yards. Cutting spiraled grooves inside the barrel gave the projectile a spin and much greater accuracy after Frenchman Claude Minie and the American James Burton developed a new kind of bullet. Civil War bullets were sizable lead slugs with a cavity at the bottom that expanded on firing so that the bullet "took" the rifling and flew accurately. With these bullets, rifles were accurate at 400 yards and useful up to 1,000 yards.

This meant that soldiers assaulting a position defended by riflemen were in greater peril than ever before. Although Civil War rifles were cumbersome to load, advancing soldiers were repeatedly exposed to accurate rifle fire. Because medical knowledge was rudimentary, even minor wounds often led to amputation and to death through infection. Never before in Europe or America had such massive forces pummeled each other with weapons of such destructive power.

At the outset of the war, racism in the Union Army was strong. Most white soldiers wanted noth-

THE BLACK SOLDIER'S FIGHT FOR MANHOOD

ing to do with black people and regarded them as inferior. "I never came out here for to free the black devils," wrote one soldier. For many, acceptance of black troops grew only because they could do heavy labor and "stop Bullets as well as white people."

But among some, a change occurred. White officers who volunteered to lead black units only to gain promotion found that the experience altered their opinions. After just one month with black troops, a white captain informed his wife, "I have a more elevated opinion of their abilities than I ever had before. I know that many of them are vastly the superiors of those . . . who would condemn them all to a life of brutal degradation." One general reported that his "colored regiments" possessed "remarkable aptitude for military training." Another observer said, "They fight like fiends."

Black troops created this change through their own dedication. They had a mission to destroy slavery and demonstrate their equality. Corporal James Henry Gooding of Massachusetts's black Fifty-fourth Regiment explained that his unit intended "to live down all prejudice against its color, by a determination to do well in any position it is put." After an engagement, he was proud that "a regiment of white men gave us three cheers as we were passing them," because "it shows that we did our duty as men should."

African American soldiers displayed courage despite persistent discrimination. Off-duty black soldiers were sometimes attacked by northern mobs; on duty, they did most of the heavy labor. The Union government, moreover, paid white privates $13 per month plus a clothing allowance of $3.50, whereas black privates earned only $10 per month less $3 for clothing. Congress eventually remedied the inequity. In this instance, at least, the majority of legislators agreed with a white private that black troops had

"proved their title to manhood on many a bloody field fighting freedom's battles."

1863: The Tide of Battle Turns

The fighting in the spring and summer of 1863 did not settle the war, but it began to suggest the outcome. The campaigns began in a deceptively positive way for Confederates, as their Army of Northern Virginia performed brilliantly in battles in central Virginia.

On May 2 and 3, west of Fredericksburg, Virginia, some 130,000 members of the Union Army of the Po-

BATTLE OF CHANCELLORSVILLE

tomac bore down on fewer than 60,000 Confederates. Boldly, Lee and Stonewall Jackson divided their forces, ordering 30,000 men under Jackson on a day-long march westward for a flank attack. Jackson's seasoned "foot cavalry" found unprepared Union troops laughing, smoking, and playing cards. The Confederate attack drove the entire right side of the Union Army back in confusion. However, as Jackson and a few officers returned at twilight from reconnoitering, southern troops mistook them for federals and fired, fatally wounding their commander. The next day, Union forces left in defeat. Chancellorsville was a remarkable southern victory but costly for the loss of Stonewall Jackson.

July brought crushing defeats for the Confederacy in two critical battles—Vicksburg and Gettysburg—

SIEGE OF VICKSBURG

that severely damaged Confederate hopes for independence. Vicksburg was a vital western citadel, the last major fortification on the Mississippi River in southern hands. After months of searching through swamps and bayous, General Ulysses S. Grant found an advantageous approach to the city. He laid siege to Vicksburg in May, bottling up the defending forces. If Vicksburg fell, Union forces would control the river, cutting the Confederacy in two and gaining an open path into its interior. Meanwhile, General Lee launched a Confederate invasion of the North.

As Lee's emboldened army advanced through western Maryland and into Pennsylvania, Confederate prospects along the Mississippi darkened. Davis repeatedly wired General Joseph E. Johnston, urging him to concentrate his forces and attack Grant's army.

Johnston, however, did little. Grant's men, meanwhile, were supplying themselves from the abundant crops of the Mississippi River valley and could continue their siege indefinitely.

In such circumstances, the fall of Vicksburg was inevitable, and on July 4, 1863, its commander surrendered. The same day, a battle that had been raging for three days concluded at Gettysburg, Pennsylvania (Map 15.1). On July 1, Confederate forces hunting for a supply of shoes had collided with part of the Union Army. After heavy fighting on the second day, federal forces occupied high ground along Cemetery Ridge, enjoying the protection of a stone wall and a clear view of their foe across almost a mile of open field.

BATTLE OF GETTYSBURG

Undaunted, Lee believed his reinforced troops could break the Union line, and on July 3 he ordered a direct assault. General James Longstreet warned Lee that "no 15,000 men ever arrayed for battle can take that position." But Lee stuck to his plan. Virginians under General George E. Pickett and North Carolinians under General James Pettigrew methodically marched up the slope in a doomed assault known as Pickett's Charge. For a moment, a few hundred Confederates breached the enemy's line, but most fell in heavy slaughter. On July 4, Lee had to withdraw, his army having suffered almost 28,000 casualties.

Southern troops displayed unforgettable courage and dedication at Gettysburg, as did the Union Army, which suffered 23,000 casualties (nearly one-quarter of the force), under General George G. Meade. But the results there and at Vicksburg were disastrous for the South. The Confederacy was split in two, and its heartland lay exposed to invasion. Lee's defeat spelled the end of major southern offensive actions. Too weak to prevail in attack, the Confederacy henceforth would have to conserve its limited resources and rely on a prolonged defense.

Disunity, South, North, and West

Both northern and southern governments waged the final two years of the war in the face of increasing opposition at home. The gigantic costs of a civil war that neither side seemed able to win fed

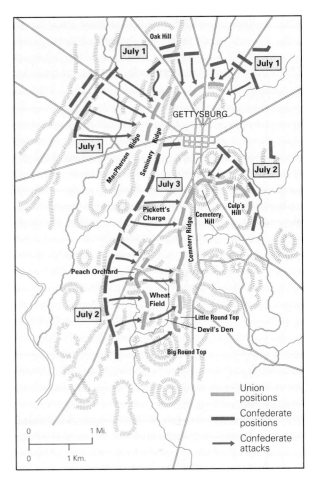

Map 15.1   Battle of Gettysburg

In the war's greatest battle, fought around a small market town in southern Pennsylvania, Lee's invasion of the North was repulsed. Union forces had the advantage of high ground, shorter lines, and superior numbers. The casualties for the two armies—dead, wounded, and missing—exceeded 50,000 men.

the unrest. But protest also arose from fundamental stresses in the social structures of North and South.

The Confederacy's problems were both more serious and more deeply rooted than the North's. One ominous development was the planters' increasing opposition to their own government. Not only did the Richmond government impose new taxes, but Confederate military authorities also impressed

DISINTEGRATION OF CONFEDERATE UNITY

slaves to build fortifications. And when Union forces advanced on plantation areas, Confederate commanders burned stores of cotton that lay in the enemy's path. Such interference with plantation routines and financial interests was not what planters had expected of their government, and they complained bitterly.

Nor were the centralizing policies of the Davis administration popular. The increasing size and power of the Richmond government startled and alarmed planters. The Confederate constitution had in fact granted substantial powers to the central government, especially in time of war. But many planters had assumed with R. B. Rhett, editor of the *Charleston Mercury,* that the Confederate constitution "leaves the States untouched in their Sovereignty, and commits to the Confederate Government only a few simple objects, and a few simple powers to enforce them."

Years of opposition to the federal government within the Union had frozen southerners in a defensive posture. Now they erected the barrier of states' rights as a defense against change. Planters sought, above all, a guarantee that their plantations and their lives would remain untouched. As secession revolutionized their world, many were not fully committed to the cause.

For ordinary southerners, hunger and suffering were becoming a reality. Food riots occurred in the

FOOD RIOTS IN SOUTHERN CITIES

spring of 1863 in Atlanta, Macon, Columbus, and Augusta, Georgia, and in Salisbury and High Point, North Carolina. On April 2 a crowd assembled in Richmond to demand relief. A passerby, noticing the excitement, asked a young girl, "Is there some celebration?" "We celebrate our right to live," replied the girl. "We are starving. As soon as enough of us get together we are going to the bakeries and each of us will take a loaf of bread." Soon they did just that, sparking a riot that Jefferson Davis himself had to quell at gunpoint.

Throughout the rural South, ordinary people resisted more quietly—by refusing to cooperate with conscription, tax collection, and impressments of food. "In all the States impressments are evaded by every means which ingenuity can suggest, and in some openly resisted," wrote a high-ranking commissary officer. Conscription officers increasingly found

no one to draft. "The disposition to avoid military service is general," observed a Georgia senator in 1864.

Such discontent was certain to affect the Confederate armies. Worried about their loved ones and resentful of what they saw as a rich

DESERTIONS FROM THE CONFEDERATE ARMY

man's war, large numbers of men deserted. The problem became especially acute after 1862. In mid-1863 it was estimated that 40,000 to 50,000 troops were absent without leave and that 100,000 were evading duty in some way. By November 1863 Secretary of War James Seddon admitted that one-third of the army could not be accounted for.

The defeats at Gettysburg and Vicksburg dealt a heavy blow to Confederate morale. In desperation, President Davis and several state governors resorted to threats and racial scare tactics to drive southern whites to further sacrifice. Despite such tactics, the internal disintegration of the Confederacy quickened. A few newspapers even began to call openly for peace.

In North Carolina a peace movement grew under the leadership of William W. Holden, a popular Democratic politician and editor. Over

ANTIWAR SENTIMENT, SOUTH AND NORTH

one hundred public meetings took place in the summer of 1863 in support of peace negotiations. In Georgia early in 1864, Governor Joseph E. Brown and Alexander H. Stephens, vice president of the Confederacy, led a similar effort. Ultimately these movements came to naught. Politically, the lack of a two-party system allowed any criticism of the government to be colored with the taint of dishonor and disloyalty.

But by 1864, much of the opposition to the war had moved entirely outside the political sphere. Southerners were simply giving up the struggle and withdrawing their cooperation from the government. Deserters dominated whole towns and counties. Secret societies favoring reunion sprang up. Active dissent was particularly common in upland and mountain regions. The government was losing the support of its citizens.

In the North, opposition to the war was similar but less severe. Alarm intensified over the growing centralization of government, and by 1863, war-weariness was widespread. Resentment of the draft sparked protest, especially among poor citizens, and the Union Army struggled with a desertion rate as high as the Confederates'. But the Union was so much richer than the South in human resources that fresh recruits were always available.

Also, Lincoln possessed a talent that Davis lacked: he knew how to stay in touch with the ordinary citizen. Through letters to newspapers and to soldiers' families, he reached the common people and demonstrated that he had not forgotten them. The daily carnage, the tortuous political problems, and the ceaseless criticism weighed heavily on him. But this self-educated man of humble origins was able to communicate his suffering with words that helped contain northern discontent.

Much of the wartime protest in the North was political in origin. The Democratic Party fought to regain power by blaming Lincoln for

PEACE DEMOCRATS

the war's death toll, the expansion of federal powers, inflation and the high tariff, and the emancipation of blacks. Appealing to tradition, its leaders called for an end to the war and reunion on the basis of "the Constitution as it is and the Union as it was." The Democrats denounced conscription and martial law and defended states' rights. In the 1862 congressional elections, the Democrats made a strong comeback, and peace Democrats, who would go much further than others in the party to end the war, had influence in New York State and majorities in the legislatures of Illinois and Indiana.

Led by outspoken men like Representative Clement L. Vallandigham of Ohio, the peace Democrats made themselves highly visible. Vallandigham criticized Lincoln as a dictator who had suspended the writ of habeas corpus without congressional authority and had arrested thousands of innocent citizens. He condemned both conscription and emancipation. Vallandigham stayed carefully within legal bounds, but his attacks seemed so damaging to the war effort that military authorities arrested him for treason. Lincoln wisely decided against punishment—and martyr's status—for the Ohioan and exiled him to the Confederacy.

Lincoln believed that antiwar Democrats were linked to secret traitorous organizations that encouraged draft resistance, discouraged enlistment, sabotaged communications, and plotted to aid the Confederacy. Likening such groups to a poisonous snake, Republicans sometimes branded them—and by extension the peace Democrats—as "Copperheads." Although some Confederate agents were active in the North and Canada, they never genuinely threatened the Union war effort.

More violent opposition to the government arose from ordinary citizens facing the draft, which became

NEW YORK CITY DRAFT RIOTS

law in 1863. Under the law, a draftee could stay at home by providing a substitute or paying a $300 commutation fee. Many wealthy men, and some of modest means, chose these options, and in response to popular demand, clubs, cities, and states provided the money for others to escape conscription. The urban poor and immigrants in strongly Democratic areas were especially hostile to conscription. The poor viewed the commutation fee as discriminatory, and many immigrants suspected (wrongly, on the whole) that they were called in disproportionate numbers.

As a result, there were scores of disturbances and melees. Enrolling officers received rough treatment, and riots occurred in many states from New Jersey to Wisconsin. By far the most serious outbreak of violence was in July 1863 in New York City, a Democratic stronghold where racial, ethnic, and class tensions ran high. Working-class New Yorkers feared an inflow of black labor from the South and regarded blacks as the cause of the war. Poor Irish workers resented having to serve in the place of others who could afford to avoid the draft. When these tensions erupted, seventy-four people died during three days of rioting. Blacks became the special target of rioters, who rampaged through African American neighborhoods, beating residents and destroying an orphan asylum.

A civil war of another kind raged on the Great Plains and in the Southwest. By 1864 U.S. troops under Colonel John Chivington waged

WAR AGAINST INDIANS IN THE FAR WEST

full-scale war against the Sioux, Arapahos, and Cheyennes to eradicate Indian title to all of eastern Colorado. Indian chiefs sought peace, but American commanders had orders to "burn villages and kill Cheyennes whenever and wherever found." A Cheyenne chief, Black Kettle, was told by the U.S. command his people would find a safe haven by moving to Sand Creek, Colorado. But on November 29, 1864, 700 cavalrymen, many drunk, attacked the Cheyenne village. With most of the men absent hunting, 105 Cheyenne women and children and 28 men were slaughtered.

In New Mexico and Arizona Territories, the Apaches and the Navajos had for generations raided the Pueblo Indians and Hispanic peoples of the region. During the Civil War years, Anglo-American farms also became Indian targets. In 1863 the New Mexico Volunteers, commanded by former mountain man Kit Carson, defeated the Mescalero Apaches and forced them onto the Bosque Redondo Reservation.

The area's Navajos resisted from the canyons and high deserts where they lived. After Carson carried out a "scorched earth" campaign against them, three-quarters of the twelve thousand Navajos were rounded up in 1864 and forced to march 400 miles (the "Long Walk") to Bosque Redondo, suffering malnutrition and death along the way. Permitted to return to a fraction of their homelands later that year, the Navajos carried with them searing memories of the federal government's ruthless policies toward Indian peoples.

Back east, war-weariness reached a peak in the summer of 1864, when the Democratic Party nominated the popular General George B. McClellan for president, inserted a peace plank into its platform, and made racist appeals to white insecurity. Lincoln concluded that it was "exceedingly probable that this Administration will not be reelected." Although relatively unified, the Republican Party faced the horrible casualty lists and battlefield stalemate of summer 1864.

ELECTION OF 1864

The fortunes of war soon changed the electoral situation. With the fall of Atlanta and Union victories in the Shenandoah valley by early September, Lincoln's prospects rose. Decisive in the election was that Lincoln won an extraordinary 78 percent of the soldier vote. With the president taking 55 percent of the total popular vote, Lincoln's reelection—a referendum on the war and emancipation—had a devastating impact on southern morale. Without this political outcome in 1864, a Union military victory may never have been possible.

1864–1865: The Final Test of Wills

During the final year of the war, the Confederates could still have won their version of victory if military stalemate and northern antiwar sentiment had forced a negotiated settlement to end the war. But events and northern determination prevailed.

From the outset, the North had pursued one paramount diplomatic goal: to prevent recognition of the Confederacy by European nations. Foreign recognition would belie Lincoln's claim to be fighting an illegal rebellion and would open the way to financial and military aid. Both England and France stood to benefit from a divided and weakened America. Thus, to achieve their goal, Lincoln and Secretary of State William H. Seward needed to avoid both serious military defeats and controversies with the European powers.

NORTHERN DIPLOMATIC STRATEGY

Aware that the textile industry employed one-fifth of the British population directly or indirectly, southerners banked on British recognition of the Confederacy. But at the beginning of the war, British mills had a 50 percent surplus of cotton on hand, and later they found new sources of supply in India, Egypt, and Brazil. Refusing to be stampeded into recognition of the Confederacy, the British government kept its eye on the battlefield. France, though sympathetic to the South, was unwilling to act independent of Britain.

More than once, the Union strategy nearly broke down. An acute crisis occurred in 1861 when the overzealous commander of an American frigate stopped the British steamer *Trent* and removed two Confederate ambassadors. The British interpreted this action as a violation of freedom of the seas and demanded the prisoners' release. Lincoln and Seward waited until northern public opinion cooled and then released the two southerners.

Then the sale to the Confederacy of warships constructed in England sparked vigorous U.S. protest. A few English-built ships, notably the *Alabama*, reached open water to serve the South. Over twenty-two months, the *Alabama* destroyed or captured more than sixty Union ships.

The Civil War in Britain

Because of the direct reliance of the British textile industry on cut-off southern cotton, as well as the many ideological and familial ties between the two nations, the American Civil War was decisive in Britain's economy and domestic politics. The British aristocracy and most cotton mill owners were solidly pro-Confederate and proslavery, while a combination of clergymen, shopkeepers, artisans, and radical politicians worked for the causes of Union and emancipation. Most British workers saw their futures at stake in a war for slave emancipation. "Freedom" to the huge British working class (who could not vote) meant basic political and civil rights, and the "cotton famine" threw millhands out of work.

English aristocrats saw Americans as untutored, wayward cousins and took satisfaction in America's troubles. Conservatives believed in the superiority of the British system of government and looked askance at America's leveling tendencies. And some aristocratic British Liberals also saw Americans through their class bias and sympathized with the Confederacy's demand for "order" and independence. English racism also intensified in these years, exemplified by the popularity of minstrelsy and the employment of science in racial theory.

The intensity of the British debate over the American conflict is evident in the huge public meetings organized by both sides with cheering and jeering, competing banners, carts and floats, orators and resolutions. In a press war, the British argued over whether rebellion or secession was justified or legal, whether slavery was at the heart of the conflict, and especially over the democratic image of America. This bitter debate over America's trial became a test over reform in Britain: those eager for a broadened franchise and increased democracy were pro-Union, and those who preferred to preserve Britain's class-ridden political system favored the Confederacy.

In the end, the British government did not recognize the Confederacy, and by 1864, the English cotton lords had found new sources in Egypt and India. But in this link between America and its English roots, the Civil War was a transformation of international significance.

Some southern leaders pronounced that cotton was "king" and would bring Britain to their cause. This British cartoon shows King Cotton brought down in chains by the American eagle, anticipating the cotton famine to follow and the intense debate in Great Britain over the nature and meaning of the American Civil War. (The Granger Collection)

On the battlefield, the northern victory was far from won in 1864. General Nathaniel Banks's Red River campaign, designed to capture more of Louisiana and Texas, quickly fell apart, and the capture of Mobile Bay in August did not cause the fall of Mobile. Union general William Tecumseh Sherman commented that the North had to "keep the war South until they are not only ruined, exhausted, but humbled in pride and spirit."

BATTLEFIELD STALEMATE AND A UNION STRATEGY FOR VICTORY

Military authorities throughout history have agreed that deep invasion is highly risky: the farther an army penetrates enemy territory, the more vulnerable are its own communications and supply lines. General Grant, by now in command of all the federal armies, decided to test this assertion—and southern will—with a strategic innovation of his own: raids on a massive scale. Grant proposed to use whole armies to destroy Confederate railroads, thus ruining the enemy's transportation and damaging the South's economy. Abandoning their lines of support, Union troops would live off the land while laying waste all resources useful to the military and to the civilian population. After General George H. Thomas's troops won the Battle of Chattanooga in November 1863 by ignoring orders and charging up Missionary Ridge, the heartland of Georgia lay open. Grant entrusted General Sherman with 100,000 men for an invasion deep into the South, toward the rail center of Atlanta.

Jefferson Davis countered by positioning the army of General Joseph E. Johnston in Sherman's path. Davis hoped that southern resolve would lead to Lincoln's defeat and the election of a president who would sue for peace. When General Johnston slowly but steadily fell back toward Atlanta, Davis grew anxious and sought assurances that Atlanta would be held. From a purely military point of view, Johnston maneuvered skillfully, but when he continued to retreat, Davis replaced him with the one-legged General John Hood, who knew his job was to fight. Hood attacked but was beaten, and Sherman's army occupied Atlanta on September 2, 1864. The victory buoyed northern spirits, ensured Lincoln's reelection, and cleared the way for Sherman's march from Atlanta to the sea (see Map 15.2).

FALL OF ATLANTA

Sherman's army was an unusually formidable force, composed almost entirely of battle-tested veterans, tanned, bearded, tough, and unkempt, who were determined, as one put it, "to Conquer this Rebellien or Die." As Sherman's men moved across Georgia, they cut a path 50 to 60 miles wide and more than 200 miles long. The destruction they caused was awesome. A Georgia woman described the "Burnt Country" this way: "The fields were trampled down and the road was lined with carcasses of horses, hogs, and cattle that the invaders, unable either to consume or to carry with them, had wantonly shot down to starve our people. . . . The stench in some places was unbearable." Such devastation sapped the South's will to resist. Indeed, the lack of popular resistance in Georgia and South Carolina indicated that southern whites had lost the will to continue the struggle.

SHERMAN'S MARCH TO THE SEA

Online Study Center Improve Your Grade
Interactive Map: Grant's Campaign Against Lee

In Virginia, too, the path to victory proved protracted and ghastly. Throughout the spring and summer of 1864, intent on capturing Richmond, Grant hurled his troops at Lee's army in Virginia and suffered appalling losses: almost 18,000 casualties in the Battle of the Wilderness, more than 8,000 at Spotsylvania, and 12,000 in the space of a few hours at Cold Harbor.

VIRGINIA'S BLOODY SOIL

Before the assault at Cold Harbor (which Grant later admitted was a grave mistake), Union troops pinned scraps of paper bearing their names and addresses to their backs, certain they would be mowed down as they rushed Lee's trenches. In four weeks in May and June, Grant lost as many men as were enrolled in Lee's entire army. Though costly, and testing northern morale to its limits, these battles prepared the way for eventual victory: Lee's army shrank until offensive action was no longer possible, while Grant's army kept replenishing its forces with new recruits.

The end finally came in the spring of 1865. From its trenches besieging Petersburg, Grant's army kept battering Lee, who tried but failed to break through the Union line. With the numerical superiority of Grant's army now greater than two to one, Confederate defeat was

SURRENDER AT APPOMATTOX

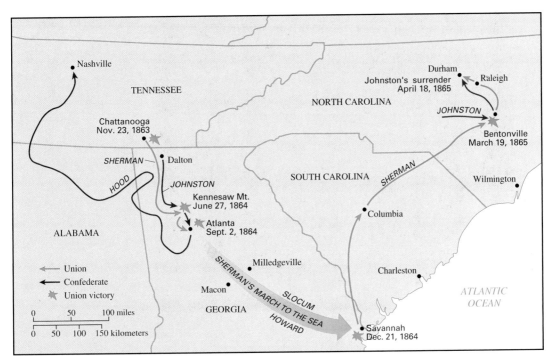

Map 15.2   Sherman's March to the Sea

The West proved a decisive theater at the end of the war. From Chattanooga, Union forces drove into Georgia, capturing Atlanta. Following the fall of Atlanta, General Sherman embarked on his march of destruction through Georgia to the coast and then northward through the Carolinas.

inevitable. On April 2 Lee abandoned Richmond and Petersburg. On April 9, hemmed in by Union troops, short of rations, and with fewer than thirty thousand men left, Lee surrendered at Appomattox Court House. Grant treated his rival with respect and paroled the defeated troops. The war was over at last. Within weeks, Confederate forces under Johnston surrendered, and Davis was captured in Georgia.

With Lee's surrender, Lincoln knew that the Union had been preserved, yet he lived to see but a few days of the war's aftermath. On the evening of Good Friday, April 14, he accompanied his wife to Ford's Theatre in Washington to enjoy a popular comedy. There, John Wilkes Booth, an embittered southern sympathizer, shot the president in the head at point-blank range. The Union had lost its wartime leader, and millions publicly mourned the martyred chief executive. Relief at the war's end mingled

hauntingly with a renewed sense of loss and anxiety about the future.

Property damage and financial costs were enormous, though difficult to tally. U.S. loans and taxes during the conflict totaled almost $3 billion, and interest on the war debt was $2.8 billion. The Confederacy borrowed over $2 billion but lost far more in the destruction of homes, crops, livestock, and other property. In southern war zones, the landscape was desolated. Over wide regions, fences and crops were destroyed; houses, barns, and bridges burned; and fields abandoned and left to erode. Factories had been looted, and two-thirds of the South's railroad system was out of service.

Estimates of the total cost of the war exceed $20 billion—five times the total expenditures of the federal government from its creation to 1861. By 1865

FINANCIAL TALLY

■ The death of President Lincoln caused a vast outpouring of grief in the North. As this Currier and Ives print shows, Lincoln's funeral train stopped at several cities on its way to Illinois to allow local services to be held.   (Anne S. K. Brown Military Collection, Brown University Library)

the federal government's spending had soared to twenty times the prewar level and accounted for over 26 percent of the gross national product. Many of these changes were more or less permanent, as wartime measures left the government deeply involved in manufacturing, banking, and transportation. If southerners had hoped to remove government from the economy, the war had now irrepressibly bound them together.

The human costs of the Civil War were staggering. The total number of military casualties on both sides exceeded 1 million—a frightful toll for a nation of 31 million people. Approximately 360,000 Union soldiers died. Another 275,175 were wounded. On the Confederate side, an estimated 260,000 lost their lives, and almost as many suffered wounds. More men died in the Civil War than in all other American wars combined until Vietnam.

DEATH TOLL

Summary   *Online Study Center* ACE the Test

The Civil War altered American society forever. During the war, women in both North and South took on new roles. Industrialization and large economic enterprises grew in power. The character and extent of government power changed markedly. Under Republican leadership, the federal government had expanded its power not only to preserve the Union but also to extend freedom. A social revolution and government authority emancipated the slaves. A republic desperately divided against itself had survived, but in new constitutional forms yet to take shape during Reconstruction.

In the West, two civil wars raged, the second resulting in conquest of southwestern Indians by U.S. troops and land-hungry settlers. On the diplomatic front, the Union government had delicately managed to keep Great Britain and other foreign powers out of the war. Dissent flourished in both North and South, playing a crucial role in the ultimate collapse of the Confederacy, while the Union cause was only marginally affected.

It was unclear how or whether the nation would use its power to protect the rights of the former slaves. Secession was dead, but whether Americans would continue to embrace a centralized nationalism remained to be seen. How would white southerners, embittered and impoverished, respond to efforts to reconstruct the nation? How would the country care for the maimed, the orphans, the farming women without men to work their land, and all the dead who had to be found and properly buried? What would be the place of black men and women in American life? In the Civil War, Americans had undergone a transformation like nothing before in their history. The war and all its drama, sacrifice, and social and political changes left a compelling memory in American hearts and minds for generations.

LEGACY FOR A PEOPLE AND A NATION
The Confederate Battle Flag

The most widespread and controversial symbol to emerge from the Civil War era is the Confederate flag. Rather than the official flag of the Confederacy, it was a flag that soldiers carried to mark the center of a unit's position in the confusion of combat. Over time, this flag has taken on powerful emotional meanings.

At Confederate veterans' reunions and parades from the 1870s to well into the twentieth century, the flag was an emblem of the South's Lost Cause. Increasingly, Confederate remembrance merged with white supremacy at the turn of the twentieth century, and African Americans resented the flag.

In the late 1940s the flag became a fixture of popular culture with heightened racial meanings. In 1948 it was a symbol of the States' Rights ("Dixiecrat") Party. By the 1950s, waving the Confederate flag expressed defiance among southern whites against the civil rights revolution.

This flag is a loaded symbol that can be interpreted in opposite ways. Some southern whites argue that it is merely a marker of regional pride and identity. But to most blacks and many whites, it expresses racism. Some claim it represents the "nobility" of southern military tradition; others conclude that it stands for the hatred embodied in the Ku Klux Klan.

In recent times, the Confederate flag has been the center of legal and political disputes emanating from city councils, high schools, and universities over public and private uses of the flag. Most visible of all have been the debates in Georgia, South Carolina, Alabama, and Mississippi over whether to cease flying the Confederate flag at official sites or as part of state flags. At issue are important questions: free speech, equal protection under law, perception versus reality, official government endorsement of collective symbols, the significance of race and racism in our national memory, and the meaning of the Civil War itself.

RECONSTRUCTION: AN UNFINISHED REVOLUTION 1865–1877

*a*fter a prolonged Union bombardment, the lower half of Charleston, South Carolina, the seedbed of secession, lay burning and in ruin when most of the white population evacuated on February 18, 1865. Among the first Union troops to enter Charleston was the Twenty-first U.S. Colored Regiment, which received the surrender of the city from its mayor. In symbolic celebrations, black Charlestonians, most of whom were former slaves, proclaimed their freedom and announced their rebirth.

Still, in Charleston, as elsewhere, death demanded attention. During the final year of the war, the Confederates had converted the planters' Race Course, a horseracing track, into a prison, where Union soldiers were kept in terrible conditions without shelter. The 257 who died of exposure and disease were buried in a mass grave behind the judges' stand. After the fall of the city, Charleston's blacks organized to create a proper burial ground for the Union dead. During April, more than twenty black workmen reinterred the dead in marked graves.

Then, on the morning of May 1, 1865, a procession of ten thousand people marched around the planters' Race Course, led by three thousand children carrying armloads of roses and singing "John Brown's Body." They were followed by black women and men, members of black and white Union regiments, and white missionaries and teachers. All who could fit assembled at the gravesite; five black ministers read from Scripture, and a black children's choir sang. When the ceremony ended, the large crowd retired to the Race Course for speeches, picnics, and military festivities.

The war was over in Charleston, and "Decoration Day"—now Memorial Day, the day to remember the war dead and decorate their graves—had been founded by African Americans. Black people had created an American tradition. In their vision, they were creating the Independence Day of a Second American Revolution.

Wartime Reconstruction

The Meanings of Freedom

Johnson's Reconstruction Plan

The Congressional Reconstruction Plan

Reconstruction Politics in the South

Reconstruction Reversed

LINKS TO THE WORLD
The Grants' Tour of the World

LEGACY FOR A PEOPLE AND A NATION
The Fourteenth Amendment

Online Study Center
This icon will direct you to interactive map and primary source activities on the website http://college.hmco.com/pic/nortonbrief7e

C H R O N O L O G Y

1865 • Johnson begins rapid and lenient Reconstruction
• Confederate leaders regain power
• White southern governments pass restrictive black codes
• Congress refuses to seat southern representatives
• Thirteenth Amendment ratified, abolishing slavery

1866 • Congress passes Civil Rights Act and renewal of Freedmen's Bureau over Johnson's veto
• Congress approves Fourteenth Amendment
• Most southern states reject Fourteenth Amendment
• In *Ex parte Milligan* the Supreme Court reasserts its influence

1867 • Congress passes Reconstruction Acts and Tenure of Office Act
• Seward arranges purchase of Alaska
• Constitutional conventions called in southern states

1868 • House impeaches Johnson; Senate acquits him
• Most southern states readmitted to the Union under Radical plan
• Fourteenth Amendment ratified
• Grant elected president

1869 • Congress approves Fifteenth Amendment (ratified in 1870)

1871 • Congress passes second Enforcement Act and Ku Klux Klan Act

1872 • Amnesty Act frees almost all remaining Confederates from restrictions on holding office
• Grant reelected

1873 • *Slaughter-House* cases limit power of Fourteenth Amendment
• Panic of 1873 leads to widespread unemployment and labor strife

1874 • Democrats win majority in House of Representatives

1875 • Several Grant appointees indicted for corruption
• Congress passes weak Civil Rights Act
• Democratic Party increases control of southern states with white supremacy campaigns

1876 • *U.S. v. Cruikshank* further weakens Fourteenth Amendment
• Presidential election disputed

1877 • Congress elects Hayes president
• "Home rule" returns to three remaining southern states not yet controlled by Democrats; Reconstruction considered over

Reconstruction would bring revolutionary circumstances, but revolutions can go backward. The Civil War and its aftermath wrought unprecedented changes in American society, law, and politics, but the underlying realities of economic power, racism, and judicial conservatism limited Reconstruction's revolutionary potential.

Nowhere was the turmoil of Reconstruction more evident than in national politics. Lincoln's successor, Andrew Johnson, fought bitterly with Congress over

the shaping of Reconstruction policies. Though a southerner, Johnson had always been a foe of the South's wealthy planters, and his first acts as president suggested that he would be tough on "traitors." Before the end of 1865, however, Johnson's policies changed direction. Jefferson Davis stayed in prison for two years, but Johnson quickly pardoned other rebel leaders and allowed them to occupy high offices. He also ordered the return of plantations to their original owners.

Johnson imagined a lenient and rapid "restoration" of the South to the Union rather than the fundamental "reconstruction" that Republican congressmen favored. Between 1866 and 1868, the president and the Republican leadership in Congress engaged in a bitter power struggle over how to put the United States back together again. Before it ended, Congress had impeached the president, enfranchised the freedmen, and given them a role in reconstructing the South. The nation also adopted the Fourteenth and Fifteenth Amendments. But little was done to open the doors of economic opportunity to black southerners. Moreover, by 1869, the Ku Klux Klan employed extensive terror to thwart Reconstruction and undermine black freedom.

As the 1870s advanced, industrial growth accelerated, creating new opportunities and priorities. The West, with its seemingly limitless potential and its wars against Indians, drew American resources and consciousness like never before. Political corruption became a nationwide scandal, bribery a way of doing business.

Thus, Reconstruction became a revolution eclipsed. White southerners' desire to take back control of their states and of race relations overwhelmed the national interest in stopping them. But Reconstruction left enduring legacies the nation has struggled with ever since. ■

Wartime Reconstruction

*R*econstruction of the Union was an issue as early as 1863. The very idea of Reconstruction raised many questions: How would the nation be restored and southern states and leaders treated? What was the constitutional basis for readmission of states to the Union? More specifically, four vexing problems compelled early thinking and would haunt the Reconstruction era. One, who would rule in the South once it was defeated? Two, who would rule in the federal government: Congress or the president? Three, what were the dimensions of black freedom, and what rights under law would the freedmen enjoy? And four, would Reconstruction be a preservation of the old republic or a second revolution, a reinvention of a new republic?

Online Study Center **Improve Your Grade**
Interactive Map: The Reconstruction

Abraham Lincoln had never been antisouthern. In his Second Inaugural Address, he had promised "malice toward none; with charity for all" as Americans strove to "bind up the nation's wounds." Lincoln planned early for a swift and moderate Reconstruction process. In his "Proclamation of Amnesty and Reconstruction," issued in December 1863, he proposed to replace majority rule with "loyal rule" as a means of reconstructing southern state governments. He proposed pardoning all ex-Confederates except the highest-ranking military and civilian officers. As soon as 10 percent of the voting population in the 1860 election in a given state had taken an oath and established a government, the new state would be recognized. Lincoln did not consult Congress in these plans, and "loyal" assemblies (known as "Lincoln governments") were created in Louisiana, Tennessee, and Arkansas in 1864, states largely occupied by Union troops.

LINCOLN'S 10 PERCENT PLAN

Congress responded with great hostility to Lincoln's moves to readmit southern states in what seemed such a premature manner. Many Radical Republicans considered the 10 percent plan a "mere mockery" of democracy. Thaddeus Stevens of Pennsylvania advocated a "conquered provinces" theory, and Charles Sumner of Massachusetts employed an argument of "state suicide." Both contended that by seceding, southern states had destroyed their status as states. They therefore must be treated as "conquered foreign lands" and revert to the status of "unorganized territories" before Congress could entertain any process of readmission.

CONGRESS AND THE WADE-DAVIS BILL

In July 1864, the Wade-Davis bill, named for its sponsors, Senator Benjamin Wade of Ohio and Congressman Henry W. Davis of Maryland, emerged from Congress with three specific conditions for southern readmission: one, it demanded a "majority" of white male citizens participating in the creation of a new government; two, to vote or be a delegate to constitutional conventions, men had to take an "iron-clad" oath (declaring they had never aided the Confederate war effort); and three, all officers above the rank of lieutenant and all civil officials in the Confederacy would be disfranchised and deemed "not a citizen of the United States." Lincoln pocket-vetoed the bill and announced that he would not be inflexibly committed to any "one plan" of Reconstruction.

This exchange came during Grant's bloody campaign in Virginia against Lee, when the outcome of the war and Lincoln's reelection were still in doubt. Radical members of his own party, indeed, were organizing a dump-Lincoln campaign for the 1864 election. What emerged in 1864–1865 was a clear-cut debate and a potential constitutional crisis. Lincoln saw Reconstruction as a means of weakening the Confederacy and winning the war; the Radicals saw it as a longer-term transformation of the political and racial order of the country.

In early 1865, Congress and Lincoln joined in two important measures that recognized slavery's

THIRTEENTH
AMENDMENT

centrality to the war. On January 31, with strong administration backing, Congress passed the Thirteenth Amendment, which had two provisions: it abolished involuntary servitude everywhere in the United States, and it declared that Congress shall have power to enforce this outcome by "appropriate legislation."

The Thirteenth Amendment had emerged from a long congressional debate and considerable petitioning and public advocacy. One of the first and most remarkable petitions for a constitutional amendment abolishing slavery was submitted early in 1864 by Elizabeth Cady Stanton, Susan B. Anthony, and the Women's Loyal National League. Women throughout the Union accumulated thousands of signatures, even venturing into staunchly pro-Confederate regions of Kentucky and Missouri to secure supporters. It was a long road from the Emancipation Proclamation to the Thirteenth Amendment, but the logic of winning the war by crushing slavery, and of securing a new beginning for the nation that so many had now died to save, won the day.

Potentially as significant, on March 3, 1865, Congress created the Bureau of Refugees, Freedmen, and

FREEDMEN'S
BUREAU

Abandoned Lands—the Freedmen's Bureau, an unprecedented agency of social uplift, necessitated by the ravages of the war. In the mere four years of its existence, the Freedmen's Bureau supplied food and medical services, built over four thousand schools and some colleges, negotiated several hundred thousand employment contracts between freedmen and their former masters, and tried to manage confiscated land.

The Bureau would be a controversial aspect of Reconstruction, both within the South, where whites generally hated it, and within the federal government, where politicians divided over its constitutionality. The war had forced into the open an eternal question of republics: What are the social welfare obligations of the state toward its people, and what do people owe their governments in return?

The Meanings of Freedom

E ntering life after slavery with hope and circumspection, freed men and women tried to gain as much as they could from their new circumstances. Often the changes they valued the most were personal: alterations in location, employer, or living arrangements.

Online Study Center Improve Your Grade
Primary Source: Black Testimony on the
Aftermath of Enslavement

For America's former slaves, Reconstruction had one paramount meaning: a chance to explore freedom.

THE FEEL OF
FREEDOM

Former slaves remembered singing far into the night after federal troops, who confirmed rumors of their emancipation, reached their plantations. The slaves on a Texas plantation shouted for joy, their leader proclaiming, "We is free—no more whippings and beatings." One man recalled that he and others "started on the move," either to search for family members or just to exercise the human right of mobility.

Many freed men and women reacted more cautiously and shrewdly, taking care to test the boundaries of their new condition. "After the war was over," explained one man, "we was afraid to move. Just like terrapins or turtles after emancipation. Just stick our heads out to see how the land lay." As slaves they had learned to expect hostility from white people, and they did not presume it would instantly disappear. Life in freedom might still be a matter of what was allowed, not what was right. One sign of

■ *The Armed Slave,* William Sprang, oil on canvas, c. 1865. This remarkable painting depicts an African American veteran soldier, musket with fixed bayonet leaning against the wall, cigar in hand indicating a new life of safety and leisure, reading a book to demonstrate his embrace of education and freedom. The man's visage leaves the impression of satisfaction and dignity.   (Courtesy of The Civil War Library and Underground Railroad Museum of Philadelphia)

wife, child, or parent. Some succeeded in their quest, sometimes almost miraculously. Others never found their loved ones.

Husbands and wives who had belonged to different masters established homes together for the first time, and, as they had under slavery, parents asserted the right to raise their own children. A mother bristled when her old master claimed a right to whip her children. She informed him that "he warn't goin' to brush none of her chilluns no more." The freed men and women were too much at risk to act recklessly, but as one man put it, they were tired of punishment and "sure didn't take no more foolishment off of white folks."

BLACKS' SEARCH FOR INDEPENDENCE

To avoid contact with overbearing whites who were used to supervising them, blacks abandoned the slave quarters and fanned out to distant corners of the land they worked. Some described moving "across the creek" or building a "saplin house . . . back in the woods." Others established small all-black settlements that still exist today along the back roads of the South.

FREEDPEOPLE'S DESIRE FOR LAND

In addition to a fair employer, what freed men and women most wanted was the ownership of land. Land represented self-sufficiency and a chance to gain compensation for generations of bondage. In February 1865 General Sherman ordered 400,000 acres in the Sea Islands region set aside for the exclusive settlement of the freedpeople. But President Johnson ordered them removed in October and returned the land to its original owners under army enforcement.

Most members of both political parties opposed genuine land redistribution to the freedmen. Even northern reformers showed little sympathy for black aspirations. The former Sea Island slaves wanted to establish small, self-sufficient farms. Northern soldiers, officials, and missionaries insisted that they grow cotton, emphasizing profit, cash crops, and the values of competitive capitalism.

"The Yankees preach nothing but cotton, cotton" complained one Sea Island black. "We wants land," wrote another, but tax officials "make the lots too big, and cut we out." Indeed, the U.S. government sold thousands of acres in the Sea Islands, 90 percent of which went to wealthy investors from the North.

their caution was the way freedpeople evaluated potential employers, wandering in search of better circumstances. A majority of blacks eventually settled as agricultural workers back on their former farms or plantations. But they relocated their houses and did their utmost to control the conditions of their labor.

REUNION OF AFRICAN AMERICAN FAMILIES

Throughout the South, former slaves devoted themselves to reuniting their families, separated during slavery or by dislocation during the war. With only shreds of information to guide them, thousands of freedpeople embarked on odysseys in search of a husband,

Ex-slaves reached out for valuable things in life that had been denied them, including education. Blacks

THE BLACK EMBRACE OF EDUCATION

of all ages hungered for the knowledge in books that had been permitted only to whites. With freedom, they started schools and filled classrooms. On log seats and dirt floors, freed men and women studied their letters in old almanacs and discarded dictionaries. Young children brought infants to school with them, and adults attended at night or after "the crops were laid by."

The federal government and northern reformers of both races assisted this pursuit of education through Freedmen's Bureau schools and others founded by private northern philanthropy. More than 600,000 African Americans were enrolled in elementary school by 1877.

Blacks and their white allies also saw the need for colleges and universities to train teachers, ministers, and professionals for leadership. The American Missionary Association founded seven colleges, including Fisk and Atlanta Universities, between 1866 and 1869. The Freedmen's Bureau helped to establish Howard University in Washington, D.C., and northern religious groups supported dozens of seminaries and teachers' colleges.

During Reconstruction, African American leaders often were highly educated individuals; many were from the prewar elite of free people of color and often blood relatives of wealthy whites; some planters had given their mulatto children an outstanding education. Francis Cardozo, who held various offices in South Carolina, had attended universities in Scotland and England. The two black senators from Mississippi, Blanche K. Bruce and Hiram Revels, possessed privileged educations. These men and many self-educated former slaves brought to political office not only fervor but useful experience.

Freed from the restrictions and regulations of slavery, blacks could build their own institutions as

GROWTH OF BLACK CHURCHES

they saw fit. The secret churches of slavery came into the open; throughout the South, ex-slaves "started a brush arbor," which was "a sort of . . . shelter with leaves for a roof," but the freed men and women worshiped in it enthusiastically. Within a few years, however, independent branches of the Methodist and

Baptist denominations had attracted the great majority of black Christians in the South.

The desire to gain as much independence as possible also shaped the former slaves' economic arrange-

RISE OF THE SHARECROPPING SYSTEM

ments. Since most of them lacked the money to buy land, they preferred the next best thing: renting the land they worked. But the South had a cash-poor economy with few sources of credit. Therefore, black farmers and white landowners turned to sharecropping, a system in which farmers kept part of their crop and gave the rest to the landowner while living on his property. The landlord or a merchant "furnished" food and supplies needed before the harvest. Although landowners tried to set the laborers' share at a low level, black farmers had some bargaining power, at least at first. Sharecroppers would hold out, or move and try to switch employers from one year to another. As the system matured during the 1870s and 1880s, most sharecroppers worked "on halves"—half for the owner and half for themselves.

The sharecropping system originated as a desirable compromise. It eased landowners' problems with cash and credit and provided them a permanent, dependent labor force; blacks accepted it because it gave them more freedom from daily supervision. Instead of working in the hated gangs under a white overseer, as in slavery, they farmed their own plot of land in family groups. But sharecropping later proved to be a disaster. Owners and merchants developed a monopoly of control over the agricultural economy, and sharecroppers found themselves riveted into ever-increasing debt. Moreover, southern farmers concentrated on cotton, and cotton prices began a long decline.

Johnson's Reconstruction Plan

*W*hen Reconstruction began under President Andrew Johnson, many former slaveowners, as well as northern Radicals, had reason to believe that he would deal sternly with the South. Throughout his career in Tennessee, he had criticized the wealthy planters and championed the small farmers. When one Radical suggested the exile or execution of ten or twelve leading rebels to set an example, Johnson replied, "How are you going to pick out so small a number?"

Like his martyred predecessor, Johnson followed a path in antebellum politics from obscurity to power.

ANDREW
JOHNSON OF
TENNESSEE

With no formal education, he became a tailor's apprentice. But from 1829, while in his early twenties, he held nearly every office in Tennessee politics, including two terms as governor, and he was a U.S. senator by 1857. Although elected as a southern Democrat, Johnson was the only senator from a seceded state who refused to follow his state out of the Union. Lincoln appointed him war governor of Tennessee in 1862, hence, his symbolic place on the ticket in the president's bid for reelection in 1864.

Although a staunch Unionist, Johnson was also an ardent states' rightist. And while he vehemently opposed secession, he advocated limited government. His philosophy toward Reconstruction may be summed up in the slogan he adopted: "The Constitution as it is, and the Union as it was."

Through 1865, Johnson alone controlled Reconstruction policy, for Congress recessed shortly before he became president and did not reconvene until December. In the following eight months, Johnson put into operation his own plan, forming new state governments in the South by using his power to grant pardons.

Although never a planter, Johnson had owned house slaves. He accepted emancipation as a result of

JOHNSON'S
RACIAL VIEWS

the war, but he did not favor black civil and political rights and was a thoroughgoing white supremacist. Johnson believed that black suffrage could never be imposed on a southern state by the federal government, and that set him on a collision course with the Radicals. In perhaps the most blatantly racist official statement ever delivered by an American president, Johnson declared in his annual message of 1867 that blacks possessed less "capacity for government than any other race of people."

Such racial views had an enduring effect on Johnson's policies. Where whites were concerned, however, Johnson seemed to be pursuing changes in class relations. He proposed rules that would keep the wealthy planter class at least temporarily out of power.

White southerners were required to swear an oath of loyalty as a condition of gaining amnesty or

JOHNSON'S
PARDON POLICY

pardon, but Johnson barred several categories of people from taking the oath: former federal officials, high-ranking Confederate officers, and political leaders or graduates of West Point or Annapolis who had joined or aided the Confederacy. To this list Johnson added another important group: all ex-Confederates whose taxable property was worth more than $20,000. These individuals had to apply personally to the president for pardon and restoration of their political rights. It thus appeared that the leadership class of the Old South would be removed from power.

Johnson appointed provisional governors who began the Reconstruction process by calling constitutional conventions. The delegates chosen for these conventions had to draft new constitutions that eliminated slavery and invalidated secession. After ratification of these constitutions, new governments could be elected, and the states would be restored to the Union with full congressional representation. But only those southerners who had taken the oath of amnesty and been eligible to vote on the day the state seceded could participate in this process. Thus, unpardoned whites and former slaves were not eligible.

If Johnson intended to strip the old elite of its power, he did not hold to his plan. Surprisingly, he

PRESIDENTIAL
RECONSTRUCTION

started pardoning aristocrats and leading rebels. These pardons, plus the rapid return of planters' abandoned lands, restored the old elite to power.

Why did Johnson allow the planters to regain power? In part, he was determined to implement a rapid Reconstruction to deny the Radicals the opportunity for the more thorough racial and political changes they desired in the South. Johnson also needed southern support in the 1866 elections. Hence, he declared Reconstruction complete only eight months after Appomattox, and in December 1865 many Confederate leaders, including the vice president of the Confederacy, traveled to Washington to claim seats in the U.S. Congress.

The election of such prominent rebels troubled many northerners. So did other results of Johnson's

BLACK CODES

program. Some of the state conventions were slow to repudiate secession; others admitted only grudgingly that slavery was dead. Furthermore, to define the status of freed men and women and control their labor, some legislatures merely revised large sections of the slave codes by substituting the word *freedmen* for *slaves*. The new black codes compelled the former slaves to carry passes, observe a curfew, live in housing provided by a landowner, and give up hope of entering many desirable occupations. Stiff vagrancy laws and restrictive labor contracts bound freedpeople to plantations.

It seemed to northerners that the South was intent on returning African Americans to servility. Thus, the Republican majority in Congress decided to call a halt to the results of Johnson's plan. On reconvening, the House and Senate considered the credentials of the newly elected southern representatives and decided not to admit them. Instead, they bluntly challenged the president's authority and established a joint committee to investigate a new direction for Reconstruction.

The Congressional Reconstruction Plan

*N*orthern congressmen were hardly unified, but they did not doubt their right to shape Reconstruction policy. The Constitution mentioned neither secession nor reunion, but it gave Congress the primary role in the admission of states. Moreover, the Constitution declared that the United States shall guarantee to each state a republican form of government. This provision, legislators believed, gave them the authority to devise policies for Reconstruction.

They soon found that other constitutional questions affected their policies. What, for example, had rebellion done to the relationship between southern states and the Union? Lincoln had always insisted that states could not secede—they had engaged in an "insurrection"—and that the Union remained intact. Not even Andrew Johnson, however, accepted the southern position that state governments of the Confederacy could simply reenter the nation. Congressmen who favored vigorous Reconstruction measures argued that the war had broken the Union and that the South was subject to the victor's will. Moderate congressmen held that the states had forfeited their rights through rebellion and thus had come under congressional supervision.

These theories mirrored the diversity of Congress itself. Northern Democrats denounced any idea of racial equality and supported John-son's policies. Conservative Republicans favored a limited federal role in

THE RADICALS

Reconstruction. The Radical Republicans wanted to transform the South. Although a minority in their party, they had the advantage of clearly defined goals. They believed it was essential to democratize the South, establish public education, and ensure the rights of freedpeople. They favored black suffrage, supported some land confiscation and redistribution, and were willing to exclude the South from the Union for several years if necessary to achieve their goals. A large group of moderate Republicans did not want to go as far as the Radicals but opposed Johnson's leniency.

Ironically, Johnson and the Democrats sabotaged the possibility of a conservative coalition. They refused to cooperate with conservative or moderate Republicans and insisted that Reconstruction was over, that the new state governments were legitimate, and that southern representatives should be admitted to Congress. Among the Republicans, the Radicals' influence grew in proportion to Johnson's intransigence.

Trying to work with Johnson, Republicans believed a compromise had been reached in the spring of 1866. Under its terms, Johnson would agree to two modifications of his program: extension of the life of the Freedmen's Bureau for another year and passage of a civil rights bill to counteract the black codes. This bill would force southern courts to practice equality before the law by allowing federal judges to remove from state courts cases in which blacks were treated unfairly. Its provisions applied to public, not private, acts of discrimination. The civil rights bill of 1866 was the first statutory definition of the rights of American citizens.

CONGRESS VS. JOHNSON

Johnson destroyed the compromise by vetoing both bills (they later became law when Congress overrode the president's veto). All hope of presidential-congressional cooperation was now dead. In 1866 newspapers reported daily violations of blacks' rights in the South and carried alarming accounts of antiblack violence. In Memphis, for instance, forty blacks were killed and twelve schools burned by white mobs. Such violence convinced Republicans, and the northern public, that more needed to be done. A new Republican plan took the form of the Fourteenth Amendment to the Constitution, forged out of a compromise between radical and conservative elements of the party.

Of the four parts of the Fourteenth Amendment, the first would have the greatest legal significance in

FOURTEENTH AMENDMENT

later years. It conferred citizenship on the freedmen and prohibited states from abridging their constitutional "privileges and immunities." It also barred any state from taking a person's life, liberty, or property "without due process of law" and from denying "equal protection of the laws." These resounding phrases became powerful guarantees of African Americans' and all other citizens' civil rights in the twentieth century.

Nearly universal agreement emerged among Republicans on the amendment's second and third provisions. The second declared the Confederate debt null and void and guaranteed the war debt of the United States. The third provision barred Confederate leaders from holding state and federal office. Only Congress, by a two-thirds vote of each house, could remove the penalty.

The fourth part of the amendment dealt with representation and embodied the compromises that produced the document. Emancipation made every former slave a full person rather than three-fifths of a person, which would increase southern representation. Thus, the postwar South stood to gain power in Congress, and if white southerners did not allow blacks to vote, former secessionists would derive the political benefit from emancipation. So Republicans determined that if a southern state did not grant black men the vote, its representation would be reduced proportionally. This compromise avoided a direct enactment of black suffrage but would deliver future black voters to the Republican Party.

The Fourteenth Amendment specified for the first time that voters were "male," but it ignored female citizens, black and white. For this reason, it provoked a strong reaction from the women's rights movement. Prominent leaders such as Elizabeth Cady Stanton and Susan B. Anthony ended their alliance with abolitionists and fought more determinedly for themselves. Thus, the amendment infused new life into the women's rights movement and caused considerable strife among old allies.

In 1866 the major question in Reconstruction politics was how the public would respond to the

THE SOUTH'S AND JOHNSON'S DEFIANCE, 1866

congressional initiative. Johnson did his best to block the Fourteenth Amendment in both North and South. Condemning Congress for its refusal to seat southern representatives, the president urged state legislatures in the South to vote against ratification. Every southern legislature except Tennessee's rejected the amendment by a wide margin.

To present his case to northerners, Johnson boarded a special train for a "swing around the circle" that carried his message into the Northeast, the Midwest, and then back to Washington. In city after city, he criticized the Republicans in a ranting, undignified style. Increasingly audiences rejected his views and hooted and jeered at him.

The elections of 1866 were a resounding victory for Republicans in Congress. Radicals and moderates whom Johnson had denounced won reelection by large margins, and the Republican majority grew to two-thirds of both houses of Congress. The North had spoken clearly: Johnson's policies were prematurely giving the advantage to rebels and traitors. Thus, Republican congressional leaders won a mandate to pursue their Reconstruction plan.

After some embittered debate, Congress passed the First Reconstruction Act in March 1867. This

RECONSTRUCTION ACTS OF 1867–1868

plan, under which the southern states were readmitted to the Union, incorporated only a part of the Radical program. Union generals, commanding small garrisons of troops and charged with supervising all elections, assumed control in five military districts in the South (see Map 16.1). Confederate leaders designated in the Fourteenth Amendment were barred from voting until new state constitutions were ratified. The act guaranteed freedmen the right to vote in elections for state constitutional conventions and in subsequent elections. In addition, each southern state was required to ratify the Fourteenth Amendment, ratify its new constitution by majority vote, and submit it to Congress for approval. The Second, Third, and Fourth Reconstruction Acts, passed between March 1867 and March 1868, provided the details of operation for voter registration boards, the adoption of constitutions, and the administration of "good faith" oaths on the part of white southerners.

In the words of one historian, the Radicals succeeded in "clipping Johnson's wings." But they had

FAILURE OF LAND REDISTRIBUTION

hoped Congress could do much more. Thaddeus Stevens, for example, argued that economic opportunity

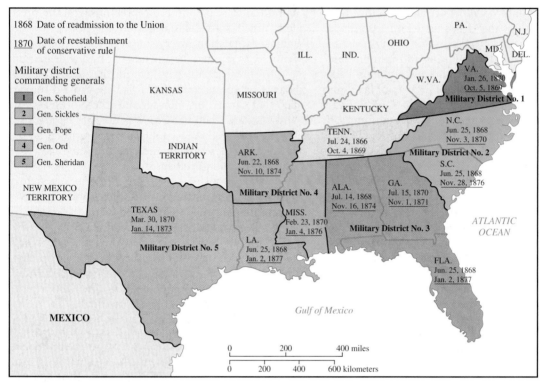

Map 16.1   The Reconstruction

This map shows the five military districts established when Congress passed the Reconstruction Act of 1867. As the dates within each state indicate, conservative Democratic forces quickly regained control of government in four southern states. So-called Radical Reconstruction was curtailed in most of the others as factions within the weakened Republican Party began to cooperate with conservative Democrats.

was essential to the freedmen. Stevens therefore drew up a plan for extensive confiscation and redistribution of land. Only one-tenth of the land affected by his plan was earmarked for freedmen, in forty-acre plots. The rest was to be sold to generate money for Union veterans' pensions, compensation to loyal southerners for damaged property, and payment of the federal debt.

But plans for property redistribution were unpopular measures, and virtually all failed. Northerners were accustomed to a limited role for government, and the business community staunchly opposed any interference with private property rights, even for former Confederates.

Congress's quarrels with Johnson grew more bitter. To restrict Johnson's influence and safeguard its plan, Congress passed a number of controversial laws. First, it limited Johnson's power over the army by requiring the president to issue military orders through the General of the Army, Ulysses S. Grant, who could not be dismissed without the Senate's consent. Then Congress passed the Tenure of Office Act, which gave the Senate power to approve changes in the president's cabinet. Designed to protect Secretary of War Edwin M. Stanton, who sympathized with the Radicals, this law violated the tradition that a president controlled ap-

CONSTITUTIONAL CRISIS

pointments to his own cabinet. These measures, as well as each of the Reconstruction Acts, were passed by a two-thirds override of presidential vetoes.

Johnson took several belligerent steps of his own. He issued orders to military commanders in the South limiting their powers and increasing the powers of the civil governments he had created in 1865. Then he removed military officers who were conscientiously enforcing Congress's new law, preferring commanders who allowed disqualified Confederates to vote. Finally, he tried to remove Secretary of War Stanton. With that attempt the confrontation reached its climax.

Twice in 1867, the House Judiciary Committee had considered impeachment of Johnson, rejecting the idea once and then having its recommendation by a 5-to-4 vote decisively defeated by the House. After Johnson tried to remove Stanton, a third attempt to impeach the president carried easily in early 1868. The indictment concentrated on his violation of the Tenure of Office Act, though many modern scholars regard his efforts to impede enforcement of the Reconstruction Act of 1867 as a far more serious offense.

IMPEACHMENT OF PRESIDENT JOHNSON

Johnson's trial in the Senate began promptly and lasted more than three months. The prosecution attempted to prove that Johnson was guilty of "high crimes and misdemeanors." But they also argued that the trial was a means to judge Johnson's performance, not a judicial determination of guilt or innocence. The Senate ultimately rejected such reasoning, which could have made removal from office a political weapon against any chief executive who disagreed with Congress. Although a majority of senators voted to convict Johnson, the prosecution fell one vote short of the necessary two-thirds majority. Johnson remained in office, politically weakened and with only a few months left in his term.

In the 1868 presidential election Ulysses S. Grant, running as a Republican, defeated Horatio Seymour, a New York Democrat. Grant was not a Radical, but his platform supported congressional Reconstruction and endorsed black suffrage in the South. (Significantly, Republicans stopped short of endorsing it in the North.) The Democrats vigorously denounced Reconstruction.

ELECTION OF 1868

Participating in their first presidential election ever on a wide scale, blacks voted en masse for General Grant.

In office Grant acted as an administrator of Reconstruction but not as its enthusiastic advocate. He vacillated in his dealings with the southern states, sometimes defending Republican regimes and sometimes currying favor with Democrats. On occasion Grant called out federal troops to stop violence or enforce acts of Congress. But he never imposed a true military occupation on the South. The later legend of "military rule," so important to southern claims of victimization during Reconstruction, was steeped in myth.

In 1869, in an effort to write democratic principles into the Constitution, the Radicals passed the Fifteenth Amendment. This measure forbade states to deny the right to vote "on account of race, color, or previous condition of servitude." Such wording did not guarantee the right to vote. It deliberately left states free to restrict suffrage on other grounds so that northern states could continue to deny suffrage to women and certain groups of men—Chinese immigrants, illiterates, and those too poor to pay poll taxes. Although several states outside the South refused to ratify, three-fourths of the states approved the measure, and the Fifteenth Amendment became law in 1870.

FIFTEENTH AMENDMENT

With passage of the Fifteenth Amendment, many Americans, especially supportive northerners, considered Reconstruction essentially completed. "Let us have done with Reconstruction," pleaded the *New York Tribune* in April 1870. "The country is tired and sick of it. . . . Let us have Peace!"

Reconstruction Politics in the South

From the start, Reconstruction encountered the resistance of white southerners. In the black codes and in private attitudes, many whites stubbornly opposed emancipation, and the former planter class proved especially unbending. In 1866 a Georgia newspaper frankly observed that "most of the white citizens believe that the institution of slavery was right, and . . . they will believe that the condition, which comes nearest to slavery, that can now be established will be the best."

Fearing loss of control over their slaves, some planters attempted to postpone freedom by denying or misrepresenting events. Former slaves reported that their owners "didn't tell them it was freedom" or "wouldn't let [them] go." To hold onto their workers, some landowners claimed control over black children and used guardianship and apprentice laws to bind black families to the plantation. Whites also blocked blacks from acquiring land. After President Johnson encouraged the South to resist congressional Reconstruction, some white conservatives worked hard to capture the new state governments, while others boycotted the polls in an attempt to defeat Congress's plans.

WHITE RESISTANCE

Very few black men stayed away from the polls. Enthusiastically and hopefully, they voted Republican. Most agreed with one man who felt he should "stick to the end with the party that freed me." Illiteracy did not prohibit blacks (or uneducated whites) from making intelligent choices. A Mississippi black testified that he and his friends had no difficulty selecting the Republican ballot. "We stood around and watched," he explained. "We saw D. Sledge vote; he owned half the county. We knowed he voted Democratic so we voted the other ticket so it would be Republican."

BLACK VOTERS AND THE SOUTHERN REPUBLICAN PARTY

Thanks to a large black turnout and the restrictions on prominent Confederates, a new southern Republican Party came to power in the constitutional conventions of 1868–1870. Republican delegates consisted of a sizable contingent of blacks (265 out of the total of just over 1,000 delegates throughout the South), some northerners who had moved to the South, and native southern whites who favored change. The new constitutions were more democratic. They eliminated property qualifications for voting and holding office, and they turned many appointed offices into elective posts. They provided for public schools and institutions to care for the mentally ill, the blind, the deaf, the destitute, and the orphaned.

The conventions broadened women's rights in property holding and divorce. Usually the goal was not to make women equal to men but to provide relief to thousands of suffering debtors. In families left

■ Thomas Nast, in this 1868 cartoon, pictured the combination of forces that threatened the success of Reconstruction: southern opposition and the greed, partisanship, and racism of northern interests.
(Library of Congress)

poverty stricken by the war and weighed down by debt, it was usually the husband who had contracted the debts. Thus giving women legal control over their own property provided some protection to their families. The goal of some delegates, however, was to elevate women with the right to vote.

Under these new constitutions, the southern states elected Republican-controlled governments. For the first time, the ranks of state legislators in 1868 included some black southerners. But in most states, whites were in the majority, and former slaveowners controlled the

TRIUMPH OF REPUBLICAN GOVERNMENTS

best land and other sources of economic power. James Lynch, a leading black politician from Mississippi, explained why African Americans shunned the "folly" of disfranchisement of ex-Confederates. Unlike northerners who "can leave when it becomes too uncomfortable," landless former slaves "must be in friendly relations with the great body of the whites in the state."

Far from being vindictive toward the race that had enslaved them, most southern blacks treated leading rebels with generosity and appealed to white southerners to adopt a spirit of fairness and cooperation. In this way, the South's Republican Party condemned itself to defeat if white voters would not cooperate. Within a few years, Republicans were reduced to the embarrassment of making futile appeals to whites while ignoring the claims of their strongest supporters, blacks. But for a time, some propertied whites accepted congressional Reconstruction as a reality and declared themselves willing to compete under the new rules. All sides found an area of agreement in economic policies.

Reflecting northern ideals and southern necessity, the Reconstruction governments enthusiastically promoted industry. Reconstruction

INDUSTRIALIZATION legislatures encouraged investment with loans, subsidies, and exemptions from taxation for periods up to ten years. The southern railroad system was rebuilt and expanded, and coal and iron mining made possible steel plants in Birmingham, Alabama. Between 1860 and 1880, the number of manufacturing establishments in the South nearly doubled. This emphasis on big business, however, produced higher state debts and taxes, drew money away from schools and other programs, and multiplied possibilities for corruption.

Policies appealing to African American voters never went beyond equality before the law. In fact, the

REPUBLICANS AND RACIAL EQUALITY whites who controlled the southern Republican Party were reluctant to allow blacks a share of offices proportionate to their electoral strength. Aware of their weakness, black leaders did not push very far for revolutionary economic or social change. In every southern state, they led efforts to establish public schools, although they did not press for integrated facilities.

Economic progress was uppermost in the minds of most freedpeople. Black southerners needed land, and much land did fall into state hands for nonpay-

ment of taxes and was offered for sale in small lots. But most freedmen had too little cash to bid against investors or speculators. Any widespread redistribution of land had to arise from Congress, which never supported such action. The lack of genuine land redistribution remained the significant lost opportunity of Reconstruction.

Within a few years, as centrists in both parties met with failure, white hostility to congressional Reconstruction began to dominate.

MYTH OF "NEGRO RULE" Taking the offensive, conservatives charged that the South had been turned over to ignorant blacks and deplored "black domination," which became a rallying cry for a return to white supremacy.

Such inflammatory propaganda was part of the growing myth of "Negro rule." African Americans participated in politics but hardly dominated or controlled events. They were a majority in only two out of ten state constitution–writing conventions (transplanted northerners were a majority in one). In the state legislatures, only in the lower house in South Carolina did blacks ever constitute a majority; among officeholders, their numbers generally were far fewer than their proportion in the population. Sixteen blacks won seats in Congress before Reconstruction was over, but none was ever elected governor. Only eighteen served in a high state office such as lieutenant governor, treasurer, superintendent of education, or secretary of state. However, elected officials, such as Robert Smalls in South Carolina, labored tirelessly for cheaper land prices, better health care, access to schools, and the enforcement of civil rights for their people.

Conservatives also assailed the allies of black Republicans. Their propaganda denounced whites from

CARPETBAGGERS AND SCALAWAGS the North as "carpetbaggers," greedy crooks planning to pour stolen tax revenues into their sturdy luggage made of carpet material. In fact, most northerners who settled in the South had come seeking business opportunities, as schoolteachers, or to find a warmer climate and never entered politics. Those who did enter politics generally wanted to democratize the South and introduce northern ways, such as industry, public education, and the spirit of enterprise.

Conservatives also coined the term *scalawag* to discredit any native white southerner who cooperated with the Republicans. A substantial number did so. Most scalawags were yeoman farmers, men from mountain areas and nonslaveholding districts who saw that they could benefit from the education and opportunities promoted by Republicans. Banding together with freedmen, they pursued common class interests and hoped to make headway against the power of long-dominant planters. A majority of scalawags, however, did not support racial equality. The black-white coalition was thus vulnerable on the race issue.

Taxation was a major problem for the Reconstruction governments. Republicans wanted to maintain prewar services, repair the war's destruction, stimulate industry, and support important new ventures such as public schools. But the Civil War had destroyed much of the South's tax base. Thus, an increase in taxes was necessary even to maintain traditional services, and new ventures required still higher taxes. Republican tax policies aroused strong opposition, especially among yeomen.

TAX POLICY AND CORRUPTION AS POLITICAL WEDGES

Corruption was another serious charge levied against the Republicans. Unfortunately, it often was true. Many carpetbaggers and black politicians engaged in fraudulent schemes, sold their votes, or padded expenses, taking part in what scholars recognize was a nationwide surge of corruption. Corruption carried no party label, but the Democrats successfully pinned the blame on unqualified blacks and greedy carpetbaggers among southern Republicans.

All these problems hurt the Republicans, but in many southern states the deathblow came through violence. The Ku Klux Klan began in Tennessee in 1866; it spread through the South and rapidly evolved into a terrorist organization. Violence against African Americans occurred from the first days of Reconstruction but became far more organized and purposeful after 1867. Klansmen sought to frustrate Reconstruction and keep the freedmen in subjection. Nighttime harassment, whippings, beatings, rapes, and murder became common, and terrorism dominated some counties and regions.

KU KLUX KLAN

The Klan's main purpose was political. Lawless nightriders targeted active Republicans. Leading white and black Republicans were killed in several states. After freedmen who worked for a South Carolina scalawag started voting, terrorists visited the planta-

tion and, in the words of one victim, "whipped every nigger man they could lay their hands on." Klansmen also attacked Union League clubs—Republican organizations that mobilized the black vote—and schoolteachers who aided the freedmen.

Klan violence was not a spontaneous outburst of racism; very specific social forces shaped and directed it. In North Carolina, for example, the sites of the worst Klan violence were Alamance and Caswell Counties. There, slim Republican majorities rested on cooperation between black voters and white yeomen, who together had ousted officials long entrenched in power. The wealthy and powerful men who had lost their accustomed political control then organized a deliberate campaign of terror. The campaign of intimidation and murder weakened the Republican coalition and restored a Democratic majority.

Klan violence injured Republicans across the South. One in ten of the black leaders who had been delegates to the 1867–1868 state constitutional conventions was attacked, seven fatally. A single attack on Alabama Republicans in the town of Eutaw left four blacks dead and fifty-four wounded. According to historian Eric Foner, the Klan "made it virtually impossible for Republicans to campaign or vote in large parts of Georgia."

Thus, a combination of difficult fiscal problems, Republican mistakes, racial hostility, and terror brought down the Republican regimes. In most southern states, "Radical Reconstruction" lasted only a few years (see Map 16.1).

FAILURE OF RECONSTRUCTION

The most enduring failure of Reconstruction, however, was not political; it was that Reconstruction failed to alter the South's social structure or its distribution of wealth and power. Without land of their own, freedpeople were at the mercy of white landowners. Armed only with the ballot, they had little chance to effect significant changes.

Reconstruction Reversed

Northerners had always been more interested in suppressing rebellion than in aiding southern blacks, and by the early 1870s the North's commitment to bringing about change in the South weakened. In one southern state after another, Democrats regained control. And for one of only a few times in American history, violence and terror emerged as a tactic in normal politics.

In 1870 and 1871, the violent campaigns of the Ku Klux Klan forced Congress to pass two Enforcement Acts and an anti-Klan law.

POLITICAL IMPLICATIONS OF KLAN TERRORISM

These laws made actions by individuals against the civil and political rights of others a federal criminal offense for the first time. They also provided for election supervisors and permitted martial law and suspension of the writ of habeas corpus to combat murders, beatings, and threats by the Klan. Federal prosecutors used the laws rather selectively. In 1872 and 1873, Mississippi and the Carolinas saw many prosecutions, but in other states where violence flourished, the laws were virtually ignored. Southern juries sometimes refused to convict Klansmen.

Some conservative but influential Republicans opposed the anti-Klan laws. Rejecting other Republicans' arguments that the Thirteenth, Fourteenth, and Fifteenth Amendments had made the federal government the protector of citizens' rights, these dissenters echoed an old Democratic charge that Congress was infringing on states' rights. This opposition foreshadowed a more general revolt within Republican ranks in 1872.

Disenchanted with Reconstruction, a group calling itself the Liberal Republicans bolted the party in 1872 and nominated Horace Greeley, the well-known editor of the *New York Tribune*, for president.

LIBERAL REPUBLICAN REVOLT

The Liberal Republicans were a varied group, including civil service reformers, foes of corruption, and advocates of a lower tariff. Normally such disparate elements would not cooperate, but two popular and widespread attitudes united them: distaste for federal intervention in the South and an elitist desire to let market forces and the "best men" determine events, in both the South and Washington. The Democrats also gave their nomination to Greeley in 1872. The combination was not enough to defeat Grant, who won reelection, but it reinforced Grant's desire to avoid confrontation with white southerners.

Dissatisfaction with Grant's administration grew during his second term. Strong-willed but politically naive, Grant made a series of poor appointments. His secretary of war, his private secretary, and officials in the Treasury and Navy Departments were involved in bribery or tax-cheating scandals. Instead of exposing the corruption, Grant defended the culprits. In 1874, as Grant's popularity and his party's prestige declined, the Democrats recaptured the House of Representatives.

The effect of Democratic gains in Congress was to weaken legislative resolve on southern issues. Already,

A GENERAL AMNESTY

in 1872, Congress had adopted a sweeping Amnesty Act, which pardoned most of the remaining rebels, lifting the political disabilities of the Fourteenth Amendment, and left only five hundred barred from political office. In 1875 Congress passed a Civil Rights Act purporting to guarantee black people equal accommodations in public places, such as inns and theaters, but the bill was watered down and contained no effective provisions for enforcement. And by 1876, the Democrats had regained control in all but three southern states. Meanwhile, new concerns were capturing the public's attention.

Both industrialization and immigration were surging, hastening the pace of change in national life.

RECONCILIATION AND INDUSTRIAL EXPANSION

Within only eight years, postwar industrial production increased by an impressive 75 percent. For the first time, nonagricultural workers outnumbered farmers, and only Britain's industrial output was greater than that of the United States. Lured by employment prospects in the expanding economy, 3 million immigrants entered the country between 1865 and 1873.

Then the Panic of 1873 ushered in over five years of economic contraction. Three million people lost their jobs, and the clash between labor and capital became the major issue of the day. Class attitudes diverged, especially in large cities. Debtors and the unemployed sought easy-money policies to spur economic expansion. Businessmen, disturbed by the widespread strikes and industrial violence that accompanied the panic, fiercely defended property rights and demanded "sound money" policies. The chasm between farmers and workers and wealthy industrialists grew ever wider.

Nowhere did the new complexity and violence of American race relations play out so vividly as in the

THE WEST, RACE, AND RECONSTRUCTION

West. Across the West, the federal government pursued a policy of containment against Native Americans. In California, where white

The Grants' Tour of the World

On May 17, 1877, two weeks after his presidency ended, Ulysses S. Grant and his wife, Julia, embarked from Philadelphia on a grand tour of the world that would last twenty-six months. Portrayed as a private vacation, the trip was a very public affair. The small entourage included John Russell Young, a reporter for the *New York Herald* who recorded the journeys in the two-volume illustrated *Around the World with General Grant.*

The Grants spent many months in England attending a bewildering array of banquets, one with Queen Victoria. In Newcastle, thousands of workingmen conducted a massive parade in Grant's honor. Grant was viewed as a warrior statesman, the savior of the American nation, the liberator of slaves, and a celebrity—a measure of the American presence on the world stage. On the European continent, the pattern continued as every royal or republican head of state hosted the Grants.

The Grants next went to Egypt, where they rode donkeys into remote villages along the Nile. They traveled by train to the Indian Ocean and embarked for India. They encountered British imperialism in full flower in Bombay and that of the French in Saigon. Northward in Asia, the grand excursion went to China and Japan. In Canton, Grant passed before an assemblage of young men who, according to a reporter, "looked upon the barbarian with . . . contempt in their expression, very much as our young men in New York would regard Sitting Bull or Red Cloud."

"I am both homesick and dread going home," Grant wrote in April 1879. Sailing across the Pacific, the Grants landed in San Francisco in late June. The former president would spend his final years a war hero and a national symbol. No American president would again establish such personal links to the world until Woodrow Wilson at the end of World War I.

On their tour of the world, Ulysses and Julia Grant sat here with companions and guides in front of the Great Hypostyle Hall at the Temple of Amon-Ra in Karnak in Luxor, Egypt, 1878. The Grants' extraordinary tour included many such photo opportunities, often depicting the plebeian American president, and now world celebrity, in exotic places with unusual people. (Library of Congress)

farmers and ranchers often forced Indians into captive labor, some civilians practiced a more violent form of "Indian hunting." By 1880, thirty years of such violence left an estimated 4,500 California Indians dead at the hands of white settlers.

In Texas and the Southwest, the rhetoric of national expansion still deemed Mexicans and other mixed-race Hispanics to be debased, "lazy," and incapable of self-government. And in California and other states of the Far West, thousands of Chinese immigrants became the victims of brutal violence. Few whites had objected to the Chinese who did the dangerous work of building railroads through the Rocky Mountains. But when the Chinese began to compete for urban, industrial jobs, great conflict emerged. Anticoolie clubs appeared in California in the 1870s, seeking laws against Chinese labor and organizing vigilante attacks on Chinese workers and the factories that employed them. Western politicians sought white votes by pandering to prejudice, and in 1879 the new California constitution denied the vote to Chinese.

During Reconstruction, America was undergoing what one historian has called a "reconstruction" of the very idea of "race" itself. And as it did so, tumbling into some of the darkest years of American race relations, the turbulence of the expanding West reinforced a resurgent white supremacy, a new nationalism, and the reconciliation of North and South.

Following the Civil War, pressure for expansion reemerged, and in 1867 Secretary of State William H.

FOREIGN EXPANSION

Seward arranged the purchase of Alaska from the Russian government. Opponents ridiculed Seward's $7.2 million venture, but he convinced important congressmen of Alaska's economic potential, and other lawmakers favored the dawning of friendship with Russia.

Also in 1867 the United States took control of the Midway Islands, a thousand miles northwest of Hawai'i. And in 1870 President Grant tried unsuccessfully to annex the Dominican Republic.

Meanwhile, the Supreme Court played its part in the northern retreat from Reconstruction. During the

JUDICIAL RETREAT FROM RECONSTRUCTION

Civil War, the Court had been cautious and inactive. Reaction to the *Dred Scott* decision (1857) had been so violent, and the Union's wartime emergency so great, that the Court avoided interference with government actions. In 1866, however, *Ex parte Milligan* reached the Court.

Lambdin P. Milligan of Indiana had plotted to free Confederate prisoners of war and overthrow state governments. For these acts, a military court sentenced Milligan, a civilian, to death. Milligan claimed that he had a right to a civil trial. The Supreme Court declared that military trials were illegal when civil courts were open and functioning, and its language indicated that the Court intended to reassert its authority.

In the 1870s the Court successfully renewed its challenge to Congress's actions when it narrowed the meaning and effectiveness of the Fourteenth Amendment. The *Slaughter-House* cases (1873) began in 1869, when the Louisiana legislature granted one company a monopoly on the slaughtering of livestock in New Orleans. Rival butchers in the city promptly sued. Their attorney argued that the Fourteenth Amendment had revolutionized the constitutional system by bringing individual rights under federal protection. This argument articulated an original goal of the Republican Party: to nationalize civil rights and guard them from state interference.

The Court rejected the argument and thus dealt a stunning blow to the scope and vitality of the Fourteenth Amendment. State citizenship and national citizenship were separate, the Court declared. National citizenship involved only matters such as the right to travel freely from state to state and to use the nation's navigable waters, and only these narrow rights were protected by the Fourteenth Amendment.

The Supreme Court also concluded that the butchers who sued had not been deprived of their rights or property in violation of the amendment's due-process clause. The Court's majority declared that the framers of the recent amendments had not intended to "destroy" the federal system, in which the states exercised "powers for domestic and local government, including the regulation of civil rights." Thus, the justices severely limited the amendment's potential for securing and protecting the rights of black citizens—its original intent.

The next day the Court decided *Bradwell v. Illinois*, a case in which Myra Bradwell, a female attorney, had been denied the right to practice law in Illinois on account of her gender. Pointing to the Fourteenth Amendment, Bradwell's attorneys contended that the state had unconstitutionally abridged her "privileges and immunities" as a citizen. The Supreme Court rejected her claim, alluding to women's traditional role in the home.

In 1876 the Court weakened the Reconstruction era amendments even further by emasculating the enforcement clause of the Fourteenth Amendment and revealing deficiencies inherent in the Fifteenth Amendment. In *U.S. v. Cruikshank* the Court overruled the conviction under the 1870 Enforcement Act of Louisiana whites who had attacked a meeting of blacks and conspired to deprive them of their rights. The justices ruled that the Fourteenth Amendment did not give the federal government power to act against these whites. The duty of protecting citizens' equal rights, the Court said, "rests alone with the States." Such judicial conservatism had a profound impact down through the next century, blunting the revolutionary potential in the Civil War amendments.

The 1876 presidential election confirmed that the nation was increasingly focused on economic issues

DISPUTED ELECTION OF 1876 AND THE COMPROMISE OF 1877

and that the North was no longer willing to pursue the goals of Reconstruction. Samuel J. Tilden, the Democratic governor of New York, ran strongly in the South and needed only one more electoral vote to triumph over Rutherford B. Hayes, the Republican nominee. Nineteen electoral votes from Louisiana, South Carolina, and Florida (the only southern states yet "unredeemed" by Democratic rule) were disputed; both Democrats and Republicans claimed to have won in those states despite fraud committed by their opponents. One vote from Oregon was undecided because of a technicality (see Map 16.2).

To resolve this unprecedented situation Congress established a fifteen-member electoral commission, with membership to be balanced between Democrats and Republicans. Since the Republicans held the majority in Congress, they prevailed 8 to 7 on every attempt to count the returns, along strict party lines. Hayes would become president if Congress accepted the commission's findings.

Congressional acceptance was not certain, and many citizens worried that the nation had entered a major constitutional crisis and would slip once again into civil war. The crisis was resolved when Democrats acquiesced in the election of Hayes based on a

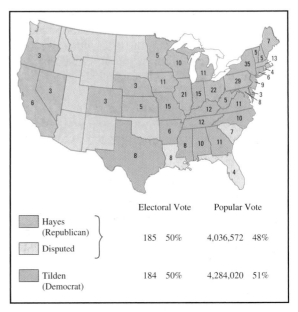

	Electoral Vote		Popular Vote	
Hayes (Republican)	185	50%	4,036,572	48%
Disputed				
Tilden (Democrat)	184	50%	4,284,020	51%

Map 16.2 Presidential Election of 1876 and the Compromise of 1877

In 1876 a combination of solid southern support and Democratic gains in the North gave Samuel Tilden the majority of popular votes, but Rutherford B. Hayes won the disputed election in the electoral college, after a deal satisfied Democratic wishes for an end to Reconstruction.

"deal" cut in a Washington hotel between Hayes's supporters and southerners who wanted federal aid to railroads, internal improvements, federal patronage, and removal of troops from southern states. Northern and southern Democrats simply decided they could not win and did not contest the election of a Republican who was not going to continue Reconstruction. Thus, Hayes became president.

Southern Democrats rejoiced, but African Americans grieved over the betrayal of their hopes for

BETRAYAL OF BLACK RIGHTS

equality. To many of these people, the only hope lay outside the South. Thus, from South Carolina, Louisiana, Mississippi, and other southern states, thousands gathered up their possessions and migrated to Kansas. They were called Exodusters, disappointed people still searching for their share in the American dream. Even in Kansas they met disillusionment as the welcome extended by the state's governor soon gave way to hostility among many whites.

Blacks now had to weigh their options, which were not much wider than they had ever been. Frederick Douglass looked back on fifteen years of unparalleled change for his people and worried about the hold of white supremacy on America's historical memory: "If war among the whites brought peace and liberty to the blacks, what will peace among the whites bring?" Douglass's question would echo down through American political culture for decades.

Summary *Online Study Center* ACE the Test

*R*econstruction left a contradictory record. It was an era of tragic aspirations and failures, but also of unprecedented legal, political, and social change. The Union victory brought about an increase in federal power, stronger nationalism, sweeping federal intervention in the southern states, and landmark amendments to the Constitution. But northern commitment to make these changes endure had eroded, and the revolution remained unfinished.

The North embraced emancipation, black suffrage, and constitutional alterations strengthening the central government. But it did so to defeat the rebellion and secure the peace. As the pressure of these crises declined, strong underlying continuities emerged and placed their mark on Reconstruction. The American people and the courts maintained a preference for state authority and a distrust of federal power. The ideology of free labor dictated that property should be respected and that individuals should be self-reliant. Racism endured and transformed into the even more virulent forms of Klan terror. Concern for the human rights of African Americans was strongest when their plight threatened to undermine the interests of whites, and reform frequently had less appeal than moneymaking in an individualistic, enterprising society.

In the wake of the Civil War, Americans faced two profound tasks: the achievement of healing and the dispensing of justice. Both had to occur, but they never developed in historical balance. Making sectional reunion compatible with black freedom and equality overwhelmed the imagination in American political culture, and the nation still faced much of this dilemma more than a century later.

LEGACY FOR A PEOPLE AND A NATION
The Fourteenth Amendment

Before the Civil War, no definition of civil rights existed in America. Reconstruction legislation, especially the Fourteenth Amendment, changed that forever. Approved by Congress in 1866, the Fourteenth Amendment enshrined in the Constitution the ideas of birthright citizenship and equal rights. The Fourteenth Amendment was designed to secure and protect the rights of the freedpeople. But over time, the "equal protection of the law" clause has been used at times to support the rights of states, cities, corporations, immigrants, women, religious organizations, gays and lesbians, students, and labor unions. It has advanced both tolerance and intolerance, affirmative action and anti-affirmative-action programs. It provides the legal wellspring for the generations-old civil rights movement in the United States.

The amendment as originally written required individuals to pursue grievances through private litigation, alleging state denial of a claimed federal right. At first, the Supreme Court interpreted it conservatively, especially on racial matters, and by 1900, the idea of color-blind liberty in America was devastated by Jim Crow laws, disfranchisement, and unpunished mob violence.

But Progressive reformers used the equal-protection clause to advocate government support of health, union organizing, municipal housing, and the protection of woman and child laborers. In the 1920s and 1930s, a judicial defense of civil liberties and free speech took hold. The Supreme Court expanded the amendment's guarantee of equality by a series of decisions upholding the rights of immigrant groups to resist "forced Americanization," especially Catholics in their creation of parochial schools. And from its inception in

1910, the National Association for the Advancement of Colored People waged a long campaign to reveal the inequality of racial segregation in schooling and every other kind of public facility. Led by Charles Houston and Thurgood Marshall, this epic legal battle culminated in the *Brown v. Board of Education* desegregation decision of 1954. In the Civil Rights Act of 1964, the equal-protection tradition was reenshrined into American law. Since 1964, Americans have lived in a society where the Fourteenth Amendment's legacy is the engine of expanded liberty for women and all minorities, as well as a political battleground for defining the nature and limits of human equality, and for redistributing justice long denied.

THE DEVELOPMENT OF THE WEST 1877–1900

*I*n 1893 young historian Frederick Jackson Turner delivered a stunning lecture at the Columbian Exposition in Chicago. In it, Turner expounded a theory that would preoccupy the textbooks for several generations. Titled "The Significance of the Frontier in American History," the paper argued that the existence of "free land, its continuous recession, and the advancement of American settlement westward" had created a distinctively American spirit of democracy and egalitarianism. The conquest of a succession of frontier Wests explained American progress and character.

Across the street, the folk character Buffalo Bill Cody staged two performances daily of an extravaganza, "The Wild West," dramatizing his version of the conquest of frontiers. Where Turner described a relatively peaceful settlement of empty land, Cody portrayed violent conquest of territory occupied by savage Indians. Turner's heroes were farmers who tamed the wilderness with plows. Buffalo Bill's heroes were rugged scouts who defeated Indians with firepower. Turner used images of wagon trains and wheat fields to argue that the frontier fashioned a new, progressive race. Cody depicted the West as a place of brutal aggression and heroic victory.

Despite exaggerations and inaccuracies, both Turner and Cody were correct to some degree. The American West inspired progress and witnessed the domination of one group over another and over the environment. Both men believed that by the 1890s, the frontier era had ended. Over time, Turner's theory was abandoned (even by Turner himself) as too simplistic, and Buffalo Bill was relegated to the gallery of rogues and showmen. Still, their versions of the West persist in the romance of American history, partially obscuring the complex truth of western development in the late nineteenth century.

Much of the West was never empty, however, and its inhabitants used its resources in different ways. On the Plains, for example, Pawnee Indians planted crops in the spring, left their fields in summer to hunt buffalo, then returned for harvesting. They sometimes battled with Cheyennes and

The Economic Activities of Native Peoples

The Transformation of Native Cultures

The Extraction of Natural Resources

Irrigation and Transportation

Farming the Plains

LINKS TO THE WORLD
The Australian Frontier

The Ranching Frontier

LEGACY FOR A PEOPLE AND A NATION
The West and Rugged Individualism

Online Study Center
This icon will direct you to interactive map and primary source activities on the website http://college.hmco.com/pic/nortonbrief7e

C H R O N O L O G Y

1862 • Homestead Act grants free land to citizens who live on and improve the land
• Morrill Land Grant Act gives states public land to finance agricultural and industrial colleges

1864 • Chivington's militia massacres Black Kettle's Cheyennes at Sand Creek

1869 • First transcontinental railroad completed, with connection at Promontory Point, Utah

1872 • Yellowstone becomes first national park

1873 • Barbed wire invented, enabling western farmers to enclose and protect fields cheaply

1876 • Sioux annihilate Custer's federal troops at Little Big Horn

1877 • Nez Percé Indians under Young Joseph surrender to U.S. troops

1878 • Timber and Stone Act allows citizens to buy timberland cheaply but also enables large companies to acquire huge tracts of forest land

1879 • Carlisle School for Indians established in Pennsylvania

1880–81 • Manypenny's *Our Indian Wards* and Jackson's *A Century of Dishonor* influence public conscience about poor government treatment of Indians

1881 • Shootout at OK Corral between Clantons and Earps

1881–82 • Chinese Exclusion Acts prohibit Chinese immigration to the United States

1883 • National time zones standardized

1884 • U.S. Supreme Court first defines Indians as wards under government protection

1887 • Dawes Severalty Act ends communal ownership of Indian lands and grants land allotments to individual Native American families
• Hatch Act provides for agricultural experiment stations in every state
• California passes law permitting farmers to organize into districts

1886–88 • Devastating winters on Plains destroys countless livestock and forces farmers into economic hardship

1890 • Final suppression of Plains Indians by U.S. Army at Wounded Knee
• Census Bureau announces closing of the frontier
• Yosemite National Park established

1892 • Muir helps found Sierra Club

1893 • Turner presents "frontier thesis" at Columbian Exposition

1896 • Rural Free Delivery made available

1902 • Newlands Reclamation Act passed

Arapahos over access to hunting grounds. For Pawnees, concepts of private property and profit had little meaning.

To white Americans, however, the expanses of land and water should be used for economic gain. They excavated the earth for valuable minerals, felled forests for construction, linked markets with railroads, and dammed rivers and plowed soil with crop machines. Their goal: opening markets nationally and internationally through corporate big business. As they transformed the landscape, the triumph of market economies transformed the nation.

By 1870, the West spanned from the Mississippi River to the Pacific Ocean and consisted of several regions of varying economic potential. Abundant rainfall along the northern Pacific coast fed huge forests. California's woodlands and grasslands provided fertile valleys for vegetable fields and orange groves. Eastward, the deserts and plateaus from the Cascades and Sierra Nevada to the Rocky Mountains contained gold, silver, and other buried minerals. East of the Rockies, the Great Plains could support grain crops and livestock with its semiarid western side of few trees and tough buffalo grass and eastern sector of ample rainfall and tall grasses.

The West had long been the scene of great migrations. Before contact with whites, Indian peoples had moved around the region, warring, trading, and negotiating with each other as they searched for food and shelter. In parts of the Southwest, Native Americans built towns, farms, and ranches. After the Civil War, white migration overwhelmed the native peoples, swelling the population between 1870 and 1890 from 7 million to nearly 17 million.

The West's abundance of exploitable land and raw materials filled white Americans with faith that anyone eager and persistent enough could succeed. This confidence rested on a belief that white people were somehow special and asserted itself at the expense of people of color, the poor, and the environment. By 1890 farms, ranches, mines, towns, and cities could be found in almost every corner of the present-day continental United States. Though of symbolic importance, the fading of the frontier had little impact on people's behavior. As long as vast stretches of land remained unsettled, pioneers who failed in one locale merely tried again somewhere else. A surplus of seemingly uninhabited land led Americans to believe they would always have a second chance. This belief, more than Turner's theory of frontier democracy or Cody's heroic reenactments, left a deep imprint on the American character. ∎

The Economic Activities of Native Peoples

*H*istorians once defined the American frontier as "the edge of the unused," implying, as Turner had, that the frontier was barren before whites arrived. Scholars now recognize that Native Americans settled and developed the West for centuries before others migrated there. Nevertheless, almost all native economic systems weakened in the late nineteenth century.

Western Indian cultures varied. Some Indians lived in permanent settlements; others were nomadic.

SUBSISTENCE CULTURES

Still, most Indians engaged in and were affected by the large-scale flow of goods, culture, language, and disease carried by migrating groups.

Indian economies were based to differing degrees on four activities: crop growing; livestock raising; hunting, fishing, and gathering; and trading and raiding. Corn was the most common crop; sheep and horses, acquired from Spanish colonizers and from other Indians, were the livestock; and buffalo (American bison) were the primary prey of hunts. Indians raided one another for food, tools, hides, and horses, which they then traded with other Indians and whites. Indians sought a balanced economic system, subsisting on crops when a buffalo hunt failed and hunting buffalo, trading livestock, or stealing food and horses in a raid when crops failed.

For Indians on the Great Plains, life focused on the buffalo. They cooked and preserved buffalo meat; fashioned hides into clothing, shoes, and blankets; used sinew for thread and bowstrings; and carved tools from bones and horns. Buffalo were so valuable that the village-dwelling Pawnees and nomadic Lakotas often struggled over access to herds. To feed their herds, Plains Indians periodically set fire to tall-grass prairies, which burned away dead plants and facilitated the growth of new grass so horses could feed all summer.

In the Southwest, Indians herded sheep, goats, and horses. Old Man Hat, a Navajo, explained, "The herd is money. . . . You know that you have some good clothing; the sheep gave you that. And you've just eaten different kinds of food; the sheep gave that food to you. Everything comes from the sheep." He was not speaking of money in a business sense, but rather in terms of status and security. Like many other Indians, the Navajos emphasized generosity and distrusted private property. Within the family, sharing was expected; outside the family, gifts and reciprocity governed relationships. Southwestern Indians too altered the environment, building elaborate irrigation systems to maximize use of scarce water supplies.

What buffalo were to the Plains Indians and sheep were to Southwestern Indians, salmon were to Indians of the Northwest. Before the mid-nineteenth century, the Columbia River and its tributaries supported the densest population of native peoples in North America. The Clatsops, Klamathets, and S'Klallam applied their technology of stream diversion, platform construction over the water, and special baskets to better harvest fish.

On the Plains and areas of the Southwest, this native world began to dissolve after 1850 when whites competed with Indians over natural resources. Perceiving buffalo and Indians as hindrances, whites endeavored to eliminate both. Railroads sponsored buffalo hunts in which eastern sportsmen shot at the bulky targets from slow-moving trains. The army refused to enforce treaties that reserved hunting grounds for exclusive Indian use.

SLAUGHTER OF BUFFALO

What neither Indians nor whites realized was that a combination of circumstances doomed the buffalo before the slaughter of the late 1800s. Indians depleted herds by increasing their kills to trade with whites and other Indians. Also, in generally dry years in the 1840s and 1850s, Indians moved to more fertile river basins, thereby pushing the bison out of important grazing territory to face starvation. Whites too settled in basin areas, further forcing buffalo away. At the same time, lethal animal diseases such as anthrax and brucellosis, brought in by white-owned livestock, decimated buffalo, already weakened by malnutrition and drought. Increased numbers of horses, oxen, and sheep owned by white newcomers and some Indians devoured grasses that buffalo required. The mass killing after 1850 struck the final blow. By the 1880s, only a few hundred remained of the 25 million bison estimated on the Plains in 1820.

In the Northwest, salmon suffered a similar fate. White commercial fishermen and canneries moved into the Columbia and Willamette River valleys during the 1860s and 1870s, and by the 1880s had greatly

DECLINE OF SALMON

diminished the salmon runs. Numerous salmon running upriver to spawn were being caught before they laid their eggs, preventing the fish supply from replenishing. By the twentieth century, the construction of dams on the river and its tributaries further impeded salmon reproduction. The government protected Indian fishing rights, and hatcheries helped restore some of the fish supply, but the need for electrical power from dams, combined with overfishing and pollution, curtailed the salmon supply.

The Transformation of Native Cultures

Buffalo slaughter and salmon reduction undermined Indian subsistence, but human demography also contributed. Throughout the nineteenth century, white migrants were overwhelmingly young, single males in their twenties and thirties, the age when they were most prone to violence. In 1870 white men outnumbered white women by three to two in California, two to one in Colorado, and two to one in Dakota Territory. The whites whom Indians were most likely to come into contact with first were explorers, traders, trappers, soldiers, prospectors, and cowboys—almost all of whom possessed guns and had few qualms about using them against animals and humans who got in their way.

Moreover, these men subscribed to prevailing attitudes that Indians were primitive, lazy, devious, and cruel. Such contempt made exploiting and killing native peoples easier, further "justified" by claims of preempting threats to life and property. When Indians raided white settlements, they sometimes mutilated bodies, burned buildings, and kidnapped women, acts that were embellished in campfire stories and popular fiction—reinforcing images of Indians as savages. In saloons, men boasted about fighting Indians and showed off trophies of scalps and other body parts taken from victims.

Indian warriors were also young, armed, and prone to violence and similarly boasted of fighting white interlopers. But Indian communities contained large groups of women and children, making native bands less mobile and therefore vulnerable to attack. They also were vulnerable to the bad habits of the bachelor white society, bingeing on whiskey and prostitution. The syphilis and gonorrhea that Indian men contracted from Indian women infected by whites killed many and impaired reproduction, a consequence that their population, already declining from smallpox and other white diseases, could not afford. Thus, the age and gender structure of the white frontier population, combined with racial contempt, threatened Indian existence in the West further.

Government policy reinforced efforts to remove Indians. North American native peoples were organized

LACK OF NATIVE UNITY

not into tribes, as whites believed, but rather into bands and confederacies. Two hundred distinct languages and dialects separated these groups, making it difficult for Indians to unite against white invaders. Although a language group could be defined as a tribe, separate bands and clans had their own leaders, and seldom did a tribal chief hold widespread power. Moreover, bands usually spent more time quarreling among themselves than with white settlers.

After the Treaty of Greenville in 1795, American officials regarded Indian tribes as nations with which

TERRITORIAL TREATIES

they could make pacts, ensuring peace and defining land boundaries. But the U.S. government did not understand that a chief who agreed to a treaty did not speak for everyone and that the group might not abide by it. Moreover, whites seldom accepted treaties as guarantees of Indians' future land rights. In the Northwest, whites considered treaties protecting Indians' fishing rights on the Columbia River as nuisances and ousted Indians from the best locations. On the Plains, whites settled wherever they wished, typically commandeering choice farmlands.

From the 1860s to the 1880s, the federal government tried to force western Indians onto reservations

RESERVATION POLICY

under the guise of "civilizing" them. Reservations usually consisted of those areas of a group's previous territory that were least desirable to whites. In exchange, the government promised protection from white encroachment along with food, clothing, and other necessities.

The reservation policy helped make way for the market economy. Early on, trade had benefited both Indians and whites equally. Indians acquired clothing, guns, and horses in return for furs, jewelry, and sometimes military assistance to whites against other

Indians. Over time, however, Indians became more dependent, and whites increasingly dictated trade. For example, white traders persuaded Navajo weavers in the Southwest to produce heavy rugs for eastern customers and to adapt colors and designs to boost sales. Meanwhile, Navajos raised fewer crops and were forced to buy food. Soon they were selling land and labor to whites, and their dependency made it easier to force them onto reservations.

Indians had no voice concerning their own affairs on reservations. Supreme Court decisions in 1884 and 1886 defined them as wards (falling, like helpless children, under government protection) and denied them the right to become U.S. citizens. Thus, they were unprotected by the Fourteenth and Fifteenth Amendments, which had extended citizenship to African Americans. Second, pressure from white farmers, miners, and herders who sought Indian lands made it difficult for the government to preserve reservations intact. Third, the government ignored native history, even combining on the same reservation Indian bands that habitually warred against each other. Rather than serving as civilizing communities, reservations weakened Indian life.

Not all Indians succumbed to market forces and reservation restrictions. Pawnees in the Midwest, for

NATIVE RESISTANCE AND INDIAN WARS

example, resisted disadvantageous deals. Some Native Americans preserved their cultures even as they became dependent on whites. Pawnees left their Nebraska homelands for a reservation in the hope that they could hunt buffalo and grow corn their way.

Online Study Center Improve Your Grade
Interactive Map:
Major Indian-White Clashes in the West

Whites responded to western Indian defiance with military aggression. In 1864, for example, in the Sand Creek region of Colorado, a militia led by Methodist minister John Chivington attacked a Cheyenne band under Black Kettle, killing almost every Indian. In 1877 four detachments of troops, aided by Crow and Cheyenne scouts, chased 800 Nez Percé Indians in the Northwest, finally killing many before one of their leaders, Young Joseph, surrendered.

The most infamous Indian battle occurred in June 1876 when 2,500 Lakotas led by Chiefs Rain-in-the-Face, Sitting Bull, and Crazy Horse annihilated

256 government troops led by the rash General Geoerge A. Custer near the Little Big Horn River in southern Montana. Though Indians demonstrated military skill, supply shortages and relentless pursuit by U.S. soldiers eventually overwhelmed Indian resistance. Native Americans were not so much conquered as they were harassed and starved into submission.

In the 1870s and 1880s, officials and reformers sought peaceful means of dealing with Native Americans. Instead of battling Indians, whites would "civilize" them through landholding and education. The U.S. government pressured Indians to abandon their traditional cultures and adopt values of the American work ethic: ambition, thrift, and materialism. Other forces argued for sympathetic—and sometimes patronizing—

REFORM OF INDIAN POLICY

treatment. Reform treaties, such as George Manypenny's *Our Indian Wards* (1880) and Helen Hunt Jackson's *A Century of Dishonor* (1881), and unfavorable comparison with Canada's more sympathetic management of Indian affairs aroused the American conscience.

In the United States, the two most active Indian reform organizations were the Women's National Indian Association (WNIA) and the Indian Rights Association (IRA). The WNIA, composed mainly of white women using domestic skills to help needy people, urged gradual assimilation of Indians. The influential IRA, which had few Native American members, supported Indian citizenship and landholding. Most reformers believed Indians were culturally inferior and could succeed economically only by embracing middle-class values of diligence and education.

■ Plains Indians did not write books or letters as whites did, but they did tell stories and spread news through art. They painted scenes on hides and notebooks to represent events such as this one, which depicts the Indians' annihilation of General George A. Custer's soldiers at Little Big Horn in 1876.

(National Anthropological Archives, Smithsonian Institution [72-3934])

Reformers particularly deplored Indians' sexual division of labor. Women seemed to do all the work—tending crops, raising children, cooking, curing hides, making tools and clothes—while being servile to men, who hunted but were otherwise idle. WNIA, IRA, and others wanted Indian men to bear more responsibilities, treat Indian women respectfully, and resemble male heads of white middle-class households. But when Indian men and women adopted the model of white society, Indian women lost much of the economic independence and power over daily life that they once had.

In 1887 Congress reversed its reservation policy and passed the Dawes Severalty Act, which achieved *DAWES SEVERALTY ACT* the reformers' goal of ending community-owned property in favor of individual family land grants. The government held that land in trust for twenty-five years, so families could not sell their allotments. The law also awarded citizenship to those accepting allotments (a 1906 act of Congress delayed citizenship for those Indians who had not yet taken their allotment). And it entitled the government to sell unallocated land to whites. Undergirding the Dawes Act was the belief that private property would more easily integrate Indians into the larger society. Officials also believed that Indians would abandon their "barbaric" habits more quickly if their children were educated away from the reservations.

The Dawes Act reflected a Euro-American and Christian worldview that a society of families headed by men was most desirable. Professional educators similarly saw schools as tools to create a patriotic, industrious citizenry. In 1879, educators established the Carlisle School in Pennsylvania as the flagship of the government's Indian school system based on the Hampton Institute founded ten years earlier in Virginia to educate newly freed slaves. Boarding schools imposed white-defined sex roles: boys were taught farming and carpentry, while girls learned sewing, cleaning, and cooking.

With active resistance suppressed, Lakotas and other groups turned to the Ghost Dance as a spiritual *GHOST DANCE* means of preserving culture. The Ghost Dance involved movement in a circle until the dancers reached a trancelike state and envisioned dead ancestors. Involving several days of dancing and meditation, the Ghost Dance expressed a messianic vision of a day when buffalo would return to the Plains and all elements of white civilization, including guns and whiskey, would be buried.

Ghost Dancers forswore violence, but as the religion spread, government agents worried about the possibility of renewed Indian uprisings. Charging that the cult was anti-Christian, they arrested Ghost Dancers. Late in 1890, the government sent Custer's former regiment, the Seventh Cavalry, to detain Lakotas moving toward Pine Ridge, South Dakota. Although the Indians were starving, the army assumed they were armed for revolt. Overtaking the band at Wounded Knee Creek, the troops massacred an estimated three hundred men, women, and children in the snow.

The Dawes Act effectively accomplished what whites wanted and Indians feared: it reduced native *LOSING THE WEST* control over land. Between 1887 and the 1930s, Indian landholdings dwindled from 138 million acres to 52 million. Land-grabbing whites were particularly cruel to the Ojibwas of the northern plains. In 1906 Senator Moses E. Clapp of Minnesota attached a rider to an Indian appropriations bill declaring that mixed-blood adults were "competent" (meaning educated in white ways) enough to sell their land without the Dawes Act's twenty-five-year waiting period. When the bill became law, speculators duped many Ojibwas into signing away their land in return for counterfeit money and worthless merchandise. The Ojibwas lost more than half their original holdings and were ruined economically.

Ultimately, political and ecological crises overwhelmed most western Indian groups. Buffalo extinction, enemy raids, and disease, in addition to white military force, weakened subsistence culture so that Native Americans had no alternative but to yield their lands to market-oriented whites. Believing their culture superior, whites determined to transform Indians into successful farmers by teaching them the value of private property, educating them in American ideals, and eradicating their "backward" languages, lifestyles, and religions. Indians tried to retain their culture, but by century's end, they had lost control of the land and faced increasing pressure to shed their group identity.

The Extraction of Natural Resources

nlike Indians, who used natural resources primarily for subsistence and small-scale trading, most whites who migrated to the West and the Great Plains saw the vast territory as an untapped source of wealth (see Map 17.1). Extracting its rich resources advanced settlement, created new markets at home and abroad, and fueled revolutions in transportation, agriculture, and industry across the United States. At the same time, extraction of nature's wealth led to environmental

Map 17.1   The Development and Natural Resources of the West

By 1890, mining, lumbering, and cattle ranching had penetrated many areas west of the Mississippi River, and railroads had linked together the western economy. These characteristics, along with the spread of agriculture, contributed to the Census Bureau's announcement in 1890 that the frontier had disappeared; yet as the map shows, large areas remained undeveloped.

wastefulness and fed habits of racial and sexual oppression.

In the mid-1800s, the mining frontier advanced rapidly, drawing thousands of people to Nevada, Idaho, Montana, Utah, and Colorado in search of gold, silver, timber, and copper. California's gold rush populated the thriving state with over 300,000 people by 1860 and furnished many of the miners moving on to nearby states in search of riches. Others followed traditional routes, moving from the East to the West.

MINING AND LUMBERING

Prospectors climbed mountains and trekked across deserts in search of precious metals. They shot game for food and financed their explorations by convincing merchants to advance credit for equipment in return for a share of the as-yet-undiscovered lode. Unlucky prospectors whose credit ran out took jobs and saved up for another search.

Digging for and transporting minerals was expensive, so prospectors who discovered veins sold their claims to large mining syndicates such as the Anaconda Copper Company. Financed by eastern capital, these companies brought in engineers, heavy machinery, railroad lines, and work crews, making mining as corporate as eastern manufacturing. Although discoveries of gold and silver first drew attention to the West, mining companies usually exploited equally lucrative lead, zinc, tin, quartz, and copper.

Midwest and southern lumber companies headed west, spurred by the demand for the rich timber resources there and the depletion of forests at home. The Timber and Stone Act of 1878 sought to stimulate settlement in California, Nevada, Oregon, and Washington, by allowing private citizens to buy, at low prices, 160-acre plots "valuable chiefly for timber." Lumber companies grabbed millions of these acres by hiring seamen from waterfront boarding houses to register private claims to timberland and then transfer those claims to the companies. By 1900 most of the 3.5 million acres believed to be sold to private citizens in truth belonged to corporations.

At the same time, oil companies were beginning to drill in the Southwest. In 1900 most of the nation's petroleum came from the Appalachians and the Midwest, but rich oil reserves had been discovered in southern California and eastern Texas. Although oil and kerosene were still used mostly for lubrication and lighting, Southwest oil would become a vital new fuel source.

The West became a rich multiracial society, comprising Native Americans, native-born white migrants, Hispanics, African Americans, and Asians. A crescent borderland from western Texas through New Mexico and Arizona to northern California supported Hispanic ranchers and sheepherders, descendants of the early Spanish settlers. In New Mexico, Spaniards mixed with Indians to form a *mestizo* population. Throughout the Southwest, Mexican immigrants moved into American territory to find work. Some returned to Mexico seasonally; others stayed.

A COMPLEX POPULATION

Before federal law excluded them in 1881 and 1882, 200,000 Chinese immigrants—mostly young, single males—came to the United States, building communities in California, Oregon, and Washington. The state's fertile fields and citrus groves demanded a huge migrant work force, and by the 1870s, Chinese composed half of California's agricultural laborers.

Japanese, Mexican, and European immigrants also moved around, working in mining and agricultural communities. The region consequently developed its own migrant economy, with workers relocating as they took short-term jobs.

African Americans tended to congregate in the West, many of them "Exodusters" who inhabited all-black towns. Nicodemus, Kansas, for example, was founded in 1877 by African American migrants from Lexington, Kentucky, and grew to six hundred residents within two years, surviving challenging times with the aid of food, firewood, and staples from nearby Osage Indians.

Although unmarried men numerically dominated the frontier, some white women also came to find fortune. But they usually accompanied a husband or father and seldom prospected themselves. With their labor as a resource, many women earned money cooking, laundering, and in some cases working in houses of prostitution. In the Northwest, they worked in canneries, cleaning and salting fish.

For white settlers, race became a vital means of controlling labor and social relations. They usually identified four nonwhite races, all ascribed with demeaning characteristics: Indians, Mexicans (including

SIGNIFICANCE OF RACE

Mexican Americans and immigrants), "Mongolians" (referring to Chinese), and "Negroes." Through these categories, whites imposed racial distinctions on people who, with the possible exception of African Americans, had never considered themselves to be a "race" and then deemed them permanently inferior. In 1878, for example, a federal judge in California ruled that Chinese could not become U.S. citizens because they were not "white persons."

Racial minorities occupied the bottom half of a two-tiered labor system and encountered prejudice as whites sought to reserve the West's riches for themselves. Whites dominated the top tier of managerial and skilled labor positions, while Irish, Chinese, and Mexicans held unskilled jobs in mines, railroad construction, and as agricultural and domestic laborers. Indians barely participated in the labor system at all. Anti-Chinese violence erupted during hard times. When the Union Pacific Railroad tried to replace white workers with lower-waged Chinese in Rock Springs, Wyoming, in 1885, whites burned down the Chinese part of town and killed twenty-eight. Mexicans, many of whom had been the original landowners, saw their property claims ignored or stolen by whites. In California, many Mexicans moved to cities, where they could get only unskilled, low-paying jobs.

Because so many white male migrants were single, intermarriage with Mexican and Indian women was common. Such intermarriage was acceptable for white men, but not for white women, especially with Asian immigrants. Most miscegenation laws passed by western legislatures were intended to prevent Chinese and Japanese men from marrying white women.

Protestant missions had long sponsored benevolent activities abroad, such as in China, and had aided the settlement of Oregon in the 1840s. But in the mid-nineteenth century, a number of women broke away from male-dominated organizations and established missionary societies in the United States. In the West, they built homes to rescue women—unmarried mothers, Mormons, Indians, and Chinese—who they believed had fallen prey to men lacking Christian virtue.

Questions about natural resources caught Americans between a desire for progress and a fear of spoiling the land. After the Civil War, people eager to protect the natural landscape organized a conservation movement. Sports hunters, concerned about loss of wildlife, lobbied state legislatures

CONSERVATION MOVEMENT

to regulate commercial hunting. Artists and tourists in 1864 persuaded Congress to preserve the beautiful Yosemite Valley by granting it to California for public use. In 1872 Congress designated the Yellowstone River region in Wyoming as the first national park. And in 1891, conservationists, led by naturalist John Muir, pressured Congress to authorize President Benjamin Harrison to create forest reserves—public lands protected from private-interest cutting. Despite Muir's activism and efforts by the Sierra Club (which Muir helped found in 1892) and corporations supporting rational resource development, opposition was loudest in the West, where people remained eager to exploit nature's bounty. Moreover, national parks induced some spoiling of the land they intended to preserve, as tourist services necessitated the building of roads, hotels, restaurants, and sewers in the wilderness.

Online Study Center
Improve Your Grade
Primary Source:
John Muir on the Dominion of Nature

Development of mining and forest regions brought western territories to the threshold of statehood (see Map 17.1). In 1889 Republicans seeking to solidify control of Congress passed a bill granting statehood to North Dakota, South Dakota, Washington, and Montana. Wyoming and Idaho, which allowed women to vote, were admitted the next year. Congress denied statehood to Utah until 1896, awaiting assurances from the Mormons, a majority of the territory's population and leaders, that they would abandon polygamy.

ADMISSION OF NEW STATES

Mining towns and lumber camps spiced American folklore and fostered a go-getter optimism that distinguished the American spirit. The lawlessness of places such as Deadwood in Dakota Territory and Tombstone in Arizona Territory gave the West notoriety and romance. Cowboys especially captivated popular imagination in the United States and Europe.

Arizona's mining towns, with their free-flowing cash and loose law enforcement, attracted gamblers, thieves, and opportunists who came to stand for the Wild West. Near Tombstone, the infamous Clanton family and their partner, John Ringgold (known as Johnny Ringo), engaged in smuggling and cattle rustling. The Earp brothers—Wyatt, Jim, Morgan, Virgil, and Warren—and their friends William ("Bat")

Masterson and John Henry ("Doc") Holliday operated on both sides of the law as gunmen, gamblers, and politicians. A feud between the Clantons and Earps climaxed on October 26, 1881, in a shootout at the OK Corral, where three Clantons were killed and Holliday and Morgan Earp were wounded.

Mark Twain, Bret Harte, and other writers captured for posterity the drama of western life, and characters like Buffalo Bill, Annie Oakley, Wild Bill Hickok, Poker Alice, and Bedrock Tom became folk heroes. But in reality, most miners and lumbermen worked long hours, often for corporations rather than as rugged individuals, and they had little time or money for gambling, carousing, or gunfights. Women worked hard too, as teachers, laundresses, storekeepers, and housewives. Only a few were sharpshooters or dance-hall queens. For most, western life was a matter of survival.

Irrigation and Transportation

*W*estern economic development is the story of how public and private interests used technology and organization to develop the region's river basins and make the land agriculturally productive. For centuries, Indians had irrigated southwestern lands for subsistence farming. When the Spanish arrived, they irrigated farms in southwest Texas, New Mexico, and California. Later they channeled water to the California mission communities of San Diego and Los Angeles. The first Americans of northern European ancestry to practice extensive irrigation were the Mormons. Arriving in Utah in 1847, they diverted streams and rivers into networks of canals, enabling them to farm the hard-baked soil. By 1890 Utah boasted over 263,000 irrigated acres, supporting more than 200,000 people.

Irrigation in Colorado and California raised controversies over rights to the precious streams that flowed through the West. Americans had inherited the English common-law principle of riparian rights, which held that the stream itself belonged to God; those who lived near it could take water as needed but were not to diminish the river. Intended to protect nature, this principle discouraged economic development by prohibiting property owners from damming or diverting water at the expense of neighbors along the banks.

RIGHTS TO WATER

Westerners, taking cues from eastern Americans who had diverted waterways to power mills, asserted the doctrine of prior appropriation: water, like other natural resources, existed to serve human needs, so anyone intending a "reasonable" (economically productive) use of river water should have the right to appropriation. The courts generally agreed.

Under appropriation, those who dammed and diverted water often reduced its flow downstream. People disadvantaged by it could protect their interests by either suing or establishing a public authority to regulate water use. Thus, in 1879 Colorado created several water divisions. In 1890 Wyoming added a constitutional provision declaring that the state's rivers were public property subject to state supervision.

California maintained a mixed legal system that upheld riparianism while allowing for some appropriation. This system disadvantaged irrigators, who sought to change state law. In 1887 the legislature passed a bill permitting farmers to organize into districts that would construct and operate irrigation projects. An irrigation district could use its public authority to purchase water rights, seize private property for irrigation canals, and finance projects through taxation or by issuing bonds. As a result, California became the nation's leader in irrigated acreage, with more than 1 million irrigated acres by 1890, making it the most profitable agricultural state in the country.

Still, the federal government owned most of western lands in the 1890s. Prodded by land-hungry developers, states claimed that they could make these lands profitable through reclamation and subsequent irrigation. Congress generally refused to transfer the land because of potential controversies. If one state sponsored irrigation, who would regulate waterways that flowed through more than one state? If, for example, California controlled the Truckee River, which flowed westward to the Nevada border, how would Nevadans ensure that California would give them sufficient water? Only the federal government, it seemed, could regulate regional water development.

NEWLANDS RECLAMATION ACT

In 1902, after years of debates, Congress passed the Newlands Reclamation Act. This allowed the federal government to sell western public lands to individuals in parcels of under 160 acres and to use the proceeds to finance irrigation. Often seen as sensitive to natural-resource conservation, the Newlands

Reclamation Act in fact represented a decision by the federal government to aid the agricultural and general economic development of the West.

Between 1865 and 1890, railroad construction grew from 35,000 to 200,000 miles, mostly west of the Mississippi River (see Map 17.1). By 1900, the United States contained one-third of all railroad track in the world. The Central Pacific imported seven thousand Chinese to build its tracks; the Union Pacific used mainly the Irish. Workers lived in shacks and tents that were dismantled, loaded on flatcars, and relocated every 60 miles or so. After 1880, railroads helped to boost the steel industry by switching from iron to steel rails. Railroad expansion also spawned related industries, including coal production, passenger- and freight-car manufacture, and depot construction. Transporting people and freight, lines such as the Union Pacific and Southern Pacific accelerated the growth of western hubs such as Omaha, Kansas City, Cheyenne, Los Angeles, Portland, and Seattle.

RAILROAD CONSTRUCTION

Railroads received some of the largest government subsidies in American history. Executives argued that because railroads were a public benefit, the government should give them land from the public domain, which they could sell to finance construction. During the Civil War, Congress, dominated by business-minded Republicans, was sympathetic, granting over 180 million acres to railroad corporations, mostly for interstate routes. Railroads funded construction by using the land as security for bonds or by selling it. State legislators, many of whom had financial interests in a railroad's success, granted an additional 50 million acres. Cities and towns also assisted, usually through loans or by purchasing railroad bonds or stocks.

RAILROAD SUBSIDIES

Without public help, few railroads could have prospered sufficiently to attract private investment, yet such aid was not always voluntary. Localities that could not or would not pay suffered. The Southern Pacific, for example, threatened to bypass Los Angeles unless the city paid a bonus and built a depot. Some laborers and farmers fought subsidies, arguing that companies like Southern Pacific would become too powerful. Many communities boomed, however, as railroads helped attract investment into the West and drew farmers into the market economy.

The growth of railroads required technological and organizational reforms. By the late 1880s, almost all lines had adopted standard-gauge rails allowing their tracks to connect. Air brakes, automatic car couplers, standardized handholds on freight cars, and other devices made rail transportation safer and more efficient. The need for gradings, tunnels, and bridges spurred the growth of the engineering profession. Organizational advances included systems for co-ordinating passenger and freight schedules and the adoption of uniform freight classification.

STANDARD GAUGE; STANDARD TIME

Railroads also altered conceptions of time and space. First, instead of expressing distance in miles, people began to refer to the time it took to travel from place to place. Second, railroad scheduling required nationwide standardization of time. Before railroads, local church bells and clocks struck noon when the sun was directly overhead, and people set clocks accordingly. But because the sun was not overhead at the same moment everywhere, time varied by place. Boston's clocks differed from New York's by almost twelve minutes. By 1880 there were nearly fifty different standards. In 1883 the railroads, without authority from Congress, agreed to establish four standard time zones that would regularize the country. Railroad time became national time.

Farming the Plains

*W*estern agriculture in the late nineteenth century yielded two notable achievements: the transformation of arid prairies into crop-producing land and the transformation of agriculture into big business via mechanization, transportation, and scientific cultivation. The climate and terrain of the Great Plains presented formidable challenges. Technological innovation and the mechanization enabled farmers to feed the burgeoning population and turned the United States into the world's breadbasket.

During the 1870s and 1880s, thousands of hopeful farmers streamed into the Great Plains region, cultivating more land in states such as Kansas, Nebraska, and Texas than in the entire country during the previous 250 years. The number of

SETTLEMENT OF THE PLAINS

The Australian Frontier

Australia, founded like the United States as a European colony, bred a frontier society that paralleled the American experience in its mining development, folk society, and treatment of indigenous people. Australia experienced a gold rush two years after the United States in 1851, and large-scale mining companies quickly moved into its western regions to extract lucrative mineral deposits.

A promise of mineral wealth lured thousands of immigrants, primarily males, to Australia in the late nineteenth century, many from China. As in the United States, anti-Chinese riots erupted, and beginning in 1854 Australia passed laws restricting Chinese immigration. When the country became an independent British federation in 1901, it implemented a strict literacy test that eliminated Chinese immigration for over fifty years.

While Australians lauded "white men," they considered native peoples, whom they called "Aborigines," to be savages. Christian missionaries viewed natives as pagans and tried to convert them. In 1869 the government of Victoria passed the Aborigine Protection Act, encouraging the removal of native children from their families to learn European customs in white schools. Aborigines tried in their own ways to adapt or, if they had light skin, sometimes reported themselves as white for the census. In the end, Australians resorted to reservations. Like the Americans, Australians could not find a place for Aborigines in a land of opportunity for whites.

Much like the American counterpart, the Australian frontier was populated by natives before Anglo colonists arrived. The Aborigines, as the Australian natives were called, lived in villages and used their own culture to adapt to the environment. This photo shows a native camp in the Maloga reserve. (National Library of Australia)

311

farms tripled from 2 million to over 6 million between 1860 and 1910. Several states opened offices in the East to lure migrants westward. Land-rich railroads aggressively advertised cheap land, arranged credit, and offered reduced fares. Railroad agents—often former immigrants—traveled to Denmark, Sweden, Germany, and other European nations to recruit settlers.

Most families migrated because opportunities in the West seemed to promise a better existence. Railroad expansion enabled farmers to ship produce to market, and the construction of grain elevators eased storage problems. Worldwide and national population growth fueled demand for farm products, and the prospects for commercial agriculture became increasingly favorable.

Farm life was harder than advertisements and railroad agents suggested. Migrants often encountered

HARDSHIP ON THE PLAINS

scarcities of essentials they had once taken for granted. The open prairies contained little lumber, so families built houses of sod and burned buffalo dung for heat. Water was often scarce too. Few families were wealthy enough to buy land near a stream that did not dry up in summer. Machinery for drilling wells was expensive, as were windmills for drawing water to the surface.

The weather was especially formidable. The climate between the Missouri River and the Rocky Mountains divides along a line running from Minnesota southwest through Oklahoma, then south, bisecting Texas. West of this line, annual rainfall averages less than twenty-eight inches, not enough for most crops, and even that rain was never certain.

Weather was unpredictable. In summer, weeks of heat and parching winds suddenly gave way to violent storms that washed away crops and property. Winter blizzards piled up mountainous snowdrifts that halted outdoor movement. Melting snow swelled streams, and floods threatened millions of acres. In the fall, a rainless week turned dry grasslands into

■ Posing in front of their sod house, this proud Nebraska family displays the seriousness that derived from their hard lives on the Great Plains. Although bushes and other growth appear in the background, the absence of trees is notable.   (Nebraska State Historical Society, Solomon D. Butcher Collection)

tinder, and the slightest spark could ignite a raging prairie fire. Although early Plains settlers were optimistic about a wet-weather cycle, the climate changed abruptly in 1886, beginning a four-year drought that drove many off the land.

Nature could be cruel even under good conditions. Weather that was favorable for crops was also good for breeding insects. In the 1870s and 1880s, swarms of grasshoppers devoured everything: plants, tree bark, and clothes. As one farmer lamented, the "hoppers left behind nothing but the mortgage."

Settlers also braved isolation. New England and European farmers lived in villages, traveling daily to

SOCIAL ISOLATION

nearby fields. In the Plains, the Far West, and the South, peculiarities of land division compelled rural dwellers to live far apart. The Homestead Act of 1862 and other measures offered cheap or free plots to people who would reside on and improve their property. Because most small farmers' plots were rectangles of about 160 acres, at most four families could live close by, but only if they congregated around the shared four-corner intersection. In practice, farm families lived back from their boundary lines with at least a half-mile separating farmhouses.

Letters that Ed Donnell, a young Nebraska homesteader, wrote to his family in Missouri reveal how circumstances could dull optimism. In fall 1885, Donnell rejoiced to his mother: "I like Nebr first rate. . . . I have saw a pretty tuff time a part of the time since I have been out here, but I started out to get a home and I was determined to win or die in the attempt. . . . Have got a good crop of corn, a floor in my house and got it ceiled overhead." A year and a half later, Donnell's dreams were dissolving, and still a bachelor, he was beginning to look elsewhere. He wrote to his brother, "If I sell I am going west and grow up with the country." By fall, conditions had worsened. Donnell lamented, "We have been having wet weather for 3 weeks. . . . My health has been so poor this summer. . . . If I can sell I will . . . move to town for I can get $40 a month working in a grist mill and I would not be exposed to the weather." Thousands shared Donnell's hardships and cityward migration, fueling late-nineteenth-century urban growth (see Chapter 19).

By 1900 two developments brought rural settlers into closer contact with modern consumer society

MAIL-ORDER COMPANIES AND RURAL FREE DELIVERY

(though people in sparsely settled regions west of the 28-inch-rainfall line remained isolated for several more decades). First, mail-order companies such as Montgomery Ward and Sears, Roebuck made new products available to almost everyone by the 1870s and 1880s. Ward and Sears were outlets for sociability as well. Letters from customers to Mr. Ward reported family news and sought advice on needs from gifts to childcare. A Washington man wrote, "As you advertise everything for sale that a person wants, I thought I would write you, as I am in need of a wife, and see what you could do for me."

Second, after farmers petitioned Congress for extension of the postal service, the government in 1896 widely expanded the Rural Free Delivery (RFD) it had begun in West Virginia. Farmers who previously had to pick up mail in town could receive letters, newspapers, and catalogues in roadside mailboxes almost daily. In 1913 the postal service inaugurated parcel post, reducing the cost of package delivery.

Expanded use of machinery drove the agricultural revolution. When the Civil War drew men away

MECHANIZATION OF AGRICULTURE

from farms in the upper Mississippi River valley, the women and older men who remained behind began using reapers and other mechanical implements. After the war, continued demand and high prices encouraged farmers to depend more on machines, and inventors developed new grain implements. Seeders, combines, binders, mowers, and rotary plows improved grain growing in the 1870s and 1880s. The centrifugal cream separator, patented in 1879, aided dairy farming by speeding the skimming of cream from milk.

For centuries, grain farmers could plant only as much as could be harvested by hand. Machines—driven first by animals and then by steam—significantly increased productivity. Before mechanization, a farmer could harvest about 7.5 acres of wheat; with an automatic binder that cut and bundled the grain, he could harvest 135 acres. Machines facilitated farming other crops as well.

Congress and scientists worked to improve existing crops and develop new ones. The 1862 Morrill Land

LEGISLATIVE AND SCIENTIFIC AIDS

Grant Act gave states federal lands to finance agricultural research and development. New state universities were established in Wisconsin, Illinois, Minnesota, California, and other states. A second Morrill Act in 1890 aided more schools, including some black colleges. The Hatch Act of 1887 provided for agricultural experiment stations in every state, further encouraging farming science and technology.

Science also enabled farmers to use the soil more efficiently. Researchers developed dry farming, a plowing and harrowing technique that minimized evaporation. Botanists perfected varieties of "hard" wheat whose seeds could withstand northern winters. Agriculturists also adapted new varieties of alfalfa from Mongolia, corn from North Africa, and rice from Asia. George Washington Carver, a son of slaves who became a chemist and taught at Alabama's Tuskegee Institute, created new products from peanuts, soybeans, sweet potatoes, and cotton wastes and developed industrial applications from agricultural products. Other scientists developed means of combating plant and animal diseases. Science and technology helped American farming expand productivity in the market economy.

The Ranching Frontier

Commercial farming ran headlong into one of the region's most romantic industries—ranching. Beginning in the sixteenth century, Spanish landholders raised cattle in Mexico and what would become the American Southwest. They employed Indian and Mexican cowboys, known as *vaqueros,* to tend herds and round up free-roaming cattle. American immigrant ranchers moving into Texas and California in the early nineteenth century hired *vaqueros* to train them in roping, branding, horse training, and saddle making. By the 1860s, cattle raising became increasingly profitable as population growth boosted beef demand and railroads simplified food transportation. By 1870 drovers were herding thousands of Texas cattle northward to Kansas, Missouri, and Wyoming (see Map 17.1). At the northern terminus—usually Abilene, Dodge City, or Cheyenne—the cattle were sold or loaded onto trains bound for Chicago and St. Louis slaughterhouses.

The long drive gave rise to romantic lore of bellowing cattle, buckskin-clad cowboys, and smoky campfires. But trekking over 1,000 miles for months made cattle sinewy and tough, and herds were sometimes shot at for trespassing on Indian and farmers' land. When ranchers discovered that crossing Texas longhorns with Hereford and Angus breeds produced animals better able to survive northern winters, cattle raising expanded northward. Between 1860 and 1880, the cattle population of Kansas, Nebraska, Colorado, Wyoming, Montana, and the Dakotas increased from 130,000 to 4.5 million, crowding out already declining buffalo.

Cattle raisers kept costs down through open-range ranching. It worked like this: ranchers would buy a few acres bordering a stream, and then let their herds graze on adjacent public domain land that no one wanted because it lacked water access. This way, a cattle raiser could use thousands of acres while owning considerably less. Neighboring ranchers often formed associations and allowed their herds to graze together, burning a brand into their animals' hide for identification. But as cattle production rose to meet demand, cattle began to overrun the range, making it difficult for ranchers to control the land.

THE OPEN RANGE

Meanwhile, sheepherders from California and New Mexico also were using the public domain, sparking territorial clashes. Ranchers complained that sheep ruined grassland by eating down to the roots and that cattle refused to graze where sheep had been. Cowboys and sheepherders sometimes resorted to violence rather than settle disagreements in court, where a judge might discover that both were using public land illegally.

More important, the farming frontier generated new land demands. Lacking sufficient timber and stone for fencing, western settlers could not easily mark their property. Tensions flared when farmers accused cattle ranchers of letting herds trespass on cropland and when herders charged that farmers should fence their property.

The solution was barbed wire. Invented in 1873 by Joseph F. Glidden, a DeKalb, Illinois, farmer, this inexpensive and mass-produced fencing consisted of two wires held in place by sharp spurs twisted around them. It enabled Plains homesteaders to protect their farms from grazing cattle. It also ended open-range ranching and made roundups unnecessary because it enclosed private land that had been used ille-

BARBED WIRE

■ A group of cowboys prepare for a roundup. Note the presence of African Americans, who, along with Mexicans, made up one-fourth of all cowboys. Although they rarely became trail bosses or ranch owners, black cowboys enjoyed an independence on the trails that was unavailable to them on tenant farms and city streets.   (Nebraska State Historical Society)

gally for grazing. Likewise, the development of the round silo for storing and making feed (silage) enabled cattle raisers to feed herds without grazing.

By 1890 big businesses were taking over the cattle industry and applying scientific methods of breeding and feeding. Similarly, big corpora-

RANCHING AS BIG BUSINESS

tions used technology to squeeze larger returns from meatpacking. All parts of a cow had uses: its hide became leather, and about half was salable meat. Meatpackers' largest profits came from livestock byproducts: blood for fertilizer, hooves for glue, fat for candles and soap, and the rest for sausages. But cattle processing polluted the environment, as meatpackers and leather tanners dumped what they could not sell into rivers and streams. By the late nineteenth century, the Chicago River created such a powerful stench that residents became sick.

The environment contributed to changes in ranching. The brutal winters of 1886–1888 destroyed 90 percent of some herds and drove small ranchers out

of business. Cowboys formed labor organizations and went on strike for higher pay. The myth of the cowboy's freedom and individualism lived on, but ranching quickly became a corporate business.

Summary ⚙️ *Online Study Center* **ACE the Test**

he land of the American West exerted a lasting influence on the complex mix of people who settled it. Living mostly in small groups, Indians, the original inhabitants, depended heavily on delicate resources such as buffalo herds and salmon runs. When they came into contact with commerce-minded Euro-Americans, their resistance to the market economy, diseases, and violence that whites brought into the West failed.

Migrants discovered a reciprocal relationship between human activities and the environment too. Miners, timber cutters, farmers, and builders extracted raw minerals for eastern factories, used irrigation and mechanization to yield agricultural abundance, filled pastures with cattle and sheep to expand food sources, and constructed railroads to tie the nation together. But the environment exerted its own power through climate, insects and predators, undesirable plant growths, and impenetrable barriers to agriculture.

The West's settlers employed force, violence, and greed that sustained discrimination within a multi-racial society, left many farmers feeling cheated, provoked contests over water and pastures, and sacrificed environmental balance for market profits. The region's raw materials and agricultural products improved living standards and hastened the industrial progress of the Machine Age, but not without costs.

LEGACY FOR A PEOPLE AND A NATION
The West and Rugged Individualism

Though born in New York State, Theodore Roosevelt, twenty-sixth president of the United States, thought of himself as a westerner. In 1884, at age twenty-five, he moved to Dakota Territory to ranch. In the West, Roosevelt believed, he developed "rugged individualism," an ability to conquer challenges through strength and fortitude. He once wrote that he "knew toil and hardship . . . but we felt the beat of hardy life in our veins, and ours was the glory of work and the joy of living."

Americans have long shared Roosevelt's fascination with the West. They have popularized western settings and characters in movies and on television. The film *Cimarron* (1930) was one of the first to win an Academy Award, and *Gunsmoke* held the record as one of the longest-running television series (1955–1975). Movie star John Wayne epitomized the rugged westerner in dozens of films. From *The Virginian,* published in 1902, to the recent novels of Larry McMurtry, Americans have made books about the West bestsellers. In many, a lone individual, usually male and white, overcomes danger and hardship through solitary effort.

Western reality, however, is far different from the myth of rugged individualism. Migrants traveled on railroads built with government subsidies, acquired land cheaply from the federal government under the Homestead and Timber and Stone Acts, depended on the army to remove Indians, and cut forests and diverted rivers with federal support. More recently, western politicians who oppose big government have received votes from constituents who depend on federal farm subsidies and price supports, free or subsidized water, and government-financed relief from droughts, floods, and tornadoes.

The West could not have been settled and developed without both individualism *and* government assistance—what might be called "rugged cooperation." Here was the West's true legacy.

𝒯HE MACHINE AGE 1877–1920

𝐼 n 1911, iron molders at the Watertown Arsenal, a government weapons factory near Boston, went on strike after a worker was fired. Joseph Cooney had objected to having his work timed by an efficiency expert with a stopwatch, and the molders knew they soon would be given new work routines. Iron molders union president John Frey explained, "The workman believes when he goes on strike that he is defending his job." The molders felt a property right to their labor—that jobs could not be changed or taken away without their consent.

The army officers who ran the factory, however, believed they owned the molders' labor and that output was "one-half what it should be." To increase production, managers had installed an incentive-pay system, but when that failed, they hired Dwight Merrick, an expert in the new field of "scientific management," to time workers and speed up performance.

The day Merrick began his time study, a molder named Perkins secretly timed the same task. Merrick reported that the job should take twenty-four minutes; Perkins found that to do the job right required fifty minutes. That evening, the molders discussed how they should respond to the discrepancy between Merrick's report and their own. Cooney argued for resisting scientific management; the workers drew up a petition and were ready to walk out.

Eventually the molders and their bosses reached a compromise, but this incident reveals a consequence of the industrialization that made many new products available in the late 1800s. To increase production, factories and machines divided work into minute, repetitive tasks, organized by timetables. Workers who had long thought themselves skilled now struggled to avoid becoming slaves to machines. Defenders of the new system devised theories to justify it, while laborers tried to combat what they thought were demoralizing abuses of power.

In the mid-nineteenth century, an industrial revolution swept through parts of the United States, and improved mechanization triggered a second round in the late 1800s and early 1900s. Three technological developments

Technology and the Triumph of Industrialism

LINKS TO THE WORLD
The Atlantic Cable

Mechanization and the Changing Status of Labor

Labor Violence and the Union Movement

Standards of Living

The Corporate Consolidation Movement

The Gospel of Wealth and Its Critics

LEGACY FOR A PEOPLE AND A NATION
Industrialization, Smoke, and Pollution Control

Online Study Center
This icon will direct you to interactive map and primary source activities on the website http://college.hmco.com/ pic/nortonbrief7e

CHRONOLOGY

1869 • Knights of Labor founded

1873–78 • Economic decline

1876 • Bonsack invents machine for rolling cigarettes

1877 • Widespread railroad strikes protest wage cuts

1878 • Edison Electric Light Company founded

1879 • George's *Progress and Poverty* argues against economic inequality

1881 • First federal trademark law begins spread of brand names

1882 • Standard Oil Trust formed

1884–85 • Economic decline

1886 • Haymarket riot in Chicago protests police brutality against labor demonstrators
• American Federation of Labor (AFL) founded

1890 • Sherman Anti-Trust Act outlaws "combinations in restraint of trade"

1892 • Homestead (Pennsylvania) steelworkers strike against Carnegie Steel Company

1893–97 • Economic depression causes high unemployment and business failures

1894 • Workers at Pullman Palace Car Company strike

1895 • *U.S. v. E. C. Knight Co.* limits Congress's power to regulate manufacturing

1896 • *Holden v. Hardy* upholds law regulating miners' work hours

1898 • Taylor promotes scientific management as efficiency measure in industry

1901–03 • U.S. Steel Corporation founded
• E. I. du Pont de Nemours and Company reorganized
• Ford Motor Company founded

1903 • Women's Trade Union League founded

1905 • *Lochner v. New York* overturns law limiting bakery workers' work hours and limits labor protection laws
• Industrial Workers of the World (IWW) founded

1908 • *Muller v. Oregon* upholds law limiting women to ten-hour workday
• First Ford Model T built

1911 • Triangle Shirtwaist Company fire in New York City leaves 146 workers dead

1913 • Ford begins moving assembly line

1919 • Telephone operator unions strike in New England

propelled this latter stage: the harnessing of electricity, the internal combustion engine, and new applications in the use of chemicals. Steam engines' limitations generated demand for a new power source—electricity. The railroads' mechanization spurred progress in automobile manufacture. And the textile industry's experiments with dyes, bleaches, and cleaning agents advanced chemical research.

In 1860 only one-fourth of the American labor force worked in manufacturing and transportation; by 1900, over half did so. As the twentieth century dawned, the United States was the world's largest producer of raw materials and food and the most productive industrial nation (see Map 18.1). From 1880 to 1920, labor-saving machines boosted productivity. Innovations in business organization and marketing also fueled the drive for profits.

Between 1877 and 1920, a new consumer society took shape as goods that had once been accessible to a few became available to many. Products such as canned foods and machine-made clothing became common. Industrialism furthered the extraction of natural resources and the expansion of agriculture. These processes brought together people, the environment, and technology in ways that were both constructive and destructive.   ■

Technology and the Triumph of Industrialism

*I*n 1876 Thomas A. Edison and his associates set up a laboratory in a wooden shed in Menlo Park, New Jersey. There they intended to turn out "a minor invention every ten days and a big thing every six months or so." Edison envisioned his lab as an invention factory, where creative people pooled ideas to fashion marketable products, under a systematic work ethic. But, Edison believed, if Americans wanted new products, they had to organize and work purposefully toward progress.

To many, the machine symbolized opportunity. The patent system, created by the Constitution to "promote the Progress of science and useful Arts," reveals American mechanical inventiveness. Between 1790 and 1860, the U.S. Patent Office granted a total of 36,000 patents. Between 1860 and 1930, it registered 1.5 million. Inventions in fields such as electricity, internal combustion, and industrial chemistry often sprang from the marriage of technology and business organization.

Most of Edison's more than one thousand inventions used electricity to transmit light, sound, and images. Perhaps his biggest "big thing" began in 1878 when the Edison Electric Light Company embarked on a search for a cheap, efficient means of indoor lighting. After tedious experiments, Edison perfected an incandescent bulb. He also devised a system of power generation and distribution to provide electricity conveniently to a large number of customers.

BIRTH OF THE ELECTRICAL INDUSTRY

Edison's system of direct current could transmit electric power only a mile or two, losing voltage the farther it was transmitted. Inventor George Westing-house solved the problem. He purchased European patent rights to generators that used alternating current and transformers that reduced high-voltage power to lower voltage levels, thus making long-distance transmission more efficient.

Other entrepreneurs used new business practices to market Edison's and Westinghouse's technological breakthroughs. Samuel Insull, Edison's private secretary, organized Edison power plants nationwide, amassing an electric utility empire. In the late 1880s and early 1890s financiers Henry Villard and J. P. Morgan bought up patents in electric lighting and merged small equipment-manufacturing companies into the General Electric Company. Westinghouse Electric and General Electric established research laboratories to create electrical products for everyday use.

Independent inventors continued to develop and attempt to sell their handiwork and patents—sometimes successfully, other times not—to manufacturers. Granville T. Woods, an engineer sometimes called the "black Edison," patented thirty-five devices vital to electronics and communications. Most were sold to companies such as General Electric, including an automatic circuit breaker, an electromagnetic brake, and instruments to aid communications between railroad trains.

European engineers made early innovations in the technology of the internal-combustion engine, which powers a piston by a series of explosions within a confined space. Major progress occurred in Germany in 1885, when Gottlieb Daimler built a high-speed internal-combustion engine driven by vaporized gasoline.

HENRY FORD AND THE AUTOMOBILE INDUSTRY

In the 1890s Henry Ford, an electrical engineer in Detroit's Edison Company and one of America's most visionary manufacturers, experimented with powering a vehicle using Daimler's gasoline-burning engine. Applying organizational genius to this invention, Ford spawned a massive industry.

Ford had a scheme as well as a product, declaring in 1909, "I am going to democratize the automobile. When I'm through, everybody will be able to afford one." Ford planned to mass-produce thousands of identical cars. Ford engineers set up assembly lines that drastically reduced the time and cost of production. Instead of performing numerous tasks, each worker handled only one, performed repeatedly.

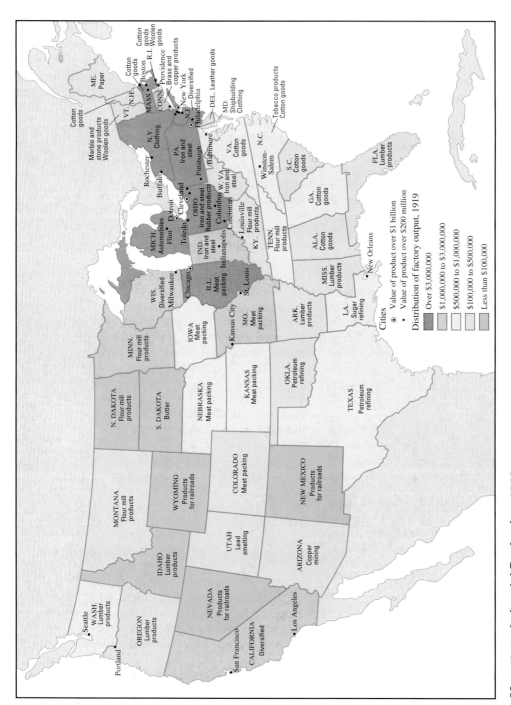

Map 18.1 Industrial Production, 1919

By the early twentieth century, each state could boast of at least one kind of industrial production. Although the value of goods produced was still highest in the Northeast, states like Minnesota and California had impressive dollar values of outputs. (Source: Data from U.S. Bureau of the Census, *Fourteenth Census of the United States, 1920*, Vol. IX, *Manufacturing* [Washington, D.C.: U.S. Government Printing Office, 1921].)

The Atlantic Cable

During the late nineteenth century, as American manufacturers expanded their markets overseas, their ability to communicate with customers and investors improved as a result of telegraph cable beneath the Atlantic Ocean. The telegraph was an American invention, and Cyrus Field, who came up with the idea of laying cable across the Atlantic, was an American. Yet most of the engineers and capitalists involved were British. In 1851 a British company laid the world's first successful undersea telegraph cable from Dover, England, to Calais, France, proving that an insulated wire could carry signals underwater. This inspired British and American businessmen to attempt a larger project across the Atlantic.

The first efforts failed, but in 1866 a British ship, funded by British investors, successfully laid a telegraph wire that operated without interruption. Thereafter, England and the United States grew more closely linked in their diplomatic relations, and citizens of both nations developed greater concern for each other. When American president James Garfield was assassinated in 1881, the news traveled almost instantly to Great Britain, and Britons mourned the death profusely.

Financially savvy individuals experienced welcome benefits as a result of the cable's link. Rapid availability of stock quotes caused the businesses of the New York and London stock exchanges to boom. Newspaper readers enjoyed learning about events on the other side of the ocean the next day instead of a week later. By 1902 underwater cables circled the globe. The age of global telecommunications had begun.

Laid by British ships across the ocean in 1866, the Atlantic cable linked the United States with England and continental Europe so that telegraph communications could be sent and received much more swiftly than ever before. Now Europeans and Americans could exchange news about politics, business, and military movements almost instantly, whereas previously such information could take a week or more to travel from one country to another. (Library of Congress)

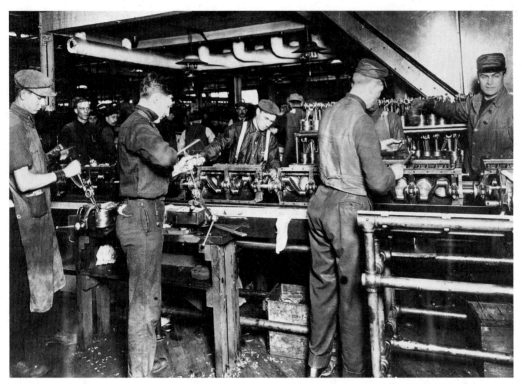

■ The assembly line broke the production process down into simple tasks that individual workers could efficiently repeat hour after hour. Here, assembly-line workers at the Ford plant in Highland Park, Michigan, outside Detroit, are installing pistons in engines of the Model T around 1914.   (From the Collections of The Henry Ford Museum and Greenfield Village)

The Ford Motor Company began operation in 1903. In 1908 Ford rolled out the Model T and sold 10,000. In 1913 the company's first full assembly line began producing automobiles outside Detroit, and the next year, 248,000 Fords were sold. Rising automobile production created more jobs, higher earnings, and greater profits in related industries such as oil, paint, rubber, and glass, which necessitated increased resources from the West and abroad. The internal-combustion engine led to the manufacture of trucks, buses, and, ultimately, airplanes. These industries, as well as many others, would not have been possible without precision machine tools creating standardized parts.

By 1914 many Ford cars cost $490, about one-fourth of their price a decade earlier, but that was still too expensive for many workers, who earned at best $2 a day. That year, Ford tried to spur productivity, reduce labor turnover, head off unionization, and better enable his workers to buy cars through his Five-Dollar-Day plan—a combination of wages and profit sharing.

The du Pont family similarly transformed the chemical industry. In 1902, fearing antitrust prosecution

The du Ponts and the Chemical Industry

for the company's near-monopoly of the explosives industry, three cousins, Alfred, Coleman, and Pierre, took over E. I. du Pont de Nemours and Company and broadened into fertilizers, dyes, and other chemical products. In 1911 du Pont scientists and engineers in the nation's first research laboratory adapted cellulose to the production of new materials such as photographic film, rubber, lacquer, textile fibers, and plastics; the innovation wrought a significant transformation in consumer products. Du Pont research into dyestuffs aided the pharmaceutical industry, and the company pioneered methods of management, accounting, and reinvestment of earnings, contributing to efficient production, better recordkeeping, and higher profits.

The South's two major staple crops, tobacco and cotton, propelled it into the machine age. Before

TECHNOLOGY AND SOUTHERN INDUSTRY

the 1870s, Americans used tobacco mainly for snuff, cigars, and chewing. But in 1876 James Bonsack, an eighteen-year-old Virginian, invented a cigarette-rolling machine. Sales soared when James B. Duke of North

Carolina began marketing cigarettes with free samples, trading cards, and billboards. By 1900 his American Tobacco Company was a nationwide business, employing Jewish immigrant cigar makers who trained laborers to mass-produce cigarettes. Cigarette factories in southern cities employed black and white workers (including women), though in segregated work rooms.

New technology helped relocate the textile industry to the South. Factories with electric looms were more efficient than New England's water-powered mills, and local investors built them in small towns along the Carolina Piedmont and wherever else cheap labor was available. Women and children earned 50 cents for twelve or more hours a day—about half the wages of northern workers. New textile machinery needed fewer workers with fewer skills, and electric lighting expanded the hours of production.

By 1900 the South had more than four hundred textile mills, with 4 million total spindles. Many companies built villages around their mills, where they controlled housing, stores, schools, and churches. Owners also banned criticism of the company and squelched union organization.

Northern and European capitalists financed other southern industries. Between 1890 and 1900, northern lumber syndicates moved into pine forests of the Gulf states, boosting production 500 percent. During the 1880s, northern investors developed southern iron and steel manufacturing, much of it in Birmingham, Alabama. With few exceptions, the South lacked technological innovations that had enabled northern industries to compete with other industrializing nations. Nevertheless, southern boosters heralded the emergence of a New South. In reality, that New South would not emerge until after the First World War.

Machines broadly altered American life. Telephones and typewriters made face-to-face communi-

CONSEQUENCES OF TECHNOLOGY

cation less important and facilitated correspondence and recordkeeping in the growing insurance, banking, and advertising firms. Electric sewing machines mass-produced clothing.

Refrigeration enabled the preservation and shipment of meat, fruit, vegetables, and dairy products. Cash registers and adding machines revamped accounting and created new clerical jobs. At the same time, American universities established programs in engineering.

Profits resulted from higher production at lower costs. As technological innovations made large-scale production more economical, owners replaced small factories with larger ones. Between 1850 and 1900, the average capital investment in a manufacturing firm increased from $700,000 to $1.9 million. Only large companies could afford complex machines. And large companies received discounts for buying raw materials and shipping in bulk—advantages that economists call "economies of scale."

Profitability also depended on how production was organized. Where once workers controlled how a product was made, by the 1890s engineers and managers with specialized knowledge planned every task to increase output. By standardizing production, they diminished workers' skills, boosting profits at the expense of worker independence.

The most influential advocate of efficient production was Frederick W. Taylor. As foreman and

FREDERICK W. TAYLOR AND EFFICIENCY

engineer for the Midvale Steel Company in the 1880s, Taylor concluded that companies could best reduce costs and increase profits by applying scientific studies of "how quickly the various kinds of work . . . ought

to be done." This meant producing more for lower cost per unit, usually by eliminating unnecessary workers.

In 1898 Taylor took his stopwatch to the Bethlehem Steel Company in Pennsylvania to illustrate his principles of scientific management. His experiments involved studying workers and devising "a series of motions which can be made quickest and best." For shoveling ore, Taylor designed fifteen kinds of shovels and prescribed the proper motions for each. He reduced a crew of 600 men to 140. Soon other companies began applying Taylor's theories.

As a result, time, as much as quality, became the measure of acceptable work, and science rather than experience determined the ways of doing things. As elements of the assembly line, employees feared that they were becoming another interchangeable part.

Mechanization and the Changing Status of Labor

y 1900, the status of labor had shifted dramatically. Technological innovation and assembly-line production created new jobs, but because most machines were labor saving, fewer workers could produce more in less time. Instead of producers, the working class now consisted mainly of employees who worked for hire. Producers had been paid based on the quality of what they produced; now, employees received wages for time spent on the job.

As mass production subdivided manufacturing into smaller, specialized tasks, workers became like

MASS PRODUCTION

machines. They no longer decided when to begin and end the workday, and what tools and techniques to use. Production experts regulated them. As a Massachusetts factory operative testified in 1879, "During working hours the men are not allowed to speak to each other . . . on pain of instant discharge. Men are hired to watch and patrol the shop."

Workers struggled to retain independence. Artisans such as cigar makers, glass workers, and coopers (barrel makers), caught in the transition from hand labor to machine production, fought to preserve their work customs, such as appointing a fellow worker to read a newspaper aloud while they worked. Immigrants in factories tried to persuade foremen to hire their relatives and friends, thus preserving on-the-job family and village ties.

Employers, concerned with efficiency and productivity, supported temperance and moral-reform societies to combat immoderate drinking and debauchery. Ford Motor Company required workers to satisfy its behavior code before becoming eligible for the profit-sharing segment of the Five-Dollar-Day plan. To in-

crease worker incentives, some employers established piecework rates, paying per item produced rather than an hourly wage. Efforts to increase productivity were intended to make workers as docile as the machines they operated.

As machines reduced the need for skilled workers, employers cut labor costs by hiring women

RESTRUCTURING OF THE WORK FORCE

and children for low-skill, low-wage jobs. Between 1880 and 1900, employed women soared from 2.6 million to 8.6 million. The proportion of women in domestic service (maids, cooks, laundresses)—the most common and lowest-paid form of female employment—dropped as jobs opened in other sectors (see Figure 18.1). In manufacturing, women usually held menial positions in textile mills and food-processing plants that paid them as little as $1.56 for seventy hours of labor. (Unskilled men received $7.00 to $10.00 for a similar workweek.) Although the number of female factory hands tripled between 1880 and 1900, the proportion of women workers remained about the same.

General expansion of the clerical and retail sectors caused the numbers and percentages of women who were typists, bookkeepers, and sales clerks to skyrocket. New inventions such as the typewriter, cash register, and adding machine simplified tasks that were formerly done by men. By 1920 women filled nearly half of all clerical jobs; in 1880 only 4 percent in these jobs had been women. Although they were paid low wages, women were attracted to sales jobs because of the respectability, pleasant surroundings, and contact with affluent customers that such positions offered. Nevertheless, sex discrimination pervaded the clerical sector. In department stores, only men were cashiers; women were seldom given responsibility for billing or counting money. Women held some low-level supervisory positions, but males dominated the managerial ranks.

Meanwhile, the number of children in nonagricultural occupations tripled between 1870 and 1900. In 1890 over 18 percent of all children between ages ten and fifteen were gainfully employed, with large numbers in textile and shoe factories. Mechanization created numerous light tasks, such as running errands and helping machine operators, that children could handle cheaply. Conditions were especially hard for child laborers in the South, where mill owners induced struggling white sharecroppers and tenant farmers to contract their children to factories at miserably low wages.

Several states, especially in the Northeast, passed laws specifying minimum ages and maximum hours for child labor. But statutes regulated only firms operating within state borders, making it easy for large companies to circumvent them. Enforcing age requirements proved difficult because many parents, needing the income, lied about their children's ages. After 1900, state laws and automation, along with compulsory school attendance laws, began to reduce the number of children employed in manufacturing. After 1910 Progressive era reformers sought federal legislation to control child labor (see Chapter 21).

Repetitive tasks using high-speed machinery dulled concentration, and the slightest mistake could

INDUSTRIAL ACCIDENTS

cause serious injury. Industrial accidents rose steadily before 1920, killing or maiming hundreds of thousands of people annually. In 1913, after factory owners had installed safety devices, 25,000 people died in industrial mishaps, and 1 million were injured. There was

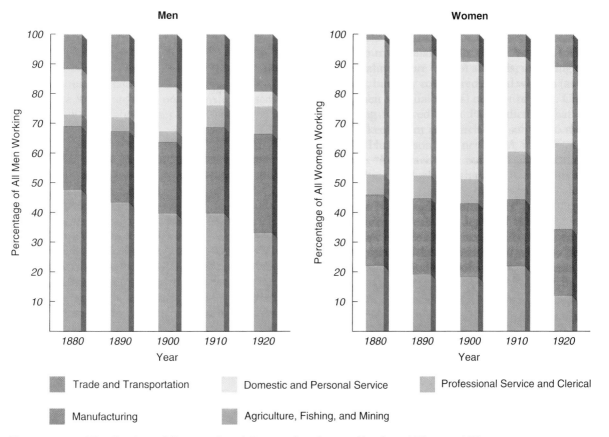

Figure 18.1 Distribution of Occupational Categories Among Employed Men and Women, 1880–1920

The changing lengths of the bar segments of each part of this graph represent trends in male and female employment. Over the forty years covered by this graph, the agriculture, fishing, and mining segment for men and the domestic service segment for women declined the most, while notable increases occurred in manufacturing for men and services (especially store clerks and teachers) for women. (Source: U.S. Bureau of the Census, *Census of the United States, 1880, 1890, 1900, 1910, 1920* [Washington, D.C.: U.S. Government Printing Office].)

no disability insurance to replace lost income, and families suffered acutely.

The most notorious tragedy was a fire at New York City's Triangle Shirtwaist Company in 1911, which killed 146 workers, most of them teenage Jewish immigrant women trapped in locked workrooms. Despite public clamor for safety regulations, free-market views hampered passage of legislation, and employers denied responsibility for their employees' well-being.

Low wages compounded the suffering. Many employers believed that wage rates should be set by sup-

"IRON LAW OF WAGES"

ply and demand. In theory, because employers competed for labor, workers would receive the highest wages an employer could afford. In reality, employers could pay as little as workers were willing to accept.

Courts regularly denied labor the right to organize and bargain collectively on grounds that wages should be individually negotiated between employee and employer. Wage earners felt trapped. A factory worker told Congress in 1879, "The market is glutted . . . and the pay is cut down; our tasks are increased, and if we remonstrate, we are told our places can be filled."

Despite reform laws regulating working conditions, the Supreme Court limited such legislation

COURT RULINGS ON LABOR REFORM

by narrowly defining which jobs were dangerous and which workers needed protection. In *Holden v. Hardy* (1896), the Court upheld regulating working hours of miners because overly long hours increased potential injuries. In *Lochner v. New York* (1905), however, the Court voided a law limiting bakery workers to a sixty-hour week and ten-hour day. It ruled that baking was not a dangerous enough occupation to justify restricting workers' right to sell their labor freely. Such restriction, according to the Court, violated the Fourteenth Amendment's guarantee that no state could "deprive any person of life, liberty, or property without due process of law."

In *Muller v. Oregon* (1908), the Court used a different rationale to uphold limiting women to a ten-hour workday in laundries. It set aside its *Lochner* argument to assert that a woman's well-being "becomes an object of public interest and care in order to preserve the strength and vigor of the race." The case represented a victory for labor reformers, who had sought government regulation of hours and working conditions. But based on *Muller*, later laws barred women from occupations such as printing and transportation that required heavy lifting, long hours, or night work, thus further confining women to low-paying, dead-end jobs.

Labor Violence and the Union Movement

*a*nxiety over the loss of independence via mechanization and a desire for better wages, hours, and working conditions pushed more workers into unions. Because trade unions dating back to the early 1800s restricted membership to skilled workers in particular crafts, their influence was limited. The National Labor Union, founded in 1866, claimed 640,000 members from a variety of industries but collapsed during the hard times of the 1870s.

In the economic slump following the Panic of 1873, which lasted until 1878, railroad managers cut

RAILROAD STRIKES OF 1877

wages, increased workloads, and laid off workers, especially union members. Workers responded with strikes and riots. The year 1877 marked a crisis for labor. In July unionized railroad workers organized a series of strikes to protest wage cuts. Violence spread from Pennsylvania and West Virginia to the Midwest, Texas, and California. State militia companies, organized and commanded by employers, broke up picket lines and fired into threatening crowds. Factory workers, wives, and merchants aided the strikers, and railroads enlisted strikebreakers to replace union men.

Pittsburgh saw the worst violence: on July 21 state troops bayoneted and fired on rock-throwing demonstrators, killing ten and wounding others. The infuriated mob drove troops into a roundhouse and set fires that destroyed 39 buildings, 104 engines, and 1,245 freight and passenger cars. The next day, the troops shot their way out and killed twenty more citizens before fleeing. After a month, President Rutherford B. Hayes sent in federal soldiers—the first significant use of the army in U.S. history to quell labor unrest.

The only broad-based labor organization to survive that depression was the Knights of Labor.

KNIGHTS OF LABOR

Founded in 1869 by Philadelphia garment cutters, the Knights began recruiting other workers in the 1870s. In 1879 Terence V. Powderly, a machinist and the mayor of Scranton, Pennsylvania, was elected grand master. Under his guidance, Knights membership grew, peaking at 730,000 in 1886. Knights welcomed unskilled and semiskilled workers, including women, immigrants, and African Americans.

The Knights sought a workers' alliance that offered an alternative to profit-oriented industrial capitalism. They believed they could eliminate labor and management conflict by establishing a cooperative society in which laborers owned the industries in which they worked. The goal, argued Powderly, was to "eventually make every man his own master—every man his own employer." The cooperative idea, attractive in the abstract, was unattainable because employers could outcompete laborers who might try to establish their own businesses. Strikes might achieve immediate goals, but Powderly and other leaders argued that strikes diverted attention from the long-term goal of a cooperative society and that workers lost more by striking than they won.

Some Knights, however, did support militant action. In 1886 railroad magnate Jay Gould refused to negotiate when Knights demanded higher wages and union recognition from Southwest Railroad. A strike began in Texas and spread to Kansas, Missouri, and Arkansas. As violence increased, Powderly met with Gould and called off the strike, hoping to reach a settlement. But Gould again rejected concessions, and the Knights gave in. Upset by Powderly's compromise, militant craft unions deserted the Knights. Membership dwindled, although the union made a brief attempt to unite with Populists in the 1890s (see Chapter 20). Craft unions replaced the Knights' broad-based but often vague appeal, and dreams of labor unity faded.

Meanwhile, several groups calling for an eight-hour workday generated the largest spontaneous labor demonstration in the country's history.

HAYMARKET RIOT

On May 1, 1886, in Chicago, over 100,000 workers turned out, including radical anarchists. In Europe, labor radicals had made May 1 a day of demonstration, and Chicago police, fearing that European radicals were transplanting their tradition of violence to the United States, mobilized against them. The day passed calmly, but two days later, police stormed an area near the McCormick reaper factory and broke up a battle between striking unionists and nonunion strikebreakers, killing two unionists and wounding several others.

The next evening, labor groups protested police brutality at Haymarket Square, near downtown Chicago. As police approached, a bomb exploded, killing seven and injuring sixty-seven. Authorities made mass arrests, and a court convicted eight anarchists of the bombing, despite questionable evidence. Four were executed, and one committed suicide in prison. The remaining three were pardoned in 1893 by Illinois governor John P. Altgeld.

Online Study Center
Improve Your Grade
Primary Source: Haymarket Trials

The Haymarket bombing, like the 1877 railroad strikes, drew attention to labor's growing discontent and heightened fear of radicalism. The participation of anarchists and socialists, many of them foreign born, heightened urgency that law and order act swiftly to prevent social turmoil. Private Chicago donors helped establish a military base at Fort Sheridan and the Great Lakes Naval Training Station. Elsewhere, governments strengthened police forces. Employer associations countered labor militancy by drawing up blacklists of union activists whom they would not employ and by hiring private detectives to suppress strikes.

The American Federation of Labor (AFL), founded in 1886, emerged from the upheavals as the

AMERICAN FEDERATION OF LABOR

major workers' organization. An alliance of national craft unions, the AFL had about 140,000 members, most of them skilled workers. Led by Samuel Gompers, a pragmatic immigrant who headed the Cigar Makers' Union, the AFL pressed for higher wages, shorter hours, and the right to bargain collectively. In contrast to the Knights, the AFL accepted the industrial system and worked to improve conditions within it. It avoided party politics, adhering to Gompers's dictum to support labor's friends and oppose its enemies, regardless of party.

AFL membership grew to 1 million by 1901 and 2.5 million by 1917, when it represented 111 national unions and 27,000 local unions. Member unions tried to protect skilled workers by organizing by craft rather than by workplace and had little interest in recruiting unskilled workers or women. Of 6.3 million employed women in 1910, fewer than 2 percent belonged to unions. Male unionists rationalized women's exclusion by insisting that women should not be employed. According to one labor leader, "The mental and physical makeup of woman is in revolt against wage service. She is competing with the man who is her father or husband or is to become her husband." Mostly, unionists worried that because women were paid less than men, their own wages would be lowered or their jobs given to cheaper female laborers.

Organized labor also excluded most immigrant and African American workers, fearing that they would depress wages. Some trade unions welcomed skilled immigrants, but only the more radical unions had explicit policies of accepting immigrants and blacks. Blacks were prominent in the coal miners' union and were partially unionized in trades such as construction, barbering, and dock work, which had large numbers of African American workers. But they could belong only to segregated local unions in the South.

Online Study Center **Improve Your Grade**
Interactive Map: Percent of Foreign-Born Whites and Native Whites of Foreign or Mixed Parentage in Total Populations, by Counties, 1910

The AFL and the labor movement suffered setbacks in the early 1890s, when labor violence stirred public fears. In July 1892, the AFL-affiliated Amalgamated Association of Iron and Steelworkers went on strike against pay cuts in Homestead, Pennsylvania. Henry C. Frick, president of Carnegie Steel Company, then closed the plant. Shortly after, Frick tried to protect the plant by hiring three hundred guards from the Pinkerton Detective Agency and floating them in by barge under cover of darkness. Lying in wait, angry workers attacked and routed the guards. State troops intervened, and after five months, the strikers gave in. By then, public opinion had turned against the union.

HOMESTEAD STRIKE

In 1894 workers at the Pullman Palace (railroad passenger) Car Company walked out over exploitative policies at the company town near Chicago. The

PULLMAN STRIKE

paternalistic George Pullman provided everything for the twelve thousand residents of the so-called model town named after him. His company owned and controlled all land and buildings, the school, the bank, and the water and gas systems. It paid wages, fixed rents, and spied on disgruntled employees.

One thing Pullman would not do was negotiate with workers. When hard times hit in 1893, Pullman protected profits by cutting wages 25 to 40 percent while holding firm on rents and prices. Hard-pressed workers sent a committee to Pullman to protest. He reacted by firing three members of the committee. When enraged workers called a strike, Pullman closed the factory. The railway union, led by Eugene V. Debs, refused to handle Pullman cars attached to any trains. The railroad owners' association then enlisted aid from U.S. Attorney General Richard Olney, a former railroad attorney, who obtained a court injunction to prevent the union from "obstructing the railways and holding up the mails." President Grover Cleveland ordered federal troops to Chicago. Within a month, strikers gave in, and Debs was jailed for defying the injunction. The Supreme Court upheld Debs's six-month sentence, arguing that the federal government had the power to remove obstacles to interstate commerce.

Colorado miners engaged in several bitter strikes. In 1905 they helped form a new, radical labor organization, the Industrial Workers of the World (IWW). The IWW strove like the Knights to unite all laborers, including the unskilled and African Americans. Its motto was "An injury to one is an injury to all." But the "Wobblies," as IWW members were known, exceeded the Knights by espousing violence and sabotage.

IWW

Embracing the rhetoric of class conflict and socialism, Wobblies believed workers should seize and run the nation's industries. "Mother" Jones, an Illinois coalfield union organizer; Elizabeth Gurley Flynn, a fiery orator known as the "Joan of Arc of the labor movement"; and William D. (Big Bill) Haywood, the brawny, one-eyed founder of the Western Federation of Miners, led a series of strikes. Although the Wobblies' anticapitalist goals and aggressive tactics attracted publicity, union membership never exceeded 150,000. The organization collapsed during the First World War when federal prosecution sent many of its leaders to jail and local police forces violently harassed IWW members.

Although excluded from the general union movement, female workers had formed their own labor associations. Some, such as the 1860s *WOMEN UNIONISTS* Collar Laundry Union of Troy, New York, had successfully struck for higher wages. The "Uprising of the 20,000" in New York City, a 1909 strike by male and female immigrant members of the International Ladies Garment Workers Union (ILGWU), was one of the country's largest strikes. Female trade-union membership swelled during the 1910s, but men monopolized national trade-union leadership.

Women did dominate one union: the Telephone Operators' Department of the International Brotherhood of Electrical Workers. Organized in Montana and San Francisco early in the twentieth century, the union spread throughout the Bell system, the nation's monopolistic telephone company and single largest employer of women. To promote solidarity among their mostly young members, union leaders organized dances, excursions, and bazaars, as well as educational programs. The union resisted scientific management and increased supervision. In 1919 several militant union branches paralyzed phone service in five New England states, but the union collapsed after a failed strike there in 1923.

The first women's organization promoting interests of laboring women was the Women's Trade Union League (WTUL), founded in 1903 and patterned after a similar organization in England. The WTUL sought workplace protective legislation and reduced hours for female workers, sponsored educational activities, and campaigned for women's suffrage. It helped telephone operators organize, and in 1909 it supported the ILGWU's massive strike against New York City sweatshops. Initially the union's highest offices were held by sympathetic middle-class women, but control shifted in the 1910s to working-class leaders, notably Agnes Nestor, a glove maker, and Rose Schneiderman, a cap maker. The WTUL advocated opening apprenticeship programs to women and training female workers for leadership. It served as a vital link between the labor and women's movements into the 1920s.

Despite the visibility of struggles in the second half of the nineteenth century, only a small fraction of *THE EXPERIENCE OF WAGE WORK* American workers belonged to unions. In 1900 about 1 million out of a total of 27.6 million workers were unionized. By 1920, union membership had grown to 5 million, just 13 percent of the work force. Unionization was strong in construction trades, transportation, communications, and, to a lesser extent, manufacturing. For many workers, getting and holding a job took priority over wages and hours. Job instability and the seasonal nature of work seriously hindered union-organizing efforts. Few companies employed workers year-round; most hired laborers during peak seasons and laid them off during slack periods.

The millions of men, women, and children who were not unionized tried to cope with pressures of the machine age. Many native-born and immigrant workers turned to fraternal societies such as the Polish Roman Catholic Union and the Jewish B'nai B'rith. Widespread by the early twentieth century, these organizations provided life insurance, sickness benefits, and funeral expenses for small contributions.

The machine age had mixed benefits. Industrial wages rose between 1877 and 1914, boosting purchasing power and creating a mass market for standardized goods. Yet in 1900, most employees worked sixty hours a week at wages averaging 20 cents an hour for skilled work and 10 cents an hour for unskilled. Even as wages rose, living costs increased even faster.

Standards of Living

The expansion of railroad, postal, and telephone service drew even isolated communities into the consumer-oriented society. American ingenuity combined with mass production and marketing to make available myriad goods that previously had not existed or had been the province of the wealthy. The new material well-being blended Americans of differing status into consumer communities and accentuated differences between those who could afford goods and services and those who could not.

If a society's affluence can be measured by the conversion of luxuries into commonplace articles, the *COMMONPLACE LUXURIES* United States was indeed becoming affluent from 1880 and 1920. By 1899, manufactured goods and perishable foodstuffs had become increasingly available. That year Americans bought 2 billion machine-produced cigarettes and 151,000 pairs of silk stockings, consumed oranges at the rate of 100 crates for every 1,000 people, and spent an average of 63 cents per person on soap. In 1921 Americans smoked 43 billion cigarettes (403 per person), bought 217 million pairs of silk stockings, ate 248 crates of oranges per 1,000 people, and spent $1.40 on soap.

Data for the period also show that incomes rose broadly, spawning massive fortunes and creating a new industrial elite. By 1920, the richest 5 percent of the population received almost one-fourth of all earned income. Incomes also rose among the growing middle class. Average pay for clerical workers rose 36 percent between 1890 and 1910 (see Table 18.1). At the turn of the century, federal employees averaged $1,072 a year (between $20,000 and $25,000 in modern dollars). The middle class could afford relatively comfortable housing. A six- or seven-room house cost around $3,000 to buy (about $85,000 to $90,000 in current dollars) and from $15 to $20 per month ($450 to $550 in current dollars) to rent.

TABLE 18.1

American Living Standards, 1890–1910

	1890	1910
Income and earnings		
Annual income		
Clerical worker	$848	$1,156
Public school teacher	256	492
Industrial worker	486	630
Farm laborer	233	336
Hourly wage		
Soft-coal miner	0.18[a]	0.21
Iron worker	0.17[a]	0.23
Shoe worker	0.14[a]	0.19
Paper worker	0.12[a]	0.17
Labor statistics		
Number of people in labor force	28.5 million	41.7 million[b]
Average workweek in manufacturing	60 hours	51 hours

a. 1892
b. 1920

Although industrial wages increased, jobs were not always secure, and workers had to expend a disproportionate sum on necessities. Annual wages of factory workers rose about 30 percent, from $486 in 1890 (about $12,000 to $14,000 in modern dollars) to $630 in 1910 (about $15,000 to $17,000 in current dollars). In industries with large female work forces, hourly rates remained lower than in male-dominated industries. Nevertheless, as Table 18.1 shows, most wages moved upward.

Wage increases mean little, however, if living costs rise as fast or faster. The weekly cost of living for a typical family of four rose over 47 percent between 1889 and 1913. Goods that cost $6.78 in 1889 increased, after a slight dip in the mid-1890s, to $10.00 by 1913. In few working-class occupations did income rise as fast as cost of living.

COST OF LIVING

How could working-class Americans afford goods and services? Many could not. The daughter of a textile worker, recalling her school days, described how "some of the kids would bring bars of chocolate, others an orange. . . . I suppose they were richer than a family like ours. My father used to buy a bag of candy and a bag of peanuts every payday. . . . And that's all we'd have until the next payday."

Still, a family could raise its income and partake modestly in consumer society by sending children and women to work outside the home. Where a father might earn $600 a year, wages of other family members might lift total family income to $800 or $900. Many also rented rooms to boarders, yielding up to $200 a year and providing housewives with vital economic roles. Workers were thus able to improve their living standards, but not without sacrifices.

SUPPLEMENTS TO FAMILY INCOME

More than ever before, American workers existed within a wage economy. Between 1890 and 1920, the labor force increased by 50 percent, from 28 million workers to 42 million. These figures represent a change in the nature of work as much as an increase in the number of available jobs. Most Americans, male and female, had always worked. In the rural society of the nineteenth century, women and children performed the crucial jobs of cooking, cleaning, planting, and harvesting—labor typically absent from employment figures. As the nation industrialized and the agricultural sector declined, wage labor became more common. The proportion of Americans who worked probably did not increase markedly. What was new was the increase in paid employment, making purchases of consumer goods and services more affordable.

Medical advances, better diets, and improved housing sharply reduced death rates and extended life.

HIGHER LIFE EXPECTANCY
Between 1900 and 1920, life expectancy rose by six years, and the death rate dropped 24 percent. Notable declines occurred in deaths from typhoid, diphtheria, influenza (except for a harsh pandemic in 1918 and 1919), tuberculosis, and intestinal ailments. There were, however, significantly more deaths from cancer, diabetes, and heart disease, afflictions of an aging population and of new environmental factors such as smoke and chemical pollution. Homicides and automobile-related deaths, too, increased dramatically.

Not only were luxuries more available, but upward mobility seemed more accessible as well. Public education, aided by new school construction and laws requiring children to stay in school to age fourteen, equipped young people to achieve a higher living standard than their parents'. The creation of managerial and sales jobs in service industries helped counter downward mobility when mechanization pushed skilled workers out of their crafts. And mass-produced goods made life more convenient for all workers.

The toilet stood at the vanguard of a revolution in American lifestyles. The chain-pull washdown

FLUSH TOILETS
water closet, invented in England around 1870, reached the United States in the 1880s. Shortly after 1900, the flush toilet appeared. Before 1880, only luxury hotels and estates had private indoor bathrooms. By the 1890s, the germ theory of disease had raised fears about carelessly disposed human waste as a source of infection and water contamination. Americans began including water closets in middle-class urban houses. By the 1920s, they were prevalent in working-class homes too. Edward and Clarence Scott, who produced white tissue in perforated rolls, provided Americans a more convenient form of toilet paper than the rough paper they had previously used. Bodily functions took on an un-pleasant image, and the home bathroom became a place of utmost privacy.

Before the mid-nineteenth century, Americans typically ate only foods that were in season. Drying, smoking, and salting could preserve meat

PROCESSED AND PRESERVED FOODS
for a short time, but the availability of fresh meat and fresh milk was limited. A French inventor developed the cooking-and-sealing process of canning around 1810, and in the 1850s, an American man named Gail Borden devised a means of condensing and preserving milk. Availability of canned goods and condensed milk increased during the 1860s. By the 1880s, inventors had fashioned machines to peel fruits and vegetables, process salmon, and mass-produce cans from tin plate. Now, people everywhere could readily consume tomatoes, milk, oysters, and other alternatives to previously monotonous diets.

Other inventions broadened Americans' diets. Growing urban populations sparked demand for more produce. Railroad refrigerator cars enabled growers and meatpackers to ship perishables greater distances and preserve them for longer periods. By the 1890s, northern city dwellers could enjoy southern and western strawberries, grapes, and tomatoes for several months. Home iceboxes enabled middle-class families to store perishables.

The availability of new foods also inspired health reformers to correct the American diet. In the 1870s

DIETARY REFORM
John H. Kellogg, a nutritionist and manager of the Western Health Reform Institute in Battle Creek, Michigan, began serving patients new health foods, including peanut butter and wheat flakes. Several years later, his brother, William K. Kellogg, invented corn flakes, and Charles W. Post introduced Grape-Nuts, replacing eggs, potatoes, and meat with ready-to-eat cereal. Growing numbers of published cookbooks and cooking schools reflected heightened interest in food and its possibilities for health and enjoyment.

As in the past, the poorest people still consumed cheap foods, heavy in starches and carbohydrates, and could seldom afford meat. Now, though, many could purchase previously unavailable fruits, vegetables, and dairy products. Workers spent almost half of a breadwinner's wages on food, but they never suffered the malnutrition that plagued other developing nations.

Before 1850, nearly all Americans wore clothes made at home or by seamstresses and tailors, depending on social status. Then in the

READY-MADE CLOTHING

1850s, the sewing machine, invented in Europe but refined by Americans Elias Howe Jr. and Isaac M. Singer, came into use in clothing and shoe manufacture. By 1890 annual retail sales of machine-made garments reached $1.5 billion. Mass production enabled manufacturers to turn out quality apparel at relatively low cost and to standardize sizes. By 1900, only the poorest families could not afford "ready-to-wear" clothes. Tailors and seamstresses were relegated to repair work. Many women continued to make clothing at home, but commercial dress patterns injected another form of standardization into everyday life.

As women became more active outside the home, dress designers began emphasizing comfort. In the 1890s, sleeves and skirt hemlines receded, and high-boned collars disappeared. Women began wearing tailored blouses called shirtwaists. Designers used less fabric; by the 1920s a dress required three yards of material instead of ten.

Men's clothes too became lightweight. Before 1900, men in the middle class and well-off working classes would have owned two suits—one for Sundays and special occasions and one for everyday. After 1900, manufacturers began to produce garments from fabrics of different weights for different seasons. Men replaced derbies with felt hats and stiff collars with soft ones; somber, dark-blue serge gave way to lighter shades and more intricate weaves.

Department and chain stores helped to create and serve this new consumerism. Between 1865 and

DEPARTMENT AND CHAIN STORES

1900, Macy's in New York, Wanamaker's in Philadelphia, Marshall Field in Chicago, and Rich's in Atlanta became urban landmarks. Previously, working classes had bought goods in stores with limited inventories, and wealthier people patronized fancy shops; price, quality of goods, and social custom discouraged each from the other's establishments. Now, department stores, with their open displays, offered not only a wide variety but also home deliveries, exchange policies, and charge accounts.

Meanwhile, the Great Atlantic Tea Company, founded in 1859, became the first grocery chain. Renamed the Great Atlantic and Pacific Tea Company in 1869 (and known as A&P), the stores bought in volume and sold to the public at low prices. By 1915, there were eighteen hundred A&P stores, and twelve thousand more over the next ten years.

In 1881 Congress passed a trademark law enabling producers to register and protect brand names. Thou-

ADVERTISING

sands of companies registered products as varied as Hires Root Beer and Carter's Little Liver Pills. Advertising agencies—a service industry pioneered by N. W. Ayer & Son of Philadelphia—in turn offered expert advice to companies seeking to cultivate brand loyalty. In 1865 retailers spent about $9.5 million on advertising; that sum reached $95 million

■ Advertising, which developed into a powerful medium in the late nineteenth century, used explicit and implicit domestic images to reinforce a wife's role as homemaker. This ad implies that a devoted wife lovingly assumes tasks such as sewing and mending clothing, guided into her role by a strong and superior husband. (Library of Congress)

by 1900 and nearly $500 million by 1919. Newspapers served as the prime instrument for advertising. More than ever before, people read newspapers to find out what was for sale as well as what was happening.

Outdoor billboards and electrical signs were also important advertising organs. Signs in railroad and subway stations and billboards on city buildings and alongside roads promoted national products such as Gillette razors, Kodak cameras, and Wrigley chewing gum. In the mid-1890s, electricity made lighted billboards more dynamic and appealing. The flashing electric signs on New York City's Broadway gave the street its label "the Great White Way."

The Corporate Consolidation Movement

*N*either new products nor new marketing techniques could mask unsettling factors in the American economy. The huge capital investment in new technology meant that factories had to operate at near capacity to recover costs. But the more manufacturers produced, the more they had to sell, which meant reducing prices. To compensate for price drops, they expanded production and often cut wages. To expand, they borrowed money. And to repay loans, they had to produce and sell even more. This spiraling process strangled small firms and thrust workers into constant uncertainty.

In this environment, optimism could dissolve at the hint that debtors could not meet their obligations. Financial panics afflicted the economy during every decade in the late nineteenth century. Economic declines that began in 1873, 1884, and 1893 lingered for several years. Some business leaders blamed overproduction; others pointed to underconsumption; still others blamed lax credit and investment practices. Either way, businesspeople sought to combat these boom-and-bust business cycles, often through centralized forms of business organization, notably corporations, pools, trusts, and holding companies.

Industrialists never questioned the capitalist system and embraced the incorporation laws adopted by states in the early 1800s to spur commerce and industry. Under such laws, anyone could start a company

RISE OF CORPORATIONS

and raise money by selling stock to investors. Stockholders shared in profits without personal risk because laws limited their liability for company debts to the amount of their investment. And responsibility for a firm's day-to-day operation rested with its managers.

By 1900 two-thirds of all goods manufactured in the United States were produced by corporations such as General Electric and the American Tobacco Company. In the 1880s and 1890s, the Supreme Court ruled that corporations, like individuals, are protected by the Fourteenth Amendment. That is, states could not deny corporations equal protection under the law and could not deprive them of rights or property without due process of law. Such rulings insulated corporations against government interference.

As downward business cycles threatened profits, corporations sought greater economic concentration. Between the late 1880s and early 1900s, business consolidation produced massive conglomerates that have since dominated the economy. At first, such alliances were informal, consisting of cooperative agreements, called pools, among firms manufacturing the same product or offering the same service. Competing companies tried to control the market by agreeing how much each should produce and sharing profits. Used by railroads, steel producers, and whiskey distillers, pools depended on members' honesty. But during slow periods, pool members secretly reduced prices or sold more than the agreed quota. The strategy was already fading by the time the Interstate Commerce Act of 1887 outlawed pools among railroads (discussed in Chapter 20).

POOLS

John D. Rockefeller, boss of Standard Oil, called pools undependable. In 1879 his lawyer, Samuel Dodd, devised another means of market domination. Because state laws prohibited one corporation from holding stock in another corporation, Dodd adapted an old device called a trust, a legal arrangement whereby a responsible individual would manage the financial affairs of a person unable to handle them alone. Dodd reasoned that one company could control an industry by luring stockholders of smaller companies to cede their stock "in trust" to the larger company's board of trustees. This allowed Rockefeller to achieve horizontal integration—the acquisition of several similar companies—of the profitable petroleum industry in 1882 by combining his

TRUSTS

Standard Oil Company of Ohio with other refineries he bought up.

In 1888 New Jersey adopted laws allowing corporations chartered there to own property in other states and stock in other corporations. This facilitated creation of the holding company, which owned a partial or complete interest in other companies. Holding companies could merge their assets (buildings, equipment, inventory, and cash) as well as their management. Rockefeller's holding company, Standard Oil of New Jersey, merged forty refining companies. By 1898 Standard Oil refined 84 percent of all oil produced in the nation, controlled most pipelines, and engaged in natural-gas production and ownership of oil-producing properties.

HOLDING COMPANIES

To dominate their markets, many holding companies sought control over all aspects of their operations, including raw materials, manufacturing, and distribution. A model of such vertical integration was Gustavus Swift's meat-processing operation. During the 1880s, Swift invested in livestock, slaughterhouses, refrigerator cars, and marketing to ensure profits from the sale of his beef at prices he could control.

Mergers provided order and profits. Between 1889 and 1903, three hundred combinations were formed, most of them trusts and holding companies. The most spectacular was U.S. Steel Corporation, financed by J. P. Morgan in 1901. Made up of iron-ore properties, freight carriers, wire mills, and other firms, it was capitalized at over $1.4 billion. In 1896 fewer than a dozen corporations were worth over $10 million; by 1903 three hundred were worth that much, and seventeen had assets exceeding $100 million. These huge companies ruthlessly put thousands of competitors out of business.

The merger movement created a new species of businessman, whose vocation was financial organizing. Shrewd operators sought opportunities for combination, formed a holding company, and then persuaded producers to sell their firms to the new company. These financiers raised money by selling stock and borrowing from banks. Investment bankers like J. P. Morgan and Jacob Schiff piloted the merger movement, inspiring awe with their financial power.

FINANCIERS

Growth of corporations in the late nineteenth century turned stock and bond exchanges into hubs of activity. In 1886 trading on the New York Stock Exchange passed 1 million shares a day. By 1914, the number of industrial stocks traded reached 511, compared with 145 in 1869. Between 1870 and 1900, foreign investment in American companies rose from $1.5 billion to $3.5 billion. Assets of savings banks, concentrated in the Northeast and West Coast, rose by 700 percent between 1875 and 1897, to a total of $2.2 billion. States loosened regulations to enable banks to invest in railroads and industrial enterprises.

The Gospel of Wealth and Its Critics

Business leaders used corporate consolidation to minimize competition, and justified their tactics through the doctrine of Social Darwinism. Social Darwinism loosely grafted Charles Darwin's theory of the survival of the fittest onto laissez faire, the doctrine that government should not interfere in private economic affairs. Social Darwinists reasoned that in an unconstrained economy, power and wealth would flow naturally to the most capable people. In this view, monopolies represented the natural accumulation of economic power by those best suited for wielding it.

Social Darwinists believed that wealth carried moral responsibilities. Steel baron Andrew Carnegie asserted "the Gospel of Wealth": that as guardians of society's wealth, he and other industrialists had a duty to serve society. Over his lifetime, Carnegie donated more than $350 million to libraries, schools, peace initiatives, and the arts. Such philanthropy, however, also enabled benefactors to define what was necessary for society; it did not translate into paying workers decent wages.

Leaders in the corporate consolidation movement extolled individual initiative but also pressed for government assistance. While denouncing efforts to legislate maximum working hours or factory conditions as interference, they lobbied forcefully and successfully for subsidies, loans, and tax relief to encourage business growth. Grants to railroads (see

GOVERNMENT ASSISTANCE TO BUSINESS

Chapter 17) were one form of such assistance. When Congress imposed high tariffs on foreign goods such as kerosene, steel rails, woolen goods, and tin plate, American producers could raise prices on theirs to just under what comparable foreign goods would sell. Industrialists argued that tariff protection encouraged the development of new products and enterprises. But tariffs also forced consumers to pay artificially high prices.

Critics charged that trusts and other forms of big business stifled opportunity and originated from greed. Such charges by farmers, workers, and intellectuals reflected an ardent fear of monopoly—the domination of an economic activity (such as oil refining) by one powerful company (such as Standard Oil). Those who feared monopoly believed that large corporations fixed prices, exploited workers by cutting wages, destroyed opportunity by crushing small businesses, and threatened democracy by corrupting politicians—all of which was not only unnatural, they said, but immoral.

DISSENTING VOICES

By the mid-1880s, a number of intellectuals began to challenge Social Darwinism and laissez-faire economics. In *Dynamic Sociology* (1883), sociologist Lester Ward argued that a system guaranteeing survival only to the fittest was wasteful and brutal. Instead, Ward reasoned, cooperative activity fostered by government intervention was moral. Economists Richard Ely, John R. Commons, and Edward Bemis agreed that natural forces should be harnessed for the public good.

Others more directly questioned why the United States had so many poor people while a few became fabulously wealthy. Henry George was a San Francisco printer and writer who had fallen into poverty during the depression of the 1870s. He believed that inequality stemmed from the ability of a few to profit from rising land values, which made speculators rich simply because of increased demand for living and working space, especially in cities. To prevent profiteering, George proposed replacing all taxes with a "single tax" on the "unearned increment"—the rise in property values caused by increased demand rather than owners' improvements. Argued forcefully in *Progress and Poverty* (1879), this popular scheme almost won George the mayoralty of New York City in 1886.

Several states took steps to prohibit monopolies and regulate business. By 1900, fifteen states, mostly in the agricultural South and West, had constitutional provisions outlawing trusts, and twenty-seven had laws forbidding pools. But state governments lacked staff and judicial support for an effective attack on big business, and corporations found ways to evade restrictions.

ANTITRUST LEGISLATION

Congress moved hesitantly toward national legislation but in 1890 passed the Sherman Anti-Trust Act. Introduced by Senator John Sherman of Ohio, the law made illegal "every contract, combination in the form of trust or otherwise, or conspiracy in the restraint of trade." Those found guilty faced fines and jail terms, and those wronged by illegal combinations could sue for triple damages. However, the law, watered down by pro-business eastern senators, was left purposely vague. It did not clearly define "restraint of trade" and consigned interpretation of its provisions to the sometimes business-friendly courts.

Judges used the law's vagueness to blur distinctions between reasonable and unreasonable restraints of trade. When in 1895 the federal government prosecuted the so-called Sugar Trust for owning 98 percent of the nation's sugar-refining capacity, eight of nine Supreme Court justices ruled in *U.S. v. E. C. Knight Co.* that control of manufacturing did not necessarily mean control of trade. According to the Court, the Constitution empowered Congress to regulate interstate commerce, but not manufacturing.

Between 1890 and 1900, the federal government prosecuted only eighteen cases under the Sherman Anti-Trust Act. Ironically, the act equipped the government to break up labor unions: courts that did not consider monopolistic production a restraint on trade willingly applied antitrust provisions to boycotts encouraged by striking unions.

Summary   *Online Study Center* ACE the Test

Mechanization and new inventions thrust the United States into the vanguard of industrial nations and immeasurably altered daily life between 1877 and 1920. But aggressive consolidation changed the nature of work from individual activity by skilled producers to mass production by wage earners. Laborers fought to retain control of their work and struggled to develop unions. The outpouring of products created a mass society based on consumerism and dominated by technology and the communications media.

The problems of enforcing the Sherman Anti-Trust Act reflected the uneven distribution of power. Corporations consolidated to control resources, production, and politics. Laborers and reformers had numbers and ideas but lacked influence. In factories and homes, some people celebrated the industrial transformation while others struggled with the dilemma of industrialism: whether a system based on ever-greater profits was the best way to fulfill the nation's democratic destiny.

Industrial expansion proved impossible to stop, because so many powerful and ordinary people were benefiting from it. Moreover, waves of people pouring into the nation's cities increasingly provided both workers and consumers for America's expanding productive capacity.

LEGACY FOR A PEOPLE AND A NATION
Industrialization, Smoke, and Pollution Control

Coal fueled the steel mills and iron foundries of America's industrial era. Skies over cities such as Pittsburgh and St. Louis became clogged with choking pollution from factories, coal-burning railroads, steamboats, and home furnaces. The heaviest smoke came from burning soft, bituminous coal, which is cheaper and more plentiful than cleaner-burning anthracite coal. Prior to the First World War, the United States used four times as much bituminous coal as anthracite coal. New chemical plants began spewing other pollutants into the air as well.

Many Americans assumed that air was a free resource and accepted air pollution as a necessary nuisance. But others began campaigns to curb the worst pollution. By 1900, doctors reported a link between coal smoke and respiratory diseases such as bronchitis and pneumonia. Women's groups and health reformers argued that air contamination undermined efforts to keep cities clean. As early as 1881, Chicago and a few other cities passed anti-smoke legislation and hired smoke inspectors, but courts often declared such laws unconstitutional, and judges were reluctant to enforce regulations that remained on the books.

As the twentieth century advanced, air pollution from coal decreased as technological innovations reduced smoke output. By midcentury, many industries had converted to natural gas and petroleum, but governments refrained from emissions control because industries and citizens were reluctant to pay any added costs. And automobile emissions were creating pollution problems that may have seemed more innocuous but were just as dangerous.

In the late 1960s, air pollution became the defining issue of the new environmental reform movement. The Clean Air Act amendment of 1970 recognized for the first time that pollution was a national problem subject to federal authority. That act and subsequent legislation established air quality standards and prompted states and cities to pass laws. Since then, business interests and environmentalists have scuffled over regulations, often bouncing air pollution between health and cleanliness, on one hand, and economic progress, convenience, and jobs, on the other. Thus, an unwanted legacy of industrial progress—air pollution—remains unresolved.

The Vitality and Turmoil of Urban Life 1877–1920

*R*ahel Gollop grew up in a shtetl, a Jewish village in western Russia. Her father, facing anti-Jewish pogroms (violent persecutions by Russian officials), left his family in 1890 to find a better life. Arrested by Russian soldiers, he escaped to Germany and found passage on a steamship bound for New York City. After two and a half years in the United States, he had saved enough to bring the rest of the family to America.

Rahel's first impression of New York was awe. "I looked with wonder at the tall houses, the paved streets, the street lamps," she recalled. "I thought these things true only of America." But the Gollops' landlady, an immigrant who had arrived years earlier, gave Rahel a dose of reality. Rahel wrote:

> When we praised our new homeland, that landlady smiled a queer smile. "Life here is not all that it appears to the 'green horn' (new immigrant)," she said. ". . . where you used to live. You had your own house, and most of the food came from the garden. Here you will have to pay for everything; the rent!" she sighed, "for every grain of barley."

To help out, Rahel, only twelve years old, worked in a garment sweatshop. She witnessed—and experienced—many of the travails suffered by immigrants, including the beating of eastern European Jews on election night and the harassment of street vendors by drunken nativists. Like other immigrants, Rahel sought security with her own kind, rarely mingling with strangers.

Gradually Rahel broke away. She learned to read English and acquired an education. Rejecting the man whom her parents had selected for her husband, she married a grocer and became a writer. She published her autobiography in 1918 and died in 1925 at the age of forty-five, possibly of suicide.

Though it ended tragically, Rahel Gollop's story illustrates many themes characterizing American urban life in the late nineteenth and early twentieth centuries. Where to live, where to work, how to support the family, the

Growth of the Modern City

Urban Neighborhoods

Living Conditions in the Inner City

Managing the City

Family Life

The New Leisure and Mass Culture

LINKS TO THE WORLD
Japanese Baseball

LEGACY FOR A PEOPLE AND A NATION
Ethnic Food

Online Study Center
This icon will direct you to interactive map and primary source activities on the website
http://college.hmco.com/pic/nortonbrief7e

CHRONOLOGY

1867 • First law regulating tenements passes, in New York State

1870 • One-fourth of Americans live in cities

1876 • National League of Professional Baseball Clubs founded

1880s • "New" immigrants from eastern and southern Europe begin to arrive in large numbers

1883 • Brooklyn Bridge completed
 • Pulitzer buys *New York World* and creates a major vehicle for yellow journalism

1885 • Safety bicycle invented

1886 • First settlement house opens, in New York City

1889 • Edison invents the motion picture and viewing device

1890s • Electric trolleys replace horse-drawn mass transit

1893 • Columbian Exposition opens in Chicago

1895 • Hearst buys the *New York Journal,* another major popular yellow-journalism newspaper

1898 • Race riot erupts in Wilmington, North Carolina

1900–10 • Immigration reaches peak
 • Vaudeville rises in popularity

1903 • Boston beats Pittsburgh in first baseball World Series

1905 • Intercollegiate Athletic Association, forerunner of the National College Athletic Association (NCAA), is formed and restructures the rules of football

1915 • Griffith directs *Birth of a Nation,* one of the first major technically sophisticated movies

1920 • Majority (51.2 percent) of Americans live in cities

cash-based economy, ethnic consciousness and big-otry, the quest for independence and respectability—these made cities places of hope, frustration, comfort, and conflict.

Not until the 1880s did the United States become an urban nation. The technological innovations of the late nineteenth century fueled widespread economic and geographical expansion that funneled millions of people into cities. By 1920, a majority of Americans (51.2 percent) lived in cities (settlements with more than 2,500 people) for the first time.

Online Study Center **Improve Your Grade**
Interactive Map: Urbanization, 1880 and 1929

Cities served as marketplaces and forums, bringing together the people, resources, and ideas responsible for changes in neighborhoods, politics, commerce, and leisure. By 1900, a network of cities spanned every section of the country. Some people relished the opportunities cities offered; others found them disquieting. Either way, cities had become central to American life. ∎

Growth of the Modern City

In the late nineteenth century, cities became the main arenas for industrial growth. As labor, transportation, and communication hubs, cities supplied everything factories needed. Capital accumulated by mercantile enterprises fed industrial investment. Residents also acted as consumers for new products. The further industrialization advanced, the more opportunities it created for jobs and investment. Increased opportunities drew more people to cities; as workers and as consumers, they fueled yet more industrialization.

Within cities, industrial product specialization gradually became common. Mass production of cloth-

INDUSTRIAL DEVELOPMENT
ing concentrated in New York, shoes in Philadelphia, textiles in New England cities. Other cities processed products from surrounding agricultural regions: flour in Minneapolis, cottonseed oil in Memphis, beef and pork in Chicago. Still others processed natural resources: gold and copper in Denver, fish and lumber in Seattle, coal and iron in Pittsburgh and Birmingham, oil in Houston and Los Angeles. Such activities made cities a magnet for people in search of employment.

Urban and industrial growth freed the United States from dependence on European capital and goods. By 1900, urban development helped convert America from a debtor agricultural nation into an industrial, financial, and exporting power.

At the same time, the compact city of the early nineteenth century, where residences mingled among shops, factories, and warehouses, expanded. No longer did different social groups live close together. Instead, cities subdivided into distinct districts: working-class and ethnic neighborhoods, downtown, and a ring of suburbs. Two forces were responsible for this: mass transportation, which propelled people and enterprises outward, and economic change, which drew human and material resources inward.

Mass transportation moved people faster and farther. By the 1870s, horse-drawn vehicles began shar-

MECHANIZATION OF MASS TRANSPORTATION
ing city streets with motor-driven conveyances. At first, commuter railroads carried commuters to and from outlying communities; then cable cars did the job. In the 1890s, electric-powered streetcars began replacing horse cars and cable cars. Between 1890 and 1902, total electrified track grew from 1,300 to 22,000 miles. In Boston, New York, and Philadelphia, transit firms dug underground subway tunnels to avoid traffic congestion. Subways and elevated railroads were expensive, appearing in only the few cities with enough riders to ensure profits.

Mass transit created a commuting public. Those who could afford the fare—usually 5 cents—could

URBAN SPRAWL
live beyond the crowded central city and travel there for work, shopping, and entertainment. Working-class families, who needed every cent, found streetcars unaffordable. But the growing middle class could escape to quiet, tree-lined neighborhoods on the outskirts. Real-estate development boomed around city borders. Between 1890 and 1920, for example, developers in the Chicago area opened 800,000 new lots—enough to house at least three times the city's 1890 population.

When consumers moved outward, companies followed, with business centers emerging near trolley lines and railway stations. Branches of department stores and banks joined groceries, theaters, taverns, and shops to create neighborhood shopping centers. Meanwhile, the urban core became a work zone, where tall buildings loomed over streets clogged with people, horses, and vehicles.

Between 1870 and 1920, the number of Americans living in cities increased from 10 million to 54

POPULATION GROWTH
million. During this period, the number of cities with more than 100,000 people swelled from fifteen to sixty-eight; the number with more than 500,000 rose from two to twelve (see Map 19.1).

American urban growth came from the annexation of bordering land and net migration (excess of in-migrants over out-migrants). The most notable such enlargement occurred in 1898 when New York City, formerly only Manhattan and the Bronx, merged with Brooklyn, Staten Island, and part of Queens and doubled to 3 million people. Suburbs often desired annexation for the schools, water, fire protection, and sewer systems that cities could provide. In the 1880s, Chicago, Minneapolis, and Los Angeles incorporated hundreds of undeveloped square miles into their borders to accommodate future residential growth.

In-migration from the countryside and immigration from abroad made by far the greatest contribu-

URBAN IN-MIGRATION
tion to urban population growth. Urban newcomers arrived from two major sources: the American countryside and Europe. Smaller numbers of immigrants also came from Asia, Canada, and Latin America.

Rural populations declined as urban populations burgeoned. Low crop prices and high debts drove white farmers toward opportunities that cities seemed to offer. Such migration peopled major cities such as Detroit, Chicago, and San Francisco but also secondary cities such as Indianapolis, Salt Lake City, Nashville,

Map 19.1   Urbanization, 1880 and 1920

In 1880 the vast majority of states were heavily rural. By 1920, only a few had less than 20 percent of their population living in cities.

and San Diego. Despair drove farm boys to cities, but for every four men who migrated cityward, five women did the same, often to escape unhappy home life or to enjoy the independence that urban employment offered.

In the 1880s and 1890s, thousands of rural African Americans also moved cityward, seeking better employment and fleeing crop liens, ravages of the boll weevil on cotton crops, racial violence, and political oppression. Though black migration accelerated after 1915, thirty-two cities already had more than ten thousand black residents by 1900. Because few factories would employ African Americans, most found jobs in the service sector—cleaning, cooking, and driving. Since service jobs were traditionally female, black women outnumbered black men in cities. In the South, African Americans migrating from the countryside became an important source of unskilled labor in growing cities. By 1900 almost 40 percent of the total population of Atlanta, Georgia, and Charlotte, North Carolina, were blacks.

In the West, Latino migrants followed a similar pattern. They took unskilled construction and grading jobs previously held by Chinese laborers who had been driven from southern California cities. In some Texas cities, native Mexicans (called *Tejanos*) held most of the unskilled jobs. In places such as Los Angeles, males often left home for long periods to take temporary agricultural jobs, leaving behind female heads of household.

Foreign immigrants fled villages and cities in Europe, Asia, Canada, and Latin America for the

FOREIGN IMMIGRATION

United States. Many wanted only to earn enough money to return home and live in greater comfort. For every hundred foreigners who came to the United States, thirty ultimately left. Still, most of the 26 million immigrants arriving between 1870 and 1920 remained, settling largely in cities, where they helped reshape American culture.

Population pressures, land redistribution, and industrialization induced millions of peasants, small

THE NEW IMMIGRATION

farmers, and craftsmen to leave Europe and Asia for Canada, Australia, Brazil, and Argentina, as well as the United States. Religious persecution, too, particularly the merciless pogroms that Jews suffered in eastern Europe, also forced people to escape across the Atlantic.

Immigrants from northern and western Europe had long made the United States their main destination, but after 1880, economic and demographic changes propelled immigrants from other regions. Two-thirds of newcomers in the 1880s came from Germany, England, Ireland, and Scandinavia; between 1900 and 1909, two-thirds came from Italy, Austria-Hungary, and Russia. By 1910, arrivals from Mexico outnumbered arrivals from Ireland, and numerous Japanese had moved to the West Coast and Hawai'i. Foreign-born blacks, chiefly from the West Indies, also came.

Many long-settled Americans feared these so-called new immigrants, whose customs, Catholic and Jewish faiths, and poverty made them seem especially alien. Unlike earlier arrivals from Great Britain and Ireland, new immigrants did not speak English and typically worked in low-skilled occupations. Family connections aided both old and new immigrants. New arrivals usually knew where to go and how to get there from relatives who had already immigrated. Workers often helped kin obtain jobs, and family members pooled resources to improve their standard of living.

In-migrants and immigrants rarely stayed put. Each year millions of families packed up and moved.

GEOGRAPHIC AND SOCIAL MOBILITY

More than half the families residing in a city at any one time were gone ten years later. Even within a city, it was not uncommon for a family to live at three or more addresses over a ten-year period. One in every three or four families moved every year (compared to one in five today).

Migration offered one path to improved opportunity; occupational change offered another. An advance up the employment hierarchy was mostly available to white males. Thousands of businesses were needed to supply goods and services to burgeoning urban populations, and as corporations grew and centralized operations, they required new managerial personnel. Knowledge of accounting could qualify one for white-collar jobs with higher incomes than manual labor. And an aspiring merchant could open a saloon or shop for a few hundred dollars.

Although advancement occurred often, only a very few could accumulate large fortunes. The vast majority of the era's wealthiest businessmen began their careers with distinct advantages: American birth, Protestant religion, superior education, and relatively

■ The Caribbean as well as Europe sent immigrants to the United States. Proud and confident on arrival from their homeland of Guadeloupe, these women perhaps were unprepared for the double disadvantage they faced as both blacks and foreigners. (William Williams Papers, Manuscripts & Archives Division, The New York Public Library, Astor, Lenox and Tilden Foundations)

affluent parents. Yet considerable movement occurred along the road from poverty to moderate success, from manual to nonmanual jobs.

Rates of upward occupational mobility were slow but steady between 1870 and 1920. In fast-growing cities such as Atlanta, Los Angeles, and Omaha, approximately one in five white manual workers rose to white-collar or owner's positions within ten years. In older cities such as Boston and Philadelphia, upward mobility averaged closer to one in six workers in ten years. Some men slipped from a higher to lower rung on the occupational ladder, but rates of upward movement usually doubled those of downward movement.

What constitutes a better job, however, depends on one's definition of improvement. People with traditions of pride in manual skills considered nonmanual jobs demeaning and discouraged their children from them. As one Italian tailor explained, "I learned the tailoring business in the old country. Over here, in America, I never have trouble finding a job. . . . I want that my oldest boy learn my trade because I tell him that you could always make at least enough for the family."

Many manual workers sought security rather than mobility, preferring a steady wage to the risks of ownership. Failure rates were high among small proprietors in working-class neighborhoods because the low incomes of their customers made business uncertain.

Many women held paying jobs, but the chief means to improve their status was by marrying men with wealth or potential. Laws limited what women could inherit; educational institutions blocked their training in professions such as medicine and law; and prevailing assumptions attributed higher aptitude for manual skills and business to men. Assigned to lowest-paying occupations by prejudice, African Americans, American Indians, Mexican Americans, and Asian Americans could make even fewer gains.

A person might also achieve social mobility by acquiring property, not an easy task. Banks and savings-and-loan institutions had strict lending practices, and mortgage loans carried high interest rates and short repayment periods. Nevertheless, many families were able to amass enough savings for down payments on homes. Ownership rates varied regionally—higher in western cities, lower in eastern cities—but 36 percent of all urban American families owned their homes in 1900, the highest homeownership rate of any western nation except for Denmark, Norway, and Sweden.

Thus, while cities frustrated the hopes of some, they offered opportunities to others. The possibilities for upward mobility seemed to temper people's dissatisfaction with the frustrations of city life. For every story of rags to riches, a multitude of small triumphs mixed with disappointment occurred. Although the gap between the very rich and the very poor widened, the expanding economies of American cities created room for those in between.

Online Study Center **Improve Your Grade**
Primary Source: Theory of the Leisure Class

Urban Neighborhoods

*a*merican cities were characterized by collections of subcommunities where people, most of whom had migrated from somewhere else, coped with daily challenges to their cultures. Rather than yield completely to assimilation, migrants and immigrants interacted with the urban environment to retain their identity while altering both their outlook and the social structure of cities themselves.

In their new surroundings, immigrants first anchored their lives to what they knew best: their culture.

CULTURAL RETENTION AND CHANGE

Old World customs persisted in immigrant districts. Orthodox Jewish men from eastern Europe grew earlocks, women wore wigs, and children attended afternoon religious training. Newcomers re-created mutual aid societies they had known in their homelands. For example, Japanese transferred *ken* societies, which organized social celebrations and relief services, and Chinese used loan associations, called *whey*, to help members acquire businesses. Chinese also transplanted associations called *fongs*, which rented apartments for homeless members, and *tongs*, which were secret aid societies that often acted as gangs extorting protection money from businesses. Southern Italians transplanted the system whereby a *padrone* (boss) found jobs for unskilled workers by negotiating with—and receiving a payoff from—an employer.

In industrial cities such as Chicago, Philadelphia, and Detroit, European immigrants initially clustered

URBAN BORDERLANDS

in inner-city neighborhoods where low-skill jobs and cheap housing were most available. These were typically multiethnic neighborhoods, places historians have called "urban borderlands," where people of diverse backgrounds coexisted. Even within districts identified with a certain group, such as Little Italy, Jewtown, Polonia, or Greektown, rapid mobility constantly undermined residential homogeneity as new inhabitants moved in and older ones left. Despite increasing ethnic mixes, businesses and institutions, such as the bakeries, and churches—operated by and for one ethnic group—gave a neighborhood its identity.

Some ethnic groups often tried to exclude outsiders from their neighborhoods. For example, Italians, Jews, and Poles deliberately maintained separate religious, linguistic, and cultural lifestyles. For such groups, neighborhoods acted as havens until individuals were ready to move into the majority society.

But these borderland experiences often dissolved. The expansion of mass transportation and factories enticed people to relocate, where they interspersed with families of their own socioeconomic class but not necessarily of their own ethnicity. European immigrants did encounter prejudice, such as the exclusion of Jews from certain neighborhoods, professions, and clubs, but discrimination was rarely complete. For people of color, however—African Americans, Asians, and Mexicans—discrimination made the borderlands increasingly less multiethnic over time.

Where small numbers of African Americans may have lived near or among whites in the eighteenth and early nineteenth centuries, by the late nineteenth century, rigid racial discrimination forced them into highly segregated areas later labeled ghettos. By 1920 in Chicago, Detroit, Cleveland, and other cities, two-thirds or more of the total African American population inhabited only 10 percent of the residential area. The only way blacks could relieve overcrowding was to expand residential borders into surrounding, previously white neighborhoods, a process often resulting in harassment and attacks by white residents who feared that black neighbors would cause property values to decline.

RACIAL SEGREGATION IN CITIES

African Americans nurtured cultural institutions to ease urban life: shops, schools, clubs, theaters, dance halls, newspapers, and saloons. Churches, particularly the Baptist and African Methodist Episcopal (AME) branches of Protestantism, were especially influential. Pittsburgh boasted twenty-eight such churches in the early 1900s, and membership in Cincinnati's black Baptist churches doubled between 1870 and 1900. Black religious activity dominated urban local life and represented cooperation across class and regional lines.

Asians encountered similar isolation. Although Chinese immigrants often preferred to live apart from Anglos in the Chinatowns of San Francisco, Los Angeles, and New York City, where they created their own business, government, and protective institutions, Anglos made every effort to keep them separated. Using the slogan "The Chinese must go," Irish immigrant Dennis Kearney and his followers intimidated San Francisco employers into refusing to hire Chinese and drove hundreds of Asians out of the city. San Francisco's government prohibited Chinese laundries from locating in white neighborhoods and banned the wearing of queues, the traditional Chinese hair braid. In 1882 Congress passed the Chinese Exclusion Act, which suspended Chinese immigration and prohib-

ited naturalization of those Chinese already residing in the United States. And in 1892, Congress approved the Geary Act, which extended immigration restriction and required Chinese Americans to carry certificates of residence issued by the Treasury Department. It was upheld by the U.S. Supreme Court in 1893. Similarly prevented from becoming U.S. citizens, Japanese immigrants, called *Issei*, developed separate communities.

Mexicans in southwestern cities experienced more complex residential patterns. In places such as Los Angeles, Santa Barbara, and Tucson, Mexicans had been the original inhabitants, and Anglos were migrants who pushed Mexicans out, where they became increasingly isolated in adjoining districts called *barrios*. Frequently real-estate covenants reinforced this trend as property owners pledged not to sell homes to Mexicans (or to African Americans, or to Jews). Instead, they were confined to segregated areas away from the central-city multiethnic borderlands that housed European immigrants.

MEXICAN BARRIOS

Immigrants struggled to maintain their native languages and customs. But English, taught in schools and needed on the job, soon penetrated nearly every community. Foreigners fashioned homeland garments from American fabrics. Italians went to American doctors but still carried traditional amulets to ward off evil spirits. Music especially revealed adaptations. Polka bands blended American and Polish folk music; once dominated by violins, bands added accordions, clarinets, and trumpets so they could play louder. Mexican ballads acquired new themes that described border crossing and hardships in the United States.

CULTURAL ADAPTATION

The influx of so many immigrants between 1870 and 1920 transformed the United States from a basically Protestant nation into a diverse collection of Protestants, Catholics, Orthodox Christians, Jews, Buddhists, and Muslims. Newcomers from Italy, Hungary, Polish lands, and Slovakia joined Irish and Germans to boost the proportion of Catholics in many cities. German and Russian immigrants gave New York City one of the largest Jewish populations in the world.

Many Catholics and Jews tried to accommodate their faiths to the new environment. Catholic and

Jewish leaders from earlier immigrant groups supported liberalizing trends—use of English in sermons, phasing out of Old World rituals such as saints' feasts, and a preference for public over religious schools.

Newcomers usually resisted and held on to familiar practices, whether the folk Catholicism of southern Italy or the Orthodox Judaism of eastern Europe. Despite church attempts to make American Catholicism more uniform, bishops acceded to pressures from predominantly Polish congregations for Polish priests. Eastern European Jews, convinced that Reform Judaism sacrificed too much to American ways, established the Conservative branch, which retained traditional ritual but abolished the segregation of women in synagogues and allowed English prayers.

The cities nurtured rich cultural variety: American folk music and literature, Italian and Mexican cuisine, Irish comedy, Yiddish theater, African American jazz and dance, and much more. Newcomers changed their environment as much as they were changed by it.

Living Conditions in the Inner City

*T*he central sections of American cities were plagued by poverty, disease, crime, and other unpleasant conditions that occur when large numbers of people live close together. City dwellers coped as best they could, and technology, private enterprise, and public authority achieved some remarkable successes.

In spite of massive construction in the 1880s and early 1900s, population growth outpaced housing supplies. Lack of inexpensive housing especially afflicted working-class families who,

INNER-CITY HOUSING

because of low wages, had to rent their living quarters. As cities grew, landlords took advantage of shortages by splitting up existing buildings to house more people, constructing multiple-unit tenements, and hiking rents. Low-income families adapted to high costs and short supply by sharing space and expenses. A one-family apartment was often occupied by up to three families or by a single family plus several boarders.

The result was unprecedented crowding. In 1890 New York City's immigrant-packed Lower East Side, where the Gollop family lived, averaged 702 people per acre, one of the highest population densities in the world. Inside, conditions were harsh. The largest rooms were barely ten feet wide, and interior rooms lacked windows or opened onto narrow shafts that bred vermin and rotten odors. Few buildings had indoor plumbing; the only source of heat was dangerous, polluting coal-burning stoves.

Housing problems sparked widespread reform campaigns. New York State took the lead by applying light, ventilation, and safety codes for new tenement

HOUSING REFORM

buildings with laws passed in 1867, 1879, and 1901. A few reformers, such as journalist Jacob Riis and humanitarian Lawrence Veiller, advocated "model tenements," with more spacious rooms and better facilities for low-income families. Model tenements meant lower profits, a sacrifice few landlords were willing to make. Both reformers and public officials opposed government financing, fearing that it might undermine private enterprise. Still, new housing codes and regulatory commissions strengthened the power of local government to oversee construction.

Technology radically changed home life. Advanced systems of central heating (furnaces), artificial lighting, and modern indoor plumbing created a new kind

NEW HOME TECHNOLOGY

of consumption, first for middle-class households and later for most others. Whereas formerly families bought coal or chopped wood for cooking and heating, made candles, and hauled bath water, they increasingly connected to outside pipes and wires for gas, electricity, and water. Moreover, these utilities helped create new attitudes about privacy. Middle-class bedrooms and bathrooms became comfortable private retreats, while indoor plumbing replaced the unpleasant experiences of the outhouse.

Better housing for the poor came later, but scientific and technological advances enabled the nation to live better. By the 1880s, doctors had begun to accept the theory that microorganisms (germs) cause disease. Cities developed more efficient water purification and sewage disposal, which helped to control dread diseases such as cholera, typhoid fever, and diphtheria.

■ Inner-city dwellers used not only indoor space as efficiently as possible but also what little outdoor space was available to them. Scores of families living in this cramped block of six-story tenements in New York strung clotheslines behind the buildings. Notice that there is virtually no space between buildings, so only rooms at the front and back received daylight and fresh air.   (Library of Congress)

Meanwhile, street paving, modernized firefighting equipment, and electric street lighting spread rapidly across urban America. Steel-frame construction, which relies on a metal skeleton rather than masonry walls, made possible the erection of skyscrapers—and thus more efficient vertical use of scarce urban land. Electric elevators and steam-heating systems serviced these buildings. Steel-cable suspension bridges, developed by John A. Roebling and epitomized by his Brooklyn Bridge (completed in 1883), linked metropolitan sections more closely.

None of these improvements, however, lightened the burden of poverty. Since colonial days, Americans have disagreed about public responsibility for poor relief. According to

POVERTY RELIEF

traditional beliefs, still widespread by the early twentieth century, anyone could escape poverty through hard work and clean living; indigence was linked to moral weakness. Some people feared that granting aid to the poor encouraged them to rely on public support rather than their own efforts. As poverty increased, this attitude hardened, and city governments discontinued direct grants of food, fuel, and clothing to needy families. Instead, cities provided relief in return for work on public projects and sent special cases to state-run almshouses, orphanages, and homes for the blind, deaf, and mentally ill.

Between 1877 and 1892, philanthropists in ninety-two cities formed Charity Organization Societies to make social welfare (like business) more efficient by merging disparate charity groups into coordinated units. Believing poverty to be caused by defects such as alcoholism and laziness, members of these organizations visited the poor to determine if they were "deserving" and encourage them to be thriftier and more virtuous.

Close observation of the poor, however, prompted some humanitarians to conclude that people's environments, not their shortcomings, caused poverty. They believed poverty would be reduced by improving housing, education, sanitation, and job opportunities. This fueled campaigns for building codes, factory regulations, and public health measures in the Progressive era of the early twentieth century (covered in Chapter 21). Still, most middle- and upper-class Americans continued to endorse the creed that only the unfit were poor and that poverty relief should be tolerated but never encouraged.

Crime and disorder, as much as crowding and poverty, nurtured fears that cities and their slums

CRIME AND VIOLENCE

threatened the nation. While homicide rates declined in other industrialized nations, America's rose alarmingly, from 25 murders per million people in 1881 to 107 per million in 1898. Pickpockets, swindlers, and burglars roamed every city. Urban outlaws, such as Rufus Minor, acquired as much notoriety as western desperadoes. Short, stocky, and bald, Minor resembled a shy clerk, but one police chief labeled him "one of the smartest bank sneaks in America." Minor was implicated in bank heists in New York City, Cleveland, Detroit, Providence, Philadelphia, Albany, Boston, and Baltimore—all between 1878 and 1882.

In reality, urban crime may simply have become more visible rather than more prevalent. To be sure, concentrations of wealth and the mingling of different peoples provided opportunities for larceny, vice, and assault. But urban lawlessness probably did not exceed that of backwoods mining camps and southern plantations. Nativists were quick to blame immigrants for crime, but the criminal rogues' gallery included native-born Americans as well as foreigners.

The cityward movement of African Americans especially sparked white violence, and as the twentieth century dawned, a series of race riots spread across the nation. In 1898 citizens of Wilmington, North Carolina, resenting African Americans' involvement in local politics, rioted and killed dozens of blacks, ex-

pelled black officeholders, and instituted voting restrictions. An influx of African American unskilled laborers and strikebreakers into East St. Louis, Illinois, heightened racial tensions, and violence erupted in 1917 when blacks fired back at a car whose occupants they believed had shot into their homes. When whites discovered that the blacks had mistakenly killed two policemen in the car, a riot erupted, ending only after nine whites and thirty-nine blacks had been killed and over three hundred buildings destroyed. Domestic violence, muggings, and gang fights also made cities turbulent.

Managing the City

*B*urgeoning populations and business expansion created urgent needs for sewers, police and fire protection, schools, parks, and other services. Such needs strained municipal resources and city governments beyond their capacities. Legislative and administrative responsibilities for health, public works, and poverty relief were typically scattered among a mayor, city council, and independent boards. Philadelphia at one time had thirty different boards, plus a mayor and council. Also, state governments often interfered in local matters, appointing board members and limiting cities' abilities to levy taxes and borrow money.

Finding sources of clean water and a way to dispose of waste became increasingly urgent challenges.

WATER SUPPLY AND SEWAGE DISPOSAL

Earlier in the nineteenth century, urban households used privies (outdoor toilets) to dispose of human excrement, and factories dumped untreated sewage into nearby rivers, lakes, and bays. By the late nineteenth century, the installation of sewer systems and flush toilets, plus use of water as a coolant in factories, overwhelmed waterways and contaminated drinking water sources. The stench of rivers was often unbearable, and pollution bred disease. Memphis and New York experienced yellow-fever epidemics in the 1870s and 1880s, and typhoid fever threatened many cities.

Acceptance in the 1880s of the germ theory of disease prompted cities to reduce chances that human waste and other pollutants would endanger water supplies. Some states prohibited discharge of raw sewage into rivers and streams, and a few cities began the expensive process of chemically treating sewage. Gradually, water managers installed mechanical filters, and cities, led by Jersey City, began purifying water supplies by adding chlorine. These efforts dramatically reduced death rates from typhoid fever.

But waste disposal remained a thorny problem. Experts in 1900 estimated that every New Yorker generated annually some 160 pounds of garbage (food and bones), 1,200 pounds of ashes (from stoves and furnaces), and 100 pounds of rubbish (shoes, furniture, and other discarded items). Solid waste from factories and businesses included tons of scrap metal, wood, and other materials. Each of the estimated 3.5 million horses in American cities in 1900 dropped about 20 pounds of manure and a gallon of urine daily—a serious environmental problem. By the twentieth century, such debris were health and safety hazards.

Citizen groups, led by women's organizations, began discussing the dilemma in the 1880s and 1890s,

URBAN
ENGINEERS

and by the turn of the century, urban governments hired sanitary engineers to develop garbage collection and disposal systems, mostly in incinerators and landfills. The American engineering profession developed new systems and standards of worldwide significance in such areas as street lighting, bridge and street construction, fire protection, and other urban needs that required technological creativity. Elected officials came to depend on the expertise of engineers in supervising urban expansion. Insulated within bureaucratic agencies and party politics, engineers made some of the most lasting contributions to urban management.

After the mid-nineteenth century, urban dwellers increasingly depended on professional police to protect life and property, but law enforcement became controversial as various groups differed about how laws should be enforced. Ethnic and racial minorities were more likely to be arrested, and police officers applied the law less harshly to members of their own ethnic groups as well as to those offering bribes.

LAW
ENFORCEMENT

Often poorly trained and prone to corruption, police officers were caught between demands for swift and severe action on one hand and leniency on the other. As urban society diversified, some people clamored for crackdowns on drunkenness, gambling, and

prostitution, while others objected to the violation of civil liberties. Achieving balance between criminal law and individual freedom grew increasingly difficult.

Out of the apparent confusion surrounding urban management arose political machines, organizations whose main goals were the rewards—money, influence, and prestige—of getting and keeping power. Machine politicians routinely used fraud and bribery to further their ends. But they also provided relief, security, and services to voters who kept them in power.

POLITICAL
MACHINES

Machines bred leaders, called bosses, who catered to urban working classes and especially to new immigrant voters, who provided their power base. Most bosses had immigrant backgrounds and had grown up in the inner city; they knew their constituents' needs firsthand and secured their loyalty by tending to problems of everyday life. In return for votes, bosses provided jobs, built parks and bathhouses, distributed food and clothing to the needy, and helped when someone ran afoul of the law. Pittsburgh's Christopher Magee gave his city a zoo and a hospital. Brooklyn's Hugh McLaughlin provided free burial services. Never before had public leaders assumed such responsibility for people in need. Bosses attended weddings and wakes, joined clubs, and held open house in saloons where neighborhood folk could speak to them personally. According to George Washington Plunkitt, a neighborhood boss in New York City, "As a rule [the boss] has no business or occupation other than politics. He plays politics every day and night . . . and his headquarters bears the inscription, 'Never closed.'"

To finance their activities, bosses exchanged favors for votes and money. Power over local government enabled machines to control who received public contracts, utility and streetcar franchises, and city jobs. Recipients of these favors were expected to repay the machine with a portion of their profits or salaries and to cast supporting votes on election day. Critics called this process graft; bosses called it gratitude.

Bosses such as Philadelphia's "Duke" Vare, Kansas City's Tom Pendergast, and New York's Richard Croker lived like kings, though their official incomes were slim. Yet machines were rarely as dictatorial or corrupt as critics charged. Rather, several machines, like businesses, evolved into highly organized political structures, such as New York's Tammany Hall organization (named after a society that originally began as a patriotic and fraternal club), that wedded public accomplishments with personal gain. The system rested on a popular base and was held together by loyalty and service. But most machines were coalitions of smaller organizations that derived power directly from inner-city neighborhoods. Machine-led governments constructed urban infrastructures—public buildings, sewer systems, schools, bridges, and mass-transit lines—and expanded urban services—police, firefighting, and public health departments.

Machine politics, however, was not always fair. Racial minorities and new immigrant groups such as Italians and Poles received only token jobs and nominal favors, if any. And bribes and kickbacks made machine projects and services costly to taxpayers. Cities could not ordinarily raise enough revenue for their construction projects from taxes and fees, so they financed expansion with loans from the public in the form of municipal bonds—which caused public debts and taxes to soar. In addition, payoffs from gambling, prostitution, and illicit liquor traffic became important sources of machine revenue. But bosses were no more guilty of discrimination and self-interest than were business leaders who exploited workers, spoiled the landscape, and manipulated government in pursuit of profits.

Many middle- and upper-class Americans feared that immigrant-based political machines menaced democracy and wasted municipal finances. Anxious over the poverty, crowding, and disorder that accompanied city growth and convinced that urban services were making taxes too high, civic reformers organized to elect more responsible leaders.

CIVIC REFORM

Business-minded reformers believed government should run like a company. Thus, they advocated reducing city budgets, making public employees work more efficiently, and cutting taxes.

To implement business principles in government, civic reformers supported structural changes such as city-manager and commission forms of government, which would place administration in the hands of experts rather than politicians, and nonpartisan, citywide rather than neighborhood-based election of officials. The reformers' goal was to weaken bosses' power bases in the neighborhoods.

A few reform mayors addressed social problems too. Hazen S. Pingree of Detroit, Samuel "Golden Rule" Jones of Toledo, and Tom Johnson of Cleveland worked to provide jobs to poor people, reduce charges by transit and utility companies, and promote governmental responsibility for the welfare of all citizens. They also supported public ownership of gas, electric, and telephone companies, quasi-socialist reforms that alienated their business allies. Civic reformers achieved some successes but rarely held office for very long.

Driven to improve as well as manage society, social reformers—mostly young and middle class—sought to solve urban problems. Housing reformers pressed local governments for building codes ensuring safety in tenements. Educational reformers pressed to use public schools to prepare immigrant children for citizenship by teaching them American values.

SOCIAL REFORM

Perhaps the most ambitious urban reform movement was the settlement house. Located in inner-city neighborhoods and run mostly by young, middle-class women who lived and worked among the poor to bridge the gulf between social classes, settlements sponsored programs for better education, jobs, and housing. The first American settlement, patterned after London's Toynbee Hall, opened in New York City in 1886, and others quickly appeared across the country. Early settlement leaders included Jane Addams, founder of Hull House in Chicago in 1889 and one of the country's most influential women, and Florence Kelley, who pioneered laws protecting consumers and working women.

Their efforts to involve national and local governments in the solution of social problems put settlements in the vanguard of the Progressive era, when a reform spirit swept the nation. Moreover, settlement-house programs created new professional opportunities for women in social work, public health, and child welfare. These professions enabled female reformers to wield influence over social policy and make valuable contributions to national as well as inner-city life.

Still, the settlement-house movement was segregated. Middle-class white women lobbied for government programs to aid mostly white immigrant and native-born working classes. Black women reformers, excluded from white settlements, raised funds from private donors and promoted racial advancement by founding schools, old-age homes, and hospitals, as well as protecting black women from sexual exploitation. Their ranks included Jane Hunter, who founded a home for unmarried black working women in Cleveland in 1911 and inspired the establishment of similar homes in other cities.

Male reformers joined female activists' improvement efforts with their own City Beautiful campaign.

THE CITY BEAUTIFUL MOVEMENT Inspired by the Columbian Exposition of 1893, a dazzling world's fair held in Chicago, architects and planners aimed to redesign the urban landscape. City Beautiful advocates built civic centers, parks, and boulevards that would make cities economically efficient as well as beautiful, with projects in Chicago, San Francisco, and Washington, D.C., in the early 1900s. Yet neither government nor private businesses could finance large-scale projects, and planners disagreed among themselves and with social reformers over whether beautification would truly solve urban problems.

Urban reformers wanted to save cities, but they often failed to recognize the diversity of people and opinions about reform. To civic reformers, appointing government workers based on civil service exams rather than party loyalty meant progress, but to working-class men, civil service signified reduced employment opportunities. Moral reformers believed that restricting the sale of alcohol would prevent working-class breadwinners from squandering wages, but immigrants saw it as interference. Planners saw new streets and buildings as modern necessities, but such structures often displaced the poor. Well-meaning humanitarians criticized immigrant mothers for the way they dressed, did housework, and raised children, without recognition of their limited finances. Thus, urban reform merged idealism with naiveté and insensitivity.

Family Life

*U*rbanization and industrialization put strains on family life. New institutions—schools, social clubs, political organizations, unions—increasingly competed with the family to provide nurture, education, and security. Clergy and journalists warned that the growing separation between home and work, rising divorce rates, the entrance of women into the work force, and loss of parental control over children spelled peril for home and family. Yet the family remained a cushion in an uncertain world.

Since colonial times, most American households (75 to 80 percent) have consisted of nuclear families—

FAMILY AND HOUSEHOLD STRUCTURES usually a married couple, with or without children. About 15 to 20 percent of households have consisted of extended families—usually a married couple, with or without children, plus one or more relatives. About 5 percent of households have consisted of people living alone or in boarding houses and hotels. Despite slight variations, this pattern held relatively constant among ethnic, racial, and socioeconomic groups.

Several factors explain this pattern. Because immigrants tended to be young, the American population as a whole was young. In 1880 the median age was under twenty-one, and by 1920 it was still only twenty-five. (Median age at present is about thirty-three.) Moreover, in 1900 the death rate among people aged forty-five to sixty-four was double what it is today. Only 4 percent of the population was over sixty-five, versus about 13 percent today. Thus, few families could form extended three-generation households, and fewer children than today had living grandparents. Migration split up families, and the ideal of homeownership encouraged nuclear household organization.

Most of Europe and North America experienced falling birth rates in the nineteenth century. In 1880

DECLINING BIRTH RATES the birth rate was 40 live births per 1,000 people in the United States; by 1900 it had dropped to 32; by 1920 to 28. Although fertility was higher among blacks, immigrants, and rural people, birth rates of all groups fell. Several factors explain this decline.

First, the United States was becoming an urban nation, and birth rates are historically lower in cities than in rural areas. On farms, each child born represented an addition to the family work force. In the wage-based urban economy, children could not contribute significantly to the family income for many years, so a new child represented another mouth to feed. Second, infant mortality fell as diet and medical care improved, and families did not have to bear many children to ensure that some would survive. Third, awareness that smaller families meant improved quality of life seems to have stimulated decisions to limit family size—either by abstaining from sex during the wife's fertile period or through contraception and abortion. Families with three or four children instead of six or eight became the norm. Birth-control technology—diaphragms and condoms—had been used for centuries, but in this era, new materials made devices more convenient and dependable.

The process of leaving home to work altered household composition. Middle- and working-class families commonly took in boarders

BOARDING for additional income. Immigrants such as Rahel Gollop often lodged with relatives and fellow villagers until they could establish themselves. By 1900, as many as 50 percent of city residents had lived either as, or with, boarders at some point during their lifetime. Housing reformers charged that boarding caused overcrowding and loss of privacy.

For people on the move, boarding was a transitional stage, providing a quasi-family environment until they set up their own households. Especially in communities where housing was expensive or scarce, newlyweds sometimes lived temporarily with one spouse's parents. Families also took in widowed parents or unmarried siblings.

At a time when welfare agencies were rare, the family was the institution to which people could turn in times of need. Relatives often resided nearby and aided one another with childcare, meals, shopping, advice, and consolation. They also obtained jobs for each other. According to one new arrival, "After two days my brother took me to the shop he was working in and his boss saw me and he gave me the job."

But obligations of kinship were not always welcome. Immigrant families pressured last-born children to stay at home to care for aging parents, a practice that stifled opportunities for education, marriage, and economic independence. Tensions also developed when immigrant parents and American-born children clashed over the abandonment of Old World ways or the amount of wages children should contribute to the household. Nevertheless, kinship helped people cope with the stresses of urban-industrial society.

Large numbers of city dwellers were unmarried. In 1890 almost 42 percent of adult American men and 37 percent of women were single, almost twice as high as in 1960

UNMARRIED
PEOPLE
but slightly lower than today. About half still lived with parents, but others inhabited rented rooms. Mostly young, these men and women constituted a separate subculture that supported institutions like dance halls, saloons, cafés, and the Young Men's Christian Association (YMCA) and Young Women's Christian Association (YWCA).

Some unmarried people were part of the homosexual populations in large cities like New York, San Francisco, and Boston. Though numbers are difficult to estimate, gay men had their own subculture of clubs, restaurants, coffeehouses, theaters, and support networks. A number of same-sex couples, especially women, formed lasting marital-type relationships, sometimes called "Boston marriages." People in this subculture were categorized more by how they acted—men acting like women, women acting like men—than by who their sexual partners were. The term *homosexual* was not used. Men who dressed and acted like women were called "fairies." Gay women remained largely hidden, and a visible lesbian subculture was rare until the 1920s.

Before the late nineteenth century, stages of life were less distinct than they are today. Childhood, for instance, had been regarded as a

STAGES OF LIFE period during which young people prepared for adulthood by gradually assuming more responsibilities. The subdivisions of youth—toddlers, schoolchildren, teenagers, and the like—were not recognized. Because married couples had more children over a longer time span, active parenthood occupied most of adult life. Older children who cared for younger siblings might begin parenting even before reaching adulthood. And older people were not isolated from other age groups.

In the late nineteenth century, demographic and social changes altered these patterns. Decreasing birth rates shortened the period of parental responsibility, so more middle-aged couples experienced an "empty nest" once their children grew up and left home. Longer life expectancy and a tendency by employers to force aged workers to retire separated the old from the young. As states passed compulsory school-attendance laws in the 1870s and 1880s, childhood and adolescence became distinct from adulthood. People's roles in school, in the family, on the job, and in the community came to be determined by age more than any other characteristic.

Thus, by 1900, new institutions were assuming tasks formerly performed by the family. Schools made education a community responsibility. Employment agencies, personnel offices, and labor unions were taking responsibility for employee recruitment and job security. Age-based peer groups exerted greater influence over people's values and activities. Migration and divorce seemed to be splitting families apart. Yet kinship remained a dependable though not always appreciated institution.

An emphasis on family togetherness became especially visible at holiday celebrations. Middle-class

HOLIDAY CELEBRATIONS

moralists helped make Thanksgiving, Christmas, and Easter special times for family reunion and child-centered activities. Birthdays too took on an increasingly festive quality as a milestone for measuring the age-related norms that accompanied life stages. In 1914 President Woodrow Wilson signed a proclamation designating the second Sunday in May as Mother's Day, capping a six-year campaign by schoolteacher Anna Jarvis, who believed grown children were neglecting their mothers. Ethnic and racial groups adapted national celebrations to their cultures, preparing special ethnic foods, and engaging in unique ceremonies. For many, holiday celebrations were a testimony to the vitality of family life.

The New Leisure and Mass Culture

*O*n December 2, 1889, as workers paraded through Worcester, Massachusetts, seeking shorter working hours, a group of carpenters hoisted a banner proclaiming, "Eight Hours for Work, Eight Hours for Rest, Eight Hours for What We Will." That last phrase laid claim to a segment of daily life belonging to the individual. Increasingly, leisure activities filled this time.

By the late 1800s, technology had become truly time-saving. Mechanization and assembly-line produc-

INCREASE IN LEISURE TIME

tion cut the average manufacturing workweek from sixty-six hours in 1860 to sixty in 1890 and forty-seven in 1920, which meant shorter workdays and freer weekends. White-collar employees spent eight to ten hours a day on the job and often worked only half a day or not at all on weekends. As the economy changed, more Americans engaged in a variety of diversions, and a substantial segment of the economy provided for—and profited from—leisure.

After the Civil War, amusement became a commercial activity. Production of games, toys, and musical instruments expanded. Improvements in printing and paper production and the rise of manufacturers such as Milton Bradley and Parker Brothers increased the popularity of board games. Significantly, the content of board games shifted from moral lessons to topics involving transportation, finance, and sports. Also, by the 1890s, middle-class families were buying mass-produced pianos and sheet music that made singing of popular songs a common form of home entertainment. The vanguard of new leisure pursuits, however, was sports. Formerly a fashionable indulgence of elites, organized sports became a favored pastime of all classes.

The most popular organized sport was baseball. Derived from older bat, ball, and base-circling games,

BASEBALL

baseball was formalized in 1845 by the Knickerbocker Club of New York. By 1860 at least fifty baseball clubs existed. The National League of Professional Baseball Clubs, founded in 1876, gave the sport a stable, businesslike structure. As early as 1867 a "color line" excluded black players from professional teams. By the 1880s professional baseball was big business. In 1903 the National League and competing American League (formed in 1901) began a World Series between their championship teams. The Boston Red Sox beat the Pittsburgh Pirates in that first series.

Baseball appealed mostly to men. But croquet, which also swept the nation, attracted both sexes.

CROQUET AND CYCLING

Middle- and upper-class people held croquet parties and night contests that increased opportunities for social contact between the sexes.

■ Amusement centers such as Luna Park, at Coney Island in New York City, became common and appealing features of the new leisure culture. One of the most popular Coney Island attractions was a ride called Shooting the Chutes, which resembled modern giant water slides. In 1904 Luna Park staged an outrageous stunt when an elephant slid down the chute. It survived, apparently unfazed.   (Picture Research Consultants and Archives)

Meanwhile, cycling achieved popularity rivaling that of baseball, especially after 1885, when the cumbersome velocipede, with its huge front wheel and tall seat, gave way to safety bicycles with pneumatic tires and wheels of identical size. By 1900 Americans owned 10 million bicycles, and clubs petitioned state governments to build more paved roads. Organized cycle races brought international fame to professional riders such as Major Taylor, an African American. Moreover, the bicycle helped free women from constraints of Victorian fashions. In order to ride the dropped-frame female models, women had to wear divided skirts and simple undergarments. As the 1900 census declared, "Few articles . . . have created so great a revolution in social conditions as the bicycle."

American football, as an intercollegiate competition, mostly attracted players and spectators wealthy enough to have access to higher education. By the late nineteenth cen-

FOOTBALL

tury, however, the game was appealing to a broader audience. The 1893 Princeton-Yale game drew fifty thousand spectators, and informal games were played in yards and playgrounds throughout the country.

But college football's violence and use of "tramp athletes," nonstudents hired to help teams win, sparked a national scandal. Critics accused football of mirroring undesirable features of American society. An editor of *The Nation* charged in 1890 that "the lack of moral scruple which pervades the struggles of the business world meets with temptations equally irresistible in the miniature contests of the football field."

The scandals climaxed in 1905, when 18 players died from game-related injuries and over 150 were seriously injured. President Theodore Roosevelt, a strong advocate of athletics, convened a White House conference to discuss ways to eliminate brutality and foul play. The gathering founded the Intercollegiate

Japanese Baseball

Baseball, the "American pastime," was one of the new leisure-time pursuits that Americans took with them to different parts of the world. The Shanghai Base Ball Club was founded by Americans in China in 1863, but was denounced by the Imperial Court as spiritually corrupting. However, when Horace Wilson, an American teacher, taught the rules of baseball to his Japanese students around 1870, the game received enthusiastic welcome as a reinforcement of traditional virtues and quickly became an entrenched aspect of Japanese culture.

During the 1870s, Japanese high schools and colleges organized baseball games, and in 1883 Hiroshi Hiraoka, a railroad engineer who had studied in Boston, founded the first official local team, the Shimbashi Athletic Club Athletics.

Prior to baseball, the Japanese had no team sports or recreational athletics. When they learned about baseball, they found that the idea of a team sport fit into their culture very well. But to the Japanese, baseball was serious business, often involving brutal training. Practices at Ichiko, one of Japan's two great high-school teams in the late nineteenth century, were dubbed "Bloody Urine" because many players passed blood after a day of drilling. There was a spiritual quality as well, linked to Buddhist values. According to one Japanese coach, "Student baseball must be the baseball of self-discipline, or trying to attain the truth, just as in Zen Buddhism." This attitude prompted Japanese to consider baseball as a new method to pursue the spirit of Bushido, the way of the samurai.

When Americans played baseball in Japan, the Japanese appreciated their talent, but found them lacking in discipline and respect. Americans insulted the Japanese by refusing to remove their hats and bow when they stepped up to bat. An international dispute occurred in 1891 when William Imbrie, an American professor at Meijo University in Tokyo, arrived late for a local game and climbed over the fence. The fence, however, was sacred, and Japanese fans attacked him for his sacrilege, causing him facial injuries. Americans assumed that their game would encourage Japanese to become like westerners, but the Japanese transformed the American pastime into a uniquely Japanese expression of discipline and nationalism.

Replete with bats, gloves, and uniforms, this Japanese baseball team of 1890 very much resembles its American counterpart of that era. The Japanese adopted baseball soon after Americans became involved in their country, but added their cultural qualities to the game.
(Japanese Baseball Hall of Fame)

Athletic Association (renamed the National College Athletic Association in 1910) to police college sports. In 1906 the association altered the game to make it less violent and more open.

As more women enrolled in college, they participated in sports such as rowing, track, and swimming. Eventually women made basketball their most popular intercollegiate sport. Invented in 1891 as a winter sport for men, basketball received women's rules (which limited dribbling and running and encouraged passing) from Senda Berenson of Smith College.

American show business also became a mode of leisure created by and for common people. After the

***CIRCUSES,
POPULAR
DRAMA,
AND MUSICAL
COMEDY***

Civil War, railroads enabled circuses to reach towns across the country. Circuses offered two main attractions: oddities of nature, both human and animal, and the temptation and conquest of death.

Three branches of American show business—popular drama, musical comedy, and vaudeville—matured with the growth of cities. Theatrical performances offered audiences escape into melodrama, adventure, and comedy. For urban people unfamiliar with the frontier, popular plays made the mythical Wild West and Old South come alive through stories of Davy Crockett, Buffalo Bill, and the Civil War. Virtue and honor always triumphed in melodramas such as *Uncle Tom's Cabin* and *The Old Homestead,* reinforcing faith that goodness would prevail.

The American musical derived from Europe's lavishly costumed operettas. George M. Cohan, a spirited singer, dancer, and songwriter born into an Irish family of entertainers, became master of American musical comedy after the turn of the century. Drawing on patriotism and traditional values in songs like "Yankee Doodle Boy" and "You're a Grand Old Flag," Cohan bolstered morale during World War I. American comic operas initially imitated European musicals, but by the early 1900s, composers like Victor Herbert were writing themes appealing directly to American audiences.

Because of its variety, vaudeville was probably the most popular mass entertainment in early-twentieth-

VAUDEVILLE

century America. Shows included, in rapid succession, acts of jugglers, pantomimists, magicians, puppeteers, acrobats, comedians, singers, and

dancers. Shrewd entrepreneurs made vaudeville a big business. The famous producer Florenz Ziegfeld brilliantly packaged shows in a stylish format—the Ziegfeld Follies—and gave the nation a new model of femininity, the Ziegfeld Girl, whose graceful dancing and alluring costumes suggested a haunting sensuality.

Show business provided new opportunities for female, African American, and immigrant performers, but it also encouraged stereotyping and exploitation. Comic opera diva Lillian Russell, vaudeville singer-comedienne Fanny Brice, and burlesque queen Eva Tanguay attracted intensely loyal fans and commanded handsome fees. In contrast to the demure Victorian female, they conveyed an image of pluck and creativity. There was something both shocking and confident about Eva Tanguay singing "It's All Been Done Before But Not the Way I Do It." But lesser female performers and showgirls (called "soubrettes") were often exploited by male promoters and theater owners, who wanted to profit by titillating the public with scantily clad women.

Before the 1890s, the chief form of commercial entertainment employing African Americans was the minstrel show, but vaudeville opened new opportunities to them. Pandering to prejudices of white audiences, composers and performers of both races ridiculed blacks. As songs like "He's Just a Little Nigger, But He's Mine All Mine" confirm, blacks were demeaned on stage much as they were in society. Burt Williams, a highly paid black performer, achieved success by playing stereotypical roles but was tormented by the humiliation he had to suffer.

Immigrants occupied the core of American show business. Vaudeville in particular used ethnic humor, exaggerated dialects, and other national traits. Skits and songs reinforced stereotypes, but such distortions were more sympathetic than those directed at blacks. A typical scene involving Italians, for example, highlighted a character's uncertain grasp of English, which caused him to confuse *mayor* with *mare, diploma* with the *plumber,* and *pallbearer* with *polar bear.* The conditions of African Americans, however, were subject to more vicious jokes.

Shortly after 1900, live entertainment began to yield to motion pictures. Perfected by Thomas Edison

MOVIES

in the 1880s, movies began as slot-machine peepshows in penny arcades and billiard parlors. Eventually images were projected onto a screen for large audiences. At first, subjects of films hardly mattered; scenes of speeding trains, acrobats, and writhing belly dancers were thrilling enough.

Producers soon discovered that a film could tell a story in exciting ways, and motion pictures became a distinct art form. D. W. Griffith's *Birth of a Nation* (1915), an epic film about the Civil War and Reconstruction, fanned racial prejudice by depicting African Americans as threats to white moral values. The National Association for the Advancement of Colored People (NAACP), formed in 1909, led organized protests against it. But the film's innovative techniques—close-ups, fade-outs, and battle scenes—heightened the drama. By 1920, movies appealed to all classes, and audiences idolized film stars such as Mary Pickford, Lillian Gish, and Charlie Chaplin.

By mass-producing sound and images, technology made entertainment a desirable consumer good. The still camera, modernized by inventor George Eastman, enabled ordinary people to record visual images and preserve family memories. The phonograph, another Edison invention, brought musical performances into the home. News also became a consumer product. Using high-speed printing presses, cheap paper, and profits from growing advertisement revenues, shrewd publishers created a much-desired medium. Increased leisure time seemed to nurture a fascination with the sensational, and from the 1880s onward, popular urban newspapers increasingly whetted that appetite.

Joseph Pulitzer, a Hungarian immigrant who bought the *New York World* in 1883, pioneered journalism as a branch of mass culture.

YELLOW JOURNALISM

Pulitzer filled the *World* with stories of disasters, crimes, and scandals and printed screaming headlines, set in large bold type like that used for advertisements. *World* reporter Nellie Bly (real name, Elizabeth Cochrane) faked her way into an insane asylum and wrote a brazen exposé of the sordid conditions she found. Pulitzer also popularized comics, and the yellow ink they were printed in gave rise to the term *yellow journalism* as a synonym for sensationalism.

In one year the *World*'s circulation increased from 20,000 to 100,000, and by the late 1890s it reached 1 million. Soon other publishers, such as William Randolph Hearst, who bought the *New York Journal*

in 1895 and started a newspaper empire, adopted Pulitzer's techniques. Pulitzer, Hearst, and their rivals boosted circulation further by emphasizing sports and women's news. Newspapers had previously reported sporting events, but yellow-journalism papers gave such stories greater prominence with separate, expanded sports pages. Newspapers also added special sections devoted to household tips, fashion, decorum, and club news to capture female readers.

By the early twentieth century, mass-circulation magazines overshadowed expensive elitist journals of earlier eras. Publications such as

OTHER MASS-MARKET PUBLICATIONS

McClure's, Saturday Evening Post, and *Ladies' Home Journal* offered human-interest stories, exposés, fiction, photographs, colorful covers, and eye-catching ads. Meanwhile, the total number of published books more than quadrupled between 1880 and 1917. This reflected growing literacy. Between 1870 and 1920, the proportion of Americans over age ten who could not read or write fell from 20 percent to 6 percent.

Other forms of communication also expanded. In 1891 there was less than 1 telephone for every 100 people in the United States; by 1901 the number reached 2.1, and by 1921 it swelled to 12.6. In 1900 Americans used 4 billion postage stamps; in 1922 they bought 14.3 billion. More than ever before, people in different parts of the country knew about and discussed the same news event. America was becoming a mass society where the same products, technology, and information dominated everyday life, regardless of region.

To some extent, the cities' new amusements allowed ethnic and social groups to share common experiences. Yet different consumer groups used parks, ball fields, movies, and newspapers to reinforce their own cultural habits. To the dismay of reformers who hoped that public recreation and holidays would assimilate newcomers and teach them habits of restraint, immigrants used picnics for special ethnic gatherings and Fourth of July celebrations for boisterous drinking and sometimes violent behavior. Young working-class men and women resisted parents' and moralists' warnings and frequented urban dance halls, where they explored their own forms of courtship and sexual behavior. Thus, leisure—like work and politics—was shaped by the pluralistic forces that thrived in urban life.

Summary *Online Study Center* ACE the Test

*a*merican cities experienced an "unheralded triumph" by the early 1900s. Amid corruption and political conflict, urban engineers modernized local infrastructures with sewer, water, and lighting services, and urban governments made the environment safer by expanding professional police and fire departments. When native inventiveness met the traditions of European, African, and Asian cultures, a new kind of society emerged. The jumble of social classes, ethnic and racial groups, political organizations, and professional experts sometimes lived in harmony, sometimes not.

Amid bewildering diversity, native-born whites tried to Americanize and uplift immigrants, but newcomers stubbornly protected their cultures. Optimists had envisioned the American nation as a melting pot, where various nationalities would fuse into a unified people. Instead, many ethnic groups proved unmeltable, and racial minorities got burned on the bottom of the pot. Instead, the United States became a pluralistic society—more like a salad bowl, where ingredients retained their original flavor and occasionally blended.

Pluralism and interest-group loyalties enhanced the importance of politics, with different groups competing for power, wealth, and status. By 1920, immigrants outnumbered the native-born in many cities, and the national economy depended on these new workers and consumers. Migrants and immigrants transformed the United States into an urban nation. They gave American culture its varied texture, and they laid the foundations for the liberalism that characterized American politics in the twentieth century.

LEGACY FOR A PEOPLE AND A NATION
Ethnic Food

The American taste for ethnic food has a complicated history. Since the nineteenth century, the food business has offered immigrant entrepreneurs lucrative opportunities, many of which involved products unrelated to their own ethnic background. The industry is replete with success stories such as Hector Boiardi (Chef Boyardee), William Gebhardt (Eagle Brand chili and tamales), Jeno Paulucci (Chun-King), and Alphonse Biardot (Franco-American), all of whom immigrated to the United States in the late nineteenth or early twentieth century. But Americans have also supported unheralded local immigrant merchants and restaurateurs who have offered special and regional fare—German, Chinese, Italian, Tex-Mex, "soul food," or Thai—in every era.

The evolution of American eating habits was one of the true melting pots. Occasionally criticisms developed, such as when dietitians and reformers in the early twentieth century charged that the rich foods of eastern European Jews made them overly emotional and less capable of assimilating. But as historian Donna Gabaccia has observed, relatively conflict-free sharing and borrowing have characterized American food ways far more than intolerance. And mass marketers have been quick to capitalize.

As each wave of immigrants has entered the nation—and especially as these newcomers have occupied the cities, where cross-cultural contact has been inevitable—food has given them certain ways of becoming American, of finding some group acceptance, while also confirming their identity.

GILDED AGE POLITICS 1877–1900

*K*nown to friends as the "People's Joan of Arc" and to enemies as the "Kansas Pythoness," Mary Elizabeth Lease was an electrifying orator who, one observer said, could "set a crowd hooting and harrahing at her will." Born in 1853 in Pennsylvania, she lived most of her adult life in Kansas. Married at age twenty, Lease bore five children, took in washing, and studied law by pinning her notes above her washtub.

In 1885, Lease became the first woman admitted to the Kansas bar and an ardent activist. Joining the Women's Christian Temperance Union and the Farmers' Alliance, she became a spokesperson for the Populist party, making over 160 speeches in 1890 on behalf of downtrodden farmers and laboring people. She later ran for the U.S. Senate, but damaged her party's fortune by refusing to unite with Democrats in opposition to big business and political corruption. "This is a nation of inconsistencies," proclaimed Lease, who backed prohibition, women's suffrage, and birth control. "We fought England for our liberty and put chains on four million blacks. We wiped out slavery and [then] by our tariff laws and national banks began a system of white wage slavery worse than the first."

Lease's turbulent career paralleled an eventful era, characterized by three themes: special-interest ascendancy, legislative accomplishment, and political exclusion. When she attacked the railroads and big business for exploiting farmers, she expressed the growing dissatisfaction with the greed and abuses of power exerted by large corporations and wealthy individuals. The era's venality seemed so widespread that when, in 1874, Mark Twain and Charles Dudley Warner satirized America as a land of shallow money grubbers in their novel *The Gilded Age*, the name stuck.

At the same time, Lease's rhetoric obscured economic and political accomplishments at the state and national levels. Between 1877 and 1900, Congress achieved legislative landmarks in railroad regulation, tariff and currency reform, and civil service despite partisan and regional rivalries. Meanwhile, the judiciary actively supported big business by defending property

The Nature of Party Politics

Issues of Legislation

LINKS TO THE WORLD
Missionaries

The Presidency Restrengthened

Discrimination, Disfranchisement, and Response

Agrarian Unrest and Populism

The Depression and Protests of the 1890s

The Silver Crusade and the Election of 1896

LEGACY FOR A PEOPLE AND A NATION
Interpreting a Fairy Tale

Online Study Center
This icon will direct you to interactive map and primary source activities on the website http://college.hmco.com/pic/nortonbrief7e

C H R O N O L O G Y

1873 • Congress ends coinage of silver dollars

1873–78 • Economic hard times hit

1876 • Hayes elected president

1878 • Bland-Allison Act requires Treasury to buy between $2 and $4 million in silver each month

1880 • Garfield elected president

1881 • Garfield assassinated; Arthur assumes the presidency

1883 • Pendleton Civil Service Act introduces merit system
• Supreme Court strikes down 1875 Civil Rights Act

1884 • Cleveland elected president

1886 • *Wabash* case declares that only Congress can limit interstate commerce rates

1887 • Farmers' Alliances form
• Interstate Commerce Commission begins regulating rates and practices of interstate shipping

1888 • B. Harrison elected president

1890 • McKinley Tariff raises tariff rates
• Sherman Silver Purchase Act commits Treasury to buying 4.5 million ounces of silver each month

• "Mississippi Plan" uses poll taxes and literacy tests to prevent African Americans from voting
• National American Woman Suffrage Association formed

1892 • Populist convention in Omaha draws up reform platform
• Cleveland elected president

1893 • Sherman Silver Purchase Act repealed

1893–97 • Major economic depression hits United States

1894 • Wilson-Gorman Tariff passes
• Coxey's army marches on Washington, D.C.

1895 • Cleveland deal with bankers saves gold reserves

1896 • McKinley elected president
• *Plessy v. Ferguson* establishes separate-but-equal doctrine

1899 • *Cummins v. County Board of Education* applies separate-but-equal doctrine to schools

1900 • Gold Standard Act requires all paper money to be backed by gold
• McKinley reelected president

rights against state and federal regulation. The presidency was occupied by respectable men who prepared the office for its more activist character after the turn of the century. Even so, exclusion—the third phenomenon—prevented the majority of Americans—including women, southern blacks, Indians, uneducated whites, and unnaturalized immigrants—from access to the tools of democracy.

Until the 1890s, special interests, accomplishment, and exclusion existed within a delicate political equilibrium characterized by a stable party system and balance of power among geographical sections. Then in the 1890s, rural discontent rumbled through the West and South, and a deep economic depression bared flaws in the industrial system. The 1896 presidential campaign stirred Americans with near-religious fervor. A new party arose, old parties split, sectional unity dissolved, and fundamental disputes about the nation's future climaxed. ■

The Nature of Party Politics

*P*ublic interest in elections reached an all-time high between 1870 and 1896, with around 80 percent of eligible voters (white and black males in the North, somewhat lower rates among mostly white males in the South) consistently voting. (Under 50 percent typically do so today.) Politics served as a form of recreation, more popular than baseball, and included parades, picnics, and speeches.

As different groups competed for power and wealth, they formed coalitions. With some exceptions, groups who opposed govern-

CULTURAL-
POLITICAL
ALIGNMENTS

ment interference in personal liberty identified with the Democratic Party; those who believed government could be an agent of moral reform identified with the Republican Party. Democrats included immigrant Catholics and Jews; Republicans consisted mostly of native-born Protestants. Democrats would restrict government power. Republicans believed in direct government action.

Adherents battled over how much government should control people's lives. The most contentious issues were use of leisure time and celebration of Sunday, the Lord's day. Protestant Republicans wanted to keep the Sabbath holy through legislation that would close bars, stores, and commercial amusements on Sundays. Immigrant Democrats, accustomed to feasting after church, fought saloon closings and other restrictions.

Allegiances to national parties and candidates were so evenly divided that no faction gained control for very long. Between 1877 and 1897, Republicans held the presidency for three terms, Democrats for two. Rarely did one party control the presidency and Congress simultaneously. From 1876 through 1892, presidential elections were extremely close. The outcome often hinged on the popular vote in a few populous northern states—Connecticut, New York, New Jersey, Ohio, Indiana, and Illinois.

Internal quarrels split both the Republican and Democratic parties. Among Republicans, New York's

PARTY FACTIONS

pompous senator Roscoe Conkling led one faction, known as "Stalwarts," and worked the spoils system to win government jobs for his supporters. The Stalwarts' rivals were the "Half

Breeds," led by James G. Blaine, who pursued influence as blatantly as Conkling did. On the sidelines stood more idealistic Republicans, or "Mugwumps" (supposedly an Indian term meaning "mug on one side of the fence, wump on the other"). Mugwumps such as Senator Carl Schurz of Missouri believed that only righteous men should govern. Meanwhile, Democrats subdivided into white-supremacy southerners, immigrant-stock and working-class urban political machines, and business-oriented advocates of low tariffs.

In each state, one party usually dominated, and often the state "boss" was a senator who parlayed his state power into national influence. Until the Seventeenth Amendment to the Constitution was ratified in 1913, state legislatures elected U.S. senators, and a senator could wield enormous influence with his command of federal jobs, and many brazenly did so.

Issues of Legislation

*W*ell into the 1880s, bitter hostilities from the Civil War and Reconstruction continued to divide Americans. Republicans capitalized on war memories by "waving the bloody shirt." As one Republican orator harangued in 1876, "Every man that tried to destroy this nation was a Democrat. . . . Soldiers, every scar you have on your heroic bodies was given you by a Democrat." In the South, Democratic candidates also waved the bloody shirt, calling Republicans traitors to white supremacy and states' rights.

The Grand Army of the Republic, an organization of 400,000 Union Army veterans, allied with the Republican Party and cajoled Congress into generous pensions for former Union soldiers and their widows. The Union Army spent $2 billion to fight the Civil War; veterans' pensions ultimately cost $8 billion, one of the largest welfare commitments the federal government has ever made. By 1900 soldiers' pensions accounted for roughly 40 percent of the federal budget. Confederate veterans received none of this money, though some southern states funded small pensions and built old-age homes for ex-soldiers.

The practice of awarding government jobs to party workers regardless of their qualifications, known

CIVIL SERVICE
REFORM

as the spoils system, predated the Civil War and flourished afterward. As the postal service and other

During the Gilded Age, American Christians contributed more money toward missionary work than toward other popular political and social causes. First intended to teach native peoples about the Bible, missionary projects focused increased attention overseas as the nineteenth century progressed, sending funds and volunteers to every part of the globe, including the Middle East, Africa, and China. Expanding beyond pure preaching, mission organizations sponsored construction of schools and hospitals and taught secular subjects as well as biblical learning.

American missionaries altered the educational climate in several countries. In Syria, they opened the American University of Beirut (first called the Syrian Protestant College), and the school soon developed departments of medicine, pharmacy, and commerce. Its nursing program was one of the few places where Middle Eastern women could receive technical training. Missionaries' efforts in the Middle East also increased interest in Arabic literature. Their use of Arabic printing presses to translate the Bible advanced the mass production of books for Middle Easterners.

In Africa, almost all leaders of the earliest independent African states had been educated in schools founded and taught by European and American missionaries, many of whom were African American. Protestant denominations believed that African American missionaries would be more effective than white missionaries in Africa.

By 1890, there were one hundred missionary physicians in China, who brought American medical techniques to 350,000 patients per year. Many other missionaries to China were unmarried American women whose feminist impulses fueled their opposition to practices such as foot binding, which they considered debasing to women.

American foreign missionaries in the late nineteenth century did not come close to realizing their goal of converting the world to Christ. When they tried to impose western customs, they were often rejected and sometimes persecuted. Yet they established churches that lasted for decades and schools that influenced native educational efforts. In the United States, divisions between liberals and fundamentalists in the 1920s destroyed the evangelical unity that previously made large missionary societies possible, and by the 1930s the heyday of American foreign missions was over.

Missionary work enabled American women to undertake humanitarian projects in foreign lands. Using both her gentility and her strength of character, Dr. Kate Woodall, shown in this photo from 1895, carried out her missionary work in China by training female medical students. (ABCFM Picture Collection: Individuals, Woodhull, Kate C., Houghton Library, Harvard College Library)

government agencies expanded, the number of federal jobs tripled, from 53,000 in 1865 to 166,000 in 1891. Elected officials scrambled to control these jobs to benefit themselves and their party. In return for comparatively short hours and high pay, appointees to federal positions pledged votes and a portion of their earnings to their patrons.

Shocked by such corruption, especially after the revelation of scandals in the Grant administration, some reformers began advocating appointments based on merit. Civil service reform accelerated in 1881 with the formation of the National Civil Service Reform League. That year, the assassination of President James Garfield by a distraught job seeker hastened the drive for change. The Pendleton Civil Service Act, which Congress passed in 1882 and President Chester Arthur signed in 1883, created the Civil Service Commission to oversee competitive examinations for government positions. The act gave the commission jurisdiction over only 10 percent of federal jobs, though the president could expand the list. Because the Constitution barred Congress from interfering in state affairs, civil service at the state and local levels developed more haphazardly.

But economic policy furnished the main issue of the Gilded Age. Railroads particularly provoked controversy. In their quest for customers, railroads engaged in rate wars, which hurt profits and angered shippers with inconsistent freight charges. On noncompetitive routes, railroads often boosted charges to compensate for unprofitably low rates on competitive routes. Railroads also played favorites, reducing rates to large shippers and offering free passenger passes to preferred customers and politicians.

Such favoritism stirred farmers, small merchants, and reform politicians to demand rate regulation. By 1880 fourteen states had established commissions to limit freight and storage charges of state-chartered lines. Railroads fought back, arguing that the Constitution guaranteed them freedom to acquire and use property without government restraint. But in 1877, in *Munn v. Illinois*, the Supreme Court upheld state regulation, declaring that grain warehouses owned by railroads acted in the public interest and therefore must submit to regulation for "the common good."

RAILROAD REGULATION

But only the federal government could limit rates involving interstate commerce, as affirmed by the Supreme Court in the *Wabash* case of 1886. In 1887 Congress passed the Interstate Commerce Act. The law prohibited pools, rebates, and long-haul/short-haul rate discrimination, and created the Interstate Commerce Commission (ICC), the nation's first regulatory agency, to investigate railroad rate-making methods and issue cease-and-desist orders against illegal practices. The legislation's weak provisions for enforcement, however, left railroads room for evasion, and federal judges chipped away at ICC powers. In the *Maximum Freight Rate* case (1897), the Supreme Court ruled that the ICC lacked power to set rates, and in the *Alabama Midlands* case (1897), it overturned prohibitions against long-haul/short-haul discrimination. Even if weakened, regulation remained in force.

In 1816 Congress initially created a tariff, which levied duties (taxes) on imported goods, to protect American products from European competition. But tariffs quickly became a tool by which special interests could enhance their profits. By the 1880s, these interests had succeeded in obtaining tariffs on more than four thousand items. A few economists and farmers argued for free trade, but most politicians still insisted that tariffs were necessary to support industry and preserve jobs.

TARIFF POLICY

The Republican Party put protective tariffs at the core of its agenda. Democrats complained that tariffs made prices artificially high by keeping out less expensive foreign goods, thereby benefiting domestic manufacturers while hurting farmers whose crops were not protected and consumers.

During the Gilded Age, revenues from tariffs and other levies created a surplus in the federal budget. Most Republicans, being businessmen, liked the idea that the government was earning more than it spent and hoped to keep the extra money as a Treasury reserve or for projects that would aid commerce. Democrats acknowledged a need for protection of some manufactured goods and raw materials, but they favored lower tariff duties to encourage foreign trade and reduce the Treasury surplus.

Manufacturers and their congressional allies firmly controlled tariff policy. The McKinley Tariff of 1890 boosted already-high rates by another 4 percent. When House Democrats passed a bill to trim tariffs in 1894, Senate Republicans added six hundred amendments restoring most cuts (Wilson-Gorman

Tariff). In 1897 the Dingley Tariff raised rates further. Attacks on duties made tariffs a symbol of privileged business in the public mind.

MONETARY
POLICY

Monetary policy inflamed stronger emotions than tariffs. When increased industrial and agricultural production caused prices to fall after the Civil War, debtors and creditors had opposing reactions. Farmers suffered because their incomes dropped. And because high demand for a relatively limited amount of available money raised interest rates on loans, it was costly for them to borrow to pay off mortgages and other debts. They favored the coinage of silver to increase the amount of currency in circulation, which would reduce interest rates. Small businessmen agreed. Large businesses and bankers favored a stable, limited money supply backed only by gold, fearing that anything else would fluctuate and threaten investors' confidence in the U.S. economy.

Creditor-debtor tension translated into class divisions between haves and have-nots. The debate also reflected sectional cleavages: western silver-mining areas and agricultural regions of the South and West against the industrial Northeast.

By the 1870s, the currency controversy boiled down to gold versus silver. Previously, the government had bought gold and silver to back the national currency at a ratio that made a gold dollar worth sixteen times more than a silver dollar. The gold rush of 1848, however, increased the gold supply and lowered its market price relative to that of silver. Consequently, silver dollars disappeared as owners hoarded them. In 1873 Congress officially stopped coining them. The United States and many of its trading partners unofficially adopted the gold standard, meaning that their currency was backed chiefly by gold.

But within a few years, new mines in the American West began to flood the market with silver, and its price dropped. Because gold now was relatively less plentiful, it became worth more than sixteen times silver (the ratio reached twenty to one by 1890). Silver producers now wanted the government to resume buying silver at the old sixteen-to-one ratio.

Congress tried to compromise. The Bland-Allison Act (1878) authorized the Treasury to buy between $2 million and $4 million worth of silver monthly, and the Sherman Silver Purchase Act (1890) increased the government's silver purchase by specifying weight (4.5 million ounces) rather than dollars. Neither group was satisfied, however. Creditors wanted the government to stop buying silver, while debtors felt the legislation failed to expand the money supply satisfactorily. The issue would intensify during the 1896 presidential election.

LEGISLATIVE
ACCOMPLISHMENTS

In the Gilded Age, senators and representatives earned small salaries yet had to maintain residences in their home district and in Washington. They had no private offices, worked long hours, wrote their own speeches, and paid for staff out of their own pockets.

■ Taking advantage of the new fad of bicycling (see Chapter 19), a cartoonist in an 1886 issue of the humor magazine *Puck* illustrates the controversy over silver coinage. Depicting two uncoordinated wheels, one a silver coin and the other a gold coin, the illustration conveys the message of how hard it was to proceed with conflicting kinds of currency. (Private Collection)

The Presidency Restrengthened

*O*perating under the cloud of Andrew Johnson's impeachment, Grant's scandals, and doubts about the legitimacy of the 1876 election (see Chapter 16), American presidents between 1877 and 1900 moved to restore authority to their office. Proper and honest, Presidents Rutherford Hayes (1877–1881), James Garfield (1881), Chester Arthur (1881–1885), Grover Cleveland (1885–1889 and 1893–1897), Benjamin Harrison (1889–1893), and William McKinley (1897–1901) tried to act as legislative as well as administrative leaders. Each president initiated legislation and used the veto to guide national policy.

Rutherford B. Hayes had been a Union general and an Ohio congressman and governor before his

HAYES,
GARFIELD,
AND ARTHUR

disputed election to the presidency, which prompted opponents to label him "Rutherfraud." Hayes saw himself as reformer and conciliator, emphasizing national harmony over sectional rivalry. He tried to overhaul the spoils system by appointing civil service reformer Carl Schurz and battling New York's patronage king, Senator Conkling.

When Hayes declined to run for reelection in 1880, Republicans nominated another Ohio congressman and Civil War hero, James A. Garfield, who won by just 40,000 votes out of 9 million cast. By winning the pivotal states of New York and Indiana, however, Garfield carried the electoral college by 214 to 155. Garfield hoped to reduce the tariff, develop economic relations with Latin America, and fight patronage. But his chance to make lasting contributions ended in July 1881 when Charles Guiteau shot him in a Washington railroad station. Garfield lingered for seventy-nine days before dying.

Garfield's successor was Vice President Chester A. Arthur, a New York spoilsman whom Hayes had fired in 1878. Arthur became a temperate executive. He signed the Pendleton Civil Service Act, urged Congress to modify outdated tariff rates, and supported federal regulation of railroads. But congressional partisans frustrated his plans for reducing the tariff and strengthening the navy. Arthur lost the 1884 presidential nomination to James G. Blaine at the Republican National Convention.

Democrats nominated New York governor Grover Cleveland, a bachelor who had tainted his reputation when he admitted to fathering an illegitimate son. On election day Cleveland won by only 29,000 popular votes; his tiny margin of 1,149 votes in New York secured that state's 36 electoral votes, enough for a 219-to-182 victory in the electoral college. Cleveland may have won New York due to remarks by a Protestant minister, who equated Democrats with "rum, Romanism, and rebellion." Democrats eagerly publicized the slur among New York's large Irish Catholic population, urging voters to protest by supporting Cleveland.

Cleveland, the first Democratic president since James Buchanan (1857–1861), expanded civil service,

CLEVELAND
AND HARRISON

vetoed hundreds of private pension bills, and urged Congress to cut tariff duties. When advisers worried about his chances for reelection, the president retorted, "What is the use of being elected or reelected, unless you stand for something?" But when Democrats renominated Cleveland for the presidency in 1888, businessmen in the party convinced him to moderate his attacks on tariffs.

Republicans in 1888 nominated Benjamin Harrison, former senator from Indiana and grandson of President William Henry Harrison (1841). Bribery and multiple voting helped Harrison win Indiana by 2,300 votes and New York by 14,000, ensuring his victory. (Democrats also indulged in such cheating, but Republicans proved more successful at it.) Although Cleveland outpolled Harrison by 90,000 popular votes, Harrison secured 233 electoral votes to Cleveland's 168.

The first president since 1875 whose party had majorities in both houses of Congress, Harrison influenced legislation with threats of vetoes, informal dinners, and consultations with politicians. The Congress of 1889–1891 passed 517 bills, 200 more than the average passed by Congresses between 1875 and 1889. Harrison appointed reformer Theodore Roosevelt as civil service commissioner. But under pressure from special interests, he signed the Dependents' Pension Act, which doubled the number of welfare recipients from 490,000 to 966,000 by providing pensions for disabled Union veterans and aid to their widows and minor children.

The Pension Act and other appropriations in 1890 pushed the federal budget past $1 billion for the first time. Voters reacted by unseating seventy-eight Republicans in the 1890 congressional elections. Seeking to capitalize on voter unrest, Democrats nominated Grover Cleveland to run against Harrison again in 1892. With large contributions from business, Cleveland beat Harrison by 370,000 popular votes (3 percent of the total) and won the electoral vote.

In office again, Cleveland's actions reflected political weakness and the power of business interests. Cleveland campaigned on sweeping tariff reform, but he failed to line up support in the Senate, where protectionists undercut his efforts. And when 120,000 boycotting railroad workers paralyzed commerce in the Pullman strike of 1894, Cleveland bowed to requests from railroad managers to send in troops (see Chapter 18).

Discrimination, Disfranchisement, and Response

Issues of race gave a peculiar quality to politics in the South. There, poor whites feared that newly enfranchised African American men would challenge their political and social superiority (real and imagined). Wealthy white landowners and merchants fanned these fears, using racism to divide whites and blacks from protesting their similar economic subjugation.

Most African Americans lived in the South and worked in agriculture. In 1880, 90 percent of all southern blacks worked in farming or personal and domestic service— just as they had as slaves. Weapons, including a gun commonly known as a "nigger killer," were plentiful, and whites used them. Between 1889 and 1909, over seventeen hundred African Americans were lynched in the South, typically in sparsely populated districts where whites felt threatened by an influx of migrant blacks. Most lynching victims were accused of assault—rarely proved— on a white woman.

VIOLENCE AGAINST AFRICAN AMERICANS

Protests arose on several fronts. In Memphis, for example, Ida B. Wells, a teacher in an African American school, reacted by establishing an antilynching newspaper in 1892, *The Free Speech and Headlight*. She urged local blacks to migrate to the West and fled to England to escape death threats. But she soon returned and wrote *A Red Record* (1895), which tabulated statistics on racial lynchings and served as a foundation for further protest campaigns.

Despite threats and intimidation, blacks formed the backbone of the southern Republican Party and won numerous elective offices, even after Reconstruction. In North Carolina, for example, eleven African Americans served in the state Senate and forty-three in the House between 1877 and 1890. White politicians sought restrictions that would disfranchise blacks, or deprive them of their right to vote. Beginning with Tennessee in 1889 and Arkansas in 1892, southern states levied poll taxes of $1 to $2, prohibitive to most blacks, who were poor and deep in debt. Other schemes disfranchised blacks who could not read.

DISFRANCHISEMENT

The Supreme Court determined in *U.S. v. Reese* (1876) that Congress had no control over local and state elections other than upholding the Fifteenth Amendment, which prohibits states from denying the vote "on account of race, color, or previous condition of servitude." State legislatures found other ways to exclude black voters. For instance, an 1890 state constitutional convention established the "Mississippi Plan," requiring voters to pay a poll tax eight months before each election, to present the tax receipt at election time, and to prove that they could read and interpret the state constitution. Registration officials applied stiffer standards to blacks, even declaring black college graduates ineligible on grounds of illiteracy.

Such restrictions proved highly effective. In South Carolina, for example, 70 percent of eligible blacks voted in the 1880 presidential election; by 1896 the rate had dropped to 11 percent. By the 1900s, African Americans had effectively lost political rights in the South. Disfranchisement also affected poor whites, few of whom could meet poll tax, property, and literacy requirements. Thus, the total number of eligible voters in Mississippi shrank from 257,000 in 1876 to 77,000 in 1892.

Racial discrimination and legal segregation expanded. In a series of cases during the 1870s, the

LEGAL SEGREGATION

Supreme Court opened the door to discrimination by ruling that the Fourteenth Amendment protected citizens' rights only against infringement by state governments but not from individuals or organizations. If blacks wanted legal protection from individual prejudice, the Court said, they must seek it from state laws because under the Tenth Amendment, states retained all powers not specifically assigned to Congress. These rulings climaxed in 1883 when the Court struck down the 1875 Civil Rights Act, which prohibited segregation in public facilities such as streetcars, theaters, and parks.

States, however, still could segregate on a "separate-but-equal" basis, as upheld by the Supreme Court in the famous case of *Plessy v. Ferguson* (1896). This case began in 1892 when the Citizens Committee, an organization of prominent New Orleans African Americans, chose Homer Plessy, a dark-skinned Creole, to stage a sit-in in a whites-only railroad car. The Citizens Committee hoped to challenge the law through Plessy's arrest. But in upholding Plessy's conviction, the Court stated that a state law providing for separate facilities for the two races was not unconstitutional because "a distinction which is founded in the color of the two races, and which must always exist so long as white men are distinguished from the other race by color—has no tendency to destroy the legal equality of the two races." In 1899 the Court legitimated school segregation in *Cummins v. County Board of Education,* until it was overturned by *Brown v. Board of Education* in 1954.

Segregation laws—known as Jim Crow laws—multiplied throughout the South, reminding African Americans of their inferior status. State and local statutes restricted them to the rear of streetcars, separate public drinking fountains and toilets, and separate sections of hospitals and cemeteries. Mobile, Alabama, passed a curfew requiring blacks to be off the streets by 10:00 P.M., and Atlanta mandated separate Bibles for swearing in black witnesses in court.

African American women and men challenged discrimination. Some boycotted racist businesses; others considered moving to Africa. Still

AFRICAN AMERICAN ACTIVISM

others promoted "Negro business enterprise." In 1898 Atlanta University professor John Hope urged blacks to become their own employers and supported Negro Business Men's Leagues. In the optimistic days following Reconstruction, many blacks saw higher education as a means of elevating their status. In all-black teachers' colleges, men and women sought opportunities for themselves and their race.

While disfranchisement pushed African American men out of public life, African American women used traditional roles as mothers, educators, and moral guardians to seek services and reforms. They successfully lobbied southern local and state governments for cleaner city streets, better public health, expanded charity services, and vocational education. Ida B. Wells moved to Chicago and continued her equal rights crusade by founding the Women's Era Club, the first civic organization for African American women. While black and white women sometimes united to improve the general community, white women often joined men in white supremacy campaigns.

In the North, white women sought equality through the vote; their successes, however, were lim-

WOMAN SUFFRAGE

ited. Prior to 1869, each state determined who was qualified to vote. That year, the Fifteenth Amendment forbade states from denying the vote "on account of race, color or previous condition" but omitted any reference to sex. For the next twenty years, two organizations—the National Woman Suffrage Association (NWSA) and the American Woman Suffrage Association (AWSA)—crusaded for female suffrage. The NWSA, led by Elizabeth Cady Stanton and Susan B. Anthony, advocated women's rights in courts and workplaces as well as at the ballot box. The AWSA, led by former abolitionists Lucy Stone and Thomas Wentworth Higginson, focused narrowly on suffrage.

In 1878 Anthony persuaded Senator A. A. Sargent of California to introduce a constitutional amendment stating that the right to vote "shall not be denied or abridged by the United States or by any state on account of sex." A Senate committee killed the bill, but the NWSA had it reintroduced repeatedly over the next eighteen years. On the few occasions it did reach the Senate floor, it was rejected with the claim that suffrage would interfere with women's family obligations.

Meanwhile, the AWSA worked to amend state constitutions. (The groups merged in 1890 to form the National American Woman Suffrage Association.)

■ Livingstone College in North Carolina was one of several institutions of higher learning established by and for African Americans in the late nineteenth century. With a curriculum that emphasized training for educational and religious work in the South and in Africa, these colleges were coeducational, operating on the belief that both men and women could have public roles. (Courtesy of Heritage Hall, Livingstone College, Salisbury, North Carolina)

Between 1870 and 1910, eleven states (mostly in the West) legalized limited woman suffrage. By 1890 nineteen states allowed women to vote on school issues, and three granted suffrage on tax and bond issues. Just as important, these campaigns helped train a corps of female leaders in political organizing and public speaking.

Agrarian Unrest and Populism

*E*conomic inequities sparked a mass movement that would shake American society. The agrarian revolt began in Grange organizations in the early 1870s and accelerated within a decade as Farmers' Alliances formed in Texas and across the Cotton Belt and Great Plains. The movement flourished where tenancy, debt, weather, and insects endangered struggling farmers and inspired visions of a truly cooperative and democratic society.

Southern agriculture did not benefit much from mechanization (see Chapter 17). Tobacco and cotton,

SHARECROPPING AND TENANT FARMING IN THE SOUTH

the principal southern crops, required constant hoeing and weeding by hand. Tobacco could not be harvested all at once because the leaves matured at different rates and stems were too fragile for machines. Thus, after the Civil War, southern landlords employed sharecroppers and tenant farmers to replace slaves.

Sharecropping and tenant farming entangled millions of black and white southerners in a web of debt and humiliation, at whose center stood the crop lien. Most farmers, too poor to have ready cash, borrowed to buy necessities, offering their future crop as collateral. After the crop was harvested and brought to market, the lender claimed the portion of the crop that would satisfy the loan. But often the debt exceeded the crop's value. So the farmer would pay off part of the debt, but borrow more for food and supplies for the coming year, sinking even deeper into debt.

Merchants frequently took advantage by inflating prices and charging interest ranging from 33 to 200 percent. Farmers, having pledged more than their crop's worth against such debts, often fell behind in payments and never recovered.

In the southern backcountry, farmers now devoted all of their land to cotton and had to purchase supplies such as flour, potatoes, and corn that they had grown prior to the Civil War. This shift toward commercial farming came about for two reasons: debts incurred during the war and Reconstruction forced farmers to grow crops that would bring in cash, and railroads enabled them to transport cotton to markets more easily than before. As they grew fewer subsistence crops, backcountry yeomen found themselves frequently at the mercy of merchants.

Online Study Center **Improve Your Grade**
Interactive Map:
  The Expansion of Agriculture, 1860–1900

In the Midwest, as growers cultivated more land, as mechanization boosted productivity, and as foreign competition increased, supplies of agricultural products exceeded worldwide demand, leading to steady price drops for staple crops. A bushel of wheat that sold for $1.45 in 1866 brought only 80 cents in the mid-1880s and 49 cents by the mid-1890s. Meanwhile, transportation and storage fees remained high. In order to buy necessities and pay bills, farmers had to produce more, but the more they produced, the lower crop prices dropped.

HARDSHIP IN THE MIDWEST AND WEST

The West suffered special hardships. In Colorado absentee capitalists seized control of technology as well as access to transportation and water. Charges of monopolistic control by railroads echoed among farmers, miners, and stockmen in Wyoming and Montana. In California, Washington, and Oregon, wheat and fruit growers found their opportunities blocked by railroads' control of transportation and storage rates.

With aid from Oliver H. Kelley, a clerk in the Department of Agriculture, farmers in almost every state during the 1860s and 1870s founded local organizations called Granges. By 1875 the Grange had twenty thousand branches and a mil-

GRANGE MOVEMENT

lion members. Strongest in the Midwest and South, Granges first served a social function, sponsoring meetings and educational events to relieve the loneliness of farm life. Family-oriented, local Granges welcomed women's participation.

As membership flourished, Granges turned to economic and political action. Local branches formed cooperative associations to buy supplies and market crops and livestock. Some Grangers operated farm-implement factories and insurance companies. Most enterprises failed, however, because farmers lacked capital for large-scale buying and because large manufacturers undercut them.

Granges declined in the late 1870s, after convincing states to establish agricultural colleges, electing sympathetic legislators, and securing state laws regulating transportation and storage rates. But corporations won court support to overturn Granger laws in the *Wabash* case of 1886. Disavowing party politics, Granges did not challenge business interests within the two major parties. As a result, Granges again became farmers' social clubs.

In the Southwest, migrations of English-speaking ranchers into Mexican pastureland sparked another agrarian protest. In the late 1880s, a group calling itself Las Gorras Blancas, or White Hats, struggled to control ancestral lands, harassing Anglo ranchers and destroying fences on public land. Their cause, however, could not halt Anglos from legally buying and using public land, and by 1900 many Hispanics had given up farming to work as agricultural laborers or migrate into the cities.

THE WHITE HATS

By 1890, two networks of Farmers' Alliances—one in the Great Plains, one in the South—became the center of rural activism. The first Farmers' Alliances arose in Texas, where hard-pressed small farmers rallied against crop liens, merchants, and railroads. Using traveling lecturers to build membership, the southern Alliance extended into other states and boasted 2 million members by 1889. A separate Colored Farmers' National Alliance claimed 1 million black members. The Plains movement in the late 1880s organized 2 million members in Kansas, Nebraska, and the Dakotas.

FARMERS' ALLIANCES

Farmers' Alliances fostered loyalty through rallies, educational meetings, and cooperative buying and selling agreements, and encouraged women's participation.

They also proposed a subtreasury plan to relieve the most serious rural problems: shortages of cash and credit. The plan first called for the federal government to construct warehouses where farmers could store nonperishable crops while awaiting higher prices; the government would then loan farmers Treasury notes valued at 80 percent of the market price of stored crops. Farmers could use these notes for debts and purchases. Once the crops were sold, farmers would repay the loans plus small interest and storage fees, thereby avoiding the exploitative crop-lien system.

The subtreasury plan's second part would provide low-interest government loans to farmers to buy land.

PROBLEMS IN ACHIEVING ALLIANCE UNITY These loans, along with the Treasury notes for stored crops, would inject cash into the economy and encourage the kind of inflation that advocates hoped would raise crop prices without raising other prices.

If Farmers' Alliances had been able to unite, they could have made a formidable force, but racial and sectional differences and personality clashes thwarted such attempts. Racist voting restrictions weakened potential Alliance voter strength. Also, racism impeded acceptance of blacks by white Alliances. Many poor white farmers came from families that had supported the Ku Klux Klan during Reconstruction. Some had owned slaves, considered African Americans inferior, and took comfort in the belief that there always would be people worse off than they were.

Northern and southern Alliances favored government regulation of transportation and communications, equitable taxation, currency reform, and prohibition of landownership by foreign investors, but regional differences further prevented unity. Northern farmers, mostly Republicans, wanted protective tariffs to keep out foreign grain. White southerners, mostly Democrats, wanted low tariffs to hold down costs of foreign manufactured goods.

Online Study Center **Improve Your Grade**
Primary Source:
Tom Watson Indicts Corporate Plunder

Growing membership drew Alliances into politics. By 1890 farmers had elected several officeholders sympathetic to their cause, especially in the South, where Alliances controlled four governorships, eight state legislatures, and forty-seven seats in

RISE OF POPULISM

Congress (forty-four in the House, three in the Senate). In the Midwest, Alliance candidates often ran on third-party tickets, with some success in Kansas, Nebraska, and the Dakotas. Leaders crisscrossed the country to solidify support for a new party. In summer 1890, the Kansas Alliance held a "convention of the people" and nominated candidates who swept the state's fall elections. Formation of this People's, or Populist, Party gave a title to Alliance political activism. (Populism is the political doctrine that asserts the rights and powers of the common people in their struggle with the privileged elite.) By 1892 southern Alliance members joined northern counterparts in St. Louis in summoning a People's Party convention in Omaha, Nebraska, on July 4 to draft a platform and nominate a presidential candidate.

As its presidential candidate, the party nominated James B. Weaver of Iowa, a former Union general and supporter of an expanded money supply. Charging that inequality (between white classes) threatened to splinter American society, the new party's platform declared, "The fruits of the toil of millions are boldly stolen to build up colossal fortunes for a few." Claiming that "wealth belongs to him that creates it," the document addressed three central sources of rural unrest: transportation, land, and money. Frustrated with weak regulation, Populists demanded government ownership of railroad and telegraph lines. The monetary plank called for the government to make more money available for farm loans and to base money on free and unlimited coinage of silver. Other planks advocated a graduated income tax, postal savings banks, direct election of U.S. senators, and a shorter workday.

The Populist campaign featured dynamic personalities such as Mary Elizabeth Lease and "Sockless Jerry" Simpson, an unschooled but canny rural reformer who got his nickname after he ridiculed wealthy people for their silk stockings, causing a reporter to carp that Simpson probably wore no stockings at all. The South produced leaders such as Texas's Charles W. Macune, Georgia's Tom Watson, and North Carolina's Leonidas Polk. Minnesota's Ignatius Donnelly, pseudoscientist and writer of apocalyptic novels, became chief ideologue of the northern plains and penned the platform's thunderous language.

POPULIST SPOKESPEOPLE

Not since 1856 had a third party done so well in its first national effort. Weaver garnered 8 percent of the popular vote in 1892, majorities in four states, and twenty-two electoral votes. Nevertheless, the party faced a dilemma of whether to stand by its principles or compromise to gain power. Populist candidates were mainly successful in the West. The vote-rich Northeast ignored Weaver, and Alabama was the only southern state that gave Populists as much as one-third of its votes.

Still, Populism gave rural southerners and westerners faith in the future, especially the 1896 presidential election. Amid hardship, millions of people came to believe that a cooperative democracy in which government would ensure equal opportunity could overcome corporate power.

The Depression and Protests of the 1890s

In 1893, shortly before Grover Cleveland's second presidency, the Philadelphia and Reading Railroad, once profitable, went bankrupt. Like other railroads, it had borrowed heavily to lay track and build stations and bridges. Overexpansion cut into profits, and ultimately the company was unable to pay its debts.

Similar problems beset manufacturers. For example, output at McCormick farm machinery factories was nine times greater in 1893 than in 1879, but revenues had only tripled. The company bought more equipment and squeezed more work out of fewer laborers, but it only enlarged debt and unemployment. Jobless workers also could not pay their bills, and banks suffered when customers defaulted. The failure of the National Cordage Company in May 1893 sparked a chain reaction of business and bank closings: five hundred banks and sixteen hundred businesses failed by year's end. Between 1893 and 1897, the nation suffered a devastating economic depression.

Nearly 20 percent of the labor force was jobless during the depression. Falling demand caused prices to drop between 1892 and 1895, but layoffs and wage cuts more than offset declining living costs. Many people could not afford basic necessities. The New York police estimated that twenty thousand homeless and jobless people roamed city streets.

As the depression deepened, the currency dilemma reached a crisis. The Sherman Silver Purchase Act of 1890 had committed the government to use Treasury notes (silver certificates) to buy 4.5 million ounces of silver each month. Recipients could redeem these certificates for gold, at the ratio of one ounce of gold for every sixteen ounces of silver. But a western mining boom increased silver supplies, causing its market value to fall and prompting holders of Sherman silver notes and Civil War greenbacks to exchange their notes for more valuable gold. As a result, the nation's gold reserve dwindled, falling below $100 million in early 1893.

Continuing Currency Problems

If investors believed that the country's gold reserve was disappearing, they would lose confidence in America's economic stability and refrain from investing. British capitalists, for example, owned some $4 billion in American stocks and bonds and were likely to stop investing if dollars were to depreciate. The lower the gold reserve dropped, the more people rushed to redeem their money. Panic spread, causing more bankruptcies and unemployment.

To protect the gold reserves, President Cleveland called a special session of Congress to repeal the Sherman Silver Purchase Act. Repeal passed in late 1893, but the run on gold continued through 1894. In early 1895 reserves fell to $41 million, and Cleveland accepted an offer of 3.5 million ounces of gold for $65 million in federal bonds from a banking syndicate led by financier J. P. Morgan. When the bankers resold the bonds, they made a $2 million profit. Cleveland claimed that he had saved the reserves, but discontented farmers, workers, silver miners, and some of Cleveland's Democratic allies saw only his humiliation at the hands of businessmen.

The deal between Cleveland and Morgan did not end the depression. After improving slightly in 1895, the economy plunged again. Farm income, declining since 1887, continued to slide; factories closed; banks restricted withdrawals. The tight money supply depressed housing construction and dried up jobs. Cities such as Detroit allowed citizens to cultivate "potato patches" on vacant land to alleviate food shortages. Urban police stations filled up nightly with vagrants who had no other place to stay.

In the final years of the century, gold discoveries in Alaska, good harvests, and industrial growth brought relief. But the downturn hastened the crumbling of the old economic system and the emergence of a new one. The American economy had become national rather than sectional. When farmers in the West fell into debt, they affected the economic health of railroads, farm-implement manufacturers, and banks in other regions. Moreover, the corporate consolidation that characterized the new business system was beginning to solidify as the depression hit. When contraction occurred, companies that had expanded too rapidly were dragged down by their reckless debts, and they pulled other industries with them.

CONSEQUENCES OF THE DEPRESSION

A new global marketplace was emerging, forcing American farmers to contend not only with discriminatory transportation rates and falling crop prices at home, but also with Canadian and Russian wheat growers, Argentine cattle ranchers, Indian and Egyptian cotton manufacturers, and Australian wool producers. And the glutted domestic market persuaded American businessmen to seek new markets abroad (discussed in Chapter 22).

The depression exposed fundamental tensions in the industrial system. Technological and organizational changes had been widening the gap between employees and employers for half a century (see Chapter 18). Protests began with the railroad strikes of 1877. The vehemence of those strikes, and their support by working-class people, raised fears that the United States would experience a popular uprising like the one in Paris six years earlier, which had briefly overturned the government and introduced communist principles. The Haymarket riot of 1886, a general strike in New Orleans in 1891, and the prolonged strike at the Carnegie Homestead Steel plant in 1892 heightened anxieties. In 1892 violence erupted at a silver mine in Coeur d'Alene, Idaho, where striking miners, angered by wage cuts and a lockout, seized the mine and battled federal troops.

DEPRESSION-ERA PROTESTS

In 1894 there were over thirteen hundred strikes and countless riots. Contrary to accusations of business leaders, few protesters were anarchists or communists. Instead, they were men and women who believed that in a democracy their voices should be heard.

Small numbers of socialists did participate in these and other confrontations. Furthermore, personal experience convinced many workers who never became socialists to agree with Karl Marx (1818–1883), the German philosopher and father of communism, that whoever controls the means of production determines how well people live. Marx wrote that industrial capitalism generates profits by paying workers less than the value of their labor and that mechanization and mass production alienate workers from their labor. According to Marx, only by abolishing the return on capital—profits—could labor receive its true value, possible only if workers owned the means of production. Marx predicted that workers worldwide would revolt and seize factories, farms, banks, and transportation lines. This revolution would establish a socialist order of justice and equality.

SOCIALISTS

In America, socialism suffered from lack of strong leadership and disagreement over how to achieve Marx's vision. Much of the movement consisted of ideas brought by immigrants—first Germans, later Russian Jews, Italians, Hungarians, and Poles. It splintered into small groups, such as the Socialist Labor Party, which failed to attract the mass of unskilled laborers because it often focused on doctrine while ignoring workers' everyday needs. Social mobility and the philosophy of individualism also undermined socialist aims. Workers hoped to benefit through education, through property acquisition, or by becoming their own boss; thus, most American workers sought individual advancement rather than the betterment of all.

In 1894 an inspiring Socialist leader arose in response to the government's quashing of the Pullman strike and of the newly formed American Railway Union. Eugene V. Debs converted to socialism while serving a six-month prison term for defying an injunction against the strike. Once released, he became the leading spokesman for American socialism, combining visionary Marxism with Jeffersonian and Populist antimonopolism. Debs captivated audiences with indignant attacks on the free-enterprise system. "Many of you think you are competing," he would lecture. "Against whom? Against Rockefeller?

EUGENE V. DEBS

About as I would if I had a wheelbarrow and competed with the Santa Fe [railroad] from here to Kansas City." By 1900 the group soon to be called the Socialist Party of America was uniting around Debs.

In 1894 Debs shared public attention with Jacob S. Coxey, a quiet businessman from Massillon, Ohio.

COXEY'S ARMY   Coxey believed that the government should aid debtors by issuing $500 million of "legal tender" paper money, making low-interest loans to local governments, and using the loaned money to pay the unemployed to build roads and other public works. He planned to publicize his scheme by leading a march from Massillon to Washington, D.C., gathering a "petition in boots" of unemployed workers along the way.

Coxey's army, about 200 strong, left in March 1894. Moving across Ohio into Pennsylvania, the marchers received food and housing in depressed industrial towns and rural villages and added new recruits. A dozen similar marches from places such as Seattle, San Francisco, and Los Angeles also began the trek eastward. Sore feet prompted some to commandeer trains, but most processions were law-abiding.

Coxey's band of 500, including women and children, entered Washington on April 30. The next day (May Day, a date traditionally associated with socialist demonstrations), the group, armed with "war clubs of peace," marched to the Capitol. When Coxey and a few others vaulted the wall surrounding the Capitol grounds, mounted police routed the crowd. Police dragged Coxey away as he tried to speak from the Capitol steps. As arrests and clubbings continued, Coxey's dream demonstration of 400,000 jobless workers dissolved.

Unlike socialists, who wished to replace the capitalist system, Coxey's troops merely wanted more jobs and better living standards. The brutal reactions of officials, however, reveal how threatening dissenters such as Coxey and Debs were to the existing social order.

The Silver Crusade and the Election of 1896

ocial protest and economic depression made the presidential election of 1896 seem pivotal. Debates over money and power were climax-

ing, Democrats and Republicans battled to control Congress and the presidency, and the Populist party stood at the center of the political whirlwind.

As late as 1894, Populist candidates made good showings in western and southern elections, but the

POPULIST PARTY   party was underfinanced and underorganized. It had strong candidates, but not enough of them to effectively challenge the major parties and convince voters to abandon the Republicans or Democrats.

The Populist crusade against "money power" settled on the issue of silver, which many believed would solve the nation's complex ills.

FREE SILVER   To them, free coinage of silver symbolized an end to special privileges for the rich and the return of government to the people by lifting common people out of debt, increasing the cash in circulation, and reducing interest rates.

As the election of 1896 approached, Populists had to decide whether to join with sympathetic factions of the major parties, thus risking a loss of identity, or remain an independent third party. Except in mining areas of the Rocky Mountain states, where free coinage of silver had strong support, Republicans were unlikely allies because their support for the gold standard and big business represented what Populists opposed.

Alliance with northern and western Democrats was more plausible, since there the Democratic Party retained vestiges of antimonopoly ideology and sympathy for a looser currency system despite the influence of "gold Democrats" such as President Cleveland and Senator David Hill of New York. Fusion with southern Democrats seemed less likely, since there the party constituted the very power structure against which farmers had revolted in the late 1880s. Whatever they chose to do, Populists ensured that the election of 1896 would be the most issue oriented since 1860.

Each party was divided. For a year, Ohio industrialist Marcus A. Hanna had been maneuvering to

REPUBLICAN NOMINATION OF McKINLEY   win the Republican nomination for Ohio's governor, William McKinley, and had corralled enough delegates to succeed. The Republicans' only distress occurred when they adopted a moderate platform supporting gold, rejecting a prosilver stance proposed by Colorado senator Henry M. Teller. Teller, who had been among the party's founders forty years earlier, walked out in tears, taking a small group of silver Republicans with him.

At the Democratic convention, prosilver delegates wearing silver badges and waving silver banners paraded through the Chicago Amphitheatre. A *New York World* reporter remarked that "all the silverites need is a Moses." They found one in William Jennings Bryan.

Bryan, age thirty-six, arrived at the Democratic convention as a member of a contested Nebraska

WILLIAM JENNINGS BRYAN

delegation. A former congressman whose support for coinage of silver had annoyed President Cleveland, Bryan found the depression's impact on midwestern farmers distressing. Shortly after the convention seated Bryan, he joined the resolutions committee and helped write a platform calling for free coinage of silver. Bryan addressed the full convention, and his now-famous words ignited the delegates:

> Having behind us the producing masses of this nation and the world, supported by the commercial interests, the laboring interests, and the toilers everywhere, we will answer [the wealthy classes'] demand for a gold standard by saying to them: You shall not press down upon the brow of labor this crown of thorns, you shall not crucify mankind upon a cross of gold.

After that speech, delegates had no trouble supporting Bryan as presidential nominee. In accepting the silverite goals of southerners and westerners and repudiating Cleveland's policies, the Democratic Party became more attractive to discontented farmers. But it too alienated a dissenting minority wing of gold Democrats, who withdrew and nominated their own candidate.

Bryan's nomination presented the Populist party convention with a dilemma. Should Populists join Democrats in support of Bryan, or should they nominate their own candidate? Some reasoned that supporting a different candidate would split the anti-McKinley vote and guarantee a Republican victory. The convention compromised, first naming Tom Watson as its vice-presidential nominee to preserve party identity (Democrats had nominated Maine

shipping magnate Arthur Sewall for vice president) and then nominating Bryan for president.

The campaign, as Kansas journalist William Allen White observed, "took the form of religious frenzy." Bryan preached that "every great economic question is in reality a great moral question." Republicans countered Bryan's attacks on privilege by predicting chaos if he won. Hanna invited thousands of people to McKinley's home in Canton, Ohio, where the candidate plied them with homilies on moderation and prosperity, promising something for everyone. In an appeal to working-class voters, Republicans stressed the new jobs that a protective tariff would create.

The election revealed that the political standoff had finally ended. McKinley, symbol of urban and

ELECTION RESULTS

corporate ascendancy, beat Bryan by over 600,000 popular votes and won in the electoral college by 271 to 176.

Bryan worked hard to rally the nation, but obsession with silver undermined his effort and prevented Populists from building the urban-rural coalition that would have expanded their political appeal. Urban workers, who might have benefited from Populist goals, shied away from the silver issue out of fear that free coinage would shrink the value of their wages. Labor leaders such as the AFL's Samuel Gompers, though partly sympathetic, would not commit themselves fully because they viewed farmers as businessmen, not workers. And socialists such as Daniel DeLeon denounced Populists as "retrograde" because they believed in free enterprise. Although Populists and fusion candidates won a few state and congressional elections, the Bryan-Watson ticket of the Populist party polled only 222,600 votes nationwide. Thus, the Populist crusade collapsed.

As president, McKinley signed the Gold Standard Act (1900), requiring that all paper money be backed

THE MCKINLEY PRESIDENCY

by gold. A seasoned politician, McKinley had guided passage of record-high tariff rates in 1890 when he was a congressman from Ohio. He accordingly supported the Dingley Tariff of 1897, which raised duties even higher. An upward swing of the business cycle and a money supply enlarged by gold discoveries in Alaska, Australia, and South Africa helped restore prosperity. To sustain prosperity at home, McKinley encouraged imperialistic ventures in Latin America and the Pacific (covered in Chapter 22). Good times and victory in the Spanish-American War enabled him to beat Bryan again in 1900.

Summary ⚙ *Online Study Center* **ACE the Test**

Politicians during the Gilded Age prepared the nation for the twentieth century. Laws encouraging economic growth with some principles of regulation, measures expanding government agencies while reducing crass patronage, federal intervention in trade and currency issues, and a more active presidency all evolved during the 1870s and 1880s.

True to Mary Lease's characterization, the United States remained a "nation of inconsistencies." Those who supported disfranchisement of African Americans and continued discrimination against blacks and women still polluted politics. Nor could the system tolerate radical views such as those expressed by socialists, Coxey, or Populists.

The 1896 election realigned national politics. The Republican Party, founded in the 1850s amid a crusade against slavery, became the majority party by emphasizing government aid to business, attracting urban workers, and playing down its moralism. The Democratic Party miscalculated on the silver issue and held its traditional support only in the South. After 1896, suspicion of party politics increased, and voter participation rates declined.

Populism failed because the political system lacked the ability to accept third parties. The structure of Congress gave the two-party system enormous power, making it difficult for the few Populist representatives to speak, let alone serve on committees and promote reform legislation.

Nevertheless, by 1920, many Populist goals were achieved, including regulation of railroads, banks, and utilities; shorter workdays; a variant of the subtreasury plan; a graduated income tax; direct election of senators; and the secret ballot. These reforms succeeded because immigration, urbanization, and industrialization had transformed the United States into a pluralistic society in which compromise had become a political fact of life. As the Gilded Age ended, business was still in the ascendancy, and large segments of the population were still excluded from political and economic opportunity. But the winds of reform had begun to blow more strongly.

LEGACY FOR A PEOPLE AND A NATION
Interpreting a Fairy Tale

The Wizard of Oz, one of the most popular movies of all time, began as a work of juvenile literature by journalist L. Frank Baum in 1900. Originally titled *The Wonderful Wizard of Oz*, the story used memorable characters to create an adventurous quest.

Adults, however, were tempted to search for hidden meanings. In 1964 one scholar, Henry M. Littlefield, asserted that Baum really intended to write a Populist parable about the conditions of overburdened farmers and laborers. Dorothy symbolized the well-intentioned common person; the Scarecrow, the struggling farmer; the Tin Man, the industrial worker. Hoping for a better life, these friends, along with the Cowardly Lion (William Jennings Bryan), followed a yellow brick road (the gold standard) that led nowhere. The Emerald City they find is presided over by a wizard. A typical politician, the wizard tries to be all things to all people, but Dorothy reveals him as a fraud. Dorothy is able to leave this muddled society and return to her simple Kansas farm family of Aunt Em and Uncle Henry by using her magical silver slippers (representing coinage of silver, though the movie made them red).

Subsequent theorists found additional supportive symbols, such as Oz being the abbreviation for ounces (oz.), the chief measurement of gold; the Wicked Witch of the East—who, Baum wrote, made the little people (Munchkins) "slaves for her night and day"—could represent industrial capitalism.

But in 1983, historian William R. Leach asserted that Baum's masterpiece actually was a celebration of urban consumer culture. Its language exalted the opulence of Emerald City, which to Leach resembled the "White City" of the Chicago World's Fair of 1893. Baum's career supported this new interpretation. Before he was a writer, he designed display windows and was involved in theater— activities that gave him an appreciation of modern urban life.

The real legacy of *The Wonderful Wizard of Oz* has been its ability to provoke differing interpretations. Baum's fairy tale, the first real American work of this sort, has bequeathed many fascinating images about the diversity and contradictions of American culture.

*T*HE PROGRESSIVE ERA 1895–1920

a coworker once described Florence Kelley as a "guerrilla warrior" in the "wilderness of industrial wrongs." A commanding woman, Kelley was a leader in guiding the United States out of the tangled swamp of unregulated industrial capitalism into the twentieth-century welfare state.

The daughter of a Republican congressman from Philadelphia, Kelley graduated from Cornell University in 1883. She prepared to study law but was denied admission to the University of Pennsylvania because she was female. Instead, she traveled to Europe and joined a group of socialists in Zurich, who alerted her to the plight of the underprivileged. She married a socialist Russian medical student and returned to New York City in 1886. When the marriage collapsed from debts and physical abuse, Kelley took her three children to Chicago in 1891. She moved into Hull House, a settlement-house residence in the slums where middle-class reformers lived, while assisting and learning from working-class immigrants.

Until the 1890s, Kelley's life had been male oriented, influenced first by her father, then by her husband. At Hull House, Kelley entered a female-dominated environment, where women applied helping skills to better society.

Over the next decade, Kelley became the nation's most ardent advocate of improved conditions for working-class women and children. She investigated and publicized the exploitative sweatshop system in Chicago's garment industry, lobbied for laws prohibiting child labor and regulating women's working hours, and served as Illinois's first factory inspector. Her work helped create new professions for women in social service, and her strategy of investigating and crusading for action became a model for reform.

During the 1890s, economic depression, labor violence, political upheaval, and foreign entanglements shook the nation. By 1900, however, the political tumult had calmed, and economic depression seemed to be over. The nation emerged victorious from a war against Spain (covered in Chapter 22), and a new era of dynamic political leaders such as Theodore Roosevelt and Woodrow Wilson was dawning. A sense of renewal both intensified anxiety

The Varied Progressive Impulse

Governmental and Legislative Reform

LINKS TO THE WORLD
Russian Temperance

New Ideas in Social Institutions

Challenges to Racial and Sexual Discrimination

Theodore Roosevelt and the Revival of the Presidency

Woodrow Wilson and the Extension of Reform

LEGACY FOR A PEOPLE AND A NATION
Margaret Sanger, Planned Parenthood, and the Birth-Control Controversy

Online Study Center
This icon will direct you to interactive map and primary source activities on the website
http://college.hmco.com/pic/nortonbrief7e

CHRONOLOGY

1895 • Booker T. Washington gives Atlanta Compromise speech
• National Association of Colored Women founded

1898 • *Holden v. Hardy* upholds limits on miners' working hours

1900 • McKinley reelected

1901 • McKinley assassinated; T. Roosevelt assumes the presidency

1904 • T. Roosevelt elected president
• *Northern Securities* case dissolves railroad trust

1905 • *Lochner v. New York* removes limits on bakers' working hours

1906 • Hepburn Act tightens ICC control over railroads
• Meat Inspection Act passed
• Pure Food and Drug Act passed

1908 • Taft elected president
• *Muller v. Oregon* upholds limits on women's working hours

1909 • NAACP founded

1910 • Mann-Elkins Act reinforces ICC powers
• White Slave Traffic Act (Mann Act) prohibits transportation of women for "immoral purposes"

1911 • Society of American Indians founded

1912 • Woodrow Wilson elected president

1913 • Sixteenth Amendment ratified, legalizing federal income tax
• Seventeenth Amendment ratified, providing for direct election of U.S. senators
• Underwood Tariff institutes income tax
• Federal Reserve Act establishes central banking system

1914 • Federal Trade Commission created to investigate unfair trade practices
• Clayton Anti-Trust Act outlaws monopolistic business practices

1916 • Wilson reelected
• Adamson Act mandates eight-hour workday for railroad workers

1919 • Eighteenth Amendment ratified, establishing prohibition of alcoholic beverages

1920 • Nineteenth Amendment ratified, giving women the vote in federal elections

over continuing social and political problems and raised hopes that democracy could be reconciled with capitalism.

Between 1895 and 1920, a series of complex reform movements emerged, seeking to restore American society, values, and institutions. By the 1910s reformers were calling themselves "Progressives," and two years later they formed a political party. Historians have used the term *Progressivism* to refer to the

era's spirit while disagreeing over its meaning and over which groups and individuals actually were Progressive.

The reform impulse indeed had many sources. Industrial capitalism had created awesome technology, unprecedented productivity, and vast consumer goods. But it also brought harmful overproduction, domineering monopolies, labor strife, and the spoiling of natural resources. Burgeoning cities facilitated cultural amenities but also bred poverty, disease, and crime. Rising immigration and a new professional class reconfigured the social order. And the depression of the 1890s led many leaders to conclude that the central promise of American life was not being kept; equality of opportunity was a myth.

Progressives organized around three goals. First, they sought to end abuses of power. Progressives made trustbusting, consumers' rights, and good government compelling political issues.

Second, Progressives aimed to supplant corrupt power with humane institutions such as schools and medical clinics. They abandoned notions that hard work and good character guaranteed success and that the poor were responsible for their plight. Instead, Progressives acknowledged that society bore responsibility for improving individual lives, and they believed that government must protect the common good and elevate public interest above self-interest. Their attitude challenged entrenched views on women's roles, race relations, education, legal and scientific thought, and morality.

Third, Progressives wanted to establish bureaus of experts that would end wasteful competition and promote social and economic order. Just as corporations applied scientific method—planning, control, and predictability—to ensure economic efficiency, Progressives advocated expertise and planning to achieve social and political efficiency.

Progressives had faith in the ability of humankind to create a better world. Rising incomes, new educational opportunities, and increased availability of goods and services inspired confidence that social improvement would follow. Judge Ben Lindsey of Denver, who spearheaded juvenile delinquency reform, expressed the Progressive creed when he wrote, "In the end the people are bound to do the right thing, no matter how much they fail at times." ■

The Varied Progressive Impulse

*a*s the twentieth century dawned, party loyalty eroded and voter turnout declined. In northern states, voter participation in presidential elections dropped from Gilded Age levels of 80 percent to less than 60 percent. In southern states, where poll taxes and literacy tests excluded most African Americans and many poor whites from voting, it fell below 30 percent. At the same time, the political system was opening to new interest groups, each championing its own cause.

Many local voluntary organizations became national after 1890 and tried to shape public policy.

NATIONAL ASSOCIATIONS AND FOREIGN INFLUENCES

These organizations included professional associations such as the American Bar Association; women's organizations such as the National American Woman Suffrage Association, issue-oriented groups such as the National Consumers League, civic clubs such as the National Municipal League, and minority associations such as the National Negro Business League. Because they were usually independent from political parties, these groups made politics more fragmented and issue driven than in earlier eras.

American reformers transferred foreign ideas for reorganizing society to America. Some were introduced by Americans such as Florence Kelley who had observed reforms in England, France, and Germany, and others by foreigners traveling in the United States. The settlement-house model was directly copied from England; other reforms, such as old-age insurance, subsidized workers' housing, city planning, and rural reconstruction, were modified to suit America. Although Populist, rural-based goals of moral regeneration, political democracy, and antimonopolism lingered, the Progressive quest for social justice and educational and legal reform had a largely urban bent.

The new middle class—men and women in law, medicine, engineering, settlement house and social work, religion, teaching, and business—formed the vanguard of Progressive reform. Offended by inefficiency and immorality in business and government, these people sought to apply the rationalism of their professions to social problems.

THE NEW MIDDLE CLASS AND MUCKRAKERS

Progressive views were conveyed by journalists whom Theodore Roosevelt dubbed muckrakers (after a character in the Puritan allegory *Pilgrim's Progress* who, rather than looking heavenward at beauty, looked downward and raked the muck to find what was wrong with life). Muckrakers fed public taste for scandal by exposing social, economic, and political wrongs. Investigative articles in popular magazines attacked adulterated foods, fraudulent insurance, prostitution, and political corruption. Lincoln Steffens hoped his exposés of bosses' misrule in *McClure's* (later published as *The Shame of the Cities* in 1904) would inspire mass outrage and reform. Other well-known muckraking works included Upton Sinclair's novel *The Jungle* (1906), highlighting the perils of the meatpacking industry; and Ida M. Tarbell's critical history of Standard Oil (first published in *McClure's*, 1902–1904).

Progressives advocated nominating candidates through direct primaries instead of party caucuses. To make officeholders more responsible, they urged adoption of the initiative permitting voters to propose new laws; the referendum, which enabled voters to accept or reject a law; and the recall, which allowed voters to remove offending officials from office.

The Progressive spirit also attracted some businessmen and wealthy women. Executives like Alexander

UPPER-CLASS REFORMERS

Cassatt of the Pennsylvania Railroad supported some government regulation to protect their interests from more radical reformers. Others, like E. A. Filene, founder of a Boston department store, were humanitarians who worked unselfishly for social justice. Business-dominated organizations like the Municipal Voters League and U.S. Chamber of Commerce thought that running schools, hospitals, and local government like efficient businesses would stabilize society. Elite women led organizations like the Young Women's Christian Association (YWCA), which aided unmarried working women, and they joined middle- and working-class women in many causes of the Woman's Christian Temperance Union (WCTU), the largest women's organization of its time.

Vital elements of what became modern American liberalism derived from working-class urban experiences. By 1900 many urban workers were pressing for "bread-and-butter reforms" such as safe factories,

WORKING-CLASS REFORMERS

shorter workdays, workers' compensation, and better housing. Often these were the same people who supported political bosses, but bossism was not necessarily at odds with humanitarianism. "Big Tim" Sullivan, an influential boss in New York City's Tammany Hall political machine, said he supported shorter workdays for women because "I had seen me sister go out to work when she was only fourteen and . . . we ought to help these gals by giving 'em a law which will prevent 'em from being broken down while they're still young."

After 1900, urban working-class voters elected Progressive legislators trained in machine politics. New York's Alfred E. Smith and Robert F. Wagner, Massachusetts's David I. Walsh, and Illinois's Edward F. Dunne—all from immigrant backgrounds—wanted government to alleviate the hardships of urban-industrial growth. But as protectors of individual liberty, they opposed reforms such as prohibition, Sunday closing laws, civil service, and nonpartisan elections.

Disillusioned immigrant intellectuals, industrial workers, miners, and women's rights activists wanted

SOCIALISTS

a different society altogether and turned to socialism. They wanted the United States to follow the example of Germany, England, and France, where the government sponsored low-cost housing, social insurance and old-age pensions, public ownership of municipal services, and labor reform. Rarely did these reforms gain wide acceptance. Labor unions, for example, opposed social insurance because it would increase taxes.

Most socialists united behind Eugene V. Debs, the American Railway Union organizer who drew nearly 100,000 votes as the Socialist Party's presidential candidate in 1900. A spellbinding spokesman for causes such as peace and antimaterialism, Debs polled over 900,000 votes in 1912 at the pinnacle of his party's career. With rebukes of unfair privilege, socialists won over some Progressives, such as Florence Kelley. But most Progressives had too large a stake in capitalism. Municipal ownership of public utilities represented their limit of drastic change.

Progressive reform in the South similarly focused on railroad and utility regulation, factory safety, and

SOUTHERN PROGRESSIVISM

pure food and drug legislation. The South pioneered some reforms: the direct primary originated in North

■ Though their objectives sometimes differed from those of middle-class
Progressive reformers, socialists also became a more active force in the early
twentieth century. Socialist parades on May Day, such as this one in 1910,
were meant to express the solidarity of all working people.   (Library of Congress)

Carolina; the city commission plan arose in Galveston, Texas; and the city manager plan began in Staunton, Virginia. Progressive governors introduced business regulation that rivaled that of their northern counterparts.

Yet racial discrimination tainted southern Progressivism. The disenfranchisement of black men through poll taxes, literacy requirements, and other means meant that electoral reforms affected only white men with enough cash and education to satisfy voting prerequisites.

Southern women's reform efforts also remained racially distinct. White women crusaded against child labor, founded social service organizations, and challenged unfair wages. African American women, using a guise as homemakers and religious leaders, which was more acceptable to whites than political activism, advocated street cleaning, better education, and health reforms.

It would be a mistake to assume that a Progressive spirit captured all of American society between 1895 and 1920. Defenders **OPPONENTS OF** of free enterprise opposed regulatory **PROGRESSIVISM** measures, believing government programs undermined the individual initiative and competition central to a free-market system. "Old guard" Republicans like Senator Nelson W. Aldrich of Rhode Island and House Speaker Joseph Cannon of Illinois championed the notion that government intervention contradicted the natural law of survival of the fittest.

Moreover, prominent Progressives were not always progressive. Governor Hiram Johnson of California promoted discrimination against Japanese Americans, New Jersey's Woodrow Wilson had no sympathy for African Americans, and northern settlement houses segregated blacks and whites.

Nevertheless, Progressive reformers generally occupied the center of the ideological spectrum, believing on one hand that laissez faire was obsolete and on the other that a radical departure from free enterprise was dangerous. Like Thomas Jefferson, they expressed faith in the conscience and will of the people; like Alexander Hamilton, they desired a strong central government to act in the interest of conscience.

Governmental and Legislative Reform

*T*raditionally, mistrust of tyranny had prompted most Americans to believe that government should interfere in private affairs only in extreme circumstances. In the late 1800s, this viewpoint weakened when economic problems led corporations to pursue government aid for their enterprises. Discontented farmers sought government regulation of railroads and monopolistic businesses. And city dwellers, accustomed to the favors of political machines, expected government to act on their behalf.

Progressive reformers endorsed the principle that government should ensure justice and counteract exploitation. But to use such power

RESTRUCTURING GOVERNMENT

effectively, activists would have to reclaim government from politicians whose greed they believed had soiled the democratic system. Between 1870 and 1900, opponents of urban bosses tried to restructure government through such reforms as civil service, nonpartisan elections, and tight scrutiny of public expenditures. After 1900, reform campaigns installed city-manager and commission forms of government (in which urban officials were chosen for professional expertise rather than political connections) and public ownership of utilities (to prevent gas, electric, and transit companies from profiting at public expense).

Reformers found the city too small an arena, however, and saw greater legislative opportunities in state and federal governments. In the Plains and West, reformers sought railroad regulation and government control of natural resources. In the South, they continued the Populist crusade against big business and autocratic politicians. In the Northeast and Midwest, they attacked corrupt politics and unsafe labor conditions.

Faith in a fair-minded executive prompted Progressives to support a number of skillful governors,

ROBERT M. LA FOLLETTE

particularly Wisconsin's Robert M. La Follette. A small-town lawyer, La Follette rose through the state Republican Party to become governor in 1900. There, he initiated direct primaries, more equitable taxes, and regulation of railroad rates. After three terms, La Follette was elected to the U.S. Senate. "Battling Bob" asserted that his "goal was not to 'smash' corporations, but to drive them out of politics."

Political reformers achieved a major goal in 1913 with the Seventeenth Amendment, which provided for direct election of U.S. senators (they previously had been elected by state legislatures, which Progressives suspected were corrupt). By 1916 all but three states had direct primaries, and many had adopted the initiative, referendum, and recall. But party bosses were still able to control elections. Efforts to use the initiative, referendum, and recall often failed because special-interest groups spent large sums to influence the voting.

Middle- and working-class reformers sometimes united around labor laws. A coalition of the middle

LABOR REFORM

and working classes pushed many states to use their constitutional police power to protect public health and enact factory inspection laws. By 1916 nearly two-thirds of the states required victims' compensation for industrial accidents. Some legislatures even granted aid to mothers with dependent children. Under pressure from the National Child Labor Committee, nearly every state set minimum employment ages (varying from twelve to sixteen) and prohibited employers from making children work more than eight or ten hours a day. Such laws had a limited effect, though, because they seldom provided for the close inspection of factories that enforcement required. And families needing extra income encouraged children to lie about their ages.

Several groups united to achieve restricted working hours for women. After the Supreme Court, in *Muller v. Oregon*, upheld Oregon's ten-hour limit in 1908 (see Chapter 18), more states passed laws protecting female workers. In 1914 the American Association for Old Age Security secured old-age pensions in Arizona. Judges struck down the law, but demand for pensions continued, and in the 1920s many states enacted such laws.

Russian Temperance

When American temperance advocates secured nationwide prohibition with the 1919 constitutional amendment, they were five years behind Russia. Vodka and other spirits had been outlawed there since 1914, when Czar Nicholas II decreed nationwide prohibition, following a twenty-seven-year effort launched when author Leo Tolstoy started a temperance society.

While American reformers feared the moral and economic consequences of drunkenness, some Russians linked alcohol to deficiencies in strength and valor, believing Russia had lost the war with Japan in 1905 because excessive drinking made their soldiers unfit. Both Russians and Americans agreed that alcohol had negative effects on health. Adopting American treatments, Russian doctors opened clinics to help alcoholics overcome their addiction.

In contrast to the United States, where the Woman's Christian Temperance Union spearheaded alcohol reform, Russian women never formed a temperance society. Upper-class Russian women were more interested in obtaining the vote, and working-class women opted for personal persuasion. One group of peasant women installed a lock on the village liquor store door to prevent their husbands from buying vodka. Moreover, all women worried about how a ban on alcohol might undermine Russian hospitality, which required a hostess to serve vodka and wine.

When Bolsheviks seized power in 1917, they extended prohibition. But as in the United States, Russians who wanted to drink found substitutes, some of them dangerous, such as wood alcohol or varnish. Eventually the Bolshevik regime abandoned prohibition just as Americans would, because they needed the tax revenues from alcoholic beverage sales.

In 1925 Russia restored the state vodka monopoly, which guaranteed the government a steady flow of income. Alcohol abuse increased, as did alcohol-related diseases such as liver cancer and fetal alcohol syndrome, problems that remain today. On a lesser scale, similar difficulties resulted after Americans ended prohibition with the Twenty-first Amendment in 1933. The dilemma of excessive drinking and alcoholism linked the United States to Russia, but both discovered that prohibition would not fight alcohol's resulting problems.

Like Americans, other people—in this instance, Ukrainians—used posters as propaganda for a cause. Here, the temperance movement in the Ukraine in the early twentieth century depicted a dissolute alcoholic with bottle in hand, and the text links his drinking with the work of the Devil. (© Rykoff Collection/CORBIS)

Reformers did not always agree about whether states should regulate drinking and sexual behavior. The Anti-Saloon League, formed in 1893, allied with the Woman's Christian Temperance Union (founded in 1874) to publicize alcoholism's role in health problems like liver disease. Reformers successfully shifted temperance from individual responsibility to the alleged link between drinking and accidents, poverty, and reduced productivity.

TEMPERANCE AND PROHIBITION

The war on saloons prompted many areas to restrict liquor consumption. By 1900 almost one-fourth of the nation's population lived in "dry" communities, prohibiting liquor sales. But alcohol consumption, especially beer, increased after 1900, convincing prohibitionists that a nationwide ban was the best solution. In 1918 Congress passed the Eighteenth Amendment (ratified in 1919 and implemented in 1920), outlawing the manufacture, sale, and transportation of intoxicating liquors. Although not all prohibitionists were Progressives and vice versa, the Eighteenth Amendment embodied the Progressive strategy of using legislation to protect the family and workplace.

Moral outrage erupted when muckraking journalists charged that international gangs were kidnapping young women and forcing them into prostitution, a practice called "white slavery." More imagined than real, these charges alarmed moralists, who falsely perceived a link between immigration and prostitution. Reformers prodded governments to investigate and pass corrective legislation. The Chicago Vice Commission, for example, undertook a "scientific" survey and published its findings as *The Social Evil in Chicago* in 1911. The report concluded that poverty, gullibility, and desperation drove women into prostitution.

PROSTITUTION AND WHITE SLAVERY

Investigations found rising numbers of prostitutes but failed to prove that criminal organizations deliberately lured women into "the trade." Reformers nonetheless believed they could attack prostitution by punishing its promoters. In 1910 Congress passed the White Slave Traffic Act (Mann Act), prohibiting interstate and international transportation of a woman for immoral purposes. By 1915 nearly every state had outlawed brothels and solicitation of sex. Such laws failed to address the more serious problem of sexual violence that women suffered from family, presumed friends, and employers.

New Ideas in Social Institutions

reoccupation with efficiency and scientific management infiltrated education, law, religion, and the social sciences. Darwin's theory of evolution had challenged traditional beliefs in a God-created world, immigration had created complex social diversity, and technology had made old habits of production obsolete. Professionals grappled with how to embrace progress yet preserve the best of the past.

As late as 1870, when families needed children to work on farms, Americans attended school only a few months a year for four years on average. By 1900, however, laws required children to attend school to age fourteen. The number of public high schools grew from five hundred in 1870 to ten thousand in 1910. In the late nineteenth century, psychologist G. Stanley Hall and philosopher John Dewey asserted that in modern education, personal development should be the focus of the curriculum.

JOHN DEWEY AND PROGRESSIVE EDUCATION

Progressive education, based on Dewey's *The School and Society* (1899) and *Democracy and Education* (1916), stressed that learning should involve real-life problems and that children should be taught to use ingenuity to control their environments. Dewey and his wife, Alice, practiced these ideas in their Laboratory School at the University of Chicago.

Making curriculum practical similarly drove higher-education reform. Previously American colleges had resembled their European counterparts in training a select few for careers in law, medicine, and religion. But in the late 1800s, institutions of higher learning multiplied, aided by land grants. Between 1870 and 1910, the number of colleges and universities in the United States grew from 563 to nearly 1,000. Educators sought to make learning more appealing and to keep up with technological and social changes. Harvard University, under President Charles W. Eliot, pioneered new teaching methods and substituted electives for required courses. Many schools, private

GROWTH OF COLLEGES AND UNIVERSITIES

and public, considered athletics vital to a student's growth, and intercollegiate sports became a permanent fixture.

Southern states set up segregated land-grant colleges for blacks and whites. Although African Americans continued to suffer from inferior educational opportunities, they found intellectual stimulation in all-black colleges and used their education to help uplift their race.

Between 1890 and 1910, the number of women in colleges swelled from 56,000 to 140,000. Of these, 106,000 attended coeducational institutions (mostly state universities); the rest enrolled in women's colleges. By 1920, 283,000 women attended college, accounting for 47 percent of total enrollment. But discrimination lingered. Women were encouraged (and usually sought) to take home economics and education courses, and most medical schools and many private institutions refused to admit them. Instead they attended separate schools, most of which were founded in the late nineteenth century—such as Women's Medical College of Philadelphia and Smith College.

By 1920, 78 percent of children ages five to seventeen were enrolled in public schools; another 8 percent attended private and parochial schools. There were 600,000 college and graduate students in 1920 versus 52,000 in 1870. Yet critical analysis seldom tested the faith that schools could promote equality and justice as well as personal growth and responsible citizenship.

Oliver Wendell Holmes Jr., associate justice of the Supreme Court between 1902 and 1932, led the attack on the traditional view of law as universal and unchanging, arguing instead that law should reflect society's needs. Louis D. Brandeis, a lawyer who later joined Holmes on the Supreme Court, insisted that judges' opinions be based on scientifically gathered information about social realities. Using this Progressive approach, Brandeis collected extensive data on the harmful effects of long working hours to convince the Supreme Court, in *Muller v. Oregon* (1908), to uphold Oregon's ten-hour limit on women's workday.

PROGRESSIVE LEGAL THOUGHT

Judges raised on laissez-faire economics and strict interpretation of the Constitution overturned laws Progressives thought necessary for reform. In 1905 the Supreme Court, in *Lochner v. New York*, revoked a New York law limiting bakers' working hours. The Court's majority argued that the Fourteenth Amendment protected an individual's right to make contracts without government interference.

Several decisions beginning with *Holden v. Hardy* (1898), in which the Supreme Court sustained a Utah law regulating miners' hours, confirmed the use of state police power to protect health, safety, and morals. Judges also affirmed federal police power and Congress's authority over interstate commerce by upholding federal legislation such as the 1906 Pure Food and Drug Act, the Meat Inspection Law, and the Mann Act.

But even if one agreed that laws should address society's needs, whose needs should prevail in a diverse nation? In many localities, a native-born Protestant majority imposed Bible reading in public schools (offending Catholics and Jews), required businesses to close on Sundays, limited women's rights, restricted religious practices of Mormons and other groups, prohibited interracial marriage, and enforced racial segregation. Justice Holmes asserted that laws should be made for "people of fundamentally differing views," but were such laws possible?

Social science—the study of society and its institutions—underwent changes of its own. Young economics scholars used statistics to argue that laws governing economic relationships were not timeless but should reflect prevailing social conditions. A new breed of sociologists led by Lester Ward, Albion Small, and Edward A. Ross agreed, adding that citizens should work to cure social ills rather than wait for problems to solve themselves.

SOCIAL SCIENCE

Meanwhile, Progressive historians Frederick Jackson Turner, Charles A. Beard, and Vernon L. Parrington examined the past to explain present American society. Beard, like other Progressives, believed that the Constitution was a flexible document. His influential *Economic Interpretation of the Constitution* (1913) argued that merchants and lawyers created the Constitution to defend private property. If the Constitution had served special interests in one age, it could be changed to serve broader interests in another age.

In public health, organizations such as the National Consumers League (NCL) joined physicians and social scientists to secure far-reaching Progressive reforms. Founded by Florence Kelley in 1899, NCL activities included woman suffrage, protection of female and child laborers, and elimination of health hazards. Local branches united with women's clubs to advance consumer protection measures such as the licensing of food vendors and inspection of dairies and urged city governments to provide medical care to the poor.

Much of Progressive reform rested on religious underpinnings. A movement known as the Social Gospel, led by Protestant ministers Walter Rauschenbusch, Washington Gladden, and Charles Sheldon, would counter the brutality of competitive capitalism by interjecting Christian churches into worldly matters such as arbitrating industrial harmony and improving the environment of the poor. Believing that service provided individual salvation and God's kingdom on earth, Social Gospelers actively participated in social reform.

THE SOCIAL GOSPEL

The Social Gospel served as a response to Social Darwinism, the application of biological natural selection and survival of the fittest to human interactions. But another movement, eugenics, sought to apply Darwinian principles to society scientifically. The brainchild of Francis Galton, an English statistician and cousin of Charles Darwin, eugenics rested on the belief that human character could be inherited, including bad traits such as criminality, insanity, and what some people called feeblemindedness. Eugenicists believed society had an obligation to prevent the reproduction of the mentally defective, the criminally inclined, and the generally inferior. Inevitably such ideas targeted immigrants and people of color.

EUGENICS

Eugenicists advocated two basic means to prevent the proliferation of people who might threaten American progress: sterilization and immigration restrictions. In 1907 Indiana enacted the country's first statute permitting involuntary sterilization of "confirmed criminals, idiots, imbeciles, and rapists." By 1915 thirteen states had such laws, and by 1930 the number reached thirty. Meanwhile, Madison Grant's *The Passing of the Great Race* (1916) strongly bolstered theories that immigrants from southern and eastern Europe threatened to weaken American society because they were inferior mentally and morally

to earlier Nordic immigrants. Thus, many people, including some Progressives, wanted new laws to curtail the influx of Poles, Italians, Jews, and other eastern and southern Europeans, as well as Asians. In the 1920s restrictive legislation did just that.

Challenges to Racial and Sexual Discrimination

*T*he white male reformers of the Progressive era dealt primarily with politics and institutions, and ignored issues directly affecting former slaves, nonwhite immigrants, American Indians, and women. Yet activists within these groups made strides toward their own advancement. Their efforts, however, posed a dilemma. Should women and nonwhites seek to be on a par with white men, or was there something unique about racial and sexual cultures that they should preserve at the risk of broader gains?

In 1900 nine-tenths of African Americans lived in the South, where repressive Jim Crow laws had multiplied in the 1880s and 1890s. In 1910 only 8,000 out of 970,000 high-school-age blacks in the South were enrolled in high schools. Denied voting rights and officially segregated, blacks met with relentless intimidation and violence, including lynching.

CONTINUED DISCRIMINATION FOR AFRICAN AMERICANS

Many African Americans moved north in the 1880s, accelerating their migration after 1900. Although conditions were better, job discrimination, inferior schools, and segregated housing prevailed in the North too. White authorities confined blacks to separate and inferior schools, hospitals, and other institutions. And most whites still believed that blacks were inferior and incapable of citizenship.

African American leaders differed sharply over how—and whether—to pursue assimilation. In the wake of emancipation, ex-slave Frederick Douglass urged "ultimate assimilation through self-assertion." Others supported emigration to Africa or the establishment of all-black communities in Oklahoma Territory and Kansas. Others, as bitter as white racists, advocated militancy, believing, as one writer stated, "Our people must die to be saved."

■ Booker T. Washington's Tuskegee Institute helped train young African Americans in useful crafts such as shoemaking and shoe repair, as illustrated here. At the same time, Washington's intentions and the Tuskegee curriculum reinforced what many whites wanted to believe: that blacks were unfit for anything except manual labor. (Tuskegee University Library)

Most blacks could neither escape nor conquer white society. Self-help, a strategy articulated by educator Booker T. Washington, offered one popular alternative. Born into slavery in backcountry Virginia in 1856, Washington obtained an education and in 1881 founded Tuskegee Institute in Alabama, an all-black vocational school. There he developed a philosophy that blacks' best hopes lay in at least temporarily accommodating to whites. Washington counseled African Americans to work hard, acquire property, and prove they were worthy of respect. "Dignify and glorify common labor," he urged in a speech at the Atlanta

BOOKER T. WASHINGTON AND SELF-HELP

Exposition in 1895, which became known as the Atlanta Compromise. Washington observed that "in all things that are purely social we can be as separate as the fingers, yet one as the hand in all matters essential to mutual progress."

Because he said what they wanted to hear, white businesspeople, reformers, and politicians welcomed Washington as representative of all African Americans. Washington never argued that blacks were inferior to whites; he asserted that they could enhance their dignity through self-improvement.

Some blacks concluded that Washington favored a degrading second-class citizenship. In 1905 a group of "anti-Bookerites" convened near Niagara Falls and pledged militant pursuit of unrestricted voting, economic opportunity, integration, and equality before the law. Representing the Niagara movement was W. E. B. Du Bois, an outspoken critic of the Atlanta Compromise.

Online Study Center Improve Your Grade
Primary Source: Atlanta Exposition Address

A New Englander and the first black to receive a Ph.D. degree from Harvard, Du Bois was both a

W. E. B. DU BOIS AND THE "TALENTED TENTH"

Progressive and a member of the black elite. While a faculty member at Atlanta University, Du Bois compiled sociological studies of black urban life and wrote in support of civil rights. He treated Booker T. Washington politely but could not accept white domination.

Du Bois believed that an intellectual vanguard of highly trained blacks, the "Talented Tenth," could use their skill to pursue racial equality. In 1909 he joined with white liberals similarly discontent with Washington's accommodationism to form the National Association for the Advancement of Colored People (NAACP). Du Bois and his allies wanted the organization to end racial discrimination and obtain voting rights through legal redress in the courts. By 1914 the NAACP had fifty branch offices and six thousand members.

African Americans who managed to acquire property and education encountered continued oppression. Woodrow Wilson, a southerner, condoned segregation. During his presidency, southern cabinet members preserved racial separation in restrooms, restaurants, and government office buildings and balked at hiring black workers.

African Americans struggled with questions about their place in white society. Du Bois voiced this dilemma, observing that "one ever feels his twoness— an American, a Negro, two souls, two thoughts, two unreconciled strivings, two warring ideals in one dark body." As he wrote in 1903, a black "would not bleach his Negro soul in a flood of white Americanism, for he knows that Negro blood has a message for the world. He simply wishes to make it possible for a man to be both a Negro and an American."

In 1911 educated middle-class Indians formed their own association, the Society of American Indi-

SOCIETY OF AMERICAN INDIANS

ans (SAI), to work for better education, civil rights, and healthcare. It also sponsored "American Indian Days" to cultivate pride and offset images of savage peoples promulgated in Wild West shows.

The SAI's emphasis on racial pride, however, was squeezed between pressures for assimilation from one side and tribal allegiance on the other. Its small membership did not fully represent the diverse and unconnected Indian nations. Individual hard work was not enough to overcome white prejudice and condescension, and attempts to redress grievances through legal action faltered for lack of funds. Ultimately the SAI had to rely on rhetoric and moral exhortation, which had little effect on poverty-stricken Indians. Torn by internal disputes, the association folded in the early 1920s.

Women's groups shared similar questions about the tactics they should use to achieve equality. Could

"THE WOMAN MOVEMENT"

women achieve equality with men and at the same time change male-dominated society?

The answers that women found involved a subtle but important shift in women's politics. Before 1910, women's rights advocates called themselves "the woman movement." Often middle class, these women sought to move beyond the household into higher education and paid professions in social welfare, and argued that legal and voting rights were indispensable to such moves. They claimed that women's special, even superior, traits as guardians of family and morality would humanize all of society. Settlement-house founder Jane Addams, for example, endorsed woman suffrage by asking, "If women have in any sense been responsible for the gentler side of life which softens and blurs some of its harsher conditions, may not they have a duty to perform in our American cities?"

Originating as middle-class literary and educational organizations, women's clubs began taking

WOMEN'S CLUBS

stands on public affairs in the late nineteenth century. They asserted traditional female responsibilities for home and family as the rationale for reforming society through an enterprise called social housekeeping. These women worked for factory inspection, regulation of children's and women's labor, improved housing and education, and consumer protection.

African American women had their own club movement, including the Colored Women's Federation, which sought to establish a training school for "colored girls." Founded in 1895, the National Association of Colored Women was the nation's first African American social service organization; it concentrated on establishing nurseries, kindergartens, and retirement homes. Black women also developed reform organizations within black Baptist and African Methodist Episcopal churches.

Around 1910 some of those concerned with women's place in society began using the term

FEMINISM

feminism to represent their ideas. Whereas the woman movement spoke of duty and moral purity, feminists emphasized rights and self-development. On one hand, feminists argued that all women should unite in the struggle for rights because of their shared disadvantages as women. On the other hand, feminists insisted that sex typing—treating women differently from men—must end because it resulted in discrimination.

Feminism focused primarily on economic and sexual independence. Charlotte Perkins Gilman, a major figure in the movement, declared in her book *Women and Economics* (1898) that domesticity was obsolete and attacked men's monopoly on economic opportunity. Arguing that paid employees should handle domestic chores, Gilman asserted that modern women must take jobs in industry and the professions to secure independence.

Feminists also supported a single standard of behavior for men and women, and several feminists joined the birth-control movement

MARGARET SANGER'S CRUSADE

led by Margaret Sanger. A former visiting nurse, Sanger helped reverse state and federal "Comstock laws"— named after a nineteenth-century New York moral reformer—that had banned distribution of information about sex and contraception. Despite opposition from those who saw birth control as a threat to family, Sanger formed the American Birth Control League in 1921, successfully enlisting physicians and social workers to convince judges to allow distribution of birth-control information. Most states still prohibited the sale of contraceptives, but Sanger succeeded in initiating public debate.

Online Study Center Improve Your Grade
Interactive Map: Woman Suffrage Before 1920

During the Progressive era, a generation of feminists, represented by Harriot Stanton Blatch, daughter of nineteenth-century suffragist

WOMAN SUFFRAGE

Elizabeth Cady Stanton, carried on women's battle for the vote. Blatch, whose chief goal was improvement of women's working conditions, saw the vote as the means to achieve such improvement. Thus, women would exercise the vote to promote and protect their economic roles.

Nine states, all in the West, allowed women to vote in state and local elections by 1912 (see Map 21.1). Suffragists' tactics ranged from moderate but persistent letter-writing and publications of the National American Woman Suffrage Association, led by Carrie Chapman Catt, to spirited meetings and militant marches of the National Woman's Party, led by Alice Paul. More decisive was women's service during the First World War as factory laborers, medical volunteers, and municipal workers. Legislators, who could no longer deny that women could shoulder public responsibilities, passed the national suffrage amendment (the Nineteenth) in 1920.

The Progressive era helped women clarify issues that concerned them, but major reforms were not achieved until later. Women's clubs, feminists, and suffragists failed to create an interest group united enough to overcome men's political, economic, and social control. As feminist Crystal Eastman observed in the aftermath of suffrage, "Men are saying perhaps, 'Thank God, this everlasting women's fight is over!' But women, if I know them, are saying, 'Now at last we can begin.' . . . Now they can say what they are really after, in common with all the rest of the struggling world, is freedom."

Theodore Roosevelt and the Revival of the Presidency

*T*he Progressive era's reform efforts focused on the federal government as the foremost agent of change. Though the federal government had notable accomplishments during the Gilded Age (see Chapter 20), its role was mainly to support rather than

Map 21.1   Woman Suffrage Before 1920

Before Congress passed and the states ratified the Nineteenth Amendment, woman suffrage already existed, but mainly in the West. Several midwestern states allowed women to vote only in presidential elections, but legislatures in the South and Northeast generally refused such rights until forced to do so by constitutional amendment.

control economic expansion. Then, in September 1901, the assassination of President William McKinley by anarchist Leon Czolgosz vaulted Theodore Roosevelt, the vigorous young vice president, into the White House. As governor of New York, Roosevelt had angered Republican bosses by showing sympathy for regulatory legislation. He would become the nation's most forceful president since Lincoln and would bestow the office with much of its twentieth-century character.

Driven throughout his life by an obsession to overcome the physical limitations of asthma and near-sightedness that plagued his youth, *THEODORE ROOSEVELT* Roosevelt exerted a zest for action and display of courage that contemporaries called "manliness." In his

teens, he became an expert marksman and horseman and later competed on Harvard's boxing and wrestling teams. In the 1880s he lived on a Dakota ranch, roping cattle and brawling with cowboys. Roosevelt had wealth, but he also inherited a sense of civic responsibility that guided him into public service. He served three terms in the New York State Assembly, ran for mayor of New York City in 1886 (finishing third), sat on the federal Civil Service Commission, served as New York City's police commissioner, was assistant secretary of the navy, and earned a reputation as a combative, crafty leader. In 1898 Roosevelt thrust himself into the Spanish-American War by organizing a volunteer cavalry brigade, called the Rough Riders, to fight in Cuba. Although his dramatic act had little impact on the war's outcome, it made him a media hero.

Only forty-two years old when he assumed the presidency in 1901, Roosevelt carried his youthful exuberance into the White House. A Progressive, he concurred with allies that a small, uninvolved government would not suffice in the industrial era. Instead, he believed that economic development necessitated a government powerful enough to guide national affairs broadly. Especially in economic matters, he wanted the government to decide when big business was good and when it was bad.

The federal economic regulation that characterized twentieth-century America began with Roosevelt's

REGULATION OF TRUSTS

presidency. Although labeled a "trustbuster," Roosevelt actually considered business consolidation an efficient means toward material progress. He believed in distinguishing between good and bad trusts and preventing bad ones from manipulating markets. Thus, he instructed the Justice Department to use antitrust laws to prosecute railroad, meatpacking, and oil trusts, which he believed unscrupulously exploited the public. Roosevelt triumphed in 1904 when the Supreme Court ordered the breakup of Northern Securities Company, the huge railroad combination created by J. P. Morgan and his business allies (the *Northern Securities* case). Roosevelt did not attack other trusts, such as U.S. Steel, another of Morgan's creations.

When prosecution of Northern Securities began, Morgan reportedly asked Roosevelt, "If we have done anything wrong, send your man to my man and they can fix it up." The president refused but was more sympathetic to cooperation between business and government than it might seem. He urged the Bureau of Corporations (part of the newly created Department of Labor and Commerce) to assist companies to merge and expand. Through investigation and cooperation, the administration cajoled businesses to regulate themselves.

Roosevelt also supported regulatory legislation. After a year of wrangling, Roosevelt persuaded Congress to pass the Hepburn Act (1906), which gave the Interstate Commerce Commission (ICC) greater authority to set railroad freight and storage rates, though it did allow courts to overturn rate decisions. Progressive senator Robert La Follette complained that Roosevelt had compromised to ensure the bill's

passage. But Roosevelt focused on achievable regulation rather than idealistic objectives.

Roosevelt was also willing to compromise to secure pure food and drug legislation. For decades

PURE FOOD AND DRUG LAWS

reformers had sought government regulation of processed meat and patent medicines. Public outrage flared in 1906 when Upton Sinclair published *The Jungle*, a fictionalized exposé of Chicago meatpacking plants. Sinclair, a socialist who sought to improve working conditions, shocked the public with vivid descriptions:

> There would be meat stored in great piles in rooms; and the water from the leaky roofs would drip over it, and thousands of rats would race about on it. It was too dark in these storage places to see well, but a man could run his hand over these piles of meat and sweep off handfuls of dried dung of rats. These rats were a nuisance, and the packers would put poisoned bread out for them; they would die, and then rats, bread, and meat would go into the hoppers together.

Roosevelt ordered an investigation, and finding Sinclair's descriptions accurate, he supported the Meat Inspection Act (1906). This law required government agents to monitor the quality of processed meat. But as part of a compromise to pass the bill, the government had to finance inspections, and meatpackers could appeal adverse decisions. Nor were companies required to provide date-of-processing information on canned meats. Most large meatpackers benefited because the legislation helped them force out smaller competitors and restored foreign confidence in American meat products.

The Pure Food and Drug Act (1906) also addressed abuses in the patent medicine industry. Makers of tonics and pills had long been making exaggerated claims about their products' effects and liberally using alcohol and narcotics as ingredients. The law required that labels list the ingredients, a goal consistent with Progressive confidence that with the truth, people would make wiser purchases.

In Roosevelt's mind, there were good and bad labor organizations (socialists, for example, were bad), just as there were good and bad business combinations. When the United Mine Workers struck against Pennsylvania coal mine owners in 1902 over an eight-hour workday and higher pay, the president employed investigation and arbitration. Owners refused to recognize the union or arbitrate grievances. As winter approached and fuel shortages loomed, Roosevelt threatened to use federal troops to reopen the mines, thus forcing management to accept arbitration. The arbitration commission supported higher wages and reduced hours and required management to deal with grievance committees, but it did not mandate recognition of the union. The settlement embodied Roosevelt's belief that the president or his representatives should determine which labor demands were legitimate and which were not.

Roosevelt's Progressive impulse for efficiency and love for the outdoors inspired lasting contributions to

CONSERVATION

resource conservation. Government establishment of national parks had begun in the late nineteenth century (see Chapter 17). Roosevelt advanced the movement by favoring conservation over preservation. Thus, he not only exercised presidential power to declare national monuments of natural wonders such as the Grand Canyon in Arizona but also backed a policy of "wise use" of forests, waterways, and other resources. Previously, the government had transferred ownership of natural resources on federal land to the states and private interests, but Roosevelt believed the federal government should retain management over lands in the public domain.

Roosevelt exerted federal authority over resources by protecting waterpower sites from sale to private interests and charging permit fees for those who wanted to produce hydroelectricity. He also supported the Newlands Reclamation Act of 1902, which controlled sale of irrigated federal land in the West. He tripled the number of national forests and supported conservationist Gifford Pinchot in creating the U.S. Forest Service.

As principal advocate of the "wise use" policy, Pinchot promoted scientific management of the nation's

GIFFORD
PINCHOT

woodlands. He obtained Roosevelt's support for transferring management of the national forests from the Interior Department to his bureau in the Agriculture Department. The Forest Service charged fees for grazing livestock within the national forests, supervised bidding for the cutting of timber, and hired university-trained foresters as federal employees.

Pinchot and Roosevelt did not seek to lock up—preserve—resources permanently; rather they wanted to guarantee—conserve—their efficient use and prevent big corporations from demanding more federal land. Many of those involved in natural-resource exploitation welcomed such a policy because it enabled them to minimize overproduction and restrict competition. As a result of new federal policies, the West and its resources fell under the Progressive spell of management.

In 1907 a financial panic caused by reckless speculation forced some New York banks to close to pre-

PANIC OF 1907

vent frightened depositors from withdrawing money. J. P. Morgan helped stem the panic by persuading financiers to stop dumping their stocks. In return for Morgan's aid, Roosevelt approved a deal allowing U.S. Steel to absorb the Tennessee Iron and Coal Company—a deal at odds with Roosevelt's trustbusting aims.

During his last year in office, Roosevelt retreated from the Republican Party's friendliness to big business. He supported stronger business regulation and heavier taxation of the rich. Promising he would not seek reelection, Roosevelt backed Secretary of War William Howard Taft in 1908. Taft handily defeated third-time Democratic nominee William Jennings Bryan by 1.25 million popular votes and a 2-to-1 margin in the electoral college.

Taft faced political problems that Roosevelt had postponed: foremost, excessively high tariffs. Honor-

TAFT
ADMINISTRATION

ing Taft's pledge to cut rates, the House passed a bill providing numerous reductions. Protectionists in the Senate prepared to amend the House bill and revise rates upward. But Senate Progressives organized a stinging attack on the tariff, trapping Taft between reformers who claimed to be preserving Roosevelt's antitrust campaign and protectionists who still dominated the Republican Party. In the end, Senator Aldrich and other protectionists restored many of the cuts, and Taft signed what became known as the Payne-Aldrich Tariff (1909). In the eyes of Progressives, Taft had failed to fill Roosevelt's shoes.

In reality, Taft was as sympathetic to reform as Roosevelt. He prosecuted more trusts than Roosevelt; expanded national forest reserves; signed the Mann-Elkins Act (1910), which bolstered regulatory powers of the ICC; and supported labor reforms such as the eight-hour workday and mine safety legislation. The Sixteenth Amendment, which legalized the federal income tax as a permanent part of federal power, and the Seventeenth Amendment, which provided for direct election of U.S. senators, were initiated during Taft's presidency (and ratified in 1913). Like Roosevelt, Taft compromised with big business, but unlike Roosevelt, he lacked the ability to manipulate the public with spirited rhetoric. Roosevelt had expanded presidential power. Taft, by contrast, believed in the strict restraint of law. He had been a successful lawyer and judge and returned to the bench as chief justice of the United States between 1921 and 1930.

In 1910, when Roosevelt returned from a hunting trip in Africa boasting three thousand animal trophies, he found his party fragmented. While one wing remained loyal to Taft, reformers formed the National Progressive Republican League and rallied behind Robert La Follette for president in 1912, though many hoped Roosevelt would run. Disappointed by Taft, Roosevelt spoke out in favor of "the welfare of the people" and stronger regulation of business. When La Follette became ill early in 1912, Roosevelt, proclaiming himself fit as a "bull moose," sought the Republican presidential nomination.

Split of the Republican Party

Taft's supporters controlled the Republican convention and nominated him for a second term. In protest, Roosevelt's supporters formed a third party—the Progressive, or Bull Moose, Party—and nominated the fifty-three-year-old former president. Democrats took forty-six ballots to select New Jersey's Progressive governor Woodrow Wilson. Socialists, by now a growing party, again nominated Eugene V. Debs.

Central to Roosevelt's campaign was a scheme called the "New Nationalism." Roosevelt foresaw an era of national unity in which government would coordinate and regulate economic activity. He would not destroy big business, but instead would establish regulatory commissions of experts to protect citizens' interests and ensure wise use of economic power.

New Nationalism Versus New Freedom

Dubbing his program the "New Freedom," Wilson argued that concentrated economic power threatened individual liberty and that monopolies should be broken up to ensure a free marketplace. But he would not restore laissez faire. Like Roosevelt, Wilson would enhance government authority to protect and regulate. "Without the watchful . . . resolute interference of the government, there can be no fair play between individuals and such powerful institutions as the trust," he declared. Wilson stopped short, however, of advocating the cooperation between business and government that characterized Roosevelt's New Nationalism.

Roosevelt and Wilson stood closer than their rhetoric implied. Both believed in individual freedom. Both supported equality of opportunity (chiefly for white males), conservation of natural resources, fair wages, and social betterment for all. And both would expand government through strong leadership and bureaucratic reform.

The popular vote was inconclusive. The victorious Wilson won just 42 percent, though he did capture 435 out of 531 electoral votes. Roosevelt received 27 percent of the popular vote and 88 electoral votes; Taft polled 23 percent of the popular vote and 8 electoral votes. Debs won 901,000 votes, 6 percent of the total, but no electoral votes. Three-quarters of the electorate supported alternatives to Taft's view of restrained government.

Woodrow Wilson and the Extension of Reform

*D*espite receiving a minority of the total vote in 1912, Wilson interpreted the election as a mandate to subdue trusts and broaden the government's role in social reform. On inauguration day in 1913, he proclaimed, "The feelings with which we face this new age of right and opportunity sweep across our heartstrings like some air out of God's own presence, where justice and mercy are reconciled and the judge and the brother are one."

Born in Virginia in 1856 and raised in the South, Wilson was the son of a Presbyterian minister. He earned a B.A. degree at Princeton University, studied law at the University of Virginia, received a Ph.D. degree from Johns Hopkins University, and became a professor of his-

Woodrow Wilson

tory, jurisprudence, and political economy. Between 1885 and 1908, he published several respected books on American history and government.

A superb orator, Wilson could inspire loyalty with religious imagery and eloquent expressions of American ideals. In 1902 he became president of Princeton and upset tradition with curricular reforms and battles against aristocratic elements. In 1910 New Jersey's Democrats, eager for respectability, nominated Wilson for governor. Once elected, Wilson repudiated the party bosses and promoted Progressive legislation. A poor administrator, he often lost his temper, but his accomplishments nevertheless won him the Democratic nomination for president in 1912.

As president, Wilson blended New Freedom competition with New Nationalism regulation. His

WILSON'S POLICY ON BUSINESS REGULATION

administration sought to prevent corporate abuses with passage in 1914 of the Clayton Anti-Trust Act and a bill creating the Federal Trade Commission (FTC). The Clayton Act corrected deficiencies of the Sherman Anti-Trust Act of 1890 (see Chapter 18) by outlawing such practices as price discrimination (efforts to destroy competition by lowering prices in some regions but not in others) and interlocking directorates (management of two or more competing companies by the same executives). The FTC could investigate and issue cease-and-desist orders against unfair trade practices.

Wilson expanded banking regulation with the Federal Reserve Act (1913), which established the nation's first central banking system since 1836. The act intended to break the power that banking syndicates held over money supply and credit. It created twelve district banks supervised by the Federal Reserve Board to lend money to member banks at low interest rates called the "discount rate." By adjusting this rate (and thus the amount a bank could afford to borrow), district banks could increase or decrease the amount of money in circulation, enabling the Federal Reserve Board to loosen or tighten credit as needed. Monetary affairs no longer would depend on the gold supply, and interest rates would be fairer.

Wilson attempted to restore competition with the Underwood Tariff, passed in 1913. By the 1910s,

TARIFF AND TAX REFORM

prices for some consumer goods had become unnaturally high because tariffs discouraged the importation of cheaper foreign goods. By reducing or eliminating certain tariff rates, the Underwood Tariff encouraged imports. To replace revenues lost because of tariff reductions, the act levied a graduated income tax on U.S. residents. Incomes under $4,000 were exempt; thus, almost all factory workers and farmers escaped taxation. Individuals and corporations earning between $4,000 and $20,000 had to pay a 1 percent tax; thereafter, rates rose to a maximum of 6 percent on earnings over $500,000.

By 1916, the First World War, raging in Europe since 1914, and that year's upcoming presidential election prompted Wilson to support stronger reforms. He backed the Federal Farm Loan Act, which created twelve federally supported banks (not to be confused with the Federal Reserve banks) that could lend money at moderate interest to farmers who belonged to credit institutions—a watered-down version of the Populists' subtreasury plan proposed a generation earlier.

To forestall railroad strikes, Wilson in 1916 pushed passage of the Adamson Act, which mandated eight-hour workdays and time-and-a-half overtime pay. He pleased Progressives by appointing Louis Brandeis, the "people's advocate," to the Supreme Court, though anti-Semitism almost blocked Senate approval of the Court's first Jewish justice. Wilson also backed laws regulating child labor and providing workers' compensation for federal employees who suffered work-related injuries or illness.

Republicans snubbed Theodore Roosevelt as their candidate in 1916, choosing Charles Evans Hughes,

ELECTION OF 1916

Supreme Court justice and former reform governor of New York. Aware of the First World War's impact on national affairs, Wilson ran on a platform of peace, Progressivism, and preparedness; his slogan was "He Kept Us Out of War." Republicans could not muzzle Roosevelt, whose bellicose speeches suggested that Republicans would drag Americans into war. Wilson received 9.1 million votes to Hughes's 8.5 million and barely won in the electoral college, 277 to 254. The Socialist candidate drew only 600,000 votes, down from 901,000 in 1912, largely because Wilson's reforms had won over some socialists and because the ailing Debs was no longer the party's standard-bearer.

During Wilson's second term, U.S. involvement in the First World War increased government regulation of the economy. Mobilization for war, he came to believe, required coordination of production and cooperation between the public and private sectors. The War Industries Board exemplified this cooperation: private businesses submitted to the board's control on condition that their profit motives would be satisfied. After the war, Wilson's administration dropped these measures, including farm price supports, guarantees of collective bargaining, and high taxes. This retreat from regulation stimulated an era of business ascendancy in the 1920s.

Summary *Online Study Center* ACE the Test

*B*y 1920 a quarter-century of reform had wrought momentous changes. In their efforts to end abuses of power, Progressives established the principle of public intervention to ensure fairness, health, and safety. For every American who suffered some form of poverty or deprivation, three or four enjoyed unprecedented material comforts. Although Progressive values lingered after the First World War, growing affluence and a mass-consumer society refocused people's attention away from reform to materialism.

Multiple and sometimes contradictory goals characterized the Progressive era because there was no single Progressive movement. Programs on the national level ranged from Roosevelt's faith in big government as a coordinator of big business to Wilson's promise to dissolve economic concentrations and legislate open competition. At state and local levels, reformers pursued causes as varied as neighborhood improvement, government reorganization, public ownership of utilities, and better working conditions. New consciousness about identity confronted women and African Americans, and although women made some inroads into public life, both groups still found themselves in confined social positions.

Their remarkable successes aside, the failure of many Progressive initiatives indicates the strength of the opposition, as well as weaknesses within the reform movements. Courts asserted constitutional and liberty-of-contract doctrines in striking down key Progressive legislation, notably the federal law prohibiting child labor. On the federal level, regulatory agencies rarely had enough resources for thorough

investigations and had to depend on information from the very companies they policed. In 1920, as in 1900, government remained under the influence of business.

Yet Progressive era reforms reshaped the national outlook. Trustbusting, however faulty, forced industrialists to become more sensitive to public opinion. Progressive legislation equipped government with tools to protect consumers against price fixing and dangerous products. The income tax, created to redistribute wealth, also became a source of government revenue. Although the questions they raised about American life remained unresolved, Progressives made the nation acutely aware of its principles and promises.

LEGACY FOR A PEOPLE AND A NATION

Margaret Sanger, Planned Parenthood, and the Birth-Control Controversy

Some reforms of the Progressive era illustrate how earnest intentions can become tangled in divisive issues of morality. Such is the legacy of birth-control advocate Margaret Sanger. In 1912 Sanger wrote an advice column on sex education in the *New York Call* titled "What Every Girl Should Know." Censors accused her of writing obscene literature because she discussed venereal disease publicly. She counseled poor women on New York's Lower East Side about how to avoid the pain of frequent childbirth, miscarriage, and bungled abortion. In 1914 Sanger launched *The Woman Rebel*, a radical monthly advocating a woman's right to birth control. Indicted for distributing obscenity through the mails, Sanger fled to England, where she gave speeches promoting birth control.

Back in the United States, Sanger opened the first birth-control clinic in Brooklyn in 1916. She was arrested and jailed, but when a court exempted physicians from a law prohibiting distribution of contraceptive information, she set up a doctor-run clinic in 1923. Staffed by female doctors and social workers, the Birth Control Clinical Research Bureau became a model for other clinics. Sanger organized the American Birth Control League (1921) and tried to win support from medical and social reformers, including the eugenics movement, for legalized birth control. After a falling-out with some of her allies, she resigned from the American Birth Control League in 1928.

The movement continued, however, and in 1938, the American Birth Control League and the Birth Control Clinical Research Bureau merged to form the Birth Control Federation of America, renamed the Planned Parenthood Federation of America (PPFA) in 1942. The organization's name defined its mission to strengthen the family and stabilize society rather than to protect a woman's right to voluntary motherhood. Throughout the 1940s, PPFA emphasized family planning through increased availability of contraceptives. In 1970 it began receiving federal funds.

In the 1960s, feminist agitation for women's rights and rising concerns about overpopulation expanded issues of birth control to include abortion. The intense debate between a woman's "choice" and an unborn child's "right to life" drew PPFA into the fray, especially after 1973, when the Supreme Court validated women's right to abortion in *Roe v. Wade*. PPFA fought legislative and court attempts to make abortions illegal and helped organize a women's march on Washington in 1989. But some Latino and African American groups attacked PPFA's stance, charging that abortion was a kind of eugenics program meant to reduce births among nonwhite races.

Because of PPFA's involvement in abortion politics, several of its clinics have been targets of picketing and even violence by those who believe abortion is immoral. PPFA now operates nearly nine hundred health centers providing medical services and education. But birth control's legacy includes disagreement over whose rights and whose morality should prevail.

THE QUEST FOR EMPIRE 1865–1914

"Foreign devil!" they shouted at Lottie Moon. The Southern Baptist missionary, half a world from home in the 1880s, braced herself against the Chinese "rabble" she came to convert to Christianity. She walked "steadily and persistently" through the hecklers, vowing silently to win their acceptance and their souls.

Born in 1840 in Virginia and educated at what is now Hollins College, Charlotte Diggs Moon volunteered in 1873 for "woman's work" in northern China. There she taught and proselytized, largely among women and children until her death in 1912.

Lottie Moon (Mu Ladi, or 幕拉第) made sometimes dangerous evangelizing trips in the 1870s and 1880s to isolated Chinese hamlets. Curious peasant women pinched her, purring, "How white her hand is!" They questioned: "How old are you?" and "Where do you get money to live on?" Speaking in Chinese, she held high a picture book on Jesus Christ, drawing attention to the "foreign doctrine" that she hoped would displace Confucianism, Buddhism, and Taoism.

In the 1890s a "storm of persecution" against foreigners swept China, and missionaries became targets. One missionary conceded that by "believing Jesus," girls and women alarmed men, who worried that "disobedient wives and daughters" would no longer "worship the idols when told." In the village of Shaling in early 1890, Lottie Moon's Christian converts were beaten. For months in 1900, during the violent Boxer Rebellion, she had to leave China altogether.

Lottie Moon and thousands of other missionaries managed to convert to Christianity only a small minority of the Chinese people. Although she, like other missionaries, probably never shed the Western view that she represented a superior religion and culture, she felt great affection for the Chinese. In letters and articles directed to a U.S. audience, she lobbied to recruit "a band of ardent, enthusiastic, and experienced Christian women," to stir up "a mighty wave of enthusiasm for Woman's Work for Woman."

Imperial Dreams

Ambitions and Strategies

Crises in the 1890s: Hawai'i, Venezuela, and Cuba

The Spanish-American War and the Debate over Empire

Asian Encounters: War in the Philippines, Diplomacy in China

LINKS TO THE WORLD
The U.S. System of Education in the Philippines

TR's World

LEGACY FOR A PEOPLE AND A NATION
The Status of Puerto Rico

Online Study Center
This icon will direct you to interactive map and primary source acivities on the website
http://college.hmco.com/pic/nortonbrief7e

CHRONOLOGY

1861–69 • Seward sets expansionist course

1867 • United States acquires Alaska and Midway

1876 • Pro-U.S. Díaz begins thirty-four-year rule in Mexico

1878 • U.S. gains naval rights in Samoa

1885 • Strong's *Our Country* celebrates Anglo-Saxon destiny of dominance

1887 • U.S. gains naval rights to Pearl Harbor, Hawai'i

1890 • Alfred Thayer Mahan publishes *The Influence of Sea Power upon History*
   • McKinley Tariff hurts Hawaiian sugar exports

1893 • Economic crisis leads to business failures and mass unemployment
   • Pro-U.S. interests stage successful coup against Queen Lili'uokalani of Hawai'i

1895 • Cuban revolution against Spain begins
   • Japan defeats China in war, annexes Korea and Formosa (Taiwan)

1898 • United States formally annexes Hawai'i
   • U.S. battleship *Maine* blows up in Havana harbor
   • United States defeats Spain in Spanish-American War

1899 • Treaty of Paris enlarges U.S. empire
   • United Fruit Company forms and becomes influential in Central America
   • Philippine insurrection breaks out, led by Emilio Aguinaldo

1901 • McKinley assassinated; Theodore Roosevelt becomes president

1903 • Panama grants canal rights to United States
   • Platt Amendment subjugates Cuba

1904 • Roosevelt Corollary declares U.S. a hemispheric "police power"

1905 • Portsmouth Conference ends Russo-Japanese War

1906 • San Francisco School Board segregates Asian schoolchildren
   • U.S. invades Cuba to quell revolt

1907 • "Great White Fleet" makes world tour

1910 • Mexican revolution threatens U.S. interests

1914 • U.S. troops invade Mexico
   • First World War begins
   • Panama Canal opens

Like many other Americans who went overseas in the late nineteenth and early twentieth centuries, Lottie Moon helped spread American culture abroad. Some adopted and others rejected American ways. American participants likewise became transformed. Lottie Moon, for example, strove to understand the Chinese and learn their language. She abandoned derogatory phrases like "heathen Chinese" and assumed Chinese dress. She reminded less sensitive missionaries that the Chinese rightfully took pride in their own ancient history.

Lottie Moon also changed—in her own words—from "a timid self-distrustful girl into a brave self-reliant woman." As she questioned the Chinese confinement of women, most conspicuous in arranged marriages, foot binding, and sexual segregation, she advanced women's rights. She also challenged the male domination of America's religious missions. When the Southern Baptist Foreign Mission Board denied women missionaries the right to vote in meetings, she resigned in protest. The board soon reversed itself.

In later decades, critics labeled missionaries' activities as "cultural imperialism," accusing them of subverting indigenous traditions and sparking cultural clashes. Defenders of missionary work have celebrated their efforts to break down cultural barriers. Either way, Lottie Moon's story illustrates how Americans in the late nineteenth century interacted with the rest of the world, how the categories "domestic" and "foreign" intersected, and how they expanded abroad not only to seek land, trade, investments, and strategic bases but also to promote American culture.

Between the Civil War and the First World War, an expansionist United States joined the great world powers. Before the Civil War, Americans had extended the frontier: they pushed Indians out of the path of white migration, seized California and other areas from Mexico, and acquired southern parts of present-day Arizona and New Mexico from Mexico in the Gadsden Purchase. Americans had also developed international trade and promoted American culture everywhere.

By the 1870s, Europe's powers were carving up Africa and large parts of Asia and Oceania. By 1900 they had conquered over 10 million square miles (one-fifth of the earth's land) and 150 million people. As the century turned, France, Russia, and Germany were spending heavily on modern steel navies, challenging an overextended Great Britain. In Asia, a rapidly modernizing Japan expanded at the expense of both China and Russia.

Engineering advances altered the world's political geography through the Suez Canal (1869), the British Trans-Indian railroad (1870), and the Russian Trans-Siberian Railway (1904), while steamships, machine guns, telegraphs, and malaria drugs facilitated the imperialists' task. Simultaneously, Europe's optimism of the 1850s and 1860s gave way to a pessimistic sense of impending warfare informed by notions of racial conflict and survival of the fittest.

Observant Americans argued that the United States risked being "left behind" if it failed to join the scramble for territory and markets. Republican senator Henry Cabot Lodge of Massachusetts advised that "the United States must not fall out of the line of march," because "civilization and the advancement of the [Anglo-Saxon] race" were at stake. Such thinking enticed Americans to reach beyond the continental United States for more land, markets, cultural influence, and power.

By 1900 the United States had emerged as a great power with particular clout in Latin America, especially as Spain declined and Britain disengaged from the Western Hemisphere. In the Pacific, the new U.S. empire included Hawai'i, American Samoa, and the Philippines. In the decade that followed, President Theodore Roosevelt would seek to consolidate this power.

Most Americans applauded expansionism—the outward movement of goods, ships, dollars, people, and ideas. But many became uneasy when it gave way to imperialism—the imposition of control over other peoples and the undermining of their sovereignty. Abroad, native nationalists, commercial competitors, and other imperial nations tried to block the spread of U.S. influence. ■

Imperial Dreams

*a*t the end of the nineteenth century, Americans shifted from internal emphases on industrialization, railroad construction, and western settlement to foreign policy. Political and business leaders began to advocate a more activist approach to world affairs. The motives of these expansionists were complex, but all emphasized the supposed benefits to the country's domestic health.

The leaders who guided America's expansionism also guided the economic development of the machine age, forged the transcontinental railroad, built America's bustling cities and giant corporations, and shaped a mass culture. They unabashedly believed that the United States was an exceptional nation, different from and superior to others because of its Anglo-

Saxon heritage and its God-favored and prosperous history.

Along with exceptionalism, the American march toward empire embraced nationalism, capitalism, Social Darwinism, and a paternalistic attitude toward foreigners. "They are children and we are men in these deep matters of government," the future president Woodrow Wilson announced in 1898. His words reveal the gender and age bias of American attitudes. Where these attitudes intersected with foreign cultures, the result was often tension and rejection.

Foreign policy is usually dominated by what scholars have labeled the "foreign policy elite"—opinion leaders in politics, journalism, business, agriculture, religion, education, and the military. Better read and better traveled than most other Americans and more politically active in the post–Civil War era, this small group, whom Secretary of State Walter Q. Gresham called "the thoughtful men of the country," believed that U.S. prosperity and security depended on exerting U.S. influence abroad. Increasingly in the late nineteenth century, the expansionist-minded elite urged both formal and informal imperialism. They often met in Washington, D.C., at the homes of the historian Henry Adams and the writer and diplomat John Hay (who became secretary of state in 1898) or at the Metropolitan Club. They talked about building a bigger navy and digging a canal across Panama, Central America, or Mexico; establishing colonies; and selling surpluses abroad. Theodore Roosevelt, appointed assistant secretary of the navy in 1897, was among them; so were Senator Henry Cabot Lodge, who joined the Foreign Relations Committee in 1896, and the corporate lawyer Elihu Root, who later would serve as both secretary of war and secretary of state.

FOREIGN POLICY ELITE

These American leaders believed that selling, buying, and investing in foreign marketplaces were important to the United States. One reason was profits from foreign sales. Another was that foreign markets could offset American economic imbalances, particularly since the nation's farms and factories produced more than Americans could consume, especially during the 1890s depression. By exporting surpluses, foreign commerce might relieve overproduction, unemployment, economic depression, and the social tension that arose from them. Economic ties also enabled Americans to exert political influence abroad and helped spread the American way of life, especially capitalism.

Foreign trade contributed to the United States's tremendous economic growth after the Civil War. Foreign commerce stimulated the building of a larger navy, the professionalization of the foreign service, calls for more colonies, and a more interventionist foreign policy. In 1865 U.S. exports totaled $234 million; by 1900 they topped $1.5 billion (see Figure 22.1). By 1914, exports had reached $2.5 billion. In 1874 the United States reversed its historically unfavorable balance of trade (importing more than it exported) and began to enjoy a long-term favorable balance. Most of America's products went to Britain, continental Europe, and Canada, but increasing amounts flowed to new markets in Latin America and Asia. And direct American investments abroad reached $3.5 billion by 1914, placing the United States among the top four investor countries.

FOREIGN TRADE EXPANSION

Agricultural goods accounted for about three-fourths of total exports in 1870 and about two-thirds in 1900, with grain, cotton, meat, and dairy products topping the list. Farmers' livelihoods thus became tied to world-market conditions and foreign wars. Wisconsin cheesemakers shipped to Britain; the Swift and Armour meat companies exported refrigerated beef to Europe.

In 1913 manufactured goods led U.S. exports for the first time (see Figure 22.1). America's steel, copper, and petroleum were sold abroad, making many workers in those industries dependent on American exports.

In expanding U.S. influence overseas, officials championed sometimes racist notions of American supremacy. For decades, the Western scientific establishment had classified humankind by race, and students of physical anthropology drew on phrenology and physiognomy—the measurement of skull size and the comparison of facial features—to produce a hierarchy of superior and inferior races. One prominent French researcher claimed that blacks represented a "female race" and "like the woman, the black is deprived of political and scientific intelligence. . . . But on the other hand he has great virtues of sentiment. Like women he also likes jewelry, dancing, and singing."

RACE THINKING AND THE MALE ETHOS

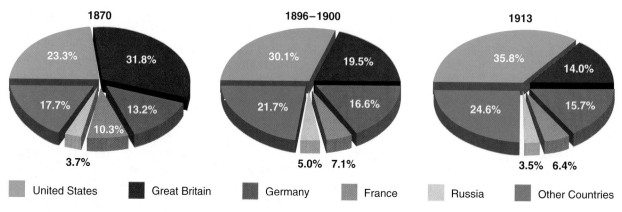

Figure 22.1   The Rise of U.S. Economic Power in the World

These pie charts showing percentage shares of world manufacturing production for the major nations of the world demonstrate that the United States came to surpass Great Britain in this significant economic measurement of power.   (Source: League of Nations data presented in Aaron L. Friedberg, *The Weary Titan: Britain and the Experience of Relative Decline, 1895–1905* [Princeton, N.J.: Princeton University Press, 1988], p. 26.)

The language of U.S. leaders was also weighted with words such as *manliness* and *weakling*. The warrior and president Theodore Roosevelt viewed people of color (or "darkeys," as he called them) as effeminate weaklings who lacked the ability to govern themselves and could not cope with world politics. Americans regularly debased Latin Americans as half-breeds needing supervision or distressed damsels begging for manly rescue. The gendered imagery prevalent in U.S. foreign relations joined race thinking to place women, people of color, and nations weaker than the United States low in the hierarchy of power and, hence, in a necessarily dependent status justifying U.S. dominance.

"As America goes, so goes the world," declared Reverend Josiah Strong, author of the influential *Our Country* (1885), which celebrated an Anglo-Saxon race destined to lead others. Social Darwinists saw Americans as a superior people certain to overcome all competition. Secretary of State Thomas F. Bayard (1885–1889) applauded the "overflow of our population and capital" into Mexico to "saturate those regions with Americanism."

Race thinking—popularized in world's fairs, magazine cartoons, postcards, school textbooks, museums, and political orations—reinforced notions of American greatness, influenced the way U.S. leaders dealt with other peoples, and obviated the need to think about the subtle textures of other societies. *National Geographic*, which published its first issue in 1888, featured pictures of exotic, premodern people who had not yet become "Western" and regularly pictured women with naked breasts. Fairs also put so-called uncivilized people of color on display in the "freaks" or "midway" section. Dog-eating Filipinos aroused comment at the 1904 St. Louis World's Fair. Such racism downgraded diplomacy and justified domination and war, because self-proclaimed superiors do not negotiate with people ranked as inferiors.

Similar thinking permeated attitudes toward immigrants, whose entry into the United States was first restricted in these years. Although the Burlingame Treaty (1868) had provided for free immigration between the United States and China, riots against Chinese immigrants continuously erupted in the American West. A new treaty in 1880 permitted Congress to suspend Chinese immigration. But hostility continued: in 1885 white coal miners and railway workers in Rock Springs, Wyoming, massacred at least twenty-five Chinese.

In 1906 the San Francisco School Board ordered the segregation of all Chinese, Koreans, and Japanese in special schools. Tokyo protested this discrimination, and President Roosevelt quieted the crisis by striking a "gentleman's agreement" with Tokyo restricting the inflow of Japanese immigrants. San Francisco then rescinded its segregation order. Relations with Tokyo were jolted again in 1913 when the California legislature denied Japanese residents the right to own property.

Expansionists believed that empire benefited both Americans and those who came under their control. When the United States intervened in weaker states, Americans claimed they were extending liberty and prosperity to less fortunate people. William Howard Taft, as civil governor of the Philippines (1901–1904), described the U.S. mission in its new colony as lifting up Filipinos "to a point of civilization" that will make them "call the name of the United States blessed." Later, Taft said about the Chinese that "the more civilized they become . . . the wealthier they become, and the better market they become for us."

THE "CIVILIZING" IMPULSE

Missionaries dispatched to Asia and Africa helped spur the transfer of American culture and power abroad—"the peaceful conquest of the world," as Reverend Frederick Gates put it. In 1915 10,000 American missionaries worked overseas. In China, by 1915 over 2,500 American Protestant missionaries, most of them female, labored to preach the gospel, teach, and administer medical care.

■ As part of "Anthropology Days" during the 1904 St. Louis World's Fair, organizers put on a series of athletic events showing "primitive" people participating in games such as running, high-jumping, archery, and spear throwing. In this photo by Jessie Tarbox Beals, Igorots from the Philippines compete in a spear-throwing contest. The winners were given American flags. Meanwhile, the 1904 Olympic Games took place on an irregular basis during the fair featuring white "civilized" athletes (the vast majority from the United States) who received gold medals for their victories.   (Special Collections, St. Louis Public Library)

Ambitions and Strategies

The U.S. empire grew gradually, sometimes haltingly, as American leaders defined guiding principles and built institutions to support overseas ambitions. William H. Seward, one of its chief architects, argued relentlessly for extension of the American frontier as senator from New York (1849–1861) and secretary of state (1861–1869). Seward envisioned a large U.S. empire encompassing Canada, the Caribbean, Cuba, Central America, Mexico, Hawai'i, Iceland, Greenland, and the Pacific islands. This empire would be the result of a natural process of gravitation toward the United States. Commerce would hasten the process, as would a canal across Central America, a transcontinental American railroad, and a telegraph system to speed communications.

Most of Seward's grandiose plans did not reach fruition in his lifetime. In 1867 a treaty with Denmark to buy the Danish West Indies (Virgin Islands) was scuttled by his political foes in the Senate and a hurricane in St. Thomas. The Virgin Islanders, who had voted for annexation, would gain official U.S. status in 1917. Seward's scheme with unscrupulous Dominican Republic leaders to gain a Caribbean naval base at Samaná Bay similarly failed. The corruption surrounding this deal foiled President Ulysses S. Grant's initiative in 1870 to buy the island nation.

SEWARD'S QUEST FOR EMPIRE

Anti-imperialism blocked Seward. Senator Carl Schurz and E. L. Godkin, editor of *The Nation*, argued that creating a showcase of democracy and prosperity on unsettled land at home would best persuade other peoples to adopt American ways. Some anti-imperialists, sharing the racism of the times, opposed the annexation of territory populated by dark-skinned people.

Seward did enjoy some successes. In 1866, citing the Monroe Doctrine (see Chapter 10), he sent troops to the Mexican border and demanded that France abandon its puppet regime there. Also facing angry Mexican nationalists, Napoleon III abandoned the Maximilian monarchy that he forcibly installed three years earlier. In 1867 Seward paid Russia $7.2 million for the 591,000 square miles of Alaska—resource rich and twice the size of Texas. That same year,

Seward claimed the Midway Islands (two small islands and a coral atoll northwest of Hawai'i).

In 1866, through the efforts of financier Cyrus Field, an underwater transatlantic cable linked European and American telegraph networks. Backed by J. P. Morgan, communications pioneer James A. Scrymser strung telegraph lines to Latin America, entering Chile in 1890. In 1903 a submarine cable spanned the Pacific to the Philippines; three years later it reached Japan and China. Wire telegraphy—like radio (wireless telegraphy) later—shrank the globe. Nellie Bly, a reporter for the *New York World*, accented the impact of new technology in 1890 when she completed a well-publicized trip around the world in seventy-two days. Drawn closer through improved communications and transportation, nations found that faraway events had greater impact on their prosperity and security.

INTERNATIONAL COMMUNICATIONS

Increasingly, American diplomats negotiated with their European counterparts as equals, signaling that the United States had arrived on the international stage. Seward's successor, Hamilton Fish (1869–1887), for example, achieved a diplomatic victory in resolving tensions with Great Britain, which had built the *Alabama* and other vessels for the Confederacy during the Civil War to prey on Union shipping. Senator Charles Sumner demanded that Britain pay $2 billion in damages or cede Canada to the United States. But in 1871, Fish's negotiations led to the Washington Treaty, whereby Britain apologized and agreed to the creation of a tribunal, which later awarded the United States $15.5 million.

Washington officials also squared off with European powers over Samoa, South Pacific islands 4,000 miles from San Francisco on the trade route to Australia. In 1878 the United States gained exclusive right to a coaling station at Samoa's coveted port of Pago Pago. Eyeing the same prize, Britain and Germany began to cultivate ties with Samoan leaders. Tensions grew, and war seemed possible. Britain, Germany, and the United States met in Berlin in 1889 and, without consulting the Samoans, devised a three-part protectorate that limited Samoa's independence. Ten years later, the three powers partitioned Samoa: the United States received Pago Pago through annexation of part of the islands (now called American Samoa), Germany took what is today independent Western Samoa, and

Britain obtained the Gilbert Islands and Solomon Islands.

Calling attention to the naval buildup by the European powers, notably Germany, U.S. expansion-ists argued for a bigger, modernized

ALFRED T.
MAHAN AND
NAVALISM

navy that would add the "blue wa-ter" command of the seas to its traditional role of coastline defense. Captain Alfred Thayer Mahan, a major popularizer for this "New Navy," whose ideas were published in *The Influence of Sea Power upon History* (1890), argued that be-cause foreign trade was essential, the nation required an efficient navy to protect its shipping; in turn, a navy required colonies for bases. Theodore Roosevelt and Henry Cabot Lodge consulted Mahan, sharing his belief in the links between trade, navy, and colonies and his alarm over "the aggressive military spirit" of Germany.

Moving toward modernization, Congress in 1883 authorized construction of the first steel-hulled war-ships. American factories produced steam engines, high-velocity shells, powerful guns, and precision in-struments. The navy shifted from sail power to steam and from wood construction to steel. New ships such as the *Maine, Oregon,* and *Boston* earned the United States naval prominence.

Crises in the 1890s: Hawai'i, Venezuela, and Cuba

*I*n the depression-plagued 1890s, crises in Hawai'i and Cuba and the belief that the fron-tier had closed at home buoyed the expansion-ist argument. In 1893 historian Frederick Jackson Turner postulated that the expanding continental frontier, which had shaped the American character, was gone. He did not say that a new frontier had to be found overseas, but he did claim that "American energy will continually demand a wider field for its exercise."

Hawai'i, the Pacific Ocean archipelago of eight major islands located 2,000 miles from the U.S. West

ANNEXATION OF
HAWAI'I

Coast, emerged as America's new frontier. The Hawaiian Islands had long commanded American

attention—commercial, religious missionary, naval, and diplomatic. By 1881 Secretary of State James Blaine had declared the Hawaiian Islands "essentially a part of the American system." By 1890 Americans owned about three-quarters of Hawai'i's wealth and subordinated its economy to that of the United States through sugar exports that entered the U.S. market-place duty free.

In Hawai'i's multiracial society, Chinese and Japanese nationals far outnumbered Americans, who represented just 2.1 percent of the population. Promi-nent Americans on the islands organized secret clubs and military units to contest the royal government. In 1887 they forced the king to accept a constitution that allowed foreigners to vote and shifted decision making from the monarchy to the legislature. The same year, Hawai'i granted the United States naval rights to Pearl Harbor. Many native Hawaiians be-lieved that the *haole* (foreigners), especially Ameri-cans, were taking their country from them.

The native government was further undermined when the McKinley Tariff of 1890 eliminated the duty-free status of Hawaiian sugar exports in the United States. Suffering declining sugar prices, the American island elite pressed for annexation by the United States, thereby classifying their sugar as domestic. When Princess Lili'uokalani assumed the throne in 1891, she sought to roll back the political power of the *haole*. The next year, the white oligarchy—questioning her moral rectitude and fearing Hawaiian nationalism—formed the subversive Annexation Club.

The annexationists struck in January 1893 in collusion with John L. Stevens, the chief American diplomat in Hawai'i, who dispatched troops from the U.S.S. *Boston* to occupy Honolulu. The queen, ar-rested and confined, surrendered. Rather than yield to the new provisional regime, headed by Sanford B. Dole, son of missionaries and a prominent attorney, she relinquished authority to the U.S. government. President Benjamin Harrison hurried an annexation treaty to the Senate.

Sensing foul play, incoming President Grover Cleveland ordered an investigation, which confirmed a conspiracy and revealed that most Hawaiians op-posed annexation. But when Hawai'i proved a strate-gic and commercial way station to Asia and the Philippines during the Spanish-American War, Presi-dent William McKinley maneuvered annexation through Congress on July 7, 1898. Under the Organic Act of June 1900, the people of Hawai'i became U.S. citizens with the right to vote in local elections and to send a nonvoting delegate to Congress. Statehood came in 1959.

The Venezuelan crisis of 1895 also saw the United States in an expansive mood. For decades Venezuela

VENEZUELAN BOUNDARY DISPUTE

and Great Britain had quarreled over the border between Venezuela and British Guiana, a territory containing gold deposits and a commercial gateway to South America via the Orinoco River. Venezuela sought U.S. help, and Secretary of State Richard Olney brashly lectured the British that the Monroe Doctrine prohibited European powers from denying self-government to nations in the Western Hemisphere. The British, seeking international friends to counter intensifying competition from Germany, quietly retreated. With almost no Venezuelan input, in 1896 an Anglo-American arbitration board divided the disputed territory between Britain and Venezuela. Thus, the United States displayed a typical imperialist trait: disregard for the rights of small nations.

In 1895 Cuba was the site of another crisis. From 1868 to 1878 the Cubans had battled Spain for their

REVOLUTION IN CUBA

independence, winning the end of slavery only. While the Cuban economy suffered, repressive Spanish rule continued. Insurgents committed to *Cuba libre* waited for another chance, and José Martí, one of the heroes of Cuban history, collected money, arms, and men in the United States.

Cubans of all classes settled in Baltimore, New York, Boston, and Philadelphia, and prominent Cubans on the island sent their children to school in the United States. When Cuban expatriates returned home, many spoke English, had American names, played baseball, and jettisoned Catholicism for Protestant denominations.

The Cuban and U.S. economies were also intertwined. American investments of $50 million dominated the island. Over 90 percent of Cuba's sugar was exported to the United States, and most island imports came from the United States. Havana's famed cigar factories relocated to Key West and Tampa to evade protectionist U.S. tariff laws. Martí, however,

feared that "economic union means political union," for "the nation that buys, commands" and "the nation that sells, serves."

Martí's fears were prophetic. In 1894 the Wilson-Gorman Tariff imposed a duty on Cuban sugar. The Cuban economy, highly dependent on exports, plunged into crisis, hastening the island's revolution against Spain and its further incorporation into "the American system."

From American soil, Martí launched the revolution against Spain. Rebels burned sugar-cane fields and razed mills. U.S. investments went up in smoke, and Cuban-American trade dwindled. To separate the insurgents from their supporters, Spanish general Valeriano Weyler instituted a policy of "reconcentration." Some 300,000 Cubans were herded into fortified towns and camps, where starvation and disease led to tens of thousands of deaths. As reports of atrocity made headlines in the United States, Americans sympathized with the insurrectionists. In late 1897, a new government in Madrid modified reconcentration and promised some autonomy for Cuba, but the insurgents continued to gain ground.

President William McKinley assumed office as an imperialist who advocated foreign bases for the

SINKING OF THE MAINE

New Navy, the export of surplus production, and U.S. supremacy in the Western Hemisphere. Vexed by the turmoil in Cuba, he explored purchasing it for $300 million. In January 1898, when antireform pro-Spanish loyalists and army personnel rioted in Havana, Washington ordered the battleship *Maine* to Havana harbor to demonstrate U.S. concern and protect American citizens.

On February 15 an explosion ripped the *Maine*, killing 266 of 354 American officers and crew. A week earlier, William Randolph Hearst's inflammatory *New York Journal* had published a stolen private letter written by the Spanish minister in Washington, Enrique Dupuy de Lôme, belittling McKinley and suggesting that Spain would fight on. Congress complied unanimously with McKinley's request for $50 million in defense funds. Vengeful Americans blamed Spain. (Later, official and unofficial studies attributed the sinking to an accidental internal explosion.)

Though reluctant to go to war, McKinley sent Spain an ultimatum: accept an armistice, end recon-

■ On July 1, 1898, U.S. troops stormed Spanish positions on San Juan Hill near Santiago, Cuba. Both sides suffered heavy casualties. A *Harper's* magazine correspondent reported a "ghastly" scene of hundreds killed and thousands wounded. The American painter William Glackens (1870–1938) put to canvas what he saw. Because Santiago surrendered on July 17, propelling the United States to victory in the war, and because Rough Rider Theodore Roosevelt fought at San Juan Hill and later gave a self-congratulatory account of the experience, the human toll has often gone unnoticed. (Wadsworth Atheneum Museum of Art, Hartford, CT, Gift of Henry Schnakenberg)

McKinley's Ultimatum and War Decision

centration, and designate McKinley as arbiter. Madrid made concessions. It abolished reconcentration and rejected, then accepted, an armistice. The president would no longer tolerate chronic disorder 90 miles off the U.S. coast. On April 11 McKinley asked Congress for authorization to use force "to secure a full and final termination of hostilities between . . . Spain and . . . Cuba, and to secure in the island the establishment of a stable government, capable of maintaining order."

McKinley listed the reasons for war: the "cause of humanity"; the protection of American life and property; the "very serious injury to the commerce, trade, and business of our people"; and, referring to the destruction of the *Maine*, the "constant menace to our peace." On April 19 Congress declared Cuba free and independent and directed the president to use force to remove Spanish authority. The legislators also passed the Teller Amendment, which disclaimed any U.S. intention to annex Cuba or control the island except to ensure its "pacification." Believing that the Cubans were not ready for self-government, McKinley successfully argued against recognizing the rebel government in favor of a period of American tutoring.

The Spanish-American War and the Debate over Empire

By the time the Spanish concessions were on the table, prospects for compromise appeared dim. Advancing Cuban insurgents wanted nothing less than independence, and no Spanish government could have granted that and remained in office. Nor did the United States welcome a truly independent Cuban government that might reduce U.S. interests.

McKinley's April message expressed a humanitarian impulse to stop the bloodletting and a concern for commerce and property as justification for war. Republican politicians wanted the Cuban question solved to secure the party's victory in the upcoming congressional elections. Many businesspeople and farmers believed that ejecting Spain would open new markets for surplus production.

MOTIVES FOR WAR

Imperialists saw the war as an opportunity to fulfill expansionist dreams, while conservatives, alarmed by Populism and labor strikes, welcomed it as a national unifier. One senator commented that "internal discord" was disappearing in the "fervent heat of patriotism." Assistant Secretary of the Navy Theodore Roosevelt and others too young to remember the Civil War looked on war as adventure.

More than 263,000 regulars and volunteers served in the army and 25,000 in the navy during the war. Most, however, never left the United States. The typical volunteer was young (early twenties), white, unmarried, native-born, and working class. Deaths numbered 5,462, mostly from a typhoid epidemic in Tennessee, Virginia, and Florida. Only 379 died in combat. About 10,000 African Americans, assigned to segregated regiments, found no relief from racism, even though black troops were central to the victorious battle for Santiago de Cuba. For all, food, sanitary conditions, and medical care were bad. Although Roosevelt's Rough Riders, a motley unit of Ivy Leaguers and cowboys, proved undisciplined and ineffective, Roosevelt's self-serving publicity ensured that they received good press.

The first war news came not from Cuba but the Spanish colony of the Philippine Islands, where Filipinos were also seeking independence. On May 1, 1898, Commodore George Dewey's ship *Olympia* led an American squadron into Manila Bay and wrecked the Spanish fleet. Dewey received orders from Washington in February to attack the islands if war broke out. Manila was a choice harbor, and the Philippines sat on the way to China's potentially huge market.

DEWEY IN THE PHILIPPINES

Facing Americans and rebels in Cuba and the Philippines, Spanish resistance collapsed rapidly. U.S.

ships blockaded Cuban ports, and insurgents cut off supplies from the countryside, causing starvation and illness for Spanish soldiers. American troops landed near Santiago de Cuba on June 22 and laid siege to the city. On July 3, U.S. warships sank the Spanish Caribbean squadron in Santiago harbor. American forces then assaulted the Spanish colony of Puerto Rico, winning another Caribbean naval base and pushing Madrid to defeat.

On August 12, 1898, Spain and the United States signed an armistice, and in December, they agreed on the peace terms: independence for Cuba and cession of the Philippines, Puerto Rico, and the Pacific island of Guam to the United States in exchange for $20 million. The U.S. empire now stretched deep into Asia, and the annexation of Wake Island (1898), Hawai'i (1898), and Samoa (1899) gave American traders, missionaries, and naval promoters other steppingstones to China.

TREATY OF PARIS

During the war, the *Washington Post* detected that "the taste of empire is in the mouth of the people." But anti-imperialists such as author Mark Twain, Nebraska politician William Jennings Bryan, reformer Jane Addams, and industrialist Andrew Carnegie argued against annexation of the Philippines. Their concern that a war to free Cuba had led to empire stimulated a debate over American foreign policy.

Imperial control could be imposed either formally (by military occupation, annexation, or colonialism) or informally (by economic domination, political manipulation, or the threat of intervention). Anti-imperialist ire focused mostly on formal imperial control. Some critics cited the Declaration of Independence and the Constitution, arguing that the conquest of people against their wills violated the right of self-determination.

ANTI-IMPERIALIST ARGUMENTS

Online Study Center Improve Your Grade
Primary Source:
American Anti-Imperialist League Program

Other anti-imperialists feared that the American character was being corrupted by imperialist zeal. Seeing children play war games on Chicago streets, Jane Addams noted that they were not freeing Cubans but slaying Spaniards. Hoping to build a foreign policy constituency from women's organizations, Addams and others championed peace and an end to imperial conquest.

Some anti-imperialists protested that the United States was practicing a double standard—"offering liberty to the Cubans with one hand, cramming liberty down the throats of the Filipinos with the other, but with both feet planted upon the neck of the negro," as an African American politician from Massachusetts put it. Still other anti-imperialists warned that annexing people of color would undermine Anglo-Saxon purity and supremacy at home.

For Samuel Gompers and other anti-imperialist labor leaders, the issue was jobs. Might not the new colonials be imported as cheap labor to drive down American wages? Would not exploitation of the weak abroad lead to further exploitation at home?

The anti-imperialists never launched an effective campaign. Although they organized the Anti-Imperialist League in November 1898, they differed so profoundly on domestic issues that it was difficult to speak with one voice on a foreign question.

The imperialists appealed to patriotism, destiny, and commerce. They envisioned American greatness:

IMPERIALIST ARGUMENTS merchant ships plying the waters to boundless Asian markets, naval vessels cruising the Pacific to protect American interests, missionaries uplifting inferior peoples. It was America's duty, they insisted, quoting a then-popular Rudyard Kipling poem, to "take up the white man's burden." Furthermore, Filipino insurgents were beginning to resist U.S. rule, and it seemed cowardly to pull out under fire, especially with Germany and Japan ready to seize them. National honor dictated that Americans keep what they had shed blood to take.

In February 1899, by a 57-to-27 vote (just 1 more than the minimum two-thirds majority), the Senate passed the Treaty of Paris, ending the war with Spain. Most Republicans voted yes and most Democrats no. An amendment promising independence once the Filipinos formed a stable government lost only by the tie-breaking ballot of the vice president.

Asian Encounters: War in the Philippines, Diplomacy in China

he Philippine crisis was far from over. Emilio Aguinaldo, the Philippine nationalist leader who had been battling the Spanish for years, believed that American officials had promised independence for his country. But after the victory, U.S. officers ordered Aguinaldo out of Manila. In early 1899, he proclaimed an independent Philippine Republic and took up arms.

Both sides fought viciously: American soldiers burned villages and tortured captives, while Filipinos staged brutal hit-and-run guerrilla ambushes. U.S. troops introduced a variant of the Spanish reconcentration policy. In the province of Batangas, for instance, U.S. troops forced residents to live in designated zones to separate insurgents from local supporters. Poor sanitation, starvation, and malaria and cholera killed thousands. Outside secure areas, Americans destroyed food supplies to starve out the rebels. At least one-quarter of the population of Batangas died or fled.

PHILIPPINE INSURRECTION AND PACIFICATION

Before the Philippine insurrection was suppressed in 1902, over 200,000 Filipinos and 5,000 Americans lay dead. Resistance to U.S. rule, however, continued. When the fiercely independent, often violent Muslim Filipinos of Moro Province refused to knuckle under, the U.S. military threatened extermination. In 1906, 600 of them, including women and children, were slaughtered at the Battle of Bud Dajo.

U.S. officials soon tried to Americanize the Philippines, including a new education system with English as the primary language. Architect Daniel Burnham, leader of the City Beautiful movement (see Chapter 19), planned modern Manila. The Philippine economy grew as an American satellite, and a sedition act sent U.S. critics to prison. In 1916 the Jones Act vaguely promised independence once the Philippines established a "stable government," but the United States did not end its rule until 1946.

McKinley had greater success with negotiations in China. Outsiders had been pecking away at China since the 1840s. The major powers took advantage of the Qing (Manchu) dynasty's weakness and carved out spheres of influence (regions over which they claimed political control and exclusive commercial privileges): Germany in Shandong; Russia in Manchuria; France in Yunnan and Hainan; Britain in Kowloon and Hong Kong. Then, in 1895, Japan claimed victory over China in a short war and assumed control of Formosa, Korea,

CHINA AND THE OPEN DOOR POLICY

The U.S. System of Education in the Philippines

In the Philippines, U.S. officials moved swiftly after 1898 to create a school system based on the American notion of universal education. Under the Spanish, education had been limited and run largely by the Catholic Church. U.S. leaders hoped improved schools would be a show of goodwill. By 1901, a national education system had been established. Most instruction would be in English rather than native Philippine languages (only a small minority spoke Spanish), which rankled many Filipinos.

To overcome a teacher shortage, the United States recruited thousands of young American educators. Over a thousand arrived in 1901–1902 alone. One ship, the U.S.S. *Thomas,* carried 540 teachers, both male and female, who opened local schoolhouses across the country.

American officials also helped promising Filipinos attend universities in the United States. After returning, these students provided a cadre of well-trained medical doctors, engineers, and other professionals in the public and private sectors. Other Filipinos earned degrees at home, many at the University of the Philippines, founded in 1908.

Public schools for boys and girls, and higher education for women—at home and in the United States—allowed women to qualify as professionals for the first time. Many seized the chance, earning degrees, entering the public sphere, and founding their own colleges. Although male students outnumbered females initially, women outnumbered men at the university level by the end of the twentieth century.

But the U.S. goal of universal education never became a complete reality. Schools varied widely in quality, and Filipino elites proved better able than the less privileged to take advantage of the system. The result was a widening gap between the entitled few and the masses in the decades of U.S. colonial rule (which ended in 1946) and postcolonial independence.

Still, for millions in the Philippines, the arrival of the Americans linked the two countries through education. The irony was not lost on educated Filipinos, who knew they owed their schooling partly to the colonial power.

Boys in Normal High School, Manila, Philippines, 1900.   (Library of Congress)

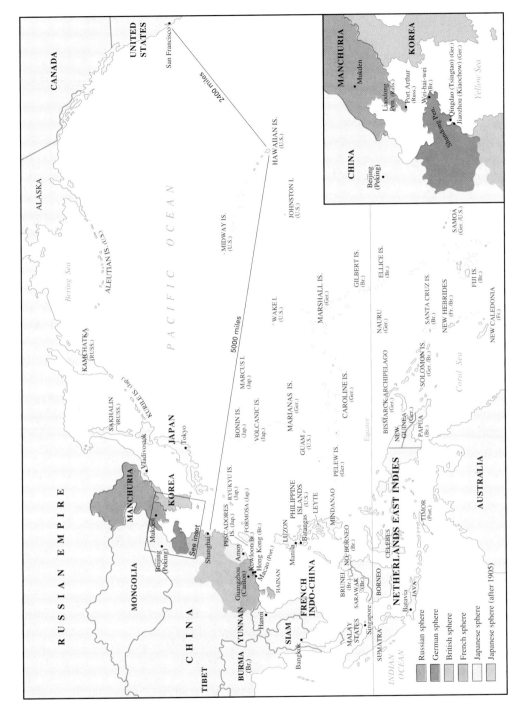

Map 22.1   Imperialism in Asia: Turn of the Century

China and the Pacific region had become imperialist hunting grounds by the turn of the century. The European powers and Japan controlled more areas than the United States, which nonetheless participated in the imperial race by annexing the Philippines, Wake, Guam, Hawai'i, and Samoa; announcing the Open Door policy; and expanding trade. As the spheres of influence in China demonstrate, that besieged nation succumbed to outsiders despite the Open Door policy.

and parts of China proper (see Map 22.1). American religious and business leaders petitioned Washington to halt the dismemberment of China before they were closed out.

Secretary of State John Hay knew that missionaries had become targets of Chinese nationalist anger and that American oil and textile companies had been disappointed with their investments there. Thus, in September 1899 Hay sent nations with spheres of influence in China a note seeking their respect for the principle of equal trade opportunity—an Open Door. The recipients sent evasive replies, privately complaining that the United States was seeking for free in China the trade rights that they had gained at considerable cost.

The next year, the Boxers, a Chinese secret society (so named in the Western press because some members were martial artists), sought to expel foreigners. They rioted, killing many outsiders and laying siege to the foreign legations in Beijing. The United States joined other imperialist powers in sending troops. Hay also sent a second Open Door note instructing other nations to preserve China's territorial integrity and honor "equal and impartial trade." China continued for years to be fertile soil for foreign exploitation, especially by the Japanese.

The Open Door policy became a cornerstone of U.S. diplomacy. While the United States had long opposed barriers to its international commerce, after 1900, when it emerged as the premier world trader, the Open Door policy became an instrument first to pry open markets and then to dominate them. The Open Door also developed several tenets: first, that America's domestic well-being required exports; second, that foreign trade would suffer interruption unless the United States intervened abroad; and third, that the closing of any area to American products, citizens, or ideas threatened the survival of the United States.

TR's World

Theodore Roosevelt played an important role in shaping U.S. foreign policy in the McKinley administration. As assistant secretary of the navy (1897–1898), as a Spanish-American War hero, and then as vice president in McKinley's second term, Roosevelt worked to build U.S. global prominence.

Long fascinated by power, he also relished hunting and killing. After an argument with a girlfriend in his youth, he vented his anger by shooting a neighbor's dog. Roosevelt justified the slaughtering of American Indians, if necessary, and took his Rough Riders to Cuba, desperate to get in on the fighting.

Like many Americans of his day, Roosevelt took for granted the superiority of Protestant Anglo-American culture and believed in using American power to shape world affairs. In TR's view, there were "civilized" and "uncivilized" nations; the former, primarily white and Anglo-Saxon or Teutonic, had a duty to intervene in the affairs of the latter (generally non-white, Latin, or Slavic, and therefore "backward") to preserve order, even if that included violence.

Roosevelt's love of the good fight made many rue his ascension to the presidency after McKinley's assassination in September 1901. But this "cowboy" was also an astute analyst of foreign policy. TR understood that American power, though growing year by year, remained limited, and in many parts of the world the United States would have to rely on diplomacy to achieve satisfactory outcomes.

PRESIDENTIAL AUTHORITY

Roosevelt sought to centralize foreign policy in the White House, believing the president should lead foreign relations as he did domestic priorities. Congress was too large and unwieldy, and he saw public opinion as "the voice of the devil, or what is still worse, the voice of the fool." Most presidents who followed TR shared the notion that foreign policy belonged in the executive branch.

Roosevelt's first efforts focused on Latin America, where U.S. economic interests and power towered (see Map 22.2), and on Europe, where repeated tensions persuaded Americans to develop friendlier relations with Great Britain while avoiding the continent's troubles, which Americans blamed largely on Germany.

As U.S. economic interests expanded in Latin America, so did U.S. political influence. Exports to Latin America rose from over $50 million in the 1870s to more than $120 million in 1901, and they reached $300 million in 1914. Investments by U.S. citizens in Latin America climbed to $1.26 billion in 1914. In 1899 two large banana importers had merged to form the United Fruit Company, owning much of the land in Central America (more than 1

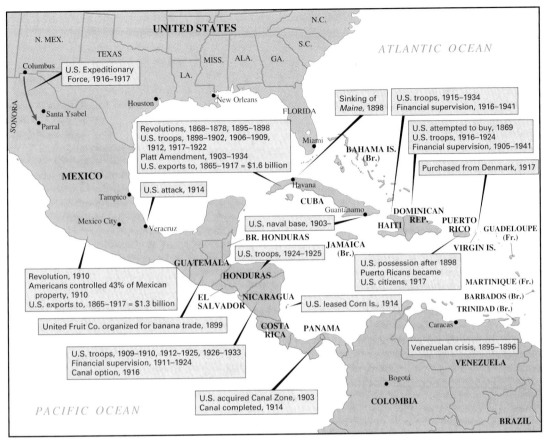

Map 22.2 U.S. Hegemony in the Caribbean and Latin America

Through many interventions, territorial acquisitions, and robust economic expansion, the United States became the predominant power in Latin America in the early twentieth century. The United States often backed up the Roosevelt Corollary's declaration of a "police power" in 1904 by dispatching troops to Caribbean nations, where they met nationalist opposition.

million acres in 1913) and the railroad and steamship lines.

After the war in Cuba, U.S. business interests dominated the island's economy, controlling the sugar, mining, tobacco, and utilities industries and most of the rural lands. Private U.S. investments grew from $50 million before the revolution to $220 million by 1913, and U.S. exports rose from $26 million in 1900 to $196 million in 1917. The Teller Amendment outlawed the annexation of Cuba, but Washington offi-

CUBA AND THE PLATT AMENDMENT

cials used its call for "pacification" to justify U.S. control and keeping troops there until 1902.

U.S. authorities restricted voting rights largely to propertied Cuban males, excluding two-thirds of adult men and all women. American officials also forced Cubans to add the Platt Amendment to their constitution in 1903. This statement prohibited Cuba from making treaties that might impair its independence; in practice, it meant that all treaties required U.S. approval. Most important, the Platt Amendment granted the United States "the right to intervene" to preserve the island's independence and maintain order. Finally, it required Cuba to lease a naval base to the United States (at Guantánamo Bay, still under U.S. jurisdiction today). Formalized in a 1903 treaty, the amendment governed Cuban-American relations until 1934.

Cubans widely protested the Platt Amendment, and a rebellion in 1906 prompted another U.S. invasion. The marines stayed until 1909; they returned briefly in 1912 and again from 1917 to 1922. U.S. officials helped develop a transportation system, expand the public schools, establish a national army, and increase sugar production. When Dr. Walter Reed's experiments, based on the theory of Cuban physician Carlos Juan Finlay, proved that mosquitoes transmitted yellow fever, sanitary engineers eradicated the disease.

Puerto Rico, the Caribbean island taken as a spoil of war in the Treaty of Paris, at first welcomed the United States as an improvement over Spain. But the U.S. military governor, General Guy V. Henry, disdained Puerto Ricans as children who needed "kindergarten instruction in controlling themselves without allowing them too much liberty." Some residents warned against the "Yankee peril"; others applauded the "Yankee model" and futilely anticipated statehood (see the end of this chapter).

Panama meanwhile became the site of a bold U.S. expansionist venture. In 1869 the world had marveled

PANAMA CANAL   when the newly completed Suez Canal facilitated travel between the Indian Ocean and Mediterranean Sea and enhanced the power of the British Empire. Surely that feat could be duplicated in the Western Hemisphere, possibly in Panama, a province of Colombia. Business interests joined politicians, diplomats, and navy officers in insisting that the United States control such an interoceanic canal.

The trouble was that the Clayton-Bulwer Treaty with Britain (1850) had provided joint control of a canal. The British, recognizing their diminishing influence and cultivating friendship with the United States as a counterweight to Germany, permitted a solely U.S.-run canal in the Hay-Pauncefote Treaty (1901). When Colombia resisted Washington's terms, Roosevelt encouraged Panamanian rebels to declare independence and ordered American warships to back them.

In 1903 the new Panama awarded the United States a canal zone and long-term rights to its con-

trol, and Panama received its independence. (In 1922 the United States paid Colombia $25 million in "conscience money" but did not apologize.) A technological achievement, the Panama Canal was completed in 1914.

Online Study Center **Improve Your Grade**
Interactive Map:
The Panama Canal

Worried that Latin American nations' defaults on debts owed to European banks were provoking European intervention, Theodore Roo-

ROOSEVELT   sevelt in 1904 issued the Roosevelt
COROLLARY   Corollary to the Monroe Doctrine. The corollary warned Latin Americans to stabilize their politics and finances, or risk "intervention by some civilized nation." Roosevelt's declaration provided the rationale for frequent U.S. interventions in Latin America.

From 1900 to 1917, U.S. presidents ordered American troops to Cuba, Panama, Nicaragua, the Dominican Republic, Mexico, and Haiti to quell civil wars, thwart challenges to U.S. influence, gain ports and bases, and forestall European meddling (see Map 22.2). U.S. authorities ran elections, trained national guards, and shifted foreign debts to U.S. banks. They also controlled tariff revenues and government budgets (as in the Dominican Republic, from 1905 to 1941).

U.S. officials focused particular attention on Mexico, where long-time dictator Porfirio Díaz (1876–

U.S.-MEXICO   1910) aggressively recruited foreign
RELATIONS   investors through tax incentives and land grants. In the 1890s, the United States dominated Mexico's foreign trade. By 1910 Americans controlled 43 percent of Mexican property and produced over half the country's oil; in the state of Sonora, 186 of 208 mining companies were American owned. The Mexican revolutionaries who ousted Díaz in 1910 wanted to end their economic dependence on the United States.

The revolution descended into a bloody civil war with strong anti-Yankee overtones, and the Mexican government intended to nationalize American-owned properties. President Woodrow Wilson twice ordered troops to Mexican soil: once in 1914, at Veracruz, to overthrow President Victoriano Huerta, and again in 1916, in northern Mexico, where General John J. "Black Jack" Pershing spent months pursuing Mexican rebel Pancho Villa for raiding an American border town. Failing to capture Villa and facing another nationalistic government, U.S. forces departed in January 1917.

As the United States demonstrated the power to enforce the Monroe Doctrine, European nations reluctantly honored U.S. hegemony in Latin America. In turn, the United States continued to stand outside European embroilments. Theodore Roosevelt did help settle a Franco-German clash over Morocco by mediating a settlement at Algeciras, Spain (1906), but he drew American criticism for this involvement. Americans endorsed the Hague peace conferences (1899 and 1907) and negotiated arbitration treaties but generally stayed outside the European arena, except for trade.

In East Asia, Roosevelt and his successor, William Howard Taft, sought to preserve the Open Door and contain Japan's rising power. The United States gradually made concessions to Japan to protect the Philippines and sustain the Open Door policy. Japan continued to plant interests in China and then smashed the Russians in the Russo-Japanese War (1904–1905). President Roosevelt mediated the negotiations at the Portsmouth Conference in New Hampshire in 1905 and won the Nobel Peace Prize for helping to preserve a balance of power in Asia.

PEACEMAKING IN EAST ASIA

In 1905, in the Taft-Katsura Agreement, the United States conceded Japanese hegemony over Korea in return for Japan's respect for the U.S. position in the Philippines. Three years later, in the Root-Takahira Agreement, Washington recognized Japan's interests in Manchuria, and Japan again pledged the security of the U.S. Pacific possessions and endorsed the Open Door in China. Roosevelt also deterred the Japanese with reinforced naval power; in late 1907 he sent the navy's "Great White Fleet" on a world tour. Impressed, the Japanese expanded their navy.

President Taft hoped to counter Japanese advances in Asia through dollar diplomacy—the use of private funds to serve American diplomatic goals while simultaneously garnering profits for American financiers. Taft induced American bankers to join an international consortium building a railway in China. But it seemed only to embolden Japan to extend its holdings in China.

DOLLAR DIPLOMACY

In 1914, when the First World War broke out in Europe, Japan seized Shandong and some Pacific islands from the Germans. In 1915 Japan issued its Twenty-One Demands, insisting on hegemony over China. The United States lacked power in Asia to block Japan's imperialism. A new president, Woodrow Wilson, worried about how the "white race" could blunt the rise of the "yellow race."

British officials shared this concern, though their attention focused on rising tensions in Europe. Anglo-American cooperation blossomed in the TR-Taft years. The intense German-British rivalry and the rise of the United States to world power furthered London's quest for friendship with Washington. Americans not only shared their language and respect for private property rights, but also appreciated British support in the 1898 war and the Hay-Pauncefote Treaty, London's endorsement of the Roosevelt Corollary, and withdrawal of British warships from the Caribbean.

ANGLO-AMERICAN RAPPROCHEMENT

British-American trade and U.S. investment in Britain also secured ties. By 1914 over 140 American companies operated in Britain, including H. J. Heinz's processed foods and F. W. Woolworth's "penny markets." Many decried an Americanization of British culture. But such exaggerated fears gave way to cooperation, especially in 1917 when the United States entered the First World War supporting Britain against Germany.

Summary ⁂*Online Study Center*   **ACE the Test**

B y 1914 Americans held extensive economic, strategic, and political interests across the globe.

The outward reach of U.S. foreign policy from Seward to Wilson sparked opposition from domestic critics, other imperial nations, and foreign nationalists, but expansionists prevailed, and the trend toward empire endured.

Economic and strategic needs motivated and justified expansion. The belief that the U.S. economy needed foreign markets to absorb surplus production joined missionary zeal to reform other societies through American influence. Notions of racial and male supremacy and appeals to national greatness also fed the appetite for foreign adventure. The greatly augmented navy became a primary means for satisfying America's expansionist impulses.

Revealing the diversity of America's intersection with the rest of the world, missionaries, generals, companies, and politicians carried American ideas, guns, and goods abroad to a mixed reception. When world war broke out in August 1914, the United States's self-proclaimed greatness and political isolation from Europe were put to the test.

LEGACY FOR A PEOPLE AND A NATION
The Status of Puerto Rico

Since the U.S. invasion of their island in July 1898 and subsequent transfer from Spain to the United States, Puerto Ricans have debated their status. Colony? Territory? Nation? State? Or the "Commonwealth of Puerto Rico" that the U.S. Congress designated in 1952? A small island with 3.8 million people, Puerto Rico has held nonbinding plebiscites in 1967, 1993, and 1998, each time rejecting statehood and independence in favor of commonwealth. The U.S. Congress, which holds constitutional authority over Puerto Rico, is similarly uneasy with the ambivalence of commonwealth status.

Puerto Ricans remain troubled by their incomplete political status. The island governs itself, and Puerto Ricans are U.S. citizens (made so by the Jones Act of 1916). They pay no federal income taxes, but contribute to Social Security, and they cannot elect representatives to Congress or vote in U.S. elections. In 1999 many Puerto Ricans marched against the U.S. Navy's decades-long use of its Vieques islands as a bombing range. Two years later, President George W. Bush announced plans to vacate that installation by May 2003.

Puerto Ricans have rejected statehood because they fear it would mean forfeiting their Latin American culture and Spanish language. Most Puerto Ricans today, although bilingual, prefer Spanish over English and oppose mandatory English courses. Puerto Rico's concerns are a legacy of the era of empire building. Then as now, the issue centered on self-determination—in this case, the right of a people to sustain their own culture.

AMERICANS IN THE GREAT WAR 1914–1920

On May 7, 1915, Secretary of State William Jennings Bryan was having lunch with cabinet members in Washington when he received a bulletin: the British luxury ocean liner *Lusitania* had been sunk, apparently by a German submarine. He rushed to his office and at 3:06 P.M. received confirmation from London: "THE LUSITANIA WAS TORPEDOED OFF THE IRISH COAST AND SANK IN HALF AN HOUR." In truth, the giant vessel sank in just eighteen minutes: 1,198 people died, including 128 Americans. With Europe at war, Bryan had feared such a calamity. Britain had imposed a naval blockade against Germany, and the Germans responded with submarine warfare against Allied shipping, proclaiming the North Atlantic a danger zone and then sinking numerous British and Allied ships. As a passenger liner, the *Lusitania* was supposed to be spared, but German officials had warned Americans in newspaper ads that they traveled on British or Allied ships at their own risk: passenger liners suspected of carrying munitions or other contraband were subject to attack. For weeks Bryan had urged President Woodrow Wilson to stop Americans from booking passage on British ships; Wilson had refused.

The *Lusitania,* it soon emerged, was carrying munitions. Desperate to keep the United States out of the war, Bryan urged Wilson to condemn Germany and Britain equally and to ban Americans from traveling on belligerent ships. Others, including former president Theodore Roosevelt, called the sinking "an act of piracy" and pressed for war. Wilson did not want war, but disagreed with Bryan. He sent a strong note to Berlin, insisting Germany end its submarine warfare.

As Bryan pressed his case, he became increasingly isolated within the administration. When in early June Wilson refused to ban Americans from belligerent ships and sent a second protest note to Germany, Bryan resigned.

Americans were similarly divided over Europe's war. Eastern newspapers charged Bryan with stabbing the country in the back. In the Midwest and

Precarious Neutrality

The Decision for War

Winning the War

Mobilizing the Home Front

LINKS TO THE WORLD
The Influenza Pandemic of 1918

Civil Liberties Under Challenge

Red Scare, Red Summer

The Defeat of Peace

LEGACY FOR A PEOPLE AND A NATION
Freedom of Speech and the ACLU

Online Study Center
This icon will direct you to interactive map and primary source activities on the website
http://college.hmco.com/pic/nortonbrief7e

CHRONOLOGY

1914 • First World War begins in Europe

1915 • Germans sink *Lusitania* off the coast of Ireland

1916 • After torpedoing the *Sussex*, Germany pledges not to attack merchant ships without warning
    • National Defense Act expands military

1917 • Germany declares unrestricted submarine warfare
    • Russian Revolution ousts the czar; Bolsheviks later take power
    • United States enters the First World War
    • Selective Service Act creates the draft
    • Espionage Act limits First Amendment rights
    • Race riot breaks out in East St. Louis, Illinois

1918 • Wilson announces Fourteen Points for new world order
    • Sedition Act further limits free speech

    • U.S. troops at Château-Thierry help blunt German offensive
    • U.S. troops intervene in Russia against Bolsheviks
    • Spanish flu pandemic kills 20 million worldwide
    • Armistice ends the First World War

1919 • Paris Peace Conference punishes Germany and launches League of Nations
    • May Day bombings help instigate Red Scare
    • American Legion organizes for veterans' benefits and antiradicalism
    • Wilson suffers stroke after speaking tour
    • Senate rejects Treaty of Versailles and U.S. membership in League of Nations
    • *Schenck v. U.S.* upholds Espionage Act

1920 • Palmer Raids round up suspected radicals

South, however, Bryan won praise from pacifists and German American groups. A few weeks later, speaking to fifteen thousand people at Madison Square Garden in New York City, Bryan was loudly applauded when he warned against "war with any of the belligerent nations." Although many Americans agreed with Wilson that honor was more important than peace, others shared Bryan's position that some sacrifice of neutral rights was reasonable to keep the country out of the fighting.

To many, war seemed unthinkable. The new machine guns, howitzers, submarines, and dreadnoughts were awesome death engines; one social reformer lamented that using them would mean "civilization is all gone, and barbarism come."

For almost three years, Wilson kept America out of the war while protecting U.S. trade interests and improving the nation's military posture. But American property, lives, and neutrality fell victim to British and German naval warfare. When the president fi-

nally asked Congress for a declaration of war, two years after the *Lusitania* went down, he insisted America would not just win the war but "make the world safe for democracy."

A year and a half later, the Great War was over. Some 10 million soldiers perished. Europeans suffered the destruction of ideals and goodwill, not to mention immense economic damage. The Great War toppled four empires of the Old World—German, Austro-Hungarian, Russian, and Ottoman Turkish—and left two others, British and French, drastically weakened.

Losses for the United States were comparatively small, yet American involvement tipped the scales in favor of the Allies with the infusion of troops, supplies, and loans. The war years also witnessed a massive international transfer of wealth from Europe across the Atlantic, as the United States went from being the world's largest debtor nation to the largest creditor. The conflict marked the United States as a world power.

At home, though, World War I intensified social divisions. Racial tensions accompanied the northward migration of southern blacks, and pacifists and German Americans were harassed. The federal government trampled on civil liberties to promote patriotism and silence critics. And after Russia's communist revolution, a Red Scare in America repressed radicals and tarnished its democratic image. Although reformers continued to devote themselves to issues such as prohibition and woman suffrage, the war splintered the Progressive movement.

Abroad, Americans who had marched to battle grew disillusioned with the peace process. They recoiled from the victors' squabbling over the spoils and chided Wilson for failing to deliver his promised "peace without victory." Americans again debated foreign policy. After negotiating the Treaty of Versailles at Paris following World War I, the president urged U.S. membership in the new League of Nations, which he believed would reform world politics. The Senate rejected his appeal (the League nonetheless organized without U.S. membership) because many Americans feared that the organization might threaten the U.S. empire and entangle America in Europe's problems. ■

Precarious Neutrality

*W*orld War I grew from years of European competition over trade, colonies, allies, and armaments. Two powerful alliance systems had formed: the Triple Alliance of Germany, Austria-Hungary, and Italy and the Triple Entente of Britain, France, and Russia. All had imperial holdings and wanted more, but as Germany challenged Britain for world leadership, many Americans saw Germany as an excessively militaristic nation that threatened U.S. interests in the Western Hemisphere.

Crises in the Balkans triggered a chain of events that shattered Europe's delicate balance of power.

OUTBREAK OF THE FIRST WORLD WAR Slavic nationalists sought to enlarge independent Serbia by annexing regions such as Bosnia, then a province of the Austro-Hungarian Empire. On June 28, 1914, Archduke Franz Ferdinand, heir to the Austro-Hungarian throne, was assassinated by a Serbian nationalist while in Sarajevo, the capital of Bosnia. Austria-Hungary consulted its Triple Alliance partner Germany, which urged toughness. When Serbia called on its Slavic friend Russia for help, Russia looked for backing from its ally France. In late July, Austria-Hungary declared war against Serbia. Russia began to mobilize its armies.

Germany struck first, declaring war against Russia on August 1 and against France two days later. When German forces slashed into neutral Belgium to get France, London declared war against Germany on August 4. Eventually Turkey (the Ottoman Empire) joined Germany and Austria-Hungary as the Central Powers, and Italy (switching sides) and Japan teamed up with Britain, France, and Russia as the Allies. Japan seized Shandong, Germany's sphere of influence in China.

President Wilson at first distanced America by proclaiming neutrality, the traditional U.S. policy toward European wars. Privately, the president worried that without neutrality, "our mixed populations would wage war on each other."

Despite Wilson's appeal for unity at home, ethnic groups did take sides. Many German Americans and anti-British Irish Americans (Ireland was trying to break free from British rule) cheered for the Central Powers. Americans with roots in Allied nations championed the Allied cause. Germany's attack on Belgium confirmed for many that it was the archetype of unbridled militarism.

TAKING SIDES

The pro-Allied sympathies of Wilson's administration also weakened the U.S. neutrality proclamation. Wilson shared the conviction with British leaders that a German victory would destroy free enterprise and government by law. If Germany won the war, he prophesied, "it would change the course of our civilization and make the United States a military nation."

U.S. economic ties with the Allies also rendered neutrality difficult, if not impossible. England, a long-time customer, flooded America with new orders, especially for arms. Sales to the Allies helped end an American recession. Between 1914 and 1916, American exports to England and France grew 365 percent, from $753 million to $2.75 billion. Largely because of Britain's naval blockade, exports to Germany dropped by more than 90 percent, from $345 million to only $29 million. Loans to Britain and France from private American banks—totaling $2.3 billion during neutrality—financed much of U.S. trade with the Allies. Germany received only $27 million in the same period.

To Germans, the huge U.S. trade with the Allies was an act of unneutrality that had to be stopped. Americans, however, worried that cutting their economic ties with Britain would constitute an unneutral act in favor of Germany. Under international law, Britain—which controlled the seas—could buy both contraband (war-related goods) and noncontraband from neutrals. It was Germany's responsibility, not America's, to stop such trade as international law prescribed by blockading the enemy's territory, seizing contraband from neutral (American) ships, or confiscating goods from belligerent (British) ships.

"Wilsonianism," the cluster of ideas Wilson espoused, consisted of traditional American principles (such as democracy and the Open Door) and a vision of the United States as a beacon of freedom. Only the United States could lead the convulsed world into a peaceful era of unobstructed commerce, free-market capitalism, democratic politics, and open diplomacy.

WILSONIANISM

"America had the infinite privilege of fulfilling her destiny and saving the world," Wilson claimed. Critics, however, charged that Wilson often violated his own credos while forcing them on others—as his military interventions in Mexico in 1914, Haiti in 1915, and the Dominican Republic in 1916 testified. Nonetheless, his ideals served American commercial purposes.

To say that American neutrality was never a possibility given ethnic loyalties, economic ties, and Wilsonian preferences is not to say that Wilson sought to enter the war. In early 1917, the president remarked, "We are the only one of the great white nations that is free from war today, and it would be a crime against civilization for us to go in." What, then, finally brought the United States into the war?

The short answer is that Americans got caught in the Allied–Central Power crossfire. The British sought to cripple the German economy by severing neutral trade. They seized cargo and defined a broad list of contraband (including foodstuffs) that they prohibited neutrals from ship-

VIOLATIONS OF NEUTRAL RIGHTS

ping to Germany. Furthermore, to counter German submarines, the British flouted international law by arming their merchant ships and flying neutral (sometimes American) flags. Wilson frequently protested Britain's actions, but London deflected Washington's criticism by paying for confiscated cargoes, while German provocations made British behavior appear less offensive by comparison.

Germany looked for victory at sea by using its submarines. In February 1915 Berlin declared a war zone around the British Isles, warned neutral vessels to stay away so as not to be mistakenly attacked, and advised passengers to stay off Allied ships. Wilson informed Germany that it would be accountable for any losses of American life and property.

Wilson held a strict interpretation of international law and expected Germans to warn passenger or merchant ships before attacking, so that passengers and crew could disembark safely into lifeboats. The Germans thought that surfacing its slender and sluggish *Unterseebooten* (U-boats) would risk their advantage and leave them vulnerable to attack. Berlin protested that Wilson was denying it the one weapon that could break the British economic stranglehold, disrupt the Allies' substantial connection with U.S. producers and bankers, and win the war. To British, Germans, and Americans, naval warfare became a matter of life and death.

Online Study Center **Improve Your Grade**
Interactive Map:
The War in Europe, 1914–1918

The Decision for War

In early 1915 German U-boats sank ship after ship, notably the *Lusitania* on May 7. Germany's subsequent brief promise to refrain from attacking passenger liners ended in mid-August when another British vessel, the *Arabic*, was sunk off Ireland, claiming three Americans' lives. The Germans quickly pledged that an unarmed passenger ship would never again be attacked without warning. But the *Arabic* incident led critics to ask why Americans could not be required to sail on American craft. After all, from August 1914 to March 1917, 190 Americans were killed on belligerent ships in contrast to 3 deaths on an American ship (the tanker *Gulflight*, sunk by a German U-boat in May 1915).

■ Initially underestimated as a weapon, the German U-boat proved to be frighteningly effective against Allied ships. At the beginning of the war, Germany had about twenty operational submarines in its High Seas Fleet, and officials moved swiftly to speed up production. This photograph shows a German U-boat under construction in 1914. (Bibliothek für Zeitgeschichte, Stuttgart)

In March 1916, a U-boat attack on the *Sussex,* a French vessel crossing the English Channel, injured four more Americans. Wilson threatened Berlin that the United States would sever diplomatic relations if the attacks continued. Again the Germans retreated. At the same time, U.S.-British relations soured after Britain's crushing response to the Easter Rebellion in Ireland and further British restriction of U.S. trade with the Central Powers.

PEACE ADVOCATES

As the United States became more entangled in the war, many Americans urged Wilson to keep the peace. In early 1915, Jane Addams, Carrie Chapman Catt, and other suffragists helped found the Woman's Peace Party, the U.S. section of the Women's International League for Peace and Freedom. "The mother half of humanity," claimed women peace advocates, had a special role as "the guardians of life." Later that year, pacifist Progressives organized the antiwar American Union Against Militarism. Businessmen Andrew Carnegie and Henry Ford financed peace efforts, as did socialists such as Eugene Debs.

Antiwar advocates emphasized that war drained a nation of its youth, resources, and reform impulse; that it fostered repression at home; that it violated Christian morality; and that wartime business barons reaped huge profits at the expense of the people. Militarism and conscription, Addams pointed out, were what millions of immigrants had left behind in Europe. Although the peace movement was splintered, it articulated several ideas that Wilson, who campaigned on a peace platform in 1916, shared. Wilson futilely labored to bring the belligerents to the conference table, urging them in early 1917 to temper their acquisitive war aims and embrace "peace without victory."

In Germany, Wilson's overture went unheeded. Since August 1916, leaders in Berlin had debated whether to resume the unrestricted U-boat campaign. Opponents feared a break with the United States, but proponents claimed that only through an all-out attack on Britain's supply shipping could Germany win the war. True, the United States might enter the war, but victory might be achieved before U.S. troops crossed the Atlantic. Consequently, in early February 1917, Germany launched unrestricted submarine warfare, attacking all warships and merchant

UNRESTRICTED SUBMARINE WARFARE

vessels—belligerent or neutral—in the declared war zone. Wilson then broke diplomatic relations with Berlin.

In late February, British intelligence intercepted and passed to U.S. officials a telegram addressed to the German minister in Mexico from German foreign secretary Arthur Zimmermann. Its message was that if Mexico joined an alliance against the United States, Germany would help Mexico recover the territories it had lost in 1848. Zimmermann hoped to "set new enemies on America's neck—enemies which give them plenty to take care of over there."

Although Mexico City rejected Germany's offer, Wilson judged Zimmermann's telegram "a conspiracy against this country." The prospect of a German-Mexican collaboration helped turn the tide of opinion in the American Southwest, where antiwar sentiment had been strong.

Soon afterward, Wilson asked Congress for "armed neutrality" to defend American lives and commerce, seeking authority, for example, to arm American merchant ships. Antiwar senators Robert M. La Follette and George Norris, among others, saw the armed-ship bill as a blank check for the president to move the country to war, and they filibustered it to death. Wilson armed America's commercial vessels anyway, but acted too late to prevent the sinking of several American ships. War cries heightened. In late March, Wilson called Congress into special session.

On April 2, 1917, the president stepped before a hushed Congress and enumerated U.S. grievances: Germany's violation of freedom of the seas, disruption of commerce, interference with Mexico, and breach of human rights by killing innocent Americans. Congress declared war against Germany on April 6 by a vote of 373 to 50 in the House and 82 to 6 in the Senate. (This vote was for war against Germany only; a declaration of war against Austria-Hungary came several months later, on December 7.) Montana's Jeannette Rankin, the first woman in Congress, cast a ringing "no" vote.

WAR MESSAGE AND WAR DECLARATION

For principle, for morality, for honor, for commerce, for security, for reform—for all of these reasons, Wilson took the United States into the Great War. The submarine was certainly the culprit that drew a reluctant president and nation into the maelstrom. Critics blamed Wilson's rigid definition of in-

ternational law and his contention that Americans should be entitled to travel anywhere, even on a belligerent ship loaded with contraband. Most Americans came to accept Wilson's view that the Germans had to be checked to ensure an open, orderly world in which U.S. principles and interests would be safe.

America went to war to reform world politics, not to destroy Germany. By early 1917 the president concluded that America would be unable to claim a seat at the postwar peace conference unless it became a combatant. At the peace conference, Wilson intended to promote the principles he thought essential to a stable world order, to advance democracy and the Open Door, and to outlaw revolution and aggression. In designating the United States an "Associate" rather than an Allied nation, Wilson tried to preserve part of his country's neutral status, but to no avail.

Winning the War

*E*ven before the U.S. declaration of war, the Wilson administration strengthened the military under the banner of "preparedness." The National Defense Act of 1916 provided for increases in the army and National Guard and for summer training camps modeled on the one in Plattsburgh, New York, where some of America's social and economic elite had trained in 1915 as "citizen soldiers." The Navy Act of 1916 started the largest naval expansion in American history.

To raise an army, Congress in May 1917 passed the Selective Service Act, requiring all males between the ages of twenty-one and thirty (later changed to eighteen and forty-five) to register. National service, proponents believed, would prepare the nation for battle and instill patriotism and respect for democracy and personal sacrifice. Critics, however, feared it would lead to the militarization of American life.

THE DRAFT AND THE SOLDIER

On June 5, 1917, more than 9.5 million men signed up for the "great national lottery." By war's end, 24 million had been registered by local draft boards. The typical soldier was in his early to mid-twenties, white, single, American born, and poorly educated (most had not attended high school, and perhaps 30 percent could not read or write). Tens of thousands of women enlisted in the army Nurse Corps, served as "hello girls" (volunteer bilingual telephone operators) in the army Signal Corps, and became clerks in the navy and Marine Corps.

Some 400,000 African Americans also served in the military. Many southern politicians feared arming African Americans, but the army drafted them into segregated units and assigned them to menial labor; they endured miserable conditions. Ultimately over 42,000 blacks would see combat in Europe, and several black units served with distinction in the French army. The all-black 369th Infantry Regiment, for example, spent more time in the trenches—191 days— and received more medals than any other American outfit.

Although French officers had their share of racial prejudice and often treated the soldiers from their own African colonies poorly, black Americans serving with the French reported a degree of respect lacking in the American army. The irony was not lost on African American leaders such as W. E. B. Du Bois, who had endorsed the National Association for the Advancement of Colored People's (NAACP) support for the war and urged blacks to volunteer to help make the world safe for democracy.

Approximately 3 million men evaded draft registration. Some were arrested, others fled to Mexico or Canada, but most stayed at home and were never discovered. Another 338,000 men who had registered— mostly lower-income agricultural and industrial laborers—never showed up for induction. Nearly 65,000 draftees applied for conscientious-objector (CO) status (refusing to bear arms for religious or pacifistic reasons), but some changed their minds or failed preinduction examinations. Quakers and Mennonites were numerous among the 4,000 inductees classified as COs. COs who refused noncombat service, such as in the medical corps, faced imprisonment.

U.S. General John J. Pershing, head of the American Expeditionary Forces (AEF), insisted that his

TRENCH WARFARE

"sturdy rookies" remain a separate army. He refused to turn over his "doughboys" (so termed, apparently, because the large buttons on American uniforms in the 1860s resembled a deep-fried bread of that name) to Allied commanders, who favored deadly trench warfare. Since the fall of 1914, zigzag trenches fronted by barbed wire and mines stretched across France. Between the muddy, stinking trenches lay "no man's

land," denuded by artillery fire. Soldiers would charge enemy trenches, only to face machine-gun fire and poison gas.

First used by the Germans in April 1915, chlorine gas stimulated overproduction of fluid in the lungs, leading to death by drowning. Gas in various forms (mustard and phosgene, in addition to chlorine) would continue in use throughout the war, sometimes blistering, sometimes incapacitating, often killing.

The death toll in trench warfare was immense. At the Battle of the Somme in 1916, the British and French suffered 600,000 dead or wounded to earn only 125 square miles; the Germans lost 400,000 men. At Verdun that same year, 336,000 Germans perished, while at Passchendaele in 1917, over 370,000 British men died to gain about 40 miles of mud and barbed wire.

Not long after arriving on the French front, American soldiers faced the horrors caused by advanced

SHELL SHOCK

weaponry. Some suffered shell shock, a form of mental illness also known as war psychosis. Symptoms included a fixed, empty stare; violent tremors; paralyzed limbs; listlessness; jabbering; screaming; and haunting dreams. The illness could strike anyone; even soldiers appearing courageous cracked after days of incessant shelling and inescapable human carnage. Providing some relief were Red Cross canteens, staffed by women volunteers, which offered haircuts, food, and recreation.

In Paris, where forty large houses of prostitution thrived, venereal disease became such a problem

AMERICAN UNITS IN FRANCE

that French prime minister Georges Clemenceau offered licensed, inspected prostitutes in "special houses" to the American army. Still, by war's end, about 15 percent of America's soldiers had contracted venereal disease, costing the army $50 million and 7 million days of active duty. Periodic inspections, chemical prophylactic treatments, and the threat of court-martial kept the problem from being greater.

Overseas soldiers filled their diaries and letters with descriptions of "ancient" architecture and noted how the war-torn French countryside bore little resemblance to the groomed landscapes they had seen in paintings. "Life in France for the American soldier meant marching in the dirt and mud, living in cellars in filth, being wet and cold and fighting," the chief of staff of the Fourth Division remarked, ". . . but these French people did not seem to appreciate him at all."

With both sides virtually exhausted, the Americans tipped the balance toward the Allies. But not at first. Initially, the U.S. Navy battled submarines and escorted troop carriers; pilots in the U.S. Air Service, flying mostly British and French aircraft, saw limited action. American "aces" such as Eddie Rickenbacker defeated their German counterparts in aerial "dogfights" and became heroes, as much in France as at home. But only ground troops could make a decisive difference, and American units did not engage in much combat until after the harsh winter of 1917–1918.

The military and diplomatic situation changed dramatically as a result of the Bolshevik Revolution

THE BOLSHEVIK REVOLUTION

in Russia. In November 1917, the liberal-democratic government of Aleksander Kerensky, which had led the country since the czar's abdication early in the year, was overthrown by V. I. Lenin's radical socialists. Lenin vowed to change world politics and end imperial rivalries on terms that challenged Wilson's. To Lenin, the war signaled the impending end of capitalism and the rise of a global revolution of workers. For Western leaders, the prospect of Bolshevik-style revolutions worldwide was too frightening to contemplate.

In the weeks following their takeover, the Bolsheviks attempted to embarrass the capitalist governments and incite world revolution by publishing several Allied secret agreements for dividing up the colonies and other territories in the event of an Allied victory. Wilson confided to Colonel House that he wanted to tell the Bolsheviks to "go to hell," but he accepted the colonel's argument that he would have to address Lenin's claims that there was little to distinguish the two warring sides and that socialism represented the future.

In the Fourteen Points, unveiled in January 1918, Wilson reaffirmed America's commitment to an inter-

FOURTEEN POINTS

national system governed by laws and renounced territorial gains as a legitimate war aim. The first five points called for diplomacy "in the public view," freedom of the seas, lower tariffs, reductions in armaments, and the decolonization of empires. The next eight points specified the evacuation of foreign troops from Russia, Belgium, and France and appealed for self-determination for

nationalities in Europe, such as the Poles. For Wilson, the fourteenth point was the mechanism for achieving the others: "a general association of nations," or League of Nations.

Lenin was unimpressed and called for an immediate end to the fighting, the eradication of colonialism, and self-determination for all peoples. He also made a separate peace with Germany—the Treaty of Brest-Litovsk, signed on March 3, 1918. The deal erased centuries of Russian expansion, as Poland, Finland, and the Baltic states were taken from Russia and Ukraine was granted independence. One of Lenin's motives was to allow Russian troops loyal to the Bolsheviks to return home to fight anti-Bolshevik forces attempting to oust his government.

In March 1918, the Germans launched a major offensive, transferring troops from the Russian front

AMERICANS IN BATTLE

to France, and by May they were within 50 miles of Paris. U.S. First Division troops helped blunt the German advance at Cantigny (see Map 23.1). In June the Third Division and French forces held positions along the Marne River at Château-Thierry, and the Second Division attacked the Germans in the Belleau Wood. American soldiers won the battle after three weeks of fighting, but thousands died or were wounded in sacrificial frontal assaults against German machine guns.

Allied victory in the Second Battle of the Marne in July 1918 stemmed German advances. In September, French and American forces took St. Mihiel in a ferocious battle. Then, in the Meuse-Argonne offensive, over 1 million Americans joined British and French troops in weeks of combat in which some 26,000 Americans were killed before the Allies claimed the Argonne Forest on October 10. For Germany— its ground and submarine war stymied, its troops and cities mutinous, its allies Turkey and Austria dropping out, its kaiser having abdicated—peace became imperative. The Germans accepted a punishing armistice effective November 11, 1918.

The cost of the war is impossible to compute: the belligerents counted 10 million soldiers and 6.6 mil-

CASUALTIES

lion civilians dead and 21.3 million people wounded. Fifty-three thousand American soldiers died in battle and another 62,000 from disease, mainly a virulent strain of influenza in late 1918. Economic damage was colossal and output dwindled,

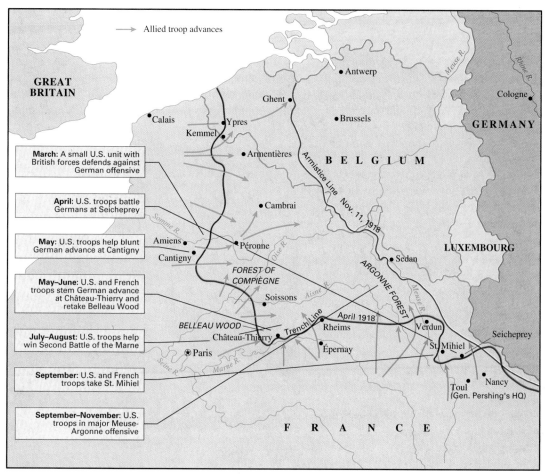

March: A small U.S. unit with British forces defends against German offensive

April: U.S. troops battle Germans at Seicheprey

May: U.S. troops help blunt German advance at Cantigny

May–June: U.S. and French troops stem German advance at Château-Thierry and retake Belleau Wood

July–August: U.S. troops help win Second Battle of the Marne

September: U.S. and French troops take St. Mihiel

September–November: U.S. troops in major Meuse-Argonne offensive

Map 23.1   American Troops at the Western Front, 1918

America's 2 million troops in France met German forces head-on, ensuring the defeat of the Central Powers in 1918.

contributing to widespread starvation in Europe during the winter of 1918–1919.

The German, Austro-Hungarian, Ottoman, and Russian empires were no more. For a time it appeared that the Bolshevik Revolution might spread westward, as communist uprisings shook Germany and parts of central Europe. Even before the armistice, revolutionaries temporarily took power in the German cities of Bremen, Hamburg, and Lübeck. In Moscow, the new Soviet state sought to consolidate its power.

Mobilizing the Home Front

*T*he war had a tremendous impact on America. The federal government expanded its power to meet war needs and intervened in American life. The enlarged Washington bureaucracy managed the economy, labor force, military, public opinion, and more. Federal expenditures increased as the government spent more than $760 million a month from April 1917 to August 1919. As tax revenues lagged, the administration resorted to deficit spending. To

The Influenza Pandemic of 1918

In the summer and fall of 1918, as World War I neared its end, an outbreak of influenza swept the earth. It claimed more than twice as many as the Great War itself—somewhere between 25 and 40 million lives. In the United States, 675,000 people died.

The first cases were identified in midwestern military camps in early March. At Fort Riley, Kansas, 48 men died. Soldiers shipped out to Europe in large numbers (84,000 in March), some unknowingly carrying the virus. The illness appeared on the western front in April, and by June, an estimated 8 million Spaniards were infected.

In August, after a midsummer lull, a deadlier form of the influenza erupted simultaneously in three cities on three continents: Freetown, Sierra Leone, in Africa; Brest, France, the port of entry for many American soldiers; and Boston, Massachusetts. In September, the disease swept down the East Coast, killing 12,000 Americans.

People could be healthy at the start of the weekend and dead by the end of it. Some experienced a rapid accumulation of fluid in the lungs and literally drowned. Others died slowly. Mortality rates were highest for twenty- to twenty-nine-year-olds—the same group dying in the trenches.

In October, the epidemic hit full force, spreading to Japan, India, Africa, and Latin America and claiming 200,000 American lives. There was a nationwide shortage of caskets and gravediggers, and funerals were limited to fifteen minutes. Bodies were left in gutters or on front porches, to be picked up by trucks that drove the streets.

Suddenly, for reasons still unclear, the epidemic eased in November, though the dying continued into 1919. In England and Wales, the final toll was 200,000. Samoa lost a quarter of its population, and in India, the epidemic may have claimed a staggering 20 million. It was, in historian Roy Porter's words, "the greatest single demographic shock mankind has ever experienced." Americans, accustomed to thinking that two great oceans could isolate them, were reminded that they were immutably linked to the rest of humankind.

A nurse at a special camp for influenza victims on the grounds of Correy Hill Hospital in Brookline, Massachusetts, September 1918. The gauze mask she and countless others wore that autumn proved to be useless: the microbe could pass right through it.
(© Underwood & Underwood/CORBIS)

Progressives of the New Nationalist persuasion (see Chapter 21), the wartime expansion and centralization of government power were welcome, but others worried about the dangers of concentrated federal power.

The federal government and private business became partners during the war. Early on, the government relied on industrial committees for advice on purchases and prices. But evidence of self-interested businesspeople cashing in on the national interest aroused public protest. The head of the aluminum advisory committee, for example, was also president of the largest aluminum company. Consequently, the committees were replaced in July 1917 with a single manager, the War Industries Board. The government also suspended antitrust laws and signed cost-plus contracts, guaranteeing companies healthy profits and a means to head off labor strikes with higher wages. Competitive bidding was virtually abandoned, and big business grew bigger.

BUSINESS-GOVERNMENT COOPERATION

Hundreds of new government agencies, staffed primarily by businesspeople, used economic controls to shift the nation's resources to the Allies, the AEF, and war-related production. The Food Administration, led by engineer and investor Herbert Hoover, urged Americans to grow "victory gardens" and eat meatless and wheatless meals, but it also regulated prices and distribution. The Railroad Administration took over the railway industry; the Fuel Administration controlled coal supplies and rationed gasoline. When strikes threatened the telephone and telegraph companies, the federal government seized and ran them.

The largest of the superagencies was the War Industries Board (WIB), headed by the financier Bernard Baruch. This Wall Streeter threatened Henry Ford that he would dispatch the military to seize his plants unless the automaker accepted WIB limits on car production. Designed as a clearing-house to coordinate the national economy, the WIB made purchases, allocated supplies, and fixed prices at levels that business requested. The WIB also ordered the standardization of goods to streamline production. The varieties of automobile tires, for example, were reduced from 287 to 3.

About a quarter of all American production was diverted to war needs. As farmers enjoyed boom years, they put more acreage into production and mechanized. Gross farm income from 1914 to 1919 increased

ECONOMIC PERFORMANCE

over 230 percent. Although manufacturing output leveled off in 1918, wartime demand fueled substantial growth for some industries such as steel, which enjoyed a peak production of 45 million tons in 1917, twice the prewar figure. Overall, the gross national product in 1920 stood 237 percent higher than in 1914.

There were mistakes in the rush to production. Weapons deliveries fell short, and the bloated bureaucracy of the War Shipping Board failed to build enough ships. In the severe winter of 1917–1918, coal companies withheld production to raise prices; railroads did not have enough coal cars; and harbors froze, closing out coal barges. People died from pneumonia and freezing. A Brooklyn man went to forage for coal in the morning and returned to find his two-month-old daughter frozen to death in her crib.

To pay its wartime bills, the government dramatically increased taxes. The Revenue Act in 1916 started by raising the surtax on high incomes and corporate profits, imposing a federal tax on large estates, and significantly increasing the tax on munitions manufacturers. Still, the government financed only one-third of the war through taxes. The other two-thirds came from loans, including Liberty bonds sold to the American people. The War Revenue Act of 1917 provided for a more steeply graduated personal income tax, a corporate income tax, an excess-profits tax, and increased excise taxes on alcoholic beverages, tobacco, and luxury items.

Although these taxes did curb excessive corporate profiteering, there were loopholes. Sometimes companies inflated costs to conceal profits. Corporate net earnings for 1913 totaled $4 billion; in 1917 they reached $7 billion; and in 1918, after the tax bite and the war's end, they still stood at $4.5 billion. The abrupt cancellation of billions of dollars' worth of contracts at war's end, however, caused a brief economic downturn, a short boom, and then an intense decline (discussed in Chapter 24).

For American workers, the full-employment wartime economy increased earnings. With the higher cost of living, however, workers saw minimal improvement in their economic standing. Turnover rates escalated as workers switched jobs, seeking better pay and conditions. Some employers sought to overcome labor shortages by expanding welfare and social programs and establishing personnel departments.

LABOR SHORTAGE

To meet the labor crisis, the Department of Labor's U.S. Employment Service matched laborers with job vacancies, attracting workers from the South and Midwest to war industries in the East. The department also temporarily relaxed the literacy-test and head-tax provisions of immigration law to attract farm labor, miners, and railroad workers from Mexico. As workers crammed into cities, the U.S. Housing Corporation and Emergency Fleet Corporation built row houses in Newport News, Virginia, and Eddystone, Pennsylvania.

The tight wartime labor market meant new work opportunities for women. In Connecticut, a special motion picture, *Mr. and Mrs. Hines of Stamford Do Their Bit*, appealed to housewives' patriotism, urging them to take factory jobs. Although the total number of working women increased slightly, the real story was that many moved into formerly male domains. Some white women left domestic service for factories, shifted from clerking in department stores to stenography and typing, or departed textile mills for firearms plants. For the first time, department stores employed black women as elevator operators and cafeteria waitresses. But most working women were single and remained concentrated in the sex-segregated occupations of typists, nurses, teachers, and domestic servants.

Women also participated in the war effort as volunteers, making clothing for refugees and soldiers, serving at Red Cross facilities, and teaching French to nurses assigned to the war zone. Many worked for the Women's Committee of the Council of National Defense, a network of state and local organizations publicizing government mobilization programs, encouraging home gardens, sponsoring drives to sell Liberty bonds, and promoting social welfare reforms. This patriotic work improved prospects of passing the Nineteenth Amendment granting woman suffrage (see Chapter 21). "We have made partners of women in this war," Wilson said in 1918. "Shall we admit them only to a partnership of suffering and sacrifice . . . and not to a partnership of privilege and right?"

War mobilization encouraged a great migration of southern blacks to northern cities to work in railroad yards, packinghouses, steel mills, shipyards, and coal mines. Between 1910 and 1920, Cleveland's black population swelled by more than 300 percent, Detroit's by more than 600 percent, and Chicago's by

150 percent, with most of it occurring between 1916 and 1919. All told, about a half-million African Americans moved to the North, with families pooling savings or selling household goods to pay for the journey. Most of the migrants were unmarried and skilled or semiskilled males in their early twenties. Northern wartime jobs provided an escape from low wages, sharecropping, tenancy, crop liens, debt peonage, lynchings, and political disfranchisement. One African American wrote to a friend in Mississippi: "I just begin to feel like a man. . . . I don't have to humble to no one. I have registered. Will vote the next election."

To keep factories running smoothly, Wilson instituted the National War Labor Board (NWLB) in early 1918. The NWLB discouraged strikes and lockouts and urged management to negotiate with existing unions. In July, after the Western Union Company fired eight hundred union members for trying to organize the firm's workers, the president nationalized the telegraph lines and put the laborers back to work. But in September the NWLB ordered striking Bridgeport, Connecticut, machinists back to munitions factories, threatening to revoke the draft exemptions they received for working in an "essential" industry.

NATIONAL WAR LABOR BOARD

Many labor leaders hoped the war would lead to recognition and better pay through partnership with government. Samuel Gompers threw the AFL's loyalty to Wilson, promising to deter strikes. He and other moderate labor leaders accepted appointments to federal agencies. The antiwar Socialist Party blasted the AFL for becoming a "fifth wheel on [the] capitalist war chariot," but union membership climbed from roughly 2.5 million in 1916 to more than 4 million in 1919.

The AFL, however, could not curb strikes by the radical Industrial Workers of the World (IWW, also known as "Wobblies") or rebellious AFL locals, especially those controlled by socialists. In the nineteen war months, more than six thousand strikes expressed workers' demands for a "living wage" and improved working conditions. Unions sought to create "industrial democracy," a more representative workplace with a role for labor in determining job categories and content. Defying the AFL, labor parties had sprung up in twenty-three states by 1920.

Civil Liberties Under Challenge

*W*ilson and his advisers enjoyed the support of newspapers, religious leaders, and public officials, but they were less certain about ordinary Americans. An official and unofficial campaign soon began to silence dissenters who were questioning Wilson's decision for war or protesting the draft. The Wilson administration had one of the worst civil liberties records in American history.

The targets of governmental and quasi-vigilante repression included hundreds of thousands of antiwar Americans and aliens: pacifists, conscientious objectors, socialists, radical labor groups, the debt-ridden Oklahoma tenant farmers who staged the Green Corn Rebellion against the draft, the Non-Partisan League, reformers such as Robert La Follette and Jane Addams, and countless others. In the wartime debate over democratic free speech, the concept of "civil liberties" emerged for the first time as a major public policy issue (see the end of this chapter).

Spearheading the administration's war campaign was the Committee on Public Information (CPI),

COMMITTEE ON PUBLIC INFORMATION

formed in April 1917 and headed by Progressive journalist George Creel. Employing talented writers and scholars, the CPI used propaganda to shape public opinion. Pamphlets and films demonized the Germans, and CPI "Four-Minute Men" spoke at movie theaters, schools, and churches to pump up patriotism. Encouraged by the CPI, film companies and the National Association of the Motion Picture Industry produced documentaries, newsreels, and anti-German movies such as *The Kaiser, the Beast of Berlin* (1918).

The committee also urged the press to practice "self-censorship" and encouraged people to spy on their neighbors. Ultrapatriotic groups such as the Sedition Slammers and the American Defense Society used vigilantism. In Hilger, Montana, citizens burned history texts mentioning Germany. To avoid trouble, the Kaiser-Kuhn grocery in St. Louis changed its name to Pioneer Grocery. Germantown, Nebraska, became Garland, and the townspeople in Berlin, Iowa, henceforth hailed from Lincoln. The German shepherd became the Alsatian shepherd.

Towns had Liberty Loan quotas and sometimes bullied "slackers" into purchasing bonds. Nativist advocates of "100% Americanism" exploited the atmosphere to exhort immigrants to throw off their Old World cultures. Companies offered English-language and naturalization classes and refused jobs and promotions to those who did not learn English fast enough.

Even institutions that had long practiced tolerance were contaminated. Wellesley College economics professor Emily Greene Balch was fired for her pacifist views (she won the Nobel Peace Prize in 1946). Three Columbia University students were apprehended in mid-1917 for circulating an antiwar petition. Columbia fired Professor J. M. Cattell, a distinguished psychologist, for his antiwar stand. His colleague Charles Beard, a prowar historian, resigned in protest. Local school boards also dismissed teachers who questioned the war.

The Wilson administration guided through an obliging Congress the Espionage Act (1917) and the

ESPIONAGE AND SEDITION ACTS

Sedition Act (1918), giving the government wide latitude to crack down on critics. The first statute forbade "false statements" designed to impede the draft or promote military insubordination, and it banned from the mails materials considered treasonous. The Sedition Act made it unlawful to obstruct the sale of war bonds and to use "disloyal, profane, scurrilous, or abusive" language to describe the government, the Constitution, the flag, or the military uniform. More than two thousand people were prosecuted under the acts, with many others intimidated into silence.

Progressives and conservatives used the war emergency to throttle the Industrial Workers of the World and the Socialist Party. Government agents raided IWW meetings, and the army put down IWW strikes. By war's end, most of the union's leaders were in jail. In summer 1918, Socialist Party leader Eugene V. Debs was arrested by federal agents for an oration extolling socialism and freedom of speech—including the freedom to criticize Wilson on the war. Debs told the court what many thought of the Espionage Act: it was "a despotic enactment in flagrant conflict with democratic principles and with the spirit of free institutions." Handed a ten-year sentence, Debs remained in prison until he was pardoned in late 1921.

The Supreme Court endorsed such convictions. In *Schenck v. U.S.* (1919), the Court unanimously upheld the conviction of a Socialist Party member who had mailed pamphlets urging draft resistance. In war, Justice Oliver Wendell Holmes wrote, the First Amendment could be restricted: when words "are of such a nature as to create a clear and present danger that they will bring about the substantial evils that Congress has a right to prevent," free speech could be limited.

Red Scare, Red Summer

*T*he line between wartime suppression of dissent and the postwar Red Scare is not easily drawn. Together they stabbed at the Bill of Rights and wounded radicalism in America. But where wartime fears focused on subversion, after the armistice it was revolution; and where the prewar target was often German Americans, in 1919 it was frequently organized labor. Already alarmed by the Russian Revolution and communist uprisings in Europe, American fears grew in 1919 when the Soviet leadership formed the Communist International (or Comintern) to export revolution throughout the world. Terrified conservatives sought out pro-Bolshevik sympathizers (or "Reds," from the red flag used by communists) in the United States, especially in immigrant groups and labor unions.

Labor union leaders emerged from the war determined to secure higher wages for workers and retain wartime bargaining rights, while employers rescinded benefits they had been forced to grant during the war, including recognition of unions. The result was more than thirty-three hundred strikes involving 4 million laborers nationwide. On May 1, a day of celebration for workers around the world, bombs were sent to prominent Americans, though they were intercepted and dismantled. Police never captured the conspirators, but many blamed anarchists and others bent on destroying the American way of life. When the Boston police went on strike in September, some claimed a Bolshevik conspiracy, but others thought it ridiculous to label Boston's Irish American Catholic cops "radicals."

LABOR STRIKES

Unrest in the steel industry in September stirred more fears of Bolshevism. Many steelworkers worked twelve hours a day, seven days a week, and lived in squalid housing, counting on the National Committee for Organizing Iron and Steel Workers to improve their lives. When postwar industry unemployment climbed and the U.S. Steel Corporation refused to meet with committee representatives, some 350,000 workers walked off the job demanding the right to collective bargaining, a shorter workday, and a living wage. The steel barons hired strikebreakers and sent agents to club strikers. The strike collapsed in early 1920.

Business and political leaders dismissed the steel strike as a foreign threat orchestrated by American radicals. There was no conspiracy, and the American left was badly splintered. Two defectors from the Socialist Party, John Reed and Benjamin Gitlow, founded the Communist Labor Party in 1919. The rival Communist Party of the United States of America, composed largely of aliens, was launched the same year. But their combined membership did not exceed seventy thousand, and in 1919 the harassed Socialist Party could muster barely thirty thousand members.

Although divisiveness signified weakness, both Progressives and conservatives interpreted the rise of new communist parties as strengthening the radical menace. Organized in May 1919 to lobby for veterans' benefits, the American Legion soon preached an antiradicalism that fueled the Red Scare. By 1920, 843,000 Legion members, mostly middle and upper class, embraced an Americanism demanding conformity.

AMERICAN LEGION

Wilson's attorney general, A. Mitchell Palmer, also insisted that Americans think alike. A Progressive reformer, Quaker, and ambitious politician, Palmer appointed J. Edgar Hoover to head the Radical Division of the Department of Justice. Hoover compiled index cards naming allegedly radical individuals and organizations. During 1919 agents jailed IWW members; Palmer also made sure that 249 alien radicals, including anarchist Emma Goldman, were deported to Russia.

States passed peacetime sedition acts and arrested hundreds of people. Vigilante groups flourished, their numbers swelled by returning veterans. In November 1919 in Centralia, Washington, American Legionnaires broke from a parade to storm the IWW hall. Several were wounded, others were arrested, and one Wobbly, an ex-soldier, was taken from jail by a mob, then beaten, castrated, and shot. The New York State legislature expelled five duly elected Socialist Party members in early 1920.

The Red Scare reached a climax in January 1920 in the Palmer Raids. Planned and directed by Hoover,

PALMER RAIDS government agents in thirty-three cities broke into meeting halls and homes without search warrants, jailing over four thousand people and denying them counsel. In Boston some four hundred people were detained on bitterly cold Deer Island: two died of pneumonia, one leaped to his death, and another went insane. Because of court rulings and the courageous efforts of Assistant Secretary of Labor Louis Post, most of the arrestees were released, although nearly six hundred were deported in 1920–1921.

Palmer's disregard for elementary civil liberties drew criticism, with many charging that his tactics violated the Constitution. When Palmer called for a peacetime sedition act, he alarmed both liberal and conservative leaders. His dire prediction that pro-Soviet radicals would incite violence on May Day 1920 proved mistaken, as the day remained peaceful. Palmer, who had called himself the "Fighting Quaker," was jeered as the "Quaking Fighter."

Palmer also blamed communists for the racial violence that gripped the nation in these years,

RACIAL UNREST though the charge was equally baseless. African Americans realized well before the war ended that their participation did little to change discriminatory white attitudes. Segregation remained social custom. The Ku Klux Klan was reviving, and racist films such as D. W. Griffith's *The Birth of a Nation* (1915) fed prejudice with its celebration of the Klan and its demeaning depiction of blacks. Despite wartime declarations of humanity, 382 blacks were lynched in America between 1914 and 1920, some of them in military uniform.

Northern whites who resented "the Negro invasion" rioted, as in East St. Louis, Illinois, in July 1917 (see Chapter 19) and a month later in Houston. During the bloody "Red Summer" of 1919 (so named by black author James Weldon Johnson for the blood that was spilled), race riots rocked two dozen cities and towns. The worst violence occurred in Chicago, a favorite destination for migrating blacks. In the hot days of July 1919, a black youth swimming at a segregated white beach was hit by a rock and drowned. Soon blacks and whites were battling one another. Stabbings, burnings, and shootings continued for days until state police restored calm. Thirty-eight people died, twenty-three African Americans and fifteen whites. A disillusioned W. E. B. Du Bois vowed a struggle: "We return. We return from fighting. We return fighting." And poet Claude McKay put it this way in his poem, "If We Must Die":

Like men we'll face the murderous cowardly pack.
Pressed to the wall, dying, but fighting back.

Du Bois and McKay reflected a newfound militancy among black veterans and northern black

BLACK MILITANCY communities. Editorials in African American newspapers subjected white politicians to increasingly harsh criticism and implored readers to embrace their own prowess and beauty. The NAACP stepped up its campaign for civil rights and equality, vowing in 1919 to publicize the terrors of lynching and seek legislation against it. Other blacks, doubting the potential for equality, turned instead to charismatic Jamaican immigrant Marcus Garvey, who called on African Americans to seek a separate black nation (as detailed in Chapter 24).

The crackdown on laborers and radicals and the resurgence of racism in 1919 dashed wartime hopes. Although the passage of the Nineteenth Amendment in 1920, guaranteeing women the right to vote, showed that reform could happen, it was the exception. Unemployment, inflation, racial conflict, labor upheaval, a campaign against free speech—all inspired disillusionment in the immediate postwar years.

The Defeat of Peace

President Wilson seemed more focused on confronting the threat of radicalism abroad than at home. In mid-1918, he revealed his ardent anti-Bolshevism when he ordered five thousand American troops to northern Russia and ten thousand more to Siberia, where they joined other Allied contingents in fighting what was now a Russian civil war. Wilson did not consult Congress. He said the military expeditions would guard Allied supplies and Russian railroads from German seizure and would also rescue a group of Czechs who wished to fight the Germans.

Seeking to smash the infant Bolshevik government, Wilson backed an economic blockade of Russia, sent arms to anti-Bolshevik forces, and refused to recognize Lenin's government. The United States also secretly passed military information to anti-Bolshevik forces and used food relief to shore up Soviet opponents in the Baltic region. Later, at the Paris Peace Conference, Russia was denied a seat. U.S. troops did not leave Siberia until spring 1920, after the Bolsheviks had demonstrated their staying power.

Wilson faced a monumental task in securing a postwar settlement, though some observers suggested he underestimated his task. During the 1918 congressional elections, Wilson misstepped in suggesting that patriotism required the election of a Democratic Congress; Republicans blasted the president for questioning their love of country and gained control of both houses. This was trouble because a peace treaty would require approval from a potentially hostile Senate and because the election results diminished Wilson's stature in the eyes of foreign leaders. Wilson aggravated his political problems by not naming a senator to his advisory American Peace Commission and refusing to bring any prominent Republicans with him or to consult with the Senate Foreign Relations Committee before the Paris Peace Conference.

Wilson was greeted by adoring crowds in Paris, London, and Rome, but their leaders—Georges Clemenceau of France, David Lloyd George of Britain, and Vittorio Orlando of Italy (with Wilson, the Big Four)—became formidable adversaries. After four years of horrible war, the Allies were not about to be cheated out of the fruits of victory. The late-arriving Americans had not suffered as France and Great Britain had. Germany would have to pay big for the calamity it had caused.

The Big Four tried to work out an agreement at the conference. The victors demanded that Germany (which had been excluded from the proceedings) pay a huge reparations bill. Wilson instead called for a small indemnity, fearing that an economically hobbled Germany might turn

PARIS PEACE CONFERENCE

to Bolshevism. Unable to moderate the Allied position, the president reluctantly agreed to a clause blaming the war on the Germans and to the creation of a commission to determine reparations (later set at $33 billion). Wilson acknowledged that the peace terms were "hard," but he also came to believe that "the German people must be made to hate war."

As for dismantling empires and the principle of self-determination, Wilson could achieve only some of his goals. Creating a League-administered "mandate" system, the conferees gave Japan authority over Germany's colonies in the Pacific, while France obtained what became Lebanon and Syria and Britain received the three former Ottoman provinces that became Iraq. Britain also secured Palestine, on the condition that it promote "the establishment in Palestine of a national home for the Jewish people" without prejudice to "the civil and religious rights of existing non-Jewish communities"—the so-called Balfour Declaration of 1917.

Elsewhere in Europe, Wilson's prescriptions fared better. Out of Austria-Hungary and Russia came the newly independent states of Austria, Hungary, Yugoslavia, Czechoslovakia, and Poland. Wilson and his colleagues also built a *cordon sanitaire* (buffer zone) of new westward-looking nations (Finland, Estonia, Latvia, and Lithuania) around Russia to quarantine the Bolshevik contagion.

Wilson worked hardest on the charter for the League of Nations, the centerpiece of his plans for the postwar world. He envisioned the League as having power over all disputes among states; as such, it could transform international relations. Even so, the great powers would have preponderant say: the organization would have an influential council of five permanent members and elected delegates from smaller states, an assembly of all members, and a World Court.

LEAGUE OF NATIONS AND ARTICLE 10

Wilson identified Article 10 as the "kingpin" of the League covenant: "The Members of the League undertake to respect and preserve as against external aggression the territorial integrity and existing political independence of all Members of the League." Wilson insisted the League charter become part of the peace treaty, arguing that there could be no future peace without a league to oversee it.

German representatives at first refused to sign the punitive treaty but submitted in June 1919. They gave up 13 percent of Germany's territory, 10 percent of its population, all of its colonies, and a huge portion of its national wealth. Many people wondered how the League could function in the poisoned postwar atmosphere of humiliation and revenge.

In March 1919, thirty-nine senators (enough to deny the treaty the necessary two-thirds vote) signed

CRITICS OF THE TREATY

a petition stating that the League's structure did not adequately protect U.S. interests. Wilson denounced his critics as "pygmy" minds, but persuaded the peace conference to exempt the Monroe Doctrine and domestic matters from League jurisdiction. But Wilson would budge no more. Could his critics not see that League membership would give the United States "leadership in the world"?

By summer, criticism intensified: Wilson had bastardized his own principles. He had conceded Shandong to Japan and killed a provision affirming the racial equality of all peoples. The treaty ignored freedom of the seas, and tariffs were not reduced. Reparations on Germany promised to be punishing. Critics on the left protested that the League would perpetuate empire. Conservative critics feared it would limit American freedom of action in world affairs, stymie U.S. expansion, and intrude on domestic questions. And Article 10 raised serious questions: Would the United States be *obligated* to use armed force to ensure collective security? And would the League feel compelled to crush colonial rebellions, such as in Ireland or India?

Henry Cabot Lodge of Massachusetts led the Senate opposition. A Harvard-educated Ph.D. and partisan Republican who intensely disliked Wilson, Lodge packed the Foreign Relations Committee with critics and introduced several reservations to the treaty, most importantly that Congress had to approve any obligation under Article 10.

In September 1919 Wilson embarked on a speaking tour of the United States. Growing more exhausted, he dismissed his antagonists as "contemptible quitters." While doubts about Article 10 multiplied, Wilson highlighted neglected features of the League charter—such as the arbitration of disputes and an international conference to abolish child labor. In Colorado, the president awoke to nausea and uncontrollable facial twitching. A few days later, he suffered a massive stroke that paralyzed his left side. He

became peevish and even more stubborn, increasingly unable to conduct presidential business. Advised to placate Lodge and other senatorial critics so the Versailles treaty might receive congressional approval, Wilson rejected "dishonorable compromise."

Twice in November the Senate rejected the Treaty of Versailles and thus U.S. membership in the

SENATE REJECTION OF THE TREATY AND LEAGUE

League. In March 1920 the Senate again voted; this time, a majority (49 for and 35 against) favored the treaty with reservations, but the tally fell short of the two-thirds needed. Had Wilson permitted Democrats to compromise—to accept reservations—he could have achieved his fervent goal of membership in the League, which came into being without the United States.

At the core of the debate lay a basic issue in American foreign policy: whether the United States would endorse collective security or continue the more solitary path articulated in George Washington's Farewell Address and the Monroe Doctrine. In a world dominated by imperialist states unwilling to subordinate their strategic ambitions to an international organization, Americans preferred their traditional nonalignment and freedom of choice over binding commitments to collective action. Wilson countered that the League promised something better than the status quo for the United States and the rest of the world: collective security in place of the frail protection of alliances and the instability of a balance of power.

World War I did not make the world safe for democracy, but it did make the United States an even

AN UNSAFE WORLD

greater world power. By 1920 the United States was the leading global economic power, producing 40 percent of the world's coal, 70 percent of its petroleum, and half of its pig iron. It also ranked first in world trade. American companies used the war to nudge the Germans and British out of foreign markets, especially in Latin America. Meanwhile, the United States shifted from a debtor to a creditor nation, becoming the world's leading banker.

After the disappointment of Versailles, the peace movement revitalized, and the military became more professional. The Reserve Officers Training Corps (ROTC) became permanent; military "colleges" provided upper-echelon training; and the Army Industrial College, founded in 1924, pursued business-military cooperation in logistics and planning. The National Research Council, created in 1916 with government money and Carnegie and Rockefeller funds, continued as a defense research alliance. Tanks, quick-firing guns, armor-piercing explosives, and oxygen masks for pilots were among the technological advances emerging from the First World War.

The international system born in these years was unstable. Nationalist leaders active during the First World War, such as Ho Chi Minh of Indochina and Mohandas K. Gandhi of India, vowed independence for their peoples. Communism became a disruptive force in world politics, and the Soviets bore a grudge against those who had tried to thwart their revolution. The new states in central and eastern Europe proved weak. Germans bitterly resented the harsh peace settlement, and German war debts and reparations dogged international order for years.

Summary   *Online Study Center*   **ACE the Test**

*T*he war years marked the emergence of the United States as a world power, and Americans could take justifiable pride in their contribution to the Allied victory. But the war exposed deep divisions among Americans: white versus black, nativist versus immigrant, capital versus labor, men versus women, radical versus Progressive and conservative, pacifist versus interventionist, nationalist versus internationalist.

During the war, the federal government intervened in the economy and influenced people's everyday lives as never before. Although the Wilson administration shunned reconversion plans (war housing projects, for example, were sold to private investors) and quickly dismantled the many governmental agencies, the World War I experience of the activist state served as guidance for reformers battling the Great Depression in the 1930s (the topic of Chapter 25). The partnership of government and business in managing the wartime economy advanced the development of a mass society through the standardization of products and the promotion of efficiency. Wilsonian wartime policies also nourished the concentration of corporate ownership by suspending antitrust laws. Business

power dominated the next decade, while labor entered lean years.

Although the disillusionment of Versailles did not cause the United States to adopt isolationism (as discussed in Chapter 26), skepticism about America's ability to right wrongs abroad marked the nation's postwar mood. People recoiled from photographs of shell-shocked faces and bodies dangling from barbed wire. American soldiers, tired of idealism, craved regular jobs. Many Progressives lost their enthusiasm for crusades, disgusted by the bickering of the victors.

By 1920 idealism had faded at home and abroad. Americans were unsure what their country's new-found status as a world power meant for the future. With uneasiness and a mixed legacy from the Great War, the country entered the 1920s.

LEGACY FOR A PEOPLE AND A NATION
Freedom of Speech and the ACLU

Before World War I, those with radical views often received harsh treatment for exercising their freedom of speech. During the war, however, the Wilson administration's suppression of dissidents led some Americans to reformulate the traditional definition of allowable speech. Roger Baldwin, a conscientious objector, and women's suffrage activist Crystal Eastman were among the first to advance the idea that the content of political speech could be separated from the identity of the speaker and that patriotic Americans could—indeed, should—defend the right of others to express political beliefs abhorrent to their own. After defending conscientious objectors, Baldwin and Eastman—joined by activists such as Jane Addams, Helen Keller, and Norman Thomas—formed the American Civil Liberties Union (ACLU).

Since 1920 the ACLU, which today has some 300,000 members, has aimed to protect the civil liberties of all Americans. It has been involved in almost every major civil liberties case in U.S. courts, among them the John Scopes "monkey trial" (1925) concerning the teaching of evolution at a Tennessee school and the landmark *Brown v. Board of Education* case (1954) that ended federal tolerance of racial segregation.

Conservatives have long criticized the ACLU for its opposition to official prayers in public schools and its support of abortion, as well as its decisions on whose freedom of speech to defend. ACLU proponents counter that it has also defended those on the right, such as Oliver North, a key figure in the Iran-contra scandal of the 1980s.

Either way, the principle of free speech is today broadly accepted by Americans, so that even ACLU bashers take it for granted. Ironically, the Wilson administration's crackdown on dissent produced an expanded commitment to freedom of speech for a people and a nation.

THE NEW ERA 1920–1929

*E*ager to win $25,000 offered by a hotel owner to the first person to fly nonstop between New York and Paris, three different airplane crews at Roosevelt Airfield accepted the challenge in the spring of 1927. One man, Charles A. Lindbergh, young, handsome, and the only one piloting solo, risked drizzly weather to start the trip on May 20. For thirty-three hours, his craft, *The Spirit of St. Louis,* bounced across the Atlantic skies. The flight captivated Americans as newspaper and telegraph reports followed Lindbergh's progress. When he landed at Le Bourget Airfield, the nation rejoiced. President Calvin Coolidge dispatched a warship to bring "Lucky Lindy" home. Celebrants sent Lindbergh 55,000 telegrams and feted him during a triumphant homecoming parade.

Although his was not the first transatlantic flight (in 1919, two men had piloted a plane from Newfoundland to Ireland), Lindbergh's venture turned him into one of the most celebrated heroes in American history. One newspaper exclaimed that he had accomplished "the greatest feat of a solitary man in the history of the human race." Lindbergh received the Distinguished Flying Cross and the Congressional Medal of Honor. Promoters offered him millions of dollars for a world air tour and $700,000 for a movie contract. Texas named a town after him.

The celebration and publicity surrounding Lindbergh's flight reveal the impact of commercialism, technology, and mass entertainment on American culture. Lindbergh epitomized achievement, self-reliance, and courage—old-fashioned values that vied for public allegiance in a new era.

During the 1920s, consumerism flourished. Although poverty beset small farmers, workers in declining industries, and nonwhites in inner cities, most others enjoyed a high standard of living relative to previous generations. Spurred by advertising and installment buying, Americans acquired radios, automobiles, real estate, and stocks. As in the Gilded Age, government maintained a favorable climate for business. And in contrast to the Progressive era, few people worried about abuses of power. Still, state and local governments undertook important reforms.

Big Business Triumphant

Politics and Government

Materialism Unbound

Cities, Migrants, and Suburbs

New Rhythms of Everyday Life

LINKS TO THE WORLD
Pan American Airways

Lines of Defense

The Age of Play

Cultural Currents

The Election of 1928 and the End of the New Era

LEGACY FOR A PEOPLE AND A NATION
Intercollegiate Athletics

Online Study Center
This icon will direct you to interactive map and primary source activities on the website
http://college.hmco.com/pic/nortonbrief7e

CHRONOLOGY

1920 • Nineteenth Amendment ratified, legalizing the vote for women in federal elections
  • Harding elected president
  • KDKA transmits first commercial radio broadcast

1920–21 • Postwar deflation and depression occurs

1921 • Federal Highway Act funds national highway system
  • Emergency Quota Act establishes immigration quotas
  • Sacco and Vanzetti convicted
  • Sheppard-Towner Act allots funds to states to set up maternity and pediatric clinics

1922 • Economic recovery raises standard of living
  • *Coronado Coal Company v. United Mine Workers* rules that strikes may be illegal actions in restraint of trade
  • *Bailey v. Drexel Furniture Company* voids restrictions on child labor
  • Federal government ends strikes by railroad shop workers and miners
  • Fordney-McCumber Tariff raises rates on imports

1923 • Harding dies; Coolidge assumes the presidency
  • *Adkins v. Children's Hospital* overturns a minimum-wage law affecting women

1923–24 • Government scandals (Teapot Dome) exposed

1924 • National Origins Act revises immigration quotas
  • Coolidge elected president

1925 • Scopes trial highlights battle between religious fundamentalists and modernists

1927 • Sacco and Vanzetti executed
  • Lindbergh pilots solo transatlantic flight
  • Ruth hits sixty home runs
  • *The Jazz Singer,* the first movie with sound, is released

1928 • Stock market soars
  • Hoover elected president

1929 • Stock market crashes; Great Depression begins

As Lindbergh's adventure reveals, it was an era of contrast and complexity. Fads and frivolities coincided with creativity in the arts and advances in science and technology. Changes in work habits, family responsibilities, and healthcare fostered new uses of time and new attitudes about behavior. Material bounty and leisure enticed Americans into new amusements. The era's modernism and materialism were appealing to many but unsettling to those who embraced tradition and scorned liberal ideas.

The glitter of consumer culture blinded Americans to rising debts and uneven prosperity. They were thoroughly unprepared when a devastating depression brought the era to a close. ■

Big Business Triumphant

The 1920s began with economic decline. After the First World War ended, industrial output dropped and unemployment rose as wartime orders dried up, consumer spending dwindled, and demobilized soldiers flooded the work force. Unemployment, around 2 percent in 1919, passed 12 percent in 1921. Railroads and mining industries suffered, and New England textile companies abandoned outdated factories for the convenient raw materials and cheap labor of the South.

Electric energy prompted a recovery in 1922 that continued unevenly until 1929.

NEW ECONOMIC EXPANSION By decade's end, factories using electric motors dominated industry, increasing productivity. Most urban households now had electric lighting and could use new appliances such as refrigerators and vacuum cleaners.

As Americans acquired spending money and leisure time, service industries such as restaurants, beauty salons, and movie theaters boomed. Installment, or time-payment, plans drove the new consumerism. Of 3.5 million automobiles sold in 1923, 80 percent were bought on credit.

Although Progressive era trustbusting reined in big business, it had not eliminated oligopoly, the control of an industry by a few large

OLIGOPOLIES AND "NEW LOBBYING" firms. By the 1920s oligopolies dominated production, marketing, distribution, and finance. In industries such as steel and electrical equipment, a few companies, such as U.S. Steel and General Electric, predominated.

Business and professional organizations also expanded in the 1920s. Retailers and manufacturers formed trade associations to swap information. Farm bureaus promoted scientific agriculture and tried to stabilize markets. These special-interest groups participated in the "new lobbying." With government playing an increasingly influential role, hundreds of organizations sought to convince legislators to support their interests.

Government policies helped business thrive, and legislators came to depend on lobbyists' expertise. Congress cut taxes on corporations and wealthy individuals in 1921, and the next year raised tariff rates in the Fordney-McCumber Tariff Act. Presidents Warren G. Harding, Calvin Coolidge, and Herbert Hoover appointed cabinet officers who were favorable toward business. Regulatory agencies such as the Federal Trade Commission and Interstate Commerce Commission cooperated with, rather than regulated, corporations.

Key Supreme Court decisions sheltered business from government regulation and hindered organized labor. In *Coronado Coal Company v. United Mine Workers* (1922), Chief Justice William Howard Taft, the former president, ruled that a striking union, like a trust, could be prosecuted for illegal restraint of trade. Yet in *Maple Floor Association v. U.S.* (1929), the Court decided that trade associations that distributed anti-union information were not acting in restraint of trade. The Court also voided restrictions on child labor (*Bailey v. Drexel Furniture Company*, 1922)

and overturned a minimum-wage law affecting women because it infringed on liberty of contract (*Adkins v. Children's Hospital,* 1923).

Public opinion turned against organized labor in the 1920s, linking it with communism brought to

SETBACKS FOR ORGANIZED LABOR America by radical immigrants. Using Red Scare tactics, the Harding administration in 1922 obtained a sweeping court injunction to quash a strike by 400,000 railroad shop workers. State and federal courts issued injunctions to prevent strikes and permitted businesses to sue unions for damages suffered from labor actions.

Some corporations countered the appeal of unions by offering pensions, profit sharing (which amounted to withholding wages for later distribution), and company-sponsored picnics and sporting events—a policy known as welfare capitalism. State legislators aided employers by prohibiting closed shops (workplaces where union membership was mandatory) and permitting open shops (which could discriminate against unionized workers). As a result of these efforts, union membership fell from 5.1 million in 1920 to 3.6 million in 1929.

Agriculture suffered during the 1920s, as farmers faced international competition and tried to increase productivity by investing in new ma-

LANGUISHING AGRICULTURE chines such as harvesters and tractors. Debt increased, while overproduction and foreign competition depressed crop and livestock prices, in turn reducing incomes. Early in the decade, for example, the price of cotton dropped by two-thirds, and that of hogs and cattle fell by half. Farm income never recovered. Many farmers became tenants because they lost their land; more quit farming altogether.

Politics and Government

a series of Republican presidents extended Theodore Roosevelt's government-business cooperation, but they made government a compliant coordinator rather than the active manager Roosevelt had advocated. President Warren G. Harding, elected in 1920, was a symbol of government's goodwill toward business. He captured 16 million popular votes to 9 million for the Democratic nominee, Ohio governor James M. Cox. (The total vote in the 1920 presidential election increased 36 percent over 1916, reflecting the participation of women voters for the first time.)

A small-town newspaperman and senator from Ohio, Harding appointed assistants who promoted business growth, notably Secretary of State Charles Evans Hughes, Secretary of Commerce Herbert Hoover, Secretary of the Treasury Andrew Mellon, and Secretary of Agriculture Henry C. Wallace. Harding also backed reforms such as the Budget and Accounting Act of 1921 to streamline federal spending, and he supported antilynching legislation and efforts to assist farm cooperatives and liberalize farm credit.

Harding was plagued by problems, among them his extramarital affairs. For example, in 1917, he

SCANDALS OF HARDING ADMINISTRATION

began a relationship with Nan Britton, thirty-one years his junior, that resulted in a daughter in 1919. Britton reputedly visited Harding in the White House, although Harding never acknowledged his illegitimate offspring.

Of greater consequence, Harding often appointed cronies who used government positions for personal gain. Charles Forbes of the Veterans Bureau went to federal prison, convicted of fraud and bribery in connection with government contracts. Most notorious, a congressional inquiry in 1923 and 1924 revealed that Secretary of the Interior Albert Fall had accepted bribes to lease oil-rich government property to private oil companies. He was fined $100,000 and spent a year in jail for his role in the so-called Teapot Dome scandal, named for the oil reserve he turned over to the Mammoth Oil Company.

By mid-1923, Harding had become disillusioned. On a speaking tour, he became ill and died in San Francisco on August 2. Although his death preceded revelation of the Teapot Dome scandal, some speculated that Harding committed suicide to avoid impeachment or was poisoned by his wife. Most evidence, however, points to death from natural causes, probably a heart attack. Vice President Calvin Coolidge, who now became president, was more aloof than Harding. As governor of Massachusetts, Coolidge had attracted national attention in 1919 with his stand against striking Boston policemen, winning him business support and the vice-presidential nomination in 1920.

Respectful of private enterprise and aided by Andrew Mellon, who was retained as secretary of

COOLIDGE PROSPERITY

the treasury, Coolidge's administration reduced federal debt, lowered income-tax rates (especially for the wealthy), and began a national highway system. Meanwhile, with farm prices falling, Congress twice passed bills to establish government-backed price supports for staple crops (the McNary-Haugen bills of 1927 and 1928). Resembling the Farmers' Alliances' subtreasury scheme of the 1890s (see Chapter 20), these bills would have established a system whereby the government would buy surplus farm products and either hold them until prices rose or sell them abroad. Coolidge, however, vetoed the measures as improper government interference in the market economy.

"Coolidge prosperity" was the decisive issue in the presidential election of 1924. Both major parties ran candidates who favored private initiative over government intervention. At their national convention, Democrats voted 542 to 541 against condemning the revived Ku Klux Klan, and deadlocked for 103 ballots between southern prohibitionists, who supported former secretary of the treasury William G. McAdoo, and antiprohibition easterners, backing New York's governor Alfred E. Smith. They compromised on John W. Davis, a New York corporation lawyer.

Remnants of the Progressive movement, along with various farm, labor, and socialist groups, formed a new Progressive Party and nominated Robert M. La Follette, the aging Wisconsin reformer. The new party stressed public ownership of utilities, aid to farmers, rights for organized labor, and regulation of business. Coolidge beat Davis by 15.7 million to 8.4 million popular votes and 382 to 136 electoral votes. La Follette received 4.8 million popular votes and only 13 electoral votes.

The urgency for political and economic reform that inspired the previous generation faded in the

EXTENSIONS OF PROGRESSIVE REFORM

1920s, with important reforms continuing primarily at state and local levels. Following pre–World War I initiatives, thirty-four states instituted or expanded workers' compensation laws in the 1920s. Many states established employee-funded old-age pensions and welfare programs for the indigent. By 1926 every major city and many smaller ones had planning and zoning commissions to harness physical growth to the common good. Statehouses, city halls, and universities trained a new generation of reformers who later influenced national affairs.

Organizations such as the Indian Rights Association, the Indian Defense Association, and the General

INDIAN AFFAIRS Federation of Women's Clubs worked to obtain justice and social services for Native Americans, including better education and return of tribal lands. But like other minorities, Indians generally met discrimination and pressure to assimilate. Severalty, the policy created by the Dawes Act of 1887 of allotting land to individuals rather than to tribes, failed to make Indians self-supporting. Deeply attached to their land, even struggling Indian farmers were unlikely to move to cities. Whites still hoped to convert native peoples into "productive" citizens, typically ignoring indigenous cultures. Reformers were especially critical of Indian women, who refused to adopt middle-class homemaking habits and balked at sending their children to boarding schools.

Citizenship remained unclear. The Dawes Act had conferred citizenship on Indians who accepted land allotments but not those who remained on reservations. After several court challenges, Congress passed a law in 1924 granting citizenship to all Indians. President Herbert Hoover's administration reorganized the Bureau of Indian Affairs and increased expenditures for health, education, and welfare. Much of the money, however, went to enlarge the bureaucracy rather than to Indians.

Ratification of the Nineteenth Amendment in 1920 gave women the vote, but they nonetheless remained

WOMEN AND POLITICS outside local and national power structures. Instead, they worked through voluntary associations to lobby legislators on issues such as birth control, peace, education, Indian affairs, or opposition to lynching.

Women's groups persuaded Congress to pass the Sheppard-Towner Act (1921), granting funds to states to create maternity and pediatric clinics. (The measure ended in 1929, when Congress, under pressure from private physicians, canceled funding.) The Cable Act of 1922 reversed the law under which an American woman who married a foreigner assumed her husband's citizenship, allowing her to retain U.S.

citizenship. At state levels, women achieved rights, such as the ability to serve on juries.

As new voters, however, most women pursued diverging interests. Women in the National Association of Colored Women, for example, fought for the rights of minorities. Other groups, such as the National Woman's Party, pressed for an equal rights amendment (ERA) to ensure women's equality under the law. But the ERA alienated organizations such as the National Consumers League, the Women's Trade Union League, and the League of Women Voters, which supported special protective legislation to limit the hours and improve conditions for employed women.

Materialism Unbound

Between 1919 and 1929, the gross national product—the total value of all goods and services produced in the United States—swelled by 40 percent. Wages and salaries also grew, while the cost of living remained relatively stable. People enjoyed greater purchasing power (see Table 24.1). By 1929 two-thirds of all Americans had electricity at home, compared with one-sixth in 1912. In 1929 one-fourth of all families owned vacuum cleaners. Many could afford such goods as radios, washing machines, and movie tickets only because several family members worked or because the breadwinner took a second job. Nevertheless, new products and services were available to more than just the rich.

During the 1920s automobile registrations soared from 8 million to 23 million, and by 1929 there

EFFECTS OF THE AUTOMOBILE was one car for every five Americans. Mass production and competition made cars affordable. A Ford Model T cost less than $300, and a Chevrolet sold for $700 by 1926—when factory workers earned about $1,300 a year and clerical workers about $2,300. At those prices, people could consider the car a necessity rather than a luxury.

Cars altered American life. City streets became cleaner as autos replaced the horses that had dumped tons of manure every day. Women who learned to drive achieved newfound independence, traveling by themselves or with female friends. By 1927 most au-

TABLE 24.1

Consumerism in the 1920s

1900

2 bicycles	$ 70.00
wringer and washboard	5.00
brushes and brooms	5.00
sewing machine (mechanical)	25.00
TOTAL	$ 105.00

1928

automobile	$ 700.00
radio	75.00
phonograph	50.00
washing machine	150.00
vacuum cleaner	50.00
sewing machine (electric)	60.00
other electrical equipment	25.00
telephone (per year)	35.00
TOTAL	$1,145.00

From *Another Part of the Twenties,* by Paul Carter. Copyright 1977 by Columbia University Press. Reprinted by permission of the author.

Note: These figures, taken from an article in *Survey Magazine* in 1928, contrast one family's expenditures on consumer goods in 1900 with those of 1928.

tos were enclosed (they previously had open tops), creating new private space for courtship and sex. Most important, the car was the ultimate symbol of social equality. As one writer observed in 1924, "It is hard to convince Steve Popovich, or Antonio Branca, or plain John Smith that he is being ground into the dust by Capital when at will he may drive the same highways, view the same scenery, and get as much enjoyment from his trip as the modern Midas."

After the First World War, motorists joined farmers and bicyclists in their decades-old campaign for improved roads. In 1921 Congress passed the Federal Highway Act, providing funds for state roads, and in 1923 the Bureau of Public Roads planned a national highway system. Road building inspired technological developments such as mechanized road graders and concrete mixers, and mass-produced tires and plate

glass. The oil refining industry, aided by chemistry, became vast and powerful, with the United States producing about 65 percent of the world's oil in 1920. Public officials paid more attention to traffic control, with General Electric Company producing the first timed stop-and-go traffic light in 1924.

By 1929 more money was spent on advertising than on formal education. Blending psychological theory with practical cynicism, advertising theorists asserted that people's tastes could be manipulated. For example, cosmetics manufacturers such as Max Factor and the African American entrepreneur Madame C. J. Walker used movie stars and beauty advice in magazines to entice female customers. Baseball star Babe Ruth was hired to endorse food and sporting goods.

ADVERTISING

Radio became an influential advertising medium. By 1929 over 10 million Americans owned radios, spending $850 million annually on radio equipment. In the early 1920s, Congress decided that radio should be a private enterprise, not a tax-supported public service as in Great Britain. American programming focused on entertainment—such as Lindbergh's flight—rather than on educational content because of the larger audiences—and therefore advertising profits. Station KDKA in Pittsburgh, at first noncommercial, pioneered broadcasting in 1920. In 1922 an AT&T-run station in New York ran advertisements—"commercials." Other stations followed, and by 1922 there were 508 commercial stations.

RADIO

Radio transformed political culture when both parties broadcast their presidential nominating conventions for the first time in 1924. And radio's mass marketing and standardized programming blurred ethnic boundaries and created—at least in one way—a homogeneous "American" culture, which television and other mass media extended throughout the twentieth century.

Some new trends benefited the working classes, especially in cities. Indoor plumbing and electricity became more common, and canned foods and ready-made clothes were more affordable. A little cash and a lot of credit enabled many wage earners to purchase an automobile. Spending became a national pastime.

■ During the 1920s, the desire to own an automobile spread to members of all classes, races, and ethnic groups. Low prices and available credit enabled this family from Beaumont, Texas, to own a "touring car." (Tyrrell Historical Library, Beaumont, Texas)

Cities, Migrants, and Suburbs

*T*he 1920 federal census revealed that for the first time, a majority of Americans lived in urban areas (defined as places with 2,500 or more people). Growth in manufacturing and services helped propel urbanization. Industries such as steel, oil, and auto production energized Birmingham, Houston, and Detroit; services and retail trades boosted expansion in Seattle, Atlanta, and Minneapolis.

During the 1920s, 6 million Americans left their farms for the city. Irrigation and mechanization made large-scale farming so efficient that fewer farmers could produce more crops. As a result, crop prices plummeted, and small landholders could not make a living. Midwesterners, particularly young single people, moved to regional centers like Kansas City and Indianapolis or to the West. Between 1920 and 1930, California's population increased 67 percent, and California be-

came one of the most urbanized states while retaining its status as a leading agricultural state.

African Americans, in what is called the Great Migration, made up a sizable portion of people on the move. Pushed from cotton farming by a boll weevil plague and lured by industrial jobs, 1.5 million blacks moved cityward during the 1920s, doubling the African American populations of New York, Chicago, Detroit, and Houston. Forced by low wages and discrimination to seek cheap housing, black newcomers squeezed into low-rent ghettos. The only way to expand their housing opportunities was to spill into nearby white neighborhoods, which sparked resistance and violence. Fears of such "invasion" prompted white neighborhood associations to adopt restrictive covenants, whereby homeowners pledged not to sell or rent property to blacks.

AFRICAN AMERICAN MIGRATION

In response to discrimination and violence, thousands of urban blacks joined movements that glorified racial independence. The most

Marcus Garvey influential was the Universal Negro Improvement Association (UNIA), headed by Marcus Garvey, a Jamaican immigrant who believed blacks should separate from corrupt white society. *Negro World*, Garvey's newspaper, refused to publish ads for products foreign to black culture, such as hair straightening and skin-lightening cosmetics, and he founded the Black Star shipping line to help blacks emigrate to Africa.

The UNIA declined in the mid-1920s after ten UNIA leaders were arrested on charges of anarchism, and Garvey was deported for mail fraud involving the bankrupt Black Star line; the company's main problem was that unscrupulous dealers had sold it dilapidated ships. Black leaders like W. E. B. Du Bois opposed the UNIA, fearing its extremism would undermine their efforts. Nevertheless, in big cities, the organization attracted a large following (contemporaries estimated 500,000; Garvey claimed 6 million), and Garvey's speeches instilled many African Americans with a heightened sense of racial pride.

The newest immigrants to American cities came from Mexico and Puerto Rico, where declining fortunes pushed people off the land.

Newcomers from Mexico and Puerto Rico During the 1910s, Anglo farmers' associations encouraged Mexican immigration to provide cheap agricultural labor, and by the 1920s, Mexican migrants made up three-fourths of farm labor in the American West. Growers treated Mexican laborers as slaves, providing them low wages and poor healthcare. Though some achieved middle-class status, most crowded into low-rent districts plagued by poor sanitation, poor police protection, and poor schools. Mexicans moved back and forth across the border, creating a way of life that Mexicans called *sin fronteras*—without borders.

The 1920s also witnessed an influx of Puerto Ricans to the mainland as a shift in the island's economy from sugar to coffee production created a labor surplus. Attracted by contracts from employers seeking cheap labor, most Puerto Rican migrants moved to New York City, where they created *barrios* (communities) in Brooklyn and Manhattan and found jobs in manufacturing, hotels, restaurants, and domestic service.

Puerto Ricans and Mexicans practiced traditional customs and developed businesses—*bodegas* (grocery stores), cafés, boarding houses—and social organizations to help them adapt to American society. Educated elites—doctors, lawyers, business owners—often became community leaders.

Prosperity and automobile transportation in the 1920s made suburbs more accessible to those wishing

Growth of Suburbs to flee congested urban neighborhoods. Between 1920 and 1930, suburbs of Chicago (such as Oak Park and Evanston), Cleveland (Shaker Heights), and Los Angeles (Burbank and Inglewood) grew five to ten times faster than nearby central cities. Los Angeles builders alone opened 3,200 subdivisions and erected 250,000 homes. Most suburbs were middle- and upper-class bedroom communities; some, like Highland Park (near Detroit), were industrial satellites.

Suburbanites wanted to escape big-city crime, grime, and taxes, and they fought urban annexation efforts, preserving control over their own police, schools, and water and gas services. Particularly in the Northeast and Midwest, the suburbs' independence prevented central cities from accessing the resources and tax bases of wealthier suburban communities. Moreover, population dispersal spread the environmental problems of city life—trash, pollution, noise—across the entire metropolitan area.

Most of the consumers who jammed movie houses and sporting arenas and who embraced fads like crossword puzzles, miniature golf, and marathon dancing lived in or around cities. People there defied law and tradition by patronizing speakeasies (illegal saloons during prohibition), wearing outlandish clothes, and listening to jazz, while moralists strained to resist modernism, and many reminisced about the simplicity of a world gone by.

New Rhythms of Everyday Life

*a*mid changes, people increasingly split daily life into distinct compartments: work, family, and leisure. Increased mechanization and higher productivity enabled many employers to shorten the workweek for industrial laborers from six days to

Pan American Airways

Air transportation and air mail service between the United States and Latin America began in the 1920s, but anti-American hostility in the region made it difficult. In 1926 the U.S. government, fearful that German aircraft might drop bombs on the Panama Canal in future conflicts, signed a treaty with Panama giving American airplanes exclusive rights to Panamanian airports. Charles Lindbergh and a formerly obscure pilot, Juan Trippe, played key roles in expanding American air service to Latin America.

With help from his father-in-law, Trippe established Pan American Airways (informally known as Pan Am) in 1927 and won a contract to carry mail between Florida and Cuba. In December of that year, Lindbergh charmed the Mexicans into accepting airline links to the United States. The next year, Lindbergh joined Pan Am and helped Trippe initiate mail and passenger service to Panama, Mexico, and other Latin American countries in 1929. Trippe advertised to wealthy Americans the opportunity to escape prohibition and enjoy Caribbean beaches.

Pan Am built airports that became essential connections between Latin America and the rest of the world. Pan Am air service also helped unite parts of Latin America that previously were divided by impenetrable mountain ranges. But to build an airport, Pan Am cooperated with dictators, engaged in bribery, and violated human rights, in one case helping Bolivian police corral Indians behind barbed wire for days to clear a new airport.

Still, Pan Am facilitated global travel. In 1942 its aircraft became the first to fly around the world. In the 1940s, the company began offering flights to Europe and Africa. Until its demise in 1991, Pan Am provided a leading link between the United States and the rest of the world.

Providing air transport connections to the Caribbean, Central America, and South America, Pan American Airways established the first major passenger and cargo links between the United States and other nations. By the early 1930s, flights were so numerous that the timetable announced in this illustration consisted of twelve pages. (The Pan American Heritage Web Site)

five and a half. White-collar employees often worked a forty-hour week, enjoyed a full weekend off, and received annual vacations.

Family size decreased between 1920 and 1930 as birth control became more widely practiced. Over half the women married in the 1870s and 1880s had five or more children; only 20 percent of their counterparts marrying in the 1920s had similar childbirth patterns. The divorce rate jumped from 1 divorce for every 7.5 marriages in 1920 to 1 in 6 by 1929. With longer life expectancy, lower birth rates, and more divorce, adults devoted a smaller portion of their lives to child rearing.

Although housework was still arduous, machines lightened some household chores. Especially in middle-

HOUSEHOLD MANAGEMENT

class households, electric irons and washing machines simplified housewives' toil. Gas- and oil-powered central heating and hot-water heaters eliminated hauling wood, coal, and water; keeping up a kitchen fire; and removing ashes.

But technology and economic change also created new demands on women's time. The availability of washing machines, hot water, vacuum cleaners, and commercial soap put greater pressure on wives to keep everything clean. No longer a producer of food and clothing as her ancestors were, a housewife now also became the chief shopper. And the automobile also made her the family's chauffeur. One survey found that urban housewives spent 13 percent of their work time, seven and a half hours per week, driving to shop and to transport children.

Nutrition added a scientific dimension to housewives' responsibilities. With the discovery of vitamins between 1915 and 1930, nutrition-

HEALTH AND LIFE EXPECTANCY

ists began advocating certain foods to prevent illness, and giant food companies advertised their products as filled with vitamins and minerals. Other companies made lofty claims that were hard to dispute because little was known about these invisible, tasteless ingredients. Welch's Grape Juice, for example, avoided mentioning its excess of sugars when it advertised that it was "Rich in Health Values," containing vitamins, minerals, and "the laxative properties you cannot do without."

Better diets and improved hygiene made Americans healthier. Life expectancy at birth increased from fifty-four to sixty years between 1920 and 1930, and

infant mortality decreased by two-thirds. Public sanitation and research in bacteriology and immunology reduced life-threatening diseases such as tuberculosis and diphtheria. But infant mortality rates were 50 to 100 percent higher among nonwhites, and tuberculosis in inner-city slums remained alarmingly common. Nevertheless, the total population over age sixty-five grew 35 percent between 1920 and 1930.

Industrialism put premiums on youth and agility, pushing older people into poverty from forced re-

OLDER AMERICANS AND RETIREMENT

tirement and reduced income. Most European countries established state-supported pension systems in the early 1900s. Many Americans, however, believed pensions smacked of socialism and that individuals should prepare for old age by saving in their youth.

Most inmates in state poorhouses were older people, and almost one-third of Americans age sixty-five and older depended financially on someone else. Few employers, including the federal government, provided for retired employees. Resistance to pension plans finally broke at the state level in the 1920s. Led by Isaac Max Rubinow and Abraham Epstein, reformers persuaded voluntary associations, labor unions, and legislators to endorse old-age assistance. By 1933 almost every state provided at least minimal support to needy elderly people, opening the door to a national program of old-age insurance.

New cultural influences altered habits and values. Women and men wore more casual and gaily colored clothes than their parents' genera-

SOCIAL VALUES

tion. The line between acceptable and inappropriate behavior blurred as smoking, drinking, swearing, and frankness about sex became fashionable. Birth-control advocate Margaret Sanger, who a decade earlier had been accused of promoting race suicide, gained a large following. Newspapers, motion pictures, and popular songs (such as "Hot Lips" and "Burning Kisses") made certain that Americans did not suffer from "sex starvation."

Because child-labor laws and compulsory-attendance rules kept children in school longer than in the past, peer groups played a more influential role in socializing youngsters. Graded school classes, sports, and clubs constantly brought together children of the same age, separating them from the company and influence of adults. Meanwhile, parents relied less on traditions of childcare and more on experts who wrote manuals on successful child rearing.

Online Study Center **Improve Your Grade**
Primary Source: Wild Young People

After the First World War, women continued to stream into the labor force. By 1930, 10.8 million women held paying jobs, an increase of 2 million since war's end. Most notably, the proportion of women working in agriculture shrank, while it grew or held steady in urban job categories (see Figure 24.1). Sex segregation persisted; most women took jobs that men seldom sought. Over 1 million women worked as professionals, primarily teachers and nurses. Some 2.2 million women were typists, bookkeepers, and filing clerks, a tenfold increase since 1920. Although almost 2 million women worked in manufacturing, their numbers hardly grew over the decade. Women's wages seldom exceeded half of those paid to men.

WOMEN IN THE WORK FORCE

Family economic needs were paramount among women's reasons for working. Consumerism provided an additional push. Although the majority of married women did not work outside the home (only 12 percent were employed in 1930), married women as a proportion of the work force rose by 30 percent, and the number of employed married women swelled from 1.9 million to 3.1 million.

Minority women were twice as likely to be employed as white women. Often they entered the labor force because their husbands were unemployed or underemployed. The majority of employed African American women held domestic jobs doing cooking, cleaning, and laundry. The few working in factories performed the least desirable, lowest-paying tasks. Some opportunities opened for educated black women in social work, teaching, and nursing, but even these women faced discrimination and low incomes.

EMPLOYMENT OF MINORITY WOMEN

Next to black women, Japanese American women were the most likely to have paying jobs, similarly working as field hands and domestics facing racial bias and low pay. Economic necessity also drew thousands of Mexican women into wage labor, although

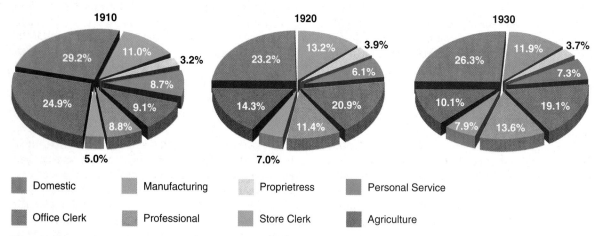

Figure 24.1   Changing Dimensions of Paid Female Labor, 1910–1930

These charts reveal the extraordinary growth in clerical and professional occupations among employed women and the accompanying decline in agricultural labor in the early twentieth century. Notice that manufacturing employment peaked in 1920 and that domestic service fluctuated as white immigrant women began to move out of these jobs and were replaced by women of color.

their tradition resisted female employment. Most worked as field laborers, operatives in garment factories, and domestic servants.

Many women cast aside previous images of femininity that included heavy, floor-length dresses and
long hair, opting instead for the independence and sexual freedom of the 1920s "flapper" with her short skirts and bobbed hair. Although few women lived the flapper life, office workers, store clerks, and college coeds adopted the look. New models of female behavior included movie temptresses like Clara Bow, known as the "It Girl," and Gloria Swanson, notorious for love affairs on and off the screen. Women increasingly asserted a new social equality with men. One observer described "the new woman" as intriguingly independent:

> She takes a man's point of view as her mother never could. . . . She will never make you a hatband or knit you a necktie, but she'll drive you from the station . . . in her own little sports car. . . . [S]he'll dive as well as you, perhaps better, she'll dance as long as you care to, and she'll take everything you say the way you mean it.

The era's sexual openness enabled the underground homosexual culture to surface. In nontradi-
tional city neighborhoods, such as New York's Greenwich Village and Harlem, cheap rents and an apparent tolerance attracted gays and lesbians who patronized dance halls, speakeasies, and cafés. Still, gay establishments remained targets for police raids, demonstrating that there was little acceptance by the rest of society.

These trends represented a break with the more restrained culture of the nineteenth century. But social change rarely proceeds smoothly. As the decade proceeded, groups mobilized to defend older values.

Lines of Defense

*E*arly in 1920 the leader of a newly formed organization hired two public relations experts to recruit members. The experts, Edward Clarke and Elizabeth Tyler, canvassed the South, Southwest,

and Midwest, where they found thousands of men eager to pay a $10 membership fee and $6 for a white uniform. Clarke and Tyler pocketed $2.50 from each membership and secured 5 million members by 1923.

This was the Ku Klux Klan, a revived version of the hooded order that had terrorized southern communities after the Civil War. It appealed to fear, vowing to protect female, racial, and ethnic purity.

As one pamphlet declared, "Every criminal, every gambler, every thug, every libertine, every girl ruiner, every home wrecker, every wife beater, every dope peddler, every moonshiner, every white slaver, every Rome-controlled newspaper, every black spider—is fighting the Klan. . . . Which side are you on?"

Reconstituted in 1915 by William J. Simmons, an Atlanta evangelist and insurance salesman, the Klan revived the hoods, intimidating tactics, and mystical terminology of its forerunner (its leader was the Imperial Wizard, its book of rituals the Kloran). But the new Klan fanned outward from the Deep South, wielding power in places as diverse as Oregon, Oklahoma, and Indiana. Members included many from the middle class who were fearful of losing social and economic gains and nervous about a new youth culture that eluded family control. An estimated half-million women joined.

One phrase summed up Klan goals: "Native, white, Protestant supremacy." Native meant no immigration, no "mongrelization" of American culture. According to Imperial Wizard Hiram Wesley Evans, "The world has been so made so that each race must fight for its life, must conquer, accept slavery, or die." Evans accused the Catholic Church of discouraging assimilation and enslaving people to a foreign pope.

Using threatening assemblies, violence, and political and economic pressure, Klansmen meted out vigilante justice to suspected bootleggers, wife beaters, and adulterers; forced schools to adopt Bible reading and stop teaching the theory of evolution; campaigned against Catholic and Jewish political candidates; and fueled racial tensions against Mexicans in Texas border cities. Klan women both promoted native white Protestantism and worked for women's rights. By 1925, scandal undermined its moral base. Indiana Grand Dragon David Stephenson was convicted of second-degree murder after he kidnapped and raped a woman who later died. More generally,

Marginal terms:

ALTERNATIVE IMAGES OF FEMININITY

HOMOSEXUAL CULTURE

KU KLUX KLAN

the Klan's negative, exclusive brand of patriotism could not compete in a pluralistic society.

The KKK was not alone. Intolerance pervaded American society in the 1920s. Nativists charged that Catholic and Jewish immigrants clogged city slums, flouted community norms, and stubbornly held to alien religious and political beliefs. Naturalist Madison Grant, whose study of zoology fueled his belief that certain human races, mainly Nordics, were superior, wrote in *The Passing of the Great Race* (1916): "These immigrants adopt the language of the native American, they wear his clothes, they steal his name and they are beginning to take his women, but they seldom adopt his religion or understand his ideals."

Efforts to restrict immigration gathered support. Labor leaders warned that aliens would depress wages

IMMIGRATION QUOTAS

and raise unemployment. Business executives, who formerly desired cheap immigrant laborers, now realized that they could keep wages low by mechanizing and by hiring blacks. In response to these pressures, Congress set yearly immigration quotas for each nationality. By restricting annual immigration of a given nationality to 3 percent of the number of immigrants from that nation residing in the United States in 1910, the Emergency Quota Act of 1921 favored northern and western Europeans and discriminated against immigrants from southern and eastern Europe, whose numbers were comparatively small in 1910.

In 1924 Congress replaced the Quota Act with the National Origins Act. This law limited the influx to 150,000 people by setting quotas at 2 percent of each nationality residing in the United States in 1890, except for Asians, who were banned completely. The act further restricted southern and eastern Europeans, since fewer of those groups lived in the United States in 1890 than in 1910, though it allowed wives and children of U.S. citizens to enter as nonquota immigrants. As a result, the 1921 quotas for southern and eastern Europeans fell by 84 percent, while those for northern and western Europeans dropped by only 29 percent. Revisions beginning in 1929 redefined quotas to be distributed among European countries in proportion to the "national origins" (country of birth or descent) of American inhabitants in 1920. People from Canada, Mexico, and Puerto Rico did not fall under the quotas (except for those whom the Labor Department defined as potential paupers) and became the largest immigrant groups (see Figure 24.2).

Fear of immigrant radicalism was evident in 1921 when a court convicted Nicola Sacco and Bartolomeo Vanzetti, two immigrant an-

SACCO AND VANZETTI CASE

archists, of murdering a guard and paymaster during a robbery in South Braintree, Massachusetts. Though evidence failed to prove their guilt, Judge Webster Thayer openly sided with the prosecution and privately called the defendants "anarchist bastards." Appeals failed to win a new trial, and the prisoners were executed in 1927, touching off protests in Europe, Asia, and South America and leaving doubts that the United States truly nurtured freedom of belief.

The pursuit of spiritual purity stirred religious fundamentalists as millions sought salvation from

FUNDAMENTALISM

what they perceived as the irreverence of a materialistic, hedonistic society. Resolutely believing that God's miracles created earth and its life, they rejected Darwin's theory of evolution as speculation. Where fundamentalists constituted a majority, as they did throughout the South, they sought to determine what schools taught. Their enemies were "modernists," who interpreted "truths" critically, believing that biblical accuracy was less important than the historical relevance of God in culture and the role of science in advancing knowledge.

In 1925 Christian fundamentalism clashed with modernism when the Tennessee state legislature outlawed public schools from teaching

SCOPES TRIAL

the theory that humans had evolved from lower forms of life rather than descended from Adam and Eve. High-school teacher John Thomas Scopes volunteered to serve in a test case and was arrested for violating the law. William Jennings Bryan, former secretary of state and three-time presidential candidate, argued for the prosecution, and civil liberties lawyers headed by Clarence Darrow represented the defense. News correspondents crowded into town, and radio stations broadcast the trial.

Scopes was convicted—clearly he had broken the law—but modernists claimed victory in showing the illogic of fundamentalism. The trial's climax occurred when Bryan took the witness stand as an expert on

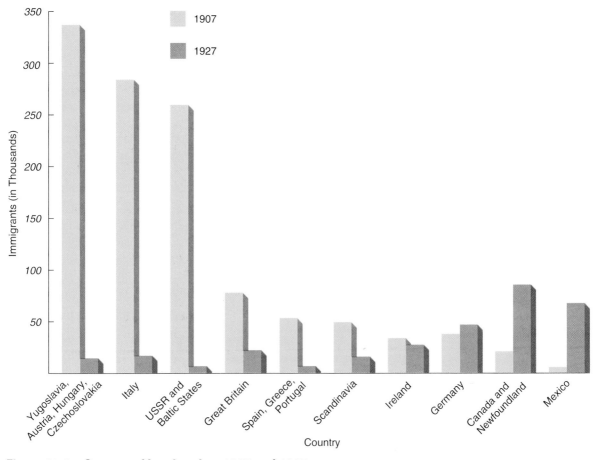

Figure 24.2   Sources of Immigration, 1907 and 1927

Immigration peaked in 1907 and 1908, when newcomers from southern and eastern Europe poured into the United States. After immigration restriction laws were passed in the 1920s, the greatest number of immigrants came from the Western Hemisphere (Canada and Mexico), which was exempted from the quotas, and the number coming from eastern and southern Europe shrank.

religion and science. He asserted that Eve really had been created from Adam's rib, that the Tower of Babel was responsible for the diversity of languages, and that a biblical "day" could have lasted thousands of years. Spectators in Dayton cheered Bryan, but the liberal press mocked him. Nevertheless, fundamentalists convinced school boards to ban the teaching of evolution and influenced the content of high-school biology books. They also created an independent subculture of schools, camps, radio ministries, and missionary societies.

Klan rallies, immigration restriction, and fundamentalist literalism might appear as last gasps of a rural society struggling against modern urban-industrial values. Yet half the Klan's members lived in cities, especially in working-class neighborhoods. Even urban reformers backed immigration restriction as a means of controlling poverty and assimilating immigrants.

Urban Pentecostal churches attracted blacks and whites struggling with economic insecurity, nervous about modernism's attack on old-time religion, and swayed by the notion of a personal God. Using modern advertising and elaborately staged services broadcast on radio, magnetic preachers such as Aimee Semple McPherson of Los Angeles, former baseball player Billy Sunday, and Father Divine (George Baker, an African American who amassed an interracial following especially in eastern cities) stirred revivalist fervor. Clergy of all faiths condemned drinking, dancing, new dress styles, and sex in movies and in parked cars. Many urban dwellers supported prohibition, believing that it would win the battle against poverty, vice, and corruption. Yet most people sincerely wanted balance as they tried to adjust to the modern order in one way or another. Americans sought fellowship in civic organizations. Membership swelled in Rotary, Elks, and women's clubs, and the number of Community Chests—associations that coordinated local welfare projects—grew from 12 in 1919 to 361 in 1930. Perhaps most important, more people were finding release in recreation and leisure time.

Saving Old-Fashioned Values

The Age of Play

americans embraced commercial entertainment, spending $2.5 billion on leisure in 1919; by 1929, it topped $4.3 billion. Spectator amusements—movies, music, and sports—accounted for 21 percent of the 1929 total; the rest involved participatory recreation, such as games, hobbies, and travel.

Entrepreneurs fed this appetite for fads, fun, and "ballyhoo." Games and fancies particularly attracted newly affluent middle-class families; early in the 1920s, mahjong, a Chinese tile game, was the craze. In the mid-1920s, crossword puzzles, printed in mass-circulation newspapers and magazines, were the rage, and by 1930 the nation boasted thirty thousand miniature golf courses. Dance crazes like the Charleston and recorded music on radio boosted the growing popularity of jazz.

Americans also enjoyed watching movies and sports. In total capital investment, motion pictures became one of the nation's leading industries. In 1922 movies attracted 40 million viewers weekly; by

Movies and Sports

decade's end, nearly 100 million—at a time when the nation's population was 120 million and total weekly church attendance was 60 million. Between 1922 and 1927, the Technicolor Corporation developed a means to produce movies in color. That, along with the introduction of sound in *The Jazz Singer* in 1927, made movies more exciting.

The most popular films were spectacles such as Cecil B. DeMille's *The Ten Commandments* (1923); lurid dramas such as *A Woman Who Sinned* (1924); and slapstick comedies starring Fatty Arbuckle, Harold Lloyd, and Charlie Chaplin. Ironically, comedies, with their poignant satires of the human condition, carried the most thought-provoking messages. In 1927 movie producers, bowing to political pressure, instituted self-censorship, forbidding nudity, rough language, and plots that did not end with justice and morality triumphant.

Spectator sports also boomed. Gate receipts from college football surpassed $21 million by the late 1920s, as sports provided the drama people craved. Newspapers and radio magnified this tension, glorifying events with such unrestrained narrative that promoters did not need advertising.

Baseball's drawn-out suspense, variety of plays, and potential for keeping statistics attracted a huge following. After the "Black Sox scandal" of 1919, when eight members of the Chicago White Sox were banned for allegedly throwing the World Series to the Cincinnati Reds (even though a jury acquitted them), baseball transformed itself. Discovering that home runs excited fans, the leagues redesigned the ball. A record 300,000 people attended the six-game 1921 World Series between the New York Giants and New York Yankees. Millions enjoyed professional games on the radio.

As technology and mass society made the individual less significant, people clung to sports, movie, and news heroes as a means of identifying with the unique. Bill Tilden in tennis, Gertrude Ederle in swimming (the first woman to swim across the English Channel), and Bobby Jones in golf were famous. But boxing, football, and baseball produced the most popular sports heroes. Heavyweight champion Jack Dempsey, the "Manassa (Colorado) Brawler," attracted the first of several million-dollar gates in his fight with French boxer Georges Carpentier in 1921.

Baseball's foremost hero was George Herman "Babe" Ruth, who began his career as a pitcher but

Sports Heroes

broke records hitting home runs. He hit twenty-nine in 1919, fifty-four in 1920 (the year the Boston Red Sox traded him to the New York Yankees), fifty-nine in 1921, and sixty in 1927. Known for overindulgence in food, drink, and sex, he nonetheless charmed fans with public appearances and visits to hospitalized children.

Americans fulfilled a yearning for romance and adventure through movie idols. One of the decade's
MOVIE STARS AND PUBLIC HEROES
most ballyhooed personalities was Rudolph Valentino, whose image exploited the era's sexual liberalism. In his most famous film, Valentino played a passionate sheik who carried away beautiful women to his tent. When he died at age thirty-one of complications from ulcers and appendicitis, the press turned his funeral into a public extravaganza.

The Eighteenth Amendment (1919) and ensuing federal law (1920) prohibited the manufacture, sale,
PROHIBITION
and transportation of alcoholic beverages (see Chapter 21), and prohibition worked well at first. Per capita consumption of liquor dropped, as did arrests for drunkenness. But it was hardly enforced: in 1922 Congress gave the Prohibition Bureau just three thousand employees and less than $7 million for nationwide enforcement.

After 1925, prohibition broke down as thousands made their own wine and bathtub gin, and bootleg importers easily evaded the few patrols that existed. Moreover, drinking was a business with willing customers, and criminal organizations capitalized on public demand. The most notorious of such mobs belonged to Al Capone, who seized control of illegal liquor and vice in Chicago, maintaining his grip on politicians and the business through intimidation, bribery, and violence. Americans wanted liquor, and until 1931 when a federal court convicted and imprisoned him for income-tax evasion (the only charge for which authorities could obtain hard evidence), Capone supplied them.

Cultural Currents

 ntellectuals exposed the era's hypocrisy. Writers and artists felt at odds with society, and their rejection of conformity was biting and bitter.

Several writers from the so-called Lost Generation, including novelist Ernest Hemingway and poets
LITERATURE OF ALIENATION
Ezra Pound and T. S. Eliot, abandoned the United States for Europe. Others, such as novelists William Faulkner and Sinclair Lewis, remained in America but expressed disillusionment with the materialism they witnessed. F. Scott Fitzgerald's *This Side of Paradise* (1920) and *The Great Gatsby* (1925) and Eugene O'Neill's plays derided Americans' preoccupation with money. Edith Wharton explored the clash of old and new moralities in novels such as *The Age of Innocence* (1920).

Inspired by spiritual discontent, middle-class, educated black writers rejected white culture and exalted
HARLEM RENAISSANCE
the militantly assertive "New Negro." In the "Negro Mecca" of New York's Harlem, black intellectuals and artists, aided by a few white patrons, celebrated black culture and created the Harlem Renaissance.

The popular 1921 musical comedy *Shuffle Along* is often credited with launching the Harlem Renaissance and showcased African American artists such as composer Eubie Blake and singer Josephine Baker. Harlem also fostered gifted writers, including Langston Hughes, Countee Cullen, Zora Neale Hurston, Jessie Fauset, and Alain Locke.

Though cherishing their African heritage, these artists and intellectuals realized that blacks had to make peace with themselves as Americans. Langston Hughes wrote, "We younger Negro artists who create now intend to express our individual dark-skinned selves without fear or shame. If white people are pleased, we are glad. If they are not, it doesn't matter. We know we are beautiful."

The Jazz Age, as the 1920s is sometimes called, owes its name to the music of black culture. Evolving
JAZZ
from African and black American folk music, early jazz communicated exuberance, humor, and authority that African Americans seldom experienced in their public and political lives. Jazz's emotional rhythms and improvisation blurred the distinction between composer and performer. Music recorded by black artists—among them trumpeter Louis Armstrong and blues singer Bessie Smith—and aimed at black consumers (sometimes called "race records") gave African Americans a place in consumer

culture. More important, jazz endowed America with its most distinctive and popular art form.

In many ways, the 1920s were the nation's most creative years. Artists such as Georgia O'Keeffe, Aaron Douglas, and John Marin forged a uniquely American style of painting. Composers such as Henry Cowell pioneered electronic music, and Aaron Copland built orchestral works around native folk motifs. George Gershwin blended jazz rhythms, classical forms, and folk melodies in serious compositions (*Rhapsody in Blue,* 1924, and the Piano Concerto in F, 1925) and hit tunes such as "Someone to Watch Over Me." In architecture the skyscraper boom drew worldwide attention to American forms. The "emotional and aesthetic starvation" that essayist Harold Stearn lamented at the beginning of the decade were long gone by the end.

The Election of 1928 and the End of the New Era

Intellectuals' uneasiness about materialism seldom affected the confident rhetoric of politics. Herbert Hoover voiced that confidence when he accepted the Republican nomination for president in 1928. "We in America today," Hoover boasted, "are nearer to the final triumph over poverty than ever before in the history of any land."

As the Republican candidate in 1928 (Coolidge did not seek reelection), Hoover fused individual hard

HERBERT HOOVER

work with modern emphasis on collective action. A Quaker from Iowa, orphaned at age ten, Hoover put himself through Stanford University and became a wealthy mining engineer. During and after the First World War, he distinguished himself as U.S. food administrator.

As secretary of commerce under Harding and Coolidge, Hoover practiced "associationalism." Recognizing that nationwide associations dominated commerce and industry, Hoover sought business and government cooperation by making the Commerce Department a center for the promotion of business, encouraging the formation of trade associations, holding conferences, and issuing reports, all aimed at improving productivity, marketing, and profits.

In sharp contrast, Democrats chose New York's governor Alfred E. Smith as their candidate. Hoover

AL SMITH

had rural, native-born, Protestant, business roots and had never before run for public office. Smith was an urbane politician of immigrant stock with a career embedded in New York City's Tammany Hall political machine, who relished the give-and-take of city streets.

Smith was the first Roman Catholic to run for president on a major party ticket. His religion enhanced his appeal among urban ethnics, who voted in increasing numbers, but intense anti-Catholic sentiments lost him southern and rural votes. Smith had a strong record on Progressive reform and civil rights, but his campaign stressed issues like opposition to prohibition that alienated many farmers and city dwellers.

Hoover won the popular vote by 21 million to 15 million, the electoral vote by 444 to 87. Smith carried the nation's twelve largest cities, formerly Republican strongholds, and he lured millions of foreign-stock voters to the polls for the first time. For the next forty years or so, the Democratic Party solidified this urban base, which in conjunction with its traditional strength in the South, made the party a formidable force in national elections.

At his inaugural, Hoover proclaimed a New Day, "bright with hope." His cabinet featured mostly

HOOVER'S ADMINISTRATION

businessmen, including six millionaires. In low-ranking posts, Hoover appointed young professionals who similarly believed that scientific methods could solve national problems. Americans widely agreed that individuals were responsible for their own success and that poverty suggested personal weakness. Prevailing opinion also held that ups and downs of the business cycle were natural and not to be tampered with by government.

This trust dissolved in the fall of 1929 when stock market prices suddenly plunged after soaring in

STOCK MARKET CRASH

1928, and on October 24, "Black Thursday," panic set in. Prices of many stocks hit record lows; some sellers could find no buyers. At noon, leading bankers put up $20 million and ceremoniously began buying stocks. The mood brightened, and some stocks rallied, lifting hopes. But as news spread, panicked investors sold off stock to avoid further losses. On "Black Tuesday," October 29, prices plummeted again. Hoover assured Americans that "the crisis will be over in sixty days." He shared the popular assumptions that the economy was strong enough to endure until the market righted itself. Instead, the crash fueled a devastating depression.

The economic weakness that underlay the Great Depression had several interrelated causes. Since mid-1928, demand for new housing had faltered, reducing sales of building materials and increasing unemployment. Growth industries such as automobiles and electric appliances also saw demand level off, but initially frenzied expansion continued. Consequently, unsold inventories stacked up in warehouses, and laborers were laid off. Retailers also had amassed large inventories and in turn started ordering less. Farm prices continued to sag, leaving farmers with less income for new machinery and goods. As wages and purchasing power stagnated, workers could not afford to buy consumer products. Thus, by 1929, a sizable population of underconsumers was causing serious repercussions.

DECLINING DEMAND

The widening divisions in income distribution meant the rich grew richer, while middle- and lower-income Americans barely made modest gains. Although average per capita disposable income (income after taxes) rose about 9 percent between 1920 and 1929, the income of the wealthiest 1 percent rose 75 percent. Much of this increase was put into stock market investments, not consumer goods.

Furthermore, many businesses overloaded themselves with debt. To obtain loans, they misrepresented their assets in ways that weakened their ability to repay. Overlooked by lending agencies, this practice put the nation's banking system on precarious footing.

CORPORATE DEBT

The depression also resulted from risky stock market speculation. Individuals bought heavily on margin, meaning that they purchased stock with a down payment of only a fraction of the stock's price and then used these stocks as collateral for more stock purchases. When stock prices stopped rising, people tried to unload what they bought on margin, but as numerous investors sold simultaneously, prices dropped. Brokers

STOCK MARKET SPECULATION

then demanded full payment for stocks bought on margin. Bankers in turn needed cash and pressured businesses to pay back their loans. The more obligations went unmet, the more banks and investment companies collapsed.

International economic woes also contributed. During and after the First World War, Americans loaned billions to European nations. By the late 1920s, however, American investors instead opted for the more lucrative U.S. stock market. Europeans, unable to borrow more or sell goods in America because of high tariffs, bought less from the United States. Moreover, the Allied nations depended on German war reparations to pay their debts to the United States, and the German government depended on American bank loans to pay those war reparations. When the crash cut off American loans, the world economy ground to a halt.

INTERNATIONAL ECONOMIC TROUBLES

The government refrained from regulating wild speculation. In supporting business expansion, the Federal Reserve Board pursued easy credit policies, charging low discount rates (interest on loans to member banks) even though easy money was financing the speculative mania.

FAILURE OF FEDERAL POLICIES

Neither the experts nor people on the street realized what really had happened in 1929. Conventional wisdom, based on previous depressions, held that downturns simply had to run their course. Farmers in the country's midsection, where drought parched some of the lands that would become the Dust Bowl of the 1930s, had already begun to feel the pinch of hard times. But in 1929 most people waited, never realizing that the era of expansion and frivolity had come to an end.

Online Study Center Improve Your Grade
Interactive Map: The Dust Bowl

Summary **Online Study Center** ACE the Test

*T*wo disturbing events, the end of the First World War and the beginning of the Great Depression, marked the boundaries of the 1920s. After the war, traditional customs weakened as many women and men replaced old-fashioned values with new liberation. Modern science and technology touched rich and poor alike through the mass media, movies, automobiles, and electric appliances. Moreover, the decade's prosperity and freewheeling attitudes enabled ordinary Americans to emulate wealthier people by consuming more and speculating in the stock market.

Beneath the "era of excess," prejudice and intergroup tensions resurfaced, tainting the American Dream. Prohibitionists, Klansmen, and immigration restrictionists encouraged discrimination against racial minorities and ethnic groups. Meanwhile, the distinguishing forces of twentieth-century life—technological change, bureaucratization, mass culture, and growth of the middle class—accelerated, making the decade truly a "new era."

LEGACY FOR A PEOPLE AND A NATION
Intercollegiate Athletics

In 1924 brutality, academic fraud, and illegal payments to recruits prompted the Carnegie Foundation for the Advancement of Higher Education to undertake a five-year investigation of college sports. Its 1929 report condemned coaches and alumni supporters, but had minimal impact. Football was big, and other sports followed as universities built stadiums to attract spectators, bolster alumni allegiance, and enhance revenues.

For most of the twentieth century, intercollegiate athletics ranked as a major national commercial entertainment. Still, American colleges struggled to reconcile conflicts between the commercialism of athletic competition and the restraints of educational missions. The economic potential of college sports coupled with burgeoning athletic departments—including administrators, staffs, and tutors as well as coaches and trainers—has created programs that compete with and sometimes overshadow an institution's academic operations.

Since the 1920s, recruiting scandals, cheating incidents, and academic fraud in college sports have sparked continual controversy. In 1952, after revelations of point-shaving (fixing the outcome) of basketball games at several colleges, the American Council on Education undertook its own study. Its recommendations, including the abolition of football bowl games, went largely unheeded. In 1991 further abuses prompted the Knight Foundation Commission on Intercollegiate Athletics to urge college presidents to reform intercollegiate athletics. After a follow-up study in 2001, few significant changes resulted, though by 2005 the NCAA had attempted to bolster the importance of academics.

The most sweeping reforms followed court rulings in the 1990s mandating that women's sports be treated equally under Title IX of the Educational Amendments Act of 1972. Enforcement, however, provoked a backlash that resulted in changes to prevent men's teams from being cut. With millions of dollars involved, the system established in the 1920s has withstood most pressures for change.

*T*HE GREAT DEPRESSION AND THE NEW DEAL 1929–1941

*I*n 1931 the rain stopped in the Great Plains. As temperatures reached 115 degrees in Iowa, the soil baked. Farmers watched rich black dirt turn to gray dust.

Then the winds began to blow. Farmers had stripped the Plains of native grasses in the 1920s, using tractors to put millions of acres into production. Now, with nothing to hold the earth, it began to blow away. The dust storms began in 1934 and worsened in 1935. Cattle, blinded by blowing grit, ran in circles until they died. Boiling clouds of dust filled and darkened the skies over Kansas, Colorado, Oklahoma, Texas, and New Mexico—the Dust Bowl.

In late 1937 on a farm near Stigler, Oklahoma, Marvin Montgomery counted up his assets: $53 and a car—a 1929 Hudson he had just bought. On December 29, 1937, Montgomery and his wife and four children—along with their furniture, bedding, pots, and pans—squeezed into the Hudson. Traveling on Route 66, the Montgomerys headed for California.

At least a third of farms in the Dust Bowl were abandoned in the 1930s, and many families headed west, lured by advertisements promising work in California fields. The plight of families like the Montgomerys, captured in the federal government–sponsored Farm Security Administration (FSA) photographs, came to represent the suffering of the Great Depression.

The Montgomerys ran out of money in Arizona and worked the cotton fields there for five weeks, before traveling on to California. There, the wages were low, and migrant families found little welcome. Because they took over agricultural labor formerly done by Mexicans and Mexican Americans, rural Californians regarded these migrants as forfeiting their "whiteness." "Negroes and 'Okies' upstairs," read a sign in a San Joaquin valley movie theater.

While most migrants lived in squalid makeshift camps, the Montgomerys secured housing provided by the federal Farm Security Administration (FSA).

Hoover and Hard Times: 1929–1933

Franklin D. Roosevelt and the Launching of the New Deal

Political Pressure and the Second New Deal

Labor

Federal Power and the Nationalization of Culture

LINKS TO THE WORLD *The 1936 Olympic Games*

The Limits of the New Deal

LEGACY FOR A PEOPLE AND A NATION *Social Security*

Online Study Center
This icon will direct you to interactive map and primary source activities on the website http://college.hmco.com/pic/nortonbrief7e

CHRONOLOGY

1929 • Stock market crash (Oct.); Great Depression begins

1930 • Hawley-Smoot Tariff raises rates on imports

1931 • "Scottsboro Boys" arrested in Alabama

1932 • Banks fail throughout nation
• Bonus Army marches on Washington
• Hoover's Reconstruction Finance Corporation tries to stabilize banks, insurance companies, and railroads
• Roosevelt elected president

1933 • 13 million Americans unemployed
• "First Hundred Days" of Roosevelt administration offers major legislation for economic recovery and poor relief
• National bank holiday halts run on banks
• Agricultural Adjustment Act (AAA) encourages decreased farm production
• National Industrial Recovery Act (NIRA) attempts to spur industrial growth
• Tennessee Valley Authority established

1934 • Long starts Share Our Wealth Society
• Townsend proposes old-age pension plan
• Indian Reorganization (Wheeler-Howard) Act restores lands to tribal ownership

1935 • National Labor Relations (Wagner) Act guarantees workers' right to unionize
• Social Security Act establishes insurance for the aged, the unemployed, and needy children
• Works Progress Administration creates jobs in public works projects
• Revenue (Wealth Tax) Act raises taxes on business and the wealthy

1936 • 9 million Americans unemployed
• United Auto Workers win sit-down strike against General Motors

1937 • Roosevelt's court-packing plan fails
• Memorial Day massacre of striking steelworkers
• "Roosevelt recession" begins

1938 • 10.4 million Americans unemployed
• 80 million movie tickets sold each week

1939 • Marian Anderson performs at Lincoln Memorial
• Social Security amendments add benefits for spouses and widows

The FSA camp had 240 tents and 40 small houses. The Montgomerys' experience shows the human costs of the Great Depression, but statistics are necessary to give a sense of its magnitude. Between 1929 and 1933, the U.S. gross national product was cut in half. Corporate profits fell from $10 billion to $1 billion; 100,000 businesses shut their doors. Four million workers were unemployed in January 1930; by November the number had jumped to 6 million. When President Herbert Hoover left office in 1933, 13 million workers—about one-fourth of the labor force—were idle, and millions more had only part-time work. There was no national safety net: no welfare system, no unemployment compensation, no Social Security. And as thousands of banks failed, with no federally guaranteed deposit insurance, families' savings disappeared.

Herbert Hoover, who had been elected president in the prosperous late 1920s, looked first to private enterprise for solutions. By the end of his term, he had extended the federal government's role in managing an economic crisis further than his predecessors had. Yet the depression continued to deepen. The economic catastrophe exacerbated existing racial and class tensions. In Germany, the international economic crisis propelled Adolf Hitler to power. By late 1932 many feared the depression was a crisis of capitalism, and even of democracy itself.

In 1932 voters replaced Hoover with a man who promised a New Deal. Franklin Delano Roosevelt seemed willing to experiment, and although he did not end the depression (only the massive mobilization for World War II did that), New Deal programs did alleviate suffering. For the first time, the federal government assumed responsibility for the nation's economy and the welfare of its citizens, thus strengthening its power in relation to the states.

As it transformed the role and power of the federal government, the New Deal nevertheless maintained America's existing economic and social systems. Although some Americans saw the economic crisis as an opportunity for major economic change—even revolution—Roosevelt's goal was to save capitalism. New Deal programs increased federal regulation of the economy without altering the capitalist system or the distribution of wealth. And despite pressure (even within his administration) to attack racist discrimination, Roosevelt never directly challenged legal segregation in the South—in part because he relied on southern white Democrats to pass New Deal legislation.

Despite its limits, the New Deal preserved America's democratic experiment through a time of uncertainty and crisis. By the end of the decade, the widening force of world war shifted America's focus from domestic to foreign policy. But the changes set in motion by the New Deal continued to transform the United States for decades to come. ■

Hoover and Hard Times: 1929–1933

*a*s the depression deepened in the early 1930s, tens of millions of Americans were desperately poor. In cities, the hungry lined up at soup kitchens. In West Virginia and Kentucky, wide-

spread hunger and limited resources meant that the American Friends Service Committee distributed food only to those who were 10 percent below the normal weight for their height. In November 1932, *The Nation* told readers that one-sixth of the American population risked starvation over the coming winter. In Albany, New York, a ten-year-old girl died of starvation in her elementary school classroom.

Families, unable to pay rent, were evicted. The new homeless poured into shantytowns, called "Hoovervilles" in ironic tribute to the formerly popular president. Over a million men took to the road or the rails in search of work. The average marriage age rose by over two years during the 1930s. Married people delayed having children, and in 1933 the birth rate sank below replacement rates. (Contraceptive sales, with condoms costing at least $1 per dozen, did not fall during the depression.) More than 25 percent of women who were between the ages of twenty and thirty during the Great Depression never had children.

FARMERS AND INDUSTRIAL WORKERS The agricultural sector, which employed almost a quarter of American workers and did not share in 1920s prosperity, was hit hard by the depression. As urbanites spent less and foreign competitors dumped agricultural surpluses into the global market, farm prices hit bottom. Farmers tried to compensate for lower prices by producing more, thus adding to the surplus and further depressing prices. By 1932, a bushel of wheat that cost North Dakota farmers 77 cents to produce brought only 33 cents. Cash-strapped farmers could not pay their property taxes or mortgages. Banks, facing their own ruin, foreclosed. In Mississippi, on a single day in April 1932, approximately one-fourth of all farmland was being auctioned off to meet debts. By the middle of the decade, the ecological crisis of the Dust Bowl would drive thousands of farmers from their land.

America's industrial workers had seen their standard of living improve during the 1920s, and their consumer spending had bolstered the nation's economic growth. But as Americans had less money to spend, sales of manufactured goods plummeted and factories closed: more than seventy thousand had gone out of business by 1933. As car sales dropped from 4.5 million in 1929 to 1 million in 1933, Ford laid off more than two-thirds of its Detroit workers. Almost a quarter of industrial workers were unemployed,

■ This 1939 photograph, titled "Mother and Children on the Road," was taken in Tule Lake, California, by Farm Security Administration photographer Dorothea Lange. The FSA used photos like this one to build public support for New Deal programs to assist migrant workers and the rural poor.   (Library of Congress)

and those with jobs saw the average wage fall by almost one-third.

For workers on the lowest rungs of the employment ladder, the depression was a crushing blow. In

MARGINAL
WORKERS

the South, positions most white men had considered undignified before the depression—street cleaners, bellhops, garbage collectors—became desirable as other jobs disappeared, thereby increasing pressure for "Negro removal." In 1930 a short-lived fascist-style organization, the Black Shirts, recruited forty thousand members with the slogan, "No Jobs for Niggers Until Every White Man Has a Job!" Northern blacks did not fare much better. An Urban League survey of 106 cities found black unemployment rates averaged 30 to 60 percent higher than whites'. By 1932, African American unemployment reached almost 50 percent.

Mexican Americans and Mexican nationals in the American Southwest also felt the twin impacts of depression and racism. Their wages on California farms fell from a miserable 35 cents an hour in 1929 to a cruel 14 cents an hour by 1932. Throughout the Southwest, campaigns against "foreigners" hurt not only Mexican immigrants but also American citizens of Hispanic background whose families had lived in the Southwest for centuries, long before the land belonged to the United States. In 1931 the Labor Department announced plans to deport illegal immigrants to free jobs for Americans. The policy hit people of Mexican origin hardest, since even those who immigrated legally often lacked full documentation, and officials ignored that children born in the United States were U.S. citizens. The U.S. government deported eighty-two thousand Mexicans between 1929 and 1935, but almost half a million people repatriated to Mexico during the 1930s. Some left voluntarily, but many were coerced into believing they had no choice.

Even before the economic crisis, women were barred from many jobs and were paid significantly less than men. As the economy worsened, discrimination heightened. With widespread male unemployment, it was easy to believe that women who worked took jobs from men. In fact, men laid off from U.S. Steel would not have been hired as teachers, secretaries, "sales girls," or maids. Nonetheless, when a 1936 Gallup poll asked whether wives should work if their husbands had jobs, 82 percent (including 75

percent of the women) answered no. Such beliefs translated into policy. In 1930 and 1931, 77 percent of urban school systems refused to hire married women as teachers, and 63 percent fired female teachers who married.

At first, women lost jobs more quickly than men did. Women in low-wage manufacturing jobs were laid off before male employees, who were presumed to be supporting families. Middle-class families economized by firing household help. Almost a quarter of women in domestic service—a high percentage of them African American—were unemployed by January 1931. And as jobs disappeared, women of color lost even poorly paid positions to white women. But as the depression progressed, "women's jobs," such as teaching, clerical work, and switchboard operators, were not hit as hard as "men's jobs" in heavy industry, and women—including married women who previously did not work for wages—increasingly sought employment. Still, by 1940 only 15.2 percent of married women worked outside the home.

Although unemployment climbed to 25 percent, most Americans did not lose their homes or jobs dur-

MIDDLE-CLASS
WORKERS AND
FAMILIES

ing the depression. Professional and white-collar workers did not fare as badly as industrial workers and farmers. Many middle-class families, however, made do with less. "Use it up, wear it out, make it do, or do without," the saying went, and middle-class women cut back on household expenses by canning food or making their own clothes. Although most families' incomes fell, the impact was cushioned by declining prices of consumer goods, especially food. But even for the relatively affluent, the human toll of the depression was visible everywhere, and no one took economic security for granted any more.

Although Herbert Hoover, "the Great Engineer," had a reputation as a problem solver, no one knew

HOOVER'S
LIMITED
SOLUTIONS

what to do about the crisis. Experts disagreed about the causes of the depression and about the proper course of action. Many prominent business leaders believed that financial panics and depressions, no matter how painful, were part of a natural and ultimately beneficial "business cycle." Economic depressions, according to this theory, brought down inflated prices and cleared the way for real economic growth.

Herbert Hoover disagreed. "The economic fatalist," he said, "believes that these crises are inevitable.... I would remind these pessimists that exactly the same thing was once said of typhoid, cholera, and smallpox." Hoover had faith in "associationalism": business and professional organizations coordinated by the federal government and working together to solve the nation's problems. The federal government's role was limited to serving as a clearinghouse for ideas and plans that state and local governments, along with private industry, could voluntarily choose to implement.

While many Americans thought Hoover was doing nothing to fight the downturn, in truth he stretched his beliefs about the role of government to their limit. He tried voluntarism, exhortation, and limited government intervention. First, he sought voluntary pledges from business groups to keep wages stable and renew investment. But when they looked at their bottom lines, few could keep those promises.

As unemployment climbed, Hoover continued his focus on volunteerism, creating the President's Organization on Unemployment Relief (POUR) to generate private contributions to aid the destitute. Although 1932 saw record charitable contributions, they were inadequate. By mid-1932, one-quarter of New York's private charities, funds exhausted, had closed their doors. State and city officials found their treasuries drying up too.

Hoover held firm, fearing that government "relief" would destroy self-reliance in the poor. Thus, he authorized federal funds to feed drought-stricken livestock but rejected a smaller grant providing food for impoverished farm families. Many Americans were angry at Hoover's seeming insensitivity. When Hoover, trying to restore confidence, said, "What this country needs is a good big laugh," the resulting jokes were not what he expected. "Business is improving," one man tells another. "Is Hoover dead?" asks his companion. Two years after his election, Hoover was the most hated man in America.

Hoover eventually endorsed limited federal action to combat the crisis, but it was too little. Federal public works projects, such as the Grand Coulee Dam in Washington, created some jobs. The Federal Farm Board, created in 1929, supported crop prices by lending money to cooperatives to buy crops and keep them off the market. But the board soon ran short of money, and unsold surpluses jammed warehouses.

Hoover also signed into law the Hawley-Smoot Tariff (1930) to support American farmers and manufacturers by raising import duties to a staggering 40 percent. Instead it hampered international trade as other nations created their own protective tariffs. And as other nations sold less to the United States, they had less money to repay their U.S. debts or buy American products. Fearing the collapse of the international monetary system, Hoover in 1931 announced a moratorium on the payment of First World War debts and reparations.

In January 1932, the administration took its most forceful action with the Reconstruction Finance Corporation (RFC). It provided federal loans to banks, insurance companies, and railroads, which Hoover hoped would shore up those industries and halt disinvestment in the American economy. Hoover compromised his principles: this was direct government intervention, not "voluntarism." If he would support assistance to private industries, why not direct relief to the millions of unemployed?

More and more Americans had begun to ask that question. As the depression deepened, social unrest and violence began to surface. Increasing

Protest and Social Unrest

violence raised the specter of popular revolt, and Chicago mayor Anton Cermak told Congress that if the federal government did not send his citizens aid, it would have to send troops instead.

Throughout the nation, tens of thousands of farmers took the law into their own hands. Angry crowds forced auctioneers to accept just a few dollars for foreclosed property and then returned it to the original owners. In August 1932 a new group, the Farmers' Holiday Association, encouraged farmers to hold back agricultural products to limit supply and drive prices up. In the Midwest, farmers barricaded roads to stop other farmers' trucks and then dumped the contents in roadside ditches.

In cities, the most militant actions came from Unemployed Councils, local groups similar to unions for unemployed workers that were created and led by Communist Party members. Communist leaders believed that the depression demonstrated capitalism's failure and offered an opportunity for revolution. Few of the quarter-million Americans joining local

Unemployed Councils sought revolution, but they did demand action. "Fight, Don't Starve," read banners in a Chicago demonstration.

As social unrest spread, so did racial violence. Vigilante committees offered bounties to force African Americans off the Illinois Central Railroad's payroll: $25 for maiming and $100 for killing black workers. Ten men were murdered and at least seven wounded. The Ku Klux Klan reemerged, and at least 140 attempted lynchings were recorded between January 1930 and February 1933. In most cases, local authorities were able to prevent the lynchings, but white mobs tortured, hung, and mutilated thirty-eight black men during the early years of the Great Depression. Racial violence was not restricted to the South; lynchings took place in Pennsylvania, Minnesota, Colorado, and Ohio as well.

The worst confrontation occurred in summer 1932. More than fifteen thousand unemployed World

BONUS ARMY

War I veterans and their families converged on the nation's capital as Congress debated a bill authorizing immediate payment of cash "bonuses" that veterans had been scheduled to receive in 1945. Calling themselves the Bonus Army, they set up a "Hooverville" shantytown across the river from the Capitol. Concerned about the federal budget, President Hoover opposed the bill, and the Senate voted it down.

Most of the Bonus Marchers left Washington, but several thousand stayed. Calling them "insurrectionists," the president set a deadline for their departure. On July 28, Hoover sent in General Douglas MacArthur and four infantry companies, four troops of cavalry, a machine-gun squadron, and six tanks. What followed shocked the nation: men and women chased by horsemen; children teargassed; shacks set afire. The next day, newspapers carried photographs of U.S. troops attacking their own citizens.

Many worried about an even greater danger in the growing disillusionment with democracy. As the depression worsened, the appeal of a strong leader—someone who would take action, unencumbered by constitutionally mandated checks and balances—grew. In February 1933 the U.S. Senate passed a resolution calling for newly elected president Franklin D. Roosevelt to assume "unlimited power." The rise to power of Hitler and his National Socialist Party in depression-ravaged Germany was an obvious parallel.

Franklin D. Roosevelt and the Launching of the New Deal

In the presidential campaign of 1932, Democratic challenger Franklin Delano Roosevelt insisted that the federal government had to play a much greater role than the limited federal intervention Hoover espoused. Roosevelt supported direct relief payments for the unemployed, declaring that such government aid was "a matter of social duty." During the campaign, he was never explicit about the outlines of his "New Deal." His most concrete proposals, in fact, were sometimes contradictory. But all understood that he had committed to use the power of the federal government to combat the paralyzing economic crisis. Roosevelt's 22.8 million popular votes far outdistanced Hoover's 15.8 million. Third-party Socialist candidate Norman Thomas drew nearly 1 million votes.

Franklin Roosevelt, the twentieth-century president most beloved by America's "common people,"

FRANKLIN D. ROOSEVELT

was born into upper-class privilege. After graduating from Harvard College and Columbia Law School, he married Eleanor Roosevelt, Theodore Roosevelt's niece and his own fifth cousin, once removed. He served in the New York State legislature, was appointed assistant secretary of the navy by Woodrow Wilson, and at age thirty-eight ran for vice president in 1920 on the Democratic Party's losing ticket.

In 1921 Roosevelt was stricken with polio and was bedridden for two years. He lost the use of his legs but gained, according to his wife, Eleanor, a new strength of character. By 1928 Roosevelt was sufficiently recovered to run for—and win—the governorship of New York, and then the Democratic Party's presidential nomination in 1932.

Elected in November 1932, Roosevelt did not take office until March 4, 1933. (The Twentieth Amendment to the Constitution shifted all future inaugurations to January 20.) In this long interregnum, the American banking system reached the verge of collapse.

The origins of the banking crisis lay in the flush years of World War I and the 1920s, when American

BANKING CRISIS banks made risky loans. After real-estate and stock market bubbles burst in 1929 and agricultural prices collapsed, many of these loans soured. As a result, banks lacked sufficient funds to cover their customers' deposits. Fearful of losing their savings, depositors pulled money out of banks and put it into gold or under mattresses. "Bank runs," in which crowds of angry customers demanded their money, became common.

By the 1932 election, the bank crisis was escalating rapidly. Hoover, the lame-duck president, refused to take action without Roosevelt's support, while Roosevelt refused to endorse actions he could not control. By Roosevelt's March 4 inauguration, every state had either suspended banking operations or restricted depositors' access to their money. The new president understood that the collapse of the U.S. banking system would threaten the nation's survival.

Standing in a cold rain on the Capitol steps, Roosevelt vowed in his inaugural address to face the crisis "frankly and boldly." The lines we remember from his speech are words of comfort: "The only thing we have to fear is fear itself—nameless, unreasoning, unjustified terror." But the only loud cheers came when Roosevelt asserted that, if need be, "I shall ask the Congress for the one remaining instrument to meet the crisis—broad Executive power to wage a war against the emergency, as great as the power that would be given to me if we were in fact invaded by a foreign foe."

The next day Roosevelt, using powers legally granted by the World War I "Trading with the Enemy" Act, closed the nation's banks for a four-day "holiday" and summoned Congress to an emergency session. He immediately introduced the Emergency Banking Relief Bill, which was passed sight unseen by unanimous House vote, approved 73 to 7 in the Senate, and signed into law the same day. It provided federal authority to reopen solvent banks and reorganize the rest, and authorized federal money to shore up private banks. Roosevelt had attacked "unscrupulous money changers," and many critics of the failed banking system had hoped he planned to remove the banks from private hands. Instead, Roosevelt's banking policy was much like Hoover's—a fundamentally conservative approach that upheld the status quo.

The banking bill could save the U.S. banking system only if Americans were confident enough to deposit money in the reopened banks. In the first of his radio "Fireside Chats," the president reached out to the people. "We have provided the machinery to restore our financial system," he said. "It is up to you to support and make it work." The next morning when the banks opened, people lined up—this time, most of them to deposit money. In his first action as president, Roosevelt demonstrated that he was not as radical as some wished or as others feared.

During the ninety-nine-day-long special session of Congress, which journalists dubbed "The First

FIRST HUNDRED DAYS Hundred Days," the federal government took on dramatically new roles. Roosevelt set out to revive the economy, aided by advisers—lawyers, university professors, and social workers, collectively nicknamed "the Brain Trust"—and by the enormously capable First Lady. These "New Dealers" had no coherent plan, and Roosevelt alternated between attempts to balance the budget and massive deficit spending (spending more than is taken in in taxes and borrowing the difference). But with a strong mandate for action and the support of a Democrat-controlled Congress, the administration produced a flood of legislation. Two basic strategies emerged: New Dealers experimented with national economic planning, and they created a range of "relief" programs to help the needy.

At the heart of the New Deal experiment in planning were the National Industrial Recovery Act (NIRA)

NATIONAL INDUSTRIAL RECOVERY ACT and the Agricultural Adjustment Act (AAA). The NIRA was based on the belief that "destructive competition" had worsened industry's economic woes. Skirting antitrust regulation, the NIRA authorized competing businesses to cooperate in crafting industrywide "codes." Thus, automobile manufacturers, for example, would cooperate to limit production and establish industrywide prices and wages. With wages and prices stabilized, the theory went, consumer spending would increase, thereby allowing industries to rehire workers.

Administered by the National Recovery Administration (NRA), participation was voluntary—with one catch. Businesses that adhered to the industrywide "codes" could display the NRA "Blue Eagle" symbol; the government urged consumers to boycott businesses without the Blue Eagle. Still, this voluntary program, while larger than previous efforts, was not very different from Hoover-era "associationalism."

As small-business owners had feared, big business easily dominated the NRA-mandated cartels. NRA staff lacked the training to stand up to the representatives of corporate America. The twenty-six-year-old NRA staffer who oversaw the creation of the petroleum industry code was "helped" by twenty highly paid oil industry lawyers. The majority of the 541 codes approved by the NRA reflected the interests of major corporations, not small-business owners, labor, or consumers. Most fundamental, the NRA did not deliver economic recovery. In 1935 the Supreme Court put an end to the fragile, floundering system when it found that the NRA extended federal power past its constitutional bounds.

The Agricultural Adjustment Act (AAA) had a more enduring effect. Establishing a national system of crop controls, it offered subsidies to farmers who agreed to limit production of specific crops. (Overproduction drove crop prices down.) The subsidies would ideally provide farmers the same purchasing power they had had during the prosperous period before World War I. In 1933 the nation's farmers destroyed 8.5 million piglets and plowed under crops in the fields. Millions of hungry Americans found it difficult to understand this waste of food.

AGRICULTURAL ADJUSTMENT ACT

AAA crop control policies hurt tenant farmers and sharecroppers, who were turned off the land as landlords cut production. In the South the number of sharecropper farms dropped by almost a third between 1930 and 1940. The result was a homeless population of dispossessed Americans—many of them African American—heading to cities and towns. But the subsidies did help many. In the Dakotas, government payments accounted for almost three-quarters of the total farm income for 1934.

In 1936 the Supreme Court found that the AAA, like the NRA, was unconstitutional. But the AAA (unlike the NRA) was too popular with its constituency, American farmers, to disappear. The legislation was rewritten to meet the Supreme Court's objections, and farm subsidies continued into the twenty-first century.

Roosevelt also moved quickly to implement poor relief, with $3 billion in federal funds allocated in

RELIEF PROGRAMS

1935. New Dealers, like many other Americans, disapproved of direct relief payments. Thus, New Deal programs emphasized "work relief." By January 1934, the Civil Works Administration gave jobs to 4 million people, most earning $15 a week. And the Civilian Conservation Corps (CCC) paid unmarried young men $1 a day to do hard outdoor labor: building dams and reservoirs, creating trails in national parks. The program was segregated by race but brought together young men from very different backgrounds. By 1942 the CCC had employed 2.5 million men, including 80,000 Native Americans working on western Indian reservations.

The Public Works Administration (PWA), created by Title II of the National Industrial Recovery Act, appropriated $3.3 billion for public works in 1933. PWA workers built the Grand Coulee Dam (begun during Hoover's administration) and the Triborough Bridge in New York City, as well as hundreds of public buildings. But the PWA's main purpose was to pump federal money into the economy. This huge appropriation shows the Roosevelt administration's willingness to use the controversial deficit spending to stimulate the economy.

In the three months until Congress adjourned on June 16, 1933, Roosevelt delivered fifteen messages to Congress proposing major legislation, and Congress had passed fifteen significant laws (see Table 25.1). The United States had rebounded from near collapse. As these and other New Deal programs were implemented, unemployment fell from 13 million in 1933 to 9 million in 1936. Farm prices rose, along with wages and salaries, and business failures abated (see Figure 25.1).

Political Pressure and the Second New Deal

The unprecedented popular and congressional support for Roosevelt's New Deal did not last. The dramatic actions of the First Hundred Days were possible as responses to a national emergency, but once the immediate crisis was averted, the struggle over solutions began in earnest. Some sought to stop the expansion of government power; others

TABLE 25.1

New Deal Achievements

Year	Labor	Agriculture and Environment	Business and Industrial Recovery	Relief	Reform
1933	Section 7(a) of NIRA	Agricultural Adjustment Act Farm Credit Act	Emergency Banking Relief Act Economy Act Beer-Wine Revenue Act Banking Act of 1933 (guaranteed deposits) National Industrial Recovery Act	Civilian Conservation Corps Federal Emergency Relief Act Home Owners Refinancing Act Public Works Administration Civil Works Administration	Tennessee Valley Authority Federal Securities Act
1934	National Labor Relations Board	Taylor Grazing Act			Securities Exchange Act
1935	National Labor Relations (Wagner) Act	Resettlement Administration Rural Electrification Administration		Works Progress Administration National Youth Administration	Social Security Act Public Utility Holding Company Act Revenue Act (wealth tax)
1937		Farm Security Administration			
1938	Fair Labor Standards Act	Agricultural Adjustment Act of 1938		National Housing Act	

Source: Adapted from Charles Sellers, Henry May, and Neil R. McMillen, *A Synopsis of American History*, 6th ed. Copyright © 1985 by Houghton Mifflin Company. Reprinted by permission.

pushed for increased governmental action to combat continuing poverty and inequality.

Many wealthy business leaders criticized the New Deal. Some charged that there was too much

BUSINESS
OPPOSITION

taxation and government regulation. Others condemned the deficit financing of relief and public works. In 1934 several corporate leaders joined former presidential candidate Al Smith and disaffected conservative Democrats to establish the American Liberty League and campaigned against New Deal "radicalism." In an attempt to turn southern whites against the New Deal and splinter

the Democratic Party, the Liberty League secretly channeled funds to a racist group in the South, which circulated incendiary pictures of the First Lady with African Americans.

Meanwhile, other Americans (sometimes called populists) thought the government favored business

DEMAGOGUES
AND POPULISTS

over the common people. Unemployment had decreased, but 9 million people were still jobless. In 1934 a wave of strikes hit the nation, affecting 1.5 million workers. In 1935 dust storms enveloped the southern plains states, killing livestock and driving families from their land. As

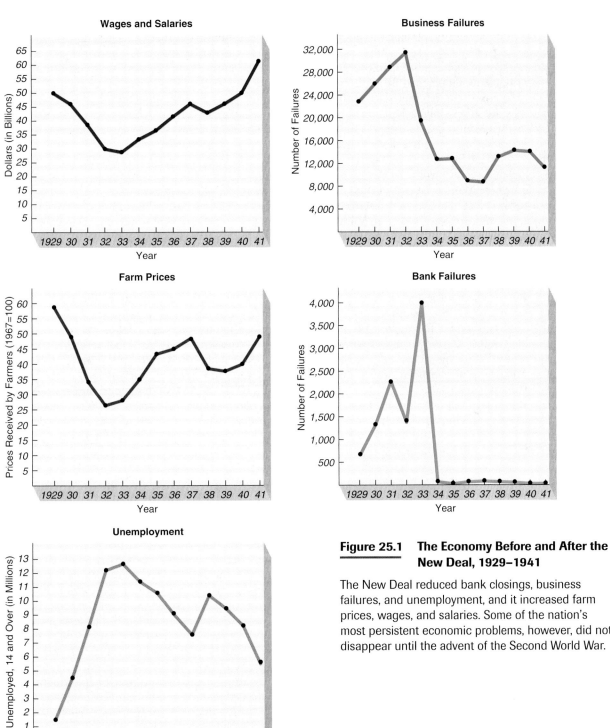

Figure 25.1   The Economy Before and After the New Deal, 1929–1941

The New Deal reduced bank closings, business failures, and unemployment, and it increased farm prices, wages, and salaries. Some of the nation's most persistent economic problems, however, did not disappear until the advent of the Second World War.

dissatisfaction mounted, so did the appeal of dema-gogues, who sought power by playing to people's prejudices.

Father Charles Coughlin, a Roman Catholic priest whose weekly radio sermons reached 30 million lis-teners, appealed to people who felt they'd lost control of their lives to distant elites. Increasingly anti–New Deal, he was also anti-Semitic, telling listeners that an international conspiracy of Jewish bankers caused their problems.

Another challenge came from Dr. Francis E. Townsend, a public health officer in Long Beach, Cal-ifornia, who lost his job at age sixty-seven with only $100 in savings. His situation was common. With so-cial welfare left to the states, only about 400,000 of the 6.6 million elderly Americans received a state-supplied pension. As employment and savings disap-peared, many older people fell into poverty. Townsend proposed that Americans over the age of sixty receive a government pension of $200 a month, financed by a new "transaction" (sales) tax. Townsend's plan was fiscally impossible (almost three-quarters of working Americans earned just $200 a month or less). Nonethe-less, 20 million Americans, or one in five adults, signed petitions supporting this plan.

Then there was Huey Long, perhaps the most suc-cessful populist demagogue in American history. As a U.S. senator, Long initially supported the New Deal, but later believed Roosevelt had fallen captive to big business. Long countered in 1934 with the Share Our Wealth Society, advocating the seizure (by taxation) of all income exceeding $1 million a year and of wealth in excess of $5 million per family. From these funds, the government would provide each American family an annual income of $2,000 and a one-time home-stead allowance of $5,000. (Long's plan was fiscally impossible too.) By mid-1935, Long's movement claimed 7 million members. An assassin's bullet ex-tinguished his ambition in September 1935.

The political left also gained ground. In Wisconsin the left-wing Progressive Party reelected Robert La Follette Jr. to the Senate in 1934,

LEFT-WING CRITICS provided seven of the state's ten rep-resentatives to Congress, and placed La Follette's brother Philip in the governorship. Muckraker and social-ist Upton Sinclair won the Democratic gubernatorial nomination in California in 1934. Disclaiming any intention to overthrow the U.S. government, the U.S.

Communist Party proclaimed that "Communism Is Twentieth Century Americanism," and cooperated with left-wing labor unions, student groups, and writ-ers' organizations in a "Popular Front" against fascism abroad and racism at home. In 1938, at its high point, the party had fifty-five thousand members.

Owing to Eleanor Roosevelt's influence, the administration included activists committed to pro-gressive causes. Frances Perkins,

SHAPING THE SECOND NEW DEAL America's first woman cabinet mem-ber, came from a social work back-ground, as did Roosevelt's close adviser, Harold Ickes. Women ac-tivists in government and the Dem-ocratic Party, attached to Eleanor Roosevelt, were strong advocates for social reform. In 1936 at least fifty African Americans held relatively important po-sitions in New Deal agencies and cabinet-level de-partments. Journalists called these officials—who met on Friday evenings at the home of Mary McLeod Bethune, Director of Negro Affairs for the National Youth Administration—the "black cabinet."

Roosevelt also drew political lessons from populist demagogues and leftist politicians. Many Americans hit hard by the depression looked to the New Deal for help. Other Americans with a tenuous hold on the middle class were afraid of continued disorder and wanted stability. Still others, frightened by the populist promises of Long and Coughlin, wanted the New Deal to preserve American capitalism. In the 1936 presiden-tial election, Roosevelt took initiative once more.

During the period historians call "the Second New Deal," Roosevelt introduced progressive programs aimed at providing "greater security for the average man than he has ever known before." The first tri-umph of the Second New Deal was a law Roosevelt called "the Big Bill." The Emergency Relief Appro-priation Act provided $4 billion in new deficit spend-ing, primarily for massive public works programs for the jobless. Programs included the Resettlement Ad-ministration, which resettled destitute families and organized rural homestead communities and subur-ban greenbelt towns for low-income workers; the Rural Electrification Administration, which brought elec-tricity to isolated areas; and the National Youth Ad-ministration, which sponsored work-relief programs for young adults.

The largest and best-known program was the Works Progress Administration (WPA), later renamed

WORKS PROGRESS ADMINISTRATION the Work Projects Administration. The WPA employed over 8.5 million people who built 650,000 miles of highways and roads and 125,000 public buildings, as well as bridges, reservoirs, irrigation systems, sewage treatment plants, parks, playgrounds, and swimming pools nationwide. WPA workers built or renovated schools and hospitals, operated nurseries for preschool children, and taught 1.5 million adults to read and write.

The WPA also sponsored cultural programs, which provided employment for artists, musicians, writers, and actors and offered art to the people. The WPA's Federal Theater Project brought vaudeville, circuses, and theater, including African American and Yiddish plays, to cities and towns; its Arts Project hired painters and sculptors to teach their crafts in rural schools and commissioned artists to decorate post office walls with murals depicting ordinary life in America. Perhaps the most ambitious was the WPA's Federal Writers Project (FWP), which hired authors such as John Steinbeck and Richard Wright to create guidebooks for every state and write about the people of the United States. More than two thousand elderly former slaves told their stories to FWP writers as "slave narratives." Life stories of sharecroppers and textile workers were published as *These Are Our Lives* (1939). WPA projects were controversial, for many of the artists, performers, and writers sympathized with the struggles of workers and farmers, and some of the artists were communists. However, the goal of this "Popular Front" culture was not to overthrow the government, but to remember and celebrate artistically the lives and labor of America's plain folk.

Big Bill programs offered a short-term "emergency" strategy, but Roosevelt's long-term strategy **SOCIAL SECURITY ACT** centered around the Social Security Act, which created for the first time a federal system to provide for the social welfare of American citizens. Its key provision was a federal pension system in which eligible workers paid mandatory Social Security taxes on their wages and their employers contributed an equivalent amount; these workers then received federal retirement benefits. The Social Security Act also created several welfare programs, including a cooperative federal-state system of unemployment compensation and Aid to Dependent Children (later renamed Aid to Families with Dependent Children, AFDC) for needy children in families without fathers present.

Compared with systems of social security already available in most western European nations, U.S. Social Security was fairly conservative. First, the government did not pay for old-age benefits; workers and their employers did. Second, the tax was regressive in that the more workers earned, the less they were taxed proportionally. Finally, the law did not cover agricultural labor, domestic service, and "casual labor not in the course of the employer's trade or business" (for example, janitorial work at a hospital). Thus, a disproportionally high number of people of color, who worked as farm laborers, domestic servants, and service workers, received no benefits. The act also excluded public sector employees, so many teachers, nurses, librarians, and social workers, the majority of whom were women, went uncovered. (Although the original Social Security Act provided no retirement benefits for spouses or widows of covered workers, Congress added these benefits in 1939.) Despite these limitations, with its passage, the federal government took responsibility for the economic security of the aged, the temporarily jobless, dependent children, and people with disabilities.

As the 1936 election approached, Roosevelt adopted the populist language of his critics. Denouncing the "unjust concentration of **ROOSEVELT'S POPULIST STRATEGIES** wealth and power," he proposed that government should "cut the giants down to size" through antitrust suits and heavy corporate taxes. He also supported the Wealth Tax Act, which helped slightly redistribute income by raising income taxes of the wealthy. It imposed a new tax on business profits and increased taxes on inheritances, large gifts, and profits from the sale of property.

Roosevelt won by a landslide, defeating the Republican nominee, Governor Alf Landon of Kansas, by a margin of 27.8 million votes to 16.7 million. The Democrats also won majorities in the House and Senate. Roosevelt had forged a powerful "New Deal coalition" consisting of the urban masses—especially immigrants from southern and eastern Europe—organized labor, the eleven states of the Confederacy (the "Solid South"), and northern blacks. African Americans in northern cities now constituted voting blocks, and the New Deal drew them away from the

Republican Party, which they had long supported as the party of Lincoln. With the New Deal coalition, the Democratic Party would occupy the White House for most of the next thirty years.

Labor

During the worst years of the depression, American workers continued to struggle for the rights of labor. Management, however, resisted unionization vigorously, with some refusing to negotiate with union representatives and others hiring armed thugs to intimidate workers. When workers walked off the job, employers replaced them with strikebreakers. Workers tried to keep the strikebreakers from crossing picket lines, and the situation often turned violent. Local police or National Guard troops frequently intervened for management. As strikes spread, violence erupted in the steel, automobile, and textile industries, among lumber workers in the Pacific Northwest, and among teamsters in the Midwest.

The Roosevelt administration responded with the 1935 National Labor Relations (Wagner) Act, guaranteeing workers the right to organize unions and bargain collectively. It outlawed "unfair labor practices" such as firing workers who joined unions, prohibited management from sponsoring company unions, and required employers to bargain with labor's elected union representatives to set wages, hours, and working conditions. Critically important, it also created a mechanism for enforcement: the National Labor Relations Board (NLRB). By decade's end, the NLRB played a key role in mediating disputes. Union membership grew: in 1929, it stood at 3.6 million; in mid-1938, it surpassed 7 million.

The Wagner Act further alienated business leaders. The business-sponsored Liberty League insisted that the Supreme Court would soon find the Wagner Act unconstitutional.

The rapid growth and increasing militancy of the labor movement exacerbated an internal division

RIVALRY BETWEEN CRAFT AND INDUSTRIAL UNIONS

between "craft" and "industrial" unions. Craft unions represented labor's elite—the skilled workers in a particular trade, such as carpentry. Industrial unions represented all the workers, skilled and unskilled, in a given industry, such as automobile

manufacture. In the 1930s, industrial unions grew dramatically.

Craft unions dominated the American Federation of Labor, the powerful union umbrella organization. Most AFL leaders offered little support for industrial organizing, and many looked down on industrial workers, disproportionately immigrants from southern and eastern Europe—"the rubbish at labor's door," in the words of the Teamsters' president. Conservative craft unionists were alarmed at what they saw as the radicalism of industrial unions.

In 1935 John L. Lewis, head of the United Mine Workers and the nation's most prominent labor leader, resigned as vice president of the AFL. He and other industrial unionists created the Committee for Industrial Organization (CIO); the AFL suspended CIO unions. In 1938 the slightly renamed Congress of Industrial Organizations had 3.7 million members, slightly more than the AFL's 3.4 million. Unlike the AFL, the CIO included women and people of color, giving these "marginal" workers greater employment security and the benefits of collective bargaining.

The most decisive labor conflict came when the United Auto Workers (UAW) demanded recognition

SIT-DOWN STRIKES

from General Motors (GM), Chrysler, and Ford. When GM refused, on December 30, 1936, workers at the Fisher Body plant in Flint, Michigan, responded with a sit-down strike *inside* the Fisher One factory, thus immobilizing a key part of the GM production system. GM tried to force the workers out by turning off the heat. When the police tried tear gas, strikers turned the plant's water hoses on the police.

As the sit-down strike spread, production plummeted. General Motors obtained a court order to evacuate the plant, but the strikers stood firm, risking imprisonment and fines. Michigan's governor refused to send in the National Guard. After forty-four days, GM agreed to recognize the union, and Chrysler followed. Ford held out until 1940.

On Memorial Day 1937, picnicking workers and their families marched toward the Republic Steel plant

MEMORIAL DAY MASSACRE

in Chicago, intending to support strikers there. Police ordered them to disperse. A marcher threw something, and the police attacked. Ten men were killed, seven of them shot in the back. Thirty marchers were wounded, including a woman and three children. Many Americans, fed up with labor strife, showed little sympathy for the workers.

Gradually the violence receded as the National Labor Relations Board proved effective in mediating disputes. Unionized workers—about 23 percent of the nonagricultural work force—saw their standards of living rise.

Federal Power and the Nationalization of Culture

*I*n the 1930s, the expansion of federal power meant government policies played an increasingly important role in the lives of Americans from different regions, classes, and ethnic backgrounds. During the depression, political power moved from the state and local levels to the White House and Congress. By the end of the 1930s, almost 35 percent of the population had received some federal benefit, whether crop subsidies through the AAA or a WPA job. As political analyst Michael Barone argues, "The New Deal changed American life by changing the relationship between Americans and their government." Americans now expected the federal government to play an active role in the life of the nation.

The New Deal changed the American West more than any other region, as federally sponsored construction of dams and other public works projects reshaped the region's economy and environment. During the 1930s, the federal Bureau of Reclamation, an obscure agency created in 1902, expanded its mandate dramatically to build large multipurpose dams that controlled entire river systems. The Boulder Dam (later renamed for Herbert Hoover) harnessed the Colorado River, providing water to southern California municipalities and using hydroelectric power to produce electricity for Los Angeles and southern Arizona.

NEW DEAL IN THE WEST

The water from these dams opened new areas to agriculture and allowed western cities to expand; the cheap electricity they produced attracted industry. After the completion of Washington State's Grand Coulee Dam in 1941, the federal government controlled a great deal of water and hydroelectric power

in the region—which meant control over the region's future.

The federal government also brought millions of acres of western land under its control in the 1930s, limiting agricultural production to keep prices from falling further and to combat the environmental disaster of the Dust Bowl. In 1934 the Taylor Grazing Act imposed new restrictions on ranchers' use of public lands for grazing stock. Federal livestock reduction programs probably saved the western cattle industry, but they destroyed the traditional economy of the Navajos by forcing them to reduce the size of their sheep herds on federal reservation lands. The large farms and ranches of the West benefited from federal subsidies and crop supports through the AAA, but such programs also increased federal government control in the region.

New federal activism included Native Americans. Previous federal policy toward Native Americans, especially those on western Indian reservations, had been disastrous. The Bureau of Indian Affairs (BIA) was riddled with corruption; in its attempts to "assimilate" Native Americans, it had separated children from their parents, suppressed native languages, and outlawed tribal religious practices. Division of tribal lands failed to promote individual landownership. In the early 1930s, Native Americans were the poorest group in the nation, with an infant mortality rate twice that of white Americans.

NEW DEAL FOR NATIVE AMERICANS

In 1933 Roosevelt named one of the BIA's most vocal critics to head the agency. John Collier, founder of the American Indian Defense Agency, sought to reverse the failed course of Indian policy. The Indian Reorganization Act (IRA, 1934) worked toward ending forced assimilation and restoring Indian lands to tribal ownership. Indian tribes had regained their status as semisovereign nations, guaranteed "internal sovereignty" in matters not limited by acts of Congress.

Some Indians rejected the IRA as a "back-to-the-blanket" measure based on romantic notions of "authentic" Indian culture. The tribal government structure specified by the IRA was perplexing to tribes such as the Papagos, whose language had no word for "representative." The Navajo nation also refused to ratify the IRA, especially since the vote occurred during the federally mandated destruction of Navajo sheep herds. Eventually, however, 181 tribes organized under the IRA, which laid the groundwork for future economic development and limited political autonomy among native peoples.

Online Study Center **Improve Your Grade**
Primary Source: Economic Conditions of the South

Well before the Great Depression, the South was mired in debilitating poverty. In 1929 the South's per capita income of $365 per year was less than half of the West's $921. More than half of southern farm families were tenants or sharecroppers with no land of their own. Almost 15 percent of South Carolina's people could not read or write.

NEW DEAL IN
THE SOUTH

The largest federal intervention in the South was the Tennessee Valley Authority (TVA), authorized by Congress during Roosevelt's First Hundred Days in 1933. The TVA was created to develop a water and hydroelectric power project similar to the multipurpose dams of the West. However, confronted with the poverty of the Tennessee River Valley region (which included parts of Virginia, North Carolina, Tennessee, Georgia, Alabama, Mississippi, and Kentucky), the TVA broadened to promote economic development, bring electricity to rural areas, restore fields worn out from overuse, and fight malaria.

Though an economic miracle, the TVA proved a monumental environmental disaster over time. TVA strip mining caused soil erosion. Its coal-burning generators released sulfur oxides, which combined with water vapor to produce acid rain. Above all, the TVA degraded the water by dumping untreated sewage, toxic chemicals, and metal pollutants from strip mining into streams and rivers.

Online Study Center **Improve Your Grade**
Interactive Map: The Tennessee Valley Authority

Southern senators benefited from the flow of federal dollars to their states but were suspicious of federal intervention. When federal action threatened the South's racial hierarchy, they resisted passionately. As the nation's poorest and least educated region, the South would not easily be integrated into the national culture and economy. But New Deal programs began

that process and improved the lives of at least some of the region's people.

America's national popular culture played a critical role in the life of Americans throughout the 1930s. The national mass medium of radio broke down regional boundaries, fostered national connections, and helped millions survive hard times. Manufacturers rushed to produce cheaper models, and by 1937 Americans were buying radios at the rate of twenty-eight a minute. By the end of the decade 27.5 million households owned radios, and families listened on average five hours a day.

MASS MEDIA
AND POPULAR
CULTURE

In a time of uncertainty, radio gave citizens immediate access to political news and the actual voices of their elected leaders. It also offered escape: for children, the adventures of *Flash Gordon,* and for housewives, the new soap operas such as *The Romance of Helen Trent.* Families gathered to listen to the comedy of ex-vaudevillians George Burns and Gracie Allen, and Jack Benny.

Listeners were carried to New York City for performances of the Metropolitan Opera on Saturday afternoons; to the Moana Hotel on the beach at Waikiki through the live broadcast of *Hawaii Calls;* to major league baseball games (begun by the St. Louis Cardinals in 1935) in distant cities. Millions shared the horror of the kidnapping of aviator Charles Lindbergh's son in 1932; black Americans in the urban North and the rural South shared the triumphal moment when African American boxer Joe Louis knocked out white heavyweight champion James Braddock in 1937. Radio lessened the isolation of individuals and helped to create a more homogeneous mass culture.

The shared popular culture of 1930s America also centered around Hollywood movies. Although the film industry suffered in the initial years of the depression—almost one-third of all movie theaters closed, and ticket prices fell from 30 cents to 20 cents—it rebounded after 1933. In a nation of fewer than 130 million people, 80 to 90 million movie tickets were sold weekly by the mid-1930s. Comedies were especially popular, from the slapstick of the Marx Brothers to the sophisticated banter of *My Man Godfrey.*

Finally, federal policies intended to channel jobs to male heads of households strengthened the power of national popular culture. During Roosevelt's first two years in office, 1.5 million youths lost jobs and

The 1936 Olympic Games

GERMANY
XIth OLYMPIC GAMES
1936
1st—16th AUGUST
BERLIN

The 1936 Olympic Games scheduled to take place in Berlin, under the Nazi regime, created a dilemma for the United States and other nations. Would participation in the Nazi-orchestrated spectacle lend credence to Hitler? Or would victories by other nations undermine Hitler's claims about the superiority of Germany's "Aryan race"?

From the first Olympic Games in 1896, international politics were always near the surface. Germany was excluded in 1920 and 1924 following its defeat in World War I. The International Olympic Committee's choice (in 1931) of Berlin for the XI Olympiad was intended to welcome Germany back into the world community. However, with Hitler's rise to power in 1933, Germany determined to use the games as propaganda for the Nazi state. Soon after, campaigns to boycott the Berlin Olympics emerged in several nations, including the United States.

Americans were divided over the boycott. Some U.S. Jewish groups led campaigns against U.S. participation in Berlin, while many African Americans hoped to demonstrate on the fields of Berlin just how wrong Hitler's notions of Aryan superiority were.

The debate over the Berlin Olympics also revealed pockets of American anti-Semitism. Faced with the prospect of a boycott, the president of the American Olympic Committee (AOC), Avery Brundage, attributed the boycott movement to a "conspiracy" of Jews and communists.

In the end, the United States sent 312 athletes to Berlin, including eighteen African Americans, who won fourteen medals, or almost one-quarter of the U.S. total of fifty-six. Track and field star Jesse Owens earned four gold medals.

Despite the initial controversy, the XI Olympiad was a public relations triumph for Germany in the United States. As participants and spectators flocked to swastika-bedecked Berlin, Hitler's vow that the Olympic Games would thereafter take place in Germany "for all time to come" seemed suddenly possible. The vision of nations linked in peaceful athletic competition hit a low point at the 1936 Olympics. The 1940 Olympic Games, scheduled for Tokyo, were cancelled because of the escalating world war.

The eleventh summer Olympic Games in Berlin were carefully crafted as propaganda for the Nazi state. And the spectacle of the 1936 games, as represented in this poster, was impressive. But on the athletic fields, Nazi claims of Aryan superiority were challenged by athletes such as African American Jesse Owens, who is shown breaking the Olympic record in the 200-meter race.
(Above: © Leonard de Selva/ CORBIS; left: © Bettmann/CORBIS)

■ Radio provided the backdrop for family life and household chores during the 1930s, with programs ranging from operas to soap operas. The largest audience for any single program during the decade listened to the Joe Louis–Max Schmeling boxing match in June 1938.
(AP/Wide World Photo)

many young people who would have gone to work at the age of fourteen in better times decided to stay in school. By the end of the decade, three-quarters of American youth went to high school—up from one-half in 1920—and graduation rates doubled. As more young people went to high school, more participated in national youth culture, increasingly listening to the same music and adopting the same styles of clothing, dance, and speech. Paradoxically, the hard times of the depression caused youth culture to spread more widely among America's young.

The Limits of the New Deal

*R*oosevelt began his second term with a strong mandate for reform. Almost immediately, however, the president's actions undermined his New Deal agenda. Labor strife and racial issues divided America. As fascism spread in Europe, domestic initiatives lost ground to foreign affairs and defense. By late 1938, New Deal reform had ground to a halt.

In safeguarding his progressive agenda in 1936, Roosevelt perceived the Supreme Court as the great-

COURT-PACKING PLAN

est danger to his programs. In ruling unconstitutional both the National Industrial Recovery Act (in 1935) and the Agricultural Adjustment Act (in 1936), the Court rejected not only specific provisions of New Deal legislation but the expansion of presidential and federal power. Only three of the nine justices were consistently sympathetic to New Deal "emergency" measures, and Roosevelt was convinced the Court would invalidate most of the Second New Deal legislation. Citing the advanced age and heavy workload of the nine justices, he asked Congress for authority to appoint up to six new justices. But in an era that had seen the rise to power of Hitler, Mussolini, and Stalin, many Americans saw Roosevelt's plan as an attack on constitutional government. Congress rebelled, and Roosevelt experienced his first major congressional defeat.

During the long public debate over court packing, key swing-vote justices began to favor liberal, pro–New Deal rulings. The Court upheld both the Wagner Act (*NLRB v. Jones & Laughlin Steel Corp.*), ruling that Congress's power to regulate interstate commerce also involved regulating the production of goods for interstate commerce, and the Social Security Act. Moreover, a new judicial pension program encouraged older judges to retire, and the president appointed seven new associate justices, including notables such as Hugo Black, Felix Frankfurter, and William O. Douglas. In the end, Roosevelt got what he wanted, but the court-packing plan damaged his political credibility.

Another New Deal setback was the recession of 1937–1939, sometimes called the "Roosevelt recession." In 1937, confident that the depression had largely been cured, Roosevelt cut back government spending. At the same time, the Federal Reserve Board, concerned about a 3.6 percent inflation rate, tightened credit. The actions sent the economy into a tailspin: unemployment climbed from 7.7 million in 1937 to 10.4 million in 1938.

ROOSEVELT RECESSION

New Dealers struggled over the direction of liberal reform. Some urged trustbusting; others advocated the resurrection of national economic planning as it had existed under the National Recovery Administration. But Roosevelt chose deficit financing to stimulate consumer demand and create jobs. And in 1939, with conflict over the world war in Europe commanding more of the nation's attention, the New Deal came to an end.

No president had ever served more than two terms, and many Americans speculated whether Franklin Roosevelt would run for a third term in 1940. Roosevelt seemed undecided until spring, when Adolf Hitler's military advances convinced him to stay on. Roosevelt expanded military contracts, thereby reducing unemployment. Roosevelt also promised Americans, "Your boys are not going to be sent into any foreign wars."

ELECTION OF 1940

On election day, the New Deal did not deliver the landslide victory it had in the 1936 election. Roosevelt again won in the cities, primarily among blue-collar workers, ethnic Americans, and African Americans, and carried every state in the South.

While many Americans benefited, the New Deal fell short of equality for people of color. Over and over, national New Deal programs lost to local custom in the South and the West. In the South, African Americans received lower relief payments than whites and were paid

RACE AND THE LIMITS OF THE NEW DEAL

less for WPA jobs. In Tucson, Arizona, Federal Emergency Relief Agency officials divided applicants into four groups—Anglos, Mexican Americans, Mexican immigrants, and Indians—and allocated relief payments in descending order.

The case of the Scottsboro Boys illustrates the power of racism in the conflict between local and national power in 1930s America. One night in March 1931, young black and white "hobos" fought on a Southern Railroad freight train as it passed through Alabama. The black youths tossed the whites off the train. A posse stopped the train and threw the black youths in the Scottsboro, Alabama, jail. Two white women "riding the rails" claimed these young men had raped them. The youths were barely saved from a lynch mob. Medical evidence later showed that the women were lying. But within two weeks, eight of the so-called Scottsboro Boys were convicted of rape by all-white juries and sentenced to death. The ninth, a boy of thirteen, was saved from the death penalty by one vote. The case, clearly a product of southern racism, became a cause célèbre, both nationally and, through the Communist Party, around the world.

The Supreme Court intervened, ruling that Alabama deprived black defendants of equal protection under the law by systematically excluding African Americans from juries and that the defendants had been denied counsel. Alabama staged new trials, however, convicting five of the young men, who spent almost two decades in prison. On issues of race, the South would not yield easily to federal power.

Roosevelt could not secure passage of his New Deal without southern Democrats, and they were willing to hold him hostage over race. For example, in 1938, southern Democrats blocked an antilynching bill with a six-week-long filibuster in the Senate. Roosevelt refused to use his political capital to break the filibuster and pass the bill. He knew that blacks would not desert the Democratic Party, but without southern senators, his legislative agenda was dead. Roosevelt wanted all Americans to enjoy the benefits of democracy, but he had no strong commitment to civil rights.

African Americans supported Roosevelt and the New Deal, despite discriminatory policies, because it helped them. By the end of the 1930s, almost one-third of African American households survived on income from a WPA job. African Americans held significant positions in the Roosevelt administration.

When the acclaimed black contralto Marian Anderson was barred from performing in Washington's Constitution Hall by the Daughters of the American Revolution, First Lady Eleanor Roosevelt arranged for Anderson to sing at the Lincoln Memorial on Easter Sunday, 1939. Such public commitment to equality was enormously important to African Americans.

With the New Deal's limits, some blacks concluded that self-help and direct-action movements were the only road to equality. In 1934 black tenant farmers and sharecroppers joined with poor whites to form the Southern Tenant Farmers' Union. In the North, African American consumers began to boycott white merchants who refused to hire blacks. Their slogan was "Don't Buy Where You Can't Work." And the Brotherhood of Sleeping Car Porters, under the leadership of A. Philip Randolph, fought for black workers. Such actions helped to improve the lives of black Americans during the 1930s.

Assessments of Roosevelt varied widely during his presidency: he was passionately hated and just as passionately loved. When he spoke to Americans in his Fireside Chats, thousands wrote to him, asking for his help and offering their advice.

AN ASSESSMENT OF THE NEW DEAL

Eleanor Roosevelt, the nation's First Lady, played an unprecedented role in the Roosevelt administration. She worked tirelessly for social justice, bringing reformers, trade unionists, and advocates for the rights of women and African Americans to the White House. Sometimes described as the conscience of the New Deal, she took public positions—especially on African American civil rights—far more progressive than those of her husband's administration. In some ways, she deflected criticism from her husband to herself; in others, she cemented allegiances of groups such as African Americans to the New Deal.

Most scholars consider Franklin Roosevelt a truly great president, citing his courage and self-confidence, his willingness to experiment, and his capacity to inspire the nation. Some who see the New Deal as a squandered opportunity for true change charge that Roosevelt lacked vision. They judge Roosevelt by goals that were not his own: Roosevelt was a pragmatist whose goal was to preserve the system. But even critics agree that he transformed the presidency.

During his more than twelve years in office, Roo-sevelt strengthened the presidency and the federal government. Through New Deal programs, the government greatly added to its regulatory responsibilities, including overseeing the nation's financial systems. For the first time, the federal government offered relief to the jobless and the needy and used deficit spending to stimulate the economy. Millions of Americans benefited from programs that are still operating today, among them, Social Security.

As late as 1939, more than 10 million men and women were still jobless, and the nation's unemployment rate stood at 19 percent. In 1941, as a result of mobilization for war, unemployment declined to 10 percent, and in 1944, at the height of the war, only 1 percent of the labor force was jobless. World War II, not the New Deal, would reinvigorate the American economy.

Summary Online Study Center ACE the Test

In the 1930s, a major economic crisis threatened the nation. By 1933, almost a quarter of America's workers were unemployed, and millions were homeless and hungry. Herbert Hoover, elected president in 1928, believed that government should play only a limited role in managing the economy. He tried to solve the nation's economic problems through a voluntary partnership of businesses and the federal government known as associationalism. In the 1932 presidential election, voters turned to the candidate who promised them a "New Deal."

The New Deal was a liberal reform program that developed within the parameters of America's capitalist and democratic system, expanding the power of the federal government. New Deal reforms forced banks, utilities, stock markets, farms, and most businesses to operate within federal guidelines. The government guaranteed workers' right to join unions, and federal law required employers to negotiate with unions to set wages, hours, and working conditions. Many unemployed workers, elderly and disabled Americans, and dependent children were protected by a national welfare system, administered through the federal government.

The New Deal had its detractors. Business leaders attacked New Deal regulations and support of organized labor. As the federal government expanded its role, tensions between national and local authority sometimes flared, and differences in regional ways of life and social and economic structures presented challenges to national policymakers. Both the West and the South were transformed by federal government action, but citizens of both regions were suspicious of federal intervention, and white southerners resisted challenges to the racial system of Jim Crow. The political realities of a fragile New Deal coalition and strong opposition shaped—and limited—New Deal programs of the 1930s and the social welfare systems Americans still live with today.

LEGACY FOR A PEOPLE AND A NATION
Social Security

The New Deal's Social Security system resulted in a secure old age for millions of Americans. Although Social Security initially excluded some of America's neediest citizens, such as farm and domestic workers, amendments expanded eligibility. Today, almost 99 percent of American workers are covered by Social Security.

The Social Security system faces an uncertain future, and its troubles are due in part to decisions made during the 1930s. President Franklin Roosevelt did not want Social Security to be confused with poor relief and instead created a system financed by payments from workers and their em-

ployers. But if benefits came from their own contributions, workers who began receiving payments in 1940 would have received less than a dollar a month. Therefore, Social Security payments from current workers covered the benefits of those already retired.

Over time, this financing system has become increasingly unstable. In 1935 average life expectancy was under sixty-five years, the age one could collect benefits. Today, on average, American men live to over eighty, and women live nearly twenty years past retirement age. In 1935 there were 16 workers paying into the system for each person receiving benefits. In 2000 there were fewer than 3.5 workers per retiree. Unless the system is reformed, many argue, the retirement of 77 million baby boomers born from the 1940s to the 1960s could bankrupt the system.

While the stock market soared in the 1990s, some proposed that since Social Security paid only a fraction of what individuals might have earned by investing their Social Security tax payments in the stock market, Americans be allowed to do just that. Opponents declared this proposal too risky; others argued that if current workers kept their money to invest, where would benefits for current retirees come from? Debates over Social Security would play a crucial role in the second term of President George W. Bush.

*P*EACESEEKERS AND WARMAKERS: AMERICANS IN THE WORLD 1920–1941

*I*n 1921 the Rockefeller Foundation dedicated several million dollars for projects to control yellow fever in Latin America, beginning with Mexico. Transmitted by mosquitoes, the virus causes severe headaches, vomiting, jaundice (yellow skin), and often death. Learning from the pioneering work of Carlos Juan Finlay of Cuba, Oswaldo Cruz of Brazil, and U.S. Army surgeon Walter Reed, scientists sought to destroy the mosquito in its larval stage, before it became an egg-laying adult.

U.S. diplomats, military officers, and business executives agreed that the disease threatened public health, which in turn disturbed political and economic order. When outbreaks occurred, ports were closed and quarantined, disrupting trade and immigration. The infection struck American officials, merchants, investors, and soldiers abroad and incapacitated workers. Insufficient official attention to epidemics stirred public discontent against regimes the United States supported. When the Panama Canal opened in 1914, leaders feared that the disease would spread, even reinfecting the United States, which suffered its last epidemic in 1905.

Gradually overcoming local anti-U.S. feelings, Rockefeller personnel inspected breeding places and deposited larvae-eating fish in public waterworks. In 1924 La Fundación Rockefeller declared yellow fever eradicated in Mexico. Elsewhere in Latin America, the foundation's antimosquito campaign proved successful in maritime and urban areas but less so in rural and jungle regions. Politically, Rockefeller Foundation efforts in the 1920s and 1930s strengthened central governments by providing a public health infrastructure and diminishing anti-U.S. sentiment.

The Rockefeller Foundation's program offers insights into Americans' fervent but futile efforts to build a stable international order after the First

Searching for Peace and Order in the 1920s

The World Economy, Cultural Expansion, and Great Depression

U.S. Dominance in Latin America

The Course to War in Europe

Japan, China, and a New Order in Asia

U.S. Entry into World War II

LINKS TO THE WORLD
Radio News

LEGACY FOR A PEOPLE AND A NATION
Presidential Deception of the Public

Online Study Center
This icon will direct you to interactive map and primary source activities on the website
http://college.hmco.com/pic/nortonbrief7e

C H R O N O L O G Y

1921–22 • Washington Conference limits naval arms
• Rockefeller Foundation begins battle against yellow fever in Latin America

1922 • Mussolini comes to power in Italy

1924 • Dawes Plan eases German reparations

1928 • Kellogg-Briand Pact outlaws war

1929 • Great Depression begins
• Young Plan reduces German reparations

1930 • Hawley-Smoot Tariff raises duties

1931 • Japan seizes Manchuria

1933 • Adolf Hitler becomes chancellor of Germany
• United States extends diplomatic recognition to Soviet Union
• U.S. announces Good Neighbor policy for Latin America

1934 • Fulgencio Batista comes to power in Cuba

1935 • Italy invades Ethiopia
• Congress passes first Neutrality Act

1936 • Germany reoccupies the Rhineland
• Spanish Civil War breaks out

1937 • Sino-Japanese War breaks out
• Roosevelt makes "quarantine speech" against aggressors

1938 • Mexico nationalizes American-owned oil companies
• Munich Conference grants part of Czechoslovakia to Germany

1939 • Germany and Soviet Union sign nonaggression pact
• Germany invades Poland, and Second World War begins

1940 • Germany invades Denmark, Norway, Belgium, the Netherlands, and France
• Selective Training and Service Act starts first U.S. peacetime draft

1941 • Lend-Lease Act gives aid to Allies
• Germany attacks Soviet Union
• U.S. freezes Japanese assets
• Roosevelt and Churchill sign Atlantic Charter
• Japanese flotilla attacks Pearl Harbor, Hawai'i, and U.S. enters Second World War

World War. Despite the "isolationist" label sometimes applied to U.S. foreign relations during the interwar decades, Americans remained active in world affairs in the 1920s and 1930s—from gunboats on Chinese rivers, to negotiations in European financial centers, to marine occupations in Haiti and Nicaragua, to oil wells in the Middle East, to campaigns against diseases in Africa and Latin America. President Wilson said after the First World War that the United States had "become a determining factor in the history of mankind."

Notwithstanding the nation's overseas projects—colonies, spheres of influence, naval bases, investments, trade, missionary activity, humanitarian efforts—many Americans did think of themselves as isolationists, meaning that they wanted no part of Europe's political squabbles, military alliances and interventions, or the League of Nations, which might drag them into war. Internationalist-minded Americans, including most senior officials, also wanted to steer clear of future European war but were more willing than isolationists to attempt to reshape the world.

A stable world would better facilitate American prosperity and security. In the interwar years, American diplomats increasingly exercised U.S. power through conferences, humanitarian programs, cultural penetration ("Americanization"), calls for peace, non-recognition of disapproved regimes, arms control, and economic and financial ties under the Open Door principle.

But a stable world order proved elusive. Public health projects saved lives but could not address staggering poverty across the globe. World War I debts and reparations bills bedeviled the 1920s. The Great Depression shattered world trade and threatened America's prominence in international markets. It also spawned political extremism, militarism, and war in Europe and Asia. As Nazi Germany marched to war, the United States adopted a policy of neutrality. The United States also defended its interests in Asia against Japanese aggression by invoking the Open Door policy.

After the outbreak of European war in September 1939, many Americans agreed with President Franklin D. Roosevelt that Germany and Japan imperiled U.S. interests because they were building self-sufficient spheres of influence based on military and economic domination. Roosevelt first pushed for American military preparedness and then favored aiding Britain and France. A German victory, he reasoned, would destroy traditional economic ties, threaten U.S. influence in the Western Hemisphere, and place at the pinnacle of European power Adolf Hitler, whose ambitions and barbarities seemed limitless.

At the same time, Japan seemed determined to dismember America's friend China, destroy the Open Door principle, and endanger a U.S. colony: the Philippines. To deter the Japanese, the United States cut off supplies of vital American products such as oil. Japan's surprise attack on Pearl Harbor, Hawai'i, in December 1941 finally brought the United States into the Second World War. ∎

Searching for Peace and Order in the 1920s

he First World War left Europe in shambles. Between 1914 and 1921, Europe suffered tens of millions of casualties from world war, civil wars, massacres, epidemics, and famine. Germany and France lost 10 percent of their workers. The American Relief Administration and private charities delivered food to needy Europeans, including Russians wracked by famine in 1921 and 1922. Through their generosity, Americans also hoped to dampen any appeal political radicalism might have. Secretary of State Charles Evans Hughes and other leaders expected American economic expansion to promote international stability—a prosperity that would render unnecessary ideological extremes, revolution, arms races, aggression, and war.

Collective security, as envisioned by Woodrow Wilson (see Chapter 23), elicited little enthusiasm among Republican leaders. Senator Henry Cabot Lodge gloated in 1920 that "we have destroyed Mr. Wilson's League of Nations." The Geneva-headquartered League of Nations, envisioned as a peacemaker, proved feeble, not just because the United States did not join but because members failed to use it to settle disputes. Still, starting in the mid-1920s, American officials participated discreetly in League meetings on public health, prostitution, drug and arms trafficking, counterfeiting of currency, and other issues. American jurists served on the Permanent Court of International Justice (World Court). The Rockefeller Foundation donated $100,000 a year to the League's public health efforts.

During the interwar years, peace groups drew widespread support. Women gravitated to their own

PEACE GROUPS organizations because they lacked influence in the male-dominated groups and because of the popular assumption that women—as nurturing mothers—had a unique aversion to war. Carrie Chapman Catt's moderate National Conference on the Cure and Cause of War, formed in 1924, and the U.S. Section of the Women's International League for Peace and Freedom (WILPF), organized in 1915 by Jane Addams and Emily Greene Balch, became the largest women's peace groups. When Addams won the Nobel Peace Prize in 1931, she gave her award money to the League of Nations.

Peace groups differed over strategies to ensure world order. Some urged cooperation with the League of Nations and the World Court. Others championed arbitration, disarmament and arms reduction, the outlawing of war, and strict neutrality during wars. The WILPF called for an end to U.S. economic imperialism, which, it claimed, compelled the United States to intervene militarily in Latin America to protect U.S. business interests. The Women's Peace Union (organized in 1921) lobbied for a constitutional amendment requiring a national referendum on a declaration of war. Quakers, YMCA officials, and Social Gospel clergy in 1917 created the American Friends Service Committee to identify pacifist alternatives to warmaking.

Peace advocates influenced Warren G. Harding's administration to convene the Washington Naval

WASHINGTON NAVAL CONFERENCE

Conference of November 1921–February 1922. Delegates from Britain, Japan, France, Italy, China, Portugal, Belgium, and the Netherlands joined a U.S. team to discuss limiting naval armaments. American leaders worried that huge military spending endangered economic rehabilitation and that an expansionist Japan, with the world's third largest navy, would overtake the United States, ranked second behind Britain.

Secretary of State Charles Evans Hughes opened the conference with the stunning proposal to scrap thirty major U.S. ships, totaling 846,000 tons. He urged the British and Japanese delegations to do away with smaller amounts. The final limit was 500,000 tons each for the Americans and the British, 300,000 tons for the Japanese, and 175,000 tons each for the French and Italians, as agreed to in the Five-Power Treaty. The treaty set a ten-year moratorium on building capital ships (battleships and aircraft carriers). The governments also pledged not to build new fortifications in their Pacific possessions (such as the Philippines).

Next, the Nine-Power Treaty reaffirmed the Open Door in China, recognizing Chinese sovereignty. Finally, in the Four-Power Treaty, the United States, Britain, Japan, and France agreed to respect one another's Pacific possessions. These treaties did not limit submarines, destroyers, or cruisers, and did not provide enforcement powers for the Open Door. Still, Hughes achieved arms limitation and improved America's strategic position in the Pacific regarding Japan.

Peace advocates also welcomed the Locarno Pact of 1925, a set of agreements among European na-

KELLOGG-BRIAND PACT

tions that sought to reduce tensions between Germany and France, and the Kellogg-Briand Pact of 1928. In

the latter document, sixty-two nations agreed to "condemn recourse to war for the solution of international controversies, and renounce it as an instrument of national policy." The accord passed the Senate 85 to 1, but it lacked enforcement provisions. The Kellogg-Briand Pact reflected popular opinion that war was barbaric and stimulated public discussion on the topic. But arms limitations, peace pacts, and efforts by peace groups failed to eradicate war, which fed on the economic troubles that upended world order.

The World Economy, Cultural Expansion, and Great Depression

*W*hile Europe struggled after the First World War, the international economy wobbled. Then, in the 1930s, the Great Depression set off a political chain reaction that carried the world to war. Cordell Hull, secretary of state from 1933 to 1944, argued that political extremism and militarism sprang from maimed economies. Hull proved right.

Because of World War I, the United States became a creditor nation and the financial capital of the world

ECONOMIC AND CULTURAL EXPANSION

(see Figure 26.1). From 1914 to 1930, private investments abroad grew fivefold to more than $17 billion. By the late 1920s, the United States produced nearly half of the world's industrial goods and ranked first among exporters ($5.2 billion worth of shipments in 1929). Britain and Germany lost ground to American businesses in Latin America, where Standard Oil operated in eight nations and the United Fruit Company became a huge landowner.

With America's economic prominence, cultural exportation easily followed. Hollywood movies saturated the global market and stimulated interest in American ways and products. Although some foreigners warned against "Americanization," others aped American mass-production methods and modernization. Coca-Cola opened a bottling plant in Essen, Germany, and Ford built an automobile plant in Cologne.

Germans marveled at Henry Ford's industrial techniques ("Fordismus"). In the 1930s, Nazi leader Adolf Hitler sent German car designers to Detroit

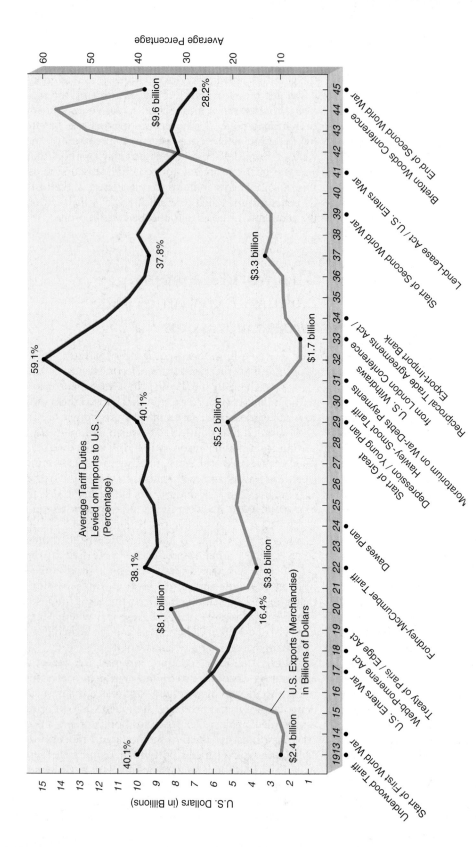

Figure 26.1   The United States in the World Economy

In the 1920s and 1930s, global depression and war scuttled the United States's hope for a stable economic order. This graph suggests, moreover, that high American tariffs meant lower exports, further impeding world trade. The Reciprocal Trade Agreements program initiated in the early 1930s was designed to ease tariff wars with other nations.   (Source: U.S. Bureau of the Census, *Historical Statistics of the United States, Colonial Times to 1970* [Washington, D.C., 1975].)

before launching the Volkswagen. The Phelps-Stokes Fund further adverted the American capitalist model, exporting to black Africa Booker T. Washington's Tuskegee philosophy of education, while the Rockefeller Foundation supported colleges training doctors in Lebanon and China and funded medical research and nurses' training in Europe.

The U.S. government assisted this expansion. The Webb-Pomerene Act (1918) excluded from antitrust prosecution those combinations set up for export trade; the Edge Act (1919) permitted American banks to open foreign-branch banks; and the overseas offices of the Department of Commerce distributed valuable market information. The federal government also stimulated foreign loans by American investors. U.S. government support for the expansion of the telecommunications industry helped International Telegraph and Telephone (IT&T), Radio Corporation of America (RCA), and the Associated Press (AP) become international giants by 1930.

Europeans branded the United States stingy for its handling of World War I debts and reparations.

WAR DEBTS AND GERMAN REPARATIONS
Twenty-eight nations were involved in inter-Allied government debts, totaling $26.5 billion ($9.6 billion of it owed to the U.S. government). Europeans owed private American creditors another $3 billion and urged Americans to erase the government debts as a magnanimous contribution to the war effort. During the war, they angrily charged, Europe had bled while America profited. American leaders insisted on repayment, some pointing out that the victorious European nations had gained vast territory and resources as war spoils.

The debts question became linked to Germany's $33 billion reparations bill—which some believed Germany had the capacity but not the willingness to pay. When Germany defaulted on its payment, American bankers loaned millions to keep the nation afloat and forestall the radicalism that might thrive on economic troubles. A triangular relationship developed: American investors' money flowed to Germany, Germany paid reparations to the Allies, and the Allies then paid some of their debts to the United States. The American-crafted Dawes Plan of 1924 reduced Germany's annual payments, extended the repayment period, and provided more loans. The United States also gradually scaled down Allied obligations, cutting the debt by half during the 1920s.

But everything hinged on continued German borrowing in the United States, and in 1928 and 1929, American lending abroad dropped sharply as funds shifted to more lucrative opportunities in the stock market (see Chapters 24 and 25). The U.S.-negotiated Young Plan of 1929, which reduced Germany's reparations, salvaged little as the world economy sputtered and collapsed. By 1931, the Allies had paid back only $2.6 billion. Staggered by the Great Depression—an international catastrophe—they defaulted on the rest. Annoyed, Congress in 1934 passed the Johnson Act, which forbade U.S. government loans to foreign governments in default to the United States.

As the depression deepened, tariff wars reinvigorated economic nationalism. By 1932 twenty-five

DECLINE IN TRADE
nations retaliated against rising American tariffs (created in the Fordney-McCumber Act of 1922 and the Hawley-Smoot Act of 1930) by imposing higher tariffs on foreign imports. From 1929 to 1933, world trade declined by 40 percent. Exports of American merchandise slumped from $5.2 billion to $1.7 billion.

For Secretary of State Hull, finding a way out of the crisis depended on reviving world trade, which he believed would also boost the chances for global peace. He successfully pressed Congress to pass the Reciprocal Trade Agreements Act in 1934, which empowered the president to reduce U.S. tariffs by up to 50 percent through special agreements with foreign countries. The act's central feature was the most-favored-nation principle, whereby the United States was entitled to the lowest tariff rate set by any nation with which it had an agreement.

In 1934 Hull also helped create the Export-Import Bank, a government agency providing loans to foreigners purchasing American goods. The bank stimulated trade and became a diplomatic weapon, allowing the United States to exact concessions by approving or denying loans. In the short term, Hull's ambitious programs brought mixed results.

The Roosevelt administration's move to extend diplomatic recognition to the Soviet Union was also

U.S. RECOGNITION OF THE SOVIET UNION
economically driven. Throughout the 1920s, the Republicans refused diplomatic relations with the Soviet government, which had failed to pay $600 million for confiscated American-owned property and repudiated

preexisting Russian debts. Nonetheless, in the late 1920s, American businesses such as General Electric and International Harvester entered the Soviet marketplace, and Henry Ford signed a contract to build an automobile plant there. By 1930 the Soviet Union had become the largest buyer of American farm and industrial equipment.

Roosevelt speculated that closer Soviet-American relations might help the economy while deterring Japanese expansion. In 1933 Roosevelt granted U.S. diplomatic recognition to the Soviet Union in return for Soviet agreement to discuss its debts, forgo subversive activities in the United States, and grant Americans in the Soviet Union religious freedom and legal rights.

U.S. Dominance in Latin America

Through the Platt Amendment, the Roosevelt Corollary, the Panama Canal, military intervention, and economic preeminence, the United States had thrown an imperial net over Latin America in the early twentieth century (see Chapter 22). U.S. dominance in the hemisphere grew after the First World War. A prominent State Department officer patronizingly remarked that Latin Americans were of "low racial quality" and therefore "very easy people to deal with if properly managed."

American-made schools, roads, telephones, and irrigation systems dotted Central America and the Caribbean. American "money doctors" in Colombia and Peru helped reform tariff and tax laws and invited U.S. companies to build public works. Washington forced private high-interest loans on the Dominican Republic and Haiti. Republican administrations curtailed U.S. military intervention in the hemisphere, temporarily withdrawing troops from the Dominican Republic (1924) and Nicaragua (1925). But the marines returned to Nicaragua in 1926 to end fighting between conservative and liberal Nicaraguans and protect American property. In Haiti, the U.S. troop commitment made under Woodrow Wilson in 1915 lasted until 1934, the soldiers there to keep pro-Washington governments in power.

By 1929 direct American investments in Latin America (excluding bonds and securities) totaled $3.5 billion, while U.S. exports dominated the region's trade. Country after country experienced the repercussions of U.S. economic and political decisions. For example, the price that Americans set for Chilean copper determined the health of Chile's economy.

Latin American nationalists protested that their resources were being drained away by U.S. companies, leaving many nations in a dependent state. Unapologetic Americans believed that they were bringing material improvements and the blessings of liberty to Latin American neighbors.

DEPENDENCY STATUS

Criticism of U.S. imperialism in the region mounted in the interwar years. In 1928, at the Havana Inter-American conference, U.S. officials unsuccessfully tried to kill a resolution stating that "no state has a right to intervene in the internal affairs of another." Two years later, a Chilean newspaper warned that the American "Colossus" had "financial might" and that its aim was "Americas for the Americans—of the North." In the United States, Senator William Borah of Idaho urged that Latin Americans be granted the right of self-determination, to decide their own futures. Business leaders feared that Latin American nationalists would direct their anti-Yankee feelings against American-owned property.

Renouncing unpopular military intervention, the United States switched strategies to maintain its influence in Latin America: Pan-Americanism (a fifty-year-old concept strengthening ties between North and South America), support for strong local leaders, the training of national guards, economic and cultural penetration, Export-Import Bank loans, financial supervision, and political subversion. Dubbed the Good Neighbor policy by Franklin Roosevelt in 1933, it meant that the United States would be less blatant in its domination—avoiding exploitative business practices and military expeditions and consulting with Latin Americans.

GOOD NEIGHBOR POLICY

Most notably, Roosevelt ordered home the U.S. military forces stationed in Haiti (since 1915) and Nicaragua (since 1912, with a hiatus in 1925–1926), and he restored some sovereignty to Panama and increased that nation's income from the canal. Roosevelt's popularity in Latin America grew when, in a series of pan-American conferences, he joined in pledging that no nation in the hemisphere would intervene in the "internal or external affairs" of any other.

But Roosevelt promised more than he could deliver. His administration continued to bolster dictators in the region, believing that they would preserve U.S. economic interests. And when a revolution brought a radical government to power in Cuba in 1933, FDR instructed the American ambassador in Havana to work with conservative Cubans to replace the new government with one friendlier to U.S. interests. With Washington's support, army sergeant Fulgencio Batista took power in 1934.

During the Batista era (which ended when he was dethroned by Fidel Castro in 1959), Cuba protected U.S. investments and aligned itself with U.S. foreign policy. In return, the United States provided military aid and Export-Import Bank loans, abrogated the unpopular Platt Amendment, and gave Cuban sugar a favored position in the United States. American tourists flocked to Havana's night life of rum, rumba, prostitution, and gambling. Nationalistic Cubans protested that their nation had become a mere extension of the United States.

In Mexico, Roosevelt again showed a level of restraint that his predecessors had lacked. Since

CLASH WITH MEXICAN NATIONALISM

Woodrow Wilson sent troops to Mexico in 1914 and again in 1916, U.S.-Mexican relations had faltered as the two governments wrangled over economic interests. Still, by 1934, the United States accounted for 61 percent of Mexico's imports and received 52 percent of its exports. That year, however, a new government under Lázaro Cárdenas pledged "Mexico for the Mexicans" and strengthened trade unions to strike against foreign corporations.

In 1937 workers struck foreign oil companies for higher wages and recognition, but the companies, including Standard Oil, rejected union appeals, hoping to send a message across the hemisphere that economic nationalism could never succeed. The following year, the Cárdenas government boldly expropriated the property of all foreign-owned petroleum companies, calculating that the approaching war in Europe would restrain the United States from attacking Mexico. The United States countered by reducing purchases of Mexican silver and promoting a multinational business boycott. But Roosevelt rejected appeals to intervene militarily, fearing that Mexicans would increase oil sales to Germany and Japan. Tense negotiations led to a compromise in 1942 whereby the United States conceded that Mexico owned and could control its raw materials, and Mexico compensated the companies for their lost property.

While the United States remained the dominant power in the hemisphere, the Good Neighbor policy under Roosevelt filled Latin Americans with hope that a new era had dawned. The more sober-minded nationalists in the region knew that deepening tensions in Europe and Asia might have influenced Washington's restraint. But these threats also created a sense that nations in the Western Hemisphere should stand together.

The Course to War in Europe

On March 5, 1933, one day after Roosevelt's inauguration, Germany's parliament granted dictatorial powers to the new chancellor, Adolf Hitler, leader of the Nazi Party. It was a stunning rise to power for Hitler, whose Nazis would probably have remained a fringe party had the Great Depression not hit Germany so hard. Production plummeted 40 percent, and unemployment ballooned to 6 million, meaning that two of every five workers were jobless. The disintegrating banking system, which robbed millions of their savings, and widespread resentment over the post–World War I Versailles settlement further fueled mass discontentment. While the communists preached a workers' revolution, German businessmen and property owners supported Hitler, believing they could manipulate him once he thwarted the communists. They were wrong.

Like Benito Mussolini, who gained control of Italy in 1922, Hitler was a fascist. Fascism (called Nazism, or National Socialism, in Germany) celebrated supremacy of the state over the individual; dictatorship over democracy; authoritarianism over freedom of speech; a state-regulated economy over the free market; and militarism over peace. The Nazis vowed to revive Germany, cripple communism, and "purify" the German "race" by destroying Jews and others, such as homosexuals and Gypsies, whom Hitler deemed inferior. The Nuremberg Laws of 1935 stripped Jews of citizenship and outlawed intermarriage with Germans. Half of all German Jews were without work.

Determined to get out from under the Versailles treaty, Hitler withdrew Germany from the League

GERMAN
AGGRESSION
UNDER HITLER

of Nations, ended reparations payments, and began to rearm. While secretly laying plans to conquer neighboring states, he watched admiringly as Mussolini's troops invaded Ethiopia in 1935. The next year Hitler ordered his own troops into the Rhineland, an area demilitarized by the Versailles treaty.

In 1936 Italy and Germany formed an alliance called the Rome-Berlin Axis. Shortly after, Germany and Japan united against the Soviet Union in the Anti-Comintern Pact. Britain and France responded with a policy of appeasement, hoping to curb Hitler's expansionism by permitting him a few territorial gains. Instead, the German leader continually raised his demands.

Online Study Center   **Improve Your Grade**
Interactive Map:
German and Italian Expansion, 1933–1942

The Spanish Civil War in 1936 made matters worse. Beginning in July, about three thousand American volunteers, known as the Abraham Lincoln Battalion of the "International Brigades," joined Spanish Loyalists in defending Spain's elected republican government against Francisco Franco's fascist movement. The Soviet Union also backed the Loyalists. Hitler and Mussolini sent military aid to Franco, who won in 1939, tightening fascism's grip on the European continent.

Early in 1938 Hitler again tested European tolerance when he sent soldiers to annex his birth nation, Austria. In September he seized the

THE MUNICH
CONFERENCE

Sudeten region of Czechoslovakia. France and Britain, without consulting the Czechs, agreed to allow Hitler this territorial bite, in exchange for a pledge that he would not take more. British prime minister Neville Chamberlain returned home to proclaim "peace in our time." In March 1939 Hitler swallowed the rest of Czechoslovakia.

Many Americans sought to maintain distance from Europe's tumult by embracing isolationism, either because they abhorred war

ISOLATIONIST
VIEWS IN THE
UNITED STATES

or because they opposed U.S. alliances with other nations. Americans learned powerful lessons from the First World War: that war dam-

ages reform movements, undermines civil liberties, dangerously expands federal power, disrupts the economy, and accentuates racial and class tensions (see Chapter 23). In a 1937 Gallup poll, nearly two-thirds said U.S. participation in World War I was a mistake.

Conservative isolationists feared higher taxes and increased executive power if the nation went to war again. Liberal isolationists worried that domestic problems might go unresolved with increased military spending. Many isolationists predicted that in attempting to spread democracy abroad, Americans would lose their freedoms at home. The vast majority of isolationists opposed fascism, but they did not think the United States should do what Europeans refused to do: block Hitler.

A congressional committee headed by Senator Gerald P. Nye held hearings from 1934 to 1936 on the

NYE COMMITTEE
HEARINGS

role of business in the U.S. decision to enter the First World War. The Nye committee did not prove that American munitions makers dragged the nation into war, but it uncovered evidence that corporations had bribed foreign politicians to bolster arms sales in the 1920s and 1930s.

Isolationists grew suspicious of American business ties with Nazi Germany and fascist Italy. Twenty-six of the top American corporations, including DuPont, Standard Oil, and General Motors, had contracts in 1937 with German firms. And after Italy attacked Ethiopia in 1935, American petroleum, copper, scrap iron, and steel exports to Italy increased substantially, despite Roosevelt's call for a moral embargo. Other businesses, such as the Wall Street law firm of Sullivan and Cromwell, severed ties with Germany to protest the Nazi persecution of Jews.

Roosevelt signed a series of neutrality acts. Congress meanwhile outlawed the kinds of contacts that

NEUTRALITY
ACTS

had compromised U.S. neutrality during World War I. The Neutrality Act of 1935 prohibited arms shipments to either side in a war once the president had declared the existence of belligerency. The Neutrality Act of 1936 forbade loans to belligerents. The Neutrality Act of 1937 introduced the cash-and-carry principle: warring nations would have to pay cash for nonmilitary purchases and carry the goods from U.S. ports in their own ships. The act also forbade Americans from traveling on the ships of belligerent nations.

President Roosevelt shared isolationist views in the early 1930s. Although prior to World War I

ROOSEVELT'S EVOLVING VIEWS

he was an expansionist and interventionist like his cousin Theodore, during the interwar period FDR talked more about the horrors of war. In a passionate speech in August 1936 at Chautauqua, New York, Roosevelt appealed to pacifist voters in the upcoming election. The United States, he promised, would remain unentangled in the European conflict. During the crisis over Czechoslovakia in 1938, Roosevelt endorsed appeasement.

All the while, Roosevelt grew troubled by the arrogance of Germany, Italy, and Japan—aggressors he tagged the "three bandit nations." He condemned Nazi persecution of the Jews and the Japanese slaughter of Chinese civilians. In November 1938, Hitler launched *Kristallnacht* (or "Crystal Night," named for the shattered glass that littered streets after the attack on Jewish synagogues, businesses, and homes) and sent tens of thousands of Jews to concentration camps. Shocked, Roosevelt recalled the U.S. ambassador and allowed fifteen thousand refugees on visitor permits to remain longer in the United States. But he would not break trade relations with Hitler or push Congress to loosen immigration laws. Congress rejected all measures, including a bill to admit twenty thousand children under age fourteen. Motivated by economic concerns and widespread anti-Semitism, over 80 percent of Americans supported Congress's decision to uphold immigration restrictions.

Even the tragic voyage of the *St. Louis* did not change government policy. The vessel left Hamburg in mid-1939 carrying 930 desperate Jewish refugees. Denied entry to Havana, the *St. Louis* headed for Miami, where Coast Guard cutters prevented it from docking and forced its return to Europe. Some refugees took shelter in countries that later were overrun by Hitler's legions.

Quietly, though, Roosevelt began readying for war. In early 1938 he successfully pressured the House of Representatives to defeat a constitutional amendment that would require a majority vote in a national referendum before a congressional declaration of war could take effect (unless the United States were attacked). Later, in the wake of the Munich crisis, Roosevelt asked Congress for funds to fortify the air force, which he believed essential to deter aggression. In January 1939 the president secretly decided to sell bombers to France. Although these five hundred combat planes did not deter war, French orders spurred growth of the U.S. aircraft industry.

Hitler's swallowing of Czechoslovakia in March 1939 proved a turning point for Western leaders. Until then, they could explain away Hitler's actions by saying he was only trying to reunite German-speaking peoples. Now they knew it would require force to stop him. When Hitler began eyeing Poland, London and Paris stood by the Poles. Undaunted, Berlin signed a nonaggression pact with Moscow in August 1939, including a top-secret protocol that carved eastern Europe into German and Soviet zones, and let the Soviets grab the eastern half of Poland and the Baltic states of Lithuania, Estonia, and Latvia, formerly part of the Russian Empire.

Early on September 1, 1939, German tanks rolled into Poland while fighting planes covered them, thereby

POLAND AND THE OUTBREAK OF WORLD WAR II

launching a new type of warfare, the *blitzkrieg* (lightning war)—highly mobile land forces and armor combined with tactical aircraft. Within forty-eight hours, Britain and France declared war on Germany.

With Europe at war, Roosevelt declared neutrality and pressed for repeal of the arms

REPEAL OF THE ARMS EMBARGO

embargo. After much debate, Congress in November lifted the embargo on contraband and approved cash-and-carry exports of arms. Using "methods short of war," Roosevelt thus began to aid the Allies. Hitler sneered that a "half Judaized, half negrified" United States was "incapable of conducting war."

Japan, China, and a New Order in Asia

In Asia, Japan flexed its muscle. The United States had interests at stake in Asia: the Philippines and Pacific islands, religious missions, trade and investments, and the Open Door in China. In missionary fashion, Americans believed that they were China's friend and protector. Pearl Buck's best-selling novel and later film *The Good Earth* (1931) countered prevailing images of the "heathen Chinee" by representing the Chinese as noble, persevering peasants. By contrast, the aggressive Japan loomed as a threat to American interests. The Tokyo government seemed bent on subjugating China and unhinging the Open Door doctrine of equal trade and investment.

The Chinese were uneasy about the U.S. presence in Asia and shared Japan's interest in reducing Western influence. The Chinese Revolution of 1911 still rumbled in the 1920s as antiforeign riots damaged American property and imperiled American missionaries. Chinese nationalists criticized Americans for extraterritoriality (the exemption of foreigners from Chinese legal jurisdiction) and demanded an end to this affront to Chinese sovereignty.

In the late 1920s, civil war broke out in China when Jiang Jieshi (Chiang Kai-shek) ousted Mao

JIANG JIESHI

Zedong and his communist followers from the ruling Guomindang Party. Americans applauded this anti-Bolshevism and Jiang's conversion to Christianity in 1930. Jiang's new wife, American-educated Soong Meiling, won their hearts with her flawless English and Western fashion. Warming to Jiang, U.S. officials signed a treaty in 1928 restoring control of tariffs to the Chinese. U.S. gunboats and marines still remained in China to protect American citizens and property.

The Japanese grew suspicious of U.S. ties with China. In the early twentieth century, Japanese-American relations deteriorated as Japan gained influence in Manchuria, Shandong, and Korea. The Japanese sought to dominate Asian territories that produced the raw materials that their import-dependent island nation required. The Japanese also resented the discriminatory immigration law of 1924, which excluded them from emigrating to the United States. Secretary Hughes called the law "a lasting injury" to Japanese-American relations. Although Japanese-American trade was twice that of Chinese-American trade, commercial rivalry strained relations between Japan and the United States.

Relations further soured in 1931 after the Japanese military seized Manchuria from China (see Map 26.1). Larger than Texas, Manchuria

MANCHURIAN CRISIS

served Japan as a buffer against the Soviets and was a vital source of coal, iron, timber, and food. More than half of Japan's foreign investments rested in Manchuria. Although the seizure of Manchuria violated the Nine-Power Treaty and the Kellogg-Briand Pact, the United States could not compel Japanese withdrawal, and the League of Nations merely condemned the Tokyo government. The American response came as a moral lecture known as the Stimson Doctrine: the United States would not recognize any impairment of China's sovereignty or of the Open Door policy, Secretary Stimson declared in 1932.

Japan continued to pressure China, leading to the Sino-Japanese War in 1937. Japanese forces seized Beijing and cities along the coast. The gruesome bombing of Shanghai intensified anti-Japanese sentiment in the United States. In an effort to help China by permitting it to buy American arms, Roosevelt refused to declare the existence of war, thus avoiding activation of the Neutrality Acts.

In a speech on October 5, 1937, the president called for a "quarantine" to curb the "epidemic of

ROOSEVELT'S QUARANTINE SPEECH

world lawlessness." People who thought Washington had been too gentle with Japan cheered. Isolationists feared that Roosevelt was edging toward war. On December 12 Japanese aircraft sank the American gunboat *Panay,* an escort for Standard Oil Company tankers on the Yangtze River. Two American sailors died. Roosevelt was relieved when Tokyo apologized and offered to pay for damages.

Japan's declaration of a "New Order" in Asia, in the words of one American official, "banged, barred, and bolted" the Open Door. Alarmed, the Roosevelt administration during the late 1930s gave loans and sold military equipment to Jiang's Chinese government, while embargoing airplane shipments to Japan. In mid-1939, the United States abrogated its trade treaty with Tokyo, yet Americans continued to ship oil, cotton, and machinery to Japan. The administration hesitated to initiate sanctions because it might spark a Japanese-American war when Germany posed a more serious threat and the United States was unprepared for war. That left Japanese-American relations stalemated when Europe's war erupted in 1939.

U.S. Entry into World War II

a stalemate was fine with many Americans if it kept the United States out of war. Roosevelt remarked in 1939 that the United States could not "draw a line of defense around this country and

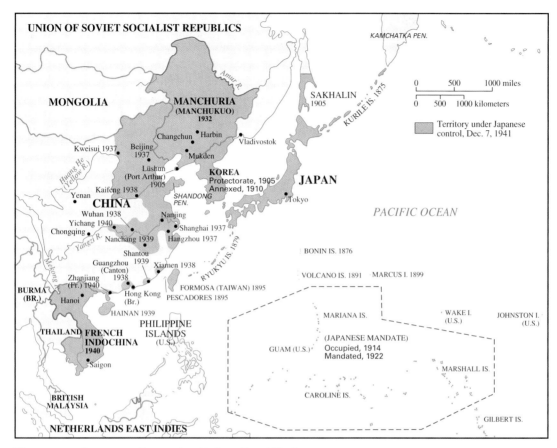

Map 26.1   Japanese Expansion Before Pearl Harbor

The Japanese quest for predominance began at the turn of the century and intensified in the 1930s. China suffered the most at the hands of Tokyo's military. Vulnerable U.S. possessions in Asia and the Pacific proved no obstacle to Japan's ambitions for a Greater East Asia Co-Prosperity Sphere.

live completely and solely to ourselves" or remain insulated from world war. Polls showed that Americans favored the Allies and supported aid to Britain and France, but the great majority emphatically wanted the United States to remain at peace. Troubled by this conflicting advice—oppose Hitler, aid the Allies, but stay out of the war—the president gradually moved the nation from neutrality to undeclared war against Germany and then, after the Japanese attack on Pearl Harbor, to full-scale war.

Unprecedented numbers of Americans spoke out on foreign affairs and joined organizations addressing foreign policy from 1939 through 1941. The widespread use of radio, the nation's chief source of news,

helped stimulate public interest, as did ethnic affiliations with the various belligerents and victims. The American Legion, the League of Women Voters, labor unions, and local chapters of the Committee to Defend America by Aiding the Allies and the isolationist America First Committee amassed citizen participation in the national debate. African American churches organized anti-Italian boycotts to protest Mussolini's pummeling of Ethiopia.

In March 1940 the Soviet Union invaded Finland. In April Germany conquered Denmark and Norway (see Map 26.2). On May 10, 1940,

FALL OF FRANCE Germany attacked Belgium, the Netherlands, and France, ultimately pushing French and British forces back to the English Channel. At Dunkirk, France, between May 26 and June 6, more than 300,000 Allied soldiers frantically escaped to Britain on a flotilla of small boats. The Germans occupied Paris a week later. A new French government in the town of Vichy collaborated with the Nazis and, on June 22, surrendered France to Berlin. The German Luftwaffe (air force) launched massive bombing raids against Great Britain.

Online Study Center   **Improve Your Grade**
Primary Source:
Propaganda in Films

Alarmed by the swift defeat of one European nation after another, Americans shed their isolationism. Insisting that New Deal reforms would not be sacrificed for military preparedness, the president began to aid the beleaguered Allies to prevent the fall of Britain. In May 1940 he ordered the sale of old surplus military equipment to Britain and France. In July he cultivated bipartisan support by naming Republicans Henry L. Stimson and Frank Knox, backers of aid to the Allies, secretaries of war and the navy, respectively. In September, the president traded fifty over-age American destroyers for leases to eight British military bases, including Newfoundland, Bermuda, and Jamaica.

Map 26.2   The German Advance, 1939–1942

Hitler's drive to dominate Europe pushed German troops deep into France and the Soviet Union. Great Britain took a beating but held on with the help of American economic and military aid before the United States itself entered the Second World War in late 1941.

Radio News

In radio's early years, network executives believed their job was to entertain Americans and left current affairs to newspapers. Yet radio had the revolutionary potential of reporting events as they happened.

Franklin Roosevelt was among the first to grasp radio's promise. As governor of New York he occasionally went on the air, and after becoming president he commenced his Fireside Chats, reassuring Americans during the depression that the government was working hard to help them. The broadcasts were so successful that one journalist remarked, "The President has only to look toward a radio to bring Congress to terms."

Across the Atlantic, Adolf Hitler also used radio to carry speeches directly to the German people. His message: Germany had been wronged by enemies abroad and by Marxists and Jews at home. But under Hitler, the Nazis promised to restore the country's former greatness. As "Sieg Heil!" thundered over the airwaves, millions of Germans saw Hitler as their salvation.

In 1938, as events abroad escalated, American radio networks increased news coverage. When Hitler annexed Austria in March, NBC and CBS broke into scheduled programs to deliver bulletins. Then, on March 13, CBS broadcast the first international news roundup, a half-hour show featuring live reports. A new era in American radio was born. In the words of author Joseph Persico, what made the broadcast revolutionary "was the listener's sensation of being on the scene" in far-off Europe.

When leaders from France and Britain met with Hitler in Munich later that year, millions of Americans eagerly listened to live radio updates. Correspondents became well known, in particular, Edward R. Murrow of CBS. During the Nazi air blitz of London in 1940–1941, Murrow's understated, nicotine-scorched voice kept Americans spellbound as he tried to "report suffering to people [Americans] who have not suffered."

Without a doubt Murrow's reports strengthened interventionist voices in Washington by emphasizing Winston Churchill's greatness and England's bravery. Furthermore, radio reports from Europe made Americans feel closely linked to people living an ocean away.

Edward R. Murrow at his typewriter in wartime London. (Library of Congress)

Two weeks later Roosevelt signed the hotly debated and narrowly passed Selective Training and

FIRST PEACETIME MILITARY DRAFT

Service Act, the first peacetime military draft in American history. The law called for the registration of all men between the ages of twenty-one and thirty-five, with over 16 million men signing up. Meanwhile, Roosevelt won reelection in November 1940 with promises of peace: "Your boys are not going to be sent into any foreign wars."

Roosevelt claimed that the United States could avoid war by enabling the British to win. In January 1941 Congress debated the president's Lend-Lease bill. Because Britain was broke, the president explained, the United States should lend rather than sell weapons. In March 1941, with pro-British sentiment running high, the House passed the Lend-Lease Act by 317 votes to 71; the Senate followed with a 60-to-31 tally. The initial appropriation was $7 billion, but by war's end, it reached $50 billion, more than $31 billion of it for Britain.

To ensure delivery of Lend-Lease goods, Roosevelt ordered the U.S. Navy to patrol halfway across the Atlantic and sent American troops to Greenland. In July, the president dispatched marines to Iceland, arguing that it was essential for safeguarding the Western Hemisphere. He also sent Lend-Lease aid to the Soviet Union, which Hitler had attacked in June (thereby shattering the 1939 Nazi-Soviet nonaggression pact). If the Soviets could hold off two hundred German divisions in the east, Roosevelt calculated, Britain would gain some breathing space.

In August 1941 Roosevelt and British prime minister Winston Churchill met for four days on a British

ATLANTIC CHARTER

battleship off the coast of Newfoundland. The two leaders issued the Atlantic Charter, a set of war aims reminiscent of Wilsonianism (see Chapter 23): collective security, disarmament, self-determination, economic cooperation, and freedom of the seas. Churchill later recalled that the president told him that he could not ask Congress to declare war against Germany but "he would wage war" and "become more and more provocative."

On September 4, a German submarine launched torpedoes at (but did not hit) the American destroyer *Greer.* Henceforth, Roosevelt said, the U.S. Navy would shoot on sight. He also made good on a promise to Churchill: American warships would convoy British merchant ships across the ocean. Thus, the United States entered into an undeclared naval war with Germany. When in October the destroyer *Reuben James* went down with the loss of more than one hundred American lives, Congress scrapped the cash-and-carry policy and revised the Neutrality Acts to permit transport of munitions to Britain on armed American merchant ships. The United States was very close to being a belligerent.

It seems ironic that the Second World War came to the United States by way of Asia. Roosevelt had

U.S. DEMANDS ON JAPAN

wanted to avoid war with Japan to concentrate on defeating Germany. In September 1940, after Germany, Italy, and Japan had signed the Tripartite Pact (to form the Axis powers), Roosevelt slapped an embargo on shipments of aviation fuel and scrap metal to Japan. After Japanese troops occupied French Indochina in July 1941, Washington froze Japanese assets in the United States, virtually ending trade (including oil) with Japan. "The oil gauge and the clock stood side by side" for Japan, wrote one observer.

Tokyo recommended a summit between President Roosevelt and Prime Minister Prince Konoye, but American officials insisted that the Japanese first agree to respect China's sovereignty and honor the Open Door policy. Roosevelt supported Secretary Hull's hard line against Japan's pursuit of the Greater East Asia Co-Prosperity Sphere—the name Tokyo gave to the Asian region it intended to dominate.

Roosevelt told his advisers to string out ongoing Japanese-American talks to gain time to fortify the Philippines and check the fascists in Europe. By deciphering intercepted messages, American officials learned that Tokyo's patience was dissipating. In late November the Japanese rejected American demands to withdraw from Indochina. An intercepted message on December 3 instructed the Japanese embassy in Washington to burn codes and destroy cipher machines—a step suggesting that war was coming.

In a daring raid on Pearl Harbor in Hawai'i, an armada of sixty Japanese ships, including six carriers

SURPRISE ATTACK ON PEARL HARBOR

bearing 360 airplanes, crossed 3,000 miles of the Pacific Ocean, maintaining radio silence to avoid detection. Early on December 7, some 230 miles northwest of Honolulu, the carriers unleashed their planes, dropping torpedoes and bombs on the unsuspecting American naval base and nearby airfields.

The battleship U.S.S. *Arizona* fell to a Japanese bomb that ignited explosives below deck, killing over one thousand sailors. The U.S.S. *Nevada* tried to escape by heading out to sea but was hit. Altogether the invaders sank or damaged eight battleships, many smaller vessels, and more than 160 aircraft on the ground. A total of 2,403 died; 1,178 were wounded. Even so, from the perspective of the war's outcome the Pearl Harbor tragedy amounted to a military inconvenience more than a disaster.

American cryptanalysts may have broken Japanese code, but the intercepted messages offered few details: there were no specifics on Japan's military plans and no mention of Pearl Harbor. Roosevelt did not, as some critics charged, conspire to leave the fleet vulnerable so that the United States could enter the Second World War through the "back door" of Asia. The base at Pearl Harbor was not on red alert because a message from Washington warning of the imminence of war was transmitted by a slow method and had arrived too late. Base commanders believed Hawai'i was

EXPLAINING
PEARL HARBOR

■ The stricken U.S.S. *West Virginia* was one of eight battleships caught in the surprise Japanese attack at Pearl Harbor, Hawai'i, on December 7, 1941. In this photograph, sailors on a launch attempt to rescue a crew member from the water as oil burns around the sinking ship.   (U.S. Army)

too far from Japan to be a target. Like Roosevelt's advisers, they expected an assault against British Malaya, Thailand, or the Philippines (see Map 26.1). The Pearl Harbor calamity stemmed from mistakes and insufficient information, not from conspiracy.

Roosevelt described the December 7 attack as "a date which will live in infamy," and the next day asked Congress for a declaration of war against Japan. He noted that the Japanese had also attacked Malaya, Hong Kong, Guam, the Philippines, Wake, and Midway. A unanimous vote in the Senate and a 388-to-1 vote in the House thrust America into war. Representative Jeannette Rankin of Montana voted no, as she had for World War I. Britain declared war on Japan, but the Soviet Union did not. Three days later, Germany and Italy, honoring the Tripartite Pact they had signed with Japan in September 1940, declared war against the United States.

At the core, the war resulted from a fundamental clash of systems. Germany and Japan preferred a world divided into closed spheres of influence. The United States sought a liberal capitalist world order. American principles manifested respect for human rights; fascists in Europe and militarists in Asia did not. The United States prided itself on democracy; Germany and Japan embraced authoritarian regimes. When the United States protested against German and Japanese expansion, Berlin and Tokyo charged that Washington conveniently ignored its sphere of influence in Latin America and its history of military and economic aggrandizement. These incompatible objectives obstructed diplomacy and made war likely.

Summary ⟳ *Online Study Center* ACE the Test

*I*n the 1920s and 1930s, America could not create a peaceful and prosperous world order. The Washington Conference treaties failed to curb a naval arms race or protect China, and both the Dawes Plan and the Kellogg-Briand Pact were ineffective. U.S. trade policies, shifting from protectionist tariffs to reciprocal trade agreements, only minimally improved U.S. or international commerce during the Great Depression. Recognition of the Soviet Union had little effect. Most ominous, the aggressors Germany and Japan ignored repeated U.S. protests. Even where American policies seemed to satisfy

Good Neighbor goals—in Latin America—nationalist resentments simmered and Mexico challenged U.S. dominance.

During the late 1930s and early 1940s, President Roosevelt hesitantly but steadily moved the United States from neutrality to aiding the Allies, to belligerency, and finally to war after the attack on Pearl Harbor. Congress gradually revised and retired the Neutrality Acts in the face of growing danger.

The Second World War offered another opportunity for Americans to set things right. As the publisher Henry Luce wrote in *American Century* (1941), the United States must "exert upon the world the full impact of our influence." Isolationists joined the president's call for victory when he said, "We are going to win the war, and we are going to win the peace that follows."

LEGACY FOR A PEOPLE AND A NATION
Presidential Deception of the Public

Before U-652 launched two torpedoes at the *Greer*, heading for Iceland on September 4, 1941, the U.S. destroyer stalked the German submarine for hours. After the attack, which missed its mark, the *Greer* also released depth charges. But when President Roosevelt described the encounter in a radio Fireside Chat on September 11, he declared that the German submarine had fired the first shot and accused Germany of violating freedom of the seas.

Roosevelt misled the American people about the events of September 4. The incident had little to do with freedom of the seas—which related to neutral merchant ships, not to U.S. warships in a war zone. Roosevelt's words were a call to arms, yet he never asked Congress for a declaration of war against Germany. The president believed that deceiving the public would move hesitant Americans toward war as noble and necessary. The practice worked: public opinion polls soon demonstrated that most Americans approved Roosevelt's shoot-on-sight policy after the *Greer* incident.

While some defended Roosevelt and accused the public of being shortsighted, his critics—even those agreeing that Nazi Germany had to be stopped—have seen in his methods a danger to the democratic process, which cannot work with dishonesty and a usurping of congressional powers. In the 1960s, during America's descent into the Vietnam War, Senator J. William Fulbright of Arkansas recalled the *Greer* incident: "FDR's deviousness in a good cause made it easier for LBJ to practice the same kind of deviousness in a bad cause." Indeed, during the Tonkin Gulf crisis of 1964, President Lyndon B. Johnson shaded the truth to gain from Congress wide latitude in waging war.

Since Roosevelt, presidents have found it easier to distort, withhold, or lie about foreign relations to garner public support. The result: the growth of the "imperial presidency"—grabbing power from Congress and using questionable means to reach presidential objectives. The practice of deception—even for a noble end—was one of Roosevelt's legacies for a people and a nation.

THE SECOND WORLD WAR AT HOME AND ABROAD 1941–1945

*W*illiam Dean Wilson was sixteen in 1942 when U.S. Marine Corps recruiters came to Shiprock, New Mexico, where he attended the Navajo boarding school. Five years too young to be drafted and a year too young to volunteer for the marines, he lied about his age. He also removed the note reading "Parents will not consent" from his recruiting file and was inducted into the Marine Corps.

Wilson and fellow Navajo recruits trained for a crucial project. Battles were won or lost because nations broke the codes enemies used to transmit messages, and the marines wanted a code based on the highly complex Navajo language, Diné. In 1942 there was no written form, and fewer than thirty non-Navajos worldwide—none of them Japanese—understood it. Unlike written ciphers, this code promised to be unbreakable. Navajo words represented the first letter of their English translations; thus *wol-la-chee* ("ant") stood for the letter *A*. The Navajo "code-talkers" memorized words representing 413 basic military terms and concepts. *Dah-he-tih-hi* ("hummingbird") meant fighter plane; *ne-he-mah,* "our mother," was the United States; *beh-na-ali-tsosie,* "slant-eye," stood for Japan.

Beginning with the Battle of Guadalcanal, Wilson and the other 420 code talkers participated in every marine assault in the Pacific from 1942 to 1945. Usually two code talkers were assigned to a battalion, one going ashore with assault forces and the other receiving messages on ship. Often under hostile fire, code talkers set up their equipment and began transmitting enemy sightings and directing shelling by American detachments. "Were it not for the Navajos," declared Major Howard Conner, Fifth Marine Division signal officer, "the Marines would never have taken Iwo Jima. . . . Six Navajo radio sets operating around the clock . . . sent and received over eight hundred messages without error."

The United States at War

The Production Front and American Workers

Life on the Home Front

The Limits of American Ideals

LINKS TO THE WORLD
War Brides

Life in the Military

Winning the War

LEGACY FOR A PEOPLE AND A NATION
Atomic Waste

Online Study Center
This icon will direct you to interactive map and primary source activities on the website
http://college.hmco.com/pic/nortonbrief7e

CHRONOLOGY

1941 • Government war-preparedness study concludes U.S. not ready for war before June 1943
- Roosevelt issues Executive Order No. 8802, forbidding racial discrimination by defense industry
- Japan attacks Pearl Harbor
- United States enters World War II

1942 • War Production Board created to oversee conversion to military production
- Millions of Americans move to take jobs in war industries
- Allies losing war in Pacific to Japan; U.S. victory at Battle of Midway in June is turning point
- Office of Price Administration creates rationing system for food and consumer goods
- U.S. pursues "Europe First" war policy; Allies reject Stalin's demands for a second front and invade North Africa
- West Coast Japanese Americans relocated to internment camps
- Manhattan Project set up to create atomic bomb
- Congress of Racial Equality established

1943 • Soviet army defeats German troops at Stalingrad
- Congress passes War Labor Disputes (Smith-Connally) Act following coal miners' strike
- Zoot suit riots in Los Angeles; race riots break out in Detroit, Harlem, and forty-five other cities
- Allies invade Italy
- Roosevelt, Churchill, and Stalin meet at Teheran Conference

1944 • Allied troops land at Normandy on D-Day, June 6
- Roosevelt elected to fourth term as president
- U.S. retakes Philippines

1945 • Roosevelt, Stalin, and Churchill meet at Yalta Conference
- British and U.S. forces firebomb Dresden, Germany
- Battles of Iwo Jima and Okinawa result in heavy Japanese and American losses
- Roosevelt dies; Truman becomes president
- Germany surrenders; Allied forces liberate Nazi death camps
- Potsdam Conference calls for Japan's "unconditional surrender"
- U.S. uses atomic bombs on Hiroshima and Nagasaki
- Japan surrenders
- More than 55 million people worldwide have perished in WWII

Wartime service changed the Navajo code talkers' lives, broadening their horizons and often deepening their ambitions. William Dean Wilson, for example, later became a tribal judge. Most Navajo veterans were happy to return to their traditional culture in 1945, participating in purification ceremonies to dispel battlefield ghosts and invoke blessings for the future.

The Second World War marked a turning point for millions of Americans and also in the history of the United States. For forty-five months, Americans fought abroad. Although the war began badly for the United States, the Allies halted the Axis powers' advance by mid-1942. In June 1944, American troops, together with Canadian, British, and Free French units, launched a massive invasion across the English Channel, landing at Normandy and pushing into Germany the following spring. Battered by bombing raids, leaderless after Adolf Hitler's suicide, and pressed by a Soviet advance, the Nazis capitulated in May 1945. In the Pacific, Americans drove Japanese forces back, island by island. America's devastating conventional bombing of Japanese cities, followed by the atomic bombs that demolished Hiroshima and Nagasaki in August 1945, led to the surrender of Japan. Throughout the war, the "Grand Alliance"—Britain, the Soviet Union, and the United States—united in defeating Germany but disagreed about how best to fight and how to shape the postwar world. Prospects for postwar international cooperation seemed bleak.

Although the war was fought far from the United States, it had a major impact on American society. America's leaders committed the United States to become the "arsenal of democracy," producing vast quantities of arms. All sectors of the economy were mobilized for victory. America's big businesses got even bigger, as did its central government, labor unions, and farms. The federal government had the monumental task of coordinating these spheres and two new ones: higher education and science.

During the war, nearly one of every ten Americans moved permanently to another state, most heading for war-production centers in the North and West Coast cities. Japanese Americans were rounded up by the army and placed in internment camps. And while the war encouraged African Americans to demand citizenship rights, competition for jobs and housing sparked race riots. For women, the war offered new job opportunities in the armed forces and war industries.

On the home front, Americans supported the war by collecting scrap iron, rubber, and newspapers for recycling and planting "victory gardens." At war's end, although many Americans grieved for lost loved ones and worried about the postwar order, the United States enjoyed unprecedented power and prosperity. ■

The United States at War

merican antiwar sentiment evaporated as Japanese bombs fell in the U.S. territory of Hawai'i and Franklin Roosevelt responded

by declaring war with Japan on December 8. When Germany formally declared war on the United States three days later, America joined British and Soviet Allied nations in the ongoing war against the Axis powers of Japan, Germany, and Italy. The American public's shift from caution—even isolationism—to fervent support for war seemed dramatic. But in truth, the U.S. entry into World War II had been coming. America's embargo of shipments to Japan and refusal to accept Japan's expansionist policies brought the two nations to the brink of war, and the United States was deeply involved in an undeclared naval war with Germany well before Japan's attack on Pearl Harbor. By December 1941, Roosevelt had long since instituted a peacetime draft, created war mobilization agencies, and commissioned war plans for simultaneous struggle in Europe and the Pacific.

Nonetheless, the nation was not militarily ready for war. Throughout the 1930s, military funding had

A NATION UNPREPARED   been a low priority. In September 1939 (when Hitler invaded Poland and began the Second World War), the U.S. army ranked forty-fifth in size among the world's armies and could fully equip only one-third of its 227,000 men. A peacetime draft instituted in 1940 expanded the U.S. military to 2 million men, but Roosevelt's 1941 survey of war preparedness estimated that the United States could not be ready to fight before June 1943.

In December 1941, the Allies were losing (see Map 26.2). Hitler claimed Austria, Czechoslovakia, Poland, the Netherlands, Denmark, and Norway. Romania was lost, then Greece and Bulgaria. France had fallen in 1940. Britain fought on, but German planes rained bombs on London. More than 3 million German soldiers penetrated deep into the Soviet Union and Africa. German U-boats controlled the Atlantic from the Arctic to the Caribbean and in 1942 sank 216 vessels, some so close to American shores that residents could see the glow of burning ships.

In the Pacific, the war was largely America's. The Soviets had not declared war on Japan, and there

WAR IN THE PACIFIC   were too few British troops protecting England's Asian colonies to make much difference. By late spring 1942, Japan had captured most of the European colonial possessions in Southeast Asia. The Japanese attacked the Philippines hours after Pearl Harbor and destroyed U.S. air capability in the region. American and Filipino troops retreated to the Bataan Peninsula, hoping to hold the main island, Luzon, but Japanese forces were superior. In March 1942, General Douglas MacArthur, the commander of U.S. forces in the Far East, departed the Philippines for Australia, proclaiming, "I shall return."

Left behind were almost eighty thousand American and Filipino troops. Starving and decimated by disease, they held on for nearly a month before surrendering. The Japanese troops, lacking supplies themselves, were unprepared to deal with such a large number of prisoners, and most believed the prisoners had forfeited honorable treatment by sur-

rendering. In what came to be known as the Bataan Death March, the Japanese force-marched their captives to prison camps 80 miles away, denying them food and water and bayoneting or beating to death those who fell behind. As many as ten thousand Filipinos and six hundred Americans died. Tens of thousands of Filipino refugees and prisoners died under Japanese occupation.

The United States struck back. On April 18, sixteen American B-25s released bombs above Tokyo and other cities. The Doolittle raid (named after the mission's leader) did little harm to Japan, but the image of American bombers so close pushed Japanese commander Yamamoto to bold action: attempting to

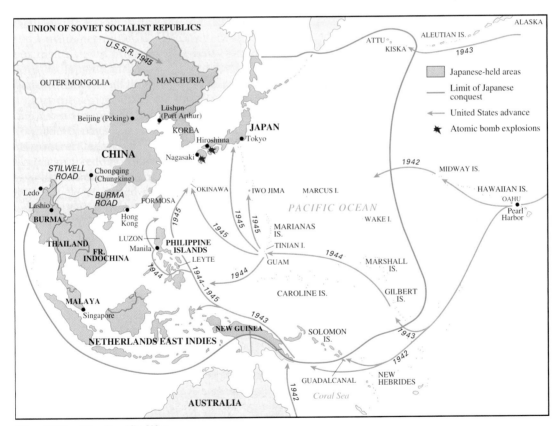

Map 27.1   The Pacific War

The strategy of the United States was to "island-hop"—from Hawai'i in 1942 to Iwo Jima and Okinawa in 1945. Naval battles were also decisive, notably the Battles of the Coral Sea and Midway in 1942. The war in the Pacific ended with Japan's surrender on August 15, 1945 (V-J Day).   (Source: Thomas G. Paterson, J. Garry Clifford, Kenneth J. Hagan, *American Foreign Policy: A History,* vol. 2, 3d ed. Copyright © 1991 by D. C. Heath Company. Used by permission of Houghton Mifflin Company.)

lure the weakened United States into a "decisive battle." The target was Midway—two tiny islands about 1,000 miles northwest of Honolulu, where the U.S. Navy had a base. If Japan could take Midway—not implausible, given Japan's string of victories—it would have a secure defensive perimeter far from the home islands (see Map 27.1). By using Guam, the Philippines, and perhaps even Australia as hostages, Japan could dictate a negotiated peace with the United States.

What General Yamamoto did not know was that America's codebreaking machines were deciphering Japanese messages. When the Japanese fleet arrived, it found the U.S. Navy lying in wait. The Battle of Midway in June 1942 was a turning point in the Pacific war. Japan's hope of forcing the United States to withdraw, leaving Japan to control the Pacific, vanished. Now Japan was on the defensive.

Despite the importance of these early Pacific battles, America's war strategy was "Europe First." U.S. military leaders believed that if Germany conquered the Soviet Union, it might directly threaten the United States. Roosevelt also feared that the Soviet Union, suffering almost unimaginable losses, might pursue a separate peace with Germany and so destroy the coalition of Allies. Thus, America would work with Britain and the USSR to defeat Germany, then deal with an isolated Japan.

"Europe First" Strategy

British prime minister Winston Churchill and Soviet premier Joseph Stalin disagreed over strategy. By late 1941, German troops had nearly reached Moscow and Leningrad (present-day St. Petersburg) and slashed deeply into Ukraine, claiming the lives of over a million Soviet soldiers. Stalin pressed for British and American troops to attack Germany from the west to draw Germans away from the Soviet front. Roosevelt agreed and promised to open a second front before the end of 1942. Churchill, however, blocked this plan. He argued that it was essential to win control of the North Atlantic shipping lanes first, and promoted air attacks on Germany and a smaller, safer attack on Axis positions in North Africa. Churchill meant to halt the Germans in North Africa to protect British possessions in the Mediterranean and the oil-rich Middle East.

Against his advisers' advice, Roosevelt accepted Churchill's plan. The U.S. military was not yet ready for a major campaign, and Roosevelt needed to demonstrate wartime success to the American public before the end of 1942. Thus, instead of helping the USSR, the British and Americans made a joint landing in North Africa in November 1942, winning quick victories in Algeria and Morocco. In Egypt, the British confronted General Erwin Rommel and his Afrika Korps in a struggle over the Suez Canal and Middle East oil fields, with Rommel's army surrendering after six months. Meanwhile, the Soviet army, fighting block by block for control of Stalingrad in the deadly cold, defeated the German Sixth Army. By the spring of 1943, Germany, like Japan, was on the defensive. Relations among the Allies remained precarious as the United States and Britain continued to resist Stalin's demand for a second front.

The Production Front and American Workers

*a*lthough the war would be fought on the battlefields of Europe and the Pacific, the nation's strategic advantage lay on the "production front" at home. America would serve as the world's "great arsenal of democracy," making the machines that would win the war for the Allies.

Goals for military production were staggering. In 1940 American factories built only 3,807 airplanes. Following Pearl Harbor, Roosevelt asked for 60,000 aircraft in 1942 and double that in 1943. Plans called for the manufacture of 16 million tons of shipping and 120,000 tanks. During the war, military production took precedence over civilian goods. Automobile plants built tanks and airplanes instead of cars; dress factories sewed military uniforms. The War Production Board, established by Roosevelt in early 1942, had allocated resources and coordinated production among thousands of independent factories.

During the war, American businesses overwhelmingly cooperated with government war-production plans. Patriotism was one reason, but generous incentives were another. In 1940, as the United States produced armaments for the Allies, the American economy began to recover from the depression. Auto

Businesses, Universities, and the War Effort

manufacturers, for example, expected to sell 4 million cars in 1941, a 25 percent increase over 1939. The massive retooling necessary to produce planes or tanks instead of cars would be expensive and leave manufacturers dependent on a single client—the federal government.

The federal government, however, paid for retooling and factory expansions; it guaranteed profits by allowing corporations to charge it production costs plus a fixed profit; it created tax write-offs and exemptions from antitrust laws. Consequently, corporations doubled their net profits between 1939 and 1943.

Most military contracts went to America's largest corporations, which had the facilities to guarantee rapid, efficient production. From mid-1940 through September 1944, the government awarded contracts totaling $175 billion, with two-thirds going to the top one hundred corporations. General Motors alone received 8 percent of the total. This approach made sense for a nation that wanted enormous quantities of war goods manufactured in the shortest possible time; most small businesses lacked the necessary capacity. However, wartime government contracts further consolidated American manufacturing in the hands of a few giant corporations.

Wartime needs also created a new relationship between science and the U.S. military. Federally sponsored research programs developed new technologies of warfare, such as radar, and millions of dollars went to fund research at America's largest universities. The most important government-sponsored scientific research was the Manhattan Project, a $2 billion secret effort to build an atomic bomb. Roosevelt was convinced by scientists fleeing the Nazis in 1939 that Germany was creating an atomic weapon, and he resolved to beat them to it. The Manhattan Project achieved the world's first sustained nuclear chain reaction at the University of Chicago in 1942, and in 1943 the government established a secret community for atomic scientists and their families at Los Alamos, New Mexico. Although the expression "military-industrial complex" had not yet been coined (president and former five-star general Dwight Eisenhower would do so in 1961), the web of military-business-university interdependence had begun.

MANHATTAN PROJECT

America's new defense factories required millions of workers. At first they were plentiful: 9 million Americans were unemployed in 1940 when war mobilization began. But the armed forces took 16 million men, forcing industry to look elsewhere for workers. Women, African Americans, Mexican Americans, and poor whites from Appalachia and the Deep South streamed into defense plant jobs.

NEW OPPORTUNITIES FOR WORKERS

But many industries refused to hire African Americans. A. Philip Randolph, head of the Brotherhood of Sleeping Car Porters, proposed a march on Washington, D.C., to demand equal access to defense jobs. Roosevelt, fearing race riots, offered the March on Washington movement a deal: in exchange for canceling the march, he issued Executive Order No. 8802, which prohibited discrimination in war industries and government jobs. With this federal protection, more than 1.5 million black Americans migrated from the South to the industrial cities of the North and West during the war.

Mexican workers also filled wartime jobs in the United States. About 200,000 Mexican farm workers, or *braceros*, were offered short-term agricultural contracts as Americans shifted to more lucrative war work. Mexican and Mexican American workers faced discrimination and segregation, but they seized these new economic opportunities. In 1941 not a single Mexican American worked in the Los Angeles shipyards; by 1944, seventeen thousand were employed there.

At first, employers insisted that women were not suited for industrial jobs. But as labor shortages loomed, employers did an about-face: posters and billboards urged women to "Do the Job HE Left Behind." The government's War Manpower Commission glorified the invented worker "Rosie the Riveter," who was featured on posters, in magazines, and in recruitment jingles.

WOMEN AT WORK

Rosie the Riveter was an inspiring, albeit inaccurate, image of working women. Only 16 percent of women workers held jobs in defense plants, and only 4.4 percent of the so-called skilled jobs (such as riveting). Nonetheless, during the war, over 6 million women entered the labor force, and the number of working women increased by 57 percent. More than 400,000 African American women abandoned domestic service for higher-paying industrial jobs with union benefits. Seven million women moved to war-production areas, such as Willow Run, Michigan, and southern California. Women workers in all fields kept the American economy going.

Workers in defense plants were often expected to work ten days for every day off or accept difficult night shifts. Businesses and the federal government provided new support to keep workers on the job. The West Coast Kaiser shipyards offered high pay, child-care, subsidized housing, and healthcare. The federal government also funded childcare centers and before- and after-school programs, with 130,000 preschoolers and 320,000 school-age children enrolled during the programs' peak.

The federal government attempted to ensure that labor strikes, so common in the 1930s, would

ORGANIZED LABOR DURING WARTIME

not interrupt wartime production. Days after Pearl Harbor, a White House labor-management conference agreed to a no-strike/no-lockout pledge. In 1942 Roosevelt created the National War Labor Board (NWLB) to settle disputes. The NWLB forged a temporary compromise between union demands for a "closed shop," in which only union members could work, and management's desire for "open" shops. Workers could not be required to join a union, but unions could enroll as many members as possible. Between 1940 and 1945, union membership ballooned from 8.5 million to 14.75 million.

The government did restrict union power if it threatened war production. When coal miners in the United Mine Workers union went on strike in 1943, following an NWLB attempt to limit wage increases to a cost-of-living adjustment, lack of coal halted railroads and shut down steel mills essential to war production. Congress responded with the War Labor Disputes (Smith-Connally) Act, granting the president authority to seize and operate any strike-bound plant deemed necessary to national security.

For nearly four years, American factories operated twenty-four hours a day, seven days a week,

SUCCESS ON THE PRODUCTION FRONT

turning out roughly 300,000 airplanes, 102,000 armored vehicles, 77,000 ships, 20 million small arms, 40 billion bullets, and 6 million tons

of bombs. By war's end, the United States was producing 40 percent of the world's weaponry. This feat depended on transforming formerly skilled work into assembly-line mass production. Henry Ford, now seventy-eight years old, created a massive bomber plant not far from Detroit, with assembly lines almost a mile long turning out one B-24 Liberator bomber every hour. On the West Coast, William Kaiser cut construction time for Liberty ships—the huge, 440-foot-long cargo ships transporting tanks, guns, and bullets overseas—from 355 to 56 days. The ships were not well made; welded hulls sometimes split in rough seas. However, as the United States struggled to produce cargo ships faster than Germans could sink them, production speed surpassed quality in importance.

Life on the Home Front

*a*mericans worried about family and friends fighting in distant places and grieved the loss of loved ones. And although their lives were disrupted, the United States was protected by two oceans, and thereby spared the war that other nations experienced. Bombs did not fall on American cities; invading armies did not burn and rape and kill. Instead, war mobilization ended the Great Depression and brought prosperity. American civilians experienced the paradox of good times amid global conflagration.

Still, the war was a constant presence for Americans on the home front. Families planted 20 million

SUPPORTING THE WAR EFFORT

"victory gardens" to free up food supplies for the military. Housewives saved cooking fat and returned it to butchers, because it yielded glycerin to make black powder used in bullets. Children collected scrap metal: the iron in one old shovel blade was enough for four hand grenades, and tin cans helped make a tank or ship.

Many consumer goods were rationed or unavailable during the war. To save wool for military use, the War Production Board (WPB) redesigned men's suits, narrowing lapels, shortening jackets, and eliminating vests and pant cuffs. Bathing suits, the WPB specified, must shrink by 10 percent. When silk and nylon were diverted from stockings to parachutes, women used makeup on their legs. The Office of Price Administration (OPA), created by Congress in 1942, established a nationwide rationing system. Every citizen—regardless of age—received two ration books each month with 48 blue stamps for canned fruits and vegetables and 54 red points for meat, fish, and dairy. Sugar was tightly rationed, and people saved for months to make a birthday cake. Feeding a family required complex calculations. A black market existed, but most Americans understood that sugar produced alcohol for weapons manufacture and meat went to feed "our boys" overseas.

Despite widespread support, government leaders worried that in a long war, public willingness to sacrifice might lag. To boost public support, in 1942 Roosevelt created the Office of War Information (OWI), which hired Hollywood filmmakers and New York copywriters to sell the war at home. OWI posters exhorted Americans to save and sacrifice and reminded them to watch what they said, for "loose lips sink ships."

PROPAGANDA AND POPULAR CULTURE

Popular culture reinforced wartime messages. A vacuum cleaner advertisement in the *Saturday Evening Post* urged women war workers to fight "for freedom and all that means to women everywhere. You're fighting for a little house of your own, and a husband to meet every night at the door." Songs urged Americans to "Remember December 7th" or to "Accentuate the Positive." Others made fun of America's enemies ("You're a sap, Mr. Jap / You make a Yankee cranky").

Movies drew 90 million viewers a week in 1944—out of a total population of 132 million. Hollywood sought to meet Eleanor Roosevelt's challenge to "Keep 'em laughing." *A WAVE, a WAC, and a Marine* promised "no battle scenes, no message, just barrels of fun and jive to make you happy you're alive." Others, such as *Bataan* or *Wake Island*, portrayed actual—if sanitized—events in the war. Even in comedies, however, the war was always present. Theaters held "plasma premieres," offering free admission to those who donated a half-pint of blood to the Red Cross. Audiences sang "The Star Spangled Banner," then watched newsreels with censored combat footage. In movie theaters, Americans saw the horror of Nazi death camps in May 1945.

Although Americans made sacrifices, American per capita income rose from $691 to $1,515 between 1939 and 1945. Price controls kept inflation down so wage increases didn't disappear to higher costs. With little to buy, savings rose.

WARTIME PROSPERITY

World War II cost approximately $304 billion (more than $3 trillion in today's dollars), which the United States financed through deficit spending, borrowing money by selling war bonds. The national debt grew from $49 billion in 1941 to $259 billion in 1945 (the debt was not paid off until 1970). However, wartime revenue acts increased the number of Americans paying personal income tax from 4 million to 42.6 million—at rates ranging from 6 to 94 percent—and introduced a new system where employers "withheld" taxes from employee paychecks. For the first time, individuals paid more taxes than corporations did.

Online Study Center **Improve Your Grade**
Interactive Map: The Home Front

Despite hardships and fears, the war also offered home-front Americans new opportunities. More than 15 million civilians moved during the war. People who had never traveled before found themselves on the other side of the country—or the world, moving for defense jobs or to be near loved ones at stateside military posts.

A NATION IN MOTION

The rapid influx of war workers to cities and small towns strained resources. Migrants crowded into substandard housing, such as woodsheds, tents, or cellars or into trailer parks without adequate sanitary facilities. Disease spread: scabies and ringworm, polio, tuberculosis. Many native citizens found the war workers—especially the unmarried men—a rough bunch.

In and around Detroit, where car factories were producing tanks and planes, established residents called war workers from southern Appalachia "hillbillies" and "white trash." Many migrants knew little about urban life. One young man from rural Tennessee, unfamiliar with traffic lights and street signs, navigated by counting the number of trees between his home and the war plant where he worked. Some Appalachian "trailer-ites" appalled neighbors by building outdoor privies or burying garbage in their yards.

As people from different backgrounds confronted one another, tensions rose and racism flared. In 1943 almost 250 racial conflicts exploded in forty-seven cities. In June in Detroit, white mobs, undeterred by police, roamed the city attacking

RACIAL CONFLICTS

blacks. Blacks hurled rocks at police and dragged whites off streetcars. After thirty hours of rioting, twenty-five blacks and nine whites lay dead.

In Los Angeles in 1943, young Mexican American gang members, or *pachucos*, wore zoot suits: long jackets with wide shoulders, loose pants "pegged" below the knee, and wide-brimmed hats. With cloth rationed, wearing pants requiring five yards of fabric was a purposeful rejection of wartime sacrifice. Although a high percentage of Mexican Americans served in the military, many white servicemen believed otherwise. Racial tensions fueled rumors that *pachucos* had attacked white sailors, and violence resulted. For four days, mobs of white men—mainly soldiers and sailors—attacked and stripped zoot-suiters. Los Angeles outlawed zoot suits, but the riots ended only when naval personnel were removed from the city.

The war changed family life. Despite policies initially exempting married men and fathers from the draft, almost 3 million families were broken up. The divorce rate of 16 per 1,000 marriages in 1940 almost doubled to 27 per 1,000 in 1944. At the same time, the marriage rate climbed. Some couples scrambled to marry before the man went overseas; others married and had children for military deferments. Total births rose from about 2.4 million in 1939 to 3.1 million in 1943. Many were "goodbye babies," conceived to guarantee the continuation of the family if the father died in battle.

FAMILIES IN WARTIME

On college campuses, women complained along with song lyrics, "There is no available male." But other young women enjoyed male company, sparking concern about wartime threats to sexual morality. *Youth in Crisis,* a newsreel shown nationwide in 1943, featured a girl with "experience far beyond her age" necking with a soldier. These "victory girls" or "cuddle bunnies" allegedly supported the war by giving their all to men in uniform. Many young men and women behaved as they never would in peacetime, which often meant hasty marriages to virtual strangers, especially if a baby was on the way. Wartime mobility created opportunities for young men and women to explore same-sex attraction, and gay communities grew in such cities as San Francisco.

In many ways, the war reinforced traditional gender roles weakened by the depression, restoring a pseudo-breadwinner role with men defending the nation while women "kept the home fires burning."

Some women took "men's jobs," but those who were motivated by patriotism rather than need understood it to be "for the duration." Either way, women who worked were blamed for creating an "epidemic" of juvenile delinquency. Nonetheless, millions of women took on new responsibilities and enjoyed greater independence, and many husbands returned to find that the lives of their wives and children seemed complete without them.

The Limits of American Ideals

The U.S. government worked hard to explain the reasons for citizens' wartime sacrifices. In 1941 Roosevelt pledged America to defend "four essential human freedoms"—freedom of speech, freedom of religion, freedom from want, and freedom from fear—and government-sponsored films contrasted democracy and totalitarianism, freedom and fascism, equality and oppression.

As America fought the totalitarian regimes of the Axis powers, the nation confronted difficult questions. What limits on civil liberties were justified in the interest of national security? How freely could information flow without revealing military secrets and costing American lives? How could the United States protect itself against spies or saboteurs, especially from German, Italian, or Japanese citizens living in the United States? And what about America's ongoing problem of race? The answers revealed tensions between the nation's democratic ideals and its wartime practices.

In civil liberties, American leaders mostly embraced a "strategy of truth," declaring that citizens required a truthful accounting of the war's progress. However, the government closely controlled military information, as seemingly unimportant details might tip off enemies about troop movements. While government-created propaganda sometimes dehumanized the enemy, such hate mongering was used much less frequently than during the First World War.

More complex was how to handle dissent and guard against the possibility that enemy agents were operating within the nation's borders. The Alien Registration (Smith) Act, passed in 1940, made it unlawful to advocate the overthrow of the U.S. government by force or violence. After Pearl Harbor, the government arrested thousands of Germans, Italians, and

War Brides

During and immediately after World War II, more than 60,000 American servicemen married women from other nations. The U.S. government promised servicemen that it would deliver their wives and babies home, free of charge.

Beginning in Britain in 1946, the U.S. Army's "Operation War Bride" eventually transported more than 70,000 women and children. The first group—455 British women and their 132 children—arrived in the United States on February 4, 1946. As the former WWII transport *Argentina* sailed into New York harbor in the predawn darkness, the Statue of Liberty was specially illuminated. Women who had sung "There'll Always Be an England" as they set sail from Southampton, England,

gathered on the deck to attempt "The Star Spangled Banner." These women, many of them teenagers, had left their homes and families behind to join their new husbands in a strange land.

Women from war-destroyed cities were impressed by America's material abundance and the warm welcome they received. But America's racial prejudice shocked Shanghai native Helen Chia Wong, wife of Staff Sgt. Albert Wong, when she and her husband were refused rental of a house with the explanation, "The neighbors wouldn't like it." It wasn't always easy, but most war brides settled into their new communities, becoming part of their new nation and helping to forge an intimate link between America and other nations of the world.

The army's "Operation War Bride" (sometimes called "Operation Mother-in-Law" or "the Diaper Run") began in Britain in early 1946. Employing eleven former World War II troopships, including the *Queen Mary*, the U.S. government relocated the wives and babies of U.S. servicemen from dozens of nations to the United States. These English war brides, with babies their fathers have not yet seen, are waiting to be reunited with their husbands in Massachusetts, Missouri, and Iowa. (Bettmann/CORBIS)

other Europeans suspected as spies and potential traitors. The government interned 14,426 Europeans in Enemy Alien Camps and prohibited ten thousand Italian Americans from living or working in restricted zones along the California coast.

In March 1942, Roosevelt ordered that all 112,000 foreign-born Japanese and Japanese Americans living in California, Oregon, and the state of Washington (the vast majority of the mainland population) be removed from the West Coast to "relocation centers." There were no individual charges as was the case with Germans and Italians; Japanese and Japanese Americans were imprisoned solely because they were of Japanese descent.

INTERNMENT OF JAPANESE AMERICANS

Anger at Japan's "sneak attack" on Pearl Harbor fueled calls for internment, as did fears that West Coast cities might come under enemy attack. Long-standing racism also played a critical role, and people in economic competition with Japanese Americans were among the strongest supporters of internment. Although Japanese nationals were forbidden to gain U.S. citizenship, American-born Nissei (second generation) and Sansei (third generation) were increasingly successful in business and agriculture. The relocation order forced Japanese Americans to sell property valued at $500 million for a fraction of its worth.

The internees were sent to flood-damaged lands at Relocation, Arkansas; to the intermountain terrain of Wyoming and the desert of western Arizona; and to other arid and desolate spots in the West. The camps were bleak: behind barbed wire, entire families lived in a single room in tar-papered wooden barracks with cots, blankets, and a bare light bulb. Toilets, bathing, and dining facilities were communal; privacy was almost nonexistent. People nonetheless attempted to sustain community life, setting up schools and clubs to battle monotony.

Feeling betrayed, almost 6,000 internees renounced U.S. citizenship and demanded to be sent to Japan. Some Japanese Americans sought legal remedy, but the Supreme Court upheld the government's action in *Korematsu v. U.S.* (1944). Others sought to

■ In February 1942 President Franklin D. Roosevelt ordered that all Japanese Americans living on the West Coast be rounded up and placed in prison camps. These families were awaiting a train to take them to an assembly center in Merced, California; from there, they would be sent to relocation camps in remote inland areas. (National Archives)

demonstrate their loyalty. The all–Japanese American 442nd Regimental Combat Team, drawn heavily from internees, was the most decorated unit of its size, receiving a Congressional Medal of Honor, 47 Distinguished Service Crosses, 350 Silver Stars, and more than 3,600 Purple Hearts. In 1988 Congress issued a public apology and symbolic payment of $20,000 each to the 60,000 surviving Japanese American internees.

Meanwhile, African American leaders wanted the nation to confront the parallels between the Nazi

AFRICAN AMERICANS AND "DOUBLE V"

racist doctrines and the persistence of Jim Crow segregation in the United States. Proclaiming a "Double V" campaign (victory at home and abroad), groups such as the National Association for the Advancement of Colored People (NAACP) hoped "to persuade, embarrass, compel and shame our government and our nation . . . into a more enlightened attitude toward a tenth of its people." The NAACP, 50,000 strong in 1940, had 450,000 members by 1946. In 1942 civil rights activists founded the Congress of Racial Equality (CORE), which stressed "nonviolent direct action" and staged sit-ins to desegregate restaurants and movie theaters in northern cities and Washington, D.C.

Military service was a key issue for African Americans, who understood the link between duty and citizenship. But the U.S. military remained segregated by race and resisted using black units as combat troops. As late as 1943, less than 6 percent of the armed forces were African American: the marines initially refused to accept African Americans at all, and the navy approximated segregation by assigning black men to service positions in which they would rarely interact with nonblacks as equals or superiors.

The U.S. federal government and War Department decided that the world war was not the time to

A SEGREGATED MILITARY

integrate the armed forces. The majority of Americans (approximately 89 percent of Americans were white) opposed integration. Racism was so entrenched that the Red Cross segregated blood plasma during the war. In southern states, racial segregation was the law. Integration of military installations, the majority of which were in the South, would have provoked a crisis as federal power contradicted state law. Pointing to outbreaks of racial violence in southern training camps, government and military officials argued that wartime integration would provoke more racial violence and hinder America's war effort. General Marshall proclaimed that it was not the army's job to "solve a social problem that has perplexed the American people throughout the history of this nation." Hopes for racial justice were another casualty of the war.

Despite discrimination, African Americans stood up for their rights. Lt. Jackie Robinson refused to move to the back of the bus at the army's Camp Hood, Texas, in 1944—and faced court-martial, even though military regulations forbade racial discrimination on military vehicles. Black sailors disobeyed orders to return to work after an explosion that destroyed two ships and killed 320 men—an explosion caused by navy practice of assigning untrained black stevedores to load bombs onto Liberty ships. When they were court-martialed for mutiny, future Supreme Court justice and chief counsel for the NAACP Thurgood Marshall asked why only black sailors did this work. He proclaimed: "This is the Navy on trial for its whole vicious policy toward Negroes."

African American servicemen did eventually fight on the front lines. The Marine Corps commandant in the Pacific proclaimed that "Negro Marines are . . . Marines, period." The "Tuskegee Airmen," trained at the Tuskegee Institute in Alabama, saw heroic service in all-black units such as the Ninety-ninth Pursuit Squadron, which won eighty Distinguished Flying Crosses. After the war, African Americans called on their wartime service to claim the full rights of citizenship and shared fully in veterans' benefits under the GI Bill (discussed in Chapter 29). The war was a turning point for equal rights.

America failed to live up to its democratic ideas in refusing to assist European Jews and others attempting to flee Hitler's Germany.

AMERICA AND THE HOLOCAUST

In 1942 American papers reported the "mass slaughter" of Jews and other "undesirables" (Gypsies, homosexuals, the physically and mentally disabled) under Hitler. Roosevelt knew about Nazi death camps capable of killing two thousand people an hour using the gas Zyklon-B. Still, American leaders did not divert airpower from principal German targets to destroy the camps.

British and American representatives met in Bermuda in 1943 but took no action. Appalled,

Secretary of the Treasury Henry Morgenthau Jr. charged that the State Department made the United States an accessory to murder. Early in 1944, stirred by Morgenthau, Roosevelt created the War Refugee Board, establishing refugee camps in Europe and helping to save 200,000 Jews. But, it came too late. By war's end, the Nazis had systematically murdered almost 11 million people.

Life in the Military

More than 16 million men and approximately 350,000 women served in the U.S. armed forces during World War II. Eighteen percent of American families had a father, son, or brother in the armed forces. Some men (and all of the women) volunteered. But over 10 million were draftees. The World War II draft extended fairly equitably across the population. Almost 10,000 Princeton students or alumni served—as did all four of the Roosevelts' sons.

The Selective Service Act provided for deferments, but the small number of college deferments was offset

SELECTIVE SERVICE by deferments for many "critical occupations," including war workers and almost 2 million agricultural workers. Most deferments were for those deemed physically or mentally unqualified for military service. Army physicians discovered the impact of the depression as draftees arrived with rotted teeth and deteriorated eyesight—signs of malnutrition. Army dentists pulled 15 million teeth; optometrists prescribed 2.5 million pairs of glasses. Up to one-third of African American draftees were functionally illiterate. Forty-six percent of African Americans and almost a third of European American draftees were classified "4-F"—unfit for service.

Nonetheless, almost 12 percent of America's total population served in the military. Regional differences were profound, and northerners and southerners often could not understand one another. Ethnic differences complicated things further. Although African Americans and Japanese Americans served in separate units, Hispanics, Native Americans—including the Navajo code talkers—and Chinese Americans served in "white" units. Furthermore, the differences among "whites"—the "Italian" kid from Brooklyn and the one from rural Mississippi (or rural

Montana)—were profound. The result was often tension, but many became less prejudiced as they served with men unlike themselves.

Military service was widespread, but the burdens of combat were not equally shared. Women's roles in

FIGHTING THE WAR the U.S. military were much more restricted than in the British or Soviet militaries. In the United States, the recruiting slogan for the WACs (Women's Army Corps) was "Release a Man for Combat," with women typically serving as nurses, in communications offices, and as typists or cooks. However, most men never saw combat either; one-quarter never left the United States. One-third of U.S. military personnel served in clerical positions, with educated men most likely slotted into noncombat positions. African Americans, though assigned dirty and dangerous tasks, were largely kept from combat. Lower-class, less-educated white men bore the brunt of the fighting.

Combat in World War II was horrible. Hollywood war films depicted men dying bravely, shot cleanly and comforted by buddies in their last moments. In reality, fewer than 10 percent of casualties were from bullets; most were killed or wounded by mortars, bombs, or grenades. Seventy-five thousand American men remained missing at the end of the war, blown into fragments too small to identify. Combat meant using flamethrowers that burned at 2,000 degrees Fahrenheit on other human beings. It meant being violently ill on a landing craft steering through floating body parts of those who had gone ahead, knowing that if you tripped, you would likely drown under the sixty-eight-pound weight of your pack, and that if you made it ashore, you would likely be blown apart by artillery. Service was "for the duration" of the war. Only death, serious injury, or victory offered release.

In forty-five months of war, close to 300,000 American servicemen died in combat, and nearly 1 million were wounded, half of them seriously. Medical advances, such as penicillin and the use of blood plasma to prevent shock, helped wounded men survive—but many never fully recovered. Between 20 and 30 percent of combat casualties were psychoneurotic. The federal government strictly censored images of American combat deaths for most of the war, consigning them to a secret file called "the chamber of horrors." Americans at home rarely understood what combat was like, and many men never talked about their experiences in the war.

Winning the War

*a*xis hopes for victory depended on a short war. Leaders in Germany and Japan recognized that if the United States had time to fully mobilize, the war was lost. Hitler, blinded by racial arrogance, stated shortly after declaring war on the United States, "I don't see much future for the Americans. . . . It's a decayed country. . . . American society [is] half Judaized, and the other half Negrified. How can one expect a State like that to hold together." By mid-1942 Axis powers realized that they had underestimated American resolve and the willingness of other Allies to sacrifice their citizens to stop the Axis advance (see Map 27.2). The chance of an Axis victory grew slim as months passed, and although the outcome was virtually certain after spring 1943, two more years of bloody fighting lay ahead.

The Allies' suspicions of one another undermined cooperation. The Soviets continued to press Britain and the United States to open a sec-

TENSIONS AMONG THE ALLIES

ond front to draw German troops away from the USSR. The English-speaking Allies, however, continued to delay. When Italy surrendered in September 1943 to American and British officers, Stalin grumbled that the arrangement smacked of a separate peace.

With the alliance badly strained, the three Allied leaders met in Teheran, Iran, in December 1943. Stalin dismissed Churchill's justifications for delaying the second front. Roosevelt also rejected Churchill's proposal for another peripheral attack, this time through the Balkans to Vienna. The three agreed to launch Operation Overlord—the cross-Channel invasion of France—in early 1944. And the Soviet Union promised to aid the Allies against Japan once Germany was defeated.

The second front opened in the dark morning hours of June 6, 1944—D-Day. In the largest am-

WAR IN EUROPE

phibious landing in history, 200,000 Allied troops commanded by American general Dwight D. Eisenhower scrambled ashore at Normandy, France. Landing craft and soldiers immediately en-

countered the enemy; they triggered mines and were pinned down by fire from cliffside pillboxes. Although heavy aerial and naval bombardment and the clandestine work of saboteurs had softened the German defenses, the fighting was ferocious.

Allied troops spread across the countryside, liberating France and Belgium and entering Germany in September. In December, German armored divisions counterattacked in Belgium's Ardennes Forest, hoping to get to Antwerp and halt Allied supplies through that Belgian port. After weeks of heavy fighting in what has come to be called the Battle of the Bulge, the Allies gained control in late January 1945. Meanwhile, Soviet troops marched through Poland and cut a path to Berlin. American forces crossed the Rhine River in March 1945 and captured the industrial Ruhr valley. Several units peeled off to enter Austria and Czechoslovakia, where they met up with Soviet soldiers.

Allied leaders began planning the peace in early 1945. Franklin Roosevelt, by this time very ill, called

YALTA CONFERENCE

for a summit meeting. The three Allied leaders convened at Yalta, in the Russian Crimea, in February 1945, each with definite goals for the postwar world. Britain, its formerly powerful empire now vulnerable and shrinking, sought to protect its colonial possessions and limit Soviet power, in part by insisting that France be included in plans for postwar control of Germany, thus reducing the Soviet sphere of influence from one-third to one-quarter. The Soviet Union, with 21 million dead, wanted reparations from Germany for its massive rebuilding effort. The Soviets hoped to expand their sphere of influence throughout eastern Europe and guarantee their national security; Germany, Stalin insisted, must be permanently weakened so it could never again attack the Soviet Union.

The United States also wanted to expand its influence and control the peace. Roosevelt lobbied for the United Nations Organization, approved in principle the previous year at Dumbarton Oaks in Washington, D.C., and through which the United States hoped to exercise influence. The United States sought to avoid the debts-reparations fiasco that had plagued Europe after the First World War. U.S. goals included self-determination for liberated peoples; gradual and orderly decolonization; and management of world affairs by the Soviet Union, Great Britain, the United

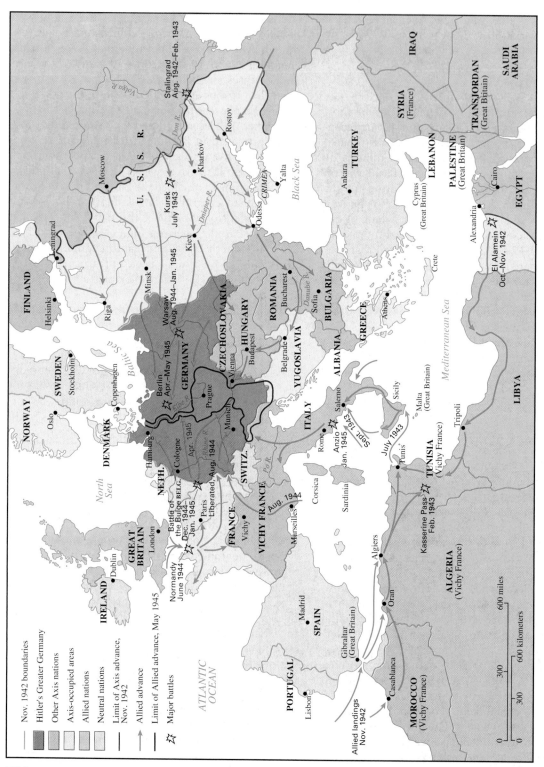

Map 27.2   The Allies on the Offensive in Europe, 1942–1945

The United States pursued a "Europe First" policy: first defeat Germany, then focus on Japan. American military efforts began in North Africa in late 1942 and ended in Germany in 1945 on May 8 (V-E Day).

Nov. 1942 boundaries
Hitler's Greater Germany
Other Axis nations
Axis-occupied areas
Allied nations
Neutral nations
Limit of Axis advance, Nov. 1942
Allied advance
Limit of Allied advance, May 1945
Major battles

States, and China. (Roosevelt hoped China might help stabilize Asia after the war; the United States abolished the Chinese Exclusion Act in 1943 to consolidate ties between the two nations.) The United States was also determined to limit Soviet influence in the postwar world.

Military positions during the Yalta Conference helped shape negotiations. Soviet troops occupied eastern European countries, including Poland, where Moscow installed a pro-Soviet regime despite a British-supported Polish government-in-exile in London.

With Soviet troops in place, Britain and the United States were limited in negotiating the future of eastern Europe. The Big Three agreed that some eastern German territory would be transferred to Poland and the remainder divided into four zones (the fourth to be administered by France). Berlin, within the Soviet zone, would also be divided among the four victors. In exchange for U.S. promises to support Soviet claims on territory lost to Japan in the Russo-Japanese War of 1904–1905, Stalin agreed to a treaty of friendship with Jiang Jieshi (Chiang Kai-shek), America's ally,

■ The three Allied leaders—Winston Churchill, Franklin D. Roosevelt, and Joseph Stalin—met at Yalta in February 1945. Having been president for twelve years, Roosevelt showed signs of age and fatigue. Two months later, he died of a massive cerebral hemorrhage. (Franklin D. Roosevelt Library)

rather than with the communist Mao Zedong (Mao Tse-tung), and to declare war on Japan within three months of Hitler's defeat.

Franklin D. Roosevelt, reelected to an unprecedented fourth term in November 1944, did not live to

HARRY TRUMAN

see the war's end. He died on April 12, making Vice President Harry S Truman president. Truman, who had replaced former vice president Henry Wallace as Roosevelt's running mate in 1944, was inexperienced in foreign policy and was not informed about the top-secret atomic weapons project until after he became president. Eighteen days into Truman's presidency, Adolf Hitler killed himself in a bunker in bomb-ravaged Berlin. On May 8 Germany surrendered.

As the great powers jockeyed for influence after Germany's surrender, the Grand Alliance began to crumble. At the Potsdam Conference in mid-July, Truman—a novice at international diplomacy—was less patient with the Soviets than Roosevelt had been. Truman also was emboldened by learning during the conference that a test of the new atomic weapon had been successful; the United States no longer needed or wanted the Soviet Union in the Pacific war. The Allies did agree that Japan must surrender unconditionally. But with the end of the European war, the wartime bonds between the Allies were strained.

With Hitler defeated, the Pacific war continued. Since the Battle of Midway in June 1942, American

WAR IN
THE PACIFIC

strategy had been to "island-hop" toward Japan, skipping the most fortified islands and taking the weaker ones, aiming to strand the Japanese armies on their island outposts. To cut off supplies, Americans also attempted to sink the Japanese merchant marine. By 1944 Allied troops—from the United States, Britain, Australia, and New Zealand—had secured the Solomon, Gilbert, Marshall, and Mariana Islands. General Douglas MacArthur landed at Leyte to retake the Philippines for the United States in October 1944.

In February 1945, U.S. and Japanese troops battled for Iwo Jima, an island less than 5 miles long, about 700 miles south of Tokyo. Twenty-one thousand Japanese defenders occupied the island's high ground. Hidden in caves, trenches, and underground tunnels, they were protected from the aerial bombardment U.S. forces used to make way for an am-

phibious landing. The island offered no cover, and marines were slaughtered as they came ashore. For twenty days, U.S. forces fought their way up Mount Suribachi, the highest and most heavily fortified point on Iwo Jima. Iwo Jima claimed 6,821 Americans and more than 20,000 Japanese—some of whom committed suicide rather than surrender. Only 200 Japanese survived.

A month later, American troops landed on Okinawa, an island at the southern tip of Japan, from which Allied forces planned to invade the main Japanese islands. Fighting raged for two months. The monsoon rains began in May, turning battlefields into seas of mud with decaying corpses. The supporting fleet endured waves of mass *kamikaze* (suicide) attacks, in which Japanese pilots intentionally crashed bomb-laden planes into American ships. On Okinawa, 7,374 American soldiers died, and nearly the entire Japanese garrison of 100,000 was killed. Approximately 80,000 civilians—about one-quarter of the population—perished.

With American forces just 350 miles from Japan's main islands, a powerful military faction was

BOMBING
OF JAPAN

nonetheless determined to avoid the humiliation of an unconditional surrender and to preserve the emperor's sovereignty. On March 9, 1945, 333 American B-29 Superfortresses dropped a mixture of explosives and incendiary devices on a 4-by-3-mile area of Tokyo. They created a firestorm, a fierce blaze that sucked all the oxygen from the air, creating hurricane-force winds and growing hot enough to melt concrete and steel. Almost 100,000 people were incinerated, suffocated, or boiled to death hiding in canals. Over the following five months, American bombers attacked sixty-six Japanese cities, leaving 8 million people homeless and killing almost 900,000.

Meanwhile, Japan was attempting to bomb the U.S. mainland. Thousands of bomb-bearing high-altitude balloons, constructed by schoolgirls of rice paper and flour-potato paste, were launched into the jetstream. As General Yamamoto had realized at the war's beginning, American resources would far outlast Japan's.

Early in the summer of 1945, Japan sent out peace feelers through the Soviets. Japan was not, however, willing to accept the "unconditional surrender" terms that Allied leaders had agreed to at Potsdam, and Truman chose not to pursue a negotiated peace. U.S. troops were mobilizing to invade the Japanese home islands, highly aware of the death tolls on Iwo Jima and Okinawa. The Manhattan Project offered another option, and Truman took it. Using atomic bombs on Japan, Truman believed, would end the war quickly and save American lives.

Historians still debate Truman's decision to use the atomic bomb rather than negotiate surrender terms. Was Japan on the verge of an unconditional surrender, as some argue? Or was the antisurrender faction of Japanese military leaders strong enough to prevail? Truman knew the bomb could give the United States real and psychological power in negotiating the peace. How much did his desire to demonstrate the bomb's power to the Soviet Union influence him? Did racism or retaliation play any role? No matter the answers to these ongoing debates, bombing (whether conventional or atomic) fit the established U.S. strategy of using machines rather than men whenever possible.

The decision to use the bomb did not seem as momentous to Truman as it does in retrospect. The moral line had already been crossed with the bombing of civilian populations: the Japanese bombed Shanghai, China, in 1937; Germans "terror-bombed" Warsaw, Rotterdam, and London. British and American bombers created firestorms in German cities, killing 225,000 people in Dresden. The American bombing of Japanese cities with conventional weapons had killed nearly 1 million people and destroyed 56 square miles of Tokyo alone. What distinguished the atomic bombs from conventional bombs was their power and their efficiency—not that they killed huge numbers of innocent civilians in unspeakably awful ways.

Online Study Center
Primary Source: Effects of the Atomic Bomb

On July 26, 1945, the Allies delivered an ultimatum to Japan: promising that the Japanese people would not be "enslaved," the Potsdam Declaration called for unconditional surrender or "prompt and utter destruction." Tokyo radio announced that the government would respond with *mokusatsu* (literally, "kill with silence," or ignore the ultimatum). On August 6, 1945, the B-29 bomber *Enola Gay* dropped an atomic bomb above the city of Hiroshima, killing 130,000 people. Tens of thousands more would suffer radiation poisoning.

On August 8, the Soviet Union declared war on Japan. On August 9, Americans dropped a second atomic bomb on Nagasaki, killing 60,000 people. Five days later, Japan surrendered. The Allies promised that the Japanese emperor could remain as the nation's titular head. The Second World War was over.

Summary   ### Online Study Center   ACE the Test

*H*itler once prophesied, "We may be destroyed, but if we are, we shall drag a world with us."

World War II devastated much of the globe. In Asia and Europe, people wandered through rubble, searching for food. One out of nine people in the Soviet Union had perished: at least 21 million civilians and military were dead. The Chinese lost 10 million; the Germans and Austrians 6 million; the Japanese 2.5 million. Almost 11 million people had been murdered in Nazi death camps. Across the globe, the Second World War killed at least 55 million people.

War required Allied nations with very different goals to cooperate. Tensions remained high as Stalin unsuccessfully pushed the United States and Britain to open a second front to draw German soldiers away from the Soviet Union. The United States, meanwhile, was fighting the Japanese in the Pacific. When Japan surrendered in August 1945, the strains between the Soviet Union and its English-speaking Allies made postwar stability unlikely.

American servicemen covered the globe, while on the home front, Americans worked around the clock to make weapons. Despite wartime sacrifices, including almost 300,000 lives, many Americans found that the war improved their lives. Mobilization ended the Great Depression. Americans moved in huge numbers to job-rich war-production centers. The influx strained the resources of existing communities and sometimes led to social friction and violence. But many Americans—African Americans, Mexican Americans, women, poor whites from the South—found new opportunities in well-paid war jobs.

The federal government became a stronger presence—regulating business and employment, overseeing the military, and even controlling what people could buy to eat or wear. The Second World War was a powerful engine of social change.

At war's end, only the United States had the economic resources to spur international recovery; only the United States was more prosperous than when war began. In the struggle to fashion a new world, soon to be called the Cold War, the United States held a commanding position. For better or worse, the Second World War was a turning point in the nation's history.

LEGACY FOR A PEOPLE AND A NATION
Atomic Waste

Victory in the Second World War may have been sweet to Americans, but the war's environmental legacy proved noxious, not to mention toxic and deadly. War industries fouled the water and the soil with both solid and petrochemical wastes. The production of synthetic rubber spewed forth sulfur dioxide, carbon monoxide, and other dangerous gases. Air pollution—smog—was first detected in Los Angeles in 1943, the result of rapid wartime industrialization and widespread automobile dependence.

No wartime or postwar weapons program became more threatening to the environment than the atomic bomb. Many of its ingredients—notably, plutonium, beryllium, and mercury—are highly toxic contaminants. Radioactive waste was initially stored at Oak Ridge, Tennessee, and Hanford, Washington, where plutonium was produced. During the postwar arms race, the United States opened other production facilities—for example, at Rocky Flats in Colorado and on the Savannah River in South Carolina. There, radioactive waste seeped from leaky barrels into the soil and water, threatening human life and killing wildlife. Nuclear testing between 1945 and 1963 killed an estimated 800,000 Americans from cancers attributable to radioactive fallout.

The biggest problem of the new millennium remains how to dispose of radioactive materials. Scientists are skeptical that current technology is up to the task of cleaning soil and water at the nuclear weapons sites. "The technology . . . used to remediate contaminated sites," said the chairman of a National Resource Council task force that studied the problem, "is simply ineffective and unable to accomplish the massive job that needs to be done."

THE COLD WAR AND AMERICAN GLOBALISM 1945–1961

*O*n July 16, 1945, the "Deer" Team leader parachuted into northern Vietnam. Colonel Allison Thomas and the five members of his Office of Strategic Services (OSS) unit followed their mission: to work with the Vietminh, a nationalist Vietnamese organization, to sabotage Japanese forces that in March had seized Vietnam from France. A banner proclaimed, "Welcome to Our American Friends." Ho Chi Minh, head of the Vietminh, greeted the OSS team. The next day Ho denounced the French but added, "We welcome 10 million Americans." "Forget the Communist Bogy," Thomas radioed OSS headquarters in China.

A communist dedicated to winning his nation's independence from France, Ho joined the French Communist Party after World War I. For the next two decades, living in China, the Soviet Union, and elsewhere, Ho planned and fought to free his nation from French colonialism. During World War II, Ho's Vietminh warriors harassed French and Japanese forces and rescued downed American pilots. In March 1945 Ho met with U.S. officials in China. Receiving no aid from ideological allies in the Soviet Union, Ho hoped the United States would favor his nation's quest for liberation.

Other OSS personnel soon parachuted into Kimlung, including a male nurse who diagnosed Ho's ailments as malaria and dysentery; quinine and sulfa drugs restored his health, but Ho remained frail. Everywhere the Americans went, impoverished villagers thanked them with gifts of food and clothing, interpreting the foreigners' presence as a sign of U.S. anticolonial and anti-Japanese sentiments. In early August, the Deer Team gave Vietminh soldiers weapons training. Ho said he hoped young Vietnamese could study in the United States and that American technicians could help build an independent Vietnam. Ho remarked that "your statesmen make eloquent speeches about . . . self-determination. We are self-determined. Why not help us?"

A second OSS unit, the "Mercy" Team, headed by Captain Archimedes Patti, arrived in Hanoi on August 22. But unbeknown to these OSS members,

From Allies to Adversaries

Containment in Action

The Cold War in Asia

The Korean War

Unrelenting Cold War

LINKS TO THE WORLD
The People-to-People Campaign

The Struggle for the Third World

LEGACY FOR A PEOPLE AND A NATION
The National Security State

Online Study Center
This icon will direct you to interactive map and primary source activities on the website
http://college.hmco.com/pic/nortonbrief7e

CHRONOLOGY

1945 • Roosevelt dies; Truman becomes president
     • Atomic bombings of Japan

1946 • Kennan's "long telegram" criticizes USSR
     • Vietnamese war against France erupts

1947 • Truman Doctrine seeks aid for Greece and Turkey
     • Marshall offers Europe economic assistance
     • National Security Act reorganizes government

1948 • Communists take power in Czechoslovakia
     • Truman recognizes Israel
     • U.S. organizes Berlin airlift

1949 • NATO founded as anti-Soviet alliance
     • Soviet Union explodes atomic bomb
     • Mao's communists win power in China

1950 • NSC-68 recommends major military buildup
     • Korean War starts in June; China enters in fall

1951 • U.S. signs Mutual Security Treaty with Japan

1953 • Eisenhower becomes president
     • Stalin dies
     • U.S. helps restore shah to power in Iran
     • Korean War ends

1954 • Geneva accords partition Vietnam
     • CIA-led coup overthrows Arbenz in Guatemala

1955 • Soviets create Warsaw Pact

1956 • Soviets crush uprising in Hungary
     • Suez crisis sparks war in Middle East

1957 • Soviets fire first ICBM and launch *Sputnik*

1958 • U.S. troops land in Lebanon
     • Berlin crisis

1959 • Castro ousts Batista in Cuba

1960 • Eighteen African colonies become independent
     • Vietcong organized in South Vietnam

---

who believed that President Franklin D. Roosevelt's sympathy for eventual Vietnamese independence remained U.S. policy, the new Truman administration wanted France to decide Vietnam's fate. That policy shift explains why Ho never received answers to the several letters and telegrams he sent to Washington beginning August 30, 1945.

On September 2, 1945, with OSS personnel present, an emotional Ho Chi Minh read his declaration of independence for the Democratic Republic of Vietnam: "All men are created equal; they are endowed by their Creator with certain unalienable Rights; among these are Life, Liberty, and the pursuit of Happiness." Having borrowed from the internationally renowned 1776 American document, Ho then itemized Vietnamese grievances against France.

In a last meeting with Captain Patti, Ho expressed his sadness that the United States had armed the French to reestablish their colonial rule in Vietnam. Sure, Ho said, U.S. officials in Washington judged him a "Moscow puppet" because he was a communist. But Ho claimed that he drew inspiration from the American struggle for independence. If necessary, Ho insisted, the Vietnamese would go it alone. And they did—first against the French and eventually against more than half a million U.S. troops in what became America's longest war.

Because Ho Chi Minh and his nationalist followers declared themselves communists, U.S. leaders rejected their appeal. Endorsing the containment doctrine against communism, American presidents from Truman to George H. W. Bush believed that a ruthless Soviet Union directed a worldwide communist conspiracy against peace, free-market capitalism, and democracy. Soviet leaders from Joseph Stalin to Mikhail Gorbachev protested that a militarized, economically aggressive United States sought world domination. This protracted contest between the United States and the Soviet Union acquired the name "Cold War."

The primary feature of world affairs for over four decades, the Cold War was fundamentally a contest between the United States and the Soviet Union over spheres of influence. The face-off between the capitalist "West" and the communist "East" dominated international relations and eventually took the lives of millions, cost trillions of dollars, spawned fears of doomsday, and destabilized several nations. On occasion the two superpowers negotiated and signed agreements to temper their dangerous arms race; at other times they went to the brink of war and armed allies to fight vicious Third World conflicts. Sometimes these allies had their own ambitions and resisted pressure from one or both superpowers.

Vietnam was part of the Third World, a general term for nations that during the Cold War era wore neither the "West" (the "First World") nor the "East" (the "Second World") label. Sometimes called "developing countries," Third World nations on the whole were nonwhite, nonindustrialized, and located in the southern half of the globe—in Asia, Africa, the Middle East, and Latin America. Many had been colonies of European nations or Japan and were vulnerable to the Cold War rivalry. U.S. leaders often interpreted their anticolonialism as Soviet inspired rather than as expressions of indigenous nationalism. Vietnam became one among many sites where Cold War fears and Third World aspirations intersected, prompting American intervention and a globalist foreign policy that regarded the entire world as the appropriate sphere for America's influence.

Critics in the United States challenged Cold War exaggerations of threats from abroad, meddlesome interventions in the Third World, and the militarization of foreign policy. But when leaders such as Truman described the Cold War as a life-and-death struggle against a monstrous enemy, critics' questions were drowned out by charges that dissenters were "soft on communism," if not un-American. U.S. leaders successfully cultivated a Cold War consensus that stifled debate and shaped the mindset of generations of Americans. ∎

From Allies to Adversaries

*T*he Second World War unsettled the international system. At its end, Germany was in ruins; Great Britain was overstrained and exhausted; after five years of Nazi occupation, France was rent by internal division; and Italy was drastically weakened. Japan was decimated and under occupation, and China was headed toward a renewed civil war. Throughout Europe and Asia, factories, transportation, and communications links were reduced to rubble, and agricultural production plummeted. The United States and the Soviet Union, though they had been allies in the war, proposed very different solutions. The collapse of Germany and Japan, moreover, created power vacuums that drew the two major powers into collision over former Axis-influenced countries. For example, in Greece and China, where civil wars raged between leftists and conservative regimes, the two powers supported different sides.

With empires disintegrating, a new Third World was created, especially as financial constraints and

DECOLONIZATION nationalist rebellions forced the imperial states to set their colonies free. Britain exited India (and Pakistan) in 1947 and Burma and Sri Lanka (Ceylon) in 1948. The Philippines gained independence from the United States in 1946. After four years of battling nationalists in Indonesia, the Dutch left in 1949. In the Middle East, Lebanon (1943), Syria (1946), and Jordan (1946) gained independence, while in Palestine, British officials faced pressure from Zionists intent on creating a Jewish homeland and from Arab leaders opposed to it. In Iraq, nationalist agitation increased against the British-installed government. Washington and Moscow regarded these new or emerging Third World states as potential allies that might provide military bases, resources, and markets.

However, some new nations stayed out of the Cold War.

The United States and the Soviet Union assessed their most pressing tasks in very different terms. The Soviets, though committed to victory over the capitalist countries, were most concerned about preventing another invasion of their homeland. The USSR land mass was three times larger than the United States, but it had only 10,000 miles of seacoast, which was under ice much of the year. Russian leaders before and after the revolution had made increased maritime access a chief foreign policy aim.

STALIN'S AIMS

Worse, the USSR's geographical frontiers were hard to defend. Siberia, vital for its mineral resources, lay 6,000 miles east of Moscow and was vulnerable to encroachment by Japan and China. In the west, the border with Poland had generated violent clashes since World War I. With World War II claiming at least 20 million lives and causing massive physical destruction, Soviet leaders wanted no dangers along their western borders.

Overall, however, Soviet territorial objectives were limited. Although many Americans compared Stalin to Hitler, Stalin's aims resembled those of czars before him: he wanted the USSR's borders to include the Baltic states of Estonia, Latvia, and Lithuania, as well as the eastern part of prewar Poland. To the south, Stalin wanted a presence in northern Iran, and he pressed the Turks for naval bases and free access out of the Black Sea. Economically suspicious of their European neighbors, the Soviets did not promote rapid rebuilding of the war-ravaged economies of the region or expanded world trade.

The United States, by contrast, came out of the war secure of its borders. Separated from other world powers by two oceans, the American home base had been virtually immune from attack during the fighting. American casualties were fewer than any of the other major combatants. With its fixed capital intact, its resources more plentiful than ever, and in lone possession of the atomic bomb, the United States was the strongest world power at war's end.

U.S. ECONOMIC AND STRATEGIC NEEDS

But Washington officials guarded against complacency. Some other power—almost certainly the USSR—could take advantage of instability in war-torn Europe and Asia and seize control of these areas, with dire implications for America's security. Therefore Washington officials sought bases overseas to keep an airborne enemy at bay. To enhance U.S. security, American planners sought the quick reconstruction of nations—including former enemies Germany and Japan—and a world economy based on free trade.

The Soviets refused to join the new World Bank and International Monetary Fund (IMF), created at the July 1944 Bretton Woods Conference by forty-four nations to stabilize trade. They held that the United States dominated both institutions and used them to promote private investment and open international commerce, which Moscow saw as capitalist tools of exploitation. With the United States as its largest donor, the World Bank opened in 1945 and made loans to finance members' reconstruction projects; the IMF, also heavily U.S. backed, helped members meet balance-of-payments through currency loans.

Joseph Stalin, though hostile to the Western powers and capable of ruthlessness against his own people (his periodic purges since the 1930s had taken the lives of millions), did not want war. He was aware of his country's weakness in relation to the United States and believed he could achieve his aspirations through cooperation with the Americans and British. But Stalin believed that Germany and Japan would eventually threaten the USSR again, and his suspicion of capitalist powers was boundless. Many suspected Stalin was clinically paranoid. As historian David Reynolds has noted, this paranoia, coupled with Stalin's xenophobia (fear of anything foreign) and his Marxist-Leninist ideology, created in him a mental map of "them" versus "us" that decisively influenced his approach to world affairs.

STALIN AND TRUMAN

To a lesser degree, Harry Truman too was prone to a "them" versus "us" worldview. He often glossed over ambiguities and counterevidence, preferring the simple, decisive answer. Truman exaggerated, as when he declared in his undelivered farewell address that he had "knocked the socks off the communists" in Korea. When Truman protested in 1945 that the Soviets were not fulfilling the Yalta agreement on Poland, the Soviet commissar of foreign affairs, V. M. Molotov, stormed out of their meeting. Truman self-consciously developed what he called his "tough method," and his toughness became a trademark of American Cold War diplomacy.

There are no precise dates for the beginning of the Cold War. It resulted more from an ongoing process

THE BEGINNING OF THE COLD WAR

that arguably began in 1917 with the Bolshevik Revolution and Western powers' hostile response, but which in a more meaningful sense began in mid-1945 as World War II ended. By spring 1947, certainly, the struggle was underway.

One of the first Soviet-American clashes came in Poland in 1945, when the Soviets blocked the Polish government-in-exile in London from participating in the communist government that Moscow sponsored. The Soviets also extinguished civil liberties in Romania, arguing that the United States similarly manipulated Italy. Moscow initially allowed free elections in Hungary and Czechoslovakia, but as the Cold War accelerated and U.S. influence in Europe expanded, the Soviets encouraged communist coups in Hungary (1947) and Czechoslovakia (1948). Yugoslavia was unique: its independent communist government, led by Josip Broz Tito, successfully broke with Stalin in 1948.

To defend their actions, Moscow officials noted that the United States was reviving their traditional enemy, Germany, and was meddling in eastern Europe. The Soviets cited clandestine American meetings with anti-Soviet groups, repeated calls for elections likely to produce anti-Soviet regimes, and the use of loans to gain political influence (financial diplomacy). Moscow charged that the United States was pursuing a double standard—intervening in eastern Europe but demanding that the Soviet Union stay out of Latin America and Asia. Americans called for free elections in the Soviet sphere, Moscow noted, but not in the U.S. sphere in Latin America.

The Soviets believed that the United States was practicing "atomic diplomacy"—maintaining a nu-

ATOMIC DIPLOMACY

clear monopoly to scare the Soviets into diplomatic concessions. Secretary of State James F. Byrnes thought the atomic bomb could deter Soviet expansion, but Secretary of War Henry L. Stimson disagreed in 1945. If Americans continued to have "this weapon rather ostentatiously on our hip," he warned Truman, the Soviets' "suspicions and their distrust of our purposes and motives will increase."

In this tense atmosphere, Truman refused to turn over the weapon to an international authority. In 1946 he backed the Baruch Plan, named after its author, financier Bernard Baruch, which provided for U.S. abandonment of its atomic monopoly only after the world's fissionable materials were controlled by an international agency. The Soviets retorted that it would require them to shut down their atomic-bomb development project while the United States continued its own. Washington and Moscow soon became locked in a frightening nuclear arms race.

By mid-1946, the Soviets and Americans clashed on numerous fronts. When the United States declined a Soviet reconstruction loan but gave Britain a loan, Moscow upbraided Washington for using its dollars to manipulate foreign governments. The two Cold War powers also backed different groups in Iran, where the United States helped bring the pro-West shah to the throne. Unable to agree on the unification of Germany, the former allies built up their zones independently.

After Stalin gave a speech in February 1946 depicting the world as threatened by capitalist acquisi-

WARNINGS FROM KENNAN AND CHURCHILL

tiveness, the American chargé d'affaires in Moscow, George F. Kennan, sent a pessimistic "long telegram" to Washington. His widely circulated report fed a growing belief among American officials that only toughness would work with the Soviets. The following month, in Fulton, Missouri, former British prime minister Winston Churchill warned that a Soviet-erected "iron curtain" had cut off eastern European countries from the West. With an approving Truman nearby, Churchill called for Anglo-American partnership to resist the new menace.

The growing Soviet-American tensions had major implications for the United Nations. The delegates who gathered in San Francisco in April 1945 to sign the U.N. charter agreed on an organization that included a General Assembly of all member states and a smaller Security Council spearheading peace and security issues. Five great powers were given permanent seats on the council—the United States, the Soviet Union, Great Britain, China, and France—and could exercise a veto against any proposed action. To be effective, therefore, the U.N. needed great-power cooperation. Of the fifty-one founding states, twenty-two came from the Americas and another fifteen from Europe, which effectively gave the United States a majority in the assembly. In retaliation, Moscow exercised its veto in the Security Council.

Some high-level U.S. officials were dismayed by the administration's harsh anti-Soviet posture. Secretary of Commerce Henry A. Wallace charged that Truman's get-tough policy substituted atomic and economic coercion for diplomacy. Wallace told a Madison Square Garden audience in September 1946 that "'getting tough' never brought anything real and lasting—whether for schoolyard bullies or businessmen or world powers." Truman fired Wallace, blasting him privately as "a real Commy."

East-West tensions escalated further in early 1947, when the British requested American help

TRUMAN DOCTRINE

defending their conservative client-government (a government that is dependent on the economic or military support of a more powerful country) in Greece in a civil war against leftists. Truman requested $400 million in aid from Congress. The Republican Eightieth Congress wanted less spending, and many had little respect for the Democratic president after voters in the 1946 elections gave the GOP ("Grand Old Party," the Republican Party) majorities in both houses of Congress. Republican senator Arthur Vandenberg of Michigan, a bipartisan leader, told the president he would have to "scare hell out of the American people" to gain congressional approval.

With that in mind, the president delivered a speech laced with alarmist language outlining America's role in the postwar world. Truman claimed that communism imperiled the world. "If Greece should fall under the control of an armed minority," he concluded in an early version of the domino theory (discussed later in this chapter), "the effect upon its neighbor, Turkey, would be immediate and serious. Confusion and disorder might well spread throughout the entire Middle East." Truman articulated what became known as the Truman Doctrine: "I believe that it must be the policy of the United States to support free peoples who are resisting attempted subjugation by armed minorities or by outside pressures."

Critics correctly pointed out that the Soviet Union was little involved in the Greek civil war, that the communists in Greece were more pro-Tito than pro-Stalin, and that the resistance movement had non-communist as well as communist members. Truman countered that should communists gain control of Greece, they might open the door to Soviet power in the Mediterranean. The Senate approved Truman's

request by 67 to 23 votes. Using U.S. dollars and military advisers, the Greek government defeated the insurgents in 1949, and Turkey became a staunch U.S. ally on the Soviets' border.

Months after Truman's speech, the term *Cold War* slipped into the lexicon as a description of

INEVITABLE COLD WAR?

the Soviet-American relationship. Within two years of the victory over the Axis powers, the two Grand Alliance members were locked in a struggle for world dominance that would last almost half a century. Even before World

■ On March 5, 1946, former British prime minister Winston S. Churchill (1874–1965) delivered a speech, which he intended for a worldwide audience, at Westminster College in Fulton, Missouri. President Harry S Truman (*right*) had encouraged Churchill (*seated*) to speak on two themes: the need to block Soviet expansion and the need to form an Anglo-American partnership. Always eloquent and provocative, Churchill denounced the Soviets for drawing an "iron curtain" across eastern Europe. This speech became one of the landmark statements of the Cold War.   (Terry Savage/Harry S Truman Presidential Library)

War II ended, perceptive observers anticipated that the United States and the USSR would seek to fill the power vacuum. The two countries had a history of tension and were militarily powerful. Most of all, they were divided by sharply differing political economies with divergent needs and a deep ideological chasm.

Far less clear is that the conflict had to result in a cold war. The "cold peace" that had prevailed through World War II could conceivably have been maintained into the postwar years. Neither side's leadership wanted war. Both hoped, at least initially, that a spirit of cooperation could be maintained. The Cold War resulted from decisions by individual human beings who might have done more, for example, to maintain diplomatic dialogue and negotiated solutions to complex international problems. For decades, Americans would wonder if the high price they were paying for victory in the superpower confrontation was necessary.

Containment in Action

To counter Soviet and communist expansion, the Truman team relied on a policy of containment. George Kennan, now at the State Department in Washington, published an influential statement of the containment doctrine, under the pseudonym "Mr. X," in the July 1947 issue of *Foreign Affairs* magazine. Kennan advocated a "policy of firm containment, designed to confront the Russians with unalterable counterforce at every point where they show signs of encroaching upon the interests of a peaceful and stable world." Such counterforce, Kennan argued, would foster a "mellowing" of Soviet behavior. Kennan's "X" article joined the Truman Doctrine as another key manifesto of Cold War policy.

The veteran journalist Walter Lippmann took issue with the containment doctrine in his slim but powerful book *The Cold War* (1947), calling it a "strategic monstrosity" that failed to distinguish between areas vital and peripheral to U.S. security. Nor did Lippmann share Truman's conviction that the Soviet Union wanted to take over the world. Ironically, Kennan agreed with much of Lippmann's critique and soon distanced himself from the doctrine he had helped to create.

LIPPMANN'S CRITIQUE

Invoking the containment doctrine, the United States in 1947 and 1948 began to build an international economic and defensive network to protect American prosperity and advance U.S. hegemony. In western Europe, the region of primary concern, American diplomats pursued economic reconstruction; the ouster of communists from governments, as occurred in 1947 in France and Italy; and blockage of "third force," or neutralist, tendencies. U.S. officials kept the decolonization of European empires orderly. Meanwhile, American culture—consumer goods, music, consumption ethic, and production techniques—permeated European societies, and while some resisted, transatlantic ties were strengthened.

Online Study Center   Improve Your Grade
Interactive Map: Divided Europe

Americans, who already had spent billions of dollars on European relief and recovery by 1947, remembered all too well the troubles of the 1930s: global depression, political extremism, and war born of economic discontent. Such cataclysms could not be allowed to happen again; communism must not replace fascism. Hence, in June 1947, Secretary of State George C. Marshall announced that the United States would finance a massive European recovery program. Launched in 1948, the Marshall Plan sent $12.4 billion to western Europe until 1951 (see Map 28.1). To stimulate business at home, the legislation required that Europeans spend this aid on American-made products. The Marshall Plan proved a mixed success: it caused inflation, failed to solve a balance-of-payments problem, took only tentative steps toward economic integration, and further divided Europe between "East" and "West." But the program spurred impressive western European industrial production and investment, started the region toward self-sustaining economic growth, and contained communism.

MARSHALL PLAN

Truman streamlined U.S. defense by working with Congress on the National Security Act of July 1947. The act created the Office of Secretary of Defense (which became the Department of Defense two years later) to oversee the armed services, the National Security Council (NSC) of high-level officials to advise the president, and the Central Intelligence Agency (CIA) to conduct spy and

NATIONAL SECURITY ACT

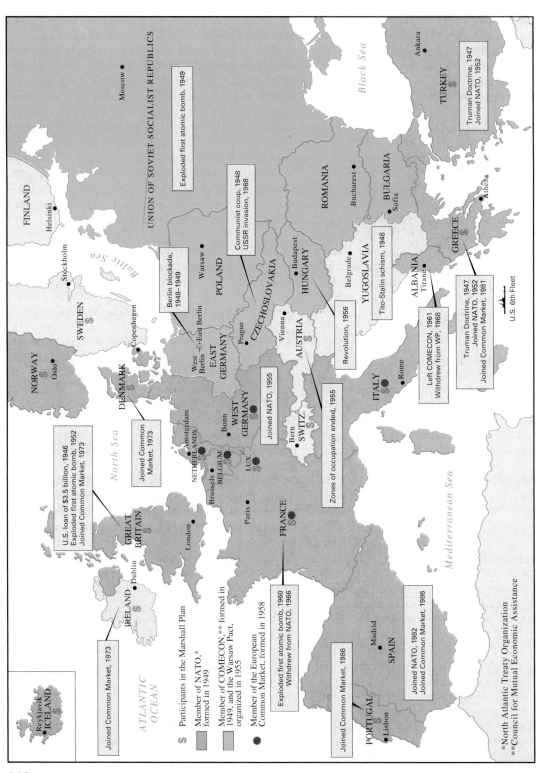

Map 28.1 Divided Europe

After the Second World War, Europe broke into two competing camps. When the United States launched the Marshall Plan in 1948, the Soviet Union countered with its own economic plan the following year. When the United States created the North Atlantic Treaty Organization (NATO) in 1949, the Soviet Union answered with the Warsaw Pact in 1955. On the whole, these two camps held firm until the late 1980s.

UNION OF SOVIET SOCIALIST REPUBLICS

Moscow •

Exploded first atomic bomb, 1949

*North Atlantic Treaty Organization
**Council for Mutual Economic Assistance

$ Participants in the Marshall Plan

Member of NATO,*
formed in 1949

Member of COMECON,** formed in
1949, and the Warsaw Pact,
organized in 1955

● Member of the European
Common Market, formed in 1958

FINLAND
Helsinki •

Baltic Sea

SWEDEN
Stockholm •

NORWAY $
Oslo •

DENMARK
Copenhagen •

POLAND
Warsaw •

Berlin blockade,
1948–1949

West Berlin—East Berlin
EAST GERMANY

Prague •
CZECHOSLOVAKIA

Communist coup, 1948
USSR invasion, 1968

HUNGARY
Budapest •

Revolution, 1956

Vienna •
AUSTRIA $

Zones of occupation ended, 1955

ROMANIA
Bucharest •

Black Sea

BULGARIA
Sofia •

YUGOSLAVIA
Belgrade •

Tito-Stalin schism, 1948

TURKEY
Ankara •

Truman Doctrine, 1947
Joined NATO, 1952

GREECE $
Athens •

Truman Doctrine, 1947
Joined NATO, 1952
Joined Common Market, 1981

ALBANIA
Tiranë •

Left COMECON, 1961
Withdrew from WP, 1968

U.S. 6th Fleet

North Sea

GREAT BRITAIN $
London •

U.S. loan of $3.5 billion, 1946
Exploded first atomic bomb, 1952
Joined Common Market, 1973

IRELAND $
Dublin •

ICELAND $
Reykjavík •

ATLANTIC OCEAN

Joined Common Market, 1973

NETHERLANDS
Amsterdam •

BELGIUM
Brussels •

LUX. $

Joined Common Market, 1973

WEST GERMANY $
Bonn •

Joined NATO, 1955

SWITZ. $
Bern •

FRANCE $
Paris •

Exploded first atomic bomb, 1960
Withdrew from NATO, 1966

ITALY $
Rome •

Mediterranean Sea

SPAIN
Madrid •

Joined NATO, 1982
Joined Common Market, 1986

PORTUGAL $
Lisbon •

Joined Common Market, 1986

518

information gathering overseas. By the early 1950s the CIA had expanded to include covert (secret) operations aimed at overthrowing unfriendly foreign leaders. The National Security Act gave the president increased powers regarding foreign policy.

In response, Stalin forbade communist satellite governments in eastern Europe to accept Marshall Plan aid and ordered communist parties in western Europe to work to thwart it. He also created the Cominform, an organization designed to coordinate communist activities around the world. Whereas American planners saw the Marshall Plan as protecting their European friends against a potential Soviet threat, to Stalin it raised anew the specter of capitalist penetration. He tightened his grip on eastern Europe—most notably, engineering a coup in Czechoslovakia in February 1948 that ensured Soviet control—which heightened anxiety in the United States.

In June 1948, the Americans, French, and British agreed to fuse their German zones and integrate

BERLIN BLOCKADE AND AIRLIFT

West Germany (the Federal Republic of Germany) into the western European economy. Fearing a resurgent Germany tied to the American Cold War camp, the Soviets cut off access to the jointly occupied city of Berlin inside the Soviet zone. President Truman then ordered a massive airlift of food, fuel, and other supplies to Berlin. The Soviets finally lifted the blockade in May 1949 and founded the German Democratic Republic, or East Germany.

The successful airlift may have saved Truman's political career: he narrowly defeated Republican Thomas E. Dewey in the November 1948 presidential election. Truman next formalized the military alliance among the United States, Canada, and western Europe. In April 1949, twelve nations signed a mutual defense treaty, agreeing that an attack on one of them would be considered an attack on all, and establishing the North Atlantic Treaty Organization (NATO) (see Map 28.1).

Not since 1778 had the United States entered a formal European military alliance, and some critics, such as Senator Robert A. Taft, Republican of Ohio, claimed that NATO would provoke rather than deter war. Administration officials responded that should the Soviets ever probe westward, NATO would bring the full force of the United States to bear on the Soviet Union. Truman officials also hoped that NATO

would keep western Europeans from embracing communism or even neutralism in the Cold War. The Senate ratified the treaty by 82 votes to 13, and the United States began spending billions of dollars under the Mutual Defense Assistance Act.

By the summer of 1949, Truman and his advisers were basking in the successes of their foreign policy. Containment was working, West Germany was on the road to recovery, the Berlin blockade had been defeated, and NATO had been formed. True, there was trouble in China, where the communists under Mao Zedong were winning a civil war. But that struggle would likely wax and wane for years to come. Just possibly, some dared to think, Harry Truman was on his way to winning the Cold War.

Then, suddenly, in late September, came the "twin shocks," two momentous developments that made

TWIN SHOCKS

Americans feel in greater danger than ever before. First, an American reconnaissance aircraft detected unusually high radioactivity in the atmosphere: the Soviets had exploded an atomic bomb. With the American nuclear monopoly erased, western Europe seemed more vulnerable. The communists in China completed their conquest sooner than many expected. Now the world's largest and most populous countries were ruled by communists, and one of them had the atomic weapon. Rejecting appeals for high-level negotiations, Truman in early 1950 gave the go-ahead for production of a hydrogen bomb, the "Super." Kennan bemoaned the militarization of the Cold War and was replaced at the State Department by Paul Nitze. The National Security Council delivered to the president in April 1950 a significant top-secret document tagged NSC-68. Predicting continued tension with expansionistic communists, the report, authored primarily by Nitze, urged a much enlarged military budget and the mobilization of public support. The Cold War was about to become vastly more expensive and far-reaching.

The Cold War in Asia

sia gradually became ensnared in the Cold War. Indeed, the consequences of an expansive containment doctrine would exact its heaviest price on the United States in large-scale wars in Korea and Vietnam. Though less important to both superpowers than Europe, Asia was where the Cold War turned hot.

From the start, Japan was crucial to U.S. strategy. The United States monopolized Japan's reconstruction through a military occupation directed by General Douglas MacArthur. Truman disliked "Mr. Prima Donna, Brass Hat" MacArthur, but MacArthur wrote a democratic constitution, gave women voting rights, revitalized the economy, and destroyed the nation's weapons. U.S. authorities Americanized Japan by censoring films critical of the United States (for the destruction of Hiroshima, for example) or depicting Japanese customs such as suicide, arranged marriages, and swordplay. In 1951, against Soviet protests, the United States and Japan signed a separate peace that restored Japan's sovereignty and ended the occupation. The Mutual Security Treaty that year provided for U.S. forces in Japan, including a base on Okinawa.

The administration had less success in China. The United States had long backed the Nationalists

CHINESE CIVIL WAR

of Jiang Jieshi (Chiang Kai-shek) against Mao Zedong's communists. But after the Second World War, Generalissimo Jiang's government had become corrupt, inefficient, and out of touch with discontented peasants, whom the communists enlisted with promises of land reform. Jiang also subverted American efforts to negotiate a cease-fire and a coalition government. American officials divided on the question of whether Mao was an Asian Tito—communist but independent—or, as most believed, part of an international communist movement that might give the Soviets a springboard into Asia. Thus, when the Chinese communists made secret overtures to the United States for diplomatic talks in 1945 and 1949, American officials declined. Mao leaned to the Soviet side in the Cold War. Because of China's fierce independence, however, a Sino-Soviet schism opened.

With his victory in September 1949, Mao proclaimed the People's Republic of China (PRC). Truman hesitated to extend diplomatic recognition to the new government. U.S. officials became alarmed by the 1950 Sino-Soviet Treaty and the harassment of Americans in China. Truman also chose nonrecognition because vocal Republican critics, the so-called China lobby, pinned Jiang's defeat on Truman. The president argued that despite billions of dollars in American aid, Jiang proved a poor instrument of containment. Not until 1979 did official Sino-American relations resume.

Mao's victory in China drew urgent American attention to Indochina, the southeast Asian peninsula

VIETNAM'S QUEST FOR INDEPENDENCE

held by France for nearly a century. The Japanese wrested control over Indochina during World War II, but still the Vietnamese nationalist movement grew. Their leader, Ho Chi Minh, hoped to use Japan's defeat to assert Vietnamese independence and sought U.S. support. American officials rejected Ho's appeals over restoring French rule. Paris warned that American support of Vietnamese independence would strengthen the French Communist Party, perhaps even drive France into the arms of the USSR. In addition, the Truman administration feared that Ho Chi Minh was an "agent of international communism," who would assist Soviet and, after 1949, Chinese expansionism. Overlooking the native roots of the nationalist rebellion against French colonialism, Washington interpreted events in Indochina through a Cold War lens.

When war between the Vietminh and France broke out in 1946, the United States initially took a hands-off approach. But after Jiang's regime collapsed in China three years later, the Truman administration in February 1950 recognized the French puppet government of Bao Dai, a playboy and former emperor. To many Vietnamese, the United States thus became an ally of the hated French. Second, in May, the administration agreed to send weapons and military advisers to sustain the French. From 1945 to 1954, the United States gave $2 billion of the $5 billion that France spent to keep Vietnam within its empire—to no avail. How Vietnam ultimately became the site of America's longest war, covered in Chapters 30 and 31, is one of the most tragic stories of modern history.

The Korean War

Early on June 25, 1950, a large military force of the Democratic People's Republic of Korea (North Korea) moved into the Republic of Korea (South Korea). Colonized by Japan since 1910, Korea was split in two after Japan's defeat in 1945.

Although the Soviets armed the North and Americans armed the South (U.S. aid reached $100 million a year), the Korean War began as a civil war. Since its division, the two parts had been skirmishing while antigovernment (and anti-U.S.) guerrilla fighting flared in the South.

Both the North's communist leader, Kim Il Sung, and the South's president, Syngman Rhee, sought to reunify their nation. Kim's military especially gained strength when tens of thousands returned home in 1949 after serving in Mao's army. President Truman claimed that the Soviets had masterminded the North Korean attack.

Actually, Stalin reluctantly approved the attack only after Kim predicted an easy, early victory and after Mao backed Kim. When the U.N. Security Council voted to defend South Korea, the Soviet representative was not present because the Soviets were boycotting the United Nations for its refusal to admit the People's Republic of China. During the war, Moscow gave limited aid to North Korea and China, reneging on promised Soviet airpower. Aware of his strategic inferiority in relation to the United States, Stalin did not want war.

STALIN'S DOUBTS

The president first ordered General Douglas MacArthur to send arms and troops to South Korea. He did not seek congressional approval—fearing lawmakers would initiate a lengthy debate—and thereby set the precedent of waging war on executive authority alone. After the Security Council voted to assist South Korea, MacArthur became commander of U.N. forces in Korea. Sixteen nations contributed troops, but 40 percent were South Korean and 50 percent American. In the early weeks, North Korean tanks and superior firepower sent the South Korean army into retreat. The first American soldiers, taking heavy casualties, could not stop the North Koreans from pushing them and the South Koreans and Americans into the tiny Pusan perimeter at the tip of South Korea.

U.S. FORCES INTERVENE

General MacArthur planned a daring amphibious landing at heavily fortified Inchon, several hundred miles behind North Korean lines. After U.S. bombs pounded Inchon, marines sprinted ashore on September 15, 1950, liberating the South Korean capital of Seoul and pushing the North Koreans back.

Truman meanwhile redefined the U.S. war goal from the containment of North Korea to the reunification of Korea by force.

In September U.S. troops drove deep into North Korea, and American aircraft began strikes against bridges on the Yalu River, the border between North Korea and China. Mao publicly warned that China could not permit the bombing of its transportation links with Korea and would not accept the annihilation of North Korea. MacArthur shrugged off the warnings, and Washington officials agreed, confident that the Soviets were not preparing for war.

CHINESE ENTRY INTO THE WAR

MacArthur was right about the Soviets, but wrong about the Chinese. On October 25 Mao sent Chinese soldiers into the war near the Yalu. Perhaps to lure American forces into a trap or signal willingness to negotiate, they pulled back after a successful offensive against South Korean troops. Then, on November 26, tens of thousands of Chinese troops surprised American forces and drove them southward. One U.S. officer described "the men of a whole United States Army fleeing from a battlefield, abandoning their wounded, running for their lives."

Online Study Center   Improve Your Grade
Primary Source:
MacArthur Outlines His Objectives in Korea

By 1951 the front stabilized around the 38th parallel. Both Washington and Moscow welcomed negotiations, but MacArthur called for an attack on China and Jiang's return. Denouncing limited war (war without nuclear weapons, confined to one place), MacArthur hinted that the president was practicing appeasement. In April, backed by the Joint Chiefs of Staff, Truman fired MacArthur, who nonetheless returned home a hero. Truman's popularity sagged as he weathered scattered demands for his impeachment.

TRUMAN'S FIRING OF MACARTHUR

Armistice talks began in July 1951, but the fighting continued for two years. Defying the Geneva Prisoners of War Convention (1949), U.S. officials announced that only North Korean and Chinese prisoners of war (POWs) who wished to go home would be returned. While Americans resisted forced repatriation, the

North Koreans denounced forced retention. Both sides undertook "reeducation" or "brainwashing" on POWs.

As the POW issue stalled negotiations, U.S. officials made deliberately vague public statements about

PEACE
AGREEMENT

using atomic weapons in Korea. Casualties on all sides mounted. Not until July 1953 was an armistice signed. Stalin's death in March and a more conciliatory Soviet government helped enable a settlement that the Chinese especially welcomed. The combatants agreed to hand the POW question to a special panel of neutral nations, which gave prisoners the choice to stay or leave. The North Korean–South Korean borderline was set near the 38th parallel, the prewar boundary, and a demilitarized zone was created between them.

American casualties totaled 54,246 dead and 103,284 wounded. Nearly 5 million Asians died: 2 million North Korean civilians and 500,000 soldiers; 1 million South Korean civilians and 100,000 soldiers; and at least 1 million Chinese soldiers—ranking Korea as one of the costliest wars of the twentieth century.

The Korean War carried major domestic political consequences. The failure to achieve victory and

CONSEQUENCES
OF THE WAR

the public's impatience undoubtedly helped elect Republican Dwight Eisenhower to the presidency in 1952, as this former general promised to end the war. The powers of the presidency grew as Congress repeatedly deferred to Truman. The president never asked Congress for a declaration of war, believing that as commander-in-chief, he had the authority to send troops wherever he wished. He saw no need to consult Congress—except to get the $69.5 billion Korean War bill paid. In addition, Republican lawmakers, including Wisconsin senator Joseph McCarthy, accused Truman and Secretary of State Dean Acheson of being "soft on communism," which pushed the administration into an uncompromising position in the negotiations.

The Sino-American hostility generated by the war made U.S. reconciliation with the Beijing government impossible and made South Korea and Formosa major recipients of American foreign aid. The alliance with Japan strengthened as its economy boomed after filling large U.S. procurement orders. Australia and New Zealand joined the United States in a mutual defense agreement, the ANZUS Treaty (1951). The United States sent four army divisions to Europe and initiated plans to rearm West Germany. The military budget jumped from $14 billion in 1949 to $44 billion in 1953; it remained between $35 billion and $44 billion a year throughout the 1950s. The Soviet Union matched this military buildup, resulting in an arms race. Truman's legacy was a highly militarized U.S. foreign policy on a global scale.

Unrelenting Cold War

President Eisenhower and Secretary of State John Foster Dulles largely sustained Truman's Cold War foreign policies. As a World War II general, Eisenhower had traveled in Europe, Asia, and Latin America and had negotiated with world leaders. After the war, he had served as army chief of staff and NATO supreme commander. Dulles had been closely involved with U.S. diplomacy since the first decade of the century.

Eisenhower and Dulles accepted the Cold War consensus about the threat of communism and the

EISENHOWER
AND DULLES

need for global vigilance. Although Democrats promoted an image of Eisenhower as a bumbling, aging hero, the president in fact commanded the policymaking process and occasionally tamed the more hawkish proposals of Dulles and Vice President Richard Nixon. Even so, the secretary of state was influential. Few Cold Warriors rivaled Dulles's anticommunism, often expressed in biblical terms. A graduate of Princeton and George Washington Universities, Dulles had assisted Woodrow Wilson at Versailles and later became a senior partner in a prestigious Wall Street law firm and an officer of the Federal Council of Churches. He struck people as arrogant and averse to an essential ingredient in successful diplomacy: compromise. But his assertion that neutrality was an "immoral and short-sighted conception" did not sit well with Third World leaders, who resented being told they had to choose between East and West.

Dulles conceded much to the anticommunist McCarthyites, who claimed that the State Department was infested with communists (discussed in the next chapter). The State Department's chief security officer targeted homosexuals and other "incompatibles," making few distinctions between New Dealers and communists. Dulles thus forced many talented officers out of the Foreign Service, among them, Asia specialists. "The wrong done," the journalist Theodore A. White wrote, "was to poke out the eyes and ears of the State Department on Asian affairs, to blind American foreign policy."

Considering containment too defensive, Dulles called instead for "liberation," freeing eastern Europe from Soviet control. "Massive retaliation" was the administration's plan for the nuclear obliteration of the Soviet state or its assumed client, the People's Republic of China, if either one took aggressive action.

"MASSIVE RETALIATION"

In the military, Eisenhower and Dulles emphasized airpower and nuclear weaponry. The president's preference for heavy weapons stemmed in part from his desire to trim the federal budget ("more bang for the buck," as the saying went). Galvanized by the successful test of the world's first hydrogen bomb in November 1952, Eisenhower oversaw a massive stockpiling of nuclear weapons—from 1,200 at the start of his presidency to 22,229 at the end. With this huge arsenal, the United States could practice "brinkmanship": not backing down, even if it took the nation to the brink of war. Eisenhower also popularized the "domino theory": that small, weak nations would fall to communism like a row of dominoes unless they were backed by the United States.

Eisenhower increasingly used the Central Intelligence Agency as an instrument of foreign policy. The CIA put foreign leaders (such as King Hussein of Jordan) on its payroll; subsidized foreign labor unions, newspapers, and political parties; planted false stories in newspapers through "disinformation" projects; and trained foreign military officers. It hired American journalists and professors, used business executives as "fronts," and conducted experiments on unsuspecting Americans to determine the effects of "mind control" drugs (the MKULTRA program). The CIA also launched covert operations (including assassination schemes) to subvert governments in the Third World, helping to overthrow the governments of Iran (1953) and Guatemala (1954).

CIA AS FOREIGN POLICY INSTRUMENT

The American intelligence community embraced the principle of plausible deniability: covert operations should be conducted in such a way, and the decisions that launched them concealed so well, that the president could deny any knowledge of them. Thus, Eisenhower disavowed any U.S. role in Guatemala, even though he had ordered the operation. He and his successor, John F. Kennedy, also denied instructing the CIA to assassinate Cuba's Fidel Castro, whose regime after 1959 became stridently anti-American.

Leaders in Moscow quickly became aware of Eisenhower's covert actions, as well as his stockpiling of nuclear weapons. The Soviets increased their intelligence and tested their first H-bomb in 1953. Four years later, they fired the world's first intercontinental ballistic missile (ICBM) and propelled the satellite *Sputnik* into outer space. Americans felt more vulnerable to air attack, even though in 1957 the United States had 2,460 strategic weapons and a nuclear stockpile of 5,543, compared with the Soviet Union's 102 and 650, respectively. The administration deployed intermediate-range missiles in Europe, targeted against the Soviet Union. At the end of 1960, the United States added Polaris missile–bearing submarines to its navy. To foster future technological advancement, the National Aeronautics and Space Administration (NASA) was created in 1958.

NUCLEAR BUILDUP

Overall, though, Eisenhower sought to avoid military confrontation with the Soviet Union and China, content to follow Truman's containment of communism. Eisenhower declined to use nuclear weapons and proved more reluctant than other Cold War presidents to send soldiers into battle. Convinced that the struggle against Moscow would be largely decided by international public opinion, he wanted to win the "hearts and minds" of people overseas. The "People-to-People" campaign, launched in 1956, used ordinary Americans and nongovernmental organizations to enhance the international image of the United States and its people.

Sometimes the propaganda war was waged on the Soviets' turf. In 1959 Vice President Richard Nixon traveled to Moscow for an American products fair. In the display of a modern American kitchen, Nixon extolled capitalist consumerism, while Soviet premier Nikita Khrushchev, Stalin's successor, touted

The People-to-People Campaign

Just after the start of the Cold War, U.S. officials determined that the Soviet-American confrontation was as much psychological and ideological as military and economic. One result was the People-to-People campaign, a state-private venture initiated by the U.S. Information Agency (USIA) in 1956 that aimed to win the "hearts and minds" of people around the world. American propaganda experts used ordinary Americans, businesses, civic organizations, labor groups, and women's clubs to promote confidence abroad in American goodness. The People-to-People campaign, one USIA pamphlet said, made "every man an ambassador."

Campaign activities resembled the home-front mobilization efforts of World War II. Americans were told that thirty dollars could send a ninety-nine-volume portable library of American books to schools and libraries overseas. Publishers donated magazines and books for free distribution to foreign countries. People-to-People committees organized sister-city affiliations and pen-pal letter exchanges, hosted exchange students, and organized traveling "People-to-People delegations." The travelers were urged to behave like goodwill ambassadors and "help overcome any feeling that America is a land that thinks money can buy everything."

Camp Fire Girls in over three thousand communities took photographs on the theme "This is our home. This is how we live. These are my People." The photographs were sent to girls in Latin America, Africa, Asia, and the Middle East. The Hobbies Committee connected people with interests in radio, photography, coins, stamps, and horticulture.

The persistence to this day of the widespread impression that Americans are a provincial, materialistic people promotes skepticism about the People-to-People campaign's success. But alongside this negative image is a positive one that sees Americans as open, friendly, optimistic, and pragmatic. Whatever role the People-to-People campaign played in the larger Cold War struggle, it certainly linked ordinary Americans more closely to other parts of the world.

This Alice Nast painting of two girls—one from the United States and one from Taiwan—was commissioned by the Kansas City chapter of People to People and the Kansas City, Tainan Sister City Commission. The painting was presented by Zelma Millman, Chairman of the Kansas City / Tainan Sister City Commission to the mayor of Tainan in September 1994, prior to the 11th Worldwide Conference of People-to-People International. (The Cover of 40th Anniversary issue is reprinted with permission of Alice Nast, Artist / Courtesy of *People to People International* Magazine)

communism. The encounter became famous as the "kitchen debate."

In February 1956, Khrushchev called for "peaceful coexistence" between capitalists and communists,

REBELLION IN HUNGARY

denounced Stalin, and suggested that Moscow would tolerate different brands of communism. Testing Khrushchev, revolts erupted in Poland and Hungary. After a new Hungarian government in 1956 withdrew from the Warsaw Pact (the Soviet military alliance formed in 1955 with communist countries of eastern Europe), Soviet troops and tanks crushed the rebellion.

Although the Eisenhower administration's propaganda encouraged liberation efforts, U.S. officials could not aid the rebels without igniting a world war. Instead, they promised only to welcome more Hungarian immigrants than American quota laws allowed. The West could have reaped some propaganda advantage had not British, French, and Israeli troops—U.S. allies—invaded Egypt during the Suez crisis just before the Soviets smashed the Hungarian uprising (detailed in the next section).

The turmoil had barely subsided when the divided city of Berlin again became a Cold War flash point. The Soviets railed against American bombers capable of carrying nuclear warheads in West Germany and complained that West Berlin had become an escape route for East Germans. In 1958 Khrushchev announced that the Soviet Union would recognize East German control of all of Berlin unless the United States and its allies began talks on German reunification and rearmament. The United States refused; Khrushchev backed down but promised to press the issue again.

Two weeks before a summit in Paris on May 1, 1960, a U-2 spy plane carrying high-powered cameras

U-2 INCIDENT

crashed 1,200 miles inside the Soviet Union. Moscow admitted shooting down the plane and promptly displayed captured CIA pilot Francis Gary Powers and the pictures he had been snapping of Soviet military sites. Khrushchev demanded an apology for violation of Soviet airspace. When Washington refused, the Soviets walked out of the Paris summit.

Meanwhile, both sides kept an eye on the People's Republic of China. Despite evidence of a widening Sino-Soviet split, most American officials treated communism as a monolithic world movement. In 1954,

in a dispute over Jinmen (Quemoy) and Mazu (Matsu), two tiny islands off the Chinese coast, the United States and China lurched toward the brink. Taiwan's Jiang Jieshi used these islands to raid the mainland. Communist China bombarded the islands in 1954. Thinking U.S. credibility was at stake, Eisenhower defended the outposts, even hinting he might use nuclear weapons. "Let's keep the Reds guessing," advised Dulles.

In early 1955, Congress passed the Formosa Resolution, authorizing the president to deploy troops to

FORMOSA RESOLUTION

defend Formosa and adjoining islands. In so doing, Congress formally surrendered to the president what it had informally given up in the 1950 Korea decision: the constitutional power to declare war. The crisis passed, but war loomed again in 1958 over Jinmen and Mazu. This time, as Jiang withdrew some troops, China relaxed its bombardments. But Eisenhower's nuclear threats persuaded the Chinese that they too needed nuclear arms. In 1964 China exploded its first nuclear bomb.

The Struggle for the Third World

In much of the Third World, the process of decolonization that began during the First World War accelerated after the Second World War, when the economically wracked imperial countries proved incapable of resisting their colonies' demands for freedom. A cavalcade of new nations cast off their colonial bonds (see Map 28.2). From 1943 to 1994, 125 countries, including 18 in Africa in 1960 alone, became independent (the figure includes the former Soviet republics that departed the USSR in 1991). The emergence of so many new states in the 1940s shook the foundations of the international system. In the traditional U.S. sphere of influence, Latin America, nationalists once again challenged Washington's dominance.

By the late 1940s, Soviet-American rivalry shifted increasingly to the Third World. The new nations

INTERESTS IN THE THIRD WORLD

could buy American goods, supply raw materials, and invite investments (more than one-third of America's private foreign investments were in

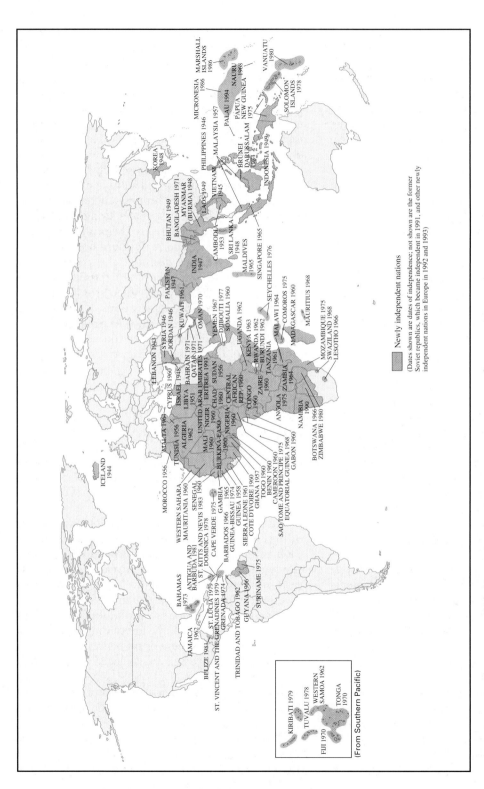

Map 28.2 The Rise of the Third World: Newly Independent Nations Since 1943

Accelerated by the Second World War, decolonization liberated many peoples from imperial rule. New nations emerged in the postwar international system dominated by the Cold War rivalry of the United States and the Soviet Union. Many newly independent states became targets of great-power intrigue but chose nonalignment in the Cold War.

Third World countries in 1959). Both great powers looked to these new states for votes in the United Nations and military and intelligence bases. But many new nations wanted to end the economic, military, and cultural hegemony of the West and set the two superpowers against each other to garner more aid and arms. U.S. interventions in the Third World, American leaders believed, became necessary to impress Moscow with Washington's might against threats to American interests.

To thwart nationalist, radical, and communist challenges, over 90 percent of U.S. foreign aid went to developing nations by 1961. Washington also allied with undemocratic but anticommunist regimes, meddled in civil wars, and unleashed CIA covert operations. When some of the larger Third World states—notably India, Ghana, Egypt, and Indonesia—refused to take sides in the Cold War, Secretary of State Dulles declared that neutralism was a step on the road to communism, insisting with Eisenhower that every nation take sides.

American leaders argued that technologically "backward" Third World countries needed Western-induced capitalist development to enjoy economic growth and political moderation. Often U.S. officials ascribed stereotyped race- and gender-based characteristics to Third World peoples, seeing them as dependent, emotional, and irrational, and therefore dependent on the fatherly tutelage of the United States. American officials also suggested that Third World countries were "weak women"—passive and servile, unable to resist the menacing communists. Eisenhower condescendingly described neutralist India as a place where "emotion rather than reason seems to dictate policy."

Racism influenced U.S. relations with Third World countries. In 1955 G. L. Mehta, the Indian ambassador to the United States, was refused service in the whites-only section of a restaurant at Houston International Airport. The insult stung deeply, as did many similar indignities experienced by other Third World diplomats. Dulles apologized to Mehta and thought U.S. racial segregation was a "major international hazard."

RACISM AND SEGREGATION AS U.S. HANDICAPS

Thus, developments in race relations (covered in the next chapter) came into play. When the Supreme Court announced its decision in *Brown v. Board of Education* in 1954, the government quickly broadcast news of the desegregation order around the world in thirty-five languages on its Voice of America overseas radio network. But the problem did not go away. For example, after the 1957 Little Rock crisis, Dulles remarked that racial bigotry was "ruining our foreign policy." Still, when a State Department office countered Soviet anti-American race propaganda with a 1958 World's Fair exhibit in Brussels titled "The Unfinished Work"—on U.S. strides toward desegregation—southern conservatives kicked up such a furor that the Eisenhower administration closed the display.

U.S. hostility toward revolution also obstructed its quest for influence in the Third World. In the twentieth century, the United States opposed revolutions in Mexico, China, Russia, Cuba, Vietnam, Nicaragua, and Iran, largely because many Third World revolutions rose against America's Cold War allies and threatened American investments, markets, and military bases. Preferring to maintain the status quo, the United States usually supported its European allies or the conservative, propertied classes in the Third World during revolutionary crises.

Yet idealism also drove U.S. policy. Believing that Third World peoples craved modernization and the American economic model of private enterprise, American policymakers launched various "development" projects. Such projects held out the promise of sustained economic growth, prosperity, and stability, which the benefactors hoped would undermine radicalism. In the 1950s the Carnegie, Ford, and Rockefeller Foundations worked with the U.S. Agency for International Development (AID) to sponsor the Green Revolution promoting agricultural production. The Rockefeller Foundation supported foreign universities' efforts to train national leaders committed to nonradical development.

DEVELOPMENT AND MODERNIZATION

To persuade Third World peoples against radical doctrines, American leaders created propaganda campaigns. The U.S. Information Agency (USIA), founded in 1953, used films, radio broadcasts, the magazine *Free World*, exhibitions, and libraries (in 162 cities worldwide by 1961) to trumpet the "People's Capitalism." Citing America's economic success—contrasted with "slave-labor" conditions in the Soviet Union—it showcased well-paid American workers, political democracy, and religious freedom. To counter ugly pictures of segregation, the USIA applauded success stories of individual African Americans, such as the boxers Floyd Patterson and Sugar Ray Robinson. In 1960 some 13.8 million people visited U.S. pavilions abroad.

Undoubtedly, the American way of life had appeal for some Third World peoples. Hollywood movies offered enticing glimpses of middle-class materialism, as American films dominated many overseas markets. Blue jeans, advertising billboards, and soft drinks flooded foreign societies. Foreigners both envied and resented Americans for wasting so much while poorer peoples went without. The people of many countries, moreover, resented the profits that U.S. corporations extracted from them. Americans were often blamed for the persistent poverty in the developing world, even though leaders of those nations made decisions hindering their own progress, such as pouring millions of dollars into their militaries while their people needed food. Anti-American resentments materialized in the late 1950s attacks on USIA libraries in Calcutta, India; Beirut, Lebanon; and Bogotá, Colombia.

When the more benign techniques of containment—aid, trade, cultural relations—proved

INTERVENTION IN GUATEMALA

insufficient to prompt Third World nations to the American side, the Eisenhower administration pressed harder. Guatemala was an early test case. In 1951 the leftist Jacobo Arbenz Guzmán was elected president of Guatemala, a poor country whose largest landowner was the powerful American-owned United Fruit (UF) Company, which held 3 million acres across Latin America and operated railroads, ports, ships, and telecommunications facilities. Arbenz expropriated UF's uncultivated land and offered compensation. The company declined and charged that Arbenz posed a communist threat. The CIA began a secret plot to overthrow Arbenz, who turned to Moscow for military aid, thus reinforcing American suspicions. The CIA airlifted arms into Guatemala, and in mid-1954, CIA-supported Guatemalans struck from Honduras. U.S. planes bombed the capital city, driving Arbenz from power. The new pro-American regime returned United Fruit's land, but an ensuing civil war staggered the nation for decades.

Eisenhower was apprehensive as turmoil gripped Cuba in the late 1950s. In early 1959 Fidel Castro's rebels, or *barbudos* ("bearded ones"), driven by anti-American nationalism, ousted Fulgencio Batista, a

THE CUBAN REVOLUTION AND FIDEL CASTRO

long-time U.S. ally whose corrupt regime had turned Havana into a haven for gambling, prostitution, and organized crime. Cubans had resented U.S. domination since the early twentieth century, when the Platt Amendment compromised their independence. Castro sought to break the U.S. grasp on Cuban trade and roll back American business, which invested some $1 billion on the island.

In early 1960, after Cuba signed a trade treaty with the Soviet Union, Eisenhower ordered the CIA to organize Cuban exiles to overthrow the Castro government. The agency also began to plot an assassination of the Cuban leader. When the president drastically cut U.S. sugar purchases, Castro seized all North American–owned companies that had not yet been nationalized. Castro appealed to the Soviet Union, which offered loans and expanded trade. Before leaving office in early 1961, Eisenhower broke diplomatic relations with Cuba and advised president-elect John F. Kennedy to advance plans for the invasion.

In the Middle East, meanwhile, ongoing tensions between Arabs and Jews posed additional challenges (see Map 33.1). Before the end of

ARAB-ISRAELI CONFLICT

World War II, only France and Britain had been much concerned with this region. But the dissolution of empires and the rise of Cold War tensions drew Washington in, as did trouble in British-held Palestine. From 1945 to 1947, Britain tried to enlist U.S. officials to help resolve how to split Palestine between the Arabs and Jews. The Truman administration declined, and the British in 1947 turned the issue over to the United Nations, which voted to partition Palestine into separate Arab and Jewish states. Arab leaders opposed the decision, but in May 1948, Jewish leaders announced the creation of Israel.

The United States, which lobbied to secure the U.N. vote, extended recognition to the new state minutes after the act of foundation. A moral conviction that Jews deserved a homeland and that Zionism would create a democratic Israel influenced Truman, as did the belief that Jewish votes might swing some states to the Democrats in the 1948 election. These beliefs trumped concerns on the part of some senior officials that Arab oil producers might turn against the United States. The Soviet Union recognized the new nation, but Israel kept Moscow at arm's length. Palestinian Arabs, displaced from land they considered theirs, joined with Israel's Arab neighbors to make immediate war on the new state. The Israelis fought for six months until a U.N.-backed truce was called.

Thereafter, American Middle East policy centered on ensuring Israel's survival and cementing ties with Arab oil producers. American companies produced about half of the region's petroleum in the 1950s. Oil-rich Iran became a special friend, as its shah granted American oil companies a 40 percent interest in a new petroleum consortium in return for CIA help in the successful overthrow, in 1953, of his rival, Mohammed Mossadegh.

American officials faced a formidable foe in Egypt's Gamal Abdul Nasser, a towering figure in a pan-Arabic movement who vowed to expel the British from the Suez Canal and the Israelis from Palestine. The United States wished neither to anger the Arabs, for fear of losing valuable oil supplies, nor to alienate its ally Israel, supported at home by politically active American Jews. When Nasser declared neutrality in the Cold War, Dulles lost patience.

In 1956 the United States abruptly reneged on its offer to Egypt to help finance the Aswan Dam, a

SUEZ CRISIS

project to provide inexpensive electricity and water for Nile valley farmland. Nasser responded by nationalizing the British-owned Suez Canal, intending to use its profits to build the dam. Fully 75 percent of western Europe's oil came from the Middle East, most of it through the Suez. Fearing an interruption in trade, the British and French conspired with Israel to bring down Nasser. On October 29, 1956, the Israelis invaded Suez, joined two days later by British and French forces.

Eisenhower fumed. America's allies had not consulted him, and the president feared the invasion would cause Nasser to seek help from the Soviets, inviting them into the Middle East. Eisenhower sternly demanded that London, Paris, and Tel Aviv pull their troops out, and they did. Egypt took possession of the canal, the Soviets built the Aswan Dam, and Nasser became a hero. The United States countered Nasser by supporting the notoriously corrupt King Ibn Saud of Saudi Arabia, who renewed America's lease of an air base.

Washington officials worried that a vacuum existed in the Middle East and that the Soviets might fill

EISENHOWER DOCTRINE

it. To protect American interests there, the president proclaimed in the 1957 Eisenhower Doctrine that the United States would intervene in the Middle East if any government threatened by a communist takeover asked for help. In 1958 fourteen thousand American troops scrambled to quell a political dispute in Lebanon that Washington feared might be exploited by pro-Nasser groups or communists.

Cold War concerns also drove Eisenhower's policy in Vietnam. Despite substantial U.S. aid, the French

NATIONALIST VICTORY IN VIETNAM

lost steadily to the Vietminh. Finally, in early 1954, Ho's forces surrounded the French fortress at Dienbienphu in northwest Vietnam (see Map 30.1). The United States had advised and bankrolled the French, but had not committed troops to the war.

Eisenhower pressed the British to help form a coalition to address the Indochinese crisis, but they refused. At home, influential members of Congress—including Lyndon Baines Johnson of Texas, who as president would wage large-scale war in Vietnam—told Eisenhower they wanted "no more Koreas" and warned him against any U.S. military commitment. The issue became moot on May 7, when French defenders at Dienbienphu surrendered.

Peace talks, already under way in Geneva, brought Cold War and nationalist contenders together—the

GENEVA ACCORDS

United States, the Soviet Union, Britain, the People's Republic of China, Laos, Cambodia, and the competing Vietnamese regimes of Bao Dai and Ho Chi Minh. The 1954 Geneva accords, signed by France and Ho's Democratic Republic of Vietnam, temporarily divided Vietnam at the 17th parallel; Ho's government was confined to the North, Bao Dai's to the South. The 17th parallel was meant to serve as a military truce line; the country was scheduled to be reunified after national elections in 1956. In the meantime, neither North nor South was to join a military alliance or permit foreign bases on its soil.

Sure that the Geneva agreements would spell communist victory, the United States tried to undermine them. Soon after the conference, a CIA team undertook secret operations against the North, including commando raids across the 17th parallel. In the South, the United States helped Ngo Dinh Diem push Bao Dai aside and inaugurate the Republic of Vietnam. Diem was a dedicated nationalist and anticommunist, but he had little mass support. When Ho and some in the world community pressed for national elections, Diem and Eisenhower refused, fearing that the popular Vietminh leader would win. From 1955 to 1961, the Diem government received more than $1 billion in American aid, most of it military. American advisers organized and trained Diem's army, and American agriculturalists improved crops. Diem's Saigon regime became dependent on the United States for its very existence.

Diem proved a difficult ally. He abolished elections and appointed people beholden to him. He threw

NATIONAL LIBERATION FRONT

dissenters in jail and shut down newspapers criticizing him. Noncommunists and communists alike began to strike back at Diem's repressive government. In Hanoi, Ho's government in the late 1950s sent aid to southern insurgents, who assassinated hundreds of Diem's village officials. In late 1960, southern communists, at Hanoi's direction, organized the National Liberation Front (NLF), known as the Vietcong. The Vietcong in turn attracted other anti-Diem groups in the South. The Eisenhower administration, aware of Diem's shortcomings, affirmed its commitment to an independent, noncommunist South Vietnam.

Summary   *Online Study Center*   **ACE the Test**

The United States emerged from the Second World War as the preeminent world power. But Washington officials worried that the unstable international system, an unfriendly Soviet Union, and the decolonizing Third World could upset American plans for the postwar peace. Locked with the Soviet Union in a "Cold War," U.S. leaders marshaled their nation's superior resources to influence other countries. Foreign economic aid, atomic diplomacy, military alliances, client states, covert operations, propaganda, and cultural infiltration became the instruments of the Cold War, which began as a conflict over Europe's future but soon encompassed the globe.

America's international leadership was welcomed by those who feared Soviet intentions. The reconstruction of former enemies Japan and (West) Germany helped those nations recover swiftly and become staunch members of the Western alliance. But U.S. policy also sparked resistance. Communist countries condemned financial and atomic diplomacy, while Third World nations sought to undermine America's European allies and sometimes identified the United States as an imperial co-conspirator. On occasion, even America's allies bristled at a United States that boldly proclaimed itself economic master and global policeman and haughtily touted its hegemonic status.

At home, critics protested that Presidents Truman and Eisenhower exaggerated the communist threat, wasting U.S. assets on immoral foreign ventures. Still, these presidents and their successors held firm to the mission of creating a nonradical, capitalist, free-trade international order. Determined to contain Soviet expansion, fearful of domestic charges of being "soft on communism," they enlarged the U.S. sphere of influence and held the line against the Soviet Union and the People's Republic of China, and revolution everywhere. One consequence was a dramatic increase in presidential power over foreign affairs—what historian Arthur M. Schlesinger Jr. called "the Imperial Presidency"—as Congress ceded constitutional power.

The globalist perspective of the United States prompted Americans to interpret troubles in the developing world as Cold War conflicts, inspired, if not directed, by Soviet-backed communists. The intensity of the Cold War obscured for Americans the indigenous roots of most Third World troubles, as the wars in Korea and Vietnam attested. Nor could the United States abide developing nations' drive for economic independence—for gaining control of their own raw materials and economies. Intertwined in the global economy as importer, exporter, and investor, the United States read challenges from this "periphery" as threats to the American standard of living.

LEGACY FOR A PEOPLE AND A NATION
The National Security State

For decades, America's Cold War religion has been national security; its texts the Truman Doctrine, the "X" article, and NSC-68; and its cathedral the national security state. During the Cold War, embracing preparedness for total war, the U.S. government transformed itself into a huge military headquarters that interlocked with corporations and universities.

Overseen by the president and his National Security Council, the national security state's core, once called the National Military Establishment, in 1949 became the Department of Defense. This department ranks as a leading employer; its payroll by 2000 included 1.3 million people on active duty and almost 600,000 civilian personnel, giving it more employees than ExxonMobil, Ford, General Motors, and GE combined. Almost a quarter of a million of these troops and civilians served overseas, in 130 countries. Although national defense spending declined after the Cold War, it never fell below $290 billion. In the aftermath of the terrorist attacks of September 11, 2001, the military budget rose again, reaching $400 billion in 2003.

Joining the Department of Defense as instruments of national security policy were the Joint Chiefs of Staff, Central Intelligence Agency, and dozens more government bodies. The focus of all of these entities was finding the best means to combat real and potential threats from foreign governments. But what about threats from within? The terrorist attacks of September 2001 made starkly clear that enemies existed who, while perhaps beholden to a foreign entity, launched their attacks from inside the nation's borders. In 2002 President George W. Bush created the Department of Homeland Security, which would have 170,000 employees and would encompass all or part of twenty-two agencies, including the Coast Guard, the Customs Service, the Federal Emergency Management Administration, and the Internal Revenue Service. It would involve the biggest overhaul of the federal bureaucracy since the Department of Defense was created, and it signified a more expansive notion of national security.

In 1961 President Eisenhower had warned against a "military-industrial complex," while others feared a "warfare state." Despite the warnings, the national security state remained vigorous in the early twenty-first century, a lasting legacy of the early Cold War period for a people and a nation.

*A*MERICA AT MIDCENTURY 1945–1960

*E*venings after supper, when the sticky heat of the Georgia summer days ebbed, families on Nancy Circle enjoyed a walk. Parents stood chatting as children played.

In 1959 the twenty houses on Nancy Circle were a couple of years old. They stood on land once belonging to the Cherokees, in a development carved from the old Campbell plantation, along the route General William Tecumseh Sherman had taken in his march to the sea during the Civil War. Slaves picked cotton there a century before, but no African Americans lived in those homes.

Nancy Circle was part of a new suburban development in Smyrna, Georgia, northwest of Atlanta, but few residents worked in the city. Most traveled to the massive Lockheed Georgia airplane plant created, in large part, by Cold War defense spending. With three bedrooms for about $17,000, the houses were affordable to young families.

Children ran in and out of each other's houses and women gathered to drink coffee in the mornings after the men left for work. There were aerospace engineers, three career military men, an auto mechanic, and a musician. Only two women held paid jobs: one had almost-grown children and taught second grade, and the other was divorced and worked as a secretary. People were suspicious of her but liked her sister, born with dwarfism, who had left her job in a North Carolina textile mill to help care for her nephew. Two war brides—one Japanese and one German—lived in the neighborhood. The Japanese woman spoke little English; the German woman taught the girls in the neighborhood to crochet.

The people who lived on Nancy Circle read magazines criticizing the homogeneity and conformity of suburban life, but that wasn't their experience. On this single street, people from deep Appalachia lived next to people who had grown up in city tenement apartments, and women who'd done graduate work baked Christmas cookies with women who had not finished high school. These new suburbanites were creating for themselves a new world and a new

Shaping Postwar America

Domestic Politics in the Cold War Era

Cold War Fears and Anticommunism

The Struggle for Civil Rights

Creating a Middle-Class Nation

Men, Women, and Youth at Midcentury

LINKS TO THE WORLD
Barbie

The Limits of the Middle-Class Nation

LEGACY FOR A PEOPLE AND A NATION
The Pledge of Allegiance

Online Study Center
This icon will direct you to interactive map and primary source activities on the website
http://college.hmco.com/pic/nortonbrief7e

CHRONOLOGY

1945 • World War II ends

1946 • Marriage and birth rates skyrocket, creating baby boom
• More than 1 million veterans enroll in colleges under GI Bill
• More than 5 million U.S. workers go on strike

1947 • Taft-Hartley Act limits power of unions
• Truman orders loyalty investigation of 3 million government employees
• Mass-production techniques used to build Levittown houses

1948 • Truman issues executive order desegregating armed forces and federal government
• Truman elected president

1949 • Soviet Union explodes atomic bomb
• National Housing Act promises decent housing for all Americans

1950 • Korean War begins
• McCarthy alleges communists in government
• "Treaty of Detroit" creates model for new labor-management relations

1952 • Eisenhower elected president

1953 • Korean War ends
• Congress adopts termination policy for Native American tribes
• Rosenbergs executed as atomic spies

1954 • *Brown v. Board of Education* decision reverses "separate-but-equal" doctrine
• Senate condemns McCarthy

1955 • Montgomery bus boycott begins

1956 • Highway Act launches interstate highway system
• Eisenhower reelected
• Elvis Presley appears on *Ed Sullivan Show*

1957 • King elected first president of Southern Christian Leadership Conference
• School desegregation crisis in Little Rock, Arkansas
• Congress passes Civil Rights Act
• Soviet Union launches *Sputnik*

1958 • Congress passes National Defense Education Act

middle-class culture. Having grown up with the Great Depression and world war, these new suburbanites believed they had found good lives.

The United States had emerged from World War II stronger and more prosperous. Europe and Asia had been devastated, but America's farms, cities, and factories were intact. U.S. production capacity increased during the war, and the fight against fascism gave Americans a unity of purpose. Victory seemed to confirm their struggles. But memories of sixteen years of depression and war would continue to shape the choices Americans made in their private lives, domestic policies, and relations with the rest of the world.

In the postwar era, the actions of the federal government and the choices individual Americans made

began a profound reconfiguration of American society. Postwar social policies that sent millions of veterans to college on the GI Bill, linked the nation with interstate highways, fostered the growth of suburbs and the Sunbelt, and disrupted regional isolation helped to create a national middle-class culture encompassing an unprecedented majority of the nation's citizens. Countless individual decisions—to go to college, marry young, have a large family, move to the suburbs, start a business—were made possible by federal initiatives. Americans in the postwar era defined a new American Dream: one that centered on the family, a new level of material comfort and consumption, and a shared sense of belonging to a common culture.

Nevertheless, almost a quarter of Americans did not share in the postwar prosperity—but they were invisible to the middle-class majority. Rural poverty continued, and inner cities became increasingly impoverished as more affluent Americans moved to the suburbs and new migrants—poor black and white southerners, new immigrants from Mexico and Puerto Rico, Native Americans resettled by the federal government from tribal lands—arrived.

As class and ethnicity became less important in suburbia, race continued to divide Americans. The 1950s saw important federal actions to protect the civil rights of African Americans, including the Supreme Court's school desegregation decision in *Brown v. Board of Education*. African Americans increasingly took direct action, and in 1955, the year-long Montgomery bus boycott launched the modern civil rights movement.

The economic boom that began with the end of the war lasted twenty-five years. Although fears—of nuclear war, of returning hard times—lingered, new prosperity bred complacency by the late 1950s. The most significant domestic political ferment, in fact, was a byproduct of the Cold War: a ferocious anti-communism that narrowed the boundaries of acceptable dissent. Instead, by decade's end, people sought satisfaction in their families and in the consumer pleasures newly available to so many. ∎

Shaping Postwar America

*a*t the end of World War II, many Americans feared that the economy would plunge back into depression—and in the immediate aftermath of the war, unemployment rose and a wave of strikes rocked the nation. But dire predictions were wrong: the economy flourished, and Americans' standard of living improved. The GI Bill and other federal programs created new opportunities that fundamentally changed the nation.

As the end of the war approached and the American war machine slowed, factories began to lay off workers. Ten days after the victory over Japan, 1.8 million people nationwide received pink slips, and 640,000 filed for unemployment compensation. More than 15 million GIs awaited demobilization.

POSTWAR ECONOMIC UNCERTAINTY

In the spring of 1944—a year before V-E Day—Congress, anticipating a postwar crisis, unanimously passed the Servicemen's Readjustment Act, known as the GI Bill of Rights. It showed the nation's gratitude but also attempted to keep demobilized veterans from swamping the U.S. economy: year-long unemployment benefits meant they could be gradually absorbed into civilian employment, and higher-education benefits would keep men out of the job market. In winter 1945, congressional Democrats introduced the Full Employment Act guaranteeing work through public sector employment if necessary. By the time Truman signed it into law in early 1946, key provisions guaranteeing work had virtually disappeared. But the act reaffirmed the federal government's responsibility for managing the economy and created the Council of Economic Advisors to help prevent economic downturns.

Conversion to a peacetime economy hit workers hard, especially as the inflation rate skyrocketed. More than 5 million workers walked off the job the first year. Unions shut down the coal, automobile, steel, and electric industries and halted railroad and maritime transportation. So disruptive were the strikes that Americans began hoarding food and gasoline.

POSTWAR STRIKES AND THE TAFT-HARTLEY ACT

By spring 1946, Americans grew impatient with the strikes. When unions threatened a national railway strike, President Truman announced that if strikers in an industry vital to national security refused a presidential order to return to work, he would ask Congress to draft them into the armed forces. The Democratic Party would not offer unlimited support to organized labor.

Then, in 1947, the Taft-Hartley Act permitted states to enact right-to-work laws that outlawed "closed shops," in which all workers were required to join the union if a majority of their number favored a union shop. The law also mandated an eighty-day cooling-off period before unions initiated strikes imperiling national security. These restrictions limited unions' ability to expand their membership. Truman did not want to see union power so limited, but Congress passed the Taft-Hartley Act over Truman's veto.

Despite initial difficulties, the economy recovered quickly, fueled by consumer spending. Although Americans had brought home steady pay-

ECONOMIC GROWTH

checks during the war, they had had little on which to spend them. No new cars, for example, had been built since 1942. When new cars and appliances appeared at war's end, Americans were ready to buy. Because most factories around the world were in ruins, U.S. corporations expanded their global dominance and grew dramatically in size. America's ten largest corporations were in automobiles (GM, Ford, Chrysler), oil (Standard Oil of New Jersey, Mobil, Texaco), and electronics and communications (GE, IBM, IT&T, AT&T).

In the agricultural sector, new machines, such as mechanical cotton-, tobacco-, and grape-pickers and crop-dusting planes, revolutionized farming, and the increased use of fertilizers and pesticides raised the total value of farm output from $24.6 billion in 1945 to $38.4 billion in 1961. Large investors were drawn to agriculture by its increased profitability, and the average size of farms increased from 195 to 306 acres.

Economic growth was also fueled by government programs. By 1949, veterans received close to $4 billion in unemployment compensation, low-interest loans for homes or businesses, and—perhaps most significant—money for higher education.

Before the war, only about 7.5 percent of young Americans had gone to college. With GI benefits, almost half of America's returning veterans sought higher education. The resulting increase in the number of well-educated or technically trained workers benefited the American economy. And the flood of students and federal dollars into the nation's colleges and universities created a golden age for higher education.

Education created social mobility: children of barely literate menial laborers became white-collar professionals. The GI Bill fostered the emergence of a national middle-class culture, for as colleges exposed people to new ideas and experiences, students became less rooted in ethnic or regional cultures.

The end of the war brought a boom in marriage and birth rates. In 1946 the U.S. marriage rate was

BABY BOOM

higher than that of any other record-keeping nation (except Hungary). The birth rate soared, reversing the downward trend of the past 150 years. "Take the 3,548,000 babies born in 1950," wrote Sylvia F. Porter in her syndicated newspaper column. "Bundle them into a batch. . . . What do you get? Boom. The biggest, boomiest boom ever known in history. Just imagine how much these extra people, these new markets, will absorb—in food, clothing, in gadgets, in housing, in services." Although the baby boom peaked in 1957, more than 4 million babies were born every year until 1965 (see Figure 29.1). As this vast cohort

Figure 29.1   Birth Rate, 1945–1964

The birth rate began to rise in 1942 and 1943, but it skyrocketed during the postwar years beginning in 1946, reaching its peak in 1957. From 1954 to 1964, the United States recorded more than 4 million births every year. (Source: Adapted from U.S. Bureau of the Census, *Historical Statistics of the United States, Colonial Times to 1970,* Bicentennial Edition [Washington, D.C.: U.S. Government Printing Office, 1975], p. 49.)

grew older, it had successive impacts on housing, schools, fads, popular music, the job market, and retirement funds, including Social Security.

Scarcely any new housing had been built since the 1920s. Almost 2 million families were doubled up with relatives in 1948; 50,000 people were living in Quonset huts, and housing was so tight in Chicago that 250 used trolley cars were sold as homes.

In the postwar years, white Americans moved to the suburbs. Some escaped crowded cities. People from rural areas moved closer to city jobs. Some white families left urban neighborhoods because African American families were moving in. Most, however, simply wanted to own their own homes, and suburban developments offered affordable housing. Although suburban development predated World War II, the massive migration of 18 million Americans to the suburbs between 1950 and 1960 was on a wholly different scale (see Table 29.1).

SUBURBANIZATION

In 1947 builder William Levitt adapted Henry Ford's assembly-line methods to revolutionize home building. By 1949, instead of 4 or 5 custom homes per year, Levitt's company built 180 houses a week. They were very basic: four and a half rooms on a 60-by-100-foot lot, all with identical floor plans disguised by four different exteriors. By rotating seven paint colors, Levitt guaranteed that only one in every twenty-eight houses would be identical. The basic house sold for $7,990. Other homebuilders quickly adopted Levitt's techniques.

Suburban development happened on such a large scale because federal policies encouraged it. The Federal Housing Administration (FHA) offered low-interest mortgages. New highways also promoted suburban development. Congress authorized construction of a 37,000-mile chain of highways in 1947 and in 1956 passed the Highway Act to create a 42,500-mile interstate highway system. Intended to facilitate commerce and rapid mobilization of the military, highways allowed workers to live farther from their jobs in central cities.

Postwar federal programs did not benefit all Americans equally. First, federal policies often assisted men at the expense of women. As industry laid off civilian workers to make room for veterans, women lost their jobs at a rate 75 percent higher than men. Many stayed in the work force but were pushed into lower-paying jobs. Universities made room for veterans on the GI Bill by excluding qualified women students.

INEQUALITY IN BENEFITS

Inequities were also based on race. African American, Native American, Mexican American, and Asian American veterans, like European American veterans, received educational benefits and hiring preference in civil service jobs. But war workers from these groups were among the first laid off. Federal loan officers and bankers often labeled African American or racially mixed neighborhoods "high risk," denying mortgages to racial minorities regardless of individual credit-worthiness. This practice, called "redlining" because such neighborhoods were outlined in red on lenders' maps, kept African Americans and many Hispanics from enjoying the economic explosion of the postwar era, as white families who bought homes with federally guaranteed mortgages saw their small investments grow dramatically over the years.

Domestic Politics in the Cold War Era

lthough the major social and economic transformations in postwar America were largely due to federal policies and programs, foreign affairs were politically paramount, given the challenges of the expanding Cold War. Domestically, Truman attempted to build on the New Deal's liberal

TABLE 29.1

Geographic Distribution of the U.S. Population, 1930–1970 (in Percentages)

Year	Central Cities	Suburbs	Rural Areas and Small Towns
1930	31.8%	18.0%	50.2%
1940	31.6	19.5	48.9
1950	32.3	23.8	43.9
1960	32.6	30.7	36.7
1970	31.4	37.6	31.0

Source: Adapted from U.S. Bureau of the Census, *Decennial Censuses, 1930–1970* (Washington, D.C.: U.S. Government Printing Office).

agenda, while Eisenhower called for balanced budgets and business-friendly policies. But neither administration approached the legislative activism of the New Deal.

HARRY S TRUMAN AND POSTWAR LIBERALISM

Harry Truman, a former haberdasher from Missouri, never expected to be president. In 1944, when Franklin Roosevelt asked him to be his vice-presidential candidate, he almost refused. But with the war in its fourth year, the busy president had little time for his new vice president and left Truman in the dark about everything from the Manhattan Project to plans for postwar domestic policy. When Roosevelt died suddenly in April 1945, Truman was unprepared to take his place.

Truman nevertheless stepped forward, placing a sign on his desk: "The Buck Stops Here." Most of Truman's presidency focused on foreign relations, as he led the nation through the end of World War II into the Cold War with the Soviet Union. Domestically, he oversaw reconversion from war to peace and attempted to keep a liberal agenda—the legacy of Roosevelt's New Deal—alive.

In his 1944 State of the Union address, Roosevelt offered Americans a "Second Bill of Rights": the right to employment, healthcare, education, food, and housing. This notion of government responsibility was the cornerstone of postwar liberalism. Truman proposed an increase in the minimum wage and national housing legislation offering loans for mortgages, and he supported the Full Employment Act. To pay for his proposed social welfare programs, he gambled that full employment would generate sufficient tax revenue and that consumer spending would fuel economic growth.

The gamble paid off, but the conservative coalition of Republicans and southern Democrats that stalled Roosevelt's New Deal legislation in the late 1930s was less inclined to support Truman. Congress gutted the Full Employment Act, refused to raise the minimum wage, and passed the anti-union Taft-Hartley Act. With powerful congressional opposition, Truman had little chance of major legislative accomplishments. As Truman presided over the rocky transition from a wartime to a peacetime economy, he faced massive inflation (briefly hitting 35 percent), shortages of consumer goods, and a wave of strikes that slowed production and drove prices up. His ap-

proval rating plunged from 87 percent in late 1945 to 32 percent in 1946.

1948 ELECTION

By 1948 it seemed that Republicans would win the White House in November, and the party nominated Thomas Dewey, the man Roosevelt defeated in 1944, as its candidate. Republicans hoped schisms in the Democratic Party would ensure victory. Former New Dealer Henry Wallace ran for president on the Progressive Party ticket, advocating friendly relations with the Soviet Union, racial desegregation, and nationalization of basic industries. A fourth party, the Dixiecrats (States' Rights Democratic Party), was organized by white southerners who left the 1948 Democratic convention when it adopted a pro–civil rights plank. They nominated the fiercely segregationist governor of South Carolina, Strom Thurmond.

Truman refused to give up. He resorted to red-baiting, denouncing "Henry Wallace and his communists." Most important, he appealed to the burgeoning population of African American voters in northern cities, becoming the first presidential candidate to campaign in Harlem. In the end, Truman prevailed. Roosevelt's New Deal coalition—African Americans, union members, northern urban voters, and most southern whites—had endured.

TRUMAN'S FAIR DEAL

In his 1949 State of the Union message, Truman stated, "I expect to give every segment of our population a fair deal." Unlike Roosevelt, Truman pushed legislation supporting the civil rights of African Americans, including antilynching laws. He proposed national health insurance and federal aid for education. However, southern conservatives in Congress destroyed his civil rights legislation. The American Medical Association denounced his health insurance plan as "socialized medicine," and the Roman Catholic Church opposed educational assistance because it would not include parochial schools.

When Truman ordered troops to Korea in June 1950 (see Chapter 28), Americans grumbled as the nation again mobilized for war. People remembered the shortages of the previous war and stocked up on sugar, coffee, and canned goods. Fueled by panic buying, inflation rose again. An unpopular war and charges of influence peddling by Truman's cronies pushed the president's public approval rating to an all-time low of 23 percent in 1951, where it stayed for a year.

"It's Time for a Change" was the Republican campaign slogan in 1952, and voters agreed. Americans hoped that candidate General

EISENHOWER'S DYNAMIC CONSERVATISM

Dwight D. Eisenhower, the immensely popular World War II hero, could end the Korean War. Eisenhower appealed to moderates in both parties (the Democrats tried to recruit him as their presidential candidate).

Smiling Ike, with his folksy style, garbled syntax, and frequent escapes to the golf course, was no stranger to hard work. His low-key style played down his role as politician and highlighted his role as chief of state. Relying heavily on his staff, Eisenhower delegated authority to cabinet members and sometimes appeared out of touch with his own government, but he was not, and he remained a popular president.

With a Republican in the White House for the first time in twenty years, conservatives hoped to roll back New Deal programs such as Social Security. Instead, Eisenhower adopted what he called "dynamic conservatism": being "conservative when it comes to money and liberal when it comes to human beings." In 1954 Eisenhower signed into law amendments to the Social Security Act that raised benefits and added 7.5 million workers, mostly self-employed farmers, to its rolls. His administration, motivated by Cold War fears, also increased government funding for education. When the Soviet Union launched *Sputnik,* the first earth-orbiting satellite, in 1957 (and America's first launch exploded seconds after liftoff), education became an issue of national security. Congress responded in 1958 with the National Defense Education Act (NDEA), which funded enrichment of school programs in mathematics, foreign languages, and the sciences and offered fellowships and loans to college students.

Overall, Eisenhower's administration was an ally of business and industry. The Eisenhower tax reform

GROWTH OF THE MILITARY-INDUSTRIAL COMPLEX

bill raised business depreciation allowances, and the Atomic Energy Act of 1954 allowed private companies to own reactors and nuclear materials to produce electricity. Eisenhower balanced only three of his eight budgets, turning to deficit spending to cushion the impact of three recessions (in

1953–1954, 1957–1958, and 1960–1961) and fund America's global activities. In 1959 federal expenditures climbed to $92 billion, about half of which went to the military, mostly for developing new weapons.

Before leaving office in 1961 at the end of his second term, Eisenhower delivered his farewell address. Because of the Cold War, he observed, the United States had a large standing army—3.5 million men—and spent ever greater percentages of its budget developing weapons. Condemning the new "conjunction of an immense military establishment and a large arms industry," Eisenhower warned, "The total influence—economic, political, even spiritual—is felt in every city, every statehouse, every office of the federal government" and threatened the nation's democratic process. Eisenhower, former five-star general and war hero, urged Americans to "guard against . . . the military-industrial complex."

Cold War Fears and Anticommunism

International relations had a profound influence on America's domestic politics in the years following World War II. Americans were frightened by Cold War tensions between the United States and the Soviet Union, and their reasonable fears spilled over into anticommunist demagoguery and witch hunts, allowing the trampling of civil liberties, the suppression of dissent, and the persecution of innocent Americans.

Anticommunism was not new: a "red scare" had swept the nation following the Russian Revolution of 1917, and opponents of America's labor movement had used charges of communism to block unionization through the 1930s. Many saw the Soviet Union's virtual takeover of eastern Europe after World War II as an alarming parallel to Nazi Germany's takeover of neighboring states. People remembered the failure of "appeasement" at Munich and worried about being "too soft" toward the Soviet Union.

In addition, American intelligence officers in a top-secret project code-named "Venona" decrypted

ESPIONAGE AND NUCLEAR FEARS

almost three thousand Soviet telegraphic cables that proved spies had infiltrated U.S. government agencies and nuclear programs. (The United

States also had spies within the Soviet Union.) To prevent the Soviets from realizing their codes were compromised, intelligence officials withheld this evidence from the American public.

Fear of nuclear war contributed to American anticommunism. When the Soviet Union joined the United States in possessing atomic weapons in 1949, President Truman initiated a national atomic civil defense program, advising: "I cannot tell you when or where the attack will come or that it will come at all. I can only remind you that we must be ready when it does come." Children practiced "duck-and-cover" positions in school classrooms, learning how to shield their faces from the atomic flash. *Life* magazine featured backyard fallout shelters. Americans worried that the United States was vulnerable to attack.

American leaders did not always draw a sufficient line between prudent attempts to prevent Soviet

THE POLITICS OF ANTICOMMUNISM

spies from infiltrating government agencies and anticommunist scaremongering. Republican politicians effectively used red-baiting against Democratic opponents, eventually targeting the Truman administration. In 1947 President Truman ordered investigations into the loyalty of more than 3 million government employees. As anticommunist hysteria grew, the government discharged people deemed "security risks," among them alcoholics, homosexuals, and debtors thought susceptible to blackmail. In most cases, there was no evidence of disloyalty.

Leading the anticommunist crusade was the House Un-American Activities Committee (popularly known as HUAC). Created in 1938 to investigate "subversive and un-American propaganda," the committee lost credibility by charging that film stars, including eight-year-old Shirley Temple, were Communist Party dupes. By 1947, HUAC attacked Hollywood again, using Federal Bureau of Investigation (FBI) files and testimony of people such as Screen Actors Guild president Ronald Reagan (a secret informant for the FBI). Screenwriters and directors known as the "Hollywood Ten" were sent to prison when they refused to "name names" of suspected communists. At least a dozen others committed suicide. Studios blacklisted screenwriters, directors, and even makeup artists suspected of communist affiliations. With no evidence of wrongdoing, careers were ruined.

University professors were targeted in 1949, when HUAC demanded lists of the textbooks used at

MCCARTHYISM AND THE GROWING "WITCH HUNT"

eighty-one universities. When the board of regents at the University of California, Berkeley, instituted a loyalty oath and fired twenty-six faculty members resisting on principle, protests nationwide forced the regents to back down. But many professors began to downplay controversial material in their courses. In the labor movement, the CIO expelled eleven unions, over 900,000 members, for alleged communist domination. The red panic reached its nadir in February 1950, when Joseph R. McCarthy of Wisconsin, a relatively obscure U.S. senator, charged that the U.S. State Department was "thoroughly infested with Communists." McCarthy first claimed there were 205 communists in the State Department, then 57, then 81. He had a severe drinking problem and a record of dishonesty as a lawyer and judge. But McCarthy crystallized Americans' anxieties, and anticommunist excesses came to be known as "McCarthyism."

The anticommunist crusade was embraced by labor union officials, religious leaders, and the media, as well as by politicians. Women in New York who lobbied for the continuation of wartime daycare programs were denounced as communists by the *New York World Telegram*.

In such a climate, most public figures found it too risky to stand up against McCarthyist tactics. In 1950,

ANTICOMMUNISM IN CONGRESS

with bipartisan support, Congress passed the Internal Security (McCarran) Act, which required members of "Communist-front" organizations to register with the government and prohibited them from holding government jobs or traveling abroad. In 1954 the Senate passed the Communist Control Act sponsored by Senator Hubert H. Humphrey of Minnesota, which effectively made membership in the Communist Party illegal.

In 1948 Congressman Richard Nixon of California, a member of HUAC, was propelled onto the national stage when he accused former State Department official Alger Hiss of espionage. In 1950 Hiss was convicted of lying about his contacts with Soviet agents. That same year, Ethel and Julius Rosenberg were arrested for passing atomic secrets to the Soviets;

they were found guilty of treason and executed in 1953. For decades, many historians believed that the Rosenbergs were victims of a witch hunt, but there was evidence of Julius Rosenberg's guilt in cables decrypted by the Venona Project. They were not presented at trial for national security reasons and remained top secret until 1995.

The excesses of Cold War anticommunism waned when Senator McCarthy was discredited on national

THE WANING OF THE RED SCARE

television in 1954. McCarthy was a master at using the press and making sensational accusations—front-page material—just before reporters' deadlines. When McCarthy's charges proved untrue, retractions appeared in the back pages of the newspapers.

But McCarthy's crucial mistake was charging on television that the army was shielding communists, citing the case of one army dentist. The so-called Army-McCarthy hearings, held by a Senate subcommittee in 1954, became a showcase for the senator's abusive treatment of witnesses. McCarthy, apparently drunk, alternately ranted and slurred his words. When army counsel Joseph Welch protested, "Have you no sense of decency, sir?" the gallery erupted in applause. In December 1954, the Senate voted to "condemn" McCarthy for sullying the dignity of Congress. He remained a senator, but exhaustion and alcohol took their toll, and he died in 1957 at the age of forty-eight. With McCarthy discredited, the most virulent anticommunism had run its course.

≈ **Online Study Center**   **Improve Your Grade**

Primary Source: Army-McCarthy Hearings

The Struggle for Civil Rights

*T*he Cold War also shaped African American struggles for social justice and the nation's responses to them. As the Soviet Union pointed out, the United States could hardly pose as the leader of the free world or condemn the denial of human rights in eastern Europe while practicing segregation. Nor could the United States convince new African and Asian nations of its dedication to human rights if African Americans were subjected to segregation, discrimination, disfranchisement, and racial violence. Many Americans, however, viewed such criticism as a

Soviet-inspired attempt to weaken the United States. The FBI and local law enforcement commonly used anticommunist fears to justify attacking civil rights activists. In this heated environment, African Americans struggled to seize the political initiative.

African Americans who had helped win the Second World War were determined to enjoy better lives in

GROWING BLACK POLITICAL POWER

postwar America. Politicians such as Harry Truman were paying attention to black aspirations, especially as black voters in some urban-industrial states began to influence the balance of power.

President Truman had compelling political reasons for supporting African American civil rights and genuinely believed that every American, regardless of race, should enjoy full citizenship. Truman was disturbed by a resurgence of racial terrorism, as a revived Ku Klux Klan burned crosses and murdered blacks seeking civil rights after World War II. But what really horrified Truman was the report that police in Aiken, South Carolina, had gouged out the eyes of a black sergeant just three hours after his army discharge. In December 1946, Truman signed an executive order establishing the President's Committee on Civil Rights. Its report, *To Secure These Rights*, would become the civil rights movement agenda for the next twenty years. It called for antilynching and antisegregation legislation and for laws guaranteeing voting rights and equal employment opportunity. For the first time since Reconstruction, a president had acknowledged the federal government's responsibility to protect blacks and strive for racial equality.

In 1948 Truman issued two executive orders ending racial discrimination in the federal government. One proclaimed a policy of "fair employment throughout the federal establishment" and created the Employment Board of the Civil Service Commission to hear discrimination charges. The other ordered the racial desegregation of the armed forces. Segregated units were phased out by the Korean War.

At the same time, African Americans challenged racial discrimination in the courts. In 1939 the

SCHOOL DESEGREGATION AND SUPREME COURT VICTORIES

NAACP established its Legal Defense and Education Fund under Charles Hamilton Houston and Thurgood Marshall. By the 1940s, Marshall (who in 1967 would become the first African American

Supreme Court justice) and his colleagues worked to destroy the separate-but-equal doctrine established in *Plessy v. Ferguson* (1896). Because of NAACP lawsuits, African Americans gained admission to professional and graduate schools at many formerly segregated state universities. The NAACP also won victories through the Supreme Court in *Smith v. Allwright* (1944), which outlawed the whites-only primaries held by the Democratic Party in some southern states; *Morgan v. Virginia* (1946), which struck down segregation in interstate bus transportation; and *Shelley v. Kraemer* (1948), which held that racially restrictive covenants (private agreements among white homeowners not to sell to blacks) could not legally be enforced.

Changing social attitudes accompanied these gains. Gunnar Myrdal's social science study *An American Dilemma* (1944) and Richard Wright's novel *Native Son* (1940) and his autobiography, *Black Boy* (1945), increased white awareness of racial injustice. A new and visible black middle class emerged, composed of college-educated activists, veterans, and union workers. Blacks and whites worked together in CIO unions and service organizations such as the National Council of Churches. In 1947 a black baseball player, Jackie Robinson, broke the major league color barrier and electrified Brooklyn Dodgers fans.

Even so, blacks continued to suffer disfranchisement, job discrimination, and violence, including the bombing murder in 1951 of the Florida state director of the NAACP and his wife. But in 1954 the NAACP won a historic victory. *Brown v. Board of Education of Topeka*, which Thurgood Marshall argued, incorporated school desegregation cases from several states. Written by Chief Justice Earl Warren, the Court's unanimous decision concluded that "in the field of public education the doctrine of 'separate but equal' has no place. Separate educational facilities are inherently unequal." But the ruling that overturned *Plessy v. Ferguson* did not demand immediate compliance. A year later the Court ordered school desegregation, but without a timetable, southern states resisted.

The forces of white resistance urged southern communities to defy the Court. The Klan experienced

WHITE RESISTANCE

another resurgence, and white violence against blacks increased. In 1955 Emmett Till, a fourteen-year-old from Chicago, was murdered by white men in Mississippi who took offense at the way he spoke to a white woman. Business and professional people created White Citizens' Councils, known familiarly as "uptown Ku Klux Klans," and used economic power against black civil rights activists. When FBI director J. Edgar Hoover briefed President Eisenhower on southern racial tensions in 1956, he warned of communist influences among civil rights activists, and even suggested that Citizens' Councils might "control the rising tension."

White resistance also mounted in northern cities, such as Chicago, where the African American population increased due to migration from 275,000 to 800,000 between 1940 and 1960. The newcomers found good jobs and enjoyed political power, but faced housing segregation. So racially divided was Chicago that the U.S. Commission on Civil Rights in 1959 described it as "the most residentially segregated city in the nation." Other northern cities were not far behind.

Although President Eisenhower disapproved of racial segregation, he objected to "compulsory federal

FEDERAL AUTHORITY AND STATES' RIGHTS

law," believing instead that race relations would improve "only if [desegregation] starts locally." He also feared that the ugly public confrontations over desegregation would jeopardize Republican inroads in the South. Thus, Eisenhower did not state forthrightly that the federal government would enforce the *Brown* decision as law.

Events in Little Rock, Arkansas, forced the president to get involved. In September 1957 Arkansas governor Orval E. Faubus defied court-ordered desegregation for Little Rock's Central High School, saying on television that "blood would run in the streets" if black students tried to enter the high school. Eight black teenagers tried to enter Central High but were turned away by the Arkansas National Guard. The ninth was surrounded by jeering whites and narrowly escaped the mob with the help of a sympathetic white woman.

The "Little Rock Nine" entered Central High more than two weeks later, after a federal judge intervened. Television broadcast the scene to the world. Eisenhower, fearing violence, nationalized the Arkansas National Guard (placing it under federal, not state, control) and dispatched one thousand army paratroopers to guard the students for the rest of the year. Eisenhower's use of federal power was a critical step toward racial equality, directly confronting the conflict between federal authority and states' rights. However, the state triumphed the following year when Faubus closed all public high schools in Little Rock rather than desegregate them.

By the mid-1950s, African Americans were increasingly engaged in a grassroots struggle for civil rights. In 1955 Rosa Parks, a department store seamstress and long-time NAACP activist, was arrested when she refused to give up her seat to a white man on a public bus in Montgomery, Alabama. Her arrest enabled local black women's organizations and civil rights groups to organize a boycott of the city's bus system. They selected Martin Luther King Jr., a recently ordained minister, as their leader. King launched the boycott declaring, "If we are wrong, the Constitution is wrong. If we are wrong, God Almighty is wrong. . . . If we are wrong, justice is a lie."

MONTGOMERY BUS BOYCOTT

Martin Luther King Jr. was a twenty-six-year-old Baptist minister with a recent Ph.D. from Boston University. Schooled in the teachings of India's leader Mohandas K. Gandhi, King believed in nonviolent civil disobedience as a vehicle to focus the nation's attention on the immorality of Jim Crow.

During the year-long Montgomery bus boycott, blacks rallied in their churches. They maintained their boycott through heavy rains and steamy summer heat, often walking miles a day. With the bus company near bankruptcy and downtown merchants hurt by declining sales, city officials adopted harassment tactics to end the boycott. But the black people of Montgomery persevered: thirteen months later, the Supreme Court declared Alabama's bus segregation laws unconstitutional.

The boycott propelled King to the forefront of a new grassroots civil rights activism, with black churches playing a major role. In 1957 he became the first president of the Southern Christian Leadership Conference (SCLC), organized to coordinate civil rights activities. That same year, Congress passed the first Civil Rights Act since Reconstruction, creating the Commission on Civil Rights to investigate sys-

■ In 1957 white teenagers in Little Rock, Arkansas, angrily confront African American students who, under federal court order, are attempting to enter, and thus desegregate, Central High School. The Supreme Court's *Brown* decision of 1954 was resisted by whites throughout the South. (AP/Wide World Photos, Inc.)

tematic discrimination, such as in voting. This measure proved ineffective; however, with success in Montgomery and gains in the Supreme Court, African Americans were poised for a major civil rights movement in the decade to come.

Creating a Middle-Class Nation

Despite resistance to civil rights in the 1950s, the United States was becoming increasingly inclusive. National prosperity offered more Americans material comfort and economic security—entrance into an economic middle class. Old European ethnic identities faded as an ever smaller percentage of America's people were first- or second-generation immigrants. In the new suburbs, people from different backgrounds worked together to create communities. Middle-class Americans increasingly looked to national media for advice on matters ranging from how to celebrate Thanksgiving to how to raise children. New opportunities for consumption—whether teenage fads or suburban ranch-style homes—also tied disparate Americans together. In the postwar years, a new middle-class way of life was transforming the United States.

During the 1950s, sustained economic growth created unprecedented levels of prosperity and economic security. In great part, the boom was driven by consumer spending, as Americans eagerly bought goods unavailable during the war, and industries expanded production. As the Cold War deepened, government spending for defense created jobs and further stimulated the economy.

Prosperity for More Americans

A new era of peaceful labor relations helped bring prosperity to more Americans. By 1950, the United Auto Workers (UAW) and General Motors led the way for other corporations in providing workers with health insurance, pension plans, and guaranteed cost-of-living adjustments, or COLAs. The 1950 agreement gave GM's workers a five-year contract with regular wage increases tied to corporate productivity. With wage increases linked to productivity, labor cast its lot with management: workplace stability and efficiency, not strikes, would boost wages. During the 1950s, wages and benefits propelled union families into the ranks of the middle class.

During World War II, new defense plants and military training camps channeled federal money to the South, stimulating economic growth. In the postwar era, massive defense spending continued to shift economic development to the South and Southwest—the Sunbelt (see Map 29.1). Government actions—including generous tax breaks for oil companies, siting of military bases, and defense and aerospace contracts—were crucial to the region's new prosperity.

The Sunbelt and Economic Growth

The Sunbelt's spectacular growth was due to agribusiness, the oil industry, real-estate development, and recreation. Sunbelt states aggressively—and successfully—sought foreign investment and drew industry with lower taxes and heating bills as well as right-to-work laws outlawing closed shops. The development of air-conditioning was also crucial, making bearable even the hottest summer days. Houston, Phoenix, Los Angeles, San Diego, Dallas, and Miami all boomed, and by 1963 California was the most populous state in America.

Cold War military and aerospace spending created a need for highly educated scientists, engineers, and other white-collar professionals. By the early 1960s, universities and academic researchers received several billion dollars in space program research funding alone. Their research transformed American industry and society with inventions like the transistor in the 1950s, which sparked the computer revolution, and everyday consumer goods like the transistor radio.

By the 1950s, America was becoming a middle-class nation. Unionized blue-collar workers gained middle-class incomes, and veterans with GI Bill college educations swelled the growing managerial and professional class. In 1956, for the first time, the United States had more white-collar workers than blue-collar workers, and most families—60 percent—had incomes in the middle-class range (approximately $3,000 to $9,000 a year in the mid-1950s).

A New Middle-Class Culture

Paradoxically, the strength of unions in the postwar era contributed to a decline in working-class identity: as large numbers of blue-collar workers participated in suburban middle-class culture, the lines separating working class and middle class seemed less important. Increasingly, a family's standard of living mattered more than what sort of work made the

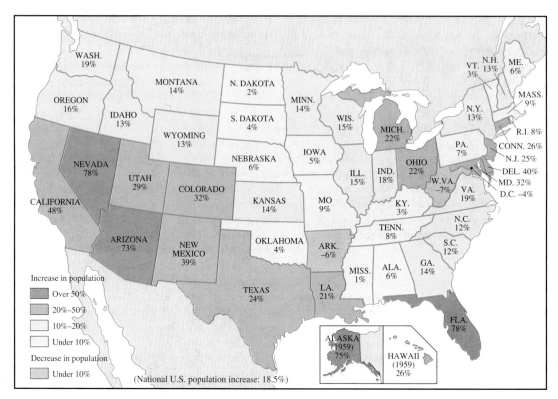

Map 29.1   Rise of the Sunbelt, 1950–1960

The years after the Second World War saw a continuation of the migration of
Americans to the Sunbelt states of the Southwest and the West Coast.

standard of living possible. Although people of color
did not share equally in America's postwar prosperity,
many middle-income African Americans, Latinos, and
Asian Americans did participate in middle-class culture.

The emergence of a national middle-class culture
was possible, in part, because America's population

*WHITENESS AND
NATIONAL
CULTURE*

was more homogeneous in the 1950s
than before or since. In the nineteenth and early twentieth centuries,
the United States had restricted or
prohibited immigration from Asia,
Africa, and Latin America while accepting millions of Europeans to America's shores.
This large-scale European immigration was shut off
in the 1920s, so that by 1960, only 5.7 percent of
Americans were foreign born (compared with approximately 15 percent in 1910 and 10 percent in
2000). In 1950, 88 percent of Americans were of Eu-

ropean ancestry (compared with 69 percent in 2000),
10 percent of the population was African American,
2 percent was Hispanic, and Native Americans and
Asian Americans each accounted for about one-fifth
of 1 percent.

Although the new suburbs were peopled mostly
by white families, these suburbs were more diverse
than the communities from which their residents had
come. America's small towns and urban ethnic enclaves
were homogeneous and intolerant of challenges to
traditional ways. In the suburbs, paradoxically, many
people encountered different customs and beliefs, but
new suburbanites frequently adopted the norms of
the developing national middle class.

Because many white Americans were new to the
middle class, they were uncertain about what was ex-

TELEVISION

pected of them and turned to the
national mass media for answers.

Women's magazines helped housewives replace the ethnic and regional dishes with "American" recipes created from national brand-name products—such as casseroles made with Campbell's cream of mushroom soup. Television also fostered America's shared national culture. Although televisions cost about $300—the equivalent of $2,000 today—almost half of American homes had them by 1953, and ownership rose to 90 percent by 1960.

On television, suburban families such as the Andersons (*Father Knows Best*) and the Cleavers (*Leave It to Beaver*) ate at a properly set dining room table. June Cleaver did housework in carefully ironed dresses. Every crisis was resolved through paternal wisdom. These popular family situation comedies reinforced the suburban middle-class ideal many American families sought.

The "middle-classness" of television programming was due in part to advertising. Corporations buying airtime did not want to offend potential consumers. Thus, while African American musician Nat King Cole drew millions of viewers to his NBC show, it could not find a sponsor because companies feared that being linked to a black performer would hurt sales among whites, especially in the South. Since African Americans made up only about 10 percent of the population and often had little disposable income, they did not influence advertising decisions. The *Nat King Cole Show* was canceled within a year; it was a decade before the networks again anchored a show around a black performer.

With only three TV networks available—ABC, CBS, and NBC—at any one time 70 percent or more of all viewers might be watching the same popular program. (In the early twenty-first century, the most popular shows might attract 12 percent of the viewing audience.) Television gave Americans a shared set of experiences and helped create a homogeneous, white-focused, middle-class culture.

Americans also found common ground in a new abundance of consumer goods. After decades of scarcity, Americans had a dazzling array of consumer goods from which to choose, and even utilitarian objects got two-tone paint jobs or rocket-ship details. People used consumer choices to express personal identities and claim status. Cars, more than anything else, embodied consumer fantasies. Expensive Cadillacs were the

CONSUMER CULTURE

first to develop tailfins, soon added to midrange Chevys, Fords, and Plymouths. Americans spent $65 billion on automobiles in 1955—equivalent to almost 20 percent of the gross national product. To pay for cars, suburban houses, and modern appliances, consumer debt rose from $5.7 billion in 1945 to $58 billion in 1961.

The uncertainties of the nuclear age likely contributed to the resurgence of religion, as church membership doubled (primarily in mainline Christian churches) between the end of World War II and the early 1960s. The media played a role, as preachers such as Billy Graham created national congregations from television audiences, preaching a message that combined salvation with Cold War patriotism. Local churches and synagogues offered new suburbanites a sense of community, celebrating life's rituals and supporting the sick and bereaved, who were often far from their extended families and old communities.

RELIGION

Men, Women, and Youth at Midcentury

*H*aving survived the Great Depression and a world war, many Americans pursued "the good life" and sought refuge from the Cold War through homes and families. They saw their familial commitment as an expression of faith in the future. Yet despite the satisfactions many Americans found in family life, both men and women felt limited by social pressures to conform to narrowly defined gender roles.

During the 1950s, few Americans remained single, and most people married very young. By 1959, almost half of American brides were younger than nineteen; their husbands were usually only a year or so older. Early marriage was endorsed by experts and approved by most parents, in part to prevent premarital sex. As Americans accepted psychotherapeutic insights, they worried not only that premarital sex might leave the young woman pregnant but that the experience could damage her psychologically so she would never adjust to "normal" marital relations. One popular women's

MARRIAGE AND FAMILIES

magazine argued, "When two people are ready for sexual intercourse at the fully human level they are ready for marriage. . . . And society has no right to stand in their way."

Many young couples found freedom from parental authority by marrying. Most newlyweds quickly had babies—an average of three—completing their families in their twenties. Birth control (condoms and diaphragms) was widely available and used, as couples planned the size of their families. Two children were the American ideal in 1940; by 1960, most couples wanted four. About 88 percent of children under age eighteen lived with two parents (in 2000, the figure was 69 percent), and fewer were born outside marriage; only 3.9 percent of births were to unmarried women in 1950 (compared with more than one-third of births in 2000). As late as 1960, there were only 9 divorces per 1,000 married couples.

In fifties families, men and women usually adopted distinct roles, with male breadwinners and female homemakers. Contemporary commentators insisted this was based on essential differences between the sexes. In fact, the economic structure and cultural values of postwar America determined the choices available to men and women.

GENDER ROLES IN FIFTIES FAMILIES

During the 1950s, it was possible for many families to live in modest middle-class comfort on one (male) salary. Good childcare was rarely available, and fewer families lived close to relatives. Childcare experts, including Dr. Spock, whose 1946 *Baby and Child Care* sold millions of copies, insisted that a mother's full-time attention was necessary to her child's well-being. Because of hiring discrimination, women who could afford to stay home often didn't find the jobs available to them attractive enough to justify juggling cooking and housework too. Instead, America's schools and religious institutions benefited immensely from women's volunteer labor.

Suburban domesticity left many women feeling isolated from the larger world their husbands inhabited. The popular belief that one should find complete emotional satisfaction in private life put unrealistic pressures on marriages. And despite near-universal celebration of women's domestic roles, many women were manag-

WOMEN AND WORK

ing both job and family responsibilities (see Figure 29.2). Twice as many women were employed in 1960 as in 1940, including 39 percent of women with children between the ages of six and seventeen. Most worked part time for a specific family goal, like a new car or college tuition. These jobs were in service to the family, not a means to independence from it.

Figure 29.2   Marital Distribution of the Female Labor Force, 1944–1970

The composition of the female labor force changed dramatically from 1944 to 1970. In 1944, 41 percent of women in the labor force were single; in 1970, only 22 percent were single. During the same years, the percentage of the female labor force who had a husband in the home jumped from 34 to 59. The percentage who were widowed or divorced remained about the same from 1944 to 1970.   (Source: Adapted from U.S. Bureau of the Census, *Historical Statistics of the United States, Colonial Times to 1970*, Bicentennial Edition [Washington, D.C.: U.S. Government Printing Office, 1975], p. 133.)

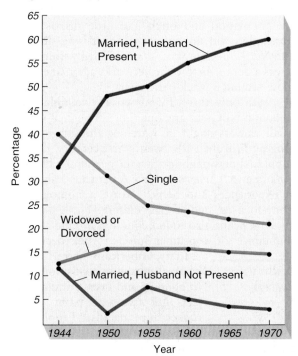

Women nonetheless faced discrimination in the work force. Want ads were divided into "Help Wanted—Male" and "Help Wanted—Female" categories. Female full-time workers earned, on average, 60 percent of what men were paid and were restricted to lower-paid "female" fields: maids, secretaries, teachers, and nurses. A popular book, *Modern Woman: The Lost Sex,* claimed that ambitious women and "feminists" suffered from "penis envy." College psychology textbooks warned women not to "compete" with men, and magazine articles described "career women" as a "third sex." Medical schools limited female admissions to 5 percent of each class. In 1960 less than 4 percent of lawyers and judges were female. When future Supreme Court Justice Ruth Bader Ginsburg graduated at the top of her Columbia Law School class in 1959, she could not find a job.

Academics and mass media critics devoted equal attention to the plight of the American male. American men faced a "crisis of masculinity,"

"THE CRISIS OF MASCULINITY" proclaimed the nation's mass-circulation magazines. In a best-selling book, sociologist William H. Whyte explained that postwar corporate employees had become "organization men," succeeding through cooperation and conformity, not through initiative and risk. And experts insisted women's "natural" desire for security and comfort was stifling men's natural instincts for adventure. Men who did not conform to standards of male responsibility—husband, father, breadwinner—were also condemned. Some linked concerns about masculinity to the Cold War, arguing that unless men recovered masculinity diminished by white-collar work or a family-centered existence, the nation's future was at risk.

Sexuality was complicated terrain in postwar America. Only heterosexual intercourse within marriage was socially acceptable. Women

SEXUALITY who became pregnant outside marriage were often ostracized by friends and family and expelled from school. Homosexuality was grounds for job dismissal, expulsion from college, even jail. In his works on human sexuality, *Sexual Behavior in the Human Male* (1948) and *Sexual Behavior in the Human Female* (1953), Dr. Alfred Kinsey, director of the Institute for Sex Research at Indiana University, noted that while 80 percent of his female sample disapproved of premarital

sex, half of them had had premarital sex. He also reported that 37 percent of American men had had "some homosexual experience." The *Chicago Tribune* called him a "menace to society." While Kinsey's samples did not provide a complete picture of American sexual behavior, they told many Americans they were not alone in breaking certain rules.

Another challenge to sexual norms came when Hugh Hefner launched *Playboy* magazine in 1953. Within three years, it had a circulation of 1 million. Hefner saw *Playboy* as an attack on America's "ferocious anti-sexuality" and his nude "playmates" as a means for men to combat the increasingly "blurred distinctions between the sexes" in suburban culture.

The sheer numbers of "baby boom" youth made them a force in American society. As this group moved

YOUTH CULTURE from childhood to youth, a distinct youth culture developed. Its customs and rituals were created within peer groups and were shaped by national media—teen magazines, movies, radio, advertising, music—targeted toward this huge potential audience. America's corporations quickly learned the power of youth, as children's fads launched multimillion-dollar industries. Mr. Potato Head, probably the first toy advertised on television, had $4 million in sales in 1952. In the mid-1950s, when Walt Disney's television show *Disneyland* featured Davy Crockett, "King of the Wild Frontier," every child in America *had* to have a coonskin cap. As these baby boom children grew up, their buying power shaped American popular culture.

By 1960, America's 18 million teenagers were spending $10 billion a year. Seventy-two percent of movie tickets in the 1950s were sold to teenagers, and Hollywood created a flood of teen films, ranging from forgettable B-movies to controversial films such as James Dean's *Rebel Without a Cause.* Adults worried about teens' copying the delinquency romanticized by the film, and teenage boys did emulate Dean's rebellious look. The film, however, blamed parents for teenage confusion, drawing heavily on popular psychological theories about sexuality and the "crisis of masculinity."

Nothing defined youth culture as much as its music. Young Americans were electrified by the driving energy of Bill Haley and the Comets, Chuck Berry, Little Richard, and Buddy Holly. Elvis Presley's 1956 appearance on TV's *Ed Sullivan Show* touched off a

Barbie

Barbie, the "All-American Doll," is—like many Americans—an immigrant. Though introduced in 1959 by the American toy company Mattel, Barbie's origins lie in Germany, where she was called Lilli.

The German Lilli doll was based on a character that cartoonist Reinhard Beuthien drew to fill space in the June 24, 1952, edition of the German tabloid *Das Bild*. Lilli was so popular that she became a regular feature. Soon Lilli appeared in three-dimensional form as *Bild* Lilli, an eleven-and-a-half-inch-tall blonde doll—with the figure Barbie would make famous (equivalent to 39-21-31 in human proportions). Dressed in a variety of sexy outfits, Lilli was sold in tobacco shops and bars as a "novelty gift" for men, not girls.

Lilli came to America with Ruth Handler, one of the founders of the Mattel toy corporation. When she glimpsed Lilli while vacationing in Europe, Handler bought three—one for her daughter Barbara, after whom Lilli would be renamed. Mattel bought the rights to Lilli (the doll and the cartoon, which Mattel quietly retired) and unveiled "Barbie" in March 1959. Despite mothers' hesitations about a doll that looked like Barbie, within the year Mattel had sold 351,000 Barbies at $3 each (or about $17 in 2000 dollars). The billionth Barbie was sold in 1997.

In 2002 labor-rights groups called for a boycott of Barbie. They cited studies showing that half of all Barbies are made by exploited young women in mainland China: of the $10 retail cost of an average Barbie, Chinese factories receive only 35 cents to cover their costs, including labor. But the eleven-and-a-half-inch doll remains popular, selling in over 150 countries. Today the average American girl has ten Barbies—and the typical German girl owns five.

Before Barbie became an American child's toy, she was "Lilli," a German sex symbol. Mattel transformed the doll into a wholesome American teenager with a new wardrobe to match.   (Spielzeug Museum, Munich)

frenzy of teen adulation—and a flood of letters from parents scandalized by his "gyrations." Though few white musicians acknowledged it, the roots of rock 'n' roll lay in African American rhythm and blues. The raw energy and sometimes sexually suggestive lyrics of early rock music faded as the music industry sought white performers, such as Pat Boone, to do blander, more acceptable "cover" versions of music by black artists.

The distinct youth culture of the 1950s made many adults uneasy. Parents worried that "going steady" might encourage teens to "go too far" sexually. Juvenile delinquency was a major concern. Crime rates for young people had risen dramatically after World War II, but much juvenile delinquency was "status" crimes (activities that were criminal only because of the person's age): curfew violations, sexual experimentation, and underage drinking. Congress held extensive hearings on juvenile delinquency, with experts testifying to the corrupting power of youth-oriented popular culture, comic books in particular. Most youthful behavior, however, fit squarely into the consumer culture that youth shared with their parents.

The Limits of the Middle-Class Nation

*D*uring the 1950s, America's popular culture and mass media celebrated new opportunities. But influential critics condemned middle-class culture as a wasteland of conformity, homogeneity, and ugly consumerism.

Some of the most popular fiction of the postwar era, such as J. D. Salinger's *The Catcher in the Rye* (1951) and Norman Mailer's *The Naked and the Dead* (1948), was profoundly critical of American society, and Americans devoured them. They even made bestsellers of difficult academic works such as David Riesman's *The Lonely Crowd* (1950) and William H. Whyte's *The Organization Man* (1955), both of which criticized conformity in American life. Versions of these critiques also appeared in mass-circulation magazines like *The Ladies' Home Journal* and *Reader's Digest*. Steeped in such cultural criticism, many Americans under-

CRITICS OF CONFORMITY

stood *Invasion of the Body Snatchers*—a 1956 film in which zombie-like aliens grown in pods gradually replace a town's human inhabitants—as criticism of the bland homogeneity of postwar culture.

Americans did lose some autonomy at work as large corporations replaced smaller businesses; they experienced the homogenizing force of mass production and a national consumer culture; they saw distinctions among ethnic groups and socioeconomic classes decline in importance. Critics were often elitist and antidemocratic, seeing only bland conformity and sterility in the emerging middle-class suburban culture. However, identical houses did not produce identical souls; instead, inexpensive suburban housing provided healthier, and perhaps happier, lives to millions who had grown up in dank, dark tenements or ramshackle farmhouses without indoor plumbing.

The new consumer culture encouraged wastefulness and harmed the environment. *Business Week* noted that corporations need not rely on "planned obsolescence," purposely designing a product to wear out. Americans replaced products because they were "out of date," not because they didn't work; hence, automakers revamped designs annually. By the 1960s the United States, with only 5 percent of the world's population, consumed more than one-third of the world's goods and services.

ENVIRONMENTAL DEGRADATION

The rapid economic growth that made the middle-class consumer culture possible exacted environmental costs. Steel mills, coal-powered generators, and car engines burning lead-based gasoline polluted the atmosphere and imperiled people's health. As suburbs spread farther from jobs and neighborhoods were built without public transportation, Americans relied on private automobiles, consuming the nonrenewable resources of oil and gasoline and filling cities and suburbs with smog. Water was diverted from lakes and rivers to service burgeoning Sunbelt cities, including the swimming pools and golf courses that dotted parched Arizona and southern California.

Defense contractors and farmers were among the country's worst polluters. Refuse from nuclear weapons facilities at Hanford, Washington, and at Colorado's Rocky Flats arsenal poisoned soil and water resources. Agriculture used pesticides and other chemicals. DDT, a chemical used during the war to kill mosquitoes and lice on Pacific islands, was used widely in the United States until 1962, when wildlife biologist Rachel Carson specifically indicted DDT for the deaths of mammals, birds, and fish in her best-selling book *Silent Spring*.

The nation was moving toward a postindustrial economy in which providing goods and services to consumers was more important than manufacturing goods. Therefore, although union members prospered during the 1950s, union membership grew slowly—as most new jobs were created in the union-resistant white-collar service trades. Technological advances increased productivity and also pushed people from relatively well-paid blue-collar jobs into the growing and less-well-paid service sector.

Even as fewer Americans were excluded because of ethnic identities, racial discrimination remained largely unchallenged in most of 1950s America. Suburbs, both North and South, were almost always racially segregated. Many white Americans had little or no contact in their daily lives with people of different races, partly because the relatively small populations of nonwhite Americans were not equally dispersed nationwide. In 1960 there were 68 people of Chinese descent and 519 African Americans in Vermont; 181 Native Americans lived in West Virginia; Mississippi had just 178 Japanese American residents. Most white Americans in the 1950s, especially those outside the South, gave little thought to race. Instead, they regarded the emerging middle-class culture not as "white," but as "American," marginalizing people of color in image as in reality.

CONTINUING RACISM

In an age of abundance, more than one in five Americans still lived in poverty. One-fifth of the poor were people of color, including almost half of the nation's African American population and more than half of all Native Americans. Two-thirds lived in households headed by a person with an eighth-grade education or less, one-fourth in households headed by a single woman. More than one-third were under age eighteen. One-fourth were over age sixty-five; Social Security payments helped, but many retirees were not yet covered, and in the years before Medicare, medical costs drove many older Americans into poverty.

As millions of Americans (most of them white) settled in the suburbs, the poor concentrated in inner

POVERTY IN AN AGE OF ABUNDANCE

cities. African American migrants were joined by poor whites from the southern Appalachians, moving to Chicago, Cincinnati, Baltimore, and Detroit. Latin Americans arrived in growing numbers from Mexico, the Dominican Republic, Colombia, Ecuador, and Cuba. According to the 1960 census, over a half-million Mexican Americans had migrated to the Los Angeles–Long Beach area since 1940. And New York City's Puerto Rican population exploded from 70,000 in 1940 to 613,000 in 1960.

Because of the strong economy, many newcomers gained the higher standard of living they sought. But discrimination limited their advances, and they endured crowded and decrepit housing and poor schools. In addition, the federal programs that helped middle-class Americans sometimes made the lives of the poor worse. For example, the National Housing Act of 1949, passed to make available "a decent home . . . for every American family," provided for "urban redevelopment." Redevelopment meant slum clearance, replacing the only housing many poor people had with high-rise buildings, parking lots, or highways.

The growth of large "agribusinesses" pushed more tenant farmers and small farmers off the land. From 1945 to 1961 the nation's farm population declined from 24.4 million to 14.8 million. When the harvesting of cotton in the South was mechanized in the 1940s and 1950s, more than 4 million people were displaced. Southern tobacco growers dismissed tenant farmers, bought tractors to plow the land, and hired migratory workers. In the West and Southwest, Mexican citizens served as cheap migrant labor under the *bracero* program. Almost 1 million Mexican workers came legally to the United States in 1959. Entire families labored, enduring conditions little better than in the Great Depression of the 1930s.

Native Americans were America's poorest people, with an average annual income barely half that of the poverty level. Conditions were worsened by "termination," a federal policy implemented during the Eisenhower administration. "Termination" reversed the Indian Reorganization Act of 1934, allowing Indians to terminate their tribal status and so remove reservation lands from federal protection prohibiting their sale. Sixty-one tribes were terminated between 1954 and 1960. Termination could take place only with a tribe's agreement, but pressure was sometimes intense, especially when reservation land was rich in natural resources. Enticed by cash payments, almost four-fifths of the Klamaths of Oregon voted to sell their shares of the forest land. Many Indians left reservation land for the city. By the time termination ceased in the 1960s, observers compared the situation of Native Americans to the devastation of their forebears in the nineteenth century.

Online Study Center **Improve Your Grade**

Interactive Map: American Indian Reservations

Overall, Americans enjoyed relative prosperity in the postwar era. But those who made it to the comfortable middle class often ignored the plight of those left behind. It would be their children—the generation of the baby boom—who would see racism, poverty, and the self-satisfaction of postwar suburban culture as a failure of American ideals.

Summary *Online Study Center* **ACE the Test**

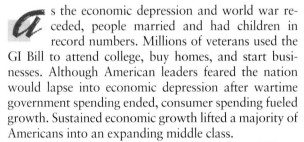

s the economic depression and world war receded, people married and had children in record numbers. Millions of veterans used the GI Bill to attend college, buy homes, and start businesses. Although American leaders feared the nation would lapse into economic depression after wartime government spending ended, consumer spending fueled growth. Sustained economic growth lifted a majority of Americans into an expanding middle class.

The Cold War presidencies of Truman and Eisenhower focused more on international relations than on domestic politics. Within the United States, Cold War fears provoked an extreme anticommunism that stifled political dissent and diminished Americans' civil liberties and freedoms.

The continuing African American struggle for civil rights drew national attention during the Montgomery bus boycott. African Americans won victories in the Supreme Court, including the landmark *Brown v. Board of Education*. Truman and Eisenhower used federal power to guarantee the rights of black Americans as a national civil rights movement began to coalesce.

Despite continued racial divisions, the United States became a more inclusive nation in the 1950s as a majority of Americans participated in a national, consumer-oriented, middle-class culture. This culture largely ignored the poverty in the nation's cities and rural areas. For the growing number in the middle class, the American Dream seemed a reality.

LEGACY FOR A PEOPLE AND A NATION
The Pledge of Allegiance

The Pledge of Allegiance Americans recite today was shaped by the Cold War. Congress added the phrase "under God" to the pledge in 1954 to emphasize the difference between the God-fearing United States and the "godless communists" of the Soviet Union.

The Pledge of Allegiance was not always an important part of American public life. The original version was written in 1892 by Francis Bellamy, editor of *The Youth's Companion*, to commemorate the four hundredth anniversary of Columbus's arrival in North America. In 1942 Congress officially adopted a revised version as an act of wartime patriotism. The Supreme Court ruled in 1943, however, that schoolchildren could not be forced to say the "Pledge to the Flag."

During the Cold War years, the pledge became an increasingly important symbol of U.S. loyalty. Cold War fears fueled a campaign by the Knights of Columbus, a Catholic men's service organization, to include "under God" in the pledge. Supporting the bill, President Eisenhower proclaimed that

in this way we shall constantly strengthen those spiritual weapons which forever will be our country's most powerful resource in peace and war. From this day forward, the millions of our schoolchildren will daily proclaim in every city and town, every village and every rural schoolhouse, the dedication of our nation and our people to the Almighty.

Some Americans, citing the doctrine of separation of church and state, have protested including "under God." In June 2002, the Ninth District Court (covering California and eight other western states) sparked a controversy by ruling that the 1954 version of the pledge was unconstitutional because it conveyed "state endorsement" of a religious belief. Questions about the proper role of religion in American life remain controversial, a legacy for a people and a nation becoming more diverse in the twenty-first century.

THE TUMULTUOUS SIXTIES 1960–1968

*I*t was late, and Ezell Blair had an exam the next day. But he and friends in the dormitory sat talking—as they often did—about injustice, about living in a nation that proclaimed equality for all but denied full citizenship to some because of the color of their skin. They were complaining about all the do-nothing adults, condemning the black community of Greensboro, when Franklin McCain said, "It's time to fish or cut bait." Joe McNeil and McCain's roommate, David Richmond, agreed they should do something. Blair hesitated. "I was thinking about my grades," he said later, just "trying to deal with that architecture and engineering course I was taking."

But the next day, February 1, 1960, after their classes at North Carolina Agricultural and Technical College, the four freshmen walked into town. At the F. W. Woolworth's on South Elm Street, one of the most profitable stores in the national chain, each bought a few small things. Then, nervously, they sat down at the lunch counter and tried to order coffee. These seventeen- and eighteen-year-olds were prepared to be arrested, even physically attacked. The counter help just ignored them, until one worker said, "We don't serve colored here." An elderly white woman told the boys how proud she was of them. Still nothing happened. The store closed; the manager turned out the lights. After forty-five minutes, the four men who had begun the sit-in movement left.

The next day they returned with twenty fellow students. By February 3, sixty-three of the sixty-five seats were taken. On February 4, the sit-in spread to the S. H. Kress store across the street. By February 7, there were sit-ins in Winston-Salem; by February 8, in Charlotte; by February 9, in Raleigh. By the third week in February, students were picketing Woolworth's stores in the North. On July 26, 1960, F. W. Woolworth's ended segregation in all its stores.

The sit-in at the Greensboro Woolworth's signaled the beginning of a decade of public activism as millions of Americans—many of them young—marched for civil rights or against the war in Vietnam. Passion over contemporary issues

Kennedy and the Cold War

Marching for Freedom

Liberalism and the Great Society

Johnson and Vietnam

A Nation Divided

1968

LINKS TO THE WORLD
The British Invasion

LEGACY FOR A PEOPLE AND A NATION
The Immigration Act of 1965

Online Study Center

This icon will direct you to interactive map and primary source activities on the website http://college.hmco.com/pic/nortonbrief7e

CHRONOLOGY

1960 • Sit-ins begin in Greensboro
- Birth-control pill approved for contraceptive use
- John F. Kennedy elected president
- Young Americans for Freedom write Sharon Statement
- Freedom Rides protest segregation in transportation

1962 • Students for a Democratic Society issues Port Huron Statement
- Cuban missile crisis courts nuclear war

1963 • Civil rights March on Washington for Jobs and Freedom draws more than 250,000
- John F. Kennedy assassinated; Lyndon B. Johnson becomes president

1964 • Civil Rights Act outlaws discrimination in hiring and public accommodation
- Race riots break out in first of the "long, hot summers"
- Free Speech Movement begins at UC Berkeley
- Lyndon B. Johnson elected president

1965 • Lyndon Johnson launches Great Society programs
- Voting Rights Act outlaws practices that prevent most African Americans from voting in southern states
- Immigration and Nationality Act lowers barriers to immigration from Asia and Latin America
- Malcolm X assassinated
- Watts riot leaves thirty-four dead

1967 • Summer of Love in San Francisco's Haight-Ashbury district
- Race riots erupt in Newark, Detroit, and other cities

1968 • Tet Offensive causes fear of losing war in Vietnam
- Martin Luther King Jr. assassinated
- Robert Kennedy assassinated
- Antiwar protests escalate
- Violence erupts at Democratic National Convention
- Richard Nixon elected president

revitalized democracy—and threatened to tear the nation apart.

John F. Kennedy, the nation's youngest president, told Americans as he took office in 1961: "The torch has been passed to a new generation." But Kennedy had only modest success implementing his domestic agenda. In his third year as president, however, Kennedy offered greater support for civil rights and proposed more ambitious domestic policies. When he was assassinated in November 1963, his death seemed to many the end of an era of hope.

Lyndon Johnson, Kennedy's successor, summoned the memory of the martyred president to launch an ambitious program of civil rights and other liberal legislation. Calling his vision the Great Society, John-

son intended to use federal power to eliminate poverty and guarantee equal rights to all Americans.

Despite liberal triumphs, social tensions escalated during the mid-1960s. A revitalized conservative movement emerged, and Franklin Roosevelt's old New Deal coalition fractured as white southerners abandoned the Democratic Party. Angry that discrimination and poverty persisted even with landmark civil rights laws, many African Americans, especially in the North, rioted. White youth culture increasingly rejected the values and lifestyle of its elders, creating "the generation gap."

Meanwhile, after the 1962 Cuban missile crisis brought the Soviet Union and the United States close to nuclear disaster, Kennedy and Khrushchev deescalated tensions in 1963 and lessened Cold War pressures in Europe. Everywhere else, however, the superpowers competed frantically. Throughout the 1960s, the United States tried a variety of approaches—including foreign aid, CIA covert actions, military assaults, cultural penetration, economic sanctions, and diplomacy—to win the Cold War. In Vietnam, Kennedy expanded U.S. involvement significantly. Johnson increased U.S. troops to more than half a million in 1968.

By 1968, the Vietnam War divided Americans and undermined Johnson's Great Society. With the assassinations that spring of Martin Luther King Jr. and Robert Kennedy, two of America's brightest leaders, cities in flames, and tanks on Chicago streets in August, the fate of the nation hung in the balance. ∎

Kennedy and the Cold War

*Y*oung, handsome, and intellectually inquisitive, John F. Kennedy brought wit and sophistication to the White House. His Irish American grandfather had been mayor of Boston, and his millionaire father, Joseph P. Kennedy, served as ambassador to Great Britain. In 1946 the young Kennedy returned from the Second World War a naval hero (the boat he commanded was sunk by a Japanese destroyer in 1943, and Kennedy saved his crew) and campaigned to represent Boston in the U.S. House of Representatives. He served three terms in the House and in 1952 was elected to the Senate.

As a Democrat, Kennedy inherited the New Deal commitment to America's social welfare system. He

JOHN FITZGERALD KENNEDY generally voted with the pro-labor sentiments of his low-income, blue-collar constituents, but avoided controversial issues such as civil rights. Kennedy won a Pulitzer Prize for his *Profiles in Courage* (1956), a study of principled politicians, but he shaded the truth in claiming sole authorship, when it was written largely by aide Theodore Sorensen (from over a hundred pages of notes dictated by Kennedy). In foreign pol-

icy, Senator Kennedy endorsed the Cold War policy of containment. Despite an unimpressive legislative record, he enjoyed an enthusiastic following, especially after his landslide Senate reelection in 1958.

Kennedy cultivated an image as a happy and healthy family man. But he was a chronic womanizer, even after his 1953 marriage to Jacqueline Bouvier. As a child he had almost died of scarlet fever and developed severe back problems, which worsened during World War II. After the war, Kennedy was diagnosed with Addison's disease, an adrenalin deficiency causing chronic pain that required daily cortisone injections. As president he would require plenty of bed rest and frequent therapeutic swims in the White House pool.

Kennedy beat Republican Richard Nixon in 1960 by a narrow 118,000 votes out of nearly 69 million.

ELECTION OF 1960 Kennedy achieved mixed success in the South, but ran well in the Northeast and Midwest. His Roman Catholic faith hurt him in states where voters feared he would take direction from the pope, but helped in states with large Catholic populations. As the sitting vice president, Nixon had to answer for sagging economic figures and the Soviet downing of a U-2 spy plane (see Chapter 28). Perhaps worse, when asked to list Nixon's significant decisions as vice president, Eisenhower replied, "If you give me a week, I might think of one."

The new president surrounded himself with mostly young advisers; the writer David Halberstam called them "the best and the brightest." Secretary of Defense Robert McNamara (age forty-four) had been an assistant professor at Harvard at twenty-four and later the whiz-kid president of the Ford Motor Company. Kennedy's special assistant for national security affairs, McGeorge Bundy (age forty-one), had become a Harvard dean at thirty-four with only a bachelor's degree. Secretary of State Dean Rusk, at fifty-two the oldest, had been a Rhodes scholar in his youth. Kennedy was only forty-three, and his brother Robert, the attorney general, was thirty-five.

Kennedy gave top priority to the Cold War. In the campaign he accused Eisenhower of an unimaginative foreign policy that failed to reduce the threat of nuclear war with the Soviet Union and of weakening America's standing in the Third World.

Once in office, Kennedy understood sooner than his advisers the limits of American power abroad.

NATION BUILDING AND COUNTER-INSURGENCY
More than his predecessor, he proved willing to initiate dialogue with the Soviets, sometimes using his brother Robert as a secret channel to Moscow. Yet Kennedy also sought victory in the Cold War. After Soviet leader Nikita Khrushchev endorsed "wars of national liberation" such as the one in Vietnam, Kennedy called for "peaceful revolution" based on nation building. The administration helped developing nations with aid to improve agriculture, transportation, and communications. Kennedy oversaw the creation of the multibillion-dollar Alliance for Progress in 1961 to spur economic development in Latin America. That year, too, he created the Peace Corps, dispatching American teachers, agricultural specialists, and health workers, many of them recent graduates, to assist in developing nations.

Cynics then and later dismissed the Alliance and Peace Corps as Kennedy's Cold War tools for countering anti-Americanism and defeating communism in the developing world. True enough, but they were also humanitarian. As historian Elizabeth Cobbs Hoffman has written, "the Peace Corps broached an age-old dilemma of U.S. foreign policy: how to reconcile the imperatives and temptations of power politics with the ideals of freedom and self-determination for all nations."

Although Kennedy and his aides were supportive of social revolution in the Third World, they could not accept communist involvement in these uprisings. Therefore, the administration also relied on counterinsurgency to defeat revolutionaries who challenged pro-American Third World governments. American military and technical advisers trained native troops and police to quell unrest.

The Alliance for Progress was only partly successful; infant mortality rates improved, but Latin American economies registered unimpressive growth, and class divisions widened, exacerbating political unrest. Although many foreign peoples welcomed U.S. economic assistance and American material culture, they resented meddling by outsiders. And because aid was usually funneled through a self-interested elite, it often never reached the poor. To people who preferred the quick fix of a managed economy, moreover, the American emphasis on private enterprise seemed inappropriate.

The administration's first year witnessed little movement on controlling the nuclear arms race or even getting a superpower ban on

SOVIET-AMERICAN TENSIONS
testing nuclear weapons in the atmosphere or underground. Kennedy and Soviet leader Nikita Khrushchev could not agree on these issues or other preconditions for peace at a summit in Vienna in June 1961. Instead, both superpowers continued testing and accelerated their arms production. In 1961 the U.S. military budget shot up 15 percent; by mid-1964, U.S. nuclear weapons had increased by 150 percent. Government advice to citizens to build fallout shelters in their backyards intensified public fear of devastating war.

If war occurred, many expected Berlin would be the proximate cause. In mid-1961 Khrushchev demanded an end to Western occupation of West Berlin and a reunification of East and West Germany. Kennedy replied that the United States would honor its commitment to West Germany. In August the Soviets, at the urging of the East German regime, erected a concrete and barbed-wire barricade to halt the exodus of East Germans into the more prosperous and politically free West Berlin. The Berlin Wall inspired protests throughout the noncommunist world, but Kennedy privately sighed that "a wall is a hell of a lot better than a war."

Kennedy knew that Khrushchev would continue to press elsewhere, and he was particularly rankled by growing Soviet assistance to Fidel

BAY OF PIGS INVASION
Castro's Cuban government. The Eisenhower administration had contested the Cuban revolution and bequeathed to Kennedy a partially developed CIA plan to overthrow Castro (see Chapter 28): CIA-trained Cuban exiles would land and secure a beachhead; the Cuban people would rise up against Castro and welcome a new U.S.-backed government.

The attack took place on April 17, 1961, as twelve hundred exiles landed at the swampy Bay of Pigs in Cuba. Instead of discontented Cubans, they were greeted by Castro's loyal troops and were quickly captured. Kennedy tried to keep U.S. participation in the operation hidden, but the CIA's role swiftly became public. Anti-American sentiments swept the region. Castro, concluding that the United States might launch another invasion, looked increasingly toward the Soviet Union for military and economic assistance.

Embarrassed, Kennedy vowed to bring Castro down. The CIA soon hatched a project called Operation Mongoose to disrupt the island's trade, support raids on Cuba from Miami, and plot to kill Castro. The agency's assassination schemes included providing Castro with cigars laced with explosives and deadly poison. The United States also tightened its economic blockade and undertook military maneuvers in the Caribbean. The Joint Chiefs of Staff sketched plans to spark a rebellion in Cuba that would be followed by an invasion of U.S. troops.

Both Castro and Khrushchev believed an invasion was coming, which partly explains the Soviet leader's risky decision in 1962 to secretly deploy nuclear missiles in Cuba as a deterrent. But Khrushchev also hoped the move would improve the Soviet position in the nuclear balance of power and force Kennedy to finally resolve the German problem. Khrushchev worried that Washington might provide West Germany with nuclear weapons, and believed he could prevent it by putting Soviet missiles just 90 miles off the coast of Florida. The world soon faced a frightening example of brinkmanship.

CUBAN MISSILE CRISIS

In mid-October 1962 a U-2 plane flying over Cuba photographed the missile sites. The president immediately organized a special executive committee of advisers to find a way to force the missiles and their nuclear warheads out of Cuba. Options considered ranged from full-scale invasion to limited bombing to quiet diplomacy. Defense Secretary McNamara proposed a solution acceptable to the president: a naval quarantine of Cuba.

Kennedy addressed the nation on October 22, demanding that the Soviets retreat. U.S. warships began crisscrossing the Caribbean, while B-52s with nuclear bombs took to the skies. Khrushchev agreed to withdraw the missiles if the United States pledged never to attack Cuba and promised to remove American Jupiter missiles aimed at the Soviet Union from Turkey. For several days, the world teetered on the brink of disaster. Then, on October 28, came a compromise: the United States agreed to Soviet demands

in exchange for the withdrawal of Soviet offensive forces from Cuba. Fearing Castro might make matters worse, Khrushchev settled without consulting the Cubans.

Many observers then and later called it Kennedy's finest hour, although critics claimed Kennedy may have triggered the crisis with his anti-Cuban projects. Either way, the Cuban missile crisis was a watershed in the Soviet-American relationship. Both Kennedy and Khrushchev acted with greater prudence in its aftermath, taking steps toward improved relations. In August 1963 the adversaries signed a treaty banning nuclear tests in the atmosphere, the oceans, and outer space. They also installed a coded wire-telegraph "hot line" staffed around the clock to allow near-instant communication between the capitals. Both sides refrained from further confrontation in Berlin.

Together, these small steps began to build mutual trust. By the autumn of 1963, the Cold War in Europe was drawing to a close, as both sides accepted the status quo of a divided continent and a fortified border. But the arms race continued and accelerated, and the superpower competition in the Third World continued.

Marching for Freedom

While President Kennedy saw the Cold War as the most important issue Americans faced, many African Americans believed civil rights should become a national priority. In the early 1960s, young civil rights activists seized the national stage and demanded that the federal government mobilize behind them.

In 1960, six years after the *Brown* decision declared "separate but equal" unconstitutional, little had changed for African Americans in the South. Fewer than 7 percent of black students attended integrated schools. Water fountains were still labeled "White Only" and "Colored Only." One year after the young men had sat down at the all-white lunch counter in Greensboro, more than seventy thousand Americans—most of them college students—participated in sit-ins.

STUDENTS AND THE MOVEMENT

The young people who created the Student Nonviolent Coordinating Committee (SNCC) in the spring of 1960 to coordinate the growing movement were committed to nonviolence. In years to come, SNCC stalwarts—including activist Diane Nash; future NAACP chair Julian Bond; future Washington, D.C., mayor Marion Barry; and future member of the U.S. House of Representatives John Lewis—would risk their lives in the struggle for social justice.

On May 4, 1961, thirteen members of the Congress of Racial Equality (CORE), a nonviolent civil rights organization (see Chapter 27), purchased bus tickets in Washington, D.C., for a 1,500-mile trip through the South to New Orleans. Calling themselves Freedom Riders, this racially mixed group sought to demonstrate that despite Supreme Court rulings ordering the desegregation of interstate buses, Jim Crow still ruled the South. They knew they were risking their lives, and some suffered serious injuries. One bus was firebombed outside Anniston, Alabama. Riders were badly beaten in Birmingham, and in Montgomery, a thousand whites attacked riders with baseball bats and steel bars. Police stayed away.

FREEDOM RIDES

News of the violent attacks made headlines worldwide. Soviet commentators decried the "savage nature of American freedom and democracy." One southern business leader, in Tokyo to promote Birmingham as a site for international business development, saw Japanese interest evaporate once photos of the Birmingham attacks appeared in Tokyo newspapers.

In America, the violence forced many to confront racial discrimination and hatred in their nation. Middle- and upper-class white southerners had resisted integration following the *Brown* decision. The Freedom Rides made some think differently. Even the *Atlanta Journal* editorialized: "It is time for the decent people . . . to muzzle the jackals." The national and international outcry pushed a reluctant President Kennedy to send federal marshals to safeguard Freedom Riders in Alabama. But bowing to white southern pressure, he allowed Freedom Riders to be arrested in Mississippi.

Beginning in 1961, thousands of SNCC volunteers, many of them high-school and college students, risked their lives encouraging African Americans in rural Mississippi and Georgia to resist segregation and register to vote. They formed Freedom Schools, teaching literacy and constitutional rights. Some SNCC volunteers were white and some were from the North, but many were black southerners who understood firsthand the impact of racism, powerlessness, and poverty.

These efforts achieved national attention during the Freedom Summer of 1964. Because Mississippi laws made it almost impossible for blacks to vote, the Freedom Summer volunteers created a racially integrated grassroots political party, the Mississippi Freedom Democratic Party. Project workers were arrested over a thousand times and were shot at, bombed, and beaten. Local black activist James Cheney and two white volunteers, Michael Schwerner and Andrew Goodman, were murdered by a Klan mob. That summer, black and white activists risked their lives together.

FREEDOM SUMMER

The Freedom Riders had captured the attention of the nation and the larger Cold War world, and had forced the hand of the president. Martin Luther King Jr., having risen through the Montgomery bus boycott to leadership in the movement, concluded that only by provoking a crisis would the civil rights struggle advance. King and the SCLC planned a 1963 campaign in the most violently racist city in America: Birmingham, Alabama. Anticipating a violent response to their nonviolent protests, they called their plan "Project C"—for "confrontation." King wanted all Americans to see the racist hate and violence that marred their nation.

BIRMINGHAM AND THE CHILDREN'S CRUSADE

In a controversial action, King and the parents of Birmingham put children on the front lines. As about a thousand black children, some as young as six, marched, police commissioner Eugene "Bull" Connor ordered his police to train "monitor" water guns—powerful enough to strip bark from a tree at 100 feet—on them. The water guns mowed down the children, and then police loosed attack dogs as the nation watched in horror on television. President Kennedy demanded that Birmingham's white business and political elite negotiate a settlement. The Birmingham movement won and, more important, pushed civil rights to the fore of Kennedy's political agenda.

Kennedy was sympathetic—though not terribly committed—to the civil rights movement, and he knew that racial oppression hurt the United States in the Cold War struggle for international opinion. Domestically, however, he knew that if he alienated conservative southern Democrats in Congress, his legislative programs would

KENNEDY AND CIVIL RIGHTS

founder. Thus, he appointed five die-hard segregationists to the federal bench in the Deep South and delayed issuing an executive order forbidding segregation in federally subsidized housing (a pledge made in the 1960 campaign) until late 1962. He allowed FBI director J. Edgar Hoover to harass Martin Luther King and other activists, using wiretaps and surveillance to gather personal information and circulating rumors of communist connections and personal improprieties to discredit them.

But grassroots civil rights activism—and the violence of white mobs—forced Kennedy's hand. In September 1962, the president ordered 500 U.S. marshals to protect James Meredith, the first African American to attend the University of Mississippi. Thousands of whites attacked the marshals with guns, gasoline bombs, bricks, and pipes, killing two and seriously wounding 160. Neither the marshals nor James Meredith backed down.

The following spring, Kennedy confronted the defiant Alabama governor, George C. Wallace, who promised to "bar the schoolhouse door" to prevent the desegregation of the University of Alabama. With Wallace vowing, "Segregation now, segregation tomorrow, segregation forever!" Kennedy committed

the federal government to guarantee racial justice—even over the opposition of individual states. In a televised address Kennedy said: "Now the time has come for this nation to fulfill its promise." That night, civil rights leader Medgar Evers was murdered in his driveway in Jackson, Mississippi. A week later, the president asked Congress to pass a comprehensive civil rights bill ending racial discrimination in the entire United States.

On August 28, 1963, a quarter of a million Americans gathered on the Washington Mall to show

MARCH ON WASHINGTON

support for Kennedy's civil rights bill. Behind the scenes, organizers from the major civil rights groups—SCLC, CORE, SNCC, the NAACP, the Urban League, and A. Philip Randolph's Brotherhood of Sleeping Car Porters—grappled with growing tensions. SNCC activists saw Kennedy's legislation as too little, too late, and wanted radical action. King and other older leaders counseled moderation. The movement was splintering.

What Americans saw, however, was a celebration of unity. Black and white celebrities joined hands; folk singers sang freedom songs. Television aired Martin Luther King Jr.'s prophesy of a day when "all

■ A historic moment for the civil rights movement was the March on Washington on August 28, 1963. The Reverend Martin Luther King Jr. (*center*) joined a quarter of a million black people and white people in their march for racial equality. Addressing civil rights supporters, and the nation, from the steps of the Lincoln Memorial, King delivered his "I Have a Dream" speech.   (R. W. Kelley/ Getty Images)

God's children, black men and white men, Jews and Gentiles, Protestants and Catholics, will be able to join hands and sing in the words of the old Negro spiritual, 'Free at last! Free at last! Thank God Almighty, we are free at last!'" The 1963 March on Washington for Jobs and Freedom was a triumph, powerfully demonstrating African Americans' commitment to equality and justice. Days later, white supremacists bombed the Sixteenth Street Baptist Church in Birmingham, killing four black girls.

Liberalism and the Great Society

B y 1963, Kennedy seemed to be taking a new path. Campaigning in 1960, he promised to lead America into a "New Frontier," with the federal government working to eradicate poverty, guarantee healthcare to the elderly, and ensure decent schools for all children. But few of Kennedy's initiatives were passed into law. Lacking a popular mandate in the election and fearful of alienating southern Democrats in Congress, Kennedy let his social policy agenda languish.

Instead, Kennedy focused on the economy, believing that continued prosperity would solve America's social problems. Kennedy's vision was perhaps best realized in America's space program. As the Russians moved ahead in the space race, Kennedy vowed in 1961 to put a man on the moon before the decade's end. With billions in new funding, the National Aeronautics and Space Administration (NASA) began the Apollo program. And in February 1962, astronaut John Glenn orbited the earth in the space capsule *Friendship Seven*.

On November 22, 1963, Kennedy visited the home state of Vice President Lyndon Johnson. Riding with

THE KENNEDY ASSASSINATION his wife, Jackie, in an open-top limousine, Kennedy was cheered by thousands along the motorcade's route. Suddenly gunshots rang out. The president crumpled, shot in the head. Tears ran down the cheeks of CBS anchorman Walter Cronkite as he announced to the nation later that day that the president was dead.

That same day, police captured a suspect: Lee Harvey Oswald, a former U.S. Marine (dishonorably discharged) who had once attempted to gain Soviet citizenship. Two days later, television cameras rolled

as Oswald was shot dead by nightclub owner Jack Ruby. Was Ruby silencing Oswald to prevent him from implicating others? Americans wondered. The seven-member Warren Commission, headed by U.S. Supreme Court Chief Justice Earl Warren, concluded that Oswald acted alone. But debates still rage over whether Kennedy's death was a conspiracy.

Millions of Americans watched their president's funeral on television: the brave young widow; a riderless horse; three-year-old "John-John" saluting his father's casket. People would remember Kennedy less for any specific accomplishment than for his inspirational rhetoric and the romance he brought to American political life. In the post-assassination grief, Lyndon Johnson invoked Kennedy's memory to push through the most ambitious legislative program since the New Deal.

Whereas Kennedy had been raised with wealth and was educated at Harvard, Johnson had grown

JOHNSON AND THE GREAT SOCIETY up in modest circumstances in the Texas hill country and graduated from Southwest Texas State Teachers' College. He was as earthy as Kennedy was elegant, prone to colorful curses, and willing to use his physical size to his advantage. Johnson had a long political career, beginning when he filled an empty congressional seat from Texas in 1937. As Senate majority leader from 1954 to 1960, he learned how to manipulate people and wield power, and in the presidency, he used these skills to unite the nation.

Johnson, a liberal in the style of Franklin D. Roosevelt, believed the federal government should actively improve the lives of Americans. In a 1964 commencement address at the University of Michigan, he described his vision of "abundance and liberty for all . . . demand[ing] an end to poverty and racial injustice . . . where every child can find knowledge to enrich his mind and to enlarge his talents." Johnson called this vision "The Great Society."

Johnson signed into law the Civil Rights Act of 1964, ending legal discrimination on the basis of

CIVIL RIGHTS ACT race, color, religion, national origin, and sex in federal programs, voting, employment, and public accommodation. The original bill did not include discrimination on the basis of sex; that was added by a southern congressman who hoped it would torpedo the bill. But a bipartisan group of women members of the House of Representatives ensured it was passed. The Civil Rights Act of 1964 gave the government enforcement power, including the authority to withhold federal funds from public agencies or federal contractors that discriminated and establishing the Equal Employment Opportunity Commission (EEOC) to investigate and judge claims of job discrimination.

Many Americans did not believe it was the federal government's job to end racial discrimination or poverty. White southerners resented federal intervention, and millions of conservative Americans believed that since the New Deal, the federal government had been overstepping its constitutional boundaries and wanted a return to local control and states' rights. In the 1964 election, this vision was championed by the Republican candidate, Arizona senator Barry Goldwater.

Goldwater not only voted against the 1964 Civil Rights Act; he opposed the national Social Security system. Like many conservatives, he

THE ELECTION OF 1964

believed that individual liberty, not equality, mattered most. Goldwater also believed that the United States needed a more powerful national military to fight communism; in campaign speeches, he suggested that the United States should use tactical nuclear weapons against its enemies.

Goldwater's campaign slogan, "In your heart you know he's right," was turned against him by Johnson supporters: "In your heart you know he's right . . . far right," one punned. Johnson campaigned on a record unemployment rate below 4 percent and economic growth above 6 percent. But his civil rights support severed the New Deal coalition and, he told an aide, "delivered the south to the Republican Party for my lifetime and yours."

Tensions mounted at the 1964 Democratic National Convention. Two delegations arrived from Mississippi, each demanding to be seated. The Democratic Party's official delegation was exclusively white; the Mississippi Freedom Democratic Party (MFDP) was racially mixed. White southern delegates threatened to leave if the MFDP delegates were seated. MFDP delegate Fannie Lou Hamer told the convention's credentials committee about the threats and violence she'd faced when she tried to register to vote. Johnson sought a compromise, but the MFDP declined. "We didn't come all this way

for no two seats," Hamer said, and the delegation walked out.

Though Johnson won the election by a landslide, he lost the Deep South—the first Democrat since the Civil War to do so. But voters also elected the most liberal Congress in history. With a record 61.1 percent of the popular vote, Johnson launched his Great Society. Congress responded in 1965 and 1966 with the most sweeping reform legislation since 1935.

Johnson signed the 1965 Voting Rights Act, which outlawed practices that prevented most blacks in the Deep South from voting and provided for federal oversight of elections. Within two years, the percentage of African Americans registered to vote in Mississippi jumped from 7 percent to more than 60 percent. Black elected officials became increasingly common in southern states over the following decade.

Seeking to improve the quality of American life, the Johnson administration established new student

IMPROVING AMERICAN LIFE

loan and grant programs to help low- and moderate-income Americans attend college and created the National Endowment for the Arts and the National Endowment for the Humanities. The Immigration Act of 1965 ended racially based quotas. And Johnson supported consumer protection legislation, including the 1966 National Traffic and Motor Vehicle Safety Act, inspired by Ralph Nader's exposé of the automobile industry, *Unsafe at Any Speed* (1965). Johnson signed "preservation" legislation protecting America's wilderness and addressing environmental pollution.

At the heart of Johnson's Great Society was the War on Poverty, which included major legislation beginning in 1964 (see Table 30.1).

WAR ON POVERTY

Johnson and other liberals believed that in a time of affluence, the nation should use its resources to end "poverty, ignorance and hunger as intractable, permanent features of American society."

Johnson's goal was "to offer the forgotten fifth of our people opportunity, not doles." Billions of federal dollars were channeled to municipalities and school districts to improve opportunities for the poverty stricken, from preschoolers (Head Start) to high schoolers (Upward Bound) to young adults (Job Corps). The Model Cities program offered federal funds to upgrade employment, housing, education, and health in targeted urban neighborhoods, and

TABLE 30.1

Great Society Achievements, 1964–1966

	1964	1965	1966
Civil Rights	Civil Rights Act Equal Employment Opportunity Commission Twenty-fourth Amendment	Voting Rights Act	
War on Poverty	Economic Opportunity Act Office of Economic Opportunity Job Corps Legal Services for the Poor VISTA		Model Cities
Education		Elementary and Secondary Education Act Head Start Upward Bound	
Environment		Water Quality Act Air Quality Act	Clean Water Restoration Act

New Government Agencies		Department of
		    Housing and Urban
		    Development
		National Endowments for
		    the Arts and Humanities
			Department of
			    Transportation

Miscellaneous		Medicare and Medicaid Immigration and Nationality Act	

The Great Society of the mid-1960s saw the biggest burst of reform legislation since the New Deal of the 1930s.

Community Action Programs involved the poor in creating local grassroots antipoverty programs.

The Johnson administration also expanded the Food Stamp program and earmarked billions for constructing public housing and subsidizing rents. Two massive federal programs provided healthcare: Medicare for those sixty-five and older and Medicaid for the poor. Finally, Aid to Families with Dependent Children (AFDC), the welfare program created during the New Deal, increased benefits and eligibility.

The War on Poverty was controversial. Leftists believed the government was doing too little to change structural inequality. Conservatives argued that Great Society programs created dependency among America's poor. Policy analysts noted that specific programs were ill conceived and badly implemented.

Decades later, most historians judge the War on Poverty a mixed success. It did alleviate poverty, directly addressing debilitating housing, health, and nutritional deficiencies that hurt America's poor. Between 1965 and 1970, federal spending for Social Security, healthcare, welfare, and education more than doubled. By 1975, the number of Americans receiving food stamps had increased from 600,000 (in 1965) to 17 million. Poverty among the elderly fell from about 40 percent in 1960 to 16 percent in 1974, due largely to increased Social Security benefits and Medicare (see Figure 30.1).

But War on Poverty programs less successfully addressed the root causes of poverty. Neither the Job Corps nor Community Action Programs showed significant results. Economic growth largely sparked the

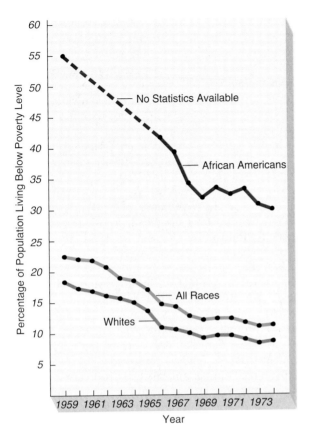

Figure 30.1   Poverty in America for Whites, African Americans, and All Races, 1959–1974

Because of rising levels of economic prosperity, combined with the impact of Great Society programs, the percentage of Americans living in poverty in 1974 was half as high as in 1959. African Americans still were far more likely than white Americans to be poor. In 1959 more than half of all blacks (55.1 percent) were poor; in 1974 the figure remained high (30.3 percent). The government did not record data on African American poverty for the years 1960 through 1965.

dramatic decrease in poverty rates during the 1960s—from 22.4 percent of the population in 1959 to 11 percent in 1973. Unchanged was the fact that 11 million Americans in female-headed households remained poor—the same number in 1969 as in 1963.

Political compromises created long-term problems. For example, Congress accommodated doctors and hospitals in Medicare legislation by allowing federal reimbursements of hospitals' "reasonable costs" and doctors' "reasonable charges" in treating elderly patients. With no incentives to hold prices down, national healthcare expenditures as a percentage of the gross national product rose by almost 44 percent from 1960 to 1971. Nevertheless, problems aside, Johnson's Great Society marked the moment in which many Americans believed they could and should eliminate poverty, disease, and discrimination.

Johnson and Vietnam

In foreign policy, Johnson held firmly to ideas about U.S. superiority and the menace of communism. But international affairs held little interest for him, and he had little appreciation for foreign cultures. At the Taj Mahal in India, Johnson tested the monument's echo with a Texas cowboy yell. And on a trip to Senegal, he ordered that an American bed, a special showerhead, and cases of Cutty Sark be sent along with him. "Foreigners," Johnson quipped early in his administration, only half-jokingly, "are not like the folks I am used to."

Online Study Center   **Improve Your Grade**
Interactive Map: The Vietnam War, 1954–1975

Yet Johnson knew that foreign policy, especially regarding Vietnam, would demand his attention. Since the late 1950s, hostilities in Vietnam had increased, as Ho Chi Minh's North assisted Vietcong guerrillas in the South in reunifying the country under a communist government. President Kennedy had increased aid to the Diem regime in Saigon, airdropped more raiding teams in North Vietnam, and launched herbicide crop destruction to starve the Vietcong. Kennedy also strengthened the U.S. military presence in South Vietnam: by 1963 over sixteen thousand military advisers were there, some authorized to join the U.S.-equipped Army of the Republic of Vietnam (ARVN) in combat.

KENNEDY'S LEGACY IN VIETNAM

Meanwhile, opposition to Diem's repressive regime increased. Peasants objected to being removed from their villages, and Buddhist monks, protesting the Roman Catholic Diem's religious persecution, poured gasoline and ignited themselves in the streets of Saigon. Although Diem was honest, he countenanced corruption in his government and jailed critics. Eventually U.S. officials encouraged ambitious South Vietnamese generals to remove Diem; they murdered him on November 1, 1963.

The timing of Kennedy's assassination a few weeks later ensured that Vietnam would be the most controversial aspect of his legacy. He had expanded U.S. involvement and approved a coup against Diem, but despite the urgings of top advisers, he had refused to commit American ground forces. Over time he became skeptical about South Vietnam's prospects and hinted he would end the American commitment after winning reelection in 1964. Kennedy arrived in Dallas that fateful day uncertain about how to proceed in solving the Vietnam problem.

With the 1964 election looming, Lyndon Johnson did not want to do anything in Vietnam that could keep him from winning the presidency, and so he kept Vietnam on the back burner. Yet Johnson also sought victory there, and throughout 1964, the administration secretly considered expanding the war to North Vietnam.

TONKIN GULF INCIDENT AND RESOLUTION

In early August 1964, U.S. destroyers reported coming under attack from North Vietnamese patrol boats in the Gulf of Tonkin twice in three days (see Map 30.1). Despite conflicting evidence as to whether the second attack occurred, Johnson ordered retaliatory air strikes against North Vietnamese patrol boat bases and an oil depot. By a vote of 416 to 0 in the House and 88 to 2 in the Senate, Congress quickly passed the Gulf of Tonkin Resolution, giving the president the authority to "take all necessary measures to repel any armed attack against the forces of the United States and to prevent further aggression." In so doing, Congress essentially surrendered its warmaking powers to the executive branch.

President Johnson also appreciated how the Gulf of Tonkin affair boosted his public approval ratings and effectively removed Vietnam as a campaign issue for GOP presidential nominee Barry Goldwater. On the ground in South Vietnam, however, the outlook remained grim, as the Vietcong made gains. U.S. officials secretly planned to escalate American involvement.

DECISION FOR ESCALATION

In February 1965, in response to Vietcong attacks on American installations in South Vietnam that killed thirty-two Americans, Johnson ordered Operation Rolling Thunder, a bombing program that continued until October 1968. On March 8, the first U.S. combat battalions came ashore near Danang. The North Vietnamese hid in shelters and increased infiltration into the South. In Saigon, meanwhile, coups and countercoups by self-serving military leaders undermined U.S. efforts.

In July 1965, Johnson convened high-level discussions about U.S. war policy, partially to manipulate the historical record to show him agonizing over a decision he had in truth already made about America's open-ended involvement. On July 28, Johnson publicly announced a significant troop increase, with others to follow. By the end of 1965, more than 180,000 U.S. ground troops were in South Vietnam; in 1966 there were 385,000; and in 1968 U.S. troop strength reached 536,100. In 1967 alone, U.S. warplanes flew 108,000 sorties and dropped 226,000 tons of bombs on North Vietnam. Each American escalation brought a new North Vietnamese escalation, and increased material assistance to the Hanoi government from the Soviet Union and China.

Rolling Thunder and the U.S. troop commitment "Americanized" the war, transforming it from a civil war between North and South into an American war against the communist Hanoi government. Not everyone embraced the decision. Democratic leaders in the Senate, major newspapers such as the *New York Times* and the *Wall Street Journal,* and prominent columnists like Walter Lippmann warned against deepening involvement, as did Vice President Hubert H. Humphrey and Undersecretary of State George W. Ball. Abroad, virtually all of America's allies—including France, Britain, Canada, and Japan—cautioned against escalation and urged a political settlement. Remarkably, many top U.S. officials knew that the odds of success were small, but hoped the new measures would cause Hanoi to end the insurgency in the South.

OPPOSITION TO AMERICANIZATION

Leaders feared that if the United States failed in Vietnam, other countries would find American power less credible. The Soviets and Chinese would challenge U.S. interests elsewhere, and allied governments might conclude they could not depend on Washington. Johnson worried that failure in Vietnam would harm his domestic agenda and feared the personal humiliation. As for helping a South Vietnamese ally

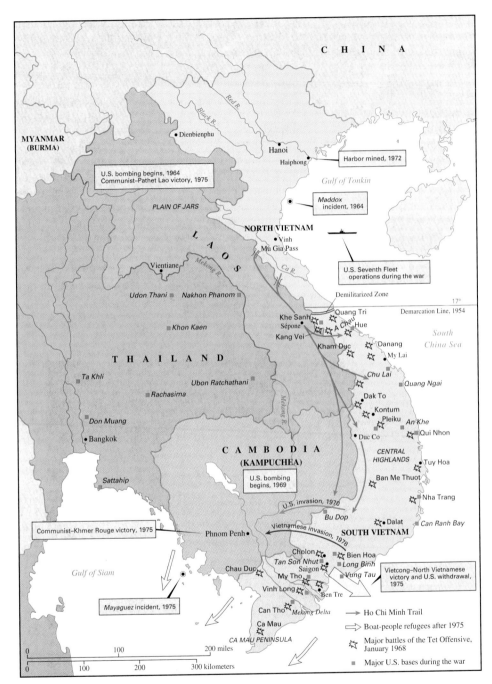

Map 30.1   Southeast Asia and the Vietnam War

To prevent communists from coming to power in Vietnam, Cambodia, and Laos in the 1960s, the United States intervened massively in Southeast Asia. The interventions failed, and the remaining American troops made a hasty exit from Vietnam in 1975, when the victorious Vietcong and North Vietnamese took Saigon and renamed it Ho Chi Minh City.

repulse external aggression, that did not figure into the equation as much as it would have if the Saigon government—wracked with infighting and possessing little popular support—had done more in its own defense.

To minimize publicity about the war, Johnson refused to call up reserve units. This forced the military to rely heavily on the draft, which made Vietnam a young man's war—the average age of soldiers was twenty-two, compared with twenty-six in World War II. It also became a war of the poor and the working class. Through the years of heavy escalation (1965–1968), college students could get deferments, as could teachers and engineers. (In 1969 the draft was changed so that some students were called up through a lottery system.) The armed services recruited hard in poor communities, many of them heavily African American and Latino, advertising the military as an avenue of training and advancement. Once in uniform, those with fewer skills were far more likely to see combat, and hence to die.

AMERICAN SOLDIERS IN VIETNAM

Infantrymen maneuvered into thick jungles, where booby traps and land mines were a constant threat. The enemy was hard to find, often burrowed into elaborate underground tunnels or melded into the population, where any Vietnamese might be a Vietcong.

The entry of American forces into the conflict in 1965 helped stave off a South Vietnamese defeat, thereby achieving Americanization's most immediate and basic objective. But as the North Vietnamese matched each American escalation with one of their own, the war became a stalemate. The U.S. commander, General William Westmoreland, mistakenly believed that a strategy of attrition represented the key to victory. Thus, the measure of success became the "body count"—the number of North Vietnamese and Vietcong corpses found after battle. But the counts were manipulated by officers eager to demonstrate an

■ Wounded American soldiers after a battle in Vietnam.   (Larry Burrows/Getty Images)

operation's success. Worse, the American reliance on massive military technology—including carpet bombing, napalm (jellied gasoline), and crop defoliants that destroyed forests—alienated many South Vietnamese and brought new recruits to the Vietcong.

As television coverage brought the war—its body bags, burned villages, and weeping refugees—into homes nightly, opposition grew. College professors and students organized debates and lectures on American policy, which became a form of protest, called "teach-ins" after the sit-ins of the civil rights movement. Pacifist groups such as the American Friends Service Committee and the Women's International League for Peace and Freedom also organized early protests.

DIVISIONS AT HOME

In early 1966 Senator William Fulbright held televised hearings on whether the national interest was being served by pursuing the war. To the surprise of some, George F. Kennan testified that his containment doctrine was meant for Europe, not volatile Southeast Asia. America's "preoccupation" with Vietnam, Kennan asserted, was undermining its global obligations. Fulbright provoked Americans to think about the conflict and the nation's role in it and illustrated deep divisions among public officials.

Defense Secretary Robert McNamara, who championed the Americanization of the war in 1965, became increasingly troubled by the killing and destructiveness of the bombing. As early as November 1965, he expressed skepticism that victory could ever be achieved. American credibility was suffering, McNamara feared. But Johnson was determined to prevail in Vietnam. Although on occasion he halted the bombing to encourage Ho Chi Minh to negotiate, such pauses often were accompanied by increases in American troop strength. The North demanded a complete suspension of bombing raids before negotiating. And Ho rejected American terms, which amounted to abandonment of his dream of an independent, unified Vietnam.

A Nation Divided

s Johnson struggled with Vietnam, his Great Society faced challenges at home. America was fracturing not only over the Vietnam war, but also along many different lines: black and white, youth and age, radical and conservative.

Shortly after President Johnson signed into law the 1964 landmark Civil Rights Act, racial violence erupted in northern cities. Angry residents of Harlem took to the streets after a white police officer shot a black teenager in July 1964. The following summer, in the predominantly black Watts section of Los Angeles, crowds burned, looted, and battled police for five days and nights. The riot, which began when a white police officer attempted to arrest a black resident on suspicion of drunken driving, left thirty-four dead and more than one thousand injured. In July 1967 twenty-six people were killed in street battles between African Americans and police and army troops in Newark, New Jersey. A week later, in Detroit, forty-three died as 3 square miles went up in flames. In 1967 there were 167 violent outbreaks in 128 cities.

URBAN UNREST

The "long, hot summers" of urban unrest in the 1960s differed from almost all previous race riots. Where past riots were typically started by whites, now black residents exploded in anger over the lack of opportunity in their lives. They looted and burned stores, most of them white owned, while also devastating their own neighborhoods.

In 1968 the National Advisory Commission on Civil Disorders, chaired by Governor Otto Kerner of Illinois, warned that America was "moving towards two societies, one white, one black—separate and unequal," and blamed white racism for the riots. "What white Americans have never fully understood—but what the Negro can never forget—is that white society is deeply implicated in the ghetto. White institutions created it, white institutions maintain it, and white society condones it," concluded the Kerner Commission. Some white Americans disagreed, while others wondered why African Americans were venting their frustration just when they were making real progress.

Online Study Center **Improve Your Grade**
Primary Source:
The Negro Family: The Case for National Action

The answer stemmed, in part, from regional differences. The civil rights movement focused mostly on fighting legal discrimination in the South and ignored problems in the North. Increasingly concentrated in deteriorating inner-city ghettos, most northern

African Americans faced discrimination in housing, credit, and employment. The median income of northern blacks was roughly half that of whites, and their unemployment rate was twice as high. Many northern blacks had given up on both the civil rights movement and the Great Society.

In this climate, the voice of Malcolm X, one-time pimp and street hustler who converted in prison to

BLACK POWER

the Nation of Islam faith, carried a powerful message, urging blacks to seize their freedom "by any means necessary." Members of the Nation of Islam, commonly known as Black Muslims, espoused black pride and separatism from white society. Their faith combined traditional Islam with a belief that whites were subhuman "devils" whose race would soon be destroyed. By the early 1960s, Malcolm X had become the Black Muslims' chief spokesperson. But his murder in 1965 by members of the Nation of Islam who felt betrayed when he started his own more racially tolerant organization, transformed Malcolm X into a powerful symbol of black defiance and self-respect.

A year after Malcolm X's death, Stokely Carmichael, SNCC chairman, denounced "the betrayal of black dreams by white America." To end white oppression, Carmichael proclaimed, blacks had to "stand up and take over" by electing black candidates and organizing their own schools and institutions. "Black Power," his listeners chanted. That year, SNCC expelled its white members and repudiated both nonviolence and integration. CORE followed in 1967.

The best-known black radicals were the Black Panthers, formed in Oakland, California, in 1966. Blending black separatism and revolutionary communism, the Panthers focused on destroying capitalism and its "military arm," the police. Male Panthers dressed in commando gear, carried weapons, and talked about killing "pigs"—and did kill eleven officers by 1970. Police responded in kind; most infamously, Chicago police murdered Panther leader Fred Hampton in his bed. However, the group—led by female members—also worked to improve their neighborhoods by instituting free breakfast and healthcare for ghetto children, offering courses in African American history, and demanding jobs and housing. Before the end of the decade, a vocal minority of America's young of varying races and ethnicities would also call for revolution.

By the mid-1960s, 41 percent of the American population was under age twenty. These young

YOUTH AND POLITICS

people spent more time with peers than any previous generation, as three-quarters of them graduated from high school (up from one-fifth in the 1920s) and almost half attended college (up from 16 percent in 1940). As this large baby boom generation came of age, many believed they must provide democratic leadership for their nation. Inspired by the sit-in movement started at black colleges, white students committed themselves to changing the system.

In the fall of 1960, a group of conservative college students met at William F. Buckley's estate in Sharon, Connecticut, to create Young Americans for Freedom (YAF). Their manifesto, the "Sharon Statement," endorsed Cold War anticommunism and a vision of limited government directly opposed to New Deal liberalism. The YAF planned to capture the Republican Party and move it to the political right; Goldwater's selection as the Republican candidate for president in 1964 demonstrated their early success.

At the other end of the political spectrum, an emerging New Left also rejected liberalism. While conservatives believed liberalism's activist government encroached on individual liberty, the New Left believed liberalism was not enough to bring equality to all Americans. Meeting in Port Huron, Michigan, in 1962, founding members of Students for a Democratic Society (SDS) drafted their "Port Huron Statement," condemning racism, poverty in the midst of plenty, and the Cold War. Calling for "participatory democracy," SDS sought to wrest power from the corporations, the military, and the politicians and return it to "the people."

The rise of white youth activism crystallized at the University of California, Berkeley in fall 1964,

FREE SPEECH MOVEMENT

when the university banned political activity—including recruiting volunteers for civil rights work in Mississippi—from its traditional place along a university-owned sidewalk. When police tried to arrest a CORE worker who defied the order, some four thousand students surrounded the police car. Berkeley graduate student and Mississippi Freedom Summer veteran Mario Savio encouraged the students: "You've got to put your bodies upon the levers . . . [and] you've got to indicate to the people who run it . . . that unless you're free, the machine will be prevented from working at all."

Student political groups, left and right, united to create the Free Speech Movement (FSM). The FSM won back the right to political speech, but not before state police arrested almost eight hundred student protesters. Many saw the administration's actions as a failure of America's democratic promises, but the FSM's victory also demonstrated to students their potential power. By decade's end, the activism born at Berkeley would spread to hundreds of colleges and universities.

Student protesters sought greater control over their education, demanding more relevant classes, more freedom in course selection, and a greater voice in the running of universities. A major target was the doctrine of in loco parentis, which until the late 1960s put universities legally "in the place of parents," allowing control over student behavior that went beyond the law. In loco parentis fell heaviest on women, who had strict curfew regulations called *parietals*, while men did not. Along with an end to sex discrimination, protesters like those at the University of Kansas wanted administrators to explain how statements that "college students are assumed to have maturity of judgment necessary for adult responsibility" squared with the minute regulation of students' nonacademic lives. One man complained that "a high school dropout selling cabbage in a supermarket" had more rights and freedoms than successful university students.

STUDENT ACTIVISM

But it was the war in Vietnam that truly mobilized a national student movement. Believing that learning and speaking out about issues was their civic duty, university students and faculty held teach-ins about U.S. involvement in Vietnam in 1965. SDS sponsored the first major antiwar march that year, drawing twenty thousand protesters to Washington, D.C. On campuses nationwide, students borrowed from civil rights movement strategies, picketing ROTC buildings and protesting military research and recruiting on their

YOUTH AND THE WAR IN VIETNAM

campuses. Despite the antiwar protests' visibility, most students did not yet oppose the war: in 1967 only 30 percent of male college students were antiwar, while 67 percent supported the war. But as the war escalated, more students distrusted the government as well as the seemingly arbitrary authority of university administrations.

During the 1960s, the large baby boom generation would change the nation's culture more than its politics. While many protested the war, most did not, and radicalism did not replace fraternities and sororities. And while there was some crossover, black, white, and Latino youth had different cultural styles, clothes, and music. Collectively, as potential consumers, young people exercised tremendous cultural authority and drove American popular culture in the late 1960s.

YOUTH CULTURE AND THE COUNTERCULTURE

The most unifying element of youth culture was music. The Beatles electrified American teenagers: 73 million viewers watched their first television appearance on the *Ed Sullivan Show* in 1964. Bob Dylan promised revolutionary answers in "Blowin' in the Wind"; Janis Joplin brought the sexual power of the blues to white youth; James Brown and Aretha Franklin proclaimed black pride; and the psychedelic rock of the Jefferson Airplane and the Grateful Dead— along with hallucinogenic drugs—redefined reality. And at the Woodstock Festival in upstate New York in 1969, over 400,000 people reveled in the power of music, coexisting in rain and mud for four days without shelter and without violence.

Some hoped to turn youth rebellion into a social revolution, rejecting what they saw as hypocritical middle-class values. Instead, they crafted an alternative way of life, or "counterculture," liberated from competitive materialism and celebrating pleasure. "Sex, Drugs, and Rock 'n' Roll" became a mantra of sorts, offering these "hippies," or "freaks," a path to a new consciousness. Many did the hard work of creating communes and intentional communities, whether in cities or in hidden stretches of rural America. Although the New Left criticized the counterculture as apolitical, many hippies did envision revolutionary change through mind-altering drugs, sex, or music.

The nascent counterculture first entered the national consciousness during the summer of 1967, when tens of thousands poured into the Haight-Ashbury district of San Francisco, the heart of America's psychedelic culture, for the "Summer of Love." As an older generation of "straight" (or Establishment) Americans watched with horror, white youth adopted aspects of the counterculture. Coats and ties disappeared, as did stockings—and bras. Young men grew long hair, and parents complained, "You can't tell the boys from the girls." Millions experimented with marijuana or hallucinogenic drugs, read underground newspapers, and thought of themselves as alienated from "straight" culture even though as high-school or college students, they were not completely "dropping out."

Some of the most lasting cultural changes involved sexual attitudes. The mass media were fascinated with "Free Love," and while some enjoyed promiscuous sexuality, most were glad that premarital sex no longer destroyed a woman's "reputation." The birth-control pill, distributed since 1960, greatly lessened the risk of unplanned pregnancy, and venereal diseases were easily cured by a basic course of antibiotics. The number of couples living together increased 900 percent from 1960 to 1970. While many young people no longer hid that they were sexually active, 68 percent of adults disapproved of premarital sex in 1969. The adult generation that grew up in the hard decades of depression and war did not understand how promising young people could risk their futures by having sex without marriage, taking drugs, or opposing the war in Vietnam.

1968

By early 1968, the nation was increasingly fragmented. Divided over the war in Vietnam, disillusioned with the prospect of social change, or angry about racial violence, the nation faced the most serious domestic crisis of the postwar era.

On January 31, 1968, the first day of the Vietnamese New Year (Tet), Vietcong and North Vietnamese forces struck South Vietnam, capturing provincial capitals. During the carefully planned offensive, the Saigon airport, the presidential palace, and the ARVN headquarters were attacked. The American embassy was occupied by Vietcong soldiers for six hours. U.S. and South

THE TET OFFENSIVE

Vietnamese units eventually regained ground, inflicting heavy casualties and devastating numerous villages.

Although the Tet Offensive ultimately counted as a U.S. military victory, the heavy fighting called into question American military leaders' confident predictions in earlier months that the war would soon be won. Had not the Vietcong and North Vietnamese demonstrated that they could strike when and where they wished? If America's airpower, dollars, and half a million troops could not now defeat the Vietcong, could they ever do so?

Top presidential advisers sounded notes of despair. Clark Clifford, the new secretary of defense, told Johnson the war could not be won, even with the 206,000 additional soldiers Westmoreland wanted. Aware that the nation was suffering a financial crisis prompted by rampant deficit spending, they knew that taking the initiative in Vietnam would cost billions more, further derail the budget, panic foreign owners of dollars, and wreck the economy.

Controversy over the war split the Democratic Party, just as a presidential election loomed in November. Senator Eugene McCarthy of Minnesota and Robert F. Kennedy (now a senator from New York), both strong opponents of Johnson's war policies, forcefully challenged the president in early primaries. During a March 31 television address, Johnson changed course: he announced a halt to most of the bombing, asked Hanoi to begin negotiations, and then stunned his listeners by withdrawing from the presidential race. His presidency had become a casualty of the war. Peace talks began in May in Paris, but the war ground on.

JOHNSON'S EXIT

Days after Johnson's shocking announcement, Martin Luther King Jr. was murdered in Memphis. It remains unclear why James Earl Ray, a white forty-year-old drifter and petty criminal, shot King—or whether he acted alone. By 1968 King, the senior statesman of the civil rights movement, had become an outspoken critic of the Vietnam War and of American capitalism. Most Americans mourned his death, even as black rage and grief exploded into riots in 130 cities throughout the nation. The violence provoked a backlash from whites, primarily urban, working-class people who were quickly losing sympathy for black Americans' increasingly

ASSASSINATIONS

The British Invasion

The British invasion began in earnest on February 7, 1964. Three thousand screaming American teenagers were waiting when Pan Am's Yankee Clipper touched down at Kennedy Airport with four British "moptops" aboard. "I Want to Hold Your Hand" was already at the top of the U.S. charts, and 73 million people—the largest television audience in history—watched them on the *Ed Sullivan Show* the following Sunday night.

Although the Beatles led the invasion, they did not conquer America alone. The Rolling Stones' first U.S. hit single also came in 1964. The Dave Clark Five appeared on *Ed Sullivan* eighteen times. And there were many others: Herman's Hermits, the Animals, the Hollies, the Kinks, Gerry and the Pacemakers, Petula Clark.

The British invasion was, at least in part, a triumphant homecoming of American music, a transatlantic exchange that reinvigorated both nations. American rock 'n' roll had lost much of its energy by the early 1960s, and the London-centered popular music industry was pumping out a saccharine version of American pop. But by the late 1950s, young musicians in England's provincial cities were listening to the music of African American bluesmen Muddy Waters and Howlin' Wolf and the early rock 'n' roll of Buddy Holly and Chuck Berry. None of this music had a large following in the United States, where *Billboard* magazine's number one hit for 1960 was Percy Faith's "Theme from *A Summer Place*" (a movie starring Sandra Dee and Troy Donahue).

Young British musicians, including John Lennon, Eric Clapton, and Mick Jagger, re-created American musical forms and reinvented rock 'n' roll. By the mid-1960s, the British invasion bands were at the heart of a youth culture that transcended the boundaries of nations. This music connected not only Britain and America but young people throughout the world.

The Beatles perform on the *Ed Sullivan Show* in February 1964. Although Britain's Queen Mother thought the Beatles "young, fresh, and vital," American parents were appalled when the "long" Beatles haircut swept the nation. (AP/Wide World Photos)

radical demands. In Chicago, Mayor Richard Daley ordered police to shoot rioters.

An already shaken nation watched in disbelief only two months later when antiwar Democratic presidential candidate Robert Kennedy was shot and killed after winning the California primary. His assassin, Sirhan Sirhan, an Arab nationalist, targeted Kennedy because of his support for Israel.

Violence erupted again in August at the Democratic National Convention in Chicago. Thousands

CHICAGO DEMOCRATIC NATIONAL CONVENTION

of protesters converged on the city: students who'd gone "Clean for Gene," cutting long hair and donning "respectable" clothes for antiwar candidate Eugene McCarthy; members of the counterculture drawn by the anarchist Yippies' promise of a "Festival of Life" to counter the "Convention of Death"; antiwar groups. Chicago's mayor assigned twelve thousand police to twelve-hour shifts and had twelve thousand army troops with bazookas, rifles, and flamethrowers as backup. Police attacked peaceful antiwar protesters and journalists. "The Whole World Is Watching," chanted the protesters, as police indiscriminately beat people to the ground and Americans gathered around their television sets, despairing over their nation's future.

Upheavals spread around the world that spring and summer. In France, university students protested

GLOBAL PROTEST

rigid academic policies and the Vietnam War. They received support from French workers, who occupied factories and paralyzed public transport; the turmoil contributed to the collapse of Charles de Gaulle's government the following year. In Italy, Germany, England, Ireland, Sweden, Canada, Mexico, Chile, Japan, and South Korea, students held similar protests. In Czechoslovakia, hundreds of thousands of demonstrators flooded Prague streets, demanding democracy and an end to Soviet repression. This so-called Prague Spring developed into a full-scale national rebellion before being crushed by Soviet tanks.

Why so many uprisings occurred simultaneously is unclear. The postwar baby boom produced by the late 1960s a huge mass of teenagers and young adults, many of whom had grown up in relative prosperity with high expectations for the future. Technological advances allowed the nearly instantaneous transmittal of televised images worldwide, so protests in one country could readily inspire similar actions in others.

The 1968 presidential election did little to heal the nation. Democratic nominee Hubert Humphrey,

NIXON'S ELECTION

Johnson's vice president, seemed a continuation of the old politics. Republican candidate Richard Nixon appealed to a nation tired of violence with calls for "law and order." He reached out to those he called "the great, quite forgotten majority—the nonshouters and the nondemonstrators." On Vietnam, Nixon vowed to "end the war and win the peace." Governor George Wallace of Alabama, a vehement segregationist who proposed using nuclear weapons on Vietnam, ran as a third-party candidate. Wallace carried five southern states, drawing almost 14 percent of the popular vote, and Nixon was elected president with the slimmest of margins.

On Christmas Eve 1968, *Apollo 8* entered lunar orbit, in a step toward fulfilling Kennedy's pledge at the start of the tumultuous decade. Looking down on a troubled world, the astronauts read aloud the opening passages of Genesis: "In the beginning, God created the heaven and the earth . . . and God saw that it was good." Many listeners were moved to tears.

Summary   *Online Study Center* ACE the Test

The 1960s began with high hopes for a more democratic America. Civil rights volunteers, often risking their lives, carried the quest for racial equality across the nation. The passage of the Civil Rights Act of 1964 and the Voting Rights Act of 1965 were major milestones. America was shaken by the assassination of President John Kennedy in 1963, but under President Johnson, the liberal vision of government working to improve citizens' lives inspired a flood of legislation designed to create a Great Society.

The Cold War between the United States and the USSR intensified during the 1960s, and a nuclear war nearly happened in the 1962 Cuban missile crisis. Determined not to let Vietnam "fall" to communists, the United States became increasingly involved in the war in Vietnam, sending military forces to prevent communist Vietnamese nationalists led by Ho Chi Minh from succeeding in that nation's civil war. By 1968 there were more than half a million American ground troops in Vietnam, which ultimately divided the country, undermined Great Society domestic programs, and destroyed Lyndon Johnson's presidency.

Despite civil rights gains, many African Americans turned away from the movement, seeking more immediate change. Poor African American neighborhoods burned as riots spread through the nation. Vocal young people—and some of their elders—questioned whether democracy truly existed in the United States. Large numbers of the nation's white youth rebelled by embracing a "counterculture" that rejected white middle-class respectability. With great passion, Americans struggled over the future of their nation.

1968 was a year of crisis, of assassinations and violence in the streets. The decade that started with such promise ended in fierce political polarization.

LEGACY FOR A PEOPLE AND A NATION
The Immigration Act of 1965

When President Johnson signed the 1965 Immigration Act in a ceremony at the foot of the Statue of Liberty, he believed it was important because it "repair[ed] a very deep and painful flaw in the fabric of American justice" by ending national origins quotas that had all but excluded "Polynesians, Orientals, and Negroes" (as Hawai'i's senator Hiram Fong pointed out in 1963). But the president and his advisers mistakenly saw it as primarily symbolic. In fact, this act may have had greater long-term impact on Americans than any other Great Society legislation.

The architects of the Immigration Act did not expect the nature of immigration to change. Attorney General Robert Kennedy argued that abolishing immigration restrictions for Asia and the Pacific would probably produce about five thousand new immigrants before subsiding. But rapid population growth in many poorer nations created a large pool of potential immigrants.

Immigration rates skyrocketed, and by the 1990s, immigration accounted for almost 60 percent of America's population growth. By 2000, more Americans were foreign born than at any time since the 1930s. The majorities came from Mexico, the Philippines, Vietnam, China, the Dominican Republic, Korea, India, the USSR, Jamaica, and Iran.

More than two-thirds of the new immigrants settled in six states: New York, California, Florida, New Jersey, Illinois, and Texas. By the late twentieth century, Spanish-language signs appeared in South Carolina, and Hmong farmers from Southeast Asia offered their produce at the farmers' market in Missoula, Montana. The legacy of the 1965 Immigration Act was unintended but profound: the United States is a more diverse nation today than it otherwise would have been.

CONTINUING DIVISIONS AND NEW LIMITS 1969–1980

*I*n 1969 Daniel Ellsberg was a thirty-eight-year-old former aide to Assistant Secretary of Defense John McNaughton. At the Pentagon, Ellsberg worked on a top-secret study of U.S. decision making in Vietnam. When he left office after Richard Nixon's election, he accessed a copy of the study stored at the Rand Corporation, where he would resume his pregovernment research career. He spent six months poring over the seven thousand pages that made up the so-called Pentagon Papers.

Initially supportive of U.S. intervention in Vietnam, Ellsberg had grown disillusioned. A Harvard-trained Ph.D., former marine officer, and Cold Warrior, he spent 1965 to 1967 in South Vietnam, assessing the war's progress for Washington. He had gone on combat patrols and interviewed military officials, U.S. diplomats, and Vietnamese leaders. The war, he concluded, was in military, political, and moral respects a lost enterprise.

Loyal to the president, Ellsberg was initially reluctant to act. But in 1969 when it became clear that Nixon had no intention of ending the war, Ellsberg boldly decided to risk imprisonment by making the Pentagon Papers public. The study, he believed, showed that presidents had escalated America's presence in Vietnam despite pessimistic estimates from advisers—and that they repeatedly lied to the public about their actions and the results. Ellsberg hoped disclosure would generate sufficient uproar to force a dramatic policy change.

Aided by a Rand colleague, Ellsberg surreptitiously photocopied the study, then spent months pleading with antiwar senators and representatives to release it. When they refused, he went to the press. On June 13, 1971, the *New York Times* published a front-page exposé on the Pentagon Papers. Numerous other newspapers soon published excerpts as well.

Ellsberg's leak became intensely controversial. Nixon tried to stop the papers' publication—the first effort to muzzle the press since the American

The New Politics of Identity

The Women's Movement and Gay Liberation

The End in Vietnam

Nixon, Kissinger, and the World

Presidential Politics and the Crisis of Leadership

LINKS TO THE WORLD
OPEC and the 1973 Oil Embargo

Economic Crisis

An Era of Cultural Transformation

Renewed Cold War and Middle East Crisis

LEGACY FOR A PEOPLE AND A NATION
Human Rights

Online Study Center
This icon will direct you to interactive map and primary source activities on the website
http:college.hmco.com/
pic/nortonbrief7e

CHRONOLOGY

1966 • National Organization for Women founded

1969 • Stonewall Inn uprising begins gay liberation movement
   • *Apollo 11* astronaut Neil Armstrong becomes first person to walk on moon's surface
   • National Chicano Liberation Youth Conference held in Denver
   • "Indians of All Tribes" occupy Alcatraz Island
   • Nixon administration begins affirmative-action plan

1970 • United States invades Cambodia
   • Students at Kent State and Jackson State Universities shot by National Guard troops
   • First Earth Day celebrated
   • Environmental Protection Agency created

1971 • Pentagon Papers published

1972 • Nixon visits China and Soviet Union
   • CREEP stages Watergate break-in
   • Congress approves ERA and passes Title IX, which creates growth in women's athletics

1973 • Peace agreement in Paris ends U.S. involvement in Vietnam
   • OPEC increases oil prices, creating U.S. "energy crisis"
   • *Roe v. Wade* legalizes abortion
   • Agnew resigns; Ford named vice president

1974 • Nixon resigns under threat of impeachment; Ford becomes president

1975 • In deepening economic recession, unemployment hits 8.5 percent
   • New York City saved from bankruptcy by federal loan guarantees
   • Congress passes Indian Self-Determination and Education Assistance Act in response to Native American activists

1976 • Carter elected president

1978 • *Regents of the University of California v. Bakke* outlaws quotas but upholds affirmative action
   • California voters approve Proposition 13

1979 • Three Mile Island nuclear accident raises fears
   • Camp David accords signed by Israel and Egypt
   • American hostages seized in Iran
   • Soviet Union invades Afghanistan
   • Consumer debt doubles from 1975 to hit $315 billion

Revolution—and to discredit Ellsberg and deter other leakers through the illegal actions of a group of petty operatives. Many saw Ellsberg as a hero who acted to shorten an illegitimate war. To others, he was a publicity-seeking traitor.

The 1970s would be a decade of division for Americans. The violence and chaos of 1968 continued in Nixon's early presidency. Antiwar opposition intensified, and as government deceptions were exposed, Americans were increasingly polarized over Vietnam. The movements for racial equality and social justice also became more radical by the 1970s. While some worked for integration, many embraced cultural nationalism, which sought separatist cultures and societies. Even the women's movement, the strongest and most successful movement of the 1970s, had a polarizing effect. Opponents, many of them women, understood feminism as an attack on their way of life and responded with a conservative grassroots movement.

This divided America faced great challenges. Richard Nixon and his national security adviser, Henry Kissinger, understood that the United States and the Soviet Union, weakened by the costs of their competition and challenged by other nations, faced a world where power was diffused. Accordingly, Nixon and

Kissinger sought improved relations with the People's Republic of China and the Soviet Union in an effort to maintain world order and reduce the threat of great-power war.

Ultimately, however, Richard Nixon's illegal acts in the political scandal known as "Watergate" shook the faith of Americans. By the time Nixon, under threat of impeachment, submitted his resignation, Americans were cynical about politics. Neither of Nixon's successors, Gerald Ford or Jimmy Carter, though both honorable men, could restore that lost faith. Carter's presidency was undermined by international events beyond his control. In the Middle East, a region of increasing importance in U.S. foreign policy, Carter helped broker peace between Egypt and Israel but proved powerless to end a hostage crisis in Iran. The Soviet invasion of Afghanistan in 1979 meanwhile revived Cold War tensions.

A deepening economic crisis added to Carter's woes. In the 1970s, middle-class Americans saw unemployment skyrocket and their savings disappearing to double-digit inflation. The downturn was largely triggered by changes in the global economy and international trade, made worse by the oil embargo launched by Arab members of the Organization of Petroleum Exporting Countries in 1973. Americans recognized their vulnerability to decisions made in far-off lands. ■

The New Politics of Identity

By the end of the 1960s, divisions among Americans deepened. The civil rights movement, begun in a quest for equal rights and integration, splintered as many young African Americans rejected nonviolence and integration for separatism and embraced a distinct African American culture. Mexican Americans and Native Americans, inspired by civil rights, created powerful "Brown Power" and "Red Power" movements by the early 1970s. They too demanded equal rights and cultural

recognition. These movements fueled a new "identity politics," which stressed that differences among racial and ethnic groups were critically important foundations for political action.

AFRICAN AMERICAN CULTURAL NATIONALISM

By 1970, most African American activists no longer sought political power and racial justice by emphasizing the shared humanity of all people. Instead, an emphasis on the distinctiveness of black culture attracted a large following. Many black Americans were disillusioned by the racism that outlasted the end of legal segregation and believed that integration would mean subordination in a white-dominated society.

In the early 1970s, though mainstream groups such as the NAACP continued to seek equality through the courts and ballot boxes, many African Americans looked to culture for social change. Rejecting current European American standards of beauty, young people let their hair grow into "naturals" and "Afros." Seeking strength in their own histories, black college students and faculty fought successfully to create black studies departments in American universities. African traditions were reclaimed—or sometimes created. The new holiday Kwanzaa, created in 1966 by Maulana Karenga, professor of black studies at California State University, Long Beach, united African Americans in celebrating a shared heritage.

MEXICAN AMERICAN ACTIVISM

In 1970 the nation's 9 million Mexican Americans (4.3 percent of America's total population) were heavily concentrated in the Southwest and California. Although the U.S. Census classified all Hispanics as white, discrimination in hiring, pay, housing, schools, and the courts was commonplace. In cities, poor Mexican Americans lived in rundown barrios. Almost half of Mexican Americans were functionally illiterate. By the 1970s, although more Mexican Americans were middle class, almost one-quarter of Mexican American families remained below the poverty level. The national Mexican American movement for social justice began with migrant workers. From 1965 through 1970, labor organizers César Chávez and Dolores Huerta led migrant workers in a strike (huelga) against grape growers in California's San Joaquin valley. Chávez and the AFL-CIO-affiliated United Farm Workers (UFW) drew national attention to the working conditions of migrant laborers, who received 10 cents an hour (the minimum wage in 1965 was $1.25) and were often housed by employers in squalid conditions without running water or indoor toilets. A national consumer boycott of table grapes brought the growers to the bargaining table, and in 1970 the UFW won better wages and working conditions. The union resembled nineteenth-century Mexican *mutualistas,* or cooperative associations. Its members founded cooperative groceries, a Spanish-language newspaper, and a theater group.

During the same period in northern New Mexico, Reies Tijerina created the Alianza Federal de Mercedes (Federal Alliance of Grants). The group wanted the return of land belonging to local *hispano* villagers, whose ancestors occupied the territory before the United States claimed it under the 1848 Treaty of Guadalupe Hidalgo. In Denver, former boxer Rudolfo "Corky" Gonzáles drew more than one thousand Mexican American youth to his "Crusade for Justice" at the National Chicano Liberation Youth Conference in 1969. They adopted a manifesto, *El Plan Espiritual de Aztlán,* condemning the "brutal 'Gringo' invasion of our territories."

CHICANO MOVEMENT

These young activists called for the liberation of "La Raza" (from "La Raza de Bronze," the brown people) from oppressive American society, not for equal rights. They also rejected a hyphenated "Mexican-American" identity. The "Mexican American," they explained in *El Plan Espiritual de Aztlán,* "lacks respect for his culture." Instead, they called themselves "Chicanos" or "Chicanas"—barrio slang associated with *pachucos,* hip and sometimes criminal young men who symbolized what "respectable" Mexican Americans despised.

Many middle-class Mexican Americans and members of the older generations never embraced the term *Chicano* or the separatist agenda of *el movimiento.* Younger activists succeeded in introducing Chicano studies into local high-school and college curricula and in creating a unifying cultural identity for Mexican American youth. Politically, La Raza Unida (RUP), a Southwest-based political party, registered thousands of voters and won local elections. Although never as influential as the African American civil rights movement, the Chicano movement effectively challenged discrimination on the local level and created a basis for political action.

■ Calling their movement "Red Power," these American Indian activists dance in 1969 while "reclaiming" Alcatraz Island in San Francisco Bay. Arguing that an 1868 Sioux treaty entitled them to possession of unused federal lands, the group occupied the island until mid-1971.   (Ralph Crane/Getty Images)

Between 1968 and 1975, Native American activists forced American society to reform U.S. government policies affecting them. Young Native American activists were greatly influenced by cultural nationalist beliefs, and seeking a return to the "old ways," they joined with "traditionalists" to challenge tribal leaders advocating assimilation.

NATIVE AMERICAN ACTIVISM

In November 1969 a small group of activists, calling themselves "Indians of All Tribes," occupied Alcatraz Island in San Francisco Bay and demanded that the land be returned to native peoples for an Indian cultural center. The protest, which lasted nineteen months and eventually involved more than four hundred people from fifty different tribes, marked the consolidation of a "pan-Indian" approach to activism. Before Alcatraz, protests were reservation based and local. Although the protesters did not reclaim Alcatraz Island, they drew national attention to the growing "Red Power" movement. In 1972 the radical American Indian Movement occupied a Bureau of Indian Affairs office in Washington, D.C., and then in 1973 a trading post at Wounded Knee, South Dakota, where U.S. Army troops had massacred three hundred Sioux men, women, and children in 1890.

Meanwhile, moderate activists, working through pan-tribal organizations such as the National Congress of American Indians and the Native American Rights Fund, lobbied Congress for greater resources to govern themselves. In response, Congress and the federal courts returned millions of acres of land, and in 1975 Congress passed the Indian Self-Determination and Education Assistance Act. Still, during the 1970s and 1980s, American Indians had a higher rate of tuberculosis, alcoholism, and suicide than any other group. Nine of ten lived in substandard housing, with 40 percent unemployment.

As activists made Americans increasingly aware of discrimination and inequality, policymakers struggled to frame remedies. As early as 1965,

AFFIRMATIVE ACTION President Johnson acknowledged the limits of civil rights legislation, calling for "not just legal equality . . . but equality as a fact and equality as a result." Here Johnson joined his belief that the federal government must help individuals attain competitive skills to a new concept: that equality could be measured by group outcomes or results.

Practical issues also contributed to the shift in emphasis from individual opportunity to group outcomes. The 1964 Civil Rights Act had outlawed discrimination but seemingly had stipulated that action could be taken only when an employer "intentionally engaged" in discrimination. The tens of thousands of cases filed suggested a pervasive pattern of racial and sexual discrimination in education and employment, but each required proof of "intentional" actions against an individual before the Equal Employment Opportunity Commission (EEOC) could respond. Consequently, some people argued that it was possible to prove discrimination by "results"—by the relative number of African Americans or women, for example, an employer had hired or promoted.

In 1969 the Nixon administration implemented the first major government affirmative-action programs. The Philadelphia Plan (so called because it targeted government contracts in that city) required businesses contracting with the federal government to show "affirmative action to meet the goals of increasing minority employment" and set specific numerical "goals," or quotas, for employers. Affirmative action for women and racial and ethnic minorities was soon required by all major government contracts, and many corporations and educational institutions launched their own programs.

Supporters saw affirmative action as a remedy for the lasting effects of past discrimination. Critics argued that creating proportional representation for women and minorities meant discrimination against others who had not created past discrimination, and that group-based remedies violated the principle that individuals should be judged on their own merits. As affirmative action affected hiring and university admissions, bringing members of underrepresented groups into college classrooms, law firms, police stations, and companies nationwide, a deepening recession made jobs scarce. Thus, increasing the number of minorities and women hired often meant reducing the number of white men hired, which triggered their resentment.

The Women's Movement and Gay Liberation

During the 1960s, a second wave of the American women's movement emerged, and by the 1970s mainstream and radical activists joined to wage a multifront battle for "women's liberation."

One event that rejuvenated the women's movement was the popularity of Betty Friedan's 1963 book, *The Feminine Mystique.* Writing as a housewife and mother (though she had a long history of political activism), Friedan described "the problem with no name," the dissatisfaction of educated, middle-class wives and mothers like herself, who—looking at their homes and families—wondered guiltily if that was all there was to life. Instead of blaming women for failing to adapt to women's proper role as 1950s magazines often did, Friedan blamed the role itself and the society that created it.

The organized, liberal wing of the women's movement emerged in 1966 with the founding of the National Organization for Women (NOW). Comprising primarily educated women, NOW was a lobbying group seeking to pressure the EEOC into enforcing the 1964 Civil Rights Act. With racial discrimination its priority, sex discrimination fell to the bottom of the EEOC's list. By 1970, NOW had one hundred chapters and over three thousand members nationwide.

LIBERAL AND RADICAL FEMINISM

Another strand of the women's movement developed from the nation's radical social justice movements. In 1968 a group of women protested the Miss America Pageant in Atlantic City as a "degrading mindless-boob girlie symbol." Though nothing was burned, the pejorative 1970s term for feminists, "bra-burners," came from this event, in which women threw items of "enslavement" (girdles, high heels, curlers, and bras) into a "Freedom Trashcan." Many of these women, and others who created a radical feminist movement, had been active in the antiwar or civil rights movements, and those experiences led them to analyze women's roles in American society.

The feminism embraced by these young activists was never a single, coherent set of beliefs. Most radical feminists, however, practiced what they called "personal politics," believing, as feminist author Charlotte Bunch explained, that "there is no private domain of a person's life that is not political, and there is no political issue that is not ultimately personal." In the early 1970s, women throughout the nation came together in suburban kitchens, college dorm rooms, and churches or synagogues to create "consciousness-raising" groups, exploring topics such as power relationships in romance and marriage, sexuality, abortion, healthcare, work, and family.

During the 1970s, the women's movement claimed significant achievements. On March 22, 1972, after massive lobbying by women's organizations, Congress approved the Equal Rights Amendment (ERA) to the Constitution. It stated simply that "equality of rights under the law shall not be denied or abridged by the United States or by any State on account of sex." By the end of the year, twenty-two states (of the thirty-eight necessary to amend the Constitu-

ACCOMPLISHMENTS OF THE WOMEN'S MOVEMENT

tion) had ratified the ERA. Also in 1972, Congress passed Title IX of the Higher Education Act, which prevented federal funds from going to any college or university discriminating against women. As a result, universities began to channel money to women's athletics, and women's participation in sports boomed.

At the state and local levels, women challenged understandings of rape that blamed the victim for the attack. By the end of the decade, activists established rape crisis centers, educated local police and hospital officials about procedures protecting rape survivors, and even changed laws.

Challenging the medical establishment, *Our Bodies, Ourselves* was a book created by the Boston Women's Health Collective in 1971 to help women understand—and take control over—their own sexual and reproductive health. Women who sought the right to safe and legal abortions won a major victory in 1973 when the Supreme Court, in a 7–2 decision on *Roe v. Wade,* ruled that privacy rights protected a woman's choice to end a pregnancy.

Women greatly increased their roles in religious organizations, and some denominations ordained women. In 1970 only 8.4 percent of medical school graduates and 5.4 percent of law school graduates were women; by 1979, those figures had climbed to 23 percent and 28.5 percent, respectively. Colleges and universities also established women's studies departments, with thirty thousand college courses focused on women or gender relations by 1980.

The women's movement was met by opposition, much of it from women. Many had no desire to be "equal" if it meant giving up traditional gender roles in marriage or working at low-wage, exhausting jobs. African American women and Chicanas, many of whom were active in movements for the liberation of their peoples and some of whom helped create second-wave feminism, often regarded feminism as a "white" movement that ignored their cultural traditions and diverted attention from the fight for racial equality.

OPPOSITION TO THE WOMEN'S MOVEMENT

Organized opposition to feminism came primarily from conservative, often religiously motivated men and women. As one conservative Christian writer claimed, "The Bible clearly states that the wife is to submit to her husband's leadership." These beliefs, along with fears about changing gender roles, fueled the

STOP-ERA movement led by Phyllis Schlafly, a lawyer and prominent conservative political activist. Schlafly attacked the women's movement as "a total assault on the role of the American woman as wife and mother." Schlafly's group argued that the ERA would decriminalize rape, force Americans to use unisex toilets, and make women subject to the military draft.

In fighting the ERA, tens of thousands of women became politically experienced and fed a growing grass-roots conservative movement that would come into its own in the 1980s. By the mid-1970s, the STOP-ERA movement stalled the Equal Rights Amendment. Despite a congressional deadline extension, the amendment would fall three states short of ratification and expire in 1982.

GAY LIBERATION

In the early 1970s, gay men and lesbians faced widespread discrimination. Consensual, same-sex sexual intercourse was illegal in almost every state, and until 1973 homosexuality was labeled a mental disorder by the American Psychiatric Association. Homosexual couples did not receive partnership benefits such as health insurance; they could not marry or adopt children. Gay men and women remained targets of discrimination in hiring and endured public ridicule, harassment, and physical attacks.

There were small "homophile" organizations, such as the Mattachine Society and the Daughters of Bilitis, that had worked for gay rights since the 1950s. But the symbolic beginning of the gay liberation movement came on June 28, 1969, when New York City police raided the Stonewall Inn, a gay bar in Greenwich Village. (New York City law made it illegal for more than three homosexual patrons to occupy a bar at the same time.) That night, for the first time, patrons stood up to the police. The next morning, a new slogan was spray-painted on neighborhood walls: "Gay Power."

Inspired by the Stonewall riot, some people worked openly and militantly for gay rights. They focused on a dual agenda: legal equality and the promotion of Gay Pride. Some rejected the notion of fitting into straight (heterosexual) culture and helped create distinctive gay communities. By 1973, there were about eight hundred gay organizations in the United States. Centered in big cities and on college campuses, most organizations created supportive environments encouraging gay men and lesbians to come "out of the closet" and push for reform. By decade's end, gay men and lesbians were a public political force in several cities, especially New York, Miami, and San Francisco.

The End in Vietmam

*N*o division pervaded American politics as did the war in Vietnam. Although Richard Nixon said he was going to end the war fast so it would not ruin his political career as it had Johnson's, he did not. Like Johnson, he feared that a precipitous withdrawal would harm American credibility on the world stage. Anxious to get American troops out of Vietnam, Nixon was equally committed to preserving an independent, noncommunist South Vietnam. Hence, he adopted a policy that at once contracted and expanded the war.

INVASION OF CAMBODIA

Nixon's policy centered on "Vietnamization": building up South Vietnamese forces to replace U.S. troops. Accordingly, the president decreased American forces from 543,000 in the spring of 1969 to 156,800 by the end of 1971, and to 60,000 by the fall of 1972. Vietnamization helped quiet domestic dissent—as did the replacement of the military draft with a lottery system, by which only those nineteen-year-olds with low lottery numbers would be subject to conscription—but it did nothing to end the stalemate in the Paris peace talks underway since 1968. Nixon therefore intensified the bombing of North Vietnam and enemy supply depots in neighboring Cambodia, hoping to pound Hanoi into concessions.

The expanded bombing of neutral Cambodia commenced in March 1969 with fourteen months of B-52 pilots flying 3,600 missions and dropping over 100,000 tons of bombs, initially in secret. When the North Vietnamese refused to buckle, Nixon turned up the heat: in April 1970 South Vietnamese and U.S. forces invaded Cambodia. The president publicly said he would not allow "the world's most powerful nation" to act "like a pitiful, helpless giant."

PROTESTS AND COUNTERDEMON- STRATIONS

Instantly, the antiwar movement rose up; students on about 450 college campuses went out on strike, and hundreds of thousands of demonstrators protested the administration's policies in various cities. The crisis atmosphere intensified on May 4 when National Guardsmen in Ohio fired at fleeing students at Kent State University, killing four young people. Ten days later, police armed with automatic weapons blasted a women's dormitory at historically black Jackson State University in Mississippi, killing two and wounding nine others. Police claimed they had been shot at, but no evidence could be found. Nixon's widening of the war sparked congressional outrage, and in June the Senate terminated the 1964 Tonkin Gulf Resolution. After two months, U.S. troops withdrew from Cambodia.

Although a majority of Americans told pollsters they thought the original troop commitment to Vietnam was a mistake, 50 percent said they accepted Nixon's claim that invading Cambodia would shorten the war, and some were angered by demonstrating college students. In New York City, construction workers organized counterdemonstrations against the antiwar protests. Nevertheless, the tumult over the invasion reduced Nixon's options on the war. Henceforth, solid majorities opposed any new missions for U.S. ground troops in Southeast Asia.

Online Study Center **Improve Your Grade**
Primary Source: Gayle Smith's Private War

Equally troubling was that morale and discipline among troops had been on the decline before Nixon

MORALE
PROBLEMS IN
MILITARY

took office. There were growing reports of drug addiction, desertion, racial discord, even the murder of unpopular officers by enlisted men (a practice called "fragging"). The 1971 court-martial and conviction of Lieutenant William Calley, charged with overseeing the killing of over three hundred unarmed South Vietnamese civilians in My Lai in 1968, got particular attention when an army photographer captured the horror in graphic pictures.

The Nixon administration meanwhile stepped up its efforts to pressure Hanoi into a settlement. When

CEASE-FIRE
AGREEMENT

the North Vietnamese launched a major offensive into South Vietnam in March 1972, Nixon responded with a massive aerial onslaught. In December 1972, after an apparent peace agreement collapsed, the United States launched another air strike on the North—the so-called Christmas bombing.

A diplomatic agreement was close. Kissinger and his North Vietnamese counterpart in the negotiations, Le Duc Tho, resolved many of the outstanding issues. Most notably, Kissinger agreed that North Vietnamese troops could remain in the South after the settlement, while Tho abandoned Hanoi's insistence that the Saigon government of Nguyen Van Thieu be removed. On January 27, 1973, Kissinger and Le Duc Tho signed a cease-fire agreement, and Nixon compelled a reluctant Thieu to accept it by threatening to cut off U.S. aid. The United States promised to withdraw its troops within sixty days. North Vietnamese troops could stay in South Vietnam, and a coalition government that included the Vietcong would be formed in the South.

The United States pulled its troops out of Vietnam, leaving behind some military advisers. Soon, full-scale war erupted again. Just before the South Vietnamese surrendered, hundreds of Americans and Vietnamese advocates were hastily evacuated from Saigon. On April 29, 1975, the South Vietnamese government collapsed, and Vietnam was reunified under a communist government in Hanoi. Saigon was renamed Ho Chi Minh City for the persevering patriot who had died in 1969.

More than 58,000 Americans and between 1.5 and 3 million Vietnamese died in the war. Civilian

COSTS OF THE
VIETNAM WAR

deaths in Cambodia and Laos reached hundreds of thousands. The war cost the United States at least $170 billion, and billions more in subsequent veterans' benefits. With funds shifted from domestic programs, the nation suffered inflation, political schism, and abuses of executive power. The war also delayed accommodation with the Soviet Union and the People's Republic of China, fueled friction with allies, and alienated Third World nations.

In 1975 communists established repressive governments in Vietnam, Cambodia, and Laos, but beyond Indochina, the domino effect once predicted by U.S. officials never occurred. Acute hunger afflicted the people of those devastated lands. Soon refugees—"boat people"—crowded aboard unsafe vessels to escape. Many emigrated to the United States, where they were received with mixed feelings by Americans reluctant to be reminded of defeat and their responsibility for the plight of the Southeast Asian peoples.

As historian William Appleman Williams observed, Americans had had their overseas sphere of

DEBATE OVER THE LESSONS OF VIETNAM

influence pushed back for the first time. Hawkish observers claimed that failure in Vietnam undermined the nation's credibility. They pointed to a "Vietnam syndrome"—an American suspicion of foreign entanglements—that they feared would inhibit the future exercise of U.S. power. America lost in Vietnam, they asserted, because Americans had lost their guts at home.

Dovish analysts blamed the war on an imperial presidency that permitted strong-willed men to act without restraint and a weak Congress that conceded too much power to the executive branch. Make the president adhere to the checks-and-balances system—make him go to Congress for a declaration of war—these critics counseled. This view found expression in the War Powers Act of 1973, which limited the president's warmaking freedom and require congressional approval before committing U.S. forces to combat lasting more than sixty days.

Veterans' calls for help in dealing with posttraumatic stress disorder, which afflicted thousands

VIETNAM VETERANS

of the 2.8 million Vietnam veterans, also stimulated public discussion. Doctors reported that the disorder, which included nightmares and extreme nervousness, stemmed from soldiers' having seen many children, women, and elderly people killed. Some GIs inadvertently killed these people; some killed them vengefully and later felt guilt. Other veterans publicized their deteriorating health from the defoliant Agent Orange and other herbicides they handled or were accidentally sprayed with in Vietnam.

Nixon, Kissinger, and the World

The difficulties of the Vietnam War signified to Nixon and Kissinger that American power was limited and, in relative terms, in decline. This reality necessitated a new approach to the Cold War. In particular, they believed the United States had to adapt to a new multipolar international system, one no longer defined simply by the Soviet-American rivalry. Western Europe was becoming a major player

in its own right, as was Japan. The Middle East loomed increasingly large. Above all, Americans had to come to grips with China by rethinking the policy of hostile isolation.

Nixon and Kissinger were an unlikely duo—the reclusive, ambitious Californian, born of Quaker parents, and the sociable, dynamic Jewish intellectual who fled Nazi Germany as a child. Nixon, ten years older, was a career politician, while Kissinger had made his name as a Harvard professor and foreign policy consultant. What the two men shared was a paranoia about rivals and a capacity to think in large conceptual terms about America's place in the world.

In July 1969 Nixon and Kissinger acknowledged the limits of American power and resources in the

NIXON DOCTRINE

Nixon Doctrine. The United States, they said, would provide economic aid to allies, but they should not count on American troops. Washington could no longer afford to sustain its overseas commitments and would have to rely on regional allies, including authoritarian regimes, to maintain an anticommunist world order. Nixon's doctrine partially retreated from the 1947 Truman Doctrine's promise to support noncommunist governments facing threats.

The other pillar of the new foreign policy was détente: measured cooperation with the Soviets

DÉTENTE

through negotiations within an environment of rivalry. Détente's primary purpose, like that of the containment doctrine, was to check Soviet expansion and arms buildup, but through diplomacy and mutual concessions. The second part of the strategy sought to curb revolution and radicalism in the Third World and quash threats to American interests. More specifically, expanded trade with friendlier Soviets and Chinese might reduce the huge U.S. balance-of-payments deficit. And improving relations with both communist giants, at a time when Sino-Soviet tensions were increasing, might weaken communism.

The Soviet Union too found that the Cold War drained its resources, with defense and consumer demands increasingly at odds. Improved relations with Washington would also allow the USSR to focus on the threat from China and might generate progress on outstanding European issues, including the status of Germany and Berlin. In May 1972 the two nations agreed to slow the arms race by limiting the construction and deployment of intercontinental ballistic missiles and antiballistic missile defenses.

Meanwhile, the United States took dramatic steps to end two decades of Sino-American hostility. The

OPENING
TO CHINA

Chinese wanted to spur trade and hoped that friendlier Sino-American relations would make their one-time ally and now enemy, the Soviet Union, more cautious. In early 1972 Nixon made a historic trip to "Red China," where he and the venerable Chinese leaders Mao Zedong and Zhou Enlai agreed to disagree on many issues, except one: the Soviet Union should not be permitted to make gains in Asia. Sino-American relations improved slightly, and official diplomatic recognition came in 1979.

In the Third World, too, Nixon and Kissinger sought stability, though there they hoped to achieve it by maintaining the status quo. As it happened, events in the Third World would provide the Nixon-Kissinger approach with its greatest test.

In the Middle East the situation had grown more volatile in the aftermath of the Arab-Israeli Six-Day

WARS IN THE
MIDDLE EAST

War in 1967. Israel scored victories against Egypt and Syria, seizing the Sinai Peninsula and the Gaza Strip from Egypt, the West Bank and East Jerusalem from Jordan, and the Golan Heights from Syria (see Map 33.1). Instantly, Israel's regional position was transformed as it gained 28,000 square miles and could henceforth defend itself against invading forces. But with Gaza and the West Bank as the ancestral homeland to hundreds of thousands of Palestinians and refugees, Israel found itself governing large numbers of people who wanted to see it destroyed (see Chapter 28). When the Israelis established Jewish settlements in their newly won areas, Arab resentment grew. Terrorists associated with the Palestinian Liberation Organization (PLO) made hit-and-run raids on Jewish settlements, hijacked jetliners, and murdered Israeli athletes at the 1972 Olympic Games in Munich, West Germany. The Israelis retaliated by assassinating PLO leaders.

In October 1973, on the Jewish High Holy Day of Yom Kippur, Egypt and Syria attacked Israel, primarily seeking revenge for the 1967 defeat. Surprised, Israel reeled before launching an effective counteroffensive. To punish Americans for their pro-Israel

stance, the Organization of Petroleum Exporting Countries (OPEC), a group of mostly Arab nations that had joined together to raise the price of oil, embargoed oil shipments to the United States and other Israeli supporters. An energy crisis rocked the nation. Kissinger arranged a cease-fire, but OPEC did not lift the embargo until March 1974. The next year Kissinger persuaded Egypt and Israel to accept a U.N. peacekeeping force in the Sinai. But Arabs still vowed to destroy Israel, and Israelis built more Jewish settlements in occupied lands.

In Latin America, the Nixon administration thwarted leftist challenges to authoritarian rule. When

ANTIRADICALISM
IN LATIN
AMERICA
AND AFRICA

voters in Chile elected Marxist president Salvador Allende in 1970, the CIA secretly encouraged military officers to stage a coup. In 1973 a military junta ousted Allende and installed an authoritarian regime under General Augusto Pinochet. (Allende was subsequently murdered.) Washington publicly denied any role.

In Africa, too, Washington preferred the status quo, backing a white-minority regime in Rhodesia (now Zimbabwe), and activated the CIA in a failed effort to defeat a Soviet- and Cuban-backed faction in Angola's civil war. In South Africa, Nixon tolerated the white rulers who imposed segregationist apartheid on blacks and mixed-race "coloureds" (85 percent of the population), keeping them poor, disfranchised, and ghettoized in prisonlike townships. After the leftist government came to power in Angola, however, Washington paid attention to Africa, building economic ties and sending arms to friendly black nations such as Kenya and the Congo, while distancing the United States from the white governments of Rhodesia and South Africa.

Presidential Politics and the Crisis of Leadership

*R*ichard Nixon's foreign policy accomplishments were overshadowed by his domestic failures. He betrayed the public trust and broke laws. That, combined with Americans' belief that leaders had repeatedly lied about the war in Vietnam, shook their faith in government. This new mistrust joined

OPEC and the 1973 Oil Embargo

If one date can mark the decline of American power in the Cold War era and the arrival of the Arab nations as important players on the world stage, it would be October 20, 1973. That day, Arab members of the Organization of Petroleum Exporting Countries (OPEC)—Saudi Arabia, Iraq, Kuwait, Libya, and Algeria—imposed an embargo on oil shipments to the United States and other Israeli allies. The move was in retaliation against U.S. support of Israel in the two-week-old Yom Kippur War. The embargo followed an OPEC price hike days earlier, from $3.01 to $5.12 per barrel. In December, the five Arab countries, joined by Iran, raised prices again, to $11.65 per barrel, almost a fourfold increase from early October.

Gasoline prices surged across America, and some dealers ran low on supplies. Frustrated Americans endured endless lines at the pumps and shivered in underheated homes. When the embargo was lifted in April 1974, oil prices stayed high, and the aftereffects of the embargo would linger through the decade. It confirmed how much America's economic destiny was beyond its control.

In the early 1950s, Americans produced all the oil they needed at home. By the early 1960s the picture changed, as America depended on foreign sources for one out of every six barrels of oil. By 1972, the figure had gone up to about two out of six, or more than 30 percent. But few Americans worried and were shocked by the embargo. As author Daniel Yergin put it, "The shortfall struck at fundamental beliefs in the endless abundance of resources . . . that a large part of the public did not even know, up until October 1973, that the United States imported any oil at all."

When the embargo ended, Americans resumed their wastefulness, but in a changed world: the United States had become a dependent nation, its economic future linked to decisions by Arab sheiks half a world away.

In 1976 OPEC sharply raised the price of oil a second time, prompting this editorial cartoon by Don Wright of the *Miami News*. (Copyright, Tribune Media Services, Inc. All rights reserved. Reprinted with permission)

with conservatives' traditional suspicion of big, activist government to create a crisis of leadership and undermine liberal policies that had governed the nation since the New Deal. Nixon's successors, Gerald Ford and James Earl Carter, were limited by the public's suspicion of government.

Richard Nixon was brilliant, driven, politically cunning, yet also crude, prejudiced against Jews and African Americans, happy to use dirty tricks against his enemies, and driven by a resentment that bordered on paranoia. The son of a grocer from an agricultural region of southern California, Nixon loathed the liberal establishment, which loathed him back, and his presidency was driven by that as much as by a philosophical commitment to conservative principles.

NIXON'S
DOMESTIC
AGENDA

Nixon's domestic policy initiatives often appeared oddly liberal, even progressive. The Nixon administration pioneered affirmative action and doubled the budgets of the National Endowment for the Humanities (NEH) and National Endowment for the Arts (NEA). Nixon supported the ERA, signed major environmental legislation, created the Occupational Safety and Health Administration, actively used deficit spending to manage the economy, and even proposed a guaranteed minimum income for all Americans.

At the same time, Nixon pursued a conservative agenda that involved "devolution," or shifting federal government authority to states and localities. He promoted revenue-sharing programs that distributed federal funds back to the states, thus appealing to those who saw high taxes as supporting liberal "giveaway" programs for poor and minority Americans. Nixon worked to equate the Republican Party with law and order and the Democrats with permissiveness, crime, drugs, radicalism, and the "hippie lifestyle." He used his outspoken vice president, Spiro Agnew, to attack protesters and critics as "naughty children." He appointed four conservative justices to the Supreme Court (Chief Justice Warren Burger, Harry Blackmun, Lewis Powell Jr., and William Rehnquist); ironically, Nixon's appointees did not always vote as he would have wished.

But most of Nixon's "liberal" agenda was not so much liberal as tricky—a term commonly applied to Nixon at the time. Instead of attacking liberal programs, Nixon attempted to undermine them while appearing to offer support. For example, when Nixon proposed a guaranteed minimum income for all Americans, his larger goal was to dismantle the federal welfare system and destroy its liberal bureaucracy of social workers.

Nixon additionally sought to attract white southerners to the Republican Party. He nominated two southerners for the Supreme Court—one of whom had a segregationist record. When Congress declined to confirm either nominee, Nixon protested angrily. After the Supreme Court upheld a school desegregation plan requiring a highly segregated North Carolina school system to achieve racial integration by busing both black and white children throughout the county (*Swann v. Charlotte-Mecklenburg*, 1971), Nixon denounced busing.

Nixon was almost sure of reelection in 1972. His Democratic opponent was George McGovern, a progressive senator from South Dakota and strong opponent of the Vietnam War who declared, "I am not a centrist candidate." Alabama governor George Wallace, running on a third-party ticket, withdrew from the race after an assassination attempt at a Maryland shopping center left him paralyzed. The Nixon campaign, however, was taking no chances. On June 17, five men from the Committee to Re-elect the President, known as CREEP, were caught breaking into the Democratic National Committee's offices at the Watergate apartment and office complex in Washington, D.C. The break-in got little attention, and Nixon was swept into office in November with 60 percent of the popular vote. McGovern carried only Massachusetts and the District of Columbia. But even as Nixon triumphed, his downfall had begun.

ENEMIES AND
DIRTY TRICKS

From the beginning of his presidency, Nixon obsessively believed he was surrounded by enemies. He made "enemies lists" that included all black members of Congress and the presidents of most Ivy League universities. On Nixon's order, his aide Charles Colson formed a secret group called the Plumbers. Their first job was to break into the office of the psychiatrist treating Daniel Ellsberg, the former Pentagon employee responsible for making the Pentagon Papers public, looking for material to discredit him. During the 1972 presidential campaign, the Plumbers bugged phones, infiltrated campaign staffs, and wrote anonymous letters falsely accusing Democratic candidates of sexual misconduct. They were going back to plant more surveillance at the Democratic National Committee offices when they were caught by D.C. police at the Watergate complex.

Nixon was not directly involved in the Watergate affair, but instead of distancing himself and firing the people involved, he covered up their connection to the break-ins. He had the CIA stop the FBI's investigation, claiming national security. At this point, Nixon had obstructed justice—a felony and an impeachable crime—but he had also halted the investigation. However, two relatively unknown reporters for the *Washington Post*, Carl Bernstein and Bob Woodward, stayed on the story. Aided by an anonymous, highly placed government official code-named Deep Throat (the title of a notorious 1972 X-rated film), they followed a money trail leading to the White House. (In June 2005, it was revealed that Deep Throat was Mark Felt, a high-ranking FBI official at the time of Watergate.)

WATERGATE COVER-UP AND INVESTIGATION

From May to August 1973, the Senate held televised hearings on the Watergate affair. White House counsel John Dean, fearful that he was becoming the fall guy for the Watergate fiasco, gave damning testimony. On July 13, a White House aide told the Senate Committee that Nixon regularly recorded his conversations in the Oval Office. Nixon refused to turn the tapes over to Congress.

Nixon's problems continued. In October 1973, Vice President Spiro Agnew resigned following charges that he accepted bribes while governor of Maryland. Nixon appointed and Congress approved Michigan's Gerald Ford, the House minority leader, as Agnew's replacement. Meanwhile, Nixon's staff was increasingly concerned about his excessive drinking and seeming mental instability. Then, on October 24, 1973, the House of Representatives began impeachment proceedings.

IMPEACHMENT AND RESIGNATION

Under court order, Nixon released portions of the Oval Office tapes. Though the first tapes revealed nothing criminal, the public was shocked by Nixon's obscenities and racism. In July 1974, the Supreme Court ruled that Nixon must release all the tapes. Despite "mysterious" erasures on two key tapes, the House Judiciary Committee found evidence to im-

■ Resigning in disgrace as impeachment for his role in the Watergate cover-up became a certainty, Richard Nixon flashes the "V for victory" sign as he leaves the White House for the last time. (Nixon Presidential Materials Project, National Archives and Record Administration)

peach Nixon on three grounds: obstruction of justice, abuse of power, and contempt of Congress. On August 9, 1974, facing certain impeachment and conviction, Richard Nixon became the first president of the United States to resign.

The Watergate scandal shook the confidence of American citizens in their government and prompted Congress to pass several bills aimed at restricting presidential power, including the War Powers Act.

Gerald Ford, the nation's first unelected president, faced a cynical nation. The presidency was discredited; the nation's economy was in

FORD'S PRESIDENCY

decline. Ford was an honorable man who tried to end "the long national nightmare." But when he issued a full pardon to Richard Nixon, his approval ratings plummeted from 71 to 41 percent. Some suggested, though with no evidence, that he had struck a deal with Nixon.

Ford accomplished little domestically during his two and a half years in office. The Democrats gained a large margin in the 1974 congressional elections, and after Watergate, Congress was willing to exercise its power. Ford almost routinely vetoed its bills—thirty-nine in one year—but Congress often overrode his veto. During the course of his brief presidency, Ford was constantly portrayed as a buffoon and klutz in political cartoons, comedy monologues, and especially on the hit television show *Saturday Night Live*. Ford caught the fallout of disdain from Nixon's actions. No longer would respect for the presidency prevent the mass media from reporting presidential stumbles or misconduct.

Jimmy Carter, who was elected in 1976 by a slim margin, initially benefited from Americans' suspicion of politicians. Carter was a one-term

CARTER AS "OUTSIDER" PRESIDENT

governor of Georgia, one of the new southern leaders committed to racial equality. He grew up on his family's peanut farm in rural Plains, Georgia; graduated from the Naval Academy; then served as an engineer in the navy's nuclear submarine program. A born-again Christian, Carter promised America, "I will never lie to you," underscoring his distance from Washington's recent political corruption.

From his inauguration, when he broke with the conventional motorcade and walked down Pennsylvania Avenue holding hands with his wife and close adviser Rosalynn and their daughter, Amy, Carter emphasized his populist, outsider appeal. But his outsider status proved one of his greatest problems as president. Though an astute policymaker, he scorned the deal making that was necessary to pass legislation in Congress.

Carter faced problems that would have challenged any leader: continued economic downturn, unabated energy shortages, public distrust of government. More than any other postwar American leader, Carter was willing to tell Americans things they did not want to hear. As shortages of natural gas forced schools and businesses to close during the bitterly cold winter of 1977, Carter, wearing a cardigan sweater, called for "sacrifice" and implemented energy conservation at government buildings. In a defining speech, Carter told Americans that the nation suffered from a crisis of the spirit. He talked about the false lures of "self-indulgence and consumption." He called for a "new commitment to the path of common purpose." But he had few solutions for the national malaise.

Carter did ease burdensome government regulations without destroying consumer and worker safeguards, and created the Departments of Energy and Education. He also established a $1.6 billion "Superfund" to clean up abandoned chemical-waste sites and placed over 100 million acres of Alaskan land under federal protection as national parks, forests, and wildlife refuges.

Economic Crisis

Since World War II, except for a few brief downturns, prosperity had dominated American life. Prosperity made possible the great liberal initiatives of the 1960s and improved the lives of America's poor and elderly citizens. But in the early 1970s, that long period of economic expansion ended. In 1974 alone, the gross national product dropped two percentage points. Industrial production fell 9 percent. Inflation—the increase in costs of goods and services—skyrocketed, and unemployment grew.

Throughout the 1970s, the U.S. economy floundered in what economists dubbed "stag-flation":

STAGFLATION AND ITS CAUSES

a stagnant economy characterized by high unemployment and out-of-control inflation. Stagflation was almost impossible to manage with traditional economic remedies. When the federal government increased spending to stimulate the economy and so reduce unemployment, inflation grew. When it tried to halt inflation by cutting government spending or tightening the money supply, the recession deepened and unemployment skyrocketed.

The causes of the economic crisis were complex. President Johnson had created inflationary pressure by waging an expensive war in Vietnam while greatly expanding domestic spending in his Great Society programs. But fundamental problems also came from America's changing role in the global economy. By the early 1970s, both of America's major World War II adversaries, Japan and Germany, had become major economic powers—and competitors in global trade that the United States once exclusively dominated. In 1971, for the first time since the nineteenth century, the United States imported more goods than it exported, beginning an era of American trade deficits.

Corporate decisions also contributed to growing trade imbalances. During the years of global dominance, few American companies improved production techniques or educated workers. Consequently, American productivity—the average output of goods per hour of labor—declined. But wages rarely did. The combination of falling productivity and high labor costs meant that American goods became increasingly expensive. And American companies allowed the quality of their goods to decline. From 1966 to 1973, for example, American car and truck manufacturers recalled almost 30 million vehicles because of serious defects.

America's global economic vulnerability was driven home by the energy crisis in 1973. The country depended on imported oil for almost one-third of its energy. When OPEC cut off oil shipments to the United States, prices rose 350 percent and increased heating costs, shipping costs, and manufacturing costs, as well as the cost of goods and services. Inflation jumped from 3 percent in 1973 to 11 percent in 1974. Sales of gas-guzzling American cars plummeted as people switched to energy-efficient subcompacts from Japan and Europe. General Motors laid off 6 percent of its domestic work force and put larger numbers on rolling unpaid leaves. As the ailing automobile industry quit buying steel, glass, and rubber, manufacturers of these goods laid off workers, too.

American leaders tried desperately to manage the economic crisis, but their actions often exacerbated it instead. As America's rising trade deficit undermined international confidence in the dollar, the Nixon administration ended the dollar's link to the gold standard; free-floating exchange rates increased the price

ATTEMPTS TO
FIX THE
ECONOMY

of foreign goods and stimulated inflation. Following the monetary theory, which held that with less money available to "chase" the supply of goods, price increases would slow and end the inflationary spiral, Ford curbed federal spending and encouraged the Federal Reserve Board to tighten credit—prompting the worst recession in forty years. In 1975 unemployment climbed to 8.5 percent.

Carter's larger economic policies, including his 1978 deregulation of airline, trucking, banking, and communications industries, would eventually foster economic growth—but not soon enough. After almost a decade of decline, Americans were losing faith in the American economy and the ability of their political leaders to manage it.

The economic crisis of the 1970s accelerated the transition from an industrial to a service economy. During the 1970s, the American economy "deindustrialized," as auto companies laid off workers and steel plant closings left communities devastated. Other manufacturing concerns moved overseas, seeking lower labor costs and fewer government regulations. New jobs were created—27 million of them—overwhelmingly in what economists called the "service sector": retail sales, restaurants, and other service providers. Jobs there, such as warehouse work or retail sales, for example, paid much lower wages than union manufacturing positions and often lacked benefits such as healthcare.

IMPACTS OF
THE ECONOMIC
CRISIS

Formerly successful blue-collar workers saw their middle-class standards of life slipping away. More married women joined the work force because they had to. High-school and college graduates in the 1970s, raised with high expectations, found limited possibilities—if they found jobs at all.

As the old industrial regions of the North and Midwest went into decline, people headed for the Sunbelt, where the jobs were (see Map 31.1). The federal government had invested heavily in the South and West during the postwar era, especially in military and defense industries. The Sunbelt was primed for the rapid growth of modern industries and services: aerospace, defense, electronics, transportation, research, banking and finance, and leisure. City and state governments competed for business dollars, in part by preventing the growth of unions. Like Atlanta and Houston, many southern cities marketed them-

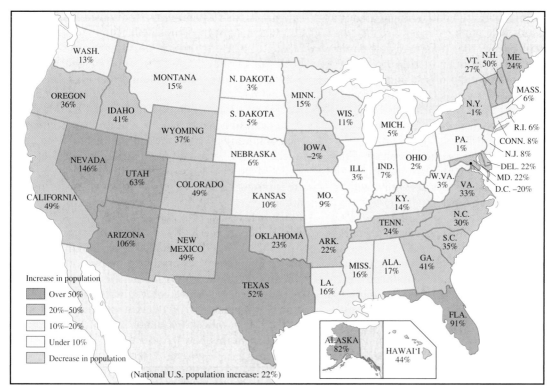

Map 31.1   The Continued Shift to the Sunbelt in the 1970s and 1980s

Throughout the 1970s and 1980s, Americans continued to leave economically declining areas of the North and East in pursuit of opportunity in the Sunbelt. States in the Sunbelt and in the West had the largest population increases.   (Source: "Shift to the Sunbelt," *Newsweek,* September 10, 1990.)

selves as cosmopolitan and racially tolerant; they bought sports teams and built museums.

Online Study Center **Improve Your Grade**
Interactive Map: Population Increase in the Sunbelt States, 1950–1994

Population shifts created disaster in northern and midwestern cities. New York City, near financial collapse by late 1975, was saved only when the House and Senate Banking Committees approved federal loan guarantees. Cleveland defaulted on its debts in 1978, the first major city to do so since Detroit declared bankruptcy in 1933.

Meanwhile, a "tax revolt" movement grew in the West. In California, inflation had driven property taxes up rapidly, hitting middle-class tax-

TAX REVOLTS   payers hard. Instead of calling for

wealthy citizens and corporations to pay a larger share of taxes, voters rebelled against taxation itself. California's Proposition 13, passed by a landslide in 1978, rolled back property taxes and restricted future increases. Thirty-seven states similarly cut property taxes, and twenty-eight lowered their state income-tax rates.

The impact of Proposition 13 and similar initiatives was originally cushioned by state budget surpluses, but as those surpluses turned to deficits, states cut services—closing fire stations and libraries, ending or limiting mental health services and programs for the disabled. Public schools were hit especially hard.

Before the runaway inflation of the 1970s, home mortgages and auto loans were the only major debt

CREDIT AND   most Americans had. National
INVESTMENT   credit cards had become common
only in the late 1960s, and few

Americans—especially those who remembered the Great Depression—were willing to spend money they did not have. In the 1970s, double-digit inflation rates made it economically smarter to buy goods before prices went up—even if it meant borrowing the money. Since debt was paid off later with devalued dollars, the consumer came out ahead. In 1975 consumer debt hit a high of $167 billion; it almost doubled, to $315 billion, by 1979.

In the 1970s, Americans became investors rather than savers. Because banking regulations capped the interest paid on individual savings accounts, with inflation, an account bearing 5 percent interest actually *lost* more than 20 percent of its value from 1970 through 1980. That same money, invested at market rates, would have grown dramatically. Fidelity Investments, a mutual fund company, saw an opportunity: its money market accounts combined many smaller investments to purchase large-denomination treasury bills and certificates of deposit, thus providing small investors the high interest rates normally available only to major investors. Money market investments grew from $1.7 billion in 1974 to $200 billion in 1982. Deregulation of the New York Stock Exchange spawned discount brokerage houses, whose low commission rates were affordable to middle-class investors.

An Era of Cultural Transformation

a s Americans struggled with economic recession, governmental betrayal, and social division, major strands of late-twentieth-century culture were developed. The current environmental movement, a "therapeutic culture" and the growth of born-again Christianity, contemporary forms of sexuality and the family, and America's emphasis on diversity have roots in this decade, sandwiched between the political vibrancy of the 1960s and the conservatism of the 1980s.

A series of ecological crises drove home the fragility of the environment. In 1969 a major oil spill

ENVIRONMENTALISM took place off the coast of Santa Barbara, California; that same year the polluted Cuyahoga River, flowing through Cleveland,

caught fire. In 1979 human error contributed to a nuclear accident at the Three Mile Island nuclear power plant near Harrisburg, Pennsylvania, and in 1980 President Carter declared a federal emergency at New York State's Love Canal, a dump site for a local chemical manufacturer, after it was discovered that 30 percent of local residents had suffered chromosome damage. Public activism produced major environmental initiatives, from the Environmental Protection Agency (EPA), created (under strong public pressure) in 1970 by the Nixon administration, to eighteen environmental laws enacted by Congress during the decade.

When almost 20 million Americans—half of them schoolchildren—celebrated the first Earth Day on April 22, 1970, they signaled the triumph of a new environmentalism. Central to this movement was a recognition that earth's resources were finite and must be conserved and protected. Many also identified rapid global population growth as a problem, and state public health offices frequently dispensed contraceptives to stem this new "epidemic."

During these years, Americans became increasingly uneasy about the science and technology that had

TECHNOLOGY been a source of America's might. Americans watched with pride as astronaut Neil Armstrong stepped onto the moon on July 20, 1969, stating, "One small step for man, one giant step for mankind." But technology seemed unable to cope with earthbound problems of poverty, crime, pollution, and urban decay. The failure of technological warfare to deliver victory in Vietnam happened as antiwar protesters were questioning the morality of such technology. But in the 1970s, the foundation was laid for America's computer revolution, with the creation of the integrated circuit in 1970, and mail-order processors later in the decade.

Americans increasingly sought spiritual fulfillment. Methodist, Presbyterian, and Episcopalian churches

RELIGION AND THE THERAPEUTIC CULTURE lost members during this era, while evangelical and fundamentalist Christian churches grew dramatically. Protestant evangelicals described themselves as "born again" and emphasized the immediate, daily presence of God in their lives. Even some Catholics, such as the Mexican Americans who embraced the *cursillo* movement (a "little course" in faith), sought a more personal relationship with God. Other Americans embraced the New Age movement, which drew from and combined non-Western spiritual and religious practices, including Zen Buddhism, yoga, and shamanism, along with insights from Western psychology and spiritually oriented environmentalism.

Also in the 1970s, America saw the emergence of a "therapeutic" culture. Although some were disgusted with the self-centeredness of the "Me-Decade," best-selling books by therapists and self-help gurus insisted that individual feelings offered the ultimate measure of truth. Self-help titles such as *I'm OK—You're OK* (first published in 1967, it became a best-seller in the mid-1970s) made up 15 percent of all best-selling books.

Sex became far more visible in American culture during the 1970s as network television loosened its regulation of sexual content. At the beginning of the 1960s, married couples in television shows were required to occupy twin beds; in the 1970s, hit shows included *Three's Company*, a comedy based on the then-scandalous premise that a single man shared an apartment with two female roommates—and got away with it by pretending to their suspicious landlord that he was gay. Donna Summers's 1975 disco hit, "Love to Love You Baby," contained sixteen minutes of sexual moaning. And though few Americans participated in heterosexual orgies at New York City's Plato's Retreat, many read about them in *Time* magazine.

SEXUALITY AND THE FAMILY

Sexual behaviors also changed. The seventies was the era of singles bars and gay bathhouses, but for most Americans, "sexual revolution" meant a broader public acceptance of premarital sex and a limited acceptance of homosexuality, especially among more educated Americans. More heterosexual young people "lived together" without marriage during the 1970s; the Census Bureau even coined the term "POSSLQ" (persons of opposite sex sharing living quarters) to describe the relationship.

Changes in sexual mores and women's roles altered the family structure as well. Men and women married later, and women had fewer children. By the end of the 1970s, the birth rate dropped almost 40 percent from its 1957 peak. Almost a quarter of young single women in 1980 said they did not plan to have children. And a steadily rising percentage of babies were born to unmarried women, as the number of families headed by never-married women rose 400 percent. The divorce rate also rose, in part because states implemented "no-fault" divorce, which did not require evidence of adultery, physical cruelty, abandonment, or other wrongdoing. Americans also developed a greater acceptance of various family forms (the blended family of television's *Brady Bunch*, for example).

DIVERSITY

The racial justice and identity movements of the late 1960s and 1970s made Americans more aware of differences among the nation's peoples—an awareness strengthened by new immigrants from Latin America and Asia. The challenge was figuring out how to acknowledge the new importance of "difference" in public policy. The solution was the idea of "diversity." Difference was not a problem but a strength; the nation should seek to foster the "diversity" of its schools, workplaces, and public culture.

The 1978 Supreme Court decision *Regents of the University of California v. Bakke* was a crucial early step. Allan Bakke, a thirty-three-year-old white man with a strong academic record, was denied admission to the medical school of the University of California at Davis. Bakke sued, charging that he had been denied "equal protection" because the medical school's affirmative-action program reserved 16 percent of its slots for racial-minority candidates, who were held to lower standards than other applicants. In 1978 the Supreme Court, in a split decision, decided in favor of Bakke. Four justices argued that any race-based decision violated the Civil Rights Act of 1964; four saw affirmative-action programs as constitutionally acceptable. The deciding vote, though for Bakke, contained an important qualification: a "diverse student body," Justice Lewis Powell wrote, is "a constitutionally permissible goal for an institution of higher education." To achieve "diversity," educational institutions could consider race in admissions.

Renewed Cold War and Middle East Crisis

 hen Jimmy Carter took office in 1977, he asked Americans to abandon their "inordinate fear of communism." Carter vowed to reduce the U.S. military presence overseas, cut back arms sales, and slow the nuclear arms race. More than 400,000 American military personnel were stationed abroad, the United States had military links with ninety-two nations, and the CIA was active on every continent. Carter promised to avoid new Vietnams and give more attention to environmental issues. He especially determined to improve human rights abroad—the freedom to vote, worship, travel, speak out, and get a fair trial. Like his predecessors, however, Carter identified revolutionary nationalism as a threat to America's global prominence.

Carter spoke and acted inconsistently, in part because in the post-Vietnam years, no consensus existed in foreign policy and in part because his advisers squabbled among themselves. One source of the problem was the stern-faced Zbigniew Brzezinski, a Polish-born political scientist who became Carter's national security adviser. An old-fashioned Cold Warrior, Brzezinski blamed foreign crises on Soviet expansionism. Carter gradually listened more to Brzezinski than to Secretary of State Cyrus Vance, an experienced public servant who advocated quiet diplomacy. Under Carter, détente deteriorated, and the Cold War deepened. Initially, Carter maintained fairly good relations with Moscow and managed some foreign policy successes. The United States signed two treaties with Panama in 1977. One provided for the return of the Canal Zone to Panama in 2000, and the other guaranteed the United States the right to defend the canal after that time (see Chapter 22). With conservatives denouncing a retreat from greatness, the Senate narrowly endorsed both agreements in 1978. The majority agreed with Carter that relinquishing the canal would improve U.S. relations with Latin America.

CARTER'S DIVIDED ADMINISTRATION

The crowning accomplishment of Carter's presidency was the Camp David accords, the first mediated peace treaty between Israel and an Arab nation. In September 1978, the president persuaded Israel and Egypt to agree to a peace treaty, gained Israel's promise to withdraw from the Sinai Peninsula, and forged an agreement that provided for continued negotiations on the future status of Palestinians in the occupied territories of Jordan's West Bank and Egypt's Gaza Strip (see

CAMP DAVID ACCORDS

Map 33.1). Other Arab states denounced the agreement for not requiring Israel to relinquish all occupied territories and not guaranteeing a Palestinian homeland. But the treaty, signed on March 26, 1979, by Israeli prime minister Menachem Begin and Egyptian president Anwar al-Sadat, at least ended warfare along one frontier.

Meanwhile, relations with Moscow deteriorated. U.S. and Soviet officials sparred over the Kremlin's reluctance to lift restrictions on Jewish emigration and over the Soviet decision to deploy new intermediate-range ballistic missiles aimed at western Europe. Then, in December 1979, the Soviets invaded Afghanistan, a remote country whose strategic position made it a source of great-power conflict. Following World War II, Afghanistan struggled with ongoing ethnic and factional squabbling; in the 1970s, it spiraled into anarchy. In late 1979 the Red Army bludgeoned into Afghanistan to shore up a faltering communist government under siege by Muslim rebels. Moscow officials calculated they could be in and out before anyone noticed, including the Americans.

SOVIET INVASION OF AFGHANISTAN

Carter not only noticed but reacted forcefully. He suspended shipments of grain and high-technology equipment to the Soviet Union, withdrew a major arms control treaty from Senate consideration, and initiated an international boycott of the 1980 Summer Olympics in Moscow. He also secretly authorized the CIA to distribute aid, including arms and military support, to the Mujahidin (Islamic guerrillas) fighting the communist government and sanctioned military aid to their backer, Pakistan. Announcing the Carter Doctrine, the president asserted that the United States would intervene, unilaterally and militarily, should Soviet aggression threaten the petroleum-rich Persian Gulf. Carter warned aides that the Soviets, unless checked, would likely attack elsewhere in the Middle East, but declassified documents confirm what contemporary critics said: that the Soviet invasion was largely defensive and did not presage a push to the Persian Gulf.

Carter simultaneously faced a foreign policy test in Iran. The shah, long favored by America, was dethroned by a coalition of Iranians who resented the dislocation of their traditional ways by the shah's mod-

IRANIAN HOSTAGE CRISIS

ernization. Riots led by anti-American Muslim clerics erupted in late 1978. The shah went into exile, and in April 1979 Islamic revolutionaries, led by the Ayatollah Khomeini, an elderly cleric who denounced the United States as the stronghold of capitalism and Western materialism, proclaimed a Shi'ite Islamic Republic. In November, with the exiled shah in the United States for medical treatment, mobs stormed the U.S. embassy in Teheran. They took American personnel as hostages, demanding the return of the shah to stand trial. The Iranians eventually released a few American prisoners, but fifty-two others suffered solitary confinement, beatings, and terrifying mock executions.

Unable to gain the hostages' freedom through diplomatic intermediaries, Carter took steps to isolate Iran economically, freezing Iranian assets in the United States. When the hostage takers paraded their blindfolded captives before television cameras, Americans felt taunted and humiliated. In April 1980, Carter broke diplomatic relations with Iran and ordered a daring rescue mission. But equipment failed and two aircraft collided, killing eight American soldiers. The hostages were not freed until January 1981, just after Carter left office.

The Iranian revolution, together with the rise of the Mujahidin in Afghanistan, signified the emergence of Islamic fundamentalism as a force in world affairs. Socialism and capitalism, the answers that the two superpowers offered to the problems of modernization, failed to solve the problems in Central Asia and the Middle East. Consequently, Islamic orthodoxy found growing support for its message: that secular leaders such as Nasser in Egypt and the shah in Iran had taken their peoples down the wrong path, necessitating a return to conservative Islamic values and Islamic law. The Iranian revolution expressed a complex mixture of discontents within Islamic societies.

U.S. officials took some consolation from the avowedly secular government in Iraq. Ruled by the

RISE OF SADDAM HUSSEIN

Ba'athist Party, Iraq won favor in Washington for its pursuit and execution of Iraqi communists. When a Ba'athist leader named Saddam Hussein took over as president of Iraq in 1979 and threatened the Teheran government, U.S. officials thought Saddam could offset the Iranian danger in the Persian Gulf. As border clashes escalated into

war in 1980, Washington policymakers were officially neutral but tilted toward Iraq.

Jimmy Carter earned some diplomatic successes in the Middle East, Africa, and Latin America, but the revived Cold War and prolonged Iranian hostage crisis hurt the administration politically. Contrary to Carter's goals, more American military personnel were stationed overseas in 1980 than in 1976; the defense budget climbed, and arms sales grew to $15.3 billion in 1980. On human rights, the president practiced a double standard, applying the human-rights test to some nations (the Soviet Union, Argentina, and Chile) but not to U.S. allies. Still, Carter's human-rights policy saved the lives of some political prisoners and institutionalized concern for human rights worldwide. But his inability to restore economic and military dominance helped dash his reelection hopes: he lost in 1980 to the hawkish Ronald Reagan, former Hollywood actor and governor of California.

Summary *Online Study Center*   **ACE the Test**

From the crisis year of 1968 on, Americans were extremely polarized—over the war in Vietnam, over the best path to racial equality and equal rights, and over the meaning of America itself. As many activists turned to "cultural nationalism," or group-identity politics, notions of American unity seemed a relic of the past. And while a new women's movement won victories against sex discrimination, powerful opposition arose in response.

During this era, Americans became increasingly disillusioned with politics. Richard Nixon's abuses of power in the Watergate scandal and cover-up, combined with the realization that the administration had lied repeatedly about America's role in Vietnam, produced a profound suspicion of government. A major economic crisis ended the post–World War II expansion, and Americans struggled with the effects of stagflation: rising unemployment rates coupled with high rates of inflation.

Overseas, a string of setbacks—defeat in Vietnam, the oil embargo, and the Iranian hostage crisis—signified the waning of American power. Détente with the Soviet Union flourished for a time; however, by 1980, Cold War tensions escalated. Meanwhile, the Middle East became an increasing focus of U.S. foreign policy.

Plagued by political, economic, and foreign policy crises, America's age of liberalism was over; the elements for a conservative resurgence were in place.

LEGACY FOR A PEOPLE AND A NATION
Human Rights

Human rights—the notion that people worldwide are entitled to life, liberty, and the pursuit of happiness—is not new. It was expressed most famously in the American and French Revolutions.

In the twentieth century, the concept became a consistent theme in U.S. foreign policy, and in the 1970s, a central tenet of American diplomacy. In the wake of the Vietnam War, many Americans yearned to restore America's international moral position. Congress led by restricting economic or military aid to nations that engaged "in a consistent pattern of gross violations of internationally recognized human rights."

Jimmy Carter made human rights a centerpiece of his foreign policy. "Because we are free we can never be indifferent to the fate of freedom elsewhere," he declared in his inaugural address. Carter installed a Bureau of Human Rights in the State Department, monitoring governments worldwide.

The campaign encountered problems, threatening arms control negotiations, alliances, and trade. The United States denounced abuses in nations where it had minimal economic or strategic interests and was almost silent where the interests were greater.

Still, Carter's human-rights emphasis altered the international landscape. It emboldened people around the world to challenge repressive governments and brought the release of political prisoners in many countries. It improved America's image overseas. Although human-rights concerns became less central in the foreign policies of Carter's successors, they remained on the agenda. In June 1993, delegates from 180 countries met in Vienna for the first World Conference on Human Rights, indicating that human rights had established itself firmly on the international map. It proved Carter's greatest legacy, duly noted by the committee awarding him the 2002 Nobel Peace Prize.

CONSERVATISM REVIVED 1980–1992

*N*guyet Thu Ha was twenty-two years old in 1975 when South Vietnam capitulated to North Vietnamese and Vietcong forces. As the fighting neared, Ha fled with her four teenage brothers and sisters and her six-year-old nephew. She found passage on a fishing ship dangerously over-crowded with refugees and arrived in the U.S. territory of Guam, an island over 2,000 miles from Vietnam. From there, they were sent to a refugee camp in Arkansas. Eventually Nguyet Ha and the children settled in Kansas City, Missouri, where they would live throughout the 1980s.

Nguyet Ha worked seven days a week as a hotel housekeeper and waitress, saving every possible penny for a house. Ha soon had the down payment for a $16,000 house and worked to pay off the mortgage in three years. She also married and had two daughters. In 1989 the thirty-six-year-old Ha bought a laundromat, five adjoining lots, and a vacant building she hoped would eventually house the family she'd left behind in Vietnam. Pursuing her ambition to become a teacher, Ha earned two associate of arts degrees and was hired as a paraprofessional at Kansas City's Northeast High School.

For ten years, Ha filled out U.S. government forms and visited the offices of the Immigration and Naturalization Service (INS). Finally she received a call from the INS: Ha's mother, two brothers, a sister-in-law, and a niece would be arriving at Kansas City International Airport. By 1997, all eight of Ha's siblings, most with their children, were living in the United States.

Nguyet Thu Ha and her family were part of the "new immigration" beginning in the early 1970s and continuing through the 1980s, as record numbers of immigrants came to the United States from Asia, Mexico, Central and South America, and the Caribbean. But not all immigrants—or Americans—fared as well as Ha in the 1980s, when divisions between rich and poor were increasingly evident. While the urban poor struggled with social problems—drugs, violence, homelessness, the growing AIDS epidemic—those on the other side of the economic divide enjoyed an era of luxury and ostentation.

Reagan and the Conservative Resurgence

"Reaganomics"

Reagan and the World

LINKS TO THE WORLD
CNN

A Polarized People: American Society in the 1980s

The End of the Cold War and Global Disorder

LEGACY FOR A PEOPLE AND A NATION
The Americans with Disabilities Act

Online Study Center

This icon will direct you to interactive map and primary source activities on the website http:college.hmco.com/pic/nortonbrief7e

CHRONOLOGY

1980 • Reagan elected president

1981 • AIDS first observed in United States
• Economic problems continue; prime interest rate reaches 21.5 percent
• Reagan breaks air traffic controllers strike
• "Reaganomics" plan of budget and tax cuts approved by Congress

1982 • Unemployment reaches 10.8 percent, highest rate since Great Depression
• ERA dies after STOP-ERA campaign prevents ratification in key states

1983 • Reagan introduces SDI
• Terrorists kill U.S. Marines in Lebanon
• U.S. invasion of Grenada

1984 • Reagan aids contras despite congressional ban
• Economic recovery; unemployment rate drops and economy grows without inflation
• Reagan reelected
• Gorbachev promotes reforms in the USSR

1986 • Iran-contra scandal erupts

1987 • Stock market drops 508 points in one day
• Palestinian *intifada* begins

1988 • George H. W. Bush elected president

1989 • Tiananmen Square massacre in China
• Berlin Wall torn down
• U.S. troops invade Panama
• Gulf between rich and poor at highest point since 1920s

1990 • Americans with Disabilities Act passed
• Communist regimes in eastern Europe collapse
• Iraq invades Kuwait
• South Africa begins to dismantle apartheid

1991 • Persian Gulf War
• USSR dissolves into independent states
• United States enters recession

1992 • Annual federal budget deficit reaches high of $300 billion at end of Bush presidency

The election of Ronald Reagan in 1980 began a twelve-year period of Republican rule, as Reagan was succeeded by his vice president, George Bush, in 1988. Reagan was a popular president who seemed to restore the confidence shaken by the crises of the 1970s. Wealthy people liked Reagan's pro-business policies; the religious New Right embraced his vision of "God's America"; white middle- and working-class Americans were attracted by his charisma and "old-fashioned" values.

Reagan supported New Right social issues: he was anti-abortion, embraced prayer in schools, and reversed the GOP's support of the Equal Rights Amendment. Most important, Reagan appointed Supreme Court and federal judges whose rulings strengthened social-conservative agendas. Reagan's primary focus was on reducing the size and power of the federal gov-

ernment and creating favorable conditions for business and industry. The U.S. economy recovered from 1970s stagflation and rebounded through much of the 1980s. But corruption flourished in financial institutions freed from government oversight. By the end of the Reagan-Bush era, a combination of tax cuts and massive increases in defense spending increased the budget deficit fivefold.

In a single decade, the Cold War intensified and then ended. The key figure in the first development was Reagan, who promised to stand up to the Soviet Union. The central player in ending the conflict was Soviet leader Mikhail Gorbachev, who came to power in 1985 determined to end the USSR's economic decline, which required a more amicable superpower relationship. Gorbachev hoped to reform the Soviet system but lost control of events as revolutions in eastern Europe toppled one communist regime after another. In 1991 the Soviet Union itself disappeared, and the Persian Gulf War demonstrated America's unrivaled world power and the unprecedented importance of the Middle East. ■

Reagan and the Conservative Resurgence

*T*he 1970s were hard for Americans: defeat in Vietnam, the resignation of a president in disgrace, the energy crisis, economic "stagflation," and the Iranian hostage crisis. In 1980 President Carter's approval rating stood at 21 percent, lower than Richard Nixon's during the Watergate crisis. The time was ripe for a challenge to Carter's leadership, the Democratic Party, and the liberalism that had governed the United States since Franklin Roosevelt's New Deal.

In 1980 several conservative Republicans ran for the White House, including Ronald Reagan, former

RONALD REAGAN movie star and two-term governor of California. In the 1940s, as president of the Screen Actors Guild in Hollywood, Reagan was a New Deal Democrat. But in the 1950s, as a corporate spokesman for General Electric, he became conservative. In 1964 Reagan's televised speech for Republican presidential candidate Barry Goldwater catapulted him to the forefront of conservative politics.

As governor of California two years later, Reagan became known for his right-wing rhetoric: America should "level Vietnam, pave it, paint stripes on it, and make a parking lot out of it." And when student protesters occupied "People's Park" near the University of California in Berkeley, he threatened a "bloodbath," dispatching National Guard troops. But he could be pragmatic: he denounced welfare but presided over reform of the state's social welfare bureaucracy and signed one of the nation's most liberal abortion laws.

In the 1980 election, Reagan offered an optimistic vision for America's future. With his Hollywood charm,

THE NEW *CONSERVATIVE* *COALITION* he succeeded in forging very different kinds of conservatives into a new political coalition. He united political conservatives—strong anticom-

munists who sought to limit federal power and roll back the liberal social programs of the New Deal and Great Society—with less ideologically oriented economic conservatives, who sought deregulation and tax policies benefiting corporations, wealthy investors, and entrepreneurs.

Reagan united political and economic conservatives with two new constituencies. He tapped into the sentiments that fueled the tax revolt of the 1970s, drawing voters from traditionally Democratic constituencies such as labor unions and urban ethnic groups. These "Reagan Democrats" found the Republican critique of tax-funded social programs and "big government" appealing, even though Reagan's policies would benefit the wealthy at their expense.

Finally, in the largest leap, Reagan attracted the religiously based New Right. "When political conservative leaders began to . . . strike an alliance with social conservatives—the pro-life people, the anti-ERA people, the evangelical and born-again Christians, the people concerned about gay rights, prayer in the schools, sex in the movies or whatever," explained conservative fundraiser Richard Viguerie, "that's when this whole movement began to come alive."

Reagan claimed victory with 51 percent of the popular vote. Jimmy Carter carried only six states.

REAGAN'S *CONSERVATIVE* *AGENDA* Reagan served two terms as president, followed by his vice president, George Bush, who was elected in 1988.

Reagan was not especially focused on the details of governing. When Carter briefed him on foreign and domestic policy issues, Reagan took no notes. Critics argued that his lack of knowledge could prove dangerous—as when he insisted that intercontinental ballistic missiles carrying nuclear warheads could be called back once launched.

But supporters insisted that Reagan focused on the big picture. When he spoke to the American people, he offered what seemed to be simple truths. While even supporters winced at his willingness to reduce complex policy issues to basic (and often misleading) stories, Reagan was to most Americans the "Great Communicator." He won admiration for his courage after he was seriously wounded in an assassination attempt sixty-nine days into his presidency.

Most important, Reagan had a clear vision for America's future. He and his advisers wanted nothing

REAGAN

FOR PRESIDENT
Let's make America great again.

■ Ronald Reagan, the Republican presidential candidate in 1980, campaigned for "family values," an aggressive anti-Soviet foreign and military policy, and tax cuts. He also exuded optimism and appealed to Americans' patriotism. This poster, issued by the Republican National Committee, included Reagan's favorite campaign slogan: "Let's make America great again." (Collection of David J. and Janice L. Frent)

lieved, funded government "handouts." Reagan fed a stereotype of welfare recipients as unwed, black, teenage mothers who kept having babies to collect larger checks.

In 1981 the administration cut social welfare funding by $25 billion. But "welfare" (Aid to Families with Dependent Children and food stamp programs) was small compared with Social Security and Medicare—welfare programs benefiting Americans of all income levels. The Reagan administration did shrink the proportion of the federal budget devoted to social welfare programs (including Social Security and Medicare) from 28 to 22 percent by the late 1980s—but a $1.2 trillion increase in defense spending, rather than budget cuts, was responsible for the shift.

Reagan also attacked federal environmental, health, and safety regulations that he believed reduced

PRO-BUSINESS POLICIES AND THE ENVIRONMENT

business profits and discouraged economic growth. Administration officials claimed that removing the stifling hand of government regulation would restore the energy and creativity of America's free-market system. However, removing them did not so much end government's role as deploy government power to aid corporate America. The president even appointed opponents of federal regulations to head agencies charged with enforcing them.

Environmentalists were appalled when Reagan appointed James Watt, a well-known antienvironmentalist, as secretary of the interior. Watt was a leader in the "Sagebrush Rebellion," which sought to return public lands in the West, such as national forests, to state control. The federal government controlled more than half of western lands—including 83 percent in Nevada, 66 percent in Utah, and 50 percent in Wyoming—and many westerners believed eastern policymakers did not understand the realities of western life. But state control was not the only issue: Watt's group wanted to open western public lands to private businesses for logging, mining, and ranching.

Telling Congress, "I don't know how many generations we can count on until the Lord returns," Watt dismissed concerns about protecting resources and public lands for future generations and allowed private corporations to acquire oil, mineral, and timber rights to federal lands for minuscule payments. He was forced to resign in 1983 after he dismissively

less than to roll back the liberalism of the past fifty years that had made government responsible for the health of the nation's economy and for the social welfare of its citizens.

Reagan, like traditional conservatives, did not think the federal government could solve social problems. But he drew support from

ATTACKS ON SOCIAL WELFARE PROGRAMS

Americans struggling to make ends meet during the economic crises of the 1970s and early 1980s who resented paying taxes that, they believed.

referred to a federal advisory panel as "a black . . . a woman, two Jews, and a cripple." Even before Watt's resignation, his appointment had backfired as his actions reenergized the nation's environmental movement and even provoked opposition from business leaders who understood that uncontrolled strip-mining and clear-cut logging of western lands could destroy lucrative tourism and recreation industries in western states.

The pro-business Reagan administration undercut organized labor's ability to negotiate wages and work-

ATTACKS ON ORGANIZED LABOR

ing conditions. Union power was already waning; labor union membership declined in the 1970s as jobs in heavy industry disappeared, and efforts to unionize the high-growth electronics and service sectors of the economy had not succeeded. Reagan intervened in a strike by the Professional Air Traffic Controllers Organization (PATCO) in August 1981. The air traffic controllers—federal employees, for whom striking was illegal—protested working conditions they believed compromised the safety of air travel. Forty-eight hours later, Reagan fired the 11,350 strikers, stipulating that they could never be rehired by the Federal Aviation Administration.

With the support of Reagan appointees to the National Labor Relations Board, businesses took an increasingly hard line with labor during the 1980s, and unions failed to mount an effective opposition. Roughly 44 percent of union families had voted for Reagan in 1980, and despite his anti-union policies, many were still drawn to his espousal of old-fashioned values and vigorous anticommunist rhetoric.

The New Right played an increasingly important role in Reagan's domestic policy, despite the adminis-

THE NEW RIGHT

tration's focus on traditional conservative political and economic goals, and Reagan endorsed New Right social issues including the anti-abortion cause and prayer in public schools.

Reagan's judicial nominations also pleased the religious New Right. While the Senate, in a bipartisan vote, refused to confirm Supreme Court nominee Robert Bork, Reagan added Antonin Scalia and Sandra Day O'Connor (the first woman) to the Court and elevated Nixon appointee William Rehnquist to chief justice.

These appointments made the Court more conservative. In 1986, for example, the Supreme Court upheld a Georgia law that punished consensual anal or oral sex between men with up to twenty years in jail (*Bowers v. Hardwick*); in 1989 justices ruled that a Missouri law restricting the right to an abortion was constitutional (*Webster v. Reproductive Health Services*), thus encouraging further challenges to *Roe v. Wade*. Still, the Reagan administration did not push a conservative social agenda as strongly as some in the new Republican coalition had hoped.

"Reaganomics"

The centerpiece of Reagan's domestic agenda was the economic program that took his name: Reaganomics. The U.S. economy was foundering in the early 1980s. Stagflation proved resistant to traditional remedies: when the government increased spending to stimulate the economy, inflation skyrocketed; when it cut spending or tightened the money supply to reduce inflation, the economy plunged deeper into recession and unemployment rates jumped.

Reagan offered a simple answer. Instead of focusing on the complexities of global competition, deindustrialization, and OPEC's control of oil, Reagan argued that U.S. economic problems were caused by intrusive government regulation of business and industry, expensive social programs giving "handouts" to nonproductive citizens, high taxes, and deficit spending—in short, by government itself. Reagan proposed to "unshackle" the free-enterprise system from government regulation and control, slash social programs, and balance the budget by reducing the role of the federal government.

Reagan's economic policy was based largely on "supply-side economics," the theory that tax cuts

"SUPPLY-SIDE ECONOMICS"

(rather than government spending) stimulate growth. Economist Arthur Laffer had proposed one key hypothesis—his soon-to-be famous "Laffer curve." It stated that at some point, rising tax rates discourage people from engaging in taxable activities (such as investing their money): if profits from investments disappear to taxes, what is the incentive to invest? As people invest less, the economy slows and there is less tax revenue to collect. Cutting taxes, in contrast, reverses the cycle.

Although economists at the time accepted the larger principle behind Laffer's curve, almost none believed U.S. tax rates approached the point of disincentive. Even conservative economists were highly suspicious of supply-side principles. Reagan and his staff, however, sought a massive tax cut, arguing that American corporations and individuals would invest funds freed up by lower tax rates, producing new plants, new jobs, and new products. And as prosperity returned, the profits at the top would "trickle down" to the middle classes and even the poor.

David Stockman, head of the Office of Management and Budget, proposed a five-year plan to balance the federal budget through economic growth (created by tax cuts) and deep cuts, primarily in social programs. Congress cooperated with a three-year, $750 billion tax cut, the largest in history. But Stockman's plan required $100 billion in cuts from government programs, including Social Security and Medicare, which Congress rejected. Reagan, meanwhile, canceled out domestic spending cuts by dramatically increasing defense spending.

With major tax cuts, big increases in defense spending, and small cuts in social programs, the federal budget deficit exploded—from $59 billion in 1980, to more than $100 billion in 1982, to almost $300 billion by the end of George H. W. Bush's presidency in 1992. The federal government borrowed to make up the difference, transforming the United States from the world's largest creditor nation to its largest debtor at almost $3 trillion.

Meanwhile, in 1981, the Federal Reserve Bank, an autonomous federal agency, raised interest rates for bank loans to an unprecedented 21.5 percent, battling inflation by tightening the money supply and slowing the economy. The nation plunged into recession. By year's end, the gross national product (GNP) fell 5 percent, and sales of cars and houses dropped sharply. Unemployment soared to 8 percent.

HARSH MEDICINE FOR INFLATION

By late 1982, unemployment reached 10.8 percent, the highest rate since 1940; for African Americans, it was 20 percent. Reagan promised that consumers would lift the economy out of the recession by spending their tax cuts. But as late as April 1983, unemployment remained at 10 percent, and people were angry. Agriculture too was faltering as farmers suffered from falling crop prices, floods and droughts, and burdensome debts at high interest rates. Many lost their property through mortgage foreclosures; others filed for bankruptcy. As the recession deepened, poverty rose to its highest level since 1965.

It was harsh medicine, but the Federal Reserve Bank's plan to end stagflation worked. High interest rates helped drop inflation from 12 percent in 1980 to less than 7 percent in 1982. The economy also benefited from OPEC's 1981 decision to increase oil production, thus lowering prices. In 1984 the GNP rose 7 percent, the sharpest increase since 1951, and midyear unemployment fell to a four-year low of 7 percent.

Reagan got credit for the recovery, though it had little to do with his supply-side policies. Insisting that the escalating budget deficit would have dire consequences for the economy, the 1984 Democratic presidential candidate, former vice president Walter Mondale, said he would raise taxes. Mondale emphasized fairness and compassion: not all Americans, Mondale said, were prospering in Reagan's America. Reagan, in contrast, proclaimed, "It's morning again in America." He won in a landslide, with 59 percent of the vote. Mondale (with running mate Geraldine Ferraro, the first woman vice-presidential candidate) carried only his home state of Minnesota.

"MORNING IN AMERICA"

Deregulation, started by Jimmy Carter and dramatically expanded by Reagan, also transformed America's economy in the 1980s by creating new opportunities for business. The 1978 deregulation of the airline industry lowered ticket prices; airline tickets cost almost 45 percent less in the early twenty-first century (in constant dollars) than in 1978. Deregulation of telecommunications industries created serious competition for the giant AT&T, and long-distance calling became inexpensive.

DEREGULATION

The Reagan administration loosened regulation of American banking and finance industries and purposely cut the enforcement ability of the Securities and Exchange Commission (SEC). In the early 1980s, Congress deregulated the nation's savings-and-loan institutions (S&Ls), organizations previously required to invest depositors' savings in thirty-year, fixed-rate mortgages secured by property within a 50-mile radius of the S&L's main office. The 1980s legislation created conditions for a collapse. By ending government oversight of investment practices, while covering losses from bad S&L investments, Congress left no penalties for failure. S&Ls increasingly put depositors' money into high-risk investments and engaged in shady—even criminal—deals.

Risky investments typified Wall Street as well, as Michael Milken, a reclusive bond trader for the firm Drexel Firestone, pioneered the "junk bond" industry and created lucrative investment possibilities. Milken offered financing to debt-ridden corporations unable to get traditional low-interest bank loans, using bond issues that paid investors high interest rates because they were high risk (thus "junk" bonds). Many of these corporations were attractive targets for takeover by other corporations or investors, who in turn could finance takeovers with junk bonds. Such "predators" could use the first corporation's existing debt as a tax write-off, sell off unprofitable units, and lay off employees to create a more efficient—and thus more profitable—corporation. Investors in the original junk bonds could make huge profits by selling their shares to the corporate raiders.

JUNK BONDS AND "MERGER MANIA"

By the mid-1980s, hundreds of major corporations—including giants Walt Disney and Conoco—fell prey to "merger mania" and "hostile takeovers." Profits for investors were staggering, and by 1987 Milken, the guru of junk bonds, was earning $550 million a year—about $1,046 a minute.

Deregulation helped smaller, often innovative, corporations challenge the virtual monopolies of giants in fields like telecommunications. And the American economy boomed. Although the stock market plunged 508 points on a single day in October 1987—losing 22.6 percent of its value, or almost double that of the 1929 crash—it rebounded quickly. But the high-risk boom of the 1980s had costs. Corporate downsizing meant layoffs for white-collar workers and management personnel, many of whom had difficulty finding comparable positions. The wave of mergers and takeovers left American corporations as a whole increasingly burdened by debt. It also helped to consolidate sectors of the economy—such as media—under the control of an ever smaller number of players.

The 1980s boom, furthermore, was rotten with corruption. By the late 1980s, insider trading scandals—in which people used "inside" information not available to the general public to make huge profits trading stocks—rocked financial markets

THE RICH GET RICHER

and sent some prominent Wall Street figures to jail. Savings and loans lost billions in bad investments, sometimes fraudulently covering them up. Scandal reached the White House: Vice President Bush's son Neil was involved in shady S&L deals. The Reagan-Bush administration's bailout of the S&L industry cost taxpayers half a trillion dollars.

During the 1980s, the rich got richer and the poor got poorer (see Figure 32.1). The number of Americans reporting an annual income of $500,000 increased tenfold between 1980 and 1989, and the salary and benefits of corporate chief executive officers increased from 30 times that of the average factory worker in 1980 to 130 times greater by 1989. In 1987 the United States had forty-nine billionaires—up from one in 1978. Middle-class incomes, however, were stagnant.

Reagan's economic policies benefited the wealthy at the expense of other Americans. Reagan's tax policies decreased the "total effective tax rates"—income taxes plus Social Security taxes—for the top 1 percent of American families by 14.4 percent. But they increased taxes for the poorest 20 percent of families by 16 percent. By 1990, the richest 1 percent controlled 40 percent of the nation's wealth, with 80 percent of wealth controlled by the top 20 percent.

Reagan and the World

a key element in Reagan's winning strategy in the 1980 election was his call for the United States to reassert itself in the world. Although he lacked a firm grasp of world issues, history, and geography, Reagan adhered to a few core principles. One was a deep and abiding anticommunism; a second was an underlying optimism about America's power and ability to positively affect the world. Together, these elements help explain both Reagan's aggressively anticommunist foreign policy and his positive response in his second term to Soviet leader Mikhail Gorbachev's call for "new thinking" in world affairs.

Initially embracing the strident anticommunism of early Cold War U.S. foreign policy, Reagan and his advisers rejected both Nixon's détente and Carter's emphasis on human rights. Where Nixon and Carter saw an increasingly multipolar

SOVIET-AMERICAN TENSION

CNN

When Ted Turner launched CNN, his Cable News Network, on June 1, 1980, few people took it seriously. With a staff of three hundred—mostly young, mostly inexperienced—CNN operated out of the basement of a converted Atlanta country club. CNN was initially known for its on-air errors, as when a cleaning woman emptied anchor Bernard Shaw's trash during a live newscast. But by 1992, CNN was seen in over 150 nations worldwide, and *Time* magazine named Ted Turner its "Man of the Year."

Throughout the 1980s, CNN built relations with local news outlets throughout the world. CNN reported live from Tiananmen Square and from the Berlin Wall in 1989. Millions watched as CNN reporters broadcast live from Baghdad in the early hours of the Gulf War in 1991. When the Soviet Union wanted to denounce the 1989 U.S. invasion of Panama, officials called CNN's Moscow bureau instead of the U.S. embassy. During the Gulf War, Saddam Hussein reportedly kept televisions in his bunker tuned to CNN, and U.S. generals used its broadcasts to judge the effectiveness of missile attacks.

Despite its global mission, CNN's American origins were often apparent. During the U.S. invasion of Panama, CNN cautioned correspondents not to refer to the American military forces as "our" troops. What CNN offered was not international news but a global experience: people throughout the world collectively watching the major moments in contemporary history as they unfolded. But as *Time* magazine noted (while praising Turner as the "Prince of the Global Village"), such connections "did not produce instantaneous brotherhood, just a slowly dawning awareness of the implications of a world transfixed by a single TV image."

The "Boys of Baghdad"—CNN reporters Bernard Shaw, John Holliman, and Peter Arnett—broadcast live by satellite from Suite 906 of the Al Rashid Hotel as Allied bombs fell on Baghdad throughout the night of January 16, 1991. Despite their dramatic reporting on the first night of the war, critics charged that continuing network coverage of Operation Desert Storm, with distant shots of cruise missiles seeking targets and heavy use of animation, graphics, and even theme music, made the war appear more like a video game than a bloody conflict. (CNN)

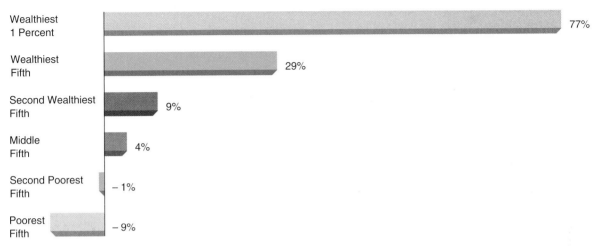

Percentage Increase in Pretax Income, 1977–1989

Wealthiest 1 Percent	77%
Wealthiest Fifth	29%
Second Wealthiest Fifth	9%
Middle Fifth	4%
Second Poorest Fifth	−1%
Poorest Fifth	−9%

Figure 32.1   While the Rich Got Richer in the 1980s, the Poor Got Poorer

Between 1977 and 1989, the richest 1 percent of American families reaped most of the gains from economic growth. In fact, the average pretax income of families in the top percentage rose 77 percent. At the same time, the typical family saw its income edge up only 4 percent. And the bottom 40 percent of families had actual declines in income.   (Source: Data from the *New York Times,* March 5, 1992.)

international system, the Reagan team reverted to a bipolar perspective defined by the Soviet-American relationship. In his first presidential press conference, Reagan described a malevolent Soviet Union. When Poland's pro-Soviet leaders in 1981 cracked down on an independent labor organization, Solidarity, Washington restricted Soviet-American trade and hurled angry words at Moscow. In March 1983, Reagan told evangelical Christians in Florida that the Soviets were "an evil empire." That year Reagan restricted commercial flights to the Soviet Union after a Soviet fighter pilot mistakenly shot down a South Korean commercial jet straying 300 miles off course into Soviet airspace, killing 269 passengers.

Reagan believed that substantial military buildup would thwart the Soviet threat and launched the largest peacetime arms buildup in history. In 1985, when the military budget hit $294.7 billion (double that of 1980), the Pentagon spent an average $28 million an hour. Assigning low priority to arms control talks, Reagan announced in 1983 his desire for a space-based defense shield against incoming ballistic missiles: the Strategic Defense Initiative (SDI). His critics tagged it "Star Wars" and said such a system could never work scientifically—some enemy missiles would get through the shield. Moreover, the critics warned, SDI would elevate the arms race to dangerous new levels. SDI research and development consumed tens of billions of dollars.

Attributing Third World disorders to Soviet intrigue, the president declared the Reagan Doctrine: the United States would openly support *REAGAN* anticommunist movements—"free-*DOCTRINE* dom fighters" battling the Soviets or Soviet-backed governments. In Afghanistan, Reagan continued providing covert assistance, through Pakistan, to the Mujahidin rebels fighting Soviet occupation. When the Soviets stepped up the war in 1985, the Reagan administration sent more high-tech weapons, particularly anti-aircraft Stinger missiles. Easily transportable and fired by a single soldier, the Stingers turned the tide by making Soviet jets and helicopters vulnerable below fifteen thousand feet.

Senior White House officials also believed that the Soviets and Castro's Cuba were fomenting disorder in the Caribbean and Central America (see Map 32.1). In October 1983 the president sent troops into the tiny island of Grenada to oust a pro-Marxist government. In El Salvador, he provided military and economic assistance to a military-dominated government struggling with left-wing revolutionaries. The regime used right-wing death squads, which by decade's end killed forty thousand dissidents and citizens as well as several American missionaries. In January 1992 the Salvadoran combatants finally negotiated a U.N.-sponsored peace.

The Reagan administration also meddled in the Nicaraguan civil war. In 1979 leftist insurgents in Nicaragua overthrew Anastasio Somoza, a long-time U.S. ally. The revolutionaries called themselves Sandinistas in honor of César Augusto Sandino—who had headed the anti-imperialist opposition against U.S. occupation in the 1930s and was finally assassinated by Somoza henchmen. When the Sandinistas aided rebels in El Salvador, bought Soviet weapons, and invited Cubans to help reorganize the Nicaraguan army, Reagan officials charged that Nicaragua was becoming a Soviet client. In 1981 the CIA began to train, arm, and direct more than ten thousand counterrevolutionaries, known as contras, to overthrow the Nicaraguan government.

CONTRA WAR IN NICARAGUA

Many Americans, however, including Democratic leaders in Congress, were skeptical about the communist threat and warned that Nicaragua could become another Vietnam. Congress in 1984 voted to stop U.S. military aid to the contras. Secretly, the Reagan administration lined up other countries, including Saudi Arabia, Panama, and South Korea, to funnel money and weapons to the contras, and in 1985 Reagan imposed an economic embargo against Nicaragua. The president rejected a plan by Costa Rica's president, Oscar Arias Sánchez, in 1987 to obtain a cease-fire in Central America through negotiations and cutbacks in military aid to all rebel forces. (Arias won the 1987 Nobel Peace Prize.) Three years later, Central American presidents brokered a settlement; in the national election that followed, the Sandinistas lost to a U.S.-funded party. After nearly a decade of civil war, thirty thousand Nicaraguans had died, and the ravaged economy was one of the poorest in the hemisphere.

Reagan's obsession with defeating the Sandinistas almost caused his political undoing. In November 1986 it became known that the president's national security adviser, John M. Poindexter, and an aide, marine lieutenant colonel Oliver North, in collusion with CIA director William Casey, covertly sold weapons to Iran in an unsuccessful attempt to win the release of Americans held hostage by Islamic fundamentalist groups. Washington condemned Iran as a terrorist nation and demanded that America's allies cease trading there. More damaging was the revelation that money from the Iran arms deal had been illegally diverted to aid the contras. North later admitted that he illegally destroyed government documents and lied to Congress to keep the operation clandestine.

IRAN-CONTRA SCANDAL

Although Reagan survived the scandal, his popularity declined, and Congress reasserted its authority over foreign affairs. In late 1992 outgoing president George Bush pardoned several former government officials convicted of lying to Congress. Critics smelled a cover-up, for Bush himself, as vice president, participated in high-level meetings on Iran-contra deals. As for North, his conviction was overturned on a technicality.

U.S. foreign policy placed increased importance on the Middle East and terrorism. The main U.S. goals in the Middle East were to preserve access to oil and support ally Israel, while checking Soviet influence. In the 1980s, though, American leaders faced new pressures from a deepened Israeli-Palestinian conflict and an anti-American and anti-Israeli Islamic fundamentalist movement that spread after the ouster of the shah of Iran in 1979.

U.S. INTERESTS IN THE MIDDLE EAST

The 1979 Camp David accords between Israel and Egypt raised hopes of a lasting settlement involving self-government for the Palestinian Arabs in the Israeli-occupied Gaza Strip and West Bank. Instead, Israel and the Palestinian Liberation Organization (PLO) remained at odds. In 1982, in retaliation for Palestinian shelling of Israel from Lebanon, Israeli troops invaded Lebanon. The beleaguered PLO and various Lebanese factions called on Syria to contain the Israelis. Soon after Reagan sent U.S. Marines to Lebanon to join a peacekeeping force, American

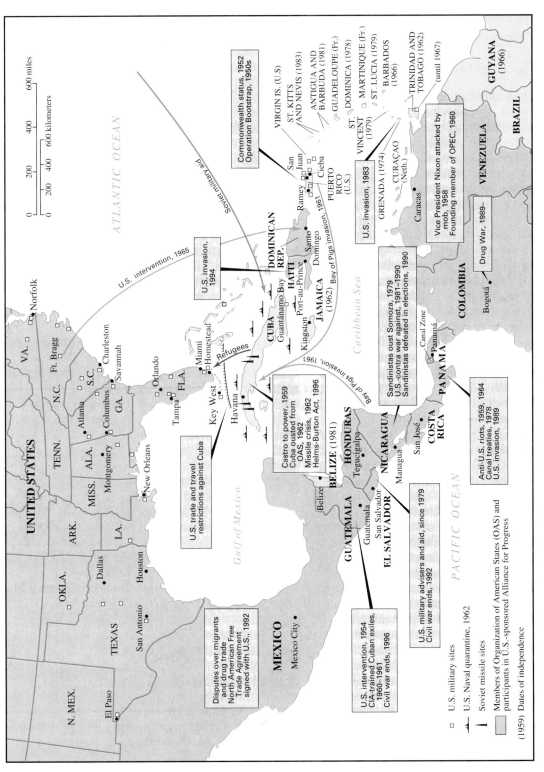

Map 32.1 The United States in the Caribbean and Central America

The United States often has intervened in the Caribbean and Central America. Geographical proximity, economic stakes, political disputes, security links, trade in illicit drugs, and Cuba's alliance with the Soviet Union and defiance of the United States have kept North American eyes fixed on events in the region.

605

troops became embroiled in a war between Lebanese factions. In October 1983 terrorist bombs demolished a barracks, killing 241 American servicemen. Four months later, Reagan pulled the remaining marines out.

The attack on the marine barracks made the danger of terrorism increasingly real to the United

TERRORISM

States and other Western countries. In the 1980s, numerous otherwise powerless groups, many of them associated with the Palestinian cause or with Islamic fundamentalism, relied on terrorism to further their aims. Often they targeted American citizens and property, because of Washington's support of Israel and involvement in the Lebanese civil war. Of the 690 hijackings, kidnappings, bombings, and shootings around the world in 1985, for example, 217 were against Americans, most originating in Iran, Libya, Lebanon, and the Gaza Strip. Three years later, a Pan American passenger plane was destroyed over Scotland, probably by pro-Iranian terrorists.

Washington proposed peace plans persuading the Israelis to give back occupied territories and the Arabs to stop trying to push the Jews out of the Middle East. As the peace process stalled in 1987, Palestinians in the West Bank began an *intifada* (Arabic for "uprising") against Israeli forces. Israel refused to negotiate, but the United States talked with PLO chief Yasir Arafat after he renounced terrorism and accepted Israel's right to live in peace. For the PLO to recognize Israel and the United States to recognize the PLO were major developments in the Arab-Israeli conflict.

In South Africa too, American diplomacy became more aggressive. At first, the Reagan administration

SOUTH AFRICA

followed a policy of "constructive engagement"—asking the government to reform its white supremacist apartheid system. But many Americans demanded cutting off imports from South Africa and pressuring 350 American companies to cease operations there. Some American cities and states passed divestment laws, withdrawing investment dollars from American companies active in South Africa. Public protest and congressional legislation forced the Reagan administration in 1986 to impose economic restrictions. Within two years, about half of the American companies in South Africa left.

American conservatives disliked the South Africa sanctions policy. Rabid anticommunists among them

ENTER GORBACHEV

also balked when Reagan, his popularity declining, entered negotiations with the Soviet Union. At a 1985 Geneva summit meeting between Reagan and new Soviet leader Mikhail Gorbachev, the president agreed in principle with Gorbachev's contention that strategic weapons should be substantially reduced, and at a 1986 Reykjavik, Iceland, meeting, they came close to a major reduction agreement. SDI stood in the way: Gorbachev insisted it should be shelved, and Reagan refused.

But Reagan and Gorbachev got on well. As General Colin Powell commented, while the Soviet leader was far superior to Reagan in mastery of specifics, he recognized that Reagan was, as Powell put it, "the embodiment of his people's down-to-earth character, practicality, and optimism." And Reagan toned down his strident anti-Soviet rhetoric.

The turnaround in Soviet-American relations stemmed more from changes abroad than from Reagan's decisions. Under Gorbachev, a

PERESTROIKA AND GLASNOST

younger generation of Soviet leaders came to power in 1985. They modernized the highly bureaucratized, decaying economy through reforms known as *perestroika* ("restructuring") and liberalized the authoritarian political system through *glasnost* ("openness"). For these reforms to work, Soviet military expenditures had to be reduced.

In 1987 Gorbachev and Reagan signed the Intermediate-Range Nuclear Forces (INF) Treaty banning all land-based intermediate-range nuclear missiles in Europe. About 2,800 missiles were destroyed. Gorbachev also unilaterally reduced his nation's armed forces, helped settle regional conflicts, and began the withdrawal of Soviet troops from Afghanistan. The Cold War was coming to an end.

A Polarized People: American Society in the 1980s

s the Cold War waned, so too did the power of the belief in an America united by shared, middle-class values. By the 1980s, after years of social struggle and division, few Americans believed in the reality of that vision; many rejected it as undesirable. And although the 1980s were never as contentious as the 1960s and early 1970s, deep cultural divides nonetheless prevailed. A newly powerful group of Christian conservatives challenged the secular majority. A growing class of affluent Americans seemed a society apart from the urban poor that sociologists and journalists began calling "the underclass." At the same time, the composition of the American population was changing dramatically as people immigrated to the United States from more nations than ever before.

Since the 1960s, America's mainline liberal Protestant churches—Episcopalian, Presbyterian,

GROWTH OF THE RELIGIOUS RIGHT

Methodist—had been losing members, while Southern Baptists and other denominations offering the spiritual experience of being "born again" through belief in Jesus Christ and the literal truth of the Bible (fundamentalism) had grown rapidly. Fundamentalist preachers reached out through television: by the late 1970s, televangelist Oral Roberts drew 3.9 million viewers. Close to 20 percent of Americans identified themselves as fundamentalist Christians in 1980.

Most fundamentalist Christian churches stayed out of the social and political conflicts of the 1960s and early 1970s, concentrating on preaching the gospel instead. But in the late 1970s some influential preachers mobilized their flocks for political struggle. In a "Washington for Jesus" rally in 1980, fundamentalist leader Pat Robertson told crowds, "We have enough votes to run the country." The Moral Majority, founded in 1979 by Jerry Falwell, sought a "Christian America," in part by supporting political candidates. Falwell's defense of socially conservative "family values" and his condemnation of feminism (he called NOW the "National Order of Witches"), homosexuality, pornography, and abortion resonated with many Americans.

Throughout the 1980s, conservative Christians known as the New Right campaigned against America's secular culture. Rejecting multiculturalism—that different cultures and lifestyle choices were equally valid—the New Right wanted what they believed to be "God's law" as the basis for American society. Concerned Women for America, founded by Beverly La-

■ The Reverend Jerry Falwell, an evangelical preacher whose *Old Time Gospel Hour* program reached 15 million Americans, founded the Moral Majority in 1979. This conservative political action group drew support from fundamentalist Christians and played a major role in the political elections of the 1980s.
(Dennis Brack/Black Star/Stockphoto.com)

Hayes in 1979, wanted elementary school readers containing "unacceptable" religious beliefs (including excerpts from *The Diary of Anne Frank* and *The Wizard of Oz*) removed from classrooms. Fundamentalist Christian groups again challenged the teaching of evolution in public schools. The Reagan administration frequently turned to James Dobson, founder of the conservative Focus on the Family, for policy advice. Conservative Christians also joined with Roman Catholics, Mormons, and other groups in the anti-abortion or "prolife" movement.

Many Americans vigorously opposed the New Right's seeming intolerance and threat to basic

"CULTURE WARS"

freedoms—including the freedom of religion for those whose beliefs differed from the conservative

Christianity of the New Right. In 1982 the politically progressive television producer Norman Lear, influential former congresswoman Barbara Jordan, and other prominent figures in business, religion, politics, and entertainment founded People for the American Way to support American civil liberties, the separation of church and state, and the values of tolerance and diversity. This struggle between the religious right and their opponents for the future of the nation came to be known as the "culture wars."

Many beliefs of Christian fundamentalists ran counter to the ways most Americans lived, especially regarding women's roles. By the 1980s, a generation of girls had grown up with the benefits of the women's movement, expecting freedoms and opportunities their mothers never had. Legislation such as the Civil Rights Act of 1964 and Title IX opened academic and athletic programs to females. In 1960 there were 38 male lawyers for every 1 female lawyer in the United States; by 1983, the ratio was 5.5 to 1. By 1985, more than half of married women with children under age three worked outside the home. The religious right's insistence that women's place was in the home, subordinated to her husband, contradicted the gains made toward sexual equality and the reality of many women's lives.

The racialized nature of poverty also divided the nation. A 1988 national report on race relations looked

The New Inequality

back to the 1968 Kerner Commission report, claiming, "America is again becoming two separate societies," white and black. Although the majority of America's poor were white and the black middle class was expanding, people of color were much more likely to be poor. In 1980, 33 percent of blacks and 26 percent of Latinos lived in poverty, compared with 10 percent of whites (see Figure 32.2).

Reasons for poverty varied. The legacies of racism played a role. The changing job structure was partly responsible; the well-paid jobs for unskilled workers disappeared, replaced by lower-paid service jobs. New York alone had 234,000 fewer blue-collar workers in 1980 than in 1970. In addition, families headed by a single mother were five times more likely to be poor than families headed by a married couple. By 1992, 59 percent of African American children and 17 percent of white children lived in female-headed households, and almost half of black children lived in poverty.

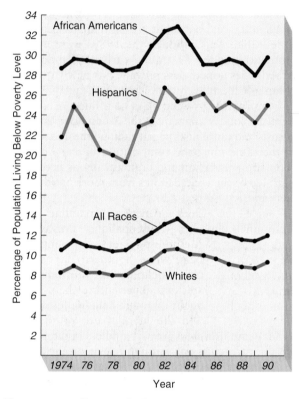

Figure 32.2   Poverty in America by Race, 1974–1990

Poverty in America rose in the early 1980s but subsided afterward. Many people of color, however, experienced little relief during the decade. Notice that the percentage of African Americans living below the poverty level was three times higher than that for whites. It also was much higher for Hispanics.   (Source: Adapted from U.S. Bureau of the Census, *Statistical Abstract of the United States* [Washington, D.C., 1992], p. 461.)

In impoverished inner-city neighborhoods, violent crime—particularly homicides and gang warfare—grew

Social Crises in American Cities

alarmingly, as did school dropout rates, general crime rates, and child abuse. Some poverty-stricken people tried to find escape in hard drugs, especially crack, a derivative of cocaine, which first struck New York City's poorest neighborhoods in 1985. Gang shootouts over drugs were deadly: the toll in Los Angeles in 1987 was 387 deaths, more than half of them innocent bystanders.

Many states instituted mandatory prison sentences for possessing small amounts of crack, making penalties for 1 gram of crack equivalent to those for 100 grams of cocaine, the drug favored by more affluent white Americans. Such policies increased America's prison population almost fourfold from 1980 to the mid-1990s, with black and Latino youth arrested in disproportionate numbers. By 2000, young black men were more likely to have been arrested than to have graduated from a four-year college.

Rates of homelessness also grew during the 1980s. Some were impoverished families; many had drug or alcohol problems. About a third of the homeless were former psychiatric patients discharged under "deinstitutionalization." By 1985, 80 percent of the total number of beds in state mental hospitals had been eliminated on the premise that small neighborhood programs would be more responsive to people's needs—though these programs failed to materialize. Consequently, many of America's mentally ill citizens wandered the streets.

Another social crisis in the 1980s was the global spread of autoimmune deficiency syndrome, or AIDS.

THE AIDS EPIDEMIC Caused by the human immunodeficiency virus (HIV), AIDS leaves its victims susceptible to deadly infections and cancers. The human immunodeficiency virus itself is spread through the exchange of blood or other body fluids, often through sexual intercourse or needle sharing by intravenous drug users.

AIDS was first observed in the United States in 1981. Of the fifty-seven thousand AIDS cases reported between 1981 and 1988, nearly thirty-two thousand resulted in death. Politicians were slow to devote resources to AIDS, in part because it was perceived initially as exclusively a "gay man's disease." "A man reaps what he sows," declared Jerry Falwell of the Moral Majority. AIDS, along with other sexually transmitted diseases such as genital herpes and chlamydia, ended an era defined by penicillin and "the pill," in which sex was freed from the threat of disease or unwanted pregnancy.

For the rich, the 1980s marked an era of ostentation. "Greed is all right," Wall Street financier Ivan

AN ERA OF OSTENTATION Boesky told students at the University of California, Berkeley, the center of 1960s campus protest, and he was met with cheers and laughter.

New York entrepreneur Donald Trump's $29 million yacht had gold-plated bathroom fixtures. Publisher Malcolm Forbes flew eight hundred guests to Morocco for his seventieth birthday; the party cost $2 million.

Nineteen eighty-four was the "Year of the Yuppie"—Young Urban Professional—proclaimed *Newsweek* magazine. A derogatory term, *Yuppie* (and *Buppie*, for black urban professional) described ambitious and successful young Americans in demanding careers who enjoyed a consumer-driven lifestyle: BMWs, Sub-Zero refrigerators, Armani suits, Häagen-Dazs ice cream. Americans in the 1980s seemed fascinated with tales of the super-rich (making *Dallas* a top-rated television show) and with Yuppie lifestyles (chronicled on the popular show *thirtysomething*). But Yuppies also represented those who got ahead without caring about those left behind. As Yuppies gentrified urban neighborhoods, displacing poorer residents, graffiti appeared in New York: "Die, Yuppie Scum."

America was further polarized by the arrival of new immigrants who did not fit cleanly into old racial

NEW IMMIGRANTS FROM ASIA categories. Between 1970 and 1990, the United States absorbed more than 13 million arrivals, most from Latin America and Asia. Before the immigration reforms of 1965, Americans of Asian ancestry made up less than 1 percent of the nation's population; by 1990, that figure was 3 percent.

Before 1965, the majority of Asian Americans were of Japanese ancestry (about 52 percent in 1960), followed by Chinese and Filipino. In the 1960s and 1970s, the highest rates of immigration were from nations not previously represented in the United States. There were only 603 Vietnamese residents in 1964. By 1990, the United States had absorbed almost 800,000 refugees from Indochina, many casualties of the Vietnam War. Immigrants flooded in from South Korea, Thailand, India, Pakistan, Bangladesh, Indonesia, Singapore, Laos, Cambodia, and Vietnam. Japanese Americans were now only 15 percent of the Asian American population.

Immigrants from Asia tended to be either highly skilled or unskilled. Unsettled conditions in the Philippines in the 1970s and 1980s created an exodus of well-educated Filipinos to the United States. Korea, Taiwan, India, and China also lost skilled and educated workers to the United States. Other Chinese immigrants, however, had few job skills and spoke little or no English. Large numbers crowded into neighborhoods like New York's Chinatown, where women worked under terrible conditions in the city's nonunion garment industry. Immigrants from Southeast Asia were the most likely to be unskilled and to live in poverty in the United States.

But even highly educated immigrants found their options limited. A 1983 study revealed that Korean Americans owned three-quarters of the approximately twelve hundred greengroceries in New York City. Though often cited as a success story, Korean greengrocers usually had descended the professional ladder: 78 percent of them had college or professional degrees.

Unprecedented immigration rates coupled with a high birth rate made Latinos the fastest-growing group of Americans. In 1970 Latinos made

THE GROWING LATINO POPULATION

up 4.5 percent of the nation's population; that percentage jumped to 9 percent by 1990, when one out of three Los Angelenos and Miamians were Hispanic, as was 70 percent of El Paso. Mexican Americans, concentrated in California and the Southwest, made up most of this population, but Puerto Ricans, Cubans, Dominicans, and other Caribbean immigrants also lived in the United States, clustered principally in East Coast cities.

During the 1980s, people from Guatemala and El Salvador fled civil war and government violence for the United States. Although the U.S. government commonly refused them political asylum (about 113,000 Cubans received political refugee status during the 1980s, compared with fewer than 1,400 El Salvadorians), a national "sanctuary movement" of Christian churches defied the law to protect refugees from deportation to places where they risked violence or death. Economic troubles in Mexico and Central and South America also produced a flood of undocumented workers who crossed the poorly guarded 2,000-mile border between the United States and Mexico, seeking economic opportunities. Some moved back and forth across the border; a majority meant to stay.

Many Americans believed new arrivals threatened jobs and economic security, and nativist violence and bigotry increased during the 1980s. In 1982 twenty-seven-year-old Vincent Chin was beaten to death in Detroit by an unemployed auto worker and his uncle. American auto plants were losing to Japanese imports, and the two men seemingly mistook the Chinese

American Chin for Japanese. In New York, Philadelphia, and Los Angeles, African Americans boycotted Korean groceries. Riots broke out in Los Angeles schools between black students and newly arrived Mexicans. In Dade County, Florida, voters passed an "antibilingual" measure that removed Spanish-language signs from public transportation, while at the state and national levels, people debated declaring English the "official" language of the United States.

Concerned about the flow of illegal aliens, Congress passed the Immigration Reform and Control (Simpson-Rodino) Act in 1986. The act's purpose was to discourage illegal immigration by imposing sanctions on employers who hired undocumented workers, but it also provided amnesty to millions who had immigrated illegally before 1982.

Online Study Center
Improve Your Grade
Primary Source: Rosa Maria Urbina and Jose Luis Describe Life as Illegals

The End of the Cold War and Global Disorder

*T*he end of Reagan's presidency coincided with world events that would replace the Cold War with a new international system. Reagan's vice president, George Herbert Walker Bush, would become president and oversee the transition. The son of a Wall Street banker and U.S. senator from Connecticut, Bush had attended an exclusive boarding school and then Yale. He had the advantage in seeking the Republican presidential nomination in having been a loyal vice president. And he possessed a formidable résumé: he had been ambassador to the United Nations, chairman of the Republican Party, special envoy to China, and director of the CIA. He also had been a war hero, flying fifty-eight combat missions in the Pacific in World War II and receiving the Distinguished Flying Cross.

Bush entered the 1988 presidential campaign trailing his Democratic opponent, Massachusetts governor Michael Dukakis, by a wide margin.

1988 PRESIDENTIAL CAMPAIGN

Republicans turned that around by waging one of the most negative campaigns in American history. Most notorious, the Bush camp aired a television commercial featuring a black convicted murderer, Willie Horton, who terrorized a Maryland couple, raping the woman, while on weekend furlough—a temporary release program begun under Dukakis's Republican predecessor. The Republicans also falsely suggested that Dukakis had a history of psychiatric problems. Dukakis, though not personally attacking Bush, ran an uninspired campaign. On election day, Bush won by eight percentage points in the popular vote and received 426 electoral votes to Dukakis's 112. The Democrats, however, retained control of both houses of Congress.

Bush focused his attention on foreign policy. He envisioned the United States as the supreme power in a unipolar world. Yet he also knew that the Cold War was drawing to a close. Mikhail Gorbachev's cascading changes in the Soviet Union were now stimulating reforms in eastern Europe that ultimately led to revolution. In 1989 people in East Germany, Poland, Hungary, Czechoslovakia, and Romania startled the world by repudiating their communist governments and staging mass protests against a despised ideology. In November 1989, Germans scaled the Berlin Wall and tore it down; the following October, the two Germanys reunited. By then, other regional communist governments had fallen or were on the verge.

Other communist challenges were less successful. In June 1989 Chinese armed forces stormed into Beijing's

TIANANMEN SQUARE

Tiananmen Square, slaughtering hundreds—perhaps thousands—of unarmed students and citizens who for weeks had held peaceful pro-democracy rallies. The Chinese government emphatically rejected political liberalization; henceforth, the "Chinese solution" came to mean repression in response to popular calls for freedom.

Elsewhere, however, the forces of democratization proved too powerful to resist. In South Africa, a new government under F. W. De Klerk began a cautious retreat from apartheid. In February 1990 De Klerk legalized all political parties in South Africa, including the African National Congress, the chief black party, and released Nelson Mandela, a hero to black South Africans, after a twenty-seven-year imprisonment. Then the government repealed its apartheid laws over several years, allowing all citizens to vote regardless of color. Mandela, who became South Africa's first black president in 1994, called the transformation "a small miracle."

The same phrase could be used to describe what happened in the Soviet Union. In 1990 the Baltic states

COLLAPSE OF SOVIET POWER

of Lithuania, Latvia, and Estonia declared independence from Moscow's rule; the following year, the Soviet Union ceased to exist, disintegrating into independent successor states—Russia, Ukraine, Tajikistan, and many others. Muscled aside by Russian reformers who thought he was moving too slowly toward democracy and free-market economics, Gorbachev lost power. The breakup of the Soviet empire, the dismantling of the Warsaw Pact (the Soviet military alliance formed in 1955 with communist countries of eastern Europe), the repudiation of communism by its own leaders, German reunification, and a significantly reduced risk of nuclear war signaled the end of the Cold War and the Soviet-American rivalry. The United States and its allies had won. The containment policy followed by nine presidents—from Truman through Bush—had had many critics over the years, but it had succeeded at containing communism for four-plus decades without blowing up the world or obliterating freedom at home. Over time, the Soviet socialist economy proved less able to compete with the American free-market one, less able to cope with the demands of the Soviet and eastern European citizenry.

Yet the Soviet empire might have survived longer had it not been for Gorbachev, one of the most influential figures of the twentieth century. Through a series of unexpected overtures and decisions, Gorbachev fundamentally transformed the superpower relationship in a way that could scarcely have been anticipated before. Ronald Reagan's role was less central but vitally important because of his later willingness to negotiate and treat Gorbachev more as a partner than as an adversary. Just as personalities mattered in starting the Cold War, so they mattered in ending it.

Online Study Center **Improve Your Grade**
Interactive Map:
 The End of the Cold War Changes the Map of
 Europe

The victory in the Cold War elicited little celebration among Americans. The confrontation may never

COSTS OF VICTORY

have become a hot war, but the period after 1945 nevertheless witnessed numerous Cold War–related conflicts claiming millions of lives.

In the Vietnam War alone, at least 1.5 million people died, more than 58,000 of them Americans. Military budgets had eaten up billions of dollars, thereby shortchanging domestic programs. Some Americans wondered whether the communist threat had ever been as grave as officials claimed.

As the Cold War closed, the Bush administration signed important arms reduction treaties with the Soviet Union in 1991, and with the postbreakup Russia in 1993, but the United States sustained a large defense budget and continued to station large numbers of military forces overseas. As a result, Americans were denied the "peace dividend" they hoped would reduce taxes and free up funds for domestic problems.

In Central America, the Bush administration cooled the zeal with which Reagan had meddled, but showed no reluctance to intervene in the region to further U.S. aims. In December 1989, American troops invaded Panama to oust the military leader Manuel Noriega. A long-time drug trafficker, Noriega had stayed in Washington's favor in the mid-1980s by providing logistical support for the Nicaraguan contras. When exposés of Noriega's sordid record provoked protests in Panama, however, Bush decided to dump the dictator. Noriega was captured and taken to Miami, where, in 1992, he was convicted of drug trafficking and imprisoned. Devastated Panama meanwhile became increasingly dependent on the United States.

The strongest test of Bush's foreign policy came in the Middle East. The Iran-Iraq War ended inconclusively in August 1988, after eight years and almost 400,000 dead. The Reagan administration assisted the Iraqis with weapons and intelligence, as had many NATO countries. In mid-1990, Iraqi president Saddam Hussein, facing massive war debts, invaded neighboring Kuwait, hoping to enhance his regional power and his oil revenues. George Bush condemned the invasion and vowed to defend Kuwait, in part fearing that Iraq might threaten U.S. oil supplies in Kuwait and petroleum-rich Saudi Arabia next door.

SADDAM HUSSEIN'S GAMBLE

Within weeks, Bush convinced every important government, including most Arab and Islamic states, to commit to an economic boycott of Iraq. Then, in Operation Desert Shield, Bush dispatched more than 500,000 U.S. forces to the region, joined by over 200,000 from the allies. Likening Saddam to Hitler

and declaring the moment the first post–Cold War "test of our mettle," Bush rallied a deeply divided Congress to authorize "all necessary means" to oust Iraq from Kuwait (a vote of 250 to 183 in the House and 52 to 47 in the Senate). Many Americans believed that economic sanctions should be given more time to work, but Bush would not wait. Victory would come swiftly and cleanly.

Operation Desert Storm began on January 16, 1991, with the greatest air armada in history pummeling Iraqi targets. American missiles reinforced around-the-clock bombing raids on Baghdad, Iraq's capital. It was a television war, in which CNN reporters broadcast live from a Baghdad hotel as bombs were falling. In late February, coalition forces launched a ground war that quickly routed the Iraqis from Kuwait. When the war ended on March 1, at least 40,000 Iraqis had been killed; the death toll for allied troops stood at 240 (148 of them Americans).

OPERATION DESERT STORM

Bush rejected a call from advisers to take Baghdad and topple Hussein's regime. Coalition members would not have agreed to such a plan, and it was not clear who would replace the dictator. So Saddam Hussein remained, though with his power curtailed. The U.N. maintained an arms and economic embargo, and the Security Council issued Resolution 687, demanding full disclosure of Iraq's program to develop weapons of mass destruction and ballistic missiles. In Resolution 688, the Security Council condemned a brutal crackdown by the Iraqi regime against Kurds in northern Iraq and Shia Muslims in the south and demanded access for humanitarian groups. The United States, Britain, and France seized on Resolution 688 to create a northern "no-fly zone" prohibiting Iraqi aircraft flights. A similar no-fly zone was set up in southern Iraq in 1992 and expanded in 1996.

Though later many would question Bush's decision to stop short of Baghdad, initially there were few objections. In the wake of Desert Storm, the president's popularity soared to 91 percent, beating the record 89 percent set by Harry Truman in June 1945 after Germany's surrender. Cocky advisers thought Bush could ride his popularity through the 1992 election and beyond. Bush could also claim domestic achievements

DOMESTIC PROBLEMS

that seemed to affirm his pledge to lead a "kinder, gentler nation."

In 1990, for example, Bush signed the Americans with Disabilities Act, banning job discrimination, in companies with twenty-five or more employees, against the blind, deaf, mentally disabled, and physically impaired, as well as against those who are HIV positive or have cancer. The act, which covered 87 percent of all wage earners, also required that "reasonable accommodations," such as wheelchair ramps, be made available to people with disabilities. Also in 1990, the president signed the Clean Air Act, which sought to reduce acid rain by limiting emissions from factories and automobiles.

Yet Bush's poll numbers started falling and kept falling, largely because of his ineffectual response to the weakening economy. He was slow to grasp the implications of the heavy national debt and massive federal deficit. When the nation entered a full-fledged recession after the Gulf War, Bush merely proclaimed that things were not really *that* bad.

Business shrank, despite low interest rates that theoretically should have encouraged investment. Real-estate prices plummeted. American products faced steadily tougher competition from overseas competitors, especially Japan and elsewhere in Asia. As unemployment climbed to 8 percent, consumer confidence sank. By late 1991, fewer than 40 percent of Americans felt comfortable with the way the country was going.

Bush's credibility was diminished further by confirmation hearings for Clarence Thomas, his Supreme Court nominee, in the fall of 1991. The Bush administration hoped that those who opposed the nomination of another conservative to the high court might nonetheless support an African American justice. But in October, Anita Hill, an African American law professor at the University of Oklahoma, charged that Thomas had sexually harassed her when she worked for him during the early 1980s. The Judiciary Committee hearings, carried on television, turned ugly, and some Republican members suggested that Hill was either lying or mentally ill. Thomas described himself as the "victim" of a "high-tech lynching." However, Hill's testimony focused the nation's attention on issues of power, gender, sex, and the workplace. And the Senate's confirmation of Thomas, along with the

CLARENCE THOMAS NOMINATION

attacks on Hill, angered many, further increasing the gender gap in American politics.

Summary *Online Study Center* **ACE the Test**

When Ronald Reagan left the White House in 1988, the *New York Times* wrote: "Ronald Reagan leaves no Vietnam War, no Watergate, no hostage crisis. But he leaves huge question marks—and much to do." George H. W. Bush fulfilled the foreign policy promises of the 1980s, as the Soviet Union collapsed and America won the Cold War. He also led the United States into war with Iraq, which ended in swift victory but left Saddam Hussein in power.

During the 1980s, the United States moved from recession to economic prosperity. However, deep tax cuts and massive increases in defense spending created huge budget deficits, increasing the national debt from $994 billion to more than $2.9 trillion. Probusiness policies, such as deregulation, created opportunities for economic growth but also opened the door to corruption. Policies that benefited the wealthy at the expense of middle-class or poor Americans widened the gulf between the rich and everyone else. Drug addiction, crime, and violence grew, especially in the most impoverished areas.

The 1980s also saw the beginning of the "culture wars" between fundamentalist Christians who sought to "restore America to God" and opponents who championed separation of church and state. The nation shifted to the right politically, though the coalitions of economic and social conservatives that supported Reagan were fragile.

Finally, during the 1980s, the nation's Latino population grew in size and visibility, and new immigrants from Asia arrived in large numbers. During the Reagan-Bush years, America had become both more polarized and more diverse.

The Americans with Disabilities Act (ADA), passed by large bipartisan majorities in Congress and signed into law by President George Bush on July 26, 1990, built on the legacy of America's civil rights movement. Beyond banning discrimination, the ADA mandated that public and private entities—schools, stores, restaurants and hotels, government buildings, and public transportation authorities—provide "reasonable accommodations" allowing people with disabilities to participate fully in their communities and the nation.

The equal-access provisions of the ADA have changed the landscape of America. Steep curbs and stairs once blocked access to wheelchair users; now ramps and lifts are common. Buses "kneel" for passengers with limited mobility; crosswalks and elevators use audible signals for those with sight impairments; schools and universities offer qualified students a wide range of assistance. People with a whole spectrum of disabilities have traveled into the Grand Canyon, thanks to National Park Service "accessibility" programs.

At the same time, ADA regulations covering employment have generated difficult legal questions. Which conditions are covered by the ADA? (The Supreme Court has ruled that asymptomatic HIV infection is a covered disability and carpal tunnel syndrome is not.) Employers may not discriminate against qualified people who can, with "reasonable" accommodation, perform the "essential" tasks of a job—but what is "reasonable" and "essential"? The specific provisions of the ADA will likely continue to be contested and redefined in the courts, but as Attorney General Janet Reno noted on the ADA's tenth anniversary, its true legacy is the determination "to find the best in everyone and to give everyone equal opportunity."

GLOBAL BRIDGES IN THE NEW MILLENNIUM
America Since 1992

*a*t 8:46 A.M. on that fateful Tuesday morning, Jan Demczur, a window washer, stepped into an elevator in the North Tower of the World Trade Center in New York City. Before the elevator reached its next landing, one of the six occupants recalled, "We felt a muted thud. The whole building shook. And the elevator swung from side to side like a pendulum." None of the occupants knew it, but American Airlines Flight 175 had just crashed into the building at a speed of 440 miles per hour.

The elevator started plunging. Someone pushed the emergency stop button. Then a voice came over the intercom: there had been an explosion. As smoke seeped through the elevator's doors, several men used the wooden handle of Demczur's squeegee to force open the doors, but discovered they were on the fiftieth floor, where this elevator did not stop. In front of them was a wall.

Demczur, a Polish immigrant who once worked as a builder, saw that the wall was made of Sheetrock, a plasterboard that could be cut. The six men took turns scraping and poking at it, and an hour later burst through to a men's bathroom. Startled firefighters guided them to a stairwell. They reached the street at 10:23 A.M. Five minutes later the tower collapsed.

It was September 11, 2001.

Later that day, Demczur learned that terrorists had hijacked four airliners and turned them into missiles. Two were flown into the World Trade Center, one slammed into the Pentagon in Washington, D.C., and one crashed in a field in Pennsylvania after passengers tried to retake the plane from the hijackers. Both World Trade Center towers collapsed, killing nearly three thousand people.

It was the deadliest attack the United States had ever suffered on its soil, and it would dramatically change American life. The events of the day sent shock waves around the globe, revealing how interconnected the world had become. At the World Trade Center, nearly five hundred foreigners from more

Social Strains and New Political Directions

"The New Economy" and Globalization

Paradoxes of Prosperity

September 11 and the War on Terrorism

Americans in the New Millennium

LINKS TO THE WORLD
The Global AIDS Epidemic

Summary

LEGACY FOR A PEOPLE AND A NATION
The Internet

Online Study Center

This icon will direct you to interactive map and primary source activities on the website http:college.hmco.com/ pic/nortonbrief7e

C H R O N O L O G Y

1992 • Violence erupts in Los Angeles over Rodney King verdict
• Major economic recession
• Clinton elected president
• U.S. sends troops to Somalia

1993 • Congress approves North American Free Trade Agreement (NAFTA)
• U.S. withdraws from Somalia

1994 • Contract with America helps Republicans win majorities in House and Senate
• Genocide in Rwanda
• U.S. intervention in Haiti

1995 • Domestic terrorist bombs Oklahoma City federal building
• U.S. diplomats broker peace for Bosnia

1996 • Welfare reform bill places time limits on welfare payments
• Clinton reelected

1998 • House votes to impeach Clinton

1999 • Senate acquits Clinton of impeachment charges

• NATO bombs Serbia over Kosovo crisis
• Antiglobalization demonstrators disrupt World Trade Organization (WTO) meeting in Seattle

2000 • Nation records longest economic expansion in its history
• Supreme Court settles contested presidential election in favor of Bush

2001 • Economy dips into recession; begins period of low growth and high unemployment
• Bush becomes president
• Al Qaeda terrorists attack World Trade Center and Pentagon
• PATRIOT Act passed by Congress
• Enron business scandal results in Justice Department investigation
• U.S. attacks Al Qaeda positions in Afghanistan, topples ruling Taliban regime

2003 • U.S. invades Iraq, ousts Saddam Hussein regime

than eighty countries lost their lives: sixty-seven Britons, twenty-one Jamaicans, twenty-seven Japanese, seventeen Mexicans, thirty-four Indians, sixteen Canadians, fifteen Australians, and seven Haitians. Many of the victims were, like Demczur, immigrants who sought a better life for themselves and their families; others were on temporary work visas. But all made the World Trade Center a global city within a city, where some 50,000 people worked and another 140,000 visited daily.

An emblem of U.S. financial power, the World Trade Center towers also symbolized the globalization of world trade that marked the 1980s and 1990s. The towers housed the offices of more than four hundred businesses, including some of the world's leading financial institutions: the Bank of America, Switzerland's Credit Suisse Group, Germany's Deutsche Bank, and Japan's Dai-Ichi Kangyo Bank.

Globalization was a 1990s buzzword and went beyond trade and investment to include connections in commerce, communications, and culture. While the terrorists—the radical Islamic group Al Qaeda— sought to bring down globalization, their attack used the same international technological, economic, and travel infrastructure that had fueled global integration. Cell phones, computers, and intercontinental air travel were crucial in the terrorists' plot to turn four modern jetliners into lethal weapons.

Islamic militants had struck the World Trade Center before, in 1993, bombing its underground parking garage. But Americans at the time paid only fleeting attention. President Bill Clinton took office in 1993 concentrating less on foreign policy and more on domestic issues such as healthcare and deficit reduction. Clinton also sought to harness globalization to America's benefit.

For most Americans, the 1990s offered good times. The stock market soared, unemployment dropped, and more Americans than ever before owned their own homes. But the decade was also marked by violence and cultural conflict: the first multiethnic uprising in Los Angeles, domestic terrorism in Oklahoma City, school shootings, and hate crimes.

These were also politically volatile years. Republicans blocked Democrats' legislative programs. With a conservative agenda of limited government and "family values"—spelled out in his "Contract with America"—House minority whip Newt Gingrich led a "Republican Revolution" that routed Democrats in the 1994 midterm elections. But Republicans alienated voters by shutting down the federal government during the winter of 1995–1996 in a budget standoff, and Clinton was reelected in 1996. However, scandal plagued the Clinton White House, and in 1999 Clinton was impeached by the House of Representatives, alleging he committed perjury and obstructed justice. The Senate failed to convict him, and Clinton's popularity remained high, but his leadership was compromised.

Clinton's successor, George W. Bush, successful in an extremely controversial election, was galvanized by the 9/11 attacks, declaring a "war on terrorism." Bush ordered U.S. forces into large-scale military action, first in Afghanistan where Al Qaeda was headquartered with the blessing of the Taliban regime, then in Iraq to oust Saddam Hussein's government. Militarily, the Taliban and Iraqi government were quickly beaten. Al Qaeda, however, remained a threat, and Iraq endured postwar instability. At home, Bush enjoyed high approval ratings, despite a weak economy and ballooning budget deficit. Bush had declared his a "war presidency," and Americans, following the pattern of many previous wars, rallied around the flag and around the president. ∎

Social Strains and New Political Directions

*a*lthough the 1990s would be remembered for relative peace and prosperity, the decade did not start that way. Scourges of drugs, homelessness, and crime plagued America's cities. Racial tensions had worsened; the gulf between rich and poor had grown more pronounced. The economy tipped into recession. Public disillusion with political leaders ran strong. As the 1992 presidential campaign began, Americans wanted a change.

Racial tensions erupted in Los Angeles in spring 1992. To some, the April 29 violence in South Central L.A. was a riot; to others, a rebellion. The immediate cause: a jury (with no African American members) acquitted four white police officers charged with beating a black man, Rodney King, who had fled pursuing police at over 110 miles per hour. A bystander captured the beating on videotape, and CNN, the new twenty-four-hour news network, replayed it so frequently that the local event became national news.

VIOLENCE IN LOS ANGELES

The roots of this violence, however, went deeper. Well-paid jobs disappeared in the deindustrialization of the 1970s and 1980s, as a hundred manufacturing and industrial plants shut their doors. By the early 1990s, almost a third of South Central residents lived in poverty—a rate 75 percent higher than for the entire city.

Tensions increased as new immigrants arrived: Latinos from Mexico and Central America who competed with African Americans for jobs; Koreans establishing small businesses such as grocery stores. Street gangs struggled over territory in South Central as the crack epidemic further decimated the neighborhood and homicide rates soared. Many African American and Latino residents saw high prices in Korean-owned shops as exploitation, while Korean shopkeepers complained of frequent shoplifting, robberies, even beatings.

The violence in Los Angeles left at least fifty-three people dead. Almost $1 billion in property was destroyed, including twenty-three hundred stores owned by Koreans or Korean Americans. More than sixteen thousand people were arrested, half of them Latinos.

During the administration of George H. W. Bush, the economy had grown slowly or not at all. Thirty states were in financial trouble in the early 1990s; some local governments faced bankruptcy. In 1978 California's Proposition 13—the first in a series of "tax revolts" nationwide—cut property taxes while the population boomed, and the state government, out of money in mid-1992, paid workers and bills in IOUs. Many businesses closed down or cut back. By 1992, several million Americans were unemployed. In 1991 median household incomes hit the most severe decline since the 1973 recession; in 1992 the number of poor people in America reached the highest level since 1964.

ECONOMIC TROUBLES AND THE 1992 ELECTION

As economic woes continued, President Bush's approval rating fell—to half its high point of 91 percent after the Persian Gulf War. Despite the credit Bush gained for the end of the Cold War and the quick victory in the Gulf War, economic difficulties and a belief that he was out of touch with Americans' problems left him vulnerable in the 1992 presidential election.

Democratic nominee and Arkansas governor Bill Clinton offered a profound contrast to Bush. Clinton's campaign headquarters bore signs with the reminder: "It's the economy, stupid." In a town-hall-format presidential debate, a woman asked how the economic troubles had affected each candidate, and Clinton replied, "Tell me how it's affected you again?" George Bush was caught on camera looking at his watch.

Third-party candidate Ross Perot, a Texas billionaire, was certainly insulated by his vast fortune from the problems of most Americans. Nevertheless, his appeals to common sense and folksy populism attracted many who were fed up with Washington.

On election day, Americans denied George Bush a second term. Ross Perot claimed almost 20 percent of the popular vote but did not carry a single state. Clinton, with 43 percent of the popular vote, swept all of New England, the West Coast, and much of the industrial Midwest, even making inroads into the South and drawing "Reagan Democrats" back to the fold. Although Democrats controlled both houses, incumbents did not fare well. The 103rd Congress had 110 new representatives and 11 new senators. Many were—like Clinton—baby boomers in their forties.

A journalist described the paradoxical Bill Clinton in a 1996 *New York Times* article as "one of the biggest, most talented, articulate, intelligent, open, colorful characters ever to inhabit the White House," while also noting that he could be "an undisciplined, fumbling, obtuse, defensive, self-justifying rogue." Clinton was a born politician from a small town called Hope who wanted to be president most of his life. At Georgetown University in Washington, D.C., during the 1960s, he'd protested the Vietnam War and maneuvered to keep himself out of it. Clinton won a Rhodes scholarship to Oxford, earned his law degree from Yale, and returned to his home state of Arkansas, where he was elected governor in 1978 at age thirty-two.

WILLIAM JEFFERSON CLINTON

In 1975 Clinton married Hillary Rodham, whom he met when both were law students at Yale. Rodham Clinton was the first First Lady with a significant career of her own, and she spoke of balancing her professional and family life. But Rodham Clinton was attacked by conservatives and antifeminists. After she told a hostile interviewer, "I suppose I could have stayed home and baked cookies and had teas," the *New York Post* called her "an insult to most women."

Politically, Bill Clinton was a "new Democrat," advocating a more centrist—though still socially progressive—position for the Democratic Party. Clinton and his colleagues emphasized private-sector economic development rather than public jobs programs, focusing on job training and other policies to promote opportunity, not dependency. Some Democrats found Clinton too conservative. However, the political right vehemently attacked Clinton, making 1990s politics exceptionally partisan and rancorous.

A NEW DEMOCRAT'S PROMISE AND PITFALLS

Clinton began his presidency with an ambitious program of reform and revitalization, including appointing a cabinet that "looks like America" in all its diversity. But Republicans, determined not to allow Clinton the traditional "honeymoon" period, maneuvered him into fulfilling his pledge to end the ban on gays in the military before he had secured congressional or military support. Amid great controversy, Clinton accepted a "don't ask, don't tell" compromise that alienated liberals and conservatives, the gay community, and the military.

Clinton's major goal was to make healthcare affordable and accessible for all Americans. But special interests mobilized in opposition: the insurance industry worried about lost profits; the business community feared higher taxes; the medical community worried about more regulation, lower government reimbursement rates, and reduced healthcare quality. The healthcare task force, co-chaired by Hillary Rodham Clinton, could not defeat these forces. Within a year, the centerpiece of Clinton's fledgling presidency had failed.

Scandal also plagued Clinton. Rumors of his past marital infidelities circulated. The suicide of Vincent Foster, deputy White House counsel and Clinton friend, spurred wild theories of murder and conspiracy. By December 1993, Republicans wanted a special prosecutor to investigate the Clintons' involvement in Whitewater, a private Arkansas land deal that figured in one of the savings-and-loan scandals of the 1980s. In January 1994, under political pressure, Attorney General Janet Reno named a special prosecutor.

New-style Republicans challenged the beleaguered "new Democrat." In September 1994, more than three hundred Republican candidates for the House of Representatives endorsed the "Contract with America," ten policy proposals the Republicans pledged to pass. Developed under the leadership of Georgia's conservative representative, Newt Gingrich, the "Contract" promised the "end of [big] government" and "the beginning of a Congress that respects the values and shares the faith of the American family." It included a balanced-budget amendment to the Constitution, reduction of the capital gains tax, a two-year limit on welfare payments (with payments prohibited for unmarried mothers under eighteen), and increased defense spending.

THE "REPUBLICAN REVOLUTION"

In the midterm elections, the Republican Party mobilized socially conservative voters and took control of both houses of Congress for the first time since 1954. Gingrich was made Speaker of the House, and Bob Dole of Kansas became Senate majority leader. Republicans launched a counterrevolution to reverse more than sixty years of federal dominance and dismantle the welfare state.

Although many Americans applauded cutting government spending, they opposed cuts to specific programs, including Medicare and Medicaid, education and college loans, highway construction, farm subsidies, veterans' benefits, and Social Security. Republicans angered the public when they issued Clinton an ultimatum on the federal budget and forced the government to suspend all nonessential action during the winter of 1995–1996.

Such struggles led Clinton to make compromises that moved American politics to the right. For example, he signed the 1996 Personal Responsibility and Work Opportunity Act, a welfare reform measure that ended cash assistance to poor children (Aid to Families with Dependent Children) and gave each state a lump sum for its own "welfare-to-work" programs. The law mandated that heads of families on welfare must find work within two years—though states could exempt 20 percent of recipients—and limited welfare benefits to five years over an individual's lifetime. The Telecommunications Act of 1996, signed by Clinton, reduced diversity in America's media by permitting companies to own more television and radio stations.

POLITICAL COMPROMISE AND THE ELECTION OF 1996

Clinton and Al Gore were reelected in 1996 (defeating Republican Bob Dole and Reform Party candidate Ross Perot), partly because Clinton stole some of the conservatives' thunder. He declared that "the era of big government is over" and invoked family values, a centerpiece of the Republican campaign. Sometimes Clinton's actions were true compromises; other times he attempted to reclaim issues from the conservatives, as when he redefined family values as "fighting for the family-leave law." The Democrats also benefited from a strong economy and the gender gap: women were more likely to vote Democratic.

"The New Economy" and Globalization

 ust how much credit Clinton deserved for the improved economy is debatable. The roots of the 1990s boom were in the 1970s, when

American corporations began investing in new technologies, retooling plants to become energy efficient, and cutting labor costs. Specifically, companies reduced the influence of organized labor by moving operations to the union-weak South and West and to countries such as China and Mexico, where labor was cheap and pollution controls lax.

The rapid development of what came to be called "information technology"—computers, fax machines,

DIGITAL
REVOLUTION

cellular phones, and the Internet—had a huge economic impact in the 1980s and 1990s. New companies and industries sprang up, many headquartered in the "Silicon Valley" near San Francisco. By the second half of the 1990s, the *Forbes* list of the Four Hundred Richest People in America featured high-tech leaders such as Bill Gates, who became the wealthiest person in the world with a worth approaching $100 billion, as his company produced the operating software for most personal computers. The high-tech industries had considerable spillover effects, generating improved productivity, new jobs, and sustained economic growth.

The heart of this technological revolution was the microprocessor. Introduced in 1970 by Intel, the microprocessor miniaturized the central processing unit of a computer, meaning small machines could perform calculations previously requiring large machines. Computing chores that took a week in the early 1970s by 2000 took one minute, while the cost of storing 1 megabyte of information, enough for a 320-page book, fell from over $5,000 in 1975 to 17 cents in 1999.

Analysts dubbed this technology-driven sector "The New Economy," and it would have emerged no matter who was in the White House. Yet Clinton and his advisers had some responsibility for the dramatic upturn. With the U.S. budget deficit topping $500 billion, they made the politically risky move of abandoning the middle-class tax cut and making deficit reduction a top priority. White House officials rightly concluded that if the deficit could be brought under control, interest rates would drop and the economy would rebound. The budget deficit decreased (by 1997 it had been erased), leading to lower interest rates, which helped boost investment. Stock prices soared, and the gross national product rose by an average of 3.5 to 4 percent annually.

Clinton perceived early on that the technology revolution would make the world more interconnected.

GLOBALIZATION
OF BUSINESS

He was convinced that, with the demise of Soviet communism, capitalism—or at least the introduction of market forces, freer trade, and deregulation—was spreading around the globe.

The journalist Thomas L. Friedman asserted that the post–Cold War world was "the age of globalization," characterized by the integration of markets, finance, and technologies. U.S. officials lowered trade and investment barriers, completing the North American Free Trade Agreement (NAFTA) with Canada and Mexico in 1993, and in 1994 concluding the Uruguay Round of the General Agreement on Tariffs and Trade (GATT), which lowered tariffs for the seventy member nations that accounted for 80 percent of world trade. The administration also endorsed the 1995 creation of the World Trade Organization (WTO) to administer and enforce agreements made at the Uruguay Round. Finally, the president formed a National Economic Council to promote trade missions around the world.

By 2000 there were 63,000 parent companies worldwide and 690,000 foreign affiliates. Some, such as the Nike Corporation and the Gap, subcontracted production of certain merchandise to whichever developing countries had the lowest labor costs. Such arrangements created a "new international division of labor" and generated a boom in world exports, which, at $5.4 trillion in 1998, had doubled in two decades. U.S. exports reached $680 billion in 1998, but imports rose even higher, to $907 billion (for a trade deficit of $227 billion). Sometimes these multinational corporations affected foreign policy, as when Clinton in 1995 extended full diplomatic recognition to Vietnam under pressure from Coca-Cola, Citigroup, General Motors, and United Airlines, all seeking to enter that emerging market.

While the administration promoted open markets, labor unions argued that free-trade agreements

CRITICS OF
GLOBALIZATION

exacerbated the trade deficit and often exported American jobs. Average real wages for American workers declined steadily after 1973, from $320 per week to $260 by the mid-1990s. Other critics maintained that globalization widened

■ Animal protection advocates wear sea turtle costumes while carrying signs to protest what they contend are animal-harming rulings by the World Trade Organization, in Seattle Monday, Nov. 29, 1999. Protests began in earnest Monday against the WTO meetings and the conference schedule was thrown off by a security threat that temporarily closed the meeting's primary venue, the Washington State Trade and Convention Center.   (AP Photo/Beth Keiser)

the gap between rich and poor countries, creating a mass of "slave laborers" in poor countries working under conditions that would never be tolerated in the West. Environmentalists charged that globalization also exported pollution to countries unprepared to deal with it. Still other critics worried about the power of multinational corporations and the global financial markets over traditional cultures.

Antiglobalization fervor reached a peak in fall 1999 when WTO ministers met in Seattle for trade negotiations called the Millennium Round. Hundreds were arrested as thousands of protesters shut down the meeting. In the months that followed, there were smaller protests at meetings of the International Monetary Fund (IMF) and the World Bank. In July 2001, fifty thousand demonstrators protested an IMF and World Bank meeting in Genoa, Italy.

Activists also targeted corporations such as the Gap, Starbucks, Nike, and, especially, McDonald's, which by 1995 was serving 30 million customers daily in twenty thousand franchises in over one hundred countries. Critics assailed the company's slaughterhouse techniques, alleged exploitation of workers, its high-fat menu, and its contributions to creating an increasingly

TARGET:
McDONALD'S

homogeneous and sterile world culture, a so-called McWorld. For six years starting in 1996, McDonald's endured hundreds of often violent protests, including bombings in Rome, Prague, London, Macao, Rio de Janeiro, and Jakarta.

Others decried the violence and underlying arguments of the antiglobalization campaigners. True, some economists noted, statistics showed that global inequality had grown in recent years. But if one included quality-of-life measurements such as literacy and health, global inequality had actually declined. Some studies found that wage and job losses for U.S. workers were caused not primarily by globalization factors such as imports, production outsourcing, and immigration, but by technological change that made production more efficient. Other researchers saw no evidence that governments' sovereignty had been seriously compromised or that there was a "race to the bottom" in environmental standards.

As for creating a homogeneous global culture, critics noted that McDonald's, supposedly a prime mover of "McWorld," tailored its menu and operating practices to local tastes. And although American movies, TV programs, music, computer software, and other intellectual property often dominated world markets in the 1990s, foreign competition also arrived in America. Millions of American children were gripped by the Japanese fad Pokemon, and satellite television established a worldwide following for European soccer leagues.

Still, it remained true that the United States occupied a uniquely powerful position on the world stage.

CLINTON'S DIPLOMACY

The demise of the Soviet Union created a one-superpower world, in which the United States stood above other powers in terms of political and military might. Yet in his first term, Clinton was more wary in traditional aspects of foreign policy—great-power diplomacy, arms control, regional disputes—than in facilitating American cultural and trade expansion. Recalling the public's impatience in the Vietnam debacle, he was deeply suspicious of foreign military involvements.

Clinton's mistrust was cemented by the difficulties he inherited from Bush in Somalia. In 1992 Bush had sent U.S. Marines to the East African nation as part of a U.N. effort to ensure that humanitarian supplies reached starving Somalis. But in the summer of 1993, when Americans came under deadly attack, Clinton withdrew U.S. troops. And he did not intervene in Rwanda, where in 1994 the majority Hutus butchered 800,000 of the minority Tutsis in a brutal civil war.

Many administration officials argued for using America's power to contain ethnic hatreds, support human rights, and promote democracy around the world. Clinton moved cautiously. In 1991 a military coup in Haiti had overthrown the democratically elected president, Jean-Bertrand Aristide, and imposed a harsh system. Tens of thousands of Haitians fled in boats for U.S. territory, spawning an immigration crisis. In 1994 Clinton sent former president Jimmy Carter to negotiate an arrangement facilitating Aristide's return to power.

CRISIS IN HAITI

Humanitarian intervention faced a real test in the Balkans, which erupted in a series of ethnic wars where Bosnian Muslims, Serbs, and Croats were killing one another. Clinton lashed out against Serbian aggression and atrocities in Bosnia-Herzegovina, especially the Serbs' "ethnic cleansing" of Muslims through massacres and rape camps. He occasionally ordered air strikes, but he primarily emphasized diplomacy. In late 1995, American diplomats brokered a fragile peace.

But Yugoslav president Slobodan Milosevic continued the anti-Muslim and anti-Croat fervor. When Serb forces moved to violently rid Kosovo of its majority ethnic Albanians, Clinton was pressed to intervene. Reports of Serbian atrocities against the Muslim Kosovars and a major refugee crisis stirred world opinion and pushed him to act. In 1999 NATO forces led by the United States launched a massive aerial bombardment of Serbia. Milosevic withdrew his military from Kosovo, where U.S. troops joined a U.N. peacekeeping force.

KOSOVO WAR

In the Middle East, in September 1993 the PLO's Yasir Arafat and Israel's prime minister Yitzhak Rabin signed an agreement for Palestinian self-rule in the Gaza Strip and the West Bank's Jericho. The following year, Israel signed a peace accord with Jordan, further reducing the chances of another full-scale Arab-Israeli war. Radical anti-Arafat Palestinians, however, continued terrorist attacks on Israelis, while extremist Israelis killed Palestinians and, in November 1995, Rabin himself. With American-conducted negotiations and renewed violence in the West Bank, Israel agreed in early 1997 to withdraw troops from the Palestinian city of Hebron. Thereafter, the peace process sagged.

International efforts to protect the environment gathered pace in the 1990s. The Bush administration

ENVIRONMENTAL DIPLOMACY

opposed many provisions of the 1992 Rio de Janeiro Treaty protecting the diversity of plant and animal species and resisted stricter rules on global warming. Clinton, urged on by environmentalist Vice President Al Gore, signed the 1997 Kyoto Protocol, which aimed to combat emissions of carbon dioxide and other gases. But facing strong congressional opposition, Clinton never submitted it for ratification to the Republican-controlled Senate.

Meanwhile, the administration was privately but increasingly concerned about the threat to U.S. in-

BIN LADEN AND AL QAEDA

terests by Islamic fundamentalists. Senior officials worried about Al Qaeda (Arabic for "the base"), an international terrorist network led by Osama bin Laden that wanted to purge Muslim countries of what it saw as the profane influence of the West.

The son of a Yemen-born construction tycoon in Saudi Arabia, bin Laden supported the Afghan Mujahidin against Soviet occupation. He then founded Al Qaeda and began financing terrorist projects with his substantial inheritance. U.S. officials grew increasingly concerned, particularly as bin Laden focused on American targets. In 1995 a car bomb in Riyadh killed seven people, five of them Americans. In Yemen in 2000, a small boat laden with explosives hit the destroyer U.S.S. *Cole*, killing seventeen American sailors. Although bin Laden masterminded and financed these attacks, he eluded U.S. attempts to apprehend him. In 1998 Clinton approved a plan to assassinate bin Laden, but it failed.

Paradoxes of Prosperity

*F*or most Americans, the late 1990s marked unprecedented peace and prosperity, fueled by the dizzying rise of the stock market. Between 1991 and 1999, the Dow Jones Industrial Average climbed from 3,169 to a high of 11,497. The booming market benefited the middle class as well as the

wealthy, as mutual funds and other new investment vehicles drew a majority of Americans into the stock market. In 1952 only 4 percent of American households owned stocks; by the year 2000 almost 60 percent did.

At the end of the 1990s, the unemployment rate stood at 4.3 percent. Plentiful jobs made it easier for states to implement welfare reform and cut welfare rolls almost in half. Both the richest 5 percent and the least well-off 20 percent of American households saw their incomes rise almost 25 percent. But that meant an average gain of $50,000 for the top 5 percent and only $2,880 for the bottom 20 percent, further widening the gap between rich and poor. Nevertheless, by decade's end, more than two-thirds of Americans were homeowners. Teen pregnancy rates declined, infant mortality dropped, and murder rates hit a thirty-year low.

Still, new crises shook the nation. On April 19, 1995, 168 people were killed in a bomb blast that destroyed the Alfred P. Murrah Federal Building in

OKLAHOMA CITY BOMBING

downtown Oklahoma City. At first many blamed Middle Eastern terrorists. But a charred piece of truck axle two blocks away, with the vehicle identification number still legible, revealed that the bomber was Timothy McVeigh, a white American and Persian Gulf War veteran. He sought revenge for the deaths of the Branch Davidian religious sect, whom he believed the FBI deliberately slaughtered in a standoff over firearms charges two years earlier in Waco, Texas.

Online Study Center Improve Your Grade
Primary Source: Events in Waco

In subsequent months, reporters and investigators discovered networks of militias, tax resisters, and white-supremacist groups nationwide. United by distrust of the federal government, many saw gun control laws as a dangerous usurpation of citizens' right to bear arms. They believed the federal government was controlled by "sinister forces," including Zionists, corrupt politicians, cultural elitists, Queen Elizabeth, the Russians, and the United Nations.

On April 20, 1999, eighteen-year-old Eric Harris and seventeen-year-old Dylan Klebold opened fire

VIOLENCE AND HATE CRIMES

on classmates and teachers at Columbine High School in Littleton, Colorado, murdering thirteen before

■ On April 20, 1999, students evacuated Columbine High School in Littleton, Colorado, after two schoolmates went on a shooting rampage, killing twelve students and a teacher before killing themselves. (AP/Wide World Photos)

killing themselves. No clear reason why two academically successful students in a middle-class suburb would commit mass murder ever emerged. Students in Paducah, Kentucky; Springfield, Oregon; and Jonesboro, Arkansas, also massacred classmates. Disgruntled employees opened fire on coworkers; shootings by U.S. Postal Service employees inspired the phrase "going postal" as a synonym for violent outburst.

In the late 1990s, two hate crimes shocked the nation. In 1998 James Byrd Jr., a forty-nine-year-old black man, was murdered by white supremacists who dragged him by a chain from the back of a pickup truck in Jasper, Texas. Later that year, Matthew Shepherd, a gay college student, was beaten and tied to a fence in freezing Laramie, Wyoming. His killers said they were "humiliated" when he flirted with them at a bar. To some, these murders signified that bigotry remained strong in America. Others noted the horror Americans expressed and the growing support for federal legislation against hate crimes as a positive change.

Scandals plagued the Clinton White House. The independent counsel would eventually spend

SCANDAL IN THE CLINTON WHITE HOUSE

$72 million investigating allegations against Hillary and Bill Clinton. Independent counsel Kenneth Starr, a conservative Republican and former judge, was originally charged with investigating Whitewater, the Arkansas real-estate deal the Clintons participated in during the 1970s, but he never found any evidence against them. Starr did find evidence that the president committed perjury, however.

Early in Clinton's presidency, former Arkansas state employee Paula Jones brought charges of sexual harassment against the president, which were eventually dropped. But when asked before a grand jury whether he had engaged in sexual relations with twenty-two-year-old White House intern Monica Lewinsky, Clinton said no. Starr discovered evidence proving he had lied. In response, Clinton angrily declared: "I want to say one thing to the American people. . . . I did not have sexual relations with that woman, Miss Lewinsky." In fact, Clinton had at least ten sexual encounters, and fifteen "phone sex" conversations, with Lewinsky. Starr produced phone conversations recorded without Lewinsky's knowledge by her supposed friend Linda Tripp. Most infamously, Starr obtained DNA evidence against the president: a navy blue dress of Lewinsky's, stained with Clinton's semen.

In a 445-page report to Congress, Starr outlined eleven possible grounds for impeachment, including

IMPEACHMENT

lying under oath, obstruction of justice, witness tampering, and abuse of power. On December 19, 1998, the House voted on four articles of impeachment against Clinton; largely along party lines, the House passed two of the articles, one alleging that the president had committed perjury, the other that he had obstructed justice. Clinton became only the second president to face a trial in the Senate, which has the constitutional responsibility to decide (by two-thirds vote) whether to remove a president from office.

But the American people did not want Clinton removed from office. Polls showed large majorities approved of the president's job performance, even while condemning his personal behavior. And many did not believe his wrongdoing constituted the "high crimes and misdemeanors" (normally acts such as treason) required by the Constitution for impeachment. The Republican-controlled Senate, responding partly to popular opinion, voted against the charge of perjury 55–45 and voted 50–50 to clear Clinton of obstructing justice. The vote did not approach the two-thirds majority required for conviction. Clinton said he was "profoundly sorry."

Clinton was not the first president to engage in illicit sex. President Kennedy had numerous and well-

POLITICAL PARTISANSHIP, THE MEDIA, AND CELEBRITY CULTURE

known sexual affairs, including one with a nineteen-year-old intern. But after the Watergate scandals of the early 1970s, the mass media no longer turned a blind eye to presidential misconduct. The fiercely competitive news networks relied on scandal, spectacle, and crisis to lure viewers.

The partisan political wars of the 1990s created a take-no-prisoners climate. Both Republican Speaker of the House Newt Gingrich and his successor, Robert Livingston, resigned when evidence of their extramarital affairs surfaced. Finally, as former Clinton aide Sidney Blumenthal writes, the impeachment struggle was part of the "culture wars": "a monumental battle over . . . cultural mores and the position of women in American society, and about the character of the American people."

Clinton's legislative accomplishments during his two terms in office included the Family and Medical

CLINTON'S LEGISLATIVE RECORD

Leave Act, guaranteeing 91 million workers the right to take time off to care for ailing relatives or newborn children. The Health Insurance Portability and Accountability Act ensured that when Americans changed jobs, they would not lose health insurance because of preexisting medical conditions. The federal government operated efficiently with 365,000 fewer employees. Clinton created national parks and monuments that protected 3.2 million acres of American land and made unprecedented progress cleaning up toxic waste dumps.

Vice President Al Gore was initially favored in the 2000 presidential election. The son of a prominent

THE BUSH-GORE RACE

senator from Tennessee, Gore graduated cum laude from Harvard in 1969, enlisted in the army, and served in Vietnam despite his reservations about the war. He was elected to the House and to the Senate, serving six terms, and wrote a well-received book on global environmental issues. In the Clinton administration, Gore played a greater role than any previous vice president in history, and after eight years of prosperity and relative peace, he had a strong platform. But earnest and intelligent Gore appeared to many as a well-informed policy wonk rather than a charismatic leader.

Gore's Republican opponent was the son of George H. W. Bush, the forty-first president of the United States. An indifferent student, George W. Bush graduated from Yale in 1968 and pulled strings to jump ahead of a one-and-a-half-year waiting list for the Texas Air National Guard, thus avoiding service in Vietnam. After a rocky career in the oil business, Bush gave up alcohol and embraced Christianity at the age of forty. In 1994 he was elected to the first of two terms as governor of Texas.

As a presidential candidate, Bush made up for his limited foreign policy knowledge and often garbled syntax with a confident style that connected with many Americans. He spoke of his relationship with God and his commitment to conservative social values, styling himself a "compassionate conservative." Supported by Republicans and business leaders, Bush amassed the largest campaign war chest in history ($67 million, compared with Gore's $28 million).

Consumer rights activist Ralph Nader ran on the Green Party ticket. Condemning globalization and environmental despoliation, he attacked Bush and Gore, calling them "Tweedledee and Tweedledum." However, Nader drew support from left-liberal voters who might have voted for Gore and so helped tip some districts to Bush.

On election day 2000, Al Gore narrowly won the popular vote but not the presidency. It all came down to

THE CONTESTED ELECTION OF 2000

Florida (where Bush's brother Jeb was governor) and its twenty-five electoral votes. At first, television coverage declared Gore the winner, giving him the presidency. But by early morning, the election outcome was unclear. When the Florida votes were first tallied, Bush narrowly edged out Gore, but with a close margin that legally required an automatic recount. In several heavily African American counties, tens of thousands of votes went uncounted because voters failed to fully dislodge the "chads," or small perforated squares, when punching the paper ballots. Lawyers struggled over whether "hanging chads" (partially detached) and "pregnant chads" (punched but not detached) were sufficient signs of voter intent. In Palm Beach County, many elderly Jewish residents were confused by a poorly designed ballot and accidentally selected the allegedly anti-Semitic Reform party candidate Pat Buchanan instead of Gore. After thirty-six days, with court cases at the state and federal levels, the Supreme Court voted 5 to 4 along narrowly partisan lines to end the recount process. Florida's electoral votes—and the presidency—went to George Bush.

Online Study Center   **Improve Your Grade**
Interactive Map:
The Election of 2000

Gore won the West Coast, Northeast, and industrial Midwest. The South, Rocky Mountain West (except New Mexico), and heartland went to Bush. More than 90 percent of black voters selected Gore, as did 63 percent of Latinos and 55 percent of Asian Americans. Bush won 60 percent of the white vote, and, overall, 95 percent of his supporters were white. The gender gap was 12 points: 54 percent of women voted for Gore. With such divisions, Bush had no popular mandate and critics referred to him as the "president-select."

September 11 and the War on Terrorism

*W*ith the close election and bitter controversy, many believed Bush would govern from the center. Some also thought he, like his father, moved to the right only to secure conservative evangelical Christian voters. But Bush governed from the right, arguably more so than any modern administration.

The centerpiece of the Bush agenda was a massive tax cut, to be financed by the predicted budget surplus. Critics believed that a mas-

Bush's Tax Plan sive cut would wipe out the surplus

and that the Bush plan favored the wealthy, but Bush used his party's control of Congress to push through the largest tax cut in U.S. history—$1.3 trillion. To the dismay of environmentalists, he also reiterated his plan to drill for oil in America's last wilderness, the Arctic National Wildlife Refuge.

In international affairs, the administration charted a more unilateralist course. Given America's preponderant power, senior Bush officials reasoned, it did not need the help of other countries. Bush pulled the United States out of the 1972 Anti-Ballistic Missile Treaty with Russia to develop a National Missile Defense system similar to Reagan's "Star Wars." The White House also renounced the 1997 Kyoto protocol on global warming and opposed a carefully negotiated protocol to strengthen the 1972 Biological and Toxin Weapons Convention. These decisions, and the administration's hands-off policy toward the Israeli-Palestinian peace process, caused consternation in Europe.

Then came September 11. On that sunny Tuesday morning, nineteen hijackers seized control of four com-

9/11 mercial jets departing from East Coast airports. At 8:46 A.M. one plane crashed into the 110-story North Tower of the World Trade Center in New York City. At 9:03 A.M., a second plane flew into the South Tower. In less than two hours, both buildings collapsed, killing thousands of office workers, firefighters, and police officers. At 9:43, the third plane crashed into the Pentagon, leaving a huge hole in its west side. The fourth plane was also headed toward Washington, but several passengers—learning of the World Trade Center attacks through cell phones—stormed the cockpit; in the scuffle, the plane crashed in Somerset County, Pennsylvania, killing all aboard.

More than three thousand people died in the deadliest act of terrorism in history. The hijackers—fifteen Saudi Arabians, two Emiratis, one Lebanese, and, leading them, an Egyptian—had ties to Al Qaeda, Osama bin Laden's radical Islamic organization. Some officials in the Clinton and Bush administrations had warned that an Al Qaeda attack was inevitable, but neither administration made counterterrorism a top foreign policy priority.

In an instant, counterterrorism was priority one. President Bush responded quickly with military force.

Afghanistan War Al Qaeda operated out of Afghanistan with the blessing of the ruling Taliban, a repressive Islamic fundamentalist regime that gained power in 1996. In early October, the United States launched a sustained bombing campaign against Taliban and Al Qaeda positions and sent special operations forces to help resistance groups in northern Afghanistan. Within two months, the Taliban was driven from power, though bin Laden and top Taliban leaders eluded capture.

As administration officials acknowledged, military victory did not end terrorism. Bush spoke of a long and difficult war against evil forces, in which the nations of the world were either with the United States or against it. Some questioned whether a "war on terrorism" could ever be won in a meaningful sense, given that the foe was a nonstate actor with little to lose. Most Americans, however, were ready to believe. Stunned by September 11, they experienced a renewed sense of national pride. Flag sales soared, and Bush's approval ratings skyrocketed.

But the new patriotism had a dark side. Congress passed the USA PATRIOT Act (Uniting and Strength-

PATRIOT ACT

ening America by Providing Appropriate Tools Required to Intercept and Obstruct Terrorism), making it easier for law enforcement to conduct searches, wiretap telephones, and obtain electronic records on individuals. Attorney General John Ashcroft approved giving FBI agents new powers to monitor the Internet, mosques, and rallies. Civil libertarians charged that the Justice Department overstepped, and some judges ruled against the tactics. Yet according to a June 2002 Gallup poll, 80 percent of Americans were willing to give up some freedoms for security.

In surveys after the attacks, 71 percent said they felt depressed, and a third had trouble sleeping. The discovery of anthrax-laden letters in several East Coast cities heightened fears, particularly after post offices and government buildings were closed and five people died. Investigators found no evidence connecting the letters to the 9/11 hijackings, but also no good clues as to who the perpetrator might be.

Yet continuity was as evident as change. People continued shopping in malls and visiting amusement parks. Although airline bookings dropped significantly in the early weeks (causing severe problems for many airlines), people still took to the skies. In Washington, the partisanship that had disappeared after 9/11 returned, as Democrats and Republicans sparred over judicial appointments, energy policy, and the pro-

posed new Department of Homeland Security. Approved by Congress in November 2002, the department incorporated parts of eight cabinet departments and twenty-two agencies to coordinate intelligence and defense against terrorism.

Economically, the months before September 11 witnessed a collapse of the so-called dot-coms, the Internet companies that were the darlings of Wall Street in the 1990s. In 2001 some five hundred dot-coms declared bankruptcy or closed. There were other economic warning signs as well, notably a meager 0.2 percent growth rate in goods and services for the second quarter of 2001—the slowest growth in eight years. Corporate revenues were also down.

Economic concerns deepened after 9/11 with a four-day closing of Wall Street and a subsequent sharp

ENRON COLLAPSE

drop in stock prices. The Dow Jones Industrial Average plunged 14.26 percent. The markets eventually rebounded, but then a corporate scandal made headlines. Enron Corporation, a Houston-based energy company that was one of the largest commodity trading firms in the world, filed for bankruptcy. Enron's twenty thousand employees lost billions in pension plans while many executives—who had advised the White House on energy policies—allegedly raked in profits, selling their shares before the steep fall in prices.

The Enron collapse marked the biggest corporate failure in U.S. history, and it generated a Justice Department criminal investigation. Despite Bush's close relationship with Enron going back to his days as Texas governor, the president seemed largely unscathed, underscoring how 9/11 and his early responses to it strengthened his political position. Notwithstanding growing economic weakness, the general absence of a domestic agenda, and the failure to capture Osama bin Laden and top Taliban leaders, Bush's approval ratings remained high.

Bush's clout became clear in the midterm congressional elections. The GOP retook control of the

GOP MIDTERM GAINS

Senate and added to its majority in the House. The Republicans' core message—that a country at war should unite behind the president—resonated with voters. Now the Republicans not only controlled Congress, the White House, and a majority of governorships but also had appointed a majority of Supreme Court justices.

Immediately after September 11, there was an outpouring of support from people everywhere. "We are all Americans now," the French

INTERNATIONAL
RESPONSES

newspaper *Le Monde* wrote the day after the attacks. Governments across the globe announced they would cooperate with Washington in the struggle against terrorism. But by a year later, attitudes had changed dramatically. Bush's good-versus-evil stance had put off many foreign observers from the start, but they initially swallowed their objections. When the president hinted that America might unilaterally strike Saddam Hussein's Iraq or deal forcefully with North Korea or Iran—the three countries of Bush's "axis of evil"—many allied governments strongly objected.

Bush and other top officials argued that in an age of terrorism, the United States would not wait for a potential security threat to become real; henceforth, it would strike first. "In the world we have entered, the only path to safety is the path of action and this nation will act," Bush declared. Critics, among them many world leaders, called it recklessly aggressive and contrary to international law, and they wondered what would happen if dictators around the world began claiming the same right of preemption.

But Bush was determined, particularly on Iraq. Several of his top advisers, including Secretary of

REGIME CHANGE
IN IRAQ

Defense Donald Rumsfeld and Vice President Dick Cheney, had wanted to oust Saddam Hussein since the end of the Gulf War in 1991; they now folded that objective into the larger war on terrorism. Cynics wondered whether the focus on Hussein was intended to deflect attention from the poor economy and failure to capture bin Laden. In September 2002, Bush challenged the United Nations to immediately enforce its resolutions against Iraq or the United States would act on its own. In subsequent weeks, he and his aides offered shifting reasons for getting tough with Iraq. They said Hussein was a major threat to the United States and its allies, a leader who possessed and would use banned biological and chemical "weapons of mass destruction" and who sought to acquire nuclear weapons. They claimed he had ties to Al Qaeda and could be linked to the 9/11 attacks. They said he brutalized his own people.

Although Bush claimed he did not need congressional authorization for military action against Iraq, he nevertheless sought it. In early October, the House of Representatives voted 296-133 and the Senate 77–23 to authorize the use of force against Iraq. The vote was misleading: many who voted yes were unwilling to defy a president so close to a midterm election, even though they opposed military action without U.N. sanction. Critics complained that the president had not presented evidence that Saddam Hussein constituted an imminent threat or was connected to the 9/11 attacks. Bush switched to a less hawkish stance, and in early November, the U.N. Security Council unanimously approved Resolution 1441, imposing rigorous new arms inspections on Iraq.

But the Security Council was deeply divided over the next move. In late January 2003, the weapons inspector's report castigated Iraq for failing to carry out "the disarmament that was demanded of it" but also said it was too soon to tell whether the inspections would succeed. While U.S. and British officials said the time for diplomacy was up, France, Russia, and China called for more inspections. As the U.N. debate continued and as massive antiwar demonstrations took place worldwide, Bush sent about 250,000 soldiers to the region. Britain sent about 45,000 troops.

In late February the United States floated a draft resolution to the U.N. that proposed issuing an ulti-

FALL OF
BAGHDAD

matum to Iraq, but only three of the fifteen Security Council members affirmed support. Defeated, Bush abandoned the resolution and diplomatic efforts on March 17 when he ordered Saddam Hussein to leave Iraq within forty-eight hours or face an attack. Saddam ignored the ultimatum, and on March 19 the United States and Britain launched an aerial bombardment of Baghdad and other areas. A ground invasion followed days later (see Map 33.1). The Iraqis initially offered stiff resistance, but on April 9, Baghdad fell.

The military victory was swift and decisive, but stability was slow to return to Iraq, raising concerns that Washington might win the war and lose the peace. U.S. occupying forces faced frequent ambushes and hit-and-run attacks by disaffected Iraqis, indicating that a "guerrilla war" had begun. In December 2003 elite U.S. forces captured Saddam Hussein, raising hopes that the insurgency could be brought under

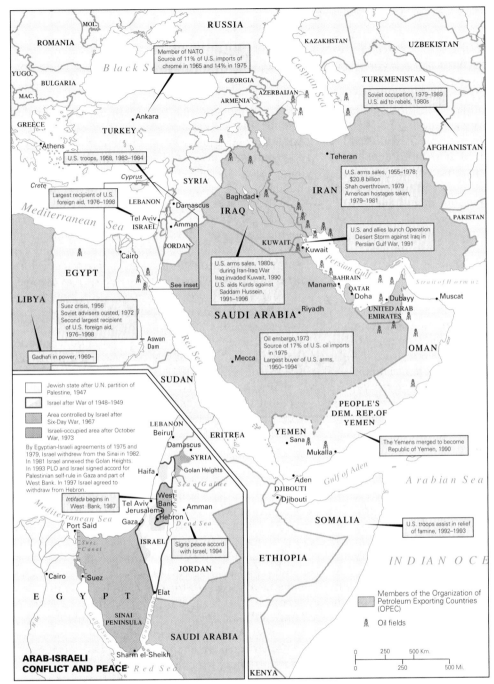

Map 33.1   The Middle East

Extremely volatile and often at war, the nations of the Middle East maintained precarious relations with the United States. To protect its interests, the United States extended large amounts of economic and military aid and sold huge quantities of weapons to the area. At times, Washington ordered U.S. troops to the region. The Arab-Israeli dispute particularly upended order, although the peace process moved forward intermittently.

control. But concerns existed about the potential costs of the postwar occupation, particularly given the uncertain economic climate at home.

Federal, state, and local governments nationwide faced severe budget shortfalls. Education and Medicaid took the brunt of the cuts, but many states also raised taxes. The governor of Missouri ordered every third light bulb unscrewed to save money. In Oklahoma, teachers doubled as janitors.

STATE ECONOMIC WOES

Americans in the New Millennium

*E*arly in the twenty-first century, the United States is a nation of extraordinary diversity. Immigration reform in the mid-1960s opened American borders to large numbers of people from a wider variety of nations than previously. New technologies—the Internet, and cable and satellite television with their proliferation of channels—replaced mass markets with niche markets. Everything from television shows to cosmetics to cars could be targeted at specific groups defined by age, ethnicity, class, gender, or lifestyle choices. These changes helped to make Americans' understandings of identity simultaneously more fluid and more complex.

For the first time in the 2000 U.S. government census, Americans could identify themselves as belonging to more than one race. The change acknowledged the growing number of Americans born to parents of different racial backgrounds. Critics, however, worried that because census data are used to gather information about social conditions in the United States and to allocate resources, the new "multiracial" option would reduce the clout of minority groups. Thus, the federal government counted those who identified both as white and members of a racial or ethnic minority as belonging to the minority group. Consequently, the official population of some groups increased. Others rejected racial and ethnic categories altogether: 20 million people identified themselves simply as "American," up more than 50 percent since 1990.

RACE AND ETHNICITY IN RECENT AMERICA

During the 1990s, the population of people of color grew twelve times as fast as the white population, fueled by immigration and birth rates. The Latino population alone more than doubled. By 2003, Latinos moved past African Americans to become the second largest ethnic or racial group (after non-Hispanic whites). Immigration from Asia also remained high, with people of Asian ancestry comprising 3.6 percent of the U.S. population in 2000.

These rapid demographic changes have altered the face of America. At a Dairy Queen in the far southern suburbs of Atlanta, 6 miles from the "Gone with the Wind Historical District," teenage children of immigrants from India and Pakistan serve Blizzards and Mister Mistys. In the small town of Ligonier, Indiana, the formerly empty main street now boasts three Mexican restaurants and a Mexican western-wear shop. Still, more than half of American counties were still at least 85 percent white in 2000, and more than half of all Latinos lived in just eight metropolitan areas (see Map 33.2).

American popular culture embraced the influences of this new multiethnic population. After all, Latino buying power exceeded $561 billion in 2000, and average income for Asian Americans topped all other groups. But audiences crossed racial and ethnic lines: Jennifer Lopez (of Puerto Rican descent) was the nation's most "bankable" musician/actress; black basketball great Michael Jordan had more commercial endorsements than any other celebrity in history. Suburban white teens took up urban rap and hip-hop culture. Golfer Tiger Woods became a symbol of this new, hybrid, multiethnic nation: of African, European, Native American, Thai, and Chinese descent, he calls himself "Cablinasian" (CAucasian-BLack-INdian-ASIAN).

A MORE DIVERSE CULTURE

Americans were divided over the meaning of changing family structure (see Figure 33.1). The number of people living together without marriage jumped 72 percent during the 1990s, to 5.5 million. Of those, at least 600,000 were same-sex couples—perhaps 1 percent of households nationwide. A third of female-partner households and one-fifth of male-partner households had children, and in 2002 the

THE CHANGING AMERICAN FAMILY

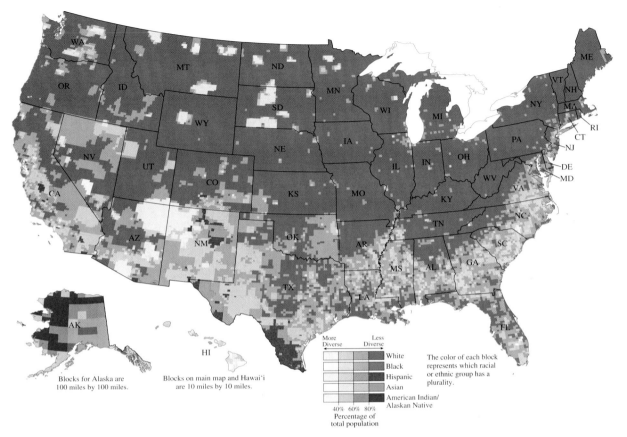

Map 33.2   Mapping America's Diversity

Aggregate figures (more than 12 percent of the U.S. population is African American and about 4 percent is Asian American, for example) convey America's ethnic and racial diversity. However, as this map shows, members of racial and ethnic groups are not distributed evenly throughout the nation.   (Source: Adapted from the *New York Times* National Edition, April 1, 2001, "Portrait of a Nation," p. 18. Copyright © 2001 by The New York Times Co. Reprinted with permission.)

American Academy of Pediatrics endorsed adoption by gay couples. A vocal antigay movement coexisted with support for the legal equality of gay, lesbian, transgendered, and bisexual Americans. While many states and private corporations extended domestic-partner benefits to gay couples, the federal Defense of Marriage Act, passed by Congress in 1996, defined marriage as "only" a union between one man and one woman.

Almost a third of all children and over two-thirds of African American babies were born outside marriage. In the majority of married-couple families with children under age eighteen, both parents held jobs. Statistically, a couple that married in the late 1990s had about a 50–50 chance of divorce. While almost a third of families with children had only one parent present—usually the mother—children also lived in blended families created by second marriages, or

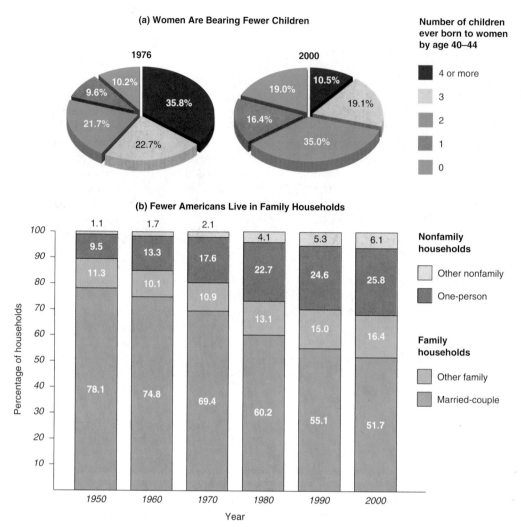

Figure 33.1   The Changing American Family

American households became smaller in the latter part of the twentieth century, as more people lived alone and women had, on average, fewer children.   (Source: Adapted from U.S. Bureau of the Census: http://www.census.gov/prod/2002pubs/censr-4.pdf and http://www.census.gov/population/pop-profile/2000/chap04.pdf)

moved back and forth between households of parents with joint custody.

Increasingly, new reproductive technologies allowed infertile women or couples to have children. In 2000 more than 100,000 attempted in vitro fertilizations—in which sperm and egg combine in a sterile dish or test tube and the fertilized egg or eggs are then transferred to the uterus—resulted in the birth of about 35,000 babies. Such techniques raised legal and ethical questions about the rights and responsibilities of sperm and egg donors, the woman who carries the fetus, and male and female prospective parents.

This field of biogenetics offers even knottier philosophical and ethical conundrums. The five- or six-cell blastocytes formed by the initial division of fertilized eggs during in vitro procedures contain stem cells,

NEW TECHNOLOGIES AND NEW CHALLENGES

unspecialized cells that can be induced to become cells with specialized functions. For example, stem cells might become insulin-producing cells of the pancreas—and thus a cure for diabetes. President Bush in 2001 acknowledged the "tremendous hope" of this research but called it "the leading edge of a series of moral hazards," including the possibility of cloning humans for spare body parts. In a highly controversial decision, Bush limited federally funded research to the existing seventy-eight stem cell lines, not all of which are viable.

The twentieth century had seen momentous changes, some bringing enormous benefits to human beings, others threatening the existence of the human species. Research in the physical and biological sciences provided deep insight into the structure of matter and the universe. Technology—the application of science—made startling advances that benefited people in nearly every aspect of life: better health, more wealth, more mobility, less drudgery, greater access to information.

CENTURY OF CHANGE

As a result, Americans at the start of the new century were more connected to the rest of humankind. And the world had shrunk to the size of an airplane ticket. In 1955, 51 million people a year traveled by plane. By the turn of the century, 1.6 billion were airborne every year, and 530 million crossed international borders—about 1.5 million each day. For millions of Americans, this permeability of national boundaries brought many benefits, as did the integration of markets and the global spread of information that occurred alongside it.

On the flip side, the rapid increase in international air travel was a particularly potent force for global disease dissemination, as flying enabled people to reach the other side of the world in less time than the incubation period for many ailments.

INFECTIOUS DISEASES

In early 2003, a respiratory illness known as severe acute respiratory syndrome (SARS) spread from Guangdong Province of China to Hong Kong to various other countries in the world, chiefly via air passengers who unwittingly carried the disease in their lungs. Public health officials also warned that increased human mobility promised more trade in illegal products and contaminated foodstuffs.

Environmental degradation also powerfully contributed to global health threats. In 2003 the World Health Organization (WHO) estimated that nearly a quarter of the global burden of disease and injury was related to environmental disruption and decline. For example, some 90 percent of diarrheal diseases (such as cholera), which were killing 3 million people a year, resulted from contaminated water. WHO also noted that in the final two decades of the twentieth century, more than thirty infectious diseases were identified in humans for the first time—including AIDS, Ebola virus, and hepatitis C and E. Environmentalists meanwhile insisted that the growing global interaction was having a deleterious impact on the ecosystem through climate change, ozone depletion, hazardous waste, and damage to fisheries.

But globalization was also essential in mobilizing the world to find solutions to health crises. Where it took centuries to identify the cause of cholera and two years to identify the virus that caused AIDS, in the case of SARS, thirteen labs in ten countries in a matter of weeks determined that the Coronavirus was responsible. Within a month, laboratories from Vancouver to Atlanta to Singapore had mapped the genome, and efforts to devise a diagnostic test for the virus began. Speed of communication allowed a coordinated international effort at finding the cause of SARS and also enabled individual countries, including the United States, to adopt measures that succeeded early on in keeping the epidemic out.

INTERNATIONAL RESPONSE TO DISEASE

Even in the interconnected world of the new millennium, then, national borders still mattered. In the wake of 9/11, the United States and other countries imposed tighter security measures on air travelers, imported goods, immigration, and information flows. Some economists predicted these measures would stall the global integration of markets; in the short term, they did, but the long-term outlook was less clear. Trade and investment shrank before September 11 due to economic slowdowns in the world's biggest economies, including the United States, Europe, and Japan. Moreover, the falloff in international economic activity in the months after the attacks was not massive.

In military and diplomatic terms, the 9/11 attacks brought home what Americans had previously only dimly perceived: that globalization had shrunk the natural buffers that distance and two oceans provided the United States. Al Qaeda used the

CONFRONTING TERRORISM

The Global AIDS Epidemic

AIDS, initially reported in the United States in 1981, has become a global epidemic. Researchers now believe that the first infection with HIV, the human immunodeficiency virus that causes AIDS, may have appeared in West Africa around 1930. HIV/AIDS spread rapidly in the late 1970s, partly as a byproduct of globalization. Increased international travel allowed for sexual transmission of HIV between populations; the international heroin trade stimulated intravenous drug use, another means of transmission; and the international circulation of blood for medical transfusions also contributed to the virus's spread. In 2003 the World Health Organization estimated that 58 million people worldwide were living with HIV/AIDS and that 23 million had died from the disease.

Globally, AIDS claims 350 lives per hour, and while altered behavior and new drug therapies have slowed the disease in North America and western Europe, infection and death rates continue to escalate in sub-Saharan Africa, eastern Europe and the former Soviet Union, and Latin America, especially the Caribbean. In the African nation of Malawi, one in six adults is HIV-positive, and the nation expects to lose almost a quarter of its work force to AIDS in the next decade. Half of current teenagers in the hardest-hit African nations will eventually die of AIDS.

The human suffering is staggering, but U.S. worries about the global spread of AIDS are not solely humanitarian. In 2000 the U.S. National Intelligence Council concluded that "these diseases will endanger U.S. citizens at home and abroad, threaten U.S. armed forces deployed overseas, and exacerbate social and political instability in key countries and regions in which the United States has significant interests." In nations already facing shortages of food and clean water and rife with conflict, AIDS has further undermined the ability to cope with crisis; political instability and social disorder result.

In 2002 U.N. Secretary General Kofi Annan estimated that between $7 billion and $10 billion are needed annually to combat the spread of AIDS—and of tuberculosis and malaria, which have reemerged as threats to world health. President Bush called for increases in U.S. spending to combat AIDS internationally, but many believe the United States should do more. With globalization, diseases do not stop at borders or respect wealth and power. The links between Americans and the rest of the world cannot be denied.

Activists protest outside Parliament in Cape Town, South Africa, calling on South Africa president Thabo Mbeki to make the struggle against AIDS a national priority. An estimated 20 percent of South Africans between the ages of fifteen and forty-nine are HIV-positive. (AP/Wide World Photos)

increasingly open, integrated, globalized world to give themselves new power and reach. They had shown that small terrorist cells could become true transnational threats without a state sponsor or home base. According to American intelligence, Al Qaeda operated in over ninety countries, including the United States.

How would one go about vanquishing such a foe? Was a decisive victory even possible? Questions like this remained open four years after the World Trade Center collapsed. Unchallenged militarily and seeing no rival great power, the United States no longer felt constrained from intervening in sensitive areas

TABLE 33.1			
U.S. Military Personnel on Active Duty in Foreign Countries, 2001[1]			
Region/Country[2]	**Personnel**	**Region/Country**	**Personnel**
United States and Territories		Singapore	160
Continental U.S.	947,955	Thailand	114
Alaska	15,926	**North Africa, Near East, and South Asia**	
Hawai'i	33,191	Bahrain	1,280
Guam	3,398	Diego Garcia	537
Puerto Rico	2,525	Egypt	665
Europe		Israel	38
Belgium*	1,554	Kuwait	4,300
Bosnia and Herzegovina	3,109	Oman	560
France*	70	Qatar	72
Germany*	71,434	Saudi Arabia	4,802
Greece*	526	United Arab Emirates	207
Greenland*	153	**Sub-Saharan Africa**	
Iceland*	1,713	Kenya	50
Italy*	11,854	South Africa	30
Macedonia	346	**Western Hemisphere**	
Netherlands*	696	Brazil	40
Norway*	187	Canada	165
Portugal*	992	Chile	30
Russia	88	Colombia	59
Serbia (includes Kosovo)	5,200	Cuba (Guantánamo)	461
Spain*	1,778	Honduras	426
Turkey*	2,170	Peru	40
United Kingdom*	11,361	Venezuela	30
East Asia and Pacific		**Total foreign countries[2]**	**255,065**
Australia	188	**Ashore**	**212,262**
China (includes Hong Kong)	54	**Afloat**	**42,803**
Indonesia (includes Timor)	48	**Total worldwide[2]**	**1,384,812**
Japan	39,691	**Ashore**	**1,242,524**
Korea, Rep. of	37,972	**Afloat**	**142,288**
Philippines	31		

*NATO countries
[1] Only countries with 30 or more U.S. military personnel are listed.
[2] Includes all regions/countries, not simply those listed.
Source: U.S. Department of Defense, *Selected Manpower Statistics,* Annual.

like the Middle East should national security interests demand it. It continued to spend vast sums on its military. (In 2003 the Pentagon spent about $400 billion, or roughly $50 million per hour.) America had taken on military commitments all over the globe, from the Balkans and Iraq to Afghanistan and Korea (see Table 33.1).

Summary *Online Study Center* ACE the Test

*T*he 1990s were good times for most Americans. A digitized revolution in communications and information was generating prosperity and transforming life in America and around the globe. The longest economic expansion in American history—from 1991 to 2001—meant that most Americans who wanted jobs had them, that the stock market boomed, that the nation had a budget surplus, and that more Americans than ever before owned homes. And with the Soviet Union gone and no other formidable rival, the United States stood as the world's lone superpower.

Yet unsettling events troubled the nation. The Cold War continued to complicate the new world order. Localized and ethnic conflicts in the Balkans, the Middle East, and Africa crowded the international agenda, as did human rights and the environment. At home, violence—the domestic terrorist attack in Oklahoma City in 1995, a rash of school shootings—captured headlines, even as the crime rate dropped. And scandal further undermined Americans' faith in their government, as President Bill Clinton was impeached by the House of Representatives.

Just minutes before midnight on December 31, 1999, President Clinton called on Americans not to fear the future but to "welcome it, create it, and embrace it." The challenges ahead would include a contested presidential election in 2000 that was decided by the Supreme Court in a partisan 5–4 vote and, in 2001, the end of the ten-year economic expansion.

Then, on September 11, 2001, radical Islamic terrorists attacked the World Trade Center and the Pentagon, killing thousands. The new president, George W. Bush, declared a "war on terrorism." While U.S. air and ground forces went after targets in Afghanistan, Congress created the Department of Homeland Security and passed the PATRIOT Act, expanding the federal government's powers of surveillance. To counter a troubled economy, Bush pressed for tax cuts in each of his first three years in office. Congress went along, but the economic impact was uncertain, and the lost revenues added to a ballooning budget deficit.

The world Americans found in the first years of the twenty-first century was much different from the one they'd imagined for the new millennium. The horror of the terror attacks of September 11 shook America to its core. Throughout the nation, people declared that life would never be the same. As Americans coped with the aftermath of 9/11, crafting new foreign and domestic policies, the resilience of the American people was clear, for Americans continued to struggle over the direction of their nation with the passion and commitment that keeps democracy alive.

LEGACY FOR A PEOPLE AND A NATION
The Internet

"Google it." The phrase, essentially unknown before the new century, had within its first years become a household expression. Google was the hugely popular Internet search engine that had gone from obscurity in the mid-1990s to responding, more or less instantly, to 200 million queries per day from around the world—almost 40 percent of all Internet searches. Google's phenomenal rise demonstrates how much the Internet had become an expected part of Americans' daily lives by the twenty-first century.

Yet the widespread use of the Internet was a recent phenomenon, although its history went back four decades. In the mid-1960s, the U.S. military's Advanced Research Projects Agency (ARPA) wanted a communications network for government and university researchers spread across the nation. In 1969 early portions of the experimental system, called ARPANET, went online at UCLA, the University of California at Santa Barbara, Stanford Research Institute, and the University of Utah. By 1971, twenty-three computers were connected, and the numbers reached close to a thousand by 1984. Renamed the Internet in the late 1980s, this system transmitted only words, but in 1990 computer scientists developed the World Wide Web to send graphic and multimedia information. Then in 1993 the first commercial "browser" to aid Web navigation hit the market. It was followed in 1994 and 1995 by two superior browsers: Netscape and Internet Explorer.

By 2003, there were nearly half a billion Internet users worldwide, including 140 million Americans. Thanks to technological advances and the new forms of "broadband" access that provided high-speed connections, these users could send and receive e-mail, join online discussion groups, book vacations, download movies and music, shop, even do their banking—all through a small computer in their home. For Americans in the new globally connected millennium, the Internet was a fitting legacy of the twentieth century.

APPENDIX

Documents

DECLARATION OF INDEPENDENCE
IN CONGRESS, JULY 4, 1776

When, in the course of human events, it becomes necessary for one people to dissolve the political bonds which have connected them with another, and to assume, among the powers of the earth, the separate and equal station to which the laws of nature and of nature's God entitle them, a decent respect to the opinions of mankind requires that they should declare the causes which impel them to the separation.

We hold these truths to be self-evident: That all men are created equal; that they are endowed by their Creator with certain unalienable rights; that among these are life, liberty, and the pursuit of happiness; that, to secure these rights, governments are instituted among men, deriving their just powers from the consent of the governed; that whenever any form of government becomes destructive of these ends, it is the right of the people to alter or to abolish it, and to institute new government, laying its foundation on such principles, and organizing its powers in such form, as to them shall seem most likely to effect their safety and happiness. Prudence, indeed, will dictate that governments long established should not be changed for light and transient causes; and accordingly all experience hath shown that mankind are more disposed to suffer, while evils are sufferable, than to right themselves by abolishing the forms to which they are accustomed. But when a long train of abuses and usurpations, pursuing invariably the same object, evinces a design to reduce them under absolute despotism, it is their right, it is their duty, to throw off such government, and to provide new guards for their future security. Such has been the patient sufferance of these colonies; and such is now the necessity which constrains them to alter their former systems of government. The history of the present King of Great Britain is a history of repeated injuries and usurpations, all having in direct object the establishment of an absolute tyranny over these states. To prove this, let facts be submitted to a candid world.

He has refused his assent to laws, the most wholesome and necessary for the public good.

He has forbidden his governors to pass laws of immediate and pressing importance, unless suspended in their operation till his assent should be obtained; and, when so suspended, he has utterly neglected to attend to them.

He has refused to pass other laws for the accommodation of large districts of people, unless those people would relinquish the right of representation in the legislature, a right inestimable to them, and formidable to tyrants only.

He has called together legislative bodies at places unusual, uncomfortable, and distant from the depository of their public records, for the sole purpose of fatiguing them into compliance with his measures.

He has dissolved representative houses repeatedly, for opposing, with manly firmness, his invasions on the rights of the people.

He has refused for a long time, after such dissolutions, to cause others to be elected; whereby the legislative powers, incapable of annihilation, have returned to the people at large for their exercise; the state remaining, in the mean time, exposed to all the dangers of invasions from without and convulsions within.

He has endeavored to prevent the population of these states; for that purpose obstructing the laws for naturalization of foreigners; refusing to pass others to encourage their migration hither, and raising the conditions of new appropriations of lands.

He has obstructed the administration of justice, by refusing his assent to laws for establishing judiciary powers.

He has made judges dependent on his will alone, for the tenure of their offices, and the amount and payment of their salaries.

He has erected a multitude of new offices, and sent hither swarms of officers to harass our people and eat out their substance.

He has kept among us, in times of peace, standing armies, without the consent of our legislatures.

He has affected to render the military independent of, and superior to, the civil power.

He has combined with others to subject us to a jurisdiction foreign to our constitution, and unacknowledged by our laws, giving his assent to their acts of pretended legislation:

For quartering large bodies of armed troops among us;

For protecting them, by a mock trial, from punishment for any murders which they should commit on the inhabitants of these states;

For cutting off our trade with all parts of the world;

For imposing taxes on us without our consent;

For depriving us, in many cases, of the benefits of trial by jury;

For transporting us beyond seas, to be tried for pretended offenses;

For abolishing the free system of English laws in a neighboring province, establishing therein an arbitrary government, and enlarging its boundaries, so as to render it at once an example and fit instrument for introducing the same absolute rule into these colonies;

For taking away our charters, abolishing our most valuable laws, and altering fundamentally the forms of our governments;

For suspending our own legislatures, and declaring themselves invested with power to legislate for us in all cases whatsoever.

He has abdicated government here, by declaring us out of his protection and waging war against us.

He has plundered our seas, ravaged our coasts, burned our towns, and destroyed the lives of our people.

He is at this time transporting large armies of foreign mercenaries to complete the works of death, desolation, and tyranny already begun with circumstances of cruelty and perfidy scarcely paralleled in the most barbarous ages, and totally unworthy the head of a civilized nation.

He has constrained our fellow-citizens, taken captive on the high seas, to bear arms against their country, to become the executioners of their friends and brethren, or to fall themselves by their hands.

He has excited domestic insurrection among us, and has endeavored to bring on the inhabitants of our frontiers the merciless Indian savages, whose known rule of warfare is an undistinguished destruction of all ages, sexes, and conditions.

In every stage of these oppressions we have petitioned for redress in the most humble terms; our repeated petitions have been answered only by repeated injury. A prince, whose character is thus marked by every act which may define a tyrant, is unfit to be the ruler of a free people.

Nor have we been wanting in our attentions to our British brethren. We have warned them, from time to time, of attempts by their legislature to extend an unwarrantable jurisdiction over us. We have reminded them of the circumstances of our emigration and settlement here. We have appealed to their native justice and magnanimity; and we have conjured them, by the ties of our common kindred, to disavow these usurpations, which would inevitably interrupt our connections and correspondence. They, too, have been deaf to the voice of justice and of consanguinity. We must, therefore, acquiesce in the necessity which denounces our separation, and hold them, as we hold the rest of mankind, enemies in war, in peace friends.

We, therefore, the representatives of the United States of America, in General Congress assembled, appealing to the Supreme Judge of the world for the rectitude of our intentions, do, in the name and by the authority of the good people of these colonies, solemnly publish and declare, that these United Colonies are, and of right ought to be, FREE AND INDEPENDENT STATES; that they are absolved from all allegiance to the British crown, and that all political connection between them and the state of Great Britain is, and ought to be, totally dissolved; and that, as free and independent states, they have full power to levy war, conclude peace, contract alliances, establish commerce, and do all other acts and things which independent states may of right do. And for the support of this declaration, with a firm reliance on the protection of Divine Providence, we mutually pledge to each other our lives, our fortunes, and our sacred honor.

ARTICLES OF CONFEDERATION

(The text of the Articles of Confederation can be found at college.hmco.com.)

CONSTITUTION OF THE UNITED STATES OF AMERICA AND AMENDMENTS*

Preamble

We the people of the United States, in order to form a more perfect union, establish justice, insure domestic tranquillity, provide for the common defense, promote the general welfare, and secure the blessings of liberty to ourselves and our posterity, do ordain and establish this Constitution for the United States of America.

Article I

Section 1 All legislative powers herein granted shall be vested in a Congress of the United States, which shall consist of a Senate and a House of Representatives.

Section 2 The House of Representatives shall be composed of members chosen every second year by the people of the several States, and the electors in each State shall have the qualifications requisite for electors of the most numerous branch of the State Legislature.

---

*Passages no longer in effect are printed in italic type.

No person shall be a Representative who shall not have attained to the age of twenty-five years, and been seven years a citizen of the United States, and who shall not, when elected, be an inhabitant of that State in which he shall be chosen.

Representatives and direct taxes shall be apportioned among the several States which may be included within this Union, according to their respective numbers, *which shall be determined by adding to the whole number of free persons, including those bound to service for a term of years and excluding Indians not taxed, three-fifths of all other persons.* The actual enumeration shall be made within three years after the first meeting of the Congress of the United States, and within every subsequent term of ten years, in such manner as they shall by law direct. The number of Representatives shall not exceed one for every thirty thousand, but each State shall have at least one Representative; *and until such enumeration shall be made, the State of New Hampshire shall be entitled to choose three, Massachusetts eight, Rhode Island and Providence Plantations one, Connecticut five, New York six, New Jersey four, Pennsylvania eight, Delaware one, Maryland six, Virginia ten, North Carolina five, South Carolina five, and Georgia three.*

When vacancies happen in the representation from any State, the Executive authority thereof shall issue writs of election to fill such vacancies.

The House of Representatives shall choose their Speaker and other officers; and shall have the sole power of impeachment.

Section 3 The Senate of the United States shall be composed of two Senators from each State, *chosen by the legislature thereof,* for six years; and each Senator shall have one vote.

Immediately after they shall be assembled in consequence of the first election, they shall be divided as equally as may be into three classes. The seats of the Senators of the first class shall be vacated at the expiration of the second year, of the second class at the expiration of the fourth year, and of the third class at the expiration of the sixth year, so that one-third may be chosen every second year; and if vacancies happen by resignation or otherwise, during the recess of the legislature of any State, the Executive thereof may make temporary appointments until the next meeting of the legislature, which shall then fill such vacancies.

No person shall be a Senator who shall not have attained to the age of thirty years, and been nine years a citizen of the United States, and who shall not, when elected, be an inhabitant of that State for which he shall be chosen.

The Vice-President of the United States shall be President of the Senate, but shall have no vote, unless they be equally divided.

The Senate shall choose their other officers, and also a President *pro tempore,* in the absence of the Vice-President, or when he shall exercise the office of President of the United States.

The Senate shall have the sole power to try all impeachments. When sitting for that purpose, they shall be on oath or affirmation. When the President of the United States is tried, the Chief Justice shall preside: and no person shall be convicted without the concurrence of two-thirds of the members present.

Judgment in cases of impeachment shall not extend further than to removal from the office, and disqualification to hold and enjoy any office of honor, trust or profit under the United States: but the party convicted shall nevertheless be liable and subject to indictment, trial, judgment and punishment, according to law.

Section 4 The times, places and manner of holding elections for Senators and Representatives shall be prescribed in each State by the legislature thereof; but the Congress may at any time by law make or alter such regulations, except as to the places of choosing Senators.

The Congress shall assemble at least once in every year, and such meeting *shall be on the first Monday in December, unless they shall by law appoint a different day.*

Section 5 Each house shall be the judge of the elections, returns and qualifications of its own members, and a majority of each shall constitute a quorum to do business; but a smaller number may adjourn from day to day, and may be authorized to compel the attendance of absent members, in such manner, and under such penalties, as each house may provide.

Each house may determine the rules of its proceedings, punish its members for disorderly behavior, and with the concurrence of two-thirds, expel a member.

Each house shall keep a journal of its proceedings, and from time to time publish the same, excepting such parts as may in their judgment require secrecy; and the yeas and nays of the members of either house on any question shall, at the desire of one-fifth of those present, be entered on the journal.

Neither house, during the session of Congress, shall, without the consent of the other, adjourn for more than three days, nor to any other place than that in which the two houses shall be sitting.

Section 6 The Senators and Representatives shall receive a compensation for their services, to be ascertained by law and paid out of the treasury of the United States. They shall in all cases except treason, felony and breach of the peace, be privileged from arrest during their attendance at the session of their respective houses, and in going to and returning from the same; and for any speech or debate in either house, they shall not be questioned in any other place.

No Senator or Representative shall, during the time for which he was elected, be appointed to any civil office under the authority of the United States, which shall have been created, or the emoluments whereof shall have been increased, during such time; and no person holding any office under the United States shall be a member of either house during his continuance in office.

Section 7 All bills for raising revenue shall originate in the House of Representatives; but the Senate may propose or concur with amendments as on other bills.

Every bill which shall have passed the House of Representatives and the Senate, shall, before it become a law, be presented to the President of the United States; if he approve he shall sign it, but if not he shall return it with objections to that house in which it originated, who shall enter the objections at large on their journal, and proceed to reconsider it. If after such reconsideration two-thirds of that house shall agree to pass the bill, it shall be sent, together with the objections, to the other house, by which it shall likewise be reconsidered, and, if approved by two-thirds of that house, it shall become a law. But in all such cases the votes of both houses shall be determined by yeas and nays, and the names of the persons voting for and against the bill shall be entered on the journal of each house respectively. If any bill shall not be returned by the President within ten days (Sundays excepted) after it shall have been presented to him, the same shall be a law, in like manner as if he had signed it, unless the Congress by their adjournment prevent its return, in which case it shall not be a law.

Every order, resolution, or vote to which the concurrence of the Senate and House of Representatives may be necessary (except on a question of adjournment) shall be presented to the President of the United States; and before the same shall take effect, shall be approved by him, or being disapproved by him, shall be repassed by two-thirds of the Senate and House of Representatives, according to the rules and limitations prescribed in the case of a bill.

Section 8 The Congress shall have power

To lay and collect taxes, duties, imposts, and excises, to pay the debts and provide for the common defense and general welfare of the United States; but all duties, imposts and excises shall be uniform throughout the United States;

To borrow money on the credit of the United States;

To regulate commerce with foreign nations, and among the several States, and with the Indian tribes;

To establish an uniform rule of naturalization, and uniform laws on the subject of bankruptcies throughout the United States;

To coin money, regulate the value thereof, and of foreign coin, and fix the standard of weights and measures;

To provide for the punishment of counterfeiting the securities and current coin of the United States;

To establish post offices and post roads;

To promote the progress of science and useful arts by securing for limited times to authors and inventors the exclusive right to their respective writings and discoveries;

To constitute tribunals inferior to the Supreme Court;

To define and punish piracies and felonies committed on the high seas and offenses against the law of nations;

To declare war, grant letters of marque and reprisal, and make rules concerning captures on land and water;

To raise and support armies, but no appropriation of money to that use shall be for a longer term than two years;

To provide and maintain a navy;

To make rules for the government and regulation of the land and naval forces;

To provide for calling forth the militia to execute the laws of the Union, suppress insurrections, and repel invasions;

To provide for organizing, arming, and disciplining the militia, and for governing such part of them as may be employed in the service of the United States, reserving to the States respectively the appointment of the officers, and the authority of training the militia according to the discipline prescribed by Congress;

To exercise exclusive legislation in all cases whatsoever, over such district (not exceeding ten miles square) as may, by cession of particular States, and the acceptance of Congress, become the seat of government of the United States, and to exercise like authority over all places purchased by the consent of the legislature of the State, in which the same shall be, for erection of forts, magazines, arsenals, dockyards, and other needful buildings; —and

To make all laws which shall be necessary and proper for carrying into execution the foregoing powers, and all other powers vested by this Constitution in the government of the United States, or in any department or officer thereof.

Section 9 *The migration or importation of such persons as any of the States now existing shall think proper to admit shall not be prohibited by the Congress prior to the year 1808; but a tax or duty may be imposed on such importation, not exceeding $10 for each person.*

The privilege of the writ of habeas corpus shall not be suspended, unless when in cases of rebellion or invasion the public safety may require it.

No bill of attainder or ex post facto law shall be passed.

No capitation, or other direct, tax shall be laid, unless in proportion to the census or enumeration herein before directed to be taken.

No tax or duty shall be laid on articles exported from any State.

No preference shall be given by any regulation of commerce or revenue to the ports of one State over those of another; nor shall vessels bound to, or from, one State, be obliged to enter, clear, or pay duties in another.

No money shall be drawn from the treasury, but in consequence of appropriations made by law; and a regular statement and account of the receipts and expenditures of all public money shall be published from time to time.

No title of nobility shall be granted by the United States: and no person holding any office of profit or trust under them, shall, without the consent of the Congress, accept of any present, emolument, office, or title, of any kind whatever, from any king, prince, or foreign state.

Section 10   No State shall enter into any treaty, alliance, or confederation; grant letters of marque and reprisal; coin money; emit bills of credit; make anything but gold and silver coin a tender in payment of debts; pass any bill of attainder, ex post facto law, or law impairing the obligation of contracts, or grant any title of nobility.

No State shall, without the consent of Congress, lay any imposts or duties on imports or exports, except what may be absolutely necessary for executing its inspection laws: and the net produce of all duties and imposts, laid by any State on imports or exports, shall be for the use of the treasury of the United States; and all such laws shall be subject to the revision and control of the Congress.

No State shall, without the consent of Congress, lay any duty of tonnage, keep troops or ships of war in time of peace, enter into any agreement or compact with another State, or with a foreign power, or engage in war, unless actually invaded, or in such imminent danger as will not admit of delay.

Article II

Section 1   The executive power shall be vested in a President of the United States of America. He shall hold his office during the term of four years, and, together with the Vice-President, chosen for the same term, be elected as follows:

Each State shall appoint, in such manner as the legislature thereof may direct, a number of electors, equal to the whole number of Senators and Representatives to which the State may be entitled in the Congress; but no Senator or Representative, or person holding an office of trust or profit under the United States, shall be appointed an elector.

The electors shall meet in their respective States, and vote by ballot for two persons, of whom one at least shall not be an inhabitant of the same State with themselves. And they shall make a list of all the persons voted for, and of the number of votes for each; which list they shall sign and certify, and transmit sealed to the seat of government of the United States, directed to the President of the Senate. The President of the Senate shall, in the presence of the Senate and House of Representatives, open all the certificates, and the votes shall then be counted. The person having the greatest number of votes shall be the President, if such number be a majority of the whole number of electors appointed; and if there be more than one who have such majority, and have an equal number of votes, then the House of Representatives shall immediately choose by ballot one of them for President; and if no person have a majority, then from the five highest on the list said house shall in like manner choose the President. But in choosing the President the votes shall be taken by States, the representation from each State having one vote; a quorum for this purpose shall consist of a member or members from two-thirds of the States, and a majority of all the States shall be necessary to a choice. In every case, after the choice of the President, the person having the greatest number of votes of the electors shall be the Vice-President. But if there should remain two or more who have equal votes, the Senate shall choose from them by ballot the Vice-President.

The Congress may determine the time of choosing the electors and the day on which they shall give their votes; which day shall be the same throughout the United States.

No person except a natural-born citizen, *or a citizen of the United States at the time of the adoption of this Constitution,* shall be eligible to the office of President; neither shall any person be eligible to that office who shall not have attained to the age of thirty-five years, and been fourteen years a resident within the United States.

In cases of the removal of the President from office or of his death, resignation, or inability to discharge the powers and duties of the said office, the same shall devolve on the Vice-President, and the Congress may by law provide for the case of removal, death, resignation, or inability, both of the President and Vice-President, declaring what officer shall then act as President, and such officer shall act accordingly, until the disability be removed, or a President shall be elected.

The President shall, at stated times, receive for his services a compensation, which shall neither be increased nor diminished during the period for which he shall have been elected, and he shall not receive within that period any other emolument from the United States, or any of them.

Before he enter on the execution of his office, he shall take the following oath or affirmation:—"I do solemnly swear (or affirm) that I will faithfully execute the office of the President of the United States, and will to the best of my ability preserve, protect and defend the Constitution of the United States."

Section 2   The President shall be commander in chief of the army and navy of the United States, and of the militia of the several States, when called into the actual service of the United States; he may require the opinion, in writing, of the principal officer in each of the executive departments, upon any subject relating to the duties of their respective offices, and he shall have power to grant reprieves and pardons for offenses against the United States, except in cases of impeachment.

He shall have power, by and with the advice and consent of the Senate, to make treaties, provided two-thirds of the Senators present concur; and he shall nominate, and by and with the advice and consent of the Senate, shall appoint ambassadors, other public ministers and consuls, judges of the Supreme Court, and all other officers of the United States, whose appointments are not herein otherwise provided for, and which shall be established by law: but Congress may by law vest the appointment of such inferior officers, as they think proper, in the President alone, in the courts of law, or in the heads of departments.

The President shall have power to fill up all vacancies that may happen during the recess of the Senate, by granting commissions which shall expire at the end of their next session.

Section 3   He shall from time to time give to the Congress information of the state of the Union, and recommend to their consideration such measures as he shall judge necessary and expedient; he may, on extraordinary occasions, convene both houses, or either of them, and in case of disagreement between them, with respect to the time of adjournment, he may adjourn them to such time as he shall think proper; he shall receive ambassadors and other public ministers; he shall take care that the laws be faithfully executed, and shall commission all the officers of the United States.

Section 4   The President, Vice-President and all civil officers of the United States shall be removed from office on impeachment for, and on conviction of, treason, bribery, or other high crimes and misdemeanors.

Article III

Section 1   The judicial power of the United States shall be vested in one Supreme Court, and in such inferior courts as the Congress may from time to time ordain and establish. The judges, both of the Supreme and inferior courts, shall hold their offices during good behavior, and shall, at stated times, receive for their services a compensation which shall not be diminished during their continuance in office.

Section 2   The judicial power shall extend to all cases, in law and equity, arising under this Constitution, the laws of the United States, and treaties made, or which shall be made, under their authority;—to all cases affecting ambassadors, other public ministers and consuls;—to all cases of admiralty and maritime jurisdiction;—to controversies to which the

United States shall be a party;—to controversies between two or more States;—*between a State and citizens of another State;*—between citizens of different States;—between citizens of the same State claiming lands under grants of different States, and between a State, or the citizens thereof, and foreign states, citizens or subjects.

In all cases affecting ambassadors, other public ministers and consuls, and those in which a State shall be party, the Supreme Court shall have original jurisdiction. In all the other cases before mentioned, the Supreme Court shall have appellate jurisdiction, both as to law and fact, with such exceptions, and under such regulations, as the Congress shall make.

The trial of all crimes, except in cases of impeachment, shall be by jury; and such trial shall be held in the State where said crimes shall have been committed; but when not committed within any State, the trial shall be at such place or places as the Congress may by law have directed.

Section 3   Treason against the United States shall consist only in levying war against them, or in adhering to their enemies, giving them aid and comfort. No person shall be convicted of treason unless on the testimony of two witnesses to the same overt act, or on confession in open court.

The Congress shall have power to declare the punishment of treason, but no attainder of treason shall work corruption of blood, or forfeiture except during the life of the person attainted.

Article IV

Section 1   Full faith and credit shall be given in each State to the public acts, records, and judicial proceedings of every other State. And the Congress may by general laws prescribe the manner in which such acts, records, and proceedings shall be proved, and the effect thereof.

Section 2   The citizens of each State shall be entitled to all privileges and immunities of citizens in the several States.

A person charged in any State with treason, felony, or other crime, who shall flee from justice, and be found in another State, shall on demand of the executive authority of the State from which he fled, be delivered up, to be removed to the State having jurisdiction of the crime.

No person held to service or labor in one State, under the laws thereof, escaping into another, shall, in consequence of any law or regulation therein, be discharged from such service or labor, but shall be delivered up on claim of the party to whom such service or labor may be due.

Section 3   New States may be admitted by the Congress into this Union; but no new State shall be formed or erected within the jurisdiction of any other State; nor any State be formed by the junction of two or more States, or parts of States, without the consent of the legislatures of the States concerned as well as of the Congress.

The Congress shall have power to dispose of and make all needful rules and regulations respecting the territory or other property belonging to the United States; and nothing in this Constitution shall be so construed as to prejudice any claims of the United States, or of any particular State.

Section 4 The United States shall guarantee to every State in this Union a republican form of government, and shall protect each of them against invasion; and on application of the legislature, or of the executive (when the legislature cannot be convened), against domestic violence.

Article V

The Congress, whenever two-thirds of both houses shall deem it necessary, shall propose amendments to this Constitution, or, on the application of the legislatures of two-thirds of the several States, shall call a convention for proposing amendments, which, in either case, shall be valid to all intents and purposes, as part of this Constitution, when ratified by the legislatures of three-fourths of the several States, or by conventions in three-fourths thereof, as the one or the other mode of ratification may be proposed by the Congress; provided *that no amendments which may be made prior to the year one thousand eight hundred and eight shall in any manner affect the first and fourth clauses in the ninth section of the first article*; and that no State, without its consent, shall be deprived of its equal suffrage in the Senate.

Article VI

All debts contracted and engagements entered into, before the adoption of this Constitution, shall be as valid against the United States under this Constitution, as under the Confederation.

This Constitution, and the laws of the United States which shall be made in pursuance thereof; and all treaties made, or which shall be made, under the authority of the United States, shall be the supreme law of the land; and the judges in every State shall be bound thereby, anything in the Constitution or laws of any State to the contrary notwithstanding.

The Senators and Representatives before mentioned, and the members of the several State legislatures, and all executive and judicial officers, both of the United States and of the several States, shall be bound by oath or affirmation to support this Constitution; but no religious test shall ever be required as a qualification to any office or public trust under the United States.

Article VII

The ratification of the conventions of nine States shall be sufficient for the establishment of this Constitution between the States so ratifying the same.

Done in Convention by the unanimous consent of the States present, the seventeenth day of September in the year of our Lord one thousand seven hundred and eighty-seven and of the Independence of the United States of America the twelfth. In witness whereof we have hereunto subscribed our names.

AMENDMENTS TO THE CONSTITUTION*

Amendment I

Congress shall make no law respecting an establishment of religion, or prohibiting the free exercise thereof; or abridging the freedom of speech, or of the press; or the right of the people peaceably to assemble, and to petition the government for a redress of grievances.

Amendment II

A well-regulated militia being necessary to the security of a free State, the right of the people to keep and bear arms shall not be infringed.

Amendment III

No soldier shall, in time of peace, be quartered in any house without the consent of the owner, nor in time of war, but in a manner to be prescribed by law.

Amendment IV

The right of the people to be secure in their persons, houses, papers, and effects, against unreasonable searches and seizures, shall not be violated, and no warrants shall issue but upon probable cause, supported by oath or affirmation, and particularly describing the place to be searched, and the persons or things to be seized.

Amendment V

No person shall be held to answer for a capital, or otherwise infamous crime, unless on a presentment or indictment of a grand jury, except in cases arising in the land or naval forces, or in the militia, when in actual service in time of war or public danger; nor shall any person be subject for the same of-

---

*The first ten Amendments (the Bill of Rights) were adopted in 1791.

fense to be twice put in jeopardy of life or limb; nor shall be compelled in any criminal case to be a witness against himself, nor be deprived of life, liberty, or property, without due process of law; nor shall private property be taken for public use without just compensation.

Amendment VI

In all criminal prosecutions, the accused shall enjoy the right to a speedy and public trial, by an impartial jury of the State and district wherein the crime shall have been committed, which district shall have been previously ascertained by law, and to be informed of the nature and cause of the accusation; to be confronted with the witnesses against him; to have compulsory process for obtaining witnesses in his favor, and to have the assistance of counsel for his defense.

Amendment VII

In suits at common law, where the value in controversy shall exceed twenty dollars, the right of trial by jury shall be preserved, and no fact tried by a jury shall be otherwise reexamined in any court of the United States, than according to the rules of the common law.

Amendment VIII

Excessive bail shall not be required, nor excessive fines imposed, nor cruel and unusual punishments inflicted.

Amendment IX

The enumeration in the Constitution, of certain rights, shall not be construed to deny or disparage others retained by the people.

Amendment X

The powers not delegated to the United States by the Constitution, nor prohibited by it to the States, are reserved to the States respectively, or to the people.

Amendment XI

[Adopted 1798]

The judicial power of the United States shall not be construed to extend to any suit in law or equity, commenced or prosecuted against one of the United States by citizens of another State, or by citizens or subjects of any foreign state.

Amendment XII

[Adopted 1804]

The electors shall meet in their respective States, and vote by ballot for President and Vice-President, one of whom, at least, shall not be an inhabitant of the same State with themselves; they shall name in their ballots the person voted for as President, and in distinct ballots the person voted for as Vice-President, and they shall make distinct lists of all persons voted for as President, and of all persons voted for as Vice-President, and of the number of votes for each, which lists they shall sign and certify, and transmit sealed to the seat of government of the United States, directed to the President of the Senate;—the President of the Senate shall, in the presence of the Senate and House of Representatives, open all the certificates and the votes shall then be counted;—the person having the greatest number of votes for President shall be the President, if such number be a majority of the whole number of electors appointed; and if no person have such majority, then from the persons having the highest numbers not exceeding three on the list of those voted for as President, the House of Representatives shall choose immediately, by ballot, the President. But in choosing the President, the votes shall be taken by States, the representation from each State having one vote; a quorum for this purpose shall consist of a member or members from two-thirds of the States, and a majority of all the States shall be necessary to a choice. And if the House of Representatives shall not choose a President whenever the right of choice shall devolve upon them, before *the fourth day of March* next following, then the Vice-President shall act as President, as in the case of the death or other constitutional disability of the President.

The person having the greatest number of votes as Vice-President shall be the Vice-President, if such number be a majority of the whole number of electors appointed; and if no person have a majority, then from the two highest numbers on the list the Senate shall choose the Vice-President; a quorum for the purpose shall consist of two-thirds of the whole number of Senators, and a majority of the whole number shall be necessary to a choice. But no person constitutionally ineligible to the office of President shall be eligible to that of Vice-President of the United States.

Amendment XIII

[Adopted 1865]

Section 1 Neither slavery nor involuntary servitude, except as a punishment for crime whereof the party shall have been duly convicted, shall exist within the United States, or any place subject to their jurisdiction.

Section 2 Congress shall have power to enforce this article by appropriate legislation.

Amendment XIV

[Adopted 1868]

Section 1 All persons born or naturalized in the United States, and subject to the jurisdiction thereof, are citizens of the United States and of the State wherein they reside. No State shall make or enforce any law which shall abridge the privileges or immunities of citizens of the United States; nor shall any State deprive any person of life, liberty, or property, without due process of law; nor deny to any person within its jurisdiction the equal protection of the laws.

Section 2 Representatives shall be apportioned among the several States according to their respective numbers, counting the whole number of persons in each State, excluding Indians not taxed. But when the right to vote at any election for the choice of Electors for President and Vice-President of the United States, Representatives in Congress, the executive and judicial officers of a State, or the members of the legislature thereof, is denied to any of the male inhabitants of such State, being twenty-one years of age and citizens of the United States, or in any way abridged, except for participation in rebellion, or other crime, the basis of representation therein shall be reduced in the proportion which the number of such male citizens shall bear to the whole number of male citizens twenty-one years of age in such State.

Section 3 No person shall be a Senator or Representative in Congress, or Elector of President and Vice-President, or hold any office, civil or military, under the United States, or under any State, who, having previously taken an oath, as a member of Congress, or as an officer of the United States, or as a member of any State legislature, or as an executive or judicial officer of any State, to support the Constitution of the United States, shall have engaged in insurrection or rebellion against the same, or given aid or comfort to the enemies thereof. Congress may, by a vote of two-thirds of each house, remove such disability.

Section 4 The validity of the public debt of the United States, authorized by law, including debts incurred for payment of pensions and bounties for services in suppressing insurrection or rebellion, shall not be questioned. But neither the United States nor any State shall assume or pay any debt or obligation incurred in aid of insurrection or rebellion against the United States, or any claim for the loss of emancipation of any slave; but all such debts, obligations, and claims shall be held illegal and void.

Section 5 The Congress shall have power to enforce, by appropriate legislation, the provisions of this article.

Amendment XV

[Adopted 1870]

Section 1 The right of citizens of the United States to vote shall not be denied or abridged by the United States or by any State on account of race, color, or previous condition of servitude.

Section 2 The Congress shall have power to enforce this article by appropriate legislation.

Amendment XVI

[Adopted 1913]

The Congress shall have power to lay and collect taxes on incomes, from whatever source derived, without apportionment among the several States, and without regard to any census or enumeration.

Amendment XVII

[Adopted 1913]

Section 1 The Senate of the United States shall be composed of two Senators from each State, elected by the people thereof, for six years; and each Senator shall have one vote. The electors in each State shall have the qualifications requisite for electors of [voters for] the most numerous branch of the State legislatures.

Section 2 When vacancies happen in the representation of any State in the Senate, the executive authority of such State shall issue writs of election to fill such vacancies: Provided, that the Legislature of any State may empower the executive thereof to make temporary appointments until the people fill the vacancies by election as the Legislature may direct.

Section 3 This amendment shall not be so construed as to affect the election or term of any Senator chosen before it becomes valid as part of the Constitution.

Amendment XVIII

[Adopted 1919; Repealed 1933]

Section 1 After one year from the ratification of this article the manufacture, sale, or transportation of intoxicating liquors within, the importation thereof into, or the exportation thereof from the United States and all territory subject to the jurisdiction thereof, for beverage purposes, is hereby prohibited.

Section 2 The Congress and the several States shall have concurrent power to enforce this article by appropriate legislation.

Section 3 This article shall be inoperative unless it shall have been ratified as an amendment to the Constitution by the legislatures of the several States, as provided by the Constitution, within seven years from the date of the submission thereof to the States by the Congress.

Amendment XIX

[Adopted 1920]

Section 1 The right of citizens of the United States to vote shall not be denied or abridged by the United States or by any State on account of sex.

Section 2 The Congress shall have power to enforce this article by appropriate legislation.

Amendment XX

[Adopted 1933]

Section 1 The terms of the President and Vice-President shall end at noon on the 20th day of January, and the terms of Senators and Representatives at noon on the 3rd day of January, of the years in which such terms would have ended if this article had not been ratified; and the terms of their successors shall then begin.

Section 2 The Congress shall assemble at least once in every year, and such meeting shall begin at noon on the 3d day of January, unless they shall by law appoint a different day.

Section 3 If, at the time fixed for the beginning of the term of the President, the President-elect shall have died, the Vice-President–elect shall become President. If a President shall not have been chosen before the time fixed for the beginning of his term, or if the President-elect shall have failed to qualify, then the Vice-President–elect shall act as President until a President shall have qualified; and the Congress may by law provide for the case wherein neither a President-elect nor a Vice-President–elect shall have qualified, declaring who shall then act as President, or the manner in which one who is to act shall be selected, and such persons shall act accordingly until a President or Vice-President shall have qualified.

Section 4 The Congress may by law provide for the case of the death of any of the persons from whom the House of Representatives may choose a President whenever the right of choice shall have devolved upon them, and for the case of the death of any of the persons from whom the Senate may choose a Vice-President whenever the right of choice shall have devolved upon them.

Section 5 Sections 1 and 2 shall take effect on the 15th day of October following the ratification of this article.

Section 6 This article shall be inoperative unless it shall have been ratified as an amendment to the Constitution by the Legislatures of three-fourths of the several States within seven years from the date of its submission.

Amendment XXI

[Adopted 1933]

Section 1 The eighteenth article of amendment to the Constitution of the United States is hereby repealed.

Section 2 The transportation or importation into any State, Territory, or Possession of the United States for delivery or use therein of intoxicating liquors, in violation of the laws thereof, is hereby prohibited.

Section 3 This article shall be inoperative unless it shall have been ratified as an amendment to the Constitution by conventions in the several States, as provided in the Constitution, within seven years from the date of submission thereof to the States by the Congress.

Amendment XXII

[Adopted 1951]

Section 1 No person shall be elected to the office of President more than twice, and no person who has held the office of President, or acted as President, for more than two years of a term to which some other person was elected President shall be elected to the office of President more than once. But this article shall not apply to any person holding the office of President when this article was proposed by the Congress, and shall not prevent any person who may be holding the office of President, or acting as President, during the term within which this article becomes operative from holding the office of President or acting as President during the remainder of such term.

Section 2 This article shall be inoperative unless it shall have been ratified as an amendment to the Constitution by the legislatures of three-fourths of the several States within seven years from the date of its submission to the States by the Congress.

Amendment XXIII

[Adopted 1961]

Section 1 The District constituting the seat of Government of the United States shall appoint in such manner as the Congress may direct:

A number of electors of President and Vice-President equal to the whole number of Senators and Representatives in Congress to which the District would be entitled if it were a State, but in no event more than the least populous State; they shall be in addition to those appointed by the States, but they shall be considered for the purposes of the election of President and Vice-President, to be electors appointed by a State; and they shall meet in the District and perform such duties as provided by the twelfth article of amendment.

Section 2 The Congress shall have the power to enforce this article by appropriate legislation.

Amendment XXIV

[Adopted 1964]

Section 1 The right of citizens of the United States to vote in any primary or other election for President or Vice-President, for electors for President or Vice-President, or for Senator or Representative in Congress, shall not be denied or abridged by the United States or any State by reason of failure to pay any poll tax or other tax.

Section 2 The Congress shall have the power to enforce this article by appropriate legislation.

Amendment XXV

[Adopted 1967]

Section 1 In case of the removal of the President from office or of his death or resignation, the Vice-President shall become President.

Section 2 Whenever there is a vacancy in the office of the Vice-President, the President shall nominate a Vice-President who shall take office upon confirmation by a majority vote of both Houses of Congress.

Section 3 Whenever the President transmits to the President pro tempore of the Senate and the Speaker of the House of Representatives his written declaration that he is unable to discharge the powers and duties of his office, and until he transmits to them a written declaration to the contrary, such powers and duties shall be discharged by the Vice-President as Acting President.

Section 4 Whenever the Vice-President and a majority of either the principal officers of the executive departments or of such other body as Congress may by law provide, transmit to the President pro tempore of the Senate and the Speaker of the House of Representatives their written declaration that the President is unable to discharge the powers and duties of his office, the Vice-President shall immediately assume the powers and duties of the office as Acting President.

Thereafter, when the President transmits to the President pro tempore of the Senate and the Speaker of the House of Representatives his written declaration that no inability exists, he shall resume the powers and duties of his office unless the Vice-President and a majority of either the principal officers of the executive department[s] or of such other body as Congress may by law provide, transmit within four days to the President pro tempore of the Senate and the Speaker of the House of Representatives their written declaration that the President is unable to discharge the powers and duties of his office. Thereupon Congress shall decide the issue, assembling within forty-eight hours for that purpose if not in session. If the Congress, within twenty-one days after receipt of the latter written declaration, or, if Congress is not in session, within twenty-one days after Congress is required to assemble, determines by two-thirds vote of both Houses that the President is unable to discharge the powers and duties of his office, the Vice-President shall continue to discharge the same as Acting President; otherwise, the President shall resume the powers and duties of his office.

Amendment XXVI

[Adopted 1971]

Section 1 The right of citizens of the United States, who are eighteen years of age or older, to vote shall not be denied or abridged by the United States or by any State on account of age.

Section 2 The Congress shall have power to enforce this article by appropriate legislation.

Amendment XXVII

[Adopted 1992]

No law, varying the compensation for the services of the Senators and Representatives, shall take effect, until an election of Representatives shall have intervened.

Presidential Elections

Year	Number of States	Candidates	Parties	Popular Vote	% of Popular Vote	Electoral Vote	% Voter Participation[a]
1789	10	**George Washington**	No party			69	
		John Adams	designations			34	
		Other candidates				35	
1792	15	**George Washington**	No party			132	
		John Adams	designations			77	
		George Clinton				50	
		Other candidates				5	
1796	16	**John Adams**	Federalist			71	
		Thomas Jefferson	Democratic-Republican			68	
		Thomas Pinckney	Federalist			59	
		Aaron Burr	Democratic-Republican			30	
		Other candidates				48	
1800	16	**Thomas Jefferson**	Democratic-Republican			73	
		Aaron Burr	Democratic-Republican			73	
		John Adams	Federalist			65	
		Charles C. Pinckney	Federalist			64	
		John Jay	Federalist			1	
1804	17	**Thomas Jefferson**	Democratic-Republican			162	
		Charles C. Pinckney	Federalist			14	
1808	17	**James Madison**	Democratic-Republican			122	
		Charles C. Pinckney	Federalist			47	
		George Clinton	Democratic-Republican			6	
1812	18	**James Madison**	Democratic-Republican			128	
		DeWitt Clinton	Federalist			89	
1816	19	**James Monroe**	Democratic-Republican			183	
		Rufus King	Federalist			34	
1820	24	**James Monroe**	Democratic-Republican			231	

Presidential Elections (continued)

Year	Number of States	Candidates	Parties	Popular Vote	% of Popular Vote	Electoral Vote	% Voter Participation[a]
		John Quincy Adams	Independent Republican			1	
1824	24	**John Quincy Adams**	Democratic-Republican	108,740	30.5	84	26.9
		Andrew Jackson	Democratic-Republican	153,544	43.1	99	
		Henry Clay	Democratic-Republican	47,136	13.2	37	
		William H. Crawford	Democratic-Republican	46,618	13.1	41	
1828	24	**Andrew Jackson**	Democratic	647,286	56.0	178	57.6
		John Quincy Adams	National Republican	508,064	44.0	83	
1832	24	**Andrew Jackson**	Democratic	701,780	54.2	219	55.4
		Henry Clay	National Republican	484,205	37.4	49	
		Other candidates		107,988	8.0	18	
1836	26	**Martin Van Buren**	Democratic	764,176	50.8	170	57.8
		William H. Harrison	Whig	550,816	36.6	73	
		Hugh L. White	Whig	146,107	9.7	26	
1840	26	**William H. Harrison**	Whig	1,274,624	53.1	234	80.2
		Martin Van Buren	Democratic	1,127,781	46.9	60	
1844	26	**James K. Polk**	Democratic	1,338,464	49.6	170	78.9
		Henry Clay	Whig	1,300,097	48.1	105	
		James G. Birney	Liberty	62,300	2.3		
1848	30	**Zachary Taylor**	Whig	1,360,967	47.4	163	72.7
		Lewis Cass	Democratic	1,222,342	42.5	127	
		Martin Van Buren	Free Soil	291,263	10.1		
1852	31	**Franklin Pierce**	Democratic	1,601,117	50.9	254	69.6
		Winfield Scott	Whig	1,385,453	44.1	42	
		John P. Hale	Free Soil	155,825	5.0		
1856	31	**James Buchanan**	Democratic	1,832,955	45.3	174	78.9
		John C. Frémont	Republican	1,339,932	33.1	114	
		Millard Fillmore	American	871,731	21.6	8	
1860	33	**Abraham Lincoln**	Republican	1,865,593	39.8	180	81.2
		Stephen A. Douglas	Democratic	1,382,713	29.5	12	
		John C. Breckinridge	Democratic	848,356	18.1	72	
		John Bell	Constitutional Union	592,906	12.6	39	
1864	36	**Abraham Lincoln**	Republican	2,206,938	55.0	212	73.8
		George B. McClellan	Democratic	1,803,787	45.0	21	

Presidential Elections (continued)

Year	Number of States	Candidates	Parties	Popular Vote	% of Popular Vote	Electoral Vote	% Voter Participation[a]
1868	37	**Ulysses S. Grant**	Republican	3,013,421	52.7	214	78.1
		Horatio Seymour	Democratic	2,706,829	47.3	80	
1872	37	**Ulysses S. Grant**	Republican	3,596,745	55.6	286	71.3
		Horace Greeley	Democratic	2,843,446	43.9	[b]	
1876	38	**Rutherford B. Hayes**	Republican	4,036,572	48.0	185	81.8
		Samuel J. Tilden	Democratic	4,284,020	51.0	184	
1880	38	**James A. Garfield**	Republican	4,453,295	48.5	214	79.4
		Winfield S. Hancock	Democratic	4,414,082	48.1	155	
		James B. Weaver	Greenback-Labor	308,578	3.4		
1884	38	**Grover Cleveland**	Democratic	4,879,507	48.5	219	77.5
		James G. Blaine	Republican	4,850,293	48.2	182	
		Benjamin F. Butler	Greenback-Labor	175,370	1.8		
		John P. St. John	Prohibition	150,369	1.5		
1888	38	**Benjamin Harrison**	Republican	5,447,129	47.9	233	79.3
		Grover Cleveland	Democratic	5,537,857	48.6	168	
		Clinton B. Fisk	Prohibition	249,506	2.2		
		Anson J. Streeter	Union Labor	146,935	1.3		
1892	44	**Grover Cleveland**	Democratic	5,555,426	46.1	277	74.7
		Benjamin Harrison	Republican	5,182,690	43.0	145	
		James B. Weaver	People's	1,029,846	8.5	22	
		John Bidwell	Prohibition	264,133	2.2		
1896	45	**William McKinley**	Republican	7,102,246	51.1	271	79.3
		William J. Bryan	Democratic	6,492,559	47.7	176	
1900	45	**William McKinley**	Republican	7,218,491	51.7	292	73.2
		William J. Bryan	Democratic; Populist	6,356,734	45.5	155	
		John C. Wooley	Prohibition	208,914	1.5		
1904	45	**Theodore Roosevelt**	Republican	7,628,461	57.4	336	65.2
		Alton B. Parker	Democratic	5,084,223	37.6	140	
		Eugene V. Debs	Socialist	402,283	3.0		
		Silas C. Swallow	Prohibition	258,536	1.9		
1908	46	**William H. Taft**	Republican	7,675,320	51.6	321	65.4
		William J. Bryan	Democratic	6,412,294	43.1	162	
		Eugene V. Debs	Socialist	420,793	2.8		
		Eugene W. Chafin	Prohibition	253,840	1.7		
1912	48	**Woodrow Wilson**	Democratic	6,296,547	41.9	435	58.8
		Theodore Roosevelt	Progressive	4,118,571	27.4	88	
		William H. Taft	Republican	3,486,720	23.2	8	
		Eugene V. Debs	Socialist	900,672	6.0		

Presidential Elections (continued)

Year	Number of States	Candidates	Parties	Popular Vote	% of Popular Vote	Elec-toral Vote	% Voter Partici-pation[a]
		Eugene W. Chafin	Prohibition	206,275	1.4		
1916	48	**Woodrow Wilson**	Democratic	9,127,695	49.4	277	61.6
		Charles E. Hughes	Republican	8,533,507	46.2	254	
		A. L. Benson	Socialist	585,113	3.2		
		J. Frank Hanly	Prohibition	220,506	1.2		
1920	48	**Warren G. Harding**	Republican	16,143,407	60.4	404	49.2
		James M. Cox	Democratic	9,130,328	34.2	127	
		Eugene V. Debs	Socialist	919,799	3.4		
		P. P. Christensen	Farmer-Labor	265,411	1.0		
1924	48	**Calvin Coolidge**	Republican	15,718,211	54.0	382	48.9
		John W. Davis	Democratic	8,385,283	28.8	136	
		Robert M. La Follette	Progressive	4,831,289	16.6	13	
1928	48	**Herbert C. Hoover**	Republican	21,391,993	58.2	444	56.9
		Alfred E. Smith	Democratic	15,016,169	40.9	87	
1932	48	**Franklin D. Roosevelt**	Democratic	22,809,638	57.4	472	56.9
		Herbert C. Hoover	Republican	15,758,901	39.7	59	
		Norman Thomas	Socialist	881,951	2.2		
1936	48	**Franklin D. Roosevelt**	Democratic	27,752,869	60.8	523	61.0
		Alfred M. Landon	Republican	16,674,665	36.5	8	
		William Lemke	Union	882,479	1.9		
1940	48	**Franklin D. Roosevelt**	Democratic	27,307,819	54.8	449	62.5
		Wendell L. Willkie	Republican	22,321,018	44.8	82	
1944	48	**Franklin D. Roosevelt**	Democratic	25,606,585	53.5	432	55.9
		Thomas E. Dewey	Republican	22,014,745	46.0	99	
1948	48	**Harry S Truman**	Democratic	24,179,345	49.6	303	53.0
		Thomas E. Dewey	Republican	21,991,291	45.1	189	
		J. Strom Thurmond	States' Rights	1,176,125	2.4	39	
		Henry A. Wallace	Progressive	1,157,326	2.4		
1952	48	**Dwight D. Eisenhower**	Republican	33,936,234	55.1	442	63.3
		Adlai E. Stevenson	Democratic	27,314,992	44.4	89	
1956	48	**Dwight D. Eisenhower**	Republican	35,590,472	57.6	457	60.6
		Adlai E. Stevenson	Democratic	26,022,752	42.1	73	
1960	50	**John F. Kennedy**	Democratic	34,226,731	49.7	303	62.8
		Richard M. Nixon	Republican	34,108,157	49.5	219	
1964	50	**Lyndon B. Johnson**	Democratic	43,129,566	61.1	486	61.7
		Barry M. Goldwater	Republican	27,178,188	38.5	52	
1968	50	**Richard M. Nixon**	Republican	31,785,480	43.4	301	60.6
		Hubert H. Humphrey	Democratic	31,275,166	42.7	191	

Presidential Elections (continued)

Year	Number of States	Candidates	Parties	Popular Vote	% of Popular Vote	Electoral Vote	% Voter Participation[a]
		George C. Wallace	American Independent	9,906,473	13.5	46	
1972	50	**Richard M. Nixon**	Republican	47,169,911	60.7	520	55.2
		George S. McGovern	Democratic	29,170,383	37.5	17	
		John G. Schmitz	American	1,099,482	1.4		
1976	50	**James E. Carter**	Democratic	40,830,763	50.1	297	53.5
		Gerald R. Ford	Republican	39,147,793	48.0	240	
1980	50	**Ronald W. Reagan**	Republican	43,904,153	50.7	489	52.6
		James E. Carter	Democratic	35,483,883	41.0	49	
		John B. Anderson	Independent	5,720,060	6.6		
		Ed Clark	Libertarian	921,299	1.1		
1984	50	**Ronald W. Reagan**	Republican	54,455,075	58.8	525	53.3
		Walter F. Mondale	Democratic	37,577,185	40.6	13	
1988	50	**George H. W. Bush**	Republican	48,886,097	53.4	426	50.1
		Michael S. Dukakis	Democratic	41,809,074	45.6	111[c]	
1992	50	**William J. Clinton**	Democratic	44,909,326	43.0	370	55.2
		George H. W. Bush	Republican	39,103,882	37.4	168	
		H. Ross Perot	Independent	19,741,048	18.9		
1996	50	**William J. Clinton**	Democratic	47,402,357	49.2	379	49.1
		Robert J. Dole	Republican	39,196,755	40.7	159	
		H. Ross Perot	Reform	8,085,402	8.4		
		Ralph Nader	Green	684,902	0.7		
2000	50	**George W. Bush**	Republican	50,455,156	47.9	271	51.2
		Albert Gore	Democratic	50,992,335	48.4	266	
		Ralph Nader	Green	2,882,955	2.7		
2004	50	**George W. Bush**	Republican	62,039,073	50.7	286	55.3
		John F. Kerry	Democratic	59,027,478	48.2	251	
		Ralph Nader	Independent	240,896	0.2		

Candidates receiving less than 1 percent of the popular vote have been omitted. Thus the percentage of popular vote given for any election year may not total 100 percent.

Before the passage of the Twelfth Amendment in 1804, the electoral college voted for two presidential candidates; the runner-up became vice president.

Before 1824, most presidential electors were chosen by state legislatures, not by popular vote.

[a]Percent of voting-age population casting ballots.

[b]Greeley died shortly after the election; the electors supporting him then divided their votes among minor candidates.

[c]One elector from West Virginia cast her electoral college presidential ballot for Lloyd Bentsen, the Democratic Party's vice-presidential candidate.

Presidents and Vice Presidents

1. President	**George Washington**	1789–1797
Vice President	John Adams	1789–1797
2. President	**John Adams**	1797–1801
Vice President	Thomas Jefferson	1797–1801
3. President	**Thomas Jefferson**	1801–1809
Vice President	Aaron Burr	1801–1805
Vice President	George Clinton	1805–1809
4. President	**James Madison**	1809–1817
Vice President	George Clinton	1809–1813
Vice President	Elbridge Gerry	1813–1817
5. President	**James Monroe**	1817–1825
Vice President	Daniel Tompkins	1817–1825
6. President	**John Quincy Adams**	1825–1829
Vice President	John C. Calhoun	1825–1829
7. President	**Andrew Jackson**	1829–1837
Vice President	John C. Calhoun	1829–1833
Vice President	Martin Van Buren	1833–1837
8. President	**Martin Van Buren**	1837–1841
Vice President	Richard M. Johnson	1837–1841
9. President	**William H. Harrison**	1841
Vice President	John Tyler	1841
10. President	**John Tyler**	1841–1845
Vice President	None	
11. President	**James K. Polk**	1845–1849
Vice President	George M. Dallas	1845–1849
12. President	**Zachary Taylor**	1849–1850
Vice President	Millard Fillmore	1849–1850
13. President	**Millard Fillmore**	1850–1853
Vice President	None	
14. President	**Franklin Pierce**	1853–1857
Vice President	William R. King	1853–1857
15. President	**James Buchanan**	1857–1861
Vice President	John C. Breckinridge	1857–1861
16. President	**Abraham Lincoln**	1861–1865
Vice President	Hannibal Hamlin	1861–1865
Vice President	Andrew Johnson	1865
17. President	**Andrew Johnson**	1865–1869
Vice President	None	
18. President	**Ulysses S. Grant**	1869–1877
Vice President	Schuyler Colfax	1869–1873
Vice President	Henry Wilson	1873–1877
19. President	**Rutherford B. Hayes**	1877–1881
Vice President	William A. Wheeler	1877–1881
20. President	**James A. Garfield**	1881
Vice President	Chester A. Arthur	1881
21. President	**Chester A. Arthur**	1881–1885
Vice President	None	
22. President	**Grover Cleveland**	1885–1889
Vice President	Thomas A. Hendricks	1885–1889
23. President	**Benjamin Harrison**	1889–1893
Vice President	Levi P. Morton	1889–1893
24. President	**Grover Cleveland**	1893–1897
Vice President	Adlai E. Stevenson	1893–1897
25. President	**William McKinley**	1897–1901
Vice President	Garret A. Hobart	1897–1901
Vice President	Theodore Roosevelt	1901
26. President	**Theodore Roosevelt**	1901–1909
Vice President	Charles Fairbanks	1905–1909
27. President	**William H. Taft**	1909–1913
Vice President	James S. Sherman	1909–1913
28. President	**Woodrow Wilson**	1913–1921
Vice President	Thomas R. Marshall	1913–1921
29. President	**Warren G. Harding**	1921–1923
Vice President	Calvin Coolidge	1921–1923
30. President	**Calvin Coolidge**	1923–1929
Vice President	Charles G. Dawes	1925–1929
31. President	**Herbert C. Hoover**	1929–1933
Vice President	Charles Curtis	1929–1933
32. President	**Franklin D. Roosevelt**	1933–1945
Vice President	John N. Garner	1933–1941
Vice President	Henry A. Wallace	1941–1945
Vice President	Harry S Truman	1945
33. President	**Harry S Truman**	1945–1953
Vice President	Alben W. Barkley	1949–1953
34. President	**Dwight D. Eisenhower**	1953–1961
Vice President	Richard M. Nixon	1953–1961

Presidents and Vice Presidents (continued)

35. President	**John F. Kennedy**	1961–1963		40. President	**Ronald W. Reagan**	1981–1989
Vice President	Lyndon B. Johnson	1961–1963		Vice President	George H. W. Bush	1981–1989
36. President	**Lyndon B. Johnson**	1963–1969		41. President	**George H. W. Bush**	1989–1993
Vice President	Hubert H. Humphrey	1965–1969		Vice President	J. Danforth Quayle	1989–1993
37. President	**Richard M. Nixon**	1969–1974		42. President	**William J. Clinton**	1993–2001
Vice President	Spiro T. Agnew	1969–1973		Vice President	Albert Gore	1993–2001
Vice President	Gerald R. Ford	1973–1974		43. President	**George W. Bush**	2001–2009
38. President	**Gerald R. Ford**	1974–1977		Vice President	Richard Cheney	2001–2009
Vice President	Nelson A. Rockefeller	1974–1977				
39. President	**James E. Carter**	1977–1981				
Vice President	Walter F. Mondale	1977–1981				

For a complete list of Presidents, Vice Presidents, and Cabinet Members, go to college.hmco.com.

Justices of the Supreme Court

	Term of Service	Years of Service	Life Span		Term of Service	Years of Service	Life Span
John Jay	1789–1795	5	1745–1829	Joseph P. Bradley	1870–1892	22	1813–1892
John Rutledge	1789–1791	1	1739–1800	Ward Hunt	1873–1882	9	1810–1886
William Cushing	1789–1810	20	1732–1810	*Morrison R. Waite*	1874–1888	14	1816–1888
James Wilson	1789–1798	8	1742–1798	John M. Harlan	1877–1911	34	1833–1911
John Blair	1789–1796	6	1732–1800	William B. Woods	1880–1887	7	1824–1887
Robert H. Harrison	1789–1790	—	1745–1790	Stanley Mathews	1881–1889	7	1824–1889
James Iredell	1790–1799	9	1751–1799	Horace Gray	1882–1902	20	1828–1902
Thomas Johnson	1791–1793	1	1732–1819	Samuel Blatchford	1882–1893	11	1820–1893
William Paterson	1793–1806	13	1745–1806	Lucius Q. C. Lamar	1888–1893	5	1825–1893
*John Rutledge**	1795	—	1739–1800	*Melville W. Fuller*	1888–1910	21	1833–1910
Samuel Chase	1796–1811	15	1741–1811	David J. Brewer	1890–1910	20	1837–1910
Oliver Ellsworth	1796–1800	4	1745–1807	Henry B. Brown	1890–1906	16	1836–1913
Bushrod Washington	1798–1829	31	1762–1829	George Shiras Jr.	1892–1903	10	1832–1924
Alfred Moore	1799–1804	4	1755–1810	Howell E. Jackson	1893–1895	2	1832–1895
John Marshall	1801–1835	34	1755–1835	Edward D. White	1894–1910	16	1845–1921
William Johnson	1804–1834	30	1771–1834	Rufus W. Peckham	1895–1909	14	1838–1909
H. Brockholst Livingston	1806–1823	16	1757–1823	Joseph McKenna	1898–1925	26	1843–1926
Thomas Todd	1807–1826	18	1765–1826	Oliver W. Holmes	1902–1932	30	1841–1935
Joseph Story	1811–1845	33	1779–1845	William D. Day	1903–1922	19	1849–1923
Gabriel Duval	1811–1835	24	1752–1844	William H. Moody	1906–1910	3	1853–1917
Smith Thompson	1823–1843	20	1768–1843	Horace H. Lurton	1910–1914	4	1844–1914
Robert Trimble	1826–1828	2	1777–1828	Charles E. Hughes	1910–1916	5	1862–1948
John McLean	1829–1861	32	1785–1861	Willis Van Devanter	1911–1937	26	1859–1941
Henry Baldwin	1830–1844	14	1780–1844	Joseph R. Lamar	1911–1916	5	1857–1916
James M. Wayne	1835–1867	32	1790–1867	*Edward D. White*	1910–1921	11	1845–1921
Roger B. Taney	1836–1864	28	1777–1864	Mahlon Pitney	1912–1922	10	1858–1924
Philip P. Barbour	1836–1841	4	1783–1841	James C. McReynolds	1914–1941	26	1862–1946
John Catron	1837–1865	28	1786–1865	Louis D. Brandeis	1916–1939	22	1856–1941
John McKinley	1837–1852	15	1780–1852	John H. Clarke	1916–1922	6	1857–1945
Peter V. Daniel	1841–1860	19	1784–1860	*William H. Taft*	1921–1930	8	1857–1930
Samuel Nelson	1845–1872	27	1792–1873	George Sutherland	1922–1938	15	1862–1942
Levi Woodbury	1845–1851	5	1789–1851	Pierce Butler	1922–1939	16	1866–1939
Robert C. Grier	1846–1870	23	1794–1870	Edward T. Sanford	1923–1930	7	1865–1930
Benjamin R. Curtis	1851–1857	6	1809–1874	Harlan F. Stone	1925–1941	16	1872–1946
John A. Campbell	1853–1861	8	1811–1889	*Charles E. Hughes*	1930–1941	11	1862–1948
Nathan Clifford	1858–1881	23	1803–1881	Owen J. Roberts	1930–1945	15	1875–1955
Noah H. Swayne	1862–1881	18	1804–1884	Benjamin N. Cardozo	1932–1938	6	1870–1938
Samuel F. Miller	1862–1890	28	1816–1890	Hugo L. Black	1937–1971	34	1886–1971
David Davis	1862–1877	14	1815–1886	Stanley F. Reed	1938–1957	19	1884–1980
Stephen J. Field	1863–1897	34	1816–1899	Felix Frankfurter	1939–1962	23	1882–1965
Salmon P. Chase	1864–1873	8	1808–1873	William O. Douglas	1939–1975	36	1898–1980
William Strong	1870–1880	10	1808–1895	Frank Murphy	1940–1949	9	1890–1949

Justices of the Supreme Court (continued)

	Term of Service	Years of Service	Life Span		Term of Service	Years of Service	Life Span
Harlan F. Stone	1941–1946	5	1872–1946	Abe Fortas	1965–1969	4	1910–1982
James F. Byrnes	1941–1942	1	1879–1972	Thurgood Marshall	1967–1991	24	1908–1993
Robert H. Jackson	1941–1954	13	1892–1954	*Warren C. Burger*	1969–1986	17	1907–1995
Wiley B. Rutledge	1943–1949	6	1894–1949	Harry A. Blackmun	1970–1994	24	1908–1998
Harold H. Burton	1945–1958	13	1888–1964	Lewis F. Powell Jr.	1972–1987	15	1907–1998
Fred M. Vinson	1946–1953	7	1890–1953	*William H. Rehnquist*	1972–2005	33	1924–2005
Tom C. Clark	1949–1967	18	1899–1977	John P. Stevens III	1975–	—	1920–
Sherman Minton	1949–1956	7	1890–1965	Sandra Day O'Connor	1981–	—	1930–
Earl Warren	1953–1969	16	1891–1974	Antonin Scalia	1986–	—	1936–
John Marshall Harlan	1955–1971	16	1899–1971	Anthony M. Kennedy	1988–	—	1936–
William J. Brennan Jr.	1956–1990	34	1906–1997	David H. Souter	1990–	—	1939–
Charles E. Whittaker	1957–1962	5	1901–1973	Clarence Thomas	1991–	—	1948–
Potter Stewart	1958–1981	23	1915–1985	Ruth Bader Ginsburg	1993–	—	1933–
Byron R. White	1962–1993	31	1917–	Stephen Breyer	1994–	—	1938–
Arthur J. Goldberg	1962–1965	3	1908–1990	John G. Roberts	2005–	—	1955–

Note: Chief justices are in italics.

*Appointed and served one term, but not confirmed by the Senate.

INDEX

A&P stores, 332
Abenakis: corn and, 16
Abolition and abolitionism, 114–115, 186–189, 216, 221, 243, 246; Wilmot Proviso and, 241; Bleeding Kansas and, 248; in Civil War, 264
Abolition of Negro Slavery (Dew), 221
Aborigines (Australia), 311, 311(illus.)
Abortion, 198, 211, 351, 395, 579, 599
Abraham Lincoln Brigade, 482
Academies: for women, 112
Acadia, *see* Nova Scotia
Accommodation policy: of Booker T. Washington, 386, 387
Acheson, Dean, 522
ACLU, *see* American Civil Liberties Union
Acoma pueblo, 22
Activism: by government, 179–180, 467–468; Jacksonian Democrats and, 190; by blacks, 215, 366. *See also* Protest(s); Revolts and rebellions
Act of Union (1800), 199
Adams, Abigail, 114
Adams, Henry, 399
Adams, John, 74, 94, 101, 136(illus.), 144; Boston Massacre and, 87–88; Declaration of Independence and, 101; presidency of, 135–137; midnight appointments by, 144–145
Adams, John Quincy, 161–163, 185, 188, 189–190
Adams, Samuel, 88, 94, 125
Adamson Act (1916), 393
Adams-Onís (Transcontinental) Treaty, 163
Addams, Jane, 349, 406, 419, 432; woman suffrage and, 387; peace efforts of, 476
Adding machines, 323, 324
Adkins v. Children's Hospital, 436
Adolescence, 352
Adoption: by gay couples, 631
Advanced Research Projects Agency (ARPA), 636
Advertising, 332–333, 332(illus.), 439
Aerospace industry, 543
Affirmative action, 578, 591
Affluence, 329–330, 607
Afghanistan: military campaign in, 141; Soviet Union and, 576, 592, 606; U.S. and, 617, 626–627
AFL, *see* American Federation of Labor (AFL)
Africa, 7–8; human origins in, 3; Portuguese in, 12; involuntary migrants from, 22, 60(map); slave trade from, 47, 49–50; British in, 79; loyalist resettlement in, 98;

Barbary pirates and, 142; cultural influences of, 216, 229–230; fugitive slave flight to, 249; American missionaries in, 361; black emigration to, 385; imperialism in, 398; independence in, 525; Nixon policy toward, 583. *See also* Slaves and slavery
African Americans, 56, 229–230, 284; population of, 59, 215, 544, 630; family and, 68, 283; Revolution and, 97–99, 104, 104(illus.), 114–116, 137–140; equality of, 110, 291; Haitian refugees and, 138; labor unions and, 174; religion and, 183, 215, 284; as abolitionists, 186–189; minstrel shows and, 207, 208(illus.); associations of, 208, 378; culture of, 216, 217, 344; in Civil War, 266, 267, 268; and 1868 election, 289; "Negro Rule" myth and, 291; as Exodusters, 296, 307; Reconstruction and, 296–297; in West, 307; as cowboys, 315(illus.); unions and, 327, 328; migration by, 341, 426, 440; settlement houses and, 349–350; vaudeville and, 355; as missionaries, 361; Jim Crow laws and, 366; women and, 366, 388, 438, 457, 498; in Progressive era, 385–387; Niagara movement and, 386–387; in Spanish-American War, 406; First World War and, 421, 429; Harlem Renaissance and, 449; jazz and, 449–450; unemployment of, 457; at 1936 Olympics, 469; New Deal and, 471; Second World War and, 485, 497, 503, 540–543; illiteracy among, 504; in postwar period, 534, 536; on television, 545; poverty of, 550, 608; sit-ins by, 553–554; King assassination and, 570–572; cultural nationalism of, 576; affirmative action and, 578; Korean immigrants and, 610; Rodney King riots and, 617–618; and 2000 election, 626. *See also* Civil rights; Civil rights movement; Free blacks; Freedpeople; Race and racism; Segregation; Slaves and slavery; Voting and voting rights
African Methodist Episcopal (AME) Church, 115, 186, 215, 224, 344, 388
African National Congress, 611
Africans: enslavement of, 12, 46–47, 51–53, 59, 60(map). *See also* Slaves and slavery
Afrika Korps, 496
Age and ageism, *see* Older Americans
Agency for International Development (AID), 527
Age of Innocence, The (Wharton), 449
Agnew, Spiro, 585, 586

Agrarian protest, 367–369
Agrarian republic, 144, 169
Agribusiness, 543, 550
Agricultural Adjustment Act, 460, 461, 462, 470
Agricultural colleges, 368
Agriculture, 3, 4, 5; in West Africa, 7; in colonies, 27, 31, 52; Indians and, 139; prizes for, 169; in California, 203; money-crop, 220; commercial, 247; mechanization of, 263; immigrant labor for, 307; in late 1800s, 313–314; exports of, 399; in First World War, 425; in 1920s, 436; after Second World War, 535. *See also* Farms and farming
Aguinaldo, Emilio, 407
AIDS, 609, 633, 634
Aid to Families with Dependent Children (AFDC), 465, 562, 598
Air force, 483, 503
Airline industry, 442, 442(illus.), 600
Airplanes, 422, 434, 496
Air pollution, 336, 510
Air traffic controllers: Reagan and, 599
Aix-la-Chapelle, Treaty of, 63
Akan States, 8
Alabama, 155, 163, 174, 177, 252, 559
Alabama (ship), 402
Alabama claims, 272
Alabama Midlands case, 362
Alamance, battle at, 71
Alamo, battle at, 195–197
Alaska, 295, 402
Albany, New York, 23, 102
Albany Congress, 76
Albemarle region, 43
Alcatraz: Indian occupation of, 577, 577(illus.)
Alcohol and alcoholism, 382, 383, 449. *See also* Temperance
Alcott, Louisa May, 211
Aldrich, Nelson W., 380, 391
Alexander VI (Pope), 13
Alfalfa, 314
Algeciras, Spain: Moroccan settlement at, 413
Algonquian Indians, 5, 28–29, 30(illus.), 35, 38, 45, 67, 76; as slaves, 39; family life of, 67, 68; polygyny among, 67
Alianza Federal de Mercedes, 577
Alien Acts (1798), 137, 144, 149
Alienation, literature of, 449
Alien Registration (Smith) Act (1940), 500–502
Allen, Richard, 186
Allende, Salvador, 583

Alliance(s): Indian, 44, 45; Washington on, 133, 135; in First World War, 417; in Second World War, 488; NATO as, 519; with Japan, 522. *See also* specific alliances
Alliance, Treaty of (1778), 103, 133, 136
Alliance for Progress, 556
Allies (First World War), 417, 430, 451, 479
Allies (Second World War), 493, 494, 496, 506(map); D-Day and, 505; end of, 508; Cold War and, 516–517
Almanac: of Banneker, 116
Almshouses, 62
Almy, William, 153
Al Qaeda, 616, 617, 623, 633–635; September 11, 2001, attacks and, 626
Alta California, 203
Alternating current system, 319
Altgeld, John P., 327
Alton, Illinois, 209
Amalgamated Association of Iron and Steelworkers, 328
Ambulance corps, 265
Amendments to Constitution: in Bill of Rights, 129; listing of, A7–A11. *See also* specific amendments
America(s), 1, 3, 13; Columbian Exchange and, 15–17
America First Committee, 485
American Airlines Flight 175, 615
American Anti-Slavery Society, 188
American Association for Old Age Security, 381
American Bar Association, 378
American Birth Control League, 388, 395
American Board of Customs Commissioners, 85, 86
American Century (Luce), 490
American Civil Liberties Union, 432–433
American Colonization Society, 186
American Council on Education: collegiate athletics and, 452
American Dilemma, An (Myrdal), 541
American Expeditionary Forces (AEF), 421
American Federation of Labor (AFL), 327–328, 426, 466
American Female Moral Reform Society, 184
American Friends Service Committee, 455, 477, 567
American Indian Defense Agency, 467
American Indian Movement (AIM), 19, 578
American Indians: Paleo-Indians and, 3; cultures of, 6(map), 7, 29, 139, 301, 302–305; religion and, 7, 13, 15; Europeans and, 13, 30(illus.), 67, 76–80; Spanish and, 15; trade and, 17–18; colonists and, 22, 45–46; Jesuits and, 23; in eastern North America, 24(map); wampum and, 26; in Jamestown, 28; Pilgrims and, 33; in Pennsylvania, 42; as slaves, 52; families of, 67–68; as servants, 68; in 1754, 78(map); in backcountry, 95–96; claims of, 120; after Revolution, 139; in Lewis and Clark expedition, 147–148; resistance by, 150–151, 175–176, 305; removal of, 155, 174, 176–179, 177(map); War of 1812 and, 155, 156, 160, 163; movement of, 166; treaties with, 175, 303; assimilation of, 176; reparations to, 234; Civil War and, 259, 271–272; wars against, 271–272; Sand Creek Massacre of, 272; containment policy against, 293–295; economic activities of, 301–302; "civilizing" of, 303, 304; Dawes Severalty Act and, 305; in West, 307; in Progressive era, 387; in 1920s, 438; in New Deal, 461, 467; Navajo code-talkers and, 492–493; population of, 544; poverty of, 550–551; in 1970s, 576; Red Power and, 577–578, 577(illus.). *See also* Land
Americanization, 413, 474, 477–479, 517, 622; of Philippines, 407; of Vietnam War, 564, 566
American League (baseball), 352
American Legion, 428, 485
American Liberty League, 462
American Missionary Association, 284
American Party, *see* Know-Nothing (American) Party
American Peace Commission, 430
American Railway Union, 371, 379
American Relief Administration, 476
American Renaissance, 203
American Revolution, 74, 99–107; allegiance in, 92–93; Indians during, 96; supporters and opponents of, 96–99; loyalist foreign settlement and, 98, 98(illus.); battles in, 99, 102–103, 105–106; in North, 102–103, 102(map); in South, 105–106, 106(map); legacy of, 108
American Samoa, 398
Americans with Disabilities Act (1990), 613, 614
American System (Clay), 190, 191
American system of manufacturing, 170
American Tobacco Company, 323, 333
American Union Against Militarism, 419
American University (Beirut), 361
American Woman Suffrage Association, 366
Amnesty Act (1872), 293
Amusement centers, 353(illus.)
Anaconda Copper Company, 307
Anaconda plan, 258
Anarchism, 327, 428, 446
Anasazi people, 4
Ancestry, 544
Anderson, Marian, 472
Andes Mountains, 3
Andros, Edmund, 53
Anglican Church, *see* Church of England
Anglo-America: covenants in, 34; growth of, 41–44; Chesapeake region and, 46; social stratification of, 51; government of, 56; economy of, 62; politics in, 69–71; after Seven Years War, 75; British taxation of, 81. *See also* Colonies and colonization; England (Britain)
Anglo-American relations, 195, 197, 413
Anglos: in Texas, 174; White Hats and, 368; Mexican labor and, 441
Angola, 59, 583
Animals, 13, 15, 301. *See also* specific animals
Annan, Kofi, 634
Annapolis Convention, 122
Annexation: of Texas, 195–197; Cuba and, 244, 245; Hawai'i and, 244, 403–404, 406; Dominican Republic and, 295; by cities, 339; of Virgin Islands, 402; of Samoa, 406; of Wake Island, 406
Antebellum period, 219–221, 229–230, 233. *See also* South

Anthony, Susan B., 282, 287, 366
Anti-Americanism, 557
Antiballistic missile defenses, 583
Anti-Ballistic Missile Treaty, 626
Anti-Bookerites, 386
Anti-Catholicism, 214
Anti-Comintern Pact, 482
Anticommunism, 522–523, 538–540, 601
Anticoolie clubs, 295
Antietam, Battle of, 260, 266
Antifederalists, 109, 125, 128, 129
Antigay movement, 631
Antiglobalization, 621–622
Anti-imperialism, 402, 406–407
Anti-Imperialist League, 407
Anti-Klan laws, 293
Antilynching newspaper, 365
Anti Masonic Almanac, 185
Antimasonry, 183, 185–186
Anti-Saloon League, 383
Anti-Semitism: Brandeis and, 393; of Coughlin, 464; in United States, 469; immigration and, 483. *See also* Jews and Judaism
Antislavery movement: international, 187; violence against, 209; Slave Power and, 241; Cuba and, 245; Republican Party and, 246, 247. *See also* Abolition and abolitionism
Antitrust laws, 335, 390
Antiwar protests: in Vietnam War, 141, 567, 569, 572, 580–581; in Civil War, 270–271; in First World War, 419; in Iraq War (2003–), 628
ANZUS Treaty, 522
Apache Indians, 68, 174, 272
Apartheid, 583, 611
Apollo 8, 572
Appalachian Mountains, 55
Appeal . . . to the Colored Citizens (Walker), 186
Appeasement: at Munich, 482, 483
Appellate courts, 129
Appleton, Nathan, 153
Appliances, 436, 438, 443
Appomattox Court House, 275
Apportionment: in Congress, 124
Apprentice laws, 290
Arabic (ship), 418
Arab-Israeli disputes, 528–529, 629(map); Six-Day War and, 583; Yom Kippur War (1973), 583
Arab world, 513, 576, 606. *See also* Arab-Israeli disputes; Oil and oil industry
Arafat, Yasir, 606, 622
Arapaho Indians, 271, 300
Arbenz Guzmán, Jacobo, 528
Arbitration, 391
Architecture: Jefferson and, 112; skyscrapers, 346
Arctic National Wildlife Refuge, 626
Arctic Ocean: Barent and, 11(illus.)
Ardennes Forest, battle in, 505
Argentina, 163, 593
Argentina (ship), 501
Argonne Forest, battle in, 422
Aristide, Jean-Bertrand, 622
Aristocracy: government by, 111; fears of, 112; American, 209; southern values and, 232–233
Arizona, 240, 308
Arizona (ship), 489
Arkansas, 174, 253, 258

Armada, 18

Armed forces, 148; in Revolution, 99–100, 104–105, 106–107; under Jefferson, 144; standing army and, 156; African Americans in, 266, 267, 268, 406, 503, 540; First World War and, 420, 422; African Americans in, 420–421; Second World War and, 494, 504–505; Japanese Americans in, 503; in Vietnam War, 566; AIDS and, 634. *See also* Military; Soldiers

Armed neutrality policy, 420

Armed Slave, The (Sprang), 283(illus.)

Armistice: Spanish-American War and, 404, 406; in First World War, 422

Arms and armaments: First World War and, 425; Washington Naval Conference and, 477; shipments of, 482, 488; Second World War and, 483, 486, 488, 496, 498; for China, 484. *See also* Weapons

Arms race, 477, 515, 522, 556, 592; missiles and, 583; INF Treaty and, 606; reduction of, 612

Armstrong, Louis, 449

Armstrong, Neil, 590

Army Industrial College, 432

Army-McCarthy hearings, 540

Army of the Republic of Vietnam (ARVN), 563

Arnett, Peter, 602(illus.)

Arnold, Benedict, 106

Around the World with General Grant (Young), 294

ARPANET, 636–637

"Arsenal of democracy," 494, 496

Art(s): republican virtues and, 111–112; in 1920s, 449

Arthur, Chester, 362, 364

Articles of Confederation, 117–120

Articles of Constitution: Article I, 90, 131, A2–A5; Article VI, 129, A7; Article IV, 240–241, A6–A7; Article II, A5–A6; Article III, A6; Article V, A7; Article VII, A7

Article 10: of League of Nations, 430, 431

Artisans, 84, 233, 324

Asante peoples, 8(illus.), 50

Ashcroft, John, 627

Asia: Portugal and, 12; route to, 13; Columbus and, 18–19; immigrants from, 341, 609–610, 630; imperialism in, 398, 407–410, 409(map); Second World War and, 483–484, 513; Cold War in, 519–520. *See also* Southeast Asia; specific countries

Asian Americans, 343, 344, 536

Asians: in West, 307; in cities, 344; segregation of, 400–401

Assassinations: of Lincoln, 275; of McKinley, 389, 410; of King, 555, 570–572; attempts against Castro, 557; of John F. Kennedy, 560, 572

Assemblies, 69–70, 81; in Virginia, 29; in Maryland, 32; in New York, 41; in Massachusetts, 85. *See also* Legislatures

Assembly lines, 319–322, 322(illus.), 324, 352

Assimilation: of Indians, 176, 387, 467; urban neighborhoods and, 343; religion and, 344–345; by African Americans, 385

Associated Press (AP), 479

Associationalism: of Hoover, 450, 461

Associations: leisure, 208; black, 215

Assumption: of state war debts, 130–131

Astor, John Jacob, 209

Astrolabe, 10

Astronomy: Mayan, 3

Aswan Dam, 529

Athletics, *see* Sports

Atlanta: Civil War in, 272, 274

Atlanta Compromise, 386, 387

Atlanta Exposition (1895), 386

Atlanta Journal, 558

Atlanta University, 284

Atlantic Charter, 488

Atlantic creoles, 46

Atlantic Ocean region, 12; exploration of, 13–14; North America and, 39–41; trade routes in, 49(map); telegraph cable in, 321, 321(illus.); Second World War in, 494

Atomic bomb, 494, 497, 508; at Hiroshima and Nagasaki, 509; environmental damage from, 510; after Second World War, 515; Soviet, 519

Atomic diplomacy, 515

Atomic Energy Act (1954), 538

Atomic waste, 510

Attorney general, 129

Auburn prison, 185

Auction in Chatham Street, 165(illus.)

Australia, 98, 204, 311, 522

Austria, 422, 482

Austria-Hungary, 341, 417, 420, 423

Autobiographies, 207

Autobiography (Franklin), 72

Automobiles, 318, 438–439, 440(illus.), 545; Ford and, 319–322; strike in, 466; Second World War and, 497, 535; Nader on, 561; in 1970s, 588; Japan and, 610

Axis powers, 482, 488, 494, 505

Ayer, N. W., & Son, 332

Azores, 12

Aztecs, 4, 15, 19

Ba'athist Party (Iraq), 593

Baby and Child Care (Spock), 546

Baby boom, 535–536, 547; Social Security and, 473

Backcountry, 61, 70–71, 95–96, 97

Back to Africa movement, 216

Bacon's Rebellion, 46

Baffin Island, 14

Baghdad, 602(illus.), 628

Bahamas: Columbus in, 13, 19

Bailey v. Drexel Furniture Company, 436

Baker, Josephine, 449

Bakke, Allan, 591

Balanced-budget amendment, 619

Balance-of-payments deficit, 582

Balance of power, 75, 359, 417–418

Balance of trade: mercantilism and, 50

Balboa, Vasco Nuñez de, 14

Balch, Emily Greene, 427, 476

Baldwin, Roger, 432

Balfour Declaration, 430

Balkan region, 417, 622

Ball, George W., 564

Ballots: in 2000 election, 626

Baltic region, 422, 483, 514, 611

Baltimore, 155, 165

Baltimore, Lords, *see* Calvert family

Baltimore and Ohio Railroad, 167–169

Bank(s) and banking, 161, 172, 192, 250, 264; investments and, 334; property ownership and, 343; 1890s depression and, 370; regulation of, 393; stock market crash and, 450–451; in Great Depression, 455, 459–460; foreign branches and, 479; in Germany, 481; Reagan and, 600

Bank of the United States, 131, 161, 164, 172

Bankruptcy: of governments, 618

Banks, Nathaniel, 274

Banneker, Benjamin, 116

Bantu-speaking peoples, 7

Bao Dai, 520, 529, 530

Baptists, 71, 183, 220, 234, 284, 344; slaves freed by, 72; Southern, 198; black, 388

Barbados, 25, 43

Barbary War, 142, 154

Barbed wire, 314–315

Barbie dolls, 548, 548(illus.)

Barents, William, 11(illus.)

Barone, Michael, 467

Barrios, 344, 441

Barton, Clara, 265

Bartram, John and William, 64–65

Baruch, Bernard, 425, 515

Baruch Plan, 515

Baseball, 207, 352, 354, 354(illus.), 448, 541

Bataan Death March, 495

Batista, Fulgencio, 481, 528

Battles, *see* Wars and warfare; specific battles and wars

Baum, L. Frank, 374–375

Bayard, Thomas E., 400

Bay of Pigs invasion, 556–557

B.C.E., 3

Beach, Moses Yale, 209

Beals, Jessie Tarbox, 401(illus.)

Beard, Charles A., 384, 427

Beatles, 569, 571, 571(illus.)

Beauregard, P. G. T., 258

Beaver pelt trade, 17–18, 22, 23

Beaver Wars, 44

Beecher family: Catharine and Mary, 210. *See also* Stowe, Harriet Beecher

Begin, Menachem, 592

Belgium, 417, 485

Bell, John, 251

Bellamy, Francis, 551

Belleau Wood, battle at, 422

Bemis, Edward, 335

Benefits: in postwar period, 536

Benevolent societies, 188

Bennitt, James and Nancy, 223

Berbers, 7

Berenson, Senda, 355

Beringia, 3

Bering Strait: land bridge at, 3

Berkeley: Free Speech Movement in, 568–569

Berkeley, John (Lord), 41

Berkeley, William, 46

Berlin: Khrushchev and, 525

Berlin, Ira, 46

Berlin airlift, 519

Berlin Wall, 556, 611

Bernard, Francis, 85

Bernstein, Carl, 585

Bethlehem Steel Company, 323

Bethune, Mary McLeod, 464
Beverages: colonial, 66, 66(illus.)
Biardot, Alphonse, 356
Bibb, Henry, 216
Bible, 579–580, 607
Bible belt, 198
Bicameral legislature, 123
Bicycles, 353
Biddle, Nicholas, 192
Big business, 335, 381; in South, 291; cattle industry and, 315; in Gilded Age, 358; Theodore Roosevelt and, 391; Taft and, 392; in 1920s, 435–436. See also Business; Corporations
Big Four: after First World War, 430
Big government, 597, 619
Bight of Biafra, 50, 59
Big Three: in Second World War, 507
Bilingualism: in Los Angeles, 207; in Puerto Rico, 414; Florida and, 610
Billboards, 332
Billionaires, 601
Bill of Rights (U.S.), 124, 125, 129. See also Amendments to Constitution; specific amendments
Bills of rights: in Northwest Ordinance, 120
Bin Laden, Osama, 623, 626, 627, 628
Biogenetics, 632–633
Biological and Toxin Weapons Convention (1972), 626
Birmingham, Alabama, 558, 560
Birney, James G., 188, 197
Birth control, 211, 226, 351, 358; movement, 388; Sanger and, 388, 394–395; clinics, 394–395; in 1920s, 443; in 1950s, 546; population growth and, 590. See also Pill, the
Birth Control Clinical Research Bureau, 395
Birth Control Federation of America, 395
Birth of a Nation, The (film), 356, 429
Birth rate: decline in, 210, 350–351; in Great Depression, 455; in Second World War, 500; from 1945 to 1964, 535(illus.); in 1970s, 591; of Hispanics, 610
Bison, see Buffalo (American bison)
Black, Hugo, 471
Black Boy (Wright), 541
"Black cabinet," 464
Black codes, 174, 285–286
Black Death, 10
Blackfish (chief), 92
Black Kettle (chief), 271–272, 303
Blacklists: of union members, 263–264, 327
Black market: in Second World War, 499
Blackmun, Harry, 585
Black Muslims, 568
Blackness: concept of, 207
Black Panthers, 568
Black Power movement, 568
Black Robes (Jesuits), 23
Blacks, 12, 31, 116. See also African Americans; Africans; Free blacks
Black Shirts (fascists): in United States, 457
Black Star line, 441
Black Thursday, 450
Black Tuesday, 451
Black vigilance committees, 243
Blaine, James G., 360, 364, 403
Blair, Ezell, 553

Blake, Eubie, 449
Bland-Allison Act (1878), 363
Blatch, Harriot Stanton, 388
Bleeding Kansas, 248
Blended families, 591, 631
Blitzkrieg (lightning war), 483
Blockades: by Royal Navy, 155; in Civil War, 258, 262; in Spanish-American War, 406; in First World War, 417; of Berlin, 519; of Cuba, 557
Blue-collar workers, 543–544, 588
Blues (music), 217, 571
Blumenthal, Sidney, 625
Bly, Nellie (Elizabeth Cochrane), 356, 402
B'nai B'rith, 208, 329
Board games, 352
Boarding process, 351
Board of Trade and Plantations, 54–55
"Boat people" (Southeast Asians), 581
Bodegas, 441
Boesky, Ivan, 609
Boiardi, Hector (Chef Boyardee), 356
Boleyn, Anne, 27
Bolshevik Revolution (1917), 422, 423, 515
Bolshevism, 382, 428–429, 430
Bombings, see Atomic bomb
Bond, Julian, 558
Bonded servants, 21, 53
Bonds: risky, 601
Bonsack, James, 323
Bonus Army, 459
Book of Mormon, 202
Books, 356; fundamentalists on, 607
Boom-and-bust cycles, 164–166, 333
Boone, Daniel, 92, 95
Boone, Pat, 549
Boonesborough, 92
Booth, John Wilkes, 275
Borah, William, 480
Borden, Gail, 331
Border(s): with Canada, 162; of Louisiana Purchase, 163; with Oregon, 163, 197; dispute over, 195; between North and South Korea, 522; illegal immigrants and, 610; international, 633
Borderlands: of New Spain, 62
Border states, 253, 258
Bork, Robert, 599
Born-again Christians, 590, 597, 607
Borrowing: by United States, 600
Bosnia: First World War and, 417
Bosnia-Herzegovina, 622
Bosnian Muslims, 622
Bosque Redondo Reservation, 272
Bosses (political), 348–349, 360, 379, 381, 393
Boston, 33; Andros in, 53; population of, 69; Stamp Act protests in, 83; confrontations in, 86–90; Committee of Correspondence in, 90; militia in, 99; free blacks in, 115; immigrants in, 213; anti-Catholicism in, 214; police strike in, 437
Boston (ship), 403
Boston Manufacturing Company, 153(illus.), 170–171
Boston marriages, 351
Boston Massacre, 86–88, 87(illus.)
Boston Red Sox, 352, 449
Boston Tea Party, 89

Boston Women's Health Collective, 579
Boulder Dam (Hoover Dam), 467
Boundaries: colonial, 81; after Revolution, 107; Rio Grande as, 240; Venezuelan dispute and, 404. See also Border(s)
Bow, Clara, 445
Bowers v. Hardwick, 599
Bowery (New York City), 208
Boxer Rebellion, 396, 410
Boxing, 207
Boycotts, 366; Stamp Act, 85–86; after Coercive Acts, 90; of British goods, 94; of Montgomery buses, 541; of table grapes, 577; of Iraq, 612
Boyne, Battle of the, 200
Bracero program, 550
Braddock, James, 468
Bradwell, Myra, 295
Bradwell v. Illinois, 295–296
Brady, Mathew, 261(illus.)
Bragg, Braxton, 260
Brain Trust, 460
Branch Davidians, 623
Brandeis, Louis D., 384, 393
Brand names, 332
Brandywine Creek, battle at, 103
Brant, Mary and Joseph, 103
Brazil, 17, 21, 25, 47
Bread-and-butter reforms, 379
Breckinridge, John C., 251, 253(illus.)
Breed's Hill, battle at, 99
Breevoort, Laura Carson and Henry, Jr., 209
Bremer, Frederick, 216
Bremer, Fredrika, 201
Br'er Rabbit folktales, 230
Brest-Litovsk, Treaty of, 422
Bretton Woods Conference (1945), 514
Brewster, Charles, 256
Brice, Fanny, 355
Bridges, 346
Briefe and True Report of the New Found Land of Virginia, A (Harriot), 18
Britain, see England (Britain)
British and Foreign Anti-Slavery Society, 187
British Empire, 53–55. See also England (Britain)
British Guiana, 404
British Trans-Indian railroad, 398
Briton, Nan, 437
Brook Farm, 203
Brooklyn Bridge, 346
Brooklyn Heights, battle at, 102
Brooks, Preston, 248
Brotherhood of Sleeping Car Porters, 472, 497, 559
Brown, Albert G., 245
Brown, James, 569
Brown, John, 237, 248, 251, 254–255
Brown, Joseph E., 270
Brown, Moses and Obadiah, 153
Brown, Noah, 155
Brown, William Hill, 111, 113
Brown, William Wells, 187, 187(illus.)
Brown Power movement, 576
Brown v. Board of Education of Topeka, 298, 366, 433, 527, 534, 541
Bruce, Blanche K., 284
Brundage, Avery, 469

Bryan, William Jennings, 373, 374, 391, 406; First World War and, 415, 416; Scopes trial and, 446–447

Brzezinski, Zbigniew, 592

Bubonic plague, *see* Black Death

Buchanan, James, 245, 248–249, 250, 364

Buchanan, Pat, 626

Buck, Pearl, 483

Buckley, William F., 568

Bud Dajo, Battle of, 407

Budget, *see* Federal budget; Spending

Budget and Accounting Act (1921), 437

Buffalo (American bison), 17, 301, 302, 305, 314

"Buffalo Bill," 299

Bulge, Battle of the, 505

Bull Moose Party, 392

Bull Run, First Battle of, 258

Bunch, Charlotte, 579

Bundy, McGeorge, 555

Bunker Hill, Battle of, 99

Buppies (black urban professionals), 609

Bureaucracy: in England, 100; in First World War, 423; Homeland Security and, 531

Bureau of Corporations, 390

Bureau of Human Rights, 594

Bureau of Indian Affairs (BIA), 438, 467, 578

Bureau of Public Roads, 439

Bureau of Reclamation, 467

Bureau of Refugees, Freedmen, and Abandoned Lands, *see* Freedmen's Bureau

Burger, Warren, 585

Burgoyne, John, 102, 103

Burlingame Treaty (1868), 400

Burma, 513

Burnham, Daniel, 407

Burns, Anthony, 244

Burnside, Ambrose, 260

Burr, Aaron, 135, 149

Burton, James, 267

Bus boycott: in Montgomery, 534, 541, 542

Bush, George H. W., 596, 597, 611–613, 618; budget and, 600; Iran-contra and, 604; Operation Desert Storm and, 612; ADA and, 613, 614; Somalia and, 622; environment and, 623

Bush, George W., 414, 531, 617; Social Security and, 473; 2000 election and, 625–626; tax plan of, 626; antiterrorism and, 626–627; stem-cell research and, 633

Bush, Neil: S&L scandal and, 601

Bushy Run, battle at, 81

Business: in market economy, 159; regulation of, 180; African Americans in, 216, 366; Civil War and, 257–258, 263; organization of, 318, 333–334; government and, 334–335, 425, 436–437; urban sprawl and, 339; silver vs. gold issue and, 363; in 1920s, 435–436; Great Depression and, 451, 457; New Deal and, 462; in Second World War, 496–497; productivity and, 588; Reaganomics and, 599; globalization of, 620; Enron collapse and, 627. *See also* Corporations

Business cycle: in Great Depression, 457

Busing, 585

Butler, Andrew P., 248

Butler, Pierce, 218

Byrd, James, Jr., 624

Byrnes, James F., 515

Cabinet: Jackson's Kitchen Cabinet and, 191; women in, 464. *See also* specific presidents

Cable Act (1922), 438

Cable cars, 339

Cabot, John, 14

Cabot, Sebastian, 14

Cabral, Pedro Álvares, 14

Cahokia, 4

Calendar: in Cahokia, 4

Calhoun, John C., 161, 191, 192, 239–240; and 1824 election, 189, 190

California, 45, 238, 240, 295, 300, 543; gold in, 203, 204, 307; Mexican Americans in, 215; sectionalism and, 241; as free state, 242; oil in, 307; irrigation in, 309; in 1920s, 440; Proposition 13 in, 589, 618

Californios, 215

Calley, William, 581

Calvert family, George and Cecilius, 31

Calvin, John, 27

Cambodia, 565(map), 580, 581

Cameron, Paul Carrington, 224

Cameroon, 50, 59

Camp David accords (1979), 592, 604

Camp Fire Girls, 524

Camp meetings, 222

"Camptown Races" (Foster), 217

Canada, 14, 36, 45; Indians in, 5, 103, 304; Norsemen in, 13–14; French settlement of, 22–23; economy of, 62; Quebec Act and, 89; loyalists in, 98; American Revolution and, 99; War of 1812 and, 154, 156; border with, 162; fugitive slave flight to, 249; immigrants from, 341

Canals, 164, 166, 167, 399

Canal Zone, 412, 592

Canary Islands, 12, 17

Cannon, Joseph ("Uncle Joe"), 380

Cantigny, battle at, 422

Cape Ann, 33

Cape Breton Island, 14, 18

Capital (city), 131. *See also* Washington, D.C.

Capital (financial), 159, 168, 323

Capital gains tax, 619

Capitalism, 399, 479; Progressives and, 379; foreign trade and, 399; Lenin on, 422; Great Depression and, 455; Third World and, 527

Capitol building (U.S.), 234

Capone, Al, 449

Caravans, 7, 12

Caravels, 11(illus.)

Cárdenas, Lázaro, 481

Cardozo, Francis, 284

Caribbean region: Columbus in, 13; Spanish in, 14; European settlement of, 20, 21, 25; sugar industry in, 25; slavery in, 47, 59, 228; economy of, 62; in Revolution, 105; Quasi-War in, 136; fugitive slave flight to, 249; immigrants from, 342(illus.), 610; U.S. hegemony in, 411(map), 412; intervention in, 604, 605(map)

Carlisle riots: over Constitution, 109

Carlisle School, 305

Carmichael, Stokely, 568

Carnegie, Andrew, 334, 406, 419

Carnegie Foundation, 527

Carnegie Steel: Homestead strike and, 328, 371

Carolinas, 42–43, 53, 70–71, 80. *See also* North Carolina; South Carolina

Carpentier, Georges, 448

Carpetbaggers, 291, 292

Carretta, Vincent, 72–73

Cars, *see* Automobiles

Carson, Kit, 272

Carson, Rachel, 550

Cartels: in New Deal, 461

Carter, James Earl ("Jimmy"), 576, 585, 587, 597; Cold War and, 591–592, 601–603; Camp David accords and, 592; Iran hostage crisis and, 592–593; human rights and, 593, 594; in Haiti, 622

Carter, Rosalynn and Amy, 587

Carter Doctrine, 592

Carteret, George, 41

Cartier, Jacques, 14

Carver, George Washington, 314

Casey, William, 604

Cash-and-carry arms sales, 483

Cash registers, 323, 324

Cass, Lewis, 241, 242

Cassatt, Alexander, 379

Castle Garden (immigrant center), 213

Castro, Fidel, 481, 523, 528, 556–557. *See also* Cuba

Casualties, *see* specific wars and battles

Catawba Indians, 76

Catcher in the Rye, The (Salinger), 549

Catell, J. M., 427

Catherine of Aragon, 27

Catholicism, *see* Roman Catholicism

Catt, Carrie Chapman, 388, 419, 476

Cattle and cattle industry, 51, 314–315. *See also* Ranching

Caucus: for nominating candidates, 186; congressional, 189

Cavalry: in Civil War, 260; in Spanish-American War, 388

Cayuga Indians, 44, 103

C.E., 3

Celts: Irish as, 213, 214

Censorship: in First World War, 427

Census, 124; in New York, 41; multiracial category on, 56; reapportionment and, 90–91; in 1790, 137; Hispanics on, 576; POSSLQ and, 591; in 2000, 630

Central America, 410–411, 605(map), 610, 612. *See also* Latin America

Central banking system, 393

Central High School, Little Rock, 541

Central Intelligence Agency (CIA), 517–519, 527, 528, 531; foreign policy and, 523; Vietnam and, 529–530; Bay of Pigs and, 556–557; in Africa, 583; Islamic guerrillas and, 592; Nicaragua and, 604

Central Pacific Railroad, 264, 310

Central Powers, 417

Century of Dishonor, A (Jackson), 304

Cermak, Anton, 458

Cessions of land, 118(map), 163, 176. *See also* American Indians; Land

Chaco Canyon, 4

Chain stores, 332

Chamberlain, Neville, 482
Champlain, Lake, 154–155
Champlain, Samuel de, 22, 26(illus.)
Chancellorsville, Battle of, 268
Chaplin, Charlie, 356
Chapman, Maria, 188
Charbonneau, Toussaint, 147
Charitable associations, 114
Charity Organization Societies, 346–347
Charles I (England), 28, 31, 41
Charles II (England), 41, 42
Charles VII (France), 10
Charles River Bridge Company, 166–167
Charles River Bridge v. Warren Bridge, 166
Charleston, 43, 84, 105, 279
Charleston Mercury, 270
Charles Town, *see* Charleston
Charlotte: A Tale of Truth (Rowson), 113
Charter(s): of Virginia, 28, 30; of Massachu-
    setts, 33, 54, 89; colonial, 53; state land claims
    and, 117–119; bank, 161, 192; corporate,
    194; of League of Nations, 430, 431
Charter grants, 167
Chase, Samuel, 145
Château-Thierry, battle at, 422
Chattanooga, Battle of, 274
Chávez, César, 576
Checks and balances, 117
Chemical industry, 318, 322–323
Cheney, Dick, 628
Cheney, James, 558
Cherokee Indians, 52, 76, 80, 120, 139, 176;
    attacks by, 96; removal of, 176–177, 178;
    Trail of Tears and, 178; Jackson and, 191; in
    Civil War, 259
Cherokee National Council, 177
Cherokee Nation v. Georgia, 177
Cherokee Phoenix, 176
Chesapeake (ship), 151–152
Chesapeake region: colonies in, 21, 28–36;
    government in, 43–44; tobacco industry in,
    46; economy of, 63; free blacks in, 115
Chesnut, Mary Boykin, 224, 226
Cheyenne Indians, 271, 299–300
Chicago, 154, 170; Columbian Exposition in,
    299, 350; Haymarket Riot in, 327, 371; real
    estate in (1890–1920), 339; Hull House in,
    349; African Americans in, 426, 541; race
    riot in (1919), 429; suburbs of, 441; postwar
    housing in, 536; Democratic National
    Convention (1968) in, 572
Chicago Vice Commission, 383
Chicago White Sox, 448
Chicanos/Chicanas, 577. *See also* Mexicans and
    Mexican Americans
Chickasaw Indians, 45, 120, 175, 176, 178
Chief justice, 145
Child, Lydia Maria, 188
Childbearing, 59, 211; by white southern
    women, 226; in 1950s, 546; by infertile
    women, 632
Childbirth: in 1920s, 443
Childcare, 498, 546
Childhood, 351
Child labor, 324–325, 436, 443–444; in textile
    mills, 323; regulation of, 325, 376, 381, 393
Children: in Chesapeake, 32; in New England,
    36; slave, 51, 68, 69, 215, 226, 228; after

Revolution, 112; on overland trails, 205;
    family size and, 211, 350–351; of freedpeople,
    290; in 1920s, 443–444; Barbie dolls and,
    548, 548(illus.); born outside marriage, 631
Chile, 163, 204, 480, 583
Chin, Vincent, 610
China, 519; Polo on, 10–11; water route to, 19;
    trade with, 119; baseball in, 354; missionaries
    in, 361, 396–397, 401; Japan and, 398, 413,
    417, 476, 485(map); communications with,
    402; and Open Door policy, 407–410,
    409(map); dollar diplomacy and, 413; sover-
    eignty of, 477; Second World War and,
    483–484, 513; Mao Zedong and, 519;
    communism in, 520; Korean War and, 521;
    Nixon and, 583; Tiananmen Square slaughter
    in, 611. *See also* Open Door policy
China lobby, 520
Chinatowns, 344, 610
Chinese Exclusion Act (1882), 344, 507
Chinese immigrants, 204, 211, 295, 307, 308,
    400; as railroad labor, 310; in Australia, 311
Chinese people: segregation of, 344, 400–401
Chinese Revolution (1911), 483
Chinook Indians, 5
Chippewa Indians, 80, 120, 155, 156
Chisholm v. Georgia, 129
Chivington, John, 271, 303
Chlorine gas, 421
Chocolate, 66
Choctaw Indians, 45, 120, 175, 176, 177–178
"Christiana riot" (1851), 242
Christianity: in Europe, 10; spread of, 11; in
    Americas, 15; Pueblo peoples and, 45;
    among slaves, 46–47, 69, 230; Indians and,
    176; fundamentalist, 198, 446–447, 590,
    607–608; in China, 396–397; in 1950s, 545;
    born-again, 590, 597, 607; conservative,
    607. *See also* Evangelicalism; Missions and
    missionaries; Religion
Chrysler: UAW and, 466
Churches: in New England, 37; in New York,
    41; colonial attendance in, 64; sex segrega-
    tion in, 65; African Americans in, 115, 215,
    216, 224, 284, 344; in Second Great Awak-
    ening, 184; in South, 220; Civil War and,
    265. *See also* Religion
Churchill, Winston, 487, 496, 507(illus.);
    Atlantic Charter and, 488; at Teheran, 505;
    on "iron curtain," 515, 516(illus.)
Church of England, 27, 32, 41, 54, 71
Church of Jesus Christ of Latter-Day Saints,
    see Mormons
CIA, *see* Central Intelligence Agency (CIA)
Cigarettes, 323, 330. *See also* Tobacco and
    tobacco industry
Cigar Makers' Union, 327
Cigars, 404
Cimarron (film), 316
Cincinnati, 172, 175
Cincinnati Daily Commercial, 249
Cincinnati Freeman, 249
CIO, *see* Committee for Industrial Organization
    (CIO)
Circular letter: as protest, 85
Circuses, 355
Cities and towns, 377–378; in Chesapeake, 31;
    coastal, 35; in Massachusetts, 35; African

Americans in, 69, 115, 223–224, 440; special-
    ization in, 171; western settlement and, 175;
    growth of, 205–209, 338–343; in 1830 and
    1860, 206(map); wealthy in, 209; slums in,
    209–210; middle class in, 210; of Confederacy,
    262; food riots in, 270; railroads and, 310;
    pollution in, 336; society and, 337–338; work
    zone in, 339; geographic mobility and, 341;
    occupational mobility in, 342; neighborhoods
    in, 343–345; sanitation in, 345; poverty in,
    346–347, 550; crime and violence in, 347;
    management of, 347–350; family life and,
    350–352; leisure, mass culture, and, 352–356;
    ethnicity in, 356, 357; government for, 380,
    381; in 1920s, 440–441; in Second World
    War, 499; in Sunbelt, 543; in South, 588–589;
    in North and Midwest, 589; social crises in,
    608–609
Citizens and citizenship: residency period for,
    137; African American, 237, 249, 287, 366;
    Supreme Court on, 295; for Indians, 303,
    305, 438; for Asians, 344; for Hawaiians,
    404; for Puerto Ricans, 414
Citizens Committee (New Orleans), 366
City Beautiful movement, 350, 407
City commission plan, 380, 381
City manager plan, 380, 381
City planning, 378
City-states: Mayan, 4; Muslim in Africa, 7
City upon a hill, 34
Civic organizations, 378, 448
Civic reform, 349
Civic rituals, 65
Civilian Conservation Corps (CCC), 461
Civilization: Mesoamerican, 3–4
"Civilizing": of Indians, 176, 303, 304
Civil liberties: First World War and, 417,
    427–428; ACLU and, 432–433; in Soviet
    Union, 515; in 1980s, 608
Civil rights: for blacks, 215–216, 232; Four-
    teenth Amendment and, 297–298; Du Bois
    and, 387; after Second World War, 540–543;
    J. Edgar Hoover on, 541; Supreme Court
    on, 541; affirmative action and, 578. *See also*
    Civil rights movement
Civil Rights Acts: of 1875, 293, 366; of 1964,
    298, 560–561, 567, 578, 579, 591, 608; of
    1957, 542
Civil rights bills: of 1866, 286; Kennedy and,
    559
Civil rights movement, 541–543; Kennedy
    and, 544; in 1960s, 557–560, 567–568;
    March on Washington and, 559–560,
    559(illus.)
Civil service, 350, 360–362, 364, 379, 381
Civil Service Commission, 362
Civil war(s): in England, 41, 43; in Latin
    America and Caribbean region, 412; in
    Mexico, 412–413; in Russia, 430; in Spain,
    482; in China (1920s), 484; in Greece, 516;
    in China (1949), 519; Korean War as, 521;
    in Rwanda, 622
Civil War (U.S.), 251–254, 256–277, 261(illus.);
    state-national powers and, 124; nullification
    and, 157–158; from 1861–1862, 258–260;
    Union naval campaign in, 259; in West,
    259–260; campaigns in, 260; casualties of,
    260, 267, 269, 274, 276; emancipation and,

265–267; in 1863, 268–269; Indians during, 271–272; in 1864–1865, 272–275; Britain and, 273; Lee's surrender in, 275; Reconstruction and, 281–282; pensions for veterans of, 360, 364
Civil Works Administration, 461
Clanton family, 308, 309
Clarissa (Richardson), 113
Clark, George Rogers, 96
Clark, William, 147–148
Clarke, Edward, 445
Classes, 62; in South, 221–226, 232–234; draft and, 262–263; in postwar period, 534. *See also* Elites; specific classes
Clay, Henry, 161, 162(map), 164, 189–190, 191, 192, 197; slavery compromise and, 241–242
Clayton Anti-Trust Act (1914), 393
Clayton-Bulwer Treaty (1850), 412
Clean Air Act: of 1970, 336; of 1990, 613
"Clear and present danger," 428
Clemenceau, Georges, 421, 430
Clergy: in 1920s, 448
Clerical positions: women in, 324
Cleveland, 426, 441, 589
Cleveland, Grover, 328, 364, 372, 373, 403; 1890s depression and, 370
Clifford, Clark, 570
Clinton, Bill, 618, 619, 622–623; globalization and, 617; impeachment of, 617, 624–625; healthcare and, 619; New Economy and, 620; on future, 636
Clinton, DeWitt, 156, 167
Clinton, George, 149, 152
Clinton, Henry, 105
Clinton, Hillary Rodham, 618, 619, 624
Closed shop, 436, 498, 534
Clothing: ready-made, 171, 319, 323, 332; of miners, 203; of Bowery youth culture, 208; of slaves, 226; cultural adaptation and, 344; in 1920s, 445; in Second World War, 498
CNN, 602, 612
Coal and coal industry, 336, 390–391, 498
Coaling stations, 244, 402
Coalitions: in Gilded Age, 360. *See also* Democratic Party; Republican Party
Cobbett, William, 127
Coca-Cola, 477
Cocaine, 608–609
Codes: in Second World War, 492–493, 496
Cody, "Buffalo Bill," 299
Coeducational colleges, 384
Coercive (Intolerable) Acts (1774), 89
Coeur d'Alene, Idaho: miners' strike at, 371
Coffee and coffeehouses, 66
Cohan, George M., 355
COLAs (cost-of-living adjustments), 543
Cold Harbor, battle at, 274
Cold War, 513, 514–520; use of term, 516–517; Eisenhower and, 522–525, 538; People-to-People campaign in, 524; national security state and, 531; domestic politics in, 536–538; anticommunism and, 538–540; in 1960s, 554–555; Kennedy and, 555–557; Nixon, Kissinger, and, 582–583; Carter and, 591–592; Reagan and, 596, 601–603; end of, 611; costs of, 611–612
Cold War, The (Lippmann), 517

Cole (ship): attack on, 623
Cole, Nat ("King"), 545
Collar Laundry Union, 329
Collective bargaining, 326, 394
Collective security, 431, 476, 488
Colleges, *see* Universities and colleges
Collier, John, 467
Colombia, 163, 412
Colonies and colonization, 20–38, 399; Portuguese, 12, 18; Spanish, 14–15, 22; English, 18, 20, 21–22, 25–37, 42(illus.), 57–58; French, 18, 22; on Providence Island, 20, 21; permanent European, 23(illus.); Dutch, 24–25; Caribbean, 25; Swedish, 25; joint-stock companies and, 28; Chesapeake, 28–32; in New England, 32–36; conflicts among, 40–41; in Restoration, 41; Quaker, 41–42; slaves in, 46–47; Navigation Acts and, 50–51; government in, 53; society in, 55; population in 1775, 59; economic growth in, 62–63, 72; cultures of, 64–67; families in, 67–69; assemblies in, 69–70; Great Awakening in, 71–72; wars in (1689–1763), 77(illus.); authority over, 81–82; George III and, 94; navalism and, 403; after First World War, 430; Vietnam and, 512; Third World nations as, 513
Colorado, 195, 240, 307, 309
"Colored Americans," 216
Colored Farmers' National Alliance, 368
Colored Women's Federation, 388
Color line: in baseball, 352, 541
Colson, Charles, 585
Colt, Samuel, 170
Columbian Exchange, 15–17
Columbian Exposition (1893), 299, 350
Columbia University: in First World War, 427
Columbine High School: murders at, 623–624, 624(illus.)
Columbus, Christopher, 13–14, 18
Columbus Day, 19
Comanche Indians, 17, 174
Comic operas, 355
Comics, 356
Commander-in-chief, 100, 124
Commerce: Dutch, 38; Atlantic slave trade and, 47–51; under Articles of Confederation, 117, 119; regulation of, 124; after Revolution, 151–152; manufacturing and, 152, 171–172; Supreme Court on, 166; Northeast, 167; Wilson and, 393; foreign, 399. *See also* Trade
Commercial farming, 169–170, 247, 314, 368
Commission on Civil Rights, 542–543
Commission plan, *see* City commission plan
Committee for Industrial Organization (CIO), 466
Committee on Public Information (CPI), 427
Committees of Correspondence, 88, 90, 93–94
Committees of observation and inspection, 94
Committee to Aid the Black Poor, 98
Committee to Defend America by Aiding the Allies, 485
Committee to Re-elect the President (CREEP), 585
Commons, John R., 335
Common Sense (Paine), 100–101
Commonwealth: in Massachusetts, 34; Puerto Rico as, 414

Commonwealth v. Hunt, 174
Communications, 356, 402; industry, 535
Communism: Marx and, 371; Red Scare (1919–1920) and, 428–429; in China, 484, 520; of Ho Chi Minh, 511, 512; policy toward, 512–513; in Greece, 516; McCarthy and, 522–523; in Vietnam, 529–530; in Southeast Asia, 581; Reagan and, 601; in eastern Europe, 611
Communist Control Act, 539
Communist Party of the United States of America, 428, 458–459, 464, 539
Communities: black, 215, 223–224, 265; "dry," 383. *See also* Utopian communities
Community Action Programs, 562
Commutation fees, 271
Commuter railroads, 339
Compulsory school-attendance laws, 325, 331, 352, 383
Computer(s), 636–637, 637
Computer revolution, 543, 590, 620
Comstock laws, 388
Concerned Women for America, 607
Concord, battle at, 99
Conestoga Indians, 95
Coney Island, 353(illus.)
Confederacies: of western Indians, 120
Confederacy (Civil War South): formation of, 252; states in, 258; defensive strategy of, 258–259; Indians and, 259; resources of, 259(illus.); centralization in, 260–261, 270; economy of, 261, 262; draft in, 262–263; Emancipation Proclamation and, 266; emancipation plan of, 267; food riots in, 270; diplomacy and, 272, 273; invasion of, 274; financial costs of war, 275–276; battle flag of, 277. *See also* Civil War (U.S.); Reconstruction; South
Confederate Congress, 261, 267
Confederate States of America (CSA), *see* Confederacy (Civil War South)
Confederation Congress, 240
Confiscation acts (1861, 1862), 265
Congo, 59, 583
Congregationalism (Puritanism), 33, 36, 41, 53, 65
Congress (U.S.): government by, 93–94, 100; Declaration of Independence and, 101–102; Articles of Confederation and, 119, 122; in Virginia Plan, 123; Constitution and, 124; powers of, 124; First, 128–129; assumption of state debts by, 131; factions in, 134; in War of 1812, 154; gag rule in, 240; Lincoln's 10 percent plan and, 281; ex-Confederates in, 285; and Andrew Johnson, 286; and 1876 election, 296; foreign affairs and, 530; 103rd, 618; Clinton and, 619. *See also* Continental Congress
Congressional Reconstruction, 286–289, 290, 291
Congress of Racial Equality (CORE), 503, 558, 559, 568
Conkling, Roscoe, 360, 364
Connecticut, 35, 53
Connecticut River region, 35, 45
Conner, Howard, 492
Connor, Eugene ("Bull"), 558
Conscientious objectors (COs): in First World War, 421

Conscription, *see* Draft (military)
Conservation, 308, 391
Conservatives and conservatism, 406, 427, 537, 585, 597–601, 625; on government regulation, 180; on War on Poverty, 562; in 1960s, 568; on Supreme Court, 599; in 1994 elections, 619
Conspiracy laws: organized labor and, 173–174
Constitution(s): state, 117; in Missouri, 164; Cherokee, 176; Lecompton, 250; Confederate, 270; in Reconstruction, 290; Cuban, 411–412
Constitution (ship), 155
Constitution (U.S.), 220; on representative apportionment, 90; drafting of, 110; events leading to, 122–123; as supreme law of the land, 124; ratification of, 124–125, 128; document, A2–A7. *See also* Amendments to Constitution; Articles of Constitution; Bill of Rights (U.S.)
Constitutional Convention (1787), 122–124
Constitutional conventions: during Reconstruction, 285, 290
Constitutional doctrines, 394
Constitutional Union Party, 251
Construction, 345, 346
Consumer goods, 329–330, 545
Consumers and consumerism, 434, 435–436, 549; colonial, 65–67, 86; stores and, 332; protection measures, 385, 561; in 1920s, 441; Great Depression and, 451; debt of, 545, 590; in 1980s, 609. *See also* Materialism
Consumer society, 313, 318–319, 329–330
Containment doctrine, 512, 517, 519; in Asia, 519–520, 567; CIA and, 528; Kennedy and, 555
Continental Army: soldiers in, 104
Continental Association, 94, 95, 100
Continental Congress, 117; First, 93–94; Second, 95, 100, 101
Continental currency, 119
Contraception, *see* Birth control
Contract with America, 617, 619
Contras, 604
Contrast, The (Tyler), 111
Convention of 1818, 162
Conventions: for secession, 252, 253
Conversion (religious): of indigenous peoples, 11, 21; by Jesuits, 22–23; in New England, 35; by Catholics and Protestants, 35–36; revivalism and, 183
Cook, James, 98
Coolidge, Calvin, 434, 436, 437
Cooney, Joseph, 317
Cooper, Peter, 167
Copland, Aaron, 450
Copley, John Singleton, 64(illus.), 74, 112(illus.)
Copper: in West, 307
Copperheads, 271
Coquette, The (Foster), 113
Coral Sea, Battle of the, 495(map)
Cordon sanitaire (buffer zone), 430
Corn (maize), 3, 4, 16, 16(illus.), 301, 314
Cornell University, 126
Cornstalk (chief), 92
Cornwallis, Charles (Lord), 106, 106(map)
Coronado, Francisco Vásquez de, 14

Coronado Coal Company v. United Mine Workers, 436
Coronavirus, 633
Corporations, 166, 179–180, 194; consolidation of, 333–334, 371; taxation of, 425; international, 479; ties with Nazi Germany, 482; in Second World War, 497; mergers by, 601; protest against, 621–622. *See also* Business
Corps of Discovery, 147–148
Corruption: during Civil War, 264; in Reconstruction, 292; in Grant administration, 293; political machines, bosses, and, 348–349; spoils system and, 360–362; Progressives and, 381; in 1980s, 596
Cortés, Hernán, 14–15
Costa Rica: Oscar Arias Sánchez in, 604
Cotton, John, 37
Cotton and cotton industry, 152; in South, 170, 220, 224, 225; commerce in, 171; in Mississippi valley, 174; Civil War and, 264, 367, 368. *See also* Textile industry
Cotton gin, 170
Coughlin, Charles (Father), 464
Council of Economic Advisors, 534
Councils: in New England, 43
Counterculture, 569–570
Counterinsurgency, 556
Counterterrorism, 626–627
"Country" interest, 55
Coureurs de bois, 45
Court-packing scheme, 470–471
"Court parties," 55
Courts: vice-admiralty, 82; creation of, 129. *See also* Supreme Court (U.S.)
Courtship: automobiles and, 439
Covenant: of League of Nations, 430, 431
Covenant Chain, 44(illus.)
Covenant idea (Massachusetts), 34
Covert operations: by CIA, 519, 523, 527, 528, 604
Cowboys, 214, 308, 314, 315, 315(illus.)
Cowell, Henry, 450
Cowpens, battle at, 106
Cox, James M., 437
Coxey, Jacob S., 372
Coxey's army, 372
Crack cocaine, 608–609
Craft unions, 174, 327, 466
Crawford, William, H., 189–190
Crazy Horse (Oglala Sioux), 303–304
Credit, 172, 440(illus.); of government, 130; economy and, 164; for settlers, 175; for land sales, 193; collapse of, 194; for farmers, 393; in 1920s, 439; in 1930s, 471; in 1970s, 588; in 1960s and 1970s, 589–590
Creditors: gold vs. silver issue and, 363
Creek Indians, 52, 80, 106, 120, 155, 175, 176; removal of, 178
Creel, George, 427
Creoles, 46, 53
Crime and criminals: punishment of, 65; urban, 209, 347; after Second World War, 549
Crisis, The (Paine), 102
Crittenden Compromise (1860), 252
Croats, 622
Croker, Richard, 348
Cromwell, Oliver, 41
Cronkite, Walter, 560

Crop-lien system, 367–368
Crops: Paleo-Indian, 3; in Columbian Exchange, 15; in South Carolina, 52; Indian, 301; southern, 367, 368; exporting of, 399; in 1920s, 440. *See also* Farms and farming; specific crops
Croquet, 352
Crosby, Alfred, 15
Cross of gold speech (Bryan), 373
Crow Indians, 17, 303
Crummell, Alexander, 188
Crusade for Justice: by Mexican Americans, 577
Crusades, 10
Cruz, Oswaldo, 474
Cryptanalysts: in Second World War, 488, 489
Crystal Palace Exhibition (London), 170
Cuba, 528; Columbus in, 13; Spanish settlement of, 25; annexation and, 244, 245; in Spanish-American War, 389; immigrants from, 404, 610; revolutions in, 404, 481; independence for, 406; U.S. hegemony in, 411–412, 411(map); Reagan and, 603–604
Cuban immigrants, 404
Cuban missile crisis, 554, 557
Cuffee, Paul, 216
Cullen, Countee, 449
Cultivation, 3
Cults: in West Africa, 8; of Virgin Mary, 15
Cultural adaptation: by immigrants, 344–345
Cultural imperialism, 398
Cultural nationalism, 575; Puerto Rico and, 414; of African Americans, 576
Culture(s): Mesoamerican, 3–4; North American, 5; pre-European, 6(map); Indian, 7, 139, 301, 302–305, 438; English and Algonquian, 29; Pequot, 38; colonial, 64–67; oral, 65; Shawnee, 176; youth, 208, 547; of German immigrants, 214; Hispanic, 214; African American, 216, 217, 344; of South, 221; yeoman folk, 222; slave, 229–231; retention in neighborhoods, 343; diversity in cities, 345; national holidays and, 352; mass, 352–356; missionaries and, 361; Americanization of, 397, 399, 401, 413, 474, 477–479, 517; media and, 439, 544–545; in 1920s, 443–444, 449–450; WPA programs and, 464; in Great Depression, 468–470; middle-class, 543–545, 549–551; whiteness and, 545–546; Mexican American, 577; transformation in 1970s, 590–593; therapeutic, 591; global, 622; population diversity and, 630. *See also* Popular culture
Culture wars, 608, 625
Cummins v. County Board of Education, 366
Currency: under Articles of Confederation, 119; during Civil War, 264; gold vs. silver, 363; 1890s depression and, 370
Currier and Ives, 276(illus.)
Cursillo movement, 590–591
Custer, George A., 304, 304(illus.), 305
Cuyahoga River: pollution of, 590
Cycling, 353
Czechoslovakia: German invasion of, 482; Franklin D. Roosevelt and, 483; after Second World War, 515; Stalin and, 519; Prague Spring in, 572; revolution in (1989), 611
Czolgosz, Leon, 389

Dahomey, 8, 50
Daimler, Gottlieb, 319
Dairy farming, 169, 313
Dakotas, 308
Daley, Richard J.: 1968 riots and, 572
Dame school, 65
Dams: in West, 467
Dance, 216, 217, 229
Darrow, Clarence: Scopes trial and, 446–447
Darwin, Charles, 334, 383, 385, 446
Daughters of Bilitis, 580
Daughters of Liberty, 86
Daughters of the American Revolution (DAR), 472
Davis, Henry W., 281
Davis, Jefferson, 248, 252, 254, 280; in Civil War, 259, 260, 261, 268, 274, 275; emancipation plan of, 267; food riots and, 270
Davis, John W., 437
Dawes, William, 99
Dawes Act (1887), 305, 438
Dawes Plan (1924), 479
D-Day, 505
DDT, 549, 550
Dean, James, 547
Dean, John, 586
Dearborn, Fort, 154
Death camps: Nazi, 503
Death rates, *see* Mortality
Debs, Eugene V., 328, 371–372, 379, 392, 393, 419; First World War and, 427
Debt: British, 75, 81; after Revolution, 107, 119; Hamilton on, 130–131; silver vs. gold issue and, 363; farming and, 368; First World War, 479; Russian, 479–480; consumer, 545; in 1960s and 1970s, 589–590
Declaration of Independence, 101–102, 110; document, A1–A2
Declaration of Rights and Grievances, 94
Declaration of Sentiments, 189
Declaratory Act, 85
Decolonization: of Third World, 525–526
Decoration Day, 279
Deep South, 167; in 1964 election, 561
Deep Throat, 586
Deere, John, 170
Defense (national), 517–519, 522; spending on, 598, 600, 603, 612, 619
Defense Department, 531
Defense industry, 497, 498, 532, 543
Defense of Marriage Act (1996), 631
Defense of the Constitutionality of the Bank (Hamilton), 131
Deferments: in Second World War, 504
Deficits: in First World War, 423–424; in Second World War, 499; under Eisenhower, 538; in balance of payments, 582; trade, 588, 620; state, 589; in Reagan-Bush era, 596; federal, 600; Clinton and, 620
Deflation: in 1800s, 164
Defoliants: in Vietnam War, 567, 582
De Gaulle, Charles, 572
Deindustrialization, 588, 617
De Klerk, F. W., 611
Delany, Martin, 216
Delaware (state), 253, 258
Delaware (Lenape) Indians, 42, 76, 122

Delaware Prophet, *see* Neolin (Delaware Prophet)
Delaware River region, 25, 102
DeLeon, Daniel, 373
Demagogues: in New Deal, 462–463
Demczur, Jan, 615–616
Democracy and Education (Dewey), 383
Democratic National Committee: break-in at, 585
Democratic National Convention: in 1964, 561; in 1968, 572
Democratic Party, 183; Jacksonians as, 190; Whigs and, 193–195; in 1844, 197; in South, 248, 293; during Civil War, 271; Klan and, 292; coalitions in, 360; factions
Democratic Party, in, 360; Populists and, 372, 373; 1896 election and, 372–374; voting base of, 450; voter coalition of, 465–466, 537; in 1960s, 554; Reagan and, 597; in 1990s, 617. *See also* Elections
Democratic-Republicans, 132, 133–134, 143; characteristics of, 134–135; Quasi-War and, 136; Virginia and Kentucky resolutions and, 137; Jefferson and, 144; after War of 1812, 161
Demographics: in 21st century, 630; of diversity, 631(map)
Demonstrations: against Vietnam War, 580–581; against WTO, 621–622, 621(illus.). *See also* Protest(s)
Dempsey, Jack, 448
Denmark, 402, 485
Departments of government, 129, 130. *See also* specific departments
Department stores, 324, 332
Dependents' Pension Act, 364, 365
Deportation: of radicals, 428, 429; in Great Depression, 457
Deposit Act (1836), 192
Depressions, 82, 180; of 1890s, 370–372, 399. *See also* Great Depression (1930s)
Deregulation, 600–601
Desegregation: foreign policy and, 527; of military, 540; of schools, 541–542, 542(illus.); Nixon and, 585. *See also Brown v. Board of Education of Topeka*
Desert Storm, *see* Operation Desert Storm (1991)
Destroyers: trade of, 486
Détente policy, 582–583, 592
Detroit, 175; Fort, 80, 154; black population of, 426; bankruptcy of, 589
Developing nations: United States as, 168; use of term, 513; foreign aid to, 527; labor costs in, 620
Dew, Thomas R., 221
Dewey, Alice, 383
Dewey, George, 406
Dewey, John, 383
Dewey, Thomas, 537
Día de la Raza, 19
Dial magazine, 203
Dias, Bartholomew, 12
Díaz, Porfirio, 412
Dickinson, John, 85, 94, 111
Dictatorships: in Latin America, 481; in 1930s, 481–482
Didier, E., 165(illus.)

Diem, Ngo Dinh, 530, 563–564
Dienbienphu, battle at, 529
Diet (food), 62; Paleo-Indian, 3; Mississippian, 4; Indian, 5; Columbian Exchange and, 15; of revolutionary army, 105; of slaves, 226; refrigeration and, 323, 331; reform in, 331–332; in 1920s, 443
Diné language, 492
Dingley Tariff (1897), 363, 373
Diplomacy: by John Quincy Adams, 162; Oregon and, 238; during Civil War, 272; racism and, 401; *Alabama* claims and, 402; status of U.S. in, 402; before Spanish-American War, 404–405; Open Door policy, 407–410, 409(map); dollar, 413; in Fourteen Points, 422; atomic, 515; Third World and, 527; human rights and, 594; Clinton and, 622; September 11, 2001, and, 633–635
Direct election: of senators, 360, 381, 392
Direct investments: American, 399
Direct primaries, 379, 381
Disabled Americans, 613, 614
Disarmament: in Rush-Bagot Treaty, 162
Discount rate, 393
Discrimination: against African Americans, 115, 215–216, 268, 385, 440, 541; in cities, 344; in voting, 365; and segregation, 365–366; against women, 384, 547; in war industries, 497; end of legal, 560–561; in employment, 578; against disabled, 613, 614
Diseases: in Columbian Exchange, 15–17; in colonies, 28, 31; in revolutionary army, 105; among Indians, 175, 303; in cities, 205; immigrants and, 213; of slaves, 228; in Civil War, 267; germ theory of, 331, 345, 347; industrialization and, 331; pollution and, 336, 347; in Spanish-American War, 406; yellow fever and, 412; First World War and, 421, 422–423, 424, 424(illus.); AIDS and, 609, in 21st century, 633
Disfranchisement: of blacks, 365, 380
Disinformation: by CIA, 523
Dissent: John Adams and, 135–136; during wartime, 140–141, 270–271
Dissenters, 27, 28, 36
Distribution of goods, 171
Distribution of wealth, 220
District banks, 393
District of Columbia: abolition of slave trade in, 242. *See also* Washington, D.C.
Diversity, 631(map); religious, 27; of New York, 41; ethnic, 59–62; in 1970s, 591; in 21st century, 630
Divine, Father (George Baker), 448
Division of labor, 5, 173
Divorce, 210, 352, 631; among Indians, 67; in 1920s, 443; during Second World War, 500; "no-fault," 591
Dix, Dorothea, 181, 184–185
Dixiecrats (States' Rights Party), 277
Dixon, Archibald, 244
Dobson, James, 607
Dodd, Samuel, 333
Doeg Indians, 46
Dole, Bob, 619
Dole, Sanford B., 403
Dollar (U.S.): gold standard and, 588

Dollar diplomacy, 413
Domestic policies, *see* specific presidents
Domestic service, 53, 324, 365
Dominican order, 15
Dominican Republic, 14, 295, 402, 412, 480;
    intervention in, 418; immigrants from, 610
Dominion of New England, 53
Domino theory, 523, 581
Donelson, Fort: in Civil War, 260
Donnell, Ed, 313
Donnelly, Ignatius, 369
Doolittle raid, 495
Double V campaign, 503
Douglas, Aaron, 449
Douglas, Stephen A., 241–242, 244, 246, 250, 251
Douglas, William O., 471
Douglass, Frederick, 185, 186(illus.), 187, 207,
    215; women's movement and, 189; on slavery,
    228; on black soldiers, 266; on white
    supremacy, 297; on assimilation, 385
Doves: in Vietnam War, 582
Dow Jones Industrial Average, 623, 627
Draft (military): in Civil War, 261, 262–263,
    263, 270, 271; in First World War,
    420–421; in Second World War, 488, 494;
    in Vietnam War, 566
Draft riots: in Civil War, 271
Dragging Canoe (chief), 96
Drake, Francis, 18, 48
Drama, 207, 208(illus.), 217, 355, 449
Dred Scott decision, 249–250, 295
Dresden: firebombings of, 509
Drinking, *see* Alcohol and alcoholism
Drugs: patent, 390; malaria and, 398; mind
    control and, 523; hallucinogenic, 569; trade
    in, 608–609; Noriega and, 612
"Dry" communities, 383
Dry farming, 314
Dual-sex principle: in Lower Guinea, 8
Du Bois, W. E. B., 387, 421, 429, 441
Duels: Hamilton-Burr, 149; in South, 232
Dukakis, Michael, 610–611
Duke, James B., 323
Duke's Laws (1665), 41
Dulles, John Foster, 522, 527
Dumbarton Oaks meeting, 505
Dunkirk, 486
Dunmore (Lord), 95, 99
Dunne, Edward F., 379
Du Pont de Nemours, E. I., and Company,
    322
Du Pont family, 322–323
Dupuy de Lôme, Enrique, 404
Duquesne, Fort, *see* Pitt, Fort
Dust Bowl, 451, 453–454, 455, 462, 467
Dutch: fur trade and, 23–25; in Caribbean
    region, 25; wampum and, 26; commerce of,
    38; slave trade and, 50; as immigrants, 213.
    See also Netherlands
Dutch Reformed Church, 41
Dutch West India Company, 14, 23, 25, 41
Duties: Townshend, 85–86; in Tariff of 1833,
    192; increase in, 458. *See also* Protective
    tariffs; Tariffs; Taxation
Dylan, Bob, 569
Dynamic conservatism: of Eisenhower, 538
Dynamic Sociology (Ward), 335
Dysentery, 267

Earl, Ralph W. E., 193(illus.)
Earp brothers, 308, 309
Earth Day (1970), 590
"East" (communist countries), 513
East (region): Indians of, 5, 178
East Africa, 7
East Asia: Japanese hegemony in, 413
Eastern Europe: immigrants from, 385; Nazi-
    Soviet pact and, 483; after Second World
    War, 505, 507; Soviets and, 515; revolutions
    in (1989), 611
Easter Rebellion (Ireland), 419
East Florida, 163
East Germany, 519, 556, 611
East India Company (Britain), 89
East Jersey, 41
Eastman, Crystal, 388
Eastman, George, 356
East St. Louis, Illinois: race riot in, 347, 429
Ebola virus, 633
Echohawk, Brummet, 178(illus.)
Ecological exchange: in colonies, 37. *See also*
    Columbian Exchange
Ecology: beaver pelt trade and, 17–18; in
    1970s, 590. *See also* Environment
Economic boom: of 1980s, 601
Economic Interpretation of the Constitution
    (Beard), 384
Economic power: of U.S., 400(illus.)
Economics: laissez faire, 334, 335; Progressives
    and, 384
Economies of scale, 323
Economy, 10; *encomienda* system and, 15;
    wampum in, 26; of Carolinas, 43; slavery
    and, 50, 220; Anglo-American, 62–63; exotic
    beverages and, 66; colonial, 72; shipping
    and, 151–152; boom-and-bust cycles and,
    164–165, 333; government intervention in,
    166, 179, 190; state governments and, 167;
    of South, 170, 218–219; mixed, 179–180;
    Jackson and, 191; of North, 218, 247; cot-
    ton and, 225; in Civil War, 261, 263; Indian,
    301–302; western irrigation and, 309–310;
    from sectional to national, 371; regulation
    of, 393–394; foreign trade and, 399; Cuba
    and, 404; of Philippines, 407; First World
    War and, 417–418, 425–426, 477–479; in
    1920s, 435–436; materialism and, 438–439;
    New Deal and, 460–461, 463(illus.); Second
    World War and, 472, 494; U.S. role in
    worldwide, 477–479, 478(illus.); in Third
    World, 527; postwar, 534; in 1950s, 543;
    middle-class culture and, 549–550; Kennedy
    and, 560; in 1970s, 587–590; Reagan and,
    596, 598, 599–601; George H. W. Bush and,
    613, 618; Clinton and, 618; globalization
    and, 619–622. *See also* Boom-and-bust cycles;
    Market economy; Panics (financial)
Ecosystem: global interaction and, 633
Ederle, Gertrude, 448
Edge Act, 479
Edison, Thomas A., 319, 355
Edison Electric Light Company, 319
Ed Sullivan Show, 547–549, 569, 571, 571(illus.)
Education, 443–444; colonial, 64, 65; for
    women, 110, 126, 210, 547; after Revolution,
    112; for Indians, 176, 305; for blacks, 234,
    284, 366, 367(illus.), 385; reform in, 349;

compulsory school-attendance laws, 352,
    383; American missionaries and, 361; in
    Progressive era, 383–384; U.S. system in
    Philippines, 408; in 1930s, 470; after
    Second World War, 535; NDEA and, 538;
    of new immigrants, 609–610. *See also* Public
    education; Schools
Educational Amendments Act (1972): Title IX
    of, 452, 608
Education Department, 587
Edwards, Jonathan, 71
Efficiency: Taylor and, 323–324; in Progressive
    era, 379
Egalitarianism: from Great Awakening, 72
Egypt, 527; Suez crisis and, 525; Camp David
    accords and, 592
Eighteenth Amendment, 382, 383, 449, A9
Eighth Amendment, 129, A8
Eight-hour workday, 352
Eisenhower, Dwight D., 505; Korean War
    and, 522; Cold War and, 522–525; military
    and, 523; Cuba and, 528; Suez crisis and,
    529; Vietnam and, 529–530; on "military-
    industrial complex," 531, 538; 1952 election
    and, 538; domestic policy of, 538; on racial
    segregation, 541; Pledge of Allegiance and,
    551–552
Eisenhower Doctrine, 529
Elections: in Virginia, 29; in New England, 43;
    of **1796**, 135; of **1800**, 144, 148, 149; of
    1804, 149; grassroots campaigning in, 149;
    of **1808**, 152; of **1812**, 156; of **1816**, 161; of
    1828, 185–186, 190–191; of **1840**, 188,
    194; of **1844**, 188, 197; of **1824**, 189–190;
    of **1836**, 192, 194; of **1856**, 237, 248–249;
    of **1848**, 241; of **1852**, 243–244; of **1854**,
    246, 247; in Kansas territory, 248; of **1860**,
    251; of **1864**, 272; of **1866**, 285, 287; of
    1868, 289; of **1872**, 293; of **1874**, 293; of
    1876, 296, 296(map), 364; of **1896**, 359,
    363, 365, 370, 372–374; **1876** to **1897**, 360;
    of senators, 360, 381, 392; of **1880**, 364;
    of **1884**, 364; of **1888**, 364; of **1890**,
    364; of **1892**, 369–370; of **1900**, 374, 379;
    voter participation in, 378; nonpartisan,
    379, 381; Progressive reforms for, 379; of
    1912, 392; of **1916**, 393; of **1918**, 430; of
    1920, 436–437; of **1924**, 437; of **1928**,
    450–451; of **1932**, 459; of **1936**, 465, 483;
    of **1952**, 522, 538; of **1948**, 537; of **1960**,
    555; of **1964**, 561; of **1968**, 572; of **1972**,
    585; of **1974**, 587; of **1980**, 593, 596; of
    1988, 596, 597, 610–611; of **1984**, 600; of
    1992, 618; of **1996**, 619; of **2000**, 625–626;
    of **2002**, 627; list of presidential, A12–A16
Electoral college, 124, 135
Electoral commission: in 1876, 296
Electoral districts: in states, 117
Electors: selection of, 189
Electricity, 318, 435–436, 438; electrical in-
    dustry and, 319; in textile industry, 323;
    nuclear power for, 538
Electric-powered streetcars, 339
Electric sewing machine, 323
Electric signs, 332
Electronics, 535
Elevated railroads, 339
Elevators, 346

Eleventh Amendment, 129, A8

Eliot, Charles W., 383

Eliot, John, 35, 39

Eliot, T. S., 449

Elites, 58, 62; colonial, 32, 64; ethnic groups and, 61–62; protests by, 84; government by, 111; after Revolution, 112; urban, 209; industrialization and, 330; foreign policy and, 399; in Philippines, 408; Hispanic, 441

Elizabeth I (England), 10, 18, 27, 48

Elkhorn Tavern, battle at, 259

Ellison, Ralph, 229

Ellsberg, Daniel, 574–575, 585

El movimiento, 577

El Paso: Hispanics in, 610

El Salvador, 604, 610

Ely, Richard, 335

Emancipation, 234, 265–267; after Revolution, 114–116; constitutional debate over, 129; gradual, 186; abolitionism and, 186–189; Lincoln and, 265; Confederate plan for, 267; Fourteenth Amendment and, 287

Emancipation Proclamation, 266, 267

Embargo: by OPEC, 576, 583, 584; against Nicaragua, 604

Embargo Act (1807), 152

Embassies: in Teheran, 593

Emergency Banking Relief Bill, 460

Emergency Fleet Corporation, 426

Emergency Quota Act (1921), 446

Emerging markets, 620

Emerson, Ralph Waldo, 203, 214, 251

Empires: Spanish, 15; English, 53–55; U.S., 398; benefits of, 401; anti-imperialists and, 402; after First World War, 423; after Second World War, 513

Employees: working class as, 324

Employers: control over workers, 324

Employment, 164; of freed people, 115; of blacks, 216; sex discrimination in, 324; trends in, 325(illus.); in government, 360–362; minimum age of, 381; in First World War, 425–426; in Second World War, 497; by Defense Department, 531; of women, 546; discrimination in, 578; Los Angeles riots and, 617. *See also* Labor

Employment Board: of Civil Service Commission, 540

Empresarios, 195

Encomienda system, 15, 22, 45

"Enemies lists": of Nixon, 585

Enemy Alien Camps, 502

Energy crisis: in 1970s, 576, 583, 584; Carter and, 587; economy and, 588

Energy Department, 587

Enforcement Acts, 293

Engineering: railroads and, 310; urban, 348; advances in, 398

England (Britain), 10, 398; and Hundred Years' War, 10; Norse voyages to, 14; colonization by, 18, 20, 21–22, 25–37, 42(illus.); Caribbean settlement by, 25; social change in, 27; Virginia colony and, 28–30; immigrants from, 31, 341; New England and, 32–36; Civil War in, 41, 43; slave trade and, 50; Navigation Acts and, 50–51; imperial reorganization and, 53–55; French wars with, 54, 76–80; in Seven Years War, 77–80;

Jay Treaty and, 134, 136; War of 1812 and, 144, 156; trade with, 151–152; technology from, 153; Oregon and, 162, 197, 238; Rush-Bagot Treaty with, 162; U.S. economy and, 168; Act of Union and, 199; Irish and, 213, 419; *Alabama* claims and, 272, 402; U.S. Civil War and, 272, 273; transatlantic cable and, 321, 321(illus.); models for reform from, 378; economic power of, 400(illus.); Samoa and, 402–403; Venezuela dispute and, 404; in China, 407, 409(map); Panama Canal and, 412; Anglo-American cooperation and, 413; in First World War, 417, 418; Munich Conference and, 482; Second World War and, 483, 486(map), 490, 513; Dunkirk withdrawal and, 486; Operation War Bride in, 501(illus.); Cold War and, 515; Palestine and, 528; Suez crisis and, 529. *See also* Anglo-America; specific colonies

English language, 344; as "official" language, 610

English Traits (Emerson), 214

Enlightenment, 64–65

Enola Gay (airplane), 509

Enron: collapse of, 627

Entertainment: in 1920s, 439. *See also* specific types

Entrepreneurs: in North and South, 220; in Civil War, 263; in Machine Age, 319

Enumerated powers, 161

Environment: of Plymouth, 33; Southwestern Indians and, 302; ranching and, 315; atomic bomb and, 510; degradation of, 549; Nixon and, 585; Reagan and, 598–599; WTO and, 621(illus.); in 1990s, 623; George W. Bush and, 626; global interaction and, 633; health and, 633

Environmentalism: in 1970s, 590

Epidemics: smallpox, 15; typhoid, 406; influenza, 422–423, 424, 424(illus.); AIDS, 609. *See also* Diseases

Epstein, Abraham, 443

Equal Employment Opportunity Commission (EEOC), 561, 578, 579

Equality, 110; Puritan philosophy of, 37; for women, 189, 579–580; Tocqueville on, 209; southern Republican Party and, 291; cultural nationalism and, 576

Equal opportunity: ADA and, 614

Equal-protection clause, 297–298

Equal rights: Second World War and, 503

Equal rights amendment (ERA), 198; of 1920s, 438; of 1970s, 579–580, 585, 596

Equiano, Olaudah, 72

Ericsson, Leif, 13–14

Erie, Lake, 155

Erie Canal, 167, 168, 168(illus.), 169

Espionage Act (1917), 427

Estonia, 430, 483, 514, 611

Ethics: biogenetics and, 632–633

Ethiopia: Italian invasion of, 482

Ethnic cleansing, 622

Ethnic groups, 59–62, 60(map); as Democratic-Republicans, 135; party affiliation and, 194; in California gold rush, 204, 204(illus.); foods of, 356; immigration quotas on, 446; in postwar period, 534; in 1950s, 550; identity politics and, 576; affirmative action for,

578; hatreds among, 622. *See also* specific groups

Eugenics, 385

Europe and Europeans: exploration by, 1–3, 11, 12–15; societies of, 9–11; in 1490, 9(map); Indians and, 13, 67, 76–80, 78(map); in North America, 17–18, 20–38, 23(illus.); settlements by, 24(map), 78(map); inter-colonial conflicts and, 40–41; migration after 1730, 59–61; Monroe Doctrine and, 163, 413; immigration from, 200, 211, 212(illus.), 307, 341; revolutions of 1848 in, 240; imperialism of, 398; Latin America and, 413; after First World War, 476–477, 479; Second World War and, 481–483, 506(map), 507–508, 513, 518(map); Nazi invasions of, 486(map); student protests in, 572

"Europe First" strategy, 496, 506(map)

Evangelicalism, 71, 183, 185; in First Great Awakening, 71–72; in Second Great Awakening, 183–184; in South, 198, 220; in 1970s, 590. *See also* Great Awakening

Evans, Hiram Wesley, 445

Everglades: Seminoles in, 179

Evers, Medgar, 559

"Evil empire": Reagan on, 603

Evolution: theory of, 383, 446–447; fundamentalist Christians on, 607

Exceptionalism, 398–399

Exchange rates: in 1970s, 588

Exclusion: in Gilded Age, 359

Executive and executive branch, 124, 129, 190–191. *See also* President and presidency

Executive departments, 130. *See also* specific departments

Executive Orders: No. 8802, 497; on racial discrimination, 540

Executive privilege, 134

Exodusters, 296, 307

Expansion and expansionism: French, 45, 56; by Spain, 45, 56; after War of 1812, 160, 162–163; of John Quincy Adams, 161–162; by Russia, 163; to Pacific, 183; manifest destiny and, 195–197; 1800–1860, 196(map); after Civil War, 295, 398; foreign policy and, 398–399; of foreign trade, 399, 400(illus.); racism and, 399–401; navalism and, 403; Hawai'i and, 403–404; Cuban crisis and, 404; Venezuelan boundary dispute and, 404; by Japan, 485(map)

Ex parte Milligan, 295

Experiments and Observations on Electricity (Franklin), 65

Exploration: Spanish, 1–2, 14–15; European, 11, 12–15; by Columbus, 13; Norse, 13–14; by Lewis and Clark, 147–148; by Zebulon Pike, 148

Export-Import Bank, 479, 480, 481

Exports, 94, 122, 152, 169, 477, 479, 620; increase in, 399, 400(illus.); of U.S. surpluses, 399; to Latin America, 410

Exposition and Protest (Calhoun), 191

Extinction: of buffalo, 305

Extraterritoriality: in China, 484

Factions, 128, 132–133; regionalism and, 134; Washington on, 135; political culture and,

Factions (*cont.*)
143; in party politics, 360. *See also* Political parties

Factor, Max, 439

Factories, 152, 173, 220; tariffs and, 191; women in, 324, 426; child labor in, 325; in Second World War, 497, 498

Factory Girl's Garland, 172

Fads: in 1920s, 441

Fair employment, 540

Fair Oaks, battle at, 260

Fallen Timbers, Battle of, 121, 121(illus.)

Falwell, Jerry, 607, 607(illus.), 609

Families: Paleo-Indian, 3; Indian, 5, 67–68; colonial, 32, 36, 67–69; use of term, 68; market economy and, 201; Mormon, 202; sizes of, 210–211, 350; urban, 210–211, 350–352; slavery and, 218, 230–231, 283; in yeoman culture, 222, 223; planter, 226; Navajo, 302; incomes of, 330; of immigrants, 341; homeownership by, 343; inner-city housing for, 345, 346(illus.); structure of, 350; boarding and, 351; stages of, 352; in Great Depression, 457; during Second World War, 500; in 1950s, 546; single-parent and blended, 591, 631; in 21st century, 630–631; changes in, 632(illus.)

Family and Medical Leave Act, 625

Family planning, 395

Family values: Reagan on, 598(illus.)

Famines: in Ireland, 200, 213

"Fancy trade," 230

Farewell Address: of Washington, 135; of Eisenhower, 538

Farmers' Alliances, 358, 367, 368–369; sub-treasury scheme of, 437

Farmers' Holiday Association, 458

Farms and farming: Indian, 5; whiskey tax and, 132; Democratic-Republicans and, 135; government policy toward, 166; by region, 169, 170, 368; commercial, 169–170, 368; by region, 170, 368; lifestyle of, 201–203; immigrants and, 213; yeomen farmers and, 221–223; in Civil War, 263; sharecropping and, 284, 367–368; irrigation for, 309; in Great Plains, 310–314; debt, silver coinage, and, 363; types of, 367–368; global market-place and, 371; credit for, 393; price supports for, 394; in 1920s, 436; Coolidge and, 437; large-scale, 440; Great Depression and, 451, 455; Dust Bowl and, 453–454; AAA and, 461; agribusiness and, 550. *See also* Agriculture; Ranching

Farm Security Administration (FSA), 453–454

Farm workers: Mexican, 441

Farragut, David, 259

Far West, *see* West

Fascists, 457, 464, 470, 481, 482. *See also* Italy; Nazi Germany

Faubus, Orval E., 541, 542

Fauset, Jessie, 449

FBI, *see* Federal Bureau of Investigation (FBI)

Federal Arts Project: of WPA, 464

Federal Aviation Administration, 599

Federal budget: tariff revenues and, 362; in 1890, 364; deficit in, 600; Clinton and deficit, 620

Federal Bureau of Investigation (FBI), 539, 627

Federal Emergency Relief Agency, 471

Federal Farm Loan Act (1916), 393

Federal government, *see* Government (U.S.); National government

Federal Highway Act (1921), 439

Federal Housing Administration (FHA), 536

Federalist, The, 125

Federalists, 109, 125, 132–133, 132(illus.), 134, 143; characteristics of, 135; Alien and Sedition Acts and, 137; France and, 137; Jefferson and, 144; Younger, 148; Older, 149; Hartford Convention and, 156–157; dissolution of, 157; nullification and, 191–192; bank controversies and, 192–193

Federal police power, 384

Federal Reserve Act (1913), 393

Federal Reserve Board, 393, 588; in 1930s, 471; stagflation controlled by, 600

Federal Theater Project, 464

Federal Trade Commission (FTC), 393, 436

Federal Writers Project (FWP), 465

Felt, Mark, 586

Female-headed households: poverty in, 563

Female Moral Reform Society, 184

Feminine Mystique, The (Friedan), 578

Femininity: in 1920s, 445

Feminism and feminists, 388, 395, 578–580, 579, 607. *See also* Women; Women's movement

Fences: barbed wire and, 314–315

Ferdinand of Aragón, 10, 13

Fern, Fanny, 207

Ferraro, Geraldine, 600

Fiction, 207; after Second World War, 549

Fiddling His Way (Johnson), 222(illus.)

Field, Cyrus, 321, 402

Fifteenth Amendment, 281, 289, 293, 296, 365, A9; citizenship rights in, 303; voting rights and, 366

Fifth Amendment, 129, 240, A7–A8

Fifth Sun, *see* Aztecs

"Fifty-four Forty or Fight," 197

Fifty-fourth Massachusetts Regiment, 268

Filene, E. A., 379

Filibuster: over antilynching bill, 471

Filipinos, 495. *See also* Philippines

Fillmore, Millard, 249

Film industry, *see* Movies and movie industry

Finances: under Articles of Confederation, 117, 119; under Hamilton, 130–132; of railroads, 310

Financial institutions, 172

Financiers, 334

Financing: in War of 1812, 155; in market economy, 159; of canals, 168; by cities, 349; of Social Security, 473; Reagan and, 600. *See also* Economy

Finland, 422, 430, 485

Finlay, Carlos Juan, 412, 474

Finney, Charles G., 183

Finnish settlers, 25

Fireside Chats, 460, 487

Firestorms, 508, 509

First Amendment, A7

First Bank of the United States, 131

First Congress, 128–129

First Continental Congress, 93–94

First Great Awakening, 71–72

First Hundred Days: of Franklin D. Roosevelt, 460, 461

First Lady, *see* specific individuals

First New Deal, 459–461

"First World," 513

First World War, 393–394; Sedition Act during, 140–141; women in, 388; Japan and, 413; American attitude toward, 415–417; United States in, 416, 420; alliances in, 417; Germany and, 417–418, 423, 430, 431; neutrality during, 417–418; soldiers in, 420–423; casualties in, 422–423; home front in, 423–426; civil liberties and, 427–428; Red Scare after, 428–429; Great Depression and, 451; Europe after, 476–477

Fish, Hamilton, 402

Fisher, Sidney George, 165

Fishing, 19, 22, 107; in Newfoundland, 14, 17

Fisk University, 284

Fitzgerald, F. Scott, 449

Five-Dollar-Day plan, 322, 324

Five Points section (New York City), 209–210

Five-Power Treaty, 477

Flag: Confederate battle, 277

Florida: Spain and, 1, 22; France and, 18, 22; slavery and, 52; after Seven Years War, 77; in War of 1812, 155; West, 162; cession to United States, 163; East, 163; statehood for, 174; Seminoles in, 178–179; fugitive slaves in, 243; secession of, 252; 2000 election and, 625–626

Flu, *see* Influenza pandemic

Flynn, Elizabeth Gurley, 328

Focus on the Family, 607

Folk culture: of yeoman farmers, 222

Folktales: slave, 229, 230

Foner, Eric, 292

Fong, Hiram, 573

Fongs (Chinese associations), 343

Food(s), 3, 5, 8(illus.); production of, 318; canned, 319, 331; refrigeration and, 323, 331; processed, 331; purity of, 390; in 1920s, 443. *See also* Agriculture; Crops; Diet (food); specific foods

Food Administration, 425

Food riots: in Confederacy, 270

Food stamps, 562, 598

Football, 353–355

Forbes, Charles, 437

Forbes, Malcolm, 609

Force Act, 192

Ford, Gerald, 576, 585, 586, 587

Ford, Henry, 319–322, 419, 477; Five-Dollar-Day plan of, 322, 324; in Second World War, 498

Ford Foundation, 527

Ford Motor Company, 322, 324; Model T and, 438; UAW and, 466; in Soviet Union, 480

Fordney-McCumber Tariff Act (1922), 436, 479

Foreign affairs: gendered imagery in, 400; presidential control over, 530; world response after September 11, 2001, 628

Foreign Affairs: Kennan article in, 517

Foreign aid, 522

Foreign-born Americans, 573

Foreign-branch banks, 479

Foreign investment, 164, 165; in U.S. companies, 334; by United States, 399; in Latin

America, 410, 411; in Mexico, 412; in Britain, 413
Foreign policy: in American Revolution, 93; French Revolution and, 133; Washington and, 135; in late 19th century, 398–399; elite, 399; anti-imperialists and, 406; Theodore Roosevelt and, 410–413; Taft and, 413; League of Nations and, 431; toward Latin America, 480–481; after Second World War, 513–517; CIA and, 523; racism and, 527; toward Israel, 528–529; of Truman, 538; Kennedy and, 555; Peace Corps and, 556; of Lyndon Johnson, 563–567; Kissinger and, 575–576; of Nixon, 575–576, 582–583; Carter and, 592; Reagan and, 601–606. *See also* Annexation; specific presidents
Foreign Relations Committee, 399
Foreign service, 399, 523
Foreign trade, 122; under Articles of Confederation, 119. *See also* Trade
Forest reserves, 308
Formosa, 407, 522. *See also* Jiang Jieshi (Chiang Kai-shek)
Formosa Resolution, 525
Fort(s): French, 76. *See also* specific forts
Forten, James, 216
Fort Wayne, Treaty of, 151
"Forty-niners," 203
Foss, John, 142
Foster, Hannah, 113
Foster, Stephen, 217
Foster, Vincent, 619
Founders, *see* Constitutional Convention (1787)
442nd Regimental Combat Team, 503
"Four-Minute Men," 427
Fourteen Points, 422
Fourteenth Amendment, 281, 286–287, 293, 326, 333, 366, 384, A8–A9; Supreme Court and, 295, 296, 297; equal-protection clause of, 297–298; citizenship rights in, 303
Fourth Amendment, 129, A7
Foxwoods Casino: Mashantucket Pequot Museum and, 38
Fragging, 581
France, 10, 398; Florida and, 18; colonization by, 20, 25; Canada and, 22–23; fur trade and, 23–25; Indians and, 44–45; slavery and, 52–53; England and, 54, 76–80; expansion of, 56; Seven Years War and, 77–80; in American Revolution, 103; Treaty of Alliance with (1778), 133; Quasi-War with, 136, 140–141; XYZ affair and, 136; Louisiana Territory and, 146; trade with, 151–152; U.S. Civil War and, 272; in Mexico, 402; China and, 407, 409(map); Morocco and, 413; First World War and, 417, 421–422, 430; black soldiers in, 421; Munich Conference and, 482; Second World War and, 483, 485–486, 513; Vietnam, 511, 512, 520, 529; Indochina and, 520; Suez crisis and, 529; student protests in, 572. *See also* specific colonies
Franciscan order, 15, 22, 45
Franco, Francisco, 482
Franco-American alliance (1778), *see* Alliance, Treaty of (1778)
Franco-American Convention (1800), 137
Frankfurter, Felix, 471
Franklin, Aretha, 569

Franklin, Benjamin, 72; Enlightenment and, 65; on British North America, 80; diplomacy of, 93, 103; Declaration of Independence and, 101; at Constitutional Convention, 123
Franz Ferdinand (Austria-Hungary), 417
Fraternal societies, 329
Free blacks: in Revolution, 104(illus.); in North, 114–115; abolitionism and, 186; in South, 223, 233. *See also* African Americans; Slaves and slavery
Freedmen's Bureau, 282, 284, 286
Freedom(s): of religion, 31, 37, 53; of speech, 69, 140–141, 188, 428, 432–433; social, 113; in states, 117; in Northwest Ordinance, 120; during Second World War, 500; New Right and, 607–608
"Freedom dues": for indentured servants, 31
Freedom Riders, 558
Freedom Schools, 558
Freedom Summer (1964), 558
Freed people: after Revolution, 115
Freedpeople (Civil War), 265, 282–284; black codes for, 285–286; land redistribution and, 288; male voting and, 290; economic progress and, 291; failure of Reconstruction and, 292
Free enterprise: Progressivism and, 380, 381; Reagan and, 599
Freeholders, 31
Free labor, 247
"Free love," 570
Free-market system: Reagan and, 598; in former Soviet Union, 611
Freemasonry, 186
Free people of color, 115, 138, 138(illus.), 215–216, 284; movement of, 174
Free silver, 372
Free-Soilers, 241, 246, 247, 248
Free Speech and Headlight, The, 365
Free Speech Movement (FSM), 568–569
Free states, 163–164, 174
Free trade, 362, 514, 620–621
Frémont, John C., 236–237, 240, 249
French and Indian War, *see* Seven Years War
French Communist Party, 520
French Indochina, 488
French Revolution, 133
Frey, John, 317
Frick, Henry C., 328
Friedan, Betty, 578
Friedman, Thomas L., 620
Friendship Seven (space capsule), 560
Frontenac, Louis de Buade de, 44
Frontier: backcountry as, 95–96; individualism along, 232; closing of, 299, 301; Turner and, 299, 403; end of, 306(map); Australian, 311, 311(illus.); ranching, 314–315
FTC cease-and-desist orders, 393
Fuel Administration, 425
Fugitive Slave Act (1850), 216, 237, 242, 244, 246; William Wells Brown and, 187
Fugitive slave law (1787): in Northwest Ordinance, 120
Fugitive slaves, 215, 231, 232; in Revolution, 107, 115; Northwest Ordinance and, 120; movement of, 174; Underground Railroad and, 243; flight to Canada, 249
Fulbright, J. William, 491, 567
Fulkes, Minnie, 229

Full Employment Act (1946), 534, 537
Fuller, Margaret, 203
Fulton, Robert, 166
Fundamental Constitutions of Carolina, 42
Fundamentalism: Christian, 198, 446–447, 590, 607–608; in 1920s, 446–447; Islamic, 615–616, 623
Fur trade, 17–18, 19, 22, 44, 76; Dutch vs. French, 23–25; England and, 77

Gabaccia, Donna, 356
Gabon, 50, 59
Gabriel's Rebellion, 138, 139–140, 231
Gadsden Purchase, 398
Gage, Thomas, 97, 99
Gag rule (Congress), 188, 240
Gallatin, Albert, 144
Galloway, Joseph, 94
Galton, Francis, 385
Gama, Vasco da, 12
Gambia, 50
Gandhi, Mohandas K., 432, 542
Gangsters, 449
Garbage, 348
Gardner, Alexander, 261(illus.)
Garfield, James A., 321, 362, 364
Garlic, Delia, 228
Garment industry: labor in, 610
Garrison, William Lloyd, 186, 188–189
Garvey, Marcus, 429, 441
Gas warfare, 421
Gates, Bill, 620
Gates, Frederick, 401
Gates, Horatio, 103
GATT, *see* General Agreement on Tariffs and Trade (GATT)
Gaugin, Michael, 213
Gay liberation, 580. *See also* Homosexuals and homosexuality
Gay Power and Gay Pride, 580
Gays, *see* Homosexuals and homosexuality
Gaza Strip, 583, 592, 604, 622
Geary Act (1892), 344
Gebhardt, William, 356
Gender and gender roles: Indians and, 5, 7, 305; in West Africa, 8; in Europe, 10; in Chesapeake colonies, 31; in New England, 37; slave trade and, 50; church segregation by, 65; African Americans and, 139; workplace division by, 173; in utopian communities, 201; in West, 307; employment discrimination and, 324; during Second World War, 500; postwar benefits and, 536; in 1950s, 546; Civil Rights Act of 1964 and, 560–561; courses in, 579. *See also* Men; Women
Gender gap, 613, 626
General Agreement on Tariffs and Trade (GATT), 620
General Court (Massachusetts), 34, 35
General Electric Company, 319, 333, 436, 439, 480
General Federation of Women's Clubs, 438
General Motors (GM), 466, 497, 543, 588
Generation gap: in 1960s, 554
Genêt, Edmond, 133
Geneva Accords (1954), 529
Geneva Prisoners of War Convention (1949), 521–522

Genizaros, 68
Genome mapping, 633
"Gentleman's agreement": with Japan, 401
Gentry, 116
Geography: of Africa, 7; of Soviet Union, 514
George II (England), 81
George III (England), 81, 94, 101–102
George, Elizabeth, 38
George, Henry, 335
Georgia, 63, 176–177, 252, 274, 275(map), 599
Germain, George, 99–100, 105
German Americans, 417, 427
German people, 208
Germantown, battle at, 103
Germany, 398; immigrants from, 61, 213, 214, 341; Samoa and, 402–403; China and, 407, 409(map); Morocco and, 413; *Lusitania* and, 415; submarine warfare by, 419–420; reparations from, 451, 479; Great Depression (1930s) in, 481; after Second World War, 513; Soviets and, 515; zones in, 515; Berlin Wall in, 556; economy of, 588; reunification of, 611. *See also* East Germany; First World War; Nazi Germany; Second World War; West Germany
Germ theory of disease, 331, 345, 347
Gershwin, George, 450
Gettysburg, Battle of, 269, 269(map), 270
Ghana, 527
Ghent, Treaty of, 155, 156, 162
Ghettos, 440
Ghost Dance, 305
Gibbons v. Ogden, 166
GI Bill of Rights, 503, 534, 535
Gibson, James F., 261(illus.)
Gilbert, Humphrey, 18
Gilbert Islands, 403
Gilded Age, 358–374, 388
Gilded Age, The (Twain and Warner), 358
Gilman, Charlotte Perkins, 388
Gilmore, William, 153
Gingrich, Newt, 617, 619, 625
Ginsburg, Ruth Bader, 547
Girls: education for, 112. *See also* Women
Gish, Lillian, 356
Gitlow, Benjamin, 428
Glackens, William, 405(illus.)
Gladden, Washington, 385
Glasnost (openness), 606
Glenn, John, 560
Glidden, Joseph F., 314
Global economy: United States in, 588
Globalization, 619–622, 633–636; use of term, 616; Clinton and, 617
Global marketplace: in 1890s, 371
Global telecommunications: transatlantic telegraph cable and, 321
Glorious Revolution (England), 53–54
GNP, *see* Gross national product (GNP)
Godkin, E. L., 402
Gold: from Americas, 14; on Cherokee land, 177; for land payment, 193; credit and, 194; in California, 203, 204; in West, 307; 1890s depression and reserves of, 370; discoveries of, 373
Gold Coast, 8, 13
Gold Democrats, 372, 373

Goldman, Emma, 428
Gold rush, 203, 204, 204(illus.), 307, 363
Gold standard, 363, 372, 373, 588
Gold Standard Act (1900), 373
Goldwater, Barry, 561, 564, 597
Gollop, Rahel, 337, 351
Gompers, Samuel, 327, 373, 407, 426
Gonorrhea: among Indians, 303
Gonzáles, Rudolfo ("Corky"), 577
Good Earth, The (Buck), 483
Gooding, James Henry, 268
Goodman, Andrew, 558
Good Neighbor policy, 480–481
Google, 636
GOP ("Grand Old Party," Republican Party), 516
Gorbachev, Mikhail, 596, 601, 606, 611
Gore, Al, 619, 623, 625–626
Gorsuch, Edward, 242
Gospel music, 217
Gospel of Wealth, 334
Gould, Jay, 327
Government: Locke and, 64; constitutional limitations on, 117; Cherokee, 176; in Kansas Territory, 248; in Confederacy, 269–270; Reconstruction, 290–292; urban, 347; civic reform and, 349; Progressives and, 379, 381; business and, 436–437; bankruptcy of local, 618. *See also* Government (colonial); Government (U.S.)
Government (colonial), 53, 69–70, 81–82, 128–129. *See also* specific colonies and regions
Government (U.S.): Congress as, 100; during Revolution, 100; republican, 109–110, 116–119; branches of, 124; supremacy over states, 161; market economy and, 164–167; farm policy of, 166; economic regulation by, 179; Jackson and, 183, 190; in Civil War, 264; Indian policy of, 303; West and, 316; assistance to business by, 334–335, 425, 436; employment in, 360–362; in First World War, 423–425; New Deal and, 455; in Great Depression, 458; power of, 467–468; South and, 468; Franklin D. Roosevelt and, 472; military contracts and, 497; fair employment by, 540; school integration and, 541–542; Nixon and, 585; Reagan and, 596, 598; under Clinton, 625. *See also* New Deal; Representative government
Government agencies: in First World War, 425
Governors: in New England, 43; colonial, 69–70; state, 117; during Reconstruction, 285; Progressive, 380, 381
Gracia Real de Santa Teresa de Mose, 52
Gradualists: on emancipation, 186–188
Graduated income tax, 393
Graft, 348
Graham, Billy, 545
Grain: demand for, 63
Grain Coast, 7
Grand Alliance, 494
Grand Army of the Republic, 360
Grand Canyon, 391
Grand Coulee Dam, 458, 461, 467
Grange movement, 367, 368
Granger laws, 368

Grant, Julia, 294
Grant, Madison, 385, 446
Grant, Ulysses S., 288, 402; in Civil War, 260, 268, 274, 275; Reconstruction and, 289; corruption and, 293; world tour by, 294, 294(illus.); civil service and, 362
Grape growers: Mexican American strike against, 576–577
Grateful Dead, 569
Great Atlantic and Pacific Tea Company (A&P), 332
Great Awakening: First, 71–72; Second, 182, 198, 201, 215
Great Basin: Indians of, 5
Great Britain, *see* England (Britain)
Great Communicator: Reagan as, 597
Great Depression (1930s): regulation and, 180; activism during, 432; causes of, 451; Hoover and, 455–459; bank crisis in, 459–460; labor during, 466–467; federal power in, 467–468; international debt default in, 479; in Germany, 481. *See also* Unemployment
Great Emancipator: Lincoln as, 266–267
Greater Antilles: Spanish in, 25
Greater East Asia Co-Prosperity Sphere, 485(map), 488
Great Gatsby, The (Fitzgerald), 449
Great Lakes Naval Training Station, 327
Great Lakes region: Indian attacks in, 80; in War of 1812, 154, 155; Erie Canal and, 167
Great Migration: of African Americans, 440
Great Plains, 17, 238, 300; farming in, 310–314; Farmers' Alliances in, 368–369; Dust Bowl in, 453–454
Great powers: in U.N., 515
Great Salt Lake region: Mormons in, 203
Great Society, 554, 560–563, 562(illus.), 567–570
Great War, The, *see* First World War
"Great White Fleet," 413
Greece, 513, 516
Greeley, Horace, 247–248, 265–266, 293
Greenbacks, 370
Green Corn Rebellion, 427
Greene, Nathanael, 106
Greenland, 13
Green Party, 625
Greensboro, North Carolina, 553–554
Greenville, Treaty of, 121, 121(illus.), 122, 150, 175, 303
Greer (ship), 488, 490–491
Grenada: invasion of, 604
Grenville, George, 81, 82
Gresham, Walter Q., 399
Griffith, D. W., 356, 429
Grimké, Angelina and Sarah, 189
Grocery chains, 332
Gross national product (GNP): after First World War, 425; in Great Depression, 454; decline in, 600; in 1990s, 620
Guadalcanal, battle at, 492
Guadalupe Hidalgo, Treaty of, 203, 240, 577
Guadeloupe, 25; immigrants from, 342(illus.)
Guam, 406, 490, 496
Guanche people, 12
Guantánamo Bay: naval base at, 412
Guardianship laws, 290

Guatemala, 3; CIA and, 523; Arbenz Guzmán in, 528; immigrants from, 610
Guerrilla warfare: in Kansas Territory, 248; in Civil War, 259; in Philippines, 407
Guilford Court House, battle at, 106
Guiteau, Charles, 364
Gulflight (ship), 418
Gulf of Mexico region, 45, 119
Gulf of Tonkin Resolution, 564
Gulf War, *see* Persian Gulf War (1991)
Gullah dialect, 51
Guns: in Iroquois-Huron war, 25; right to bear arms and, 129; interchangeable parts for, 170
Guomindang Party, 484
Gypsies: Nazis and, 503

Ha, Nguyet Thu, 595–596
Habeas corpus, writ of, 261, 264, 271, 293
Hague peace conferences (1899, 1907), 413
Haight-Ashbury district (San Francisco), 570
Haiti, 138, 418, 480, 622
Halberstam, David, 555
Hale, Stephen, 253
Haley, Bill, 217
Half Breeds, 360
Halifax, 100
Hall, G. Stanley, 383
Hallucinogenic drugs, 569
Hamer, Fannie Lou, 561
Hamilton, Alexander, 125, 130, 148, 381; domestic policy and, 130–132; France and, 137; Burr duel with, 149; on manufacturing, 152
Hammond, James Henry, 220–221
Hampton, Fred, 568
Hampton Institute, 305
Hancock, John, 86
Handler, Ruth, 548
Handsome Lake (Seneca), 139
Hanna, Marcus A., 372
Hanoi, *see* North Vietnam
Haole (foreigners), 403
Harbors, 166
Harding, Warren G., 436–437
Hard-money policies: Van Buren and, 194
Harlem: violence in, 567
Harlem Renaissance, 449
Harpers Ferry: John Brown's raid on, 251, 254
Harper's magazine, 257, 405(illus.)
Harriot, Thomas, 18, 21
Harris, Eric, 623–624
Harrison, Benjamin, 308, 364, 403
Harrison, William Henry, 151, 155, 364
Harte, Bret, 309
Hartford Convention, 156–157, 158
Hartford Female Seminary, 210
Harvard University, 64, 383
Harvest-destruction cycles, 166
Hate crimes: in 1990s, 623–624
Havana, 481, 528; Inter-American conference in, 480
Hawai'i, 204, 244, 295, 398, 495(map); annexation and, 403–404, 406; Pearl Harbor attack in, 488–489, 489(illus.)
Hawkins, John, 18
Hawks: in Vietnam War, 582

Hawthorne, Nathaniel, 203, 207
Hay, John, 399, 410
Hayes, Rutherford B., 296, 296(map), 326, 364
Haymarket Riot, 327, 371
Hayne, Robert Y.: Webster debate with, 191
Haywood, William D. (Big Bill), 328
Hay-Pauncefote Treaty (1901), 412, 413
H-bomb, *see* Hydrogen bomb (H-bomb)
Headright system, 29
Head Start program, 561
Head tax: in First World War, 426
Health: dietary reform and, 331–332; air pollution and, 336; in 21st century, 633. *See also* Diseases
Healthcare: costs of, 563; Clinton and, 619
Health Insurance Portability and Accounting Act, 625
Hearst, William Randolph, 356, 404
Hefner, Hugh, 547
Hegemony: of U.S. in Caribbean and Latin America, 411(map); 413; of Japan in East Asia, 413; of United States, 517
"Hello girls," 421
Helper, Hinton R., 233
Hemingway, Ernest, 449
Hendrick (chief), 44(illus.)
Henry VII (England), 10, 14
Henry VIII (England), 27
Henry, Edward Lamson, 168(illus.)
Henry, Fort: in Civil War, 260
Henry, Guy V., 412
Henry, Patrick, 83, 94, 125
Henry the Navigator (Portugal), 12
Hepatitis C and E, 633
Hepburn Act (1906), 390
Herbert, Victor, 355
Herbicides: in Vietnam War, 582
Hessians (German mercenaries), 102, 103
Hibernian Society, 208
Higginson, Thomas Wentworth, 366
Higher education: colonial, 64; for women, 126. *See also* Universities and colleges
Higher Education Act, 452, 579, 608
High schools, 383
High-tech industries, 620
Highway Act (1956), 536
Highways, *see* Roads and highways
Hijackings: on September 11, 2001, 626, 627
Hill, Anita, 613
Hill, David, 372
Hillsborough (Lord), 85
Hip-hop music, 217
Hiraoka, Hiroshi, 354
Hiroshima: bombing of, 494, 509
Hispanics, 214–215; Columbus Day and, 19; migration by, 174, 341; in Southwest, 201; racism against, 295; in West, 307; immigration of, 441; in postwar period, 536; percentage of, 544; Census classification of, 576; poverty of, 608; birth rate of, 610; Los Angeles riots and, 617–618; 2000 election and, 626; population growth of, 630. *See also* specific groups
Hispaniola, 15, 21, 138; Columbus in, 13; sugar in, 17; Spanish settlement of, 25
Hiss, Alger, 539
Hitler, Adolf, 454, 470, 476, 481–482, 505; 1936 Olympics and, 469; Franklin D. Roosevelt

and, 471; automobile production and, 477–479; radio use by, 487; suicide by, 493, 508. *See also* Nazi Germany
HIV, 609, 614
Hmong immigrants, 573
Hobbs, Alfred C., 170
Hobos, 471
Ho Chi Minh, 432, 511–512, 520, 529–530, 563
Ho Chi Minh City, 565(map), 581
Hoffman, Elizabeth Cobbs, 556
Hohokam peoples, 4
Holden, William W., 270
Holden v. Hardy, 326, 384
Holding company, 334
Holland: Separatists in, 33, 34(illus.). *See also* Dutch; Netherlands
Holliday, John Henry ("Doc"), 309
Holliman, John, 602(illus.)
Hollywood, *see* Movies and movie industry
"Hollywood Ten," 539
Holmes, Oliver Wendell, Jr., 384, 428
Holocaust, 503–504
Home front: in Revolution, 105; in First World War, 423–426; in Second World War, 494, 498–500
Homeland Security Department, 531
Homelessness: in 1890s depression, 370; in Great Depression, 455; in 1980s, 609
Homeownership, 343
Homestead Act (1862), 313
Homesteads, 95
Homestead strike, 328, 371
Homosexuals and homosexuality: in New England, 36–37; subculture in cities, 351; in 1920s, 445; Nazis and, 503; Kinsey on, 547; gay liberation and, 580; in 1970s, 591; Supreme Court and, 599; AIDS and, 609; in military, 619; same-sex couples and, 630–631; antigay movement and, 631
Honduras, 528
Hone, Philip, 165, 209
Hong Kong, 407, 490
Honolulu Polynesian (newspaper), 204
Hood, John, 274
Hooker, Thomas, 35
Hoover, Herbert, 425, 437, 438; business and, 436; 1928 election and, 450; Great Depression and, 454, 455, 457–458; 1932 election and, 459
Hoover, J. Edgar, 428, 429, 541, 559
Hoovervilles, 455, 459
Hope, John, 366
Hopewell treaties, 120
Horizontal integration, 333
Horses, 17
Horseshoe Bend, Battle of, 155
Horton, Willie, 611
Hospitals, 185, 265, 267
Hostage crisis (Iran), 592–593, 597, 604
Hostile takeovers, 601
House, Edward, 422
"House Divided" speech (Lincoln), 250
Households: European, 68; labor for, 173; structure of, 350; appliances for, 436; in 1920s, 443; poverty in, 550; in late 20th century, 632(illus.)
House Judiciary Committee: Andrew Johnson and, 289

House of Burgesses (Virginia), 29, 30, 32, 83
House of Delegates (Maryland), 32
House of Representatives, 123, 188
House of the Seven Gables, The (Hawthorne), 207
House Un-American Activities Committee (HUAC), 539
Housework: in 1920s, 443
Housing: in Chaco Canyon, 4; for Indians, 5; elite, 64; urban, 209–210, 211; for slaves, 226–228; on Great Plains, 312, 313(illus.); for middle class, 330; suburban, 339, 441, 532; inner-city, 345, 346(illus.); reforms in, 345, 349; subsidized workers', 378; in First World War, 426; for blacks, 440; Levitt and, 536; redlining and, 536; after Second World War, 536; Model Cities program and, 561; rent subsidies and, 561
Houston, Charles Hamilton, 298, 540
Howard University, 284
Howe, Elias, Jr., 332
Howe, William, 100, 102–103
Hudson, Henry, 14, 23
Hudson River region, 70
Hudson's Bay, 76
Huerta, Victoriano, 412
Huerto, Dolores, 576
Hughes, Charles Evans, 393, 437, 476, 477, 484
Hughes, Langston, 449
Huguenots, 22, 61
Huitzilopochtli (Aztec god), 4
Hull, Cordell, 477, 479
Hull, William, 154
Hull House, 349, 376
Humanitarian interventions, 622
Human rights, 593, 594
Humphrey, Hubert H., 539, 564, 572
Hundred Years' War, 10
Hungary: after Second World War, 515; revolt in, 525, 611
Hunger: during Great Depression, 455
Hunter, Jane, 350
Hunting: by Indians, 3, 5
Huron Indians, 25, 44
Hurston, Zora Neale, 449
Hussein (Jordan): CIA and, 523
Hutchinson, Anne Marbury, 37
Hutchinson, Thomas, 83–84, 89
Hutchinson Family, 159
Hutus: in Rwanda, 622
Hydroelectricity, 391, 467
Hydrogen bomb (H-bomb), 519, 523
Hygiene: in Civil War, 267; in 1920s, 443
Hylton v. U.S., 129

Iberian Peninsula, 12, 46
Ibn Saud (Saudi Arabia), 529
Iceland: Norse in, 14
Ickes, Harold, 464
Idaho, 307, 308
Idealism: in U.S. foreign policy, 527
Identity, 387–388
Identity politics, 576–578
Ideology: revolutionary, 115; of Republican Party, 247–248; of Confederacy, 262
"If We Must Die" (McKay), 429

Igbo people, 59
Igorot people, 401(illus.)
"I Have a Dream" speech (King), 559–560, 559(illus.)
Illegal immigrants, 610
Illinois, 96, 163, 174, 202, 203, 209
Illinois Central Railroad, 459
Illness: from pollution, 590. *See also* Diseases
Imbrie, William, 354
IMF, *see* International Monetary Fund (IMF)
Immediatists, 186–188
Immigrants and immigration, 378; in Chesapeake region, 31; in Pennsylvania, 42; 1760–1775, 61; German, 61, 214; Irish, 61, 173, 199–200, 213; Scottish, 61; traditions of, 61–62; Naturalization Act (1798) and, 137; in Lewis and Clark expedition, 147; alcohol use and, 184; Chinese, 204, 307; in cities, 205; lifestyles of, 211–215; sources of (1831–1860), 212(illus.); South and, 220; Civil War and, 271, 293; Mexican, 307, 341, 441; to Australia, 311; as workers, 324; unions and, 327, 328; urban areas and, 339, 350; old and new, 341, 573, 595–596; mobility of, 341–343; culture and, 343, 344–345; machine politics and, 349; kinship obligations and, 351; show business and, 355; party politics and, 360; socialism of, 371; eugenics and, 385; in First World War, 426, 427; labor and, 436; Klan and, 445–446, 447; national origin and, 446, 573; quotas on, 446; sources of (1907 and 1927), 447(illus.); in Great Depression, 457; by German Jews, 483; Japanese, 484; Hungarian, 525; population characteristics and, 544; Latin American, 550; in 1980s, 609–610; to Los Angeles, 617–618; in 21st century, 630; from Asia, 630. *See also* Migration; specific groups
Immigration Act (1965), 561, 573
Immigration Reform and Control Act (1986), 610
I'm OK—You're OK, 591
Impeachment: of John Pickering, 145; of Andrew Johnson, 289; of Nixon and, 585, 585(illus.); of Clinton, 617, 624–625
Impending Crisis, The (Helper), 233
Imperialism: of McKinley, 373–374; of European nations, 398; of foreign policy elite, 399; Spanish-American War and, 406; in Asia, 407–410, 409(map); in Latin America, 480. *See also* Anti-imperialism
"Imperial presidency," 491, 530
Imports, 62, 94, 191, 393, 458
Impressment, 151
Inaugural address: of Jefferson, 144
Inauguration: of Franklin D. Roosevelt, 459–460; of Carter, 587
Incandescent bulb, 319
Incas: Spanish and, 15
Inchon, battle at, 521
Income: industrialization and, 330; in 1920s, 451; during Second World War, 499; in 1990s, 623
Income tax, 392, 393, 425, 437
Incorporation laws, 333
Indentured servants, 22, 31

Independence: struggle for, 93; loyalists and, 97; Paine on, 101; Treaty of Paris (1783) and, 107; of Latin American states, 163; of Vietnam, 511–512; of Philippines, 513; after Second World War, 513; in Third World, 525; in Cold War, 526(map); of Balkan states, 611. *See also* American Revolution
Independent treasury bill, 194
India, 527; Muslim trade with, 7; Gama in, 12; British conquest of, 79(illus.); after First World War, 432; after Second World War, 513
Indiana, 96, 163, 174
Indian Defense Association, 438
Indian policy, 303; Tenskwatawa and, 151; containment policy, 293–295; in 1920s, 438
Indian Reorganization Act (1934), 467, 550
Indian Rights Association (IRA), 304–305, 438
Indians, *see* American Indians
Indian Self-Determination and Education Assistance Act (1975), 578
"Indians of All Tribes," 577
Indian Territory, 178, 179, 259. *See also* Oklahoma
Indian Trade and Intercourse Act (1793), 139
Indigo, 52, 68
Individualism, 190, 232, 316, 371
Indochina, 520; after First World War, 432; Japan and, 488; crisis in (1954), 529; immigrants from, 609. *See also* Vietnam
Indonesia, 527
Industrial accidents, 325–326, 381
Industrial capitalism, 377
Industrialization, 317–333, 378; in textile industry, 170–171; in South, 262, 291, 323; after Civil War, 293; pollution and, 336; growth of cities and, 338–339
Industrial revolution, 153, 218
Industrial unions, 466
Industrial Workers of the World (IWW, Wobblies), 328, 426, 427, 428
Industry: after Revolution, 122; Jefferson and, 152; piracy of British technology, 153; tariff and, 161; protection of, 166; workplace changes and, 173; in Civil War, 261, 262, 263; railroads and, 310; production by, 320(map); 1890s depression and, 370, 371; electricity and, 435–436; in 1920s, 436; urbanization and, 440; in suburbs, 441; Great Depression and, 451, 455–457; postwar, 535; Eisenhower and, 538; deindustrialization and, 588; in South and West, 588–589; Reaganomics and, 599; high-tech, 620
Inequality of wealth, 335
Infant mortality, 32, 350–351, 443
Inflation: in Revolution, 119; in Civil War, 262, 263; postwar, 534; after Second World War, 537; in 1970s, 576, 587, 588, 590; control of, 600
Influence of Sea Power upon History, The (Mahan), 403
Influenza pandemic, 422–423, 424, 424(illus.)
Information technology, 620
Inheritance, 209
Initiative, 379, 381
Injunctions: strikes and, 328
"In loco parentis" doctrine, 569

Inner cities, 345–347, 550

Inner light: of Quakers, 41–42

Innes, George, 202(illus.)

Inoculation, 65, 105

Insane asylums, 181, 184–185

Insider trading scandals, 601

Insull, Samuel, 319

Insurance: old-age, 443

Integrated circuit, 590

Integration, 158, 503, 540, 541–542, 542(illus.). *See also* Desegregation; Segregation

Intel, 620

Intellectual thought: Enlightenment and, 64–65; Social Darwinism and, 334; on industrialization, 335; Marx and, 371; Progressives and, 384; expansionism and, 399. *See also* Art(s); Ideology; Literature

Intelligence operations, 523. *See also* Spies and spying

Inter-Allied government debts: after World War I, 479

Inter-American conference: in Havana, 480

Interchangeable parts, 170

Intercollegiate Athletic Association, 353–355

Intercollegiate sports, 384, 452

Intercontinental ballistic missile (ICBM), 523, 583

Intercultural rituals: Indian-European, 67

Interest groups, 356

Interesting Narrative (Equiano), 72

Interlocking directorates, 393

Intermediate-Range Nuclear Forces (INF) Treaty, 606

Internal combustion engine, 318, 319, 322

Internal improvements, 164, 166; in American System, 190; under Jackson, 191

Internal Security (McCarran) Act, 539

International Brigades, 482

International Harvester, 480

International Ladies Garment Workers Union (ILGWU), 329

International Monetary Fund (IMF), 514, 621

International order: after First World War, 432, 474–475; after Second World War, 513–517

International Telephone and Telegraph (IT&T), 479

Internet, 636–637

Internet Explorer, 637

Internment: of Japanese Americans, 494, 502–503, 502(illus.); of suspected spies, 502

Interracial relations, 56, 223

Interstate commerce, 328, 335, 384, 470–471

Interstate Commerce Act (1887), 333, 362

Interstate Commerce Commission (ICC), 362, 390, 391, 436

Interstate highway system, 536

Interventions: Monroe Doctrine and, 163; and U.S. hegemony in Caribbean and Latin America, 411(map); humanitarian, 622. *See also* specific countries

Intifada (uprising), 606

Intolerable Acts, *see* Coercive (Intolerable) Acts (1774)

Inventions: piracy of, 153; patent laws and, 166; by Edison, 319; of Granville T. Woods, 319. *See also* Technology; specific inventions and inventors

Investments, 620; foreign, 164, 165, 399; in railroads, 310; in southern industry, 323; in Latin America, 410, 411, 480; in Third World, 525–527; in 1970s, 590; economy and, 599; risky, 600–601; in South Africa, 606; September 11, 2001, and, 633. *See also* Foreign investment

In vitro fertilization, 632

Involuntary migration: by slaves, 56, 59

Involuntary sterilization laws, 385

Iowa, 174

Iran: Soviets and, 514; U.S. vs. Soviets and, 515; CIA and, 523; hostage crisis in, 592–593, 597, 604

Iran-contra scandal, 433, 604

Iran-Iraq War, 612

Iraq, 513; war in (2003–), 141, 617, 628–630; Saddam Hussein in, 593; weapons inspections in, 628

Ireland: Norse in, 14; Act of Union and, 199; potato blight and famine in, 200, 213; in First World War, 419. *See also* Irish people

Irish Benevolent Society, 199

Irish people, 61, 173, 199–200, 208, 213, 214, 341, 417

Irish Republican Army, 255

Iron curtain, 515

Iron industry, 62, 323

"Iron law of wages," 326

Iroquois Confederacy, 76, 103, 139

Iroquois Indians, 22, 120; culture of, 5; Huron war with, 25; in New France, 44–45; in Seven Years War, 77

Irrigation, 440; of Hohokam, 4; in West, 309–310; Newlands Act and, 391

Isabela (settlement), 14

Isabella of Castile, 10, 13

Islam: in Africa, 7–8; orthodoxy in, 593. *See also* Muslims

Islamic fundamentalism, 623; in Iran, 604; terrorism and, 615–616. *See also* September 11, 2001, terrorist attacks; Terrorism

Island-hopping: in Pacific War, 495(map), 508

Islands: Mediterranean, 12

Isolationism, 475, 482

Israel: terrorism against, 255, 583, 622–623; Arab conflict with, 528–529; creation of, 528–529; 1972 Olympics and, 583; Six-Day War and, 583; Yom Kippur War (1973), 583, 584; Camp David accords and, 592; Lebanon invasion by, 604; *intifada* against, 606

Issei, 344

Italian immigrants, 341

Italy: First World War and, 417; in 1930s, 481; Ethiopia invaded by, 482; Second World War and, 490, 505, 513, 515

Ivy League universities, 126

Iwo Jima, 495(map); Navajo code-talkers and, 492; battle at, 508

IWW, *see* Industrial Workers of the World (IWW, Wobblies)

Jackson, Andrew, 190, 192–193, 193(illus.), 200, 248; Indians and, 155, 175, 177–178; at New Orleans, 155; Florida and, 163; on Union, 191–192; on nullification, 192; Second Bank of the United States and, 192; Texas and, 197

Jackson, Helen Hunt, 304

Jackson, Rachel, 190

Jackson, Thomas ("Stonewall"), 258, 260, 268

Jacksonians, 183, 189–191

Jackson State University: students killed at, 581

Jacobs, Harriet, 231

Jails, *see* Prisons

Jamaica: Spanish settlement of, 25

James I (England), 17, 28, 30

James II (duke of York, England), 41, 53, 54

James River, 29

Jamestown, 28

Japan: trade with, 244; immigrants from, 307, 341; baseball in, 354, 354(illus.); expansion by, 398, 413, 485(map); communications with, 402; in China, 407, 409(map), 410; in East Asia, 413; First World War and, 417, 430; Second World War and, 476, 483–484, 494, 513; Soviet-American relations and, 480; Anti-Comintern Pact and, 482; aggression by, 484; in French Indochina, 488; Pearl Harbor attack by, 488–489, 489(illus.); in Second World War, 494, 495(map), 507, 508, 509; in Cold War, 520; Indochina and, 520; alliance with, 522; economy of, 588; automobiles from, 610

Japanese Americans: reparations to, 234; employed women among, 444–445; internment of, 494, 502–503, 502(illus.); in 442nd Regimental Combat Team, 503

Japanese immigrants, 308, 344, 380, 400–401

Jarvis, Anna, 352

Jay, John, 94, 125

Jay Treaty, 134, 136

Jazz, 217

Jazz Age: in 1920s, 449–450

Jazz Singer, The (film), 448

Jefferson, Thomas, 110, 130, 131, 145(illus.), 245, 381; Declaration of Independence and, 101; and architecture, 112; on blacks, 116; whiskey tax and, 132; and 1796 election, 135; as vice president, 135; Virginia and Kentucky resolutions and, 137; as president, 143–149, 151–152; Louisiana Purchase and, 146–148; and 1800 and 1804 elections, 149; Non-Importation and Embargo acts and, 152. *See also* Democratic-Republicans

Jefferson Airplane, 569

Jeremiah, Thomas, 99

Jerseys, 41, 70. *See also* New Jersey

Jerusalem: Crusades and, 10

Jesuits, 22–23, 36

Jews and Judaism, 61, 208, 214; in Rhode Island, 37; immigration by, 337; pogroms against, 341; Orthodox, 343; religious assimilation and, 344–345; Democratic Party and, 360; on Supreme Court, 393; Balfour Declaration and, 430; 1936 Olympics and, 469; Nazi Germany and, 481, 482, 483; in Second World War, 503–504; in Soviet Union, 592. *See also* Arab-Israeli disputes; Israel

Jiang Jieshi (Chiang Kai-shek), 484, 507–508, 520

Jim Crow, 503, 558; as minstrel character, 207, 208(illus.); laws, 297, 366, 385

Jinmen (Quemoy), 525

Job Corps, 562
"John Brown's Body" (song), 254
Johnson, Andrew, 280, 284–285; Reconstruction plan of, 281; vs. Congress, 286–287; impeachment of, 289
Johnson, Eastman, 222(illus.)
Johnson, Hiram, 380
Johnson, James Weldon, 429
Johnson, Lyndon B.: Tonkin Gulf crisis and, 491; Vietnam and, 529, 563–567, 570; civil rights and, 554; Kennedy assassination and, 560; Great Society and, 560–563; 1964 election and, 561; War on Poverty and, 561–563; Immigration Act and, 573; affirmative action and, 578; inflation and, 588
Johnson, Michael, 231–232
Johnson, Tom, 349
Johnson Act (1934), 479
Johnston, Joseph E., 260, 268–269, 274, 275
Johnston, Sidney, 260
Joint Chiefs of Staff, 531
Joint-stock companies, 28, 33, 34
Jolliet, Louis, 44
Jones, Bobby, 448
Jones, Mary Harris ("Mother"), 328
Jones, Paula, 624
Jones, Samuel ("Golden Rule"), 349
Jones Act (1916), 407, 414
Jonesboro: school shootings in, 624
Joplin, Janis, 569
Jordan, 513; Israel peace accord with, 622
Jordan, Barbara, 608
Jordan, Michael, 630
Journalism: yellow, 356; muckrakers in, 379, 383
Judaism, see Jews and Judaism
Judicial review, 146
Judiciary, 124, 129, 144–145; in Massachusetts, 35; in New England, 43; in states, 117; Marshall and, 145–146; in Gilded Age, 358–359. See also Courts; Supreme Court (U.S.)
Judiciary Acts, 149; of 1789, 129, 146; of 1801, 144, 145
Jungle, The (Sinclair), 379, 390
Junk bonds, 601
Jupiter missiles: in Turkey, 557
Jury trials, 129
Justice Act (1774), 89
Justice Department, 428, 627
Juvenile delinquency, 500, 547, 549

Kaiser, William, 498
Kaiser shipyards, 498
Kamikaze attacks, 508
Kansas Alliance: Populist party and, 369
Kansas and Kansas territory, 310; Indian removal to, 176; Texas and, 195; slavery and, 237; Bleeding Kansas and, 248; Lecompton Constitution and, 250; African Americans in, 296–297, 385
Kansas Indians, 175
Kansas-Nebraska Act (1854), 244–246, 246(map)
Karenga, Maulana, 576
Kaskaskia, Illinois, 96
KDKA (radio station), 439
Kearney, Dennis, 344
Kearny, Stephen, 240

Keller, Helen, 432
Kelley, Florence, 349, 376, 378, 379, 384
Kelley, Oliver H., 368
Kellogg, John H., 331
Kellogg, William K., 331
Kellogg-Briand Pact (1928), 477, 484
Kennan, George F., 515, 517; on Southeast Asia, 567
Kennedy, Jacqueline, 560
Kennedy, John F.: as Catholic president, 198; CIA and, 523; Cuba and, 528; civil rights and, 554, 558–559; Cold War and, 554–557; health of, 555; assassination of, 560; Vietnam and, 563, 564
Kennedy, Robert F., 555, 556, 570, 572, 573
Ken societies, 343
Kent State University: students killed at, 581
Kentucky, 95, 253, 258, 260
Kentucky Resolution, 137, 157, 191
Kenya, 583
Kerensky, Aleksander, 422
Kerner, Otto, 567
Kerner Commission report (1968), 567, 608
Key, Francis Scott, 155
Khomeini (Ayatollah), 593
Khrushchev, Nikita, 523–525; Cuban missile crisis and, 554, 557; Kennedy and, 556
Kidd, William, 48
Kim Il Sung (North Korea), 521
King, Martin Luther, Jr., 541–542, 558, 559; assassination of, 555, 570–572; "I Have a Dream" speech by, 559–560, 559(illus.); March on Washington and, 559–560, 559(illus.)
King, Rodney, 617
King, Rufus, 161
King Cotton, 225
King George's War, 63, 76, 77(illus.)
King Philip's War, 39, 45
Kings and kingdoms: in West Africa, 8. See also Monarchs and monarchies; specific rulers
King's Mountain, battle at, 106
King William's War, 54, 77(illus.)
Kinsey, Alfred, 547
Kinship: Indian, 5, 68; in West Africa, 8; African American, 69, 230; urbanization and, 351, 352
Kipling, Rudyard, 407
Kissinger, Henry, 575–576, 582–583; Vietnam cease-fire and, 581
Kitchen Cabinet: of Jackson, 191
"Kitchen debate," 525
Klackner, Charles, 168(illus.)
Klamath Indians, 551
Klan, see Ku Klux Klan
Klebold, Dylan, 623
Knickerbocker Club, 207, 352
Knight Foundation Commission on Intercollegiate Athletics, 452
Knights of Labor, 327
Know-Nothing (American) Party, 236, 247, 248, 249
Knox, Frank, 486
Knox, Henry, 130, 139
Knox, Robert, 213
Konoye (Japan), 488
Korea, 407; Japan and, 413, 484; split of, 520–521. See also North Korea; South Korea

Korean immigrants, 610; segregation of, 400–401; Los Angeles riots and, 617–618
Korean War, 520–522, 537–538; consequences of, 522; desegregated military in, 540
Kosovo War, 622
Kristallnacht, 483
Ku Klux Klan, 277, 281, 292, 293, 369, 541; after First World War, 429; 1924 election and, 437; in 1920s, 445–446, 447; in Great Depression, 459; civil rights workers and, 558
Kuwait, 612
Kwanzaa holiday, 576
Kyoto protocol (1997), 623, 626

Labor: slave, 12, 21, 22, 226–229, 234; African, 15; *encomienda* system and, 15; servants as, 21, 22; in Virginia, 29; in Chesapeake, 31–32; colonial, 68; in boom-and-bust cycles, 164–165; of women, 169–170, 444, 444(illus.); workplace and, 172–174; household, 173; movement, 173–174; slave vs. free, 232; free, 247; in Civil War, 263; immigrant, 307, 441, 446, 610; in West, 308; for railroads, 310; in textile industry, 323; in tobacco industry, 323; mechanization and, 324–326; increase in wage, 330–331; reforms in, 381, 391–392; in First World War, 425–426; African American, 426; public opinion on, 436; in Great Depression, 454, 466–467; in 1970s, 588; international, 620. See also Servants; Slaves and slavery; Strikes (labor)
Labor and Commerce Department, 390
Laboratory School (University of Chicago), 383
Labor Department: in First World War, 426
Labor organizations: for women, 173
Labor-saving devices: farm implements as, 169
Labor unions, 174, 263, 379; Knights of Labor as, 327; AFL as, 327–328; IWW as, 328; membership of, 329; women and, 329; Sherman Anti-Trust Act and, 335; Theodore Roosevelt and, 390–391; anti-imperialism and, 407; in First World War, 426; prosecution of, 436; craft vs. industrial workers and, 466; in Great Depression, 466; in Second World War, 498; Taft-Hartley Act and, 534–535, 537; in 1950s, 543, 550; Reagan and, 599; free-trade agreements and, 620–621. See also Trade unions
Lackawanna Valley, The (Inness), 202(illus.)
Lady of Cofitachequi, 1
Laffer, Arthur, 599
Laffer curve, 599
La Follette, Philip, 464
La Follette, Robert M. ("Battling Bob"), 381, 390, 392; First World War and, 420
La Follette, Robert M., Jr., 464
LaHayes, Beverly, 607
Laissez faire, 179, 334, 335, 381
Lake Erie region, 76
Lakes, see specific lakes
Lakota Indians, 17, 301, 303–304, 305
Lalawethika, see Tenskwatawa ("the Prophet," Shawnee)
Land: in West Africa, 8; Indians and, 29, 76, 151, 155, 176–177, 305, 467, 551, 578; in

Massachusetts, 35; riots over, 70; under Articles of Confederation, 117–119; western claims to, 118(map); speculation in, 164, 165, 192–193, 250; surveys and settlement of, 166; prices of, 175; wealth and, 220; for colleges and railroads, 264; freedpeople and, 283; redistribution of, 288; in West, 301, 307; Dawes Severalty Act and, 305; preservation of public, 308; reclamation and irrigation for, 309; in Great Plains, 313; for cattle industry, 314; Mexican American, 577; private acquisition of, 598–599

Land bridge: Beringia as, 3

Land-grant colleges, 264, 383, 384

Land grants: in New France, 22; Dutch, 25; by James II, 41; to states, 174–175

Landless whites: in South, 223

Landlords: in inner city, 345

Landon, Alf, 465

Lange, Dorothea, 456(illus.)

Language(s), 219; cultures named by, 5; in Africa, 7; Indian, 7, 303; Gullah, 51; Cherokee, 176; English as "official," 610

L'Anse aux Meadows, Newfoundland, 14

Laos, 565(map), 581

La Raza Unida (RUP), 577

La Salle, René-Robert Cavalier de, 44

Las Gorras Blancas (White Hats), 368

Last Sale of Slaves, The (Noble), 227(illus.)

Lateen sail, 10, 11(illus.)

Latin America, 374; racial mixing in, 15; Monroe Doctrine and, 163; immigrants from, 341, 550; U.S. power in, 398, 410, 411(map), 480–481; intervention in, 410–411, 411(map), 412, 477; Roosevelt Corollary and, 411(map), 412; air travel to, 442; American business in, 477; Franklin D. Roosevelt and, 480–481; Soviet Union, 515; nationalism in, 525; United Fruit Company in, 528; Alliance for Progress and, 556; Nixon, Kissinger, and, 583; Carter and, 592. *See also* Central America; South America

Latinos, *see* Hispanics

Latitude, 10

Latvia, 430, 483, 514, 611

Law(s): in West Africa, 8; Spanish slavery and, 15; emancipation, 114–115; Constitution and, 124, 146; in West, 308; Progressives and, 379, 384

Law enforcement: in cities, 348

Lawrence, Amos A., 244

Lawrence, Kansas: sack of, 248

Lawrence, Massachusetts: anti-Catholic violence in, 214

Leach, William R., 375

League of Nations, 417, 422, 430–431, 475, 476; German withdrawal from, 482; Japanese aggression and, 484

League of Women Voters, 438, 485

Lear, Norman, 608

Lease, Mary Elizabeth, 358, 369, 374

Lebanon, 430, 513, 529; Israeli invasion of, 604; U.S. marines in, 604–606

Lecompton Constitution, 250

Le Duc Tho, 581

Lee, Ann (Mother), 201

Lee, Richard Henry, 94, 101, 125

Lee, Robert E., 260, 268, 269, 275

Left (political), 464, 562. *See also* Liberals and liberalism

Legal code: Duke's Laws as, 41

Legal Defense and Education Fund, 540

Legal rights: in nineteenth century, 210

Legal thought: Progressive, 384

Legislation: presidential veto of, 130; for working conditions, 326; antitrust, 335; pollution, 336; in Gilded Age, 358, 360–363; in New Deal, 460–461, 462; under Clinton, 625. *See also* Law(s)

Legislatures, 124; in Massachusetts, 34; in states, 117; in Constitution (U.S.), 123. *See also* Assemblies

Leisler, Jacob: rebellion by, 54

Leisure, 352–356, 436; colonial, 64; in urban areas, 207–208; party politics and, 360; in 1920s, 448–449

Le Monde: on September 11, 2001, attacks, 628

Lenape Indians, *see* Delaware (Lenape) Indians

Lend-Lease Act (1941), 488

Lenin, V. I., 422, 430

Leningrad, *see* St. Petersburg

Lennon, John, 571

Leopard (ship), 151–152

Lesbians: gay liberation movement and, 580. *See also* Homosexuals and homosexuality

Letters from a Farmer in Pennsylvania (Dickinson), 85

Letters of a Federal Farmer, 125

Levitt, William, 536

Lew, Barzillai, 104(illus.)

Lewinsky, Monica, 624

Lewis, John (civil rights activist), 558

Lewis, John L. (labor leader), 466

Lewis, Meriwether, 147–148

Lexington, battle at, 99

Liberal Republicans, 293

Liberals and liberalism, 379, 560–563, 568, 585

Liberator, The, 188

Liberator bombers, 498

Liberia, 186

Liberty, 42, 82, 247

Liberty (sloop), 86

Liberty League, 462, 466

Liberty Loans, 427

Liberty-of-contract doctrines, 394

Liberty Party, 188, 241

Liberty ships, 498

Life expectancy, 331, 351

Life of Washington (Weems), 111

Lifespan: in Chesapeake, 31, 36; in New England, 36; in 1920s, 443; Social Security and, 473

Life stages: in late 19th century, 351–352

Lifestyle: Paleo-Indian, 3; in West Africa, 7–8; European, 9–10; in Chesapeake, 30–36; in New England, 36–37; of slaves, 51, 226–229; colonial economy and, 62; in revolutionary army, 104–105; of Indians, 139, 578; in rural areas, 201–203; on Great Plains, 312; of wage workers, 329; industrialization and, 329–333, 330(illus.); of immigrants, 337; spread of American, 399; automobiles and, 438–439; of working class, 439; of Mexican workers, 441; in 1920s, 441–445; in Second World War, 498–500, 504–505; suburban, 532–534; in 1950s,

543–545; after September 11, 2001, 627. *See also* Culture(s)

Light bulb, 319

Lili'uokalani (Hawai'i), 403

Lilli doll, 548, 548(illus.)

Limited government: Jackson on, 191

Limited liability: of corporations, 166

Lincoln, Abraham, 240, 254; secession and, 157–158; on slavery in territories, 249; "House Divided" speech by, 250; and 1860 election, 251; in Civil War, 260; leadership by, 264, 271; emancipation and, 265–266; Emancipation Proclamation of, 266, 267; and 1864 election, 272; assassination of, 275, 276(illus.); 10 percent plan of, 281; Wade-Davis bill and, 282

Lincoln, Benjamin, 105

Lindbergh, Charles A., 434, 442, 468

Lindsey, Ben, 378

Lippmann, Walter, 564

Literacy, 207; Jesuit missionaries and, 23; oral cultures and, 65; newspapers and, 69; republicanism and, 111; growth in, 356; of soldiers, 504

Literacy requirements, 365, 380; in First World War, 426

Literary societies, 185

Literature: after Revolution, 111, 113; abolitionist, 188; utopians and, 203; popular, 207; *Uncle Tom's Cabin*, 242–243; about West, 309, 316; Arabic, 361; muckrakers and, 379; in 1920s, 449; after Second World War, 549. *See also* specific works

Lithuania, 430, 483, 514, 611

Little Big Horn, battle at, 304, 304(illus.)

Littlefield, Henry M., 374

Little Rock, Arkansas: school integration in, 541–542, 542(illus.)

"Little Rock Nine," 541–542

Little Turtle (Miami leader), 121, 121(illus.)

Little Women (Alcott), 211

Livestock, 15, 35; of Indians, 301. *See also* Cattle and cattle industry

Livingston, Robert, 146, 166, 625

Livingstone College, 367(illus.)

Lloyd George, David, 430

Loans: business and, 334; in First World War, 418; in Great Depression, 458; to Germany, 479; to Latin America, 480

Lobbying: in 1920s, 436

Local government(s), 54, 56; bankruptcies of, 618

Locarno Pact (1925), 477

Lochner v. New York, 326, 384

Locke, Alain, 449

Locke, John, 42, 65

Locomotives: "Tom Thumb" as, 167–169

Lodge, Henry Cabot, 398, 399, 403, 431, 476

Logan, Deborah Norris, 127

Logan, George, 127, 136

Logan Act (1799), 127–128

London: Crystal Palace Exhibition in, 170; Nazi blitz in, 487, 488(illus.)

Lonely Crowd, The (Riesman), 549

Long, Huey, 464

Longhouses, 5

"Long Walk": of Navajos, 272

Loom: water-powered, 153

Lopez, Jennifer, 630
Lord Dunmore's war, 95
Los Alamos, New Mexico, 497
Los Angeles: bilingual education and, 207; railroads in, 310; suburbs of, 441; Hispanics in, 550, 610; drug-related deaths in, 608; Rodney King riot in, 617; immigrants in, 617–618
Lost Cause ideology, 262, 277
Lost Generation: in 1920s, 449
Louis XIV (France), 54
Louis, Joe, 468, 470(illus.)
Louisbourg, 63, 77, 79
Louisiana and Louisiana Territory, 77, 143, 146, 163, 164, 174; slavery in, 52–53; secession and, 252
Louisiana Purchase, 146–148, 147(map), 174, 241; borders of, 163
Louis Philippe (France), 240
Louisville, 175
Love Canal: pollution of, 590
Lovejoy, Elijah P., 188, 209
Lowell, Francis Cabot, 153, 170–171
Lowell, James Russell, 239
Lowell, Massachusetts, 171, 172–173
Lower Guinea, 8(illus.), 49
Lower South: economy of, 63. See also South
Loyalists (Revolutionary War), 97, 98, 98(illus.), 100, 105, 119
Loyalists (Spanish Civil War), 482
Loyal Nine (Boston), 83, 84, 88
Loyalty oaths: for white southerners, 285, 287
Loyalty risk: in 1950s, 539
Lucas, Eliza, 52
Luce, Henry, 490
Luftwaffe (German air force), 486
Lumber industry, 166, 195, 306(map), 307, 323
Luna Park, 353(illus.)
Lusitania (ship), 415, 418
Luther, Martin, 27
Luxuries, 329–330; trade in, 11
Lynch, James, 291
Lynchings, 365, 385, 429, 459
Lyon, Mary, 126
Lyon, Matthew, 137

MacArthur, Douglas, 459, 495, 508, 520, 521
Machine Age, see Industrialization; Industry
Machine guns, 398
Machinery: farm, 263, 313; productivity and, 318
Machines (political), see Political machines
Machine-tool industry, 170, 322
MacIntosh, Ebenezer, 83
Mackinac Island, 154
Macon's Bill Number 2, 152
Macune, Charles W., 369
Macy's, 332
Madeira islands, 13
Madison, Dolley, 154
Madison, James, 125, 128–129, 146, 245; as "Father of the Constitution," 123; on assumption, 131; Virginia and Kentucky resolutions and, 137; and 1808 election, 152; War of 1812 and, 152–157; and 1812 election, 156; domestic policy of, 161
Magazines, 207, 356; muckraker journalism in, 379; women's, 545; mass, 549

Magee, Christopher, 348
Mahan, Alfred Thayer, 403
Mail, 356
Mailer, Norman, 549
Mail-order companies, 313
Maine, 14, 28, 35, 53, 164, 174; Indians in, 45; border dispute in, 195
Maine (battleship), 404, 405
Maize, see Corn (maize)
Malaria, 31; drugs for, 398
Malaya, 490
Malcolm X, 568
Malinche, 14
Malnutrition: among Indians, 175
Mammoth Oil Company, 437
Managed economy, 556
Management: of cities, 347–350; in Great Depression, 466. See also Scientific management
Manchuria, 407, 413, 484
Mandan, Fort, 147
Mandela, Nelson, 611
Manhattan Island, 25; battle at, 102
Manhattan Project, 497, 509
Manifest destiny, 183, 195–197
Manila, 407; British conquest of, 79; Dewey in, 406
Mann, Horace, 205
Mann Act (1910), 383, 384
Mann-Elkins Act (1910), 391
Manufacturing: in English colonies, 62; Hamilton on, 131; Embargo Act and, 152; after War of 1812, 156; commerce and, 171–172; in South, 291; growth of, 318; production and, 324, 399, 400(illus.); women in, 324; depression of 1890s and, 370; in Second World War, 497
Manumission: after Revolution, 114–116
Manypenny, George, 304
Mao Zedong, 484, 508, 519, 520, 583
Maple Floor Association v. U.S., 436
Marbury v. Madison, 145–146
March on Washington: in Second World War, 497; in 1963, 559–560, 559(illus.)
March to the sea (Sherman), 274, 275(map)
Margin buying: in Great Depression, 451
Marietta, Ohio, 121
Marin, John, 450
Marine Corps, 421; in Cuba, 412; in Latin America, 480; blacks in, 503; in Lebanon, 604–606; in Somalia, 622
Maritime trade, 10
Market(s): transportation to, 166; in West, 300; farmers and, 399; foreign, 399; emerging, 620; integration of, 620, 633
Market economy, 159–160; government and, 164–167; farming and, 169; household labor and, 173; Indians and, 175; family life and, 201, 210–211; immigrants and, 212; blacks and, 216; rural and urban life and, 216–217; in North, 218; in South, 218–219
Marketing, 318; of cigarettes, 323
Marne River: battles at, 422
Marquette, Jacques, 45
Marriages: Indian, 5; in Chesapeake, 32; interracial, 56; of blacks, 68, 231; in nineteenth century, 210, 211; in planter class, 226; Boston marriage, 351; in Great Depression, 455; in Second World War, 500, 501,

501(illus.); in 1950s, 545–546; of female labor force, 546(illus.); in 1970s, 591; age at, 591; defined, 631
Marryat, Frank, 204(illus.)
Marshall, George C., 503, 517
Marshall, James, 203, 204
Marshall, John, 145–146, 161; commerce and, 166; Cherokees and, 177
Marshall, Thurgood, 298, 503, 540–541
Marshall Plan (1948), 517, 518(map)
Martí, José, 404
Martial law: in Civil War, 261, 264; Enforcement Acts and, 293
Martín (son of Cortés and Malinche), 14
Martinique, 25
Marx, Karl, 371
Marxism-Leninism: of Stalin, 514
Maryland, 31, 53, 253; land claims by, 117–119; in Civil War, 258, 260
Masculinity: crisis of, 547
Mashantucket Pequot Museum: Foxwoods Casino and, 38
Masons, 183, 185, 186
Massachusetts, 33–36; as royal colony, 53, 54; witchcraft crisis in, 54; education in, 112, 205; Shays's Rebellion in, 122; Antifederalists in, 125; corporations in, 166–167
Massachusetts Bay Colony, 53
Massachusetts Bay Company, 33
Massachusetts Government Act (1774), 89
Massacres, see specific massacres
Massasoit (Wampanoag), 33
Mass culture, 468–470; criticisms of, 549. See also Popular culture
Massive retaliation policy, 523
Mass marketing: radio and, 439
Mass media, see Media
Mass production, 170, 171, 477; in auto industry, 319–322, 322(illus.); of cigarettes, 323; of clothing, 323, 332; in cities, 339
Mass transportation, 339, 343
Master-slave relationship, 221, 228, 229
Masterson, William ("Bat"), 308–309
Materialism: exploration and, 11; in 1920s, 438–439
Mather, Cotton, 55(illus.), 65
Matrilineal descent: Indian, 5
Mattachine Society, 580
Mattel, 548
Maximilian (Mexico), 402
Maximum Freight Rate case, 362
Mayas, 3–4, 15, 19
May Day, 372, 380(illus.)
Mayflower (ship), 33
Mayflower Compact, 33
Maysville Road bill, 191
Mazu (Matsu), 525
McAdoo, William G., 437
McAllister, Alexander, 57
McCain, Franklin, 553
McCarran Act, see Internal Security (McCarran) Act
McCarthy, Eugene, 570, 572
McCarthy, Joseph R., 522–523, 539
McClellan, George B., 258, 260, 272
McClure's (magazine), 379
McCormick, Cyrus, 170
McCormick farm machinery factories, 327, 370

McCulloch v. Maryland, 161
McDonald's: protests against, 622
McDowell, Irvin, 258
McGovern, George, 585
McHenry, Fort, 155
McKay, Claude, 429
McKinley, William, 364, 373–374, 403–404; 1896 election and, 372, 373; assassination of, 389, 410; Cuba and, 404–405; Spanish-American War and, 405–406; Open Door policy and, 407, 410
McKinley Tariff (1890), 362, 373, 403
McLaughlin, Hugh, 348
McMurtry, Larry, 316
McNamara, Robert, 555, 557, 567
McNary-Haugen bills (1927, 1928), 437
McNaughton, John, 574
McNeil, Joe, 553
McPherson, Aimee Semple, 448
McVeigh, Timothy, 623
"McWorld," 622
Meade, George G., 269
Measles, 17
Meat Inspection Act (1906), 390
Meatpacking industry, 315, 334, 379, 390
Mechanical reaper, 170
Mechanization, 159, 317–318, 441–443; of agriculture, 263, 367, 368, 440, 550; labor and, 324–326; mobility and, 331; of mass transportation, 339; leisure and, 352
Me-Decade (1970s), 591
Media, 602; cultural impact of, 439, 545–546; consolidation of, 601; diversity in, 619. *See also* specific media
Medical schools, 384
Medicare, 563; Reagan and, 598, 600
Medicine: colonial, 65; of slaves, 229; pro fessionalization of, 265; in 1920s, 443; in Second World War, 504
Mediterranean region, 10, 12
Mehta, G. L., 527
Mellon, Andrew, 437
Melodramas, 355
Melville, Herman, 203
Memorial Day, 279
Men: Indian, 7, 139, 305; West African, 8; European, 10; in New England, 32; farm life and, 201, 223; legal rights of, 210; single, 211; in West, 307; employment trends and, 325(illus.); clothing for, 332; occupational mobility and, 342–343; in homosexual sub-culture, 351; unmarried, 351; gender roles and, 546; in 1950s, 547
Menéndez de Avilés, Pedro, 22
Menlo Park, New Jersey, 319
Mennonites: as COs, 421
Mental illness, 184–185. *See also* Insane asylums
Mercantilism, 50; Townshend Acts and, 85
Meredith, James, 559
Mergers, 334; corporate, 601
Merrick, Dwight, 317
Mescalero Apache Indians, 272
Mesoamerica, 3–4; Spanish in, 15; maize in, 16, 16(illus.); wealth of, 19
Mestizos, 14, 68, 307
Metacom (King Philip), 39, 45
Methodists, 183, 220, 234, 284
Métis, 45, 68

Metropolitan Club, 399
Meuse-Argonne offensive, 422
Mexicans and Mexican Americans, 214–215, 295, 343–344, 610; in West, 308; agrarian protest by, 368; employed women among, 444–445; in Great Depression, 457, 471; in Second World War, 497; zoot suit riots and, 500; in postwar period, 536; *bracero* program and, 550; in Los Angeles–Long Beach area, 550; in 1970s, 576–577; Chicano movement and, 577; *cursillo* movement and, 590–591. *See also* Hispanics
Mexican War, 238–240, 239(map)
Mexico, 3, 44, 163; Spain and, 22, 148; Texas and, 195–196; California gold rush and, 204; fugitive slaves in, 243; immigrants from, 307, 341, 441; French in, 402; relations with, 412–413; intervention in, 418; First World War and, 420; workers from, 426; U.S. relations with, 481
Mexico City, 15, 240
Miami: Hispanics in, 610
Miami Confederacy, 121, 121(illus.)
Miami Indians, 42, 121
Michigan, 174
Microprocessor, 620
Middle class, 210, 216; industrialization and, 330; mass transit, 339; housing in, 345; in Progressive era, 378; Indians in, 387; women in, 387–388; in Great Depression, 457; black, 541; in 1950s, 543–545, 549–551; television and, 545; in 1970s, 576
Middle colonies, 47–49, 63, 169. *See also* specific colonies
Middle East, 513, 622–623, 629(map); missionaries in, 361; Cold War and, 516; Arab-Israeli conflict in, 528–529; U.S. interests in, 604–606; terrorism in, 606; national security and, 636. *See also* specific presidents
"Middle ground," 67, 68
Middle passage, 47
Midnight appointments, 144–145
Midway, Battle of, 495(map), 496, 508
Midway Islands, 295, 402, 490
Midwest, 368; agriculture in, 170; cities in, 440, 589; industrial decline in, 588
Migrant workers, 456(illus.); Mexican American activism and, 576–577
Migration, 534; of English dissenters, 28; New England and, 32, 35, 43; involuntary, 56, 59, 60(map), 175; by 1770, 57–58; from Europe, 59–61; before Revolutionary War, 95; after War of 1812, 160, 174–175; African American, 296–297, 385, 426, 497; in West, 300, 312; urban population growth and, 339–341; families and, 350, 352; in Great Depression, 453–454; in Second World War, 499; to suburbs, 536. *See also* Immigrants and immigration; Slaves and slavery
Militarism: economics and, 477
Military: in Seven Years War, 77; Quartering Act and, 89; civilian control of, 107; Federalists on, 148; labor unrest and, 326, 328; women in, 420–421, 504; U.S., in foreign countries, 480–481, 635; production for, 496; science and, 497; segregation of, 503; growth of, 519; aid to Vietnam and, 520; spending on, 522, 531, 636; Eisenhower,

Dulles, and, 523; highways and, 536; de-segregation of, 540; Reagan and, 603; gays in, 619; September 11, 2001, and, 633–635; AIDS and, 634. *See also* Armed forces; Soldiers
Military bases: in Second World War, 486; on Okinawa, 520
Military districts: in South, 287, 288(map)
Military-industrial complex, 531, 538
Military technology: in Vietnam War, 567
Militias, 95; colonial, 69; in Revolution, 99; in Constitution (U.S.), 129; in 1990s, 623
Milken, Michael, 601
Millennium Round, 621
Milligan, Lambdin P., 295
Millman, Zelma, 524(illus.)
Mills, 152; textile, 170–171, 172–173. *See also* Textile industry
Milosevic, Slobodan, 622
Minerals: in West, 307; in Australia, 311
Minie ball (bullet), 267
Minimum wage, 537, 577
Mining, 306(map), 307, 392; strikes against, 328, 371, 390–391; gold vs. silver issue, 363. *See also* Gold; Silver
Minkins, Shadrach, 242
Minor, Rufus, 347
Minorities, 308, 349, 378, 578. *See also* specific groups
Minstrel shows, 207, 208(illus.), 217, 355
Miró, Esteban Rodriguez, 138(illus.)
Miscegenation, 56, 308. *See also* Interracial relations
Miss America Pageant: protests at, 579
Missiles, 523; limiting, 583; Reagan and, 603; INF Treaty and, 606
Missions and missionaries, 15, 22–23, 203; Catholic and Protestant, 35–36; Indians and, 176; female societies of, 184; Protestant, 308; world expansion of, 361; in China, 396–397, 410, 484; cultural imperialism and, 398; American culture and, 401. *See also* specific orders
Mississippi, 163, 174, 177, 252; Freedom Summer in, 558; African American voting in, 561
Mississippian culture, 3, 4
Mississippi Freedom Democratic Party (MFDP), 558, 561
Mississippi Plan (1890), 365
Mississippi River region: Spanish closing of, 119; Louisiana Purchase and, 146–148; Civil War in, 259
Missouri, 174, 202, 209; as slave state, 163–164; secession and, 253; in Civil War, 258, 259
Missouri Compromise (1820), 162(map), 164, 241, 244, 249
Missouri Indians, 175
Mixed economy, 179–180
Mixed-race people: Indian-European, 45, 68
MKULTRA program, 523
Mobility: industrialization and, 331; of immi-grants, 341–343; in urban borderlands, 343
Mobilization: for First World War, 394
Model Cities program, 561
"Model tenements," 345
Model T Ford, 322, 322(illus.), 438

Modern Woman: The Lost Sex, 547
Mogollon peoples, 4
Mohammed, 7. *See also* Islam
Mohawk Indians, 44, 103
Molotov, V. M., 514
Moluccas, 19
Monarchs and monarchies: after Hundred
    Years' War, 10. *See also* specific rulers and
    dynasties
Mondale, Walter: 1984 election and, 600
Monetary policy: gold vs. silver, 363
Monetary system: under Articles, 119
Money: wampum as, 26; Bank of the United
    States and, 131. *See also* Currency; Mone-
    tary system; Paper money
Money supply: in 1890s depression, 370;
    under Reagan, 600
"Monkey trial," 433
Monks Mound, 4
Monopolies, 166, 167, 334, 335
Monroe, James, 146, 161, 176
Monroe Doctrine, 163, 402, 413; Venezuelan
    dispute and, 404; Roosevelt Corollary to,
    411(map), 412
Montana, 307, 308
Montauk Indians, 26
Monterrey, 240
Montezuma, *see* Motecuhzoma II (Montezuma)
Montgomery, Marvin, 453–454
Montgomery bus boycott, 534, 541, 542
Montgomery (Alabama) *Mail,* 248
Montgomery Ward (store), 313
Montreal, 22, 77, 103
Moon, Charlotte Diggs (Lottie), 396–397
Moon landing (1969), 590
Morality, 36–37, 127–128
Moral Majority, 198, 607, 607(illus.), 609
Moral reform: female reform societies and, 184;
    Antimasons and, 186; societies for, 324. *See
    also* Reform and reform movements
"Moral suasion": by Garrison, 188–189
Mordechai, Samuel, 216
Morgan, Daniel, 106
Morgan, J. P., 319, 334, 370, 390, 391, 402
Morgan, William, 185
Morgan v. Virginia, 541
Morgenthau, Henry, Jr., 504
Mormons, 184, 201, 202–203, 209, 308, 309
"Mormon War," 250
"Morning in America," 600
Morocco, 413
Moro Province, Philippines, 407
Morrill Act (1890), 314
Morrill Land Grant Act (1862), 264, 313–314
Morris, Robert, 119
Morristown, New Jersey, 102
Mortality: smallpox and, 65; Indian, 68; rates
    of, 331
Mortgages, 536
Mortgaging the Farm, 185
Moscow: in Second World War, 496
Mose, town of, *see* Gracia Real de Santa Teresa
    de Mose
Motecuhzoma II (Montezuma), 4
"Mother and Child on the Road" (Lange),
    456(illus.)
Mothers: unmarried, 591. *See also* Women
Mother's Day, 352

Mott, Lucretia, 188, 189
Mountains: in West, 300
Mt. Holyoke College, 126
Movable type, 10
Movies and movie industry, 355–356, 528;
    westerns in, 316; in First World War, 426,
    427; in 1920s, 448, 449; in 1930s, 468; in
    Second World War, 499; for teenagers, 547
"Mr. X": Kennan as, 517
Muckrakers, 379, 383
Muguet, Peter, 66(illus.)
Mugwumps, 360
Muir, John, 308
Mujahidin (Islamic guerrillas), 592, 603, 623
Mulattos: from Haiti, 138; in South, 223,
    224; from involuntary relationships, 230;
    education of, 284
Muller v. Oregon, 326, 381, 384
Multiculturalism: New Right on, 607
Multiethnicity, 630
Multiethnic neighborhoods, 343–344
Multiracial categories: on Census, 630
Multiracial people, 56
Multiracial society, 403; in West, 307
Munich Conference, 482
Municipal bonds, 349
Municipal Voters League, 379
Munn v. Illinois, 362
Murrah Federal Building: bombing of, 623
Murray, Elizabeth, 64(illus.)
Murray, Judith Sargent, 112–114, 112(illus.)
Murray, William Vans, 137
Murrow, Edward R., 487, 487(illus.)
Music, 352; African Americans and, 216, 217,
    230; African influences on, 229; in 1920s,
    450; of youth culture, 547–548; in 1960s,
    569; "British invasion" in, 571. *See also*
    specific types
Musical comedy, 355, 449
Muskogean peoples, 5–7
Muslims: European Christians and, 10; in
    Spain and Portugal, 10; Africans as, 59;
    enslaved, 69; in Philippines, 407; in
    Afghanistan, 592; Iran hostage crisis and,
    593; in Bosnia, 622. *See also* Islam
Mussolini, Benito, 470, 481, 482
Mutual aid societies, 215, 343
Mutual defense agreement: ANZUS as, 522
Mutual Defense Assistance Act, 519
Mutualistas (cooperative associations), 577
Mutual Security Treaty: with Japan, 520
My Lai massacre, 581
Myrdal, Gunnar, 541
Mystic River massacre, 35, 38

NAACP, *see* National Association for the
    Advancement of Colored People (NAACP)
Nader, Ralph, 561; 2000 election and, 625
NAFTA, *see* North American Free Trade
    Agreement (NAFTA)
Nagasaki: bombing of, 494, 509
Naked and the Dead, The (Mailer), 549
Napalm, 567
Napoleon I (France), 146, 151, 155, 156, 211
Napoleon III (France), 402
Narragansett Indians, 33, 45
NASA, *see* National Aeronautics and Space
    Administration (NASA)

Nash, Diane, 558
Nasser, Gamal Abdel, 529, 593
Nast, Alice, 524(illus.)
Nast, Thomas, 290(illus.)
Natchez Indians, 53
Nation, The, 402, 455
National Advisory Commission on Civil
    Disorders, *see* Kerner Commission report
    (1968)
National Aeronautics and Space Administration
    (NASA), 523, 560
National American Woman Suffrage Associa-
    tion, 366, 378, 388
National anthem, 155
National Anti-Slavery Standard, 188
National Association for the Advancement of
    Colored People (NAACP), 298, 356, 387,
    421, 429, 503, 540, 541, 559
National Association of Colored Women, 388,
    438
National bank: Bank of the United States as,
    131, 161; in American System, 190; system
    of, 264
National Chicano Liberation Youth Confer-
    ence (1969), 577
National Child Labor Committee, 381
National Civil Service Reform League, 362
National College Athletic Association
    (NCAA), 355, 452
National Committee for Organizing Iron and
    Steel Workers, 428
National Conference on the Cure and Cause
    of War, 476
National Congress of American Indians, 578
National Consumers League (NCL), 378,
    384–385, 438
National Cordage Company, 370
National Council of Churches, 541
National debt, 130–131, 132, 144
National Defense Act (1916), 420
National Defense Education Act (NDEA), 538
National Economic Council, 620
National Endowment for the Arts (NEA), 561,
    585
National Endowment for the Humanities
    (NEH), 561, 585
National forests, 391
National Geographic, 400
National government: states and, 117, 124;
    under Articles of Confederation, 117–119;
    Democratic-Republicans vs. Federalists on,
    143; Marshall and, 145; supremacy of, 161.
    See also Constitution (U.S.); Government
    (U.S.)
National Guard: First World War and, 420; at
    Central High School, Little Rock, 541;
    Kent State University killings by, 581
National Housing Act (1949), 550
National Industrial Recovery Act (NIRA), 460,
    461, 462, 470
National Intelligencer, 148
Nationalism, 399; after Revolution, 128; after
    War of 1812, 160, 161–164; black, 216; in
    Confederacy, 261–262; Hawaiian, 403; after
    First World War, 432; in Latin America,
    480, 525; in Mexico, 481; in China, 484; in
    Vietnam, 512; after Second World War, 513;
    in Africa, 525; cultural, 575

Nationalist Chinese, 522
Nationalities: in Europe, 422; immigration quotas on, 446. *See also* specific groups
National Labor Relations (Wagner) Act (1935), 466, 470
National Labor Relations Board (NLRB), 462, 466, 467, 599
National Labor Union, 326
National League (baseball), 352
National Liberation Front (NFL), *see* Vietcong
National Military Establishment, 531
National Missile Defense system, 626
National Municipal League, 378
National Negro Business League, 378
National Organization for Women (NOW), 579, 607
National origins: immigration quotas by, 573
National Origins Act (1924), 446
National parks, 308, 391
National Progressive Republican League, 391
National Recovery Administration (NRA), 460–461, 471
National Reparations Coordinating Committee, 234–235
National Republicans, 190
National Research Council, 432
National Road, 156, 161, 167
National security, 531
National Security Act (1947), 517–519
National Security Council: NSC-68 and, 519, 531
National Socialism, *see* Nazi Germany
National Trades Union, 174
National Traffic and Motor Vehicle Safety Act (1966), 561
National War Labor Board (NWLB), 426, 498
National Woman's Party, 388, 438
National Woman Suffrage Association (NWSA), 366
National Youth Administration, 464
Nation of Islam, 568
Native American Rights Fund, 578
Native Americans, *see* American Indians
Native Son (Wright), 541
Nativism, 209, 247; urban crime and, 347; in First World War, 427; in 1920s, 446
Nat King Cole Show, 545
NATO, *see* North Atlantic Treaty Organization (NATO, 1949)
Naturalists, 64–65
Naturalization, 216, 344. *See also* Citizens and cititizenship
Naturalization Act: of 1798, 137, 144; of 1802, 144
Natural-law doctrine, 221
Natural resources, 13, 166, 301, 306–309, 306(map); Newlands Reclamation Act and, 309–310; government management of, 381, 391; Reagan and, 598–599
Nauvoo, Illinois: Mormons in, 202–203
Navajo Indians, 68, 174, 272, 301–302, 467; trade with, 303; "code-talkers" and, 492–493
Navalism, 403
Navigation: tools of, 10
Navigation Acts (1651–1673, 1696), 50–51, 82, 85
Navy(ies): privateers and, 105; limitations of, 162; steel for, 398; of Japan, 413; in First

World War, 418; Washington Naval Conference and, 477. *See also* Navy (U.S.); Royal Navy (England); Submarines
Navy (U.S.), 148, 151–152, 154, 420; in Revolution, 148; limitations of, 162; in Civil War, 258, 259; modernization of, 403; in Spanish-American War, 406; "Great White Fleet" of, 413; Theodore Roosevelt and, 413; before Second World War, 488; Pearl Harbor attack and, 489, 489(illus.); Second World War battles by, 495(map)
Navy Act (1916), 420
Nazi Germany, 476, 481–482; 1936 Olympics and, 469, 469(illus.); Munich Conference and, 482; U.S. business ties with, 482; Jews in, 483; Poland and, 483; Soviet nonaggression pact with, 483; invasions by, 485–486, 486(map); in Second World War, 490; surrender of, 493, 508
Nazi-Soviet nonaggression pact, 488
NCAA, *see* National College Athletic Association (NCAA)
Nebraska, 310
Necessary and proper clause, 124, 131, 161
Necessity, Fort, 76–77
Negro Business Men's League, 366
Negro Convention movement, 215
"Negro Rule" myth, 291
Negro World (newspaper), 441
Neighborhoods, 339, 343–345
Neolin (Delaware Prophet), 80, 139
Nestor, Agnes, 329
Netherlands, 20, 25, 485. *See also* Dutch
Netscape, 637
Networks: television, 545
Neutrality, 476; in First World War, 417–418, 419–420; before Second World War, 485; Dulles on, 522, 527
Neutrality Acts (1935, 1936, 1937), 482, 484, 490
Neutrals: in Revolution, 97
Nevada, 240, 307
Nevada (ship), 489
New Age movement, 591
New Amsterdam, 25
Newark, New Jersey: riot in, 567
New Bern: Indians and, 52
New Brunswick, 98, 195
New Deal, 455, 463(illus.); First, 459–461; legislation in, 460–461, 462; Second, 461–466; federal power in, 467; limits of, 470–472. *See also* Social Security
"New Democrat": Clinton as, 618
New Echota, Treaty of, 178
New Economy, 620
New England, 32–37, 43; King Philip's War and, 45; trade in, 47–49; Dominion of, 53; economy of, 63; Hartford Convention in, 156–157; farming in, 169; textile industry in, 170–171
Newfoundland, 14, 17, 76, 107
New France, 22–23; fur trade and, 23–25; Iroquois and, 44–45; population of, 59; economy of, 62; British conquest of, 79. *See also* Canada
"New Freedom," 392, 393
New Frontier: of John F. Kennedy, 560
New Hampshire, 35, 53

New Haven, 35, 53
New immigrants, 341, 573, 595–596, 609–610
New Jersey, 41, 53, 102, 334
New Jersey Plan, 123
Newlands Reclamation Act (1902), 309–310, 391
New Left, 568, 569
New Lights, 71
Newly independent nations: since 1943, 526(map)
New Mexico, 45, 56, 195; Spanish in, 22; indigenous peoples in, 44; Territory of, 216, 259–260; acquisition of, 240, 242
New Mexico Volunteers, 272
New Nationalism, 392, 393, 425
New Navy, 403, 404
New Netherland, 23–24, 26, 41
"New Order": in Asia, 484
New Orleans, 146; French founding of, 45; Battle of, 155; Civil War in, 259; general strike in, 371
New Right, 596, 597, 599, 607
News, 356, 487, 602. *See also* Media; Newspapers; Television
New South, 323
New Spain, 22, 45; indigenous peoples in, 44; slavery in, 52; population in North America, 59; economy of, 62; Texas in, 148
Newspapers, 69, 207; Sedition Act and, 137; black, 215; advertising in, 332; yellow journalism and, 356
New Sweden, 25
"New woman": in 1920s, 445
New World, *see* America(s); specific countries
New York (city): blacks in, 53, 69; tea tax and, 89; in Revolution, 102–103; slavery in, 115; commerce in, 167, 171–172; prostitution in, 184; growth of, 205, 339; wealthy in, 209; immigrants in, 213; draft riots in, 271; Triangle Shirtwaist Company fire in, 326; "Great White Way" in, 332; population density in, 345; drug trade in, 608; Chinatown in, 610; Korean immigrants in, 610; economy of, 589
New York (colony), 41, 53; Leisler's rebellion in, 54; conspiracy in, 70
New York (state), 213; prisons in, 185; housing reform in, 345
New-York Evening Post, 148
New York Herald, 294
New York Journal, 356, 404
New York Stock Exchange, 334
New York Sun, 209
New York Times: Pentagon Papers and, 574–575; on Reagan, 613
New York Tribune, 265, 293
New York World, 356, 402
New York Yankees, 448–449
New Zealand: in ANZUS, 522
Nez Percé Indians, 303
Niagara, 81, 154
Niagara movement, 386–387
Niantic Indians, 26
Nicaragua, 20, 480, 604
Nicholas II (Russia), 382
Nicodemus, Kansas, 307
Nigeria, 7, 50, 59
Niña (ship), 13

Nine-Power Treaty, 477, 484

Nineteenth Amendment, 388, 426, 429, 438, A9–A10

Ninth Amendment, 129, A8

Nipmuck Indians, 45

Nitze, Paul, 519

Nixon, Richard, 523–525; as vice president, 522; Red Scare and, 539–540; 1960 election and, 555; 1968 election and, 572; foreign policy and, 575–576; affirmative action and, 578; Vietnam War and, 580; Cold War and, 582–583, 601–603; 1972 election and, 585; impeachment, resignation, and, 585, 585(illus.); Watergate and, 585–587

Nixon Doctrine, 582

NLF, see Vietcong

NLRB v. Jones & Laughlin Steel Corp., 470

Nobel Peace Prize, see specific recipients

Noble, Thomas S., 227(illus.)

"No-fault" divorce, 591

"No-fly zone": in Iraq, 612

Nomads: Paleo-Indians as, 3; in North America, 5, 7

Nonaggression pact: Nazi-Soviet, 483

Nonexportation, 94

Nonimportation, 84, 86–87, 94

Non-Importation Act (1807), 152

Non-Intercourse Act (1809), 152

Nonintervention: Monroe Doctrine and, 163

Nonpartisan elections, 381

Non-Partisan League, 427

Nonrecognition: of China, 520

Nonslaveholders: slavery's influence on, 232

Nonviolence, 503, 542, 558

Noriega, Manuel, 612

Normandy invasion, 493, 505

Norris, George, 420

Norsemen, 3, 13–14

North: Revolutionary War in, 102–103, 102(map); slavery in, 114–115, 240; Missouri Compromise and, 162(map); antislavery movement in, 188; free people of color in, 215; discrimination in, 216; market economy in, 218; South and, 219–220; cotton and, 225; Dred Scott decision and, 249; Reconstruction and, 292–293; African American migration to, 341, 385, 426; desegregation in, 541; industrial decline in, 588; cities in, 589

North (Civil War), 258, 263–265; resources of, 259(illus.); antiwar sentiment in, 270–271; diplomatic strategy of, 272. See also Civil War (U.S.)

North, Frederick (Lord), 86, 88, 89, 99–100, 106

North, Oliver, 433, 604

North Africa: in Second World War, 496, 506(map)

North America: in 1492, 5–7; native cultures of, 6(map); Cabot and, 14; Europeans in, 17–18, 20–38, 23(illus.); in Atlantic world, 39–41; worldwide links of, 79; after Seven Years War, 80–82

North American Free Trade Agreement (NAFTA), 620

North Atlantic Treaty Organization (NATO, 1949), 518(map), 519, 622

North Carolina, 43, 95, 253, 258, 585

North Carolina Agricultural and Technical College, 553–554

North Dakota, 308

Northeast region: agriculture in, 169

Northeast Trades, 12

Northern Securities case, 390

Northern Securities Company, 390

North Korea, 520–521. See also Korea; Korean War

North Vietnam, 529–530, 563. See also Vietnam War

Northwest: Indian treaties in, 303

Northwest Ordinance (1787), 120, 122

Northwest Passage, 14

Northwest Territory, 120, 240

Norway, 485

Nova Scotia, 63, 76, 77, 96

Novels, 113, 207

NOW, see National Organization for Women (NOW)

NSC-68, 519, 531

Nuclear arms race, 515

Nuclear household, 68, 350

Nuclear power, 538, 590. See also Atomic bomb

Nuclear weapons: cancers from testing, 510; after Second World War, 515; hydrogen bomb and, 519, 523; Soviets and, 519; Korean War and, 521; under Eisenhower, 523; in China, 525; anticommunism and, 539; wastes from, 549; Kennedy and, 556; in Cuba, 557

Nullification, 157–158, 191–192

Nuremberg Laws (1935), 481

Nurse Corps: in First World War, 420

Nursing: in Civil War, 265

Nutrition: in 1920s, 443. See also Diet (food)

Nye Committee, 482

Occupational Safety and Health Administration (OSHA), 585

Occupations (jobs), 341–342

Oceania: imperialism in, 398

Oceans: exploration of, 12. See also specific ocean regions

O'Connor, Sandra Day, 599

O'Connor, Thomas, 200

Officeholders: African Americans as, 290, 291, 365

Office of Management and Budget (OMB), 600

Office of Price Administration (OPA), 498–499

Office of Strategic Services (OSS): in Vietnam, 511

Office of War Information (OWI), 499

Ogden, Aaron, 166

Oglethorpe, James, 63

Ohio, 76, 202

Ohio Company, 121

Ohio Indians, 76

Ohio River region: British and French in, 76; Indians in, 80; Quebec and, 89; settlement of, 121, 122, 174; Louisiana Purchase and, 146–148; cities in, 175

Oil and oil industry, 307, 439, 543; trusts and, 333–334, 390; Arab-Israeli conflict and, 528–529; in 1970s, 576, 583, 584, 588; OPEC production and, 600; Persian Gulf War (1991) and, 612; Arctic drilling and, 626. See also Energy crisis

Oil spills, 590

Ojibwa Indians, 305

OK Corral, shootout at, 309

O'Keeffe, Georgia, 449

Okies, 453

Okinawa, 495(map), 520; battle at, 508

Oklahoma and Oklahoma Territory, 178, 195, 385

Oklahoma City: federal building bombing in, 255

Old-age assistance, 378, 381, 437. See also Pensions; Social Security

Older Americans, 351, 381; age bias and, 399; in 1920s, 443; poverty among, 550, 562

Older Federalists, 149

"Old Folks at Home" (Foster), 217

"Old Hickory": Jackson as, 190

Old immigrants, 341

Old Lights, 71

Old Man Hat (Navajo), 301

Old Northwest, 120; Indians in, 150; in War of 1812, 154, 155; family agriculture in, 169–170

Old South, see Antebellum period; South

Oligarchy: in Hawai'i, 403

Oligopolies, 436

Oliver, Andrew, 83

Olmecs, 3

Olney, Richard, 328, 404

Olympia (ship), 406

Olympic Games: of 1904, 401(illus.); of 1936, 469, 469(illus.); of 1972, 583; of 1980, 592

Omaha Indians, 175

Omaha platform: of Populists, 369

Omnibus bill: slavery compromise and, 241

Oñate, Juan de, 22

Oneida Indians, 44, 103

O'Neill, Eugene, 449

One-party system: in South, 248

Onís, Luís de, 163

Onondaga Indians, 44

Ontario, 98

OPEC, see Organization of Petroleum Exporting Countries (OPEC)

Opechancanough, 29

Open Door policy, 407–410, 409(map), 476, 477, 483, 484; Japan and, 413; before Second World War, 488

Open markets, 620

Open-range ranching, 314

Open shops, 436, 498

Operation Desert Shield, 612

Operation Desert Storm (1991), 602(illus.), 612. See also Persian Gulf War (1991)

Operation Mongoose, 557

Operation Overlord, 505

Operation Rolling Thunder, 564

Operation War Bride, 501(illus.)

Oral cultures, 65

Orange, Fort (Albany), 23

Ordinances: of 1784 and 1785, 120

Oregon, 147, 197, 216, 238, 307; occupation of, 162; border of, 163

Oregon Trail, 197, 203

Oregon Treaty (1846), 238

Organic Act (1900), 404

Organization Man, The (Whyte), 549

Organization of Petroleum Exporting Countries (OPEC), 576, 583, 584, 600
Organizations: of Progressive era, 378
Organized labor, 173–174, 534, 620. *See also* Labor; Labor unions
Orinoco River, 404
Oriskany, New York, battle at, 103
Orlando, Vittorio, 430
Orphanages: reform of, 185
Osage Indians, 45
Osceola (Seminole), 178–179
OSHA, *see* Occupational Safety and Health Administration (OSHA)
Ostend Manifesto, 245
O'Sullivan, John L., 195
Oswald, Lee Harvey, 560
Otis, Harrison Gray, 188
Otis, James, Jr., 82–83
Oto Indians, 175
Ottawa Indians, 80, 120
Ottoman Empire, 417, 423, 430
Our Bodies, Ourselves, 579
Our Country (Strong), 400
Our Indian Wards (Manypenny), 304
Outdoor billboards, 332
Overland trails: migrants on, 203–205
Overtime pay, 393
Owens, Jesse, 469, 469(illus.)
Ownership: of utilities, 381

Pachucos (gang members), 500, 577
Pacification, 405, 411
Pacific Ocean region, 300, 374; exploration of, 14, 148; expansion to, 183, 196(map); U.S. empire in, 398; U.S. claims in, 402; Japan and, 430; islands in, 483; Second World War in, 494–496, 495(map), 508
Pacifism: of Penn, 42; in Revolution, 97; First World War and, 419, 477; in Vietnam War, 567
Padlocks, 170
Padrone (boss), 343
Paducah, Kentucky: school shootings in, 624
Pago Pago, 402
Paine, Thomas, 100–101, 102
Painting, 112, 449
Paiute Indians, 5
Pakistan, 513, 603
Paleo-Indians, 3
Palestine and Palestinians, 430, 513, 528–529, 592, 622–623
Palestinian Liberation Organization (PLO), 583, 604, 606, 622
Palmer, A. Mitchell, 428, 429
Palmer Raids, 429
Palo Alto, battle at, 238
Pamela (Richardson), 113
Panama, 412, 442, 480; Isthmus of, 14; Canal Zone and, 592; invasion of, 602, 612
Panama Canal, 412, 474, 480
Pan American Airways, 442, 442(illus.), 606
Pan-Americanism, 480
Pan-Arabic movement, 529
Panay (gunboat), 484
Panics (financial): of 1837, 164–165, 168, 195, 213; of 1819, 168, 172, 190; of 1857, 250–251; of 1873, 293, 326; in late nineteenth century, 333; of 1907, 391

Pan-Indian federation, 150, 151
Paper money: Jackson and, 193
Paraguay, 163
Pardons: for Confederates, 280, 281, 285; of Nixon, 587
Parietals, 569
Paris: summit in (1960), 525
Paris, treaties of: in 1763, 77; in 1783, 107, 119; in 1898, 406, 407, 412
Paris Peace Conference: of 1849, 187; after First World War, 417, 430
Parks, Rosa, 542
Parliament (England), 106; Protestantism and, 27; English civil war and, 41; rights of, 81; protests against, 82–90
Parrington, Vernon L., 384
Partisan politics, 134–135
Party caucuses, 379
Party politics: Jacksonianism and, 183; in second party system, 193–195; in Gilded Age, 359; alignments in, 360. *See also* Political parties
Passchendaele, battle at, 421
Passing of the Great Race, The (Grant), 385, 446
Patent(s), 166, 319
Patent medicine industry, 390
Paternalism: in South, 224; toward foreigners, 399
Paterson, William, 123
Patrilineal societies: Indian, 5
PATRIOT Act, 627
Patriotism: First World War and, 417, 426, 427; Second World War and, 496; after September 11, 2001, 627
Patriots: Boston Massacre and, 87–88; in Revolution, 96–97; slaves and, 99
Patronage, 364
Patroonship, 25
Patterson, Floyd, 528
Patti, Archimedes, 511–512
Paul, Alice, 388
Paulucci, Jeno, 356
Pawnee Indians, 175, 299, 301, 303
Pawtucket: mill in, 122
Paxton Township: Conestoga massacre in, 95
Payne-Aldrich Tariff (1909), 391
Payne's Landing, Treaty of, 178–179
Peace accord: Israel-Jordan, 622
Peace Corps, 556
Peace Democrats, 271
"Peace dividend," 612
Peace groups: after First World War, 476–477
Peacekeeping: in Lebanon, 604–606; in Kosovo, 622
Peace movement: in Civil War, 270, 271
Peace of Ryswick, 54
Peace of Utrecht, 76
Peale, Charles Willson, 101(illus.), 112, 145(illus.)
Peale, Rembrandt, 145(illus.)
Pearl Harbor, 403, 488–489, 489(illus.)
Peer groups, 443
Pendergast, Tom, 348
Pendleton Civil Service Act (1883), 362, 364
Peninsula campaign, 260
Penitentiaries, *see* Prisons
Penn, William, 42

Pennington, J. W. C., 187
Pennsylvania, 42, 53; immigrants in, 61; Indians and, 76, 80–81; Whiskey Rebellion in, 132; prisons in, 185; September 11, 2001, and, 615, 626
Pensacola, 155
Pensions: for Civil War veterans, 360, 364; old-age, 381, 437, 443, 465, 473; Townsend plan for, 464; judicial, 471
Pentagon: attack on, 615, 626
Pentagon Papers, 574
Pentecostal churches, 448
People, the, 69, 110, 191
People for the American Way, 608
People of color, 56; free, 115, 138, 174, 215–216, 284; in urban borderlands, 344; eugenics movement and, 385; stereotypes of, 400, 401(illus.); New Deal and, 471; women and, 547; poverty of, 550; population of, 630
People's Party, *see* Populist party
People's Republic of China (PRC), 520, 521, 525, 576. *See also* China
People-to-people campaign, 524, 524(illus.)
Pequot Indians, 35, 38
Pequot War, 35, 38
Perestroika (restructuring), 606
Perkins, Frances, 464
Permanent Court of International Justice, *see* World Court
Perot, Ross, 618, 619
Perry, Matthew, 244
Perry, Oliver Hazard, 155
Perryville, Battle of, 260
Pershing, John J. ("Black Jack"), 412–413, 421
Persian Gulf region: Carter and, 592; Saddam Hussein in, 593
Persian Gulf War (1991), 141, 597, 612, 613, 618
Persico, Joseph, 487
Personal-liberty laws, 244
Personal Responsibility and Work Opportunity Act (1996), 619
Peru, 163
Pesticides, 549
"Pet banks," 192
Petersburg: siege of, 274, 275
Petroleum, *see* Oil and oil industry
Pharmaceutical industry, 323
Phelps-Stokes Fund, 479
Philadelphia, 42, 69, 84, 115; Continental Congress in, 93–94, 100; in Revolution, 103; Constitutional Convention in, 122–124
Philadelphia (ship), 142, 143
Philadelphia Plan: for affirmative action, 578
Philanthropy, 334, 346–347
Philippines, 398, 401, 401(illus.), 413, 477, 483, 488, 490, 494–495, 496; British in, 79; communications with, 402; Spanish-American War in, 406; Republic of, 407; independence for, 513; immigrants from, 609
Philosophy: Enlightenment and, 64; transcendentalism and, 203
Phonograph, 356
Photography: in Civil War, 261(illus.)
Physicians: as missionaries to China, 361; birth control and, 394–395. *See also* Medicine
Pickering, John, 145
Pickering, Timothy, 149

Pickett's Charge, 269
Pickford, Mary, 356
Piecework rates, 324
Pierce, Franklin, 243–244
Pike, Zebulon, 148
Pilgrims, 33
Pill, the, 570, 609
Pinchot, Gifford, 391
Pinckney, Charles Cotesworth, 149
Pinckney, Thomas, 134, 135
Pinckney's Treaty, 134, 146
Pine Ridge, South Dakota, 305
Pingree, Hazen S., 349
Pinkerton Detective Agency, 328
Pinochet, Augusto, 583
Pinta (ship), 13
Pioneers: land for, 175
Piracy, 48, 48(illus.), 142
Pitt, Fort, 76, 77, 80
Pitt, William, 77, 85
Pittigrew, James, 269
Pittsburgh: railroad strike in, 326
Pittsburgh Pirates, 352
Plague, 10
Plains Indians, 299–300, 301, 304(illus.)
Plains states, *see* Great Plains
Plan Espiritual de Aztlán, El, 577
Planned Parenthood Federation of America
  (PPFA), 395
Planning and zoning commissions, 437–438
Plan of Union, 76
Planters and plantations, 220, 224–226, 248;
  in South Carolina, 43; slaves and, 51, 59,
  68–69; classes and, 232–234; Civil War and,
  269–270. *See also* Slaves and slavery; specific
  crops
Plants: Columbus and, 13; in Columbian
  Exchange, 15; from Lewis and Clark
  expedition, 148. *See also* Crops
Platt Amendment, 411–412, 481
Playboy magazine, 547
Pledge of Allegiance, The, 551–552
Plessy, Homer, 366
Plessy v. Ferguson, 366, 541
PLO, *see* Palestinian Liberation Organization
  (PLO)
Plows, 170
Plumbers group (Watergate), 585–586
Plunkitt, George Washington, 348
Pluralism, 356
Plutonium, 510
Plymouth Colony, 33, 34(illus.), 53, 54
Pocahontas, 28
Pocket-veto: of Wade-Davis bill, 282
Poets and poetry: in 1920s, 449
Pogroms, 337, 341
Poindexter, John M., 604
Pokanoket Indians, 33, 39, 45
Poland: Russia and, 422; Hitler and, 483; after
  Second World War, 507, 514; revolt in, 525,
  611; Solidarity in, 603
Polaris missiles, 523
Police: in cities, 209, 348; in Boston, 437; in
  1968 Chicago riots, 572
Polish Roman Catholic Union, 329
Political campaigns, 149
Political cartoons, 132(illus.), 245(illus.),
  273(illus.), 290(illus.), 363(illus.)

Political conventions, *see* Elections; specific
  parties
Political culture, 143, 148–149
Political geography: engineering and, 398
Political machines, 348–349; Progressives and,
  379; Tammany Hall as, 450
Political parties, 132–133; "court parties" and
  "country" interest, 55; labor organization
  of, 173; realignment of, 247–248. *See also*
  Factions; specific parties
Political power: in colonies, 81–82; of
  Parliament, 83
Politics: Indian, 5–6; in Chesapeake, 32; colonial
  autonomy in, 53; in Anglo-America, 69–71;
  roles in, 110; factions in, 128, 132–133;
  partisanship in, 134; urban, 208; Irish immigrants in, 213; free blacks and, 215; slavery
  and, 233; sectionalism in, 246(map); in South,
  248, 289–292; machine, 348–349; pluralism,
  interest groups, and, 356; in Gilded Age,
  358–374; Farmers' Alliances in, 369;
  Progressives and, 381; world, in 1920s,
  436–438; women and, 438; radio and, 439;
  Second New Deal and, 461–466; identity
  politics and, 576–578; AIDS and, 609
Polk, James K., 195, 197, 238–240, 241, 245
Polk, Leonidas, 369
Poll taxes, 365, 380
Pollution: in cities, 205; from cattle processing,
  315; industrialization and, 336; of water, 347;
  from wartime industry, 510; in 1950s, 549–550;
  in 1970s, 590; controls of, 623
Polo, Marco, 10–11
Polygamy: among Mormons, 202, 203, 250,
  308
Polygyny, 50, 67
Ponce de León, Juan, 14
Pontiac's Uprising, 80–81, 95
Pools (business), 333, 362
Poorhouses, 443
Poor people: diet of, 331–332; Progressives
  and, 378. *See also* Poverty
Popé, 45
Popular culture: black influences on, 217; in
  1930s, 468–470; in Second World War,
  499; population diversity and, 630. *See also*
  Mass culture
Popular election: of electors, 189
Popular Front, 464, 465
Popular sovereignty, 241, 242, 244, 249, 250
Population: Indian, 5; Columbian Exchange
  and, 15, 17; and Indian wars, 45–46; of
  slaves, 47; of African Americans, 56, 215;
  growth of, 57–58, 59–62; of people of color,
  115, 630; in 1790, 137; migration and, 174;
  in cities, 205, 206(map), 339–341, 340(map),
  440; Hispanic, 215, 610; in South, 220; of
  West, 301; age of (1880–1920), 350; of
  southern black voters, 365; in schools, 384;
  in 1920s, 443; baby boom and, 535–536; distribution of (1930–1970), 536(illus.); of Sunbelt and Southwest, 543; ancestry of, 544;
  ethnic and racial groups in, 550; poverty in,
  563; immigrants in, 573; shift to Sunbelt,
  588–589, 589(map); environmentalism and,
  590. *See also* specific locations
Populism (political doctrine), 369
Populist demagogues: in New Deal, 462–463

Populist party, 327, 358, 369–370, 378; free
  silver and election of 1896, 372–374
"Porkopolis" (Cincinnati), 172
Poro cult (West Africa), 8
Porter, Roy, 424
Porter, Sylvia F., 535
Port Huron Statement, 568
Ports, *see* Seaports
Portsmouth Conference (1905), 413
Portugal, 10, 12, 18, 46, 50
POSSLQ, 591
Post, Charles W., 331
Post, Louis, 429
Postal service, 360; Rural Free Delivery (RFD)
  and, 313; employee shootings and, 624
Postmaster general, 129
Post office, 166
Posttraumatic stress disorder, 582
Postwar era, 532–536
Potato blight (Ireland): immigration and, 200
Potatoes, 3, 15
Potawatomi Indians, 80, 120, 156
Potsdam Conference, 508
Potsdam Declaration, 509
Pottawatomie Creek: John Brown and, 248
Pound, Ezra, 449
Poverty, 62; in England, 27; relief for, 62, 63,
  346–347; in cities, 209–210; in South, 223,
  262; causes of, 347, 562–563; in 1920s, 443;
  rural, 534; in 1950s, 550; War on Poverty
  and, 561–563; 1959–1974, 563(illus.); in
  1980s, 595, 608; taxation and, 601; of under-
  class, 607; reasons for, 608; homelessness
  and, 609; Los Angeles riots and, 617
Powderly, Terence V., 327
Powell, Colin, 606
Powell, Lewis, Jr., 585, 591
Power (energy): hydroelectricity and, 467. *See
  also* Electricity; Energy crisis; Oil and oil
  industry
Power (political): in states, 117; of Congress,
  124; of president, 264; of political machines,
  348; Progressives and, 377; federal, 467–468
Power loom, 153
Power of Sympathy, The (Brown), 111, 113
Power plants, 319
Powers, Francis Gary, 525
Powhatan, 28
Powhatan Confederacy, 28, 29
POWs, *see* Prisoners of war (POWs)
Prague Spring, 572
Prayer: in schools, 198
Praying Towns, 35
Precision machine tools, 322
Pre-Columbian America, 5–6
Predestination, 27
Pre-emption Act (1841), 175
Premarital sex, 547, 591. *See also* Sex and
  sexuality
Presbyterians, 198
Prescott, Samuel, 99
Preservation: vs. conservation, 391
President and presidency: in Constitution
  (U.S.), 124; title of, 130; Washington and,
  130–135; expansion of power, 264, 391, 392;
  in Gilded Age, 359, 364–365; Theodore
  Roosevelt and, 391; Franklin D. Roosevelt
  and, 472, 491; foreign affairs and, 530; after

Nixon, 587; list of elections, A12–A16; list of presidents and vice presidents, A17–A18. *See also* Elections; specific presidents

President's Organization on Unemployment Relief (POUR), 458

Presidios, 203

Presley, Elvis, 217, 547–549

Press: freedom of, 117

Price discrimination, 393

Prices, 63, 165; in 1970s, 590

Prince Hall Masons, 208

Princeton: Battle of, 101(illus.)

Princeton University, 126, 393

Printing, 10, 185, 356

Prisoners of war (POWs): as slaves, 50; in Korean War, 521–522

Prisons: reforms of, 184–185; in Civil War, 279

Privacy rights: abortion and, 579

Private enterprise, 556

Privateers, 20, 48, 105, 152

Proclamation of 1763, 81

"Proclamation of Amnesty and Reconstruction," 281

Production: machines and, 318; mass, 319–322, 322(illus.); industrial (1919), 320(map); standardization of, 323; efficiency in, 323–324; in First World War, 425; in Second World War, 496–498

Productivity, 441–443, 588

Professional Air Traffic Controllers Organization (PATCO), 599

Professionalization: of medicine, 265; of foreign service, 399

Professional organizations, 378; in 1920s, 436

Professions and professionals, 378; women and, 343, 349, 358, 408, 444, 547, 579, 608; in 1950s, 543

Profiles in Courage (Kennedy), 555

Profiteering: in Civil War, 264; in First World War, 425

Profits: production organization and, 323; from foreign sales, 399

Progress and Poverty (George), 335

Progressive era, 376–395; poverty relief and, 347; reforms and reformers in, 376, 378–379, 380, 381; associations during, 378; foreign influences on, 378; goals of, 378, 394; Socialists in, 379; in South, 379–380; temperance, prohibition, and, 382, 383; prostitution and white slavery in, 383; education in, 383–384; social institutions in, 383–385; legal thought in, 384; social science and, 384–385; African Americans in, 385–387; Indians in, 387; women during, 387–388; Margaret Sanger and birth control in, 388, 394–395; presidency in, 388–392; trustbusting in, 390; pure food and drug laws in, 390–391; conservation in, 391; business regulation in, 393; tariff and tax reform in, 393

Progressive Party, 377; of 1912 (Bull Moose Party), 392; of 1920s, 437–438; in 1934, 464; in 1948, 537

Progressives and progressivism: use of term, 377; and First World War, 419, 425, 427; in New Deal, 464

Prohibition, 358, 379, 383, 449; in Russia, 382; support for, 448

Project C, 558

Prolife movement, 607

Propaganda: in First World War, 427; in Second World War, 500; in Cold War, 523–525

Property: Algonquian and English attitudes toward, 29; liberty and, 82; as voting qualification, 114, 117, 194; social mobility and, 343. *See also* Land

Property rights: for women, 210, 226, 290; slaveholding and, 220–221

Prophet (Shawnee), *see* Tenskwatawa ("the Prophet," Shawnee)

Prophetstown, 151

Proposition 13 (California), 589, 618

Proprietary colonies, 53; Maryland as, 31; Pennsylvania as, 42

Proslavery argument: in South, 220–221

Prosperity: in 1800s, 164; under Coolidge, 437; during Second World War, 499; in 1950s, 543; in 1970s, 587; in 1990s, 623

Prostitution: reforms of, 184; white slavery and, 383; in First World War, 421

Protective tariffs, 166, 458; Hamilton on, 131; in 1816, 161; in American System, 190; South and, 191. *See also* Tariffs

Protest(s): colonial, 82–90; nonimportation as, 84, 85–86; by Committees of Correspondence, 88; against Stamp Act, 96; over whiskey tax, 132; against mill conditions, 172–173; against lynchings, 365; agrarian, 367–369; in 1890s depression, 371, 372; in Chicago, 572; by Indians, 577–578. *See also* Antiwar protests; Demonstrations

Protestant Reformation: in England, 27

Protestants and Protestantism: French, 22; in Maryland, 53; German, 61; First Great Awakening and, 71–72; revivalism and, 183; Irish and, 199–200; Catholics and, 214; missionaries and, 308; Republican Party and, 360; evangelicals and, 590; religious right and, 607. *See also* Huguenots

Providence, Rhode Island, 37

Providence Island, 20, 21, 25

Provisional governors: in Reconstruction, 285

Psychedelic drug culture, 569–570

Publications: mass-market, 356

Public debt: Hamilton on, 130–131

Public education, 112, 201; curriculum of, 205–207; accessibility of, 331; educational reform and, 349. *See also* Education; Schools

Public health and safety, 474, 476; Progressives and, 381, 384–385; regulatory measures for, 384

Public housing, 562

Public lands, 308

Public opinion: Mexican War and, 240; on labor, 436

Public ownership: of utilities, 381

Public works, 161; in Great Depression, 458, 461; in West, 467

Public Works Administration (PWA), 461

Puck (magazine), 363(illus.)

Pueblo Indians, 5–7, 22, 45, 68, 272

Pueblo Revolt, 45

Puerto Ricans, 610

Puerto Rico, 406, 412; Spanish settlement of, 25; status of, 414; immigrants from, 441, 550

Pulaski, Fort: in Civil War, 259

Pulitzer, Joseph, 356

Pullman, George, 328

Pullman Palace Car Company, 328

Pullman strike, 328, 365, 371

Punishment: colonial, 65; by Europeans and Indians, 67; Constitution on, 129; for drug possession, 609

Pure Food and Drug Act (1906), 384, 390

Puritans, 20, 27, 28; in New England, 32–33, 36; in Massachusetts, 33–36; English civil war and, 41; colonial administration and, 53

Put-in-Bay, Battle of, 155

Putting-out system, 171

Pyramids: Olmec, 3; in Teotihuacán, 3; in Cahokia, 4

Qing (Manchu) dynasty, 407

Quadrant, 10

Quakers: in East Jersey, 41; peace efforts by, 97, 477; slave trade and, 129; Indians and, 139; as COs, 421

Quality-of-life issues: global, 622

Quartering Act, 89

Quasi-War, 136, 137, 140–141

Quebec, 22, 77, 99

Quebec Act (1774), 89

Queen Anne's War, 55, 76, 77(illus.)

Queenstown, Battle of, 154

Quetzalcoatl, 3, 16

Quincy, Josiah (Congressman), 148

Quincy, Josiah, Jr.: Boston Massacre and, 87–88

Quit-rents, 70

Quotas: on women in universities, 126; on immigration, 446, 561, 573

Rabin, Yitzhak, 622

Race and racism: racial mixing and, 15; in Virginia, 46; multiracial census category and, 56; formal theory of, 115–116; manifest destiny and, 195; minstrelsy and, 207; scientific theory and, 213; immigrants and, 214, 561; in nineteenth century, 215–216; African American concept of, 229–230; slave trade and, 231; Mexican War and, 239, 240; Civil War and, 256, 268; draft riots and, 271; Confederate battle flag and, 277; Andrew Johnson and, 285; in West, 293–295, 307–308; Reconstruction and, 295; segregation in cities, 344; in Farmers' Alliance movement, 369; in Progressive era, 380, 385; southern Progressivism and, 380; classification by race, 399; expansionism and, 399–401; of anti-imperialists, 402; in Spanish-American War, 406; First World War and, 417, 421; Klan and, 445–446; in 1930s, 457, 459, 471; Second World War and, 499–500, 502–504, 540–543; Japanese American internment and, 502–503, 502(illus.); Third World relations and, 527; in postwar period, 534, 536; in 1950s, 550; identity politics and, 576; discrimination and, 578; in college admissions, 591; 1988 report on, 608; poverty and, 608, 608(illus.). *See also* Minorities; specific groups

Race Course prison camp, 279

Race riots: against immigrant labor, 308; in late 19th century, 347; anti-Chinese, 400; after First World War, 429; in Second World War, 494, 499–500; in Los Angeles, 610; Rodney King and, 617

Racial segregation, *see* Segregation
Radical feminism, 579
Radical Reconstruction, 288(map), 292. *See also* Congressional Reconstruction
Radical Republicans, 265, 281, 284, 285, 286, 289
Radicals and radicalism: after First World War, 428–429; Wilson and, 429–430; labor and, 436; Sacco-Vanzetti case and, 446; in New Deal, 462
Radio, 439; baseball on, 448; Franklin D. Roosevelt and, 460; Coughlin on, 464; in 1930s, 468, 470(illus.); news reporting on, 487, 487(illus.)
Radioactive waste, 510
Radio Corporation of America (RCA), 479
Railroad Administration, 425
Railroads, 164, 167–169, 202(illus.); lumber industry and, 166; track gauges for, 169; transportation costs and, 169; farming and, 201, 368; in South, 220, 291; transcontinental, 244, 264; speculation and, 250; in Civil War, 261, 263, 264; Chinese workers on, 295; Indians and, 302; time zones and, 310; in West, 310; western settlement and, 312; mechanization and, 318; inventions for, 319; strikes against, 326, 364, 371; Pullman strike and, 328; pools and, 333; government assistance to, 334–335; commuter, 339; elevated, 339; regulation of, 362, 381; depression of 1890s and, 370; ICC, freight and storage rates, and, 390; trusts and, 390; Adamson Act and, 393; hobos on, 471
Rain-in-the-Face (chief), 303–304
Raleigh, Walter, 18, 30(illus.)
Rancheros, 214
Ranching, 306, 314–315
Randolph, A. Philip, 472, 497, 559
Randolph, Edmund, 123
Randolph, John, 144
Rankin, Jeannette, 420, 490
Rape: of slave women, 230–231; by Klan, 292; Scottsboro Boys and, 471; women's movement and, 579
Rap music, 217
Rasière, Isaac de, 26
Rate wars: among railroads, 362
Ratification: of state constitutions, 117; of Articles of Confederation, 118, 119; of U.S. Constitution, 124–125, 128
Rationalism: in Enlightenment, 64–65
Rational self-interest, 111
Rationing system: in Second World War, 498–499
Rauschenbusch, Walter, 385
Raw materials: for Japan, 484
Ray, James Earl, 570
Reading, 207. *See also* Literacy; Literature
Ready-made clothing, 171, 332
Reagan, Ronald, 597–598, 598(illus.); 1950s anticommunism and, 539; 1980 election and, 593, 596; conservatism of, 597–601; business and, 598–599; New Right and, 599; 1984 election and, 600; foreign relations and, 601–606; Soviet Union and, 606, 611; *New York Times* on, 613
Reagan Democrats, 597, 618
Reaganomics, 599–601

Real-estate covenants: discrimination and, 344
Real-estate development, 339, 543
Real Whigs, 81–82, 88
Reapportionment: 2000 census and, 90–91
Rearmament: of Germany, 482
Rebellions, *see* Revolts and rebellions
Recall, 379, 381
Recessions: of 1937–1939, 471; under Eisenhower, 538; in 1970s, 588. *See also* Depressions
Reciprocal Trade Agreements Act (1934), 479
Reconcentration policy: in Cuba, 404, 405
Reconstruction, 279–298; freedpeople during, 282–284; presidential, 285; congressional plan for, 286–289, 290; military districts during, 288(map); Grant and, 289; reversal of, 292–297; and 1876 election, 296, 296(map); Compromise of 1877 and, 296; end to, 296, 296(map)
Reconstruction Acts (1867–1868), 287, 289
Reconstruction era amendments, *see* Fifteenth Amendment; Fourteenth Amendment; Thirteenth Amendment
Reconstruction Finance Corporation (RFC), 458
Recreation: in 1920s, 448–449; in Sunbelt, 543
Red Army, *see* Soviet Union
Red China, *see* China; People's Republic of China (PRC)
Redcoats: in Boston, 86–87. *See also* American Revolution
Red Cross, 421, 426, 503
Redlining, 536
Red Power movement, 576, 577–578, 577(illus.)
Red Record, A (Wells), 365
Red River campaign (Civil War), 274
Red Scare: in 1919–1920, 428–429; immigrant labor and, 436; in 1950s, 538–540
Reed, John, 428
Reed, Walter, 412, 474
Referendum, 379, 381
Reform and reform movements, 184–185; social problems and, 182–183, 349–350; Second Great Awakening and, 183–184; Jacksonian opposition to, 190; in 1830s and 1840s, 193; South and, 220; progressive reformers and, 297; African American female reformers, 366; Populist goals and, 374; sources of, 377–378; bread-and-butter reforms, 379; Social Gospel and, 385; in 1930s, 464, 471; in Soviet Union, 606; of welfare system, 623. *See also* Progressive era; Progressive Party; specific issues and movements
Reformed Dutch: in Democratic Party, 194
Reform Judaism, 345
Reform party, 619; in 2000 election, 626
Refrigeration, 323, 331
Refugee camps: for Jews, 504
Refugees, 138, 483, 581, 609, 610. *See also* Immigrants and immigration
Regents of the University of California v. Bakke, 591
Region(s): economies of, 62; colonial households in, 68; in West, 300. *See also* specific regions
Regionalism: factions and, 134; political campaigns and, 148; in Farmers' Alliance and, 369

Regulation: of colonial trade, 85; of commerce, 124; economic, 179, 393–394; of child labor, 325; of business, 335; of air pollution, 336; of railroads, 362; of trusts, 390; in 1920s, 436; Reagan and, 598. *See also* Deregulation
Regulators: in Carolinas, 70–71
Rehnquist, William, 585, 599
Relief programs: colonial, 62, 63; in Confederacy, 262; in late 19th century, 346–347; in Great Depression, 458–459, 461
Religion, 219; Indian, 7; freedom of, 31, 37, 117; African American, 69, 115–116, 215; First Great Awakening and, 71–72; revivalism and, 71–72, 183–186; of constitutional delegates, 123; U.S. Constitution on, 124; Second Great Awakening and, 182; women and, 189, 579; party affiliation and, 194; Bible belt and, 198; in South, 198; Catholic-Protestant riots, 209; slaves and, 220, 230; immigrants and, 343; cultural adaptation and, 344–345; Progressive reform and, 385; Klan and, 445; in 1950s, 545; Pledge of Allegiance and, 551–552; in 1970s, 590–591; New Right and, 597. *See also* specific religions
Religious fundamentalism: in 1920s, 446–447; in 1980s, 607
Religious right, *see* New Right; Religious fundamentalism
Relocation camps: for Japanese Americans, 502–503, 503(illus.)
Removal: of Indians, 155, 166, 174, 176–179, 177(map), 303
Removal Act (1830), 177
Reno, Janet, 614, 619
Reparations: to Indians, 234; to Japanese Americans, 234; for slavery, 234–235; from Germany, 451, 482; after First World War, 479; after Second World War, 505
Report on Manufactures (Hamilton), 131
Report on Public Credit (Hamilton), 131
Representation: virtual, 81; colonial, 83; taxation and, 88; census and, 90–91; under Constitution (U.S.), 123–124; apportionment of, 124; Fourteenth Amendment and, 287
Representative government: in Virginia, 29; in Maryland, 32; in New York, 41
Reproduction, *see* Birth control
Reproductive technologies, 632
Republic: Paine on, 101; virtuous, 111–114; white male leadership of, 116; Federalists on, 125
Republican governments, 116–119
Republicanism, 109–110, 200; definitions of, 111, 126; in France, 133; Jefferson and, 144; common man and, 247; southern version of, 248
Republican Party: nominating convention of, 236–237; slavery and, 238; formation of, 246–247; appeal of, 247; ideology of, 247–248; Reconstruction and, 290–292; Klan violence against, 292; coalitions in, 360; factions in, 360; in Progressive era, 391; split of, 392; African Americans and, 466; Nixon and, 585; Contract with America of, 617, 619. *See also* Elections; Liberal Republicans; Radical Republicans
Republican virtue: westward movement and, 174

Republic Steel plant (Chicago), 466–467
Resaca de la Palma, battle at, 239
Research: agricultural, 313–314; military, 497; spending on, 543; into sexual habits, 547; stem-cell, 633
Research laboratories: for electrical products, 319; Du Pont, 322–323
Reservations: policy of, 303; for Australian Aborigines, 311; termination policy and, 550–551
Reserve Officers Training Corps (ROTC), 431
Resettlement Administration, 464
Resident aliens, 137
Resistance, 305; by Indians, 150–151, 175–176; by slaves, 228, 231–232. See also Protest(s); Revolts and rebellions
Resolutions of U.N. Security Council: Resolution 688, 612; Resolution 1441, 628
Restoration colonies, 41
Restraint of trade, 335, 436
Restrictive covenants: illegality of, 541
Retailing: stores for clothing and, 171; mail-order companies and, 313; women in, 324
Retirement, 351–352; in 1920s, 443; Social Security and, 473
Reuben James (ship), 488
Reunification: of Germany, 611
Revels, Hiram, 284
Revenue Acts: of 1789, 129, 132; of 1916, 425
Revenue-sharing programs, 585
Revere, Paul, 99; Copley portrait of, 74; Boston Massacre and, 87(illus.)
Revivalism, 222; First Great Awakening and, 71; Second Great Awakening and, 183–186, 198; Southern Bible belt and, 198; in 1920s, 448
Revolts and rebellions: Pueblo, 45; by Bacon, 46; by Leisler, 54; by slaves, 69, 231–232; Shays's Rebellion, 122; Gabriel's Rebellion, 139–140; Indian resistance and, 150–151, 175–176; by Denmark Vesey, 231; by Nat Turner, 232; by John Brown, 251; Boxer, 396; in Poland and Hungary, 525; in Czechoslovakia, 572; against taxes, 589, 618; Stono Rebellion, 709
Revolution(s): Glorious Revolution, 53–54; use of term, 107–108; in Texas, 197; of 1848, 240; in Cuba, 404, 481; Bolshevik, 422, 423, 515; in China (1911), 483; U.S. hostility toward, 527; in Iran, 592–593; in eastern Europe, 611. See also American Revolution
Revolutionary War, see American Revolution
Revolvers, 170
Reykjavik, Iceland: summit meeting in, 606
Reynolds, David, 514
Rhee, Syngman (South Korea), 521
Rhett, R. B., 270
Rhode Island, 36, 37, 53
Rhodesia (Zimbabwe), 583
Rhythm and blues music, 217, 549
Rice, Thomas D., 207, 208(illus.)
Rice and rice industry, 52, 63, 314
Rice Coast, 7, 52
Richardson, Samuel, 113
Richmond, David, 553
Richmond, Virginia, 258, 262
Rich's (store), 332

Rickenbacker, Eddie, 422
Riesman, David, 549
Rifles: in Civil War, 267–268
Right (political), 562, 597. See also Conservatives and conservatism
Rights: equal, 62; colonial, 88; in states, 117; in Constitution, 125, 129; individual, 379; for women, 438; for gays, 580. See also Human rights; Protest(s)
Rights of the British Colonies Asserted and Proved (Otis), 82–83
Right-to-work laws, 534–535
Riis, Jacob, 345
Ringgold, John ("Johnny Ringo"), 308
Rio de Janeiro Treaty (1992), 623
Río de la Plata, 163
Rio Grande region, 238, 240
Riots, see Race riots; Revolts and rebellions; specific riots
Riparian rights, 309
Roads and highways, 166, 167, 439; National Road, 156, 161; improvement of, 164; suburbs and, 536
Roanoke Island, 18
Roberts, Oral, 607
Robertson, Pat, 607
Robinson, Jackie, 503, 541
Robinson, Sugar Ray, 528
Rockefeller, John D., 333
Rockefeller Foundation, 474, 476, 479, 527
Rockingham (Lord), 84–85
Rock 'n' roll music, 217, 549, 571, 571(illus.)
Rock Springs, Wyoming: violence in, 308, 400
Roebling, John A., 346
Roe v. Wade, 395, 579, 599
Rolfe, John, 28, 29
Roman Catholicism, 10, 15; in New France, 22–23; Protestant Reformation and, 27; in Maryland, 31; Puritanism compared with, 35–36; Quebec Act and, 89; alcohol use and, 184; Democratic Party and, 194, 360; John F. Kennedy and, 198, 555; Irish and, 199–200; education and, 207; immigrants and, 213; anti-Catholicism and, 214; assimilation and, 344–345; of Alfred E. Smith, 450; *cursillo* movement and, 590–591
Romania: revolution in (1989), 611
Rome-Berlin Axis, 482
Rommel, Erwin, 496
Roosevelt, Eleanor, 459, 460, 464, 472, 499
Roosevelt, Franklin D., 455, 507(illus.); power of, 472; youth culture and, 468–470; court-packing plan of, 470–471; scholarly assessment of, 472; Social Security and, 473; Second World War and, 476; Soviet recognition by, 479–480; Good Neighbor policy of, 480–481; Mexico and, 481; events leading to Second World War and, 482; Neutrality Acts and, 482; on neutrality, 484–485; military sales by, 486; radio and, 487; Atlantic Charter and, 488; Pearl Harbor attack and, 489–490; *Greer* attack and, 490–491; Japanese Americans and, 502–503, 502(illus.); at Yalta, 505; Vietnam policy of, 512; Truman and, 538
Roosevelt, Theodore, 316, 353, 376, 379, 389–390, 398, 399, 403; pure food and drugs and, 390; trusts and, 390; labor and,

390–391; conservation and, 391; Panic of 1907 and, 391; election of 1912 and, 392; people of color and, 400; "gentleman's agreement" with Japan and, 401; Spanish-American War and, 405(illus.), 406; foreign policy and, 410–413; Panama Canal and, 412; government-business cooperation and, 436
Roosevelt Corollary, 411(map), 412, 413
Root, Elihu, 399
Root-Takahira Agreement (1908), 413
Rosenberg, Ethel and Julius, 539–540
Rosie the Riveter, 497
Ross, Edward A., 384
Ross, John (Cherokee), 177
ROTC, see Reserve Officers Training Corps (ROTC)
Rough Riders, 389, 405(illus.), 406, 410
Rowlandson, Thomas, 98(illus.)
Rowson, Susanna Haswell, 113
Royal African Company, 49, 50
Royal colonies, 30, 53, 54
Royal Navy (England), 79(illus.), 151–152; in Revolution, 105; in War of 1812, 154, 155
Rubinow, Isaac Max, 443
Ruby, Jack, 560
Rudyerd, William, 20
"Rugged individualism," 316
Ruling class: in North and South, 220
Rum, 66
Rumsfeld, Donald, 628
Runaway slaves, see Fugitive slaves
Rural areas: South as, 167; lifestyle in, 201–203, 313; immigrants in, 213; population in, 339, 340(map); migration from, 339–341; discontent in, 359; poverty in, 534
Rural Electrification Administration, 464
Rural Free Delivery (RFD), 313
Rush, Benjamin, 114
Rush-Bagot Treaty, 162
Rusk, Dean, 555
Russell, Lillian, 355
Russia, 398; expansion of, 163; Alaska and, 295, 402; immigrants from, 341; temperance in, 382; Japan and, 398, 413; Trans-Siberian Railway of, 398; in China, 407, 409(map); communist revolution in, 417; First World War and, 417, 423; Bolshevik Revolution in, 422; U.S. troops in, 429–430; after Soviet Union, 611. See also Soviet Union
Russo-Japanese War, 413, 507
Ruth, George Herman ("Babe"), 439, 448–449
Ruth Hall (Fern), 207
Rwanda, 622

Sacagawea (Shoshone), 147–148
Sacco, Nicola, 446
Sachems (rulers): female, 7
al-Sadat, Anwar, 592
Saddam Hussein, 617, 628; in 1970s, 593; CNN and, 602; Kuwait invasion by, 612
Safety bicycles, 353
"Sagebrush Rebellion," 598
Saigon, see Ho Chi Minh City
Sailors, 10; Iberian, 12; impressment of, 151; black, 503. See also Ships and shipping
St. Augustine, 22

St. Christopher (St. Kitts), 25
St. Clair, Arthur, 121
St. Domingue, *see* Haiti
St. Eustatius, 25
St. Lawrence River region, 22, 77
St. Louis, 175, 213; World's Fair in, 400, 401(illus.)
St. Louis (ship), 483
St. Lucia, 105
St. Mihiel, battle at, 422
St. Patrick's Day, 199–200, 213
St. Petersburg, 496
Salary: of women, 210
Salem Village: witchcraft crisis in, 54
Salinger, J. D., 549
Salmon: Northwest Indians and, 301
Saloons, 383
Salvation, 27, 35–36, 183
Same-sex couples, 630. *See also* Homosexuals and homosexuality
Samoa, 398, 402–403, 406
San Antonio: Alamo in, 195–197
Sánchez, Oscar Arias, 604
Sanctuary movement, 610
Sand Creek Massacre, 272, 303
Sandé cult (West Africa), 8
Sandinistas (Nicaragua), 604
Sandino, Augusto, 604
San Francisco: immigrants in, 213; Chinese in, 344; counterculture in, 570
San Francisco School Board: segregation of Asians by, 400–401
Sanger, Margaret, 388, 394–395, 443
Sanitary engineers, 348
Sanitation, 205, 228, 345; flush toilets, 331, 347; in 1920s, 443. *See also* Hygiene
San Juan Hill, 405(illus.)
San Salvador: Columbus in, 13
Santa Anna, Antonio López de, 195–196
Santa Fe, 22, 56
Santa Fe Trail, 148
Santa Maria (ship), 13
Santiago, Cuba: siege of, 405(illus.), 406
Santo Domingo, 138
São Tomé, 12
Saratoga, battle at, 103, 105
SARS (severe acute respiratory syndrome), 633
Saturday Evening Post, 499
Saudi Arabia, 529
Savages: image of Indians as, 302
Savings, 164–165
Savings-and-loan institutions (S&Ls), 343, 600–601
Savings banks, 334
Savio, Mario, 569
Scalawags, 291–292
Scalia, Antonin, 599
Scandals, *see* specific scandals
Scandinavia, 213, 341
Schenck v. U.S., 427–428
Schiff, Jacob, 334
Schlafly, Phyllis, 580
Schlesinger, Arthur, Jr., 530
Schmeling, Max, 470(illus.)
Schneiderman, Rose, 329
School and Society, The (Dewey), 383
Schools: attendance in, 65; tax support for, 112; children of color in, 115; integration of, 158;

prayer in, 198; for Indians, 305; compulsory attendance in, 325, 331; legal segregation in, 366; high schools, 383; population in, 384; in 1930s, 470; budget deficits and, 589; shootings in, 623–624. *See also* Education; Universities and colleges
Schurz, Carl, 360, 364, 402
Schwerner, Michael, 558
Science, 313–314, 497, 590. *See also* Technology
Scientific agriculture, 436
Scientific management, 317, 323–324
Scientific method, 378
Scopes trial, 433, 446–447
Scotland: immigrants from, 61
Scots-Irish immigrants, 199, 213
Scott, Dred, 249
Scott, Edward and Clarence, 331
Scott, Winfield, 239(map), 240
Scottsboro Boys, 471
Screen Actors Guild, 539, 597
Scrymser, James A., 402
Seaboard cities, 167
Sea dogs, 18
Seaflower (ship), 39
Sea Islands: land for freedpeople on, 283
Seaports, 35, 63
Searches and seizures, 129
Search warrants, 117
Sears, Roebuck, 313
Seattle: WTO meeting in, 621
Secession, 264; by New England, 156–157; of South, 157, 252–253, 253(illus.)
Second Amendment, 129, A7
Second Bank of the United States, 161, 164, 172, 183, 192
Second Battle of the Marne, 422
Second Bill of Rights (1944), 538
Second Continental Congress, 95, 96, 97, 100, 101
Second front: in Second World War, 496
Second Great Awakening, 182, 189, 198, 201, 215
Second New Deal, 461–466
Second party system, 193–195
Second war for independence, 144
"Second World," 513
Second World War, 476, 484–490, 492–494; events leading to, 481–484; opening of, 483; U.S. entry into, 490; Navajo code-talkers and, 492–493; in Pacific region, 494–496, 495(map); Battle of Midway in, 496; Europe First strategy in, 496; home front in, 498–500; cost of, 499; combat in, 504; winning of, 505–509; end of, 506(map), 509; recovery after, 509–510; international system after, 513–517; Europe after, 518(map)
Sectionalism, 237, 244; and 1848 election, 241; Kansas-Nebraska Act and, 246(map); political realignment and, 247, 248; and 1860 election, 251; Panic of 1857 and, 251
Secularism: Second Great Awakening and, 184
Securities and Exchange Commission (SEC), 600
Security, 514; National Security Act and, 517–519; in 1950s, 539; after September 11, 2001, attacks, 627
Security Council (U.N.), 515; Resolution 1441 on Iraq and, 628

Seddon, James, 270
Sedition acts: of 1798, 137, 140, 144, 145, 149; of 1918, 140–141, 427
Segregation, 540; in cities, 344; in settlement-house movement, 349–349; legal, 365–366; of northern blacks, 385; of Asians in San Francisco schools, 400–401; *Brown* case and, 433; of armed forces, 503; foreign policy and, 527–528; in northern cities, 541; in 1950s, 550; sit-ins and, 553–554; in 1960s, 557–558; Kennedy and, 558–559; in Alabama, 559
Selective Service Act (1917), 420
Selective Training and Service Act (1940), 488, 504
Selectmen: in New England, 43
Self-determination, 422; anti-imperialism and, 406; Puerto Rico and, 414; for Latin America, 480; after Second World War, 505
Self-government, 34–35, 83
Self-help books: in 1970s, 591
Self-help movements: for blacks, 472
Self-help strategy: of Booker T. Washington, 386
Self-improvement: in Second Great Awakening, 183
Self-interest, 111
"Self-made men," 72–73
Seminole Indians, 163, 178–179, 243
Senate (U.S.), 123–124, 237; caning of Sumner in, 248; Andrew Johnson's trial in, 289; League of Nations and, 417; Treaty of Versailles and, 431
Senators: direct election of, 360, 381, 392; as state bosses, 360; in Gilded Age, 363
Seneca Indians, 44, 103, 139
Senegal, 50, 52
Senegambia, 59, 79
Seoul, South Korea, 521
Separate-but-equal doctrine, 366, 541
Separation of church and state: Pledge of Allegiance and, 552
Separation of powers, 124
Separatist cultures, 575
Separatists, 27, 28, 33, 37
September 11, 2001, terrorist attacks, 255, 615–616; war on terrorism and, 626–627; international responses to, 628
Sequoyah (Cherokee), 176
Serbia: First World War and, 417
Serbs, 622
Serres, Dominic, the Elder, 79(illus.)
Servants: bonded, 21; indentured, 22, 31; male, 32; female, 53; Indians as, 68
Servicemen's Readjustment Act, *see* GI Bill of Rights
Service sector: African Americans in, 341; in 1970s, 588
Settlement(s): of Americas, 3; by England, 18; of New Spain, 22; of New France, 22–23; European and Indian in eastern North American, 24(map); of New England, 35; European (1754), 78(map); of backcountry, 95; of Texas, 195; Shaker, 201–202; in Great Plains, 310–313. *See also* Colonies and colonization
Settlement houses, 349–350, 378, 380
Seven Days Battles, 260

Seventeenth Amendment, 360, 381, 392, A9

Seventh Amendment, 129, A8

Seven Years War, 75, 77–80, 77(illus.), 79(illus.)

Severalty policy, 438

Sewage disposal: in cities, 347–348

Sewall, Arthur, 373

Seward, William H., 272, 295, 402

Sewers, 205

Sewing machine, 323, 332

Sex and sexuality: Jesuit impact on Indian practices, 23; in New England, 36; myths about blacks and, 116; interracial, 223; slave women, masters, and, 226, 230–231; Progressives and, 383, 388; Margaret Sanger and, 394; automobiles and, 439; in 1920s, 443, 445; after Second World War, 545–546, 547; counterculture and, 570; in 1970s, 591; Clinton and, 624–625; John F. Kennedy and, 625

Sex roles, *see* Gender and gender roles

Sex typing, 388

Sexual Behavior in the Human Female (Kinsey), 547

Sexual Behavior in the Human Male (Kinsey), 547

Sexual discrimination, 578

Sexual division of labor, 5, 139, 305

Sexual harassment: Thomas-Hill hearings and, 613; charges against Clinton, 624

Sexually transmitted diseases, 609

Sexual revolution, 591

Sexual violence, 383

Seymour, Horatio, 289

Shah of Iran, 592–593

Shakers, 201–202

Shamans and shamanism, 23, 36, 591

Shame of the Cities, The (Steffens), 379

Shandong, China, 407, 413, 417, 484

Shanghai: Japanese bombing of, 484

Shantytowns, 455, 459

Sharecropping, 284, 367–368, 461, 468, 472

Share Our Wealth Society (Long), 464

Shaw, Bernard, 602, 602(illus.)

Shawnee Indians, 42, 76, 92, 95, 120, 121, 150, 150(illus.), 155, 156; attacks by, 96; movement of, 175–176

Shays's Rebellion, 122

Sheep: Southwestern Indians and, 301

Sheepherders: cattle and, 314

Shelburne (Lord), 107

Sheldon, Charles, 385

Shelley v. Kramer, 541

Shell shock, 421

Shenandoah valley: Civil War in, 260, 272

Shepherd, Matthew: murder of, 624

Sheppard-Towner Act (1921), 438

Sheridan, Fort, 327

Sherman, John, 335

Sherman, William Tecumseh, 274, 283, 532

Sherman Anti-Trust Act (1890), 335, 393

Sherman Silver Purchase Act (1890), 363, 370

Shi'ite Islamic Republic: in Iran, 593

Shiloh, Battle of, 260

Ships and shipping, 10, 11(illus.), 151–152, 154; European, 17; in New England, 63; immigrants and, 213; in Civil War, 264; steamships, 398; steel-hulled warships, 403;

in First World War, 415, 418; military, 477; in Second World War, 496

Shopping centers, 339

Shoshone Indians, 5

Show business: in late 19th century, 355–356

Shuffle Along (musical comedy), 449

Siberia, 514

Sierra Club, 308

Sierra Leone, 98, 98(illus.)

Signal Corps, 421

"Significance of the Frontier in American History, The" (Turner), 299

Silent Spring (Carson), 550

Silent majority, 572

Silicon Valley, 620

Silk Road, 7

Silver, 14; for land payment, 193; in West, 307; coinage of, 363, 363(illus.), 372–374; 1890s depression and, 370

Silver Republicans, 373

Simmons, William J., 445

Simpson, "Sockless Jerry," 369

Simpson-Rodino Act, *see* Immigration Reform and Control Act (1986)

Sinai Peninsula, 583

Sinclair, Upton, 379, 390, 464

Sin fronteras (without borders), 441

Singer, Isaac M., 332

"Single tax" proposal, 335

Sino-American relations, 520, 522, 583

Sino-Japanese War (1937), 484

Sino-Soviet relations, 520

Sioux Indians, 271

Sir Charles Grandison (Richardson), 113

Sirhan, Sirhan, 572

Sit-down strike: in automobile industry, 466

Sit-in movement, 553–554, 557

Six-Day War (1967), 583

Sixteenth Amendment, 392, A9

Sixteenth Street Baptist Church (Birmingham): bombing of, 560

Sixth Amendment, 129, A8

Ska music, 217

Skilled labor, 466; AFL and, 327, 328; women as, 497

Skyscrapers, 346

Slater, John, 153

Slater, Samuel, 152, 153

Slaughter-House cases, 295

Slave auctions, 218, 227(illus.)

Slave codes: in English colonies, 47

Slave colonies, 47

"Slave laborers" (workers), 621

"Slave narratives": WPA and, 465

Slave Power, 240, 241, 244, 246; Cuban annexation and, 245; *Dred Scott* decision and, 249

Slaves and slavery, 55, 56, 218–219; in West Africa, 8; Portugal and, 12; Indians and, 15, 52; sugar industry and, 17, 25; as labor force, 21; expansion of, 39, 40, 244–249, 246(map); on mainland, 46–47; prisoners of war and, 50; colonial economy and, 63; families and, 68–69, 230–231, 283; Revolution and, 97–99, 114–116; in North, 114–115; three-fifths compromise and, 124; in Constitution, 129; in Haiti, 138; Gabriel's

Rebellion and, 139–140; Missouri Compromise and, 162(map); debate over, 163–164; cotton industry and, 170; westward movement of, 174; Cherokee ownership of, 176; profitability of, 220; religion and, 220; proslavery argument and, 220–221; master relationship with, 221, 228, 229; society of, 221, 232–234; free blacks and, 223; as financial assets, 225; lifestyle and labor of, 226–229; resistance by, 228, 231–232; task system and, 228; violence against, 228; African influences and, 229–230; culture of, 229–231; reparations for, 234–235; in territories, 240–241; Wilmot Proviso and, 240–241; Compromise of 1850 and, 241–242; Fugitive Slave Act and, 242; *Uncle Tom's Cabin* and, 242–243; Underground Railroad and, 243; Kansas-Nebraska Act and, 244–246; and 1860 election, 251; areas of (1861), 252(map); Civil War and, 259, 265; colonization plan for, 265; emancipation and, 265–267; Thirteenth Amendment and, 266. *See also* Abolition and abolitionism; Africa; African Americans; Africans; Fugitive slaves; Revolts and rebellions

Slave states, 163–164, 174

Slave trade, 38, 40, 47–51, 49–50, 230; involuntary migration and, 56, 59; Constitution on, 124; Quakers and, 129; domestic, 231; in District of Columbia, 242

Slavic nationalism, 417

Slums, 209–210, 443, 550

Small, Albion, 384

Smallpox, 15, 17, 23, 65, 105

Smith, Adam, 111

Smith, Alfred E., 379, 437, 450, 462

Smith, Bessie, 449

Smith, James, 64(illus.)

Smith, John, 28

Smith, Joseph, 202–203

Smith, Kirby, 260

Smith, Thomas, 39

Smith Act, *see* Alien Registration (Smith) Act (1940)

Smith College, 384

Smith-Connally Act, *see* War Labor Disputes (Smith-Connally) Act

Smith v. Allwright, 541

Smuggling, 51

Smyrna, Georgia: housing in, 532

Soccer: European, 622

Social Darwinism, 334, 335, 385, 399, 400

Social Evil in Chicago, The, 383

Social Gospel, 385, 477

Social institutions: in Progressive era, 378, 383–385

Socialist Labor Party, 371

Socialist Party of America, 372, 379, 392, 393, 426, 427, 428, 429, 459

Socialists and socialism, 371–372, 373, 379, 380(illus.), 422, 611

Social mobility, 371

Social science, 384

Social Security, 473; Reagan and, 598, 600

Social Security Act, 465, 471; amendments to (1954), 538

Social service, 376

Society, 4; in Americas, 3, 6(map); of Teotihuacán, 3; stratification of, 51, 62; colonial,
57–58, 67–69; in backcountry, 61; mores
of, 113; freed people in, 115; reforms of,
181–183; farm, 201; southern biracial, 220;
slave, 221, 232–234; in Civil War, 256–258,
260–265, 276, 280; in West, 307–308;
industrialization and, 329–333; cities and,
337–338, 608–609; multiracial, 403; First
World War and, 417; in 1920s, 451–452;
Second World War and, 509–510, 532–534;
divisions in, 567–570, 575–576; in 1980s,
606–610; in 1990s, 617–623; in 21st century,
630–636
Society of American Indians (SAI), 387
Society of Friends, *see* Quakers
Society of the Cincinnati, 112
Sociologists: Progressive, 384
Sod houses, 312, 313(illus.)
Soil: efficient use of, 314
Soldiers: Boston Massacre and, 87–88; in
Revolution, 104–105, 106–107; African
American, 115; in Civil War, 256–258,
267–268; pensions for Union, 360; in
Spanish-American War, 406; in First World
War, 420–423; in Vietnam War, 563, 564,
581; in Iraq (2003–), 628. *See also* Armed
forces; Military
Solidarity (Poland), 603
Solid South, 465
Solomon, Job Ben, 59
Solomon Islands, 403
Somalia, 622
Somme, Battle of the, 421
Somoza, Anastasio, 604
Sons of Liberty, 84, 85, 88
Soong Meiling (Madame Jiang, China), 484
Sorensen, Theodore, 555
Soto, Hernán de, 1
Sound money policies, 293
South: economy of, 63, 543; in Revolution,
105–106, 106(map); Indians and, 120, 155,
176–179, 177(map); secession of, 157–158,
252–253, 253(illus.); transportation for, 161;
Missouri Compromise and, 162(map); cotton
in, 170, 224, 225; cities in, 175; revivalism
in, 183; antislavery movement in, 188; Bible
belt in, 198; immigrants in, 213, 214; free
people of color in, 215, 223–224; North
and, 219–220; worldview of, 220; proslavery
argument of, 220–221; slave society in, 221,
232–234; yeoman farmers in, 221–223, 233;
planters in, 224–226; Republican Party and,
247, 290–291; Democrats in, 248; black
codes in, 285–286; military districts in, 287,
288(map); "military rule" myth in, 289;
Reconstruction in, 289–292; "Negro Rule"
myth and, 291; carpetbaggers and scalawags
in, 291–292; Klan in, 292, 293; Amnesty Act
and, 293; technology and industry and, 323;
child labor in, 324–325; segregation in, 328,
384; African Americans and, 341, 365–366,
385; pensions for soldiers in, 360; farming
in, 367–368; Farmers' Alliances in, 368–369;
Progressive reform in, 379–380; in Great
Depression, 468; TVA and, 468; New Deal
in, 471; desegregation in, 541; Freedom
Riders in, 558; Nixon and, 585; growth of,

588. *See also* Civil War (U.S.); Confederacy
(Civil War South); Reconstruction; Slaves
and slavery
South Africa, 583, 606, 611
South America, 59, 610
South Carolina, 22, 43, 63; slaves in, 51; rice
in, 52; nullification in, 157, 192; secession
of, 252; Civil War in, 254, 259
South Dakota, 308
Southeast: Indians of, 5
Southeast Asia: Vietnam War and, 565(map);
Kennan on, 567; communism in, 581;
immigrants from, 609–610
Southern Baptist Foreign Mission Board, 397
Southern Baptists, 198
Southern Christian Leadership Conference
(SCLC), 541, 558, 559
Southern Europe: immigrants from, 385
Southern Pacific Railroad, 310
Southern Quarterly Review, 226
Southern Tenant Farmers' Union, 472
South Korea, 520, 522, 603. *See also* Korea;
Korean War
South Vietnam, 529, 563. *See also* Vietnam War
Southwest, 238, 301, 543, 544(map); ancient
peoples of, 4; Indians in, 5, 301; Santa Fe
Trail to, 148; Hispanics in, 174, 214–215;
expansion into, 197; oil in, 307; Las Gorras
Blancas (White Hats) in, 368; Mexican
Americans in, 610
Southwest Railroad, 327
Sovereignty: of Parliament, 88; Indian, 122;
between states and central government, 191;
Chinese, 484. *See also* Popular sovereignty;
State sovereignty doctrine
Soviet Union: policy toward, 479–480, 512;
Nazi nonaggression pact with, 483; Finland
and, 485; Lend-Lease aid to, 488; Second
World War and, 496, 505, 514; Truman
Doctrine and, 516; atomic bomb and, 519;
China and, 520; North Korea and, 521;
Third World and, 525; Cuba and, 528;
Kennedy and, 556; détente with, 582–583;
Afghanistan and, 592; Carter and, 592;
collapse of, 596–597, 611; Reagan and,
603–604, 606; arms reduction treaties with,
612. *See also* Cold War; Russia
Space exploration, 523, 538; spending for, 543;
Kennedy and, 560; *Apollo 8* and, 572; moon
landing and, 590
Spain, 1–2, 14–15, 20, 25, 56, 398; Muslims in,
10; Columbus and, 13; New Spain and, 22;
Indians and, 45; slavery and, 52; after Seven
Years War, 77; American Revolution and, 103;
after Revolution, 119; Genêt and, 133;
Pinckney's Treaty with, 134; Louisiana
Territory and, 146; Latin American inde-
pendence from, 148, 163; East Florida and,
162–163; Cuba and, 245, 404–405. *See also*
specific colonies
Spanish-American War, 374, 389–390,
405–407, 413; Hawaiian annexation and,
403–404; casualties in, 405(illus.), 406; in
Philippines, 406
Spanish Armada, 18
Spanish Civil War (1936), 482
Spanish language: bilingualism and, 610
Special interests, 362, 381

Specialization, 159–160, 164, 171–172
Specie Circular, 192–193, 194
Spectator amusements, 448
Spectator sports, 207
Speculation, 76, 165; land, 164, 175, 192–193,
305; Panic of 1857 and, 250; Panic of 1907
and, 391; Great Depression and, 451
Speech, freedom of, 69, 140–141, 188, 428,
432–433
Speed-up system, 172
Spending: in First World War, 423–424;
consumer, 438–439; in Second World War,
499; defense, 519, 531, 600, 603, 612, 619;
on Korean War, 522; military, 522, 636;
under Eisenhower, 538; by teens, 547; on
social programs, 562; in Reagan-Bush era,
596, 598; cutting, 619
Spheres of influence: in China, 407, 409(map),
410; Second World War and, 490; Soviet,
505
Spice trade, 11
Spies and spying: before Revolution, 94–95; in
Second World War, 502; in 1950s, 538–540.
See also Intelligence operations
Spinning mill: water-powered, 153
Spirit of St. Louis, The, 434
Spiritualism: exploration and, 11
Spirituals (music), 217
Spock, Benjamin, 546
Spoils system, 191, 360–362, 364
Sports: spectator, 207; organized, 352–355;
intercollegiate, 384, 452; in universities, 384;
in 1920s, 448–449, 452; women in, 579
Spotsylvania, battle at, 274
Sprang, William, 283(illus.)
Springfield, Oregon: school shootings in, 624
Sputnik, 523, 538
Squanto (Pawtuxet tribe), 33
Square rigging, 11(illus.)
Squatters, 70, 175
Sri Lanka (Ceylon), 513
Stadacona (Quebec), 22
Stagflation, 587, 597, 599, 600
Stalin, Joseph, 470, 496, 505, 507(illus.); after
Second World War, 514; Czechoslovakia
and, 519; Korean War and, 521
Stalwarts, 360
Stamp Act (1763), 82–85, 96
Stamp Act Congress, 84
Standard-gauge rails, 310
Standardization, 322, 329
Standard of living, 543–544, 550. *See also*
Lifestyle
Standard Oil Company, 333–334, 379, 477,
481
Standard time zones, 310
Standing army, 156
Stanton, Edwin M., 263, 288, 289
Stanton, Elizabeth Cady, 189, 282, 287, 366,
388
Stanwix, Fort, Treaty of, 120
Starr, Kenneth, 624
"Star-Spangled Banner, The," 155
Starvation: in Great Depression, 455
Starving time: in Jamestown, 28
State(s): slavery abolished by, 115; under Articles
of Confederation, 117–119; land claims and
cessions by, 118(map); debts of, 119–120, 132;

admission to Union, 120–121; national government and, 124, 161; representation in, 124; Constitution on, 129; federal courts and, 129; war debts of, 130–131; free and slave, 163–164, 246(map), 252(map); land grants to, 174–175; nullification by, 191; banks in, 192–193; abortion and, 211; business and, 335; disfranchisement of blacks by, 365; segregation in, 366; woman suffrage in, 366–367, 388, 389(map); elderly in, 443; new immigrants in, 573; revenue-sharing programs with, 585; deficits in, 589; tax increases in, 630

State Department, 129, 522–523, 539

Statehood, 174; slavery and, 163–164; in West, 308; Puerto Rico and, 414

State legislatures: election of senators and, 360, 381

State of the Union message, 130

State sovereignty doctrine, 240, 250

States' rights, 220, 285, 293; judicial appeals and, 129; nullification and, 157–158; Webster-Hayne debate over, 191; in Confederacy, 270

States' Rights ("Dixiecrat") Party, 277

State universities: agricultural research at, 313–314

Steamboats, 166, 175, 398

Steam engines, 318

Stearns, Harold, 450

Steel, Ferdinand L., 223

Steel and steel industry, 310, 323, 436; pools in, 333; mergers in, 334; construction with, 346; strike in, 428

Steel plow, 170

Steffens, Lincoln, 379

Steinbeck, John, 465

Stem cells: ethics of use, 632–633

Stephens, Alexander H., 270

Stephenson, David, 445

Stereotypes, 207, 208(illus.), 214, 355, 399–400

Sterilization statutes, 385

Stevens, John L., 403

Stevens, Thaddeus, 281, 287–288

Still Life of Harriet Tubman with Bible and Candle, 243(illus.)

Stimson, Henry L., 486, 515

Stimson Doctrine, 484

Stinger missiles, 603

Stock(s), 333, 334

Stock and bond exchanges, 334

Stockholders: limited liability of, 166

Stockman, David, 600

Stock market, 479; 1929 crash of, 450–451; in 1987, 601; in 1990s, 623; after September 11, 2001, 627

Stone, Lucy, 189, 366

Stonewall riot, 580

Stono Rebellion, 70

STOP-ERA movement, 580

Stowe, Harriet Beecher, 207, 242–243

Strategic Defense Initiative (SDI, "Star Wars"), 603

Strauss, Levi, 203

Stretch-out system, 172

Strict constructionism, 131

Strike(s): against mills, 172–173; in Civil War, 263, 264; in Panic of 1873, 293; at Watertown

Arsenal, 317; against railroads, 326, 327, 365, 371; Haymarket Riot and, 327, 371; Knights of Labor and, 327; Homestead strike, 328, 371; IWW and, 328; by miners, 328, 371, 390–391; Pullman strike, 328, 365, 371; by ILGWU, 329; by telephone operators, 329; in 1890s depression, 371; First World War and, 426, 428; in automobile industry, 466; in Great Depression, 466; at Republic Steel, 466–467; by coal miners, 498; in Second World War, 498; after Second World War, 534, 537; against grape growers, 576–577

Strikebreakers, 326, 327, 347; in Civil War, 264

Strip-mining, 599

Strong, Josiah, 400

Stuart, Gilbert, 112

Stuart, J. E. B., 260

Stuart dynasty (England), 28, 41

Student Nonviolent Coordinating Committee (SNCC), 557–558, 559, 568

Students: Vietnam deferments for, 566; 1960s student movement, 568–569; protests in France by, 572. *See also* Antiwar protests

Students for a Democratic Society (SDS), 568

Subcultures: of homosexuals and unmarried people, 351

Submarines: in First World War, 415, 418, 419–420, 419(illus.), 422; in Second World War, 488, 494; nuclear, 523

Sub-Saharan Africa, 7; slaves from, 46

Subsidies: to railroads, 310; to corporations, 334; for workers' housing, 378; to farmers, 461, 467; for rents, 562

Subsistence cultures: Indian, 68

Substitutes: in Civil War, 262, 271

Subtreasury plan: of Farmers' Alliances, 369, 437

Suburbs, 441; annexation of, 339; mass transit and, 339; after Second World War, 532, 536; norms of, 545–546; lifestyle in, 546

Subversives: fears of, 539

Subways, 339

Sudeten region: German invasion of, 482

Suez Canal, 398, 412, 496; crisis over (1956), 525, 529

Suffrage: for white males, 233; Fourteenth Amendment and, 287. *See also* Voting and voting rights; Woman suffrage

Suffragists, 388

Sugar Act (1764), 82

Sugar industry, 38; in São Tomé, 12; in Columbian Exchange, 17; in Brazil, 25; on Caribbean islands, 25; rum and, 66; in Hawai'i, 403; McKinley Tariff and, 403; in Cuba, 404, 481, 528

Sugar Trust, 335

Suicide bombers: in Israel, 255

Sullivan, "Big Tim," 379

Sullivan, John, 103

"Summer of Love," 570

Summit meetings: in Paris (1960), 525; in Reykjavik, 606

Sumner, Charles, 248, 281, 402

Sumter, Fort: attack on, 254

Sunbelt, 533, 543, 544(map), 588; in 1970s and 1980s, 589(map)

Sunday, Billy, 448

Sunday closing laws, 360, 379

Superfund, 587

Superpowers: arms race and, 556; U.S. as, 622

Supply-side economics, 599–600

Supreme Court (U.S.), 129; on miscegenation laws, 56; appointments to, 145–146; southern opposition to, 158; nationalism of, 161; on commerce, 166; Reconstruction and, 295–296; on Indian affairs, 303; on working conditions, 326; on interstate commerce and labor strikes, 328; on corporations, 333; on restraint of trade, 335; Chinese and, 344; railroads and, 362; blacks and, 365; segregation and, 366; Granger laws and, 368; labor reforms and, 381; Progressive legal thinking and, 384; on trusts, 390; Taft and, 392; Jews on, 393; on abortion, 395; civil liberties and, 427–428; business and, 436; AAA and, 461; NRA and, 461; Franklin D. Roosevelt and, 470–471; civil rights and, 541; Nixon and, 585; Reagan and, 599; Clarence Thomas nomination to, 613; 2000 election and, 626; list of justices, A19–A20. *See also* specific justices and decisions

Suribachi, Mount, 508

Surplus: exportation of, 399

"Susanna" (Foster), 217

Susquehannock Indians, 46

Sussex (ship), 419

Sutter's Mill: gold at, 203, 204

Swann v. Charlotte-Mecklenburg, 585

Swanson, Gloria, 445

Sweatshops, 329, 376

Swedish settlers, 25

Swift, Gustavus, 334

Swing bands, 217

Syncretism, 15

Syphilis, 17, 303

Syria, 513, 604

Taft, Robert A., 519

Taft, William Howard, 391–392, 413; on expansionism, 401; as Chief Justice, 436

Taft-Hartley Act (1947), 534–535, 537

Taft-Katsura Agreement (1905), 413

Taíno people, 13

Taiping Revolution (China, 1850), 204

Taiwan, *see* Formosa

Takeovers: corporate, 601

Taliban, 617, 626–627

Talleyrand (France), 136

Tallmadge amendment, 164

Tammany Hall, 349, 379, 450

Taney, Roger B., 167, 249

Tanguay, Eva, 355

Tanks: in Second World War, 496

Tarbell, Ida M., 379

Tariffs, 364, 436; after Revolution, 129; nullification of, 157; of 1816, 161; of 1833, 192; as government assistance to business, 335; of McKinley, 362, 373; in Gilded Age, 362–363; Taft and, 391; reform, 393; Cuba and, 404; in Great Depression, 479. *See also* Protective tariffs

Task system: among slaves, 52, 69, 228

Taxation, 53, 394; mercantilism and, 50; colonial, 69, 82–90; after Seven Years War, 75; resistance to, 94, 589, 618; for

Taxation (*cont.*)
schools, 112; in states, 117; under Articles of Confederation, 119; authority over, 124; after Revolution, 129; on whiskey, 131–132; for city services, 205; by Confederacy, 261, 269; by Reconstruction governments, 292; income tax, 392, 393; in First World War, 425; Coolidge and, 437; Huey Long on, 464; for Social Security, 473; in Second World War, 499; Nixon and, 585; Reagan and, 596, 597, 599, 601; cuts in, 600; George W. Bush and, 626; state increases in, 630
Taxation without representation, 88
Tax relief: for business, 334
Tax stamps, 82
Taylor, Frederick W., 323–324
Taylor, Major, 353
Taylor, Zachary, 238–239, 240, 241
Taylor Grazing Act (1934), 467
Tea, 66, 67; tax on, 85, 86, 88–89
Tea Act (1773), 89
Teachers: women as, 210; Klan violence against, 292; in Philippines, 408
Teach-ins, 567, 569
Teamster's Union, 466
Teapot Dome scandal, 437
Technology, 377; printing and, 10; piracy of, 153; travel times and, 169; in manufacturing, 171–172; reformers and, 185; in Civil War, 267–268; railroads and, 310; agriculture and, 314; for meatpacking industry, 315; industrialization and, 317–318, 319–324; for housing, 345–346; for movies, 355–356; international communications and, 402; road building and, 439; in 1950s, 550; in 1970s, 590; revolution in, 620; quality of life and, 622; reproductive, 632; in 20th century, 633
Tecumseh (Shawnee), 150, 150(illus.), 151, 154, 155
Teenagers: in 1950s, 547. *See also* Youth; Youth culture
Teheran: U.S. embassy in, 593
Teheran meeting (1943), 505
Tejanos, 195, 214–215, 341
Telecommunications: global, 321; deregulation of, 600, 601
Telecommunications Act (1996), 619
Telegraph, 166, 167, 321, 321(illus.), 398, 402
Telephone, 323, 356
Telephone Operators' Department of the International Brotherhood of Electrical Workers, 329
Televangelists, 607
Television, 545, 547, 591; Vietnam War and, 567; CNN and, 602
Teller, Henry M., 373
Teller Amendment (1898), 405, 411
Temperance, 184, 185(illus.), 220, 247, 324, 350, 383
Temple, Shirley, 539
Temples: of Quetzalcoatl, 3
10 percent plan, 281
Tenant farming, 367–368, 436; in West, 175; in New Deal, 461, 468; in 1930s, 472; in 1950s, 550
Tenements, 210, 345, 346(illus.)
Ten-hour day, 173

Tennessee, 174, 253, 258, 260
Tennessee Gentleman (Earl), 193(illus.)
Tennessee Iron and Coal Company, 391
Tennessee Valley Authority (TVA, 1933), 468
Tenochtitlán, 4, 14, 15
Tenskwatawa ("the Prophet," Shawnee), 150–151, 150(illus.), 176
Tenth Amendment, 129, 157, 366, A8
Tenure of Office Act, 288–289
Teotihuacán, 3, 4
Termination policy: for Native Americans, 550–551
Territories, 240–242, 244–246; free and slave, 236, 246(map), 252(map); *Dred Scott* decision and, 249; and 1860 election, 251; in West, 259
Terrorism: John Brown's legacy and, 254–255; on September 11, 2001, 255, 615–616; by Klan, 281, 292, 293; PLO and, 583, 606; in Middle East, 604–606; by Islamic fundamentalists, 615–616; against Israel, 622–623; counterterrorism and, 626–627; confronting, 633–635
Tet Offensive, 570
Texas, 45, 148, 163, 238, 310; independence of, 174; annexation of, 195–197; revolution in, 197; Mexicans in, 214–215; boundary of, 240, 242; secession of, 252; Civil War in, 259, 260; oil in, 307
Texas Revolution, 214
Textile industry, 122, 152, 153(illus.), 161, 170–171, 318; indigo and, 52; British technology for, 153; workplace in, 173; Civil War and, 272, 273; electricity and, 323; in South, 323; women in, 324
Thailand, 490
Thames, Battle of the, 150(illus.), 155
Thanksgiving (holiday), 352
Thayer, Webster, 446
Theater, *see* Drama
Therapeutic culture, 591
Thieu, Nguyen Van, 581
Third Amendment, 129, A7
Third parties, 374, 618, 619
Third World, 513; CIA covert operations in, 523; struggle for, 525–530; newly independent nations in, 526(illus.); Kennedy and, 556; Nixon, Kissinger, and, 583
Thirteen colonies, 41
Thirteenth Amendment, 266, 282, 293, A8
This Side of Paradise (Fitzgerald), 449
Thomas (ship), 408
Thomas, Allison, 511
Thomas, Clarence: nomination of, 613
Thomas, George H., 274
Thomas, Norman, 432, 459
Thoreau, Henry David, 203, 251
369th Infantry Regiment, 421
Three-fifths compromise, 124
Three Mile Island nuclear plant, 590
Tiananmen Square, 611
Ticonderoga, Fort, 99; battle at, 103
Tijerina, Reies, 577
Tilden, Bill, 448
Tilden, Samuel J., 296, 296(map)
Till, Emmett: murder of, 541
Timber and Stone Act (1878), 307
Time magazine, 602

Time zones, 310
Tippecanoe, Battle of, 151, 194
Title IX, *see* Higher Education Act
Tito, Josip Broz, 515
Tobacco and tobacco industry, 17, 29, 30–31, 46, 63, 323, 367
Tocqueville, Alexis de, 199, 209, 232
Tokyo: Doolittle bombing of, 495
Toll bridges, 167
Tolstoy, Leo, 382
Tombstone, 308
"Tom Thumb" (locomotive), 167–169
Tongs (Chinese associations), 343
Tonkin Gulf crisis, 491
Tonkin Gulf Resolution (1964), 581
Tools: Paleo-Indian, 3
Tordesillas, Treaty of, 13
Toussaint L'Ouverture (François-Dominique Toussaint), 138
Towns, *see* Cities and towns
Townsend, Francis E., 464
Townshend, Charles, 85
Townshend Acts, 85–86, 88–89
Toynbee Hall (London), 349
Trade, 10–11; in ancient America, 3; in Africa, 7; Indian-white, 17–18, 67, 303; Dutch, 23; wampum for, 26; Atlantic, 39–40, 49(map); in Pennsylvania, 42; Navigation Acts and, 50–51; in English colonies, 62, 63; exotic beverages and, 66; regulation of, 85; after Revolution, 151–152; in War of 1812, 155; South and, 170; with Japan, 244; expansion of foreign, 399; navalism and, 403; Open Door policy and, 410; Mexico and, 412; in First World War, 417–418; Great Depression and, 476, 479; Chinese- and Japanese-American, 484; free trade, 514; promotion of, 620; September 11, 2001, and, 633. *See also* Foreign trade; Fur trade; Slave trade
Trade barriers, 620
Trade deficits, 588, 620
Trademark law (1881), 332
Trade unions, 326, 328, 329
Trade winds, 12
Trading posts, 2–3, 12, 22, 49
Trail of Tears, 178, 178(illus.)
Transatlantic telegraph cable, 321, 321(illus.), 402
Transcendentalism, 203
Transcontinental railroad, 244, 264
Transcontinental Treaty, *see* Adams-Onís (Transcontinental) Treaty
Transistors, 543
Trans-Mississippi West, 146–148, 147(map)
Transportation, 159, 164, 402; in Chesapeake, 31; in South, 161; for market economy, 164; improvements in, 167–169; in West, 310; growth of, 318; engineering advances in, 398; desegregation in, 541. *See also* Mass transportation; Roads and highways; specific types
Trans-Siberian Railway (Russia), 398
Trappers, 17
Travel, 169, 213, 434, 633
Travels (Polo), 10–11
Treason, 102, 149
Treasury Department, 129, 130, 131, 194
Treaties, *see* specific treaties

Trench warfare: in First World War, 421
Trent affair, 272
Trenton, New Jersey, battle at, 102
Trial(s), 54, 117, 129
Triangle Shirtwaist Company fire, 326
Triangular trade, 47
Tribal government, 467
Tribes, *see* specific tribes
Triborough Bridge, 461
"Trickle-down" economics, 600
Tripartite Pact, 488, 490
Triple Alliance, 417
Triple Entente, 417
Tripoli, 142–143
Tripp, Linda, 624
Trippe, Juan, 442
Trollope, Frances, 222
Truman, Harry S, 508; Vietnam and, 512;
    Stalin and, 514; iron curtain and, 516(illus.);
    MacArthur and, 520, 521; Korea and, 521,
    537–538; Taft-Hartley Act and, 535;
    domestic policy of, 536–537; 1948 election
    and, 537; as vice president, 538; loyalty
    oaths and, 539
Truman Doctrine, 516
Trumbull, John, 112
Trump, Donald, 609
Trusts, 333–334, 335; Theodore Roosevelt
    and, 390; Taft and, 391; Wilson and, 393;
    antitrust prosecution and, 479
Truth, Sojourner, 188
Tubman, Harriet, 215, 243, 243(illus.)
Tudor dynasty (England), 10, 27
Turkey, 417, 422, 514, 516, 557
Turner, "Big" Joe, 217
Turner, Frederick Jackson, 299, 384, 403
Turner, Nat: slave revolt by, 232
Turner, Ted, 602
Turnpikes, 164, 191
Turnvereine, 208
Tuscarora Indians, 42, 44, 52, 103
Tuskegee Airmen, 503
Tuskegee Institute, 314, 386, 386(illus.), 479
Tutsis: in Rwanda, 622
Twain, Mark, 309, 358, 406
Twelfth Amendment, 149, A8
Twentieth Amendment, 459, A10
Twenty-fifth Amendment, A11
Twenty-first Amendment, 382, A10
Twenty-first U.S. Colored Regiment, 279
Twenty-fourth Amendment, A10–A11
Twenty-One Demands, 413
Twenty-second Amendment, A10
Twenty-seventh Amendment, A11
Twenty-sixth Amendment, A11
Twenty-third Amendment, A10
Two Treatises of Government (Locke), 65
Tyler, Elizabeth, 445
Tyler, John, 194–195, 197
Tyler, Royall, 111
Typewriters, 323, 324
Typhoid, 267, 347, 348, 406

U-boats, *see* Submarines
Ukraine, 382(illus.), 422
U.N., *see* United Nations (U.N.)
Uncle Tom's Cabin (Stowe), 207, 242–243
Underclass, 607

Underground Railroad, 231, 243
Underwood Tariff (1913), 393
Undocumented workers, 610
Unemployed Councils, 458–459
Unemployment: in Panic of 1857, 250–251;
    in Panic of 1873, 293; in 1890s depression,
    370; after First World War, 435; in Great
    Depression, 454, 461; African American,
    457; of women, 457; in New Deal, 463, 471;
    in 1939, 472; in Germany, 481; after Second
    World War, 534; under Reagan, 600; in
    1990s, 623
Unemployment compensation, 465, 534
Unification: of Germany, 611
Unilateralism, 135; of George W. Bush, 626
Union: admission to, 120–121; Jackson on,
    191–192; preservation of, 242; and 1860
    election, 251; secession and, 252–253; support
    for, 264–265. *See also* North (Civil War)
Union League clubs, 292
Union of Soviet Socialist Republics (USSR),
    see Soviet Union
Union Pacific Railroad, 264, 308, 310
Unions, *see* Labor unions
United Auto Workers (UAW), 466, 543
United Farm Workers (UFW), 576–577
United Fruit Company, 410–411, 477, 528
United Mine Workers, 390–391, 436, 466, 498
United Nations (U.N.), 505; Cold War and,
    515; China and, 521; Palestine partition
    and, 528; Persian Gulf War (1991) and, 612;
    Kosovo peacekeeping by, 622; Iraq war
    (2003–) and, 628
United States: creation of, 107–108; as developing
    nation, 168; slave and free areas (1861),
    252(map); in world economy, 477–479,
    478(illus.); after Second World War, 514
United States (ship), 155
U.S. Agency for International Development
    (USAID), 527
U.S. Chamber of Commerce, 379
U.S. Commission on Civil Rights, 541
U.S. Employment Service, 426
U.S. Forest Service, 391
U.S. Housing Corporation, 426
U.S. Information Agency (USIA), 524
United States Magazine and Domestic Review,
    195
U.S. Patent Office, 319
U.S. Sanitary Commission, 265
U.S. Steel Corporation, 334, 391, 428, 436
U.S. v. Cruikshank, 296
U.S. v. E. C. Knight Co., 335
U.S. v. Reese, 365
Universal Negro Improvement Association
    (UNIA), 441
Universities and colleges, 220, 408; colonial,
    64; women in, 126, 384, 579; land for, 264;
    for black students, 284, 314, 384; state
    schools as, 313–314; football in, 353–355;
    for African Americans, 366, 367(illus.), 384;
    agricultural, 368; growth of, 383–384; after
    Second World War, 535; *Bakke* case and,
    591
University of Alabama, 559
University of California (Berkeley): Free
    Speech Movement in, 568–569; People's
    Park in, 597

University of Chicago: Laboratory School at,
    383; nuclear chain reaction at, 497
University of Mississippi, 559
University of Philippines, 408
Unmarried people, 351, 591
Unsafe at Any Speed (Nader), 561
Unskilled labor, 328, 341, 347
Upper class, 262–263, 379
Upper Guinea, 7–8, 50
Upper South: antislavery sentiment in, 186
"Uprising of the 20,000," 329
Upward Bound program, 561
Urban areas, 58, 205–209, 313; poor-relief in,
    62; commerce in, 171–172; slums in,
    209–210; single people in, 211; in South,
    220; mass transportation and, 339; in First
    World War, 426; in 1920s, 440–441; riots in
    1960s, 567; crises in, 608–609; Hispanics in,
    630. *See also* Cities and towns
Urban borderlands, 343–344
Urban engineers, 348
Urbanization: industrialization, technology
    and, 338; 1870–1920, 338–343, 340(map);
    family life and, 350–352
Urban League, 559
Uruguay, 163
Uruguay Round: of GATT, 620
USA PATRIOT Act, *see* PATRIOT Act
USSR, *see* Soviet Union
Utah, 203, 240, 242, 250, 307, 308; irrigation
    in, 309
Ute Indians, 174
Utilities, 319, 345, 379, 381
Utopian communities, 201–203
U-2 spy plane, 525, 555

Valentino, Rudolph, 449
Vallandigham, Clement L., 271
Values: in nineteenth century, 219; in South,
    232–233; in 1920s, 448
Van Buren, Martin, 178, 194, 197, 241
Vance, Cyrus, 592
Vanzetti, Bartolomeo, 446
Vaqueros, 214, 314
Vare, "Duke," 348
Vassa, Gustavus, *see* Equiano, Olaudah
Vaudeville, 217, 355
V-E Day, 506(map)
Veiller, Lawrence, 345
Venereal disease, 421, 570
Venezuela: boundary dispute of, 404
Venona Project, 538–539, 540
Veracruz, 240, 412
Verdun, battle at, 421
Verelst, John, 44(illus.)
Verrazzano, Giovanni da, 14
Versailles Treaty, 417, 481, 482
Vertical integration, 334
Vesey, Denmark, 231
Vespucci, Amerigo, 13
Veterans: land grants to, 175; Civil War
    pensions for, 360, 364; as Bonus Army, 459;
    racism toward, 536; universities and, 536;
    after Vietnam War, 582
Vetoes, 130, 193, 286, 289, 364, 587
Vice-admiralty courts, 51, 82, 85, 88
Vice president: list of, A17–A18
Vichy government, 486

Vicksburg: siege and fall of, 268–269, 270
Victoria (England), 294
Victory gardens, 494
Vieques Island, 414
Vietcong, 530, 563, 564
Vietminh, 511, 520, 529
Vietnam, 565(map); OSS in, 511–512; independence of, 512; Cold War and, 513; France and, 520; division of, 529; Eisenhower and, 529; bombings of, 564; wounded in, 566(illus.); immigrants from, 595–596, 609; diplomatic recognition to, 620. See also Indochina
Vietnamization policy, 580
"Vietnam syndrome," 582
Vietnam War, 555, 563–567; antiwar protests in, 141; Southeast Asia and, 565(map); Tet Offensive in, 570; Pentagon Papers and, 574; end of, 580–582. See also Antiwar protests
Vigilantism: First World War and, 427, 428–429
Viguerie, Richard, 597
Vikings, see Norsemen
Villa, Francisco "Pancho," 413
Villages, see Cities and towns
Villard, Henry, 319
Vincennes, Indiana, 96
Vinland, 13, 14
Violence: against Mormons, 203; against blacks, 228, 286, 292, 365, 459, 567; against Indians, 295; against Planned Parenthood clinics, 395; in labor strikes, 466; in civil rights movement, 558. See also Riots; specific groups
Virginia, 18, 28–30, 53, 76; tobacco in, 29; Indians and, 46, 80–81; slavery in, 47; backcountry of, 95, 119; secession and, 253; in Civil War, 258, 274
Virginia Company, 29, 30, 33
Virginian, The (book), 316
Virginia Plan, 123
Virginia Resolution, 137, 157, 191
Virgin Islands: annexation of, 402
Virtual representation, 81, 83
Virtuous republic: after Revolution, 110, 111–114; women in, 127–128
Vitamins, 443
V-J Day, 495(map)
Voice of America, 527
Volkswagen, 479
Voluntary associations: in black communities, 215
Volunteerism: in Great Depression, 458
Voting: in Massachusetts, 34; republicanism and, 111; African Americans and, 114, 216, 290, 365, 466, 558; for women, 114, 308, 426, 429, 438; in states, 117; Twelfth Amendment and, 149; expansion of, 194; white manhood suffrage, 233; Fourteenth Amendment and, 287; Klan and, 292; political machines and, 348; 1870–1896, 360; in Progressive era, 378; in Cuba, 411
Voting Rights Act (1965), 561
Voyages: by Columbus, 13–14; in African slave trade, 49. See also Exploration; Sailors

Wabash case, 362, 368
WACs (Women's Army Corps), 504

Wade, Benjamin, 281
Wade-Davis bill (1864), 281–282
Wage labor, 173, 329, 330–331
Wages, 62; of Union soldiers, 268; for women, 324, 444; iron law of, 326; vs. living costs, 329; industrialization and, 330; minimum, 537, 577; in 1950s, 543
Wagner, Robert F., 379
Wagner Act, see National Labor Relations (Wagner) Act (1935)
Wake Island, 406, 490
Waldseemüller, Martin, 13
Walker, C. J., 439
Walker, David, 186
Wallace, George, 559; 1968 election and, 572; 1972 election and, 585
Wallace, Henry A., 516, 537; as vice president, 508
Wallace, Henry C., 437
Walsh, David I., 379
Waltham, Massachusetts: textile industry in, 153(illus.), 171
Wampanoag Indians, 33, 45
Wampum, 26, 26(illus.)
Wanamaker's, 332
War brides: in Second World War, 501
Ward, Lester, 335, 384
Ware v. Hylton, 129
War debts: British, 81; after Revolution, 130–131
War Department, 129, 130
War Hawks: in War of 1812, 152–154
War industries: wastes from, 510
War Industries Board (WIB), 394, 425
War Labor Disputes (Smith-Connally) Act, 498
Warner, Charles Dudley, 358
Warner, Susan, 207
War of 1812, 152–157; as second war for independence, 144; Shawnee and, 150(illus.); burning of Washington in, 155; treaty after, 155
War of the Austrian Succession, see King George's War
War of the League of Augsburg, see King William's War
War of the Spanish Succession, see Queen Anne's War
War on Poverty, 561–563
War on terrorism, 617, 626–627; invasion of Iraq (2003) and, 628
War Powers Act (1973), 582, 586
War Production Board, 496
War Refugee Board, 504
Warren, Earl, 541, 560
Warren Commission, 560
War Revenue Act (1917), 425
Wars and warfare: Mayan, 4; Indians and, 5, 25, 76–80, 95–96, 120, 303–304; colonial, 77(illus.); dissent in, 140–141; condemnation of, 477; technology and, 590; ethnic, 622. See also specific battles and wars
Warsaw Pact (1955), 518, 525, 611
War Shipping Board, 425
Warships, 403, 488
Washington (state), 307, 308
Washington, Booker T., 386–387, 386(illus.), 479
Washington, D.C., 155, 372, 395

Washington, George, 101(illus.), 105, 125; in Ohio River region, 76–77; in Revolution, 93, 100, 102, 106–107; at First Continental Congress, 94; at Constitutional Convention, 123; domestic policy under, 130–132; factions and, 133; foreign policy of, 133–135; Farewell Address of, 135
Washington Naval Conference, 477
Washington Post: Watergate and, 585
Washington Treaty (1871), 402
Wasp (ship), 155
Waste: atomic, 510. See also Sewage disposal
Water, 167; for West, 309–310; in Great Plains, 312; purification of, 347–348; diseases and, 633
Water closets, 331
Watergate scandal, 576, 585–587
Water pollution, 347
Water power, 153, 391
Watertown Arsenal, 317
Watson, Tom, 369, 373
Watt, James, 598
Watts (Los Angeles): riots in, 567
Wayne, Anthony, 121, 121(illus.)
Wealth and wealthy, 62, 209–210, 607; Spanish, 14–15, 18; intermarriage and, 58; in South, 63, 219; slavery and, 220, 232; in Civil War, 264, 271; from natural resources, 306; industrialization and, 330; Social Darwinism and, 334; intellectual thought on, 335; in 1980s, 596, 601, 603(illus.), 609; taxation of, 601; in 1990s, 623
Wealth gap: worldwide, 620–621
Weapons: Paleo-Indian, 3; in Civil War, 267–268; in Vietnam War, 567. See also Arms and armaments; specific weapons and wars
Weapons of mass destruction: Iraq war and, 628
Weaver, James B., 369, 370
Web, see World Wide Web
Webb-Pomerene Act (1918), 479
Webster, Daniel, 191, 194, 195, 242
Webster-Ashburton Treaty, 195
Webster v. Reproductive Health Services, 599
Weems, Mason Locke, 111
Welch, Joseph, 540
Welfare and welfare programs, 364, 448; AFDC and, 465, 562; Reagan and, 597, 598; cuts in, 600; reform of, 619, 623. See also Relief programs
Wellesley College, 427
Wells, Ida B., 365, 366
Welty, Eudora, 221
West, 118(map), 203–205, 247, 306(map), 316, 588; after Revolution, 120–122; Jefferson and, 146–147; Indians in, 177–178, 271–272, 301–305; slavery and, 240–241; in Civil War, 259–260, 275(map); frontier theory and, 299; resources of, 306–309, 306(map); society in, 307–308; conservation in, 308, 391; states in, 308; water in, 309–310; Hispanics in, 341; farming in, 368; anti-Chinese riots in, 400; in New Deal, 467
"West" (capitalist countries), 513
West, Benjamin, 80(illus.)
West Africa, 7–8, 49–50, 59, 60(map); black loyalists in, 98, 98(illus.)

West Bank, 583, 592, 604, 622
West Coast, 543, 544(map). *See also* Pacific Ocean region
Westerlies, 12, 14
Western Europe, 517. *See also* Eastern Europe; Europe and Europeans
Western Federation of Miners, 328
Western Health Reform Institute, 331
Western Hemisphere: Monroe Doctrine and, 163
Westerns (movies), 316
Western Samoa, 402
West Florida, 162
West Germany, 519
West Indies, 25, 47, 96, 341
Westinghouse Electric, 319
West Jersey, 41
Westmoreland, William, 566, 570
West Virginia (ship), 489(illus.)
Westward movement, 196(map), 203–205, 220; Indians and, 80; Louisiana Purchase and, 146–148; of commercial farming, 169; of slavery, 174; after War of 1812, 174–175; manifest destiny and, 195–197
Wethersfield: Pequot War and, 35
Weyler, Valeriano, 404
Wharton, Edith, 449
"What Every Girl Should Know" (Sanger), 394
Wheat, 314
Whey (Chinese loan associations), 343
Whigs, 183, 193–195, 200, 240; in Republican Party, 236; and 1848 election, 241; breakup of, 244, 246, 247. *See also* Real Whigs
Whipping: of slaves, 228, 229
Whiskey, 131–132, 333
Whiskey Rebellion, 132
White, Hugh: and 1836 election, 194
White, John, 30(illus.)
White, Richard, 67
White, Theodore A., 523
White, William Allen, 373
White Citizens' Councils, 541
White-collar workers, 352, 543–544
Whitefield, George, 71
White Hats (Las Gorras Blancas), 368
Whiteness: concept of, 207
Whites: skin color and, 116; as abolitionists, 186–188; African Americans and, 217, 365; in South, 219, 223, 232–234; Reconstruction and, 290; Indians and, 293–295, 302, 303–304; West and, 300, 306–309; migration of, 301; in Australia, 311; in Hawai'i, 403; employed women among, 444; desegregation and, 541; national culture and, 545–546; in 1950s, 550; poverty of, 608; 2000 election and, 626
White slavery, 383
White Slave Traffic Act (Mann Act, 1910), 383, 384
White supremacy, 295, 366, 624; Douglass on, 297; Progressives and, 380; in 1990s, 623
Whitewater scandal, 619, 624
Whitman, Walt, 216
Whitney, Eli, 170
WHO, *see* World Health Organization (WHO)
Whyte, William H., 547, 549

Wide, Wide, Wide World, The (Warner), 207
Wilderness, Battle of the, 274
Wildlife: conservation and, 308
Wild West, 299, 308
Wilkinson, James, 149
Willaerts, Adam, 34(illus.)
Willamette valley, 197
William and Mary (England), 53, 54, 200
Williams, Burt, 355
Williams, Roger, 37
Williams, William Appleman, 582
Wilmington: race riot in, 347
Wilmot, David, 236, 240, 241
Wilmot Proviso, 240–241, 249
Wilson, Horace, 354
Wilson, William Dean, 492–493
Wilson, Woodrow, 294, 352, 376, 380, 392–393, 399, 413, 476; racism of, 387; First World War and, 393–394, 415, 416, 417, 420, 429–431; Mexico and, 412–413, 481; Fourteen Points of, 422; civil liberties under, 427–428; League of Nations and, 430–431; Haiti and, 480
Wilson-Gorman Tariff (1894), 362–363, 404
Winds, 12, 14
Wine Islands, 12
Winstanley, William, 136(illus.)
Winthrop, John, 33–34, 35
Wire telegraphy, 402
Wirt, William, 186
Wisconsin, 174, 212, 249, 381
"Wise use" policy: of conservation, 391
Witchcraft, 43, 54, 55
Witch hunt: in 1950s, 539
Withholding taxes, 499
Wolfe, James, 77
Woman Rebel, The (Sanger), 394
Woman's Christian Temperance Union (WCTU), 358, 379, 382, 383
Woman's Peace Party, 419
Woman's Rights Convention (Seneca Falls), 189
Woman suffrage, 358, 387, 388, 426; Fourteenth Amendment and, 287; movement, 366–367; before 1920, 389(map)
Women: Indian, 5, 7, 139, 176, 304–305; in West Africa, 8; European, 10; colonial, 32, 68; Puritan, 37; African, 52; witchcraft crisis and, 54; childbearing by, 59; as Daughters of Liberty, 86; Revolution and, 104, 105, 114, 127; education for, 110, 112, 126; Abigail Adams on, 114; labor of, 169–170, 173; clothing and, 171, 332; in textile industry, 172, 323; as reformers, 181, 376, 379; revivalism and, 183, 184; as abolitionists, 186(illus.), 188–189; at Seneca Falls, 189; farm life and, 201; Shaker, 202; in West, 203–205, 307; novels by, 207; associations of, 208; poverty among, 209, 563; family size and, 210–211; black working, 216; in yeoman culture, 222; in planter class, 224, 226; property rights for, 226, 290; slavery and, 230–231; in Civil War, 262, 265; in nursing, 265; Supreme Court and, 295–296; in tobacco production, 323; employment trends and, 325(illus.); work reforms and, 326, 381, 384; unions and, 327, 328, 329; black women in service sector, 341; social mobility and, 343; in professions, 349; settlement-

house movement and, 349–350; marriage and, 351; as missionaries, 361, 361(illus.), 396–397, 401; black female reformers, 366; Farmers' Alliance and, 368; organizations of, 378; Russian temperance and, 382; prostitution and, 383; higher education for, 384; feminism and, 388; birth-control controversy and, 394–395; education for, 408; antiwar protests by, 419; in First World War, 420–421, 426; in 1920s, 443; in Great Depression workplace, 457; in Second World War, 494, 497–498, 500, 504; magazines for, 545; in 1950s, 546–547; opposition to women's movement by, 579–580; roles in 1970s, 591; sexual revolution and, 591; Christian fundamentalists and, 608; 2000 election and, 626. *See also* Gender and gender roles; Rights; Voting and voting rights
Women and Economics (Gilman), 388
Women of color, *see* People of color
Women's clubs, 387–388
Women's Committee: of Council of National Defense, 426
Women's Era Club, 366
Women's International League for Peace and Freedom (WILPF), 419, 476–477, 567
"Women's jobs": in Great Depression, 457
Women's Loyal National League, 282
Women's Medical College, 384
Women's movement, 387–388, 575; labor and, 329; of 1960s and 1970s, 578–580
Women's National Indian Association (WNIA), 304–305
Women's Peace Union, 477
Women's rights: movement in 1800s, 189; advocates for, 387; missionaries and, 397
Women's Trade Union League (WTUL), 329, 438
Wonderful Wizard of Oz, The (Baum): as Populist parable, 374–375
Wonders of the Invisible World, The (Mather), 55
Wong, Albert and Helen Chia, 501
Woodall, Kate, 361(illus.)
Woodbury, Levi, 193
Woodhenge: in Cahokia, 4
Woods, Granville T.: inventions of, 319
Woods, Tiger, 630
Woodstock Festival, 569
Woodward, Bob, 585
Woolen industry, 152, 264
Woolworth's: sit-ins at, 553–554
Worcester v. Georgia, 177
Work: availability of, 164; change in nature of, 330–331; compensation for injuries or illness and, 393. *See also* Labor
Workday, 173, 326, 352, 376, 381, 384, 392, 393, 438
Workers: and workplace, 172–174; in Civil War North, 263; mass production and, 324; industrial accidents and, 325–326; First World War and, 425–426, 428; in 1920s, 441–443; in Great Depression, 454, 455–457; layoffs of, 457, 588; marginal, 457; craft vs. industrial, 466; in Second World War, 496–498; incomes of, 601; illegal, 610; immigrant, 610. *See also* Labor; Women
Workers' compensation, 393, 437

Work force: slave, 69; women in, 169–170, 210, 216, 324, 330, 444; restructuring of, 324; increase in, 330–331
Workhouses, 62
Working class: culture of, 208; women in, 210; in Civil War, 271; as employees vs. producers, 324; industrialization and, 330; diet of, 331–332; mass transit and, 339; housing for, 345; political machines and, 348; civil service and, 350; boarders and, 351; leisure and, 356; in Progressive era, 379; lifestyle of, 439
Workplace, 172–174, 180; conditions in, 326; gender segregation in, 444; women in, 457
Work relief, 461, 464
Works Progress [Projects] Administration (WPA), 464–465
Workweek, 352; in 1920s, 443
World Bank, 514
World Conference on Human Rights, 594
World Court, 430, 476
World Health Organization (WHO), 633
World order: after First World War, 474–476
World power: United States as, 416
World Series, 352
World Trade Center, 615–616, 626
World Trade Organization (WTO), 621–622, 621(illus.)
World war: Seven Years War as, 79–80, 79(illus.). *See also* First World War; Second World War
World War I, *see* First World War

World War II, *see* Second World War
World Wide Web, 637
Wounded Knee: battle at, 305; AIM occupation of, 578
Wright, Don, 584
Wright, Richard, 465, 541
Writing system: Mayan, 3
Writs of mandamus, 146
WTO, *see* World Trade Organization (WTO)
Wyoming, 195, 240, 308, 309

XYZ Affair, 136

Yale, 126
Yalta meeting (1945), 505–507, 507(illus.), 514
Yamamoto, Isoroku, 495, 496, 508
Yamasee Indians, 52
"Yellow dog" contracts, 264
Yellow fever, 347, 412, 474
Yellow journalism, 356
Yellowstone River region, 308
Yeoman farmers, 221–223, 248, 253; in slave society, 233; as scalawags, 292; after Civil War, 368
Yergin, Daniel, 584
Yippies, 572
Yoga, 591
Yom Kippur War (1973), 583, 584
York (slave), 147, 148
York, duke of, *see* James II (duke of York, England)

Yorktown: British surrender at, 106–107
Yosemite Valley: preservation of, 308
Young, Brigham, 203, 250
Young, John Russell, 294
Young Americans for Freedom (YAF), 568
Younger Federalists, 148, 156
Young Joseph (Nez Percé Indians), 303
Young Men's Christian Association (YMCA), 351, 477
Young Plan (1929), 479
Young Women's Christian Association (YWCA), 351, 379
Youth, 208, 217, 341, 351; culture of, 468–470, 547–548, 568–570
Youth in Crisis (newsreel), 500
Yucatán Peninsula, 3
Yugoslavia, 515
Yuppies (young urban professionals), 609

Zen Buddhism, 591
Zenger, John Peter, 69
Zhou Enlai, 583
Ziegfeld, Florenz, and Ziegfeld Follies, 355
Zimmermann telegram, 420
Zionism, 513, 528
Zones: in eastern Europe, 507; in Germany, 515, 519
Zoning commissions, 438
Zoot suit riots, 500